THE WORKS OF SHAKESPEARE

Revised from the best authorities:

With a memoir, and essay on his genius,
BY BARRY CORNWALL.

ALSO,

Annotations and introductory remarks on the plays,
by many distinguished writers.

Illustrated with engravings on wood, from designs
BY KENNY MEADOWS.

VOL. II

TRAGEDIES.

Vizetelly Brothers & Co. Printers and Engravers,
Peterborough Court, 135 Fleet Street,
London.

This edition published 2009 by
Geddes & Grosset, David Dale House,
New Lanark, ML11 9DJ

Originally published by Robert Tyas,
8 Paternoster Row, London

ISBN 978 1 84205 371 3

Printed and bound in India

TRAGEDIES.

CONTENTS OF VOL. II.

TRAGEDIES.

MACBETH.

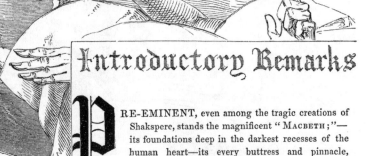

Introductory Remarks

PRE-EMINENT, even among the tragic creations of Shakspere, stands the magnificent "MACBETH;"— its foundations deep in the darkest recesses of the human heart—its every buttress and pinnacle, "jutty, frieze, and coigne of vantage," radiant with the golden light that streams in prodigal abundance from the most poetic of imaginations.

All the constituents of a perfect tragedy are here combined, with a degree of success never probably before attained, and certainly not since. In this great drama, we find incident ever changing, congruous, progressive, and interesting; character richly diversified and exquisitely portrayed; dialogue teeming with every species of excellence; and, to crown all, moral teaching of the highest and purest tendency—not obviously obtruded, like the doctor's drench, but rapturously inhaled without an effort of the will, as the infant derives sustenance from the maternal bosom, unknowing of the great results to which its instincts are subservient. Philosophy delights to dwell on the profound thought, the practical wisdom, evolved from the speakers by the various exigences to which the progress of the plot in turn exposes them; Poetry revels in contemplation of the priceless jewels here collected to enrich her treasury; while Religion, pointing to the guilt-struck murderer, "listening the fear" of the sleeping grooms (conscious the while that he himself has slept his last), proclaims the poet her beloved ally; and reading her sternest lessons by the hallowed taper of fiction, needs no stronger evidence to warn the waverer from the lures of unholy and inordinate desire.

The "great argument" of "MACBETH" is derived from Holinshed's "HISTORY OF SCOTLAND." The story in itself is highly interesting, and has been expressly pointed out by Buchanan, as forming an eligible subject for the drama. The principal incidents on which the play is founded are briefly stated by the commentators, to this effect:—Malcolm II., King of Scotland, had two daughters, the eldest married to Crinan, father of Duncan (thane of the Isles and western parts of Scotland); and on the death of Malcolm without male issue, Duncan succeeded him. The second daughter of Malcolm married Sinel (thane of Glamis), the father of Macbeth. Duncan married either the daughter or sister of Siward, Earl of Northumberland, and was murdered by his cousin-german Macbeth, in the Castle of Inverness. According to Boethius, this event took place in 1045, in the seventh year of Duncan's reign. Macbeth then usurped the crown, and was himself slain by Macduff, in conformity with the play, in 1061; having thus reigned during the long period of sixteen years. Dramatic justice, however, required that punishment should overtake his crime with swifter wing. In the chronicle, also, Shakspere found hints for the terrific character of Lady Macbeth, who is represented as strongly instigating her husband to the destruction of his sovereign, and as a woman "very ambitious, burning in unquenchable desire to bear the name of a Queen." With what surpassing power this rough material has been wrought upon, all can feel, but who can hope adequately to describe?

"MACBETH" was first printed in the original folio (1623). It is generally supposed to have been written in or about 1606. Three years previously, James I. ascended the English throne; and this circumstance possibly turned the poet's attention to Scottish history.

J. O.

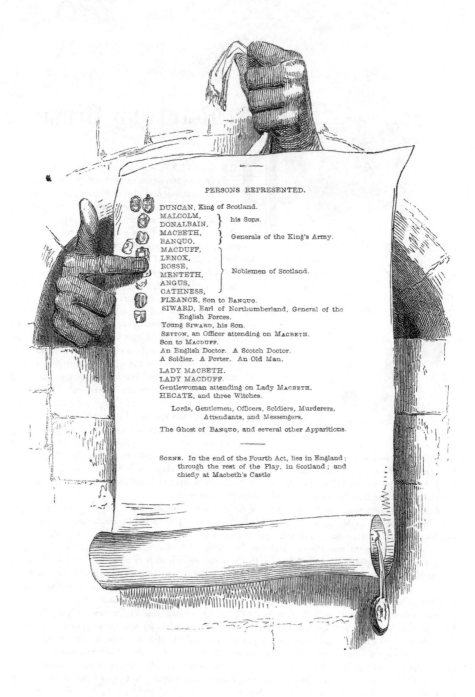

PERSONS REPRESENTED.

DUNCAN, King of Scotland.
MALCOLM,
DONALBAIN, } his Sons.
MACBETH,
BANQUO, } Generals of the King's Army.
MACDUFF,
LENOX,
ROSSE,
MENTETH, } Noblemen of Scotland.
ANGUS,
CATHNESS,
FLEANCE, Son to BANQUO.
SIWARD, Earl of Northumberland, General of the
    English Forces.
Young SIWARD, his Son.
SEYTON, an Officer attending on MACBETH.
Son to MACDUFF.
An English Doctor. A Scotch Doctor.
A Soldier. A Porter. An Old Man.

LADY MACBETH.
LADY MACDUFF.
Gentlewoman attending on Lady MACBETH.
HECATE, and three Witches.

    Lords, Gentlemen, Officers, Soldiers, Murderers,
        Attendants, and Messengers.

The Ghost of BANQUO, and several other Apparitions.

SCENE. In the end of the Fourth Act, lies in England;
    through the rest of the Play, in Scotland; and
    chiefly at Macbeth's Castle

SCENE I.—*An open Place. Thunder and Lightning.*

Enter three Witches.

1st Witch. When shall we three meet again,
In thunder, lightning, or in rain?
2nd Witch. When the hurlyburly's done,
When the battle's lost and won:

3rd Witch. That will be ere the set of sun.
1st Witch. Where the place?
2nd Witch. Upon the heath:
3rd Witch. There to meet with Macbeth.
1st Witch. I come, Graymalkin.
All. Paddock calls:—Anon.
Fair is foul, and foul is fair:
Hover through the fog and filthy air.
                    [Witches *vanish.*

5

SCENE II.—*A Camp near* Fores. *Alarum within.*

Enter KING DUNCAN, MALCOLM, DONALBAIN, LENOX, *with* Attendants, *meeting a bleeding* Soldier.

Dun. What bloody man is that? He can report,
As seemeth by his plight, of the revolt
The newest state.

    Mal.   This is the sergeant,
Who, like a good and hardy soldier, fought
'Gainst my captivity:—Hail, brave friend!
Say to the King the knowledge of the broil,
As thou didst leave it.

    Sold.   Doubtful it stood;
As two spent swimmers, that do cling together,
And choke their art. The merciless Macdonwald
(Worthy to be a rebel; for to that
The multiplying villanies of nature
Do swarm upon him) from the western isles
Of kernes and gallowglasses is supplied;
And Fortune, on his damnéd quarrel smiling,
Shewed like a rebel's whore. But all 's too weak;
For brave Macbeth (well he deserves that name),
Disdaining fortune, with his brandished steel,
Which smoked with bloody execution,
Like valour's minion, carved out his passage,
Till he faced the slave;
And ne'er shook hands, nor bade farewell to him,
Till he unseamed him from the nave to the chaps,
And fixed his head upon our battlements.

    Dun. O, valiant cousin! worthy gentleman!

    Sold. As whence the sun 'gins his reflection
Shipwrecking storms and direful thunders break;
So from that spring, whence comfort seemed to
         come,
Discomfort swells. Mark, King of Scotland,
         mark:
No sooner justice had, with valour armed,
Compelled these skipping kernes to trust their
         heels;
But the Norweyan lord, surveying vantage,
With furbished arms and new supplies of men,
Began a fresh assault.

    Dun.   Dismayed not this
Our captains, Macbeth and Banquo?

    Sold.   Yes;
As sparrows, eagles; or the hare, the lion.
If I say sooth, I must report they were
As cannons overcharged with double cracks;
So they
Doubly redoubled strokes upon the foe;
Except they meant to bathe in reeking wounds,
Or memorise another Golgotha,
I cannot tell.—
But I am faint, my gashes cry for help.

    Dun. So well thy words become thee as thy
         wounds;

They smack of honour both.—Go, get him sur-
         geons.   [*Exit* Soldier, *attended.*

Enter ROSSE.

Who comes here?

    Mal.   The worthy thane of Rosse.

    Len. What haste looks through his eyes! So
         should he look
That seems to speak things strange.

    Rosse.   God save the King!

    Dun. Whence cam'st thou, worthy thane?

    Rosse.   From Fife, great king,
Where the Norweyan banners flout the sky,
And fan our people cold.
Norway himself, with terrible numbers,
Assisted by that most disloyal traitor
The thane of Cawdor, 'gan a dismal conflict;
Till that Bellona's bridegroom, lapped in proof,
Confronted him with self-comparisons,
Point against point rebellious, arm 'gainst arm,
Curbing his lavish spirit: and, to conclude,
The victory fell on us.—

    Dun.   Great happiness!

    Rosse. That now
Sweno, the Norways' king craves composition;
Nor would we deign him burial of his men,
Till he disbursèd, at Saint Colmés' inch,
Ten thousand dollars to our general use.

    Dun. No more that thane of Cawdor shall
         deceive
Our bosom interest.—Go, pronounce his present
         death,
And with his former title greet Macbeth.

    Rosse. I 'll see it done.

    Dun. What he hath lost, noble Macbeth hath
         won.   [*Exeunt.*

SCENE III.—*A Heath.*

Thunder. Enter the three Witches.

    1st Witch. Where hast thou been, sister?

    2nd Witch. Killing swine.

    3rd Witch. Sister, where thou?

    1st Witch. A sailor's wife had chesnuts in her
         lap,
And mounched, and mounched, and mounched:—
    "Give me," quoth I:
"Aroint thee, witch!" the rump-fed ronyon cries.
Her husband 's to Aleppo gone, master o' the
         Tiger:
But in a sieve I 'll thither sail,
And, like a rat without a tail,
I 'll do, I 'll do, and I 'll do.

    2nd Witch. I 'll give thee a wind.

    1st Witch. Thou art kind.

    3rd Witch. And I another.

1st Witch. I myself have all the other;
And the very ports they blow,
All the quarters that they know
I' the shipman's card.
I will drain him dry as hay:
Sleep shall, neither night nor day,
Hang upon his penthouse lid;
He shall live a man forbid:
Weary seven nights, nine times nine,
Shall he dwindle, peak, and pine:
Though his bark cannot be lost,
Yet it shall be tempest-tossed.
Look what I have.

2nd Witch. Shew me, shew me.

1st Witch. Here I have a pilot's thumb,
Wrecked as homeward he did come.

                  [*Drum within.*

3rd Witch. A drum, a drum;
Macbeth doth come.

All. The weird sisters, hand in hand,
Posters of the sea and land,
Thus do go about, about:
Thrice to thine, and thrice to mine,
And thrice again, to make up nine.
Peace!—the charm's wound up.

       Enter MACBETH *and* BANQUO.

Macb. So foul and fair a day I have not seen.

Ban. How far is 't called to Fores?—What are
     these,
So withered, and so wild in their attire;
That look not like the inhabitants o' the earth,
And yet are on 't?—Live you? or are you aught
That man may question? You seem to understand
     me,
By each at once her choppy finger laying
Upon her skinny lips. You should be women,
And yet your beards forbid me to interpret
That you are so.

Macb.   Speak if you can: What are you?

1st Witch. All hail, Macbeth! hail to thee,
     thane of Glamis!

2nd Witch. All hail, Macbeth! hail to thee,
     thane of Cawdor!

3rd Witch. All hail, Macbeth! that shalt be
     king hereafter.

Ban. Good sir, why do you start, and seem to
     fear
Things that do sound so fair?—I' the name of
     truth,
Are ye fantastical, or that indeed
Which outwardly ye shew? My noble partner
Ye greet with present grace, and great prediction
Of noble having and of royal hope,
That he seems rapt withal: to me you speak not:
If you can look into the seeds of time,
And say which grain will grow and which will not,

Speak then to me, who neither beg, nor fear,
Your favours nor your hate.

1st Witch. Hail!

2nd Witch. Hail!

3rd Witch. Hail!

1st Witch. Lesser than Macbeth, and greater.

2nd Witch. Not so happy, yet much happier.

3rd Witch. Thou shalt get kings, though thou
     be none:
So, all hail, Macbeth and Banquo!

1st Witch. Banquo and Macbeth, all hail!

Macb. Stay, you imperfect speakers, tell me
     more!
By Sinel's death, I know I am thane of Glamis;
But how of Cawdor? the thane of Cawdor lives,
A prosperous gentleman; and to be king
Stands not within the prospect of belief,
No more than to be Cawdor. Say from whence
You owe this strange intelligence; or why
Upon this blasted heath you stop our way
With such prophetic greeting.—Speak, I charge
     you.   [*Witches vanish.*

Ban. The earth hath bubbles, as the water has,
And these are of them. Whither are they vanished?

Macb. Into the air; and what seemed corporal,
     melted
As breath into the wind. 'Would they had stayed.

Ban. Were such things here as we do speak
     about?
Or have we eaten of the insane root,
That takes the reason prisoner?

Macb. Your children shall be kings.

Ban.   You shall be king.

Macb. And thane of Cawdor too; went it not so?

Ban. To the self-same tune, and words. Who 's
     here?

       Enter ROSSE *and* ANGUS.

Rosse. The King hath happily received, Mac-
     beth,
The news of thy success: and when he reads
Thy personal venture in the rebels' fight,
His wonders and his praises do contend,
Which should be thine or his: silenced with that,
In viewing o'er the rest o' the self-same day,
He finds thee in the stout Norweyan ranks,
Nothing afeard of what thyself didst make,
Strange images of death. As thick as hail,
Came post with post; and every one did bear
Thy praises in his kingdom's great defence,
And poured them down before him.

Ang.   We are sent
To give thee, from our royal master, thanks;
Only to herald thee into his sight,
Not pay thee.

Rosse. And, for an earnest of a greater honour,
He bade me, from him, call thee thane of Cawdor:

In which addition, hail, most worthy thane!
For it is thine.

Ban.   What, can the devil speak true?

Macb. The thane of Cawdor lives: why do
            you dress me
In borrowed robes?

Ang.   Who was the thane, lives yet;
But under heavy judgment bears that life
Which he deserves to lose.   Whether he was
Combined with Norway, or did line the rebel
With hidden help and vantage, or that with both
He laboured in his country's wreck, I know not;
But treasons capital, confessed and proved,
Have overthrown him.

Macb.   Glamis, and thane of Cawdor:
The greatest is behind.—Thanks for your pains.—
Do you not hope your children shall be kings,
When those that gave the thane of Cawdor to me,
Promised no less to them?

Ban.   That, trusted home,
Might yet enkindle you unto the crown,
Besides the thane of Cawdor.   But 't is strange:
And oftentimes, to win us to our harm,
The instruments of darkness tell us truths;
Win us with honest trifles, to betray us
In deepest consequence.—
Cousins, a word, I pray you.

Macb.   Two truths are told,
As happy prologues to the swelling act
Of the imperial theme.—I thank you, gentlemen.—
This supernatural soliciting
Cannot be ill: cannot be good.   If ill,
Why hath it given me earnest of success,
Commencing in a truth? I am thane of Cawdor:
If good, why do I yield to that suggestion
Whose horrid image doth unfix my hair,
And make my seated heart knock at my ribs,
Against the use of nature?   Present fears
Are less than horrible imaginings:
My thought, whose murder yet is but fantastical,
Shakes so my single state of man, that function
Is smothered in surmise; and nothing is,
But what is not.

Ban.   Look how our partner's rapt.

Macb. If chance will have me king, why chance
            may crown me,
Without my stir.

Ban.   New honours come upon him
Like our strange garments; cleave not to their
            mould
But with the aid of use.

Macb.   Come what come may;
Time and the hour runs through the roughest day.

Ban. Worthy Macbeth, we stay upon your
            leisure.

Macb. Give me your favour: my dull brain
            was wrought

With things forgotten.   Kind gentlemen, your
            pains
Are registered where every day I turn
The leaf to read them.   Let us toward the King.—
Think upon what hath chanced; and at more time,
The interim having weighed it, let us speak
Our free hearts each to other.

Ban.   Very gladly.

Macb. Till then enough.—Come, friends.
                              [*Exeunt.*

SCENE IV.—Fores.   *A Room in the Palace.*

Flourish. Enter DUNCAN, MALCOLM, DONALBAIN,
            LENOX, *and* Attendants.

Dun. Is execution done on Cawdor?   Are not
Those in commission yet returned?

Mal.   My liege,
They are not yet come back.   But I have spoke
With one that saw him die: who did report
That very frankly he confessed his treasons;
Implored your highness' pardon; and set forth
A deep repentance.   Nothing in his life
Became him like the leaving it: he died
As one that had been studied in his death,
To throw away the dearest thing he owed,
As 't were a careless trifle.

Dun.   There 's no art
To find the mind's construction in the face:
He was a gentleman on whom I built
An absolute trust.—O worthiest cousin!

Enter MACBETH, BANQUO, ROSSE, *and* ANGUS.

The sin of my ingratitude even now
Was heavy on me: Thou art so far before,
That swiftest wing of recompense is slow
To overtake thee.   Would thou hadst less deserved;
That the proportion both of thanks and payment
Might have been mine! only I have left to say,
More is thy due than more than all can pay.

Macb. The service and the loyalty I owe,
In doing it, pays itself.   Your highness' part
Is to receive our duties: and our duties
Are, to your throne and state, children and
            servants;
Which do but what they should, by doing every-
            thing
Safe toward your love and honour.

Dun.   Welcome hither:
I have begun to plant thee, and will labour
To make thee full of growing.   Noble Banquo,
That hast no less deserved, nor must be known
No less to have done so, let me infold thee,
And hold thee to my heart.

Ban.   There if I grow,
The harvest is your own.

Dun.   My plenteous joys,
Wanton in fulness, seek to hide themselves
In drops of sorrow.—Sons, kinsmen, thanes,
And you whose places are the nearest, know,
We will establish our estate upon
Our eldest, Malcolm; whom we name hereafter,
The Prince of Cumberland: which honour must
Not, unaccompanied, invest him only,
But signs of nobleness, like stars, shall shine
On all deservers.—From hence to Inverness,
And bind us further to you.

    Macb. The rest is labour which is not used
        for you:
I'll be myself the harbinger, and make joyful
The hearing of my wife with your approach;
So, humbly take my leave.

    Dun.   My worthy Cawdor!

    Macb. The Prince of Cumberland! That is
        a step
On which I must fall down, or else o'erleap,
                        [*Aside.*
For in my way it lies. Stars, hide your fires!
Let not light see my black and deep desires:
The eye wink at the hand! yet let that be
Which the eye fears, when it is done, to see.
                        [*Exit.*

    Dun. True, worthy Banquo; he is full so valiant,
And in his commendations I am fed;
It is a banquet to me. Let us after him,
Whose care is gone before to bid us welcome:
It is a peerless kinsman.   [*Flourish. Exeunt.*

SCENE V.—Inverness. *A Room in* MACBETH's
           Castle.

Enter LADY MACBETH, *reading a letter.*

"They met me in the day of success; and I have
learned, by the perfectest report, they have more in
them than mortal knowledge. When I burned in
desire to question them further, they made themselves—air, into which they vanished. Whiles I
stood rapt in the wonder of it, came missives from
the king, who all-hailed me 'Thane of Cawdor;'
by which title, before, these weird sisters saluted
me, and referred me to the coming on of time, with,
'Hail, king that shalt be!'—This have I thought
good to deliver thee, my dearest partner of greatness; that thou mightest not lose the dues of
rejoicing, by being ignorant of what greatness is
promised thee. Lay it to thy heart, and farewell."

Glamis thou art, and Cawdor; and shalt be
What thou art promised. Yet do I fear thy
        nature;
It is too full o' the milk of human kindness,
To catch the nearest way. Thou wouldst be great;

Art not without ambition; but without
The illness should attend it. What thou wouldst
        highly,
That wouldst thou holily; wouldst not play false,
And yet wouldst wrongly win: thou'dst have,
        great Glamis,
That which cries, "Thus thou must do, if thou
        have it;
And that which rather thou dost fear to do,
Than wishest should be undone." Hie thee hither,
That I may pour my spirits in thine ear;
And chastise with the valour of my tongue
All that impedes thee from the golden round
Which fate and metaphysical aid doth seem
To have thee crowned withal.—What is your
        tidings?

Enter an Attendant.

    Atten. The King comes here to-night.

    Lady M.   Thou'rt mad to say it:
Is not thy master with him? who, wer't so,
Would have informed, for preparation,

    Atten. So please you, it is true: our thane is
        coming:
One of my fellows had the speed of him;
Who, almost dead for breath, had scarcely more
Than would make up his message.

    Lady M.   Give him tending;
He brings great news. The raven himself is hoarse
                  [*Exit* Attendant.
That croaks the fatal entrance of Duncan
Under my battlements. Come, you spirits
That tend on mortal thoughts, unsex me here;
And fill me, from the crown to the toe, topfull
Of direst cruelty! make thick my blood,
Stop up the access and passage to remorse;
That no compunctious visitings of nature
Shake my fell purpose, nor keep peace between
The effect and it! Come to my woman's breasts,
And take my milk for gall, you murdering mi-
        nisters,
Wherever in your sightless substances
You wait on nature's mischief! Come, thick night,
And pall thee in the dunnest smoke of hell!
That my keen knife see not the wound it makes;
Nor heaven peep through the blanket of the dark,
To cry, "Hold, hold!"—Great Glamis! worthy
        Cawdor!

Enter MACBETH.

Greater than both, by the all-hail hereafter!
Thy letters have transported me beyond
This ignorant present, and I feel now
The future in the instant.

    Macb.   My dearest love,
Duncan comes here to-night.

    Lady M.   And when goes hence?

Macb. To-morrow,—as he purposes.

Lady M.   O, never
Shall sun that morrow see!
Your face, my thane, is as a book, where men
May read strange matters.   To beguile the time,
Look like the time; bear welcome in your eye,
Your hand, your tongue : look like the innocent
          flower,
But be the serpent under it.   He that's coming
Must be provided for : and you shall put
This night's great business into my despatch;
Which shall to all our nights and days to come
Give solely sovereign sway and masterdom.

Macb. We will speak further.

Lady M.   Only look up clear;
To alter favour ever is to fear :
Leave all the rest to me.   [*Exeunt.*

SCENE VI.—*The same.   Before the Castle.*

Hautboys.   Servants *of* MACBETH *attending.*

Enter DUNCAN, MALCOLM, DONALBAIN, BANQUO,
LENOX, MACDUFF, ROSSE, ANGUS, & Attendants.

Dun. This castle hath a pleasant seat; the air
Nimbly and sweetly recommends itself
Unto our gentle senses.

Ban.   This guest of summer,
The temple-haunting martlet, does approve,
By his loved mansionry, that the heaven's breath
Smells wooingly here : no jutty, frieze,
Buttress, nor coigne of vantage, but this bird
Hath made his pendent bed and procreant cradle :
Where they most breed and haunt, I have observed
The air is delicate.

Enter LADY MACBETH.

Dun.   See, see ! our honoured hostess !
The love that follows us sometime is our trouble,
Which still we thank as love.   Herein I teach you,
How you shall bid God yield us for your pains,
And thank us for your trouble.

Lady M.   All our service
In every point twice done, and then done double,
Were poor and single business, to contend
Against those honours deep and broad, wherewith
Your majesty loads our house.   For those of old,
And the late dignities heaped up to them,
We rest your hermits.

Dun.   Where's the thane of Cawdor?
We coursed him at the heels, and had a purpose
To be his purveyor : but he rides well;
And his great love, sharp as his spur, hath holp him
To his home before us.   Fair and noble hostess,
We are your guest to-night.

Lady M.   Your servants ever
Have theirs, themselves, and what is theirs, in
          compt,
To make their audit at your highness' pleasure,
Still to return your own.

Dun.   Give me your hand;
Conduct me to mine host : we love him highly,
And shall continue our graces towards him.
By your leave, hostess.   [*Exeunt.*

SCENE VII.—*The same.   A Room in the Castle.*

*Hautboys and torches.   Enter and pass over the
stage, a* Sewer, *and divers* Servants *with dishes
and service.   Then enter* MACBETH.

Macb. If it were done when 'tis done, then
          't were well
It were done quickly.   If the assassination
Could trammel up the consequence, and catch
With his surcease success; that but this blow
Might be the be-all and the end-all here,
But here, upon this bank and shoal of time,—
We'd jump the life to come.   But in these cases
We still have judgment here; that we but teach
Bloody instructions, which, being taught, return
To plague the inventor : This even-handed justice
Commends the ingredients of our poisoned chalice
To our own lips.   He's here in double trust :
First, as I am his kinsman and his subject,
Strong both against the deed : then, as his host,
Who should against his murderer shut the door,
Not bear the knife myself.   Besides, this Duncan
Hath borne his faculties so meek, hath been
So clear in his great office, that his virtues
Will plead like angels, trumpet-tongued, against
The deep damnation of his taking-off :
And pity, like a naked new-born babe,
Striding the blast, or heaven's cherubim, horsed
Upon the sightless couriers of the air,
Shall blow the horrid deed in every eye,
That tears shall drown the wind.   I have no spur
To prick the sides of my intent, but only
Vaulting ambition, which o'erleaps itself,
And falls on the other—How now, what news?

Enter LADY MACBETH.

Lady M. He has almost supped : Why have
          you left the chamber?

Macb. Hath he asked for me?

Lady M.   Know you not he has?

Macb. We will proceed no further in this
          business :
He hath honoured me of late; and I have bought
Golden opinions from all sorts of people,
Which would be worn now in their newest gloss,
Not cast aside so soon.

Lady M.   Was the hope drunk
Wherein you dressed yourself? hath it slept since?
And wakes it now, to look so green and pale
At what it did so freely? From this time,
Such I account thy love. Art thou afeard
To be the same in thine own act and valour,
As thou art in desire? Wouldst thou have that
Which thou esteem'st the ornament of life,
And live a coward in thine own esteem;
Letting "I dare not" wait upon "I would,"
Like the poor cat i' the adage?
     Macb.   Pr'y thee, peace:
I dare do all that may become a man;
Who dares do more, is none.
     Lady M.   What beast was it, then,
That made you break this enterprise to me?
When you durst do it, then you were a man;
And to be more than what you were, you would
Be so much more the man. Nor time nor place
Did then adhere, and yet you would make both:
They have made themselves, and that their fit-
          ness now
Does unmake you. I have given suck; and know
How tender 't is to love the babe that milks me:
I would, while it was smiling in my face,
Have plucked my nipple from his boneless gums,
And dashed the brains out, had I so sworn
As you have done to this.

     Macb.   If we should fail,—
     Lady M.   We fail!
But screw your courage to the sticking-place,
And we'll not fail! When Duncan is asleep
(Whereto the rather shall his day's hard journey
Soundly invite him), his two chamberlains
Will I with wine and wassel so convince,
That memory, the warder of the brain,
Shall be a fume, and the receipt of reason
A limbeck only. When in swinish sleep
Their drenchéd natures lie, as in a death,
What cannot you and I perform upon
The unguarded Duncan? what not put upon
His spongy officers? who shall bear the guilt
Of our great quell.
     Macb.   Bring forth men-children only!
For thy undaunted metal should compose
Nothing but males. Will it not be received,
When we have marked with blood those sleepy two
Of his own chamber, and used their very daggers,
That they have done 't?
     Lady M.   Who dares receive it other,
As we shall make our griefs and clamour roar
Upon his death?
     Macb.   I am settled, and bend up
Each corporal agent to this terrible feat.
Away, and mock the time with fairest show:
False face must hide what the false heart doth know.
                                        [*Exeunt.*

Macbeth's Castle.

SCENE I.—*The same. Court within the Castle.*

Enter BANQUO *and* FLEANCE, *and a* Servant *with a torch before them.*

Ban. How goes the night, boy?

Fle. The moon is down; I have not heard the clock.

Ban. And she goes down at twelve.

Fle. I take 't, 'tis later, sir.

Ban. Hold, take my sword.—There 's husbandry in heaven,

Their candles are all out.—Take thee that too.

A heavy summons lies like lead upon me,

And yet I would not sleep. Merciful powers!

Restrain in me the curséd thoughts that nature

Gives way to in repose!—Give me my sword:—

Enter MACBETH, *and a* Servant *with a torch*.
Who's there?

Macb. A friend.

Ban. What, sir, not yet at rest? The King's
    a-bed:
He hath been in unusual pleasure, and
Sent forth great largess to your officers:
This diamond he greets your wife withal,
By the name of most kind hostess; and shut up
In measureless content.

Macb.   Being unprepared,
Our will became the servant to defect;
Which else should free have wrought.

Ban.   All's well.
I dreamt last night of the three weird sisters:
To you they have shewed some truth.

Macb.   I think not of them:
Yet, when we can entreat an hour to serve,
Would spend it in some words upon that business,
If you would grant the time.

Ban.   At your kindest leisure.

Macb. If you shall cleave to my consent,—
    when 'tis,
It shall make honour for you.

Ban.   So I lose none
In seeking to augment it, but still keep
My bosom franchised, and allegiance clear,
I shall be counselled.

Macb.   Good repose the while.

Ban. Thanks, sir; the like to you.
                      [*Exit* BANQUO.

Macb. Go, bid thy mistress, when my drink is
    ready,
She strike upon the bell. Get thee to bed.—
                      [*Exit* Servant.
Is this a dagger which I see before me,
The handle toward my hand? Come, let me
    clutch thee:—
I have thee not, and yet I see thee still.
Art thou not, fatal vision, sensible
To feeling as to sight? or art thou but
A dagger of the mind: a false creation,
Proceeding from the heat oppressèd brain?
I see thee yet, in form as palpable
As this which now I draw.
Thou marshall'st me the way that I was going;
And such an instrument I was to use.
Mine eyes are made the fools o' the other senses,
Or else worth all the rest. I see thee still;
And on thy blade and dudgeon gouts of blood,
Which was not so before.—There's no such thing:
It is the bloody business which informs
Thus to mine eyes.—Now o'er the one half world
Nature seems dead, and wicked dreams abuse
The curtained sleep; now witchcraft celebrates
Pale Hecate's offerings; and withered murder,
Alarumed by his sentinel, the wolf,

Whose howl's his watch, thus with his stealthy
    pace,
With Tarquin's ravishing strides, towards his de-
    sign
Moves like a ghost.—Thou sure and firm set earth,
Hear not my steps, which way they walk, for fear
The very stones prate of my whereabout,
And take the present horror from the time,
Which now suits with it. Whiles I threat, he
    lives:
Words to the heat of deeds too cold breath gives.
                    [*A bell rings.*
I go, and it is done; the bell invites me.
Hear it not Duncan; for it is a knell
That summons thee to heaven or to hell. [*Exit.*

SCENE II.—*The same.*

Enter LADY MACBETH.

Lady M. That which hath made them drunk,
    hath made me bold:
What hath quenched them, hath given me fire.
    Hark! Peace!
It was the owl that shrieked; the fatal bellman,
Which gives the stern'st good-night. He is
    about it:
The doors are open; and the surfeited grooms
Do mock their charge with snores: I have
    drugged their possets,
That death and nature do contend about them,
Whether they live or die.

Macb. [*within.*] Who's there? what, ho!

Lady M. Alack! I am afraid they have awaked,
And 'tis not done:—the attempt, and not the deed,
Confounds us. Hark! I laid their daggers ready;
He could not miss them.—Had he not resembled
My father as he slept, I had done 't.—My husband?

Enter MACBETH.

Macb. I have done the deed. Didst thou not
    hear a noise?

Lady M. I heard the owl scream, and the
    crickets cry.
Did you not speak?

Macb.   When?

Lady M.   Now.

Macb.   As I descended?

Lady M. Ay.

Macb. Hark!—
Who lies i' the second chamber?

Lady M.   Donalbain.

Macb. This is a sorry sight.
              [*Looking on his hands.*

Lady M. A foolish thought, to say a sorry sight.

Macb. There's one did laugh in his sleep, and
    one cried "Murder!"

That they did wake each other. I stood and
    heard them :
But they did say their prayers, and addressed them
Again to sleep.

Lady M.   There are two lodged together.
Macb. One cried "God bless us !" and "Amen,"
    the other ;
As they had seen me with these hangman's hands,

LADY MACBETH. Hark ! I laid their daggers ready ; he could not miss them.

Listening their fear. I could not say, "Amen,"
When they did say, "God bless us."
    Lady M. Consider it not so deeply.
    Macb. But wherefore could not I pronounce
    "Amen?"
I had most need of blessing, and "Amen"
Stuck in my throat.

Lady M.   These deeds must not be thought
After these ways ; so, it will make us mad.
    Macb. Methought I heard a voice cry, "Sleep
    no more !
Macbeth does murder sleep ; the innocent sleep ;
Sleep, that knits up the ravelled sleave of care ;
The death of each day's life, sore labour's bath,

Balm of hurt minds, great Nature's second
    course,
Chief nourisher in life's feast;"—
  Lady M. What do you mean?
  Macb. Still it cried, " Sleep no more!" to all
    the house:
" Glamis hath murdered sleep; and therefore
    Cawdor
Shall sleep no more; Macbeth shall sleep no
    more!"
  Lady M. Who was it that thus cried? Why,
    worthy thane,
You do unbend your noble strength, to think
So brainsickly of things. Go, get some water,
And wash this filthy witness from your hand.
Why did you bring these daggers from the
    place?
They must lie there: go, carry them, and smear
The sleepy grooms with blood.
  Macb.   I'll go no more:
I am afraid to think what I have done;
Look on 't again, I dare not.
  Lady M.   Infirm of purpose!
Give me the daggers. The sleeping and the
    dead
Are but as pictures: 't is the eye of childhood,
That fears a painted devil. If he do bleed,
I 'll gild the faces of the grooms withal,
For it must seem their guilt.
             [*Exit. Knocking within.*
  Macb.   Whence is that knocking?
How is 't with me, when every noise appals me?
What hands are here? Ha! they pluck out
    mine eyes!
Will all great Neptune's ocean wash this blood
Clean from my hand? No; this my hand will
    rather
The multitudinous seas incarnadine,
Making the green—one red.

      Re-enter Lady MACBETH.

  Lady M. My hands are of your colour; but
    I shame
To wear a heart so white. [*Knock.*] I hear a
    knocking
At the south entry. Retire we to our chamber.
A little water clears us of this deed:
How easy is it then? Your constancy
Hath left you unattended. [*Knocking.*] Hark!
    more knocking:
Get on your nightgown, lest occasion call us,
And shew us to be watchers. Be not lost
So poorly in your thoughts.
  Macb. To know my deed, 't were best not know
    myself.   [*Knock.*
Wake Duncan with thy knocking! I would thou
    couldst!   [*Exeunt.*

SCENE III.—*The same.*

Enter a Porter. [*Knocking within.*

  Port. Here 's a knocking, indeed! If a man
were porter of hell-gate, he should have old turning the key. [*Knocking.*] Knock, knock, knock.
Who 's there, i' the name of Beelzebub? Here 's
a farmer that hanged himself on the expectation
of plenty: Come in time; have napkins enough
about you; here you 'll sweat for 't. [*Knocking.*]
Knock, knock: who 's there i' the other devil's
name? 'Faith, here 's an equivocator, that could
swear in both the scales against either scale; who
committed treason enough for God's sake, yet
could not equivocate to heaven: O, come in,
equivocator. [*Knocking.*] Knock, knock, knock;
who 's there? Faith, here 's an English tailor
come hither, for stealing out of a French hose:
come in, tailor; here you may roast your goose.
[*Knocking.*] Knock, knock: never at quiet!
What are you?—But this place is too cold for
hell. I 'll devil-porter it no further: I had thought
to have let in some of all professions that go the
primrose way to the everlasting bonfire. [*Knocking.*] Anon, anon; I pray you, remember the
porter.   [*Opens the gate.*

Enter MACDUFF *and* LENOX.

  Macd. Was it so late, friend, ere you went to bed,
That you do lie so late?
  Port. 'Faith, sir, we were carousing till the
second cock: and drink, sir, is a great provoker
of three things.
  Macd. What three things does drink especially
provoke?
  Port. Marry, sir, nose-painting, sleep, and
urine. Lechery, sir, it provokes and unprovokes:
it provokes the desire, but it takes away the performance: therefore, much drink may be said to
be an equivocator with lechery: it makes him,
and it mars him; it sets him on, and it takes
him off; it persuades him, and disheartens him;
makes him stand to, and not stand to: in conclusion, equivocates him in a sleep, and, giving
him the lie, leaves him.
  Macd. I believe drink gave thee the lie last
    night.
  Port. That it did, sir, i' the very throat o' me:
but I requited him for his lie; and I think, being
too strong for him, though he took up my legs
sometime, yet I made a shift to cast him.
  Macd. Is thy master stirring?—
Our knocking has awaked him; here he comes.

Enter MACBETH.

  Len. Good-morrow, noble sir.
  Macb.   Good-morrow, both.

Macd. Is the King stirring, worthy thane?

Macb.   Not yet.

Macd. He did command me to call timely on
     him;

I have almost slipped the hour.

Macb.   I 'll bring you to him.

Macd. I know this is a joyful trouble to you;
But yet 't is one.

Macb. The labour we delight in, physics pain.
This is the door.

Macd.   I 'll make so bold to call,
For 't is my limited service.   [*Exit* MACDUFF.

Len. Goes the King hence to day?

Macb. He does: he did appoint so.

Len. The night has been unruly: where we lay,
Our chimneys were blown down: and, as they say,
Lamentings heard i' the air; strange screams of
     death;
And prophesying, with accents terrible,
Of dire combustion, and confused events,
New hatched to the woful time. The obscure bird
Clamoured the livelong night: some say, the earth
Was feverous, and did shake.

Macb.   'T was a rough night.

Len. My young remembrance cannot parallel
A fellow to it.

Re-enter MACDUFF.

Macd. O horror! horror! horror! Tongue, nor
     heart,
Cannot conceive, nor name thee!

Macb. }
Len. }   What 's the matter?

Macd. Confusion now hath made his master-
     piece!
Most sacrilegious murder hath broke ope
The Lord's anointed temple, and stole thence
The life o' the building.

Macb.   What is 't you say? the life?

Len. Mean you his majesty?

Macd. Approach the chamber, and destroy
     your sight
With a new Gorgon: Do not bid me speak;
See, and then speak yourselves. Awake! awake!
     [*Exeunt* MACBETH *and* LENOX.
Ring the alarum-bell:—Murder and treason!
Banquo and Donalbain! Malcolm! awake!
Shake off this downy sleep, death's counterfeit,
And look on death itself! up, up, and see
The great doom's image! Malcolm! Banquo!
As from your graves rise up, and walk like sprights,
To countenance this horror!   [*Bell rings.*

Enter LADY MACBETH.

Lady M.   What 's the business,
That such a hideous trumpet calls to parley
The sleepers of the house? speak, speak.

Macd.   O, gentle lady,
'T is not for you to hear what I can speak:
The repetition, in a woman's ear,
Would murder as it fell.—O Banquo! Banquo!

Enter BANQUO.

Our royal master 's murdered!

Lady M.   Woe, alas!
What, in our house?

Ban.   Too cruel, anywhere.
Dear Duff, I pr'y thee, contradict thyself,
And say, it is not so.

Re-enter MACBETH and LENOX.

Macb. Had I but died an hour before this chance,
I had lived a blessèd time; for, from this instant,
There 's nothing serious in mortality:
All is but toys: renown and grace is dead;
The wine of life is drawn, and the mere lees
Is left this vault to brag of.

Enter MALCOLM and DONALBAIN.

Don. What is amiss!

Macb.   You are, and do not know it:
The spring, the head, the fountain of your blood
Is stopped; the very source of it is stopped.

Macd. Your royal father 's murdered.

Mal.   O, by whom?

Len. Those of his chamber, as it seemed, had
     done 't:
Their hands and faces were all badged with blood,
So were their daggers, which, unwiped, we found
Upon their pillows: they stared, and were dis-
     tracted:
No man's life was to be trusted with them.

Macb. O, yet I do repent me of my fury,
That I did kill them.

Macd.   Wherefore did you so?

Macb. Who can be wise, amazed, temperate and
     furious,
Loyal and neutral, in a moment? No man:
The expedition of my violent love
Outran the pauser reason.—Here lay Duncan,
His silver skin laced with his golden blood;
And his gashed stabs looked like a breach in nature,
For ruin's wasteful entrance: there, the murderers,
Steeped in the colours of their trade, their daggers
Unmannerly breeched with gore: Who could re-
     frain,
That had a heart to love, and in that heart
Courage, to make his love known?

Lady M.   Help me hence, ho!

Macd. Look to the lady.

Mal.   Why do we hold our tongues,
That most may claim this argument for ours?

Don. What should be spoken here,
Where our fate, hid in an augre-hole,

May rush and seize us? Let's away; our tears
Are not yet brewed.

Mal.   Nor our strong sorrow
Upon the foot of motion.

Ban.   Look to the lady:
          [LADY MACBETH *is carried out.*
And when we have our naked frailties hid,
That suffer in exposure, let us meet,
And question this most bloody piece of work,
To know it further. Fears and scruples shake us:
In the great hand of God I stand; and thence,
Against the undivulged pretence I fight
Of treasonous malice.

Macb.   And so do I.

All.   So all.

Macb. Let's briefly put on manly readiness,
And meet i' the hall together.

All.   Well contented.
          [*Exeunt all but* MALCOLM *and* DONALBAIN.

Mal. What will you do? Let's not consort with
          them:
To shew an unfelt sorrow, is an office
Which the false man does easy. I'll to England.

Don. To Ireland, I; our separated fortune
Shall keep us both the safer: where we are,
There's daggers in men's smiles: the near in blood,
The nearer bloody.

Mal.   This murderous shaft that's shot
Hath not yet lighted; and our safest way
Is to avoid the aim. Therefore, to horse;
And let us not be dainty of leave-taking,
But shift away: there's warrant in that theft,
Which steals itself when there's no mercy left.
          [*Exeunt.*

SCENE IV.—*Without the Castle.*

Enter ROSSE *and an* Old Man.

Old M. Threescore and ten I can remember
          well:
Within the volume of which time I have seen
Hours dreadful and things strange; but this sore
          night
Hath trifled former knowings.

Rosse.   Ah, good father,
Thou see'st, the heavens, as troubled with man's act,
Threaten his bloody stage: by the clock 't is day,
And yet dark night strangles the travelling lamp.
Is it night's predominance, or the day's shame,

That darkness does the face of earth intomb,
When living light should kiss it?

Old M.   'T is unnatural,
Even like the deed that's done. On Tuesday last,
A falcon, towering in her pride of place,
Was, by a mousing owl, hawked at and killed.

Rosse. And Duncan's horses (a thing most
          strange and certain),
Beauteous and swift, the minions of their race,
Turned wild in nature, broke their stalls, flung out,
Contending 'gainst obedience, as they would make
War with mankind.

Old M.   'T is said, they eat each other.

Rosse. They did so; to the amazement of mine
          eyes,
That looked upon't. Here comes the good Macduff:

Enter MACDUFF.

How goes the world, sir, now?

Macd.   Why, see you not?

Rosse. Is't known who did this more than
          bloody deed?

Macd. Those that Macbeth hath slain.

Rosse.   Alas the day!
What good could they pretend?

Macd.   They were suborned:
Malcolm and Donalbain, the King's two sons,
Are stolen away and fled; which puts upon them
Suspicion of the deed.

Rosse.   'Gainst nature still:
Thriftless ambition, that will ravin up
Thine own life's means!—Then 't is most like
The sovereignty will fall upon Macbeth.

Macd. He is already named; and gone to Scone
To be invested.

Rosse.   Where is Duncan's body?

Macd. Carried to Colm-kill;
The sacred storehouse of his predecessors,
And guardian of their bones.

Rosse.   Will you to Scone?

Macd. No, cousin, I'll to Fife.

Rosse.   Well, I will thither.

Macd. Well, may you see things well done
          there;—adieu!—
Lest our old robes sit easier than our new!

Rosse. Farewell, father.

Old M. God's benison go with you; and with
          those
That would make good of bad, and friends of
          foes.   [*Exeunt.*

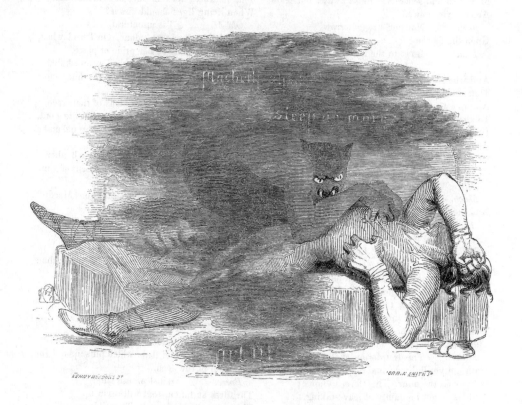

SCENE I.—*Fores.*   *A Room in the Palace.*

Enter BANQUO.

Ban. Thou hast it now, King, Cawdor, Glamis, all,
As the weird women promised; and I fear
Thou play'dst most foully for 't: yet it was said,
It should not stand in thy posterity;
But that myself should be the root and father
Of many kings. If there come truth from them
(As upon thee, Macbeth, their speeches shine),
Why, by the verities on thee made good,
May they not be my oracles as well,
And set me up in hope? But, hush; no more.

Senet sounded. Enter MACBETH, *as King;* LADY
   MACBETH, *as Queen;* LENOX, ROSSE, Lords,
   Ladies, *and* Attendants.

Macb. Here 's our chief guest.
Lady M.   If he had been forgotten,
It had been as a gap in our great feast,
And all things unbecoming.
Macb. To-night we hold a solemn supper, sir,
And I 'll request your presence.
Ban.   Let your highness

Command upon me; to the which, my duties
Are with a most indissoluble tie
For ever knit.
Macb. Ride you, this afternoon?
Ban.   Ay, my good lord.
Macb. We should have else desired your good
      advice
(Which still hath been both grave and prosperous)
In this day's council; but we 'll take to-morrow.
Is 't far you ride?
Ban. As far, my lord, as will fill up the time
'Twixt this and supper: go not my horse the better,
I must become a borrower of the night,
For a dark hour, or twain.
Macb.   Fail not our feast.
Ban. My lord, I will not.
Macb. We hear, our bloody cousins are bestowed
In England and in Ireland; not confessing
Their cruel parricide, filling their hearers
With strange invention: but of that to-morrow;
When, therewithal, we shall have cause of state,
Craving us jointly. Hie you to horse: Adieu,
Till you return at night. Goes Fleance with you?
Ban. Ay, my good lord: our time does call
      upon us.

Macb. I wish your horses swift and sure of
  foot;
And so I do commend you to their backs.
Farewell.—   [*Exit* BANQUO.
Let every man be master of his time
Till seven at night: to make society
The sweeter welcome, we will keep ourself
Till supper-time alone: while then, God be with
  you.
  [*Exeunt* LADY MACBETH, Lords, Ladies, &c.
Sirrah, a word with you: attend those men our
  pleasure?
Attend. They are, my lord, without the palace
  gate.
  Macb. Bring them before us.—[*Exit* Attendant.
  To be thus, is nothing;
But to be safely thus.—Our fears in Banquo
Stick deep; and in his royalty of nature
Reigns that which would be feared: 'tis much he
  dares;
And, to that dauntless temper of his mind,
He hath a wisdom that doth guide his valour
To act in safety.   There is none but he
Whose being I do fear: and under him
My genius is rebuked; as, it is said,
Mark Antony's was by Cæsar. He chid the sisters,
When first they put the name of King upon me,
And bade them speak to him; then, prophet-like,
They hailed him father to a line of kings:
Upon my head they placed a fruitless crown,
And put a barren sceptre in my gripe,
Thence to be wrenched with an unlineal hand,
No son of mine succeeding.   If it be so,
For Banquo's issue have I filed my mind;
For them the gracious Duncan have I murdered;
Put rancours in the vessel of my peace
Only for them; and mine eternal jewel
Given to the common enemy of man,
To make them kings; the seed of Banquo kings!
Rather than so, come fate into the list,
And champion me to the utterance! Who's there?

  Re-enter Attendant, *with two* Murderers.

Now to the door, and stay there till we call.
                              [*Exit* Attendant.
Was it not yesterday we spoke together?
  1st Mur. It was, so please your highness.
  Macb.   Well then, now
Have you considered of my speeches?   Know
That it was he, in the times past, which held you
So under fortune; which you thought had been
Our innocent self.   This I made good to you
In our last conference: passed in probation with you,
How you were borne in hand; how crossed; the
  instruments;
Who wrought with them; and all things else, that
  might,

To half a soul, and to a notion crazed,
Say, "Thus did Banquo."
  1st Mur.   You made it known to us.
  Macb. I did so; and went further, which is now
Our point of second meeting.   Do you find
Your patience so predominant in your nature,
That you can let this go? Are you so gospelled,
To pray for this good man, and for his issue,
Whose heavy hand hath bowed you to the grave,
And beggared yours for ever?
  1st Mur.   We are men, my liege.
  Macb. Ay, in the catalogue ye go for men;
As hounds, and greyhounds, mongrels, spaniels,
  curs,
Shoughs, water-rugs, and demi-wolves, are cleped
All by the name of dogs: the valued file
Distinguishes the swift, the slow, the subtle,
The housekeeper, the hunter, every one
According to the gift which bounteous Nature
Hath in him closed; whereby he does receive
Particular addition, from the bill
That writes them all alike: and so of men.
Now, if you have a station in the file,
And not in the worst rank of manhood, say it;
And I will put that business in your bosoms,
Whose execution takes your enemy off;
Grapples you to the heart and love of us,
Who wear our health but sickly in his life,
Which in his death were perfect.
  2nd Mur.   I am one, my liege,
Whom the vile blows and buffets of the world
Have so incensed, that I am reckless what
I do, to spite the world.
  1st Mur.   And I another,
So weary with disasters, tugged with fortune,
That I would set my life on any chance,
To mend it, or be rid on't.
  Macb.   Both of you
Know Banquo was your enemy.
  2nd Mur.   True, my lord.
  Macb. So is he mine: and in such bloody dis-
  tance,
That every minute of his being thrusts
Against my near'st of life: and though I could
With barefaced power sweep him from my sight,
And bid my will avouch it, yet I must not,
For certain friends that are both his and mine,
Whose loves I may not drop, but wail his fall
Whom I myself struck down: and thence it is
That I to your assistance do make love;
Masking the business from the common eye,
For sundry weighty reasons.
  2nd Mur.   We shall, my lord,
Perform what you command us.
  1st Mur.   Though our lives—
  Macb. Your spirits shine through you. With-
  in this hour, at most,

I will advise you where to plant yourselves;
Acquaint you with the perfect spy o' the time,
The moment on 't; for 't must be done to-night,
And something from the palace; always thought,
That I require a clearness: and with him
(To leave no rubs nor botches in the work),
Fleance his son, that keeps him company,
Whose absence is no less material to me
Than is his father's, must embrace the fate
Of that dark hour.   Resolve yourselves apart;
I 'll come to you anon.
   2nd Mur.   We are resolved, my lord.
   Macb. I 'll call upon you straight; abide
      within.
It is concluded:—Banquo, thy soul's flight,
If it find heaven, must find it out to-night.
                  [*Exeunt.*

SCENE II.—*The same.   Another Room.*

Enter LADY MACBETH, *and a* Servant.

   Lady M. Is Banquo gone from court?
   Serv. Ay, madam, but returns again to-night.
   Lady M. Say to the King, I would attend his
      leisure
For a few words.
   Serv.   Madam, I will.   [*Exit.*
   Lady M.   Nought 's had, all 's spent,
Where our desire is got without content:
'T is safer to be that which we destroy,
Than by destruction dwell in doubtful joy.

Enter MACBETH.

How now, my lord? why do you keep alone,
Of sorriest fancies your companions making!
Using those thoughts, which should indeed have
      died
With them they think on?   Things without all
      remedy,
Should be without regard: what 's done, is done.
   Macb. We have scotched the snake, not killed
      it:
She 'll close, and be herself; whilst our poor malice
Remains in danger of her former tooth.
But let the frame of things disjoint,
Both the worlds suffer,
Ere we will eat our meal in fear, and sleep
In the affliction of these terrible dreams
That shake us nightly: better be with the dead,
Whom we, to gain our place, have sent to peace,
Than on the torture of the mind to lie
In restless ecstasy.   Duncan is in his grave;
After life's fitful fever, he sleeps well;
Treason has done his worst: nor steel, nor poison,
Malice domestic, foreign levy, nothing,
Can touch him further.

   Lady M.   Come on:
Gentle my lord, sleek o'er your rugged looks;
Be bright and jovial 'mong your guests to-night.
   Macb. So shall I, love; and so, I pray, be
      you:
Let your remembrance apply to Banquo;
Present him eminence, both with eye and tongue:
Unsafe the while, that we
Must lave our honours in these flattering streams;
And make our faces vizards to our hearts,
Disguising what they are.
   Lady M.   You must leave this.
   Macb. O, full of scorpions is my mind, dear
      wife!
Thou know'st that Banquo and his Fleance live.
   Lady M. But in them Nature's copy 's not
      eterne.
   Macb. There 's comfort yet; they are assailable;
Then be thou jocund: ere the bat hath flown
His cloistered flight; ere, to black Hecate's sum-
      mons,
The shard-borne beetle, with his drowsy hums,
Hath rung night's yawning peal, there shall be
      done
A deed of dreadful note.
   Lady M.   What 's to be done?
   Macb. Be innocent of the knowledge, dearest
      chuck,
Till thou applaud the deed. Come, seeling night,
Skarf up the tender eye of pitiful day;
And, with thy bloody and invisible hand,
Cancel and tear to pieces that great bond
Which keeps me pale!—Light thickens; and the
      crow
Makes wing to the rooky wood:
Good things of day begin to droop and drowse,
Whiles night's black agents to their prey do rouse.
Thou marvell'st at my words: but hold thee
      still;
Things bad begun, make strong themselves by ill:
So, pr'y thee, go with me.   [*Exeunt.*

SCENE III.—*The same.   A Park or Lawn, with
a Gate leading to the Palace.*

Enter three Murderers.

   1st Mur. But who did bid thee join with us?
   3rd Mur.   Macbeth.
   2nd Mur. He needs not our mistrust; since he
      delivers
Our offices, and what we have to do,
To the direction just.
   1st Mur.   Then stand with us.
The west yet glimmers with some streaks of day:
Now spurs the lated traveller apace,

To gain the timely inn; and near approaches
The subject of our watch.

3rd Mur.   Hark! I hear horses.

Ban. [*within.*] Give us a light there, ho!

2nd Mur.   Then it is he; the rest
That are within the note of expectation,
Already are i' the court.

1st Mur.   His horses go about.

3rd Mur. Almost a mile: but he does usually,
So all men do, from hence to the palace gate
Make it their walk.

Enter BANQUO *and* FLEANCE, *a* Servant *with a
torch preceding them.*

2nd Mur.   A light, a light?

3rd Mur.   'T is he.

1st Mur. Stand to 't.

Ban. It will be rain to-night.

1st Mur.   Let it come down.

                    [*Assaults* BANQUO.

Ban. O, treachery! Fly, good Fleance, fly,
      fly, fly;
Thou mayst revenge.—O slave!

              [*Dies.* FLEANCE *and* Servant *escape.*

3rd Mur. Who did strike out the light?

1st Mur.   Was 't not the way?

3rd Mur. There 's but one down; the son is
      fled.

2nd Mur. We have lost best half of our affair.

1st Mur. Well, let 's away, and say how much
      is done.   [*Exeunt.*

SCENE IV.—*A Room of State in the Palace.
            A Banquet prepared.*

Enter MACBETH, LADY MACBETH, ROSSE, LENOX,
            Lords, *and* Attendants.

Macb. You know your own degrees; sit down:
      at first
And last, the hearty welcome.

Lords.   Thanks to your majesty.

Macb. Ourself will mingle with society,
And play the humble host.
Our hostess keeps her state; but, in best time,
We will require her welcome.

Lady M. Pronounce it for me, sir, to all our
      friends;
For my heart speaks, they are welcome.

Enter First Murderer, *to the door.*

Macb. See, they encounter thee with their
      hearts' thanks:—
Both sides are even: here I 'll sit i' the midst:
Be large in mirth; anon, we 'll drink a measure
The table round.—There 's blood upon thy face.

Mur. 'T is Banquo's, then.

Macb. 'T is better thee without, than he within.
Is he despatched?

Mur. My lord, his throat is cut; that I did
      for him.

Macb. Thou art the best o' the cut-throats: yet
      he 's good
That did the like for Fleance: if thou didst it,
Thou art the nonpareil.

Mur.   Most royal sir,
Fleance is 'scaped.

Macb. Then comes my fit again: I had else
      been perfect;
Whole as the marble, founded as the rock;
As broad and general as the casing air;
But now I am cabined, cribbed, confined, bound in
To saucy doubts and fears. But Banquo 's safe?

Mur. Ay, my good lord: safe in a ditch he bides,
With twenty trenchéd gashes on his head;
The least a death to nature.

Macb.   Thanks for that:—
There the grown serpent lies; the worm that 's fled
Hath nature that in time will venom breed;
No teeth for the present.—Get thee gone; to-
      morrow
We 'll hear ourselves again.   [*Exit* Murderer.

Lady M.   My royal lord,
You do not give the cheer: the feast is sold
That is not often vouched, while 't is a making,
'T is given with welcome. To feed were best at
      home:
From thence, the sauce to meat is ceremony;
Meeting were bare without it.

Macb.   Sweet remembrancer!—
Now, good digestion wait on appetite,
And health on both!

Len.   May it please your highness sit?

          [*The* Ghost of BANQUO *rises, and sits in
                  MACBETH's place.*

Macb. Here had we now our country's honour
      roofed,
Were the graced person of our Banquo present;
Who may I rather challenge for unkindness
Than pity for mischance!

Rosse.   His absence, sir,
Lays blame upon his promise. Please it your
      highness
To grace us with your royal company?

Macb. The table 's full.

Len. Here 's a place reserved, sir.

Macb.   Where?

Len. Here, my good lord. What is 't that
      moves your highness?

Macb. Which of you have done this?

Lords.   What, my good lord?

Macb. Thou canst not say, I did it: never shake
Thy gory locks at me.

Rosse. Gentlemen, rise; his highness is not
    well.

Lady M. Sit, worthy friends:—my lord is
    often thus,
And hath been from his youth: pray you, keep
    seat;
The fit is momentary; upon a thought
He will again be well: if much you note him,
You shall offend him, and extend his passion:
Feed, and regard him not.—Are you a man?

Macb. Ay, and a bold one, that dare look on that
Which might appal the devil.

Lady M.   O proper stuff!
This is the very painting of your fear:
This is the air-drawn dagger which, you said,
Led you to Duncan. O, these flaws and starts
(Impostors to true fear) would well become
A woman's story, at a winter's fire,
Authorised by her grandam. Shame itself!
Why do you make such faces? When all's done,
You look but on a stool.

Macb. Pr'ythee, see there! behold! look! lo!
    how say you?—
Why, what care I? If thou canst nod, speak too.—
If charnel-houses and our graves must send
Those that we bury back, our monuments
Shall be the maws of kites. [*Ghost disappears.*

Lady M.   What! quite unmanned in folly?

Macb. If I stand here, I saw him.

Lady M.   Fy, for shame!

Macb. Blood hath been shed ere now, i' the
    olden time,
Ere human statute purged the gentle weal;
Ay, and since too, murders have been performed
Too terrible for the ear: the times have been,
That, when the brains were out, the man would
    die,
And there an end: but now, they rise again,
With twenty mortal murders on their crowns,
And push us from our stools: this is more strange
Than such a murder is.

Lady M.   My worthy lord,
Your noble friends do lack you.

Macb.   I do forget:—
Do not muse at me, my most worthy friends;
I have a strange infirmity, which is nothing
To those that know me. Come, love and health
    to all;
Then I'll sit down:—Give me some wine; fill
    full:—
I drink to the general joy of the whole table,

Ghost rises.

And to our dear friend, Banquo, whom we miss;
Would he were here! to all, and him, we thirst,
And all to all.

Lords.   Our duties, and the pledge.

Macb. Avaunt, and quit my sight! Let the
    earth hide thee!
Thy bones are marrowless, thy blood is cold;
Thou hast no speculation in those eyes
Which thou dost glare with!

Lady M.   Think of this, good peers,
But as a thing of custom: 'tis no other;
Only it spoils the pleasure of the time.

Macb. What man dare, I dare:
Approach thou like the rugged Russian bear,
The armed rhinoceros, or the Hyrcan tiger;
Take any shape but that, and my firm nerves
Shall never tremble: or, be alive again,
And dare me to the desert with thy sword;
If trembling I inhibit, then protest me
The baby of a girl. Hence, horrible shadow!
          [*Ghost disappears.*
Unreal mockery, hence!—Why, so: being gone,
I am a man again.—Pray you, sit still.

Lady M. You have displaced the mirth, broke
    the good meeting,
With most admired disorder.

Macb.   Can such things be,
And overcome us like a summer's cloud,
Without our special wonder? You make me
    strange
Even to the disposition that I owe,
When now I think you can behold such sights,
And keep the natural ruby of your cheeks,
When mine are blanched with fear.

Rosse.   What sights, my lord?

Lady M. I pray you, speak not; he grows
    worse and worse;
Question enrages him. At once, good night:
Stand not upon the order of your going,
But go at once.

Len.   Good night, and better health
Attend his majesty!

Lady M.   A kind good night to all!
          [*Exeunt* Lords *and* Attendants.

Macb. It will have blood, they say; blood will
    have blood;
Stones have been known to move, and trees to
    speak;
Augurs, and understood relations, have
By magot-pies, and choughs, and rooks, brought
    forth
The secret'st man of blood.—What is the night?

Lady M. Almost at odds with morning, which
    is which.

Macb. How say'st thou, that Macduff denies
    his person,
At our great bidding?

Lady M.   Did you send to him, sir?

Macb. I hear it by the way; but I will send:
There's not a one of them, but in his house
I keep a servant fee'd. I will to-morrow

(And betimes I will) to the weird sisters:
More shall they speak; for now I am bent to
    know,
By the worst means, the worst: for mine own
    good,
All causes shall give way: I am in blood
Stept in so far, that, should I wade no more,
Returning were as tedious as go o'er:

Strange things I have in head, that will to hand;
Which must be acted ere they may be scanned.
   Lady M. You lack the season of all natures,
    sleep.
   Macb. Come, we'll to sleep. My strange and
    self-abuse
Is the initiate fear, that wants hard use:
We are yet but young in deed.   [*Exeunt.*

SCENE V.—*The Heath. Thunder.*

Enter HECATE, *meeting the three* Witches.

   1st Witch. Why, how now, Hecate? you look
    angerly.
   Hec. Have I not reason, beldams as you are,
Saucy and overbold? How did you dare
To trade and traffic with Macbeth,
In riddles and affairs of death;
And I, the mistress of your charms,
The close contriver of all harms,
Was never called to bear my part,
Or shew the glory of our art?
And, which is worse, all you have done
Hath been but for a wayward son,
Spiteful, and wrathful; who, as others do,
Loves for his own ends, not for you.
But make amends now. Get you gone,
And at the pit of Acheron
Meet me i' the morning; thither he
Will come to know his destiny.
Your vessels and your spells provide,
Your charms, and everything beside:

I am for the air; this night I'll spend
Unto a dismal and a fatal end.
Great business must be wrought ere noon:
Upon the corner of the moon
There hangs a vaporous drop profound;
I'll catch ere it come to ground:
And that, distilled by magic sleights,
Shall raise such artificial sprights,
As, by the strength of their illusion,
Shall draw him on to his confusion:
He shall spurn fate, scorn death, and bear
His hopes 'bove wisdom, grace, and fear:
And you all know, security
Is mortals' chiefest enemy.

SONG [*within*].

Come away, come away, &c.

Hark, I am called; my little spirit, see,
Sits in a foggy cloud, and stays for me. [*Exit.*
   1st Witch. Come, let's make haste; she'll soon
    be back again.   [*Exeunt.*

SCENE VI.—Fores. *A Room in the Palace.*

Enter LENOX *and another* Lord.

Len. My former speeches have but hit your
　　thoughts,
Which can interpret further: only, I say,
Things have been strangely borne. The gracious
　　Duncan
Was pitied of Macbeth:—marry, he was dead:
And the right-valiant Banquo walked too late;
Whom, you may say, if it please you, Fleance
　　killed,
For Fleance fled. Men must not walk too late.
Who cannot want the thought, how monstrous
It was for Malcolm and for Donalbain
To kill their gracious father? damnéd fact!
How it did grieve Macbeth! did he not straight,
In pious rage, the two delinquents tear,
That were the slaves of drink, and thralls of
　　sleep?
Was not that nobly done? Ay, and wisely too;
For 't would have angered any heart alive,
To hear the men deny it. So that, I say,
He has borne all things well: and I do think,
That, had he Duncan's sons under his key
(As, an 't please heaven, he shall not), they
　　should find
What 't were to kill a father: so should Fleance
But peace!—for from broad words, and 'cause
　　he failed
His presence at the tyrant's feast, I hear
Macduff lives in disgrace: sir, can you tell
Where he bestows himself?

Lord. 　　　The son of Duncan,
From whom this tyrant holds the due of birth,
Lives in the English court; and is received
Of the most pious Edward with such grace,
That the malevolence of fortune nothing
Takes from his high respect: thither Macduff
　　is gone
To pray the holy king, upon his aid,
To wake Northumberland and warlike Siward:
That, by the help of these (with Him above
To ratify the work), we may again
Give to our tables meat, sleep to our nights;
Free from our feasts and banquets bloody knives;
Do faithful homage, and receive free honours;
All which we pine for now: and this report
Hath so exasperate the King, that he
Prepares for some attempt of war.

Len. 　　　Sent he to Macduff?

Lord. He did: and with an absolute " Sir,
　　not I,"
The cloudy messenger turns me his back,
And hums; as who should say, " You 'll rue the
　　time
That clogs me with this answer."

Len. 　　　And that well might
Advise him to a caution, to hold what distance
His wisdom can provide. Some holy angel
Fly to the court of England, and unfold
His message ere he come; that a swift blessing
May soon return to this our suffering country
Under a hand accursed!

Lord. 　　　I 'll send my prayers with him!
　　　　　　　　　　　　　　[*Exeunt.*

Light thickens; and the crow makes wing to the rooky wood.

SCENE I.—*A dark Cave. In the middle,*
    a Cauldron boiling. Thunder.

        Enter the three Witches.

1st Witch. Thrice the brinded cat hath mewed.
2nd Witch. Thrice; and once the hedge-pig whined.
3rd Witch. Harper cries :—'T is time, 'tis time.
1st Witch. Round about the cauldron go ;
        In the poisoned entrails throw.—
        Toad, that under the cold stone,
        Days and nights hast thirty-one
        Sweltered venom sleeping got,
        Boil thou first i'the charmèd pot !
All.   Double, double toil and trouble ;
        Fire burn, and cauldron bubble.
2nd Witch. Fillet of a fenny snake,
        In the cauldron boil and bake :
        Eye of newt, and toe of frog,
        Wool of bat, and tongue of dog,
        Adder's fork, and blind-worm's sting,
        Lizard's leg, and owlet's wing,
        For a charm of powerful trouble,
        Like a hell-broth boil and bubble.
All.   Double, double toil and trouble ;
        Fire burn, and cauldron bubble.
3rd Witch. Scale of dragon, tooth of wolf ;
        Witch's mummy ; maw and gulf
        Of the ravined salt-sea shark ;
        Root of hemlock, digged i' the dark ;
        Liver of blaspheming Jew ;
        Gall of goat, and slips of yew
        Slivered in the moon's eclipse ;
        Nose of Turk, and Tartar's lips ;
        Finger of birth-strangled babe,
        Ditch-delivered by a drab,
        Make the gruel thick and slab :
        Add thereto a tiger's chawdron,
        For the ingredients of our cauldron.
All.   Double, double toil and trouble ;
        Fire burn, and cauldron bubble.
2nd Witch. Cool it with a baboon's blood,
        Then the charm is firm and good.

Enter HECATE, *and the other three* Witches.

Hec. O, well done! I commend your pains;
And every one shall share i' the gains.
And now about the cauldron sing,
Like elves and fairies in a ring,
Enchanting all that you put in.

SONG.

Black spirits and white,
    Red spirits and grey;
Mingle, mingle, mingle,
    You that mingle may.

2nd Witch. By the pricking of my thumbs,
Something wicked this way comes:
Open locks, whoever knocks.

Enter MACBETH.

Macb. How now, you secret, black, and mid-
            night hags?
What is 't you do?
    All.   A deed without a name.
    Macb. I cónjure you, by that which you profess
(Howe'er you come to know it), answer me:
Though you untie the winds, and let them fight
Against the churches; though the yesty waves
Confound and swallow navigation up;
Though bladed corn be lodged, and trees blown
            down;
Though castles topple on their warders' heads;
Though palaces and pyramids do slope
Their heads to their foundations; though the
            treasure
Of Nature's germins tumble all together,
Even till destruction sicken, answer me
To what I ask you.
    1st Witch.   Speak.
    2nd Witch.   Demand.
    3rd Witch.   We'll answer.
    1st Witch. Say, if thou 'dst rather hear it from
            our mouths,
Or from our masters'?
    Macb.   Call them; let me see them.
    1st Witch. Pour in sow's blood, that hath eaten
Her nine farrow; grease, that 's sweaten
From the murderer's gibbet, throw
Into the flame.
    All.   Come, high or low;
Thyself and office deftly shew.

Thunder. An Apparition of an armed Head rises.

Macb. Tell me, thou unknown power,—
    1st Witch.   He knows thy thought;
Hear his speech, but say thou nought.
    App. Macbeth! Macbeth! Macbeth! beware
            Macduff;
Beware the thane of Fife.—Dismiss me:—Enough.
                                    [*Descends.*

Macb. Whate'er thou art, for thy good caution,
            thanks;
Thou hast harped my fear aright:—But one word
            more:—
    1st Witch. He will not be commanded. Here's
            another,
More potent than the first.

Thunder. An Apparition of a bloody Child rises.

App.   Macbeth! Macbeth! Macbeth!—
    Macb. Had I three ears, I'd hear thee.
    App.   Be bloody, bold,
And resolute; laugh to scorn the power of man;
For none of woman born shall harm Macbeth.
                                    [*Descends.*
    Macb. Then live, Macduff: What need I fear
            of thee?
But yet I'll make assurance double sure,
And take a bond of fate: thou shalt not live;
That I may tell pale-hearted fear, it lies,
And sleep in spite of thunder.—What is this,

*Thunder. An Apparition of a Child crowned, with
    a tree in his hand, rises.*

That rises like the issue of a king;
And wears upon his baby brow the round
And top of sovereignty?
    All.   Listen, but speak not to 't.
    App. Be lion-mettled, proud; and take no care
Who chafes, who frets, or where conspirers are:
Macbeth shall never vanquished be, until
Great Birnam wood to high Dunsinane hill
Shall come against him.   [*Descends.*
    Macb.   That will never be:
Who can impress the forest; bid the tree
Unfix his earth-bound root? sweet bodements!
            good!
Rebellious head, rise never till the wood
Of Birnam rise; and our high-placed Macbeth
Shall live the lease of nature, pay his breath
To time and mortal custom.—Yet my heart
Throbs to know one thing: tell me (if your art
Can tell so much), shall Banquo's issue ever
Reign in this kingdom?
    All.   Seek to know no more.
    Macb. I will be satisfied: deny me this,
And an eternal curse fall on you! Let me know:—
Why sinks that cauldron? and what noise is this?
    1st Witch.   [*Hautboys.*
    2nd Witch. } Shew!
    3rd Witch. }
    All. Shew his eyes, and grieve his heart;
Come like shadows, so depart.

*Eight Kings appear, and pass over the Stage in
    order; the last with a glass in his hand;* BANQUO
    following.

Macb. Thou art too like the spirit of Banquo;
down!
Thy crown does sear mine eye-balls:—and thy air,
Thou other gold-bound brow, is like the first:—
A third is like the former:—Filthy hags!
Why do you shew me this?—A fourth?—Start,
eyes!
What! will the line stretch out to the crack of
doom?
Another yet?—A seventh?—I'll see no more:—
And yet the eighth appears, who bears a glass
Which shews me many more; and some I see
That twofold balls and treble sceptres carry:
Horrible sight!—Ay, now I see 'tis true;
For the blood-boltered Banquo smiles upon me,
And points at them for his.—What, is this so?

1st Witch. Ay, sir, all this is so: but why
Stands Macbeth thus amazédly?
Come, sisters, cheer we up his sprights,
And shew the best of our delights;
I'll charm the air to give a sound,
While you perform your antique round:
That this great king may kindly say,
Our duties did his welcome pay.

[*Music. The* Witches *dance, and vanish.*
Macb. Where are they? Gone? Let this per-
nicious hour
Stand aye accurséd in the calendar!—
Come in, without there!

Enter LENOX.

Len.   What's your grace's will?
Macb. Saw you the weird sisters?
Len.   No, my lord.
Macb. Came they not by you?
Len.   No, indeed, my lord.
Macb. Infected be the air whereon they ride;
And damned all those that trust them!—I did hear
The galloping of horse: Who was't came by?
Len 'Tis two or three, my lord, that bring you
word,
Macduff is fled to England.
Macb.   Fled to England?
Len. Ay, my good lord.
Macb. Time, thou anticipat'st my dread exploits:
The flighty purpose never is o'ertook,
Unless the deed go with it: from this moment,
The very firstlings of my heart shall be
The firstlings of my hand. And even now,
To crown my thoughts with acts, be it thought
and done:
The castle of Macduff I will surprise;
Seize upon Fife; give to the edge o' the sword
His wife, his babes, and all unfortunate souls
That trace him in his line. No boasting like a
fool;
This deed I'll do before this purpose cool:

But no more sights!—Where are these gentlemen?
Come, bring me where they are.   [*Exeunt.*

SCENE II.—Fife. *A Room in* MACDUFF's *Castle.*

Enter LADY MACDUFF, *her* Son, *and* ROSSE.

Lady Macd. What had he done, to make him
fly the land?
Rosse. You must have patience, madam.
L. Macd.   He had none:
His flight was madness: When our actions do not,
Our fears do make us traitors.
Rosse.   You know not
Whether it was his wisdom, or his fear.
L. Macd. Wisdom! to leave his wife, to leave
his babes,
His mansion, and his titles, in a place
From whence himself does fly? He loves us not;
He wants the natural touch: for the poor wren,
The most diminutive of birds, will fight
(Her young ones in her nest) against the owl.
All is the fear, and nothing is the love;
As little is the wisdom, where the flight
So runs against all reason.
Rosse.   My dearest coz,
I pray you, school yourself: but, for your husband,
He is noble, wise, judicious, and best knows
The fits o' the season. I dare not speak much
further:
But cruel are the times when we are traitors,
And do not know ourselves; when we hold rumour
From what we fear, yet know not what we fear;
But float upon a wild and violent sea,
Each way, and move.—I take my leave of you:
Shall not be long but I'll be here again:
Things at the worst will cease, or else climb up-
ward
To what they were before.—My pretty cousin,
Blessing upon you!
L. Macd. Fathered he is, and yet he's father-
less.
Rosse. I am so much a fool, should I stay longer,
It would be my disgrace, and your discomfort:
I take my leave at once.   [*Exit* ROSSE.
L. Macd.   Sirrah, your father's dead:
And what will you do now? how will you live?
Son. As birds do, mother.
L. Macd.   What, with worms and flies?
Son. With what I get, I mean; and so do they.
L. Macd. Poor bird! thou'dst never fear the
net, nor lime,
The pit-fall, nor the gin.
Son. Why should I, mother? Poor birds they
are not set for.—
My father is not dead, for all your saying.

L. Macd. Yes, he is dead; how wilt thou do
    for a father?

Son. Nay, how will you do for a husband?

L. Macd. Why, I can buy me twenty at any
    market.

Son. Then you'll buy 'em to sell again.

L. Macd. Thou speak'st with all thy wit; and
    yet, i' faith,
With wit enough for thee.

Son. Was my father a traitor, mother?

L. Macd. Ay, that he was.

Son. What is a traitor?

L. Macd. Why, one that swears and lies.

Son. And be all traitors that do so?

L. Macd. Every one that does so is a traitor,
and must be hanged.

Son. And must they all be hanged that swear
and lie?

L. Macd. Every one.

Son. Who must hang them?

L. Macd. Why, the honest men.

Son. Then the liars and swearers are fools: for
there are liars and swearers enough to beat the
honest men, and hang up them.

L. Macd. Now God help thee, poor monkey!
But how wilt thou do for a father?

Son. If he were dead, you'd weep for him: if
you would not, it were a good sign that I should
quickly have a new father.

L. Macd. Poor prattler? how thou talk'st.

Enter a Messenger.

Mess. Bless you, fair dame! I am not to you
    known,
Though in your state of honour I am perfect.
I doubt some danger does approach you nearly:
If you will take a homely man's advice,
Be not found here; hence with your little ones.
To fright you thus, methinks I am too savage;
To do worse to you were fell cruelty,
Which is too nigh your person. Heaven pre-
    serve you!
I dare abide no longer.   [*Exit* Messenger.

L. Macd.   Whither should I fly?
I have done no harm. But I remember now
I am in this earthly world; where to do harm
Is often laudable; to do good, sometime
Accounted dangerous folly: why then, alas!
Do I put up that womanly defence,
To say, I have done no harm?—What are these
    faces?

Enter Murderers.

Mur. Where is your husband?

L. Macd. I hope, in no place so unsanctified,
Where such as thou mayst find him.

Mur.   He's a traitor.

Son. Thou liest, thou shag-eared villain.

Mur.   What, you egg? [*Stabbing him.*
Young fry of treachery?

Son.   He has killed me, mother:
Run away, I pray you.   [*Dies.*
    [*Exit* Lady Macduff, *crying " Murder,"*
    and pursued by the Murderers.

Scene III.—England. *A Room in the King's Palace.*

Enter Malcolm *and* Macduff.

Mal. Let us seek out some desolate shade, and
    there
Weep our sad bosoms empty.

Macd.   Let us rather
Hold fast the mortal sword; and, like good men,
Bestride our down-fall'n birthdom: each new
    morn,
New widows howl; new orphans cry; new sor-
    rows
Strike heaven on the face, that it resounds
As if it felt with Scotland, and yelled out
Like syllable of dolour.

Mal.   What I believe, I'll wail;
What know, believe; and what I can redress,
As I shall find the time to friend, I will.
What you have spoke, it may be so perchance.
This tyrant, whose sole name blisters our tongues,
Was once thought honest: you have loved him
    well;
He hath not touched you yet. I am young; but
    something
You may deserve of him through me: and wisdom
To offer up a weak, poor, innocent lamb,
To appease an angry god.

Macd. I am not treacherous.

Mal.   But Macbeth is.
A good and virtuous nature may recoil,
In an imperial charge. But I shall crave your
    pardon;
That which you are, my thoughts cannot trans-
    pose:
Angels are bright still, though the brightest fell:
Though all things foul would wear the brows of
    grace,
Yet grace must still look so.

Macd.   I have lost my hopes.

Mal. Perchance even there where I did find
    my doubts.
Why in that rawness left you wife and child
(Those precious motives, those strong knots of
    love),
Without leave-taking?—I pray you,
Let not my jealousies be your dishonours,

But mine own safeties : you may be rightly just,
Whatever I shall think.

   Macd.   Bleed, bleed, poor country !
Great tyranny, lay thou thy basis sure,
For goodness dares not check thee ! wear thou
          thy wrongs;
Thy title is affeered !—Fare thee well, lord :
I would not be the villain that thou think'st
For the whole space that 's in the tyrant's grasp,
And the rich East to boot.

   Mal.   Be not offended :
I speak not as in absolute fear of you.
I think our country sinks beneath the yoke;
It weeps; it bleeds; and each new day a gash
Is added to her wounds : I think, withal,
There would be hands uplifted in my right;
And here, from gracious England, have I offer
Of goodly thousands. But, for all this,
When I shall tread upon the tyrant's head,
Or wear it on my sword, yet my poor country
Shall have more vices than it had before;
More suffer, and more sundry ways than ever,
By him that shall succeed.

   Macd.   What should he be?

   Mal. It is myself I mean : in whom I know
All the particulars of vice so grafted,
That, when they shall be opened, black Macbeth
Will seem as pure as snow; and the poor state
Esteem him as a lamb, being compared
With my confineless harms.

   Macd.   Not in the legions
Of horrid hell, can come a devil more damned
In evils, to top Macbeth.

   Mal.   I grant him bloody,
Luxurious, avaricious, false, deceitful,
Sudden, malicious, smacking of every sin
That has a name : but there 's no bottom, none,
In my voluptuousness : your wives, your daugh-
          ters,
Your matrons, and your maids, could not fill up
The cistern of my lust; and my desire
All continent impediments would o'erbear,
That did oppose my will. Better Macbeth,
Than such a one to reign.

   Macd.   Boundless intemperance
In nature is a tyranny; it hath been
The untimely emptying of the happy throne,
And fall of many kings. But fear not yet
To take upon you what is yours : you may
Convey your pleasures in a spacious plenty,
And yet seem cold, the time you may so hood-
          wink.
We have willing dames enough; there cannot be
That vulture in you, to devour so many
As will to greatness dedicate themselves,
Finding it so inclined.

   Mal.   With this, there grows,

In my most ill-composed affection, such
A stanchless avarice, that, were I king,
I should cut off the nobles for their lands;
Desire his jewels, and this other's house;
And my more-having would be as a sauce
To make me hunger more; that I should forge
Quarrels unjust against the good and loyal,
Destroying them for wealth.

   Macd.   This avarice
Sticks deeper; grows with more pernicious root
Than summer-seeming lust; and it hath been
The sword of our slain kings : yet do not fear;
Scotland hath foisons to fill up your will,
Of your mere own. All these are portable,
With other graces weighed.

   Mal. But I have none. The king-becoming
          graces,
As justice, verity, temperance, stableness,
Bounty, perseverance, mercy, lowliness,
Devotion, patience, courage, fortitude,
I have no relish of them; but abound
In the division of each several crime,
Acting it many ways. Nay, had I power, I should
Pour the sweet milk of concord into hell,
Uproar the universal peace, confound
All unity on earth.

   Macd.   O, Scotland ! Scotland !

   Mal. If such a one be fit to govern, speak :
I am as I have spoken.

   Macd.   Fit to govern !
No, not to live.—O, nation miserable,
With an untitled tyrant bloody-sceptered,
When shalt thou see thy wholesome days again;
Since that the truest issue of thy throne
By his own interdiction stands accursed,
And does blaspheme his breed?—Thy royal father
Was a most sainted king; the queen that bore thee,
Oftener upon her knees than on her feet,
Died every day she lived. Fare thee well !
These evils thou repeat'st upon thyself
Have banished me from Scotland.—O, my breast,
Thy hope ends here !

   Mal.   Macduff, this noble passion,
Child of integrity, hath from my soul
Wiped the black scruples, reconciled my thoughts
To thy good truth and honour. Devilish Macbeth
By many of these trains hath sought to win me
Into his power; and modest wisdom plucks me
From over-credulous haste : but God above
Deal between thee and me ! for even now
I put myself to thy direction, and
Unspeak mine own detraction; here abjure
The taints and blames I laid upon myself,
For strangers to my nature. I am yet
Unknown to woman; never was forsworn;
Scarcely have coveted what was mine own;
At no time broke my faith; would not betray

The devil to his fellow; and delight
No less in truth than life: my first false speaking
Was this upon myself: what I am truly,
Is thine, and my poor country's, to command:
Whither, indeed, before thy here-approach,
Old Siward, with ten thousand warlike men,
All ready at a point, was setting forth:
Now we'll together: and the chance of goodness
Be like our warranted quarrel!—Why are you
        silent?
    Macd. Such welcome and unwelcome things
        at once,
'Tis hard to reconcile.

Enter a Doctor.

    Mal. Well; more anon.—Comes the king
        forth, I pray you?
    Doct. Ay, sir: there are a crew of wretched
        souls
That stay his cure; their malady convinces
The great assay of art; but at his touch,
Such sanctity hath Heaven given his hand,
They presently amend.
    Mal.   I thank you, doctor. [*Exit* Doctor.
    Macd. What's the disease he means?
    Mal.   'Tis called the "evil:"
A most miraculous work in this good king;
Which often, since my here-remain in England,
I have seen him do. How he solicits Heaven,
Himself best knows: but strangely-visited people,
All swoln and ulcerous, pitiful to the eye,
The mere despair of surgery, he cures;
Hanging a golden stamp about their necks,
Put on with holy prayers: and 'tis spoken,
To the succeeding royalty he leaves
The healing benediction. With this strange virtue,
He hath a heavenly gift of prophecy;
And sundry blessings hang about his throne,
That speak him full of grace.

Enter ROSSE.

    Macd.   See, who comes here?
    Mal. My countryman; but yet I know him
        not.
    Macd. My ever-gentle cousin, welcome hither.
    Mal. I know him now: good God, betimes
        remove
The means that make us strangers!
    Rosse.   Sir, amen.
    Macd. Stands Scotland where it did?
    Rosse.   Alas, poor country;
Almost afraid to know itself! It cannot
Be called our mother, but our grave: where no-
        thing,
But who knows nothing, is once seen to smile;
Where sighs, and groans, and shrieks that rent
        the air,

Are made, not marked; where violent sorrow
        seems
A modern ecstacy; the dead man's knell
Is there scarce asked for who; and good men's
        lives
Expire before the flowers in their caps,
Dying or ere they sicken.
    Macd.   O, relation,
Too nice, and yet too true!
    Mal.   What is the newest grief?
    Rosse. That of an hour's age doth hiss the
        speaker;
Each minute teems a new one.
    Macd.   How does my wife?
    Rosse. Why, well.
    Macd.   And all my children?
    Rosse.   Well, too.
    Macd. The tyrant has not battered at their
        peace?
    Rosse. No; they were well at peace when I
        did leave them.
    Macd. Be not a niggard of your speech: how
        goes it?
    Rosse. When I came hither to transport the
        tidings
Which I have heavily borne, there ran a rumour
Of many worthy fellows that were out;
Which was to my belief witnessed the rather,
For that I saw the tyrant's power a-foot.
Now is the time of help: your eye in Scotland
Would create soldiers, make our women fight,
To doff their dire distresses.
    Mal.   Be it their comfort,
We are coming thither: gracious England hath
Lent us good Siward, and ten thousand men;
An older and a better soldier none
That Christendom gives out.
    Rosse.   'Would I could answer
This comfort with the like! But I have words
That would be howled out in the desert air,
Where hearing should not latch them.
    Macd.   What concern they?
The general cause? or is it a fee-grief,
Due to some single breast?
    Rosse.   No mind that's honest
But in it shares some woe; though the main part
Pertains to you alone.
    Macd.   If it be mine,
Keep it not from me; quickly let me have it.
    Rosse. Let not your ears despise my tongue
        for ever,
Which shall possess them with the heaviest sound
That ever yet they heard.
    Macd.   Humph! I guess at it.
    Rosse. Your castle is surprised; your wife and
        babes
Savagely slaughtered: to relate the manner,

Were, on the quarry of these murdered deer,
To add the death of you.
   Mal.   Merciful heaven!
What, man! ne'er pull your hat upon your brows;
Give sorrow words: the grief that does not speak,
Whispers the o'er-fraught heart, and bids it
     break.
   Macd. My children too?
   Rosse.   Wife, children, servants,—all
That could be found.
   Macd.   And I must be from thence!
My wife killed too?
   Rosse.   I have said.
   Mal.   Be comforted:
Let's make us medicines of our great revenge,
To cure this deadly grief.
   Macd. He has no children.—All my pretty
     ones?
Did you say, all? O, hell-kite! All?
What, all my pretty chickens, and their dam,
At one fell swoop?
   Mal. Dispute it like a man.
   Macd.   I shall do so;
But I must also feel it as a man:
I cannot but remember such things were,

That were most precious to me.—Did Heaven
     look on,
And would not take their part? Sinful Macduff,
They were all struck for thee! naught that I am,
Not for their own demerits, but for mine,
Fell slaughter on their souls: Heaven rest them
     now!
   Mal. Be this the whetstone of your sword: let
     grief
Convert to anger; blunt not the heart, enrage it.
   Macd. O, I could play the woman with mine
     eyes,
And braggart with my tongue!—But, gentle
     Heaven,
Cut short all intermission; front to front
Bring thou this fiend of Scotland and myself;
Within my sword's length set him; if he 'scape,
Heaven forgive him too!
   Mal.   This tune goes manly.
Come, go we to the king; our power is ready;
Our lack is nothing but our leave: Macbeth
Is ripe for shaking, and the powers above
Put on their instruments. Receive what cheer
     you may;
The night is long that never finds the day.
                          [*Exeunt.*

SCENE I.—Dunsinane. *A Room in the Castle.*

Enter a Doctor *of Physic, and a waiting*
Gentlewoman.

Doct. I have two nights watched with you,
but can perceive no truth in your report. When
was it she last walked?

Gent. Since his majesty went into the field, I
have seen her rise from her bed, throw her
night-gown upon her, unlock her closet, take
forth paper, fold it, write upon it, read it, afterwards seal it, and again return to bed; yet all
this while in a most fast sleep.

Doct. A great perturbation in nature! to receive
at once the benefit of sleep, and do the effects of
watching.—In this slumbry agitation, besides her
walking and other actual performances, what, at
any time, have you heard her say?

Gent. That, sir, which I will not report after her.

Doct. You may to me; and 'tis most meet you
should.

Gent. Neither to you nor any one; having no
witness to confirm my speech.

Enter LADY MACBETH, *with a taper.*

Lo you, here she comes! This is her very guise;
and, upon my life, fast asleep. Observe her; stand
close.

Doct. How came she by that light?

Gent. Why, it stood by her: she has light by
her continually; 'tis her command.

Doct. You see her eyes are open.

Gent. Ay, but their sense is shut.

Doct. What is it she does now? Look how she
rubs her hands.

Gent. It is an accustomed action with her, to
seem thus washing her hands; I have known her
continue in this a quarter of an hour.

Lady M. Yet here's a spot.

Doct. Hark, she speaks: I will set down what
comes from her, to satisfy my remembrance the
more strongly.

Lady M. Out, damned spot! out, I say!—One;
two; why, then 'tis time to do't:—Hell is
murky!—Fie, my lord, fie! a soldier and afeard?
What need we fear who knows it, when none can
call our power to account?—Yet who would have
thought the old man to have had so much blood
in him.

Doct. Do you mark that?

Lady M. The thane of Fife had a wife; where
is she now?—What, will these hands ne'er be
clean?—No more o' that, my lord, no more o' that:
you mar all with this starting.

Doct. Go to, go to; you have known what you
should not.

Gent. She has spoke what she should not, I am
sure of that: Heaven knows what she has known.

Lady M. Here's the smell of the blood still: all the perfumes of Arabia will not sweeten this little hand.   Oh! oh! oh!

Doct. What a sigh is there! The heart is sorely charged.

Gent. I would not have such a heart in my bosom, for the dignity of the whole body.

Doct. Well, well, well,—

Gent. 'Pray God it be, sir.

Doct. This disease is beyond my practice: yet

I have known those which have walked in their sleep, who have died holily in their beds.

Lady M. Wash your hands, put on your nightgown; look not so pale:—I tell you yet again, Banquo's buried; he cannot come out of his grave.

Doct. Even so?

Lady M. To bed, to bed; there's knocking at the gate. Come, come, come, come, give me your hand: what's done cannot be undone: to bed, to bed, to bed. [*Exit.*

Doct. Will she go now to bed?

Gent. Directly.

Doct. Foul whisperings are abroad: unnatural deeds
Do breed unnatural troubles: infected minds
To their deaf pillows will discharge their secrets.
More needs she the divine than the physician.
God, God, forgive us all! Look after her;
Remove from her the means of all annoyance,
And still keep eyes upon her: so, good night:
My mind she has mated, and amazed my sight:
I think, but dare not speak.

Gent. Good night, good doctor. [*Exeunt.*

SCENE II.—*The Country near* Dunsinane.

Enter, with drums and colours, MENTETH, CATHNESS, ANGUS, LENOX, *and* Soldiers.

Ment. The English power is near, led on by Malcolm,
His uncle Siward, and the good Macduff.
Revenges burn in them: for their dear causes
Would, to the bleeding, and the grim alarm,
Excite the mortified man.

Ang. Near Birnam wood
Shall we well meet them; that way are they coming.

Cath. Who knows if Donalbain be with his brother?

Len. For certain, sir, he is not: I have a file
Of all the gentry: there is Siward's son,
And many unrough youths, that even now
Protest their first of manhood.

Ment. What does the tyrant?

Cath. Great Dunsinane he strongly fortifies:
Some say, he's mad; others, that lesser hate him,
Do call it valiant fury: but, for certain,
He cannot buckle his distempered cause
Within the belt of rule.

Ang. Now does he feel
His secret murders sticking on his hands;
Now minutely revolts upbraid his faith-breach;

Those he commands, move only in command,
Nothing in love: now does he feel his title
Hang loose about him, like a giant's robe
Upon a dwarfish thief.

Ment. Who then shall blame
His pestered senses to recoil and start,
When all that is within him does condemn
Itself for being there?

Cath. Well, march we on,
To give obedience where 'tis truly owed:
Meet we the medicin of the sickly weal;
And with him pour we, in our country's purge,
Each drop of us.

Len. Or so much as it needs,
To dew the sovereign flower and drown the weeds.
Make we our march towards Birnam.
[*Exeunt, marching.*

SCENE III.—Dunsinane. *A Room in the Castle.*

Enter MACBETH, Doctor, *and* Attendants.

Macb. Bring me no more reports; let them fly all;
Till Birnam wood remove to Dunsinane,
I cannot taint with fear. What's the boy Malcolm?
Was he not born of woman? The spirits that know
All mortal consequences, have pronounced me thus:
"Fear not, Macbeth; no man that's born of woman
Shall e'er have power upon thee."—Then fly, false thanes,
And mingle with the English epicures:
The mind I sway by, and the heart I bear,
Shall never sagg with doubt, nor shake with fear.

Enter a Servant.

The devil damn thee black, thou cream-faced loon!
Where gott'st thou that goose look?

Serv. There is ten thousand—

Macb. Geese, villain?

Serv. Soldiers, sir.

Macb. Go, prick thy face, and over-red thy fear,
Thou lily-livered boy. What soldiers, patch?
Death of thy soul! those linen cheeks of thine
Are counsellors to fear. What soldiers, whey-face?

Serv. The English force, so please you.

Macb. Take thy face hence.—Seyton!—I am sick at heart,

When I behold—Seyton, I say!—This push
Will cheer me ever, or disseat me now.
I have lived long enough: my way of life
Is fall'n into the sear, the yellow leaf:
And that which should accompany old age,
As honour, love, obedience, troops of friends,
I must not look to have; but, in their stead,
Curses, not loud, but deep, mouth-honour, breath,
Which the poor heart would fain deny, but dare
      not.
Seyton!—

Enter SEYTON.

Sey. What is your gracious pleasure?
Macb.   What news more?
Sey. All is confirmed, my lord, which was re-
      ported.
Macb. I 'll fight till from my bones my flesh be
      hacked.
Give me my armour.
Sey.   'T is not needed yet.
Macb. I 'll put it on.
Send out more horses, skirr the country round;
Hang those that talk of fear. Give me mine ar-
      mour.—
How does your patient, doctor?
Doct.   Not so sick, my lord,
As she is troubled with thick-coming fancies
That keep her from her rest.
Macb.   Cure her of that:
Canst thou not minister to a mind diseased;
Pluck from the memory a rooted sorrow;
Raze out the written troubles of the brain;
And, with some sweet oblivious antidote,
Cleanse the stuffed bosom of that perilous stuff
Which weighs upon the heart?
Doct.   Therein the patient
Must minister to himself.
Macb. Throw physic to the dogs. I 'll none
      of it.—
Come, put mine armour on; give me my staff:
Seyton, send out.—Doctor, the thanes fly from
      me.—
Come, sir, despatch.— If thou couldst, doctor,
      cast
The water of my land, find her disease,
And purge it to a sound and pristine health,
I would applaud thee to the very echo,
That should applaud again.—Pull 't off, I say.—
What rhubarb, senna, or what purgative drug,
Would scour these English hence? Hearest thou
      of them?
Doct. Ay, my good lord; your royal prepara-
      tion
Makes us hear something.
Macb.   Bring it after me.—
I will not be afraid of death and bane,
Till Birnam forest come to Dunsinane. [*Exit.*

Doct. Were I from Dunsinane away and clear,
Profit again should hardly draw me here. [*Exit.*

SCENE IV.—*Country near* Dunsinane. *A Wood
      in view.*

Enter, with drums and colours, MALCOLM, Old
      SIWARD *and his* Son, MACDUFF, MENTETH,
      CATHNESS, ANGUS, LENOX, ROSSE, *and* Sol-
      diers, *marching.*

Mal. Cousins, I hope the days are near at
      hand
That chambers will be safe.
Ment.   We doubt it nothing.
Siw. What wood is this before us?
Ment.   The wood of Birnam.
Mal. Let every soldier hew him down a
      bough,
And bear 't before him: thereby shall we shadow
The numbers of our host, and make discovery
Err in report of us.
Sold.   It shall be done.
Siw. We learn no other but the confident
      tyrant
Keeps still in Dunsinane, and will endure
Our setting down before 't.
Mal.   'T is his main hope:
For where there is advantage to be given,
Both more and less have given him the revolt;
And none serve with him but constrainéd things,
Whose hearts are absent too.
Macd.   Let our just censures
Attend the true event, and put we on
Industrious soldiership.
Siw.   The time approaches
That will with due decision make us know
What we shall say we have, and what we owe.
Thoughts speculative their unsure hopes relate;
But certain issue strokes must arbitrate:
Towards which, advance the war.
                  [*Exeunt, marching.*

SCENE V.—Dunsinane. *Within the Castle.*

Enter, with drums and colours, MACBETH,
      SEYTON, *and* Soldiers.

Macb. Hang out our banners on the outward
      walls;
The cry is still, "They come." Our castle's
      strength
Will laugh a siege to scorn: here let them lie,
Till famine and the ague eat them up:

Were they not forced with those that should be
    ours,
We might have met them dareful, beard to beard,
And beat them backward home.   What is that
    noise?   [*A cry within, of women.*

  Sey. It is the cry of women, my good lord.

  Macb. I have almost forgot the taste of fears:
The time has been, my senses would have cooled
To hear a night-shriek; and my fell of hair
Would at a dismal treatise rouse, and stir
As life were in 't: I have supped full with hor-
    rors;
Direness, familiar to my slaughterous thoughts,
Cannot once start me.—Wherefore was that
    cry?

  Sey. The queen, my lord, is dead.

  Macb. She should have died hereafter;
There would have been a time for such a word.—
To-morrow, and to-morrow, and to-morrow,
Creeps in this petty pace from day to day,
To the last syllable of recorded time;
And all our yesterdays have lighted fools
The way to dusty death.   Out, out, brief candle!
Life 's but a walking shadow; a poor player,
That struts and frets his hour upon the stage,
And then is heard no more: it is a tale
Told by an idiot, full of sound and fury,
Signifying nothing.

Enter a Messenger.

Thou com'st to use thy tongue; thy story quickly.

  Mess. Gracious my lord,
I shall report that which I say I saw,
But know not how to do it.

  Macb.   Well, say, sir.

  Mess. As I did stand my watch upon the
    hill,
I looked toward Birnam, and anon, methought,
The wood began to move.

  Macb.   Liar and slave!

  Mess. Let me endure your wrath if 't be
    not so:
Within this three mile may you see it coming:
I say, a moving grove.

  Macb.   If thou speak'st false,
Upon the next tree shalt thou hang alive,
Till famine cling thee: if thy speech be sooth,
I care not if thou dost for me as much.—
I pull in resolution; and begin
To doubt the equivocation of the fiend
That lies like truth: "Fear not till Birnam
    wood
Do come to Dunsinane;" and now a wood
Comes toward Dunsinane.—Arm, arm, and
    out!—
If this which he avouches does appear,
There is nor flying hence nor tarrying here.

I 'gin to be a-weary of the sun,
And wish the estate o' the world were now
    undone.
Ring the alarum bell: Blow wind! come
    wrack!
At least we 'll die with harness on our back.
                    [*Exeunt.*

SCENE VI.—*The same.   A Plain before the
Castle.*

Enter, with drums and colours, MALCOLM, *Old
SIWARD,* MACDUFF, *&c. and their Army, with
boughs.*

  Mal. Now near enough; your leavy screens
    throw down,
And shew like those you are.—You, worthy
    uncle,
Shall, with my cousin, your right-noble son,
Lead our first battle: worthy Macduff, and we,
Shall take upon us what else remains to do,
According to our order.

  Siw.   Fare you well.
Do we but find the tyrant's power to-night,
Let us be beaten, if we cannot fight.

  Macd. Make all our trumpets speak; give them
    all breath,
Those clamorous harbingers of blood and death.
        [*Exeunt. Alarums continued.*

SCENE VII.—*The same.   Another part of the
Plain.*

Enter MACBETH.

  Macb. They have tied me to a stake; I can-
    not fly,
But, bear-like, I must fight the course.—What 's
    he
That was not born of woman?   Such a one
Am I to fear, or none.

Enter Young SIWARD.

  Yo. Siw. What is thy name?

  Macb.   Thou 'lt be afraid to hear it.

  Yo. Siw. No; though thou call'st thyself a
    hotter name
Than any is in hell.

  Macb.   My name 's Macbeth.

  Yo. Siw. The devil himself could not pro-
    nounce a title
More hateful to mine ear.

  Macb.   No, nor more fearful.

Yo. Siw. Thou liest, abhorréd tyrant; with
    my sword
I 'll prove the lie thou speak'st.
    [They fight, and Young SIWARD *is slain.*
Macb.   Thou wast born of woman.
But swords I smile at, weapons laugh to scorn,
Brandished by man that 's of a woman born.
                         [Exit.

    Alarums.   Enter MACDUFF.

Macd. That way the noise is.—Tyrant, shew
    thy face :
If thou beest slain, and with no stroke of mine,
My wife and children's ghosts will haunt me
    still.
I cannot strike at wretched kernes, whose arms
Are hired to bear their staves : either thou,
    Macbeth,
Or else my sword, with an unbattered edge,
I sheathe again undeeded. There thou shouldst
    be ;
By this great clatter, one of greatest note
Seems bruited.   Let me find him, Fortune !
And more I beg not.   *[Exit. Alarum.*

    Enter MALCOLM *and* Old SIWARD.

Siw. This way, my lord.   The castle 's gently
    rendered :
The tyrant's people on both sides do fight ;
The noble thanes do bravely in the war ;
The day almost itself professes yours,
And little is to do.
  Mal.   We have met with foes
That strike beside us.
  Siw.   Enter, sir, the castle.
                 [Exeunt. Alarums.

    Re-enter MACBETH.

Macb. Why should I play the Roman fool,
    and die
On mine own sword? Whiles I see lives, the
    gashes
Do better upon them.

    Re-enter MACDUFF.

Macd.   Turn, hell-hound, turn.
  Macb. Of all men else I have avoided thee :
But get thee back, my soul is too much charged
With blood of thine already.
  Macd.   I have no words,
My voice is in my sword ; thou bloodier villain
Than terms can give thee out !   *[They fight.*
  Macb.   Thou losest labour :
As easy mayst thou the intrenchant air
With thy keen sword impress, as make me
    bleed :
Let fall thy blade on vulnerable crests ;

I bear a charméd life, which must not yield
To one of woman born.
  Macd.   Despair thy charm ;
And let the angel whom thou still hast served,
Tell thee, Macduff was from his mother's womb
Untimely ripped.
  Macb. Accurséd be that tongue that tells me
    so,
For it hath cowed my better part of man !
And be these juggling fiends no more believed
That palter with us in a double sense ;
That keep the word of promise to our ear,
And break it to our hope.—I 'll not fight with
    thee.
  Macd.   Then yield thee, coward,
And live to be the show and gaze o' the time.
We 'll have thee, as our rarer monsters are,
Painted upon a pole ; and underwrit,
" Here may you see the tyrant."
  Macb.   I 'll not yield,
To kiss the ground before young Malcolm's feet,
And to be baited with the rabble's curse.
Though Birnam wood be come to Dunsinane,
And thou opposed, being of no woman born,
Yet I will try the last.   Before my body
I throw my warlike shield : lay on, Macduff ;
And damned be him that first cries, " Hold,
    enough."   *[Exeunt, fighting.*

Retreat. Flourish. Re-enter, with drums and co-
lours, MALCOLM, Old SIWARD, ROSSE, LENOX,
ANGUS, CATHNESS, MENTETH, *and* Soldiers.

  Mal. I would the friends we miss were safe
    arrived.
  Siw. Some must go off : and yet, by these I see,
So great a day as this is cheaply bought.
  Mal. Macduff is missing, and your noble son.
  Rosse. Your son, my lord, has paid a soldier's
    debt :
He only lived but till he was a man ;
The which no sooner had his prowess confirmed
In the unshrinking station where he fought,
But like a man he died.
  Siw.   Then he is dead ?
  Rosse. Ay, and brought off the field : your cause
    of sorrow
Must not be measured by his worth, for then
It hath no end.
  Siw.   Had he his hurts before ?
  Rosse. Ay, on the front.
  Siw.   Why then, God's soldier be he !
Had I as many sons as I have hairs,
I would not wish them to a fairer death :
And so his knell is knolled.
  Mal.   He 's worth more sorrow,
And that I 'll spend for him.
  Siw.   He 's worth no more ;

They say, he parted well, and paid his score:
So God be with him!—Here comes newer comfort.

Re-enter MACDUFF, *with* MACBETH'S *head on a pole.*

Macd. Hail, king! for so thou art: behold,
where stands
The usurper's cursèd head: the time is free:
I see thee compassed with thy kingdom's pearl,
That speak my salutation in their minds;
Whose voices I desire aloud with mine,—
Hail, King of Scotland!

All. Hail, king of Scotland! [*Flourish.*

Mal. We shall not spend a large expense of
time
Before we reckon with your several loves,
And make us even with you. My thanes and
kinsmen,
Henceforth be earls, the first that ever Scotland
In such an honour named. What's more to do,
Which would be planted newly with the time,—
As calling home our exiled friends abroad,
That fled the snares of watchful tyranny;
Producing forth the cruel ministers
Of this dead butcher and his fiend-like queen
(Who, as 'tis thought, by self and violent hands
Took off her life);—this, and what needful else
That calls upon us, by the grace of Grace,
We will perform in measure, time, and place:
So thanks to all at once, and to each one,
Whom we invite to see us crowned at Scone.

[*Flourish. Exeunt.*

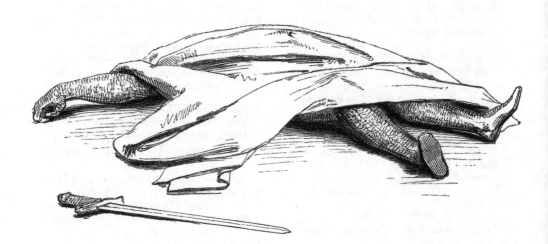

NOTES.

"When the hurlyburly's done."—Act I., Scene 1.

Peacham, in his "GARDEN OF ELOQUENCE," elevates the now vulgar phrase "hurlyburly" into one of the ornaments of language:—"Onomatopeia: when we invent, devise, feign, and make a name intimating the sound of that it signifieth; as hurlyburly, for an uproar and tumultuous stir."

"1st WITCH. I come, Graymalkin.
ALL. Paddock calls."—Act I., Scene 1.

Here, it is probable, we should suppose one familiar calling with the voice of a cat, and another with the croaking of a toad.

"Of kernes and gallowglasses is supplied."—Act I., Scene 2.

Barnaby Riche, in his "NEW IRISH PROGNOSTICATION," describes the troops here mentioned:—"The galloglas succeedeth the horseman, and he is commonly armed with a scull, a shirt of mail, and a galloglas axe." The kernes, he denounces as "the very dross and scum of the country; a generation of villains not fit to live."

"Till he disbursèd, at St. Colmés' inch."—Act I., Scene 2.

Colmes' inch, now called Inchcomb, is a small island, lying in the frith of Edinburgh, with an abbey upon it, dedicated to St. Columb; called by Camden, Inch Colm, or the Isle of Columba. Inch, or inche, in the Irish and Erse languages, signifies an island. Holinshed thus relates the circumstance alluded to in the play:—"The Danes that escaped, and got once to their ships, obtained of Macbeth, for a great sum of gold, that such of their friends as were slain might be buried in St. Colmes' inch. In memory whereof, many old sepultures are yet in the said inch there to be seen, graven with the arms of the Danes."

The rebellion of Macdonwald, and the invasion by Sweno, were not, in reality, contemporaneous events. The facts are these:—During the reign of Duncan, Banquo having been plundered, by the people of Lochaber, of some of the king's revenue, and being dangerously wounded in the affray, the parties concerned in the outrage were summoned to appear at a certain day. This led to the formidable rebellion headed by Macdonwald, which was finally suppressed by Macbeth and Banquo. It was at a subsequent period, in the last year of Duncan's reign, that Sweno, King of Norway, invaded Scotland. Duncan's successful generals were again employed. Sweno won the first battle, but was routed in the second with great slaughter, and escaped to Norway with very few followers.—Shakspere has effectively woven these two incidents together; and immediately after the defeat of Sweno, the action of the play commences.

"But in a sieve I'll thither sail,
And, like a rat without a tail."—Act I., Scene 3.

In a book "declaring the damnable life of Doctor Fian," is the following passage:—"All they (the witches) together went to sea, each one in a riddle or sieve; and went in the same very substantially, with flagons of wine, making merry and drinking by the way, in the same riddles or sieves."

"It was imagined," says Steevens, "that, though a witch could assume the form of any animal she pleased, the tail would still be wanting. This deficiency has been thus accounted for: though the hands and feet might, by an easy change, be converted into the four paws of a beast, still there was no part about a woman which corresponded to the length of tail common to almost all our four-footed animals."

"I'll give thee a wind."—Act I., Scene 3.

This was making a present of what was usually sold. In "SUMMER'S LAST WILL AND TESTAMENT," we find:—

—— "In Ireland and in Denmark both,
Witches for gold will sell a man a wind,
Which, in the corner of a napkin wrapped,
Shall blow him safe unto what coast he will."

"Weary seven nights, nine times nine,
Shall he dwindle, peak, and pine."—Act I., Scene 3.

This mischief was supposed to be effected by means of a waxen figure, which represented the person who was to be consumed by slow degrees.

"The weird sisters, hand in hand."—Act I., Scene 3.

Weird signifies prophetic. Gawin Douglas, in his translation of "VIRGIL," renders the Parcæ (or Fates) by the term weird sisters.

—— *"What are these,*
So withered, and so wild in their attire?"—Act I., Scene 3.

The circumstances attending this encounter of Macbeth and Banquo with the Witches are minutely detailed by Holinshed. Shakspere has followed the stream of the colloquy, but greatly enriched it with poetic ornament.

"By Sinel's death, I know I am thane of Cawdor."
Act I., Scene 3.

Sinel, according to Holinshed, was the name of Macbeth's father.

"Or have we eaten of the insane root,
That takes the reason prisoner?"—Act I., Scene 3.

This alludes to the qualities anciently ascribed to hemlock. In Greene's "NEVER TOO LATE," 1616, we have "You gazed against the sun, and so blemished your sight; or else you have eaten of the roots of hemlock, that makes men's eyes conceit unseen objects."

—— *"Function*
Is smothered in surmise; and nothing is,
But what is not."—Act I., Scene 3.

Dr. Johnson has thus explained this obscure passage:— "All powers of action are opposed and crushed by one overwhelming image in the mind, and nothing is present to me but that which is really future."

"We will establish our estate upon
Our eldest, Malcolm; whom we name hereafter,
The Prince of Cumberland."—Act I., Scene 4.

Cumberland was, at the time in question, held by Scotland of the crown of England, as a fief. Prince of Cumberland was the title borne by the declared successor to the throne of Scotland. A short extract from Holinshed will explain the nature of Macbeth's uneasiness on this occasion:—" Duncan having two sons, he made the elder of them (called Malcolm) Prince of Cumberland, as it was thereby to appoint him his successor in his kingdom, immediately after his decease. Macbeth, sorely troubled therewith, for that he saw by this means his hope sore hindered (where, by the old laws of the realm, the ordinance was, that if he that should succeed was not able of age to take the charge upon himself, he that was next of blood unto him should be admitted), he began to take counsel how he might usurp the kingdom by force, having a just quarrel so to do (as he took the matter), for that Duncan did what in him lay to defraud him of all manner of title and claim which he might, in time to come, pretend to the crown."

" This castle hath a pleasant seat ;" &c.—Act I., Scene 6.

Sir Joshua Reynolds has written a few remarks on this beautiful passage, which exhibit true poetic feeling. " This short dialogue," says he, " between Duncan and Banquo, as they approach Macbeth's castle, has always appeared to me a striking instance of what in painting is termed *repose*. Their conversation naturally turns upon the beauty of its situation, and the pleasantness of the air; and Banquo, observing the martlets' nests in every recess of the cornice, remarks that, where these birds most breed and haunt, the air is delicate. The subject of this quiet and easy conversation gives that repose so necessary to the mind after the tumultuous bustle of the preceding scenes, and perfectly contrasts the scene of horror that immediately succeeds. It seems as if Shakspere asked himself, ' What is a prince likely to say to his attendants on such an occasion ?' Whereas the modern writers seem, on the contrary, to be always searching for new thoughts, such as would never occur to men in the situation represented. This also is frequently the practice of Homer, who, from the midst of battles and horrors, relieves and refreshes the mind of the reader, by introducing some quiet rural image, or picture of familiar domestic life."

In his "JOURNEY TO THE WESTERN ISLANDS," Dr. Johnson says (speaking of Inverness), " Here is a castle called the Castle of Macbeth, the walls of which are yet standing. It was no very capacious edifice, but stands upon a rock so high and steep, that I think it was once not accessible, but by the help of ladders or a bridge."

———

" Court within the Castle.—Enter BANQUO & FLEANCE," &c.
Act II., Scene 1.

A graphic description of the supposed locality of this scene is given by Capell:—" A large court, surrounded all or in part by an open gallery; the gallery ascended into by stairs, open likewise; with addition of a college-like gateway, into which opens a porter's lodge—appears to have been the poet's idea of the place of this great action. The circumstances that mark it are scattered through three scenes: in the latter, the *hall* (which moderns make the scene of this action) is appointed a place of second assembly, in terms that shew it plainly distinct from that assembled in then. Buildings of this description rose in ages of chivalry, when knights rode into their courts, and paid their devoirs to ladies, viewing of their tiltings and them from this open gallery. Fragments of some of them, over the mansions of noblemen, are still subsisting in London, changed to hotels or inns. Shakspere might see them much more entire, and take his notion from them."

———" Merciful powers !
Restrain in me the cursèd thoughts that nature
Gives way to in repose."—Act II., Scene 1.

" It is apparent," says Steevens, " from what Banquo says afterwards, that he had been solicited in a dream to do something in consequence of the prophecy of the Witches, that his waking senses were shocked at; and Shakspere has finely contrasted his character with that of Macbeth. Ban-

quo is praying against being tempted to encourage thoughts of guilt, even in his sleep; while Macbeth is hurrying into temptation, and revolving in his mind every scheme, however flagitious, that may assist him to complete his purpose. The one is unwilling to sleep, lest the same phantoms should assail his resolution again; while the other is depriving himself of rest through impatience to commit the murder."

" I have drugged their possets."—Act II., Scene 2.

It was a general custom to eat possets just before bed time. Randle Holmes, in his " ACADEMY OF ARMORY," says, " Posset is hot milk poured on ale or sack, having sugar, grated biscuit, and eggs, with other ingredients, boiled in it, which goes all to a curd."

———" Had he not resembled
My father as he slept, I had done 't."
Act II., Scene 2.

This "one touch of nature" in Lady Macbeth, has called forth some able remarks from Warburton.—"This," says he, "is very artful: for, as the poet has drawn the lady and her husband, it would be thought the act should have been done by her. It is likewise highly just: for though ambition had subdued in her all the sentiments of nature towards present objects, yet the likeness of one past, which she had always been accustomed to regard with reverence, made her unnatural passions for a moment give way to the sentiments of instinct and humanity."

" To know my deed, 'twere best not know myself."—
Act II., Scene 2.

While I have the thought or recollection of this deed, I were better lost to myself; had better not have the consciousness of who I am.

" Enter a Porter."—Act II., Scene 3.

In justification of Shakspere for introducing this comical Porter at such a moment, Steevens remarks, " that a glimpse of comedy was expected by our author's audience in the most serious drama; and where else could that merriment be so happily introduced?"

———" Here lay Duncan,
His silver skin laced with his golden blood."
Act II., Scene 3.

It is not improbable that Shakspere put these forced and unnatural metaphors into the mouth of Macbeth, as a mark of artifice and dissimulation, to shew the difference between the studied language of hypocrisy and the natural outcries of sudden passion. "This whole speech," observes Dr. Johnson, "so considered, is a remarkable instance of judgment, as it consists entirely of antithesis and metaphor."

" ROSSE. Where is Duncan's body ?.
MACD. Carried to Colm-kill;
The sacred storehouse of his predecessors."
Act II., Scene 4.

This place (now called Icolm-kill) is the famous Iona, one of the Western Isles described by Dr. Johnson. Kill, in Erse, signifies a cell or chapel.

———

" Rather than so, come fate into the list,
And champion me to the utterance."
Act III., Scene 1.

The word utterance is of French origin: *à l'outrance* was a term in the law of arms, used when the combatants engaged with an *odium internecinum*, an intention to destroy each other. The sense of the passage probably is:—Let fate, that has foredoomed the exaltation of the posterity of Banquo, enter the lists against me with the utmost animosity in defence of its own decrees, which I will endeavour to invalidate, whatever be the danger.

"FLEANCE *and* Servant *escape.*"

Act III., Scene 3.

Fleance, after the assassination of his father, fled to Wales, where, by the daughter of the prince of that country, he had a son named Walter, who became Lord Steward of Scotland, and thence assumed the name of Walter Steward (or Stuart). From him, in a direct line, descended James the First of England: in compliment to whom, Shakspere has chosen to describe Banquo, who was equally concerned with Macbeth in the murder of Duncan, as innocent of that crime.

"'T *is better thee without, than he within.*"

Act III., Scene 4.

The proper reading would probably be "*him* within."—That is, I am better pleased that Banquo's blood should be on thy face than in his body. Or we may follow the present reading, by supposing the latter part of the sentence to signify "than he in this room."

——" *The feast is sold*
That is not often vouched: while 't is a making,
'T *is given with welcome.*"—Act III., Scene 4.

The meaning is, that which is not given freely and cheerfully, cannot properly be called a gift. It is like something which we are expected to pay for.

——" O, *these flaws and starts*
(*Impostors to true fear*)."—Act III., Scene 4.

The phrase "impostors to true fear," has been a source of great embarrassment to the commentators. We conceive that the word "to," must be understood in the sense of "compared to," a species of ellipsis of which many instances might be adduced from Shakspere. In the "TWO GENTLE-MEN OF VERONA," for instance, it is said of Love (act ii., scene 4), "there is no woe to his correction;" that is, compared to his correction. Lady Macbeth's meaning probably is, "True fear, the fear arising from real danger, is a rational thing; but your fears, originating solely in your own fancies, are mere impostors," and

——"Would well become
A woman's story, at a winter's fire,
Authorised by her grandam."

The same contempt of supernatural fears is expressed by this hardy woman, in the scene of the murder:—

——" The sleeping and the dead
Are but as pictures : 't is the eye of childhood
That fears a painted devil."

——" *You make me strange*
Even to the disposition that I owe."

Act III., Scene 4.

You prove to me that I am a stranger even to my own disposition, when I perceive that the very object which steals the colour from my cheek, permits it to remain in yours.

"*Augurs, and understood relations.*"—Act III., Scene 4.

By the word "relations," says Johnson, "is understood the connexion of effects with causes. To understand relations, as an augur, is to know how those things relate to each other which have no visible combination or dependence."—The word "augurs" in the text, must (according to the suggestion of Mr. Singer), be understood in the sense of "auguries."

" *How say'st thou, that Macduff denies his person,*
At our great bidding ?"—Act III., Scene 4.

"How say'st thou?" signifies here, what do you say to the circumstance? As in the "TWO GENTLEMEN OF VERONA," (act ii., scene 5): "How say'st thou, that my master is become a notable lover?"

"*Enter* HECATE, *meeting the three* Witches.*"

Act III., Scene 5.

Scott, in his "DISCOVERY OF WITCHCRAFT," mentions it as a common opinion that witches were supposed to have "nightly meetings with Herodias and the pagan gods;" and that "in the night-time they did ride abroad with Diana, goddess of the pagans." The word "Hecate," as a dissyllable, was introduced by Marlowe, in his "DOCTOR FAUSTUS."

"*And at the pit of Acheron*
Meet me i' the morning."—Act III., Scene 5.

"Shakspere," says Steevens, "seems to have thought it allowable to give the name of Acheron to any fountain, lake, or pit, through which there was vulgarly supposed to be any communication between this and the infernal world. The true original Acheron, was a river in Greece; and yet Virgil gives this name to his lake in the valley of Amsanctus, in Italy."

" *Upon the corner of the moon*
There hangs a vaporous drop profound."

Act III., Scene 5.

This "vaporous drop," seems to be of kin to the *virus lunare* of the ancients, being a foam which the moon was supposed to shed on particular herbs or other objects, when strongly solicited by enchantments. "Profound," signifies having deep or secret qualities.

"*A dark Cave. In the middle, a Cauldron boiling. Thunder.*
" *Enter the three* Witches."—Act IV., Scene 1.

Various commentators have remarked on the judgment shewn by Shakspere in detailing the infernal ceremonies of this scene. A cat was the usual interlocutor between witches and familiar spirits. A witch, who was tried about fifty years before the poet's time, was said to have had a cat named Rutterkin; and when any mischief was to be done, she would bid Rutterkin "go and fly." The common afflictions attributed to the malice of witches, were melancholy, fits, and loss of flesh. They were supposed to be very malicious to swine; one of Shakspere's hags says she has been killing swine; and Dr. Harsnet observes that, in his time, "a sow could not be ill of the measles, nor a girl of the sullens, but some old woman was charged with witchcraft." Toads have long been reproached as the abettors of witchcraft. When Vannius was seized at Toulouse, there was found in his lodgings "a great toad, shut in a phial;" upon which, those that persecuted him denounced him as a wizard. The ingredients of Shakspere's cauldron are selected according to the formularies prescribed in books of magic. Witches were supposed to take up bodies to use in enchantments. A passage from Camden explains and justifies our author in some other particulars:—" When any one gets a fall, he stands up, and turning three times to the right, digs a hole in the earth (for they imagine that there is a spirit in the ground); and if he falls sick in two or three days, they send one of their women that is skilled in that way, to the place, where she says, 'I call thee from the east, west, north, and south; from the groves, the woods, the rivers, and the fens; from the fairies, red, black, and white.'"

" *Nose of Turk, and Tartar's lips.*"—Act IV., Scene 1.

These ingredients probably owed their introduction to the detestation in which the Saracens were held, on account of the Crusades.

" *Black spirits and white,*" &c.—Act IV., Scene 1.

The right of these four metrical lines to a place in the text is certainly equivocal. Steevens introduced them from Middleton's "WITCH," on the authority of the stage direction in the first folio, which stands thus :—" *Music and a Song.*

Black Spirits, &c." Malone, however, strongly contends that "THE WITCH" was written subsequently to "MACBETH." The lines themselves have been supposed, with great probability, to be merely of a traditional nature, the production of neither Middleton nor Shakspere.

"An apparition of an armed Head rises."—Act IV., Scene 1.

It has been suggested by Mr. Upton, that the armed head represents, symbolically, Macbeth's head cut off, and brought to Malcolm by Macduff. The bloody child is Macduff, untimely ripped from his mother's womb. The child with a crown on his head, and a bough in his hand, is the royal Malcolm, who ordered his soldiers to hew down each a bough, and bear it before them to Dunsinane.

" And wears upon his baby brow the round
And top of sovereignty."—Act IV., Scene 1.

The round is that part of the crown which encircles the head; the top is the ornament that rises above it.

" And yet the eighth appears, who bears a glass
Which shews me many more; and some I see
That twofold balls and treble sceptres carry."
Act IV., Scene 1.

Magicians professed to have the power of shewing future events by means of a charmed glass, or mirror. In an extract from the penal laws against witches, it is said, "They do answer either by voice, or else do set before their eyes, in glasses, crystal-stones, &c., the pictures or images of persons or things sought for." Spenser has given a circumstantial account of the glass which Merlin made for King Ryence. A mirror of the same kind was presented to Cambuscan, in "THE SQUIRE'S TALE" of Chaucer; and in Alday's translation of Boisteau's "THEATRUM MUNDI," it is said, "A certain philosopher did the like to Pompey, the which shewed him in a glass the order of his enemies' march." The allusion, in the above extract, to the "twofold balls and treble sceptres" is a compliment to James the First, who first united the two islands and three kingdoms under one head.

———" Strangely-visited people,
All swoln and ulcerous, pitiful to the eye,
The mere despair of surgery, he cures;
Hanging a golden stamp about their necks," &c.
Act IV., Scene 3.

This miraculous power of curing the "king's evil," was claimed for seven centuries by the monarchs of England. In Laneham's account of the Entertainments of Kenilworth, given to Queen Elizabeth, it is said:—"And also, by her highness' accustomed mercy and charity, nine cured of the painful and dangerous disease called the king's evil; for that kings and queens of this realm, without other medicine (save only by handling and prayer), only do it." The practice was continued so late as Queen Anne's time; Dr. Johnson, when an infant, was touched for the evil by that princess.

The golden stamp, alluded to in the text, was the coin called an angel, value ten shillings.

" He has no children."—Act IV., Scene 3.

This is not said of Macbeth, who had children, but of Malcolm, who, having none, supposes a father can be so easily comforted.

" Hell is murky."—Act V., Scene 1.

In this great scene, Lady Macbeth is acting over again the circumstances attending the murder of Duncan. Steevens conceives her to be here addressing Macbeth, who, she supposes, has just said "Hell is murky!" (hell is a dismal place to go to in consequence of such a deed); she repeats his words in contempt:—"'Hell is murky!'—Fie, my lord, fie! a soldier, and afeard?"

" What we shall say we have, and what we owe."
Act V., Scene 4.

Meaning, when we are governed by legal kings, we shall know the limits of their claim; shall know what we have of our own, and what they have a right to take from us.

" She should have died hereafter;
There would have been a time for such a word."
Act V., Scene 5.

"Macbeth may mean," says Johnson, "that there would have been a more convenient time for such a word—for such intelligence—and so falls into the following reflection :—'To-morrow,'" &c.

" To the last syllable of recorded time."—Act V., Scene 5.

Recorded time seems to signify the time fixed in the decrees of heaven, for the period of life. The phrase may, however, be used in the sense of recording or recordable time.

" I bear a charméd life."—Act V., Scene 7.

"In the days of chivalry," says Steevens, "the champions' arms being ceremoniously blessed, each took an oath that he used no charmed weapons. Macbeth, according to the law of arms, or perhaps only in allusion to this custom, tells Macduff of the security he had in the prediction of the spirit."

" Had I as many sons as I have hairs,
I would not wish them to a fairer death :
And so his knell is knolled."—Act V., Scene 7.

This incident is thus related from Henry of Huntingdon, by Camden, in his "REMAINS:"—"When Siward, the martial Earl of Northumberland, understood that his son, whom he had sent in service against the Scotchmen, was slain, he demanded whether his wounds were in the fore part or hinder part of his body. When it was answered, in the fore part, he replied, 'I am right glad; neither wish I any other death to me or mine.'"

———" My thanes and kinsmen,
Henceforth be earls."—Act V., Scene 7.

Holinshed says, that "Malcolm, immediately after his coronation, called a parliament at Forfar, in which he rewarded them with lands and livings that had assisted him against Macbeth. Many of them, that before were thanes, were at this time made earls; as Fife, Menteth, Atholl, Lenox, Murray, Cathness, Rosse, and Angus."

TROILUS
AND
CRESSIDA

INTRODUCTORY REMARKS

DARING in its conscious strength, the genius of Shakspere turned aside from no encounter, however difficult or unpromising, that held out the most distant chance of conquest in the vast domain of human nature. In "TROILUS AND CRESSIDA" he has made a bold irruption into classic ground; and although the play does not rank among his greatest productions, he has yet shewn surprising art in rescuing the heroes and beauteous dames of Greece and Troy from the "cold obstruction" of antiquity, and placing them freshly before us as living, breathing beings, of a common nature with ourselves.

The wantonness of Cressida is from the first insinuated with consummate art, but with growing distinctness, till we are fully prepared to recognise the truth, as well as force, of the portrait of her presented by the sagacious Ulysses:—

> " Fie, fie upon her!
> There's language in her eye, her cheek, her lip;
> Nay, her foot speaks: her wanton spirits look out
> At every joint and motive of her body."

Ulysses himself is delineated with great felicity. He exhibits those manifold phases of character which afford the fairest opportunity for the manifestation of dramatic skill. He plays upon Achilles and Ajax with varied and admirable cunning; yet his craftiness is not exerted to obtain advantages peculiar to himself: his object is to make their thews and sinews subservient to the great undertaking in which his country was engaged, and which only such a head as his could have brought to so prosperous a conclusion.

The magnanimous Hector—the pleasure-tuned, good-humoured Paris—his fitting counterpart, Helen—Æneas, Agamemnon, Diomed, Nestor—indeed, all the multifarious characters who crowd the scene without encumbering it—are sketched in with every indication of vitality. We feel them to be instinct with life, and familiarly greet them on their resuscitation after a trance of so many centuries, as though all that passes were a matter of course, and they, like ourselves, were things of yesterday.

The weak good-nature of Pandarus stands in excellent contrast with the splenetic "cob-loaf," the "crusty batch of nature," Thersites; whose misanthropy, however, may claim the same palliation as Richard's—that "love foreswore him in his mother's womb." His wit, humour, and penetration make him agreeable even to those who suffer most from his sarcasm. Achilles calls him his "cheese," his "digestion;" and Ajax, although the constant object of his open and unmitigated contempt, is angry with Achilles for having inveigled him away. In these cases, we recognise the power of even misapplied intellect, forcing its way through every obstacle, and winning the regard of duller spirits, who are content to endure its scorching qualities, for the sake of sharing in the general light and brilliancy that accompany them.

"TROILUS AND CRESSIDA" was first printed in quarto (1609). There are strong grounds for believing that there was an older play on the same subject; but to what extent, or whether at all, Shakspere availed himself of it as a foundation for his own, can now be matter of conjecture only. The main incidents of the present drama were probably derived from Chaucer's tale of "TROILUS AND CRESEIDE," and the popular works of Lydgate and Caxton on the destruction of Troy.

J. O.

PERSONS REPRESENTED.

PRIAM, King of Troy.

HECTOR,
TROILUS,
PARIS, } his Sons.
DEIPHOBUS,
HELENUS,

ÆNEAS, } Trojan Commanders.
ANTENOR,

CALCHAS, a Trojan Priest, taking part with the Greeks.
PANDARUS, Uncle to CRESSIDA.
MARGARELON, a bastard Son of PRIAM.
AGAMEMNON, the Grecian General.
MENELAUS, his Brother.

ACHILLES,
AJAX,
ULYSSES, } Grecian Commanders.
NESTOR,
DIOMEDES,
PATROCLUS,

THERSITES, a deformed and scurrilous Grecian.
ALEXANDER, Servant to CRESSIDA.
Servant to TROILUS.
Servant to PARIS.
Servant to DIOMEDES.

HELEN, Wife to MENELAUS.
ANDROMACHE, Wife to HECTOR.
CASSANDRA, Daughter to PRIAM, a Prophetess.
CRESSIDA, Daughter to CALCHAS.

Trojan and Greek Soldiers, and Attendants.

SCENE. Troy, and the Grecian Camp before it.

PROLOGUE

In Troy, there lies the scene. From isles of Greece
The princes orgulous, their high blood chafed,
Have to the port of Athens sent their ships,
Fraught with the ministers and instruments
Of cruel war: sixty and nine, that wore
Their crownets regal, from the Athenian bay
Put forth toward Phrygia: and their vow is made
To ransack Troy; within whose strong immures
The ravished Helen, Menelaus' queen,
With wanton Paris sleeps; and that's the quarrel.
To Tenedos they come;
And the deep-drawing barks do there disgorge
Their warlike fraughtage: now on Dardan plains
The fresh and yet unbruiséd Greeks do pitch
Their brave pavilions: Priam's six-gated city,
Dardan, and Tymbria, Ilias, Chetas, Trojan,
And Antenorides, with massy staples,
And corresponsive and fulfilling bolts,
Sperr up the sons of Troy.
Now expectation, tickling skittish spirits,
On one and other side, Trojan and Greek,
Sets all on hazard:—and hither am I come
A prologue armed,—but not in confidence
Of author's pen, or actor's voice; but suited
In like conditions as our argument,—
To tell you, fair beholders, that our play
Leaps o'er the vaunt and firstlings of those broils,
'Ginning in the middle; starting thence away
To what may be digested in a play.
Like, or find fault; do as your pleasures are;
Now good, or bad, 'tis but the chance of war.

SCENE I.—Troy. *Before* PRIAM'S *Palace.*

Enter TROILUS *armed, and* PANDARUS.

Tro. Call here my varlet, I 'll unarm again:
Why should I war without the walls of Troy,
That find such cruel battle here within?
Each Trojan that is master of his heart,
Let him to field; Troilus, alas! hath none.

Pan. Will this geer ne'er be mended?

Tro. The Greeks are strong, and skilful to their
    strength,
Fierce to their skill, and to their fierceness va-
    liant;
But I am weaker than a woman's tear,

Tamer than sleep, fonder than ignorance;
Less valiant than the virgin in the night,
And skill-less as unpractised infancy.

Pan. Well, I have told you enough of this:
for my part, I 'll not meddle nor make no further.
He that will have a cake out of the wheat, must
tarry the grinding.

Tro. Have I not tarried?

Pan. Aye, the grinding; but you must tarry
the bolting.

Tro. Have I not tarried.

Pan. Ay, the bolting; but you must tarry the
leavening.

Tro. Still have I tarried.

Pan. Ay, to the leavening: but here's yet in the word "hereafter," the kneading, the making of the cake, the heating of the oven, and the baking; nay, you must stay the cooling too, or you may chance to burn your lips.

Tro. Patience herself, what goddess e'er she be,

Doth lesser blench at sufferance than I do.

At Priam's royal table do I sit;

And when fair Cressid comes into my thoughts—

So, traitor! when she comes!—when is she thence?

Pan. Well, she looked yesternight fairer than ever I saw her look, or any woman else.

Tro. I was about to tell thee:—When my heart,

As wedgéd with a sigh, would rive in twain;

Lest Hector or my father should perceive me,

I have (as when the sun doth light a storm)

Buried this sigh in wrinkle of a smile:

But sorrow that is couched in seeming gladness,

Is like that mirth fate turns to sudden sadness.

Pan. An her hair were not somewhat darker than Helen's (well, go to), there were no more comparison between the women—but, for my part, she is my kinswoman; I would not, as they term it, praise her; but I would somebody had heard her talk yesterday as I did. I will not dispraise your sister Cassandra's wit; but—

Tro. O, Pandarus! I tell thee, Pandarus,—

When I do tell thee, there my hopes lie drowned,

Reply not in how many fathoms deep

They lie indrenched. I tell thee, I am mad

In Cressid's love: thou answer'st, "She is fair;"

Pour'st in the open ulcer of my heart

Her eyes, her hair, her cheeks, her gait, her voice;

Handlest in thy discourse, "Oh, that her hand,

In whose comparison all whites are ink,

Writing their own reproach; to whose soft seizure

The cygnet's down is harsh, and spirit of sense

Hard as the palm of ploughman!" This thou tell'st me,

As true thou tell'st me, when I say, "I love her;"

But saying thus, instead of oil and balm,

Thou lay'st in every gash that love hath given me,

The knife that made it.

Pan.   I speak no more than truth.

Tro. Thou dost not speak so much.

Pan. 'Faith, I'll not meddle in 't. Let her be as she is: if she be fair, 't is the better for her; an she be not, she has the mends in her own hands.

Tro. Good Pandarus! How now, Pandarus?

Pan. I have had my labour for my travel: ill-thought on of her, and ill-thought on of you: gone between and between, but small thanks for my labour.

Tro. What, art thou angry, Pandarus? what, with me?

Pan. Because she is kin to me, therefore she's not so fair as Helen: an she were not kin to me, she would be as fair on Friday as Helen is on Sunday. But what care I? I care not, an she were a blackamoor; 't is all one to me.

Tro. Say I, she is not fair?

Pan. I do not care whether you do or no. She's a fool to stay behind her father; let her to the Greeks; and so I'll tell her the next time I see her: for my part, I'll meddle nor make no more in the matter.

Tro. Pandarus,—

Pan. Not I.

Tro. Sweet Pandarus,—

Pan. Pray you, speak no more to me; I will leave all as I found it, and there an end.

[*Exit* PANDARUS. *An alarum.*

Tro. Peace, you ungracious clamours! peace, rude sounds!

Fools on both sides! Helen must needs be fair,

When with your blood you daily paint her thus.

I cannot fight upon this argument;

It is too starved a subject for my sword.

But Pandarus—O gods, how do you plague me!

I cannot come to Cressid but by Pandar;

And he's as tetchy to be wooed to woo,

As she is stubborn-chaste against all suit.

Tell me, Apollo, for thy Daphne's love,

What Cressid is, what Pandar, and what we?

Her bed is India; there she lies, a pearl:

Between our Ilium and where she resides,

Let it be called the wild and wandering flood;

Ourself, the merchant; and this sailing Pandar,

Our doubtful hope, our convoy, and our bark.

Alarum. Enter ÆNEAS.

Æne. How now, prince Troilus? wherefore not afield?

Tro. Because not there. This woman's answer sorts,

For womanish it is to be from thence.

What news, Æneas, from the field to-day?

Æne. That Paris is returnéd home, and hurt.

Tro. By whom, Æneas?

Æne.   Troilus, by Menelaus.

Tro. Let Paris bleed: 't is but a scar to scorn.

Paris is gored with Menelaus' horn. [*Alarum.*

Æne. Hark! what good sport is out of town to-day!

Tro. Better at home, if "would I might" were "may."—

But, to the sport abroad:—are you bound thither?

Æne. In all swift haste.

Tro. Come, go we then together. [*Exeunt.*

SCENE II.—*The same. A Street.*

Enter CRESSIDA *and* ALEXANDER.

Cres. Who were those went by?
Alex.　　Queen Hecuba and Helen.
Cres. And whither go they?

Alex.　　Up to the eastern tower,
Whose height commands as subject all the vale,
To see the battle.　Hector, whose patience
Is, as a virtue, fixed, to-day was moved:
He chid Andromache, and struck his armourer;
And, like as there were husbandry in war,

Before the sun rose he was harnessed light,
And to the field goes he; where every flower
Did, as a prophet, weep what it foresaw
In Hector's wrath.
　Cres.　　What was his cause of anger?
　Alex. The noise goes, this: There is among
　　the Greeks
A lord of Trojan blood, nephew to Hector;
They call him Ajax.
　Cres.　　Good; and what of him?

Alex. They say he is a very man *per se*,
And stands alone.
　Cres. So do all men; unless they are drunk,
sick, or have no legs.
　Alex. This man, lady, hath robbed many beasts
of their particular additions; he is as valiant as
the lion, churlish as the bear, slow as the elephant; a man into whom nature hath so crowded
humours, that his valour is crushed into folly, his
folly sauced with discretion: there is no man hath

a virtue that he hath not a glimpse of; nor any man an attaint but he carries some stain of it. He is melancholy without cause, and merry against the hair: he hath the joints of everything; but everything so out of joint, that he is a gouty Briareus, many hands and no use; or purblind Argus, all eyes and no sight.

Cres. But how should this man, that makes me smile, make Hector angry?

Alex. They say, he yesterday coped Hector in the battle, and struck him down; the disdain and shame whereof hath ever since kept Hector fasting and waking.

Enter PANDARUS.

Cres. Who comes here?

Alex. Madam, your uncle Pandarus.

Cres. Hector's a gallant man.

Alex. As may be in the world, lady.

Pan. What's that? what's that?

Cres. Good morrow, uncle Pandarus.

Pan. Good morrow, cousin Cressid: what do you talk of?—Good morrow, Alexander.—How do you, cousin? When were you at Ilium?

Cres. This morning, uncle.

Pan. What were you talking of, when I came? Was Hector armed, and gone, ere ye came to Ilium? Helen was not up, was she?

Cres. Hector was gone; but Helen was not up.

Pan. E'en so; Hector was stirring early.

Cres. That were we talking of, and of his anger.

Pan. Was he angry?

Cres. So he says here.

Pan. True, he was so; I know the cause, too; he'll lay about him to-day, I can tell them that: and there is Troilus will not come far behind him; let them take heed of Troilus; I can tell them that too.

Cres. What, is he angry too?

Pan. Who, Troilus? Troilus is the better man of the two.

Cres. O, Jupiter! there's no comparison.

Pan. What, not between Troilus and Hector? Do you know a man if you see him?

Cres. Ay; if ever I saw him before, and knew him.

Pan. Well, I say, Troilus is Troilus.

Cres. Then you say as I say; for I am sure he is not Hector.

Pan. No, nor Hector is not Troilus, in some degrees.

Cres. 'T is just to each of them; he is himself.

Pan. Himself? Alas, poor Troilus! I would he were,—

Cres. So he is.

Pan. —'Condition I had gone barefoot to India.

Cres. He is not Hector.

Pan. Himself? no, he's not himself. 'Would 'a were himself! Well, the gods are above; Time must friend or end: well, Troilus, well, I would my heart were in her body!—No, Hector is not a better man than Troilus.

Cres. Excuse me.

Pan. He is elder.

Cres. Pardon me, pardon me.

Pan. The other's not come to't; you shall tell me another tale when the other's come to't. Hector shall not have his wit this year.

Cres. He shall not need it, if he have his own.

Pan. Nor his qualities.

Cres. No matter.

Pan. Nor his beauty.

Cres. 'T would not become him; his own's better.

Pan. You have no judgment, niece: Helen herself swore the other day, that Troilus, for a brown favour (for so 't is, I must confess)—not brown neither.

Cres. No, but brown.

Pan. 'Faith, to say truth, brown and not brown.

Cres. To say the truth, true and not true.

Pan. She praised his complexion above Paris.

Cres. Why, Paris hath colour enough.

Pan. So he has.

Cres. Then Troilus should have too much: if she praised him above, his complexion is higher than his; he having colour enough, and the other higher, is too flaming a praise for a good complexion. I had as lief Helen's golden tongue had commended Troilus for a copper nose.

Pan. I swear to you, I think Helen loves him better than Paris.

Cres. Then she's a merry Greek, indeed.

Pan. Nay, I am sure she does. She came to him the other day into a compassed window,—and you know he has not past three or four hairs on his chin.

Cres. Indeed a tapster's arithmetic may soon bring his particulars therein to a total.

Pan. Why, he is very young: and yet will he, within three pound, lift as much as his brother Hector.

Cres. Is he so young a man, and so old a lifter?

Pan. But, to prove to you that Helen loves him;—she came, and puts me her white hand to his cloven chin,—

Cres. Juno have mercy! How came it cloven?

Pan. Why, you know 't is dimpled: I think his smiling becomes him better than any man in all Phrygia.

Cres. Oh, he smiles valiantly!

Pan. Does he not?

Cres. O, yes! an 't were a cloud in autumn.

Pan. Why, go to, then. But to prove to you that Helen loves Troilus,—

Cres. Troilus will stand to the proof, if you'll prove it so.

Pan. Troilus? Why, he esteems her no more than I esteem an addle egg.

Cres. If you love an addle egg as well as you love an idle head, you would eat chickens i' the shell.

Pan. I cannot choose but laugh to think how she tickled his chin. Indeed, she has a marvellous white hand, I must needs confess.

Cres. Without the rack.

Pan. And she takes upon her to spy a white hair on his chin.

Cres. Alas, poor chin! many a wart is richer.

Pan. But there was such laughing! Queen Hecuba laughed that her eyes ran o'er.

Cres. With millstones.

Pan. And Cassandra laughed.

Cres. But there was a more temperate fire under the pot of her eyes? Did her eyes run o'er too?

Pan. And Hector laughed.

Cres. At what was all this laughing?

Pan. Marry, at the white hair that Helen spied on Troilus' chin.

Cres. An't had been a green hair, I should have laughed too.

Pan. They laughed not so much at the hair, as at his pretty answer.

Cres. What was his answer?

Pan. Quoth she, "Here's but one-and-fifty hairs on your chin, and one of them is white."

Cres. This is her question.

Pan. That's true; make no question of that. "One-and-fifty hairs," quoth he, "and one white: that white hair is my father, and all the rest are his sons." "Jupiter!" quoth she, "which of these hairs is Paris my husband?" "The forked one," quoth he; "pluck it out, and give it him." But there was such laughing! and Helen so blushed, and Paris so chafed, and all the rest so laughed, that it passed.

Cres. So let it now; for it has been a great while going by.

Pan. Well, cousin, I told you a thing yesterday; think on't.

Cres. So I do.

Pan. I'll be sworn 'tis true; he will weep you an 't were a man born in April.

Cres. And I'll spring up in his tears an 't were a nettle against May.   [*A retreat sounded.*

Pan. Hark, they are coming from the field. Shall we stand up here, and see them, as they pass towards Ilium? Good niece, do; sweet niece Cressida.

Cres. At your pleasure.

Pan. Here, here, here's an excellent place; here we may see most bravely. I'll tell you them all by their names, as they pass by; but mark Troilus above the rest.

ÆNEAS *passes over the Stage.*

Cres. Speak not so loud.

Pan. That's Æneas: is not that a brave man? he's one of the flowers of Troy, I can tell you. But mark Troilus; you shall see anon.

Cres. Who's that?

ANTENOR *passes over.*

Pan. That's Antenor; he has a shrewd wit, I can tell you; and he's a man good enough: he's one o' the soundest judgments in Troy, whosoever, and a proper man of person. When comes Troilus? I'll shew you Troilus anon; if he see me, you shall see him nod at me.

Cres. Will he give you the nod?

Pan. You shall see.

Cres. If he do, the rich shall have more.

HECTOR *passes over.*

Pan. That's Hector; that, that; look you, that. There's a fellow! Go thy way, Hector! —There's a brave man, niece. O, brave Hector. Look how he looks! there's a countenance: is't not a brave man?

Cres. O, a brave man!

Pan. Is 'a not? It does a man's heart good— Look you what hacks are on his helmet! look you yonder, do you see? look you there! There's no jesting: there's laying on; take 't off who will, as they say: there be hacks!

Cres. Be those with swords?

PARIS *passes over.*

Pan. Swords? anything, he cares not: an' the devil come to him, it's all one: by God's lid, it does one's heart good—Yonder comes Paris, yonder comes Paris: look ye yonder, niece; is't not a gallant man, too, is't not?— Why, this is brave now. Who said he came hurt home to-day? he's not hurt: why, this will do Helen's heart good now. Ha! 'would I could see Troilus now! you shall see Troilus anon.

Cres. Who's that?

HELENUS *passes over.*

Pan. That's Helenus:—I marvel where Troilus is!—that's Helenus.—I think he went not forth to-day:—that's Helenus.

Cres. Can Helenus fight, uncle?

Pan. Helenus? no;—yes, he'll fight indifferent well:—I marvel where Troilus is! Hark;

do you not hear the people cry, Troilus?—
Helenus is a priest.

Cres. What sneaking fellow comes yonder?

   TROILUS *passes over.*

Pan. Where? yonder? that's Deiphobus: 'T is
Troilus! there's a man, niece!—Hem!—Brave
Troilus! the prince of chivalry.

Cres. Peace, for shame, peace!

Pan. Mark him; note him: O brave Troilus!
Look well upon him, niece; look you how his
sword is bloodied, and his helm more hacked
than Hector's! And how he looks, and how he
goes! O admirable youth! he ne'er saw three-
and-twenty. Go thy way, Troilus, go thy way;
had I a sister were a grace, or a daughter a
goddess, he should take his choice. O admirable
man!—Paris? Paris is dirt to him; and I warrant, Helen, to change, would give an eye to
boot.

   Forces pass over the Stage.

Cres. Here come more.

Pan. Asses, fools, dolts! chaff and bran, chaff
and bran! porridge after meat! I could live and
die i' the eyes of Troilus. Ne'er look, ne'er look;
the eagles are gone; crows and daws, crows and
daws! I had rather be such a man as Troilus,
than Agamemnon and all Greece.

Cres. There is among the Greeks, Achilles; a
better man than Troilus.

Pan. Achilles! a drayman, a porter, a very
camel.

Cres. Well, well.

Pan. Well, well!—Why, have you any discretion? have you any eyes? Do you know what
a man is? Is not birth, beauty, good shape, discourse, manhood, learning, gentleness, virtue,
youth, liberality, and such like, the spice and
salt that season a man?

Cres. Ay, a minced man; and then to be
baked with no date in the pie,—for then the
man's date is out.

Pan. You are such a woman! one knows not
at what ward you lie.

Cres. Upon my back, to defend my belly;
upon my wit, to defend my wiles; upon my
secrecy, to defend mine honesty; my mask, to
defend my beauty; and you, to defend all these:
and at all these wards I lie, at a thousand watches.

Pan. Say one of your watches.

Cres. Nay, I'll watch you for that; and that's
one of the chiefest of them too: if I cannot ward
what I would not have hit, I can watch you for
telling how I took the blow; unless it swell past
hiding, and then it is past watching.

Pan. You are such another!

   Enter TROILUS' Boy.

Boy. Sir, my lord would instantly speak with you.

Pan. Where?

Boy. At your own house; there he unarms him.

Pan. Good boy, tell him I come: [*Exit* Boy.
I doubt he be hurt.—Fare ye well, good niece.

Cres. Adieu, uncle.

Pan. I'll be with you, niece, by-and-by.

Cres. To bring, uncle,—

Pan. Ay, a token from Troilus.

Cres. By the same token, you are a bawd.
        [*Exit* PANDARUS.

Words, vows, griefs, tears, and love's full sacrifice,
He offers in another's enterprise:
But more in Troilus thousand fold I see
Than in the glass of Pandar's praise may be;
Yet hold I off. Women are angels, wooing:
Things won are done, joy's soul lies in the doing:
That she, beloved, knows nought, that knows not
  this,—
Men prize the thing ungained more than it is:
That she was never yet, that ever knew
Love got so sweet, as when desire did sue:
Therefore this maxim out of love I teach,—
Achievement is command; ungained, beseech:
Then, though my heart's content firm love doth
  bear,
Nothing of that shall from mine eyes appear.
        [*Exit.*

 SCENE III.—*The* Grecian *Camp.* Before
   AGAMEMNON'S *Tent.*

Trumpets. Enter AGAMEMNON, NESTOR,
 ULYSSES, MENELAUS, *and others.*

Agam. Princes,
What grief hath set the jaundice on your cheeks?
The ample proposition that hope makes
In all designs begun on earth below,
Fails in the promised largeness: checks and
  disasters
Grow in the veins of actions highest reared;
As knots, by the conflúx of meeting sap,
Infect the sound pine, and divert his grain
Tortive and errant from his course of growth.
Nor, princes, is it matter new to us,
That we come short of our suppose so far,
That, after seven years' siege, yet Troy walls
  stand;
Sith every action, that hath gone before,
Whereof we have record, trial did draw
Bias and thwart, not answering the aim,
And that unbodied figure of the thought
That gave 't surmiséd shape. Why then, you
  princes,
Do you with cheeks abashed behold our works;

And think them shames, which are, indeed,
    nought else
But the protractive trials of great Jove,
To find persistive constancy in men?
The fineness of which metal is not found
In fortune's love: for then, the bold and coward,
The wise and fool, the artist and unread,
The hard and soft, seem all affinned and kin:
But, in the wind and tempest of her frown,
Distinction, with a broad and powerful fan,
Puffing at all, winnows the light away;
And what hath mass, or matter, by itself
Lies, rich in virtue, and unmingled.

    Nes. With due observance of thy godlike seat,
Great Agamemnon, Nestor shall apply
Thy latest words.   In the reproof of chance
Lies the true proof of men: the sea being smooth,
How many shallow bauble boats dare sail
Upon her patient breast, making their way
With those of nobler bulk!
But let the ruffian Boreas once enrage
The gentle Thetis, and, anon, behold
The strong-ribbed bark through liquid mountains
    cut,
Bounding between the two moist elements,
Like Perseus' horse: where 's then the saucy boat,
Whose weak untimbered sides but even now
Co-rivalled greatness?—either to harbour fled,
Or made a toast for Neptune.   Even so
Doth valour's show, and valour's worth, divide,
In storms of fortune: for, in her ray and brightness,
The herd hath more annoyance by the brize
Than by the tiger: but when the splitting wind
Makes flexible the knees of knotted oaks,
And flies fled under shade, why then the thing
    of courage,
As roused with rage, with rage doth sympathise,
And with an accent tuned in self-same key,
Returns to chiding fortune.
    Ulys.   Agamemnon,—
Thou great commander, nerve and bone of Greece,
Heart of our numbers, soul and only spirit,
In whom the tempers and the minds of all
Should be shut up,—hear what Ulysses speaks.
Besides the applause and approbation
The which—most mighty for thy place and sway—
                       [*To* AGAMEMNON.
And thou most reverend for thy stretched-out life—
                          [*To* NESTOR.
I give to both your speeches—which were such
As Agamemnon and the hand of Greece
Should hold up high in brass; and such, again,
As venerable Nestor, hatched in silver,
Should with a bond of air (strong as the axletree
On which heaven rides) knit all the Greekish ears
To his experienced tongue;—yet let it please both—
Thou great—and wise—to hear Ulysses speak.

    Agam. Speak, Prince of Ithaca; and be 't of
    less expect
That matter needless, of importless burden,
Divide thy lips, than we are confident,
When rank Thersites opes his mastiff jaws,
We shall hear music, wit, and oracle.

    Ulys. Troy, yet upon his basis, had been down,
And the great Hector's sword had lacked a master,
But for these instances:—
The specialty of rule hath been neglected:
And, look, how many Grecian tents do stand
Hollow upon this plain, so many hollow factions.
When that the general is not like the hive,
To whom the foragers shall all repair,
What honey is expected? Degree being vizarded,
The unworthiest shews as fairly in the mask.
The heavens themselves, the planets, and this
    centre,
Observe degree, priority, and place,
Insisture, course, proportion, season, form,
Office, and custom, in all line of order:
And therefore is the glorious planet Sol
In noble eminence enthroned and sphered
Amidst the other; whose med'cinable eye
Corrects the ill aspécts of planets evil,
And posts, like the commandment of a king,
Sans check, to good and bad: but when the planets,
In evil mixture, to disorder wander,
What plagues, and what portents; what mutiny;
What raging of the sea; shaking of earth;
Commotion in the winds; frights, changes, horrors,
Divert and crack, rend and deracinate
The unity and married calm of states
Quite from their fixture! O, when degree is
    shaked,
Which is the ladder of all high designs,
The enterprise is sick! How could communities,
Degrees in schools, and brotherhoods in cities,
Peaceful commérce from dividable shores,
The primogenitive and due of birth,
Prerogative of age, crowns, sceptres, laurels,
But by degree, stand in authentic place?
Take but degree away, untune that string,
And hark, what discord follows! each thing meets
In mere oppugnancy:—The bounded waters
Should lift their bosoms higher than the shores,
And make a sop of all this solid globe:
Strength should be lord of imbecility,
And the rude son should strike his father dead:
Force should be right; or rather, right and wrong
(Between whose endless jar justice resides)
Should lose their names, and so should justice too.
Then everything includes itself in power,
Power into will, will into appetite;
And appetite, an universal wolf,
So doubly seconded with will and power,
Must make perforce an universal prey,

And last, eat up himself.   Great Agamemnon,
This chaos, when degree is suffocate,
Follows the choking.
And this neglection of degree it is
That by a pace goes backward, with a purpose
It hath to climb.   The general's disdained
By him one step below; he, by the next;
That next, by him beneath: so every step,
Exampled by the first pace that is sick
Of his superior, grows to an envious fever
Of pale and bloodless emulation:
And 't is this fever that keeps Troy on foot,
Not her own sinews.   To end a tale of length,
Troy in our weakness stands, not in her strength.
   Nes. Most wisely hath Ulysses here discovered
The fever whereof all our power is sick.
   Agam. The nature of the sickness found, Ulysses,
What is the remedy?
   Ulys. The great Achilles, whom opinion crowns
The sinew and the forehand of our host,
Having his ear full of his airy fame,
Grows dainty of his worth, and in his tent
Lies mocking our designs: with him, Patroclus,
Upon a lazy bed, the live-long day
Breaks scurril jests;
And with ridiculous and awkward action
(Which, slanderer! he imitation calls)
He pageants us.   Sometime, great Agamemnon,
Thy topless deputation he puts on;
And, like a strutting player,—whose conceit
Lies in his hamstring, and doth think it rich
To hear the wooden dialogue and sound
'Twixt his stretched footing and the scaffoldage,—
Such to-be-pitied and o'er-wrested seeming
He acts thy greatness in: and when he speaks,
'T is like a chime a-mending; with terms un-
      squared,
Which, from the tongue of roaring Typhon
      dropped,
Would seem hyperboles.   At this fusty stuff,
The large Achilles, on his pressed bed lolling,
From his deep chest laughs out a loud applause;
Cries, " Excellent! 't is Agamemnon just.
Now play me Nestor; hem, and stroke thy beard,
As he, being 'ddressed to some oration."
That 's done—as near as the extremest ends
Of parallels; as like as Vulcan and his wife:
Yet good Achilles still cries, " Excellent!
'T is Nestor right! Now play him me, Patroclus,
Arming to answer in a night alarm."
And then, forsooth, the faint defects of age
Must be the scene of mirth; to cough, and spit,
And with a palsy-fumbling on his gorget,
Shake in and out the rivet: and at this sport
Sir Valour dies; cries, "O, enough, Patroclus;
Or give me ribs of steel! I shall split all
In pleasure of my spleen."   And in this fashion,

All our abilities, gifts, natures, shapes,
Severals and generals of grace exact,
Achievements, plots, orders, preventions,
Excitements to the field, or speech for truce,
Success, or loss, what is, or is not, serves
As stuff for these two to make paradoxes.
   Nes. And in the imitation of these twain
(Whom, as Ulysses says, opinion crowns
With an imperial voice) many are infect.
Ajax is grown self-willed; and bears his head
In such a rein, in full as proud a place
As broad Achilles; keeps his tent like him;
Makes factious feasts; rails on our state of war,
Bold as an oracle: and sets Thersites
(A slave whose gall coins slanders like a mint)
To match us in comparisons with dirt;
To weaken and discredit our exposure,
How rank soever rounded in with danger.
   Ulys. They tax our policy, and call it cow-
      ardice;
Count wisdom as no member of the war;
Forestal prescience, and esteem no act
But that of hand: the still and mental parts,—
That do contrive how many hands shall strike,
When fitness calls them on; and know, by mea-
      sure
Of their observant toil, the enemies' weight,—
Why, this hath not a finger's dignity:
They call this—bed-work, mappery, closet-war;
So that the ram that batters down the wall,
For the great swing and rudeness of his poize,
They place before his hand that made the engine;
Or those that, with the fineness of their souls,
By reason guide his execution.
   Nest. Let this be granted, and Achilles' horse
Makes many Thetis' sons.   [*Trumpet sounds.*
   Agam. What trumpet? look, Menelaus.

       Enter ÆNEAS.

   Men. From Troy.
   Agam. What would you 'fore our tent?
   Æne. Is this great Agamemnon's tent, I pray?
   Agam. Even this.
   Æne. May one, that is a herald and a prince,
Do a fair message to his kingly ears?
   Agam. With surety stronger than Achilles' arm
'Fore all the Greekish heads, which with one voice
Call Agamemnon head and general.
   Æne. Fair leave, and large security. How may
A stranger to those most imperial looks
Know them from eyes of other mortals?
   Agam. How?
   Æne. Ay: I ask, that I might waken reve-
      rence,
And bid the cheek be ready with a blush,
Modest as morning when she coldly eyes
The youthful Phœbus:

Which is that god in office, guiding men?
Which is the high and mighty Agamemnon?

Agam. This Trojan scorns us; or the men of
     Troy
Are ceremonious courtiers.

Æne. Courtiers as free, as debonair, unarmed,
As bending angels; that's their fame in peace:
But when they would seem soldiers, they have
     galls,
Good arms, strong joints, true swords; and, Jove's
     accord,
Nothing so full of heart. But peace, Æneas,
Peace, Trojan; lay thy finger on thy lips!
The worthiness of praise distains his worth,
If that the praised himself bring the praise forth:
But what the repining enemy commends,
That breath fame follows; that praise, sole pure,
     transcends.

Agam. Sir, you of Troy, call you yourself
     Æneas?

Æne. Ay, Greek, that is my name.

Agam. What's your affair, I pray you?

Æne. Sir, pardon; 'tis for Agamemnon's ears.

Agam. He hears nought privately, that comes
     from Troy.

Æne. Nor I from Troy come not to whisper him:
I bring a trumpet to awake his ear;
To set his sense on the attentive bent,
And then to speak.

Agam.   Speak frankly as the wind;
It is not Agamemnon's sleeping hour:
That thou shalt know, Trojan, he is awake,
He tells thee so himself.

Æne.   Trumpet, blow loud,
Send thy brass voice through all these lazy tents;—
And every Greek of mettle let him know,
What Troy means fairly, shall be spoke aloud.

          [*Trumpet sounds.*

We have, great Agamemnon, here in Troy
A prince called Hector (Priam is his father),
Who in this dull and long-continued truce
Is rusty grown; he bade me take a trumpet,
And to this purpose speak:—Kings, princes, lords!
If there be one, among the fair'st of Greece,
That holds his honour higher than his ease;
That seeks his praise more than he fears his peril;
That knows his valour, and knows not his fear;
That loves his mistress more than in confession
(With truant vows to her own lips he loves),
And dare avow her beauty and her worth,
In other arms than hers,—to him this challenge:—
Hector, in view of Trojans and of Greeks,
Shall make it good, or do his best to do it,
He hath a lady, wiser, fairer, truer,
Than ever Greek did compass in his arms;
And will to-morrow with his trumpet call,
Midway between your tents and walls of Troy,

To rouse a Grecian that is true in love:
If any come, Hector shall honour him;
If none, he'll say in Troy, when he retires,
The Grecian dames are sunburned, and not worth
The splinter of a lance. Even so much.

Agam. This shall be told our lovers, lord
     Æneas;
If none of them have soul in such a kind,
We left them all at home: but we are soldiers;
And may that soldier a mere recreant prove,
That means not, hath not, or is not in love!
If then one is, or hath, or means to be,
That one meets Hector: if none else, I am he.

Nes. Tell him of Nestor, one that was a man
When Hector's grandsire sucked: he is old now;
But, if there be not in our Grecian host
One noble man, that hath one spark of fire
To answer for his love, tell him from me,
I'll hide my silver beard in a gold beaver,
And in my vantbrace put this withered brawn;
And, meeting him, will tell him that my lady
Was fairer than his grandame, and as chaste
As may be in the world. His youth in flood,
I'll prove this truth with my three drops of blood.

Æne. Now heavens forbid such scarcity of
     youth!

Ulys. Amen.

Agam. Fair lord Æneas, let me touch your
     hand;
To our pavilion shall I lead you, sir.
Achilles shall have word of this intent;
So shall each lord of Greece, from tent to tent:
Yourself shall feast with us before you go,
And find the welcome of a noble foe.

          [*Exeunt all but* ULYSSES *and* NESTOR.

Ulys. Nestor,—

Nes. What says Ulysses?

Ulys. I have a young conception in my brain,
Be you my time to bring it to some shape.

Nes. What is't?

Ulys. This 'tis:
Blunt wedges rive hard knots: the seeded pride,
That hath to this maturity blown up
In rank Achilles, must or now be cropped,
Or, shedding, breed a nursery of like evil,
To overbulk us all.

Nes. Well, and how?

Ulys. This challenge that the gallant Hector
     sends,
However it is spread in general name,
Relates in purpose only to Achilles.

Nes. The purpose is perspicuous even as sub-
     stance,
Whose grossness little characters sum up:
And, in the publication, make no strain
But that Achilles, were his brain as barren
As banks of Lybia,—though, Apollo knows,

'T is dry enough,—will, with great speed of
    judgment,—
Ay, with celerity,—find Hector's purpose
Pointing on him.

Ulys. And wake him to the answer, think you?

Nes. Yes, 't is most meet: whom may you else
    oppose,
That can from Hector bring those honours off,
If not Achilles? Though 't be a sportful combat,
Yet in the trial much opinion dwells;
For here the Trojans taste our dear'st repute
With their fin'st palate: and trust to me, Ulysses,
Our imputation shall be oddly poised
In this wild action: for the success,
Although particular, shall give a scantling
Of good or bad unto the general;
And in such indexes, although small pricks
To their subséquent volumes, there is seen
The baby figure of the giant mass
Of things to come at large. It is supposed,
He that meets Hector issues from our choice,
And choice, being mutual act of all our souls,
Makes merit her election; and doth boil,
As 't were from forth us all, a man distilled
Out of our virtues; who miscarrying,
What heart receives from hence a conquering part,
To steel a strong opinion to themselves?
Which entertained, limbs are his instruments,
In no less working than are swords and bows
Directive by the limbs.

Ulys. Give pardon to my speech:—
Therefore, 't is meet Achilles meet not Hector.
Let us, like merchants, shew our foulest wares,
And think, perchance, they 'll sell; if not,

The lustre of the better shall exceed,
By shewing the worse first. Do not consent
That ever Hector and Achilles meet;
For both our honour and our shame, in this,
Are dogged with two strange followers.

Nes. I see them not with my old eyes: what
    are they?

Ulys. What glory our Achilles shares from
    Hector,
Were he not proud, we all should share with him:
But he already is too insolent;
And we were better parch in Afric sun,
Than in the pride and salt scorn of his eyes,
Should he 'scape Hector fair: if he were foiled,
Why, then we did our main opinion crush
In taint of our best man. No, make a lottery;
And, by device, let blockish Ajax draw
The sort to fight with Hector: among ourselves,
Give him allowance for the better man,
For that will physic the great Myrmidon,
Who broils in loud applause; and make him fall
His crest, that prouder than blue Iris bends.
If the dull, brainless Ajax come safe off,
We 'll dress him up in voices: if he fail,
Yet go we under our opinion still,
That we have better men. But, hit or miss,
Our project's life this shape of sense assumes,—
Ajax, employed, plucks down Achilles' plumes.

Nes. Ulysses,
Now I begin to relish thy advice;
And I will give a taste of it forthwith
To Agamemnon: go we to him straight.
Two curs shall tame each other: pride alone
Must tarre the mastiffs on, as 't were their bone.
                      [Exeunt.

ACT II.

SCENE I.—*Another part of the* Grecian *Camp.*

Enter AJAX *and* THERSITES.

Ajax. Thersites,—

Ther. Agamemnon—how if he had boils? full, all over, generally?

Ajax. Thersites,—

Ther. And those boils did run? Say so,—did not the general run then? were not that a botchy core?

Ajax. Dog!—

Ther. Then would come some matter from him; I see none now.

Ajax. Thou bitch-wolf's son! canst thou not hear? Feel, then.   [*Strikes him.*

Ther. The plague of Greece upon thee, thou mongrel beef-witted lord!

Ajax. Speak, then, thou unsalted leaven! speak: I'll beat thee into handsomeness.

Ther. I shall sooner rail thee into wit and holiness: but I think thy horse will sooner con an oration, than thou learn a prayer without book. Thou canst strike, canst thou? a red murrain o' thy jade's tricks!

Ajax. Toadstool! learn me the proclamation.

Ther. Dost thou think I have no sense, thou strikest me thus?

Ajax. The proclamation,—

Ther. Thou art proclaimed a fool, I think.

Ajax. Do not, porcupine! do not; my fingers itch.

Ther. I would thou didst itch from head to foot, and I had the scratching of thee; I would make thee the loathsomest scab in Greece. When thou art forth in the incursions, thou strikest as slow as another.

Ajax. I say, the proclamation,—

Ther. Thou grumblest and railest every hour on Achilles; and thou art as full of envy at his greatness, as Cerberus is at Proserpina's beauty; ay, that thou bark'st at him.

Ajax. Mistress Thersites!

Ther. Thou shouldst strike him.

Ajax. Cob-loaf!

Ther. He would pun thee into shivers with his fist, as a sailor breaks a biscuit.

Ajax. You whoreson cur!   [*Beating him.*

Ther. Do, do.

Ajax. Thou stool for a witch!

Ther. Ay, do, do; thou sodden-witted lord! thou hast no more brain than I have in mine elbows; an assinego may tutor thee. Thou scurvy-valiant ass! thou art here put to thrash Trojans; and thou art bought and sold among those of any wit, like a Barbarian slave. If thou use to beat me, I will begin at thy heel, and tell what thou art by inches, thou thing of no bowels, thou!

Ajax. You dog!

Ther. You scurvy lord!

Ajax. You cur!   [*Beating him.*

Ther. Mars his idiot! Do, rudeness! do, camel! do, do.

Enter ACHILLES *and* PATROCLUS.

Achil. Why, how now, Ajax, wherefore do you thus?
How now, Thersites? what's the matter, man?

Ther. You see him there, do you?

Achil. Ay; what's the matter?

Ther. Nay, look upon him.

Achil. So I do; what's the matter?

Ther. Nay, but regard him well.

Achil. Well, why I do so.

Ther. But yet you look not well upon him: for, whosoever you take him to be, he is Ajax.

Achil. I know that, fool.

Ther. Ay, but that fool knows not himself.

Ajax. Therefore I beat thee.

Ther. Lo, lo, lo, lo, what modicums of wit he utters! His evasions have ears thus long. I have bobbed his brain more than he has beat my bones: I will buy nine sparrows for a penny, and his *pia mater* is not worth the ninth part of a sparrow. This lord, Achilles, Ajax,—who wears his wit in his belly, and his guts in his head,—I 'll tell you what I say of him.

Achil. What?

Ther. I say, this Ajax,—

Achil. Nay, good Ajax.

[Ajax *offers to strike him,—* Achilles *interposes.*]

Ther. Has not so much wit—

Achil. Nay, I must hold you.

Ther. As will stop the eye of Helen's needle, for whom he comes to fight.

Achil. Peace, fool!

Ther. I would have peace and quietness, but the fool will not: he there; that he; look you there.

Ajax. O thou damned cur! I shall—

Achil. Will you set your wit to a fool's?

Ther. No, I warrant you; for a fool's will shame it.

Patr. Good words, Thersites.

Achil. What's the quarrel?

Ajax. I bade the vile owl go learn me the tenour of the proclamation, and he rails upon me.

Ther. I serve thee not.

Ajax. Well, go to, go to.

Ther. I serve here voluntary.

Achil. Your last service was sufferance, 'twas not voluntary; no man is beaten voluntary: Ajax was here the voluntary, and you as under an impress.

Ther. Even so?—a great deal of your wit too lies in your sinews, or else there be liars. Hector shall have a great catch, if he knock out either of your brains; 'a were as good crack a fusty nut with no kernel.

Achil. What, with me too, Thersites?

Ther. There's Ulysses and old Nestor—whose wit was mouldy ere your grandsires had nails on their toes—yoke you like draught oxen, and make you plough up the wars.

Achil. What, what?

Ther. Yes, good sooth:—to, Achilles! to, Ajax! to!

Ajax. I shall cut out your tongue.

Ther. 'Tis no matter; I shall speak as much as thou, afterwards.

Patr. No more words, Thersites; peace.

Ther. I will hold my peace when Achilles' brach bids me, shall I?

Achil. There's for you, Patroclus.

Ther. I will see you hanged, like clotpoles, ere I come any more to your tents; I will keep where there is wit stirring, and leave the faction of fools. [*Exit.*

Patr. A good riddance,

Achil. Marry, this, sir, is proclaimed through all our host;

That Hector, by the first hour of the sun,
Will, with a trumpet, 'twixt our tents and Troy,
To-morrow morning call some knight to arms,
That hath a stomach; and such a one, that dare
Maintain—I know not what; 'tis trash. Farewell.

Ajax. Farewell. Who shall answer him?

Achil. I know not; it is put to lottery; otherwise He knew his man.

Ajax. O, meaning you:—I'll go learn more of it. [*Exeunt.*

SCENE II.—Troy. *A Room in* PRIAM'S *Palace.*

Enter PRIAM, HECTOR, TROILUS, PARIS, *and* HELENUS.

Pri. After so many hours, lives, speeches spent,
Thus once again says Nestor from the Greeks:
"Deliver Helen; and all damage else—
As honour, loss of time, travel, expense,
Wounds, friends, and what else dear that is consumed
In hot digestion of this cormorant war—
Shall be struck off:" Hector, what say you to 't?

Hect. Though no man lesser fears the Greeks than I,
As far as toucheth my particular, yet,
Dread Priam,
There is no lady of more softer bowels,
More spongy to suck in the sense of fear,
More ready to cry out "Who knows what follows?"
Than Hector is. The wound of peace is surety,
Surety secure; but modest doubt is called
The beacon of the wise, the tent that searches
To the bottom of the worst. Let Helen go:

Since the first sword was drawn about this question,
Every tithe soul, 'mongst many thousand dismes,
Hath been as dear as Helen; I mean, of ours:
If we have lost so many tenths of ours,
To guard a thing not ours; not worth to us,
Had it our name, the value of one ten;
What merit's in that reason which denies
The yielding of her up?

Tro. Fie, fie, my brother!
Weigh you the worth and honour of a king,
So great as our dread father, in a scale
Of common ounces? will you with counters sum
The past-proportion of his infinite?
And buckle-in a waist most fathomless,
With spans and inches so diminutive
As fears and reasons? fie, for godly shame!

Hel. No marvel though you bite so sharp at reasons,
You are so empty of them. Should not our father
Bear the great sway of his affairs with reasons,
Because your speech hath none, that tells him so?

Tro. You are for dreams and slumbers, brother priest;
You fur your gloves with reason. Here are your reasons:
You know, an enemy intends you harm;
You know, a sword employed is perilous,
And reason flies the object of all harm:
Who marvels then, when Helenus beholds
A Grecian and his sword, if he do set
The very wings of reason to his heels;
And fly like chidden Mercury from Jove,
Or like a star disorbed?—Nay, if we talk of reason,
Let's shut our gates, and sleep: Manhood and honour
Should have hare hearts, would they but fat their thoughts
With this crammed reason: reason and respect
Make livers pale, and lustihood deject.

Hect. Brother, she is not worth what she doth cost The holding.

Tro. What is aught, but as 'tis valued?

Hect. But value dwells not in particular will;
It holds its estimate and dignity
As well wherein 'tis precious of itself
As in the prizer: 'tis mad idolatry
To make the service greater than the god;
And the will dotes that is attributive
To what infectiously itself affects,
Without some image of the affected merit.

Tro. I take to-day a wife, and my election
Is led on in the conduct of my will;
My will enkindled by mine eyes and ears,
Two traded pilots 'twixt the dangerous shores
Of will and judgment: How may I avoid,
Although my will distaste what it elected,
The wife I chose? there can be no evasion

To blench from this, and to stand firm by honour:
We turn not back the silks upon the merchant,
When we have soiled them; nor the remainder viands
We do not throw in unrespective sieve,
Because we now are full.   It was thought meet,
Paris should do some vengeance on the Greeks:
Your breath with full consent bellied his sails;

The seas and winds (old wranglers) took a truce,
And did him service: he touched the ports desired;
And, for an old aunt, whom the Greeks held captive,
He brought a Grecian queen, whose youth and freshness
Wrinkles Apollo's, and makes pale the morning.
Why keep we her? the Grecians keep our aunt:
Is she worth keeping? why, she is a pearl

K.M.

Whose price hath launched above a thousand ships,
And turned crowned kings to merchants.
If you'll avouch 't was wisdom Paris went
(As you must needs, for you all cried—"Go, go"),
If you'll confess he brought home noble prize
(As you must needs, for you all clapped your hands
And cried " Inestimable!"), why do you now
The issue of your proper wisdoms rate;
And do a deed that fortune never did,
Beggar the estimation which you prized
Richer than sea and land? O, theft most base;
That we have stolen what we do fear to keep!

But, thieves, unworthy of a thing so stolen,
That in their country did them that disgrace,
We fear to warrant in our native place!
    Cas. [*within.*] Cry, Trojans, cry!
    Pri.   What noise? what shriek is this?
    Tro. 'Tis our mad sister; I do know her voice.
    Cas. [*within.*] Cry, Trojans!
    Hect. It is Cassandra.

           Enter CASSANDRA, *raving.*

    Cas. Cry, Trojans, cry! lend me ten thousand eyes,
And I will fill them with prophetic tears!

Hect. Peace, sister, peace.

Cas. Virgins and boys, mid-age and wrinkled
      elders,
Soft infancy, that nothing canst but cry,
Add to my clamours! let us pay betimes
A moiety of that mass of moan to come.
Cry, Trojans, cry! practise your eyes with tears!
Troy must not be, nor goodly Ilion stand;
Our firebrand brother, Paris, burns us all.
Cry, Trojans, cry! a Helen, and a woe:
Cry, cry! Troy burns, or else let Helen go. [*Exit.*

Hect. Now, youthful Troilus, do not these high
      strains
Of divination in our sister work
Some touches of remorse? or is your blood
So madly hot, that no discourse of reason,
Nor fear of bad success in a bad cause,
Can qualify the same?

Tro.   Why, brother Hector,
We may not think the justness of each act
Such and no other than event doth form it;
Nor once deject the courage of our minds,
Because Cassandra's mad: her brain-sick raptures
Cannot distaste the goodness of a quarrel
Which hath our several honours all engaged
To make it gracious. For my private part,
I am no more touched than all Priam's sons:
And Jove forbid there should be done amongst us
Such things as might offend the weakest spleen
To fight for and maintain!

Par. Else might the world convince of levity
As well my undertakings, as your counsels:
But I attest the gods, your full consent
Gave wings to my propension, and cut off
All fears attending on so dire a project.
For what, alas, can these my single arms?
What propugnation is in one man's valour,
To stand the push and enmity of those
This quarrel would excite? Yet, I protest,
Were I alone to pass the difficulties,
And had as ample power as I have will,
Paris should ne'er retract what he hath done,
Nor faint in the pursuit.

Pri.   Paris, you speak
Like one besotted on your sweet delights:
You have the honey still, but these the gall;
So to be valiant is no praise at all.

Par. Sir, I propose not merely to myself
The pleasures such a beauty brings with it;
But I would have the soil of her fair rape
Wiped off, in honourable keeping her.
What treason were it to the ransacked queen,
Disgrace to your great worths, and shame to me,
Now to deliver her possession up
On terms of base compulsion? Can it be,
That so degenerate a strain as this
Should once set footing in your generous bosoms?

There's not the meanest spirit on our party,
Without a heart to dare, or sword to draw,
When Helen is defended; nor none so noble,
Whose life were ill bestowed, or death unfamed,
Where Helen is the subject: then, I say,
Well may we fight for her, whom, we know well,
The world's large spaces cannot parallel.

Hect. Paris and Troilus, you have both said well;
And on the cause and question now in hand
Have glozed—but superficially; not much
Unlike young men, whom Aristotle thought
Unfit to hear moral philosophy:
The reasons you allege do more conduce
To the hot passion of distempered blood,
Than to make up a free determination
'Twixt right and wrong; for pleasure and revenge
Have ears more deaf than adders to the voice
Of any true decision. Nature craves,
All dues be rendered to their owners: now,
What nearer debt in all humanity,
Than wife is to the husband? If this law
Of nature be corrupted through affection;
And that great minds, of partial indulgence
To their benumbéd wills, resist the same;
There is a law in each well-ordered nation,
To curb those raging appetites that are
Most disobedient and refractory.
If Helen then be wife to Sparta's king
(As it is known she is), these moral laws
Of nature, and of nations, speak aloud
To have her back returned: thus to persist
In doing wrong, extenuates not wrong,
But makes it much more heavy. Hector's opinion
Is this, in way of truth: yet ne'ertheless,
My sprightly brethren, I propend to you
In resolution to keep Helen still;
For 'tis a cause that hath no mean dependence
Upon our joint and several dignities.

Tro. Why, there you touched the life of our
      design:
Were it not glory that we more affected
Than the performance of our heaving spleens,
I would not wish a drop of Trojan blood
Spent more in her defence. But, worthy Hector,
She is a theme of honour and renown;
A spur to valiant and magnanimous deeds;
Whose present courage may beat down our foes,
And fame, in time to come, canónise us:
For, I presume, brave Hector would not lose
So rich advantage of a promised glory
As smiles upon the forehead of this action,
For the wide world's revénue.

Hect.   I am yours,
You valiant offspring of great Priamus.—
I have a roisting challenge sent amongst
The dull and factious nobles of the Greeks,
Will strike amazement to their drowsy spirits:

I was advértised, their great general slept,
Whilst emulation in the army crept:
This, I presume, will wake him.　　　[*Exeunt.*

SCENE III.—*The* Grecian *Camp. Before*
ACHILLES' *Tent.*

Enter THERSITES.

Ther. How now, Thersites? what, lost in the
labyrinth of thy fury? Shall the elephant Ajax
carry it thus? he beats me, and I rail at him:
O, worthy satisfaction! 'would it were otherwise;
that I could beat him, whilst he railed at me:
'sfoot, I 'll learn to conjure and raise devils, but
I 'll see some issue of my spiteful execrations.
Then there 's Achilles—a rare engineer. If Troy
be not taken till these two undermine it, the walls
will stand till they fall of themselves. O, thou
great thunder-darter of Olympus, forget that
thou art Jove, the king of gods; and Mercury,
lose all the serpentine craft of thy Caduceus;
if ye take not that little little less-than-little wit
from them that they have! which short-armed
ignorance itself knows is so abundant scarce, it
will not in circumvention deliver a fly from a
spider, without drawing their massy irons, and
cutting the web. After this, the vengeance on
the whole camp! or rather, the bone-ache! for
that, methinks, is the curse dependent on those
that war for a placket. I have said my prayers;
and devil, envy, say amen. What ho! my lord
Achilles!

Enter PATROCLUS.

Patr. Who 's there? Thersites? Good Thersites, come in and rail.

Ther. If I could have remembered a gilt counterfeit, thou wouldst not have slipped out of my
contemplation: but it is no matter; thyself upon
thyself! The common curse of mankind, folly
and ignorance, be thine in great revenue! heaven
bless thee from a tutor, and discipline come not
near thee! Let thy blood be thy direction till
thy death! then if she that lays thee out, says
thou art a fair corse, I 'll be sworn and sworn
upon 't, she never shrouded any but lazars.
Amen. Where 's Achilles?

Patr. What, art thou devout! Wast thou in
prayer?

Ther. Ay; the heavens hear me!

Enter ACHILLES.

Achil. Who 's there?
Patr. Thersites, my lord.
Achil. Where, where?— Art thou come!
Why, my cheese, my digestion, why hast thou

not served thyself into my table so many meals?
Come; what 's Agamemnon?

Ther. Thy commander, Achilles: then tell
me, Patroclus, what 's Achilles?

Patr. Thy lord, Thersites: then tell me, I
pray thee, what 's thyself?

Ther. Thy knower, Patroclus: then tell me,
Patroclus, what art thou?

Patr. Thou mayst tell, that know'st.

Achil. O, tell, tell!

Ther. I 'll decline the whole question. Agamemnon commands Achilles; Achilles is my
lord; I am Patroclus' knower; and Patroclus
is a fool.

Patr. You rascal!

Ther. Peace, fool; I have not done.

Achil. He is a privileged man. — Proceed,
Thersites.

Ther. Agamemnon is a fool; Achilles is a
fool; Thersites is a fool; and, as aforesaid,
Patroclus is a fool.

Achil. Derive this; come.

Ther. Agamemnon is a fool to offer to command Achilles; Achilles is a fool to be commanded of Agamemnon; Thersites is a fool to
serve such a fool; and Patroclus is a fool positive.

Patr. Why am I a fool?

Ther. Make that demand of the prover: it
suffices me, thou art. Look you, who comes here?

Enter AGAMEMNON, ULYSSES, NESTOR, AJAX, *and*
DIOMEDES.

Achil. Patroclus, I 'll speak with nobody:
Come in with me, Thersites.　　　[*Exit.*

Ther. Here is such patchery, such juggling,
and such knavery! all the argument is, a cuckold
and a whore: a good quarrel to draw emulous
factions, and to bleed to death upon! Now the
dry serpigo on the subject! and war and lechery
confound all!　　　　　　　　　　[*Exit.*

Agam. Where is Achilles?

Patr. Within his tent; but ill disposed, my lord.

Agam. Let it be known to him that we are here.
He shent our messengers; and we lay by
Our appertainments, visiting of him:
Let him be told so; lest perchance he think
We dare not move the question of our place,
Or know not what we are.

Patr. I shall say so to him.　　　[*Exit.*

Ulys. We saw him at the opening of his
tent; he is not sick.

Ajax. Yes, lion-sick, sick of proud heart: you
may call it melancholy, if you will favour the
man; but, by my head, 'tis pride: but why,
why? let him shew us a cause.—A word, my
lord.　　　　　　　[*Takes* AGAMEMNON *aside.*

Nes. What moves Ajax thus to bay at him?

Ulys. Achilles hath inveigled his fool from him.

Nes. Who? Thersites?

Ulys. He.

Nes. Then will Ajax lack matter, if he have lost his argument.

Ulys. No; you see he is his argument, that has his argument; Achilles.

Nes. All the better; their fraction is more our wish than their faction: But it was a strong composure a fool could disunite!

Ulys. The amity that wisdom knits not, folly may easily untie. Here comes Patroclus.

Re-enter PATROCLUS.

Nes. No Achilles with him.

Ulys. The elephant hath joints, but none for courtesy; his legs are legs for necessity, not for flexure.

Patr. Achilles bids me say—he is much sorry,
If anything more than your sport and pleasure
Did move your greatness, and this noble state,
To call upon him; he hopes it is no other,
But for your health and your digestion sake,
An after-dinner's breath.

Agam.   Hear you, Patroclus;
We are too well acquainted with these answers:
But his evasion, winged thus swift with scorn,
Cannot outfly our apprehensions.
Much attribute he hath; and much the reason
Why we ascribe it to him: yet all his virtues
(Not virtuously on his own part beheld)
Do, in our eyes, begin to lose their gloss;
Yea, like fair fruit in an unwholesome dish,
Are like to rot untasted. Go and tell him,
We come to speak with him: and you shall not sin
If you do say—we think him over-proud,
And under-honest; in self-assumption greater
Than in the note of judgment; and worthier than
          himself
Here tend the savage strangeness he puts on;
Disguise the holy strength of their command,
And underwrite in an observing kind
His humorous predominance; yea, watch
His pettish lunes, his ebbs, his flows, as if
The passage and whole carriage of this action
Rode on his tide. Go, tell him this; and add,
That if he overhold his price so much,
We'll none of him; but let him, like an engine
Not portable, lie under this report—
Bring action hither; this cannot go to war:
A stirring dwarf we do allowance give
Before a sleeping giant. Tell him so.

Patr. I shall; and bring his answer presently.
                                        [*Exit.*

Agam. In second voice we'll not be satisfied;
We come to speak with him.—Ulysses, enter you.
                                        [*Exit* ULYSSES.

Ajax. What is he more than another?

Agam. No more than what he thinks he is.

Ajax. Is he so much? Do you not think, he thinks himself a better man than I am?

Agam. No question.

Ajax. Will you subscribe his thought, and say—he is?

Agam. No, noble Ajax; you are as strong, as valiant, as wise, no less noble, much more gentle, and altogether more tractable.

Ajax. Why should a man be proud? How doth pride grow? I know not what pride is.

Agam. Your mind's the clearer, Ajax, and your virtues the fairer. He that is proud eats up himself: pride is his own glass, his own trumpet, his own chronicle; and whatever praises itself but in the deed, devours the deed in the praise.

Ajax. I do hate a proud man, as I hate the engendering of toads.

Nes. And yet he loves himself: is it not strange?
                                        [*Aside.*

Re-enter ULYSSES.

Ulys. Achilles will not to the field to-morrow.

Agam. What's his excuse?

Ulys.   He doth rely on none;
But carries on the stream of his dispose,
Without observance or respect of any,
In will peculiar and in self-admission.

Agam. Why will he not, upon our fair request,
Untent his person, and share the air with us?

Ulys. Things small as nothing, for request's sake
          only,
He makes important. Possessed he is with great-
          ness;
And speaks not to himself, but with a pride
That quarrels at self-breath: imagined worth
Holds in his blood such swoln and hot discourse,
That, 'twixt his mental and his active parts,
Kingdomed Achilles in commotion rages,
And batters down himself. What should I say?
He is so plaguy proud, that the death-tokens of it
Cry "No recovery!"

Agam.   Let Ajax go to him.—
Dear lord, go you and greet him in his tent:
'Tis said, he holds you well; and will be led,
At your request, a little from himself.

Ulys. O, Agamemnon, let it not be so!
We'll consecrate the steps that Ajax makes
When they go from Achilles. Shall the proud lord
That bastes his arrogance with his own seam,
And never suffers matter of the world
Enter his thoughts—save such as do revolve
And ruminate himself;—shall he be worshipped
Of that we hold an idol more than he?
No, this thrice-worthy and right-valiant lord
Must not so strain his palm, nobly acquired;
Nor, by my will, assubjugate his merit,

As amply titled as Achilles is,
By going to Achilles:
That were to enlard his fat-already pride,
And add more coals to Cancer, when he burns
With entertaining great Hyperion.
This lord go to him! Jupiter forbid;
And say in thunder—" Achilles, go to him."
  Nes. O, this is well; he rubs the vein of him.
                               [*Aside.*
  Dio. And how his silence drinks up this applause!   [*Aside.*
  Ajax. If I go to him, with my armed fist I'll pash him
O'er the face.
  Agam.   O, no, you shall not go.
  Ajax. An he be proud with me, I'll pheeze his pride:
Let me go to him.
  Ulys. Not for the worth that hangs upon our quarrel.
  Ajax. A paltry insolent fellow!
  Nes. How he describes himself!   [*Aside.*
  Ajax. Can he not be sociable?
  Ulys. The raven chides blackness.   [*Aside.*
  Ajax. I'll let his humours blood.
  Agam. He'll be the physician, that should be the patient.   [*Aside.*
  Ajax. An all men were o' my mind,—
  Ulys. Wit would be out of fashion.   [*Aside.*
  Ajax. He should not bear it so;
He should eat swords first: shall pride carry it?
  Nes. An 'twould, you'd carry half.   [*Aside.*
  Ulys. He'd have ten shares.   [*Aside.*
  Ajax. I'll knead him, I'll make him supple!
  Nes. He's not yet thorough warm: force him with praises:
Pour in, pour in; his ambition is dry. [*Aside.*
  Ulys. My lord, you feed too much on this dislike.   [*To* AGAMEMNON.
  Nes. Our noble general, do not do so.
  Dio. You must prepare to fight without Achilles.
  Ulys. Why, 'tis this naming of him does him harm.
Here is a man—but 'tis before his face;
I will be silent.

  Nes.   Wherefore should you so?
He is not emulous, as Achilles is.
  Ulys. Know the whole world, he is as valiant.
  Ajax. A whoreson dog, that shall palter thus with us!
'Would he were a Trojan!
  Nes. What a vice were it in Ajax now,—
  Ulys. If he were proud?
  Dio. Or covetous of praise?
  Ulys. Ay, or surly borne?
  Dio. Or strange, or self-affected?
  Ulys. Thank the heavens, lord, thou art of sweet composure;
Praise him that got thee, she that gave thee suck:
Famed be thy tutor, and thy parts of nature
Thrice-famed, beyond all erudition:
But he that disciplined thy arms to fight,
Let Mars divide eternity in twain,
And give him half: and, for thy vigour,
Bull-bearing Milo his addition yield
To sinewy Ajax. I will not praise thy wisdom,
Which like a bourn, a pale, a shore, confines
Thy spacious and dilated parts: here's Nestor,—
Instructed by the antiquary times,
He must, he is, he cannot but be wise;—
But pardon, father Nestor, were your days
As green as Ajax', and your brain so tempered,
You should not have the eminence of him,
But be as Ajax.
  Ajax.   Shall I call you father?
  Nes. Ay, my good son.
  Dio.   Be ruled by him, lord Ajax.
  Ulys. There is no tarrying here; the hart Achilles
Keeps thicket. Please it our great general
To call together all his state of war;
Fresh kings are come to Troy: to-morrow,
We must with all our main of power stand fast:
And here's a lord,—come knights from east to west,
And cull their flower, Ajax shall cope the best.
  Agam. Go we to council. Let Achilles sleep:
Light boats sail swift, though greater hulks draw deep.   [*Exeunt.*

ACT
III

Scene I.—Troy. *A Room in* Priam's *Palace.*

Enter Pandarus *and a* Servant.

Pan. Friend! you! pray you, a word: do not you follow the young lord Paris?

Serv. Ay, sir, when he goes before me.

Pan. You do depend upon him, I mean?

Serv. Sir, I do depend upon the lord.

Pan. You do depend upon a noble gentleman; I must needs praise him.

Serv. The lord be praised!

Pan. You know me, do you not?

Serv. 'Faith, sir, superficially.

Pan. Friend, know me better; I am the lord Pandarus.

Serv. I hope I shall know your honour better.

Pan. I do desire it.

Serv. You are in the state of grace.

[*Music within.*

Pan. Grace! not so, friend; honour and lordship are my titles. What music is this?

Serv. I do but partly know, sir; it is music in parts.

Pan. Know you the musicians?

Serv. Wholly, sir.

Pan. Who play they to?

Serv. To the hearers, sir.

Pan. At whose pleasure, friend?

Serv. At mine, sir, and theirs that love music.

Pan. Command, I mean, friend.

Serv. Who shall I command, sir?

Pan. Friend, we understand not one another; I am too courtly, and thou art too cunning: at whose request do these men play?

Serv. That's to't, indeed, sir: marry, sir, at the request of Paris, my lord, who is there in person; with him, the mortal Venus, the heart-blood of beauty, love's invisible soul,—

Pan. Who, my cousin Cressida?

Serv. No, sir, Helen: could you not find out that by her attributes?

Pan. It should seem, fellow, that thou hast not seen the lady Cressida. I come to speak with Paris from the prince Troilus: I will make a complimental assault upon him, for my business seeths.

Serv. Sodden business! there's a stewed phrase, indeed!

Enter Paris *and* Helen, *attended.*

Pan. Fair be to you, my lord, and to all this fair company! fair desires, in all fair measure, fairly guide them! especially to you, fair queen! fair thoughts be your fair pillow!

Helen. Dear lord, you are full of fair words.

Pan. You speak your fair pleasure, sweet queen.—Fair prince, here is good broken music.

Par. You have broke it, cousin: and, by my life, you shall make it whole again; you shall piece it out with a piece of your performance:—Nell, he is full of harmony.

Pan. Truly, lady, no.

Helen. O, sir,—

Pan. Rude, in sooth; in good sooth, very rude.

Par. Well said, my lord! well, you say so in fits.

Pan. I have business to my lord, dear queen:—My lord, will you vouchsafe me a word?

Helen. Nay, this shall not hedge us out: we'll hear you sing, certainly.

Pan. Well, sweet queen, you are pleasant with me.—But, marry, thus, my lord: my dear lord and most esteemed friend, your brother Troilus—

Helen. My lord Pandarus; honey-sweet lord,—

Pan. Go to, sweet queen, go to:—commends himself most affectionately to you.

Helen. You shall not bob us out of our melody; if you do, our melancholy upon your head!

Pan. Sweet queen, sweet queen; that's a sweet queen, i' faith.

Helen. And to make a sweet lady sad, is a sour offence.

Pan. Nay, that shall not serve your turn; that shall it not, in truth, la. Nay, I care not for such words; no, no.—And, my lord, he desires you, that, if the king call for him at supper, you will make his excuse.

Helen. My lord Pandarus,—

Pan. What says my sweet queen? my very very sweet queen?

Par. What exploit's in hand? where sups he to-night?

Helen. Nay, but my lord,—

Pan. What says my sweet queen?—My cousin will fall out with you. You must not know where he sups.

Par. I'll lay my life, with my disposer Cressida.

Pan. No, no, no such matter; you are wide: come, your disposer is sick.

Par. Well, I'll make excuse.

Pan. Ay, good my lord. Why should you say Cressida? no, your poor disposer's sick.

Par. I spy.

Pan. You spy! what do you spy?—Come, give me an instrument. Now, sweet queen.

Helen. Why, this is kindly done.

Pan. My niece is horribly in love with a thing you have, sweet queen.

Helen. She shall have it, my lord, if it be not my lord Paris.

Pan. He! no, she'll none of him; they two are twain.

Helen. Falling in, after falling out, may make them three.

Pan. Come, come, I'll hear no more of this; I'll sing you a song now.

Helen. Ay, ay, pr'y thee now. By my troth, sweet lord, thou hast a fine forehead.

Pan. Ay, you may, you may.

Helen. Let thy song be love: this love will undo us all. O, Cupid, Cupid, Cupid!

Pan. Love! ay, that it shall, i' faith.

Par. Ay, good now, love, love, nothing but love.

Pan. In good troth, it begins so:—

> Love, love, nothing but love, still more!
> 　　For, oh, love's bow
> 　　Shoots buck and doe:
> 　　The shaft confounds
> 　　Not that it wounds,
> But tickles still the sore.
>
> These lovers cry—Oh, oh, they die!
> 　　Yet that which seems the wound to kill,
> Doth turn oh, oh! to ha, ha, he!
> 　　So dying love lives still:
> Oh, oh! a while, but ha, ha, ha!
> Oh, oh! groans out for ha, ha, ha!

Hey ho!

Helen. In love, i' faith, to the very tip of the nose.

Par. He eats nothing but doves, love; and that breeds hot blood, and hot blood begets hot thoughts, and hot thoughts beget hot deeds, and hot deeds is love.

Pan. Is this the generation of love? hot blood, hot thoughts, and hot deeds? Why, they are vipers: is love a generation of vipers?—Sweet lord, who 's afield to day?

Par. Hector, Deiphobus, Helenus, Antenor, and all the gallantry of Troy: I would fain have armed to-day, but my Nell would not have it so. How chance my brother Troilus went not?

Helen. He hangs the lip at something;—you know all, lord Pandarus.

Pan. Not I, honey-sweet queen.—I long to hear how they sped to-day.—You 'll remember your brother's excuse?

Par. To a hair.

Pan. Farewell, sweet queen.

Helen. Commend me to your niece.

Pan. I will, sweet queen. 　　　　　[*Exit.*
　　　　　　　　　　　　　　　[*A retreat sounded.*

Par. They are come from field: let us to Priam's hall,
To greet the warriors. Sweet Helen, I must woo you
To help unarm our Hector: his stubborn buckles,
With these your white enchanting fingers touched,
Shall more obey than to the edge of steel,
Or force of Greekish sinews: you shall do more
Than all the island kings—disarm great Hector.

Helen. 'T will make us proud to be his servant, Paris:
Yea, what he shall receive of us in duty,
Gives us more palm in beauty than we have;
Yea, overshines ourself.

Par. Sweet, above thought I love thee. [*Exeunt.*

SCENE II.—*The same.* PANDARUS' *Orchard.*

Enter PANDARUS *and a* Servant, *meeting.*

Pan. How now? where 's thy master? at my cousin Cressida's?

Serv. No, sir; he stays for you to conduct him thither.

Enter TROILUS.

Pan. O, here he comes.—How now, how now?

Tro. Sirrah, walk off. 　　　　　[*Exit* Servant.

Pan. Have you seen my cousin?

Tro. No, Pandarus: I stalk about her door,
Like a strange soul upon the Stygian banks,
Staying for waftage. O, be thou my Charon,
And give me swift transportance to those fields,
Where I may wallow in the lily beds
Proposed for the deserver! O, gentle Pandarus,
From Cupid's shoulder pluck his painted wings,
And fly with me to Cressid!

Pan. Walk here i' the orchard; I 'll bring her
　　straight. 　　　　　[*Exit.*

Tro. I am giddy; expectation whirls me round.
The imaginary relish is so sweet,
That it enchants my sense: what will it be,
When that the watery palate tastes indeed
Love's thrice-reputed nectar? death, I fear me;
Swooning destruction; or some joy too fine,
Too subtle-potent, tuned too sharp in sweetness,
For the capacity of my ruder powers:
I fear it much; and I do fear besides,
That I shall lose distinction in my joys;
As doth a battle, when they charge on heaps
The enemy flying.

Re-enter PANDARUS.

Pan. She 's making her ready, she 'll come straight: you must be witty now. She does so blush, and fetches her wind so short, as if she were frayed with a sprite: I 'll fetch her. It is the prettiest villain:—she fetches her breath as short as a new ta'en sparrow. 　　　　　[*Exit.*

Tro. Even such a passion doth embrace my
　　bosom:
My heart beats thicker than a feverous pulse;
And all my powers do their bestowing lose,
Like vassalage at unawares encountering
The eye of majesty.

Enter PANDARUS *and* CRESSIDA.

Pan. Come, come, what need you blush? shame 's a baby.—Here she is now: swear the oaths now to her, that you have sworn to me.—What, are you gone again? you must be watched ere you be made tame, must you? Come your ways, come your ways; an you draw backward, we 'll put you i' the fills.—Why do you not speak to her?—Come, draw this curtain, and let 's see your picture. Alas the day, how loath you are to offend daylight! an 't were dark, you 'd close sooner. So, so; rub on, and kiss the mistress. How now, a kiss in fee-farm! build there, carpenter; the air is sweet. Nay, you shall fight your hearts out, ere I part you. The falcon as the tercel, for all the ducks i' the river: go to, go to.

Tro. You have bereft me of all words, lady.

Pan. Words pay no debts; give her deeds: but she 'll bereave you of the deeds too, if she call your activity in question. What, billing again? here 's "In witness whereof the parties interchangeably——." Come in, come in; I 'll go get a fire.   [*Exit.*

Cres. Will you walk in, my lord?

Tro. O, Cressida, how often have I wished me thus!

Cres. Wished, my lord?—The gods grant!—O, my lord!

Tro. What should they grant? what makes this pretty abruption? What too curious dreg espies my sweet lady in the fountain of our love?

Cres. More dregs than water, if my fears have eyes!

Tro. Fears make devils of cherubim; they never see truly.

Cres. Blind fear, that seeing reason leads, finds safer footing than blind reason stumbling without fear: to fear the worst, oft cures the worst.

Tro. O, let my lady apprehend no fear: in all Cupid's pageant, there is presented no monster.

Cres. Nor nothing monstrous neither?

Tro. Nothing, but our undertakings; when we vow to weep seas, live in fire, eat rocks, tame tigers; thinking it harder for our mistress to devise imposition enough, than for us to undergo any difficulty imposed. This is the monstruosity in love, lady,—that the will is infinite, and the execution confined; that the desire is boundless, and the act a slave to limit.

Cres. They say, all lovers swear more performance than they are able, and yet reserve an ability that they never perform; vowing more than the perfection of ten, and discharging less than the tenth part of one. They that have the voice of lions, and the act of hares, are they not monsters?

Tro. Are there such? such are not we. Praise us as we are tasted, allow us as we prove; our head shall go bare till merit crown it: no perfection in reversion shall have a praise in present: we will not name desert before his birth; and, being born, his addition shall be humble. Few words to fair faith: Troilus shall be such to Cressid, as what envy can say worst, shall be a mock for his truth; and what truth can speak truest, not truer than Troilus.

Cres. Will you walk in, my lord?

Re-enter PANDARUS.

Pan. What, blushing still? have you not done talking yet?

Cres. Well, uncle, what folly I commit, I dedicate to you.

Pan. I thank you for that; if my lord get a boy of you, you'll give him me. Be true to my lord: if he flinch, chide me for it.

Tro. You know now your hostages; your uncle's word and my firm faith.

Pan. Nay, I'll give my word for her too; our kindred, though they be long ere they are wooed, they are constant, being won: they are burs, I can tell you; they'll stick where they are thrown.

Cres. Boldness comes to me now, and brings me heart:—

Prince Troilus, I have loved you night and day
For many weary months.

Tro. Why was my Cressid, then, so hard to win?

Cres. Hard to seem won; but I was won, my lord,
With the first glance that ever—Pardon me;—
If I confess much, you will play the tyrant.
I love you now; but not, till now, so much
But I might master it:—in faith, I lie;
My thoughts were like unbridled children, grown
Too headstrong for their mother. See, we fools!
Why have I blabbed? who shall be true to us,
When we are so unsecret to ourselves?
But, though I loved you well, I wooed you not;
And yet, good faith, I wished myself a man;
Or that we women had men's privilege
Of speaking first. Sweet, bid me hold my tongue;
For, in this rapture, I shall surely speak
The thing I shall repent. See, see, your silence,

Cunning in dumbness, from my weakness draws
My very soul of council! Stop my mouth.

Tro. And shall, albeit sweet music issues thence.

Pan. Pretty, i' faith.

Cres. My lord, I do beseech you, pardon me;
'Twas not my purpose thus to beg a kiss:
I am ashamed;—O, heavens! what have I done?
For this time will I take my leave, my lord.

Tro. Your leave, sweet Cressid?

Pan. Leave! an you take leave till to-morrow morning,—

Cres. Pray you, content you.

Tro. What offends you, lady?

Cres. Sir, mine own company.

Tro. You cannot shun yourself.

Cres. Let me go and try:
I have a kind of self resides with you:
But an unkind self, that itself will leave,
To be another's fool. Where is my wit?
I would be gone. I speak I know not what.

Tro. Well know they what they speak, that
speak so wisely.

Cres. Perchance, my lord, I shew more craft
than love;
And fell so roundly to a large confession,
To angle for your thoughts. But you are wise;
Or else you love not: for to be wise, and love,
Exceeds man's might; that dwells with gods above.

Tro. O, that I thought it could be in a woman
(As, if it can, I will presume in you)
To feed for aye her lamp and flames of love;
To keep her constancy in plight and youth,
Outliving beauty's outward, with a mind
That doth renew swifter than blood decays!
Or that persuasion could but thus convince me—
That my integrity and truth to you
Might be affronted with the match and weight
Of such a winnowed purity in love:
How were I then uplifted! but, alas!
I am as true as truth's simplicity,
And simpler than the infancy of truth.

Cres. In that I'll war with you.

Tro.   O, virtuous fight,
When right with right wars, who shall be most
right!
True swains in love shall, in the world to come,
Approve their truths by Troilus:—When their
rhymes,
Full of protést, of oath, and big compare,
Want similes, truth tired with iteration,—
As true as steel, as plantage to the moon,
As sun to day, as turtle to her mate,
As iron to adamant, as earth to the centre,—
Yet, after all comparisons of truth,
As truth's authentic author to be cited,
"As true as Troilus" shall crown up the verse,
And sanctify the numbers.

Cres.   Prophet may you be!
If I be false, or swerve a hair from truth,—
When time is old and hath forgot itself;
When water-drops have worn the stones of Troy,
And blind oblivion swallowed cities up,
And mighty states chárácterless are grated
To dusty nothing; yet let memory,
From false to false, among false maids in love,
Upbraid my falsehood! when they have said—
        as false
As air, as water, wind, or sandy earth,
As fox to lamb, as wolf to heifer's calf,
Pard to the hind, or stepdame to her son;
Yea, let them say, to stick the heart of falsehood,
" As false as Cressid."
Pan. Go to, a bargain made: seal it, seal it;
I 'll be the witness.—Here I hold your hand;
here, my cousin's. If ever you prove false one
to another, since I have taken such pains to
bring you together, let all pitiful goers-between
be called to the world's end after my name;
call them all Pandars; let all constant men
be Troiluses, all false women Cressids, and all
brokers-between Pandars! say, amen.

Tro. }
Cres. } Amen.

Pan. Amen. Whereupon I will shew you a
chamber with a bed; which bed, because it shall
not speak of your pretty encounters, press it to
death: away.
And Cupid grant all tongue-tied maidens here,
Bed, chamber, Pandar to provide this gear!
                                    [*Exeunt.*

SCENE III.—*The* Grecian *Camp.*

Enter AGAMEMNON, ULYSSES, DIOMEDES, AJAX,
    NESTOR, MENELAUS, *and* CALCHAS.

Cal. Now, princes, for the service I have
        done you,
The advantage of the time prompts me aloud
To call for recompense. Appear it to your mind,
That, through the sight I bear in things, to Jove
I have abandoned Troy; left my possessions,
Incurred a traitor's name; exposed myself,
From certain and possessed conveniences,
To doubtful fortunes; sequestering from me all
That time, acquaintance, custom, and condition,
Made tame and most familiar to my nature:
And here, to do you service, am become
As new into the world, strange, unacquainted:
I do beseech you, as in way of taste,
To give me now a little benefit,
Out of those many registered in promise,
Which, you say, live to come in my behalf.

Agam. What wouldst thou of us, Trojan? make
        demand.
Cal. You have a Trojan prisoner, called Antenor,
Yesterday took: Troy holds him very dear.
Oft have you (often have you thanks therefore)
Desired my Cressid in right great exchange,
Whom Troy hath still denied: but this Antenor,
I know, is such a wrest in their affairs,
That their negociations all must slack,
Wanting his manage; and they will almost
Give us a prince of blood, a son of Priam,
In change of him: let him be sent, great princes,
And he shall buy my daughter; and her presence
Shall quite strike off all service I have done,
In most accepted pain.
Agam.   Let Diomedes bear him,
And bring us Cressid hither: Calchas shall have
What he requests of us. Good Diomed,
Furnish you fairly for this interchange:
Withal, bring word if Hector will to-morrow
Be answered in his challenge: Ajax is ready.
Dio. This shall I undertake; and 'tis a burden
Which I am proud to bear.
                    [*Exeunt* DIOMEDES *and* CALCHAS.

Enter ACHILLES *and* PATROCLUS, *before their*
                    Tent.

Ulys. Achilles stands i' the entrance of his
        tent:—
Please it our general to pass strangely by him,
As if he were forgot; and, princes all,
Lay negligent and loose regard upon him:
I will come last: 'tis like he 'll question me,
Why such unplausive eyes are bent, why turned
        on him?
If so, I have derision med'cinable,
To use between your strangeness and his pride,
Which his own will shall have desire to drink.
It may do good: pride hath no other glass
To shew itself but pride; for supple knees
Feed arrogance, and are the proud man's fees.
Agam. We 'll execute your purpose, and put on
A form of strangeness as we pass along;
So do each lord; and either greet him not,
Or else disdainfully, which shall shake him more
Than if not looked on. I will lead the way.
Achil. What, comes the general to speak with
        me?
You know my mind, I 'll fight no more 'gainst Troy.
Agam. What says Achilles? would he aught
        with us?
Nes. Would you, my lord, aught with the
        general?
Achil. No.
Nes. Nothing, my lord.
Agam. The better.
                    [*Exeunt* AGAMEMNON *and* NESTOR.

Achil. Good day, good day.

Men. How do you? how do you?   [*Exit.*

Achil. What, does the cuckold scorn me?

Ajax. How now, Patroclus?

Achil. Good morrow, Ajax.

Ajax. Ha?

Achil. Good morrow.

Ajax. Ay, and good next day too.   [*Exit.*

Achil. What mean these fellows? Know they
     not Achilles?

Patr. They pass by strangely: they were used
     to bend,

To send their smiles before them to Achilles;

To come as humbly as they used to creep

To holy altars.

Achil.   What, am I poor of late?

'T is certain, greatness, once fallen out with
     fortune,

Must fall out with men too: what the declined is,

He shall as soon read in the eyes of others,

As feel in his own fall: for men, like butterflies,

Shew not their mealy wings but to the summer;

And not a man, for being simply man,

Hath any honour; but honour for those honours

That are without him, as place, riches, favour,

Prizes of accident as oft as merit:

Which when they fall, as being slippery standers,

The love that leaned on them as slippery too,

Do one pluck down another, and together

Die in the fall. But 't is not so with me:

Fortune and I are friends; I do enjoy

At ample point all that I did possess,

Save these men's looks; who do, methinks, find out

Something not worth in me such rich beholding

As they have often given. Here is Ulysses;

I 'll interrupt his reading.—

How now, Ulysses?

Ulys.   Now, great Thetis' son?

Achil. What are you reading?

Ulys.   A strange fellow here

Writes me, that man—how dearly ever parted,

How much in having, or without, or in—

Cannot make boast to have that which he hath,

Nor feels not what he owes, but by reflection;

As when his virtues, shining upon others,

Heat them, and they retort that heat again

To the first giver.

Achil.   This is not strange, Ulysses.

The beauty that is borne here in the face,

The bearer knows not, but commends itself

To others' eyes: nor doth the eye itself

(That most pure spirit of sense) behold itself,

Not going from itself; but eye to eye opposed

Salutes each other with each other's form.

For speculation turns not to itself,

Till it hath travelled, and is married there

Where it may see itself: this is not strange at all.

Ulys. I do not strain at the position;

It is familiar; but at the author's drift:

Who, in his circumstance, expressly proves—

That no man is the lord of anything

(Though in and of him there be much consisting),

Till he communicate his parts to others:

Nor doth he of himself know them for aught,

Till he behold them formed in the applause

Where they are extended; which, like an arch,
     reverberates

The voice again; or, like a gate of steel

Fronting the sun, receives and renders back

His figure and his heat. I was much rapt in this;

And apprehended here immediately

The unknown Ajax.

Heavens, what a man is there! a very horse;

That has he knows not what. Nature, what things
     there are,

Most abject in regard, and dear in use!

What things again most dear in the esteem,

And poor in worth! Now shall we see to-morrow

(An act that very chance doth throw upon him)

Ajax renowned! O, heavens, what some men do,

While some men leave to do!

How some men creep in skittish fortune's hall,

Whiles others play the idiots in her eyes!

How one man eats into another's pride,

While pride is fasting in his wantonness!

To see these Grecian lords!—why, even already

They clap the lubber Ajax on the shoulder;

As if his foot were on brave Hector's breast,

And great Troy shrieking.

Achil. I do believe it: for they passed by me

As misers do by beggars; neither gave to me

Good word, nor look. What, are my deeds forgot?

Ulys. Time hath, my lord, a wallet at his back,

Wherein he puts alms for oblivion,

A great-sized monster of ingratitudes:

Those scraps are good deeds past; which are de-
     voured

As fast as they are made, forgot as soon

As done. Perséverance, dear my lord,

Keeps honour bright: to have done, is to hang

Quite out of fashion, like a rusty mail

In monumental mockery. Take the instant way;

For honour travels in a strait so narrow,

Where one but goes abreast: keep then the path;

For emulation hath a thousand sons,

That one by one pursue: if you give way,

Or hedge aside from the direct forthright,

Like to an entered tide, they all rush by,

And leave you hindmost;—

Or, like a gallant horse fallen in first rank,

Lie there for pavement to the abject rear,

O'er-run and trampled on: then what they do
     in present,

Though less than yours in past, must o'ertop yours:

For time is like a fashionable host,
That slightly shakes his parting guest by the
    hand;
And with his arms outstretched, as he would fly,
Grasps-in the comer. Welcome ever smiles,
And farewell goes out sighing. O, let not virtue
    seek
Remuneration for the thing it was! For beauty,
    wit,
High birth, vigour of bone, desert in service,
Love, friendship, charity, are subjects all
To envious and calumniating time.
One touch of nature makes the whole world kin—
That all, with one consent, praise new-born gawds,
Though they are made and moulded of things
    past;
And give to dust that is a little gilt,
More laud than gilt o'er-dusted.
The present eye praises the present object:
Then marvel not, thou great and cómplete man,
That all the Greeks begin to worship Ajax;
Since things in motion sooner catch the eye,
Than what not stirs. The cry went once on thee,
And still it might; and yet it may again,
If thou wouldst not entomb thyself alive,
And case thy reputation in thy tent;
Whose glorious deeds, but in these fields of late,
Made emulous missions 'mongst the gods them-
    selves,
And drave great Mars to faction.
  Achil.   Of this my privacy
I have strong reasons.
  Ulys.   But 'gainst your privacy
The reasons are more potent and heroical:
'T is known, Achilles, that you are in love
With one of Priam's daughters.
  Achil.   Ha! known?
  Ulys. Is that a wonder?
The providence that's in a watchful state,
Knows almost every grain of Plutus' gold;
Finds bottom in the uncomprehensive deeps;
Keeps place with thought, and almost, like the
    gods,
Does thoughts unveil in their dumb cradles.
There is a mystery (with whom relation
Durst never meddle) in the soul of state;
Which hath an operation more divine
Than breath or pen can give expressure to:
All the commérce that you have had with Troy,
As perfectly is ours as yours, my lord;
And better would it fit Achilles much,
To throw down Hector than Polyxena:
But it must grieve young Pyrrhus, now at home,
When fame shall in our islands sound her trump,
And all the Greekish girls shall tripping sing,
" Great Hector's sister did Achilles win;
But our great Ajax bravely beat down him.''

Farewell, my lord: I as your lover speak;
The fool slides o'er the ice that you should break.
                         [*Exit.*
  Patr. To this effect, Achilles, have I moved you:
A woman impudent and mannish grown
Is not more loathed than an effeminate man
In time of action. I stand condemned for this:
They think, my little stomach to the war,
And your great love to me, restrains you thus:
Sweet, rouse yourself; and the weak wanton Cupid
Shall from your neck unloose his amorous fold,
And, like a dewdrop from the lion's mane,
Be shook to air.
  Achil.   Shall Ajax fight with Hector?
  Patr. Ay; and, perhaps, receive much honour
    by him.
  Achil. I see my reputation is at stake;
My fame is shrewdly gored.
  Patr.   O, then beware;
Those wounds heal ill that men do give them-
    selves:
Omission to do what is necessary
Seals a commission to a blank of danger;
And danger, like an ague, subtly taints
Even then when we sit idly in the sun.
  Achil. Go call Thersites hither, sweet Patro-
    clus:
I 'll send the fool to Ajax, and desire him
To invite the Trojan lords, after the combat,
To see us here unarmed: I have a woman's
    longing,
An appetite that I am sick withal,
To see great Hector in his weeds of peace;
To talk with him, and to behold his visage,
Even to my full of view. A labour saved!

         Enter Thersites.

  Ther. A wonder!
  Achil. What?
  Ther. Ajax goes up and down the field, asking
for himself.
  Achil. How so?
  Ther. He must fight singly to-morrow with Hector; and is so prophetically proud of an heroical
cudgelling, that he raves in saying nothing.
  Achil. How can that be?
  Ther. Why, he stalks up and down like a pea-
cock, a stride and a stand: ruminates like an
hostess that hath no arithmetic but her brain to
set down her reckoning: bites his lip with a politic regard, as who should say, " There were wit in
this head, an 't would out:" and so there is; but it
lies as coldly in him as fire in a flint, which will
not shew without knocking. The man's undone
for ever; for if Hector break not his neck i' the
combat, he 'll break it himself in vain-glory. He
knows not me: I said, " Good-morrow, Ajax;"

and he replies, "Thanks, Agamemnon." What think you of this man, that takes me for the general? He is grown a very land-fish, languageless, a monster. A plague of opinion! a man may wear it on both sides, like a leather jerkin.

Achil. Thou must be my ambassador to him, Thersites.

Ther. Who, I? why, he'll answer nobody; he professes not answering; speaking is for beggars; he wears his tongue in his arms. I will put on his presence; let Patroclus make demands to me, you shall see the pageant of Ajax.

Achil. To him, Patroclus: tell him, I humbly desire the valiant Ajax to invite the most valorous Hector to come unarmed to my tent; and to procure safe conduct for his person, of the magnanimous and most illustrious, six-or-seven-times honoured captain-general of the Grecian army, Agamemnon. Do this.

Patr. Jove bless great Ajax!

Ther. Humph!

Patr. I come from the worthy Achilles,—

Ther. Ha!

Patr. Who most humbly desires you to invite Hector to his tent;—

Ther. Humph!

Patr. And to procure safe conduct from Agamemnon.

Ther. Agamemnon?

Patr. Ay, my lord.

Ther. Ha!

Patr. What say you to't?

Ther. God be wi' you, with all my heart.

Patr. Your answer, sir.

Ther. If to-morrow be a fair day, by eleven o'clock it will go one way or other; howsoever, he shall pay for me ere he has me.

Patr. Your answer, sir.

Ther. Fare you well, with all my heart.

Achil. Why, but he is not in this tune, is he?

Ther. No, but he's out o' tune thus. What music will be in him when Hector has knocked out his brains, I know not: but I am sure, none, unless the fiddler Apollo get his sinews to make catlings on.

Achil. Come, thou shalt bear a letter to him straight.

Ther. Let me bear another to his horse; for that's the more capable creature.

Achil. My mind is troubled, like a fountain stirred;
And I myself see not the bottom of it
[*Exeunt* ACHILLES *and* PATROCLUS.

Ther. 'Would the fountain of your mind were clear again, that I might water an ass at it! I had rather be a tick in a sheep, than such a valiant ignorance. [*Exit.*

SCENE I.—Troy.   *A Street.*

Enter at one side, Æneas, and Servant *with a torch; at the other,* PARIS, DEIPHOBUS, AN-TENOR, DIOMEDES, *and others, with torches.*

Par. See, ho! who is that there?

Dei. It is the lord Æneas.

Æne. Is the prince there in person?—
Had I so good occasion to lie long
As you, prince Paris, nothing but heavenly business
Should rob my bed-mate of my company.

Dio. That's my mind too.—Good morrow, lord
Æneas.

Par. A valiant Greek, Æneas; take his hand:
Witness the process of your speech, wherein
You told—how Diomed, a whole week by days,
Did haunt you in the field.

Æne.   Health to you, valiant sir,
During all question of the gentle truce:
But when I meet you armed, as black defiance
As heart can think, or courage execute.

Dio. The one and other Diomed embraces.
Our bloods are now in calm; and so long, health:
But when contention and occasion meet,
By Jove! I'll play the hunter for thy life,
With all my force, pursuit, and policy.

Æne. And thou shalt hunt a lion, that will fly
With his face backward.—In humane gentleness,
Welcome to Troy! Now, by Anchises' life,
Welcome, indeed! By Venus' hand, I swear,
No man alive can love, in such a sort,
The thing he means to kill, more excellently.

Dio. We sympathise:—Jove, let Æneas live,
If to my sword his fate be not the glory,
A thousand cómplete courses of the sun!
But, in mine emulous honour, let him die,
With every joint a wound; and that to-morrow!

Æne. We know each other well.

Dio. We do: and long to know each other worse.

Par. This is the most despiteful gentle greeting,
The noblest hateful love, that e'er I heard of.—
What business, lord, so early?

Æne. I was sent for to the king; but why, I
know not.

Par. His purpose meets you; 'twas to bring
this Greek
To Calchas' house; and there to render him,
For the enfreed Antenor, the fair Cressid.
Let's have your company; or, if you please,
Haste there before us: I constantly do think
(Or rather call my thought a certain knowledge)
My brother Troilus lodges there to-night:
Rouse him, and give him note of our approach,
With the whole quality wherefore: I fear
We shall be much unwelcome.

Æne.   That I assure you;
Troilus had rather Troy were borne to Greece,
Than Cressid borne from Troy.

Par.   There is no help;
The bitter disposition of the time
Will have it so. On, lord; we'll follow you.

Æne. Good morrow, all.   [*Exit.*

Par. And tell me noble Diomed; 'faith, tell me
true,
Even in the soul of sound good-fellowship,—
Who, in your thoughts, merits fair Helen best,
Myself or Menelaus?

Dio.   Both alike:
He merits well to have her, that doth seek her
(Not making any scruple of her soilure)
With such a hell of pain and world of charge;
And you as well to keep her, that defend her
(Not palating the taste of her dishonour)
With such a costly loss of wealth and friends:
He, like a puling cuckold, would drink up
The lees and dregs of a flat taméd piece;
You, like a lecher, out of whorish loins
Are pleased to breed out your inheritors:
Both merits poised, each weighs nor less nor more;
But he as he, the heavier for a whore.

Par. You are too bitter to your countrywoman.

Dio. She's bitter to her country: hear me, Paris:
For every false drop in her bawdy veins
A Grecian's life hath sunk; for every scruple

Of her contaminated carrion weight,
A Trojan hath been slain: since she could speak,
She hath not given so many good words breath,
As for her Greeks and Trojans suffered death.

Par. Fair Diomed, you do as chapmen do,
Dispraise the thing that you desire to buy:
But we in silence hold this virtue well,—
We 'll not commend what we intend to sell.
Here lies our way. 　　　　　　　*[Exeunt.*

SCENE II.—*The same.　Court before the House
of* PANDARUS.

Enter TROILUS *and* CRESSIDA.

Tro. Dear, trouble not yourself; the morn is cold.
Cres. Then, sweet my lord, I 'll call mine uncle
　　down;
He shall unbolt the gates.
Tro.　　　　Trouble him not;
To bed, to bed: sleep kill those pretty eyes,
And give as soft attachment to thy senses,
As infants'—empty of all thought!
Cres.　　　　Good morrow, then.
Tro. Pr'y thee now, to bed.
Cres.　　　　Are you aweary of me?
Tro. O, Cressida! but that the busy day,
Waked by the lark, hath roused the ribald crows,
And dreaming night will hide our joys no longer,
I would not from thee.
Cres.　　　　Night hath been too brief.
Tro. Beshrew the witch! with venomous wights
　　she stays
As tediously as hell; but flies the grasps of love,
With wings more momentary-swift than thought.
You will catch cold, and curse me.
Cres.　　Pr'y thee, tarry;—you men will never
　　tarry.
O, foolish Cressida! I might have still held off,
And then you would have tarried. Hark! there 's
　　one up.
Pan.[*within.*] What, are all the doors open here?
Tro. It is your uncle.

Enter PANDARUS.

Cres. A pestilence on him! now will he be
　　mocking:
I shall have such a life!
Pan. How now, how now? how go maidenheads?
Here, you maid! where 's my cousin Cressid?
Cres. Go hang yourself, you naughty mocking
　　uncle!
You bring me to do, and then you flout me too.
Pan. To do what? to do what?—Let her say
what: what have I brought you to do?
Cres. Come, come; beshrew your heart! you 'll
　　ne'er be good,
Nor suffer others.

Pan. Ha, ha! Alas, poor wretch! a poor ca-
pocchia!—hast not slept to-night? would he not,
a naughty man, let it sleep? A bugbear take
him! 　　　　　　　　　　　*[Knocking.*
Cres. Did I not tell you?—' Would he were
　　knocked o' the head!
Who 's that at door? good uncle, go and see.
My lord, come you again into my chamber:
You smile, and mock me, as if I meant naughtily.
Tro. Ha! ha!
Cres. Come, you are deceived; I think of no
　　such thing. 　　　　　　　*[Knocking.*
How earnestly they knock!—pray you, come in;
I would not for half Troy have you seen here.
　　　　　　　[Exeunt TROILUS *and* CRESSIDA.
Pan. [*going to the door*].　Who 's there?
what 's the matter? will you beat down the
door? How now? what 's the matter?

Enter ÆNEAS.

Æne. Good morrow, lord, good morrow.
Pan. Who 's there? my lord Æneas? By my
troth, I knew you not: what news with you so early?
Æne. Is not prince Troilus here?
Pan. Here! what should he do here?
Æne. Come, he is here, my lord; do not deny
　　him:
It doth import him much to speak with me.
Pan. Is he here, say you? 'tis more than I know,
I 'll be sworn: for my own part, I came in late:
What should he do here?
Æne. Who! nay, then:—
Come, come, you 'll do him wrong ere you are 'ware:
You 'll be so true to him, to be false to him:
Do not you know of him, yet go fetch him hither;
Go.

As PANDARUS *is going out, enter* TROILUS.

Tro. How now? what 's the matter?
Æne. My lord, I scarce have leisure to salute you,
My matter is so rash. There is at hand,
Paris your brother, and Deiphobus,
The Grecian Diomed, and our Antenor,
Delivered to us; and for him, forthwith,
Ere the first sacrifice, within this hour,
We must give up to Diomédes' hand,
The lady Cressida.
Tro.　　　　Is it so concluded?
Æne. By Priam, and the general state of Troy:
They are at hand, and ready to effect it.
Tro. How my achievements mock me!
I will go meet them: and, my lord Æneas,
We met by chance; you did not find me here.
Æne. Good, good, my lord; the secrets of nature
Have not more gift in taciturnity.
　　　　　　　[Exeunt TROILUS *and* ÆNEAS.
Pan. Is 't possible? no sooner got but lost?
The devil take Antenor! the young prince will

go mad. A plague upon Antenor! I would they had broke 's neck.

Enter CRESSIDA.

Cres. How now? What is the matter? Who was here?

Pan. Ah, ah!

Cres. Why sigh you so profoundly? where 's my lord?

Gone?—Tell me, sweet uncle, what 's the matter?

Pan. 'Would I were as deep under the earth as I am above!

Cres. O, the gods! what 's the matter?

Pan. Pr'y thee, get thee in: 'would thou hadst ne'er been born! I knew thou wouldst be his death: O, poor gentleman! A plague upon Antenor!

Cres. Good uncle, I beseech you on my knees, I beseech you, what 's the matter?

Pan. Thou must be gone, wench, thou must be gone; thou art changed for Antenor: thou must to thy father, and be gone from Troilus: 't will be his death; 't will be his bane; he cannot bear it.

Cres. O, you immortal gods!—I will not go.

Pan. Thou must.

Cres. I will not, uncle. I have forgot my father; I know no touch of consanguinity;
No kin, no love, no blood, no soul so near me,
As the sweet Troilus.—O, you gods divine!
Make Cressid's name the very crown of falsehood,
If ever she leave Troilus! Time, force, and death,
Do to this body what extremes you can;
But the strong base and building of my love
Is as the very centre of the earth,
Drawing all things to it.—I 'll go in, and weep;—

Pan. Do, do.

Cres. Tear my bright hair, and scratch my praiséd cheeks;
Crack my clear voice with sobs, and break my heart
With sounding Troilus. I will not go from Troy.
                                        [*Exeunt.*

SCENE III.—*The same. Before* PANDARUS' *House.*

Enter PARIS, TROILUS, ÆNEAS, DEIPHOBUS, ANTENOR, *and* DIOMEDES.

Par. It is great morning; and the hour prefixed
Of her delivery to this valiant Greek
Comes fast upon. Good my brother Troilus,
Tell you the lady what she is to do,
And haste her to the purpose.

Tro.   Walk in to her house;
I 'll bring her to the Grecian presently:
And to his hand when I deliver her,

Think it an altar; and thy brother Troilus
A priest, there offering to it his own heart. [*Exit.*

Par. I know what 't is to love;
And 'would, as I shall pity, I could help!—
Please you, walk in, my lords.   [*Exeunt.*

SCENE IV.—*The same. A Room in* PANDARUS' *House.*

Enter PANDARUS *and* CRESSIDA.

Pan. Be moderate, be moderate.

Cres. Why tell you me of moderation?
The grief is fine, full, perfect, that I taste,
And violenteth in a sense as strong
As that which causeth it: how can I moderate it?
If I could temporise with my affection,
Or brew it to a weak and colder palate,
The like allayment could I give my grief:
My love admits no qualifying dross:
No more my grief, in such a precious loss.

Enter TROILUS.

Pan. Here, here, here he comes.—Ah, sweet ducks!

Cres. O Troilus! Troilus! [*Embracing him.*

Pan. What a pair of spectacles is here! Let me embrace too: "O heart,"—as the goodly saying is,—

———— O heart, O heavy heart,
    Why sigh'st thou without breaking?

where he answers again,

    Because thou canst not ease thy smart,
        By friendship nor by speaking.

There never was a truer rhyme. Let us cast away nothing, for we may live to have need of such a verse; we see it, we see it.—How now, lambs?

Tro. Cressid, I love thee in so strained a purity,
That the blest gods—as angry with my fancy,
More bright in zeal than the devotion which
Cold lips blow to their deities—take thee from me.

Cres. Have the gods envy?

Pan. Ay, ay, ay, ay; 't is too plain a case.

Cres. And is it true that I must go from Troy?

Tro. A hateful truth.

Cres.   What, and from Troilus too?

Tro. From Troy and Troilus.

Cres.   Is it possible?

Tro. And suddenly; where injury of chance
Puts back leave-taking, justles roughly by
All time of pause, rudely beguiles our lips
Of all rejoindure, forcibly prevents
Our locked embrasures, strangles our dear vows
Even in the birth of our own labouring breath:
We two, that with so many thousand sighs
Did buy each other, must poorly sell ourselves
With the rude brevity and discharge of one.

Injurious time now, with a robber's haste,
Crams his rich thievery up, he knows not how:
As many farewells as be stars in heaven,
With distinct breath and cónsigned kisses to them,
He fumbles up into a loose adieu;
And scants us with a single famished kiss,
Distasted with the salt of broken tears.

Æne. [*within*]. My lord! is the lady ready?
Tro. Hark! you are called: Some say, the
    Genius so
Cries "Come!" to him that instantly must die.—
Bid them have patience; she shall come anon.

Pan. Where are my tears? rain, to lay this wind,
or my heart will be blown up by the root! [*Exit.*

Cres. I must then to the Grecians?
Tro.   No remedy.
Cres. A woful Cressid 'mongst the merry
    Greeks!—
When shall we see again?
Tro. Hear me, my love: Be thou but true of
    heart,—
Cres. I true! how now? what wicked deem
    is this?
Tro. Nay, we must use expostulation kindly,
For it is parting from us:
I speak not "Be thou true," as fearing thee;
For I will throw my glove to death himself,
That there's no maculation in thy heart:
But "Be thou true," say I, to fashion in
My sequent protestation: be thou true,
And I will see thee.
Cres. O, you shall be exposed, my lord, to dangers
As infinite as imminent! but I'll be true.
Tro. And I'll grow friend with danger. Wear
    this sleeve.
Cres. And you this glove. When shall I see you?
Tro. I will corrupt the Grecian sentinels,
To give thee nightly visitation.
But yet, be true.
Cres.   O heavens! "Be true," again?
Tro. Hear why I speak it, love:
The Grecian youths are full of quality;
They're loving, well composed, with gifts of nature
    flowing,
And swelling o'er with arts and exercise:
How novelty may move, and parts with person,
Alas, a kind of godly jealousy
(Which, I beseech you, call a virtuous sin)
Makes me afeard.
Cres.   O heavens! you love me not.
Tro. Die I a villain, then!
In this I do not call your faith in question,
So mainly as my merit. I cannot sing,
Nor heel the high lavolt, nor sweeten talk,
Nor play at subtle games; fair virtues all,
To which the Grecians are most prompt and preg-
    nant:

But I can tell, that in each grace of these
There lurks a still and dumb discoursive devil,
That tempts most cunningly: but be not tempted.
Cres. Do you think I will?
Tro. No.
But something may be done that we will not:
And sometimes we are devils to ourselves,
When we will tempt the frailty of our powers,
Presuming on their changeful potency.
Æne. [*within*]. Nay, good my lord,—
Tro.   Come, kiss; and let us part.
Par. [*within*]. Brother Troilus!
Tro.   Good brother, come you hither;
And bring Æneas, and the Grecian, with you.
Cres. My lord, will you be true?
Tro. Who, I? alas, it is my vice, my fault:
While others fish with craft for great opinion,
I with great truth catch mere simplicity;
Whilst some with cunning gild their copper
    crowns,
With truth and plainness I do wear mine bare.
Fear not my truth; the moral of my wit
Is "plain and true;" there's all the reach of it.

Enter ÆNEAS, PARIS, ANTENOR, DEIPHOBUS,
    and DIOMEDES.

Welcome, sir Diomed! here is the lady,
Which for Antenor we deliver you:
At the port, lord, I'll give her to thy hand;
And, by the way, possess thee what she is.
Entreat her fair; and by my soul, fair Greek,
If e'er thou stand at mercy of my sword,
Name Cressid, and thy life shall be as safe
As Priam is in Ilion.
Dio.   Fair lady Cressid,
So please you, save the thanks this prince expects;
The lustre in your eye, heaven in your cheek,
Pleads your fair usage; and to Diomed
You shall be mistress, and command him wholly.
Tro. Grecian, thou dost not use me courteously,
To shame the zeal of my petition to thee,
In praising her. I tell thee, lord of Greece,
She is as far high-soaring o'er thy praises,
As thou unworthy to be called her servant.
I charge thee, use her well, even for my charge;
For by the dreadful Pluto, if thou dost not,
Though the great bulk Achilles be thy guard,
I'll cut thy throat.
Dio.   O, be not moved, prince Troilus;
Let me be privileged by my place and message
To be a speaker free; when I am hence,
I'll answer to my lust: and know you, lord,
I'll nothing do on charge: to her own worth
She shall be prized; but that you say "be 't so,"
I speak it in my spirit and honour—no.
Tro. Come, to the port.—I tell thee, Diomed,
This brave shall oft make thee to hide thy head.

Lady, give me your hand; and, as we walk,
To our own selves bend we our needful talk.

[*Exeunt* TROILUS, CRESSIDA, *and* DIOMEDES.
[*Trumpet heard.*

Par. Hark! Hector's trumpet.

Æne.   How have we spent this morning!
The prince must think me tardy and remiss,
That swore to ride before him to the field.

Par. 'T is Troilus' fault. Come, come, to field
      with him.

Dei. Let us make ready straight.

Æne. Yea, with a bridegroom's fresh alacrity,
Let us address to tend on Hector's heels:
The glory of our Troy doth this day lie
On his fair worth and single chivalry. [*Exeunt.*

SCENE V.—*The* Grecian *Camp. Lists set out.*

Enter AJAX, *armed;* AGAMEMNON, ACHILLES,
PATROCLUS, MENELAUS, ULYSSES, NESTOR, *and
others.*

Agam. Here art thou in appointment fresh and
      fair,

Anticipating time with starting courage.
Give with thy trumpet a loud note to Troy,
Thou dreadful Ajax; that the appalléd air
May pierce the head of the great combatant,
And hale him hither.

Ajax.   Thou, trumpet, there 's my purse.
Now crack thy lungs, and split thy brazen pipe:
Blow, villain, till thy spheréd bias cheek
Outswell the colick of puffed Aquilon:
Come, stretch thy chest, and let thy eyes spout blood:
Thou blow'st for Hector.   [*Trumpet sounds.*

Ulys. No trumpet answers.

Achil.   'T is but early days.

Agam. Is not yon Diomed, with Calchas' daughter?

Ulys. 'T is he; I ken the manner of his gait;
He rises on the toe: that spirit of his
In aspiration lifts him from the earth.

Enter DIOMEDES *with* CRESSIDA.

Agam. Is this the lady Cressid?

Dio.   Even she.

Agam. Most dearly welcome to the Greeks, sweet
      lady.

Nes. Our general doth salute you with a kiss.

Ulys. Yet is the kindness but particular;
'T were better she were kissed in general.

Nes. And very courtly counsel: I 'll begin.—
So much for Nestor.

Achil. I 'll take that winter from your lips, fair
     lady:
Achilles bids you welcome.

Men. I had good argument for kissing once.

Patr. But that 's no argument for kissing now:
For thus popped Paris in his hardiment;
And parted thus you and your argument.

Ulys. O, deadly gall, and theme of all our scorns!
For which we lose our heads, to gild his horns.

Patr. The first was Menelaus' kiss;—this, mine:
Patroclus kisses you.

Men.   O, this is trim!

Patr. Paris and I kiss evermore for him.

Men. I 'll have my kiss, sir:—lady, by your
     leave.

Cres. In kissing, do you render or receive?

Patr. Both take and give.

Cres.   I 'll make my match to live,
The kiss you take is better than you give;
Therefore no kiss.

Men. I 'll give you boot, I 'll give you three for
     one.

Cres. You 're an odd man; give even, or give
     none.

Men. An odd man, lady? every man is odd.

Cres. No, Paris is not; for you know, 't is true,
That you are odd, and he is even with you.

Men. You fillip me o' the head.

Cres.   No, I 'll be sworn.

Ulys. It were no match, your nail against his
     horn.—

May I, sweet lady, beg a kiss of you?

Cres. You may.

Ulys.   I do desire it.

Cres.   Why, beg then.

Ulys. Why then, for Venus' sake, give me a kiss
When Helen is a maid again, and his.

Cres. I am your debtor; claim it when 't is due.

Ulys. Never 's my day,—and then a kiss of you.

Dio. Lady, a word: I 'll bring you to your
     father. [*Diomedes leads out* Cressida.

Nes. A woman of quick sense.

Ulys.   Fie, fie upon her!
There 's language in her eye, her cheek, her lip,
Nay, her foot speaks; her wanton spirits look out
At every joint and motive of her body.
O, these encounterers, so glib of tongue,
That give a coasting welcome ere it comes,
And wide unclasp the tables of their thoughts
To every ticklish reader! set them down
For sluttish spoils of opportunity,
And daughters of the game. [*Trumpet within.*

All. The Trojan's trumpet.

Agam. Yonder comes the troop.

Enter Hector, *armed;* Æneas, Troilus, *and
     other* Trojans, *with* Attendants.

Æne. Hail, all the state of Greece! What shall
     be done to him
That victory commands? Or do you purpose
A victor shall be known? Will you, the knights
Shall to the edge of all extremity
Pursue each other; or shall they be divided
By any voice or order of the field?
Hector bade ask.

Agam.   Which way would Hector have it?

Æne. He cares not; he 'll obey conditions.

Achil. 'T is done like Hector, but securely done;
A little proudly, and great deal misprising
The knight opposed.

Æne.   If not Achilles, sir,
What is your name?

Achil.   If not Achilles, nothing.

Æne. Therefore Achilles: but whate'er, know
     this;—
In the extremity of great and little,
Valour and pride excel themselves in Hector;
The one almost as infinite as all,
The other blank as nothing. Weigh him well,
And that which looks like pride, is courtesy.
This Ajax is half made of Hector's blood:
In love whereof, half Hector stays at home;
Half heart, half hand, half Hector, comes to seek
This blended knight, half Trojan and half Greek.

Achil. A maiden battle, then? O, I perceive you.

Re-enter Diomedes.

Agam. Here is sir Diomed:—Go, gentle knight,
Stand by our Ajax: as you and lord Æneas
Consent upon the order of their fight,
So be it; either to the uttermost,
Or else a breath: the combatants being kin,
Half stints their strife before their strokes begin.
        [Ajax *and* Hector *enter the lists.*

Ulys. They are opposed already.

Agam. What Trojan is that same that looks so
     heavy?

Ulys. The youngest son of Priam; a true knight;
Not yet mature, yet matchless; firm of word;
Speaking in deeds, and deedless in his tongue;
Not soon provoked, nor, being provoked, soon
     calmed:
His heart and hand both open, and both free;
For what he has he gives, what thinks, he shews;
Yet gives he not till judgment guide his bounty,
Nor dignifies an impair thought with breath;
Manly as Hector, but more dangerous;
For Hector, in his blaze of wrath, subscribes
To tender objects; but he, in heat of action,
Is more vindicative than jealous love:

They call him Troilus; and on him erect
A second hope, as fairly built as Hector.
Thus says Æneas: one that knows the youth
Even to his inches, and, with private soul,
Did in great Ilion thus translate him to me.

               [*Alarum.* HECTOR *and* AJAX *fight.*
Agam. They are in action.
Nes. Now, Ajax, hold thine own!
Tro. Hector, thou sleep'st: awake thee!
Agam. His blows are well disposed:—there,
      Ajax!
Dio. You must no more.   [*Trumpets cease.*
Æne.   Princes, enough, so please you.
Ajax. I am not warm yet; let us fight again.
Dio. As Hector pleases.
Hect.   Why then, will I no more:—
Thou art, great lord, my father's sister's son,
A cousin-german to great Priam's seed;
The obligation of our blood forbids
A gory emulation 'twixt us twain:
Were thy commixtion Greek and Trojan so
That thou couldst say, "This hand is Grecian all,
And this is Trojan; the sinews of this leg
All Greek, and this all Troy; my mother's blood
Runs on the dexter cheek, and this sinister
Bounds-in my father's;" by Jove multipotent,
Thou shouldst not bear from me a Greekish
      member
Wherein my sword had not impressure made
Of our rank feud: but the just gods gainsay
That any drop thou borrow'st from thy mother,
My sacred aunt, should by my mortal sword
Be drained! Let me embrace thee, Ajax:
By him that thunders, thou hast lusty arms;
Hector would have them fall upon him thus:
Cousin, all honour to thee!
   Ajax.   I thank thee, Hector:
Thou art too gentle, and too free a man:
I came to kill thee, cousin, and bear hence
A great addition earnéd in thy death.
   Hect. Not Neoptolemus so mirable
(On whose bright crest Fame with her loud'st
      "Oyes"
Cries, "This is he") could promise to himself
A thought of added honour torn from Hector.
   Æne. There is expectance here from both the
      sides,
What further you will do.
   Hect.   We'll answer it;
The issue is embracement:—Ajax, farewell.
   Ajax. If I might in entreaties find success
(As seld I have the chance), I would desire
My famous cousin to our Grecian tents.
   Dio. 'T is Agamemnon's wish: and great
      Achilles
Doth long to see unarmed the valiant Hector.
   Hect. Æneas, call my brother Troilus to me:

And signify this loving interview
To the expecters of our Trojan part;
Desire them home.—Give me thy hand, my
      cousin;
I will go eat with thee, and see your knights.
   Ajax. Great Agamemnon comes to meet us
      here.
   Hect. The worthiest of them tell me, name by
      name;
But for Achilles, my own searching eyes
Shall find him by his large and portly size.
   Agam. Worthy of arms! as welcome as to one
That would be rid of such an enemy:
But that's no welcome: understand more clear,
What's past, and what's to come, is strewed with
      husks
And formless ruin of oblivion;
But in this extant moment, faith and troth,
Strained purely from all hollow bias-drawing,
Bids thee, with most divine integrity,
From heart of very heart, great Hector, welcome.
   Hect. I thank thee, most imperious Aga-
      memnon.
   Agam. My well-famed lord of Troy, no less to
      you.   [*To* TROILUS.
   Men. Let me confirm my princely brother's
      greeting:—
You brace of warlike brothers, welcome hither.
   Hect. Whom must we answer?
   Men.   The noble Menelaus.
   Hect. O you, my lord? by Mars his gauntlet,
      thanks!
Mock not that I affect the untraded oath:
Your quondam wife swears still by Venus' glove:
She's well, but bade me not commend her to you.
   Men. Name her not now, sir; she's a deadly
      theme.
   Hect. O, pardon; I offend.
   Nes. I have, thou gallant Trojan, seen thee oft,
Labouring for destiny, make cruel way
Through ranks of Greekish youth: and I have seen
      thee,
As hot as Perseus, spur thy Phrygian steed,
And seen thee scorning forfeits and subduements,
When thou hast hung thy advanced sword i'the air,
Not letting it decline on the declined;
That I have said to some, my standers-by,
"Lo, Jupiter is yonder, dealing life!"
And I have seen thee pause, and take thy breath,
When that a ring of Greeks have hemmed thee in,
Like an Olympian wrestling: this have I seen;
But this thy countenance, still locked in steel,
I never saw till now.   I knew thy grandsire,
And once fought with him: he was a soldier good;
But by great Mars, the captain of us all,
Never like thee: let an old man embrace thee;
And, worthy warrior, welcome to our tents.

Æne. 'T is the old Nestor.

Hect. Let me embrace thee, good old chronicle,
That hast so long walked hand in hand with time :
Most reverend Nestor, I am glad to clasp thee.

Nes. I would my arms could match thee in
    contention,
As they contend with thee in courtesy.

Hect. I would they could.

Nest. Ha! by this white beard, I'd fight with
    thee to-morrow.
Well, welcome, welcome! I have seen the time—

Ulys. I wonder now how yonder city stands,
When we have here her base and pillar by us.

Hect. I know your favour, lord Ulysses, well.
Ah, sir, there's many a Greek and Trojan dead,
Since first I saw yourself and Diomed
In Ilion, on your Greekish embassy.

Ulys. Sir, I foretold you then what would ensue;
My prophecy is but half his journey yet;
For yonder walls, that pertly front your town,
Yon towers, whose wanton tops do buss the clouds,
Must kiss their own feet.

Hect.   I must not believe you:
There they stand yet; and modestly I think,
The fall of every Phrygian stone will cost
A drop of Grecian blood: the end crowns all:
And that old common arbitrator, Time,
Will one day end it.

Ulys.   So to him we leave it.
Most gentle and most valiant Hector, welcome:
After the general, I beseech you next
To feast with me, and see me at my tent.

Achil. I shall forestal thee, lord Ulysses, thou!—
Now, Hector, I have fed mine eyes on thee;
I have with exact view perused thee, Hector,
And quoted joint by joint.

Hect.   Is this Achilles?

Achil. I am Achilles.

Hect. Stand fair, I pray thee : let me look on
    thee.

Achil. Behold thy fill.

Hect.   Nay, I have done already.

Achil. Thou art too brief; I will the second time,
As I would buy thee, view thee limb by limb.

Hect. O, like a book of sport thou 'lt read me o'er;
But there's more in me than thou understand'st.
Why dost thou so oppress me with thine eye?

Achil. Tell me, you heavens, in which part of
    his body
Shall I destroy him? whether there, there, or
    there?
That I may give the local wound a name,
And make distinct the very breach whereout
Hector's great spirit flew : answer me, heavens!

Hect. It would discredit the blessed gods, proud
    man,

To answer such a question : stand again :
Think'st thou to catch my life so pleasantly,
As to prenominate in nice conjecture,
Where thou wilt hit me dead?

Achil.   I tell thee, yea.

Hect. Wert thou an oracle to tell me so,
I 'll not believe thee. Henceforth, guard thee
    well;
For I 'll not kill thee there, nor there, nor there;
But, by the forge that stithied Mars his helm,
I 'll kill thee everywhere, yea, o'er and o'er.—
You wisest Grecians, pardon me this brag;
His insolence draws folly from my lips;
But I 'll endeavour deeds to match these words,
Or may I never—

Ajax.   Do not chafe thee, cousin :
And you, Achilles, let these threats alone,
Till accident or purpose bring you to 't :
You may have every day enough of Hector,
If you have stomach; the general state, I fear,
Can scarce entreat you to be odd with him.

Hect. I pray you, let us see you in the field;
We have had pelting wars since you refused
The Grecians' cause.

Achil.   Dost thou entreat me, Hector?
To-morrow do I meet thee, fell as death;
To-night, all friends,

Hect.   Thy hand upon that match.

Agam. First, all you peers of Greece, go to my
    tent;
There in the full convive we : afterwards,
As Hector's leisure and your bounties shall
Concur together, severally entreat him.—
Beat loud the tabourines, let the trumpets blow,
That this great soldier may his welcome know.

    [*Exeunt all but* TROILUS *and* ULYSSES.

Tro. My lord Ulysses, tell me, I beseech you,
In what place of the field doth Calchas keep?

Ulys. At Menelaus' tent, most princely Troilus :
There Diomed doth feast with him to-night;
Who neither looks upon the heaven nor earth,
But gives all gaze and bent of amorous view
On the fair Cressid.

Tro. Shall I, sweet lord, be bound to you so
    much,
After we part from Agamemnon's tent,
To bring me thither?

Ulys.   You shall command me, sir.
As gentle tell me, of what honour was
This Cressida in Troy? Had she no lover there,
That wails her absence?

Tro. O, sir, to such as boasting shew their scars,
A mock is due. Will you walk on, my lord?
She was beloved, she loved; she is, and doth :
But still, sweet love is food for Fortune's tooth.

    [*Exeunt.*

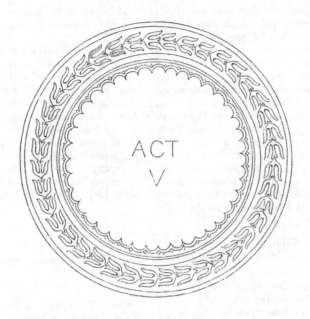

ACT
V

SCENE I.—*The* Grecian *Camp. Before* ACHILLES'
Tent.

Enter ACHILLES *and* PATROCLUS.

Achil. I 'll heat his blood with Greekish wine
to-night,
Which with my scimitar I 'll cool to-morrow.—
Patroclus, let us feast him to the height.

Patr. Here comes Thersites.

Enter THERSITES.

Achil.   How now, thou core of envy?
Thou crusty batch of nature, what 's the news?

Ther. Why, thou picture of what thou seemest,
and idol of idiot-worshippers, here 's a letter for
thee.

Achil. From whence, fragment?

Ther. Why, thou full dish of fool, from Troy.

Patr. Who keeps the tent now?

Ther. The surgeon's box, or the patient's wound.

Patr. Well said, Adversity! and what need
these tricks?

Ther. Pr'y thee be silent, boy; I profit not by
thy talk: thou art thought to be Achilles' male
varlet.

Patr. Male varlet, you rogue! what 's that?

Ther. Why, his masculine whore. Now the
rotten diseases of the south, the guts-griping,
ruptures, catarrhs, loads o' gravel i' the back,
lethargies, cold palsies, raw eyes, dirt-rotten
livers, wheezing lungs, bladders full of imposthume, sciaticas, lime-kilns i' the palm, incurable
bone-ache, and the rivelled fee-simple of the
tetter, take and take again such preposterous
discoveries!

Patr. Why, thou damnable box of envy, thou,
what meanest thou to curse thus?

Ther. Do I curse thee?

Patr. Why, no, you ruinous butt; you whoreson indistinguishable cur, no.

Ther. No? why art thou then exasperate, thou
idle immaterial skein of sleave silk, thou green
sarcenet flap for a sore eye, thou tassel of a prodigal's purse, thou? Ah, how the poor world is
pestered with such water-flies: diminutives of
nature!

Patr. Out, gall!

Ther. Finch egg!

Achil. My sweet Patroclus, I am thwarted quite
From my great purpose in to-morrow's battle.
Here is a letter from Queen Hecuba;
A token from her daughter, my fair love;
Both taxing me, and gaging me to keep
An oath that I have sworn. I will not break it:
Fall, Greeks; fail, fame; honour, or go or stay;
My major vow lies here, this I 'll obey.—
Come, come, Thersites, help to trim my tent;
This night in banqueting must all be spent.—
Away, Patroclus.

           [*Exeunt* ACHILLES *and* PATROCLUS.

Ther. With too much blood and too little brain,
these two may run mad; but if with too much
brain and too little blood, they do, I 'll be a curer
of madmen. Here 's Agamemnon—an honest

fellow enough, and one that loves quails; but he has not so much brain as ear-wax: and the goodly transformation of Jupiter there, his brother, the bull—the primitive statue and oblique memorial of cuckolds; a thrifty shoeing-horn in a chain, hanging at his brother's leg—to what form but that he is, should wit larded with malice, and malice forced with wit, turn him to? To an ass, were nothing; he is both ass and ox: to an ox, were nothing; he is both ox and ass. To be a dog, a mule, a cat, a fitchew, a toad, a lizard, an owl, a puttock, or a herring without a roe, I would not care; but to be Menelaus—I would conspire against destiny. Ask me not what I would be, if I were not Thersites; for I care not to be the louse of a lazar, so I were not Menelaus. Hey-day! spirits and fires!

Enter HECTOR, TROILUS, AJAX, AGAMEMNON, ULYSSES, NESTOR, MENELAUS, *and* DIOMEDES, *with lights.*

Agam. We go wrong, we go wrong.
Ajax. No, yonder 't is;
There, where we see the lights.
Hect. I trouble you.
Ajax. No, not a whit.
Ulys. Here comes himself to guide you.

Enter ACHILLES.

Achil. Welcome, brave Hector; welcome, princes all.
Agam. So now, fair prince of Troy, I bid good night.
Ajax commands the guard to tend on you.
Hect. Thanks and good night to the Greeks' general.
Men. Good night, my lord.
Hect. Good night, sweet lord Menelaus.
Ther. Sweet draught; sweet, quoth 'a! sweet sink, sweet sewer.
Achil. Good night, and welcome, both to those That go or tarry.
Agam. Good night.
[*Exeunt* AGAMEMNON *and* MENELAUS.
Achil. Old Nestor tarries; and you too, Diomed, Keep Hector company an hour or two.
Dio. I cannot, lord; I have important business,
The tide whereof is now.— Good night, great Hector.
Hect. Give me your hand.
Ulys. Follow his torch, he goes to Calchas' tent;
I 'll keep you company. [*Aside to* TROILUS
Tro. Sweet sir, you honour me.
Hect. And so good night.
[*Exit* DIOMEDES; ULYSSES *and* TROILUS *following.*

Achil. Come, come, enter my tent.
[*Exeunt* ACHILLES, HECTOR, AJAX, *and* NESTOR.

Ther. That same Diomed 's a false-hearted rogue, a most unjust knave; I will no more trust him when he leers, than I will a serpent when he hisses: he will spend his mouth, and promise, like Brabler the hound; but when he performs, astronomers foretel it; it is prodigious, there will come some change; the sun borrows of the moon, when Diomed keeps his word. I will rather leave to see Hector, than not to dog him: they say, he keeps a Trojan drab, and uses the traitor Calchas' tent: I 'll after.—Nothing but lechery! all incontinent varlets! [*Exit.*

SCENE II.—*The same. Before* CALCHAS' *Tent.*

Enter DIOMEDES.

Dio. What, are you up here, ho? speak.
Cal. [*within*]. Who calls?
Dio. Diomed.— Calchas, I think;— where 's your daughter?
Cal. [*within*]. She comes to you.

Enter TROILUS *and* ULYSSES, *at a distance; after them* THERSITES.

Ulys. Stand where the torch may not discover us.

Enter CRESSIDA.

Tro. Cressid come forth to him!
Dio. How now, my charge?
Cres. Now, my sweet guardian! Hark, a word with you. [*Whispers.*
Tro. Yea, so familiar!
Ulys. She will sing any man at first sight.
Ther. And any man may sing her, if he can take her clef; she 's noted.
Dio. Will you remember?
Cres. Remember?—yes.
Dio. Nay, but do then; and let your mind be coupled with your words.
Tro. What should she remember?
Ulys. List!
Cres. Sweet honey Greek, tempt me no more to folly.
Ther. Roguery!
Dio. Nay, then,—
Cres. I 'll tell you what:—
Dio. Pho, pho! come, tell a pin! you are a forsworn.
Cres. In faith, I cannot: what would you have me do?

Ther. A juggling trick, to be—secretly open.

Dio. What did you swear you would bestow on me?

Cres. I pr'y thee, do not hold me to mine oath;

Bid me do anything but that, sweet Greek.

Dio. Good night.

Tro.   Hold, patience!

Ulys.   How now, Trojan?

Cres.   Diomed,—

Dio. No, no, good night: I'll be your fool no more.

Tro. Thy better must.

Cres.   Hark! one word in your ear.

Tro. O, plague and madness!

Ulys. You are moved, prince; let us depart, I pray you,

Lest your displeasure should enlarge itself

To wrathful terms: this place is dangerous;

The time right deadly; I beseech you, go.

Tro. Behold, I pray you!

Ulys.   Now, good my lord, go off:

You flow to great destruction; come, my lord.

Tro. I pr'y thee, stay.

Ulys.   You have not patience: come.

Tro. I pray you, stay; by hell, and all hell's torments,

I will not speak a word.

Dio.   And so, good night.

Cres. Nay, but you part in anger.

Tro.   Doth that grieve thee?

O, withered truth!

Ulys.   Why, how now, lord?

Tro.   By Jove,

I will be patient.

Cres. Guardian!—why, Greek!

Dio. Pho, pho! adieu; you palter.

Cres. In faith, I do not; come hither once again.

Ulys. You shake, my lord, at something; will you go?

You will break out.

Tro.   She strokes his cheek!

Ulys.   Come, come.

Tro. Nay, stay; by Jove, I will not speak a word:

There is between my will and all offences

A guard of patience;—stay a little while.

Ther. How the devil luxury, with his fat rump and potatoe finger, tickles these together! Fry, lechery, fry!

Dio. But will you then?

Cres. In faith, I will, la; never trust me else.

Dio. Give me some token for the surety of it.

Cres. I'll fetch you one.   [*Exit.*

Ulys. You have sworn patience.

Tro.   Fear me not, sweet lord.

I will not be myself, nor have cognition

Of what I feel; I am all patience.

Re-enter CRESSIDA.

Ther. Now the pledge; now, now, now!

Cres. Here, Diomed, keep this sleeve.

Tro. O beauty! where's thy faith?

Ulys.   My lord,—

Tro. I will be patient; outwardly I will.

Cres. You look upon that sleeve; behold it well.

He loved me—O, false wench!—Give't me again.

Dio. Who was't?

Cres.   It is no matter, now I have't again.

I will not meet with you to-morrow night:

I pr'y thee, Diomed, visit me no more.

Ther. Now she sharpens; well said, whetstone.

Dio. I shall have it.

Cres.   What, this?

Dio.   Ay, that.

Cres. O, all you gods!—O, pretty, pretty pledge!

Thy master now lies thinking in his bed

Of thee and me; and sighs, and takes my glove,

And gives memorial dainty kisses to it,

As I kiss thee.—Nay, do not snatch it from me;

He that takes that, must take my heart withal.

Dio. I had your heart before; this follows it.

Tro. I did swear patience.

Cres. You shall not have it, Diomed; 'faith you shall not;

I'll give you something else.

Dio. I will have this; whose was it?

Cres.   It is no matter.

Dio. Come, tell me whose it was?

Cres. 'Twas one's that loved me better than you will.

But now you have it, take it.

Dio.   Whose was it?

Cres. By all Diana's waiting-women yonder,

And by herself, I will not tell you whose.

Dio. To-morrow will I wear it on my helm;

And grieve his spirit that dares not challenge it.

Tro. Wert thou the devil, and wor'st it on thy horn,

It should be challenged.

Cres. Well, well, 'tis done, 'tis past: and yet it is not;

I will not keep my word.

Dio. Why then, farewell;

Thou never shalt mock Diomed again.

Cres. You shall not go:—one cannot speak a word,

But it straight starts you.

Dio.   I do not like this fooling.

Ther. Nor I, by Pluto: but that that likes not you, pleases me best.

Dio. What, shall I come? the hour?

Cres.　　Ay, come:—O, Jove!
Do come:—I shall be plagued.

Dio.　　Farewell till then.

Cres. Good night. I pr'y thee, come.

　　　　　　　　　　　[*Exit* DIOMEDES.

Troilus, farewell! one eye yet looks on thee;
But with my heart the other eye doth see.
Ah! poor our sex! this fault in us I find,
The error of our eye directs our mind:
What error leads, must err: O, then conclude
Minds, swayed by eyes, are full of turpitude.

　　　　　　　　　　　　　[*Exit.*

　　Ther. A proof of strength she could not publish
　　　　more,
Unless she said, "My mind is now turned whore."

　　Ulys.　　All's done, my lord.

　　Tro.　　　　It is.

　　Ulys.　　　　　Why stay we, then?

　　Tro. To make a recordation to my soul
Of every syllable that here was spoke.
But, if I tell how these two did co-act,
Shall I not lie in publishing a truth?
Sith yet there is a credence in my heart,
An esperance so obstinately strong,
That doth invert the attest of eyes and ears!
As if those organs had deceptious functions,
Created only to calumniate.
Was Cressid here?

　　Ulys.　　I cannot conjure, Trojan.

　　Tro. She was not, sure.

　　Ulys.　　Most sure she was.

　　Tro. Why, my negation hath no taste of mad-
　　　　ness.

　　Ulys. Nor mine, my lord: Cressid was here
　　　　but now.

　　Tro. Let it not be believed for womanhood!
Think we had mothers; do not give advantage
To stubborn critics—apt, without a theme,
For depravation—to square the general sex
By Cressid's rule: rather think this not Cressid.

　　Ulys. What hath she done, prince, that can
　　　　soil our mothers?

　　Tro. Nothing at all, unless that this were she.

　　Ther. Will he swagger himself out on's own
　　　　eyes?

　　Tro. This she? no, this is Diomed's Cressida:
If beauty have a soul, this is not she;
If souls guide vows, if vows be sanctimony,
If sanctimony be the gods' delight,
If there be rule in unity itself,
This was not she. O, madness of discourse,
That cause sets up with and against itself!
Bifold authority! where reason can revolt
Without perdition, and loss assume all reason
Without revolt; this is, and is not, Cressid!
Within my soul there doth commence a fight

Of this strange nature, that a thing inseparate
Divides more wider than the sky and earth;
And yet the spacious breadth of this division
Admits no orifice for a point, as subtile
As is Arachne's broken woof, to enter.
Instance, O instance! strong as Pluto's gates;
Cressid is mine, tied with the bonds of heaven:
Instance, O instance! strong as heaven itself;
The bonds of heaven are slipped, dissolved, and
　　　　loosed;
And with another knot, five-finger tied,
The fractions of her faith, orts of her love,
The fragments, scraps, the bits, and greasy reliques
Of her o'er eaten faith, are bound to Diomed.

　　Ulys. May worthy Troilus be half attached
With that which here his passion doth express?

　　Tro. Ay, Greek; and that shall be divulgèd well
In characters as red as Mars his heart
Inflamed with Venus: never did young man fancy
With so eternal and so fixed a soul.
Hark, Greek;—as much as I do Cressid love,
So much by weight hate I her Diomed:
That sleeve is mine that he'll bear on his helm;
Were it a casque composed by Vulcan's skill,
My sword should bite it: not the dreadful spout
Which shipmen do the hurricano call,
Constringed in mass by the almighty sun,
Shall dizzy with more clamour Neptune's ear
In his descent, than shall my prompted sword
Falling on Diomed.

　　Ther. He'll tickle it for his concupy.

　　Tro. O, Cressid! O, false Cressid! false, false,
　　　　false!
Let all untruths stand by thy stainèd name,
And they'll seem glorious.

　　Ulys.　　O, contain yourself;
Your passion draws ears hither.

　　　　　　　Enter ÆNEAS.

　　Æne. I have been seeking you this hour, my lord:
Hector, by this, is arming him in Troy;
Ajax, your guard, stays to conduct you home.

　　Tro. Have with you, prince:—My courteous
　　　　lord, adieu:—
Farewell, revolted fair! and, Diomed,
Stand fast, and wear a castle on thy head!

　　Ulys. I'll bring you to the gates.

　　Tro. Accept distracted thanks.

　　　　[*Exeunt* TROILUS, ÆNEAS, *and* ULYSSES.

　　Ther. 'Would I could meet that rogue Diomed!
I would croak like a raven; I would bode, I would
bode. Patroclus will give me anything for the intelligence of this whore: the parrot will not do
more for an almond, than he for a commodious
drab. Lechery, lechery; still wars and lechery;
nothing else holds fashion: a burning devil take
them.　　　　　　　　　　　　　[*Exit.*

SCENE III.—Troy. *Before* PRIAM'S *Palace*.

Enter HECTOR *and* ANDROMACHE.

And. When was my lord so much ungently
        tempered,
To stop his ears against admonishment?
Unarm, unarm, and do not fight to-day.

Hect. You train me to offend you; get you in;
By all the everlasting gods, I 'll go.

And. My dreams will, sure, prove ominous to
        the day.

Hect. No more, I say.

Enter CASSANDRA.

Cas.   Where is my brother Hector?

And. Here, sister; armed, and bloody in intent:
Consort with me in loud and dear petition;

Pursue we him on knees; for I have dreamed
Of bloody turbulence, and this whole night
Hath nothing been but shapes and forms of
        slaughter.

Cas. O, it is true.

Hect.   Ho! bid my trumpet sound!

Cas. No notes of sally, for the heavens, sweet
        brother.

Hect. Begone, I say: the gods have heard me
        swear.

Cas. The gods are deaf to hot and peevish vows:
They are polluted offerings, more abhorred
Than spotted livers in the sacrifice.

And. O, be persuaded: Do not count it holy
To hurt by being just: it is as lawful,
For we would give much, to use violent thefts,
And rob in the behalf of charity.

Cas. It is the purpose that makes strong the
    vow;
But vows to every purpose must not hold:
Unarm, sweet Hector.
    Hect.   Hold you still, I say;
Mine honour keeps the weather of my fate:
Life every man holds dear; but the dear man
Holds honour far more precious-dear than life.

              Enter TROILUS.

How now, young man? mean'st thou to fight to-day?
    And. Cassandra, call my father to persuade.
                  [*Exit* CASSANDRA.
    Hect. No, 'faith, young Troilus; doff thy har-
    ness, youth;
I am to-day i' the vein of chivalry:
Let grow thy sinews till their knots be strong,
And tempt not yet the brushes of the war.
Unarm thee, go; and doubt thou not, brave boy,
I 'll stand, to-day, for thee, and me, and Troy.
    Tro. Brother, you have a vice of mercy in you,
Which better fits a lion than a man.
    Hect. What vice is that, good Troilus? chide
    me for it.
    Tro. When many times the captive Grecians fall,
Even in the fan and wind of your fair sword,
You bid them rise and live.
    Hect. O, 'tis fair play.
    Tro.   Fool's play, by heaven, Hector.
    Hect. How now? how now?
    Tro.   For the love of all the gods,
Let 's leave the hermit pity with our mother;
And when we have our armours buckled on,
The venomed vengeance ride upon our swords;
Spur them to ruthful work, rein them from ruth.
    Hect. Fie, savage, fie!
    Tro.   Hector, then 'tis wars.
    Hect. Troilus, I would not have you fight to-day.
    Tro. Who should withhold me?
Not fate, obedience, nor the hand of Mars
Beckoning with fiery truncheon my retire;
Not Priamus and Hecuba on knees,
Their eyes o'ergallèd with recourse of tears;
Nor you, my brother, with your true sword drawn,
Opposed to hinder me, should stop my way,
But by my ruin.

     Re-enter CASSANDRA, *with* PRIAM.

    Cas. Lay hold upon him, Priam, hold him fast;
He is thy crutch; now if thou lose thy stay,
Thou on him leaning, and all Troy on thee,
Fall all together.
    Pri.   Come, Hector, come, go back:
Thy wife hath dreamed; thy mother hath had
    visions;
Cassandra doth foresee; and I myself
Am like a prophet suddenly enrapt,

To tell thee that this day is ominous:
Therefore, come back.
    Hect.   Æneas is a-field;
And I do stand engaged to many Greeks,
Even in the faith of valour, to appear
This morning to them.
    Pri.   But thou shalt not go.
    Hect. I must not break my faith.
You know me dutiful; therefore, dear sir,
Let me not shame respect; but give me leave
To take that course by your consent and voice,
Which you do here forbid me, royal Priam.
    Cas. O Priam, yield not to him!
    And.   Do not, dear father.
    Hect. Andromache, I am offended with you:
Upon the love you bear me, get you in.
               [*Exit* ANDROMACHE.
    Tro. This foolish, dreaming, superstitious girl
Makes all these bodements.
    Cas.   O, farewell, dear Hector!
Look, how thou diest! look, how thy eye turns pale!
Look, how thy wounds do bleed at many vents!
Hark, how Troy roars! how Hecuba cries out!
How poor Andromache shrills her dolours forth!
Behold, distraction, frenzy, and amazement,
Like witless anticks, one another meet,
And all cry "Hector! Hector's dead!" O Hector!
    Tro. Away! away!
    Cas. Farewell.—Yet, soft: Hector, I take my
    leave:
Thou dost thyself and all our Troy deceive. [*Exit.*
    Hect. You are amazed, my liege, at her exclaim!
Go in, and cheer the town: we 'll forth and fight:
Do deeds worth praise, and tell you them at night.
    Pri. Farewell: the gods with safety stand about
    thee!
       [*Exeunt, severally,* PRIAM *and* HECTOR.
            Alarums.
    Tro. They are at it; hark! Proud Diomed,
    believe
I come to lose my arm, or win my sleeve.

As TROILUS *is going out, enter, from the other side,*
              PANDARUS.
    Pan. Do you hear, my lord? do you hear?
    Tro. What now?
    Pan. Here 's a letter from yon' poor girl.
    Tro. Let me read.
    Pan. A whoreson ptisick, a whoreson rascally
ptisick so troubles me, and the foolish fortune of
this girl; and what one thing, what another, that
I shall leave you one o' these days: and I have a
rheum in mine eyes too; and such an ache in my
bones, that, unless a man were cursed, I cannot
tell what to think on 't.—What says she there?
    Tro. Words, words, mere words; no matter from
    the heart;   [*Tearing the letter.*

The effect doth operate another way.—
Go, wind to wind, there turn and change toge-
    ther.—
My love with words and errors still she feeds;
But edifies another with her deeds.
                  [*Exeunt severally.*

SCENE IV.—*Between* Troy *and the* Grecian Camp.

Alarums: Excursions.   *Enter* THERSITES.

Ther. Now they are clapper-clawing one another: I 'll go look on. That dissembling abominable varlet, Diomed, has got that same scurvy
doting foolish young knave's sleeve of Troy there,
in his helm: I would fain see them meet; that
that same Trojan ass, that loves the whore there,
might send that Greekish whoremasterly villain,
with the sleeve, back to the dissembling luxurious
drab, on a sleeveless errand. O' the other side,
the policy of those crafty swearing rascals—that
stale old mouse-eaten dry cheese, Nestor, and
that same dog-fox, Ulysses—is not proved worth
a blackberry:—they set me up, in policy, that
mongrel cur, Ajax, against that dog of as bad a
kind, Achilles: and now is the cur Ajax prouder
than the cur Achilles, and will not arm to-day;
whereupon the Grecians begin to proclaim bar-
barism, and policy grows into an ill opinion.
Soft! here come sleeve, and t' other.

Enter DIOMEDES: TROILUS *following.*

Tro. Fly not; for shouldst thou take the river
    Styx,
I would swim after.
Dio.   Thou dost miscall retire:
I do not fly; but advantageous care
Withdrew me from the odds of multitude:
Have at thee!
Ther. Hold thy whore, Grecian!—now for thy
whore, Trojan!—now the sleeve, now the sleeve!
    [*Exeunt* TROILUS *and* DIOMEDES, *fighting.*

Enter HECTOR.

Hect. What art thou, Greek? art thou for Hec-
    tor's match?
Art thou of blood and honour?
Ther. No, no: I am a rascal; a scurvy railing
knave; a very filthy rogue.
Hect. I do believe thee;—live.   [*Exit.*
Ther. God-a-mercy, that thou wilt believe me;
but a plague break thy neck, for frightening me!
What 's become of the wenching rogues? I think
they have swallowed one another: I would laugh
at that miracle. Yet, in a sort, lechery eats itself. I 'll seek them.   [*Exit.*

SCENE V.—*The same.*

Enter DIOMEDES *and a* Servant.

Dio. Go, go my servant, take thou Troilus'
    horse;
Present the fair steed to my lady Cressid:
Fellow, commend my service to her beauty;
Tell her, I have chastised the amorous Trojan,
And am her knight by proof.
Serv.   I go, my lord.   [*Exit.*

Enter AGAMEMNON.

Agam. Renew, renew! The fierce Polydamus
Hath beat down Menon: bastard Margarelon
Hath Doreus prisoner;
And stands colossus-wise, waving his beam,
Upon the pashéd corses of the kings
Epistrophus and Cedius: Polixenes is slain;
Amphimachus and Thoas deadly hurt;
Patroclus ta'en or slain; and Palamedes
Sore hurt and bruised: the dreadful Sagittary
Appals our numbers: haste we, Diomed,
To reinforcement, or we perish all.

Enter NESTOR.

Nes. Go, bear Patroclus' body to Achilles;
And bid the snail-paced Ajax arm for shame.—
There is a thousand Hectors in the field:
Now here he fights on Galathé his horse,
And there lacks work; anon, he 's there afoot,
And there they fly or die, like scaléd sculls
Before the belching whale; then is he yonder,
And there the strawy Greeks, ripe for his edge,
Fall down before him, like the mower's swath:
Here, there, and everywhere, he leaves and takes;
Dexterity so obeying appetite,
That what he will, he does; and does so much,
That proof is called impossibility.

Enter ULYSSES.

Ulys. O, courage, courage, princes! great
    Achilles
Is arming, weeping, cursing, vowing vengeance.
Patroclus' wounds have roused his drowsy blood,
Together with his mangled Myrmidons,
That noseless, handless, hacked, and chipped,
    come to him,
Crying on Hector. Ajax hath lost a friend,
And foams at mouth, and he is armed, and
    at it,
Roaring for Troilus; who hath done to-day
Mad and fantastic execution;
Engaging and redeeming of himself,
With such a careless force and forceless care,
As if that luck, in very spite of cunning,
Bade him win all.

Enter AJAX.

Ajax. Troilus! thou coward Troilus! [*Exit.*
Dio.   Ay, there, there.
Nes. So, so, we draw together.

Enter ACHILLES.

Achil.   Where is this Hector?
Come, come, thou boy-queller, shew thy face;
Know what it is to meet Achilles angry.
Hector! where's Hector? I will none but Hector.
                              [*Exeunt.*

SCENE VI.—*Another part of the Field.*

Enter AJAX.

Ajax. Troilus, thou coward Troilus, shew thy
          head!

Enter DIOMEDES.

Dio. Troilus, I say! where's Troilus?
Ajax.   What wouldst thou?
Dio. I would correct him.
Ajax. Were I the general, thou shouldst have
          my office,
Ere that correction:—Troilus, I say! what,
          Troilus!

Enter TROILUS.

Tro. O, traitor Diomed!—turn thy false face,
          thou traitor,
And pay thy life thou ow'st me for my horse!
Dio. Ha! art thou there?
Ajax. I'll fight with him alone: stand, Dio-
          med.
Dio. He is my prize; I will not look upon.
Tro. Come both, you cogging Greeks; have at
          you both.   [*Exeunt, fighting.*

Enter HECTOR.

Hect. Yea, Troilus? O, well fought, my youngest
          brother!

Enter ACHILLES.

Achil. Now do I see thee:—Ha! have at thee,
          Hector.
Hect. Pause, if thou wilt.
Achil. I do disdain thy courtesy, proud Trojan.
Be happy that my arms are out of use:
My rest and negligence befriend thee now,
But thou anon shalt hear of me again;
Till when, go seek thy fortune.   [*Exit.*
Hect.   Fare thee well:
I would have been much more a fresher man,
Had I expected thee.—How now, my brother?

Re-enter TROILUS.

Tro. Ajax hath ta'en Æneas; shall it be?
No, by the flame of yonder glorious heaven,
He shall not carry him; I'll be taken too,
Or bring him off: Fate, hear me what I say!
I reck not though thou end my life to-day. [*Exit.*

Enter one in sumptuous armour.

Hect. Stand, stand, thou Greek; thou art a
          goodly mark:
No? wilt thou not?—I like thy armour well;
I'll frush it, and unlock the rivets all,
But I'll be master of it.—Wilt thou not, beast,
          abide?
Why, then, fly on; I'll hunt thee for thy hide.
                              [*Exeunt.*

SCENE VII.—*The same.*

Enter ACHILLES, *with* MYRMIDONS.

Achil. Come here about me, you my Myr-
          midons:
Mark what I say:—Attend me where I wheel:
Strike not a stroke, but keep yourselves in breath;
And when I have the bloody Hector found,
Empale him with your weapons round about;
In fellest manner execute your arms.
Follow me, sirs, and my proceedings eye:
It is decreed—Hector the Great must die.
                              [*Exeunt.*

SCENE VIII.—*The same.*

Enter MENELAUS *and* PARIS, *fighting: then*
          THERSITES.

Ther. The cuckold and the cuckold-maker are
at it. Now, bull! now, dog! 'Loo, Paris, 'loo!
now my double-henned sparrow! 'loo, Paris, 'loo!
The bull has the game:—'ware horns, ho!
                    [*Exeunt* PARIS *and* MENELAUS.

Enter MARGARELON.

Mar. Turn, slave, and fight!
Ther. What art thou?
Mar. A bastard son of Priam's.
Ther. I am a bastard too; I love bastards: I
am a bastard begot, bastard instructed, bastard
in mind, bastard in valour; in everything illegiti-
mate. One bear will not bite another, and wherefore should one bastard? Take heed; the quarrel's
most ominous to us: if the son of a whore fight for
a whore, he tempts judgment. Farewell, bastard.
Mar. The devil take thee, coward! [*Exeunt.*

SCENE IX.—*Another part of the Field.*

Enter HECTOR.

Hect. Most putrified core, so fair without,
Thy goodly armour thus hath cost thy life.
Now is my day's work done; I 'll take good
    breath :
Rest, sword; thou hast thy fill of blood and death !
    [*Puts off his helmet, and hangs his shield
    behind him.*

Enter ACHILLES *and* Myrmidons.

Achil. Look, Hector, how the sun begins to
    set;
How ugly night comes breathing at his heels :
Even with the vail and darkening of the sun,
To close the day up, Hector's life is done.

    Hect. I am unarmed; forego this 'vantage,
    Greek.

    Achil. Strike, fellows, strike; this is the man I
    seek.   [HECTOR *falls.*
So, Ilion, fall thou !   Now, Troy, sink down !
Here lies thy heart, thy sinews, and thy bone.—
On, Myrmidons; and cry you all amain,
" Achilles hath the mighty Hector slain."
                  [*A retreat sounded.*
Hark ! a retreat upon our Grecian part.

    Myr. The Trojan trumpets sound the like, my
    lord.

    Achil. The dragon wing of night o'erspreads the
    earth,
And, stickler-like, the armies separates.
My half-supped sword, that frankly would have
    fed,
Pleased with this dainty bit, thus goes to bed.—
                  [*Sheathes his sword.*
Come, tie his body to my horse's tail;
Along the field I will the Trojan trail. [*Exeun.*

SCENE X.—*The same.*

Enter AGAMEMNON, AJAX, MENELAUS, NESTOR,
    DIOMEDES, *and others, marching.*

Shouts within.

Agam. Hark ! hark ! what shout is that ?
Nes.   Peace, drums !

Voices within.

Achilles !—

Achilles !—Hector's slain !—Achilles !

    Dio. The bruit is — Hector's slain, and by
    Achilles.

    Ajax. If it be so, yet bragless let it be;
Great Hector was a man as good as he.

    Agam. March patiently along : let one be sent

To pray Achilles see us at our tent.—
If in his death the gods have us befriended,
Great Troy is ours, and our sharp wars are ended.
                  [*Exeunt, marching.*

SCENE XI.—*Another part of the Field.*

Enter ÆNEAS *and* Trojans.

    Æne. Stand, ho ! yet are we masters of the field;
Never go home; here starve we out the night.

Enter TROILUS.

Tro. Hector is slain.
All.   Hector ?—The gods forbid !
Tro. He 's dead; and at the murderer's horse's
    tail,
In beastly sort, dragged through the shameful
    field.—
Frown on, you heavens, effect your rage with
    speed !
Sit, gods, upon your thrones, and smile at Troy !
I say, at once let your brief plagues be mercy,
And linger not our sure destruction on !

    Æne. My lord, you do discomfort all the host.

    Tro. You understand me not, that tell me so :
I do not speak of flight, of fear, of death;
But dare all imminence that gods and men
Address their dangers in.   Hector is gone !
Who shall tell Priam so, or Hecuba?
Let him that will a screech-owl aye be called,
Go into Troy, and say there—" Hector 's dead :"
There is a word will Priam turn to stone;
Make wells and Niobes of the maids and wives;
Cold statues of the youth; and, in a word,
Scare Troy out of itself.   But march, away:
Hector is dead; there is no more to say.
Stay yet :—You vile abominable tents,
Thus proudly pight upon our Phrygian plains,
Let Titan rise as early as he dare,
I 'll through and through you !—And thou, great-
    sized coward !
No space of earth shall sunder our two hates;
I 'll haunt thee like a wicked conscience still,
That mouldeth goblins swift as frenzy thoughts.—
Strike a free march to Troy ! with comfort go :
Hope of revenge shall hide our inward woe.
             [*Exeunt ÆNEAS and* Trojans.

As TROILUS *is going out, enter, from the other side,*
    PANDARUS.

    Pan. But hear you, hear you !
    Tro. Hence, broker lackey ! ignomy and shame
Pursue thy life, and live aye with thy name.
                  [*Exit* TROILUS.

Pan. A goodly med'cine for my aching
    bones!—
O world! world! world! thus is the poor agent
despised! O traitors and bawds, how earnestly are
you set a'work, and how ill requited! Why should
our endeavour be so loved, and the performance so
loathed? what verse for it? what instance for it?—
Let me see:—

Full merrily the humble-bee doth sing,
    Till he hath lost his honey and his sting:
And being once subdued in arméd tail,
    Sweet honey and sweet notes together fail.

Good traders in the flesh, set this in your painted
    cloths.

As many as be here of pander's hall,
Your eyes, half out, weep out at Pandar's fall:
Or, if you cannot weep, yet give some groans,
Though not for me, yet for your aching bones.
Brethren and sisters of the hold-door trade,
Some two months hence my will shall here be made:
It should be now, but that my fear is this,—
Some galléd goose of Winchester would hiss:
Till then I'll sweat, and seek about for eases;
And, at that time, bequeath you my diseases.
                                    [*Exit.*

NOTES.

"*Call here my varlet, I'll unarm again.*"—Act I., Scene 1.

The word "varlet" anciently signified an attendant on a knight. Holinshed, speaking of the battle of Agincourt, says:—"Divers were relieved by their varlets, and conveyed out of the field."

"*Handlest in thy discourse, 'Oh, that her hand.'*"
Act I., Scene 1.

"Handlest" is here used metaphorically, with an allusion at the same time to its literal meaning. Shakspere has, on various occasions, adverted to the beauty of the female hand: as, in "ROMEO AND JULIET:"—

——"They may seize
On the white wonder of dear Juliet's hand."

In the "WINTER'S TALE," Florizel descants with equal warmth and fancy on the hand of Perdita:—

——"I take thy hand; this hand
As soft as dove's down, and as white as it;
Or Ethiopian's tooth; or the fanned snow
That's bolted by the northern blasts twice o'er."

"*She's a fool to stay behind her father.*"—Act I., Scene 1.

According to Shakspere's authority, "THE DESTRUCTION OF TROY," Calchas was "a great learned bishop of Troy," who was sent by Priam to consult the oracle of Delphi concerning the event of the war which was threatened by Agamemnon. As soon as he had made "his oblations and demands for them of Troy, Apollo answered unto him, saying, 'Calchas, Calchas, beware that thou return not back again to Troy; but go thou with Achilles unto the Greeks, and depart never from them; for the Greeks shall have victory of the Trojans, by the agreement of the gods.'" Calchas discreetly took the hint, and immediately joined the enemies of his country.

"*Between our Ilium and where she resides.*"—Act I., Scene 1.

"Ilium," or "Ilion" (it is spelled both ways), was the name of Priam's palace. According to "THE DESTRUCTION OF TROY," it was "one of the richest and the strongest that ever was in all the world. And it was of height five hundred paces, besides the height of the towers, whereof there was great plenty, and so high as that it seemed to them that saw them from far, they raught up into the heaven." There is a more particular allusion to these towers in Act IV., Scene 5. Steevens observes, that Ilium, properly speaking, is the name of the city; Troy, that of the country.

"*How now, prince Troilus? wherefore not afield?*"
Act I., Scene 1.

It appears from various lines in this play, that Shakspere pronounced "Troilus" as a dissyllable. So also in his "RAPE OF LUCRECE:"—

"Here manly Hector faints, here Troilus swounds."

Pope, in his translation of Homer, has made the same classical lapse (b. xxiv.):—

"Mestor the brave, renowned in ranks of war;
And Troilus, dreadful on his rushing car."

"*They say he is a very man per se.*"—Act I., Scene 2.

In Henrysoun's "TESTAMENT OF CRESSEIDE," we find,

"Of fair Cresseide, the flower and *a per se*
Of Troy and Greece."

"*To be baked with no date in the pie,—for then the man's date is out.*"—Act I., Scene 2.

To account for this quibble, it should be remembered that dates were a common ingredient in ancient pastry: as, in "ROMEO AND JULIET:"—

"They call for dates and quinces in the pastry."

"*Bounding between the two moist elements,
Like Perseus' horse.*"—Act I., Scene 3.

Of the allegorical horse alluded to in the text, "THE DESTRUCTION OF TROY" gives the following account:—"Of the blood that issued out [from Medusa's head], there engendered Pegasus, or the flying horse. By the flying horse that was engendered of the blood issued from her head, is understood that, of her riches issuing of that realm, he [Perseus] founded and made a ship named Pegase; and this ship was likened unto an horse flying," &c. The only flying horse of antiquity was Pegasus, who was the property not of Perseus, but Bellerophon. If the poet intended to speak literally, he has fallen into an error.

——"*The thing of courage,
As roused with rage, with rage doth sympathise.*"
Act I., Scene 3.

The "thing of courage" here alluded to is supposed to be the tiger.

"*Venerable Nestor, hatched in silver.*"—Act I., Scene 3.

"Hatched in silver" is an allusion to Nestor's white hair and beard. To hatch is a term for a particular method of engraving. The phrase is not unfrequent in writings of the same period: as, in "LOVE IN A MAZE," 1632:—

"Thy hair is fine as gold, thy chin is hatched
With silver."

To hatch in silver, was to inlay a design with lines of silver; a process often used for the hilts of swords, handles of daggers, and stocks of pistols.

"*When that the general is not like the hive.*"—Act I., Scene 3.

The meaning is, says Johnson, "When the general is not to the army like the hive to the bees—the repository of the stock of every individual; that to which each particular resorts with whatever he has collected for the good of the whole—what honey is expected? what hope of advantage?"

"*The heavens themselves, the planets, and this centre.*"
Act I., Scene 3.

By "this centre," Ulysses means the earth, which, according to the system of Ptolemy, is the centre round which the planets move.

——" *But when the planets,*
In evil mixture, to disorder wander."—Act I., Scene 3.

Meaning, in astrological phrase, when the planets form malignant configurations; when their aspects are evil towards one another. A short extract from Spenser's "FAERY QUEEN" (b. v.) will, perhaps, more accurately, as well as more pleasingly, illustrate the passage in the text:—

" For who so list into the heavens look,
And search the courses of the rolling spheres,
Shall find that from the point where they first took
Their setting forth, in these few thousand years
They all are *wandered* much; that plain appears.
For that same golden fleecy Ram, which bore
Phrixus and Helle, from their stepdames' fears,
Hath now forgot where he was placed of yore,
And shouldered hath the Bull which fair Europa bore."

" *Thou mongrel beef-witted lord !*"—Act II., Scene 1.

So in " TWELFTH NIGHT," Sir Andrew Aguecheek says, " I am a great eater of beef, and I believe that does harm to my wit." Thersites calls Ajax mongrel on account of his father being a Grecian, and his mother a Trojan.

" *Thou stool for a witch !*"—Act II., Scene 1.

In one way of trying a witch, they used to place her on a chair or stool, with her legs tied across, that all the weight of her body might rest upon her seat; and by that means, after some time, the circulation of the blood would be much stopped, and her sitting would be as painful as on the wooden horse.

" *And, for an old aunt, whom the Greeks held captive.*"
Act II., Scene 2.

The aunt alluded to was Hesione, Priam's sister, whom Hercules, being enraged at Priam's breach of faith, gave to Telamon, who by her had Ajax.

" *And do a deed that Fortune never did.*"—Act II., Scene 2.

This obscure passage is thus explained by Malone:—" Fortune was never so unjust and mutable as to rate a thing on one day above all price, and on the next to set no estimation whatsoever upon it. You are now going to do what Fortune never did."

——" *Not much*
Unlike young men, whom Aristotle thought
Unfit to hear moral philosophy."—Act II., Scene 2.

On this passage Steevens observes, " Let it be remembered, as often as Shakspere's anachronisms occur, that errors in computing time were very frequent in those ancient romances which seem to have formed the greater part of his library. Even classic authors are not exempt from such mistakes. In the fifth book of Statius's 'THEBIAD,' Amphiarus talks of the fates of Nestor and Priam, neither of whom died till long after him."

" *The elephant hath joints, but none for courtesy.*"
Act II., Scene 3.

That the elephant was incapable of bending the leg, was formerly a very prevalent error; as, in " ALL'S LOST BY LUST" (1633):—

——" *Is she pliant?*"
" Stubborn as an elephant's leg; no bending in her."

"' *Twixt his active and his mental parts,*
Kingdomed Achilles in commotion rages."—Act II., Scene 3.

This passage will be best explained by a similar one in " JULIUS CÆSAR:"—

" The genius and the mortal instruments
Are then in council; and the state of man,
Like to a little *kingdom*, suffers then
The nature of an insurrection."

" *He is so plaguy proud, that the death tokens of it*
Cry, 'No recovery!'"—Act II., Scene 3.

Alluding to the decisive spots appearing on those infected by the plague. So in Beaumont and Fletcher's " VALENTINIAN:"—

" Now, like the fearful tokens of the plague,
Are mere forerunners of their ends."

——" *For thy vigour,*
Bull-bearing Milo his addition yield."—Act II., Scene 3.

That is, yield his title, his celebrity for strength. " Addition," in legal language, is the title given to each party, shewing his degree, occupation, &c.; as, esquire, gentleman, yeoman, merchant, &c.

" *Shall I call you father?*"—Act II., Scene 3.

This alludes to a prevalent custom of the time. Ben Jonson had many who called themselves his sons. Cotton dedicated his treatise on fishing to his "father" Walton; and Ashmole, in his "DIARY," observes:—"AP. 3. Mr. Wm. Backhouse, of Swallowfield, in com. Berks, caused me to call him father henceforward."

" *I hope I shall know your honour better.*"—Act III., Scene 1.

The servant means to quibble: he hopes that Pandarus will become a better man than he is at present. In his next speech, he chooses to understand Pandarus as if he had said he wished to grow better; and hence affirms that he is in the state of grace.

" *You must be watched ere you be made tame, must you?*"
Act III., Scene 2.

Alluding to the manner of taming hawks. So, in the " TAMING OF THE SHREW:"—" To watch her as we watch these kites." Hawks were tamed by being kept from sleep.

" *So, so; rub on, and kiss the mistress.*"—Act III., Scene 2.

The allusion is to bowling. What is now termed the "jack," seems in Shakspere's time to have been called the "mistress." A bowl that kisses the "jack," or "mistress," is in the most advantageous situation. " Rub on " is a term used in the same game; as, in " NO WIT LIKE A WOMAN'S," a comedy by Middleton (1657):—

——" So, a fair riddance:
There's three rubs gone; I've a clear way to the mistress."

And in Decker's " SATIROMASTIX" (1602):—" Since he hath hit the mistress so often in the fore-game, we'll even play out the rubbers."

" *The falcon as the tercel, for all the ducks i' the river.*"
Act III., Scene 2.

Pandarus probably means that he will match his niece against her lover. The "tercel" is the male hawk; by the "falcon," is generally understood the female.

" ' *In witness whereof the parties interchangeably*——'"
Act III., Scene 2.

—" Have set their hands and seals," would complete the sentence. So, afterwards:—" Go to, a bargain made: seal it, seal it." Shakspere appears to have had here an idea in his thoughts that he has several times expressed; as, in " MEASURE FOR MEASURE:"—

" But my kisses bring again;
Seals of love, but sealed in vain."

And in his " VENUS AND ADONIS:"—

" Pure lips, sweet seals in my soft lips imprinted,
What bargains may I make, still to be sealing!"

" *That my integrity and truth to you,*
  Might be affronted with the match and weight
  Of such a winnowed purity in love."—Act III., Scene 2.

The word "affronted" was formerly used in the sense of "confronted." Dr. Johnson thus explains the passage :—
"I wish that my integrity might be met and matched with such equality and force of pure unmingled love."

" *I am as true as truth's simplicity,*
  And simpler than the infancy of truth."—Act III., Scene 2.

This (says Warburton) is fine, and means, " Ere truth, to defend itself against deceit in the commerce of the world, had, out of necessity, learned worldly policy."

" *As true as steel, as plantage to the moon.*"—Act III., Scene 2.

"As true as steel" is an ancient proverbial simile. " As plantage to the moon" alludes to the old superstitious notion of the influence of the moon over whatever was planted, sown, or grafted. An extract from Scott's " DISCOVERIE OF WITCHCRAFT" will illustrate the point :—" The poor husbandman perceiveth that the increase of the moon maketh plants fruitful; so as in the full moon they are in the best strength; decaying in the wane; and in the conjunction do utterly wither and vade."

——" *A strange fellow here*
  Writes me, that man—how dearly ever parted."
                                        Act III., Scene 3.

That is, however excellently endowed; with however dear or precious parts enriched or adorned. Ben Jonson has used the word "parted" in the same manner, in the Dramatis Personæ of " EVERY MAN OUT OF HIS HUMOUR :"—" Macilente, a man well parted, a sufficient scholar," &c.

" *And apprehended here immediately*
  The unknown Ajax."—Act III., Scene 3.

That is, Ajax who has abilities which were never brought into view or use.

" *Made emulous missions 'mongst the gods themselves,*
  And drave great Mars to faction."—Act III., Scene 3.

This alludes to the descent of deities to combat on either side before Troy. In the fifth book of "THE ILIAD," Diomed wounds Mars, who, on his return to heaven, is rated by Jupiter for having interfered in the battle.

" *'T is known, Achilles, that you are in love*
  With one of Priam's daughters."—Act III., Scene 3.

This was Polyxena; in the act of marrying whom Achilles was afterwards killed by Paris.

" *There is a mystery (with whom relation*
  Durst never meddle) in the soul of state."—Act III., Scene 3.

Meaning, probably, there is a secret administration of affairs which no history was ever able to discover.

" *Omission to do what is necessary,*
  Seals a commission to a blank of danger."—Act III., Scene 3.

That is, by neglecting our duty, we commission or enable that danger of dishonour to lay hold upon us, which could not reach us before.

————

" *Enter* PANDARUS.

" CRES. *A pestilence on him! now will he be mocking.*"
                                        Act IV., Scene 2.

The hint for this short conversation between Pandarus and Cressida appears to have been taken from Chaucer's tale on the subject (b. iii.) :—

" Pandare, a morowe which that commen was,
    Unto his necé, gan her faire to grete,
  And saied, ' All this night so rainéd it, alas !
    That all my drede is, that ye, necé swete,
    Have little leisir had to slepe and mete;
  All night (quod he) hath rain so do me wake,
  That some of us trowe ther heddis ake.'
  Cresseide answerde, ' Nevir the bet for you,
    Foxe that ye ben, God yeve your herté care ;
    God helpe me so, ye causéd all this fare.' "

" *Alas, poor wretch ! a poor capocchia.*"—Act IV., Scene 2.

This is an Italian word, used metaphorically to signify a fool or innocent.

" *But the strong base and building of my love*
  Is as the very centre of the earth."—Act IV., Scene 2.

In Shakspere's 119th Sonnet, we find a similar allusion :—
    "And ruined love, when it is built anew."

And in " ANTONY AND CLEOPATRA :"—

    " Let not the piece of virtue which is set
      Betwixt us as the cément of our love,
      To keep it builded, be the ram to batter
      The fortress of it."

" *Hark ! you are called : some say, the Genius so*
  Cries ' Come !' to him that instantly must die."
                                        Act IV., Scene 4.

Flatman has expressed a similar thought :—

    " My soul just now about to take her flight
      Into the regions of eternal night,
      Methinks I hear some gentle spirit say,
      ' Be not fearful; come away.' "

Pope is supposed to have imitated Flatman, in one of his most popular productions :—

    " Hark ! they whisper ; angels say,
      ' Sister spirit, come away.' "

" *A woful Cressid 'mongst the merry Greeks.*"—Act IV., Scene 4.

" Merry Greeks" was a proverbial expression. In " A MAD WORLD, MY MASTERS," 1640, a man gives the watchmen some money; and when they have received it, he says, " The merry Greeks understand me."

" *For I will throw my glove to death himself,*
  That there's no maculation in thy heart."—Act IV., Scene 4.

That is, " I will challenge Death himself in defence of thy fidelity."

" *Valour and pride excel themselves in Hector ;*
  The one almost as infinite as all,
  The other blank as nothing."—Act IV., Scene 5.

The meaning of this passage is thus explained by Dr. Johnson : Valour (says Æneas) is in Hector greater than valour in other men, and pride in Hector is less than pride in other men. So that Hector is distinguished by the excellence of having pride less than other pride, and valour more than other valour.

" *Not Neoptolemus so mirable.*"—Act IV., Scene 5.

The allusion here is supposed to be to Achilles himself; it could not possibly be to his son Pyrrhus Neoptolemus, who, in a former passage, is spoken of as " Young Pyrrhus, now at home." Shakspere probably thought that Neoptolemus was a family name.

" *I have, thou gallant Trojan, seen thee oft*
  Labouring for destiny."—Act IV., Scene 5.

That is, as the minister or vicegerent of destiny; so, in " CORIOLANUS :"—

    ——" His sword, death's stamp,
        Where it did mark, it took."

" Thou crusty batch of nature, what's the news ? "
Act V., Scene 1.

A "batch" signifies all that is baked at one time, without heating the oven afresh. In Ben Jonson's "CATILINE," we have,

"Except he were of the same meal and batch."

"One that loves quails."—Act V., Scene 1.

In old French, "caille" was synonymous to "fille de joie."

"Here, Diomed, keep this sleeve."—Act V., Scene 2.

This sleeve, which had been previously given by Troilus to Cressida, appears (says Malone) to have been an ornamented cuff, such as was worn by some of our young nobility at a tilt in Shakspere's age. See Spenser's "VIEW OF IRELAND" (p. 43, edit. 1633):—"Also the deep smock sleive, which the Irish women use, they say was old Spanish, and is used yet in Barbary: and yet that should seem to be rather an old English fashion; for in armoury, the fashion of the manche which is given in arms by many, being indeed nothing else but a sleive, is fashioned much like to that sleive."

" Troilus, farewell! one eye yet looks on thee;
But with my heart the other eye doth see."— Act V., Scene 2.

"One eye," says Cressida, "looks on Troilus; but the other follows Diomed, where my heart is fixed." Steevens observes that the characters of Cressida and Pandarus are more immediately formed from Chaucer than from Lydgate; for though the latter mentions them both characteristically, he does not sufficiently dwell on either to have furnished Shakspere with many circumstances to be found in this tragedy. Lydgate, speaking of Cressida, says only:—

"She gave her heart and love to Diomed,
To shew what trust there is in womankind;
For she of her new love no sooner sped,
But Troilus was clean out of her mind
As if she never had him known or seen;
Wherein I cannot guess what she did mean."

" And with another knot, five-finger tied."—Act V., Scene 2.

That is, a knot tied by giving her hand to Diomed. So, in Massinger's "FATAL DOWRY" (1632):—

" Your fingers tie my heartstrings with this touch,
In true knots, which nought but death shall loose."

"Stand fast, and wear a castle on thy head."—Act V., Scene 2.

A particular kind of close helmet was called a "castle." In the "HISTORY OF PRINCE ARTHUR" (1634, ch. 158), we find, "'Do thou thy best,' said Sir Gawaine; 'therefore hie thee fast that thou wert gone, and wit thou well we shall soon come after, and break the strongest castle that thou hast upon thy head.'"

" Brother, you have a vice of mercy in you,
Which better fits a lion than a man."—Act V., Scene 3.

In Philemon Holland's translation of "PLINY'S NATURAL HISTORY" (c. 16), we find, "The lion alone, of all wild beasts, is gentle to them that humble themselves before him, and will not touch any such upon their submission, but spareth what creature soever lieth prostrate before him." "The traditions and stories of the darker ages," says Johnson, "abounded with examples of the lion's generosity. Upon the supposition that these acts of clemency were true, Troilus reasons, that to spare against reason, by mere instinct of pity, became rather a generous beast than a wise man."

" What art thou, Greek? art thou for Hector's match?
Art thou of blood and honour ?"—Act V., Scene 4.

This idea is derived from the ancient books of chivalry. A person of superior birth might not be challenged by an inferior; or if challenged, might refuse the combat. In this spirit, Cleopatra says,

"These hands do lack nobility, that they strike
A meaner than themselves."

In "MELVIL'S MEMOIRS," we find it stated (p. 165, ed. 1735), "The laird of Grainge offered to fight Bothwell; who answered, that he was neither earl nor lord, but a baron; and so was not his equal. The like answer made he to Tullibardine. Then my Lord Lindsay offered to fight him, which he could not well refuse; but his heart failed him, and he grew cold in the business."

——*" The dreadful Sagittary*
Appals our numbers."—Act V., Scene 5.

In the "THREE DESTRUCTIONS OF TROY" we are told, that "Beyond the royalme of Amasonne came an auncyent Kynge, wyse and dyscreete, named Epystrophus, and brought a M. [thousand] Knyghtes, and a mervayllouse beste that was called Sagittayre, that behynde the myddes was an horse, and tofore a man. This beste was heery like an horse, and had his eyen red as a cole, and shotte well with a bowe. This beste made the Grekes sore aferde, and slewe many of them with his bowe."

"Now, here he fights on Galathé, his horse."—Act V., Scene 5.

The name of Hector's horse is taken from Lydgate or Caxton. In Lydgate (p. 175), we find,

"And sought, by all the means he could, to take
Galathé, Hector's horse."

"And there they fly, or die, like scaléd sculls
Before the belching whale."—Act V., Scene 5.

The term "scull" signifies what is now called a shoal of fish. In Knox's "HISTORY OF FISH" (1787), we find this passage: "The cod from the banks of Newfoundland (says a late writer) pursues the whiting, which flies before it even to the southern shores of Spain. The cachalot, a species of whale, is said in the same manner to pursue a shoal of herrings, and to swallow hundreds in a mouthful."

" He is my prize; I will not look upon."—Act V., Scene 6.

Equivalent to saying, " I will not be a looker-on;" as, in "HENRY VI.," Part 3:—

" Why stand we here—
Wailing our losses—
And look upon, as if the tragedy
Were played in jest by counterfeited actors ?"

" The dragon wing of night o'erspreads the earth,
And, stickler like, the armies separates."—Act V., Scene 9.

The business of a "stickler" was to part the combatants when victory could be determined without bloodshed. They are said to have been called "sticklers" from carrying sticks or staves in their hands, with which they interposed between the duellists. Minshew gives this explanation in his "DICTIONARY" (1617):—"A stickler between two; so called as putting a stick or staff between two fencing or fighting together."

TIMON OF ATHENS

PEN-HANDED, open-hearted Timon is the type and representative of a class too numerous with reference to their own happiness, and not enough so for the happiness and tranquillity of the world. Were all men Timons in disposition, we might soon see, in great part, the realisation of good old Glo'ster's noble wish, that "distribution should undo excess, and each man have enough." Nor could any harm result from an ultra-generosity thus universal; since, though all would be willing to give even more than they could afford, yet none would be willing to take but those who actually wanted. Beings like the crazy Misanthrope before us (for crazed he is, in his bewildering misery), feeling themselves at the outset all goodness and transparent innocence, are absolutely unfurnished with any criterion by which they can estimate the curiously-compounded clay of ordinary mortals; they have no plummet by which they may sound the depths and shoals of human nature; no diving-bell, furnished by their own consciences, by whose aid they might descend to view the "dirt and sea-weed" that lie so wondrously intermingled with "inestimable stones, unvalued jewels," at the bottom of that fearful ocean. The natural consequence is that, finding their first pure thoughts erroneous, they have no resource but to rush to the opposite extreme, and end with seeing nothing but what is base and ungenerous in the race whom they heretofore imagined to be all perfection.—The true theory appears to be, that man is naturally an imperfect being, neither all vice nor all virtue; furnished, for the most part, with a preponderating portion of good qualities, which may, under favourable circumstances, be increased to an indefinite extent: yet still, by the very law of his being, doomed to remain imperfect at the best. Those amiable enthusiasts who adopt the hypothesis that all the viler qualities of mankind are the result of vicious training, will find their conclusions no less unsound, though less pernicious, than those of the Swifts and Rochefoucaults, who would fain persuade us, in defiance both of sensation and observation—nay, in despite of their own conduct and character —that all apparent virtue is but selfishness in masquerade.

The minor characters in the present drama are all excellently adapted to bring out the one great purpose of the Poet; and we have to thank his unfailing good-nature that, in the midst of its disgust and indignation with the false friends, he has allowed the mind to repose with complacency on the tenderness and fidelity of the steward, Flavius, and the minor servants of "so noble a master" as hapless Timon.—Apemantus, the cynic, is the character second in importance to the principal, and it is delineated with equal felicity. His spontaneous misanthropy, compared with the woe-induced frenzy of the fine-natured Timon, is as the natural bitterness of the sloe to the generous grape that has been killed and withered by untimely frost; or as the sterile, branchless poplar to the noble, sheltering oak, which, in the very prime of its picturesque beauty, has been stripped and prostrated by the ruthless storm.

The story of the Misanthrope is stated, by Dr. Farmer, to be told in almost every collection of Shakspere's time; and particularly in two books with which the Poet was intimately acquainted— Painter's "PALACE OF PLEASURE," and North's translation of "PLUTARCH." Malone is of opinion that the play is founded on the following passage in the "LIFE OF ANTONY," as given in the last-named work:—"Antonius forsook the city, and company of his friends; saying that he would lead Timon's life, because he had the like wrong offered him that was offered unto Timon; and for the unthankfulness of those he had done good unto, and whom he took to be his friends, he was angry with all men, and would trust no man." Lucian's dialogue of "TIMON" is generally supposed to have had some influence over the composition of the Poet, "although," says Mr. Skottowe, "the channel through which that influence was communicated is no longer to be traced;"—as it is not known that any translation of the dialogue existed in Shakspere's age.

"TIMON OF ATHENS" was first published in the original folio, (1623). The date of its composition can be but conjectured. Malone assigns it to the year 1610.

J. O.

PERSONS REPRESENTED.

TIMON, a noble Athenian.
LUCIUS,
LUCULLUS, } Lords, and Flatterers of TIMON.
SEMPRONIUS,
VENTIDIUS, one of TIMON's false Friends.
APEMANTUS, a churlish Philosopher.
ALCIBIADES, an Athenian General.
FLAVIUS, Steward to TIMON.
FLAMINIUS,
LUCILIUS, } TIMON's Servants.
SERVILIUS,
CAPHIS,
PHILOTUS,
TITUS, } Servants to TIMON's Creditors.
LUCIUS,
HORTENSIUS,
Two Servants of VARRO.
The Servant of ISIDORE.
Two of TIMON's Creditors.
Cupid, and Maskers
Three Strangers.
Poet.
Painter.
Jeweller
Merchant.
An Old Athenian.
A Page.
A Fool.

PHRYNIA,
TIMANDRA, } Mistresses to ALCIBIADES.

Other Lords, Senators, Officers, Soldiers, Thieves,
and Attendants.

———

SCENE. Athens; and the Woods adjoining.

SCENE I.—Athens. *A Hall in* TIMON'S *House.*

Enter Poet, Painter, Jeweller, Merchant, *and others, at several doors.*

Poet. Good day, sir.
Pain.　　　I am glad you are well.
Poet. I have not seen you long; how goes the
　　world?
Pain. It wears, sir, as it grows.
Poet.　　　Ay, that's well known:
But what particular rarity? what strange,
Which manifold recórd not matches?—See,
Magic of bounty! all these spirits thy power
Hath cónjured to attend. I know the merchant.
　Pain. I know them both; the other's a jeweller.

Mer. O, 't is a worthy lord!
Jew.　　　Nay, that's most fixed.
Mer. A most incomparable man; breathed, as
　　it were,
To an untirable and continuate goodness:
He passes.
　Jew.　　　I have a jewel here.
Mer. O, pray, let's see 't: for the lord Timon,
　　sir?
Jew. If he will touch the estimate: but, for
　　that—

　　　　Poet reads.

"When we for recompense have praised the vile,
　It stains the glory in that happy verse
　Which aptly sings the good."

Mer. 'T is a good form. [*Looking at the jewel.*

Jew. And rich: here is a water, look you.

Pain. You are rapt, sir, in some work, some
         dedication

To the great lord.

Poet.   A thing slipped idly from me.

Our poesy is as a gum, which oozes

From whence 't is nourished. The fire i' the flint

Shews not till it be struck: our gentle flame

Provokes itself, and, like the current, flies

Each bound it chafes.—What have you there?

    Pain. A picture, sir.—When comes your book
         forth?

Poet. Upon the heels of my presentment, sir.—

Let's see your piece.

Pain.   'T is a good piece.

Poet. So 't is: this comes off well and excellent.

Pain. Indifferent.

Poet.   Admirable! How this grace

Speaks his own standing! what a mental power

This eye shoots forth! how big imagination

Moves in this lip! to the dumbness of the gesture

One might interpret.

    Pain. It is a pretty mocking of the life.

Here is a touch: is 't good?

    Poet.   I'll say of it,

It tutors nature: artificial strife

Lives in these touches, livelier than life.

    Enter certain Senators, *and pass over.*

    Pain. How this lord is followed!

    Poet. The senators of Athens:—happy men!

    Pain. Look; more!

    Poet. You see this confluence, this great flood of
        visitors.

I have, in this rough work, shaped out a man,

Whom this beneath world doth embrace and hug

With amplest entertainment: my free drift

Halts not particularly, but moves itself

In a wide sea of wax: no levelled malice

Infects one comma in the course I hold;

But flies an eagle flight, bold, and forth on,

Leaving no tract behind.

    Pain. How shall I understand you?

    Poet.   I will unbolt to you.

You see how all conditions, how all minds

(As well of glib and slippery creatures, as

Of grave and austere quality), tender down

Their services to lord Timon: his large fortune,

Upon his good and gracious nature hanging,

Subdues and properties to his love and tendance

All sorts of hearts; yea, from the glass-faced flatterer

To Apemantus, that few things loves better

Than to abhor himself: even he drops down

The knee before him, and returns in peace

Most rich in Timon's nod.

    Pain.   I saw them speak together.

    Poet. Sir, I have upon a high and pleasant hill

Feigned Fortune to be throned: the base o' the
        mount

Is ranked with all deserts, all kind of natures,

That labour on the bosom of this sphere

To propagate their states: amongst them all,

Whose eyes are on this sovereign lady fixed,

One do I personate of lord Timon's frame,

Whom Fortune with her ivory hand wafts to her;

Whose present grace to present slaves and servants

Translates his rivals.

Pain.   'T is conceived to scope.
This throne, this Fortune, and this hill, methinks,
With one man beckoned from the rest below,
Bowing his head against the steepy mount
To climb his happiness, would be well expressed
In our condition.

Poet.   Nay, sir, but hear me on:
All those which were his fellows but of late
(Some better than his value), on the moment
Follow his strides, his lobbies fill with tendance,
Rain sacrificial whisperings in his ear,
Make sacred even his stirrup, and through him
Drink the free air.

Pain.   Ay, marry, what of these?

Poet. When Fortune, in her shift and change of
       mood,
Spurns down her late beloved, all his dependents,
Which laboured after him to the mountain's top,
Even on their knees and hands, let him slip down,
Not one accompanying his declining foot.

Pain. 'T is common:
A thousand moral paintings I can shew,
That shall demonstrate these quick blows of
       Fortune
More pregnantly than words. Yet you do well
To shew lord Timon that mean eyes have seen
The foot above the head.

Trumpet sounds. Enter TIMON, *attended; the*
     Servant *of* VENTIDIUS *talking with him.*

Tim.   Imprisoned is he, say you?

Ven. Serv. Ay, my good lord: five talents is his
       debt;
His means most short, his creditors most strait:
Your honourable letter he desires
To those have shut him up; which failing to him,
Periods his comfort.

Tim.   Noble Ventidius! Well;
I am not of that feather to shake off
My friend when he must need me. I do know
       him
A gentleman that well deserves a help,
Which he shall have: I 'll pay the debt, and free
       him.

Ven. Serv. Your lordship ever binds him.

Tim. Commend me to him: I will send his
       ransom;
And, being enfranchised, bid him come to me:
'T is not enough to help the feeble up,
But to support him after.—Fare you well.

Ven. Serv. All happiness to your honour! [*Exit.*

Enter an Old Athenian.

Old Ath. Lord Timon, hear me speak.

Tim. Freely, good father.

Old Ath. Thou hast a servant named Lucilius.

Tim. I have so: what of him?

Old Ath. Most noble Timon, call the man be-
       fore thee.

Tim. Attends he here, or no?—Lucilius!

Enter LUCILIUS.

Luc. Here, at your lordship's service.

Old Ath. This fellow here, lord Timon, this thy
       creature,
By night frequents my house. I am a man
That from my first have been inclined to thrift;
And my estate deserves an heir more raised
Than one which holds a trencher.

Tim.   Well; what further?

Old Ath. One only daughter have I, no kin
       else,
On whom I may confer what I have got:
The maid is fair, o' the youngest for a bride,
And I have bred her at my dearest cost,
In qualities of the best. This man of thine
Attempts her love: I pr'ythee, noble lord,
Join with me to forbid him her resort;
Myself have spoke in vain.

Tim.   The man is honest.

Old Ath. Therefore he will be, Timon:
His honesty rewards him in itself,
It must not bear my daughter.

Tim.   Does she love him?

Old Ath. She is young and apt:
Our own precédent passions do instruct us
What levity 's in youth.

Tim. [*To* LUCILIUS]. Love you the maid?

Luc. Ay, my good lord, and she accepts of it.

Old Ath. If in her marriage my consent be
       missing,
I call the gods to witness, I will choose
Mine heir from forth the beggars of the world,
And dispossess her all.

Tim.   How shall she be endowed,
If she be mated with an equal husband?

Old Ath. Three talents, on the present; in
       future, all.

Tim. This gentleman of mine hath served me
       long;
To build his fortune I will strain a little,
For 't is a bond in men. Give him thy daughter:
What you bestow, in him I 'll counterpoise,
And make him weigh with her.

Old Ath.   Most noble lord,
Pawn me to this your honour, she is his.

Tim. My hand to thee; mine honour on my
       promise.

Luc. Humbly I thank your lordship: never may
That state or fortune fall into my keeping
Which is not owed to you!

       [*Exeunt* LUCILIUS *and* Old Athenian.

Poet. Vouchsafe my labour, and long live
       your lordship!

Tim. I thank you; you shall hear from me anon:
Go not away.—What have you there, my friend?

Pain. A piece of painting, which I do beseech
Your lordship to accept.

Tim.   Painting is welcome.
The painting is almost the natural man;
For since dishonour traffics with man's nature,
He is but outside: these pencilled figures are
Even such as they give out.   I like your work;
And you shall find I like it: wait attendance
Till you hear further from me.

Pain.   The gods preserve you!

Tim. Well fare you, gentlemen: give me your
hand;
We must needs dine together.—Sir, your jewel
Hath suffered under praise.

Jew.   What, my lord? dispraise?

Tim. A mere satiety of commendations.
If I should pay you for 't as 't is extolled,
It would unclew me quite.

Jew.   My lord, 't is rated
As those which sell would give: but you well
know,
Things of like value, differing in the owners,
Are prized by their masters: believe 't, dear lord,
You mend the jewel by the wearing it.

Tim.   Well mocked.

Mer. No, my good lord; he speaks the common tongue,
Which all men speak with him.

Tim. Look who comes here.   Will you be chid?

Enter APEMANTUS.

Jew. We will bear, with your lordship.

Mer.   He 'll spare none.

Tim. Good morrow to thee, gentle Apemantus.

Apem. Till I be gentle, stay for thy good morrow;
When thou art Timon's dog, and these knaves
honest.

Tim. Why dost thou call them knaves? thou
know'st them not.

Apem. Are they not Athenians?

Tim. Yes.

Apem. Then I repent not.

Jew. You know me, Apemantus.

Apem. Thou know'st, I do; I called thee by
thy name.

Tim. Thou art proud, Apemantus.

Apem. Of nothing so much as that I am not
like Timon.

Tim. Whither art going?

Apem. To knock out an honest Athenian's
brains.

Tim. That's a deed thou 'lt die for?

Apem. Right, if doing nothing be death by
the law.

Tim. How likest thou this picture, Apemantus?

Apem. The best for the innocence.

Tim. Wrought he not well that painted it?

Apem. He wrought better that made the painter;
and yet he 's but a filthy piece of work.

Pain. You are a dog.

Apem. Thy mother 's of my generation: what's
she, if I be a dog?

Tim. Wilt dine with me, Apemantus?

Apem. No; I eat not lords.

Tim. An' thou shouldst, thou 'dst anger ladies.

Apem. O, they eat lords; so they come by great
bellies.

Tim. That's a lascivious apprehension.

Apem. So thou apprehend'st it: take it for thy
labour.

Tim. How dost thou like this jewel, Apemantus?

Apem. Not so well as plain dealing, which will
not cost a man a doit.

Tim. What dost thou think 't is worth?

Apem. Not worth my thinking.—How now,
poet?

Poet. How now, philosopher?

Apem. Thou liest.

Poet. Art not one?

Apem. Yes.

Poet. Then I lie not.

Apem. Art not a poet?

Poet. Yes.

Apem. Then thou liest: look in thy last work,
where thou hast feigned him a worthy fellow.

Poet. That's not feigned; he is so.

Apem. Yes, he is worthy of thee, and to pay
thee for thy labour: he that loves to be flattered
is worthy o' the flatterer.   Heavens, that I were
a lord!

Tim. What wouldst do then, Apemantus?

Apem. Even as Apemantus does now; hate a
lord with my heart.

Tim. What, thyself?

Apem. Ay.

Tim. Wherefore?

Apem. That I had no angry wit to be a lord.—
Art not thou a merchant?

Mer. Ay, Apemantus.

Apem. Traffic confound thee, if the gods will not!

Mer. If traffic do it, the gods do it.

Apem. Traffic 's thy god, and thy god confound
thee!

Trumpets sound.   Enter a Servant.

Tim. What trumpet's that?

Serv. 'T is Alcibiades, and some twenty horse,
All of companionship.

Tim. Pray entertain them; give them guide to
us.   [*Exeunt some* Attendants.
You must needs dine with me:—Go not you hence,

Till I have thanked you; and, when dinner's
    done,
Shew me this piece.—I am joyful of your sights.

Enter ALCIBIADES, *with his company.*

Most welcome, sir!   [*They salute.*
    Apem.   So, so; there!—
Achés contract and starve your supple joints!—
That there should be small love 'mongst these sweet
    knaves,
And all this courtesy! The strain of man's bred
    out
Into baboon and monkey.
    Alcib. Sir, you have saved my longing, and I
    feed
Most hungerly on your sight.
    Tim.   Right welcome, sir.
Ere we depart, we'll share a bounteous time
In different pleasures. Pray you, let us in.
            [*Exeunt all but* APEMANTUS.

Enter two Lords.

    1st Lord. What time a day is't, Apemantus?
    Apem. Time to be honest.
    1st Lord. That time serves still.
    Apem. The most accursed thou, that still
omitt'st it.
    2nd Lord. Thou art going to lord Timon's feast.
    Apem. Ay; to see meat fill knaves, and wine
heat fools.
    2nd Lord. Fare thee well, fare thee well.
    Apem. Thou art a fool, to bid me farewell twice.
    2nd Lord. Why, Apemantus?
    Apem. Shouldst have kept one to thyself, for I
mean to give thee none.
    1st Lord. Hang thyself.
    Apem. No, I will do nothing at thy bidding;
make thy requests to thy friend.
    2nd Lord. Away, unpeaceable dog, or I'll spurn
thee hence.
    Apem. I will fly, like a dog, the heels of the ass.
            [*Exit.*
    1st Lord. He's opposite to humanity. Come,
    shall we in,
And taste lord Timon's bounty? he outgoes
The very heart of kindness.
    2nd Lord. He pours it out; Plutus, the god of
    gold,
Is but his steward: no meed, but he repays
Sevenfold above itself; no gift to him,
But breeds the giver a return exceeding
All use of quittance.
    1st Lord.   The noblest mind he carries
That ever governed man.
    2nd Lord. Long may he live in fortunes! Shall
    we in?
    1st Lord. I'll keep you company.   [*Exeunt.*

SCENE II.— *The same. A Room of State in*
         TIMON'S *House.*

*Hautboys playing loud music. A great banquet
served in;* FLAVIUS *and others attending: then
enter* TIMON, ALCIBIADES, LUCIUS, LUCULLUS,
SEMPRONIUS, *and other* Athenian Senators, *with*
VENTIDIUS, *and* Attendants. *Then comes, dropping after all,* APEMANTUS, *discontentedly.*

    Ven. Most honoured Timon, it hath pleased the
    gods to remember
My father's age, and call him to long peace.
He is gone happy, and has left me rich:
Then, as in grateful virtue I am bound
To your free heart, I do return those talents,
Doubled, with thanks, and service, from whose help
I derived liberty.
    Tim.   O, by no means,
Honest Ventidius: you mistake my love;
I gave it freely ever; and there's none
Can truly say he gives, if he receives:
If our betters play at that game, we must not dare
To imitate them: faults that are rich, are fair.
    Ven. A noble spirit!
          [*They all stand ceremoniously looking
            on* TIMON.
    Tim.   Nay, my lords,
Ceremony was but devised at first
To set a gloss on faint deeds, hollow welcomes,
Recanting goodness, sorry ere 'tis shewn;
But where there is true friendship, there needs
    none.
Pray sit; more welcome are ye to my fortunes
Than my fortunes to me.   [*They sit.*
    1st Lord. My lord, we always have confessed it.
    Apem. Ho, ho, confessed it! hanged it, have
    you not?
    Tim. O, Apemantus! you are welcome.
    Apem. No, you shall not make me welcome:
I come to have thee thrust me out of doors.
    Tim. Fie, thou art a churl; you have got a
    humour there
Does not become a man; 'tis much to blame.—
They say, my lords, "*Ira furor brevis est,*"
But yond' man's ever angry.—
Go, let him have a table by himself;
For he does neither affect company,
Nor is he fit for it, indeed.
    Apem. Let me stay at thine apperil, Timon;
I come to observe; I give thee warning on't.
    Tim. I take no heed of thee; thou art an Athe-
nian; therefore welcome. I myself would have no
power: pr'y thee, let my meat make thee silent.
    Apem. I scorn thy meat! 'twould choke me, for
    I should
Ne'er flatter thee.—O you gods! what a number
Of men eat Timon, and he sees them not!

It grieves me to see so many dip their meat
In one man's blood; and all the madness is,
He cheers them up too.
I wonder men dare trust themselves with men:
Methinks they should invite them without knives;
Good for their meat, and safer for their lives.
There's much example for't; the fellow that
Sits next him now, parts bread with him, and pledges
The breath of him in a divided draught,
Is the readiest man to kill him: it has been proved.
If I were a huge man, I should fear to drink at meals,
Lest they should spy my windpipe's dangerous
    notes:

Great men should drink with harness on their
  throats.
 Tim. My lord, in heart; and let the health go
  round.
 2nd Lord. Let it flow this way, my good lord.
 Apem. Flow this way!
A brave fellow! he keep his tides well. Timon,
Those healths will make thee, and thy state, look ill.
Here's that which is too weak to be a sinner,
Honest water, which ne'er left man i' the mire:
This and my food are equals; there's no odds.
Feasts are too proud to give thanks to the gods.

APEMANTUS'S GRACE.

Immortal gods, I crave no pelf,
I pray for no man but myself:
Grant I may never prove so fond,
To trust man on his oath or bond;
Or a harlot, for her weeping;
Or a dog that seems a sleeping;
Or a keeper with my freedom;
Or my friends, if I should need 'em.
Amen. So fall to 't:
Rich men sin, and I eat root.

[Eats and drinks.

Much good dich thy good heart, Apemantus!
 Tim. Captain Alcibiades, your heart's in the field
  now.
 Alcib. My heart is ever at your service, my lord.
 Tim. You had rather be at a breakfast of enemies,
than a dinner of friends.
 Alcib. So they were bleeding-new, my lord,
there's no meat like them; I could wish my best
friend at such a feast.
 Apem. 'Would all those flatterers were thine

enemies then; that then thou mightst kill 'em, and
bid me to 'em.
 1st Lord. Might we but have that happiness, my
lord, that you would once use our hearts, whereby
we might express some part of our zeals, we should
think ourselves for ever perfect.
 Tim. O, no doubt, my good friends, but the gods
themselves have provided that I shall have much
help from you: how had you been my friends else?
why have you that charitable title from thousands,

did you not chiefly belong to my heart? I have told
more of you to myself, than you can with modesty
speak in your own behalf; and thus far I confirm
you. O you gods! think I, what need we have any
friends, if we should never have need of them?
they were the most needless creatures living,
should we ne'er have use for them; and would
most resemble sweet instruments hung up in cases,
that keep their sounds to themselves. Why, I
have often wished myself poorer, that I might come
nearer to you. We are born to do benefits: and
what better or properer can we call our own, than
the riches of our friends? O, what a precious
comfort 't is to have so many, like brothers, commanding one another's fortunes! O joy, e'en
made away ere it can be born! Mine eyes cannot
hold out water, methinks: to forget their faults,
I drink to you.

Apem. Thou weep'st to make them drink, Timon.

2nd Lord. Joy had the like conception in our eyes,
And, at that instant, like a babe sprung up.

Apem. Ho, ho! I laugh to think that babe a
    bastard.

3rd Lord. I promise you, my lord, you moved me
    much.

Apem. Much!   [*Tucket sounded.*

Tim. What means that trump?—How now?

Enter a Servant.

Serv. Please you, my lord, there are certain ladies
most desirous of admittance.

Tim. Ladies? What are their wills?

Serv. There comes with them a forerunner, my
lord, which bears that office to signify their pleasures.

Tim. I pray, let them be admitted.

Enter Cupid.

Cup. Hail to thee, worthy Timon; and to all
That of his bounties taste!—The five best senses
Acknowledge thee their patron; and come freely
To gratulate thy plenteous bosom: the ear,
Taste, touch, smell, all pleased from thy table rise;
They only now come but to feast thine eyes.

Tim. They are welcome all; let them have kind
    admittance:
Music, make their welcome.   [*Exit* Cupid.

1st Lord. You see, my lord, how ample you are
    beloved.

Music. Re-enter Cupid, *with a masque of* Ladies
*as Amazons, with lutes in their hands, dancing
and playing.*

Apem. Hey-day, what a sweep of vanity comes
    this way!
They dance! they are mad women.
Like madness is the glory of this life,

As this pomp shews to a little oil and root.
We make ourselves fools to disport ourselves;
And spend our flatteries to drink those men
Upon whose age we void it up again,
With poisonous spite and envy.
Who lives, that's not depravéd or depraves?
Who dies, that bears not one spurn to their graves
Of their friends' gift?
I should fear those that dance before me now,
Would one day stamp upon me. It has been done:
Men shut their doors against a setting sun.

The Lords *rise from table, with much adoring of*
TIMON; *and to shew their loves, each singles out
an Amazon, and all dance, men with women, a
lofty strain or two to the hautboys, and cease.*

Tim. You have done our pleasures much grace,
    fair ladies,
Set a fair fashion on our entertainment,
Which was not half so beautiful and kind;
You have added worth unto 't, and lively lustre,
And entertained me with mine own device:
I am to thank you for it.

1st Lady. My lord, you take us even at the best.

Apem. 'Faith, for the worst is filthy; and would
not hold taking, I doubt me.

Tim. Ladies, there is an idle banquet attends
    you:
Please you to dispose yourselves.

All Ladies. Most thankfully, my lord.
        [*Exeunt* Cupid *and* Ladies.

Tim. Flavius!—

Flav. My lord.

Tim.   The little casket bring me hither.

Flav. Yes, my lord.—More jewels yet!
There is no crossing him in his humour; [*Aside.*
Else I should tell him—well—i' faith I should—
When all's spent, he 'd be crossed then, an he could.
'Tis pity bounty had not eyes behind;
That man might ne'er be wretched for his mind.
    [*Exit, and returns with the casket.*

1st Lord. Where be our men?

Serv. Here, my lord, in readiness.

2nd Lord. Our horses?

Tim.   O, my friends, I have one word
To say to you:—Look you, my good lord,
I must entreat you, honour me so much
As to advance this jewel;
Accept, and wear it, kind my lord.

1st Lord. I am so far already in your gifts,—

All. So are we all.

Enter a Servant.

Serv. My lord, there are certain nobles of the
    senate
Newly alighted, and come to visit you.

Tim. They are fairly welcome.

Flav. I beseech your honour,
Vouchsafe me a word; it does concern you near.
   Tim. Near? why then another time I'll hear
     thee:
I pr'y thee, let us be provided
To shew them entertainment.
   Flav. I scarce know how.   [*Aside.*

     Enter another Servant.

   2nd Serv. May it please your honour, the lord
     Lucius,
Out of his free love, hath presented to you
Four milk-white horses, trapped in silver.
   Tim. I shall accept them fairly: let the presents

     Enter a third Servant.

Be worthily entertained.—How now, what news?
   3rd Serv. Please you, my lord, that honourable
gentleman, lord Lucullus, entreats your company
to-morrow, to hunt with him; and has sent your
honour two brace of greyhounds.
   Tim. I'll hunt with him; and let them be re-
     ceived,
Not without fair reward.
   Flav. What will this come to? [*Aside.*
He commands us to provide, and give great gifts,
And all out of an empty coffer.—
Nor will he know his purse; or yield me this,
To shew him what a beggar his heart is,
Being of no power to make his wishes good;
His promises fly so beyond his state,
That what he speaks is all in debt; he owes
For every word: he is so kind that he now
Pays interest for't; his lands put to their books.
Well, 'would I were gently put out of office,
Before I were forced out!
Happier is he that has no friend to feed,
Than such as do even enemies exceed.
I bleed inwardly for my lord.   [*Exit.*
   Tim. You do yourselves
Much wrong, you bate too much of your own
     merits:—
Here, my lord, a trifle of our love.
   2nd Lord. With more than common thanks I
     will receive it.
   3rd Lord. O, he is the very soul of bounty!
   Tim. And now I remember me, my lord, you gave
Good words the other day of a bay courser
I rode on: it is yours, because you liked it!

   2nd Lord. I beseech you, pardon me, my lord,
     in that.
   Tim. You may take my word, my lord; I know,
     no man
Can justly praise, but what he does affect:
I weigh my friends' affection with mine own;
I'll tell you true. I'll call on you.
   All Lords. O, none so welcome.
   Tim. I take all and your several visitations
So kind to heart, 'tis not enough to give;
Methinks I could deal kingdoms to my friends,
And ne'er be weary.—Alcibiades,
Thou art a soldier, therefore seldom rich;
It comes in charity to thee: for all thy living
Is 'mongst the dead; and all the lands thou hast
Lie in a pitched field.
   Alcib. Ay, defiled land, my lord.
   1st Lord. We are so virtuously bound,—
   Tim. And so am I to you.
   2nd Lord. So infinitely endeared,—
   Tim. All to you.—Lights, more lights!
   1st Lord. The best of happiness,
Honour, and fortunes, keep with you, lord Timon!
   Tim. Ready for his friends.
     [*Exeunt* ALCIBIADES, Lords, &c.
   Apem. What a coil's here!
Serving of becks, and jutting out of bums!
I doubt whether their legs be worth the sums
That are given for 'em. Friendship's full of dregs:
Methinks false hearts should never have sound
     legs:
Thus honest fools lay out their wealth on court'sies.
   Tim. Now, Apemantus, if thou wert not sullen,
I would be good to thee.
   Apem. No, I'll nothing: for,
If I should be bribed too, there would be none left
To rail upon thee; and then thou wouldst sin the
     faster.
Thou giv'st so long, Timon, I fear me, thou
Wilt give away thyself in paper shortly:
What need these feasts, pomps, and vain glories?
   Tim. Nay, an you begin to rail on society once,
I am sworn not to give regard to you.
Farewell: and come with better music. [*Exit.*
   Apem. So; thou'lt not hear me now;—thou
     shalt not, then; I'll lock
Thy heaven from thee. O, that men's ears should
     be
To counsel deaf, but not to flattery! [*Exit.*

SCENE I.—Athens. *A Room in a* Senator's *House.*

Enter a Senator, *with papers in his hand.*

Sen. And late, five thousand (to Varro and to
        Isidore
He owes nine thousand), besides my former sum,
Which makes it five-and-twenty.—Still in motion
Of raging waste? It cannot hold; it will not.
If I want gold, steal but a beggar's dog
And give it Timon, why, the dog coins gold:
If I would sell my horse, and buy twenty more
Better than he, why, give my horse to Timon;
Ask nothing, give it him, it foals me straight,
And able horses. No porter at his gate;
But rather one that smiles, and still invites
All that pass by. It cannot hold; no reason
Can sound his state in safety. Caphis, hoa!
Caphis, I say!

Enter CAPHIS.

Caph.   Here, sir: what is your pleasure?
Sen. Get on your cloak, and haste you to lord
        Timon;
Impórtune him for my monies; be not ceased
With slight denial; nor then silenced, when—
"Commend me to your master," and the cap
Plays in the right hand thus:—but tell him, sirrah,
My uses cry to me, I must serve my turn
Out of mine own; his days and times are past,
And my reliances on his fracted dates
Have smit my credit: I love and honour him;
But must not break my back to heal his finger:
Immediate are my needs; and my relief
Must not be tossed and turned to me in words,
But find supply immediate. Get you gone:
Put on a most importunate aspéct,
A visage of demand; for I do fear,
When every feather sticks in his own wing,
Lord Timon will be left a naked gull,
Which flashes now a phœnix. Get you gone.

Caph. I go, sir.
Sen. Ay go, sir: take the bonds along with you,
And have the dates in compt.
Caph.   I will, sir.
Sen.   Go.   [*Exeunt.*

SCENE II.—*The same. A Hall in* TIMON'S *House.*

Enter FLAVIUS, *with many bills in his hand.*

Flav. No care, no stop! so senseless of expense,
That he will neither know how to maintain it,
Nor cease his flow of riot: takes no account
How things go from him; nor resumes no care
Of what is to continue: never mind
Was to be so unwise, to be so kind.
What shall be done? he will not hear, till feel:
I must be round with him, now he comes from
        hunting.
Fie, fie, fie, fie!

Enter CAPHIS, *and the* Servants *of* ISIDORE *and*
VARRO.

Caph.   Good-even, Varro: what,
You come for money?
Var. Serv.   Is't not your business too?
Caph. It is;—and yours too, Isidore?
Isid. Serv.   It is so.
Caph. 'Would we were all discharged!
Var. Serv.   I fear it.
Caph. Here comes the lord.

Enter TIMON, ALCIBIADES, *and* Lords, *&c.*

Tim. So soon as dinner's done, we'll forth again,
My Alcibiades.—With me? what is your will?
Caph. My lord, here is a note of certain dues.
Tim. Dues? whence are you?
Caph.   Of Athens here, my lord.
Tim. Go to my steward.

Caph. Please it your lordship, he hath put me off
To the succession of new days this month:
My master is awaked by great occasion,
To call upon his own; and humbly prays you,
That with your other noble parts you'll suit,
In giving him his right.

Tim.   Mine honest friend,
I pr'y thee, but repair to me next morning.

Caph. Nay, good my lord,—

Tim.   Contain thyself, good friend.

Var. Serv. One Varro's servant, my good lord,—

Isid. Serv.   From Isidore;
He humbly prays your speedy payment,—

Caph. If you did know, my lord, my master's
       wants,—

Var. Serv. 'T was due on forfeiture, my lord, six
       weeks,
And past.—

Isid. Serv. Your steward puts me off, my lord;
And I am sent expressly to your lordship.

Tim. Give me breath:—
I do beseech you, good my lords, keep on;
       [*Exeunt* ALCIBIADES *and* Lords.
I'll wait upon you instantly.—Come hither, pray
       you: [*To* FLAVIUS.
How goes the world, that I am thus encountered
With clamorous demands of date-broke bonds,
And the detention of long-since-due debts,
Against my honour?

Flav.   Please you, gentlemen,
The time is unagreeable to this business:
Your importunacy cease till after dinner;
That I may make his lordship understand
Wherefore you are not paid.

Tim.   Do so, my friends:
See them well entertained.   [*Exit.*

Flav.   I pray, draw near.   [*Exit.*

Enter APEMANTUS *and a* Fool.

Caph. Stay, stay, here comes the fool with Apemantus; let's have some sport with 'em.

Var. Serv. Hang him, he'll abuse us.

Isid. Serv. A plague upon him, dog!

Var. Serv. How dost, fool?

Apem. Dost dialogue with thy shadow?

Var. Serv. I speak not to thee.

Apem. No; 'tis to thyself.—Come away.
       [*To the* Fool.

Isid. Serv. [*To* VARRO's Servant]. There's the
fool hangs on your back already.

Apem. No, thou stand'st single; thou art not on
him yet.

Caph. Where's the fool now?

Apem. He last asked the question. — Poor
rogues, and usurers' men! bawds between gold
and want!

All Servants. What are we, Apemantus?

Apem. Asses.

All Serv. Why?

Apem. That you ask me what you are, and do
not know yourselves.—Speak to 'em, fool.

Fool. How do you, gentlemen?

All Serv. Gramercies, good fool: how does your
mistress?

Fool. She's e'en setting on water to scald such
chickens as you are. 'Would we could see you at
Corinth.

Apem. Good! gramercy!

Enter Page.

Fool. Look you, here comes my mistress' page.

Page. [*To the* Fool]. Why, how now, captain?
what do you in this wise company?—How dost
thou, Apemantus?

Apem. 'Would I had a rod in my mouth, that I
might answer thee profitably.

Page. Pr'y thee, Apemantus, read me the su-
perscription of these letters; I know not which is
which.

Apem. Canst not read?

Page. No.

Apem. There will little learning die then, that
day thou art hanged. This is to lord Timon; this
to Alcibiades. Go; thou wast born a bastard, and
thou'lt die a bawd.

Page. Thou wast whelped a dog; and thou shalt
famish—a dog's death. Answer not, I am gone.
       [*Exit* Page.

Apem. Even so thou out-runn'st grace. Fool, I
will go with you to lord Timon's.

Fool. Will you leave me there?

Apem. If Timon stay at home.—You three serve
three usurers?

All Serv. Ay; 'would they served us!

Apem. So would I,—as good a trick as ever
hangman served thief.

Fool. Are you three usurers' men?

All Serv. Ay, fool.

Fool. I think, no usurer but has a fool to his servant: my mistress is one, and I am her fool.
When men come to borrow of your masters, they
approach sadly, and go away merry; but they enter
my mistress' house merrily, and go away sadly.
The reason of this?

Var. Serv. I could render one.

Apem. Do it, then, that we may account thee a
whoremaster and a knave; which, notwithstanding, thou shalt be no less esteemed.

Var. Serv. What is a whoremaster, fool?

Fool. A fool in good clothes, and something like
thee. 'T is a spirit: sometime it appears like a
lord; sometime like a lawyer; sometime like a
philosopher, with two stones more than his artificial one: he is very often like a knight; and, gene-

rally, in all shapes that man goes up and down in,
from fourscore to thirteen, this spirit walks in.

Var. Serv. Thou art not altogether a fool.

Fool. Nor thou altogether a wise man: as much
foolery as I have, so much wit thou lackest.

Apem. That answer might have become Apemantus.

All Serv. Aside, aside: here comes lord Timon.

Re-enter TIMON *and* FLAVIUS.

Apem. Come with me, fool, come.

Fool. I do not always follow lover, elder brother, and woman; sometime, the philosopher.
                    [*Exeunt* APEMANTUS *and* Fool.

Flav. 'Pray you, walk near, I'll speak with you
        anon.   [*Exeunt* Servants.

Tim. You make me marvel: wherefore, ere this
        time,
Had you not fully laid my state before me;
That I might so have rated my expense,
As I had leave of means?

Flav.   You would not hear me,
At many leisures I proposed.

Tim. Go to:
Perchance some single vantages you took,
When my indisposition put you back;
And that unaptness made your minister
Thus to excuse yourself.

Flav.   O, my good lord!
At many times I brought in my accounts,
Laid them before you; you would throw them off,
And say, you found them in mine honesty.
When, for some trifling present, you have bid me
Return so much, I have shook my head and wept;
Yea, 'gainst the authority of manners, prayed you
To hold your hand more close: I did endure
Not seldom, nor no slight checks, when I have
Prompted you, in the ebb of your estate,
And your great flow of debts. My dear-loved lord,
Though you hear now (too late!), yet now 's a time
The greatest of your having lacks a half
To pay your present debts,

Tim.   Let all my land be sold.

Flav. 'T is all engaged, some forfeited and gone;
And what remains will hardly stop the mouth
Of present dues: the future comes apace:
What shall defend the interim? and at length
How goes our reckoning?

Tim. To Lacedæmon did my land extend.

Flav. O, my good lord, the world is but a word;
Were it all yours to give it in a breath,
How quickly were it gone!

Tim.   You tell me true,

Flav. If you suspect my husbandry, or falsehood,
Call me before the exactest auditors,
And set me on the proof. So the gods bless me,
When all our offices have been oppressed

With riotous feeders; when our vaults have wept
With drunken spilth of wine; when every room
Hath blazed with lights and brayed with min-
        strelsy;
I have retired me to a wasteful cock,
And set mine eyes at flow.

Tim.   Pr'y thee, no more.

Flav. Heavens, have I said, the bounty of this
        lord!
How many prodigal bits have slaves and peasants
This night englutted! Who is not Timon's?
What heart, head, sword, force, means, but is lord
        Timon's?
Great Timon, noble, worthy, royal Timon!
Ah! when the means are gone that buy this praise,
The breath is gone whereof this praise is made:
Feast-won, fast-lost; one cloud of winter showers,
These flies are couched.

Tim.   Come, sermon me no further:
No villanous bounty yet hath passed my heart;
Unwisely, not ignobly, have I given.
Why dost thou weep? Canst thou the conscience
        lack,
To think I shall lack friends? Secure thy heart;
If I would broach the vessels of my love,
And try the argument of hearts by borrowing,
Men, and men's fortunes, could I frankly use,
As I can bid thee speak.

Flav.   Assurance bless your thoughts!

Tim. And, in some sort, these wants of mine
        are crowned,
That I account them blessings; for by these
Shall I try friends: you shall perceive how you
Mistake my fortunes; I am wealthy in my friends.
Within there, ho!—Flaminius! Servilius!

Enter FLAMINIUS, SERVILIUS, *and other* Servants.

Serv. My lord, my lord,—

Tim. I will despatch you severally.—You to
        lord Lucius,—
To lord Lucullus you; I hunted with his
Honour to-day;—you to Sempronius:
Commend me to their loves; and, I am proud, say,
That my occasions have found time to use them
Toward a supply of money: let the request
Be fifty talents.

Flam.   As you have said, my lord.

Flav. Lord Lucius and Lucullus? humph!
                              [*Aside.*

Tim. Go you, sir [*To another* Servant], to the
        senators
(Of whom, even to the state's best health, I have
Deserved this hearing); bid 'em send o' the instant
A thousand talents to me.

Flav.   I have been bold
(For that I knew it the most general way)
To them to use your signet and your name;

But they do shake their heads, and I am here
No richer in return.

   Tim.   Is 't true ? can it be ?

   Flav. They answer, in a joint and corporate
      voice,
That now they are at fall, want treasure, cannot
Do what they would; are sorry—you are honour-
      able,—
But yet they could have wished—they know not—
Something hath been amiss—a noble nature
May catch a wrench—would all were well—'t is
      pity—
And so, intending other serious matters,
After distasteful looks, and these hard fractions,
With certain half-caps, and cold-moving nods,
They froze me into silence.

   Tim.   You gods, reward them !—
I pr'y thee, man, look cheerly. These old fellows
Have their ingratitude in them hereditary :
Their blood is caked, 't is cold, it seldom flows ;
'T is lack of kindly warmth, they are not kind ;

And nature, as it grows again towards earth,
Is fashioned for the journey, dull and heavy.—
Go to Ventidius [*To a* Servant] :—Pr'y thee, be
      not sad ;   [*To* FLAVIUS.
Thou art true and honest; ingenuously I speak,
No blame belongs to thee :—[*To* Servant] Venti-
      dius lately
Buried his father; by whose death, he 's stepped
Into a great estate : when he was poor,
Imprisoned, and in scarcity of friends,
I cleared him with five talents : greet him from
      me ;
Bid him suppose some good necessity
Touches his friend, which craves to be remembered
With those five talents :—that had [*To* FLAVIUS],
      give it these fellows
To whom 't is instant due. Ne'er speak, or think,
That Timon's fortunes 'mong his friends can sink.

   Flav. I would I could not think : that thought
      is bounty's foe ;
Being free itself, it thinks all others so. [*Exeunt.*

ACT III

SCENE I.—Athens. *A Room in LUCULLUS's House.*

FLAMINIUS *waiting.   Enter a* Servant *to him.*

Serv. I have told my lord of you; he is coming down to you.

Flam. I thank you, sir.

Enter LUCULLUS.

Serv. Here's my lord.

Lucul. [*aside*]. One of lord Timon's men? a gift, I warrant. Why, this hits right; I dreamt of a silver basin and ewer to-night.—Flaminius, honest Flaminius; you are very respectively welcome, sir.—Fill me some wine.—[*Exit* Servant. And how does that honourable, complete, freehearted gentleman of Athens, thy very bountiful good lord and master?

Flam. His health is well, sir.

Lucul. I am right glad that his health is well, sir.   And what hast thou there under thy cloak, pretty Flaminius?

Flam. 'Faith, nothing but an empty box, sir; which, in my lord's behalf, I come to entreat your honour to supply; who, having great and instant occasion to use fifty talents, hath sent to your lordship to furnish him; nothing doubting your present assistance therein.

Lucul. La, la, la, la;—"nothing doubting," says he? alas, good lord! a noble gentleman 'tis, if he would not keep so good a house.

Many a time and often I have dined with him, and told him on't; and come again to supper to him, of purpose to have him spend less: and yet he would embrace no counsel, take no warning by my coming. Every man has his fault, and honesty is his: I have told him on't, but I could never get him from it.

Re-enter Servant *with wine.*

Serv. Please your lordship, here is the wine.

Lucul. Flaminius, I have noted thee always wise. Here's to thee.

Flam. Your lordship speaks your pleasure.

Lucul. I have observed thee always for a towardly prompt spirit,—give thee thy due,—and one that knows what belongs to reason; and canst use the time well, if the time use thee well: good parts in thee.—Get you gone, sirrah.—[*To the* Servant, *who goes out.*]—Draw nearer, honest Flaminius. Thy lord's a bountiful gentleman: but thou art wise; and thou knowest well enough, although thou comest to me, that this is no time to lend money; especially upon bare friendship, without security. Here's three solidares for thee: good boy, wink at me, and say thou sawest me not.   Fare thee well.

Flam. Is't possible the world should so much differ;
And we alive, that lived? Fly, damnèd baseness,
To him that worships thee!

[*Throwing the money away.*

Lucul. Ha! now I see thou art a fool, and fit
　　for thy master.　　　[*Exit* Lucullus.
Flam. May these add to the number that may
　　scald thee!
Let molten coin be thy damnation,
Thou disease of a friend, and not himself!
Has friendship such a faint and milky heart,
It turns in less than two nights? O you gods,
I feel my master's passion! This slave
Unto his honour, has my lord's meat in him:
Why should it thrive, and turn to nutriment,
When he is turned to poison?
O, may diseases only work upon't!
And, when he is sick to death, let not that part
　　of nature
Which my lord paid for, be of any power
To expel sickness, but prolong his hour! [*Exit.*

SCENE II.—*The same.　A public Place.*

Enter Lucius, *with three* Strangers.

Luc. Who, the lord Timon? he is my very
good friend, and an honourable gentleman.

1st Stran. We know him for no less, though we
are but strangers to him.　But I can tell you one
thing, my lord, and which I hear from common
rumours; now lord Timon's happy hours are
done and past, and his estate shrinks from him.

Luc. Fie, no; do not believe it; he cannot want
for money.

2nd Stran. But believe you this, my lord, that,
not long ago, one of his men was with the lord
Lucullus, to borrow so many talents; nay, urged
extremely for 't, and shewed what necessity belonged to 't, and yet was denied.

Luc. How?

2nd Stran. I tell you, denied, my lord.

Luc. What a strange case was that? now, before the gods, I am ashamed on 't.　Denied that
honourable man? there was very little honour
shewed in 't.　For my own part, I must needs
confess I have received some small kindnesses
from him, as money, plate, jewels, and such
like trifles, nothing comparing to his; yet, had
he mistook him, and sent to me, I should ne'er
have denied his occasion so many talents.

Enter Servilius.

Ser. See, by good hap, yonder's my lord; I
have sweat to see his honour.—My honoured
lord,—　　　　　　　　　　[*To* Lucius.

Luc. Servilius! you are kindly met, sir.　Fare
thee well: commend me to thy honourable-
virtuous lord, my very exquisite friend.

Ser. May it please your honour, my lord hath
sent—

Luc. Ha! what has he sent? I am so much
endeared to that lord; he's ever sending: how
shall I thank him, think'st thou? And what has
he sent now?

Ser. He has only sent his present occasion now,
my lord; requesting your lordship to supply his
instant use with so many talents.

Luc. I know his lordship is but merry with me;
He cannot want fifty-five hundred talents.

Ser. But in the mean time he wants less, my
　　lord.
If his occasion were not virtuous,
I should not urge it half so faithfully.

Luc. Dost thou speak seriously, Servilius?

Ser. Upon my soul, 'tis true, sir.

Luc. What a wicked beast was I, to disfurnish
myself against such a good time, when I might
have shewn myself honourable! how unluckily it
happened, that I should purchase the day before
for a little part, and undo a great deal of honour!
—Servilius, now before the gods, I am not able to
do 't; the more beast, I say.　I was sending to use
lord Timon myself, these gentleman can witness;
but I would not, for the wealth of Athens, I had
done it now.　Commend me bountifully to his
good lordship; and I hope his honour will conceive the fairest of me, because I have no power
to be kind.　And tell him this from me, I count it
one of my greatest afflictions, say, that I cannot
pleasure such an honourable gentleman.　Good
Servilius, will you befriend me so far as to use
mine own words to him?

Ser. Yes, sir, I shall.

Luc. I will look you out a good turn, Servilius.
　　　　　　　　　　　　　[*Exit* Servilius.
True, as you said, Timon is shrunk, indeed;
And he that's once denied, will hardly speed.
　　　　　　　　　　　　　[*Exit* Lucius.

1st Stran. Do you observe this, Hostilius?

2nd Stran. Ay, too well.

1st Stran. Why this is the world's soul;
And just of the same piece
Is every flatterer's spirit: who can call him his friend
That dips in the same dish? for, in my knowing,
Timon has been this lord's father,
And kept his credit with his purse;
Supported his estate; nay, Timon's money
Has paid his men their wages: he ne'er drinks,
But Timon's silver treads upon his lip:
And yet (O, see the monstrousness of man,
When he looks out in an ungrateful shape!)
He does deny him, in respect of his,
What charitable men afford to beggars.

3rd Stran. Religion groans at it.

1st Stran.　　　　For mine own part,

I never tasted Timon in my life,
Nor came any of his bounties over me,
To mark me for his friend; yet, I protest,
For his right noble mind, illustrious virtue,
And honourable carriage,
Had his necessity made use of me,
I would have put my wealth into donation,
And the best half should have returned to him,
So much I love his heart: but I perceive
Men must learn now with pity to dispense;
For policy sits above conscience.   [*Exeunt.*

SCENE III.—*The same. A Room in* SEMPRONIUS'S
House.

Enter SEMPRONIUS, *and a* Servant *of* TIMON'S.

  Sem. Must he needs trouble me in 't? humph!
    'bove all others?
He might have tried lord Lucius, or Lucullus;
And now Ventidius is wealthy too,
Whom he redeemed from prison: all these
Owe their estates unto him.
  Serv.   My lord,

They have all been touched, and found base metal;
For they have all denied him.
  Sem.   How! have they denied him?
Has Ventidius and Lucullus denied him?
And does he send to me? Three? humph!—
It shews but little love or judgment in him.
Must I be his last refuge? His friends, like phy-
    sicans,
Thrice give him over: must I take the cure upon
    me?
He has much disgraced me in 't: I am angry at
    him,
That might have known my place: I see no sense
    for 't,
But his occasions might have wooed me first;
For, in my conscience, I was the first man
That e'er received gift from him:

And does he think so backwardly of me now,
That I 'll requite it last? No:
So it may prove an argument of laughter
To the rest, and 'mongst lords I be thought a fool.
I had rather than the worth of thrice the sum,
He had sent to me first, but for my mind's sake;
I had such a courage to do him good. But now
    return,
And with their faint reply this answer join;
Who bates mine honour, shall not know my coin.
                            [*Exit.*
  Serv. Excellent! Your lordship's a goodly vil-
lain. The devil knew not what he did, when he
made man politic; he crossed himself by 't: and I
cannot think but, in the end, the villanies of man
will set him clear. How fairly this lord strives to
appear foul! takes virtuous copies to be wicked;

like those that, under hot ardent zeal, would set
whole realms on fire. Of such a nature is his
politic love.
This was my lord's best hope; now all are fled,
Save the gods only. Now his friends are dead,
Doors, that were ne'er acquainted with their wards
Many a bounteous year, must be employed
Now to guard sure their master.
And this is all a liberal course allows;
Who cannot keep his wealth, must keep his house.
                                                [*Exit.*

SCENE IV.—*The same. A Hall in* TIMON'S *House.*

Enter two Servants *of* VARRO, *and the* Servant
of LUCIUS, *meeting* TITUS, HORTENSIUS, *and
other* Servants *to* TIMON'S *Creditors, waiting
his coming out.*

  Var. Serv. Well met; good-morrow, Titus and
        Hortensius.
  Tit. The like to you, kind Varro.
  Hor.   Lucius?
What, do we meet together?
  Luc. Serv.   Ay, and I think
One business does command us all; for mine
Is money.
  Tit.   So is theirs and ours.

        Enter PHILOTUS.

  Luc. Serv.   And sir
Philotus too!
  Phi.   Good-day at once.
  Luc. Serv.   Welcome, good brother.
What do you think the hour?
  Phi.   Labouring for nine.
  Luc. Serv. So much?
  Phi.   Is not my lord seen yet?
  Luc. Serv.   Not yet.
  Phi. I wonder on 't; he was wont to shine at
        seven.
  Luc. Serv. Ay, but the days are waxed shorter
        with him:
You must consider that a prodigal course
Is like the sun's; but not, like his, recoverable
I fear 'tis deepest winter in lord Timon's purse:
That is, one may reach deep enough, and yet
Find little.
  Phi.   I am of your fear for that.
  Tit. I 'll shew you how to observe a strange
        event.
Your lord sends now for money.
  Hor. Most true, he does.
  Tit. And he wears jewels now of Timon's gift,
For which I wait for money.
  Hor. It is against my heart.

  Luc. Serv.   Mark, how strange it shews,
Timon in this should pay more than he owes:
And e'en as if your lord should wear rich jewels,
And send for money for 'em.
  Hor. I am weary of this charge, the gods can
        witness:
I know my lord hath spent of Timon's wealth,
And now ingratitude makes it worse than stealth.
  1st Var. Serv. Yes, mine 's three thousand
        crowns: what 's yours?
  Luc. Serv. Five thousand mine,
  1st Var. Serv. 'Tis much deep: and it should
        seem by the sum,
Your master's confidence was above mine;
Else, surely, his had equalled.

        Enter FLAMINIUS.

  Tit. One of lord Timon's men.
  Luc. Serv. Flaminius! sir, a word: 'pray, is my
lord ready to come forth?
  Flam. No, indeed, he is not.
  Tit. We attend his lordship; 'pray, signify so
        much.
  Flam. I need not tell him that; he knows you
are too diligent.   [*Exit* FLAMINIUS.

    Enter FLAVIUS, *in a cloak, muffled.*

  Luc. Serv. Ha! is not that his steward muffled
        so?
He goes away in a cloud: call him, call him.
  Tit. Do you hear, sir?
  1st Var. Serv. By your leave, sir,—
  Flav. What do you ask of me, my friend?
  Tit. We wait for certain money here, sir.
  Flav.   Ay,
If money were as certain as your waiting,
'T were sure enough.
Why then preferred you not your sums and
        bills,
When your false masters eat of my lord's meat?
Then they could smile, and fawn upon his debts,
And take down the interest into their gluttonous
        maws.
You do yourselves but wrong to stir me up;
Let me pass quietly:
Believe 't, my lord and I have made an end;
I have no more to reckon, he to spend.
  Luc. Serv. Ay, but this answer will not serve.
  Flav. If 'twill not serve, 'tis not so base as
        you;
For you serve knaves.   [*Exit.*
  1st Var. Serv. How! what does his cashiered
worship mutter?
  2nd Var. Serv. No matter what: he 's poor, and
that 's revenge enough. Who can speak broader
than he that has no house to put his head in? such
may rail against great buildings.

Enter SERVILIUS.

Tit. O, here's Servilius; now we shall know some answer.

Ser. If I might beseech you, gentlemen, to repair some other hour, I should much derive from't: for, take 't of my soul, my lord leans wondrously to discontent. His comfortable temper has forsook him; he is much out of health, and keeps his chamber.

Luc. Serv. Many do keep their chambers are not sick:
And, if it be so far beyond his health,
Methinks, he should the sooner pay his debts,
And make a clear way to the gods.

Ser.   Good gods!

Tit. We cannot take this for an answer, sir.

Flam. [*within*]. Servilius, help!—my lord! my lord!

Enter TIMON, *in a rage;* FLAMINIUS *following.*

Tim. What, are my doors opposed against my passage?
Have I been ever free, and must my house
Be my retentive enemy, my gaol?
The place which I have feasted, does it now,
Like all mankind, shew me an iron heart?

Luc. Serv. Put in now, Titus.

Tit. My lord, here is my bill.

Luc. Serv. Here's mine.

Hor. Serv. And mine, my lord.

Both Var. Serv. And ours, my lord.

Phi. All our bills.

Tim. Knock me down with 'em: cleave me to the girdle.

Luc. Serv. Alas! my lord,—

Tim. Cut my heart in sums.

Tit. Mine, fifty talents.

Tim. Tell out my blood.

Luc. Serv. Five thousand crowns, my lord.

Tim. Five thousand drops pays that.
What yours?—and yours?

1st Var. Serv. My lord,—

2nd Var. Serv. My lord,—

Tim. Tear me, take me, and the gods fall on you!   [*Exit.*

Hor. 'Faith, I perceive our masters may throw their caps at their money: these debts may well be called desperate ones; for a madman owes 'em.   [*Exeunt.*

Re-enter TIMON *and* FLAVIUS.

Tim. They have e'en put my breath from me, the slaves:
Creditors!—devils.

Flav. My dear lord,—

Tim. What if it should be so?

Flav. My lord,—

Tim. I'll have it so.—My steward!

Flav. Here, my lord.

Tim. So, fitly.—Go, bid all my friends again,
Lucius, Lucullus, and Sempronius; all:
I'll once more feast the rascals.

Flav.   O, my lord,
You only speak from your distracted soul:
There is not so much left to furnish out
A moderate table.

Tim.   Be't not in thy care; go,
I charge thee; invite them all: let in the tide
Of knaves once more; my cook and I'll provide.
          [*Exeunt.*

SCENE V.—*The same.   The Senate-House.*

The Senate *sitting.   Enter* ALCIBIADES, *attended.*

1st Sen. My lord, you have my voice to 't;
The fault's bloody;
'Tis necessary he should die:
Nothing emboldens sin so much as mercy.

2nd Sen. Most true; the law shall bruise him.

Alcib. Honour, health, and compassion to the senate!

1st Sen. Now, captain?

Alcib. I am an humble suitor to your virtues;
For pity is the virtue of the law,
And none but tyrants use it cruelly.
It pleases time, and fortune, to lie heavy
Upon a friend of mine, who, in hot blood,
Hath stepped into the law, which is past depth
To those that, without heed, do plunge into 't.
He is a man, setting his fate aside,
Of comely virtues:
Nor did he soil the fact with cowardice
(An honour in him, which buys out his fault);
But, with a noble fury and fair spirit,
Seeing his reputation touched to death,
He did oppose his foe:
And with such sober and unnoted passion
He did behave his anger, ere 'twas spent,
As if he had but proved an argument.

1st Sen. You undergo too strict a paradox,
Striving to make an ugly deed look fair:
Your words have took such pains, as if they laboured
To bring manslaughter into form, and set quarrelling
Upon the head of valour; which, indeed,
Is valour misbegot, and came into the world
When sects and factions were newly born:
He's truly valiant that can wisely suffer
The worst that man can breathe;
And make his wrongs his outsides,
To wear them like his raiment, carelessly;

And ne'er prefer his injuries to his heart,
To bring it into danger.
If wrongs be evils, and enforce us kill,
What folly 'tis to hazard life for ill!
    Alcib. My lord,—
    1st Sen. You cannot make gross sins look clear;
To revenge is no valour, but to bear.
    Alcib. My lords, then, under favour, pardon
        me,
If I speak like a captain.—
Why do fond men expose themselves to battle,
And not endure all threats? sleep upon it,
And let the foes quietly cut their throats
Without repugnancy? If there be
Such valour in the bearing, what make we
Abroad? why then, women are more valiant,
That stay at home, if bearing carry it:
And the ass, more captain than the lion;
The fellow loaden with irons, wiser than the judge,
If wisdom be in suffering. O, my lords,
As you are great, be pitifully good:
Who cannot condemn rashness in cold blood?
To kill, I grant, is sin's extremest gust;
But in defence, by mercy, 't is most just.
To be in anger is impiety;
But who is man that is not angry?
Weigh but the crime with this.
    2nd Sen. You breathe in vain.
    Alcib.   In vain? his service done
At Lacedæmon and Byzantium
Were a sufficient briber for his life.
    1st Sen. What's that?
    Alcib. Why, I say, my lords, he has done fair
        service,
And slain in fight many of your enemies:
How full of valour did he bear himself
In the last conflict, and made plenteous wounds!
    2nd Sen. He has made too much plenty with 'em:
He is a sworn rioter: he has a sin
That often drowns him, and takes his valour pri-
        soner:
If there were no foes, that were enough
To overcome him: in that beastly fury
He has been known to commit outrages,
And cherish factions: 't is inferred to us,
His days are foul, and his drink dangerous.
    1st Sen. He dies.
    Alcib. Hard fate! he might have died in war.
My lords, if not for any parts in him
(Though his right arm might purchase his own
        time,
And be in debt to none), yet, more to move you,
Take my deserts to his, and join them both:
And, for I know your reverend ages love security,
I 'll pawn my victories, all my honour to you,
Upon his good returns.
If by this crime he owes the law his life,

Why, let the war receive 't in valiant gore;
For law is strict, and war is nothing more.
    1st Sen. We are for law; he dies: urge it no more,
On height of our displeasure: friend, or brother,
He forfeits his own blood that spills another.
    Alcib. Must it be so? it must not be. My lords,
I do beseech you, know me.
    2nd Sen. How?
    Alcib. Call me to your remembrances.
    3rd Sen. What?
    Alcib. I cannot think but your age has forgot me;
It could not else be I should prove so base,
To sue, and be denied such common grace:
My wounds ache at you.
    1st Sen.   Do you dare our anger?
'T is in few words, but spacious in effect:
We banish thee for ever.
    Alcib.   Banish me?
Banish your dotage; banish usury,
That makes the senate ugly.
    1st Sen. If, after two days' shine, Athens con-
        tain thee,
Attend our weightier judgment. And, not to swell
        our spirit,
He shall be executed presently.
                   [*Exeunt* Senators.
    Alcib. Now the gods keep you old enough; that
        you may live
Only in bone, that none may look on you!
I 'm worse than mad! I have kept back their foes,
While they have told their money, and let out
Their coin upon large interest; I myself
Rich only in large hurts:—all those, for this?
Is this the balsam that the usuring senate
Pours into captains' wounds? Banishment?
It comes not ill; I hate not to be banished;
It is a cause worthy my spleen and fury,
That I may strike at Athens. I'll cheer up
My discontented troops, and lay for hearts.
'T is honour with most lands to be at odds;
Soldiers should brook as little wrongs as gods.
                        [*Exit.*

SCENE VI.—*A magnificent Room in* TIMON's
        House.

Music. Tables set out: Servants *attending. Enter
    divers* Lords, *at several doors.*

    1st Lord. The good time of day to you, sir.
    2nd Lord. I also wish it to you. I think this
honourable lord did but try us this other day.
    1st Lord. Upon that were my thoughts tiring
when we encountered. I hope it is not so low
with him as he made it seem in the trial of his
several friends.

2nd Lord. It should not be, by the persuasion of his new feasting.

1st Lord. I should think so. He hath sent me an earnest inviting, which many my near occasions did urge me to put off; but he hath conjured me beyond them, and I must needs appear.

2nd Lord. In like manner was I in debt to my importunate business, but he would not hear my excuse. I am sorry, when he sent to borrow of me, that my provision was out.

1st Lord. I am sick of that grief too, as I understand how all things go.

2nd Lord. Every man here's so. What would he have borrowed of you?

1st Lord. A thousand pieces.

2nd Lord. A thousand pieces!

1st Lord. What of you?

2nd Lord. He sent to me, sir,—Here he comes.

Enter TIMON, *and* Attendants.

Tim. With all my heart, gentlemen both:— And how fare you?

1st Lord. Ever at the best, hearing well of your lordship.

2nd Lord. The swallow follows not summer more willing, than we your lordship.

Tim. [*aside*]. Nor more willingly leaves winter; such summer-birds are men.—Gentlemen, our dinner will not recompense this long stay: feast your ears with the music awhile, if they will fare so harshly on the trumpet's sound: we shall to 't presently.

1st Lord. I hope it remains not unkindly with your lordship, that I returned you an empty messenger.

Tim. O, sir, let it not trouble you.

2nd Lord. My noble lord,—

Tim. Ah, my good friend! what cheer?

[*The banquet brought in.*

2nd Lord. My most honourable lord, I am e'en sick of shame that, when your lordship this other day sent to me, I was so unfortunate a beggar.

Tim. Think not on 't, sir.

2nd Lord. If you had sent but two hours before,—

Tim. Let it not cumber your better remembrance.—Come, bring in all together.

2nd Lord. All covered dishes!

1st Lord. Royal cheer, I warrant you.

3rd Lord. Doubt not that, if money and the season can yield it.

1st Lord. How do you? what's the news?

3rd Lord. Alcibiades is banished: hear you of it?

1st Lord.   }
 2nd Lord. } Alcibiades banished!

3rd Lord. 'T is so, be sure of it.

1st Lord. How? how?

2nd Lord. I pray you, upon what?

Tim. My worthy friends, will you draw near?

3rd Lord. I 'll tell you more anon. Here's a noble feast toward.

2nd Lord. This is the old man still.

3rd Lord. Will 't hold? will 't hold?

2nd Lord. It does: but time will—and so—

3rd Lord. I do conceive.

Tim. Each man to his stool, with that spur as he would to the lip of his mistress: your diet shall be in all places alike. Make not a city feast of it, to let the meat cool ere we can agree upon the first place: sit, sit. The gods require our thanks.

You great benefactors, sprinkle our society with thankfulness. For your own gifts, make yourselves praised: but reserve still to give, lest your deities be despised. Lend to each man enough, that one need not lend to another: for, were your godheads to borrow of men, men would forsake the gods. Make the meat be beloved more than the man that gives it. Let no assembly of twenty be without a score of villains. If there sit twelve women at the table, let a dozen of them be—as they are.—The rest of your fees, O gods!—the senators of Athens, together with the common lag of people,—what is amiss in them, you gods, make suitable for destruction. For these my present friends, as they are to me nothing, so in nothing bless them, and to nothing are they welcome.

Uncover, dogs, and lap.

[*The dishes uncovered, are full of warm water.*

Some speak. What does his lordship mean?
Some other. I know not.

 Tim. May you a better feast never behold,
You knot of mouth-friends! smoke and lukewarm
          water
Is your perfection. This is Timon's last;
Who stuck and spangled you with flatteries,
Washes it off, and sprinkles in your faces
         [*Throwing water in their faces.*

Your reeking villany. Live loathed and long,
Most smiling, smooth, detested parasites,
Courteous destroyers, affable wolves, meek bears,
You fools of Fortune, trencher-friends, Time's flies,
Cap-and-knee slaves, vapours, and minute-jacks!
Of man, and beast, the infinite malady
Crust you quite o'er!—What, dost thou go?
Soft, take thy physic first; thou too,—and thou:—
      [*Throws the dishes at them, and drives them out.*

Stay, I will lend thee money, borrow none.—
What, all in motion? Henceforth be no feast,
Whereat a villain's not a welcome guest.
Burn, house; sink, Athens! henceforth hated be
Of Timon, man, and all humanity.   [*Exit.*

Re-enter the Lords, *with other* Lords *and* Senators.

 1st Lord. How now, my lords?
 2nd Lord. Know you the quality of lord
Timon's fury?
 3rd Lord. Pish! did you see my cap?
 4th Lord. I have lost my gown.

 3rd Lord. He's but a mad lord, and nought
but humour sways him. He gave me a jewel
the other day, and now he has beat it out of my
hat.—Did you see my jewel?
 4th Lord. Did you see my cap?
 2nd Lord. Here 'tis.
 4th Lord. Here lies my gown.
 1st Lord. Let's make no stay.
 2nd Lord. Lord Timon's mad.
 3rd Lord. I feel 't upon my bones.
 4th Lord. One day he gives us diamonds, next
    day stones.   [*Exeunt.*

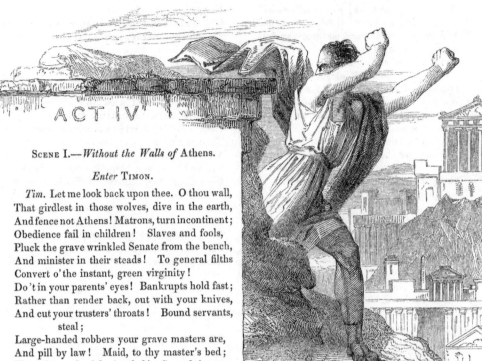

SCENE I.—*Without the Walls of* Athens.

Enter TIMON.

Tim. Let me look back upon thee. O thou wall,
That girdlest in those wolves, dive in the earth,
And fence not Athens! Matrons, turn incontinent;
Obedience fail in children! Slaves and fools,
Pluck the grave wrinkled Senate from the bench,
And minister in their steads! To general filths
Convert o' the instant, green virginity!
Do 't in your parents' eyes! Bankrupts hold fast;
Rather than render back, out with your knives,
And cut your trusters' throats! Bound servants,
    steal;
Large-handed robbers your grave masters are,
And pill by law! Maid, to thy master's bed;
Thy mistress is o' the brothel! Son of sixteen,
Pluck the lined crutch from thy old limping sire,
With it beat out his brains! Piety and fear,
Religion to the gods, peace, justice, truth,
Domestic awe, night rest, and neighbourhood,
Instruction, manners, mysteries, and trades,
Degrees, observances, customs, and laws,
Decline to your confounding contraries,
And yet confusion live!—Plagues incident to
    men,
Your potent and infectious fevers heap
On Athens, ripe for stroke! Thou cold sciatica,
Cripple our senators, that their limbs may halt
As lamely as their manners! Lust and liberty
Creep in the minds and marrows of our youth;
That 'gainst the stream of virtue they may strive,
And drown themselves in riot! Itches, blains,
Sow all the Athenian bosoms; and their crop
Be general leprosy! Breath infect breath;
That their society, as their friendship, may
Be merely poison! Nothing I 'll bear from thee
But nakedness, thou détestable town!
Take thou that too, with multiplying banns!
Timon will to the woods; where he shall find
The unkindest beast more kinder than mankind.
The gods confound (hear me, ye good gods all!)
The Athenians both within and out that wall!
And grant, as Timon grows, his hate may grow
To the whole race of mankind, high and low!
Amen.   *[Exit.*

SCENE II.—Athens.   *A Room in* TIMON'S *House.*

Enter FLAVIUS, *with two or three* Servants.

1st Serv. Hear you, master steward, where 's our
    master?
Are we undone? cast off? nothing remaining?
  Flav. Alack, my fellows, what should I say to
    you?
Let me be recorded by the righteous gods,
I am as poor as you.
  1st Serv.   Such a house broke!
So noble a master fallen! All gone! and not
One friend to take his fortune by the arm,
And go along with him!
  2nd Serv.   As we do turn our backs
From our companion, thrown into his grave,
So his familiars to his buried fortunes
Slink all away; leave their false vows with him,
Like empty purses picked: and his poor self,
A dedicated beggar to the air,
With his disease of all-shunned poverty,
Walks, like contempt, alone.—More of our fellows.

Enter other Servants.

  Flav. All broken implements of a ruined house.
  3rd Serv. Yet do our hearts wear Timon's livery,

That see I by our faces; we are fellows still,
Serving alike in sorrow.   Leaked is our bark;
And we poor mates stand on the dying deck,
Hearing the surges threat: we must all part
Into this sea of air.
 Flav. Good fellows all,
The latest of my wealth I'll share amongst you.
Wherever we shall meet, for Timon's sake,
Let's yet be fellows; let's shake our heads, and
  say,
As 'twere a knell unto our master's fortunes,
" We have seen better days." Let each take some;
       [*Giving them money.*
Nay, put out all your hands.   Not one word more:
Thus part we rich in sorrow, parting poor.
        [*Exeunt* Servants.
O, the fierce wretchedness that glory brings us
Who would not wish to be from wealth exempt,
Since riches point to misery and contempt?
Who'd be so mocked with glory? or to live
But in a dream of friendship?
To have his pomp, and all what state compounds,
But only painted, like his varnished friends?
Poor honest lord, brought low by his own heart;
Undone by goodness!   Strange, unusual blood,
When man's worst sin is, he does too much good!
Who then dares to be half so kind again?
For bounty, that makes gods, does still mar men.
My dearest lord,—blessed to be most accursed,
Rich only to be wretched,—thy great fortunes
Are made thy chief afflictions.   Alas, kind lord!
He's flung in rage from this ungrateful seat
Of monstrous friends:
Nor has he with him to supply his life,
Or that which can command it.
I'll follow, and inquire him out:
I'll ever serve his mind with my best will;
Whilst I have gold, I'll be his steward still.
           [*Exit.*

SCENE III.—*The Woods.*

Enter TIMON.

 Tim.   O blessèd breeding sun, draw from the
  earth
Rotten humidity; below thy sister's orb
Infect the air!—Twinned brothers of one womb,—
Whose procreation, residence, and birth,
Scarce is dividant,—touch them with several for-
  tunes;
The greater scorns the lesser:—not nature,
To whom all sores lay siege, can bear great fortune,
But by contempt of nature.
Raise me this beggar, and denude that lord;
The senator shall bear contempt hereditary,

The beggar native honour.
It is the pasture lards the brother's sides;
The want that makes him lean.   Who dares,—who
  dares,
In purity of manhood stand upright,
And say, " This man's a flatterer?" If one be,
So are they all; for every grize of fortune
Is smoothed by that below: the learned pate
Ducks to the golden fool: all is oblique;
There's nothing level in our cursèd natures,
But direct villany.   Therefore, be abhorred
All feasts, societies, and throngs of men!
His semblable, yea, himself, Timon disdains:
Destruction fang mankind!—Earth, yield me
  roots!   [*Digging.*
Who seeks for better of thee, sauce his palate
With thy most operant poison!—What is here?
Gold?—yellow, glittering, precious gold?—
No, gods, I am no idle votarist.
Roots, you clear heavens! Thus much of this, will
  make
Black, white; foul, fair; wrong, right;
Base, noble; old, young; coward, valiant.
Ha, you gods! why this? What this, you gods?
  Why this
Will lug your priests and servants from your sides;
Pluck stout men's pillows from below their heads:
This yellow slave
Will knit and break religions; bless the accursed;
Make the hoar leprosy adored; place thieves,
And give them title, knee, and approbation,
With senators on the bench: this is it
That makes the wappened widow wed again:
She whom the spital-house and ulcerous sores
Would cast the gorge at, this embalms and spices
To the April day again.   Come, damnèd earth,
Thou common whore of mankind, that putt'st odds
Among the rout of nations, I will make thee
Do thy right nature. [*March afar off.*] Ha! a
  drum?—Thou'rt quick,
But yet I'll bury thee.   Thou'lt go, strong thief,
When gouty keepers of thee cannot stand.—
Nay, stay thou out for earnest.
        [*Keeping some gold.*

Enter ALCIBIADES, *with drum and fife, in warlike
  manner:* PHRYNIA *and* TIMANDRA.

 Alcib. Speak, what art thou there?
 Tim. A beast, as thou art.   The canker gnaw
  thy heart.
For shewing me again the eyes of man!
 Alcib. What is thy name? Is man so hateful to
  thee,
That art thyself a man?
 Tim. I am *misanthropos,* and hate mankind.
For thy part, I do wish thou wert a dog,
That I might love thee something.

Alcib.　　　I know thee well;
But in thy fortunes am unlearned and strange.

Tim. I know thee, too; and more, than that I
　　　know thee,
I not desire to know.　Follow thy drum;
With man's blood paint the ground, gules, gules:
Religious canons, civil laws, are cruel;
Then what should war be? This fell whore of thine
Hath in her more destruction than thy sword,
For all her cherubin look.

Phry.　　　Thy lips rot off!

Tim. I will not kiss thee; then the rot returns
To thine own lips again.

Alcib. How came the noble Timon to this change?

Tim. As the moon does, by wanting light to give:
But then renew I could not, like the moon;
There were no suns to borrow of.

Alcib. Noble Timon, what friendship may I do
thee?

Tim. None, but to maintain my opinion.

Alcib. What is it, Timon?

Tim. Promise me friendship, but perform none.
—If thou wilt not promise, the gods plague thee,
for thou art a man!—if thou dost perform, confound thee, for thou 'rt a man!

Alcib. I have heard in some sort of thy miseries.

Tim. Thou saw'st them when I had prosperity.

Alcib. I see them now; then was a blesséd time.

Tim. As thine is now, held with a brace of
　　　harlots.

Timan. Is this the Athenian minion, whom the
　　　world
Voiced so regardfully?

Tim.　　　Art thou Timandra?

Timan. Yes.

Tim. Be a whore still! They love thee not that
　　　use thee;
Give them diseases, leaving with thee their lust.
Make use of thy salt hours: season the slaves
For tubs and baths: bring down rose-cheekéd
　　　youth
To the tub-fast and the diet.

Timan.　　　Hang thee, monster!

Alcib. Pardon him, sweet Timandra; for his wits
Are drowned and lost in his calamities.—
I have but little gold of late, brave Timon,
The want whereof doth daily make revolt
In my penurious band: I have heard, and grie 'd,
How curséd Athens, mindless of thy worth,
Forgetting thy great deeds, when neighbour states,
But for thy sword and fortune, trod upon them,—

Tim. I pr'y thee, beat thy drum, and get thee
　　　gone.

Alcib. I am thy friend, and pity thee, dear Timon.

Tim. How dost thou pity him whom thou dost
　　　trouble?
I had rather be alone.

Alcib.　　　Why, fare thee well:
Here's some gold for thee.

Tim.　　　Keep it; I cannot eat it.

Alcib. When I have laid proud Athens on a
　　　heap,—

Tim. Warr'st thou 'gainst Athens?

Alcib.　　　Ay, Timon, and have cause.

Tim. The gods confound them all i' thy conquest; and thee after, when thou hast conquered!

Alcib. Why me, Timon?

Tim. That, by killing of villains, thou wast born
to conquer my country.
Put up thy gold: Go on,—here's gold,—go on;
Be as a planetary plague, when Jove
Will o'er some high-viced city hang his poison
In the sick air.　Let not thy sword skip one:
Pity not honoured age for his white beard;
He's an usurer: strike me the counterfeit matron;
It is her habit only that is honest,
Herself's a bawd: let not the virgin's cheek
Make soft thy trenchant sword; for those milk-
　　　paps
That through the window-bars bore at men's eyes,
Are not within the leaf of pity writ,
But set them down horrible traitors: spare not
　　　the babe,
Whose dimpled smiles from fools exhaust their
　　　mercy;
Think it a bastard, whom the oracle
Hath doubtfully pronounced thy throat shall cut,
And mince it sans remorse: swear against objects;
Put armour on thine ears, and on thine eyes;
Whose proof, nor yells of mothers, maids, nor
　　　babes,
Nor sight of priests in holy vestments bleeding,
Shall pierce a jot. There's gold to pay thy soldiers:
Make large confusion; and, thy fury spent,
Confounded be thyself! Speak not; be gone!

Alcib. Hast thou gold yet? I'll take the gold
　　　thou giv'st me,
Not all thy counsel.

Tim. Dost thou, or dost thou not, heaven's curse
　　　upon thee!

Phry.　⎱Give us some gold, good Timon: hast
Timan.⎰　　thou more?

Tim. Enough to make a whore forswear her
　　　trade,
And to make whores, a bawd. Hold up, you sluts,
Your aprons mountant: you are not oathable,—
Although I know you'll swear, terribly swear,
Into strong shudders, and to heavenly agues,
The immortal gods that hear you,—spare your
　　　oaths;
I'll trust to your conditions.　Be whores still;
And he whose pious breath seeks to convert you,
Be strong in whore, allure him, burn him up;
Let your close fire predominate his smoke,

And be no turncoats: yet may your pains, six
    months,
Be quite contrary: and thatch your poor thin roofs
With burdens of the dead;—some that were
    hanged,
No matter;—wear them, betray with them: whore
    still;
Paint till a horse may mire upon your face:
A pox of wrinkles!
    Phry. } Well, more gold: what then?
    Timan. } Believe 't that we 'll do anything for
        gold.
    Tim. Consumption sow
In hollow bones of men; strike their sharp shins,
And mar men's spurring. Crack the lawyer's voice,
That he may never more false title plead,
Nor sound his quillets shrilly: hoar the flamen,
That scolds against the quality of flesh,
And not believes himself: down with the nose,
Down with it flat; take the bridge quite away
Of him that, his particular to foresee,
Smells from the general weal: make curled-pate
    ruffians bald;
And let the unscarred braggarts of the war
Derive some pain from you: plague all;
That your activity may defeat and quell
The source of all erection.—There 's more gold:
Do you damn others, and let this damn you,
And ditches grave you all!
    Phry. } More counsel with more money, boun-
    Timan. } teous Timon.
    Tim. More whore, more mischief, first; I have
    given you earnest.
    Alcib. Strike up the drum towards Athens.
    Farewell, Timon;
If I thrive well, I 'll visit thee again.
    Tim. If I hope well, I 'll never see thee more.
    Alcib. I never did thee harm.
    Tim. Yes, thou spok'st well of me.
    Alcib. Call'st thou that harm?
    Tim. Men daily find it. Get thee away,
And take thy beagles with thee.
    Alcib.   We but offend him.—
Strike.
    [*Drum beats. Exeunt* ALCIBIADES, PHRYNIA,
        and TIMANDRA.
    Tim. That nature, being sick of man's unkind-
    ness,
Should yet be hungry!—Common mother, thou,
                  [*Digging.*
Whose womb unmeasurable and infinite breast
Teems and feeds all; whose self-same mettle
Whereof thy proud child, arrogant man, is puffed,
Engenders the black toad and adder blue,
The gilded newt, and eyeless venomed worm,
With all the abhorréd births below crisp heaven
Whereon Hyperion's quickening fire doth shine;

Yield him who all thy human sons doth hate,
From forth thy plenteous bosom, one poor root!
Ensear thy fertile and conceptious womb;
Let it no more bring out ingrateful man!
Go great with tigers, dragons, wolves, and bears;
Teem with new monsters, whom thy upward face
Hath to the marbled mansion all above
Never presented!—O, a root; dear thanks!
Dry up thy marrows, vines, and plough-torn leas;
Whereof ingrateful man, with liquorish draughts,
And morsels unctuous, greases his pure mind,
That from it all consideration slips!

    Enter APEMANTUS.

More man? Plague! plague!
    Apem. I was directed hither: Men report
Thou dost affect my manners, and dost use them.
    Tim. 'T is, then, because thou dost not keep a
    dog
Whom I would imitate. Consumption catch thee!
    Apem. This is in thee a nature but affected;
A poor unmanly melancholy, sprung
From change of fortune. Why this spade? this
    place?
This slave-like habit? and these looks of care?
Thy flatterers yet wear silk, drink wine, lie soft;
Hug their diseased perfumes, and have forgot
That ever Timon was. Shame not these woods
By putting on the cunning of a carper.
Be thou a flatterer now, and seek to thrive
By that which has undone thee: hinge thy knee,
And let his very breath whom thou 'lt observe
Blow off thy cap; praise his most vicious strain,
And call it excellent. Thou wast told thus;
Thou gav'st thine ears, like tapsters, that bid wel-
    come
To knaves and all approachers: 'tis most just
That thou turn rascal; hadst thou wealth again,
Rascals should have 't. Do not assume my like-
    ness.
    Tim. Were I like thee, I 'd throw away myself.
    Apem. Thou hast cast away thyself, being like
    thyself;
A madman so long, now a fool. What, think'st
That the bleak air, thy boisterous chamberlain,
Will put thy shirt on warm? Will these mossed
    trees,
That have outlived the eagle, page thy heels,
And skip when thou point'st out? Will the cold
    brook,
Candied with ice, caudle thy morning taste,
To cure thy o'er-night's surfeit? Call the creatures,
Whose naked natures live in all the spite
Of wreakful heaven; whose bare unhoused trunks,
To the conflicting elements exposed,
Answer mere nature; bid them flatter thee!
O! thou shalt find,—

Tim. A fool of thee : depart.

Apem. I love thee better now than e'er I did.

Tim. I hate thee worse.

Apem. Why?

Tim. Thou flatterr'st misery.

Apem. I flatter not; but say, thou art a caitiff.

Tim. Why dost thou seek me out?

Apem. To vex thee.

Tim. Always a villain's office, or a fool's.
Dost please thyself in 't?

Apem. Ay.

Tim. What! a knave too?

Apem. If thou didst put this sour-cold habit ⸗
To castigate thy pride, 't were well : but thou
Dost it enforcedly; thou 'dst courtier be again,
Wert thou not beggar.   Willing misery
Outlives incertain pomp; is crowned before :
The one is filling still, never complete;
The other at high wish : best state, contentless,
Hath a distracted and most wretched being,
Worse than the worst, content.
Thou shouldst desire to die, being miserable.

Tim. Not by his breath that is more miserable.
Thou art a slave, whom Fortune's tender arm
With favour never clasped; but bred a dog.
Hadst thou, like us, from our first swath proceeded
The sweet degrees that this brief world affords
To such as may the passive drugs of it
Freely command, thou wouldst have plunged thy-
    self
In general riot; melted down thy youth
In different beds of lust; and never learned
The icy precepts of respect, but followed
The sugared game before thee.   But myself,
Who had the world as my confectionary;
The mouths, the tongues, the eyes, and hearts of
    men
At duty, more than I could frame employment;
That numberless upon me stuck, as leaves
Do on the oak, have with one winter's brush
Fell from their boughs, and left me open, bare
For every storm that blows;—I to bear this,
That never knew but better, is some burden.
Thy nature did commence in sufferance; time
Hath made thee hard in 't.   Why shouldst thou
    hate men?
They never flattered thee. What hast thou given?
If thou wilt curse,—thy father, that poor rag,
Must be thy subject; who, in spite, put stuff
To some she-beggar, and compounded thee,—
Poor rogue hereditary. Hence! be gone!
If thou hadst not been born the worst of men,
Thou hadst been a knave and flatterer.

Apem. Art thou proud yet?

Tim. Ay, that I am not thee.

Apem. I, that I was no prodigal.

Tim. I, that I am one now:

Were all the wealth I have shut up in thee,
I 'd give thee leave to hang it. Get thee gone.—
That the whole life of Athens were in this!
Thus would I eat it.   [*Eating a root.*

Apem.   Here; I will mend thy feast.
               [*Offering him something.*

Tim. First mend my company; take away thy-
    self.

Apem. So I shall mend mine own, by the lack
    of thine.

Tim. 'T is not well mended so; it is but botched :
If not, I would it were.

Apem. What wouldst thou have to Athens?

Tim. Thee thither in a whirlwind. If thou wilt,
Tell them there I have gold : look, so I have.

Apem. Here is no use for gold.

Tim.   The best and truest :
For here it sleeps, and does no hiréd harm.

Apem. Where ly'st o' nights, Timon?

Tim.   Under that 's above me.
Where feed'st thou o' days, Apemantus?

Apem. Where my stomach finds meat; or rather, where I eat it.

Tim. Would poison were obedient, and knew
    my mind!

Apem. Where wouldst thou send it?

Tim. To sauce thy dishes.

Apem. The middle of humanity thou never
knewest, but the extremity of both ends : when
thou wast in thy gilt and thy perfume, they
mocked thee for too much curiosity; in thy rags
thou knowest none, but art despised for the contrary. There 's a medlar for thee; eat it.

Tim. On what I hate, I feed not.

Apem. Dost hate a medlar?

Tim. Ay, though it look like thee.

Apem. An thou hadst hated meddlers sooner,
thou shouldst have loved thyself better now.
What man didst thou ever know unthrift, that
was beloved after his means?

Tim. Who, without those means thou talkest
of, didst thou ever know beloved?

Apem. Myself.

Tim. I understand thee; thou hadst some
means to keep a dog.

Apem. What things in the world canst thou
nearest compare to thy flatterers?

Tim. Women nearest; but men, men are the
things themselves. What wouldst thou do with
the world, Apemantus, if it lay in thy power?

Apem. Give it the beasts, to be rid of the men.

Tim. Wouldst thou have thyself fall in the
confusion of men, and remain a beast with the
beasts?

Apem. Ay, Timon.

Tim. A beastly ambition, which the gods grant
thee to attain to! If thou wert the lion, the fox

would beguile thee: if thou wert the lamb, the fox would eat thee: if thou wert the fox, the lion would suspect thee, when, peradventure, thou wert accused by the ass: if thou wert the ass, thy dulness would torment thee; and still thou livedst but as a breakfast to the wolf: if thou wert the wolf, thy greediness would afflict thee, and oft thou shouldst hazard thy life for thy dinner: wert thou the unicorn, pride and wrath would confound thee, and make thine own self the conquest of thy fury: wert thou a bear, thou wouldst be killed by the horse; wert thou a horse, thou wouldst be seized by the leopard; wert thou a leopard, thou wert german to the lion, and the spots of thy kindred were jurors on thy life: all thy safety were remotion; and thy defence, absence. What beast couldst thou be, that were not subject to a beast? and what a beast art thou already, that see'st not thy loss in transformation?

Apem. If thou couldst please me with speaking to me, thou mightst have hit upon it here: the commonwealth of Athens is become a forest of beasts.

Tim. How! has the ass broke the wall, that thou art out of the city?

Apem. Yonder comes a poet and a painter: the plague of company light upon thee! I will fear to catch it, and give way: when I know not what else to do, I'll see thee again.

Tim. When there is nothing living but thee, thou shalt be welcome. I had rather be a beggar's dog than Apemantus.

Apem. Thou art the cap of all the fools alive.

Tim. 'Would thou wert clean enough to spit upon.

Apem. A plague on thee, thou art too bad to curse.

Tim. All villains that do stand by thee, are pure.

Apem. There is no leprosy but what thou speak'st.

Tim. If I name thee.—
I'll beat thee,—but I should infect my hands.

Apem. I would my tongue could rot them off.

Tim. Away, thou issue of a mangy dog!
Choler does kill me, that thou art alive;
I swoon to see thee.

Apem.   'Would thou wouldst burst!

Tim.   Away,
Thou tedious rogue! I am sorry I shall lose
A stone by thee.   [*Throws a stone at him.*

Apem. Beast!

Tim. Slave!

Apem. Toad!

Tim. Rogue, rogue, rogue!
[APEMANTUS *retreats backward, as going.*
I am sick of this false world; and will love nought

But even the mere necessities upon it.
Then, Timon, presently prepare thy grave;
Lie where the light foam of the sea may beat
Thy grave-stone daily: make thine epitaph,
That death in me at others' lives may laugh.
O, thou sweet king-killer, and dear divorce
                   [*Looking on the gold.*
'Twixt natural son and sire! thou bright defiler
Of Hymen's purest bed! thou valiant Mars!
Thou ever young, fresh, loved, and delicate wooer,
Whose blush doth thaw the consecrated snow
That lies on Dian's lap! thou visible god,
That solder'st close impossibilities,
And mak'st them kiss! that speak'st with every
         tongue,
To every purpose! O, thou touch of hearts!
Think, thy slave man rebels; and by thy virtue
Set them into confounding odds, that beasts
May have the world in empire!

Apem.   'Would 't were so;
But not till I am dead!—I'll say thou hast gold:
Thou wilt be thronged to shortly.

Tim.   Thronged to?

Apem.   Ay.

Tim. Thy back, I pr'y thee.

Apem.   Live, and love thy misery!

Tim. Long live so, and so die!—I am quit.
                [*Exit* APEMANTUS.
More things like men?—Eat, Timon, and abhor
       them.

Enter Thieves.

1st Thief. Where should he have this gold? It is some poor fragment, some slender ort of his remainder: the mere want of gold, and the falling-from of his friends, drove him into this melancholy.

2nd Thief. It is noised he hath a mass of treasure.

3rd Thief. Let us make the assay upon him. If he care not for't, he will supply us easily: if he covetously reserve it, how shall's get it?

2nd Thief. True; for he bears it not about him; 'tis hid.

1st Thief. Is not this he?

Thieves. Where?

2nd Thief. 'Tis his description.

3rd Thief. He; I know him.

Thieves. Save thee, Timon.

Tim. Now, thieves?

Thieves. Soldiers, not thieves.

Tim. Both, too; and women's sons.

Thieves. We are not thieves, but men that much do want.

Tim. Your greatest want is, you want much of meat.
Why should you want? Behold, the earth hath roots;

Within this mile break forth a hundred springs:
The oaks bear mast, the briars scarlet hips;
The bounteous housewife, Nature, on each bush
Lays her full mess before you. Want? why want?

   1st Thief. We cannot live on grass, on berries,
       water,
As beasts, and birds, and fishes.

   Tim. Nor on the beasts themselves, the birds,
      and fishes;
You must eat men. Yet thanks I must you con,
That you are thieves professed; that you work not
In holier shapes: for there is boundless theft
In limited professions. Rascal thieves,
Here's gold: go, suck the subtle blood of the grape,

Till the high fever seeth your blood to froth,
And so 'scape hanging. Trust not the physician;
His antidotes are poison, and he slays
More than you rob. Take wealth and lives to-
      gether;
Do villany, do, since you profess to do 't,
Like workmen. I 'll example you with thievery:
The sun's a thief, and with his great attraction
Robs the vast sea: the moon's an arrant thief,
And her pale fire she snatches from the sun:
The sea's a thief, whose liquid surge resolves
The moon into salt tears: the earth 's a thief,
That feeds and breeds by a composture stolen
From general excrement: each thing 's a thief:

The laws, your curb and whip, in their rough power
Have unchecked theft. Love not yourselves;
      away;
Rob one another. There's more gold: cut throats;
All that you meet are thieves. To Athens go;
Break open shops: nothing can you steal
But thieves do lose it. Steal not less, for this
I give you; and gold confound you howsoever!
Amen.   [TIMON *retires to his cave.*

   3rd Thief. He has almost charmed me from
my profession, by persuading me to it,

   1st Thief. 'Tis in the malice of mankind that
he thus advises us; not to have us thrive in our
mystery.

   2nd Thief. I 'll believe him as an enemy, and
give over my trade.

   1st Thief. Let us first see peace in Athens:
there is no time so miserable but a man may be
true.   [*Exeunt* Thieves.

Enter FLAVIUS.

   Flav. O you gods!
Is yon dispised and ruinous man my lord?
Full of decay and failing? O, monument
And wonder of good deeds evilly bestowed!
What an alteration of honour has
Desperate want made!
What viler thing upon the earth than friends
Who can bring noblest minds to basest ends!
How rarely does it meet with this time's guise,
When man was wished to love his enemies!
Grant I may ever love, and rather woo
Those that would mischief me, than those that do!
He has caught me in his eye: I will present
My honest grief unto him; and, as my lord,
Still serve him with my life.—My dearest master!

     TIMON *comes forward from his cave.*

   Tim. Away! what art thou?

Flav. Have you forgot me, sir?

Tim. Why dost ask that? I have forgot all men;

Then, if thou grant'st thou 'rt a man, I have forgot thee.

Flav. An honest poor servant of yours.

Tim. Then I know thee not.

I ne'er had honest man about me, I; all
I kept were knaves, to serve in meat to villains.

Flav. The gods are witness,

Ne'er did poor steward wear a truer grief
For his undone lord, than mine eyes for you.

Tim. What, dost thou weep?—Come nearer:— then I love thee,

Because thou art a woman, and disclaim'st
Flinty mankind; whose eyes do never give
But thorough lust and laughter. Pity 's sleeping:
Strange times, that weep with laughing, not with weeping!

Flav. I beg of you to know me, good my lord,
To accept my grief, and, whilst this poor wealth lasts,

To entertain me as your steward still.

Tim. Had I a steward
So true, so just, and now so comfortable?
It almost turns my dangerous nature wild.
Let me behold thy face.—Surely this man
Was born of woman.—

Forgive my general and exceptless rashness,
Perpetual-sober gods! I do proclaim
One honest man,—mistake me not,—but one;
No more, I pray;—and he 's a steward.—
How fain would I have hated all mankind,
And thou redeem'st thyself: but all, save thee,
I fell with curses.

Methinks thou art more honest now than wise;
For, by oppressing and betraying me,
Thou mightst have sooner got another service:
For many so arrive at second masters,

Upon their first lord's neck. But tell me true
(For I must ever doubt, though ne'er so sure),
Is not thy kindness subtle, covetous,
If not a usuring kindness; and as rich men deal gifts,
Expecting in return twenty for one?

Flav. No, my most worthy master, in whose breast

Doubt and suspect, alas! are placed too late;
You should have feared false times when you did feast;
Suspect still comes where an estate is least.
That which I shew, Heaven knows, is merely love,
Duty and zeal, to your unmatchéd mind;
Care of your food and living; and believe it,
My most honoured lord,
For any benefit that points to me,
Either in hope or present, I 'd exchange
For this one wish, that you had power and wealth
To requite me, by making rich yourself.

Tim. Look thee, 'tis so!—Thou singly honest man,

Here, take:—the gods out of my misery
Have sent thee treasure. Go, live rich and happy:
But thus conditioned: thou shalt build from men;
Hate all, curse all; shew charity to none;
But let the famished flesh slide from the bone,
Ere thou relieve the beggar: give to dogs
What thou deny'st to men; let prisons swallow them,
Debts wither them to nothing: be men like blasted woods,
And may diseases lick up their false bloods!
And so farewell, and thrive.

Flav. O, let me stay and comfort you, my master!

Tim. If thou hat'st curses,
Stay not; fly while thou 'rt blessed and free:
Ne'er see thou man, and let me ne'er see thee.

[*Exeunt, severally.*

SCENE I.—*Before* TIMON'S *Cave.*

Enter Poet *and* Painter; TIMON *behind, unseen.*

Pain. As I took note of the place, it cannot be far where he abides.

Poet. What's to be thought of him? Does the rumour hold for true, that he is so full of gold?

Pain. Certain: Alcibiades reports it.; Phrynia and Timandra had gold of him: he likewise enriched poor straggling soldiers with great quantity: 't is said, he gave unto his steward a mighty sum.

Poet. Then this breaking of his has been but a try for his friends.

Pain. Nothing else: you shall see him a palm in Athens again, and flourish with the highest. Therefore, 't is not amiss we tender our loves to him, in this supposed distress of his: it will shew honesty in us; and is very likely to load our purposes with what they travel for, if it be a just and true report that goes of his having.

Poet. What have you now to present unto him?

Pain. Nothing at this time but my visitation: only I will promise him an excellent piece.

Poet. I must serve him so too; tell him of an intent that's coming toward him.

Pain. Good as the best. Promising is the very air o' the time: it opens the eyes of expectation:

performance is ever the duller for his act; and, but in the plainer and simpler kind of people, the deed of saying is quite out of use. To promise is most courtly and fashionable: performance is a kind of will or testament, which argues a great sickness in his judgment that makes it.

Tim. Excellent workman! thou canst not paint a man so bad as is thyself.

Poet. I am thinking what I shall say I have provided for him. It must be a personating of himself: a satire against the softness of prosperity; with a discovery of the infinite flatteries that follow youth and opulency.

Tim. Must thou needs stand for a villain in thine own work? wilt thou whip thine own faults in other men? Do so; I have gold for thee.

Poet. Nay, let's seek him:
Then do we sin against our own estate,
When we may profit meet, and come too late.

Pain. True;
When the day serves, before black-cornered night,
Find what thou want'st by free and offered light. Come.

Tim. I 'll meet you at the turn. What a god 's gold,
That he is worshipped in a baser temple
Than where swine feed!
'T is thou that rigg'st the bark, and plough'st the foam;
Settlest admiréd reverence in a slave:
To thee be worship! and thy saints for aye
Be crowned with plagues, that thee alone obey!
'Fit I meet them.   [*Advancing.*

Poet. Hail, worthy Timon!

Pain.   Our late noble master.

Tim. Have I once lived to see two honest men?

Poet. Sir,
Having often of your open bounty tasted,
Hearing you were retired, your friends fall'n off,
Whose thankless natures—O, abhorréd spirits!
Not all the whips of heaven are large enough—
What! to you!
Whose starlike nobleness gave life and influence
To their whole being! I am rapt, and cannot cover
The monstrous bulk of this ingratitude
With any size of words.

Tim. Let it go naked; men may see 't the better:
You that are honest, by being what you are,
Make them best seen and known.

Pain.   He and myself
Have travelled in the great shower of your gifts,
And sweetly felt it.

Tim.   Ay, you are honest men.

Pain. We are hither come to offer you our service.

Tim. Most honest men! Why, how shall I requite you?
Can you eat roots and drink cold water?—no.

Both. What we can do we 'll do, to do you service.

Tim. You are honest men. You have heard that I have gold;
I am sure you have: speak truth: you are honest men.

Pain. So it is said, my noble lord: but therefore Came not my friend nor I.

Tim. Good honest men.—Thou draw'st a counterfeit   [*To the* Painter.
Best in all Athens: thou art, indeed, the best;
Thou counterfeit'st most lively.

Pain.   So, so, my lord.

Tim. Even so, sir, as I say.—And for thy fiction,   [*To the* Poet.
Why, thy verses swell with stuff so fine and smooth,
That thou art even natural in thine art.—
But for all this, my honest-natured friends,
I must needs say, you have a little fault:
Marry, 't is not monstrous in you; neither wish I
You take much pains to mend.

Both.   Beseech your honour,
To make it known to us.

Tim.   You 'll take it ill.

Both. Most thankfully, my lord.

Tim.   Will you indeed?

Both. Doubt it not, worthy lord.

Tim. There 's ne'er a one of you but trusts a knave,
That mightily deceives you.

Both.   Do we, my lord?

Tim. Ay, and you hear him cog, see him dissemble,
Know his gross patchery, love him, feed him,
Keep in your bosom: yet remain assured
That he 's a made-up villain.

Pain. I know none such, my lord.

Poet.   Nor I.

Tim. Look you, I love you well; I 'll give you gold,
Rid me these villains from your companies:
Hang them, or stab them, drown them in a draught,
Confound them by some course, and come to me,
I 'll give you gold enough.

Both. Name them, my lord; let 's know them.

Tim. You that way, and you this; but two in company:
Each man apart, all single and alone,
Yet an arch-villain keeps him company.
If where thou art two villains shall not be,
                    [*To the* Painter.
Come not near him.—If thou wouldst not reside
                    [*To the* Poet.
But where one villain is, then him abandon.—
Hence! pack! there 's gold; ye came for gold, ye slaves:

You have work for me; there's payment: hence!
You are an alchymist; make gold of that.—
Out, rascal dogs!
            [*Exit, beating and driving them out.*

SCENE II.—*The same.*

Enter FLAVIUS *and two* Senators.

Flav. It is in vain that you would speak with
            Timon;
For he is set so only to himself,

That nothing but himself, which looks like man,
Is friendly with him.
    1st Sen.   Bring us to his cave:
It is our part, and promise to the Athenians,
To speak with Timon.
    2nd Sen.   At all times alike
Men are not still the same. 'Twas time and griefs
That framed him thus: time, with his fairer hand,
Offering the fortunes of his former days,
The former man may make him. Bring us to him,
And chance it as it may.
    Flav.   Here is his cave.—
Peace and content be here! Lord Timon! Timon!

Look out, and speak to friends. The Athenians,
By two of their most reverend senate, greet thee:
Speak to them, noble Timon.

Enter TIMON.

Tim. Thou sun, that comfort'st, burn!—Speak,
            and be hanged:
For each true word, a blister! and each false
Be as a caut'rising to the root o' the tongue,
Consuming it with speaking!
    1st Sen.   Worthy Timon,—
Tim. Of none but such as you, and you of Timon.
2nd Sen. The senators of Athens greet thee,
            Timon.

Tim. I thank them; and would send them back
            the plague,
Could I but catch it for them.
    1st Sen.   O, forget
What we are sorry for ourselves in thee.
The senators, with one consent of love,
Entreat thee back to Athens; who have thought
On special dignities, which vacant lie
For thy best use and wearing.
    2nd Sen.   They confess
Toward thee, forgetfulness too general, gross:
Which now the public body,—which doth seldom
Play the recanter,—feeling in itself
A lack of Timon's aid, hath sense withal

131

Of its own fall, restraining aid to Timon;
And send forth us to make their sorrowed render,
Together with a recompense more fruitful
Than their offence can weigh down by the dram:
Ay, even such heaps and sums of love and wealth,
As shall to thee blot out what wrongs were theirs,
And write in thee the figures of their love,
Ever to read them thine.

    Tim.   You witch me in it;
Surprise me to the very brink of tears:
Lend me a fool's heart, and a woman's eyes,
And I'll beweep these comforts, worthy senators.

    1st Sen. Therefore, so please thee to return with us,
And of our Athens (thine and ours) to take
The captainship, thou shalt be met with thanks,
Allowed with absolute power, and thy good name
Live with authority. So, soon we shall drive back
Of Alcibiades the approaches wild;
Who, like a boar too savage, doth root up
His country's peace.

    2nd Sen.   And shakes his threat'ning sword
Against the walls of Athens.

    1st Sen.   Therefore, Timon,—

    Tim. Well, sir, I will; therefore I will, sir:
        Thus,—
If Alcibiades kill my countrymen,
Let Alcibiades know this of Timon,
That Timon cares not. But if he sack fair Athens,
And take our goodly agéd men by the beards,
Giving our holy virgins to the stain
Of contumelious, beastly, mad-brained war;
Then let him know,—and tell him, Timon speaks it
In pity of our agéd and our youth,—
I cannot choose but tell him, that I care not,
And let him take't at worst: for their knives care
    not,
While you have throats to answer: for myself,
There's not a whittle in the unruly camp,
But I do prize it at my love before
The reverend'st throat in Athens. So I leave you
To the protection of the prosperous gods,
As thieves to keepers.

    Flav.   Stay not; all's in vain.

    Tim. Why, I was writing of my epitaph;
It will be seen to-morrow: my long sickness
Of health and living now begins to mend,
And nothing brings me all things. Go, live still;
Be Alcibiades your plague, you his,
And last so long enough!

    1st Sen.   We speak in vain.

    Tim. But yet I love my country; and am not
One that rejoices in the common wreck,
As common bruit doth put it.

    1st Sen.   That's well spoke.

    Tim. Commend me to my loving countrymen,—

    1st Sen. These words become your lips as they
      pass through them.

    2nd Sen. And enter in our ears like great tri-
      úmphers
In their applauding gates.

    Tim.   Commend me to them;
And tell them that, to ease them of their griefs,
Their fears of hostile strokes, their achés, losses,
Their pangs of love, with other incident throes
That nature's fragile vessel doth sustain
In life's uncertain voyage, I will some kindness do
    them:
I'll teach them to prevent wild Alcibiades' wrath.

    2nd Sen. I like this well; he will return again.

    Tim. I have a tree which grows here in my close,
That mine own use invites me to cut down,
And shortly must I fell it: tell my friends,
Tell Athens, in the sequence of degree,
From high to low throughout, that whoso please
To stop affliction, let him take his haste,
Come hither, ere my tree hath felt the axe,
And hang himself. I pray you, do my greeting.

    Flav. Trouble him no further; thus you still
      shall find him.

    Tim. Come not to me again: but say to Athens,
Timon hath made his everlasting mansion
Upon the beachéd verge of the salt flood;
Which once a day with his embosséd froth
The turbulent surge shall cover; thither come,
And let my gravestone be your oracle.—
Lips, let sour words go by, and language end:
What is amiss, plague and infection mend!
Graves only be men's works; and death their
    gain!
Sun, hide thy beams! Timon hath done his reign.
                   [*Exit* TIMON.

    1st Sen. His discontents are unremoveably
Coupled to nature.

    2nd Sen. Our hope in him is dead: let us return,
And strain what other means is left unto us
In our dear peril.

    1st Sen.   It requires swift foot. [*Exeunt.*

SCENE III.—*The Walls of* Athens.

Enter two Senators, *and a* Messenger.

    1st Sen. Thou hast painfully discovered: are his
      files
As full as thy report?

    Mess.   I have spoke the least:
Besides, his expedition promises
Present approach.

    2nd Sen. We stand much hazard, if they bring
      not Timon.

    Mess. I met a courier, one mine ancient friend;
Whom, though in general part we were opposed,
Yet our old love made a particular force,

And made us speak like friends: this man was
     riding
From Alcibiades to Timon's cave,
With letters of entreaty, which imported
His fellowship i' the cause against your city,
In part for his sake moved.

Enter Senators from TIMON

1st Sen.   Here come our brothers.
3rd Sen. No talk of Timon, nothing of him ex-
     pect.—
The enemies' drum is heard, and fearful scouring
Doth choke the air with dust.   In, and prepare;
Ours is the fall, I fear; our foes the snare. [*Exeunt.*

SCENE IV.—*The Woods.* TIMON'S *Cave, and a
Tombstone seen.*

Enter a Soldier, seeking TIMON.

Sol. By all description this should be the place.
Who's here? speak, ho!—No answer?—What is
     this?
Timon is dead, who hath outstretched his span:
Some beast reared this; there does not live a man.
Dead, sure; and this his grave.—
What's on this tomb I cannot read; the character
I'll take with wax:
Our captain hath in every figure skill;
An aged interpreter, though young in days:
Before proud Athens he's set down by this,
Whose fall the mark of his ambition is.   [*Exit.*

SCENE V.—*Before the Walls of* Athens.

Trumpets sound.   *Enter* ALCIBIADES *and Forces.*

Alcib. Sound to this coward and lascivious town
Our terrible approach.   [*A parley sounded.*

Enter Senators, on the walls.

Till now you have gone on, and filled the time
With all licentious measure, making your wills
The scope of justice; till now, myself and such
As slept within the shadow of your power,
Have wandered with our traversed arms, and
     breathed
Our sufferance vainly: now the time is flush,
When crouching marrow, in the bearer strong,
Cries of itself, "No more:" now breathless wrong
Shall sit and pant in your great chairs of ease;
And pursy indolence shall break his wind,
With fear and horrid flight.
   1st Sen.   Noble and young,

When thy first griefs were but a mere conceit,
Ere thou hadst power, or we had cause of fear,
We sent to thee; to give thy rages balm,
To wipe out our ingratitude with loves
Above their quantity.
   2nd Sen.   So did we woo
Transforméd Timon to our city's love,
By humble message and by promised means:
We were not all unkind, nor all deserve
The common stroke of war.
   1st Sen.   These walls of ours
Were not erected by their hands from whom
You have received your griefs: nor are they such,
That these great towers, trophies, and schools
     should fall
For private faults in them.
   2nd Sen.   Nor are they living
Who were the motives that you first went out:
Shame that they wanted cunning, in excess,
Hath broke their hearts.   March, noble lord,
Into our city with thy banners spread:
By decimation and a tithéd death
(If thy revenges hunger for that food
Which nature loaths), take thou the destined tenth;
And by the hazard of the spotted die,
Let die the spotted.
   1st Sen.   All have not offended;
For those that were, it is not square to take,
On those that are, revenges: crimes, like lands,
Are not inherited.   Then, dear countryman,
Bring in thy ranks, but leave without thy rage:
Spare thy Athenian cradle, and those kin
Which, in the bluster of thy wrath, must fall
With those that have offended: like a shepherd,
Approach the fold, and cull the infected forth,
But kill not all together.
   2nd Sen.   What thou wilt,
Thou rather shalt enforce it with thy smile,
Than hew to't with thy sword.
   1st Sen.   Set but thy foot
Against our rampired gates, and they shall ope;
So thou wilt send thy gentle heart before,
To say, thou'lt enter friendly.
   2nd Sen.   Throw thy glove,
Or any token of thine honour else,
That thou wilt use the wars as thy redress,
And not as our confusion, all thy powers
Shall make their harbour in our town, till we
Have sealed thy full desire.
   Alcib.   Then there's my glove:
Descend, and open your unchargéd ports.
Those enemies of Timon's, and mine own,
Whom you yourselves shall set out for reproof,
Fall, and no more: and (to atone your fears
With my more noble meaning) not a man
Shall pass his quarter, or offend the stream
Of regular justice in your city's bounds,

But shall be remedied, to your public laws,
At heaviest answer.
   Both.   'Tis most nobly spoken.
   Alcib. Descend, and keep your words.

    The Senators *descend, and open the gates.*

          Enter a Soldier.

   Sol. My noble general, Timon is dead;
Entombed upon the very hem o' the sea:
And on his gravestone this insculpture, which
With wax I brought away, whose soft impression
Interprets for my poor ignorance.

        ALCIBIADES *reads.*

" Here lies a wretched corse, of wretched soul bereft:
   Seek not my name.   A plague consume you wicked
      caitiffs left!

Here lie I, Timon; who, alive, all living men did
    hate:
   Pass by, and curse thy fill; but pass, and stay not
    here thy gait."

These well express in thee thy latter spirits:
Though thou abhorr'dst in us our human griefs,
Scorn'dst our brain's flow, and those our droplets
    which
From niggard nature fall, yet rich conceit
Taught thee to make vast Neptune weep for aye
On thy low grave, on faults forgiven.   Dead
Is noble Timon; of whose memory
Hereafter more.—Bring me into your city,
And I will use the olive with my sword:
Make war breed peace; make peace stint war;
    make each
Prescribe to other, as each other's leech.—
Let our drums strike.   *[Exeunt.*

NOTES.

"When we for recompense have praised the vile," &c.
Act I., Scene 1.

It must be here supposed, according to the suggestion of Warburton, that the Poet is busy in reading his own work; and that these three lines are the introduction to the poem addressed to Timon, of which he afterwards gives an account to the Painter.

"Our poesy is as a gum, which oozes
From whence 'tis nourished."—Act I., Scene 1.

The original folio here reads,

"Our poesy is as a gowne, which uses," &c.

Pope suggested the alteration of "gowne" to "gum," and Johnson that of "uses" to "oozes." Instances of restoration so sagacious and happy as this (and there are very many such in the received text of Shakspere), may, at least, serve to rescue the commentators generally from the common charge of utter uselessness, or something worse.

——"My free drift
Halts not particularly, but moves itself
In a wide sea of wax."—Act I., Scene 1.

The Poet means to say that his design does not stop at any single character. The phrase "sea of wax" is supposed to refer to the ancient practice of writing upon waxen tables with an iron style.

——"No levelled malice
Infects one comma in the course I hold;
But flies an eagle flight, bold, and forth on,
Leaving no tract behind."—Act I., Scene 1.

To level is to aim,—to point the shot at a mark. The meaning is, says Johnson, "My poem is not a satire with any particular view, or levelled at any single person: I fly like an eagle into the general expanse of life, and leave not, by any private mischief, the trace of my passage."

——Apemantus, that few things loves better
Than to abhor himself: even he drops down
The knee before him."—Act I., Scene 1.

Steevens remarks upon this passage, that either Shakspere meant to put a falsehood into the mouth of the Poet, or had not yet thoroughly planned the character of Apemantus; for, in the ensuing scenes, his behaviour is as cynical to Timon as to his followers. Mr. Harness, in reply, observes that the Poet, seeing that Apemantus paid frequent visits to Timon, naturally concluded that he was equally courteous with other guests.

"A thousand moral paintings I can shew,
That shall demonstrate these quick blows of Fortune
More pregnantly than words."—Act I., Scene 1.

"Shakspere seems to intend in this dialogue," says Johnson, "to express some competition between the two great arts of imitation. Whatever the Poet declares himself to have shewn, the Painter thinks he could have shewn better."

"TIM. *The man is honest.*
OLD ATH. *Therefore he will be, Timon."*—Act I., Scene 1.

"The thought," says Warburton, "is closely expressed and obscure; but the meaning seems to be, 'If the man be honest, he will be so in this, and not endeavour at the injustice of gaining my daughter without my consent.'" Coleridge thus explains this difficult passage:—"The meaning of the first line the Poet himself explains, or rather unfolds, in the second. 'The man is honest.' 'True; and for that very cause, and with no additional or extrinsic motive, he will be so. No man can be justly called honest who is not so for honesty's sake, itself including its own reward.'"

——"Never may
That state or fortune fall into my keeping
Which is not owed to you!"—Act I., Scene 1.

That is, "Let me never henceforth consider anything that I possess but as owed or due to you; held for your service, and at your disposal." In the same sense, Lady Macbeth says to Duncan,

——"Your servants ever
Have theirs, themselves, and what is theirs, in compt,
To make their audit at your highness' pleasure,
Still to return your own."

"That I had no angry wit to be a lord."—Act I., Scene 1.

This obscure expression, which is probably corrupt, has hitherto defied all satisfactory interpretation. We may, however, conclude with Johnson, that the substantial meaning is, "I should hate myself for patiently enduring to be a lord."

"I myself would have no power: pr'ythee, let my meat make thee silent."—Act I., Scene 2.

"Timon," says Mr. Tyrwhitt, "like a polite landlord, disclaims all power over his guests. His meaning is, 'I myself would have no power to make thee silent; but, pr'y thee, let my meat perform that office.'"

"I wonder men dare trust themselves with men:
Methinks they should invite them without knives."
Act I., Scene 2.

It was the custom in Shakspere's time, according to Mr. Ritson, for each guest to bring his own knife, which he occasionally whetted on a stone that hung behind the door. One of these whetstones he states to have been in Parkinson's Museum.

"Entertained me with mine own device."—Act I., Scene 2.

This mask appears to have been designed by Timon to entertain his guests.

"There is no crossing him in his humour;
Else I should tell him—well—i' faith I should—
When all's spent, he'd be crossed then, an he could."
Act I., Scene 2.

The expression here is equivocal; in the last line, the steward means to say that, in his extremity, Timon would fain have his hand crossed with money. From the circumstance of some of the old coins bearing the impress of a cross, arose the once common phrase, "I have not a cross about me."

——"*No porter at his gate;*
But rather one that smiles, and still invites
All that pass by."—Act II., Scene 1.

The word "one" in the second line does not refer to 'porter," but signifies a person. Roughness was the imputed characteristic of a porter. There appeared at Killingworth Castle, 1575, "a porter, tall of person, big of limb, and stern of countenance." The meaning of the text is, "He has no stern forbidding porter at his gate to keep people out, but a person who invites them in."

"*Good even, Varro.*"—Act II., Scene 2.

"Good even," or "good den," was the usual salutation from noon, the moment that "good morrow" became improper.

"*So soon as dinner's done, we'll forth again.*"
Act II., Scene 2.

It was formerly the custom to hunt as well after dinner as before. From Laneham's "ACCOUNT OF THE ENTERTAINMENT AT KENILWORTH CASTLE," it appears that Queen Elizabeth, while there, hunted in the afternoon:— "Monday was hot, and therefore her highness kept in till five o'clock in the evening; what time it pleased her to ride forth into the chase, to hunt the hart of force; which found anon, and after sore chased," &c. On the 18th of July, there is another entry to the same effect.

"*I have retired me to a wasteful cock,*
And set mine eyes at flow."—Act II., Scene 2.

By a "wasteful cock" is probably meant what we now call a waste-pipe; a pipe that is continually running, and thereby prevents the overflow of cisterns and other reservoirs, by carrying off their superfluous water. "This circumstance," says Steevens, "served to keep the idea of Timon's unceasing prodigality in the mind of the steward, while its remoteness from the scenes of luxury within the house, was favourable to meditation."

"*No villanous bounty yet hath passed my heart;*
Unwisely, not ignobly, have I given."—Act II., Scene 2.

"Every reader must rejoice in this circumstance of comfort which presents itself to Timon; who, although beggared through want of prudence, consoles himself with the reflection that his ruin was not brought on by the pursuit of guilty pleasures."—STEEVENS.

"*If I would broach the vessels of my love,*
And try the argument of hearts by borrowing."
Act II., Scene 2.

The contents of a poem or play were formerly called "the argument." "If I would," says Timon, "by borrowing, try of what men's hearts are composed,—what they have in them," &c.

"*(For that I knew it the most general way).*"
Act II., Scene 2.

"General" does not mean speedy, but compendious; the way to try many at a time.

——"*These old fellows*
Have their ingratitude in them hereditary."—Act II., Scene 2.

Some distempers of natural constitution being called "hereditary," Timon so calls the ingratitude of the senators.

"*And nature, as it grows again toward earth,*
Is fashioned for the journey, dull and heavy."
Act II., Scene 2.

The same thought occurs in the "WIFE FOR A MONTH" of Beaumont and Fletcher:—

"Beside, the fair soul's old too, it grows covetous;
Which shews all honour is departed from us,
And we are earth again."

"*Here's three solidares for thee.*"—Act III., Scene 1.

"Where Shakspere found this odd word," says Mr. Nares, "is uncertain. 'Solidata' is, in low Latin, the word for the daily pay of a common soldier; and 'solidare' the verb expressing the act of paying it; whence comes the word 'soldier' itself. From one or the other of these, some writer had formed the English word. Or the true reading may be 'solidate,' which is precisely 'solidata' made English."

"*The devil knew not what he did, when he made man politic; he crossed himself by it: and I cannot think but, in the end, the villanies of man will set him clear.*"
Act III., Scene 3.

The meaning of this passage appears to be, that the devil, by putting policy or cunning into the heart of man, merely intended to make him more wicked; but that this cunning has thriven so wonderfully in a congenial soil, that it will finally be turned against its bestower, and enable man to escape from the net of the devil himself.

"*Who cannot keep his wealth, must keep his house.*"
Act III., Scene 3.

That is, keep within doors for fear of duns. So in "MEASURE FOR MEASURE" (act ii., scene 2):— "You will turn good husband now, Pompey; you will keep the house."

"PHI. *All our bills.*
TIM. *Knock me down with 'em.*"—Act III., Scene 4.

This is a quibbling allusion to the weapon called the bill. In Decker's "GULL'S HORNBOOK" we find, "They durst not strike down their customers with large bills."

"*Upon that were my thoughts tiring.*"—Act III., Scene 6.

"Tiring" means fastened, as the hawk fastens its beak eagerly on its prey. So in Shakspere's "VENUS AND ADONIS:"—

"Like an empty eagle, sharp by fast,
Tires with her beak on feathers, flesh, and bone."

"2nd LORD. *Lord Timon's mad.*
3rd LORD.   *I feel't upon my bones.*
4th LORD. *One day he gives us diamonds, next day stones.*"
Act III., Scene 6.

Timon, in this mock banquet, has thrown nothing at his guests but warm water and the dishes that contained it. The mention of stones in the passage cited, may be thus plausibly accounted for:—Steevens states that Mr. Strutt, the engraver, was in possession of a MS. play on this subject, which is supposed to have been an older drama than Shakspere's. There is said to have been a scene in it resembling the banquet given by Timon in the present play. Instead of warm water, he sets before his false friends stones painted like artichokes, and afterwards beats them out of the room. He then retires to the woods, attended by his faithful steward. In the last act, he is followed by his fickle mistress, &c., after being reported to have discovered a treasure by digging. Steevens states the piece to have been a wretched composition, although apparently the work of an academic. It is possible that this production may have been of some service to Shakspere: at present, no one appears to know what has become of it.

——"*Such a house broke!*
So noble a master fallen!"—Act IV., Scene 2.

It is justly remarked by Johnson, that nothing contributes more to the exaltation of Timon's character, than the zeal and fidelity of his servants. Nothing but real virtue can be honoured by domestics; nothing but impartial kindness can gain affection from dependents.

——"*Not nature,*
To whom all sores lay siege, can bear great fortune,
But by contempt of nature."—Act IV., Scene 3.

The meaning of these and the preceding lines is probably this :—Brother, when his fortune is enlarged, will scorn brother; such is the general depravity of human nature, which, besieged as it is by misery, admonished as it is of want and imperfection, will, when elevated by fortune, despise beings of nature like its own.

——"*Like tapsters, that bid welcome*
To knaves and all approachers."—Act IV., Scene 3.

A similar satire on tapsters occurs in the poet's "VENUS AND ADONIS :"—

" Like shrill-tongued tapsters, answering every call,
Soothing the humour of fantastic wits."

——"*Will these mossed trees,*
That have outlived the eagle, page thy heels ?"
Act IV., Scene 3.

"Aquilæ senectus" is a proverb. Turberville says that the great age of this bird has been ascertained from the circumstance of its always building its eyrie, or nest, in the same place.

——"*Willing misery*
Outlives incertain pomp; is crowned before."
Act IV., Scene 3.

That is, arrives sooner at the completion of its wishes. So in a former scene of this play :—

"And in some sort these wants of mine are crowned,
That I account them blessings."

And more appositely in "CYMBELINE :"—

" My supreme crown of grief."

——"*Best state, contentless,*
Hath a distracted and most wretched being;
Worse than the worst, content."—Act IV., Scene 3.

The meaning is, that the best states without content have a wretched being compared with the worst states that are contented.

" *Hadst thou, like us, from our first swath proceeded*
The sweet degrees that this brief world affords.
Act IV., Scene 3.

"There is in this speech," says Johnson, "a sullen haughtiness and malignant dignity suitable at once to the lord and the man-hater. The impatience with which Timon bears to have his luxury reproached by one that never had luxury within his reach, is natural and graceful."

In a letter writen by the Earl of Essex (just before his execution) to another nobleman, there is a passage somewhat resembling that in the text :—"God grant your lordship may quickly feel the comfort I now enjoy in my unfeigned conversion, but that you may never feel the torments I have suffered for my long delaying it. I had none but divines to call upon me, to whom I said, ' If my ambition could have entered into their narrow breasts, they would not have been so humble; or if my delights had been once tasted by them, they would not have been so precise.' But your lordship hath one to call upon you that knoweth what it is you now enjoy, and what the greatest fruit and end is of all contentment that this world can afford."

" *The icy precepts of respect.*"—Act IV., Scene 3.

Meaning the cold admonitions of cautious prudence, that deliberately weighs the consequences of every action. So in "TROILUS AND CRESSIDA :"—

——" *Reason and respect*
Make livers pale, and lustihood deject."

——"*Have with one winter's brush*
Fell from their boughs, and left me open, bare
For every storm that blows."—Act IV., Scene 3.

The same imagery occurs in the poet's 73rd Sonnet :—

"That time of year thou mayst in me behold
When yellow leaves, or none, or few, do hang
Upon those boughs which shake against the cold;
Bare ruined choirs where late the sweet birds sang."

"*If thou hadst not been born the worst of men,*
Thou hadst been a knave and flatterer."—Act IV., Scene 3.

"Dryden has quoted two verses of Virgil," observes Johnson, "to shew how well he could write satires. Shakspere has here given a specimen of the same power, by a line bitter beyond all bitterness, in which Timon tells Apemantus that he had not virtue enough for the vices he condemns.—I have heard," continues the critic, "Mr. Burke commend the subtlety of discrimination with which Shakspere distinguishes the present character of Timon from that of Apemantus, whom, to vulgar eyes, he would now resemble."

" *When thou wast in thy gilt and thy perfume, they mocked thee for too much curiosity.*"—Act IV., Scene 3.

The word "curiosity" is here used in the sense of finical delicacy. So in Jervas Markham's "ENGLISH ARCADIA," 1606 :—"For all those eye-charming graces, of which with such curiosity she hath boasted." And in Hobby's translation of Castiglione's "CORTEGIANO," 1556 :—"A waiting-gentlewoman should flee affection or curiosity." "Curiosity" is here inserted as a synonyme to "affection," which means affectation.

" *Wert thou the unicorn, pride and wrath would confound thee, and make thine own self the conquest of thy fury.*"
Act IV., Scene 3.

The fabulous account of the unicorn states, that he and the lion being enemies by nature, as soon as the lion sees the unicorn, he betakes himself to a tree : the unicorn, in his fury, and with all the swiftness of his course, running at him, sticks his horn fast in the tree, and then the lion falls upon him and kills him.

" *Wert thou a leopard, thou wert german to the lion, and the spots of thy kindred were jurors on thy life.*"
Act IV., Scene 3.

This seems to be an allusion to Turkish policy :—
" Bear, like the Turk, no brother near the throne."—POPE.

——"*Yet thanks I must you con,*
That you are thieves professed."—Act IV., Scene 3.

To "con thanks" is a common expression of the time; as, in "PIERCE PENNILESS HIS SUPPLICATION," by Nash, 1592 :—"It is well done to practise thy wit; but I believe our lord will con thee little thanks for it."

——"*There is boundless theft*
In limited professions."—Act IV., Scene 3.

That is, in regular, orderly professions. So in "MACBETH :"—

" For 't is my limited service."

Meaning, " My appointed service, prescribed by the necessary duty and rules of my office."

"'*T is in the malice of mankind that he thus advises us ;*
not to have us thrive in our mystery."—Act IV., Scene 3.

The "malice of mankind" means here, Timon's malicious hatred of mankind. "He does not give us this advice to pursue our trade of stealing, &c., from any goodwill to us, or a desire that we should thrive in our profession, but merely from the malicious enmity that he bears to the human race."

"*Performance is ever the duller for his act; and, but in the plainer and simpler kind of people, the deed of saying is quite out of use.*"—Act V., Scene 1.

That is, the doing of that which we have said we would do,—the accomplishment and performance of our promise, is for the most part out of use.

"*It must be a personating of himself.*"—Act V., Scene 1.

The word "personating" here signifies representation. The subject of the projected satire was Timon's case, not his person.

——"*Thou draw'st a counterfeit
Best in all Athens.*"—Act V., Scene 1.

"Counterfeit" was a common term for a portrait; as, in the "MERCHANT OF VENICE:"—

——"What find I here?
Fair Portia's counterfeit."

——"*Yet remain assured
That he's a made up villain.*"—Act V., Scene 1.

Meaning, a complete or consummate villain: "omnibus numeris absolutus."

"*And send forth us, to make their sorrowed render.*"
Act V., Scene 2.

"Render" is confession. So in "CYMBELINE," (act iv., scene 4):—

——"May drive us to a render
Where we have lived."

"*Together with a recompense more fruitful
Than their offence can weigh down by the dram.*"
Act V., Scene 2.

A recompense so large that the offence they have committed, though every dram of that offence should be put into the scale, cannot counterpoise it.

——"*Thou shalt be met with thanks,
Allowed with absolute power.*"—Act V., Scene 2.

"Allowed" is licensed, privileged, uncontrolled. So of a buffoon in "LOVE'S LABOUR'S LOST," it is said that he is "allowed;" that is, at liberty to say what he will; a privileged scoffer.

"*I have a tree which grows here in my close.*"—Act V., Scene 2.

This satirical stroke appears to be founded on a passage in Plutarch's "LIFE OF ANTONY:"—" It is reported of him also, that this Timon on a time (the people being assembled in the market-place about despatch of some affairs), got up into the pulpit for orations, where the orators commonly use to speak unto the people; and silence being made, every man listening to hear what he would say, because it was a wonder to see him in that place, at length he began to speak in this manner:—' My lords of Athens, I have a little yard in my house, where there groweth a fig-tree, on the which many citizens have hanged themselves; and because I mean to make some building upon the place, I thought good to let you all understand it, that before the fig-tree be cut down, if any of you be desperate, you may there in time go hang yourselves.'"

"*Now the time is flush.*"—Act V., Scene 5.

A bird is said to be "flush" when his feathers are grown and he can leave the nest.

"*By humble message, and by promised means.*"
Act I., Scene 5.

That is, by promising him a competent subsistence. The Chief Justice says to Falstaff, "Your means are very slender, and your waste is great."

"*Here lies a wretched corse,*" &c.—Act V., Scene 5.

This epitaph is formed out of two distinct epitaphs which appear in North's "PLUTARCH." The first couplet is said by Plutarch to have been composed by Timon himself; the second to have been written by the poet Callimachus.

———

The remarks of Schlegel on this fine play are subjoined. They are worthy of the writer, although we think his estimate of the character of Timon far more severe than is warranted by the incidents of the drama:—

"Of all the works of Shakspere, 'TIMON OF ATHENS' possesses most the character of a satire: a laughing satire, in the picture of the parasites and flatterers; and a Juvenalian, in the bitterness and the imprecations of Timon against the ingratitude of a false world. The story is treated in a very simple manner, and is definitely divided into large masses. In the first act, the joyous life of Timon; his noble and hospitable extravagance, and the throng of every description of suitors of him: in the second and third acts, his embarrassment, and the trial which he is thereby reduced to make of his supposed friends, who all desert him in the hour of need: in the fourth and fifth acts, Timon's flight to the woods, his misanthropical melancholy, and his death. The only thing which may be called an episode, is the banishment of Alcibiades, and his return by force of arms. However, they are both examples of ingratitude: the one, of a state towards its defender; and the other, of private friends to their benefactor. As the merits of the general towards his fellow-citizens suppose more strength of character than those of the generous prodigal, their respective behaviours are no less different: Timon frets himself to death; Alcibiades regains his lost dignity by violence.

"If the poet very properly sides with Timon against the common practice of the world, he is, on the other hand, by no means disposed to spare Timon. Timon was a fool in his generosity; he is a madman in his discontent; he is everywhere wanting in the wisdom which enables men in all things to observe the due measure. Although the truth of his extravagant feelings is proved by his death, and though, when he digs up a treasure, he spurns at the wealth which seems to solicit him, we yet see distinctly enough that the vanity of wishing to be singular, in both parts of the play, had some share in his liberal self-forgetfulness, as well as in his anchoretical seclusion. This is particularly evident in the incomparable scene where the cynic Apemantus visits Timon in the wilderness. They have a sort of competition with each other in their trade of misanthropy: the cynic reproaches the impoverished Timon with having been merely driven by necessity to take to the way of living which *he* had been long following of his own free choice; and Timon cannot bear the thought of being merely an imitator of the cynic. As in this subject, the effect could only be produced by an accumulation of similar features, in the variety of the shades an amazing degree of understanding has been displayed by Shakspere. What a powerfully diversified concert of flatteries, and empty testimonies of devotedness! It is highly amusing to see the suitors whom the ruined circumstances of their patron had dispersed, immediately flock to him again when they learn that he has been revisited by fortune. In the speeches of Timon after he is undeceived, all the hostile figures of language are exhausted; it is a dictionary of eloquent imprecation."—

Alas! the error of hapless Timon lay not (as the critic supposes) in "the vanity of wishing to be singular," but in the humility of not perceiving that he really was so, in the boundless and unsuspecting generosity of his disposition. Timon is not to be considered an object of imitation: but it is plain, that had he not thought as well of others as of himself, he would not have been overwhelmed with horror and astonishment on the discovery of his fatal mistake.

hamlet
prince
of
denmark

Introductory Remarks

AMONG the numberless exquisite portraits delineated, for the delight and instruction of the world, by the hand of the great Dramatic Master, there is one which in a pre-eminent degree solicits and detains the universal gaze;—"the observed of all observers." It is that of a young and amiable Prince, in whom the traits of intellect and of feeling are admirably blended: his fine and varied countenance exhibits humour and sensibility, wit and philosophy, in the justest proportions: yet over all, and through all, there is still visible that "pale cast of thought," which might lead even the mere unacquainted spectator to infer, that the possessor had been burthened with a weight of mysterious care, which long oppressed, and finally overwhelmed him. This is that interesting and ever-eloquent friend, with whom we have held delightful converse from boyhood, even to the present hour; whose thoughts have penetrated to the innermost parts of our being; and whom, in despite of his occasional waywardness, weakness, and inconsistency, we have ever loved and respected as a dear and intimate personal friend.—This, in a word, is HAMLET.

Of all human compositions, there is, perhaps, not one which in the same compass contains so much just, original, and profound thought, as this gigantic effort of genius; none so suggestive, so imaginative, and yet so practical; none which in an equal degree charms alike the philosopher and the simple rustic,—the poet and the man of the world. From the hour of its first appearance, it has been the especial darling of all classes; and has thus tended, more than anything else, to shew the high capabilities of the universal human mind;—to justify the high eulogium which Hamlet himself, "the general favourite, as the general friend," pronounces so emphatically on his kindred "quintessence of dust." In reference to this point, it may be appropriately mentioned, that in the most remote eastern minor theatre —a locality which an inhabitant of more genial theatric climes would be apt to regard as a mere Bœotia, helplessly devoted to Pantomime and Melodrame—even here, the subtile wisdom and poetic beauty of the play before us, drew crowded houses, at a recent period, for upwards of sixty nights in a single season!

The main incidents on which the play of "HAMLET" is founded, are related by Saxo-Grammaticus, the Danish historian. The story is also told in the novels of Belleforest, and in a small black-letter volume, entitled "THE HISTORIE OF HAMBLETT." Shakspere's drama was first printed in 1603; a copy of this edition (supposed to be unique), was discovered of late years, and reprinted in 1825. The title runs thus:—"The Tragicall Historie of Hamlet Prince of Denmarke, by William Shake-speare. As it hath beene diverse times acted by his Highnesse servants in the Cittie of London: as also in the two Universities of Cambridge and Oxford, and elsewhere. At London, printed for N. L. and John Trundell." The title to the second quarto edition, published in 1604, states the play to have been "enlarged to almost as much againe as it was, according to the true and perfect coppie." It exhibits also some variations, both of plot and in the names of the characters, as compared with the original sketch. There were reprints of the enlarged quarto in 1605, 1609, and 1611; besides another edition without date. These various evidences of the great popularity of the play, were all precursors of the general folio collection, published by the Poet's "fellows," in 1623. Some further remarks on the different versions of "HAMLET" will be found in the Notes.

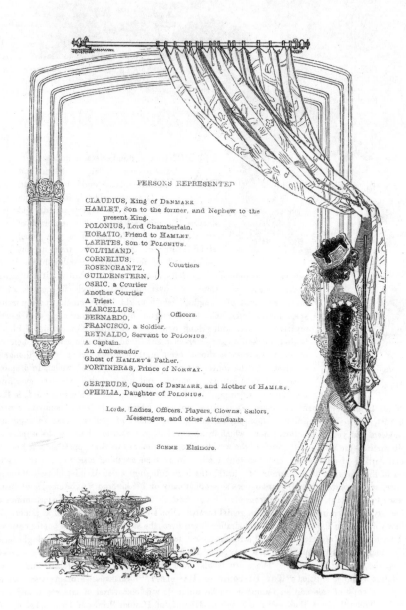

PERSONS REPRESENTED

CLAUDIUS, King of DENMARK
HAMLET, Son to the former, and Nephew to the
     present King.
POLONIUS, Lord Chamberlain.
HORATIO, Friend to HAMLET.
LAERTES, Son to POLONIUS.
VOLTIMAND,
CORNELIUS,
ROSENCRANTZ,   } Courtiers
GUILDENSTERN,
OSRIC, a Courtier
Another Courtier
A Priest.
MARCELLUS,
BERNARDO,   } Officers.
FRANCISCO, a Soldier.
REYNALDO, Servant to POLONIUS.
A Captain.
An Ambassador
Ghost of HAMLET's Father.
FORTINBRAS, Prince of NORWAY.

GERTRUDE, Queen of DENMARK, and Mother of HAMLET.
OPHELIA, Daughter of POLONIUS.

Lords, Ladies, Officers, Players, Clowns, Sailors,
     Messengers, and other Attendants.

SCENE Elsinore.

SCENE I.—Elsinore. *A Platform before the Castle.*

FRANCISCO *on his post.* *Enter to him* BERNARDO.

Ber. Who's there?

Fran. Nay, answer me: stand, and unfold
    yourself.

Ber. Long live the king!

Fran. Bernardo?

Ber. He.

Fran. You come most carefully upon your hour.

Ber. 'Tis now struck twelve; get thee to bed,
    Francisco.

Fran. For this relief, much thanks: 'tis bitter
    cold,

And I am sick at heart.

Ber. Have you had quiet guard?

Fran. Not a mouse stirring.

Ber. Well, good night.

If you do meet Horatio and Marcellus,
The rivals of my watch, bid them make haste.

Enter HORATIO *and* MARCELLUS.

Fran. I think I hear them.—Stand, ho? Who
 is there?

Hor. Friends to this ground.

Mar.   And liegemen to the Dane.

Fran. Give you good night.

Mar.   O, farewell, honest soldier:
Who hath relieved you?

Fran.   Bernardo hath my place.
Give you good night.   [*Exit.*

Mar.   Holla! Bernardo!

Ber. Say,
What, is Horatio there?

Hor.   A piece of him.

Ber. Welcome, Horatio; welcome, good Marcellus.

Hor. What, has this thing appeared again to-
 night?

Ber. I have seen nothing.

Mar. Horatio says, 't is but our fantasy;
And will not let belief take hold of him,
Touching this dreaded sight, twice seen of us:
Therefore I have entreated him along
With us to watch the minutes of this night;
That, if again this apparition come,
He may approve our eyes, and speak to it.

Hor. Tush, tush! 't will not appear.

Ber.   Sit down awhile;
And let us once again assail your ears,
That are so fortified against our story,
What we two nights have seen.

Hor.   Well, sit we down,
And let us hear Bernardo speak of this.

Ber. Last night of all,
When yon same star, that 's westward from the pole,
Had made his course to illume that part of heaven
Where now it burns, Marcellus and myself,
The bell then beating one,—

Mar. Peace, break thee off; look where it comes
 again!

Enter Ghost.

Ber. In the same figure, like the king that 's dead.

Mar. Thou art a scholar; speak to it, Horatio.

Ber. Looks it not like the king? mark it, Horatio.

Hor. Most like:—it harrows me with fear and
 wonder.

Ber. It would be spoke to.

Mar.   Question it, Horatio.

Hor. What art thou, that usurp'st this time of
 night,
Together with that fair and warlike form
In which the majesty of buried Denmark
Did sometimes march? By heaven I charge thee,
 speak!

Mar. It is offended.

Ber.   See! it stalks away.

Hor. Stay; speak: speak, I charge thee, speak!
        [*Exit* Ghost.

Mar. 'T is gone, and will not answer.

Ber. How now, Horatio? you tremble and look
 pale:
Is not this something more than fantasy?
What think you on 't?

Hor. Before my God, I might not this believe,
Without the sensible and true avouch
Of mine own eyes.

Mar.   Is it not like the king?

Hor. As thou art to thyself:
Such was the very armour he had on,
When he the ambitious Norway combated;
So frowned he once, when, in an angry parle,
He smote the sledded Polacks on the ice.
'T is strange.

Mar. Thus twice before, and just at this dead
 hour,
With martial stalk hath he gone by our watch.

Hor. In what particular thought to work, I
 know not;
But, in the gross and scope of mine opinion,
This bodes some strange eruption to our state.

Mar. Good now, sit down, and tell me, he that
 knows,
Why this same strict and most observant watch
So nightly toils the subject of the land?
And why such daily cast of brazen cannon,
And foreign mart for implements of war;
Why such impress of shipwrights, whose sore task
Does not divide the Sunday from the week:
What might be toward, that this sweaty haste
Doth make the night joint-labourer with the day;
Who is 't that can inform me?

Hor.   That can I;
At least, the whisper goes so. Our last king,
Whose image even but now appeared to us,
Was, as you know, by Fortinbras of Norway,
Thereto pricked on by a most emulate pride,
Dared to the combat; in which our valiant Hamlet
(For so this side of our known world esteemed him)
Did slay this Fortinbras; who, by a sealed compáct,
Well ratified by law and heraldry,
Did forfeit with his life, all those his lands
Which he stood seized of, to the conqueror:
Against the which, a moiety competent
Was gagéd by our king; which had returned
To the inheritance of Fortinbras,
Had he been vanquisher; as by the same cov'nant,
And carriage of the article designed,
His fell to Hamlet.—Now, sir, young Fortinbras,
Of unimprovéd mettle hot and full,
Hath in the skirts of Norway, here and there,
Sharked up a list of landless resolutes,

For food and diet, to some enterprise
That hath a stomach in 't: which is no other
(As it doth well appear unto our state)
But to recover of us, by strong hand,
And terms compulsatory, those 'foresaid lands
So by his father lost: and this, I take it,
Is the main motive of our preparations;
The source of this our watch; and the chief
   head
Of this post-haste and romage in the land.

 Ber. I think it be no other, but even so:
Well may it sort, that this portentous figure
Comes arméd through our watch; so like the king
That was, and is, the question of these wars.

 Hor. A mote it is, to trouble the mind's eye.
In the most high and palmy state of Rome,

A little ere the mightiest Julius fell,
The graves stood tenantless, and the sheeted dead
Did squeak and gibber in the Roman streets. * * *
As stars with trains of fire and dews of blood,
Disasters in the sun; and the moist star,
Upon whose influence Neptune's empire stands,
Was sick almost to doomsday with eclipse.
And even the like precurse of fierce events
(As harbingers preceding still the fates,
And prologue to the omen coming on)
Have heaven and earth together démonstrated
Unto our climatures and countrymen.—

Re-enter Ghost.

But soft; behold! lo, where it comes again!
I 'll cross it, though it blast me.—Stay, illusion!

If thou hast any sound, or use of voice,
Speak to me:
If there be any good thing to be done,
That may to thee do ease, and grace to me,
Speak to me:
If thou art privy to thy country's fate,
Which, happily, foreknowing may avoid,
O, speak!
Or, if thou hast uphoarded in thy life
Extorted treasure in the womb of earth,
For which, they say, you spirits oft walk in death,
                              [*Cock crows.*
Speak of it: stay, and speak!—Stop it, Mar-
          cellus!
  Mar. Shall I strike at it with my partizan?
  Hor. Do, if it will not stand.
  Ber. 'Tis here!
  Hor. 'Tis here!
  Mar. 'Tis gone!   [*Exit* Ghost.
We do it wrong, being so majestical,
To offer it the show of violence;
For it is, as the air, invulnerable,
And our vain blows malicious mockery.
  Ber. It was about to speak when the cock
          crew.
  Hor. And then it started, like a guilty thing
Upon a fearful summons. I have heard,
The cock, that is the trumpet to the morn,
Doth with his lofty and shrill-sounding throat
Awake the god of day; and, at his warning,
Whether in sea or fire, in earth or air,
The extravagant and erring spirit hies
To his confine: and of the truth herein
This present object made probation.
  Mar. It faded on the crowing of the cock.
Some say, that ever 'gainst that season comes
Wherein our Saviour's birth is celebrated,
This bird of dawning singeth all night long:
And then, they say, no spirit dares stir abroad;
The nights are wholesome; then no planets
          strike,
No fairy takes, nor witch hath power to charm;
So hallowed and so gracious is the time.
  Hor. So have I heard, and do in part be-
          lieve it.
But look, the morn, in russet mantle clad,
Walks o'er the dew of yon high eastern hill:
Break we our watch up; and, by my advice,
Let us impart what we have seen to-night
Unto young Hamlet: for, upon my life,
This spirit, dumb to us, will speak to him.
Do you consent we shall acquaint him with it,
As needful in our loves, fitting our duty?
  Mar. Let's do 't, I pray; and I this morning
          know
Where we shall find him most convenient.
                              [*Exeunt.*

SCENE II.—*The same. A Room of State in the
          same.*

Enter the KING, QUEEN, HAMLET, POLONIUS,
  LAERTES, VOLTIMAND, CORNELIUS, Lords, *and*
  Attendants.

  King. Though yet of Hamlet our dear brother's
          death
The memory be green; and that it us befitted
To bear our hearts in grief, and our whole kingdom
To be contracted in one brow of woe;
Yet so far hath discretion fought with nature,
That we with wisest sorrow think on him,
Together with remembrance of ourselves.
Therefore, our sometime sister, now our queen,
The imperial jointress of this warlike state,
Have we, as 't were, with a defeated joy
(With one auspicious, and one dropping eye,
With mirth in funeral, and with dirge in marriage,
In equal scale weighing delight and dole),
Taken to wife: nor have we herein barred
Your better wisdoms, which have freely gone
With this affair along:—for all, our thanks.
Now follows that you know, young Fortinbras,
Holding a weak supposal of our worth,
Or thinking, by our late dear brother's death,
Our state to be disjoint and out of frame,
Colleaguéd with this dream of his advantage,
He hath not failed to pester us with message,
Importing the surrender of those lands
Lost by his father, with all bands of law,
To our most valiant brother.—So much for him.
Now for ourself, and for this time of meeting.
Thus much the business is:—We have here writ
To Norway, uncle of young Fortinbras,—
Who, impotent and bed-rid, scarcely hears
Of this his nephew's purpose,—to suppress
His further gait herein; in that the levies,
The lists, and full proportions, are all made
Out of his subject:—and we here despatch
You, good Cornelius, and you, Voltimand,
For bearers of this greeting to old Norway;
Giving to you no further personal power
To business with the king, more than the scope
Of these dilated articles allow.
Farewell; and let your haste commend your duty.
  Cor. ⎱ In that, and all things, will we shew
  Vol. ⎰   our duty.
  King. We doubt it nothing; heartily farewell.
                    [*Exeunt* VOLTIMAND *and* CORNELIUS.
And now, Laertes, what's the news with you?
You told us of some suit: what is 't, Laertes?
You cannot speak of reason to the Dane,
And lose your voice: what wouldst thou beg,
          Laertes,
That shall not be my offer, not thy asking?
The head is not more native to the heart,

The hand more instrumental to the mouth,
Than is the throne of Denmark to thy father.
What wouldst thou have, Laertes?

Laer.   My dread lord,
Your leave and favour to return to France;
From whence, though willingly I came to Denmark,
To shew my duty in your coronation;
Yet now, I must confess, that duty done,
My thoughts and wishes bend again toward France,
And bow them to your gracious leave and pardon.

King. Have you your father's leave? what says Polonius?

Pol. He hath, my lord, wrung from me my slow leave,
By laboursome petition; and, at last,
Upon his will I sealed my hard consent:
I do beseech you, give him leave to go.

King. Take thy fair hour, Laertes; time be thine,
And thy best graces: spend it at thy will.—
But now, my cousin Hamlet, and my son:

Ham. A little more than kin, and less than kind.
                              [*Aside.*

King. How is it that the clouds still hang on you?

Ham. Not so, my lord; I am too much i' the sun.

Queen. Good Hamlet, cast thy nighted colour off,
And let thine eye look like a friend on Denmark.
Do not for ever, with thy vailéd lids,
Seek for thy noble father in the dust:
Thou know'st 't is common; all that live must die,
Passing through nature to eternity.

Ham. Ay, madam, it is common.

Queen.   If it be,
Why seems it so particular with thee?

Ham. Seems, madam! nay, it is; I know not seems.
'T is not alone my inky cloak, good mother,
Nor customary suits of solemn black,
Nor windy suspiration of forced breath,—
No, nor the fruitful river in the eye,
Nor the dejected haviour of the visage,
Together with all forms, moods, shows of grief,
That can denote me truly. These, indeed, seem;
For they are actions that a man might play:
But I have that within which passeth show;
These but the trappings and the suits of woe.

King. 'T is sweet and commendable in your nature, Hamlet,
To give these mourning duties to your father:
But, you must know, your father lost a father;
That father lost, lost his; and the survivor bound
In filial obligation, for some term
To do obsequious sorrow: but to persever
In obstinate condolement, is a course
Of impious stubbornness; 't is unmanly grief:
It shews a will most incorrect to heaven;
A heart unfortified, a mind impatient;
An understanding simple and unschooled.
For what we know must be, and is as common
As any the most vulgar thing to sense,
Why should we, in our peevish opposition,
Take it to heart? Fie! 't is a fault to heaven,
A fault against the dead, a fault to nature,
To reason most absurd; whose common theme
Is death of fathers, and who still hath cried,
From the first corse till he that died to-day,
"This must be so." We pray you, throw to earth
This unprevailing woe; and think of us
As of a father: for let the world take note,
You are the most immediate to our throne;
And with no less nobility of love
Than that which dearest father bears his son,
Do I impart towards you.—For your intent
In going back to school in Wittenberg,
It is most retrograde to our desire:
And, we beseech you, bend you to remain
Here, in the cheer and comfort of our eye,
Our chiefest courtier, cousin, and our son.

Queen. Let not thy mother lose her prayers, Hamlet:
I pray thee stay with us; go not to Wittenberg.

Ham. I shall in all my best obey you, madam.

King. Why, 't is a loving and a fair reply;
Be as ourself in Denmark.—Madam, come;
This gentle and unforced accord of Hamlet
Sits smiling to my heart: in grace whereof,
No jocund health that Denmark drinks to-day,
But the great cannon to the clouds shall tell;
And the king's rouse the heavens shall bruit again,
Re-speaking earthly thunder. Come, away!

       [*Exeunt* KING, QUEEN, Lords, &c. POLONIUS,
              and LAERTES.

Ham. O, that this too too solid flesh would melt,
Thaw, and resolve itself into a dew!
Or that the Everlasting had not fixed
His canon 'gainst self-slaughter!—O God, O God!
How weary, stale, flat, and unprofitable,
Seem to me all the uses of this world!
Fie on 't, O fie! 't is an unweeded garden,
That grows to seed; things rank and gross in nature
Possess it merely.—That it should come to this!
But two months dead! nay, not so much, not two:
So excellent a king; that was, to this,
Hyperion to a satyr: so loving to my mother,
That he might not beteem the winds of heaven
Visit her face too roughly. Heaven and earth!
Must I remember?—why, she would hang on him
As if increase of appetite had grown
By what it fed on: and yet, within a month,—

Let me not think on 't ;—Frailty, thy name is
    woman !—
A little month ; or ere those shoes were old
With which she followed my poor father's body,
Like Niobe, all tears ;—why she, even she,—
O heaven ! a beast, that wants discourse of reason,
Would have mourned longer,—married with mine
    uncle,
My father's brother ; but no more like my father
Than I to Hercules :—within a month,
Ere yet the salt of most unrighteous tears
Had left the flushing in her gallèd eyes,
She married :—O most wicked speed, to post
With such dexterity to incestuous sheets !
It is not, nor it cannot come to, good ;
But break, my heart ; for I must hold my tongue.

Enter HORATIO, BERNARDO, *and* MARCELLUS.

 Hor. Hail to your lordship !
 Ham. I am glad to see you well :
Horatio,—or I do forget myself.
 Hor. The same, my lord, and your poor ser-
  vant ever.
 Ham. Sir, my good friend ; I 'll change that
  name with you.
And what make you from Wittenberg, Horatio?—
Marcellus ?
 Mar. My good lord,—
 Ham. I am very glad to see you ; good even,
  sir.—
But what, in faith, make you from Wittenberg ?
 Hor. A truant disposition, good my lord.
 Ham. I would not hear your enemy say so ;
Nor shall you do mine ear that violence,
To make it truster of your own report
Against yourself : I know you are no truant.
But what is your affair in Elsinore ?
We 'll teach you to drink deep ere you depart.
 Hor. My lord, I came to see your father's
  funeral.
 Ham. I pray thee, do not mock me, fellow-
  student :
I think it was to see my mother's wedding.
 Hor. Indeed, my lord, it followed hard upon.
 Ham. Thrift, thrift, Horatio ! the funeral baked
  meats
Did coldly furnish forth the marriage tables.
'Would I had met my dearest foe in heaven
Ere I had ever seen that day, Horatio.
My father ! methinks I see my father.
 Hor. O, where,
My lord ?
 Ham. In my mind's eye, Horatio.
 Hor. I saw him once ; he was a goodly king.
 Ham. He was a man, take him for all in all,
I shall not look upon his like again.
 Hor. My lord, I think I saw him yesternight.

 Ham. Saw who ?
 Hor. My lord, the king your father.
 Ham. The king my father !
 Hor. Season your admiration for a while
With an attent ear ; till I may deliver,
Upon the witness of these gentlemen,
This marvel to you.
 Ham. For heaven's love, let me hear !
 Hor. Two nights together had these gentlemen,
Marcellus and Bernardo, on their watch,
In the dead waste and middle of the night,
Been thus encountered :—A figure like your
  father,
Armed at all points, exactly, cap-à-pé,
Appears before them, and, with solemn march,
Goes slow and stately by them : thrice he walked
By their oppressed and fear-surprisèd eyes,
Within his truncheon's length : whilst they, dis-
  tilled
Almost to jelly with the act of fear,
Stand dumb, and speak not to him. This to me
In dreadful secrecy impart they did ;
And I with them the third night kept the watch :
Where, as they had delivered, both in time,
Form of the thing, each word made true and good,
The apparition comes. I knew your father :
These hands are not more like.
 Ham. But where was this ?
 Mar. My lord, upon the platform, where we
  watched.
 Ham. Did you not speak to it ?
 Hor. My lord, I did ;
But answer made it none : yet once, methought,
It lifted up its head, and did address
Itself to motion, like as it would speak :
But even then the morning cock crew loud ;
And at the sound it shrunk in haste away,
And vanished from our sight.
 Ham. 'T is very strange.
 Hor. As I do live, my honoured lord, 't is true ;
And we did think it writ down in our duty,
To let you know of it.
 Ham. Indeed, indeed, sirs, but this troubles me.
Hold you the watch to-night ?
 All. We do, my lord.
 Ham. Armed, say you ?
 All. Armed, my lord.
 Ham. From top to toe ?
 All. My lord, from head to foot.
 Ham. Then saw you not his face ?
 Hor. O yes, my lord ; he wore his beaver up.
 Ham. What, looked he frowningly ?
 Hor. A countenance more
In sorrow than in anger.
 Ham. Pale, or red ?
 Hor. Nay, very pale.
 Ham. And fixed his eyes upon you ?

Hor. Most constantly.

Ham.   I would I had been there.

Hor. It would have much amazed you.

Ham.   Very like,
Very like.   Stayed it long?

Hor. While one with moderate haste might
      tell a hundred.

Mar.
Ber. } Longer, longer.

Hor. Not when I saw it.

Ham. His beard was grizzled?—no?

Hor. It was as I have seen it in his life,
A sable silvered.

Ham.   I will watch to-night;
Perchance 'twill walk again.

Hor.   I warrant it will.

Ham. If it assume my noble father's person,
I 'll speak to it, though hell itself should gape,
And bid me hold my peace.   I pray you all,
If you have hitherto concealed this sight,
Let it be tenable in your silence still;
And whatsoever else shall hap to-night,
Give it an understanding, but no tongue:
I will requite your loves.   So, fare you well:
Upon the platform, 'twixt eleven and twelve,
I 'll visit you.

All.   Our duty to your honour.

Ham. Your loves, as mine to you; farewell.

      [*Exeunt* HORATIO, MARCELLUS, *and*
            BERNARDO.

My father's spirit in arms! all is not well;
I doubt some foul play: 'would the night were
      come!
Till then, sit still my soul.   Foul deeds will rise,
Though all the earth o'erwhelm them, to men's
      eyes.   [*Exit.*

SCENE III.—*A Room in* POLONIUS' *House.*

Enter LAERTES *and* OPHELIA.

Laer. My necessaries are embarked; farewell:
And, sister, as the winds give benefit,
And convoy is assistant, do not sleep,
But let me hear from you.

Oph.   Do you doubt that?

Laer. For Hamlet, and the trifling of his favour,
Hold it a fashion and a toy in blood;
A violet in the youth of primy nature,
Forward, not permanent; sweet, not lasting;
The pérfume and suppliance of a minute;—
No more.

Oph.   No more but so?

Laer.   Think it no more:
For nature, crescent, does not grow alone
In thews and bulk; but, as this temple waxes,
The inward service of the mind and soul

Grows wide withal.   Perhaps he loves you now;
And now no soil nor cautel doth besmirch
The virtue of his will: but you must fear:
His greatness weighed, his will is not his own;
For he himself is subject to his birth:
He may not, as unvalued persons do,
Carve for himself; for on his choice depends
The safety and the health of the whole state;
And therefore must his choice be circumscribed
Unto the voice and yielding of that body
Whereof he is the head: then, if he says he loves
      you,
It fits your wisdom so far to believe it
As he in his particular act and place
May give his saying deed; which is no further
Than the main voice of Denmark goes withal.
Then weigh what loss your honour may sustain,
If with too credent ear you list his songs;
Or lose your heart; or your chaste treasure open
To his unmastered importunity.
Fear it, Ophelia; fear it, my dear sister;
And keep you in the rear of your affection,
Out of the shot and danger of desire.
The chariest maid is prodigal enough,
If she unmask her beauty to the moon:
Virtue itself scapes not calumnious strokes:
The canker galls the infants of the spring,
Too oft before their buttons be disclosed;
And in the morn and liquid dew of youth,
Contagious blastments are most imminent.
Be wary, then: best safety lies in fear:
Youth to itself rebels, though none else near.

Oph. I shall the effect of this good lesson keep,
As watchman to my heart: but good, my brother,
Do not, as some ungracious pastors do,
Shew me the steep and thorny way to heaven;
Whilst, like a puffed and reckless libertine,
Himself the primrose path of dalliance treads,
And recks not his own read.

Laer.   O, fear me not.
I stay too long: but here my father comes.

Enter POLONIUS.

A double blessing is a double grace;
Occasion smiles upon a second leave.

Pol. Yet here, Laertes! aboard, aboard, for
      shame;
The winds sits in the shoulder of your sail,
And you are stayed for: there,—my blessing
      with you:
      [*Laying his hand on* LAERTES' *head.*
And these few precepts in thy memory
Look thou chárácter.   Give thy thoughts no
      tongue,
Nor any unproportioned thought his act.
Be thou familiar, but by no means vulgar.
The friends thou hast, and their adoption tried,

Grapple them to thy soul with hoops of steel ;
But do not dull thy palm with entertainment
Of each new-hatched, unfledged comrade. Be-
  ware
Of entrance to a quarrel ; but, being in,
Bear it that the opposer may beware of thee.
Give every man thine ear, but few thy voice :
Take each man's censure, but reserve thy judg-
  ment.
Costly thy habit as thy purse can buy,
But not expressed in fancy ; rich, not gaudy :
For the apparel oft proclaims the man ;
And they in France, of the best rank and station,
Are of a most select and generous chief in that.
Neither a borrower nor a lender be :
For loan oft loses both itself and friend ;
And borrowing dulls the edge of husbandry.
This above all,—to thine ownself be true ;
And it must follow, as the night the day,
Thou canst not then be false to any man.
Farewell : my blessing season this in thee !

 Laer. Most humbly do I take my leave, my lord.
 Pol. The time invites you ; go, your servants
  tend.
 Laer. Farewell, Ophelia ; and remember well
What I have said to you.
 Oph. 'Tis in my memory locked,
And you yourself shall keep the key of it.
 Laer. Farewell.   [*Exit.*
 Pol. What is 't, Ophelia, he hath said to you?
 Oph. So please you, something touching the
  lord Hamlet.
 Pol. Marry, well bethought :
'Tis told me, he hath very oft of late
Given private time to you ; and you yourself
Have of your audience been most free and boun-
  teous :
If it be so (as so 'tis put on me,
And that in way of caution), I must tell you,
You do not understand yourself so clearly
As it behoves my daughter and your honour.
What is between you?—give me up the truth.
 Oph. He hath, my lord, of late, made many
  tenders
Of his affection to me.
 Pol. Affection? pooh ! you speak like a green girl,
Unsifted in such perilous circumstance.
Do you believe his tenders, as you call them ?
 Oph. I do not know, my lord, what I should
  think.
 Pol. Marry, I'll teach you : think yourself a
  baby ;
That you have ta'en these tenders for true pay,
Which are not sterling. Tender yourself more
  dearly ;
Or (not to crack the wind of the poor phrase,
Wronging it thus) you 'll tender me a fool.

 Oph. My lord, he hath impórtuned me with love,
In honourable fashion.
 Pol. Ay, fashion you may call it ; go to, go to.
 Oph. And hath given countenance to his
  speech, my lord,
With almost all the holy vows of heaven.
 Pol. Ay, springes to catch woodcocks. I do
  know,
When the blood burns, how prodigal the soul
Lends the tongue vows : these blazes, daughter,
Giving more light than heat,—extinct in both,
Even in their promise, as it is a making,—
You must not take for fire. From this time
Be somewhat scanter of your maiden presence ;
Set your entreatments at a higher rate
Than a command to parley. For lord Hamlet,
Believe so much in him, that he is young ;
And with a larger tether may he walk
Than may be given you. In few, Ophelia,
Do not believe his vows : for they are brokers ;
Not of that dye which their investments shew,
But mere implorators of unholy suits,
Breathing like sanctified and pious bonds,
The better to beguile. This is for all :—
I would not, in plain terms, from this time forth,
Have you so slander any moment's leisure,
As to give words or talk with the lord Hamlet.
Look to 't, I charge you ; come your ways.
 Oph. I shall obey, my lord.   [*Exeunt.*

SCENE IV.—*The Platform.*

Enter HAMLET, HORATIO, *and* MARCELLUS.

 Ham. The air bites shrewdly ; it is very cold.
 Hor. It is a nipping and an eager air.
 Ham. What hour now?
 Hor. I think it lacks of twelve.
 Mar. No, it is struck.
 Hor. Indeed ! I heard it not ; it then draws
  near the season
Wherein the spirit held his wont to walk.
  [*A flourish of trumpets, and ordnance shot
   off within.*
What does this mean, my lord ?
 Ham. The king doth wake to-night, and takes
  his rouse,
Keeps wassel, and the swaggering up-spring reels ;
And, as he drains his draughts of Rhenish down,
The kettle-drum and trumpet thus bray out
The triumph of his pledge.
 Hor. Is it a custom ?
 Ham. Ay, marry, is 't :
But to my mind,—though I am native here,
And to the manner born,—it is a custom
More honoured in the breach than the observance.

This heavy-headed revel, east and west,
Makes us traduced and taxed of other nations:
They clepe us drunkards, and with swinish phrase
Soil our addition; and indeed it takes
From our achievements, though performed at
     height,
The pith and marrow of our attribute.
So, oft it chances in particular men,
That for some vicious mole of nature in them,
As, in their birth (wherein they are not guilty,
Since nature cannot choose its origin),
By the o'ergrowth of some complexion,
Oft breaking down the pales and forts of reason;

Or by some habit that too much o'er-leavens
The form of plausive manners; that these men,
Carrying, I say, the stamp of one defect,
Being nature's livery, or fortune's star,
Their virtues else (be they as pure as grace,
As infinite as man may undergo)
Shall in the general censure take corruption
From that particular fault: the dram of base
Doth all the noble substance often dout,
To his own scandal.

          Enter Ghost.

  Hor. Look, my lord, it comes!
  Ham. Angels and ministers of grace defend us!
Be thou a spirit of health, or goblin damned,
Bring with thee airs from heaven, or blasts from
     hell,
Be thy intents wicked, or charitable,
Thou com'st in such a questionable shape,
That I will speak to thee: I'll call thee Hamlet,
King, father, royal Dane: O, answer me:
Let me not burst in ignorance; but tell,
Why thy canonised bones, hearséd in death,
Have burst their cerements! why the sepulchre,

Wherein we saw thee quietly in-urned,
Hath oped his ponderous and marble jaws,
To cast thee up again! What may this mean,
That thou, dead corse, again, in cómplete steel,
Revisit'st thus the glimpses of the moon,
Making night hideous; and we fools of nature,
So horribly to shake our disposition
With thoughts beyond the reaches of our souls?
Say, why is this? wherefore? what should we do?

Hor. It beckons you to go away with it,
As if it some impartment did desire
To you alone.

Mar.　　　Look, with what courteous action
It waves you to a more removéd ground:
But do not go with it.

Hor.　　　No, by no means.

Ham. It will not speak; then I will follow it.

Hor. Do not, my lord.

Ham.　　　Why, what should be the fear?
I do not set my life at a pin's fee;
And, for my soul, what can it do to that,
Being a thing immortal as itself?
It waves me forth again: I 'll follow it.

Hor. What, if it tempt you toward the flood, my
　　　lord,
Or to the dreadful summit of the cliff
That beetles o'er his base into the sea?
And there assume some other horrible form,
Which might deprive your sovereignty of reason,
And draw you into madness? think of it:
The very place puts toys of desperation,
Without more motive, into every brain
That looks so many fathoms to the sea,
And hears it roar beneath.

Ham.　　　It waves me still:—
Go on, I 'll follow thee.

Mar. You shall not go, my lord.

Ham.　　　Hold off your hands.

Hor. Be ruled; you shall not go.

Ham.　　　My fate cries out,
And makes each petty artery in this body
As hardy as the Némean lion's nerve.

　　　　　　　　　　[*Ghost beckons.*
Still am I called;—unhand me, gentlemen:

　　　　　　　　[*Breaking from them.*
By heaven, I 'll make a ghost of him that lets me:
I say, away!—Go on; I 'll follow thee!

　　　　　　[*Exeunt Ghost and* HAMLET.

Hor. He waxes desperate with imagination.

Mar. Let's follow; 'tis not fit thus to obey
　　　him.

Hor. Have after. To what issue will this
　　　come?

Mar. Something is rotten in the state of Den-
　　　mark.

Hor. Heaven will direct it.

Mar. Nay, let's follow him.　　　[*Exeunt.*

SCENE V.—*A more remote part of the Platform.*

　　　Re-enter Ghost *and* HAMLET.

Ham. Whither wilt thou lead me? speak; I 'll go
　　　no further.

Ghost. Mark me.

Ham.　　　I will.

Ghost.　　　　　My hour is almost come,
When I to sulphurous and tormenting flames
Must render up myself.

Ham.　　　Alas, poor ghost!

Ghost. Pity me not, but lend thy serious hearing
To what I shall unfold.

Ham. Speak; I am bound to hear.

Ghost. So art thou to revenge, when thou shalt
　　　hear.

Ham. What?

Ghost. I am thy father's spirit;
Doomed for a certain term to walk the night;
And, for the day, confined to fast in fires,
Till the foul crimes done in my days of nature
Are burnt and purged away. But that I am forbid
To tell the secrets of my prison-house,
I could a tale unfold, whose lightest word
Would harrow up thy soul; freeze thy young
　　　blood;
Make thy two eyes, like stars, start from their
　　　spheres;
Thy knotted and combinéd locks to part,
And each particular hair to stand an-end,
Like quills upon the fretful porcupine:
But this eternal blazon must not be
To ears of flesh and blood:—List, list, O list!—
If thou didst ever thy dear father love,—

Ham. O, heaven!

Ghost. Revenge his foul and most unnatural
　　　murder.

Ham. Murder?

Ghost. Murder most foul, as in the best it is;
But this most foul, strange, and unnatural.

Ham. Haste me to know it; that I, with wings
　　　as swift
As meditation, or the thoughts of love,
May sweep to my revenge.

Ghost.　　　I find thee apt;
And duller shouldst thou be than the fat weed
That rots itself in ease on Lethe wharf,
Wouldst thou not stir in this. Now, Hamlet, hear;
'T is given out that, sleeping in mine orchard,
A serpent stung me; so the whole ear of Denmark
Is by a forgéd process of my death
Rankly abused: but know, thou noble youth,
The serpent that did sting thy father's life,
Now wears his crown.

Ham. O, my prophetic soul! my uncle!

Ghost. Ay, that incestuous, that adulterate
　　　beast,

With witchcraft of his wit, with traitorous gifts,
(O wicked wit, and gifts, that have the power
So to seduce!) won to his shameful lust
The will of my most seeming virtuous queen:
O, Hamlet, what a falling-off was there!
From me, whose love was of that dignity
That it went hand in hand even with the vow
I made to her in marriage; and to decline
Upon a wretch, whose natural gifts were poor
To those of mine!
But virtue, as it never will be moved,
Though lewdness court it in a shape of heaven;
So lust, though to a radiant angel linked,
Will sate itself in a celestial bed,
And prey on garbage.
But, soft! methinks I scent the morning air;
Brief let me be:—Sleeping within mine orchard,
My custom always of the afternoon,
Upon my sécure hour thy uncle stole,
With juice of curséd hebenon in a vial,
And in the porches of mine ears did pour
The leperous distilment; whose effect
Holds such an enmity with blood of man,
That, swift as quicksilver, it courses through
The natural gates and alleys of the body;
And, with a sudden vigour, it doth posset
And curd, like aigre droppings into milk,
The thin and wholesome blood: so did it mine;
And in a most instant tetter barked about,
Most lazar-like, with vile and loathsome crust,
All my smooth body.
Thus was I, sleeping, by a brother's hand,
Of life, of crown, of queen, at once despatched:
Cut off even in the blossoms of my sin,
Unhouselled, disappointed, unanelled;
No reckoning made, but sent to my account
With all my imperfections on my head:
O, horrible! O, horrible! Most horrible!
If thou hast nature in thee, bear it not;
Let not the royal bed of Denmark be
A couch for luxury and damnéd incest.
But, howsoever thou pursuest this act,
Taint not thy mind, nor let thy soul contrive
Against thy mother aught; leave her to heaven,
And to those thorns that in her bosom lodge,
To prick and sting her. Fare thee well at once!
The glow-worm shews the matin to be near,
And 'gins to pale his uneffectual fire:
Adieu, adieu, adieu! remember me.   *[Exit.*

  Ham. O all you host of heaven! O earth! What
      else?
And shall I couple hell? O fie!—Hold, hold, my
      heart;
And you, my sinews, grow not instant old,
But bear me stiffly up!—Remember thee!
Ay, thou poor ghost, while memory holds a seat
In this distracted globe. Remember thee!

Yea, from the table of my memory
I'll wipe away all trivial fond recórds,
All saws of books, all forms, all pressures past,
That youth and observation copied there;
And thy commandment all alone shall live
Within the book and volume of my brain,
Unmixed with baser matter: yes, by heaven!
O most pernicious woman!
O villain, villain, smiling, damnéd villain!
My tables:—meet it is I set it down,
That one may smile, and smile, and be a villain;
At least, I am sure it may be so in Denmark:
                            [Writing.
So, uncle, there you are. Now, to my word;
It is, "Adieu, adieu! remember me."
I have sworn 't.
  Hor. [*within*]. My lord, my lord,—
  Mar. [*within*]. Lord Hamlet,—
  Hor. [*within*]. Heaven secure him!
  Ham. So be it!
  Mar. [*within*]. Hillo, ho, ho, my lord!
  Ham. Hillo, ho, ho, boy! come, bird, come.

        Enter HORATIO *and* MARCELLUS.

  Mar. How is 't, my noble lord?
  Hor.   What news, my lord?
  Ham. O, wonderful!
  Hor.   Good my lord, tell it.
  Ham.   No;
You will reveal it.
  Hor. Not I, my lord, by heaven.
  Mar.   Nor I, my lord.
  Ham. How say you, then; would heart of man
      once think it?
But you 'll be secret?
  Hor. }
        } Ay, by heaven, my lord.
  Mar. }
  Ham. There's ne'er a villain dwelling in all
      Denmark,
But he's an arrant knave.
  Hor. There needs no ghost, my lord, come from
      the grave,
To tell us this.
  Ham.   Why, right; you are in the right;
And so, without more circumstance at all,
I hold it fit that we shake hands and part:
You, as your business and desire shall point you;
For every man hath business and desire,
Such as it is;—and, for my own poor part,
Look you, I will go pray.
  Hor. These are but wild and whirling words, my
      lord.
  Ham. I am sorry they offend you, heartily;
Yes 'faith, heartily.
  Hor.   There's no offence, my lord.
  Ham. Yes, by St. Patrick, but there is, Horatio,
And much offence too. Touching this vision here,—

It is an honest ghost; that let me tell you:
For your desire to know what is between us,
O'ermaster it as you may. And now, good friends,
As you are friends, scholars, and soldiers,
Give me one poor request.
   Hor.   What is 't, my lord?
We will.
   Ham. Never make known what you have seen
       to-night.
   Hor. }
   Mar. } My lord, we will not.
   Ham   Nay, but swear 't.

   Hor.   In faith,
My lord, not I.
   Mar.   Nor I, my lord, in faith.
   Ham. Upon my sword.
   Mar.   We have sworn, my lord, already.
   Ham. Indeed, upon my sword; indeed.
   Ghost [*beneath*]. Swear!
   Ham. Ha, ha, boy! say'st thou so? art thou
       there, truepenny?
Come on;—you hear this fellow in the cellarage:
Consent to swear.
   Hor.   Propose the oath, my lord.

Ham. Never to speak of this that you have seen,
Swear by my sword.

    Ghost [*beneath*]. Swear !

    Ham. Hic et ubique? then we will shift our
        ground:—

Come hither, gentlemen,
And lay your hands again upon my sword:
Swear by my sword,
Never to speak of this that you have heard.

    Ghost [*beneath*]. Swear by his sword !

    Ham. Well said, old mole ! canst work i' the
        earth so fast?

A worthy pioneer !—Once more remove, good
    friends.

    Hor. O day and night, but this is wondrous
        strange!

    Ham. And therefore as a stranger give it wel-
        come.

There are more things in heaven and earth,
    Horatio,
Than are dreamt of in your philosophy.
But come :—
Here, as before, never, so help you mercy !

How strange or odd soe'er I bear myself,
As I, perchance, hereafter shall think meet
To put an antic disposition on,—
That you, at such times seeing me, never shall,
With arms encumbered thus, or this head-shake,
Or by pronouncing of some doubtful phrase,
As " Well, well, we know ; " or, " We could, an if
we would ; " or, " If we list to speak ; " or, " There
be, an if they might ; "—
Or such ambiguous giving out, to note
That you know aught of me :—this do you swear,
So grace and mercy at your most need help you !

    Ghost [*beneath*]. Swear!

    Ham. Rest, rest, perturbéd spirit ! So, gentle-
        men,

With all my love I do commend me to you;
And what so poor a man as Hamlet is
May do, to express his love and friending to you,
God willing, shall not lack. Let us go in together;
And still your fingers on your lips, I pray.
The time is out of joint ;—O cursed spite,
That ever I was born to set it right !
Nay, come, let's go together.   [*Exeunt.*

Then came each actor on his ass.

ACT II

SCENE I.—*A Room in* POLONIUS' *House.*

Enter POLONIUS *and* REYNALDO.

Pol. Give him this money, and these notes, Reynaldo.

Rey. I will, my lord.

Pol. You shall do marvellous wisely, good Rey-
naldo,
Before you visit him, to make inquiry
Of his behaviour.

Rey.   My lord, I did intend it.

Pol. Marry, well said: very well said.   Look
you, sir,
Inquire me first what Danskers are in Paris;
And how, and who, what means, and where they
keep,
What company, at what expense; and finding,
By this encompassment and drift of question,
That they do know my son, come you more nearer
Than your particular demands will touch it:
Take you, as 't were, some distant knowledge of
him;
As thus: " I know his father, and his friends,
And, in part, him." Do you mark this, Reynaldo?

Rey. Ay, very well, my lord.

Pol. "And, in part, him;—but," you may say,
" not well:
But, if 't be he I mean, he 's very wild;
Addicted so and so; "—and there put on him
What forgeries you please; marry, none so rank
As may dishonour him; take heed of that;
But, sir, such wanton, wild, and usual slips,
As are companions noted and most known
To youth and liberty.

Rey.   As gaming, my lord.

Pol. Ay, or drinking, fencing, swearing, quarrelling,
Drabbing :—you may go so far.

Rey. My lord, that would dishonour him.

Pol. 'Faith, no; as you may season it in the
charge.

You must not put another scandal on him,
That he is open to incontinency;
That 's not my meaning: but breathe his faults so
quaintly,
That they may seem the taints of liberty;
The flash and outbreak of a fiery mind;
A savageness in unreclaiméd blood,
Of general assault.

Rey.   But, my good lord,—

Pol. Wherefore should you do this?

Rey.   Ay, my lord,
I would know that.

Pol.   Marry, sir, here 's my drift;
And I believe it is a fetch of warrant:
You laying these slight sullies on my son,
As 't were a thing a little soiled i' the working,
Mark you,
Your party in convérse, him you would sound,
Having ever seen, in the prenominate crimes,
The youth you breathe of, guilty,—be assured,
He closes with you in this consequence :
"Good sir," or so; or "friend," or "gentleman,"—
According to the phrase, or the addition,
Of man and country :—

Rey.   Very good, my lord.

Pol. And then, sir, does he this,—he does—
What was I about to say?
By the mass, I was about to say something :
Where did I leave?

Rey. At " closes in the consequence."

Pol. At " closes in the consequence;" ay, marry;
He closes with you thus : " I know the gentleman;
I saw him yesterday, or t' other day,
Or then, or then; with such, or such; and, as you
say,
There was he gaming; there o'ertook in his rouse;
There falling out at tennis;" or perchance,
" I saw him enter such a house of sale"
(Videlicet, a brothel), or so forth.
See you now;
Your bait of falsehood takes this carp of truth :

And thus do we of wisdom and of reach,
With windlasses, and with assays of bias,
By indirections find directions out:
So, by my former lecture and advice,
Shall you my son:—you have me, have you not?

Rey. My lord, I have.

Pol. God be wi' you; fare you well.

Rey. Good my lord,—

Pol. Observe his inclination in yourself.

Rey. I shall, my lord.

Pol. And let him ply his music.

Rey. Well, my lord. [*Exit.*

Enter OPHELIA.

Pol. Farewell!—How now, Ophelia? what's the
matter?

Oph. O, my lord, my lord, I have been so affrighted!

Pol. With what, in the name of heaven?

Oph. My lord, as I was sewing in my closet,
Lord Hamlet,—with his doublet all unbraced;
No hat upon his head; his stockings fouled,
Ungartered, and down-gyvéd to his ancle;
Pale as his shirt; his knees knocking each other;
And with a look so piteous in purport,
As if he had been looséd out of hell,
To speak of horrors,—he comes before me.

Pol. Mad for thy love?

Oph. My lord, I do not know;
But truly I do fear it.

Pol. What said he?

Oph. He took me by the wrist, and held me hard;
Then goes he to the length of all his arm;
And, with his other hand thus o'er his brow,
He falls to such perusal of my face,
As he would draw it. Long stayed he so;
At last, a little shaking of mine arm,
And thrice his head thus waving up and down,—
He raised a sigh so piteous and profound,
As it did seem to shatter all his bulk,
And end his being. That done, he lets me go;
And, with his head over his shoulder turned,
He seemed to find his way without his eyes;
For out o' doors he went without their help,
And to the last bended their light on me.

Pol. Come, go with me; I will go seek the king.
This is the very ecstasy of love;
Whose violent property foredoes itself,
And leads the will to desperate undertakings,
As oft as any passion under heaven
That does afflict our natures. I am sorry,—
What, have you given him any hard words of late?

Oph. No, my good lord; but, as you did com-
mand,
I did repel his letters, and denied
His áccess to me.

Pol. That hath made him mad.

I am sorry that with better heed and judgment
I had not quoted him: I feared he did but trifle,
And meant to wreck thee; but, beshrew my
jealousy!
It seems it is as proper to our age
To cast beyond ourselves in our opinions,
As it is common for the younger sort
To lack discretion. Come, go we to the king:
This must be known; which, being kept close,
might move
More grief to hide, than hate to utter love.
Come. [*Exeunt.*

SCENE II.—*A Room in the Castle.*

Enter KING, QUEEN, ROSENCRANTZ, GUILDEN-
STERN, *and* Attendants.

King. Welcome, dear Rosencrantz and Guil-
denstern!
Moreover that we much did long to see you,
The need we have to use you did provoke
Our hasty sending. Something have you heard
Of Hamlet's transformation; so I call it,
Since not the exterior nor the inward man
Resembles that it was: what it should be,
More than his father's death, that thus hath put
him
So much from the understanding of himself,
I cannot deem of. I entreat you both,
That, being of so young days brought up with him,
And since so neighboured to his youth and humour,
That you vouchsafe your rest here in our court
Some little time: so by your companies
To draw him on to pleasures; and to gather,
So much as from occasion you may glean,
Whether aught, to us unknown, afflicts him thus,
That, opened, lies within our remedy.

Queen. Good gentlemen, he hath much talked of
you;
And, sure I am, two men there are not living
To whom he more adheres. If it will please you
To shew us so much gentry and good will
As to expend your time with us awhile,
For the supply and profit of our hope,
Your visitation shall receive such thanks
As fits a king's remembrance.

Ros. Both your majesties
Might, by the sovereign power you have of us,
Put your dread pleasures more into command
Than to entreaty.

Guil. But we both obey;
And here give up ourselves, in the full bent,
To lay our service freely at your feet,
To be commanded.

King. Thanks, Rosencrantz and gentle Guildenstern.

Queen. Thanks, Guildenstern and gentle
    Rosencrantz:
And I beseech you instantly to visit
My too much changéd son.—Go, some of you,
And bring these gentleman where Hamlet is.

    Guil. Heavens make our presence and our prac-
        tices
Pleasant and helpful to him!

    Queen.   Amen!
    [*Exeunt* ROSENCRANTZ, GUILDENSTERN, *and*
    some Attendants.

Enter POLONIUS.

    Pol. The ambassadors from Norway, my good
        lord,
Are joyfully returned.

    King. Thou still hast been the father of good
        news.

    Pol. Have I, my lord? Assure you, my good
        liege,
I hold my duty as I hold my soul,
Both to my God, and to my gracious king:
And I do think (or else this brain of mine
Hunts not the trail of policy so sure
As it hath used to do) that I have found
The very cause of Hamlet's lunacy.

    King. O, speak of that; that do I long to hear.

    Pol. Give first admittance to the ambassadors;
My news shall be the fruit to that great feast.

    King. Thyself do grace to them, and bring them in.
        [*Exit* POLONIUS.
He tells me, my dear Gertrude, he hath found
The head and source of all your son's distemper.

    Queen. I doubt it is no other but the main;
His father's death, and our o'er-hasty marriage.

Re-enter POLONIUS, *with* VOLTIMAND *and* COR-
    NELIUS.

    King. Well, we shall sift him.—Welcome, my
        good friends!
Say, Voltimand, what from our brother Norway?

    Volt. Most fair return of greetings and desires.
Upon our first, he sent out to suppress
His nephew's levies; which to him appeared
To be a preparation 'gainst the Polack;
But, better looked into, he truly found
It was against your highness: whereat grieved,
That so his sickness, age, and impotence,
Was falsely borne in hand, sends out arrests
On Fortinbras; which he, in brief, obeys;
Receives rebuke from Norway; and, in fine,
Makes vow before his uncle, never more
To give th' assay of arms against your majesty.
Whereon old Norway, overcome with joy,

Gives him three thousand crowns in annual fee;
And his commission to employ those soldiers,
So levied as before, against the Polack:
With an entreaty, herein further shewn,
                 [*Gives a paper.*
That it might please you to give quiet pass
Through your dominions for this enterprise;
On such regards of safety and allowance
As therein are set down.
    King.   It likes us well;
And, at our more considered time we 'll read,
Answer, and think upon this business.
Meantime, we thank you for your well-took labour.
Go to your rest; at night we 'll feast together:
Most welcome home!
           [*Exeunt* VOLTIMAND *and* CORNELIUS.
    Pol.   This business is well ended.—
My liege, and madam, to expostulate
What majesty should be, what duty is,
Why day is day, night night, and time is time,
Were nothing but to waste night, day, and time.
Therefore, since brevity is the soul of wit,
And tediousness the limbs and outward flourishes,
I will be brief:—Your noble son is mad:
Mad call I it; for to define true madness,
What is 't but to be nothing else but mad?
But let that go.
    Queen.   More matter, with less art.
    Pol. Madam, I swear I use no art at all.
That he is mad, 't is true: 't is true, 't is pity;
And pity 't is, 't is true: a foolish figure;
But farewell it, for I will use no art.
Mad let us grant him, then: and now remains
That we find out the cause of this effect;
Or rather say, the cause of this defect;
For this effect, defective, comes by cause:
Thus it remains, and the remainder thus.
Perpend:
I have a daughter; have, while she is mine;
Who, in her duty and obedience, mark,
Hath given me this: now gather, and surmise.

              Reads.
—"To the celestial, and my soul's idol, the most
beautified Ophelia;—

That 's an ill phrase, a vile phrase; "beautified" is
a vile phrase; but you shall hear. Thus:—

              Reads.
" In her excellent white bosom, these."

    Queen. Came this from Hamlet to her?
    Pol. Good madam, stay awhile; I will be
    faithful.
              Reads.
" Doubt thou the stars are fire;
     Doubt that the sun doth move;
     Doubt truth to be a liar;
     But never doubt I love.

" O dear Ophelia, I am ill at these numbers; I have
not art to reckon my groans: but that I love thee best,
O most best, believe it. Adieu!

    " Thine evermore, most dear lady, whilst this
               machine is to him, HAMLET."

This in obedience, hath my daughter shewn me;
And more above, hath his solicitings,
As they fell out by time, by means, and place,
All given to mine ear.
    King.   But how hath she
Received his love?
    Pol.   What do you think of me?
    King. As of a man faithful and honourable.
    Pol. I would fain prove so. But what might you
    think,
When I had seen this hot love on the wing
(As I perceived it, I must tell you that,
Before my daughter told me), what might you,
Or my dear majesty your queen here, think,
If I had played the desk or table-book;
Or given my heart a working mute and dumb;
Or looked upon this love with idle sight;
What might you think? No, I went round to work,
And my young mistress thus did I bespeak:
" Lord Hamlet is a prince out of thy sphere;
This must not be:" and then I precepts gave her,
That she should lock herself from his resort,
Admit no messengers, receive no tokens:
Which done, she took the fruits of my advice;
And he, repulséd (a short tale to make),
Fell into a sadness; then into a fast;
Thence to a watch; thence into a weakness;
Thence to a lightness; and, by this declension,
Into the madness wherein now he raves,
And all we mourn for.
    King.   Do you think 't is this?
    Queen. It may be, very likely.
    Pol. Hath there been such a time (I'd fain know
    that),
That I have positively said, " Tis so,"
When it proved otherwise?
    King.   Not that I know.
    Pol. Take this from this, if this be otherwise:
           [*Pointing to his head and shoulder.*
If circumstances lead me, I will find
Where truth is hid, though it were hid indeed
Within the centre.
    King.   How may we try it further?
    Pol. You know, sometimes he walks four hours
    together,
Here in the lobby.
    Queen.   So he does, indeed.
    Pol. At such a time I 'll loose my daughter to
    him:
Be you and I behind an arras then;
Mark the encounter: if he love her not,
And be not from his reason fallen thereon,

Let me be no assistant for a state,
But keep a farm, and carters.
   King.   We will try it.

        Enter HAMLET, *reading.*

   Queen. But look where sadly the poor wretch
     comes reading.

   Pol. Away, I do beseech you, both away;
I 'll board him presently:—O, give me leave.

    [*Exeunt* KING, QUEEN, *and* Attendants.

How does my good lord Hamlet?
   Ham. Well, god-'a-mercy.
   Pol. Do you know me, my lord?

   Ham. Excellent well; you are a fishmonger.
   Pol. Not I, my lord.
   Ham. Then I would you were so honest a man.
   Pol. Honest, my lord?
   Ham. Ay, sir; to be honest, as this world goes,
is to be one man picked out of ten thousand.
   Pol. That 's very true, my lord.
   Ham. For if the sun breed maggots in a dead
dog, being a god, kissing carrion——Have you a
daughter?
   Pol. I have, my lord.

   Ham. Let her not walk i' the sun : conception is
a blessing; but as your daughter may conceive,—
friend, look to 't.
   Pol. How say you by that? [*Aside.*] Still harping on my daughter : yet he knew me not at first;
he said I was a fishmonger: he is far gone, far
gone : and truly in my youth I suffered much extremity for love; very near this. I 'll speak to him
again.—What do you read, my lord?
   Ham. Words, words, words!
   Pol. What is the matter, my lord?

Ham. Between who?

Pol. I mean, the matter that you read, my lord.

Ham. Slanders, sir: for the satirical rogue says here, that old men have grey beards; that their faces are wrinkled; their eyes purging thick amber and plum-tree gum; and that they have a plentiful lack of wit, together with most weak hams. All of which, sir, though I most powerfully and potently believe, yet I hold it not honesty to have it thus set down; for you yourself, sir, should be as old as I am, if, like a crab, you could go backward.

Pol. Though this be madness, yet there's method in it [*Aside*]. Will you walk out of the air, my lord?

Ham. Into my grave.

Pol. Indeed, that is out o' the air.—How pregnant sometimes his replies are!—a happiness that often madness hits on, which reason and sanity could not so prosperously be delivered of. I will leave him, and suddenly contrive the means of meeting between him and my daughter.—My honourable lord, I will most humbly take my leave of you.

Ham. You cannot, sir, take from me anything that I will more willingly part withal; except my life, except my life, except my life.

Pol. Fare you well, my lord.

Ham. These tedious old fools!

Enter ROSENCRANTZ *and* GUILDENSTERN.

Pol. You go to seek the lord Hamlet; there he is.

Ros. God save you, sir!　　　[*To* POLONIUS.

　　　　　　　　　　　　　　　[*Exit* POLONIUS.

Guil. My honoured lord!

Ros. My most dear lord!

Ham. My excellent good friends! How dost thou, Guildenstern?—ah, Rosencrantz!—Good lads, how do ye both?

Ros. As the indifferent children of the earth.

Guil. Happy in that we are not over-happy; On Fortune's cap we are not the very button.

Ham. Nor the soles of her shoe?

Ros. Neither, my lord.

Ham. Then you live about her waist, or in the middle of her favours?

Guil. 'Faith, her privates we.

Ham. In the secret parts of Fortune? O, most true; she is a strumpet.—What news?

Ros. None, my lord; but that the world's grown honest.

Ham. Then is doomsday near: but your news is not true. Let me question more in particular: what have you, my good friends, deserved at the hands of Fortune, that she sends you to prison hither?

Guil. Prison, my lord?

Ham. Denmark's a prison.

Ros. Then is the world one.

Ham. A goodly one; in which there are many confines, wards, and dungeons; Denmark being one of the worst.

Ros. We think not so, my lord.

Ham. Why, then 'tis none to you; for there is nothing either good or bad, but thinking makes it so: to me it is a prison.

Ros. Why, then your ambition makes it one; 'tis too narrow for your mind.

Ham. O God! I could be bounded in a nutshell, and count myself a king of infinite space, were it not that I have bad dreams.

Guil. Which dreams, indeed, are ambition; for the very substance of the ambitious is merely the shadow of a dream.

Ham. A dream itself is but a shadow.

Ros. Truly; and I hold ambition of so airy and light a quality, that it is but a shadow's shadow.

Ham. Then are our beggars, bodies; and our monarchs and outstretched heroes the beggar's shadows. Shall we to the court? for, by my fay, I cannot reason.

Ros. } We'll wait upon you.
Guil. }

Ham. No such matter: I will not sort you with the rest of my servants; for, to speak to you like an honest man, I am most dreadfully attended. But, in the beaten way of friendship, what make you at Elsinore?

Ros. To visit you, my lord; no other occasion.

Ham. Beggar that I am, I am even poor in thanks; but I thank you: and sure, dear friends, my thanks are too dear, a halfpenny. Were you not sent for? Is it your own inclining? Is it a free visitation? Come, come; deal justly with me: come, come; nay, speak.

Guil. What should we say, my lord?

Ham. Anything—but to the purpose. You were sent for; and there is a kind of confession in your looks, which your modesties have not craft enough to colour. I know the good king and queen have sent for you.

Ros. To what end, my lord?

Ham. That you must teach me. But let me conjure you, by the rights of our fellowship, by the consonancy of our youth, by the obligation of our ever-preserved love, and by what more dear a better proposer could charge you withal, be even and direct with me, whether you were sent for or no?

Ros. What say you?　　　[*To* GUILDENSTERN.

Ham. Nay, then, I have an eye of you [*Aside*]. —If you love me, hold not off.

Guil. My lord, we were sent for.

Ham. I will tell you why; so shall my anticipation prevent your discovery, and your secrecy to the king and queen moult no feather. I have of late (but wherefore I know not) lost all my mirth, forgone all custom of exercises; and, indeed, it goes so heavily with my disposition, that this goodly frame, the earth, seems to me a sterile promontory; this most excellent canopy, the air, look you,—this brave o'erhanging firmament, this majestical roof fretted with golden fire,—why, it appears no other thing to me than a foul and pestilent congregation of vapours.—What a piece of work is a man! How noble in reason! how infinite in faculties! in form and moving, how express and admirable! in action, how like an angel! in apprehension, how like a god! the beauty of the world! the paragon of animals! And yet, to me, what is this quintessence of dust? man delights not me, nor woman neither; though, by your smiling, you seem to say so.

Ros. My lord, there was no such stuff in my thoughts.

Ham. Why did you laugh then, when I said, " Man delights not me!"

Ros. To think, my lord, if you delight not in man, what lenten entertainment the players shall receive from you: we coted them on the way; and hither are they coming, to offer you service.

Ham. He that plays the king shall be welcome; his majesty shall have tribute of me; the adventurous knight shall use his foil and target; the lover shall not sigh gratis; the humorous man shall end his part in peace; the clown shall make those laugh whose lungs are tickled o'the sere; and the lady shall say her mind freely, or the blank verse shall halt for't.—What players are they?

Ros. Even those you were wont to take such delight in; the tragedians of the city.

Ham. How chances it they travel? Their residence, both in reputation and profit, was better both ways.

Ros. I think their inhibition comes by the means of the late innovation.

Ham. Do they hold the same estimation they did when I was in the city? Are they so followed?

Ros. No, indeed, they are not.

Ham. How comes it? Do they grow rusty?

Ros. Nay, their endeavour keeps in the wonted pace: but there is, sir, an aiery of children, little eyases, that cry out on the top of question, and are most tyrannically clapped for't: these are now the fashion; and so berattle the common stages (so they call them), that many, wearing rapiers, are afraid of goose-quills, and dare scarce come thither.

Ham. What, are they children? who maintains them? how are they escoted? Will they pursue the quality no longer than they can sing?

will they not say afterwards, if they should grow themselves to common players (as it is most like, if their means are no better), their writers do them wrong, to make them exclaim against their own succession?

Ros. 'Faith, there has been much to do on both sides; and the nation holds it no sin to tarre them on to controversy: there was, for a while, no money bid for argument, unless the poet and the player went to cuffs in the question.

Ham. Is it possible?

Guil. O, there has been much throwing about of brains.

Ham. Do the boys carry it away?

Ros. Ay, that they do, my lord; Hercules and his load too.

Ham. It is not very strange: for my uncle is King of Denmark; and those that would make mouths at him while my father lived, give twenty, forty, fifty, an hundred ducats a-piece, for his picture in little. There is something in this more than natural, if philosophy could find it out.

[*Flourish of trumpets within.*

Guil. There are the players.

Ham. Gentlemen, you are welcome to Elsinore. Your hands. Come then: the appurtenance of welcome is fashion and ceremony: let me comply with you in this garb; lest my extent to the players, which I tell you must shew fairly outward, should more appear like entertainment than yours. You are welcome; but my uncle-father and aunt-mother are deceived.

Guil. In what, my dear lord?

Ham. I am but mad north-north-west: when the wind is southerly, I know a hawk from a hand-saw.

Enter POLONIUS.

Pol. Well be with you, gentlemen!

Ham. Hark you, Guildenstern; and you, too; at each ear a hearer: that great baby you see there, is not yet out of his swaddling-clouts.

Ros. Happily he's the second time come to them; for they say an old man is twice a child.

Ham. I will prophesy he comes to tell me of the players; mark it.—You say right, sir: o' Monday morning; 'twas then, indeed.

Pol. My lord, I have news to tell you.

Ham. My lord, I have news to tell you. When Roscius was an actor in Rome,—

Pol. The actors are come hither, my lord.

Ham. Buz, buz!

Pol. Upon my honour,—

Ham. " Then came each actor on his ass,—"

Pol. The best actors in the world, either for tragedy, comedy, history, pastoral, pastoral-comical, historical-pastoral, tragical-historical, tragi-cal-comical-historical-pastoral, scene individable, or poem unlimited: Seneca cannot be too heavy, nor Plautus too light. For the law of writ, and the liberty, these are the only men.

Ham. O Jephthah, judge of Israel, what a treasure hadst thou !

Pol. What a treasure had he, my lord?

Ham. Why,—

> " One fair daughter and no more,
> The which he loved passing well."

Pol. Still on my daughter.   [*Aside.*

Ham. Am I not i' the right, old Jephthah?

Pol. If you call me Jephthah, my lord, I have a daughter that I love passing well.

Ham. Nay, that follows not.

Pol. What follows then, my lord?

Ham. Why,

> " As by lot, God wot,"

and then you know,

> " It came to pass, As most like it was."

The first row of the pious chanson will shew you more; for look where my abridgments come.

Enter Four or Five Players.

You are welcome, masters; welcome, all:—I am glad to see thee well:—welcome, good friends.— O, old friend! why thy face is valanced since I saw thee last; comest thou to beard me in Denmark?—What, my young lady and mistress! By-'r-lady, your ladyship is nearer to heaven than when I saw you last, by the altitude of a chopine. Pray God, your voice, like a piece of uncurrent gold, be not cracked within the ring.— Masters, you are all welcome. We'll e'en to it like French falconers, fly at anything we see: we'll have a speech straight: come, give us a taste of your quality; come, a passionate speech.

1st Play. What speech, my lord?

Ham. I heard thee speak me a speech once,— but it was never acted; or, if it was, not above once: for the play, I remember, pleased not the million: 'twas caviarie to the general: but it was (as I received it, and others, whose judgments in such matters cried in the top of mine) an excellent play; well digested in the scenes, set down with as much modesty as cunning. I remember one said, there were no sallets in the lines, to make the matter savoury: nor no matter in the phrase that might indite the author of affectation: but called it, an honest method, as wholesome as sweet, and by very much more handsome than fine. One speech in it I chiefly loved: 'twas Æneas' tale to Dido; and there-about of it especially, where he speaks of Priam's

slaughter. If it live in your memory, begin at this line; let me see, let me see;—

> The rugged Pyrrhus, like the Hyrcanian beast,—

'Tis not so; it begins with Pyrrhus.

> The rugged Pyrrhus,—he, whose sable arms,
> Black as his purpose, did the night resemble,
> When he lay couchéd in the ominous horse,
> Hath now this dread and black complexion smeared
> With heraldry more dismal; head to foot
> Now is he total gules; horridly tricked
> With blood of fathers, mothers, daughters, sons;
> Baked and impasted with the parching streets,
> That lend a tyrannous and a damnéd light
> To their lord's murder: roasted in wrath and fire,
> And thus o'er-sizéd with coagulate gore,
> With eyes like carbuncles, the hellish Pyrrhus
> Old grandsire Priam seeks.

So, proceed you.

Pol. 'Fore God, my lord, well spoken; with good accent and good discretion.

1st Player.

> —— Anon he finds him
> Striking too short at Greeks; his antique sword
> Rebellious to his arm, lies where it falls,
> Repugnant to command. Unequal matched,
> Pyrrhus at Priam drives; in rage, strikes wide;
> But with the whiff and wind of his fell sword
> The unnerved father falls. Then senseless Ilium,
> Seeming to feel this blow, with flaming top
> Stoops to his base; and with a hideous crash
> Takes prisoner Pyrrhus' ear; for, lo! his sword,
> Which was declining on the milky head
> Of reverend Priam, seemed in the air to stick:
> So, as a painted tyrant, Pyrrhus stood;
> And, like a neutral to his will and matter,
> Did nothing.
> But as we often see, against some storm,
> A silence in the heavens, the rack stand still,
> The bold winds speechless, and the orb below
> As hush as death: anon, the dreadful thunder
> Doth rend the region: so, after Pyrrhus' pause,
> A rouséd vengeance sets him new a work;
> And never did the Cyclops' hammers fall
> On Mars's armour, forged for proof eterne,
> With less remorse than Pyrrhus' bleeding sword
> Now falls on Priam.—
> Out, out, thou strumpet, Fortune! All you gods,
> In general synod, take away her power;
> Break all the spokes and fellies from her wheel,
> And bowl the round nave down the hill of heaven,
> As low as to the fiends !

Pol. This is too long.

Ham. It shall to the barber's, with your beard. —Pr'ythee, say on: he's for a jig, or a tale of bawdry, or he sleeps: say on: come to Hecuba.

1st Player.

But who, ah woe ! had seen the mobled queen—

Ham. The mobled queen?
Pol. That's good; mobled queen is good.

1st Player.

Run barefoot up and down, threatening the flames
With bisson rheum; a clout upon that head
Where late the diadem stood; and, for a robe,
About her lank and all o'er-teeming loins,
A blanket, in the alarm of fear caught up ;
Who this had seen, with tongue in venom steeped,
'Gainst fortune's state would treason have pro-
            nounced :
But if the gods themselves did see her then,
When she saw Pyrrhus make malicious sport,
In mincing with his sword her husband's limbs ;
The instant burst of clamour that she made
(Unless things mortal move them not at all)
Would have made milch the burning eye of heaven,
And passion in the gods.

Pol. Look whether he has not turned his colour, and has tears in 's eyes!—Pr'y thee, no more.
Ham. 'T is well ; I 'll have thee speak out the
rest of this soon.—Good my lord, will you see
the players well bestowed? Do you hear, let
them be well used ; for they are the abstracts
and brief chronicles of the time : after your death
you were better have a bad epitaph, than their
ill report while you live.
Pol. My lord, I will use them according to
their desert.
Ham. Odd's bodikin, man, much better : use
every man after his desert, and who shall 'scape
whipping? Use them after your own honour
and dignity : the less they deserve, the more
merit is in your bounty. Take them in.
Pol. Come, sirs.

[*Exit* POLONIUS, *with some of the* Players.

Ham. Follow him, friends : we 'll hear a play
to-morrow.—Dost thou hear me, old friend ; can
you play the murder of Gonzago?
1st Play. Ay, my lord.
Ham. We 'll have it to-morrow night. You
could, for a need, study a speech of some dozen
or sixteen lines, which I would set down, and
insert in 't? could you not?
1st Play. Ay, my lord.
Ham. Very well.—Follow that lord; and look you
mock him not. [*Exit* Player]. My good friends
[*To* ROSENCRANTZ *and* GUILDENSTERN], I 'll leave
you till night : you are welcome to Elsinore.
Ros. Good my lord !

[*Exeunt* ROSENCRANTZ *and* GUILDENSTERN.

Ham. Ay, so, God be wi' you.—Now I am alone.
O, what a rogue and peasant slave am I !
Is it not monstrous, that this player here,

But in a fiction, in a dream of passion,
Could force his soul so to his own conceit,
That from her working, all his visage wanned ;
Tears in his eyes, distraction in 's aspéct,
A broken voice, and his whole function suiting
With forms to his conceit? And all for nothing !
For Hecuba !
What's Hecuba to him, or he to Hecuba,
That he should weep for her? What would he do,
Had he the motive and the cue for passion
That I have? He would drown the stage with tears,
And cleave the general ear with horrid speech ;
Make mad the guilty, and appal the free,
Confound the ignorant ; and amaze, indeed,
The very faculties of eyes and ears.
Yet I,
A dull and muddy-mettled rascal, peak,
Like John-a-dreams, unpregnant of my cause,
And can say nothing ; no, not for a king,
Upon whose property and most dear life
A damned defeat was made. Am I a coward?
Who calls me villain? breaks my pate across?
Plucks off my beard, and blows it in my face?
Tweaks me by the nose? gives me the lie i' the throat,
As deep as to the lungs? Who does me this?
Ha ! Why, I should take it : for it cannot be
But I am pigeon-livered, and lack gall
To make oppression bitter ; or, ere this,
I should have fatted all the region kites
With this slave's offal. Bloody, bawdy villain !
Remorseless, treacherous, lecherous, kindless
            villain !
Why, what an ass am I ? This is most brave ;
That I, the son of a dear father murdered,
Prompted to my revenge by heaven and hell,
Must, like a whore, unpack my heart with words,
And fall a cursing like a very drab,—
A scullion !
Fie upon 't! foh!—About, my brains !—Humph !
            I have heard,
That guilty creatures, sitting at a play,
Have by the very cunning of the scene
Been struck so to the soul, that presently
They have proclaimed their malefactions :
For murder, though it have no tongue, will speak
With most miraculous organ. I 'll have these players
Play something like the murder of my father
Before mine uncle : I 'll observe his looks ;
I 'll tent him to the quick ; if he do blench,
I know my course. The spirit that I have seen
May be a devil ; and the devil hath power
To assume a pleasing shape ; yea, and, perhaps,
Out of my weakness and my melancholy
(As he is very potent with such spirits),
Abuses me to damn me. I 'll have grounds
More relative than this : the play 's the thing
Wherein I 'll catch the conscience of the king.
                    [*Exit.*

SCENE I.—*A Room in the Castle.*

Enter KING, QUEEN, POLONIUS, OPHELIA,
ROSENCRANTZ, *and* GUILDENSTERN.

King. And can you by no drift of conference,
Get from him, why he puts on this confusion;
Grating so harshly all his days of quiet
With turbulent and dangerous lunacy?

Ros. He does confess he feels himself dis-
        tracted;
But from what cause he will by no means speak.

Guil. Nor do we find him forward to be
        sounded;
But, with a crafty madness, keeps aloof,
When we would bring him on to some confession
Of his true state.

Queen.   Did he receive you well?

Ros. Most like a gentleman.

Guil. But with much forcing of his disposi-
        tion.

Ros. Niggard of question; but, of our demands,
Most free in his reply.

Queen.   Did you assay him
To any pastime?

Ros. Madam, it so fell out that certain players
We o'er-raught on the way: of these we told
him;
And there did seem in him a kind of joy
To hear of it: they are about the court;
And, as I think, they have already order
This night to play before him.

Pol.   'T is most true:
And he beseeched me to entreat your majesties
To hear and see the matter.

King. With all my heart; and it doth much
        content me
To hear him so inclined.

Good gentlemen, give him a further edge,
And drive his purpose on to these delights.

Ros. We shall, my lord.

        [*Exeunt* ROSENCRANTZ *and* GUILDENSTERN.

King.   Sweet Gertrude, leave us too:
For we have closely sent for Hamlet hither;
That he, as 't were by accident, may here
Affront Ophelia:
Her father and myself (lawful espials)
Will so bestow ourselves, that seeing, unseen,
We may of their encounter frankly judge;
And gather by him, as he is behaved,
If 't be the affliction of his love, or no,
That thus he suffers for.

Queen.   I shall obey you:
And for your part, Ophelia, I do wish
That your good beauties be the happy cause
Of Hamlet's wildness: so shall I hope your vir-
        tues
Will bring him to his wonted way again,
To both your honours.

Oph. Madam, I wish it may. [*Exit* QUEEN.

Pol. Ophelia, walk you here:—Gracious, so
        please you,
We will bestow ourselves:—Read on this book;
        [*To* OPHELIA.
That show of such an exercise may colour
Your loneliness.—We are oft to blame in this,—
'T is too much proved,—that with devotion's
        visage,
And pious action, we do sugar o'er
The devil himself.

King.   O, 't is too true!
How smart a lash that speech doth give my con-
        science!
The harlot's cheek, beautied with plastering art,
Is not more ugly to the thing that helps it,

Than is my deed to my most painted word;
O, heavy burden!　　　　　　　　　　　[*Aside.*

　Pol. I hear him coming; let's withdraw, my
　　lord.　　[*Exeunt* KING *and* POLONIUS.

Enter HAMLET.

　Ham. To be, or not to be, that is the question:
Whether 'tis nobler in the mind to suffer
The slings and arrows of outrageous fortune;
Or to take arms against a sea of troubles,
And, by opposing, end them?—To die,—to sleep,—
No more;—and, by a sleep, to say we end
The heart-ache, and the thousand natural shocks
That flesh is heir to,—'tis a consummation
Devoutly to be wished.　To die,—to sleep;—
To sleep! perchance to dream;—ay, there's the
　　rub;
For in that sleep of death what dreams may come,
When we have shuffled off this mortal coil,
Must give us pause: there's the respect
That makes calamity of so long life:
For who would bear the whips and scorns of time,
The oppressor's wrong, the proud man's con-
　　tumely,
The pangs of déspiséd love, the law's delay,
The insolence of office, and the spurns
That patient merit of the unworthy takes,
When he himself might his quietus make
With a bare bodkin? who would fardels bear,
To grunt and sweat under a weary life;
But that the dread of something after death,—
The undiscovered country, from whose bourn
No traveller returns,—puzzles the will;
And makes us rather bear those ills we have,
Than fly to others that we know not of?
Thus conscience does make cowards of us all;
And thus the native hue of resolution
Is sicklied o'er with the pale cast of thought;
And enterprises of great pith and moment,
With this regard, their currents turn awry,
And lose the name of action.—Soft you, now!
The fair Ophelia:—Nymph, in thy orisons
Be all my sins remembered.

　Oph.　　　　Good my lord,
How does your honour for this many a day?

　Ham. I humbly thank you; well.

　Oph. My lord, I have remembrances of yours,
That I have longéd long to re-deliver;
I pray you, now receive them.

　Ham.　　　　No, not I;
I never gave you aught.

　Oph. My honoured lord, you know right well
　　you did;
And, with them, words of so sweet breath com-
　　posed
As made the things more rich: their perfume
　　lost,

Take these again; for to the noble mind,
Rich gifts wax poor when givers prove unkind.
There, my lord.

　Ham. Ha, ha! are you honest?

　Oph. My lord?

　Ham. Are you fair?

　Oph. What means your lordship?

　Ham. That if you be honest and fair, your honesty should admit no discourse to your beauty.

　Oph. Could beauty, my lord, have better commerce than with honesty?

　Ham. Ay, truly; for the power of beauty will
sooner transform honesty from what it is to a
bawd, than the force of honesty can translate
beauty into his likeness: this was some time a
paradox, but now the time gives it proof.　I did
love you once.

　Oph. Indeed, my lord, you made me believe
so.

　Ham. You should not have believed me; for
virtue cannot so inoculate our old stock, but we
shall relish of it: I loved you not.

　Oph. I was the more deceived.

　Ham. Get thee to a nunnery; why wouldst thou
be a breeder of sinners?　I am myself indifferent
honest; but yet I could accuse me of such things,
that it were better my mother had not borne me.
I am very proud, revengeful, ambitious; with
more offences at my beck than I have thoughts
to put them in, imagination to give them shape,
or time to act them in.　What should such fellows
as I do crawling between heaven and earth!　We
are arrant knaves, all; believe none of us: go thy
ways to a nunnery.　Where's your father?

　Oph. At home, my lord.

　Ham. Let the doors be shut upon him, that he
may play the fool nowhere but in's own house.
Farewell.

　Oph. O, help him, you sweet heavens!

　Ham. If thou dost marry, I'll give thee this
plague for thy dowry:—Be thou as chaste as ice,
as pure as snow, thou shalt not escape calumny.
Get thee to a nunnery; farewell: or, if thou wilt
needs marry, marry a fool; for wise men know
well enough what monsters you make of them.
To a nunnery, go; and quickly too.　Farewell.

　Oph. Heavenly powers, restore him!

　Ham. I have heard of your paintings too, well
enough; God hath given you one face, and you
make yourselves another: you jig, you amble,
and you lisp, and nickname God's creatures, and
make your wantonness your ignorance:—Go to;
I'll no more of't; it hath made me mad.　I
say we will have no more marriages: those
that are married already, all but one, shall live.;
the rest shall keep as they are.　To a nunnery,
go.　　　　　　　　　　　　　　　[*Exit.*

Oph. O, what a noble mind is here o'erthrown!
The courtier's, soldier's, scholar's, eye, tongue,
 sword;
The expectancy and rose of the fair state,
The glass of fashion, and the mould of form,
The observed of all observers! quite, quite down!
And I, of ladies most deject and wretched,
That sucked the honey of his music vows,
Now see that noble and most sovereign reason,
Like sweet bells jangled, out of tune and harsh;
That unmatched form and feature of blown youth,
Blasted with ecstasy: O, woe is me!
To have seen what I have seen, see what I see!

Re-enter KING *and* POLONIUS.

King. Love! his affections do not that way tend;
Nor what he spake, though it lacked form a little,

Was not like madness. There's something in his
 soul,
O'er which his melancholy sits on brood;
And I do doubt the hatch and the disclose
Will be some danger: which to prevent,
I have, in quick determination,
Thus set it down:—He shall with speed to Eng-
 land,
For the demand of our neglected tribute:
Haply the seas and countries different,
With variable objects, shall expel
This something-settled matter in his heart;
Whereon his brains still beating, puts him thus
From fashion of himself. What think you on 't?
 Pol. It shall do well: but yet do I believe,
The origin and commencement of his grief
Sprung from neglected love.—How now, Ophelia?

You need not tell us what lord Hamlet said;
We heard it all.—My lord, do as you please;
But, if you hold it fit, after the play,
Let his queen-mother all alone entreat him
To shew his grief; let her be round with him;
And I'll be placed, so please you, in the ear
Of all their conference: if she find him not,
To England send him: or confine him where
Your wisdom best shall think.

King. It shall be so:
Madness in great ones must not unwatched go.

[*Exeunt.*

SCENE II.—*A Hall in the same.*

Enter HAMLET, *and certain* Players.

Ham. Speak the speech, I pray you, as I
pronounced it to you, trippingly on the tongue:
but if you mouth it, as many of our players
do, I had as lief the town-crier spoke my lines.
Nor do not saw the air too much with your
hand, thus; but use all gently; for in the very
torrent, tempest, and (as I may say) whirlwind
of your passion, you must acquire and beget a
temperance that may give it smoothness. O,
it offends me to the soul, to hear a robustious
periwig-pated fellow tear a passion to tatters, to
very rags, to split the ears of the groundlings;
who, for the most part, are capable of nothing
but inexplicable dumb shows and noise: I would
have such a fellow whipped for o'er-doing Termagant; it out-herods Herod: pray you, avoid it.

1st Play. I warrant your honour.

Ham. Be not too tame neither, but let your
own discretion be your tutor: suit the action to
the word, the word to the action; with this special observance, that you o'er-step not the modesty of nature: for anything so overdone is
from the purpose of playing, whose end, both at
the first, and now, was, and is, to hold, as 't were,
the mirror up to nature; to shew virtue her
own feature, scorn her own image, and the very
age and body of the time his form and pres-
sure. Now this overdone, or come tardy off,
though it make the unskilful laugh, cannot but
make the judicious grieve; the censure of which
one, must, in your allowance, o'erweigh a whole
theatre of others. O, there be players, that I
have seen play, and heard others praise, and
that highly,—not to speak it profanely, that,
neither having the accent of christians, nor the
gait of christian, pagan, nor man, have so
strutted and bellowed, that I have thought
some of nature's journeymen had made men,
and not made them well, they imitated humanity
so abominably.

1st Play. I hope we have reformed that indifferently with us.

Ham. O, reform it altogether. And let those
that play your clowns speak no more than is set
down for them: for there be of them that will
themselves laugh, to set on some quantity of
barren spectators to laugh too; though, in the
mean time, some necessary question of the play
be then to be considered: that's villanous, and
shews a most pitiful ambition in the fool that uses
it. Go, make you ready. [*Exeunt* Players.

Enter POLONIUS, ROSENCRANTZ, *and* GUILDEN-
STERN.

How now, my lord? will the king hear this piece
of work?

Pol. And the queen too, and that presently.

Ham. Bid the players make haste.—
[*Exit* POLONIUS.
Will you two help to hasten them?

Ros. } Ay, my lord.
Guil. }

[*Exeunt* ROSENCRANTZ *and* GUILDENSTERN.

Ham. What, ho; Horatio!

Enter HORATIO.

Hor. Here, sweet lord, at your service.

Ham. Horatio, thou art e'en as just a man
As e'er my conversation coped withal.

Hor. O, my dear lord,—

Ham. Nay, do not think I flatter:
For what advancement may I hope from thee,
That no revénue hast, but thy good spirits,
To feed and clothe thee? Why should the poor
be flattered?
No, let the candied tongue lick ábsurd pomp;
And crook the pregnant hinges of the knee,
Where thrift may follow fawning. Dost thou hear?
Since my dear soul was mistress of her choice,
And could of men distinguish her election,
She hath sealed thee for herself: for thou hast been
As one, in suffering all, that suffers nothing;
A man that Fortune's buffets and rewards
Has ta'en with equal thanks: and blessed are those
Whose blood and judgment are so well co-mingled,
That they are not a pipe for Fortune's finger
To sound what stop she please: give me that man
That is not passion's slave, and I will wear him
In my heart's core, ay, in my heart of heart,
As I do thee.—Something too much of this.—
There is a play to-night before the king;
One scene of it comes near the circumstance
Which I have told thee of my father's death:
I pr'ythee, when thou seest that act a-foot,
Even with the very comment of thy soul
Observe my uncle: if his occulted guilt
Do not itself unkennel in one speech,

It is a damnéd ghost that we have seen ;
And my imaginations are as foul
As Vulcan's stithy. Give him heedful note :
For I mine eyes will rivet to his face ;
And after we will both our judgments join
In censure of his seeming.

Hor. Well, my lord :
If he steal aught the whilst this play is playing,
And 'scape detecting, I will pay the theft.

Ham. They are coming to the play ; I must
   be idle :
Get you a place.

Danish march. A Flourish. Enter KING, QUEEN,
POLONIUS, OPHELIA, ROSENCRANTZ, GUILDEN-
STERN, *and others.*

King. How fares our cousin Hamlet ?

Ham. Excellent, i' faith ; of the camelion's dish :
I eat the air, promise-crammed : you cannot feed
capons so.

King. I have nothing with this answer, Hamlet ; these words are not mine.

Ham. No, nor mine now.—My lord, you played
once in the university, you say ? [*To* POLONIUS.

Pol. That did I, my lord ; and was accounted
a good actor.

Ham. And what did you enact ?

Pol. I did enact Julius Cæsar : I was killed
i' the Capitol ; Brutus killed me.

Ham. It was a brute part of him, to kill so
capital a calf there.—Be the players ready ?

Ros. Ay, my lord ; they stay upon your patience.

Queen. Come hither, my dear Hamlet, sit
by me.

Ham. No, good mother, here 's metal more
attractive.

Pol. O, ho ! do you mark that ? [*To the* KING.

Ham. Lady, shall I lie in your lap ?

[*Lying down at* OPHELIA's *feet.*

Oph. No, my lord.

Ham. I mean, my head upon your lap ?

Oph. Ay, my lord.

Ham. Do you think I meant country matters ?

Oph. I think nothing, my lord.

Ham. That 's a fair thought to lie between
maids' legs.

Oph. What is, my lord ?

Ham. Nothing.

Oph. You are merry, my lord.

Ham. Who, I ?

Oph. Ay, my lord.

Ham. O ! your only jig-maker. What should
a man do, but be merry ? for look you how cheerfully my mother looks, and my father died within
these two hours.

Oph. Nay, 't is twice two months, my lord.

Ham. So long ? Nay, then let the devil wear
black, for I 'll have a suit of sables. O, heavens !
die two months ago, and not forgotten yet ? Then
there 's hope a great man's memory may outlive
his life half-a-year : but, by 'r-lady, he must
build churches then : or else shall he suffer not
thinking on, with the hobby-horse ; whose epitaph
is, " For O, for O, the hobby-horse is forgot ! "

Trumpets sound. The Dumb Show follows.

Enter a King *and a* Queen, *very lovingly ; the*
Queen *embracing him, and he her. She kneels, and
makes show of protestation unto him. He takes her
up, and declines his head upon her neck : lays him
down upon a bank of flowers ; she, seeing him asleep,
leaves him. Anon comes in a fellow, takes off his crown,
kisses it, and pours poison in the* King's *ears, and exit.
The* Queen *returns ; finds the* King *dead, and makes
passionate action. The poisoner, with some two or
three mutes, comes in again, seeming to lament with
her. The dead body is carried away. The poisoner
woos the* Queen *with gifts ; she seems loath and unwilling awhile, but in the end accepts his love.*

[*Exeunt.*

Oph. What means this, my lord ?

Ham. Marry, this is miching mallecho ; it
means mischief.

Oph. Belike this show imports the argument
of the play.

Enter PROLOGUE.

Ham. We shall know by this fellow : the players
cannot keep counsel ; they 'll tell all.

Oph. Will he tell us what this show meant ?

Ham. Ay, or any show that you 'll shew him :
be not you ashamed to shew, he 'll not shame to
tell you what it means.

Oph. You are naught, you are naught ; I 'll
mark the play.

PROLOGUE.

For us, and for our tragedy,
Here stooping to your clemency,
We beg your hearing patiently.

Ham. Is this a prologue, or the posy of a ring ?

Oph. 'T is brief, my lord.

Ham. As woman's love.

Enter a KING *and* QUEEN.

P. KING.

Full thirty times hath Phœbus' cart gone round
Neptune's salt wash and Tellus' orbéd ground ;
And thirty dozen moons, with borrowed sheen,
About the world have times twelve thirties been ;
Since love our hearts, and Hymen did our hands,
Unite commutual in most sacred bands.

P. Queen.

So many journeys may the sun and moon
Make us again count o'er, ere love be done!
But, woe is me, you are so sick of late,
So far from cheer, and from your former state,
That I distrust you.   Yet, though I distrust,
Discomfort you, my lord, it nothing must:
For women's fear and love hold quantity;
In neither aught, or in extremity.
Now, what my love is, proof hath made you know;
And as my love is sized, my fear is so.
. Where love is great, the littlest doubts are fear;
Where little fears grow great, great love grows there.

P. King.

'Faith, I must leave thee, love, and shortly too;
My operant powers their functions leave to do:
And thou shalt live in this fair world behind,
Honoured, beloved; and haply, one as kind
For husband shalt thou—

P. Queen.

O, confound the rest!
Such love must needs be treason in my breast:
In second husband let me be accurst!
None wed the second, but who killed the first.

Ham. That's wormword.   [*Aside.*

P. Queen.

The instances that second marriage move
Are base respects of thrift, but none of love;
A second time I kill my husband dead,
When second husband kisses me in bed.

P. King.

I do believe you think what now you speak;
But what we do determine oft we break.
Purpose is but the slave to memory;
Of violent birth, but poor validity:
Which now, like fruit unripe, sticks on the tree;
But fall unshaken when they mellow be.
Most necessary 'tis that we forget
To pay ourselves what to ourselves is debt:
What to ourselves in passion we propose,
The passion ending, doth the purpose lose.
The violence of either grief or joy
Their own enactures with themselves destroy:
Where joy most revels, grief doth most lament;
Grief joys, joy grieves, on slender accident.
This world is not for aye; nor 'tis not strange
That even our loves should with our fortunes change;
For, 'tis a question left us yet to prove,
Whether love lead fortune, or else fortune love.
The great man down, you mark, his favourite flies;
The poor advanced makes friends of enemies.
And hitherto doth love on fortune tend:
For who not needs, shall never lack a friend;
And who in want a hollow friend doth try,
Directly seasons him his enemy.
But, orderly to end where I begun,—
Our wills and fates do so contrary run,

That our devices still are overthrown;
Our thoughts are ours, their ends none of our own:
So think thou wilt no second husband wed;
But die thy thoughts, when thy first lord is dead.

P. Queen.

Nor earth to me give food, nor heaven light!
Sport and repose lock from me, day and night!
To desperation turn my trust and hope!
An anchor's cheer in prison be my scope!
Each opposite that blanks the face of joy,
Meet what I would have well, and it destroy!
Both here and hence, pursue me lasting strife,
If, once a widow, ever I be wife.

Ham. If she should break it now,—
                    [*To* Ophelia.

P. King.

'Tis deeply sworn.   Sweet, leave me here awhile;
My spirits grow dull, and fain I would beguile
The tedious day with sleep.   [*Sleeps.*

P. Queen.

Sleep rock thy brain;
And never come mischance betwéen us twain! [*Exit.*

Ham. Madam, how like you this play?

Queen. The lady doth protest too much, methinks.

Ham. O, but she'll keep her word.

King. Have you heard the argument? Is there no offence in 't?

Ham. No, no, they do but jest, poison in jest? no offence i' the world.

King. What do you call the play?

Ham. The mousetrap.   Marry, how?—tropically. This play is the image of a murder done in Vienna: Gonzago is the duke's name; his wife, Baptista; you shall see anon; 'tis a knavish piece of work: but what of that? Your majesty, and we that have free souls, it touches us not: let the galled jade wince; our withers are unwrung.

Enter Lucianus.

This is one Lucianus, nephew to the king.

Oph. You are as good as a chorus, my lord.

Ham. I could interpret between you and your love, if I could see the puppets dallying.

Oph. You are keen, my lord, you are keen.

Ham. It would cost you a groaning to take off my edge.

Oph. Still better and worse.

Ham. So you mistake your husbands.—Begin, murderer; leave thy damnable faces, and begin. Come;—
            —— The croaking raven
Doth bellow for revenge.

Lucianus.

Thoughts black, hands apt, drugs fit, and time
    agreeing;

Confederate season, else no creature seeing!
Thou mixture rank, of midnight weeds collected,
With Hecate's ban thrice blasted, thrice infected,
Thy natural magic and dire property
On wholesome life usurp immediately.

        [Pours the poison into the sleeper's ears.

  Ham. He poisons him i'the garden, for his
estate. His name's Gonzago; the story is extant, and written in very choice Italian. You
shall see anon, how the murderer gets the love
of Gonzago's wife.

  Oph. The king rises.
  Ham. What, frighted with false fire!
  Queen. How fares my lord?

  Pol. Give o'er the play.
  King. Give me some light: away!
  Pol. Lights, lights, lights!
       [Exeunt all but HAMLET *and* HORATIC
  Ham. Why, let the strucken deer go weep,
      The hart ungalléd play:
For some must watch, while some must sleep
      Thus runs the world away.—
Would not this, sir, and a forest of feathers (i
the rest of my fortunes turn Turk with me), witl
two Provencial roses on my razed shoes, get m
a fellowship in a cry of players, sir?
  Hor. Half a share.
  Ham. A whole one, I.

For thou dost know, O Damon dear,
    This realm dismantled was
Of Jove himself; and now reigns here
    A very very—peacock.

Hor. You might have rhymed.

Ham. O, good Horatio, I 'll take the ghost's word for a thousand pound.   Didst perceive?

Hor. Very well, my lord.

Ham. Upon the talk of the poisoning,—

Hor. I did very well note him.

Ham. Ah, ha!—Come, some music; come, the recorders.—

For if the king like not the comedy,
Why then, belike, he likes it not, perdy.

Enter Rosencrantz *and* Guildenstern.

Come, some music.

Guil. Good my lord, vouchsafe me a word with you.

Ham. Sir, a whole history.

Guil. The king, sir,—

Ham. Ay, sir, what of him?

Guil. Is, in his retirement, marvellous distempered.

Ham. With drink, sir?

Guil. No, my lord, with choler.

Ham. Your wisdom should shew itself more richer, to signify this to the doctor; for, for me to put him to his purgation, would perhaps plunge him into more choler.

Guil. Good my lord, put your discourse into some frame, and start not so wildly from my affair.

Ham. I am tame, sir: pronounce.

Guil. The queen, your mother, in most great affliction of spirit, hath sent me to you.

Ham. You are welcome.

Guil. Nay, good my lord, this courtesy is not of the right breed.   If it shall please you to make me a wholesome answer, I will do your mother's commandment: if not, your pardon, and my return, shall be the end of my business.

Ham. Sir, I cannot.

Guil. What, my lord?

Ham. Make you a wholesome answer; my wit's diseased: but, sir, such answer as I can make, you shall command; or rather, as you say, my mother: therefore, no more, but to the matter: My mother, you say.—

Ros. Then thus she says: your behaviour hath struck her into amazement and admiration.

Ham. O, wonderful son, that can so astonish a mother!—But is there no sequel at the heels of this mother's admiration?—impart.

Ros. She desires to speak with you in her closet, ere you go to bed.

Ham. We shall obey, were she ten times our mother.   Have you any further trade with us?

Ros. My lord, you once did love me.

Ham. And do still, by these pickers and stealers.

Ros. Good my lord, what is your cause of distemper?—you do freely bar the door of your own liberty, if you deny your griefs to your friend.

Ham. Sir, I lack advancement.

Ros. How can that be, when you have the voice of the king himself for your succession in Denmark?

Ham. Ay, sir, but "While the grass grows,"—the proverb is something musty.

Enter the Players, *with recorders.*

O, the recorders: let me see one.—To withdraw with you:—why do you go about to recover the wind of me, as if you would drive me into a toil?

Guil. O, my lord, if my duty be too bold, my love is too unmannerly.

Ham. I do not well understand that.   Will you play upon this pipe?

Guil. My lord, I cannot.

Ham. I pray you.

Guil. Believe me, I cannot.

Ham. I do beseech you.

Guil. I know no touch of it, my lord.

Ham. 'T is as easy as lying: govern these ventages with your fingers and thumb, give it breath with your mouth, and it will discourse most eloquent music.   Look you, these are the stops.

Guil. But these cannot I command to any utterance of harmony; I have not the skill.

Ham. Why, look you now, how unworthy a thing you make of me.   You would play upon me; you would seem to know my stops; you would pluck out the heart of my mystery; you would sound me from my lowest note to the top of my compass: and there is much music, excellent voice, in this little organ; yet cannot you make it speak.   S' blood, do you think I am easier to be played on than a pipe?   Call me what instrument you will, though you can fret me, you cannot play upon me.

Enter Polonius.

God bless you, sir!

Pol. My lord, the queen would speak with you, and presently.

Ham. Do you see yonder cloud, that 's almost in shape of a camel?

Pol. By the mass, and 't is like a camel, indeed.

Ham. Methinks it is like a weasel.

Pol. It is backed like a weasel.

Ham. Or like a whale?

Pol. Very like a whale.

Ham. Then will I come to my mother by-and-by.—They fool me to the top of my bent.—I will come by-and-by.

Pol. I will say so.   [*Exit* POLONIUS.

Ham. "By-and-by" is easily said.—Leave me,
friends. [*Exeunt* ROSENCRANTZ, GUILDENSTERN,
         HORATIO, &c.
'Tis now the very witching time of night;
When churchyards yawn, and hell itself breathes
     out
Contagion to this world: now could I drink hot
     blood,
And do such bitter business as the day
Would quake to look on.   Soft; now to my mo-
     ther.—
O heart, lose not thy nature: let not ever
The soul of Nero enter this firm bosom:
Let me be cruel, not unnatural:
I will speak daggers to her, but use none;
My tongue and soul in this be hypocrites:
How in my words soever she be shent,
To give them seals, never, my soul, consent!
                     [*Exit.*

SCENE III—*A Room in the same.*

Enter KING, ROSENCRANTZ, *and* GUILDENSTERN.

King. I like him not; nor stands it safe with us
To let his madness range. Therefore, prepare you;
I your commission will forthwith despatch,
And he to England shall along with you:
The terms of our estate may not endure
Hazard so near us, as doth hourly grow
Out of his lunacies.

     Guil.   We will ourselves provide:
Most holy and religious fear it is,
To keep those many many bodies safe
That live and feed upon your majesty.

     Ros. The single and peculiar life is bound,
With all the strength and armour of the mind,
To keep itself from 'noyance; but much more
That spirit upon whose weal depend and rest
The lives of many.   The cease of majesty
Dies not alone; but, like a gulph, doth draw
What's near it with it: it is a massy wheel,
Fixed on the summit of the highest mount,
To whose huge spokes ten thousand lesser things
Are mortised and adjoined; which, when it falls,
Each small annexment, petty consequence,
Attends the boisterous ruin.   Never alone
Did the king sigh, but with a general groan.

     King. Arm you, I pray you, to this speedy
         voyage;
For we will fetters put upon this fear,
Which now goes too free-footed.

     Ros. }
     Guil. }   We will haste us.

       [*Exeunt* ROSENCRANTZ *and* GUILDENSTERN.

Enter POLONIUS.

     Pol. My lord, he's going to his mother's closet:
Behind the arras I'll convey myself,
To hear the process; I'll warrant she'll tax him
     home:
And, as you said, and wisely was it said,
'Tis meet that some more audience than a mo-
     ther,
Since nature makes them partial, should o'erhear
The speech of vantage.   Fare you well, my liege:
I'll call upon you ere you go to bed,
And tell you what I know.

     King.   Thanks, dear my lord.
                    [*Exit* POLONIUS.

O, my offence is rank, it smells to heaven;
It hath the primal eldest curse upon't,
A brother's murder!—Pray can I not,
Though inclination be as sharp as will;
My stronger guilt defeats my strong intent;
And, like a man to double business bound,
I stand in pause where I shall first begin;
And both neglect.   What if this cursèd hand
Were thicker than itself with brother's blood?
Is there not rain enough in the sweet heavens
To wash it white as snow?   Whereto serves mercy
But to confront the visage of offence?
And what's in prayer but this twofold force,—
To be forestallèd ere we come to fall,
Or pardoned, being down?   Then I'll look up;
My fault is past.   But O, what form of prayer
Can serve my turn?   Forgive me my foul mur-
     der!—
That cannot be; since I am still possessed
Of those effects for which I did the murder?
My crown, mine own ambition, and my queen.
May one be pardoned and retain the offence?
In the corrupted currents of this world,
Offence's gilded hand may shove by justice;
And oft 'tis seen, the wicked prize itself
Buys out the law: but 'tis not so above:
There is no shuffling, there the action lies
In his true nature; and we ourselves compelled,
Even to the teeth and forehead of our faults,
To give in evidence.   What then? what rests?
Try what repentance can: what can it not?
Yet what can it, when one cannot repent?
O wretched state!   O bosom, black as death!
O limèd soul, that, struggling to be free,
Art more engaged!   Help, angels, make assay!
Bow, stubborn knees! and heart, with strings of
     steel,
Be soft as sinews of the new-born babe!—
All may be well!   [*Retires, and kneels.*

Enter HAMLET.

     Ham. Now might I do it, pat, now he is praying;
And now I'll do't;—and so he goes to heaven:

And so am I revenged? That would be scanned;
A villain kills my father; and for that,
I, his sole son, do this same villain send
To heaven.
Why, this is hire and salary, not revenge.
He took my father grossly, full of bread;
With all his crimes broad blown, as flush as May;
And how his audit stands who knows, save heaven?
But, in our circumstance and course of thought,
'T is heavy with him: and am I then revenged,
To take him in the purging of his soul,
When he is fit and seasoned for his passage?
No.
Up, sword; and know thou a more horrid hent:
When he is drunk, asleep, or in his rage;
Or in the incestuous pleasures of his bed;
At gaming, swearing; or about some act
That has no relish of salvation in 't:
Then trip him, that his heels may kick at heaven:
And that his soul may be as damned and black
As hell, whereto it goes.   My mother stays :—
This physic but prolongs thy sickly days. [*Exit.*

The KING *rises, and advances.*

King. My words fly up, my thoughts remain
        below :
Words without thoughts, never to heaven go.
                                        [*Exit.*

SCENE IV.—*Another Room in the same.*

Enter QUEEN *and* POLONIUS.

Pol. He will come straight. Look you lay
        home to him :
Tell him his pranks have been too broad to bear
        with;
And that your grace hath screened and stood be-
        tween
Much heat and him.   I 'll silence me e'en here.
Pray you, be round with him.
    Queen.   I 'll warrant you;
Fear me not. Withdraw; I hear him coming.
                            [POLONIUS *hides himself.*

Enter HAMLET.

Ham. Now, mother; what 's the matter?
Queen. Hamlet, thou hast thy father much
        offended.
Ham. Mother, you have my father much
        offended.
Queen. Come, come, you answer with an idle
        tongue.
Ham. Go, go, you question with a wicked
        tongue.
Queen. Why, how now, Hamlet?

Ham.   What 's the matter now?
Queen. Have you forgot me?
Ham.   No, by the rood, not so:
You are the queen, your husband's brother's wife;
And—'would it were not so—you are my mother.
    Queen. Nay, then I 'll set those to you that can
        speak.
Ham. Come, come, and sit you down; you shall
        not budge;
You go not, till I set you up a glass,
Where you may see the inmost part of you.
    Queen. What wilt thou do? thou wilt not mur-
        der me?
Help, help, ho!
    Pol. [*behind*]. What, ho! help!
    Ham.   How now! a rat?   [*Draws.*
Dead, for a ducat, dead!
            [HAMLET *makes a pass through the arras.*
    Pol. [*behind*]. O, I am slain. [*Falls and dies.*
    Queen. O me, what hast thou done?
    Ham.   Nay, I know not:
Is it the king?
    [*Lifts up the arras, and draws forth* POLONIUS.
    Queen. O, what a rash and bloody deed in this!
    Ham. A bloody deed;—almost as bad, good
        mother,
As kill a king, and marry with his brother.
    Queen. As kill a king!
    Ham.   Ay, lady, 't was my word.—
Thou wretched, rash, intruding fool, farewell!
                            [*To* POLONIUS.
I took thee for thy better; take thy fortune:
Thou find'st, to be too busy is some danger.—
Leave wringing of your hands: peace; sit you
        down,
And let me wring your heart: for so I shall,
If it be made of penetrable stuff;
If damnéd custom hath not brazed it so,
That it is proof and bulwark against sense.
    Queen. What have I done, that thou darest wag
        thy tongue
In noise so rude against me?
    Ham.   Such an act
That blurs the grace and blush of modesty;
Calls virtue hypocrite; takes off the rose
From the fair forehead of an innocent love,
And sets a blister there; makes marriage vows
As false as dicers' oaths: O, such a deed
As from the body of contraction plucks
The very soul; and sweet religion makes
A rhapsody of words: Heaven's face doth glow;
Yea, this solidity and compound mass,
With tristful visage, as against the doom,
Is thought-sick at the act,
    Queen.   Ah me, what act.
That roars so loud, and thunders in the index?
    Ham. Look here, upon this picture, and on this;

Nay, I know not: is it the king?

The counterfeit presentment of two brothers.
See what a grace was seated on this brow:
Hyperion's curls; the front of Jove himself;
An eye like Mars, to threaten and command;
A station like the herald Mercury,
New-lighted on a heaven-kissing hill;
A combination and a form, indeed,
Where every god did seem to set his seal,
To give the world assurance of a man:
This was your husband.—Look you now what
　　　follows:
Here is your husband; like a mildewed ear,
Blasting his wholesome brother. Have you eyes?
Could you on this fair mountain leave to feed,
And batten on this moor? Ha! have you eyes?
You cannot call it love: for at your age
The heyday in the blood is tame, it's humble,
And waits upon the judgment: and what judg-
　　　ment
Would step from this to this? Sense sure you
　　　have,
Else could you not have motion: but sure that
　　　sense
Is apoplexed: for madness would not err;
Nor sense to ecstasy was ne'er so thralled,
But it reserved some quantity of choice
To serve in such a difference. What devil was't
That thus hath cozened you at hoodman-blind?
Eyes without feeling, feeling without sight,

Ears without hands or eyes, smelling sans all,
Or but a sickly part of one true sense,
Could not so mope.
O shame! where is thy blush? Rebellious hell,
If thou canst mutine in a matron's bones,
To flaming youth let virtue be as wax,
And melt in her own fire: proclaim no shame
When the compulsive ardour gives the charge;
Since frost itself as actively doth burn,
And reason panders will.
　　Queen.　　　　O Hamlet, speak no more:
Thou turn'st mine eyes into my very soul;
And there I see such black and grainéd spots
As will not leave their tinct.
　　Ham.　　　　Nay, but to live
In the rank sweat of an enseaméd bed;
Stewed in corruption; honeying and making love
Over the nasty stye!
　　Queen.　　　　O, speak to me no more;
These words like daggers enter in mine ears:
No more, sweet Hamlet.
　　Ham.　　　　A murderer and a villain:
A slave, that is not twentieth part the tythe
Of your precedent lord: a vice of kings:
A cutpurse of the empire and the rule;
That from a shelf the precious diadem stole,
And put it in his pocket!
　　Queen.　　　　No more.
　　Ham. A king of shreds and patches!—

Enter Ghost.

Save me, and hover o'er me with your wings,
You heavenly guards!—What would your gracious
    figure?

  Queen. Alas! he's mad.

  Ham. Do you not come your tardy son to
    chide,
That, lapsed in time and passion, lets go by
The important acting of your dread command?
O, say!

  Ghost. Do not forget: this visitation
Is but to whet thy almost blunted purpose.
But look! amazement on thy mother sits:

O, step between her and her fighting soul;
Conceit in weakest bodies strongest works;
Speak to her, Hamlet.

  Ham.   How is it with you, lady?

  Queen. Alas, how is't with you?
That you do bend your eye on vacancy,
And with th' incorporal air do hold discourse?
Forth at your eyes your spirits wildly peep;
And, as the sleeping soldiers in th' alarm,
Your bedded hair, like life in excrements,
Starts up, and stands on end.   O, gentle son,
Upon the heat and flame of thy distemper
Sprinkle cool patience.   Whereon do you look?

Why, look you there! look how it steals away!

Ham. On him! on him!—Look you, how pale
    he glares!
His form and cause conjoined, preaching to stones,
Would make them capable.—Do not look upon
    me;
Lest, with this piteous action, you convert
My stern effects: then what I have to do
Will want true colour; tears, perchance, for blood.
    Queen. To whom do you speak this?
    Ham. Do you see nothing there?
    Queen. Nothing at all; yet all that is I see.
    Ham. Nor did you nothing hear?
    Queen. No, nothing, but ourselves.
    Ham. Why, look you there! look how it steals
    away!
My father, in his habit as he lived;
Look where he goes, even now, out at the portal!
                     [*Exit* Ghost.
    Queen. This is the very coinage of your brain:
This bodiless creation ecstasy
Is very cunning in.
    Ham. Ecstasy!
My pulse as yours doth temperately keep time,
And makes as healthful music. It is not madness
That I have uttered: bring me to the test,
And I the matter will re-word; which madness
Would gambol from. Mother, for love of grace,
Lay not that flattering unction to your soul,
That not your trespass, but my madness, speaks:
It will but skin, and film the ulcerous place;
Whiles rank corruption, mining all within,
Infects unseen. Confess yourself to heaven;
Repent what's past; avoid what is to come;
And do not spread the compost on the weeds,
To make them ranker. Forgive me this my
    virtue:
For, in the fatness of these pursy times,
Virtue itself of vice must pardon beg;
Yea, curb and woo for leave to do him good.
    Queen. O, Hamlet! thou hast cleft my heart in
    twain.
    Ham. O, throw away the worser part of it,
And live the purer with the other half.
Good night: but go not to my uncle's bed;
Assume a virtue, if you have it not.
That monster, custom, who all sense doth eat
Of habit's devil, is angel yet in this;
That to the use of actions fair and good
He likewise gives a frock or livery,
That aptly is put on. Refrain to-night:
And that shall lend a kind of easiness
To the next abstinence: the next more easy:
For use almost can change the stamp of nature,
And either curb the devil, or throw him out
With wondrous potency. Once more, good night;

And when you are desirous to be blessed,
I'll blessing beg of you.—For this same lord,
                [*Pointing to* POLONIUS.
I do repent: but heaven hath pleased it so,
To punish me with this, and this with me,
That I must be their scourge and minister.
I will bestow him, and will answer well
The death I gave him. So, again, good night!—
I must be cruel only to be kind:
Thus bad begins, and worse remains behind.—
One word more, good lady.
    Queen.   What shall I do?
    Ham. Not this, by no means, that I bid you do:
Let the bloat king tempt you again to bed:
Pinch wanton on your cheek; call you his mouse;
And let him, for a pair of reechy kisses,
Or paddling in your neck with his damned fingers,
Make you to ravel all this matter out,
That I essentially am not in madness,
But mad in craft. 'T were good you let him know:
For who, that's but a queen, fair, sober, wise,
Would from a paddock, from a bat, a gib,
Such dear concernings hide? who would do so?
No, in despite of sense and secrecy,
Unpeg the basket on the house's top,
Let the birds fly; and, like the famous ape,
To try conclusions, in the basket creep,
And break your own neck down.
    Queen. Be thou assured, if words be made of
    breath,
And breath of life, I have no life to breathe
What thou hast said to me.
    Ham. I must to England; you know that?
    Queen.   Alack,
I had forgot; 't is so concluded on.
    Ham. There's letters sealed: and my two
    schoolfellows,—
Whom I will trust as I will adders fanged,—
They bear the mandate; they must sweep my
    way,
And marshal me to knavery:—let it work;
For 't is the sport, to have the engineer
Hoist with his own petar: and it shall go hard
But I will delve one yard below their mines,
And blow them at the moon: O, 't is most sweet,
When in one line two crafts directly meet!—
This man shall set me packing.
I'll lug the guts into the neighbour room.—
Mother, good night.—Indeed, this counsellor
Is now most still, most secret, and most grave,
Who was in life a foolish prating knave.
Come, sir, to draw toward an end with you.—
Good night, mother.
           [*Exeunt severally;* HAMLET *dragging in*
            POLONIUS.

ACT IV

SCENE I.—*Elsinore.—A Room in the Castle.*

Enter KING, QUEEN, ROSENCRANTZ, *and*
GUILDENSTERN.

King. There 's matter in these sighs; these pro-
found heaves
You must translate; 't is fit we understand them:
Where is your son?
    Queen. Bestow this place on us a little while.—
      [*To* ROSENCRANTZ *and* GUILDENSTERN,
        who go out.
Ah, my good lord, what have I seen to-night!
    King. What, Gertrude?—How does Hamlet?
    Queen. Mad as the sea and wind, when both
    contend
Which is the mightier. In his lawless fit,
Behind the arras hearing something stir,
Whips out his rapier, cries, "A rat, a rat!"
And, in this brainish apprehension, kills
The unseen good old man.
    King.   O heavy deed!
It had been so with us, had we been there:
His liberty is full of threats to all;
To you yourself, to us, to every one.
Alas! how shall this bloody deed be answered?
It will be laid to us, whose providence
Should have kept short, restrained, and out of
    haunt,
This mad young man: but so much was our love,
We would not understand what was most fit;
But, like the owner of a foul disease,
To keep it from divulging, let it feed
Even on the pith of life. Where is he gone?
    Queen. To draw apart the body he hath killed:
O'er whom his very madness, like some ore
Among a mineral of metals base,
Shews itself pure; he weeps for what is done.
    King. O, Gertrude, come away!
The sun no sooner shall the mountains touch,
But we will ship him hence: and this vile deed
We must, with all our majesty and skill,
Both countenance and excuse.—Ho, Guilden-
    stern!

Enter ROSENCRANTZ *and* GUILDENSTERN.

Friends both, go join you with some further aid:
Hamlet in madness hath Polonius slain,
And from his mother's closet hath he dragged
    him:
Go, seek him out; speak fair, and bring the body
Into the chapel. I pray you, haste in this.
    [*Exeunt* ROSENCRANTZ *and* GUILDENSTERN.
Come, Gertrude, we 'll call up our wisest friends;
And let them know, both what we mean to do,
And what 's untimely done: so, haply, slander,—
Whose whisper o'er the world's diameter,
As level as the cannon to his blank,
Transports his poisoned shot,—may miss our name,
And hit the woundless air. O, come away!
My soul is full of discord and dismay. [*Exeunt.*

SCENE II.—*Another Room in the same.*

Enter HAMLET.

Ham. —— Safely stowed,—

ROSENCRANTZ, *&c., within.*

Hamlet! lord Hamlet!
    Ham. But soft; what noise? who calls on
Hamlet?—O, here they come.

Enter ROSENCRANTZ *and* GUILDENSTERN.

Ros. What have you done, my lord, with the
    dead body?
    Ham. Compounded it with dust, whereto 't is
kin.

Ros. Tell us where 't is; that we may take it
　　thence,
And bear it to the chapel.

Ham. Do not believe it.

Ros. Believe what?

Ham. That I can keep your counsel, and not
mine own. Besides, to be demanded of a sponge!
—what replication should be made by the son of
a king?

Ros. Take you me for a sponge, my lord?

Ham. Ay, sir; that soaks up the king's countenance, his rewards, his authorities. But such
officers do the king best service in the end: he
keeps them like an ape, in the corner of his jaw;
first mouthed, to be last swallowed: when he
needs what you have gleaned, it is but squeezing
you, and, sponge, you shall be dry again.

Ros. I understand you not, my lord.

Ham. I am glad of it: a knavish speech sleeps
in a foolish ear.

Ros. My lord, you must tell us where the body
is, and go with us to the king.

Ham. The body is with the king, but the king
is not with the body. The king is a thing—

Guil. A thing, my lord?

Ham. Of nothing: bring me to him. Hide fox,
and all after.　　　　　　　　　　　[*Exeunt.*

SCENE III.—*Another Room in the same.*

Enter KING, *attended.*

King. I have sent to seek him, and to find the
　　body.
How dangerous is it that this man goes loose!
Yet must not we put the strong law on him:
He 's loved of the distracted multitude,
Who like not in their judgment, but their eyes;
And where 't is so, the offender's scourge is
　　weighed,
But never the offence. To bear all smooth and
　　even,
This sudden sending him away must seem
Deliberate pause: diseases, desperate grown,
By desperate appliance are relieved,

Enter ROSENCRANTZ.

Or not at all.—How now? what hath befallen?

Ros. Where the dead body is bestowed, my
　　lord,
We cannot get from him.

King.　　　But where is he?

Ros. Without, my lord; guarded to know your
　　pleasure.

King. Bring him before us.

Ros. Ho, Guildenstern! bring in my lord.

Enter HAMLET *and* GUILDENSTERN.

King. Now, Hamlet, where 's Polonius?

Ham. At supper.

King. At supper!—where?

Ham. Not where he eats, but where he is eaten:
a certain convocation of politic worms are e'en at
him. Your worm is your only emperor for diet:
we fat all creatures else, to fat us; and we fat ourselves for maggots: your fat king, and your lean
beggar, is but variable service; two dishes, but
to one table; that 's the end.

King. Alas, alas!

Ham. A man may fish with the worm that hath
eat of a king; and eat of the fish that hath fed of
that worm.

King. What dost thou mean by this?

Ham. Nothing, but to shew you how a king may
go a progress through the guts of a beggar.

King. Where is Polonius?

Ham. In heaven; send thither to see: if your
messenger find him not there, seek him i' the other
place yourself. But, indeed, if you find him not
within this month, you shall nose him as you go up
the stairs into the lobby.

King. Go seek him there. [*To some* Attendants.

Ham. He will stay till you come.

　　　　　　　　　　[*Exeunt* Attendants.

King. Hamlet, this deed,—for thine especial
　　safety,
Which we do tender, as we dearly grieve
For that which thou hast done,—must send thee
　　hence
With fiery quickness: therefore, prepare thyself;
The bark is ready, and the wind at help,
Th' associates tend, and everything is bent
For England.

Ham. For England?

King. Ay, Hamlet.

Ham. Good.

King. So is it, if thou knew'st our purposes.

Ham. I see a cherub that sees them. But
come; for England!—Farewell, dear mother.

King. Thy loving father, Hamlet.

Ham. My mother. Father and mother is man
and wife; man and wife is one flesh; and so, my
mother. Come, for England.　　　　[*Exit.*

King. Follow him at foot; tempt him with speed
　　aboard;
Delay it not; I 'll have him hence to-night:
Away; for everything is sealed and done
That else leans on the affair: pray you, make
　　haste.

　　[*Exeunt* ROSENCRANTZ *and* GUILDENSTERN.

And, England, if my love thou hold'st at aught
(As my great power thereof may give thee
　　sense;
Since yet thy cicatrice looks raw and red

After the Danish sword, and thy free awe
Pays homage to us), thou mayst not coldly set
Our sovereign process; which imports at full,
By letters cónjuring to that effect,
The present death of Hamlet. Do it, England;
For like the hectic in my blood he rages,
And thou must cure me: till I know 'tis done,
Howe'er my haps, my joys will ne'er begin. [*Exit.*

SCENE IV.—*A Plain in* Denmark.

Enter FORTINBRAS, *and Forces, marching.*

For. Go, captain, from me, greet the Danish
　　king;
Tell him that, by his licence, Fortinbras
Craves the conveyance of a promised march
Over his kingdom. You know the rendezvous.
If that his majesty would aught with us,
We shall express our duty in his eye;
And let him know so.
　　Cap.　　I will do't, my lord.
　　For. Go softly on.

[*Exeunt* FORTINBRAS *and Forces.*

Enter HAMLET, ROSENCRANTZ, GUILDEN-
　　STERN, *&c.*

　　Ham.　　Good sir, whose powers are these?
　　Cap. They are of Norway, sir.
　　Ham.　　How purposed, sir,
I pray you?
　　Cap.　　Against some part of Poland.
　　Ham. Who commands them, sir?
　　Cap. The nephew to old Norway,—Fortinbras.
　　Ham. Goes it against the main of Poland, sir,
Or for some frontier?
　　Cap. Truly to speak, sir, and with no addition,
We go to gain a little patch of ground
That hath in it no profit but the name.
To pay five ducats, five, I would not farm it;
Nor will it yield to Norway, or the Pole,
A ranker rate, should it be sold in fee.
　　Ham. Why, then the Polack never will de-
　　　　fend it.
　　Cap. Yes, 'tis already garrisoned.
　　Ham. Two thousand souls, and twenty thou-
　　　　sand ducats,
Will not debate the question of this straw!
This is the imposthume of much wealth and
　　　peace;
That inward breaks, and shews no cause without
Why the man dies.—I humbly thank you, sir.
　　Cap. God be wi' you, sir.　　　　[*Exit.*
　　Ros.　　Will't please you go, my lord?

　　Ham. I will be with you straight. Go a little
　　　before.
　　[*Exeunt* ROSENCRANTZ *and* GUILDENSTERN.
How all occasions do inform against me,
And spur my dull revenge! What is a man,
If his chief good, and market of his time,
Be but to sleep and feed?—a beast, no more.
Sure He that made us with such large discourse,
Looking before and after, gave us not
That capability and god-like reason
To fust in us unused. Now, whether it be
Bestial oblivion, or some craven scruple
Of thinking too precisely on the event,—
A thought which, quartered, hath but one part
　　　wisdom,
And ever three parts coward,—I do not know
Why yet I live to say, " This thing's to do;"
Sith I have cause, and will, and strength, and
　　　means,
To do't. Examples gross as earth exhort me:
Witness this army of such mass and charge,
Led by a delicate and tender prince;
Whose spirit, with divine ambition puffed,
Makes mouths at the invisible event;
Exposing what is mortal and unsure
To all that fortune, death, and danger, dare,
Even for an egg-shell. Rightly to be great,
Is, not to stir without great argument;
But greatly to find quarrel in a straw,
When honour's at the stake. How stand I then,
That have a father killed, a mother stained,
Excitements of my reason and my blood,
And let all sleep? while, to my shame, I see
The imminent death of twenty thousand men,
That, for a fantasy and trick of fame,
Go to their graves like beds; fight for a plot
Whereon the numbers cannot try the cause,—
Which is not tomb enough and continent
To hide the slain!—O, from this time forth,
My thoughts be bloody, or be nothing worth!
　　　　　　　　　　　　　　　　[*Exit.*

SCENE V.—Elsinore. *A Room in the Castle.*

Enter QUEEN *and* HORATIO.

　　Queen. I will not speak with her.
　　Hor. She is importunate; indeed, distract;
Her mood will needs be pitied.
　　Queen.　　What would she have?
　　Hor. She speaks much of her father; says,
　　　she hears
There's tricks i' the world; and hems, and beats
　　　her heart;
Spurns enviously at straws; speaks things in doubt,
That carry but half sense: her speech is nothing,

Yet the unshapéd use of it doth move
The hearers to collection; they aim at it,
And botch the words up fit to their own thoughts;
Which, as her winks, and nods, and gestures yield
 them,
Indeed would make one think, there might be
 thought,
Though nothing sure, yet much unhappily.
 Queen. 'T were good she were spoken with; for
 she may strew
Dangerous conjectures in ill-breeding minds:
Let her come in.   [*Exit* HORATIO.
To my sick soul, as sin's true nature is,
Each toy seems prologue to some great amiss:
So full of artless jealousy is guilt,
It spills itself in fearing to be spilt.

 Re-enter HORATIO, *with* OPHELIA.

 Oph. Where is the beauteous majesty of Denmark?
 Queen. How now, Ophelia?

 OPHELIA *sings.*

 How should I your true love know
  From another one?
 By his cockle-hat and staff,
  And his sandal-shoon.

 Queen. Alas, sweet lady, what imports this
 song?
 Oph. Say you? nay, pray you, mark:

 Sings.

 He is dead and gone, lady,
  He is dead and gone;
 At his head a grass-green turf,
  At his heels a stone.
O, ho!
 Queen. Nay, but Ophelia,—
 Oph.   Pray you, mark:

 Sings.

White his shroud as the mountain snow,—

 Enter KING.
 Queen. Alas, look here, my lord.

 OPHELIA *sings.*
 Larded all with sweet flowers;
 Which bewept to the grave did go,
 With true-love showers.

 King. How do you do, pretty lady?
 Oph. Well, God 'ield you! They say, the owl
was a baker's daughter. Lord, we know what
we are, but know not what we may be. God be
at your table!
 King. Conceit upon her father.
 Oph. Pray let us have no words of this; but
when they ask you what it means, say you this:—

 Sings.
Good morrow, 't is St. Valentine's day,
 All in the morning betime,
And I a maid at your window,
 To be your Valentine:
Then up he rose, and donned his clothes,
 And dupped the chamber door;
Let in the maid, that out a maid
 Never departed more.

 King. Pretty Ophelia.
 Oph. Indeed, without an oath, I 'll make an
 end on 't.
 Sings.
By Gis and by Saint Charity,
 Alack and fie for shame!
Young men will do 't if they come to 't;
 By cock they are to blame.
Quoth she, before you tumbled me,
 You promised me to wed:
So would I ha' done, by yonder sun,
 An thou hadst not come to my bed.

 King. How long hath she been thus?
 Oph. I hope all will be well. We must be
patient: but I cannot choose but weep, to think
they shall lay him i' the cold ground. My brother shall know of it, and so I thank you for
your good counsel. Come, my coach! Good
night, ladies; good night, sweet ladies; good
night, good night.   [*Exit.*

King. Follow her close; give her good watch,
 I pray you,   [*Exit* HORATIO.
O, this is the poison of deep grief; it springs
All from her father's death.—O, Gertrude, Gertrude,
When sorrows come, they come not single spies,
But in battalions! First, her father slain;
Next, your son gone; and he most violent author
Of his own just remove: the people muddied,
Thick and unwholesome in their thoughts and
 whispers,
For good Polonius' death; and we have done but
 greenly,
In hugger-mugger to inter him: poor Ophelia
Divided from herself and her fair judgment;
Without the which we are pictures, or mere beasts:
Last, and as much containing as all these,
Her brother is in secret come from France;
Feeds on his wonder, keeps himself in clouds,
And wants not buzzers to infect his ear
With pestilent speeches of his father's death;
Wherein necessity, of matter beggared,
Will nothing stick our person to arraign
In ear and ear. O, my dear Gertrude, this,
Like to a murdering-piece, in many places
Gives me superfluous death. [*A noise within.*
 Queen. Alack, what noise is this?

   Enter a Gentleman.

 King. Attend:
Where are my Switzers? Let them guard the
 door:
What is the matter?
 Gent. Save yourself, my lord;
The ocean, overpeering of his list,
Eats not the flats with more impetuous haste,
Than young Laertes, in a riotous head,
O'erbears your officers! The rabble call him,
 lord;
And, as the world were now but to begin,
Antiquity forgot, custom not known,
The ratifiers and props of every word,
They cry, "Choose we; Laertes shall be king!"
Caps, hands, and tongues, applaud it to the
 clouds,
"Laertes shall be king; Laertes king!"
 Queen. How cheerfully on the false trail they
 cry;
O, this is counter, you false Danish dogs.
 King. The doors are broke. [*Noise within.*

  Enter LAERTES, *armed;* Danes *following.*

 Laer. Where is this king?—Sirs, stand you all
 without.
 Danes. No, let's come in.
 Laer. I pray you, give me leave.

 Danes. We will, we will.
    [*They retire without the door.*
 Laer. I thank you: keep the door.—O, thou
 vile king,
Give me my father.
 Queen. Calmly, good Laertes.
 Laer. That drop of blood that's calm, proclaims
 me bastard;
Cries "cuckold" to my father; brands the harlot
Even here, between the chaste unsmirchéd brow
Of my true mother.
 King. What is the cause, Laertes,
That thy rebellion looks so giant-like?
Let him go, Gertrude; do not fear our person:
There's such divinity doth hedge a king,
That treason can but peep to what it would,—
Acts little of his will.—Tell me, Laertes,
Why thou art thus incensed?—Let him go, Gertrude;—
Speak, man.
 Laer. Where is my father?
 King. Dead.
 Queen. But not by him.
 King. Let him demand his fill.
 Laer. How came he dead?—I'll not be juggled
 with:
To hell, allegiance! vows, to the blackest devil!
Conscience and grace to the profoundest pit!
I dare damnation: to this point I stand,—
That both the worlds I give to negligence,
Let come what comes; only I'll be revenged
Most throughly for my father.
 King. Who shall stay you?
 Laer. My will; not all the world:
And, for my means, I'll husband them so well,
They shall go far with little.
 King. Good Laertes,
If you desire to know the certainty
Of your dear father's death, is't writ in your revenge
That, sweepstake, you will draw both friend and
 foe,
Winner and loser?
 Laer. None but his enemies.
 King. Will you know them, then?
 Laer. To his good friends thus wide I'll ope
 my arms;
And, like the kind life-rendering pelican,
Repast them with my blood.
 King. Why, now you speak
Like a good child and a true gentleman.
That I am guiltless of your father's death,
And am most sensibly in grief for it,
It shall as level to your judgment 'pear,
As day does to your eye.
 Danes [*within*]. Let her come in.
 Laer. How now! what noise is that?

Enter OPHELIA, *fantastically dressed with straws and flowers.*

O heat, dry up my brains! tears, seven times salt,
Burn out the sense and virtue of mine eye!—
By heaven, thy madness shall be paid with weight,
Till our scale turn the beam.   O rose of May!
Dear maid, kind sister, sweet Ophelia!—
O heavens! is't possible a young maid's wits
Should be as mortal as an old man's life?

Nature is fine in love: and where 'tis fine,
It sends some precious instance of itself
After the thing it loves.

OPHELIA *sings.*

They bore him barefaced on the bier;
    Hey no nonny, nonny hey nonny:
And in his grave rained many a tear;—

Fare you well, my dove!

Laer. Hadst thou thy wits, and didst persuade
    revenge,
It could not move thus.
Oph. You must sing, "Down a-down, an you
call him a-down-a." O, how the wheel becomes
it! It is the false steward, that stole his master's
daughter.
Laer. This nothing's more than matter.
Oph. There's rosemary, that's for remembrance; pray you, love, remember: and there
is pansies, that's for thoughts.
Laer. A document in madness; thoughts and
remembrance fitted!

Oph. There's fennel for you, and columbines:
—there's rue for you; and here's some for me;
we may call it herb of grace o'Sundays: you
may wear your rue with a difference.—There's
a daisy: I would give you some violets; but
they withered all when my father died: they say
he made a good end,—

Sings.

For bonny sweet Robin is all my joy,—

Laer. Thought and affliction, passion, hell
    itself,
She turns to favour and to prettiness!

OPHELIA *sings.*

And will he not come again?
And will he not come again?
  No, no, he is dead,
  Go to thy death-bed,
He never will come again.

His beard was as white as snow,
All flaxen was his poll:
  He is gone, he is gone,
  And we cast away moan;
God 'a mercy on his soul!

And of all christian souls! I pray God. God
be wi' you!   *[Exit* OPHELIA.
  Laer. Do you see this, O God?
  King. Laertes, I must commune with your grief,
Or you deny me right.   Go but apart,
Make choice of whom your wisest friends you will,
And they shall hear and judge 'twixt you and me:
If by direct or by collateral hand
They find us touched, we will our kingdom give,
Our crown, our life, and all that we call ours,
To you in satisfaction; but if not,
Be you content to lend your patience to us,

And we shall jointly labour with your soul,
To give it due content.
  Laer.   Let this be so:
His means of death, his obscure funeral,—
No trophy, sword, nor hatchment, o'er his bones,
No noble rite, nor formal ostentation,—
Cry to be heard, as 't were from heaven to earth,
That I must call 't in question.
  King.   So you shall;
And where the offence is, let the great axe fall.
I pray you go with me.   *[Exeunt.*

SCENE VI.—*Another Room in the same.*

Enter HORATIO *and a* Servant.

  Hor. What are they that would speak with me?
  Serv. Sailors, sir; they say they have letters for you.
  Hor. Let them come in.—   *[Exit* Servant.
I do not know from what part of the world
I should be greeted, if not from lord Hamlet.

Enter Sailors.

  1st Sail. God bless you, sir.

Hor. Let Him bless thee too.

1st Sail. He shall, sir, an't please Him. There's a letter for you, sir; it comes from the ambassador that was bound for England; if your name be Horatio, as I am let to know it is.

HORATIO *reads.*

"Horatio, when thou shalt have overlooked this, give these fellows some means to the king; they have letters for him. Ere we were two days old at sea, a pirate of very warlike appointment gave us chase: finding ourselves too slow of sail, we put on a compelled valour; and in the grapple I boarded them: on the instant, they got clear of our ship; so I alone became their prisoner. They have dealt with me like thieves of mercy; but they knew what they did; I am to do a good turn for them. Let the king have the letters I have sent; and repair thou to me with as much haste as thou wouldst fly death. I have words to speak in thine ear will make thee dumb; yet are they much too light for the bore of the matter. These good fellows will bring thee where I am. Rosencrantz and Guildenstern hold their course for England; of them I have much to tell thee. Farewell.

"He that thou knowest thine, HAMLET."

Come, I will give you way for these your letters;
And do't the speedier, that you may direct me
To him from whom you brought them. [*Exeunt.*

SCENE VII.—*Another Room in the same.*

Enter KING *and* LAERTES.

King. Now must your conscience my acquittance seal,
And you must put me in your heart for friend;
Sith you have heard, and with a knowing ear,
That he which hath your noble father slain,
Pursued my life.

Laer. It well appears. But tell me
Why you proceeded not against these feats,
So crimeful and so capital in nature,
As by your safety, greatness, wisdom, all things else,
You mainly were stirred up.

King. O, for two special reasons;
Which may to you, perhaps, seem much unsinewed,
But yet to me they are strong. The queen, his mother,
Lives almost by his looks; and for myself
(My virtue, or my plague, be it either which),
She is so conjunctive to my life and soul,
That, as the star moves not but in his sphere,
I could not but by her. The other motive
Why to a public count I might not go,
Is, the great love the general gender bear him:
Who, dipping all his faults in their affection,

Work like the spring that turneth wood to stone,
Convert his gyves to graces; so that my arrows,
Too slightly timbered for so loud a wind,
Would have reverted to my bow again,
And not where I had aimed them.

Laer. And so have I a noble father lost;
A sister driven into desperate terms,
Whose worth, if praises may go back again,
Stood challenger on mount of all the age
For her perfections! but my revenge will come.

King. Break not your sleeps for that: you must not think
That we are made of stuff so flat and dull,
That we can let our beard be shook with danger,
And think it pastime. You shortly shall hear more:
I loved your father, and we love ourself;
And that, I hope, will teach you to imagine——
How now? what news?

Enter a Messenger.

Mess. Letters, my lord, from Hamlet:
This to your majesty; this to the queen.

King. From Hamlet! Who brought them?

Mess. Sailors, my lord, they say: I saw them not. They were given me by Claudio; he received them of him that brought them.

King. Laertes, you shall hear them.—Leave us.
[*Exit* Messenger.

KING *reads.*

"High and mighty, you shall know I am set naked on your kingdom. To-morrow shall I beg leave to see your kingly eyes: when I shall, first asking your pardon thereunto, recount the occasion of my sudden and more strange return.

"HAMLET."

What should this mean? Are all the rest come back?
Or is it some abuse, and no such thing?

Laer. Know you the hand?

King. 'Tis Hamlet's character. "Naked,"—
And, in a postscript here, he says, "Alone."
Can you advise me?

Laer. I am lost in it, my lord. But let him come;
It warms the very sickness in my heart,
That I shall live and tell him to his teeth,
"Thus diddest thou."

King. If it be so, Laertes,—
As how should it be so? how otherwise?—
Will you be ruled by me?

Laer. Ay, my lord;
So you will not o'errule me to a peace.

King. To thine own peace. If he be now returned,
(As checking at his voyage, and that he means
No more to undertake it), I will work him
To an exploit, now ripe in my device,
Under the which he shall not choose but fall:
And for his death no wind of blame shall breathe:

But even his mother shall uncharge the practice,
And call it accident.

   Laer.   My lord, I will be ruled;
The rather, if you could devise it so
That I might be the organ.

   King.   It falls right.
You have been talked of since your travel much,
And that in Hamlet's hearing, for a quality
Wherein they say you shine: your sum of parts
Did not together pluck such envy from him,
As did that one; and that, in my regard,
Of the unworthiest siege.

   Laer.   What part is that, my lord?

   King. A very riband in the cap of youth,
Yet needful too; for youth no less becomes
The light and careless livery that it wears,
Than settled age his sables and his weeds,
Importing health and graveness.—Two months
       since,
Here was a gentleman of Normandy,—
I have seen myself, and served against, the French,
And they can well on horseback: but this gallant
Had witchcraft in 't: he grew unto his seat;
And to such wondrous doing brought his horse,
As he had been incorpsed and demi-natured
With the brave beast: so far he topped my thought,
That I, in forgery of shapes and tricks,
Come short of what he did.

   Laer. A Norman was 't?

   King. A Norman.

   Laer. Upon my life, Lamord.

   King. The very same.

   Laer. I know him well: he is the brooch, indeed,
And gem of all the nation.

   King. He made confession of you;
And gave you such a masterly report
For art and exercise in your defence,
And for your rapier most especially,
That he cried out, 't would be a sight indeed
If one could match you: the scrimers of their nation,
He swore, had neither motion, guard, nor eye,
If you opposed them.   Sir, this report of his
Did Hamlet so envenom with his envy,
That he could nothing do but wish and beg
Your sudden coming o'er, to play with you.
Now, out of this,—

   Laer.   What out of this, my lord?

   King. Laertes, was your father dear to you?
Or are you like the painting of a sorrow,
A face without a heart?

   Laer.   Why ask you this?

   King. Not that I think you did not love your
       father;
But that I know love is begun by time;
And that I see, in passages of proof,
Time qualifies the spark and fire of it.
There lives within the very flame of love

A kind of wick, or snuff, that will abate it;
And nothing is at a like goodness still;
For goodness, growing to a pleurisy,
Dies in his own too-much: that we would do,
We should do when we would; for this "would"
       changes,
And hath abatements and delays as many
As there are tongues, are hands, are accidents;
And then this "should" is like a spendthrift sigh,
That hurts by easing. But to the quick o' the ulcer:
Hamlet comes back: what would you undertake,
To shew yourself indeed your father's son
More than in words?

   Laer.   To cut his throat i' the church.

   King. No place, indeed, should murder sanc-
       tuarise;
Revenge should have no bounds. But, good Laertes,
Will you do this,—keep close within your chamber?
Hamlet, returned, shall know you are come home:
We 'll put on those shall praise your excellence,
And set a double varnish on the fame
The Frenchman gave you; bring you, in fine, to-
       gether,
And wager on your heads: he, being remiss,
Most generous, and free from all contriving,
Will not peruse the foils; so that, with ease,
Or with a little shuffling, you may choose
A sword unbated, and, in a pass of practice,
Requite him for your father.

   Laer.   I will do 't:
And, for the purpose, I 'll anoint my sword.
I bought an unction of a mountebank,
So mortal, that but dip a knife in it,
Where it draws blood, no cataplasm so rare,
Collected from all simples that have virtue
Under the moon, can save the thing from death,
That is but scratched withal: I 'll touch my point
With this contagion; that, if I gall him slightly,
It may be death.

   King.   Let 's further think of this;
Weigh what convenience, both of time and means,
May fit us to our shape. If this should fail,
And that our drift look through our bad performance,
'T were better not assayed; therefore, this project
Should have a back, or second, that might hold,
If this should blast in proof. Soft; let me see:
We 'll make a solemn wager on your cunnings,—
I ha 't:
When in your motion you are hot and dry
(As make your bouts more violent to that end),
And that he calls for drink, I 'll have preferred him
A chalice for the nonce; whereon but sipping,
If he by chance escape your venomed stuck,
Our purpose may hold there. But stay, what noise?

                Enter QUEEN.

How now, sweet queen?

Queen. One woe doth tread upon another's heel,
So fast they follow:—Your sister's drowned,
    Laertes.
    Laer. Drowned! O, where?
    Queen. There is a willow grows ascaunt the brook,
That shews his hoar leaves in the glassy stream;
There, with fantastic garlands did she come,
Of crow-flowers, nettles, daisies, and long purples,
That liberal shepherds give a grosser name,
But our cold maids do "dead-men's fingers" call
    them:
There, on the pendent boughs her coronet weeds
Clambering to hang, an envious sliver broke;
When down her weedy trophies, and herself,
Fell in the weeping brook. Her clothes spread wide;
And, mermaid-like, awhile they bore her up:
Which time she chanted snatches of old tunes;
As one incapable of her own distress,

Or like a creature native and indued
Unto that element: but long it could not be,
Till that her garments, heavy with their drink,
Pulled the poor wretch from her melodious lay
To muddy death.
    Laer.   Alas, then, she is drowned?
    Queen. Drowned, drowned.
    Laer. Too much of water hast thou, poor Ophelia,
And therefore I forbid my tears: but yet
It is our trick; nature her custom holds,
Let shame say what it will: when these are gone,
The woman will be out.—Adieu, my lord:
I have a speech of fire, that fain would blaze,
But that this folly drowns it.   [*Exit.*
    King.   Let's follow, Gertrude:
How much I had to do to calm his rage!
Now fear I this will give it start again;
Therefore let's follow.   [*Exeunt.*

ACT V.

SCENE I.—*A Churchyard.*

Enter Two Clowns, *with spades, &c.*

1st Clo. Is she to be buried in christian burial, that wilfully seeks her own salvation?

2nd Clo. I tell thee she is; therefore make her grave straight: the crowner hath set on her, and finds it christian burial.

1st Clo. How can that be, unless she drowned herself in her own defence?

2nd Clo. Why, 'tis found so.

1st Clo. It must be *se offendendo*; it cannot be else. For here lies the point:—If I drown myself wittingly, it argues an act: and an act hath three branches; it is, to act, to do, and to perform: argal, she drowned herself wittingly.

2nd Clo. Nay, but hear you, goodman delver.

1st Clo. Give me leave. Here lies the water; good: here stands the man; good: if the man go to this water, and drown himself, it is, will he, nill he, he goes; mark you that: but if the water come to him, and drown him, he drowns not himself: argal, he that is not guilty of his own death, shortens not his own life.

2nd Clo. But is this law?

1st Clo. Ay, marry is 't; crowner's quest law.

2nd Clo. Will you ha' the truth on 't? If this had not been a gentlewoman, she should have been buried out of christian burial.

1st Clo. Why, there thou say'st: and the more pity, that great folks shall have countenance in this world to drown or hang themselves, more than their even christian. Come, my spade. There is no ancient gentlemen but gardeners, ditchers, and grave-makers; they hold up Adam's profession.

2nd Clo. Was he a gentleman?

1st Clo. He was the first that ever bore arms.

2nd Clo. Why, he had none.

1st Clo. What, art a heathen? How dost thou understand the scripture? The scripture says, Adam digged: could he dig without arms? I'll put another question to thee: if thou answerest me not to the purpose, confess thyself,—

2nd Clo. Go to.

1st Clo. What is he that builds stronger than either the mason, the shipwright, or the carpenter?

2nd Clo. The gallows-maker; for that frame outlives a thousand tenants.

1st Clo. I like thy wit well, in good faith; the gallows does well: but how does it well? it does well to those that do ill: now thou dost ill, to say the gallows is built stronger than the church: argal, the gallows may do well to thee. To 't again; come.

2nd Clo. Who builds stronger than a mason, a shipwright, or a carpenter?

1st Clo. Ay, tell me that, and unyoke.

2nd Clo. Marry, now I can tell.

1st Clo. To 't.

2nd Clo. Mass, I cannot tell.

Enter HAMLET *and* HORATIO, *at a distance.*

1st Clo. Cudgel thy brains no more about it; for your dull ass will not mend his pace with beating: and when you are asked this question next, say, a grave-maker; the houses that he makes, last till doomsday. Go, get thee to Yaughan, and fetch me a stoup of liquor.   [*Exit 2nd* Clown.

1st Clown *digs, and sings.*

In youth, when I did love, did love,
　　Methought it was very sweet,
To contract, O, the time, for, ah, my behove,
　　O, methought there was nothing meet.

Ham. Has this fellow no feeling of his business? he sings at grave-making.

Hor. Custom hath made it in him a property of easiness.

Ham. 'Tis e'en so: the hand of little employment hath the daintier sense.

1st Clown *sings.*

But age, with his stealing steps,
　　Hath clawed me in his clutch,
And hath shipped me into the land,
　　As if I had never been such.

[*Throws up a skull.*

Ham. That skull had a tongue in it, and could sing once: how the knave jowls it to the ground, as if it were Cain's jawbone, that did the first

murder! This might be the pate of a politician, which this ass now o'erreaches; one that would circumvent God; might it not?

Hor. It might, my lord.

Ham. Or of a courtier; which could say, "Good-morrow, sweet lord! How dost thou, good lord?" This might be my lord Such-a-one, that praised my lord Such-a-one's horse, when he meant to beg it; might it not?

Hor. Ay, my lord.

Ham. Why, e'en so: and now my lady Worm's; chapless, and knocked about the mazzard with a sexton's spade: here's fine revolution, an we had the trick to see 't! Did these bones cost no more the breeding, but to play at loggats with them? mine ache to think on 't.

1st Clown *sings.*

A pick-axe, and a spade, a spade,
　　For—and a shrouding sheet:
O, a pit of clay for to be made
　　For such a guest is meet.

[*Throws up a skull.*

Ham. There's another: why may not that be the skull of a lawyer? Where be his quiddits now, his quillets, his cases, his tenures, and his tricks? why does he suffer this rude knave now to knock him about the sconce with a dirty shovel, and will not tell him of his action of battery? Humph! This fellow might be in 's time a great buyer of land, with his statutes, his recognisances, his fines, his double vouchers, his recoveries. Is this the fine of his fines, and the recovery of his recoveries, to have his fine pate full of fine dirt? will his vouchers vouch him no more of his purchases, and double ones too, than the length and breadth of a pair of indentures? The very conveyances of his lands will hardly lie in this box; and must the inheritor himself have no more? ha?

Hor. Not a jot more, my lord.

Ham. Is not parchment made of sheep-skins?

Hor. Ay, my lord, and calves'-skins too.

Ham. They are sheep and calves which seek out assurance in that. I will speak to this fellow. Whose grave 's this, sirrah?

1st Clo. Mine, sir.

Sings.

O, a pit of clay for to be made
　　For such a guest is meet.

Ham. I think it be thine, indeed; for thou liest in 't.

1st Clo. You lie out on 't, sir, and therefore it is not yours: for my part, I do not lie in 't, yet it is mine.

Ham. Thou dost lie in 't, to be in 't, and say it is thine : 'tis for the dead, and not for the quick; therefore thou liest.

1st Clo. 'T is a quick lie, sir ; 't will away again, from me to you.

Ham. What man dost thou dig it for?

1st Clo. For no man, sir.

Ham. What woman, then?

1st Clo. For none, neither.

Ham. Who is to be buried in 't?

1st Clo. One that was a woman, sir ; but, rest her soul, she 's dead.

Ham. How absolute the knave is! we must speak by the card, or equivocation will undo us. By the Lord, Horatio, these three years I have taken note of it; the age is grown so picked, that the toe of the peasant comes so near the heel of the courtier, he galls his kibe. — How long hast thou been a grave-maker?

1st Clo. Of all the days i' the year, I came to 't that day that our last king Hamlet overcame Fortinbras.

Ham. How long is that since?

1st Clo. Cannot you tell that? every fool can tell that : it was that very day that young Hamlet was born; he that is mad, and sent into England.

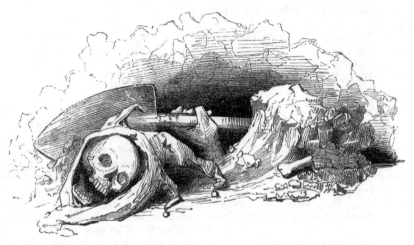

This same skull, sir, was Yorick's skull.

Ham. Ay, marry, why was he sent into England?

1st Clo. Why, because he was mad : he shall recover his wits there; or if he do not, 't is no great matter there.

Ham. Why?

1st Clo. 'T will not be seen in him there; there the men are as mad as he.

Ham. How came he mad?

1st Clo. Very strangely, they say.

Ham. How strangely?

1st Clo. 'Faith, e'en with losing his wits.

Ham. Upon what ground?

1st Clo. Why, here in Denmark. I have been sexton here, man and boy, thirty years.

Ham. How long will a man lie i' the earth ere he rot?

1st Clo. 'Faith, if he be not rotten before he die (as we have many pocky corses now-a-days, that will scarce hold the laying in), he will last you some eight year, or nine year : a tanner will last you nine year.

Ham. Why he more than another?

1st Clo. Why, sir, his hide is so tanned with his trade, that he will keep out water a great while; and your water is a sore decayer of your whoreson dead body. Here 's a skull now hath lain you i' the earth three-and-twenty years.

Ham. Whose was it?

1st Clo. A whoreson mad fellow 's it was : whose do you think it was?

Ham. Nay, I know not.

1st Clo. A pestilence on him for a mad rogue! he poured a flagon of Rhenish on my head once. This same skull, sir, was Yorick's skull, the king's jester.

Ham. This? [*Takes the skull.*

1st Clo. E'en that.

Ham. Alas, poor Yorick!—I knew him, Horatio; a fellow of infinite jest, of most excellent

fancy: he hath borne me on his back a thousand times; and now, how abhorred in my imagination it is! my gorge rises at it. Here hung those lips that I have kissed I know not how oft. Where be your gibes now? your gambols? your songs? your flashes of merriment, that were wont to set the table on a roar? Not one now, to mock your own grinning? quite chapfallen? Now get you to my lady's chamber, and tell her, let her paint an inch thick, to this favour she must come: make her laugh at that.—Pr'y thee, Horatio, tell me one thing.

Hor. What's that, my lord?

Ham. Dost thou think Alexander looked o' this fashion i' the earth?

Hor. E'en so.

Ham. And smelt so? pah!

> [*Throws down the skull.*

Hor. E'en so, my lord.

Ham. To what base uses we may return, Horatio? Why may not imagination trace the noble dust of Alexander, till he find it stopping a bunghole?

Hor. 'T were to consider too curiously, to consider so.

Ham. No, faith, not a jot; but to follow him thither with modesty enough, and likelihood to lead it:—as thus: Alexander died, Alexander was buried, Alexander returneth to dust; the dust is earth; of earth we make loam: and why of that loam whereto he was converted, might they not stop a beer-barrel?

Imperial Cæsar, dead, and turned to clay,
Might stop a hole to keep the wind away:
O, that that earth which kept the world in awe,
Should patch a wall to expel the winter's flaw!
But soft; but soft! aside:—here comes the king,

Enter Priests, *&c., in procession; the corpse of* OPHELIA; LAERTES, *and* Mourners, *following;* KING, QUEEN, *their Trains, &c.*

The queen, the courtiers: who is this they follow?
And with such maiméd rites! This doth betoken,
The corse they follow did with desperate hand
Foredo its own life.   'T was of some estate:
Couch we awhile, and mark.

> [*Retiring with Horatio.*

Laer. What ceremony else?

Ham.   That is Laertes,
A very noble youth: mark.

Laer. What ceremony else?

1st Priest. Her obsequies have been as far enlarged
As we have warranty: her death was doubtful;
And, but that great command o'ersways the order,
She should in ground unsanctified have lodged
Till the last trumpet; for charitable prayers,
Shards, flints, and pebbles, should be thrown on her;
Yet here she is allowed her virgin crants,
Her maiden strewments, and the bringing home
Of bell and burial.

Laer. Must there no more be done?

1st Priest.   No more be done!
We should profane the service of the dead,
To sing a requiem, and such rest to her
As to peace-parted souls.

Laer.   Lay her i' the earth;
And from her fair and unpolluted flesh

May violets spring!—I tell thee, churlish priest,
A ministering angel shall my sister be,
When thou liest howling.

Ham.   What, the fair Ophelia!

Queen. Sweets to the sweet: farewell!

> [*Scattering flowers.*

I hoped thou shouldst have been my Hamlet's wife:
I thought thy bride-bed to have decked, sweet maid,
And not have strewed thy grave.

Laer.   O, treble woe
Fall ten times treble on that curséd head
Whose wicked deed thy most ingenious sense
Deprived thee of!—Hold off the earth awhile,
Till I have caught her once more in mine arms:

> [*Leaps into the grave.*

Now pile your dust upon the quick and dead;
Till of this flat a mountain you have made
To o'ertop old Pelion, or the skyish head
Of blue Olympus.

Ham. [*advancing*]. What is he whose grief
Bears such an emphasis? whose phrase of sorrow
Conjures the wondering stars, and makes them stand
Like wonder-wounded hearers?   This is I,
Hamlet the Dane.   [*Leaps into the grave.*

Laer.   The devil take thy soul!

> [*Grappling with him.*

Ham. Thou pray'st not well.
I pr'y thee take thy fingers from my throat;
For though I am not splenetive and rash,
Yet have I in me something dangerous,
Which let thy wisdom fear: hold off thy hand.

King. Pluck them asunder.

Queen.   Hamlet, Hamlet!

All. Gentlemen,—

Hor.   Good my lord, be quiet.

> [*The* Attendants *part them, and they come out of the grave.*

Ham. Why, I will fight with him upon this theme,
Until my eyelids will no longer wag.

Queen. O my son! what theme?

Ham. I loved Ophelia; forty thousand brothers
Could not, with all their quantity of love,
Make up my sum.—What wilt thou do for her?

King. O, he is mad, Laertes.

Queen. For love of God, forbear him.

Ham. 'Zounds, shew me what thou 'lt do:
Would't weep? would't fight? would't fast? would't tear thyself?
Would't drink up Esil? eat a crocodile?
I'll do 't.—Dost thou come here to whine?
To outface me with leaping in her grave?
Be buried quick with her, and so will I:
And, if thou prate of mountains, let them throw

Millions of acres on us; till our ground,
Singeing his pate against the burning zone,
Make Ossa like a wart!—Nay, an thou'lt mouth,
I'll rant as well as thou.

   Queen.   This is mere madness:
And thus awhile the fit will work on him;
Anon, as patient as the female dove,
When that her golden couplets are disclosed,
His silence will sit drooping.

   Ham.   Hear you, sir:
What is the reason that you use me thus?
I loved you ever. But it is no matter;
Let Hercules himself do what he may,
The cat will mew, and dog will have his day.
                                  [Exit.

   King. I pray thee, good Horatio, wait upon
      him.—   *[Exit* HORATIO.
Strengthen your patience in our last night's
      speech;   *[To* LAERTES.
We'll put the matter to the present push.—
Good Gertrude, set some watch over your son.—
This grave shall have a living monument:
An hour of quiet shortly shall we see;
Till then, in patience our proceeding be. *[Exeunt.*

SCENE II.—*A Hall in the Castle.*

Enter HAMLET *and* HORATIO.

   Ham. So much for this, sir: now shall you see
      the other;—
You do remember all the circumstance?
   Hor. Remember it, my lord?
   Ham. Sir, in my heart there was a kind of
      fighting,
That would not let me sleep: methought I lay
Worse than the mutines in the bilboes. Rashly,
And praised be rashness for it,—let us know,
Our indiscretion sometimes serves us well,
When our deep plots do pall; and that should
      teach us,
There's a divinity that shapes our ends,
Rough-hew them how we will.
   Hor.   That is most certain.
   Ham. Up from my cabin,
My sea-gown scarfed about me, in the dark
Groped I to find out them: had my desire;
Fingered their packet; and, in fine, withdrew
To mine own room again: making so bold,
My fears forgetting manners, to unseal
Their grand commission; where I found, Horatio,
A royal knavery; an exact command,—
Larded with many several sorts of reasons,
Importing Denmark's health, and England's too,
With, ho! such bugs and goblins in my life,—
That, on the supervise, no leisure bated,

No, not to stay the grinding of the axe,
My head should be struck off.
   Hor.   Is't possible?
   Ham. Here's the commission; read it at more
      leisure.
But wilt thou hear now how I did proceed?
   Hor. Ay, 'beseech you.
   Ham. Being thus benetted round with villanies,
Ere I could make a prologue to my brains,
They had begun the play:—I sat me down;
Devised a new commission; wrote it fair:
I once did hold it, as our statists do,
A baseness to write fair, and laboured much
How to forget that learning; but, sir, now
It did me yeoman's service. Wilt thou know
The effect of what I wrote?
   Hor.   Ay, good my lord.
   Ham. An earnest conjuration from the king,—
As England was his faithful tributary;
As love between them like the palm might flourish;
As peace should still her wheaten garland wear,
And stand a comma 'tween their amities;
And many such like "As's" of great charge,—
That, on the view and knowing of these contents,
Without debatement further, more or less,
He should the bearers put to sudden death,
Not shriving-time allowed.
   Hor.   How was this sealed?
   Ham. Why, even in that was heaven ordinant:
I had my father's signet in my purse,
Which was the model of that Danish seal:—
Folded the writ up in form of the other;
Subscribed it; gave't the impression; placed it
      safely,
The changeling never known. Now, the next day
Was our sea-fight: and what to this was sequent
Thou know'st already.
   Hor. So Guildenstern and Rosencrantz go to't.
   Ham. Why, man, they did make love to this
      employment,
They are not near my conscience; their defeat
Does by their own insinuation grow:
'Tis dangerous, when the baser nature comes
Between the pass and fell incenséd points
Of mighty opposites.
   Hor.   Why, what a king is this!
   Ham. Does it not, think thee, stand me now upon?
He, that hath killed my king, and whored my
      mother;
Popped in between the election and my hopes;
Thrown out his angle for my proper life,
And with such cozenage; is't not perfect con-
      science
To quit him with this arm? and is't not to be
      damned,
To let this canker of our nature come
In further evil?

Hor. It must be shortly known to him from
　　　England
What is the issue of the business there.

Ham. It will be short: the interim is mine;
And a man's life's no more than to say, one.
But I am very sorry, good Horatio,
That to Laertes I forgot myself;
For by the image of my cause, I see
The portraiture of his.　I'll count his favours
But sure the bravery of his grief did put me
Into a towering passion.

Hor. 　　　Peace; who comes here?

Enter Osric.

Osr. Your lordship is right welcome back to
Denmark.

Ham. I humbly thank you, sir.—Dost know
this water-fly?

Hor. No, my good lord.

Ham. Thy state is the more gracious; for 'tis
a vice to know him.　He hath much land, and
fertile: let a beast be lord of beasts, and his crib
shall stand at the king's mess.　'Tis a chough;
but, as I say, spacious in the possession of dirt.

Osr. Sweet lord, if your lordship were at leisure, I should impart a thing to you from his
majesty.

Ham. I will receive it, sir, with all diligence
of spirit.　Your bonnet to his right use; 'tis for
the head.

Osr. I thank your lordship, 'tis very hot.

Ham. No, believe me, 'tis very cold; the wind
is northerly.

Osr. It is indifferent cold, my lord, indeed.

Ham. But yet, methinks, it is very sultry and
hot; or my complexion—

Osr. Exceedingly, my lord; it is very sultry,—
as 't were,—I cannot tell how.—My lord, his
majesty bade me signify to you, that he has laid
a great wager on your head: sir, this is the
matter,—

Ham. I beseech you, remember—

[HAMLET *moves him to put on his hat.*

Osr. Nay, good my lord; for my ease, in good faith. Sir, here is newly come to court, Laertes: believe me, an absolute gentleman, full of most excellent differences, of very soft society, and great showing: indeed, to speak feelingly of him, he is the card or calendar of gentry, for you shall find in him the continent of what part a gentleman would see.

Ham. Sir, his definement suffers no perdition in you;—though, I know, to divide him inventorially, would dizzy the arithmetic of memory; and yet but raw neither, in respect of his quick sail. But, in the verity of extolment, I take him to be a soul of great article; and his infusion of such dearth and rareness, as, to make true diction of him, his semblable is his mirror; and who else would trace him, his umbrage, nothing more.

Osr. Your lordship speaks most infallibly of him.

Ham. The concernancy, sir? why do we wrap the gentleman in our more rawer breath?

Osr. Sir?

Hor. Is't not possible to understand in another tongue? You will do't sir, really.

Ham. What imports the nomination of this gentleman?

Osr. Of Laertes?

Hor. His purse is empty already; all his golden words are spent.

Ham. Of him, sir.

Osr. I know you are not ignorant—

Ham. I would you did, sir.—Yet in faith, if you did, it would not much approve me.—Well, sir.

Osr. You are not ignorant of what excellence Laertes is—

Ham. I dare not confess that, lest I should compare with him in excellence; but, to know a man well, were to know himself.

Osr. I mean, sir, for his weapon; but in the imputation laid on him by them, in his meed he's unfellowed.

Ham. What's his weapon?

Osr. Rapier and dagger.

Ham. That's two of his weapons: but, well.

Osr. The king, sir, hath wagered with him six Barbary horses: against the which he has impawned, as I take it, six French rapiers and poniards, with their assigns, as girdle, hangers, and so. Three of the carriages, in faith, are very dear to fancy, very responsive to the hilts; most delicate carriages, and of very liberal conceit.

Ham. What call you the carriages?

Hor. I knew you must be edified by the margent, ere you had done.

Osr. The carriages, sir, are the hangers.

Ham. The phrase would be more german to the matter if we could carry a cannon by our sides; I would it might be hangers till then. But on: six Barbary horses against six French swords, their assigns, and three liberal-conceited carriages; that's the French bet against the Danish. Why is this impawned, as you call it?

Osr. The king, sir, hath laid, that in a dozen passes between yourself and him, he shall not exceed you three hits: he hath laid on twelve for nine; and it would come to immediate trial, if your lordship would vouchsafe the answer.

Ham. How if I answer, no?

Osr. I mean, my lord, the opposition of your person in trial.

Ham. Sir, I will walk here in the hall: if it please his majesty, it is the breathing time of day with me: let the foils be brought, the gentleman willing, and the king hold his purpose, I will win for him, if I can; if not, I will gain nothing but my shame, and the odd hits.

Osr. Shall I deliver you so?

Ham. To this effect, sir; after what flourish your nature will.

Osr. I commend my duty to your lordship.

[*Exit.*

Ham. Yours, yours.—He does well to commend it himself; there are no tongues else for's turn.

Hor. This lapwing runs away with the shell on his head.

Ham. He did comply with his dug, before he sucked it. Thus has he (and many more of the same breed, that I know the drossy age dotes on), only got the tune of the time, and outward habit of encounter; a kind of yesty collection, which carries them through and through the most fond and winnowed opinions; and do but blow them to their trial, the bubbles are out.

Enter a Lord.

Lord. My lord, his majesty commended him to you by young Osric, who brings back to him, that you attend him in the hall: he sends to know if your pleasure hold to play with Laertes, or that you will take longer time.

Ham. I am constant to my purposes; they follow the king's pleasure: if his fitness speaks, mine is ready; now or whensoever, provided I be so able as now.

Lord. The king, and queen, and all, are coming down.

Ham. In happy time.

Lord. The queen desires you to use some gentle entertainment to Laertes, before you fall to play.

Ham. She well instructs me. [*Exit* Lord.

Hor. You will lose this wager, my lord.

Ham. I do not think so; since he went into France, I have been in continual practice; I shall

win at the odds. But thou wouldst not think how
ill all's here about my heart: but it is no matter.

Hor. Nay, good my lord,—

Ham. It is but foolery; but it is such a kind of
gain-giving as would, perhaps, trouble a woman.

Hor. If your mind dislike anything, obey it: I
will forestal their repair hither, and say you are
not fit.

Ham. Not a whit; we defy augury; there is a
special providence in the fall of a sparrow. If it
be now, 'tis not to come; if it be not to come, it
will be now; if it be not now, yet it will come: the
readiness is all. Since no man, of aught he leaves,
knows, what is't to leave betimes? Let be.

Enter KING, QUEEN, LAERTES, Lords, OSRIC,
   and Attendants, *with foils,* &c.

King. Come, Hamlet, come, and take this hand
   from me.
   [*The* KING *puts the hand of* LAERTES *into
      that of* HAMLET.

Ham. Give me your pardon, sir: I have done
   you wrong;
But pardon it, as you are a gentleman.
This presence knows, and you must needs have
   heard,
How I am punished with a sore distraction.
What I have done,
That might your nature, honour, and exception,
Roughly awake, I here proclaim was madness.
Was't Hamlet wronged Laertes? Never, Hamlet:
If Hamlet from himself be ta'en away,
And when he's not himself does wrong Laertes,
Then Hamlet does it not; Hamlet denies it.
Who does it then? His madness. If't be so,
Hamlet is of the faction that is wronged;
His madness is poor Hamlet's enemy.
Sir, in this audience,
Let my disclaiming from a purposed evil
Free me so far in your most generous thoughts,
That I have shot my arrow o'er the house,
And hurt my brother.

Laer.   I am satisfied in nature,
Whose motive, in this case, should stir me most
To my revenge: but in my terms of honour
I stand aloof; and will no reconcilement,
Till by some elder masters, of known honour,
I have a voice and precedent of peace,
To keep my name ungored. But till that time,
I do receive your offered love like love,
And will not wrong it.

Ham.   I embrace it freely;
And will this brother's wager frankly play.—
Give us the foils; come on.

Laer.   Come, one for me.

Ham. I'll be your foil, Laertes; in mine ignorance

Your skill shall, like a star i' the darkest night,
Stick fiery off indeed.

Laer.   You mock me, sir.

Ham. No, by this hand.

King. Give them the foils, young Osric.—
   Cousin Hamlet,
You know the wager?

Ham.   Very well, my lord:
Your grace hath laid the odds o' the weaker side.

King. I do not fear it: I have seen you both:
But since he's bettered, we have therefore odds.

Laer. This is too heavy; let me see another.

Ham. This likes me well. These foils have
   all a length?   [*They prepare to play.*

Osr. Ay, my good lord.

King. Set me the stoups of wine upon that
   table :—
If Hamlet give the first or second hit,
Or quit in answer of the third exchange,
Let all the battlements their ordnance fire;
The king shall drink to Hamlet's better breath;
And in the cup an union shall he throw,
Richer than that which four successive kings
In Denmark's crown have worn.   Give me the
   cups;
And let the kettle to the trumpet speak,
The trumpet to the cannonier without,
The cannons to the heavens, the heaven to earth,
"Now the king drinks to Hamlet."—Come, begin;
And you, the judges, bear a wary eye.

Ham. Come on, sir,

Laer. Come, my lord.   [*They play.*

Ham. One.

Laer. No.

Ham. Judgment.

Osr. A hit, a very palpable hit.

Laer. Well,—again.

King. Stay, give me drink: Hamlet, this pearl
   is thine;
Here's to thy health.—Give him the cup.
   [*Trumpets sound; and cannon shot off within.*

Ham. I'll play this bout first; set it by awhile.
Come.—Another hit: what say you? [*They play.*

Laer. A touch, a touch, I do confess.

King. Our son shall win.

Queen. He's fat, and scant of breath.—
Here, Hamlet, take my napkin, rub thy brows:
The queen carouses to thy fortune, Hamlet.

Ham. Good madam,—

King. Gertrude, do not drink.

Queen. I will, my lord: I pray you, pardon me.

King. It is the poisoned cup; it is too late.
   [*Aside.*

Ham. I dare not drink yet, madam; by-and-by.

Queen. Come, let me wipe thy face.

Laer. My lord, I'll hit him now.

King. I do not think it.

Laer. And yet it is almost against my con-
　　science.　　　　　　　　　　　[*Aside.*
Ham. Come, for the third, Laertes. You do
　　but dally;
I pray you, pass with your best violence:
I am afeard you make a wanton of me.
Laer. Say you so? come on.　　[*They play.*
Osr. Nothing neither way.
Laer. Have at you now.
　　[LAERTES *wounds* HAMLET; *then in scuffling,
　　　　they change rapiers, and* HAMLET *wounds*
　　　　LAERTES.
King. Part them, they are incensed.
Ham. Nay, come again.　　[*The* QUEEN *falls.*
Osr. Look to the queen there, ho!
Hor. They bleed on both sides.—How is it, my
　　lord?
Osr. How is't, Laertes?
Laer. Why, as a woodcock to my own springe,
　　Osric:
I am justly killed with mine own treachery.
Ham. How does the queen?
King. She swoons to see them bleed.
Queen. No, no, the drink, the drink!—O, my
　　dear Hamlet!
The drink, the drink; I am poisoned!　　[*Dies.*
Ham. O villany! Ho! let the door be locked:
Treachery! seek it out.　　　　[LAERTES *falls.*
Laer. It is here, Hamlet. Hamlet, thou art slain;
No medicine in the world can do thee good;
In thee there is not half an hour's life;
The treacherous instrument is in thy hand,
Unbated and envenomed: the foul practice
Hath turned itself on me; lo, here I lie,
Never to rise again. Thy mother's poisoned;
I can no more;—the king, the king's to blame.
Ham. The point envenomed too!—
Then, venom to thy work.　　[*Stabs the* KING.
Osr. ⎱
Lords. ⎰ Treason! treason!
King. O, yet defend me, friends; I am but hurt.
Ham. Here, thou incestuous, murderous,
　　damnéd Dane,
Drink off this potion:—Is the union here?
Follow my mother.　　　　　　[KING *dies.*
Laer.　　　　He is justly served;
It is a poison tempered by himself.—
Exchange forgiveness with me, noble Hamlet:
Mine and my father's death come not upon thee;
Nor thine on me!　　　　　　　[*Dies.*
Ham. Heaven make thee free of it! I follow thee.
I am dead, Horatio.—Wretched queen, adieu.—
You that look pale and tremble at this chance,
That are but mutes or audience to this act,
Had I but time (as this fell sergeant, Death,
Is strict in his arrest), O, I could tell you,—
But let it be.—Horatio, I am dead;

Thou liv'st; report me and my cause aright
To the unsatisfied.
Hor.　　　　Never believe it;
I am more an antique Roman than a Dane;
Here's yet some liquor left.
Ham.　　　　As thou'rt a man,
Give me the cup; let go; by heaven I'll have it.
O, good Horatio, what a wounded name,
Things standing thus unknown, shall live behind
　　me?
If thou didst ever hold me in thy heart,
Absént thee from felicity awhile,
And in this harsh world draw thy breath in pain,
To tell my story.—[*March afar off, and shot within.*
What warlike noise is this?
Osr. Young Fortinbras, with conquest come
　　from Poland,
To the ambassadors of England gives
This warlike volley.
Ham.　　　　O, I die, Horatio;
The potent poison quite o'ercrows my spirit:
I cannot live to hear the news from England:
But I do prophesy the election lights
On Fortinbras; he has my dying voice;
So tell him, with the occurrents, more or less,
Which have solicited—The rest is silence. [*Dies.*
Hor. Now cracks a noble heart.—Good night,
　　sweet prince;
And flights of angels sing thee to thy rest!
Why does the drum come hither? [*March within.*

Enter FORTINBRAS, *the* English Ambassadors,
　　　　and others.

Fort. Where is this sight?
Hor.　　　　What is it you would see?
If aught of woe, or wonder, cease your search.
Fort. This quarry cries on havoc!—O, proud
　　Death!
What feast is toward in thine eternal cell,
That thou so many princes, at a shot,
So bloodily hast struck?
1st Amb.　　　　The sight is dismal;
And our affairs from England come too late:
The ears are senseless that should give us hearing,
To tell him his commandment is fulfilled;
That Rosencrantz and Guildenstern are dead.
Where should we have our thanks?
Hor.　　　　Not from his mouth,
Had it the ability of life to thank you;
He never gave commandment for their death.
But since, so jump upon this bloody question,
You from the Polack wars, and you from England,
Are here arrived, give order that these bodies
High on a stage be placéd to the view;
And let me speak, to the yet unknowing world,
How these things came about: so shall you hear
Of carnal, bloody, and unnatural acts;

Of accidental judgments, casual slaughters;
Of deaths put on by cunning and forced cause;
And, in this upshot, purposes mistook
Fall'n on the inventors' heads: all this can I
Truly deliver.
    Fort.   Let us haste to hear it,
And call the noblest to the audience.
For me, with sorrow I embrace my fortune:
I have some rights of memory in this kingdom,
Which now to claim my 'vantage doth invite me.
    Hor. Of that I shall have also cause to speak,
And from his mouth whose voice will draw on
      more:
But let this same be presently performed,

Even while men's minds are wild; lest more mis-
      chance,
On plots and errors, happen.
    Fort.   Let four captains
Bear Hamlet, like a soldier, to the stage;
For he was likely, had he been put on,
To have proved most royally: and, for his passage,
The soldiers' music, and the rites of war,
Speak loudly for him.—
Take up the bodies: such a sight as this
Becomes the field, but here shews much amiss.—
Go, bid the soldiers shoot.   [*A dead March.*
    [*Exeunt, marching; after which, a peal*
        of ordnance is shot off.

NOTES.

"BAR. *Who's there?*
FRAN. *Nay, answer me: stand, and unfold yourself.*"
Act I., Scene 1.

The striking and eminently dramatic opening of this great tragedy has been often praised; but never with more taste and congenial spirit, than by Mrs. Radcliffe.

"In nothing," says this very competent authority, "has Shakspere been more successful, than in selecting circumstances of manners and appearance for his supernatural beings, which, though wild and remote, in the highest degree, from common apprehension, never shock the understanding by incompatibility with themselves; never compel us, for an instant, to recollect that he has a license for extravagance.—Above every ideal being, is the ghost of Hamlet, with all its attendant incidents of time and place. The dark watch upon the remote platform; the dreary aspect of the night; the very expression of the officer on guard, 'The air bites shrewdly; it is very cold;'* the recollection of a star, an unknown world, are all circumstances which excite forlorn, melancholy, and solemn feelings, and dispose us to welcome, with trembling curiosity, the awful being that draws near; and to indulge in that strange mixture of horror, pity, and indignation, produced by the tale it reveals. Every minute circumstance of the scene between those watching on the platform, and of that between them and Horatio, preceding the entrance of the apparition, contributes to excite some feeling of dreariness, or melancholy, or solemnity, or expectation, in unison with, and leading on toward, that high curiosity and thrilling awe with which we witness the conclusion of the scene. So the first question of Bernardo, and the words in reply, 'Stand, and unfold yourself.' But there is not a single circumstance in either dialogue, not even in this short one with which the play opens, that does not take its secret effect upon the imagination. It ends with Bernardo desiring his brother officer, after having asked whether he has had 'quiet watch,' to hasten the guard if he should chance to meet them; and we immediately feel ourselves alone on this dreary ground.

"When Horatio enters, the challenge—the dignified answers, 'Friends to this ground,' 'And liegemen to the Dane'—the question of Horatio to Bernardo touching the apparition—the unfolding of the reason why 'Horatio has consented to watch with them the minutes of this night'—the sitting down together, while Bernardo relates the particulars of what they had seen for two nights—and, above all, the few lines with which he begins his story, 'Last night of all'—and the distinguishing, by the situation of 'yon same star,' the very point of time when the spirit had appeared—the abruptness with which he breaks off, 'the bell then beating one'—the instant appearance of the Ghost, as though ratifying the story for the very truth itself;—all these are circumstances which the deepest sensibility only could have suggested; and which, if you read them a thousand times, still continue to affect you almost as much as at first. I thrill with delightful awe, even while I recollect and mention them as instances of the exquisite art of the poet."

The preceding excellent remarks are extracted from a posthumous paper by Mrs. Radcliffe, on "THE SUPERNATURAL IN POETRY."

---

* This is a lapse of memory in the writer. The words here quoted are used by Hamlet at the commencement of Scene 4. The occasion, however, is similar.

"*In the most high and palmy state of Rome,*
A little ere the mightiest Julius fell," &c.
Act I., Scene 1.

The whole of this fine passage is omitted in the first folio edition of Shakspere. The second quarto (1609) is stated to be "enlarged to almost as much againe as it was;" and it is on this edition that the received text is mainly founded. It contains the passage in question, and many others of great importance which are not found in the folio. The whole of the characteristic scene in the fourth act, between Hamlet and the Captain of Fortinbras, is not in that copy: in its turn, however, it contains some valuable matter which is wanting in the quarto. Indeed, it would be highly injudicious to follow either version implicitly, although upon the whole, the quarto affords, singly considered, the most full and satisfactory text. Malone's reasons for preferring the quarto editions of those plays which did not appear for the first time in the folio, are thus stated in the preface to his edition of 1790:—"Fifteen of Shakspere's plays were printed in quarto antecedent to the first complete collection of his works, which was published by his fellow-comedians, in 1623. These plays are: 'A MIDSUMMER NIGHT'S DREAM,' 'LOVE'S LABOUR'S LOST,' 'ROMEO AND JULIET,' 'HAMLET,' the Two Parts of 'HENRY IV.,' 'RICHARD II.,' 'RICHARD III.,' 'MERCHANT OF VENICE,' 'HENRY V.,' 'MUCH ADO ABOUT NOTHING.' 'MERRY WIVES OF WINDSOR,' 'TROILUS AND CRESSIDA,' 'KING LEAR,' 'OTHELLO.'

"The players, when they mention these copies, represent them all as mutilated and imperfect; but this was merely thrown out to give an additional value to their own edition, and is not strictly true of any but two of the whole number: 'THE MERRY WIVES OF WINDSOR,' and 'HENRY V.' With respect to the other thirteen copies, though undoubtedly they were all surreptitious—that is, stolen from the playhouse, and printed without the consent of the author or proprietors—they, *in general*, are preferable to the exhibition of the same plays in the folio, for this plain reason: because, instead of printing these plays from a manuscript, the editors of the folio, to save labour, or from some other motive, printed the greater part of them from the very copies which they represented as maimed and imperfect; and frequently from a late, instead of the earliest, edition; in some instances, with additions and alterations of their own. Thus, therefore, the first folio, as far as respects the plays above enumerated, labours under the disadvantage of being, at least, a second, and in some cases a third, edition of these quartos. I do not, however, mean to say, that many valuable corrections of passages, undoubtedly corrupt in the quartos, are not found in the folio copy; or that a single line of these plays should be printed by a careful editor, without a minute examination and collation of both copies; but those quartos were in general the basis on which the folio editors built, and are entitled to our particular attention and examination as first editions.

"It is well known to those who are conversant with the business of the press, that (unless when the author corrects and revises his own works) as editions of books are multiplied, their errors are multiplied also; and that, consequently, every such edition is more or less correct, as it approaches nearer to, or is more distant from, the first."

After these remarks, the writer proceeds to give, in support of his main position, "a few instances of the gradual

199

progress of corruption:" from these instances, we will extract two, as among the most striking:—

"In the original copy of "HENRY IV.," Part I., printed in 1598 (act iv., scene 4) we find:—

'And what with Owen Glendower's absence thence,
.(Who with them was *a rated sinew* too),' &c.

"In the fourth quarto, printed in 1608, the article being omitted by the negligence of the compositor, and the line printed thus:—

'Who with them was *rated sinew* too;'

the editor of the next quarto (which was copied by the folio), instead of examining the first edition, amended the error (leaving the metre still imperfect), by reading:—

'Who with them was *rated firmly* too.' "

The instance of gradual perversion just cited, is simply curious: that which follows has the additional value of drollery:—Malone proceeds:

"'Away to heaven, respective lenity,
And *fire-eyed* fury be my conduct now!'

says Romeo, when provoked by the appearance of his rival. Instead of this, which is the reading of the quarto (1597), the line in the quarto (1599) is thus corruptly exhibited:—

'And fire *end* fury be my conduct now!'

In the subsequent quarto copy, *and* was substituted for *end;* and accordingly, in the folio, the poet's fine imagery is entirely lost, and Romeo exclaims:—

'And *fire and fury* be my conduct now!' "

From these examples, it will appear that the patient plodding of Shakspere's editors has not been the useless and ridiculous thing it is often represented. In further justice to Malone (who has, it seems to us, been somewhat harshly censured), we subjoin his statement of the praiseworthy efforts he made to secure correctness in his own edition:—

"Having often experienced the fallaciousness of collation by the eye, I determined, after I had adjusted the text in the best manner in my power, to have every proof-sheet of my work read aloud to me, while I perused the first folio for those plays which first appeared in that edition; and for all those which had been previously printed, the first quarto copy, excepting only in the instances of 'THE MERRY WIVES OF WINDSOR,' and 'HENRY V.,' which, being either sketches or imperfect copies, could not be wholly relied on. * * * I had, at the same time, before me a table which I had formed of the variations between the quarto and the folio. By this laborious process, not a single innovation, made either by the editor of the second folio, or any of the modern editors, could escape me."

" *The graves stood tenantless, and the sheeted dead
Did squeak and gibber in the Roman streets.* * * *
As stars with trains of fire and dews of blood," &c.
Act I., Scene 1.

After the word "streets," in the above quotation, a line is, with great probability, supposed to be lost, and a blank space, or a line of *dashes*, is usually left for it: we have, however, thought a minor mark of omission [* * *] sufficient for the purpose.—Something is evidently wanting to connect the passage commencing "As stars with trains of fire," &c., with that which immediately precedes it.

" *I'll cross it, though it blast me.*"—Act I., Scene 1.

It was an ancient superstition that the person who crossed the spot on which a spectre was seen, became thus subject to its malignant influence. Ferdinand, Earl of Derby, died young, in 1594; and among the reasons for supposing him to have been killed by witchcraft, was

the following:—"On Friday, there appeared a tall man, who twice crossed swiftly; and when the Earl of Derby came to the place where he saw this man, he fell sick."

" *The glowworm shews the matin to be near,
And 'gins to pale his uneffectual fire.*"—Act I., Scene 4.

In the paper by Mrs. Radcliffe, to which we have before alluded, there are some further fine observations on the Ghost scenes of Hamlet, which we subjoin, as infinitely superior in interest to mere verbal criticism:—

"I should never be weary of dwelling on the perfection of Shakspere, in his management of every scene connected with that most solemn and mysterious being, which takes such entire possession of the imagination that we hardly seem conscious we are beings of this world while we contemplate 'the extravagant and erring spirit.' The spectre departs, accompanied by natural circumstances as touching as those by which he had approached. It is by the strange light of the glowworm, which ''gins to pale his uneffectual fire;' it is at the first scent of the morning air—the living breath—that the apparition retires.

"I have sometimes thought, as I walked in the deep shade of the North Terrace of Windsor Castle, when the moon shone on all beyond, that the scene must have been present in Shakspere's mind when he drew the night scenes in Hamlet: and as I have stood on the platform, which there projects over the precipice, and have heard only the measured step of a sentinel, or the clink of his arms, and have seen his shadow passing by moonlight, at the foot of the high eastern tower, I have almost expected to see the royal shade, armed cap-à-pé, standing still on the lonely platform before me. The very star—'yon same star, that's westward from the pole'—seemed to watch over the western towers of the Terrace, whose high dark lines marked themselves upon the heavens. All has been so still and shadowy, so great and solemn, that the scene appeared fit for 'no mortal business, nor no sound that the earth owes.' Did you ever observe the fine effect of the eastern tower, when you stand near the western end of the North Terrace, and its tall profile rears itself upon the sky, from nearly the base to the battled top; the lowness of the parapet permitting this? It is most striking at night, when the stars appear at different heights, upon the tall dark line, and when the sentinel on watch moves a shadowy figure at its foot."

It is in this congenial spirit that Shakspere should be read. Such poetic associations give additional interest even to the time-honoured towers and terraces of royal Windsor.

" *My liege, and madam, to expostulate
What majesty should be, what duty is,*" &c.
Act II., Scene 2.

Johnson has discussed the conflicting qualities in the character of Polonius, in one of his best notes. "Polonius," he remarks, "is a man bred in courts; exercised in business; stored with observation; confident in his knowledge; proud of his eloquence; and declining into dotage. His mode of oratory is designed to ridicule the practice of those times, of prefaces that made no introduction, and of method that embarrassed rather than explained. This part of his character is accidental, the rest natural. Such a man is positive and confident, because he knows that his mind was once strong, and knows not that it is become weak. Such a man excels in general principles, but fails in particular application; he is knowing in retrospect, and ignorant in foresight. While he depends upon his memory, and can draw from his depositories of knowledge, he utters weighty sentences, and gives useful counsel; but as the mind in its enfeebled state cannot be kept long busy and intent, the old man is subject to the dereliction of his faculties; he loses the order of his ideas, and entangles himself in his own thoughts, till he recovers the leading principle and falls into his former train. The idea of dotage encroaching upon wisdom, will solve all the phenomena of the character of Polonius."

> "*And he, repulséd (a short tale to make),*
> *Fell into a sadness; then into a fast;*" &c.
>
> Act II., Scene 2.

It is observed by Warburton, that "the ridicule of the character of Polonius is here admirably sustained. He would not only be thought to have discovered this intrigue by his own sagacity, but to have remarked all the stages of Hamlet's disorder, from his sadness to his raving, as regularly as his physician could have done; when all the while the madness was only feigned. The humour of this is exquisite from a man who tells us, with a confidence peculiar to small politicians, that he could find—

> ' Where truth is hid, though it were hid indeed
> Within the centre.' "

"*For if the sun breed maggots in a dead dog, being a god, kissing carrion*——*Have you a daughter ?*"—Act II., Scene 2.

Hamlet, by breaking off abruptly in this sentence, has been the cause of an infinite deal of ink-shedding. The old copies read, "Being a good kissing carrion." The present reading was suggested by Warburton, and has been generally adopted, as the most plausible that has yet been proposed. His laboured comment on the passage, in which he endeavours to prove that Shakspere intended it as a vindication of the ways of Providence in permitting evil to abound in the world, has not been so well received. Malone has traced in a less exalted, though more probable strain, the train of thought in Hamlet's mind: "Hamlet has just remarked, 'that honesty is very rare in the world.' To this, Polonius assents. The prince then adds, 'that, since there is so little virtue in the world; since corruption abounds everywhere, and maggots are bred by the sun, even in a dead dog, Polonius ought to prevent his daughter from walking in the sun, lest she should prove a breeder of sinners.'"

"*Ros. Truly; and I hold ambition of so airy and light a quality, that it is but a shadow's shadow.*
Ham. Then are our beggars, bodies; and our monarchs and outstretched heroes the beggars' shadows."—Act II., Scene 2.

Meaning, according to Johnson, "If ambition is such an unsubstantial thing, then are our beggars (who at least can dream of greatness) the only things of substance; and monarchs and heroes, though appearing to fill such mighty space with their ambition, but the shadows of the beggars' dreams."

"*We coted them on the way.*"—Act II., Scene 2.

The term "coted" is derived from the french coté, the side. "In the laws of coursing," says Mr. Tollet, "a *cote* is when a greyhound goes endways by the side of his fellow, and gives the hare a turn." Instances are given of the use of the word in the sense of overtaking or passing by.

"*The clown shall make those laugh whose lungs are tickled o' the sere.*"—Act II., Scene 2.

That is, those who are troubled with a huskiness, or dry cough.

"*Ham. How chances it they travel? Their residence, both in reputation and profit, was better both ways.*
Ros. I think their inhibition comes by the means of the late innovation."—Act II., Scene 2.

The "innovation" here alluded to appears to have been the public performance of the "Children of the Revels," the "Children of St. Paul's," &c., which for a time attracted the town, and thereby in effect "inhibited" or prevented the performance of the regular players at their old stations, and compelled them to "travel." In "JACK DRUM'S ENTERTAINMENT" (1601), we find :—

> "I sawe the children of Powle's [Paul's] last night,
> And troth they pleased me prettie, prettie well ;
> The apes in time will do it handsomely."

In the first quarto edition of the play (1603), the passage stands thus :—

> "*Ham.* How comes it that they travel? do they grow restie?
> *Gil.* No, my lord ; their reputation holds as it was wont.
> *Ham.* How then?
> *Gil.* I' faith, my lord, *novelty* carries it away; for the principal public audience that came to them, are turned to private plays, and to the humour of children."

There is still, however, some obscurity connected with this matter, since we cannot be certain that the passage in the present text refers to the same period of time as the corresponding one in the earliest quarto. In June, 1600, an order of council passed "for the restraint of the immoderate use of playhouses." It prescribes that "there shall be about the city two houses, and no more, allowed for the use of the common stage plays." This order may, with some probability, be deemed the origin of the "inhibition" and "innovation" referred to in the text.

"*O Jephthah, judge of Israel, what a treasure hadst thou !*"

Act II., Scene 2.

In Percy's "RELIQUES," there is an imperfect copy of the old ballad to which Hamlet here refers. It has been since entirely recovered, and is printed entire in Mr. Evans's "COLLECTION OF OLD BALLADS" (1810). The first stanza comprises the various quotations in the text :—

> "I have heard that many years agoe,
>   When Jepha, judge of Israel,
> Had one fair daughter, and no more;
>   Whom he loved passing well.
> As by lot, God wot,
>   It came to passe most like as it was,
>   Great warrs there should be,
> And who should be the chiefe, but he, but he."

"*When he himself might his quietus make*
With a bare bodkin?"—Act III., Scene 1.

The word "quietus" signifies discharge or acquittance. Every sheriff receives his "quietus" on settling his accounts at the Exchequer. "Bodkin" was the term in use to signify a small dagger.

"*To grunt and sweat under a weary life.*"—Act III., Scene 1.

This is the true reading, according to all the old copies ; "although," as Johnson observes, "it can scarcely be borne by modern ears." On this point, Malone remarks, " I apprehend that it is the duty of an editor to exhibit what his author wrote; and not to substitute what may appear to the present age preferable. I have, therefore, though with some reluctance, adhered to the old copies, however unpleasing this word may be to the ear. On the stage, without doubt, an actor is at liberty to substitute a less offensive word. To the ears of our ancestors, it probably conveyed no unpleasing sound ; for we find it used by Chaucer and others."

"*To split the ears of the groundlings ; who, for the most part, are capable of nothing but inexplicable dumb shows and noise.*"—Act III., Scene 2.

The pit, in the early theatres, had neither floor nor benches, and was frequented by the poorer classes. Ben Jonson speaks with equal contempt of the "understanding gentlemen of the ground." Of the "dumb shows," we have a specimen in the play scene of this tragedy. "The meaner people," says Dr. Johnson, "then seem to have sat [stood] below, as they now sit in the upper gallery; who, not well understanding poetical language, were sometimes gratified by a mimical and mute representation of the drama, previous to the dialogue."

"I would have such a fellow whipped for o'er-doing Termagant; it out-herods Herod."—Act III., Scene 2.

Termagant, according to Percy, was a Saracen deity, very clamorous and violent in the Old Moralities. Herod, also, was a constant character in these entertainments, and his outrageous boasting is sometimes highly amusing. Subjoined are two short specimens. The first is from the "CHESTER WHITSUN PLAYS:"—

> "For I am kinge of all mankinde,
> I byd, I beate, I lose, I bynde;
> I master the moone;—take this in mynde,
> That I am most of mighte.
>
> I am the greatest above degree,
> That is, that was, or ever shall be;
> *The sonne it dare not shine on me,*
> And I bid him go downe."

It appears that this amiable personage had no less conceit of his "bewte" than of his "boldness." In one of his "COVENTRY PLAYS," he exclaims:—

> "Of bewte and of boldness I ber evermor the belle,
> Of mayn and of myght I master every man;
> I dynge with my dowtiness the devil down to helle,
> For both of hevyn and of earth I am kynge certayn."

"My lord, you played once in the university, you say."
Act III., Scene 2.

The practice of acting Latin plays in the universities of Oxford and Cambridge is very ancient, and continued to near the middle of the seventeenth century. They were performed occasionally for the entertainment of princes, and other great personages; and regularly at Christmas, at which time a "Lord of Misrule" was appointed at Oxford, to regulate the exhibitions, and a similar officer, with the title of "Imperator," at Cambridge. A Latin play, on the subject of Cæsar's death, was performed at Christ Church, Oxford, in 1582.

> "HAM. *Lady, shall I lie in your lap?*
> OPH. *No, my lord.*"—Act III., Scene 2.

On the publication of the original edition of this play, which had been previously unknown to the commentators or the public, some remarks upon it appeared in a morning journal, from which we select the following, as well worthy of attention, in reference to this scene, and to some other parts of Shakspere's text which the reader, without being affectedly delicate, may be pardoned for wishing away:—

"Many striking peculiarities in this edition of Hamlet tend strongly to confirm our opinion, that no small portion of the ribaldry to be found in the plays of our great poet, is to be assigned to the actors of his time, who flattered the vulgar taste with the constant repetition of many indecent, and not a few stupid jokes, till they came to be considered, and then printed, as part of the genuine text. Of these, the two or three brief but offensive speeches of Hamlet to Ophelia, in the play scene (act iii.), are not to be found in the copy of 1603; and so far are we borne out in our opinion; for it is not to be supposed that Shakspere would insert them upon cool reflection, three years after the success of his piece had been determined. Still less likely is it that a piratical printer would reject anything actually belonging to the play, which would prove pleasing to the vulgar bulk of those who were to be the purchasers of his publication."

We have no desire to be numbered among those who are in the habit of visiting the sins of Shakspere, real or imaginary, on the heads of the actors; but there is certainly something in the fact here stated that deserves consideration. In justice both to poet and players, we subjoin Mr. Campbell's judicious comment on the remarks just cited:—

"I am inclined, upon the whole, to agree with these remarks, although the subject leaves us beset with uncertainties. This copy of the play was apparently pirated; but the pirate's omission of the improper passages alluded to, is not a perfect proof that they were absent in the first representation of the piece; yet it leads to such a presumption; for, looking at the morality of Shakspere's theatre in the main, he is none of your poetical artists who resort to an impure influence over the fancy. Little sallies of indecorum he may have now and then committed; but they are few, and are eccentricities from his general character, partially pardonable on account of the bad taste of his age. What a frightful contrast to his purity is displayed among his nearest dramatic successors—love in relations of life where Nature forbids passion! Shakspere scorns to interest us in any love that is not purely natural."

"Your only jig-maker."—Act III., Scene 2.

A "jig" signified not only a dance, but also a ludicrous prose or metrical composition. Many of these jigs are entered in the books of the Stationers' Company.

"Let the devil wear black, for I'll have a suit of sables."
Act III., Scene 2.

Meaning, probably, a suit that shall be expressive of the reverse feeling to sorrow or humiliation. "A suit of sables (says Malone) was, in Shakspere's time, the richest dress worn by men in England. Wherever his scene might happen to be, the customs of his own country were still in his thoughts." By the statute of apparel (24 HEN. VIII.), it is ordained that none under the degree of an earl may use sables.

"For O, for O, the hobby-horse is forgot!"—Act III. Scene 2.

The banishment of the hobby-horse from the May games is frequently lamented in the old dramas. The line quoted by Hamlet appears to have been part of a ballad on the subject of poor Hobby. He was driven from his station by the Puritans, as an impious and pagan superstition; but restored on the promulgation of the "BOOK OF SPORTS." The hobby-horse was formed of a pasteboard horse's head, and probably a light frame made of wicker-work, to form the hinder parts; this was fastened round the body of a man, and covered with a footcloth which nearly reached the ground, and concealed the legs of the performer. Similar contrivances, in burlesque pieces, are not unusual at this day, in the London minor theatres.

> "HOR. *Half a share.*
> HAM. *A whole one, I.*"—Act III., Scene 2.

Actors, in Shakspere's time, had not annual salaries, as at present. The whole receipts of each theatre were divided into shares, of which the proprietors of the theatre, or "house-keepers," as they were called, had some; and each actor had one or more shares, or parts of a share, according to his merit.

———

"Hide fox, and all after."—Act IV., Scene 2.

This, no doubt, was the name of a juvenile sport of the poet's age; it is supposed to be the same as is now called "hide and seek."

"Where is the beauteous majesty of Denmark?"
Act IV., Scene 5.

It is remarked by Sir Joshua Reynolds, that there is no part of this play, in its representation on the stage, more pathetic than this scene; which he supposes to arise from the utter insensibility of Ophelia to her own misfortunes. "A great sensibility (says he), or none at all, seems to produce the same effect. In the latter case, the audience supply what is wanting; and with the former they sympathise."

In reference to "the sweet Ophelia," Hazlitt eloquently exclaims:—"Ophelia is a character almost too exquisitely touching to be dwelt upon. 'Oh, rose of May!' oh, flower too soon faded! Her love, her madness, her death are described with the truest touches of tenderness and pathos. It is a character which nobody but Shakspere could have drawn in the way he has done; and to the conception of which there is not the smallest approach, except in some of the old romantic ballads."

Mrs. Jameson also, in her "CHARACTERISTICS OF WOMEN," has a beautiful passage on the same pathetic theme:—"Once at Marano, I saw a dove caught in a tempest: perhaps it was young, and either lacked strength of wing to reach its home, or the instinct which teaches to shun the brooding storm: but so it was—and I watched it, pitying as it flitted, poor bird! hither and thither, with its silver pinions shining against the black thunder-cloud, till after a few giddy whirls it fell blinded, affrighted, and bewildered, into the turbid wave beneath, and was swallowed up for ever. It reminded me of the fate of Ophelia; and now, when I think of her, I see again that poor dove, beating with weary wing, bewildered amid the storm."

> "How should I your true love know
> From another one?
> By his cockle-hat and staff,
> And his sandal-shoon."—Act IV., Scene 5.

The habiliments mentioned in the last two lines were appropriated to pilgrims. Warburton remarks, "that while this kind of devotion was in favour, love intrigues were carried on under that mask. Hence the old ballads and novels made pilgrimages the subjects of their plots. The cockle-shell was an emblem of an intention to go beyond sea."

> "They say, the owl was a baker's daughter."
> Act IV., Scene 5.

This transformation is said to be a common tradition in Gloucestershire. It is thus related by Mr. Douce:—"Our Saviour went into a baker's shop where they were baking, and asked for some bread to eat: the mistress of the shop immediately put a piece of dough in the oven to bake for him; but was reprimanded by her daughter, who insisting that the piece of dough was too large, reduced it to a very small size: the dough, however, immediately began to swell, and presently became of a most enormous size, whereupon the baker's daughter cried out, 'Heugh, heugh, heugh,' which owl-like noise probably induced our Saviour to transform her into that bird, for her wickedness." The story is related to deter children from illiberal behaviour to the poor.

> "Where are my Switzers?"—Act IV., Scene 5.

The Swiss, in Shakspere's time, were already in the habit of entering as mercenaries into foreign service. In Nashe's "CHRIST'S TEARS OVER JERUSALEM" (1594), we find:—"Law, logic, and the Switzers, may be hired to fight for anybody."

> "There's such divinity doth hedge a king,
> That treason can but peep to what it would."
> Act IV., Scene 5.

For "hedge" the first quarto reads "wall."—As a genuine instance of royal confidence, an anecdote of Queen Elizabeth is quoted from Chettle's "ENGLAND'S MOURNING GARMENT:"—"While her Majesty was on the Thames, near Greenwich, a shot was fired by accident, which struck the royal barge, and hurt a waterman near her. The French ambassador being amazed, and all crying 'Treason, treason!' yet she, with an undaunted spirit, came to the open

place of the barge, and bade them never fear; for if the shot were made at her, they durst not shoot again. Such majesty had her presence, and such boldness her heart, that she despised fear, and was as all princes are, or should be, so full of *divine fulness*, that guilty mortality durst not behold her but with dazzled eyes."

> "O, how the wheel becomes it!"—Act IV., Scene 5.

The terms "wheel" and "a-down-a" both signify the round or burthen of a ballad.

> "In youth, when I did love, did love," &c.—Act V., Scene 1.

The stanzas, of which the clown gives his imperfect version, are attributed to Lord Vaux; they were published in "SONGES AND SONNETTES," by Lord Surrey and others (1575). The original runs thus:—

> "I loth that I did love,
> In youth that I thought swete,
> As time requires: for my behove
> Methinks they are not mete.
>
> *   *   *   *
>
> "For Age with steling steps
> Hath clawde me with his crowch;
> And lusty Youthe awaye he leapes,
> As there had bene none such.
>
> *   *   *   *   *
>
> "A pikeax and a spade,
> And eke a shrowding shete,
> A house of clay for to be made
> For such a guest most mete."

> "To play at loggats with them?"—Act. V., Scene 1.

"Loggats" is a game still much used in some country parts, particularly Norwich, and its vicinity. A stake is fixed in the ground, at which the loggats (small logs or pieces of wood) are thrown. The sport may be considered a rude kind of quoits.

> "It was that very day that young Hamlet was born."
> Act V., Scene 1.

This is possibly a slip of memory in the poet. It appears, from what the Gravedigger subsequently says, that Hamlet must have been at this period thirty years old; and yet, in the early part of the play, we are told of his intention to return to school at Wittenberg. In the first quarto, Yorick's skull is said to have lain in the earth *twelve* years, instead of *three-and-twenty*, as at present:—"Look you, here's a skull hath been here this dozen year; let me see, ay, ever since our last King Hamlet slew Fortinbrasse in combat:—young Hamlet's father: he that's mad."

It is probable that, in the reconstruction of the play, Shakspere perceived that the general depth of Hamlet's philosophy indicated a mind too mature for the possession of a very young man.—In reference to Hamlet's demeanour in this transcendant scene, Boswell the younger says (in his edition of Malone), "The scene with the Gravedigger shews, in a striking point of view, his good-natured affability. The reflections which follow afford new proofs of his amiable character. The place where he stands, the frame of his own thoughts, and the objects which surround him, suggest the vanity of all human pursuits; but there is nothing harsh or caustic in his satire; his observations are dictated rather by feelings of sorrow than of anger; and the sprightliness of his wit, which misfortune has repressed, but cannot altogether extinguish, has thrown over the whole a truly pathetic cast of humorous sadness. Those gleams of sunshine, which serve only to shew us the scattered fragments of a brilliant imagination, crushed and broken by calamity, are much more affecting than a long uninterrupted train of monotonous woe."

—— " Let four captains
Bear Hamlet, like a soldier to the stage,
For he was likely, had he been put on,
To have proved most royally."—Act V., Scene 2.

Many efforts have been made to render the character of Hamlet perfectly consonant with that idea of moral perfection which we are anxious to attach to him; but none, it appears to us, with perfect success; nor are such attempts necessary, except for those who are anxious to worship an idol, rather than to discuss the merits of a human being. As regards the main incident of his life, his merits and deficiencies are delineated with great delicacy and discrimination by the hand of Göethe:—" It is clear to me that Shakspere's intention was to exhibit the effects of a great action, imposed as a duty, upon a mind too feeble for its accomplishment. In this sense, I find the character consistent throughout. Here is an oak planted in a china vase, proper to receive only the most delicate flowers: the roots strike out, and the vessel flies to pieces. A pure, noble, highly moral disposition, but without that energy of soul which constitutes the hero, sinks under a load which it can neither support nor resolve to abandon altogether. *All* his obligations are sacred to him; but this alone is above his powers. An impossibility is required at his hands; not an impossibility in itself, but that which is so to him. Observe how he shifts, turns, hesitates, advances and recedes; how he is continually reminded and reminding himself of his great commission, which he, nevertheless, in the end, seems almost entirely to lose sight of; and this without ever recovering his former tranquillity."

———

In reference to the disputed question of Hamlet's sanity, Boswell makes some judicious remarks, in which he maintains that the prince's great intellect is essentially sound, though weakened and disturbed:—

"The sentiments which fall from Hamlet in his soliloquies, or in confidential communication with Horatio, evince not only a sound, but an acute and vigorous understanding. His misfortunes, indeed, and a sense of shame, from the hasty and incestuous marriage of his mother, have sunk him into a state of weakness and melancholy; but though his mind is enfeebled, it is by no means deranged. It would have been little in the manner of Shakspere to introduce two persons in the same play whose intellects were disordered; but he has rather, in this instance, as in ' KING LEAR,' a second time effected what, as far as I can recollect, no other writer has ever ventured to attempt—the exhibition on the same scene of real and fictitious madness in contrast with each other.—In carrying his design into execution, Hamlet feels no difficulty in imposing upon the King, whom he detests; or upon Polonius, and his school-fellows, whom he despises: but the case is very different indeed in his interviews with Ophelia: aware of the submissive mildness of her character, which leads her to be subject to the influence of her father and her brother, he cannot venture to entrust her with his secret. In her presence, therefore, he has not only to assume a disguise, but to restrain himself from those expressions of affection which a lover must find it most difficult to repress in the presence of his mistress. In this tumult of conflicting feelings, he is led to overact his part, from a fear of falling below it; and thus gives an appearance of rudeness and harshness to that which is, in fact, a painful struggle to conceal his tenderness."

———

Dr. Johnson's appreciation of Shakspere is, unfortunately, not in general such as to tempt us to transcribe his summary remarks on each play; but as the opening paragraph of his estimate of " HAMLET" is more lauditory than usual, we willingly give it currency:—

" If the dramas of Shakspere were to be characterised, each by the particular excellence which distinguishes it from the rest, we must allow to the tragedy of Hamlet the praise of variety. The incidents are so numerous, that the argument of the play would make a long tale. The scenes are interchangeably diversified with merriment and solemnity: with merriment that includes judicious and instructive observations; and solemnity not strained by poetical violence above the natural sentiments of man. New characters appear from time to time in continual succession, exhibiting various forms of life and particular modes of conversation. The pretended madness of Hamlet causes much mirth, the mournful distraction of Ophelia fills the heart with tenderness, and every personage produces the effect intended, from the Apparition that in the first Act chills the blood with horror, to the Fop in the last, that exposes affectation to just contempt."

———

As a specimen of the great difference between the first edition of " HAMLET" and the finished play, we subjoin a scene from the former, in which the prince's return is announced to his mother. It should be premised that, in the earlier edition, the Queen's innocence of the murder is distinctly asserted by herself; as it is also in the black-letter " HISTORIE OF HAMBLETT:"—

Enter HORATIO *and the* QUEEN.

Hor. Madam, your son is safe arrived in Denmarke,
This letter I even now received of him,
Whereas he writes how he escaped the danger
And subtle treason that the King had plotted,
Being crossed by the contention of the winds,
He found the packet sent to the King of England,
Wherein he saw himself betrayed to death,
As at his next conversion with your grace
He will relate the circumstance at full.
Queen. Then I perceive there's treason in his looks,
That seemed to sugar o'er his villanies:
But I will sooth and please him for a time,
For murderous minds are always jealous;
But know not you, Horatio, where he is?
Hor. Yes, madam, and he hath appointed me
To meet him on the east side of the city
To-morrow morning.
Queen. O fail not, good Horatio, and withal commend me
A mother's care to him, bid him awhile
Be wary of his presence, lest that he
Fail in that he goes about.
Hor. Madam, never make doubt of that;
I think by this the news be come to court
He is arrived: observe the King, and you shall
Quickly find, Hamlet being here,
Things fell not to his mind.
Queen. But what became of Gilderstone and Rossencraft?
Hor. He being set ashore, they went for England,
And in the packet there writ down that doom
To be performed on them 'pointed for him:
And by great chance he had his father's seal,
So all was done without discovery.
Queen. Thanks be to heaven for blessing of the prince.
Horatio, once again I take my leave,
With thousand mother's blessings to my son.
Hor. Madam, adieu!

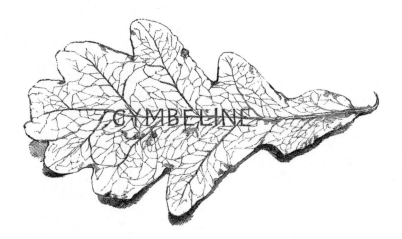

CYMBELINE

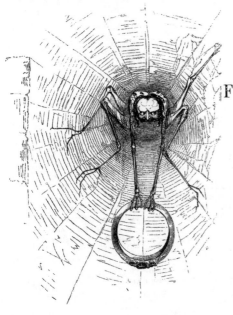

F all the loved and loving female characters of Shakspere—although some may display a lustre more intense—there is not one that cheers the eye with a more mild and modest radiance than the spotless jewel, Imogen. Harsh and difficult as sometimes is the diction of the play, the sweetness of her nature o'erinforms it with delightful associations; we think of her as of the pine-apple in its prickly enclosure; or as of the delicious milk in the husky shell of the cocoa-nut. In the clear heaven of that unclouded mind, the wearied spirit obtains glimpses of human truth and unsuspecting gentleness that well, indeed, "may make us less forlorn." No impure thought can dwell in the atmosphere that is perfumed by her breath; her bed-chamber becomes the very temple of Diana; and we not only feel the poetic beauty, but could almost believe the literal truth of Iachimo's splendid hyperbole :—

> " The flame o' the taper
> Bows toward her; and would under-peep her lids,
> To see the unclosèd lights, now canopied
> Under these windows, white and azure, laced
> With blue of heaven's own tinct."

Posthumus displays one of those respectable, but imperfect natures, whose innocence (in more senses than one) disposes them to be "as tenderly led by the nose as asses are." In yielding to the suggestions of Iachimo, to the disparagement of such a being, and one so well known to him, as Imogen, he appears, for the moment, little less guilty, and a great deal more provoking, than the villain himself. His bitter repentance, however, and general demeanour in the last Act, induce us to forgive him, were it but in humble imitation of his charming Wife : and the same feeling, founded on similar penitence and remorse, may almost be extended to the acute, unprincipled Iachimo, when we consider that the credulity of the one, combined with the scoundrelism of the other, has been the unconscious cause of so much delightful incident and poetry. The minor characters—Cymbeline and his Queen, the Brothers of Imogen, Belarius, Cloten, Lucius, and the rest—are all instinct with the life-giving power of Shakspere, although he has not put out his greatest strength in their delineation.

In order properly to enjoy this exquisite, though irregular drama, we must cast aside the "considering cap" of scientific criticism, and follow the Poet guilelessly, wherever he may choose to "wander at his own sweet will." The dim and remote era in which the action is supposed to pass, will dispose the really "gentle reader" to dispense with much of that probability, which he naturally looks for in productions of more definite pretensions. He must consider the play as a dramatic romance; and when he has mastered its occasional difficulties of versification, he will read it again, and again, and again—as all poetry should be read to be properly appreciated—and find it a "perpetual source of nectared sweets, where no crude surfeit reigns." The mountain scenes between the Brothers and their supposed Father; the instinctive affection which immediately displays itself between Imogen and the noble boys ; all the delicate and pathetic circumstances attending her supposed death; these, and a hundred other beauties in the language, breathe the very air of Nature in her loveliest aspect. They exhibit all the out-of-door sweetness and simplicity of Isaak Walton, mingled with a poetry and passion of a far higher and more recondite description.

"CYMBELINE" was first published in the original folio. Its domestic incidents appear to have been mainly derived from "BOCCACCIO'S DECAMERON" (ninth story, second day), though probably filtered through various channels before they reached the dramatist. The historic portion is founded on "HOLINSHED'S CHRONICLE ;" according to which, Cymbeline, or Kymbeline, became king of the Britons in the nineteenth year of the reign of Augustus.

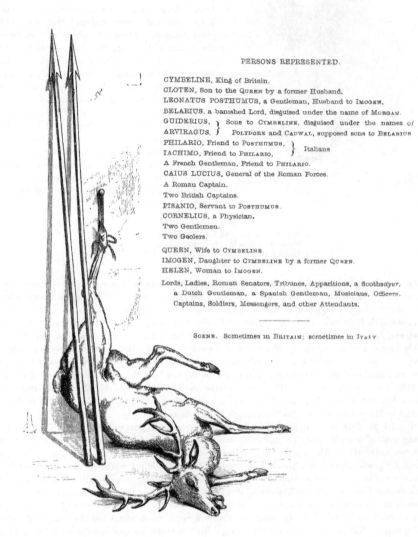

PERSONS REPRESENTED.

CYMBELINE, King of Britain.
CLOTEN, Son to the QUEEN by a former Husband.
LEONATUS POSTHUMUS, a Gentleman, Husband to IMOGEN.
BELARIUS, a banished Lord, disguised under the name of MORGAN.
GUIDERIUS, } Sons to CYMBELINE, disguised under the names of
ARVIRAGUS, } POLYDORE and CADWAL, supposed sons to BELARIUS
PHILARIO, Friend to POSTHUMUS, } Italians
IACHIMO, Friend to PHILARIO, } Italians
A French Gentleman, Friend to PHILARIO.
CAIUS LUCIUS, General of the Roman Forces.
A Roman Captain.
Two British Captains.
PISANIO, Servant to POSTHUMUS.
CORNELIUS, a Physician.
Two Gentlemen.
Two Gaolers.

QUEEN, Wife to CYMBELINE.
IMOGEN, Daughter to CYMBELINE by a former QUEEN.
HELEN, Woman to IMOGEN.

Lords, Ladies, Roman Senators, Tribunes, Apparitions, a Soothsayer,
    a Dutch Gentleman, a Spanish Gentleman, Musicians, Officers,
    Captains, Soldiers, Messengers, and other Attendants.

————————

SCENE. Sometimes in BRITAIN; sometimes in ITALY

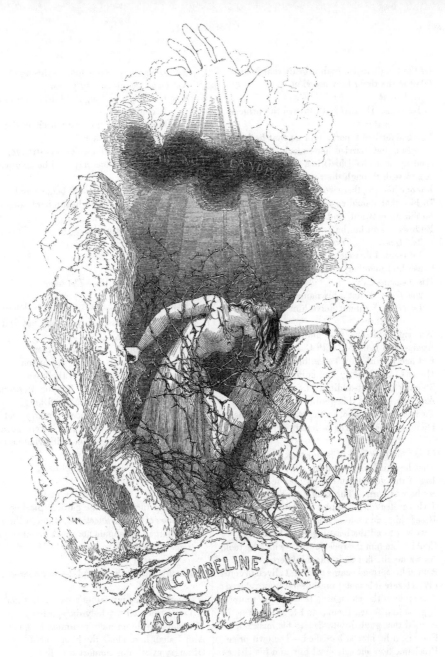

CYMBELINE

ACT II

SCENE I.—Britain. *The Garden behind* CYM-
BELINE'S *Palace.*

Enter two Gentlemen.

1st Gent. You do not meet a man but frowns:
 our bloods
No more obey the heavens than our courtiers
Still seem as does the king.
 2nd Gent.   But what's the matter?
 1st Gent. His daughter, and the heir of 's kingdom, whom

He purposed to his wife's sole son (a widow,
That late he married), hath referred herself
Unto a poor but worthy gentleman : she 's wedded ;
Her husband banished ; she imprisoned : all
Is outward sorrow ; though I think the king
Be touched at very heart.
 2nd Gent.   None but the king?
 1st Gent. He that hath lost her, too : so is the
 queen,
That most desired the match : but not a courtier,
Although they wear their faces to the bent

B B

209

Of the king's looks, hath a heart that is not
Glad at the thing they scowl at.

    2nd Gent.   And why so?

    1st Gent. He that hath missed the princess is
         a thing

Too bad for bad report: and he that hath her
(I mean, that married her—alack, good man!—
And therefore banished) is a creature such
As, to seek through the regions of the earth
For one his like, there would be something failing
In him that should compare. I do not think
So fair an outward, and such stuff within,
Endows a man but he.

    2nd Gent.   You speak him far.

    1st Gent. I do extend him, sir, within himself;
Crush him together, rather than unfold
His measure duly.

    2nd Gent. What's his name and birth?

    1st Gent. I cannot delve him to the root: his
         father

Was called Sicilius, who did join his honour
Against the Romans, with Cassibelan;
But had his titles by Tenantius, whom
He served with glory and admired success;
So gained the sur-addition, Leonatus:
And had, besides this gentleman in question,
Two other sons, who, in the wars o' the time,
Died with their swords in hand; for which their
         father
(Then old and fond of issue) took such sorrow,
That he quit being; and his gentle lady,
Big of this gentleman our theme, deceased
As he was born. The king he takes the babe
To his protection; calls him Posthumus Leonatus;
Breeds him, and makes him of his bed-chamber;
Puts him to all the learnings that his time
Could make him the receiver of,—which he took,
As we do air, fast as 't was ministered,
And in his spring became a harvest: lived in court
(Which rare it is to do) most praised, most loved:
A sample to the youngest; to the more mature,
A glass that feated them; and to the graver,
A child that guided dotards: to his mistress,
For whom he now is banished,—her own price
Proclaims how she esteemed him and his virtue;
By her election may be truly read
What kind of man he is.

    2nd Gent.   I honour him
Even out of your report. But 'pray you tell me,
Is she sole child to the king?

    1st Gent. His only child.
He had two sons (if this be worth your hearing,
Mark it): the eldest of them at three years old,
I' the swathing clothes the other, from their nursery
Were stolen; and to this hour, no guess in know-
         ledge
Which way they went.

    2nd Gent.   How long is this ago?

    1st Gent. Some twenty years.

    2nd Gent. That a king's children should be so
         conveyed!
So slackly guarded! and the search so slow,
That could not trace them!

    1st Gent.   Howsoe'er 't is strange,
Or that the negligence may well be laughed at,
Yet is it true, sir.

    2nd Gent.   I do well believe you.

    1st Gent. We must forbear: here comes the
         gentleman,
The queen, and princess.   [*Exeunt.*

SCENE II.—*The same.*

Enter the QUEEN, POSTHUMUS, *and* IMOGEN.

    Queen. No, be assured, you shall not find me,
         daughter,
After the slander of most stepmothers,
Evil-eyed unto you: you are my prisoner, but
Your gaoler shall deliver you the keys
That lock up your restraint. For you, Posthumus,
So soon as I can win the offended king,
I will be known your advocate: marry, yet
The fire of rage is in him; and 't were good
You leaned unto his sentence, with what patience
Your wisdom may inform you.

    Post.   Please your highness,
I will from hence to-day.

    Queen.   You know the peril.
I 'll fetch a turn about the garden, pitying
The pangs of barred affections: though the king
Hath charged you should not speak together. [*Exit.*

    Imo. O, dissembling courtesy! How fine this
         tyrant
Can tickle where she wounds!—My dearest hus-
         band,
I something fear my father's wrath, but nothing
(Always reserved my holy duty) what
His rage can do on me: you must be gone;
And I shall here abide the hourly shot
Of angry eyes; not comforted to live,
But that there is this jewel in the world,
That I may see again.

    Post. My queen! my mistress!
O, lady, weep no more; lest I give cause
To be suspected of more tenderness
Than doth become a man! I will remain
The loyal'st husband that did e'er plight troth.
My residence in Rome, at one Philario's,
Who to my father was a friend; to me
Known but by letter: thither write, my queen,
And with mine eyes I 'll drink the words you send,
Though ink be made of gall.

Re-enter QUEEN.

Queen.   Be brief, I pray you:
If the king come, I shall incur I know not
How much of his displeasure.—Yet I 'll move him
                              [*Aside.*
To walk this way: I never do him wrong,
But he does buy my injuries, to be friends;
Pays dear for my offences.   [*Exit.*
    Post.   Should we be taking leave
As long a term as yet we have to live,
The loathness to depart would grow: adieu!
    Imo. Nay, stay a little:
Were you but riding forth to air yourself,
Such parting were too petty.   Look here, love;
This diamond was my mother's: take it, heart;
But keep it till you woo another wife,
When Imogen is dead.
    Post. How! how! another?—
You gentle gods, give me but this I have,
And sear up my embracements from a next
With bonds of death!—Remain thou here,
                   [*Putting on the ring.*
While sense can keep it on! And sweetest, fairest,
As I my poor self did exchange for you,
To your so infinite loss; so, in our trifles
I still win of you:—for my sake, wear this;
It is a manacle of love; I 'll place it
Upon this fairest prisoner.
         [*Putting a bracelet on her arm.*
    Imo.   O, the gods!
When shall we see again?

Enter CYMBELINE *and* Lords.

    Post.   Alack, the king!
    Cym. Thou basest thing, avoid! hence from
        my sight!
If, after this command, thou fraught the court
With thy unworthiness, thou diest: away!
Thou art poison to my blood.
    Post.   The gods protect you,
And bless the good remainders of the court!
I am gone.   [*Exit.*
    Imo.   There cannot be a pinch in death
More sharp than this is.
    Cym.   O disloyal thing,
That shouldst repair my youth, thou heapest ⸗
A year's age on me!
    Imo.   I beseech you, sir,
Harm not yourself with your vexation: I
Am senseless of your wrath; a touch more rare
Subdues all pangs, all fears.
    Cym.   Past grace? obedience?
    Imo. Past hope, and in despair; that way, past
        grace.
    Cym. That mightst have had the sole son of my
        queen!

    Imo. O blessed that I might not! I chose an
        eagle,
And did avoid a puttock.
    Cym. Thou took'st a beggar; wouldst have
        made my throne
A seat for baseness.
    Imo.   No; I rather added
A lustre to it.
    Cym.   O thou vile one!
    Imo.   Sir,
It is your fault that I have loved Posthumus:
You bred him as my playfellow, and he is
A man worth any woman; overbuys me
Almost the sum he pays.
    Cym.   What! art thou mad?
    Imo. Almost, sir: Heaven restore me!—
        'Would I were
A neatherd's daughter; and my Leonatus
Our neighbour shepherd's son!

Re-enter QUEEN.

    Cym.   Thou foolish thing!—
They were again together: you have done
                  [*To the* QUEEN.
Not after our command.   Away with her,
And pen her up.
    Queen. 'Beseech your patience:—Peace,
Dear lady daughter, peace:—Sweet sovereign,
Leave us to ourselves; and make yourself some
        comfort
Out of your best advice.
    Cym.   Nay, let her languish
A drop of blood a-day; and, being aged,
Die of this folly!   [*Exit.*

Enter PISANIO.

    Queen.   Fie!—you must give way:
Here is your servant.—How now, sir? what news?
    Pisa. My lord your son drew on my master.
    Queen.   Ha!
No harm, I trust, is done?
    Pisa.   There might have been,
But that my master rather played than fought,
And had no help of anger: they were parted
By gentlemen at hand.
    Queen.   I am very glad on 't.
    Imo. Your son 's my father's friend; he takes
        his part.—
To draw upon an exile! O brave sir!
I would they were in Afric both together;
Myself by with a needle, that I might prick
The goer back.—Why came you from your master?
    Pisa. On his command: he would not suffer me
To bring him to the haven: left these notes
Of what commands I should be subject to,
When it pleased you to employ me.
    Queen.   This hath been

Your faithful servant: I dare lay mine honour
He will remain so.

Pisa. I humbly thank your highness.

Queen. Pray walk awhile.

Imo. About some half-hour hence,
I pray you, speak with me: you shall, at least,
Go see my lord aboard: for this time, leave me.
[*Exeunt.*

Scene III.—*A public Place.*

Enter Cloten *and two* Lords.

1st Lord. Sir, I would advise you to shift a
shirt; the violence of action hath made you reek
as a sacrifice. Where air comes out, air comes
in: there's none abroad so wholesome as that
you vent.

Clo. If my shirt were bloody, then to shift it—
Have I hurt him?

2nd Lord. No, faith; not so much as his patience.
[*Aside.*

1st Lord. Hurt him? his body's a passable car-
cass, if he be not hurt: it is a thoroughfare for
steel, if it be not hurt.

2nd Lord. His steel was in debt; it went o' the
backside the town. [*Aside.*

Clo. The villain would not stand me.

2nd Lord. No; but he fled forward still, toward
your face. [*Aside.*

1st Lord. Stand you! You have land enough
of your own: but he added to your having; gave
you some ground.

2nd Lord. As many inches as you have oceans.—
Puppies! [*Aside.*

Clo. I would they had not come between us.

2nd Lord. So would I, till you had measured
how long a fool you were upon the ground. [*Aside.*

Clo. And that she should love this fellow, and
refuse me!

2nd Lord. If it be a sin to make a true election,
she is damned. [*Aside.*

1st Lord. Sir, as I told you always, her beauty
and her brain go not together. She's a good
sign, but I have seen small reflection of her
wit.

2nd Lord. She shines not upon fools, lest the
reflection should hurt her. [*Aside.*

Clo. Come, I'll to my chamber. 'Would there
had been some hurt done!

2nd Lord. I wish not so; unless it had been the
fall of an ass, which is no great hurt. [*Aside.*

Clo. You'll go with us?

1st Lord. I'll attend your lordship.

Clo. Nay, come, let's go together.

2nd Lord. Well, my lord. [*Exeunt.*

Scene IV.—*A Room in* Cymbeline's *Palace.*

Enter Imogen *and* Pisanio.

Imo. I would thou grew'st unto the shores
o' the haven,
And question'dst every sail: if he should write,
And I not have it, 't were a paper lost
As offered mercy is. What was the last
That he spake to thee?

Pisa. It was, " His queen, his queen!"

Imo. Then waved his handkerchief?

Pisa. And kissed it, madam.

Imo. Senseless linen! happier therein than I!—
And that was all?

Pisa. No, madam; for so long
As he could make me with this eye or ear
Distinguish him from others, he did keep
The deck, with glove, or hat, or handkerchief,
Still waving, as the fits and stirs of his mind
Could best express how slow his soul sailed on,
How swift his ship.

Imo. Thou shouldst have made him
As little as a crow, or less, ere left
To after-eye him.

Pisa. Madam, so I did.

Imo. I would have broke mine eye-strings;
cracked them, but
To look upon him; till the diminution
Of space had pointed him sharp as my needle:
Nay, followed him till he had melted from
The smallness of a gnat to air; and then
Have turned mine eye, and wept.—But, good
Pisanio,
When shall we hear from him?

Pisa. Be assured, madam,
With his next vantage.

Imo. I did not take my leave of him, but had
Most pretty things to say! Ere I could tell him
How I would think on him, at certain hours,
Such thoughts, and such; or I could make him swear
The shes of Italy should not betray
Mine interest and his honour; or have charged him
At the sixth hour of morn, at noon, at midnight,
To encounter me with orisons, for then
I am in heaven for him; or ere I could
Give him that parting kiss, which I had set
Betwixt two charming words,—comes in my father,
And, like the tyrannous breathing of the north,
Shakes all our buds from growing.

Enter a Lady.

Lady. The queen, madam,
Desires your highness' company.

Imo. Those things I bid you do, get them despatched.—
I will attend the queen.

Pisa. Madam, I shall. [*Exeunt.*

SCENE V.—Rome. *An Apartment in* PHILARIO'S *House.*

Enter PHILARIO, IACHIMO, *a* Frenchman, *a* Dutchman, *and a* Spaniard.

Iach. Believe it, sir. I have seen him in Britain: he was then of a crescent note; expected to prove so worthy as since he hath been allowed the name of: but I could then have looked on him without the help of admiration, though the catalogue of his endowments had been tabled by his side, and I to peruse him by items.

Phi. You speak of him when he was less furnished than now he is with that which makes him, both without and within.

French. I have seen him in France: we had very many there could behold the sun with as firm eyes as he.

Iach. This matter of marrying his king's daughter (wherein he must be weighed rather by her value than his own), words him, I doubt not, a great deal from the matter.

French. And then his banishment:—

Iach. Ay, and the approbation of those that weep this lamentable divorce under her colours, are wonderfully to extend him; be it but to fortify her judgment, which else an easy battery might lay flat, for taking a beggar without more quality. But how comes it he is to sojourn with you? how creeps acquaintance?

Phi. His father and I were soldiers together; to whom I have been often bound for no less than my life.—

Enter POSTHUMUS.

Here comes the Briton: let him be so entertained amongst you as suits, with gentlemen of your knowing, to a stranger of his quality.—I beseech you all, be better known to this gentleman; whom I commend to you, as a noble friend of mine: how worthy he is I will leave to appear hereafter, rather than story him in his own hearing.

French. Sir, we have known together in Orleans.

Post. Since when I have been debtor to you for courtesies which I will be ever to pay, and yet pay still.

French. Sir, you o'errate my poor kindness. I was glad I did atone my countryman and you; it had been pity you should have been put together with so mortal a purpose as then each bore, upon importance of so slight and trivial a nature.

Post. By your pardon, sir, I was then a young traveller; rather shunned to go even with what I heard, than in my every action to be guided by others' experiences: but, upon my mended judgment (if I offend not to say it is mended), my quarrel was not altogether slight.

French. 'Faith, yes, to be put to the arbitrement of swords; and by such two that would, by all likelihood, have confounded one the other, or have fallen both.

Iach. Can we, with manners, ask what was the difference?

French. Safely, I think: 't was a contention in public, which may, without contradiction, suffer the report. It was much like an argument that fell out last night, where each of us fell in praise of our country mistresses: this gentleman at that time vouching (and upon warrant of bloody affirmation) his to be more fair, virtuous, wise, chaste, constant-qualified, and less attemptible, than any the rarest of our ladies in France.

Iach. That lady is not now living; or this gentleman's opinion, by this, worn out.

Post. She holds her virtue still, and I my mind.

Iach. You must not so far prefer her 'fore ours of Italy.

Post. Being so far provoked as I was in France, I would abate her nothing; though I profess myself her adorer, not her friend.

Iach. As fair and as good (a kind of hand-in-hand comparison), had been something too fair and too good for any lady in Britany. If she went before others I have seen, as that diamond of yours out-lustres many I have beheld, I could not but believe she excelled many: but I have not seen the most precious diamond that is, nor you the lady.

Post. I praised her as I rated her: so do I my stone.

Iach. What do you esteem it at?

Post. More than the world enjoys.

Iach. Either your unparagoned mistress is dead, or she's outprized by a trifle.

Post. You are mistaken: the one may be sold or given, if there were wealth enough for the purchase, or merit for the gift: the other is not a thing for sale, and only the gift of the gods.

Iach. Which the gods have given you?

Post. Which, by their graces, I will keep.

Iach. You may wear her in title yours; but you know strange fowl light upon neighbouring ponds: your ring may be stolen too:—so, of your brace of unprizeable estimations, the one is but frail, and the other casual; a cunning thief, or a that-way-accomplished courtier, would hazard the winning both of first and last.

Post. Your Italy contains none so accomplished a courtier, to convince the honour of my mistress; if in the holding or loss of that, you term her frail. I do nothing doubt you have store of thieves; notwithstanding, I fear not my ring.

Phi. Let us leave here, gentlemen.

Post. Sir, with all my heart. This worthy signior, I thank him, makes no stranger of me; we are familiar at first.

Iach. With five times so much conversation, I should get ground of your fair mistress; make her go back, even to the yielding; had I admittance, and opportunity to friend.

Post. No, no.

Iach. I dare thereupon pawn the moiety of my estate to your ring; which, in my opinion, o'ervalues it something: but I make my wager rather against your confidence, than her reputation: and, to bar your offence herein too, I durst attempt it against any lady in the world.

Post. You are a great deal abused in too bold a persuasion; and I doubt not you sustain what you're worthy of, by your attempt.

Iach. What's that?

Post. A repulse:—though your attempt, as you call it, deserves more; a punishment too.

Phi. Gentlemen, enough of this; it came in too suddenly; let it die as it was born, and I pray you be better acquainted.

Iach. 'Would I had put my estate, and my neighbour's, on the approbation of what I have spoke.

Post. What lady would you choose to assail?

Iach. Yours; whom in constancy you think stands so safe. I will lay you ten thousand ducats to your ring, that, commend me to the court where your lady is, with no more advantage than the opportunity of a second conference, and I will bring from thence that honour of hers which you imagine so reserved.

Post. I will wage against your gold, gold to it: my ring I hold as dear as my finger; 'tis part of it.

Iach. You are a friend, and therein the wiser. If you buy ladies' flesh at a million a dram, you cannot preserve it from tainting: but I see you have some religion in you, that you fear.

Post. This is but a custom in your tongue; you bear a graver purpose, I hope.

Iach. I am the master of my speeches; and would undergo what's spoken, I swear.

Post. Will you?—I shall but lend my diamond till your return.—Let there be covenants drawn between us. My mistress exceeds in goodness the hugeness of your unworthy thinking. I dare you to this match: here's my ring.

Phi. I will have it no lay.

Iach. By the gods it is one.—If I bring you no sufficient testimony that I have enjoyed the dearest bodily part of your mistress, my ten thou-

sand ducats are yours; so is your diamond too. If I come off, and leave her in such honour as you have trust in, she your jewel, this your jewel, and my gold are yours:—provided I have your commendation for my more free entertainment.

Post. I embrace these conditions; let us have articles betwixt us:—only, thus far you shall answer. If you make your voyage upon her, and give me directly to understand you have prevailed, I am no further your enemy; she is not worth our debate: if she remain unseduced (you not making it appear otherwise), for your ill opinion, and the assault you have made to her chastity, you shall answer me with your sword.

Iach. Your hand; a covenant. We will have these things set down by lawful counsel, and straight away for Britain, lest the bargain should catch cold, and starve. I will fetch my gold, and have our two wagers recorded.

Post. Agreed.

            [*Exeunt* POSTHUMUS *and* IACHIMO.

French. Will this hold, think you?

Phi. Signior Iachimo will not from it. Pray let us follow 'em.   [*Exeunt.*

SCENE VI.—Britain. *A Room in* CYMBELINE'S *Palace.*

Enter QUEEN, Ladies, *and* CORNELIUS.

Queen. Whiles yet the dew's on ground, gather
     those flowers:
Make haste: who has the note of them?

1st Lady.   I, madam.

Queen. Despatch.—   [*Exeunt* Ladies.
Now, master doctor, have you brought those
     drugs?

Cor. Pleaseth your highness, ay: here they are,
     madam: [*Presenting a small box.*
But I beseech your grace (without offence;
My conscience bids me ask), wherefore you have
Commanded of me these most poisonous com-
     pounds,
Which are the movers of a languishing death;
But, though slow, deadly?

Queen.   I wonder, doctor,
Thou ask'st me such a question. Have I not been
Thy pupil long? hast thou not learned me how
To make perfumes? distil? preserve? yea, so
That our great king himself doth woo me oft
For my confections? Having thus far proceeded
(Unless thou think'st me devilish), is't not meet
That I did amplify my judgment in
Other conclusions? I will try the forces
Of these thy compounds on such creatures as
We count not worth the hanging (but none
     human),

To try the vigour of them, and apply
Allayments to their act; and by them gather
Their several virtues and effects.
　　Cor.　　　　Your highness
Shall from this practice but make hard your heart:
Besides, the seeing these effects will be
Both noisome and infectious.
　　Queen.　　　O, content thee.—

Enter PISANIO.

Here comes a flattering rascal; upon him [*Aside.*
Will I first work: he's for his master,
And enemy to my son.—How now, Pisanio?—
Doctor, your service for this time is ended;
Take your own way.
　　Cor.　　　I do suspect you, madam;
But you shall do no harm.　　　　　[*Aside.*
　　Queen.　　Hark thee, a word.　[*To* PISANIO.
　　Cor. [*aside*]. I do not like her. She doth think
　　　　she has
Strange lingering poisons: I do know her spirit,
And will not trust one of her malice with
A drug of such damned nature: those she has
Will stupify and dull the sense awhile:
Which first, perchance, she'll prove on cats and
　　　　dogs;
Then afterward up higher; but there is
No danger in what show of death it makes,
More than the locking up the spirits a time,
To be more fresh, reviving. She is fooled
With a most false effect; and I the truer,
So to be false with her.
　　Queen.　　　No further service, doctor,
Until I send for thee.
　　Cor.　　　I humbly take my leave.　[*Exit.*
　　Queen. Weeps she still, say'st thou? Dost thou
　　　　think in time
She will not quench, and let instructions enter
Where folly now possesses? Do thou work:
When thou shalt bring me word she loves my son,
I'll tell thee, on the instant, thou art then
As great as is thy master: greater; for
His fortunes all lie speechless, and his name
Is at last gasp. Return he cannot, nor
Continue where he is: to shift his being,
Is to exchange one misery with another;
And every day that comes, comes to decay
A day's work in him. What shalt thou expect,
To be depender on a thing that leans?
Who cannot be new built, nor has no friends,
　[*The* QUEEN *drops a box:* PISANIO *takes it up.*
So much as but to prop him?—Thou tak'st up
Thou know'st not what; but take it for thy labour:
It is a thing I made, which hath the king
Five times redeemed from death: I do not know
What is more cordial.—Nay, I pr'y thee take it;
It is an earnest of a further good

That I mean to thee. Tell thy mistress how
The case stands with her; do't as from thyself.
Think what a chance thou changest on; but think
Thou hast thy mistress still; to boot, my son,
Who shall take notice of thee. I'll move the king
To any shape of thy preferment, such
As thou'lt desire; and then myself,—I chiefly,
That set thee on to this desert,—am bound
To load thy merit richly. Call my women:
Think on my words. [*Exit* PISANIO.]—A sly and
　　　　constant knave;
Not to be shaked: the agent for his master;
And the remembrancer of her, to hold
The hand fast to her lord. I have given him that,
Which, if he take, shall quite unpeople her
Of liegers for her sweet; and which she, after,
Except she bend her humour, shall be assured

Re-enter PISANIO and Ladies.

To taste of too.—So, so; well done, well done:
The violets, cowslips, and the primroses,
Bear to my closet.—Fare thee well, Pisanio;
Think on my words. [*Exeunt* QUEEN *and* Ladies.
　　Pisa.　　　And shall do:
But when to my good lord I prove untrue,
I'll choke myself: there's all I'll do for you. [*Exit.*

SCENE VII.—*Another Room in the same.*

Enter IMOGEN.

Imo. A father cruel, and a stepdame false;
A foolish suitor to a wedded lady,
That hath her husband banished.—O that husband!
My súpreme crown of grief! and those repeated
Vexations of it! Had I been thief-stolen,
As my two brothers, happy! but most miserable
Is the desire that's glorious. Blessed be those,
How mean soe'er, that have their honest wills,
Which seasons comfort.—Who may this be? Fie!

Enter PISANIO and IACHIMO.

Pisa. Madam, a noble gentleman of Rome;
Comes from my lord with letters.
　　Iach.　　　Change you, madam?
The worthy Leonatus is in safety,
And greets your highness dearly.
　　　　　　　　　　　　[*Presents a letter.*
　　Imo.　　　Thanks, good sir:
You are kindly welcome.
　　Iach. All of her that is out of door, most rich!
　　　　　　　　　　　　　　　[*Aside.*
If she be furnished with a mind so rare,
She is alone the Arabian bird; and I
Have lost the wager. Boldness be my friend!
Arm me, audacity, from head to foot!

Or, like the Parthian, I shall flying fight;
Rather, directly fly.

IMOGEN reads.

—— He is one of the noblest note, to whose kindnesses I am most infinitely tied. Reflect upon him
accordingly, as you value your trust.——

LEONATUS.

So far I read aloud:
But even the very middle of my heart
Is warmed by the rest, and takes it thankfully.
You are as welcome, worthy sir, as I
Have words to bid you; and shall find it so
In all that I can do.
   Iach.   Thanks, fairest lady.——
What! are men mad? Hath nature given them eyes
To see this vaulted arch, and the rich crop
Of sea and land; which can distinguish 'twixt
The fiery orbs above, and the twinned stones
Upon the numbered beach? and can we not
Partition make, with spectacles so precious,
'Twixt fair and foul?
   Imo.   What makes your admiration?
   Iach. It cannot be i' the eye; for apes and
      monkeys,
'Twixt two such shes, would chatter this way, and
Contemn with mows the other: nor i' the judg-
      ment;
For idiots, in this case of favour, would
Be wisely definite: nor i' the appetite;
Sluttery, to such neat excellence opposed,
Should make desire vomit emptiness,
Not so allured to feed.
   Imo. What is the matter, trow?
   Iach.   The cloyed will
(That satiate yet unsatisfied desire,
That tub both filled and running), ravening first
The lamb, longs after for the garbage.
   Imo.   What, dear sir,
Thus raps you? Are you well?
   Iach. Thanks, madam; well.——' Beseech you,
      sir, desire   [*To* PISANIO.
My man's abode, where I did leave him: he
Is strange and peevish.
   Pis.   I was going, sir,
To give him welcome.   [*Exit* PISANIO.
   Imo. Continues well my lord? His health,
      ' beseech you?
   Iach. Well, madam.
   Imo. Is he disposed to mirth? I hope he is.
   Iach. Exceeding pleasant; none a stranger there
So merry and so gamesome: he is called
The Briton reveller.
   Imo.   When he was here
He did incline to sadness; and ofttimes
Not knowing why.
   Iach.   I never saw him sad.

There is a Frenchman his companion, one
An eminent monsieur, that, it seems, much loves
A Gallian girl at home: he furnaces
The thick sighs from him; whiles the jolly Briton
(Your lord, I mean) laughs from 's free lungs,
      cries " O !
Can my sides hold, to think that man,—who knows
By history, report, or his own proof,
What woman is, yea, what she cannot choose
But must be,—will his free hours languish for
Assuréd bondage !"
   Imo. Will my lord say so?
   Iach. Ay, madam; with his eyes in flood with
      laughter.
It is a recreation to be by,
And hear him mock the Frenchman. But, heavens
      know
Some men are much to blame.
   Imo. Not he, I hope,
   Iach. Not he: but yet heaven's bounty towards
      him might
Be used more thankfully. In himself, 't is much;
In you,—which I count his, beyond all talents,—
Whilst I am bound to wonder, I am bound
To pity too.
   Imo.   What do you pity, sir?
   Iach. Two creatures, heartily.
   Imo.   Am I one, sir?
You look on me: what wreck discern you in me,
Deserves your pity?
   Iach.   Lamentable! What!
To hide me from the radiant sun, and solace
I' the dungeon by a snuff?
   Imo.   I pray you, sir,
Deliver with more openness your answers
To my demands. Why do you pity me?
   Iach. That others do,
I was about to say, enjoy your—But
It is an office of the gods to venge it,
Not mine to speak on 't.
   Imo.   You do seem to know
Something of me, or what concerns me. Pray you
(Since doubting things go ill, often hurts more
Than to be sure they do: for certainties
Either are past remedies; or, timely knowing,
The remedy then born), discover to me
What both you spur and stop.
   Iach.   Had I this cheek
To bathe my lips upon; this hand, whose touch,
Whose every touch, would force the feeler's soul
To the oath of loyalty; this object, which
Takes prisoner the wild motion of mine eye,
Fixing it only here: should I (damned then !)
Slaver with lips as common as the stairs
That mount the Capitol; join gripes with hands
Made hard with hourly falsehood (falsehood as
With labour); then lie peeping in an eye

Base and unlustrous as the smoky light
That's fed with stinking tallow;—it were fit
That all the plagues of hell should at one time
Encounter such revolt.
   Imo.   My lord, I fear,
Has forgot Britain.
   Iach.   And himself. Not I,
Inclined to this intelligence, pronounce
The beggary of his change; but 'tis your graces,

That from my mutest conscience, to my tongue,
Charms this report out.
   Imo.   Let me hear no more.
   Iach. O dearest soul! your cause doth strike
     my heart
With pity that doth make me sick. A lady
So fair, and fastened to an empery,
Would make the great'st king double! to be
     partnered

Let me my service tender on your lips.

With tomboys, hired with that self exhibition
Which your own coffers yield! with diseased ven-
     tures,
That play with all infirmities for gold,
Which rottenness can lend nature; such boiled
     stuff
As well might poison poison! Be revenged;
Or she that bore you was no queen, and you
Recoil from your great stock.
   Imo.   Revenged!
How should I be revenged? If this be true
(As I have such a heart that both mine ears

Must not in haste abuse),—if it be true,
How should I be revenged?
   Iach.   Should he make me
Live like Diana's priest, betwixt cold sheets,
Whiles he is vaulting variable ramps,
In your despite, upon your purse? Revenge it.
I dedicate myself to your sweet pleasure;
More noble than that runagate to your bed;
And will continue fast to your affection,
Still close as sure.
   Imo.   What ho, Pisanio!
   Iach. Let me my service tender on your lips.

Imo. Away!—I do condemn mine ears, that
  have
So long attended thee. If thou wert honourable,
Thou wouldst have told this tale for virtue, not
For such an end thou seek'st; as base as strange.
Thou wrong'st a gentleman who is as far
From thy report as thou from honour; and
Solicit'st here a lady that disdains
Thee and the devil alike.—What, ho! Pisanio!—
The king my father shall be made acquainted
Of thy assault: if he shall think it fit,
A saucy stranger in his court to mart
As in a Romish stew, and to expound
His beastly mind to us, he hath a court
He little cares for, and a daughter whom
He not respects at all.—What ho, Pisanio!

Iach. O happy Leonatus! I may say:
The credit that thy lady hath of thee
Deserves thy trust; and thy most perfect goodness
Her assured credit!—Blessèd live you long!
A lady to the worthiest sir that ever
Country called his! and you his mistress, only
For the most worthiest fit! Give me your pardon.
I have spoke this to know if your affiance
Were deeply rooted; and shall make your lord
That which he is, new o'er: and he is one
The truest mannered; such a holy witch,
That he enchants societies unto him:
Half all men's hearts are his.

Imo. You make amends.

Iach. He sits 'mongst men like a descended god:
He hath a kind of honour sets him off,
More than a mortal seeming. Be not angry,
Most mighty princess, that I have adventured
To try your taking of a false report; which hath
Honoured with confirmation your great judgment
In the election of a sir so rare,
Which you know cannot err. The love I bear him
Made me to fan you thus; but the gods made you,
Unlike all other, chaffless. Pray your pardon.

Imo. All's well, sir: take my power i' the court
  for yours.

Iach. My humble thanks. I had almost forgot
To intreat your grace but in a small request,
And yet of moment too, for it concerns
Your lord: myself, and other noble friends,
Are partners in the business.

Imo.   Pray what is't?

Iach. Some dozen Romans of us, and your lord
(The best feather of our wing), have mingled sums,
To buy a present for the emperor:
Which I, the factor for the rest, have done
In France: 'tis plate of rare device, and jewels
Of rich and exquisite form; their values great;
And I am something curious, being strange,
To have them in safe stowage. May it please you
To take them in protection?

Imo.   Willingly;
And pawn mine honour for their safety: since
My lord hath interest in them, I will keep them
In my bed-chamber.

Iach.   They are in a trunk,
Attended by my men. I will make bold
To send them to you, only for this night:
I must aboard to-morrow.

Imo.   O, no, no!

Iach. Yes, I beseech: or I shall short my word,
By lengthening my return. From Gallia
I crossed the seas on purpose, and on promise,
To see your grace.

Imo.   I thank you for your pains;
But not away to-morrow?

Iach.   O, I must, madam:
Therefore I shall beseech you, if you please
To greet your lord with writing, do't to-night.
I have outstood my time; which is material
To the tender of our present.

Imo.   I will write.
Send your trunk to me; it shall safe be kept,
And truly yielded you. You are very welcome.
                                    [*Exeunt.*

SCENE I.—*Court before* CYMBELINE'S *Palace.*

Enter CLOTEN *and two* Lords.

Clo. Was there ever man had such luck! when
I kissed the jack upon an up-cast, to be hit away!
I had an hundred pound on 't: and then a whoreson jackanapes must take me up for swearing; as
if I borrowed mine oaths of him, and might not
spend them at my pleasure.

1st Lord. What got he by that?—you have
broke his pate with your bowl.

2nd Lord. If his wit had been like him that
broke it, it would have ran all out. [*Aside.*

Clo. When a gentleman is disposed to swear,
it is not for any standers-by to curtail his oaths:
ha?

2nd Lord. No, my lord; nor [*aside*] crop the
ears of them.

Clo. Whoreson dog!—I give him satisfaction?
'Would he had been one of my rank!

2nd Lord. To have smelt like a fool. [*Aside.*

Clo. I am not more vexed at anything in the
earth.—A pox on 't! I had rather not be so noble
as I am; they dare not fight with me, because of
the queen my mother: every jack-slave hath his
belly full of fighting, and I must go up and down
like a cock that nobody can match.

2nd Lord. You are a cock and capon too; and
you crow, cock, with your comb on. [*Aside.*

Clo. Sayest thou?

1st Lord. It is not fit your lordship should
undertake every companion that you give offence to.

Clo. No, I know that; but it is fit I should
commit offence to my inferiors.

2nd Lord. Ay, it is fit for your lordship only.

Clo. Why, so I say.

1st Lord. Did you hear of a stranger that 's
come to court to-night?

Clo. A stranger! and I not know on 't!

2nd Lord. He 's a strange fellow himself, and
knows it not. [*Aside.*

1st Lord. There 's an Italian come; and, 'tis
thought, one of Leonatus' friends.

Clo. Leonatus! a banished rascal: and he 's
another, whatsoever he be.—Who told you of this
stranger?

1st Lord. One of your lordship's pages.

Clo. Is it fit I went to look upon him? Is there
no derogation in 't?

1st Lord. You cannot derogate, my lord.

Clo. Not easily, I think.

2nd Lord. You are a fool granted; therefore
your issues being foolish, do not derogate. [*Aside.*

Clo. Come, I 'll go see this Italian. What I
have lost to-day at bowls, I 'll win to-night of him.
Come, go.

2nd Lord. I 'll attend your lordship.

[*Exeunt* CLOTEN *and* First Lord.
That such a crafty devil as is his mother
Should yield the world this ass! A woman that
Bears all down with her brain; and this her son
Cannot take two from twenty for his heart,
And leave eighteen. Alas, poor princess,
Thou divine Imogen, what thou endur'st!
Betwixt a father by thy stepdame governed;
A mother hourly coining plots; a wooer
More hateful than the foul expulsion is
Of thy dear husband; than that horrid act
Of the divorce he 'd make! The heavens hold
    firm

The walls of thy dear honour; keep unshaked
That temple, thy fair mind; that thou mayst stand
To enjoy thy banished lord, and this great land!
                                                [*Exit.*

SCENE II.—*A Bed-chamber; in one part of it a trunk.*

IMOGEN, *reading in her bed; a* Lady *attending.*

Imo. Who's there? my woman Helen?

Lady.   Please you, madam.
Imo. What hour is it?
Lady.   Almost midnight, madam.
Imo. I have read three hours, then: mine eyes
     are weak.
Fold down the leaf where I have left: to bed:
Take not away the taper, leave it burning;
And if thou canst awake by four o'the clock,
I pr'ythee call me. Sleep hath seized me wholly.
                                      [*Exit* Lady.
To your protection I commend me, gods!

From fairies, and the tempters of the night,
Guard me, beseech ye!   [*Sleeps.*

IACHIMO, *from the trunk.*

The crickets sing, and man's o'erlaboured sense
Repairs itself by rest. Our Tarquin thus
Did softly press the rushes, ere he wakened
The chastity he wounded.—Cytherea,
How bravely thou becom'st thy bed! fresh lily!

And whiter than the sheets! That I might touch!
But kiss; one kiss! Rubies unparagoned,
How dearly they do't.—'Tis her breathing that
Perfumes the chamber thus: the flame o'the taper
Bows toward her; and would under-peep her lids,
To see the enclosèd lights, now canopied
Under these windows, white and azure, laced
With blue of heaven's own tinct.—But my design:
To note the chamber, I will write all down:

Such and such pictures: there the window: such
The adornment of her bed: the arras, figures,
Why, such and such; and the contents o' the
      story:
Ah, but some natural notes about her body,
Above ten thousand meaner moveables
Would testify, to enrich mine inventory.
O sleep, thou ape of death, lie dull upon her!
And be her sense but as a monument,
Thus in a chapel lying!—Come off, come off:
           [*Taking off her bracelet.*
As slippery as the Gordian knot was hard!
'Tis mine; and this will witness outwardly,
As strongly as the conscience does within,
To the madding of her lord. On her left breast,
A mole cinque-spotted, like the crimson drops
I' the bottom of a cowslip. Here's a voucher
Stronger than ever law could make: this secret
Will force him think I have picked the lock, and
      ta'en
The treasure of her honour. No more. To what
      end?
Why should I write this down, that's rivetted,
Screwed to my memory? She hath been reading
      late
The tale of Tereus: here the leaf's turned down,
Where Philomel gave up.—I have enough:
To the trunk again, and shut the spring of it.
Swift, swift, you dragons of the night! that
      dawning
May bare the raven's eye. I lodge in fear;
Though this a heavenly angel, hell is here.
           [*Clock strikes.*

One, two, three:—Time, time!
      [*Goes into the trunk.   The scene closes.*

SCENE III.—*Without the Palace, under* IMOGEN'S
Apartment.

Enter CLOTEN *and* Lords.

1st Lord. Your lordship is the most patient
man in loss, the most coldest that ever turned
up ace.

Clo. It would make any man cold to lose.

1st Lord. But not every man patient, after the
noble temper of your lordship: you are most hot
and furious when you win.

Clo. Winning would put any man into courage. If I could get this foolish Imogen, I should
have gold enough. It's almost morning, is't
not?

1st Lord. Day, my lord.

Clo. I would this music would come: I am
advised to give her music o'mornings; they say,
it will penetrate.

Enter Musicians.

Come on; tune. If you can penetrate her with
your fingering, so; we'll try with tongue too: if
none will do, let her remain; but I'll never give
o'er. First, a very excellent good-conceited thing;
after a wonderful sweet air, with admirable rich
words to it;—and then let her consider.

Hark! hark! the lark at heaven's gate sings,
  And Phœbus 'gins arise,
His steeds to water at those springs
  On chaliced flowers that lies;
And winking Mary-buds begin to ope their golden eyes:
With everything that pretty is;—My lady sweet, arise.
  Arise, arise.

So, get you gone. If this penetrate, I will consider your music the better: if it do not, it is a vice in her ears, which horsehairs and calves'-guts, nor the voice of unpaved eunuch to boot, can never amend. [*Exeunt* Musicians.

Enter CYMBELINE *and* QUEEN.

2nd Lord. Here comes the king.

Clo. I am glad I was up so late; for that's the reason I was up so early. He cannot choose but take this service I have done, fatherly.—Good-morrow to your majesty, and to my gracious mother.

Cym. Attend you here the door of our stern
    daughter?
Will she not forth?

Clo. I have assailed her with music, but she vouchsafes no notice.

Cym. The exile of her minion is too new;
She hath not yet forgot him: some more time
Must wear the print of his remembrance out
And then she's yours.

Queen. You are most bound to the king,
Who lets go by no vantages that may
Prefer you to his daughter. Frame yourself
To orderly solicits, and be friended
With aptness of the season: make denials
Increase your services: so seem, as if
You were inspired to do those duties which
You tender to her; that you in all obey her,
Save when command to your dismission tends;
And therein you are senseless.

Clo. Senseless? not so.

Enter a Messenger.

Mess. So like you, sir, ambassadors from Rome;
The one is Caius Lucius.

Cym. A worthy fellow,
Albeit he comes on angry purpose now;
But that's no fault of his: we must receive him
According to the honour of his sender;
And towards himself, his goodness forespent on
    us,
We must extend our notice.—Our dear son,

When you have given good morning to your mistress,
Attend the queen and us: we shall have need
To employ you towards this Roman.—Come, our
    queen.
      [*Exeunt* CYMBELINE, QUEEN, Lords, *and*
      Messenger.
  Clo. If she be up, I'll speak with her; if not,
Let her lie still and dream.—By your leave, ho!
      [*Knocks.*
I know her women are about her: what
If I do line one of their hands? 'T is gold
Which buys admittance; oft it doth; yea, and
    makes
Diana's rangers, false themselves, yield up
Their deer to the stand of the stealer: and 't is gold
Which makes the true man killed, and saves the
    thief;
Nay, sometime hangs both thief and true man:
    what
Can it not do, and undo? I will make
One of her women lawyer to me; for
I yet not understand the case myself.
By your leave.   [*Knocks.*

      Enter a Lady.

  Lady. Who's there that knocks?
  Clo.   A gentleman.
  Lady.   No more?
  Clo. Yes, and a gentlewoman's son.
  Lady.   That's more
Than some, whose tailors are as dear as yours,
Can justly boast of. What's your lordship's
    pleasure?
  Clo. Your lady's person: is she ready?
  Lady.   Ay,
To keep her chamber.
  Clo. There's gold for you; sell me your good
    report.
  Lady. How! my good name? or to report of you
What I shall think is good?—The princess—

      Enter IMOGEN.

  Clo. Good-morrow, fairest sister: your sweet
    hand.
  Imo. Good-morrow, sir: you lay out too much
    pains
For purchasing but trouble: the thanks I give
Is telling you that I am poor of thanks,
And scarce can spare them.
  Clo.   Still, I swear I love you.
  Imo. If you but said so, 't were as deep with me:
If you swear still, your recompence is still
That I regard it not.
  Clo.   This is no answer.
  Imo. But that you shall not say I yield, being
    silent,
I would not speak. I pray you, spare me: i' faith,

I shall unfold equal discourtesy
To your best kindness: one of your great knowing
Should learn, being taught, forbearance.
  Clo. To leave you in your madness, 't were
    my sin:
I will not.
  Imo. Fools are not mad folks.
  Clo.   Do you call me fool?
  Imo. As I am mad, I do:
If you'll be patient, I'll no more be mad;
That cures us both. I am much sorry, sir,
You put me to forget a lady's manners,
By being so verbal: and learn now, for all,
That I, which know my heart, do here pronounce,
By the very truth of it, I care not for you;
And am so near the lack of charity
(To accuse myself), I hate you: which I had rather
You felt, than make 't my boast.
  Clo.   You sin against
Obedience, which you owe your father. For
The contract you pretend with that base wretch
(One bred of alms, and fostered with cold dishes,
With scraps o' the court), it is no contract, none:
And though it be allowed in meaner parties
(Yet who than he more mean?) to knit their souls
(On whom there is no more dependency
But brats and beggary) in self-figured knot;
Yet you are curbed from that enlargement by
The consequence o' the crown; and must not soil
The precious note of it with a base slave,
A hilding for a livery, a squire's cloth,
A pantler,—not so eminent.
  Imo.   Profane fellow!
Wert thou the son of Jupiter, and no more
But what thou art besides, thou wert too base
To be his groom: thou wert dignified enough,
Even to the point of envy, if 't were made
Comparative for your virtues, to be styled
The under-hangman of his kingdom; and hated
For being preferred so well.
  Clo.   The south-fog rot him!
  Imo. He never can meet more mischance than
    come
To be but named of thee. His meanest garment
That ever hath but clipped his body, is dearer
In my respect than all the hairs above thee,
Were they all made such men.—How now, Pisanio?

      Enter PISANIO.

  Clo. His garment? Now, the devil—
  Imo. To Dorothy my woman hie thee presently:
  Clo. His garment?
  Imo.   I am sprighted with a fool;
Frighted, and angered worse:—Go, bid my woman
Search for a jewel, that too casually
Hath left mine arm; it was thy master's: 'shrew
    me,

If I would lose it for a revenue
Of any king's in Europe. I do think
I saw 't this morning: confident I am,
Last night 't was on mine arm; I kissed it.
I hope it be not gone, to tell my lord
That I kiss aught but he.

Pisa. 'T will not be lost.

Imo. I hope so: go and search. [*Exit* PISANIO.

Clo. You have abused me:
His meanest garment?

Imo. Ay; I said so, sir.
If you will make 't an action, call witness to 't.

Clo. I will inform your father.

Imo. Your mother too:
She's my good lady; and will conceive, I hope,
But the worst of me. So I leave you, sir,
To the worst of discontent. [*Exit.*

Clo. I 'll be revenged:
His meanest garment? Well! [*Exit.*

SCENE IV.—Rome. *An Apartment in* PHILARIO'S
House.

Enter POSTHUMUS *and* PHILARIO.

Post. Fear it not, sir: I would I were so sure
To win the king, as I am bold her honour
Will remain hers.

Phi. What means do you make to him?

Post. Not any; but abide the change of time;
Quake in the present winter's state, and wish
That warmer days would come. In these feared
hopes,
I barely gratify your love; they failing,
I must die much your debtor.

Phi. Your very goodness, and your company,
O'erpays all I can do. By this, your king
Hath heard of great Augustus: Caius Lucius
Will do his commission throughly. And I think
He 'll grant the tribute, send the arrearages,
Ere look upon our Romans, whose remembrance
Is yet fresh in their grief.

Post. I do believe
(Statist though I am none, nor like to be)
That this will prove a war; and you shall hear
The legions now in Gallia sooner landed
In our not-fearing Britain, than have tidings
Of any penny tribute paid. Our countrymen
Are men more ordered than when Julius Cæsar
Smiled at their lack of skill, but found their
courage
Worthy his frowning at: their discipline
(Now mingled with their courages) will make
known
To their approvers, they are people such
That mend upon the world.

Enter IACHIMO.

Phi. See! Iachimo?

Post. The swiftest harts have posted you by land;
And winds of all the corners kissed your sails,
To make your vessel nimble.

Phi. Welcome, sir.

Post. I hope the briefness of your answer made
The speediness of your return.

Iach. Your lady
Is one of the fairest that I have looked upon.

Post. And therewithal, the best; or let her
beauty
Look through a casement to allure false hearts,
And be false with them.

Iach. Here are letters for you.

Post. Their tenor good, I trust.

Iach. 'T is very like.

Phi. Was Caius Lucius in the Britain court,
When you were there?

Iach. He was expected then,
But not approached.

Post. All is well yet.—
Sparkles this stone as it was wont? or is 't not
Too dull for your good wearing?

Iach. If I have lost it,
I should have lost the worth of it in gold.
I 'll make a journey twice as far, to enjoy
A second night of such sweet shortness, which
Was mine in Britain: for the ring is won.

Post. The stone's too hard to come by.

Iach. Not a whit,
Your lady being so easy.

Post. Make not, sir,
Your loss your sport: I hope you know that we
Must not continue friends.

Iach. Good sir, we must,
If you keep covenant. Had I not brought
The knowledge of your mistress home, I grant
We were to question further: but I now
Profess myself the winner of her honour,
Together with your ring: and not the wronger
Of her or you, having proceeded but
By both your wills.

Post. If you can make 't apparent
That you have tasted her in bed, my hand
And ring is yours: if not, the foul opinion
You had of her pure honour gains or loses
Your sword or mine, or masterless leaves both
To who shall find them.

Iach. Sir, my circumstances,
Being so near the truth as I will make them,
Must first induce you to believe: whose strength
I will confirm with oath; which I doubt not
You 'll give me leave to spare, when you shall find
You need it not.

Post. Proceed.

Iach. First, her bed-chamber

(Where I confess I slept not; but profess
Had that was well worth watching), it was hanged
With tapestry of silk and silver; the story,
Proud Cleopatra, when she met her Roman,
And Cydnus swelled above the banks, or for
The press of boats, or pride: a piece of work
So bravely done, so rich, that it did strive
In workmanship and value; which I wondered
Could be so rarely and exactly wrought,
Since the true life on 't was—
    Post.   This is true;
And this you might have heard of here, by me,
Or by some other.
    Iach.   More particulars
Must justify my knowledge.
    Post.   So they must,
Or do your honour injury.
    Iach.   The chimney
Is south the chamber; and the chimney-piece,
Chaste Dian bathing: never saw I figures
So likely to report themselves; the cutter
Was as another nature, dumb; outwent her,
Motion and breath left out.
    Post.   This is a thing
Which you might from relation likewise reap;
Being, as it is, much spoke of.
    Iach.   The roof o' the chamber
With golden cherubins is fretted: her andirons
(I had forgot them) were two winking Cupids
Of silver, each on one foot standing, nicely
Depending on their brands.
    Post.   This is her honour!—
Let it be granted you have seen all this (and praise
Be given to your remembrance), the description
Of what is in her chamber, nothing saves
The wager you have laid.
    Iach.   Then, if you can,
                      [*Pulling out the bracelet.*
Be pale; I beg but leave to air this jewel: see!
And now 't is up again. It must be married
To that your diamond; I 'll keep them.
    Post.   Jove!
Once more let me behold it: is it that
Which I left with her?
    Iach.   Sir (I thank her), that:
She stripped it from her arm: I see her yet:
Her pretty action did outsell her gift,
And yet enriched it too. She gave it me, and
    said
She prized it once.
    Post.   May be she plucked it off
To send it me.
    Iach.   She writes so to you, doth she?
    Post. O, no, no, no; 't is true. Here, take this
    too;   [*Gives the ring.*
It is a basilisk unto mine eye,
Kills me to look on 't.—Let there be no honour

Where there is beauty; truth, where semblance;
    love,'
Where there 's another man. The vows of women
Of no more bondage be to where they are made,
Than they are to their virtues; which is nothing.—
O, above measure false!
    Phi.   Have patience, sir,
And take your ring again; 't is not yet won:
It may be probable she lost it; or
Who knows if one of her women, being corrupted,
Hath stolen it from her?
    Post.   Very true;
And so I hope he came by 't.—Back my ring:
Render to me some corporal sign about her,
More evident than this; for this was stolen.
    Iach. By Jupiter, I had it from her arm.
    Post. Hark you, he swears: by Jupiter he
    swears.
'T is true; nay, keep the ring—'tis true. I am sure
She would not lose it: her attendants are
All sworn, and honourable: they induced to
    steal it!
And by a stranger! No, he hath enjoyed her:
The cognizance of her incontinency
Is this; she hath bought the name of whore thus
    dearly.—
There, take thy hire; and all the fiends of hell
Divide themselves between you!
    Phi.   Sir, be patient!
This is not strong enough to be believed
Of one persuaded well of—
    Post.   Never talk on 't;
She hath been colted by him.
    Iach.   If you seek
For further satisfying,—under her breast
(Worthy the pressing) lies a mole, right proud
Of that most delicate lodging: by my life,
I kissed it; and it gave me present hunger
To feed again, though full. You do remember
This stain upon her?
    Post.   Ay, and it doth confirm
Another stain, as big as hell can hold,
Were there no more but it.
    Iach.   Will you hear more?
    Post. Spare your arithmetic: never count the
    turns;
Once, and a million!
    Iach.   I 'll be sworn,—
    Post.   No swearing.
If you will swear you have not done 't, you lie;
And I will kill thee if thou dost deny
Thou hast made me cuckold.
    Iach.   I 'll deny nothing.
    Post. O, that I had her here, to tear her limb-
    meal!
I will go there, and do 't; i' the court; before
Her father: I 'll do something—   [*Exit.*

Phi.   Quite besides
The government of patience!—You have won:
Let's follow him, and pervert the present wrath
He hath against himself.
    Iach.   With all my heart.   [*Exeunt.*

SCENE V.—*The same. Another Room in the same.*

Enter POSTHUMUS.

Post. Is there no way for men to be, but women
Must be half-workers? We are all bastards;
And that most venerable man which I
Did call my father, was I know not where
When I was stamped; some coiner with his tools
Made me a counterfeit: yet my mother seemed
The Dian of that time: so doth my wife
The nonpareil of this.—O vengeance, vengeance!
Me of my lawful pleasure she restrained,
And prayed me oft forbearance: did it with
A pudency so rosy, the sweet view on't
Might well have warmed old Saturn; that I
     thought her

As chaste as unsunned snow.—O, all the devils!
This yellow Iachimo, in an hour,—was't not?
Or less,—at first. Perchance he spoke not; but,
Like a full-acorned boar, a German one,
Cried, "O!" and mounted: found no opposition
But what he looked for should oppose, and she
Should from encounter guard. Could I find out
The woman's part in me! For there's no motion
That tends to vice in man, but I affirm
It is the woman's part:—be it lying, note it,
The woman's; flattering, hers; deceiving, hers;
Lust and rank thoughts, hers, hers; revenges,
     hers;
Ambitions, covetings, change of prides, disdain,
Nice longings, slanders, mutability,
All faults that may be named, nay, that hell knows,
Why, hers in part, or all; but rather, all:
For even to vice
They are not constant, but are changing still
One vice but of a minute old, for one
Not half so old as that. I'll write against them,
Detest them, curse them:—yet 'tis greater skill
In a true hate, to pray they have their will:
The very devils cannot plague them better. [*Exit.*

ACT III

SCENE I.—Britain. *A Room of State in* CYMBE-
LINE's *Palace.*

Enter CYMBELINE, QUEEN, CLOTEN, *and* Lords,
at one door; and at another, CAIUS LUCIUS *and*
Attendants.

Cym. Now say, what would Augustus Cæsar
    with us?

Luc. When Julius Cæsar (whose remembrance
    yet
Lives in men's eyes, and will to ears and tongues
Be theme and hearing ever) was in this Britain,
And conquered it, Cassibelan, thine uncle
(Famous in Cæsar's praises, no whit less
Than in his feats deserving it), for him
And his succession, granted Rome a tribute,
Yearly three thousand pounds; which by thee
    lately
Is left untendered.

Queen.   And, to kill the marvel,
Shall be so ever.

Clo.   There be many Cæsars,
Ere such another Julius. Britain is
A world by itself; and we will nothing pay
For wearing our own noses.

Queen.   That opportunity
Which then they had to take from us, to resume
We have again.—Remember, sir, my liege,
The kings your ancestors; together with
The natural bravery of your isle; which stands
As Neptune's park, ribbed and paled in
With rocks unscaleable, and roaring waters;
With sands that will not bear your enemies' boats,
But suck them up to the topmast. A kind of
    conquest
Cæsar made here; but made not here his brag
Of " came," and " saw," and " overcame:" with
    shame
(The first that ever touched him) he was carried

From off our coast, twice beaten; and his shipping
(Poor ignorant baubles!) on our terrible seas,
Like egg-shells moved upon their surges, cracked
As easily 'gainst our rocks: for joy whereof,
The famed Cassibelan, who was once at point
(O, giglot fortune!) to master Cæsar's sword,
Made Lud's town with rejoicing fires bright,
And Britons strut with courage.

Clo. Come, there's no more tribute to be paid.
Our kingdom is stronger than it was at that time;
and, as I said, there is no more such Cæsars:
other of them may have crooked noses; but, to
owe such straight arms, none.

Cym. Son, let your mother end.

Clo. We have yet many among us can gripe
as hard as Cassibelan: I do not say, I am one;
but I have a hand.—Why tribute? why should
we pay tribute? If Cæsar can hide the sun from
us with a blanket, or put the moon in his pocket,
we will pay him tribute for light; else, sir, no
more tribute, pray you now.

Cym. You must know,
Till the injurious Romans did extort
This tribute from us, we were free: Cæsar's am-
    bition
(Which swelled so much that it did almost stretch
The sides o' the world), against all colour, here
Did put the yoke upon us; which to shake off
Becomes a warlike people, whom we reckon
Ourselves to be. We do say, then, to Cæsar,
Our ancestor was that Mulmutius, which
Ordained our laws (whose use the sword of Cæsar
Hath too much mangled; whose repair and franchise
Shall, by the power we hold, be our good deed,
Though Rome be therefore angry): Mulmutius
    made our laws,
Who was the first of Britain which did put
His brows within a golden crown, and called
Himself a king.

Luc. I am sorry, Cymbeline,
That I am to pronounce Augustus Cæsar
(Cæsar, that hath more kings his servants than
Thyself domestic officers) thine enemy:
Receive it from me, then:—War and confusion,
In Cæsar's name, pronounce I 'gainst thee; look
For fury not to be resisted.—Thus defied,
I thank thee for myself.
    Cym.   Thou art welcome, Caius.
Thy Cæsar knighted me: my youth I spent
Much under him; of him I gathered honour;
Which he to seek of me again, perforce,
Behoves me keep at utterance. I am perfect
That the Pannonians and Dalmatians, for
Their liberties, are now in arms: a precedent
Which not to read would shew the Britons cold:
So Cæsar shall not find them.
    Luc.   Let proof speak.
    Clo. His majesty bids you welcome. Make
pastime with us a day or two, or longer: if you
seek us afterwards in other terms, you shall find
us in our salt-water girdle: if you beat us out of
it, it is yours; if you fall in the adventure, our
crows shall fare the better for you; and there's
an end.
    Luc. So, sir.
    Cym. I know your master's pleasure, and he
    mine:
All the remain is, welcome.   *[Exeunt.*

SCENE II.—*Another Room in the same.*

Enter PISANIO, *reading a letter.*

    Pisa. How! of adultery? Wherefore write you
    not
What monster's her accuser?—Leonatus!
O, master! what a strange infection
Is fallen into thy ear? What false Italian
(As poisonous tongued as handed) hath prevailed
On thy too ready hearing?—Disloyal? No:
She's punished for her truth; and undergoes,
More goddess-like than wife-like, such assaults
As would take in some virtue. O, my master!
Thy mind to her is now as low as were
Thy fortunes.—How! that I should murder her,
Upon the love, and truth, and vows which I
Have made to thy command? I, her? her blood?
If it be so to do good service, never
Let me be counted serviceable. How look I,
That I should seem to lack humanity,
So much as this fact comes to?—"Do't: the
    letter
That I have sent her, by her own command
Shall give thee opportunity." O damned paper!
Black as the ink that's on thee! Senseless bauble,

Art thou a feodary for this act, and look'st
So virgin-like without? Lo, here she comes.

Enter IMOGEN.

I am ignorant in what I am commanded.
    Imo. How now, Pisanio?
    Pisa. Madam, here is a letter from my lord.
    Imo. Who? thy lord? that is my lord? Leonatus?
O, learned indeed were that astronomer
That knew the stars as I his characters;
He'd lay the future open.—You good gods,
Let what is here contained relish of love,
Of my lord's health, of his content,—yet not
That we two are asunder; let that grieve him
(Some griefs are med'cinable; that is one of them,
For it doth physic love);—of his content,
All but in that!—Good wax, thy leave. Blessed be,
You bees, that make these locks of counsel! Lovers
And men in dangerous bonds pray not alike:
Though forfeiters you cast in prison, yet
You clasp young Cupid's tables.—Good news,
    gods!

    Reads.

    " Justice, and your father's wrath, should he take
me in his dominion, could not be so cruel to me, as
you, O the dearest of creatures, would not even renew
me with your eyes. Take notice that I am in Cambria, at Milford-Haven: what your own love will,
out of this, advise you, follow. So he wishes you
all happiness, that remains loyal to his vow, and
your, increasing in love,
                      " LEONATUS POSTHUMUS."

O, for a horse with wings!—Hear'st thou, Pisanio?
He is at Milford-Haven: read, and tell me
How far 'tis thither. If one of mean affairs
May plod it in a week, why may not I
Glide thither in a day? Then, true Pisanio
(Who long'st, like me, to see thy lord; who
    long'st,—
O, let me bate,—but not like me: yet long'st,
But in a fainter kind:—O, not like me;
For mine's beyond beyond), say, and speak thick
(Love's counsellor should fill the bores of hearing,
To the smothering of the sense), how far it is
To this same blessèd Milford: and, by the way,
Tell me how Wales was made so happy as
To inherit such a haven: but, first of all,
How we may steal from hence; and, for the gap
That we shall make in time, from our hence-going,
And our return, to excuse:—but first, how get
    hence:
Why should excuse be born or ere begot?
We'll talk of that hereafter. Pr'ythee, speak,
How many score of miles may we well ride
'Twixt hour and hour.
    Pisa.   One score, 'twixt sun and sun,
Madam, 's enough for you; and too much too.

Imo. Why, one that rode to his execution, man,
Could never go so slow: I have heard of riding
    wagers,
Where horses have been nimbler than the sands
That run i' the clock's behalf.—But this is foolery:
Go, bid my woman feign a sickness; say
She 'll home to her father; and provide me, pre-
    sently,

A riding suit; no costlier than would fit
A franklin's housewife.
   Pisa.   Madam, you 're best consider.
   Imo. I see before me, man: nor here, nor here,
Nor what ensues, but have a fog in them,
That I cannot look through. Away, I pr'y thee;
Do as I bid thee: there 's no more to say;
Accessible is none but Milford way.   [*Exeunt.*

SCENE III.—Wales. *A mountainous Country,*
        with a Cave.

Enter BELARIUS, GUIDERIUS, *and* ARVIRAGUS.

   Bel. A goodly day not to keep house, with such
Whose roof 's as low as ours! Stoop, boys: this
    gate
Instructs you how to adore the heavens; and bows
    you
To morning's holy office: the gates of monarchs
Are arched so high, that giants may jet through

And keep their impious turbands on, without
Good-morrow to the sun.—Hail, thou fair heaven!
We house i' the rock, yet use thee not so hardly
As prouder livers do.
   Gui.   Hail, heaven!
   Arv.   Hail, heaven!
   Bel. Now, for our mountain sport: up to yon
    hill,
Your legs are young; I 'll tread these flats. Con-
    sider,
When you above perceive me like a crow,

That it is place which lessens and sets off.
And you may then revolve what tales I have told
    you,
Of courts, of princes, of the tricks in war:
This service is not service, so being done,
But being so allowed: to apprehend thus,
Draws us a profit from all things we see:
And often, to our comfort, shall we find
The sharded beetle in a safer hold
Than is the full-winged eagle. O, this life
Is nobler than attending for a check;
Richer than doing nothing for a bribe;
Prouder than rustling in unpaid-for silk:
Such gains the cap of him that makes him fine,
Yet keeps his book uncrossed: no life to ours.
    Gui. Out of your proof you speak: we, poor
      unfledged,
Have never winged from view o'the nest, nor
    know not
What air's from home. Haply this life is best,
If quiet life be best: sweeter to you,
That have a sharper known; well corresponding
With your stiff age: but unto us, it is
A cell of ignorance; travelling abed;
A prison for a debtor, that not dares
To stride a limit.
    Arv.   What should we speak of,
When we are old as you? When we shall hear
The rain and wind beat dark December, how,
In this our pinching cave, shall we discourse
The freezing hours away? We have seen nothing:
We are beastly; subtile as the fox, for prey;
Like warlike as the wolf, for what we eat:
Our valour is, to chase what flies; our cage
We make a quire, as doth the prisoned bird,
And sing our bondage freely.
    Bel.   How you speak!
Did you but know the city's usuries,
And felt them knowingly: the art o'the court,
As hard to leave as keep; whose top to climb
Is certain falling, or so slippery that
The fear's as bad as falling: the toil of the war,
A pain that only seems to seek out danger
I'the name of fame and honour; which dies i'the
    search;
And hath as oft a slanderous epitaph
As record of fair act; nay, many times,
Doth ill deserve by doing well; what's worse,
Must court'sey at the censure:—O, boys, this
    story
The world may read in me: my body's marked
With Roman swords; and my report was once
First with the best of note: Cymbeline loved me;
And when a soldier was the theme, my name
Was not far off. Then was I as a tree
Whose boughs did bend with fruit: but in one
    night,

A storm, or robbery, call it what you will,
Shook down my mellow hangings, nay, my leaves,
And left me bare to weather.
    Gui.   Uncertain favour!
    Bel. My fault being nothing (as I have told you
      oft)
But that two villains, whose false oaths prevailed
Before my perfect honour, swore to Cymbeline
I was confederate with the Romans: so
Followed my banishment; and this twenty years,
This rock and these demesnes have been my
    world:
Where I have lived at honest freedom; paid
More pious debts to heaven than in all
The fore-end of my time.——But up to the moun-
    tains;
This is not hunters' language: he that strikes
The venison first shall be the lord o'the feast;
To him the other two shall minister;
And we will fear no poison, which attends
In place of greater state. I'll meet you in the
    valleys.
        [*Exeunt* GUIDERIUS *and* ARVIRAGUS.
How hard it is to hide the sparks of nature!
These boys know little they are sons to the king;
Nor Cymbeline dreams that they are alive.
They think they are mine: and, though trained
    up thus meanly
I'the cave, wherein they bow, their thoughts do
    hit
The roofs of palaces; and nature prompts them,
In simple and low things, to prince it much
Beyond the trick of others. This Polydore,——
The heir of Cymbeline and Britain, whom
The king his father called Guiderius,—Jove!
When on my three-foot stool I sit, and tell
The warlike feats I have done, his spirits fly out
Into my story: say, "Thus mine enemy fell;
And thus I set my foot on his neck;" even then
The princely blood flows in his cheek; he sweats,
Strains his young nerves, and puts himself in
    posture
That acts my words. The younger brother, Cadwal
(Once Arviragus), in as like a figure
Strikes life into my speech, and shews much more
His own conceiving. Hark! the game is roused!
O Cymbeline! heaven and my conscience knows
Thou didst unjustly banish me; whereon,
At three and two years old, I stole these babes;
Thinking to bar thee of succession, as
Thou reft'st me of my lands. Euriphile,
Thou wast their nurse; they took thee for their
    mother,
And every day do honour to her grave:
Myself, Belarius, that am Morgan called,
They take for natural father. The game is up.
        [*Exit.*

Scene IV.—*Near* Milford-Haven.

Enter Pisanio *and* Imogen.

Imo. Thou told'st me, when we came from
          horse, the place
Was near at hand: ne'er longed my mother so
To see me first, as I have now.—Pisanio! man!
Where is Posthumus? What is in thy mind,
That makes thee stare thus? Wherefore breaks
          that sigh
From the inward of thee? One but painted thus,
Would be interpreted a thing perplexed
Beyond self-explication: put thyself
Into a 'haviour of less fear, ere wildness
Vanquish my staider senses. What's the matter?
Why tender'st thou that paper to me, with
A look untender? If it be summer news,
Smile to 't before: if winterly, thou need'st
But keep that countenance still.—My husband's
          hand!
That drug-damned Italy hath out-craftied him,
And he's at some hard point.—Speak, man: thy
          tongue
May take off some extremity, which to read
Would be even mortal to me.
    Pisa.   Please you, read;
And you shall find me, wretched man! a thing
The most disdained of fortune.

Imogen *reads.*

" Thy mistress, Pisanio, hath played the strumpet
in my bed; the testimonies whereof lie bleeding in
me. I speak not out of weak surmises; but from
proof as strong as my grief, and as certain as I expect my revenge. That part thou, Pisanio, must act
for me, if thy faith be not tainted with the breach
of hers. Let thine own hands take away her life: I
shall give thee opportunity at Milford-Haven; she
hath my letter for the purpose: where, if thou fear
to strike, and to make me certain it is done, thou
art the pander to her dishonour, and equally to me
disloyal."

    Pisa. What shall I need to draw my sword? the
          paper
Hath cut her throat already.—No, 't is slander,
Whose edge is sharper than the sword; whose
          tongue
Outvenoms all the worms of Nile; whose breath
Rides on the posting winds, and doth belie
All corners of the world: kings, queens, and states,
Maids, matrons, nay, the secrets of the grave
This viperous slander enters. — What cheer,
          madam?
    Imo. False to his bed! What is it to be false?
To lie in watch there, and to think on him?
To weep 'twixt clock and clock? if sleep charge
          nature,

To break it with a fearful dream of him,
And cry myself awake? that's false to his bed,
Is it?
    Pisa. Alas, good lady!
    Imo. I false? thy conscience witness.—Iachimo,
Thou didst accuse him of incontinency;
Thou then look'dst like a villain; now, methinks
Thy favour's good enough.—Some jay of Italy,
Whose mother was her painting, hath betrayed
          him:
Poor I am stale, a garment out of fashion;
And, for I am richer than to hang by the walls,
I must be ripped: to pieces with me!—O,
Men's vows are women's traitors! All good
          seeming,
By thy revolt, O husband, shall be thought
Put on for villany; not born where 't grows,
But worn, a bait for ladies.
    Pisa.   Good madam, hear me.
    Imo. True honest men being heard, like false
          Æneas,
Were in his time thought false: and Sinon's
          weeping
Did scandal many a holy tear; took pity
From most true wretchedness: so thou, Posthu-
          mus,
Wilt lay the leaven on all proper men;
Goodly and gallant, shall be false and perjured,
From thy great fail.—Come, fellow, be thou honest;
Do thou thy master's bidding: when thou see'st
          him,
A little witness my obedience. Look!
I draw the sword myself: take it, and hit
The innocent mansion of my love, my heart:
Fear not; 't is empty of all things but grief:
Thy master is not there; who was, indeed,
The riches of it. Do his bidding; strike.
Thou mayst be valiant in a better cause;
But now thou seem'st a coward.
    Pisa.   Hence, vile instrument!
Thou shalt not damn my hand.
    Imo.   Why, I must die;
And if I do not by thy hand, thou art
No servant of thy master's: against self-slaughter
There is a prohibition so divine,
That cravens my weak hand. Come, here's my
          heart:—
Something's afore 't: soft, soft; we 'll no defence;
Obedient as the scabbard.—What is here?
The scriptures of the loyal Leonatus,
All turned to heresy? Away, away,
Corrupters of my faith! you shall no more
Be stomachers to my heart! Thus may poor fools
Believe false teachers. Though those that are be-
          trayed
Do feel the treason sharply, yet the traitor
Stands in worse case of woe:

And thou, Posthumus, thou that didst set up
My disobedience 'gainst the king my father,
And make me put into contempt the suits
Of princely fellows, shalt hereafter find
It is no act of common passage, but
A strain of rareness: and I grieve myself
To think, when thou shalt be disedged by her
That now thou tir'st on, how thy memory
Will then be panged by me.—Pr'ythee, despatch:
The lamb entreats the butcher: where's thy knife?
Thou art too slow to do thy master's bidding,
When I desire it too.
 Pisa.   O gracious lady,
Since I received command to do this business,
I have not slept one wink.
 Imo.   Do't, and to bed, then.
 Pisa. I'll wake mine eyeballs blind first.
 Imo.   Wherefore, then,
Didst undertake it? Why hast thou abused
So many miles with a pretence? this place?
Mine action, and thine own? our horses' labour?
The time inviting thee? the perturbed court,
For my being absent; whereunto I never
Purpose return? Why hast thou gone so far,
To be unbent when thou hast ta'en thy stand,
The elected deer before thee?
 Pisa.   But to win time
To lose so bad employment: in the which
I have considered of a course. Good lady,
Hear me with patience.
 Imo.   Talk thy tongue weary; speak:
I have heard I am a strumpet; and mine ear,
Therein false struck, can take no greater wound,
Nor tent to bottom that. But speak.
 Pisa.   Then, madam,
I thought you would not back again.
 Imo.   Most like;
Bringing me here to kill me.
 Pisa.   Not so, neither:
But if I were as wise as honest, then
My purpose would prove well. It cannot be
But that my master is abused:
Some villain, ay, and singular in his art,
Hath done you both this cursèd injury.
 Imo. Some Roman courtezan.
 Pisa.   No, on my life.
I'll give but notice you are dead, and send him
Some bloody sign of it; for 'tis commanded
I should do so: you shall be missed at court,
And that will well confirm it.
 Imo.   Why, good fellow,
What shall I do the while? where bide? how live?
Or in my life what comfort, when I am
Dead to my husband?
 Pisa.   If you'll back to the court,—
 Imo. No court, no father; nor no more ado
With that harsh, noble, simple nothing;

That Cloten, whose love-suit hath been to me
As fearful as a siege.
 Pisa.   If not at court,
Then not in Britain must you bide.
 Imo.   Where, then?
Hath Britain all the sun that shines? Day, night,
Are they not but in Britain? I' the world's volume
Our Britain seems as of it, but not in it;
In a great pool, a swan's nest: pr'ythee think
There's livers out of Britain.
 Pisa.   I am most glad
You think of other place. The ambassador,
Lucius the Roman, comes to Milford-Haven
To-morrow: now, if you could wear a mind
Dark as your fortune is,—and but disguise
That which, to appear itself, must not yet be
But by self-danger,—you should tread a course
Pretty and full of view: yea, haply near
The residence of Posthumus: so nigh, at least,
That though his actions were not visible, yet
Report should render him hourly to your ear,
As truly as he moves.
 Imo.   O, for such means!
Though peril to my modesty, not death on't,
I would adventure.
 Pisa.   Well, then, here's the point:
You must forget to be a woman; change
Command into obedience; fear and niceness
(The handmaids of all women, or, more truly,
Woman its pretty self), to a waggish courage;
Ready in gibes, quick-answered, saucy, and
As quarrellous as the weasel: nay, you must
Forget that rarest treasure of your cheek,
Exposing it (but, O, the harder heart!
Alack, no remedy!) to the greedy touch
Of common-kissing Titan; and forget
Your laboursome and dainty trims, wherein
You made great Juno angry.
 Imo.   Nay, be brief:
I see into thy end, and am almost
A man already.
 Pisa.   First, make yourself but like one.
Forethinking this, I have already fit
('Tis in my cloak-bag), doublet, hat, hose, all
That answer to them: would you, in their serving,
And with what imitation you can borrow
From youth of such a season, 'fore noble Lucius
Present yourself, desire his service, tell him
Wherein you are happy (which you'll make him
  know
If that his head have ear in music), doubtless
With joy he will embrace you; for he's honourable,
And, doubling that, most holy. Your means
  abroad,
You have me, rich; and I will never fail
Beginning nor supplyment.
 Imo.   Thou art all the comfort

The gods will diet me with. Pr'y thee away:
There's more to be considered, but we'll even
All that good time will give us: this attempt
I'm soldier to, and will abide it with
A prince's courage. Away, I pr'y thee.

Pisa. Well, madam, we must take a short fare-
    well;
Lest, being missed, I be suspected of
Your carriage from the court. My noble mistress,
Here is a box: I had it from the queen;
What's in 't is precious; if you are sick at sea,
Or stomach-qualmed at land, a dram of this
Will drive away distemper.—To some shade,
And fit you to your manhood. May the gods
Direct you to the best!

Imo.   Amen: I thank thee.   [*Exeunt.*

SCENE V.—*A Room in* CYMBELINE's *Palace.*

Enter CYMBELINE, QUEEN, CLOTEN, LUCIUS, *and*
    Lords.

Cym. Thus far; and so farewell.
Luc.   Thanks, royal sir.
My emperor hath wrote; I must from hence;
And am right sorry that I must report ye
My master's enemy.
Cym.   Our subjects, sir,
Will not endure his yoke; and for ourself
To shew less sovereignty than they, must needs
Appear unkinglike.
Luc.   So, sir, I desire of you
A conduct over-land, to Milford-Haven.—
Madam, all joy befal your grace, and you!
Cym. My lords, you are appointed for that office;
The due of honour in no point omit:
So farewell, noble Lucius.
Luc.   Your hand, my lord.
Clo. Receive it friendly: but from this time
    forth
I wear it as your enemy.
Luc.   Sir, the event
Is yet to name the winner: fare you well.
Cym. Leave not the worthy Lucius, good my
    lords,
Till he have crossed the Severn.—Happiness!
            [*Exeunt* LUCIUS *and* Lords.
Queen. He goes hence frowning: but it ho-
    nours us
That we have given him cause.
Clo.   'Tis all the better;
Your valiant Britons have their wishes in it.
Cym. Lucius hath wrote already to the emperor
How it goes here. It fits us therefore, ripely,
Our chariots and our horsemen be in readiness:
The powers that he already hath in Gallia

Will soon be drawn to head, from whence he moves
His war for Britain.
Queen.   'Tis not sleepy business;
But must be looked to speedily and strongly.
Cym. Our expectation that it would be thus,
Hath made us forward. But, my gentle queen,
Where is our daughter? She hath not appeared
Before the Roman, nor to us hath tendered
The duty of the day: she looks us like
A thing more made of malice than of duty:
We have noted it.—Call her before us; for
We have been too slight in sufferance.
            [*Exit an* Attendant.
Queen.   Royal sir,
Since the exile of Posthumus, most retired
Hath her life been; the cure whereof, my lord,
'Tis time must do. 'Beseech your majesty,
Forbear sharp speeches to her: she's a lady
So tender of rebukes, that words are strokes,
And strokes death to her.

Re-enter an Attendant.

Cym.   Where is she, sir? How
Can her contempt be answered?
Atten.   Please you, sir,
Her chambers are all locked; and there's no
    answer
That will be given to the loudest of noise we make.
Queen. My lord, when last I went to visit her,
She prayed me to excuse her keeping close;
Whereto constrained by her infirmity,
She should that duty leave unpaid to you
Which daily she was bound to proffer: this
She wished me to make known; but our great court
Made me to blame in memory.
Cym.   Her doors locked?
Not seen of late? Grant, heavens, that which I fear
Prove false!   [*Exit.*
Queen.   Son, I say, follow the king.
Clo. That man of hers, Pisanio, her old servant,
I have not seen these two days.
Queen.   Go, look after.—[*Exit* CLOTEN.
Pisanio, thou that stand'st so for Posthumus!
He hath a drug of mine: I pray, his absence
Proceed by swallowing that; for he believes
It is a thing most precious. But for her,
Where is she gone? Haply, despair hath seized
    her;
Or, winged with fervour of her love, she's flown
To her desired Posthumus: gone she is
To death, or to dishonour; and my end
Can make good use of either: she being down,
I have the placing of the British crown.

Re-enter CLOTEN.

How now, my son!
Clo.   'Tis certain she is fled.

Go in, and cheer the king; he rages; none
Dare come about him.

 Queen.   All the better: may
This night forestal him of the coming day! [*Exit.*

 Clo. I love, and hate her: for she 's fair and royal,
And that she hath all courtly parts more exquisite
Than lady, ladies, woman; from every one
The best she hath, and she, of all compounded,
Outsells them all: I love her, therefore: but,
Disdaining me, and throwing favours on
The low Posthumus, slanders so her judgment,
That what 's else rare is choked; and in that point
I will conclude to hate her, nay, indeed,
To be revenged upon her, For, when fools

Enter PISANIO.

Shall—Who is here? What! are you packing,
  sirrah?
Come hither: ah, you precious pander! Villain,
Where is thy lady? in a word; or else
Thou art straightway with the fiends.

 Pisa. O, good my lord!

 Clo. Where is thy lady? or, by Jupiter,
I will not ask again. Close villain,
I 'll have this secret from thy heart, or rip
Thy heart to find it. Is she with Posthumus?
From whose so many weights of baseness cannot
A dram of worth be drawn.

 Pisa.   Alas, my lord,
How can she be with him? When was she missed?
He is in Rome.

 Clo.   Where is she, sir? Come nearer;
No further halting: satisfy me home,
What is become of her?

 Pisa. O, my all-worthy lord!

 Clo.   All-worthy villain!
Discover where thy mistress is, at once,
At the next word;—no more of worthy lord:
Speak, or thy silence on the instant is
Thy condemnation and thy death.

 Pisa.   Then, sir,
This paper is the history of my knowledge
Touching her flight. [*Presenting a letter.*

 Clo. Let 's see 't.—I will pursue her
Even to Augustus' throne.

 Pisa.   Or this, or perish.
She 's far enough; and what he learns by this
May prove his travel, not her danger. [*Aside.*

 Clo.   Humph!

 Pisa. I 'll write to my lord she 's dead. O
  Imogen,
Safe mayst thou wander, safe return again!
          [*Aside.*

 Clo. Sirrah, is this letter true?

 Pisa. Sir, as I think.

 Clo. It is Posthumus' hand; I know 't.—Sirrah,
if thou wouldst not be a villain but do me true

service, undergo those employments wherein I
should have cause to use thee with a serious industry,—that is, what villany soe'er I bid thee
do, to perform it directly and truly,—I would
think thee an honest man: thou shouldst neither
want my means for thy relief, nor my voice for
thy preferment.

 Pisa. Well, my good lord.

 Clo. Wilt thou serve me? For, since patiently
and constantly thou hast stuck to the bare fortune of that beggar Posthumus, thou canst not,
in the course of gratitude, but be a diligent follower of mine. Wilt thou serve me?

 Pisa. Sir, I will.

 Clo. Give me thy hand; here 's my purse.
Hast any of thy late master's garments in thy
possession?

 Pisa. I have, my lord, at my lodging, the same
suit he wore when he took leave of my lady and
mistress.

 Clo. The first service thou dost me, fetch that
suit hither: let it be thy first service; go.

 Pisa. I shall, my lord.   [*Exit.*

 Clo. Meet thee at Milford-Haven:—I forgot
to ask him one thing; I 'll remember 't anon:—
Even there, thou villain Posthumus, will I kill
thee.—I would these garments were come. She
said upon a time (the bitterness of it I now belch
from my heart) that she held the very garment
of Posthumus in more respect than my noble and
natural person, together with the adornment of
my qualities. With that suit upon my back will I
ravish her: first kill him, and in her eyes; there
shall she see my valour, which will then be a
torment to her contempt. He on the ground, my
speech of insultment ended on his dead body,—
and when my lust hath dined (which, as I say,
to vex her, I will execute in the clothes that she
so praised), to the court I 'll knock her back,—
foot her home again. She hath despised me re-
joicingly, and I 'll be merry in my revenge.

Re-enter PISANIO, *with the clothes.*

Be those the garments?

 Pisa. Ay, my noble lord.

 Clo. How long is 't since she went to Milford-
Haven?

 Pisa. She can scarce be there yet.

 Clo. Bring this apparel to my chamber; that
is the second thing that I have commanded thee:
the third is, that thou shalt be a voluntary mute
to my design. Be but duteous, and true preferment shall tender itself to thee.—My revenge is
now at Milford; 'would I had wings to follow it!
—Come, and be true.   [*Exit.*

 Pisa. Thou bidd'st me to my loss: for, true to
  thee,

Were to prove false (which I will never be)
To him that is most true.   To Milford go,
And find not her whom thou pursu'st.   Flow, flow,
You heavenly blessings on her!   This fool's speed
Be crossed with slowness; labour be his meed!
                                  [*Exit.*

SCENE VI.—*Before the Cave of* BELARIUS.

Enter IMOGEN, *in boy's clothes.*

Imo. I see a man's life is a tedious one:
I have tired myself; and for two nights together
Have made the ground my bed.   I should be sick,
But that my resolution helps me.—Milford,
When from the mountain-top Pisanio shewed thee,
Thou wast within a ken: O Jove! I think
Foundations fly the wretched; such, I mean,
Where they should be relieved.   Two beggars
    told me
I could not miss my way: will poor folks lie,
That have afflictions on them; knowing 't is
A punishment, or trial?   Yes; no wonder,
When rich ones scarce tell true: to lapse in ful-
    ness
Is sorer than to lie for need; and falsehood
Is worse in kings than beggars.—My dear lord!
Thou art one o' the false ones: now I think on
    thee,
My hunger 's gone; but even before I was
At point to sink for food.—But what is this?
Here is a path to it: 't is some savage hold.
I were best not call; I dare not call; yet famine,
Ere clean it o'erthrow nature, makes it valiant.
Plenty and peace breeds cowards; hardness ever
Of hardiness is mother.—Ho! who's here?
If anything that 's civil, speak; if savage,
Take, or lend.—Ho!   No answer? then I 'll enter.
Best draw my sword, and if mine enemy
But fear the sword like me, he 'll scarcely look
    on 't.
Such a foe, good heavens! [*She goes into the cave.*

Enter BELARIUS, GUIDERIUS, *and* ARVIRAGUS.

Bel. You, Polydore, have proved best wood-
    man, and
Are master of the feast: Cadwal and I
Will play the cook and servant; 't is our match:
The sweat of industry would dry and die,
But for the end it works to.   Come; our stomachs
Will make what 's homely savoury: weariness
Can snore upon the flint, when resty sloth
Finds the down pillow hard.—Now peace be here,
Poor house, that keep'st thyself!
     Gui.   I am throughly weary.
     Arv. I am weak with toil, yet strong in appetite.

Gui. There is cold meat i' the cave; we 'll browse
    on that,
Whilst what we have killed be cooked.
     Bel.   Stay; come not in: [*Looking in.*
But that it eats our victuals, I should think
Here were a fairy.
     Gui.   What 's the matter, sir?
     Bel. By Jupiter, an angel! or if not,
An earthly paragon!—Behold divineness
No elder than a boy!

Enter IMOGEN.

     Imo. Good masters, harm me not:
Before I entered here I called; and thought
To have begged or bought what I have took:
    good troth,
I have stolen nought; nor would not, though I had
    found
Gold strewed o' the floor.   Here 's money for my
    meat:
I would have left it on the board, so soon·
As I had made my meal; and parted
With prayers for the provider.
     Gui.   Money, youth?
     Arv. All gold and silver rather turn to dirt!
As 't is no better reckoned, but of those
Who worship dirty gods.
     Imo.   I see you are angry:
Know, if you kill me for my fault, I should
Have died had I not made it.
     Bel. Whither bound?
     Imo. To Milford-Haven.
     Bel. What 's your name?
     Imo. Fidele, sir.   I have a kinsman, who
Is bound for Italy; he embarked at Milford;
To whom being going, almost spent with hunger,
I am fallen in this offence.
     Bel.   Pr'y thee, fair youth,
Think us no churls; nor measure our good minds
By this rude place we live in.   Well encountered!
'T is almost night: you shall have better cheer
Ere you depart; and thanks to stay and eat it.—
Boys, bid him welcome.
     Gui.   Were you a woman, youth,
I should woo hard but be your groom.   In honesty,
I bid for you as I 'd buy.
     Arv.   I 'll make 't my comfort
He is a man; I 'll love him as my brother :—
And such a welcome as I 'd give to him,
After long absence, such is yours: most wel-
    come!
Be sprightly, for you fall 'mongst friends.
     Imo.   'Mongst friends!
If brothers?—Would it had been so that they
Had been my father's sons! then had my prize
Been less; and so more equal ballasting
To thee, Posthumus.   [*Aside.*

Bel.   He wrings at some distress.
Gui.   'Would I could free 't!
Arv.   Or I; whate'er it be,
What pain it cost, what danger! Gods!
Bel.   Hark, boys.   [*Whispering.*
Imo.   Great men,
That had a court no bigger than this cave,
That did attend themselves, and had the virtue
Which their own conscience sealed them (laying
      by
That nothing gift of differing multitudes),
Could not out-peer these twain. Pardon me, gods!
I'd change my sex to be companion with them,
Since Leonatus' false.
Bel.   It shall be so:
Boys, we'll go dress our hunt.—Fair youth, come in:
Discourse is heavy, fasting; when we have supped,
We'll mannerly demand thee of thy story,
So far as thou wilt speak it.
Gui.   Pray, draw near.
Arv. The night to the owl, and morn to the lark,
    less welcome.
Imo. Thanks, sir.
Arr.   I pray, draw near.   [*Exeunt.*

SCENE VII.—Rome.

Enter two Senators *and* Tribunes.

1st Sen. This is the tenor of the emperor's
    writ;
That since the common men are now in action
'Gainst the Pannonians and Dalmatians;
And that the legions now in Gallia are
Full weak to undertake our wars against
The fall'n-off Britons; that we do incite
The gentry to this business. He creates
Lucius proconsul: and to you the tribunes,
For this immediate levy, he commands
His absolute commission. Long live Cæsar!
Tri. Is Lucius general of the forces?
2nd Sen.   Ay.
Tri. Remaining now in Gallia?
1st Sen.   With those legions
Which I have spoke of, whereunto your levy
Must be supplyant. The words of your commis-
    sion
Will tie you to the numbers, and the time
Of their despatch.
Tri.   We will discharge our duty. [*Exeunt.*

SCENE I.—*The Forest near the Cave.*

Enter CLOTEN.

Clo. I am near to the place where they should meet, if Pisanio have mapped it truly. How fit his garments serve me! Why should his mistress, who was made by him that made the tailor, not be fit too? the rather (saving reverence of the word) for 'tis said, a woman's fitness comes by fits. Therein I must play the workman. I dare speak it to myself (for it is not vain glory for a man and his glass to confer; in his own chamber, I mean), the lines of my body are as well drawn as his; no less young, more strong, not beneath him in fortunes, beyond him in the advantage of the time, above him in birth, alike conversant in general services, and more remarkable in single oppositions: yet this imperseverant thing loves him in my despite. What mortality is! Posthumus, thy head, which now is growing upon thy shoulders, shall within this hour be off; thy mistress enforced; thy garments cut to pieces before thy face; and all this done, spurn her home to her father: who may, haply, be a little angry for my so rough usage; but my mother, having power of his testiness, shall turn all into my commendations. My horse is tied up safe: out, sword, and to a sore purpose! Fortune put them into my hand! This is the very description of their meeting-place; and the fellow dares not deceive me.   [*Exit.*

SCENE II.—*Before the Cave.*

Enter, from the Cave, BELARIUS, GUIDERIUS, ARVIRAGUS, *and* IMOGEN.

Bel. You are not well [*to* IMOGEN]: remain
    here in the cave;
We'll come to you after hunting.

Arv.   Brother, stay here: [*To* IMOGEN.
Are we not brothers?

Imo.   So man and man should be;
But clay and clay differs in dignity,
Whose dust is both alike. I am very sick.

Gui. Go you to hunting; I'll abide with him.

Imo. So sick I am not;—yet I am not well:
But not so citizen a wanton, as
To seem to die ere sick. So please you, leave me;
Stick to your journal course: the breach of custom
Is breach of all. I am ill; but your being by me
Cannot amend me: society is no comfort
To one not sociable: I am not very sick,
Since I can reason of it. Pray you, trust me here;
I'll rob none but myself; and let me die,
Stealing so poorly.

Gui.   I love thee; I have spoke it:
How much the quantity, the weight as much,
As I do love my father.

Bel.   What? how, how?

Arv. If it be sin to say so, sir, I yoke me
In my good brother's fault. I know not why
I love this youth; and I have heard you say,
Love's reason's without reason: the bier at door,
And a demand who is't shall die, I'd say,
"My father; not this youth."

Bel.   O noble strain! [*Aside.*
O worthiness of nature! breed of greatness!
Cowards father cowards, and base things sire base:
Nature hath meal and bran; contempt and grace.
I'm not their father; yet who this should be
Doth miracle itself, loved before me.—
'Tis the ninth hour o' the morn.

Arv.   Brother, farewell.

Imo. I wish ye sport.

Arv.   You health.—So please you, sir.

Imo. [*aside*]. These are kind creatures. Gods,
      what lies I have heard!
Our courtiers say, all's savage but at court:
Experience, O, thou disprov'st report!
The imperious seas breed monsters; for the dish,

Poor tributary rivers as sweet fish.
I am sick still; heart sick.—Pisanio,
I 'll now taste of thy drug.

Gui. I could not stir him:
He said, he was gentle, but unfortunate;
Dishonestly afflicted, but yet honest.

Arv. Thus did he answer me: yet said, hereafter
I might know more.

Bel. To the field, to the field.—
We 'll leave you for this time; go in, and rest.

Arv. We 'll not be long away.

Bel. Pray be not sick,
For you must be our housewife.

Imo. Well or ill,
I am bound to you.

Bel. And shalt be ever. [*Exit* IMOGEN.
This youth, howe'er distressed, appears he hath
    had
Good ancestors.

Arv. How angel-like he sings!

Gui. But his neat cookery! He cut our roots
    in characters;
And sauced our broths, as Juno had been sick,
And he her dieter.

Arv. Nobly he yokes
A smiling with a sigh: as if the sigh
Was that it was, for not being such a smile;
The smile mocking the sigh, that it would fly
From so divine a temple, to commix
With winds that sailors rail at.

Gui. I do note
That grief and patience, rooted in him both,
Mingle their spurs together.

Arv. Grow, patience!
And let the stinking elder, grief, untwine
His perishing root with the increasing vine!

Bel. It is great morning. Come; away.—Who 's
    there?

Enter CLOTEN.

Clo. I cannot find those runagates; that villain
Hath mocked me.—I am faint.

Bel. Those runagates!
Means he not us? I partly know him; 't is
Cloten, the son o' the queen. I fear some ambush.
I saw him not these many years, and yet
I know 't is he. We are held as outlaws: hence.

Gui. He is but one: you and my brother search
What companies are near: pray you, away;
Let me alone with him.

[*Exeunt* BELARIUS *and* ARVIRAGUS.

Clo. Soft! what are you
That fly me thus? some villain mountaineers?
I have heard of such.—What slave art thou?

Gui. A thing
More slavish did I ne'er, than answering
" A slave" without a knock.

Clo. Thou art a robber,
A law-breaker, a villain: yield thee, thief.

Gui. To who? to thee! What art thou? Have
    not I
An arm as big as thine? a heart as big?
Thy words, I grant, are bigger; for I wear not
My dagger in my mouth. Say what thou art;
Why I should yield to thee?

Clo. Thou villain base,
Know'st me not by my clothes?

Gui. No, nor thy tailor, rascal,
Who is thy grandfather: he made those clothes,
Which, as it seems, make thee?

Clo. Thou precious varlet,
My tailor made them not.

Gui. Hence, then, and thank
The man that gave them thee. Thou art some fool;
I am loath to beat thee.

Clo. Thou injurious thief,
Hear but my name, and tremble.

Gui. What 's thy name?

Clo. Cloten, thou villain.

Gui. Cloten, thou double villain, be thy name,
I cannot tremble at it; were 't toad, or adder,
    spider,
'T would move me sooner.

Clo. To thy further fear,
Nay, to thy mere confusion, thou shalt know
I 'm son to the queen.

Gui. I 'm sorry for 't; not seeming
So worthy as thy birth.

Clo. Art not afeard?

Gui. Those that I reverence, those I fear; the
    wise:
At fools I laugh, not fear them.

Clo. Die the death:
When I have slain thee with my proper hand,
I 'll follow those that even now fled hence,
And on the gates of Lud's town set your heads:
Yield, rustic mountaineer. [*Exeunt, fighting.*

Enter BELARIUS *and* ARVIRAGUS.

Bel. No company 's abroad.

Arv. None in the world: you did mistake him,
    sure.

Bel. I cannot tell: long is it since I saw him,
But time hath nothing blurred those lines of favour
Which then he wore; the snatches in his voice,
And burst of speaking, were as his: I am absolute
'T was very Cloten.

Arv. In this place we left them:
I wish my brother make good time with him,
You say he is so fell.

Bel. Being scarce made up,
I mean to man, he had not apprehension
Of roaring terrors; for the effect of judgment
Is oft the cause of fear. But see, thy brother.

Re-enter GUIDERIUS, *with* CLOTEN's *head.*

Gui. This Cloten was a fool; an empty purse,
There was no money in 't: not Hercules
Could have knocked out his brains, for he had
   none:
Yet I not doing this, the fool had borne
My head, as I do his.

Bel.   What hast thou done?

Gui. I am perfect what: cut off one Cloten's head,
Son to the queen, after his own report;
Who called me traitor, mountaineer; and swore,
With his own single hand he 'd take us in,
Displace our heads where (thank the gods!) they
   grow,
And set them on Lud's town.

Bel.   We are all undone.

Gui. Why, worthy father, what have we to lose,
But that he swore to take, our lives? The law
Protects not us: then why should we be tender,
To let an arrogant piece of flesh threat us;
Play judge and executioner all himself;
For we do fear the law? What company
Discover you abroad?

Bel.   No single soul
Can we set eye on; but, in all safe reason,
We must have some attendants. Though his
   humour
Was nothing but mutation,—ay, and that
From one bad thing to worse,—not frenzy, not
Absolute madness, could so far have raved,
To bring him here alone. Although, perhaps,
It may be heard at court that such as we
Cave here, hunt here, are outlaws, and in time
May make some stronger head: the which he
   hearing
(As it is like him) might break out, and swear
He 'd fetch us in: yet is 't not probable
To come alone, either he so undertaking,
Or they so suffering: then on good ground we fear,
If we do fear this body hath a tail
More perilous than the head.

Arv.   Let ordinance
Come as the gods foresay it: howsoe'er,
My brother hath done well.

Bel.   I had no mind
To hunt this day: the boy Fidele's sickness
Did make my way long forth.

Gui.   With his own sword,
Which he did wave against my throat, I have ta'en
His head from him: I 'll throw 't into the creek
Behind our rock; and let it to the sea,
And tell the fishes he 's the queen's son, Cloten:
That 's all I reck.   [*Exit.*

Bel.   I fear 't will be revenged:
'Would, Polydore, thou hadst not done 't! though
   valour
Becomes thee well enough.

Arv.   'Would I had done 't,
So the revenge alone pursued me!—Polydore,
I love thee brotherly; but envy much
Thou hast robbed me of this deed. I would re-
   venges,
That possible strength might meet, would seek us
   through,
And put us to our answer.

Bel.   Well, 't is done:
We 'll hunt no more to-day, nor seek for danger
Where there 's no profit. I pr'ythee, to our rock;
You and Fidele play the cooks: I 'll stay
Till hasty Polydore return, and bring him
To dinner presently.

Arv.   Poor sick Fidele!
I 'll willingly to him: to gain his colour,
I 'd let a parish of such Clotens blood,
And praise myself for charity. [*Exit.*

Bel.   O thou goddess,
Thou divine Nature, how thyself thou blazon'st
In these two princely boys! They are as gentle
As zephyrs, blowing below the violet,
Not wagging his sweet head: and yet as rough,
Their royal blood enchafed, as the rud'st wind
That by the top doth take the mountain pine,
And make him stoop to the vale. 'Tis wonderful
That an invisible instinct should frame them
To royalty unlearned; honour untaught;
Civility not seen from other; valour,
That wildly grows in them, but yields a crop
As if it had been sowed! Yet still it 's strange
What Cloten's being here to us portends;
Or what his death will bring us.

Re-enter GUIDERIUS.

Gui.   Where 's my brother?
I have sent Cloten's clotpole down the stream,
In embassy to his mother: his body 's hostage
For his return.   [*Solemn music.*

Bel.   My ingenious instrument!
Hark, Polydore, it sounds! but what occasion
Hath Cadwal now to give it motion! Hark!

Gui. Is he at home?

Bel.   He went hence even now.

Gui. What does he mean? Since death of my
   dearest mother
It did not speak before. All solemn things
Should answer solemn accidents. The matter?
Triumphs for nothing, and lamenting toys,
Is jollity for apes, and grief for boys.
Is Cadwal mad?

Re-enter ARVIRAGUS, *bearing* IMOGEN, *as dead, in
   his arms.*

Bel.   Look, here he comes,
And brings the dire occasion in his arms,
Of what we blame him for!

Arv.   The bird is dead
That we have made so much on. I had rather
Have skipped from sixteen years of age to sixty,
To have turned my leaping time into a crutch,
Than have seen this.
    Gui.   O sweetest, fairest lily !
My brother wears thee not the one half so well,
As when thou grew'st thyself.
    Bel.   O, melancholy !
Who ever yet could sound thy bottom? find
The ooze, to shew what coast thy sluggish crare
Might easiliest harbour in ?—Thou blessèd thing !
Jove knows what man thou mightst have made ;
       but I,
Thou died'st, a most rare boy, of melancholy !—
How found you him ?
    Arv.   Stark, as you see :
Thus smiling, as some fly had tickled slumber,
Not as death's dart, being laughed at : his right
      cheek
Reposing on a cushion.
    Gui.   Where ?
    Arv.   O' the floor ;
His arms thus leagued. I thought he slept ; and put
My clouted brogues from off my feet, whose rude-
      ness
Answered my steps too loud.
    Gui.   Why, he but sleeps :
If he be gone, he 'll make his grave a bed ;
With female fairies will his tomb be haunted,
And worms will not come to thee.
    Arv.   With fairest flowers,
Whilst summer lasts, and I live here, Fidele,
I 'll sweeten thy sad grave. Thou shalt not lack
The flower that 's like thy face, pale primrose ; nor
The azured harebell, like thy veins ; no, nor
The leaf of eglantine, whom not to slander,
Out-sweetened not thy breath : the ruddock would
With charitable bill (O bill, sore-shaming
Those rich-left heirs that let their fathers lie
Without a monument !), bring thee all this ;
Yea, and furred moss besides, when flowers are
      none,
To winter-ground thy corse.
    Gui.   Pr'y thee, have done ;
And do not play in wench-like words with that
Which is so serious. Let us bury him,
And not protract with admiration what
Is now due debt.—To the grave.
    Arv.   Say, where shall 's lay him ?
    Gui. By good Euriphile, our mother.
    Arv.   Be 't so ;
And let us Polydore, though now our voices
Have got the mannish crack, sing him to the
      ground,
As once our mother ; use like note and words,
Save that Euriphile must be Fidele.

    Gui. Cadwal,
I cannot sing : I 'll weep, and word it with thee :
For notes of sorrow, out of tune, are worse
Than priests and fanes that lie.
    Arv.   We 'll speak it, then.
    Bel. Great griefs, I see, medicine the less : for
      Cloten
Is quite forgot. He was a queen's son, boys :
And, though he came our enemy, remember
He was paid for that. Though mean and mighty,
      rotting
Together, have one dust ; yet reverence
(That angel of the world) doth make distinction
Of place 't ween high and low. Our foe was
      princely ;
And though you took his life, as being our foe,
Yet bury him as a prince.
    Gui.   Pray you, fetch him hither.
Thersites' body is as good as Ajax,
When neither are alive.
    Arv.   If you 'll go fetch him,
We 'll say our song the whilst.—Brother, begin.
                [*Exit* BELARIUS.
    Gui. Nay, Cadwal, we must lay his head to the
      east ;
My father hath a reason for 't.
    Arv.   'T is true.
    Gui. Come on, then, and remove him.
    Arv.   So,—begin.

          GUIDERIUS *sings.*

Fear no more the heat o' the sun,
   Nor the furious winter's rages ;
Thou thy worldly task hast done,
   Home art gone, and ta'en thy wages :
Golden lads and girls all must,
As chimney-sweepers, come to dust.

          ARVIRAGUS *sings.*

Fear no more the frown o' the great,
   Thou art passed the tyrant's stroke ;
Care no more to clothe and eat ;
   To thee the reed is as the oak :
The sceptre, learning, physic, must
All follow this, and come to dust.

          GUIDERIUS.

Fear no more the lightning flash ;

          ARVIRAGUS.

Nor the all-dreaded thunder-stone ;

          GUIDERIUS.

Fear not slander ; censure rash :

          ARVIRAGUS.

Thou hast finished joy and moan :

          Both.

All lovers young, all lovers must
Consign to thee, and come to dust.

GUIDERIUS.

No exorciser harm thee!

ARVIRAGUS.

Nor no witchcraft charm thee!

GUIDERIUS.

Ghost unlaid forbear thee?

ARVIRAGUS.

Nothing ill come near thee!

Both.

Quiet consummation have;
And renownèd be thy grave!

Re-enter BELARIUS, *with the body of* CLOTEN.

Gui. We have done our obsequies: come lay
     him down.

Bel. Here's a few flowers; but about midnight,
     more:
The herbs that have on them cold dew o'the
     night,
Are strewings fitt'st for graves.—Upon their
     faces:—
You were as flowers, now withered: even so
These herblets shall, which we upon you strow.—
Come on, away: apart upon our knees.
The ground, that gave them first, has them
     again:
Their pleasures here are past, so is their pain.
     [*Exeunt* BELARIUS, GUIDERIUS, *and*
                    ARVIRAGUS.

Imo. [*awaking*]. Yes, sir, to Milford-Haven;
     which is the way?—
I thank you.—By yon bush? Pray, how far
     thither?
'Ods pittikens! can it be six miles yet?
I have gone all night.—'Faith, I'll lie down and
     sleep.
But soft! no bedfellow.—O, gods and goddesses!
                    [*Seeing the body.*
These flowers are like the pleasures of the world;
This bloody man the care on't.—I hope I dream;
For so I thought I was a cave-keeper,
And cook to honest creatures: but 'tis not so;
'Twas but a bolt of nothing, shot at nothing,
Which the brain makes of fumes: our very eyes
Are sometimes like our judgments, blind. Good
     faith,
I tremble still with fear: but if there be
Yet left in heaven as small a drop of pity
As a wren's eye, feared gods, a part of it!
The dream's here still: even when I wake it is
Without me, as within me; not imagined, felt.
A headless man! The garments of Posthumus!
I know the shape of his legs: this is his hand;
His foot Mercurial; his Martial thigh;
The brawns of Hercules: but his Jovial face—
Murder in heaven? How? 'tis gone.—Pisanio,
All curses madded Hecuba gave the Greeks,
And mine to boot, be darted on thee! Thou,
Conspired with that irregulous devil, Cloten,
Hast here cut off my lord.—To write and read
Be henceforth treacherous!—Damned Pisanio

Hath with his forgéd letters,—damned Pisanio,—
From this most bravest vessel of the world
Struck the main-top!—O Posthumus! alas,
Where is thy head? where's that? Ah me! where's
    that?
Pisanio might have killed thee at the heart,
And left this head on.—How should this be?
    Pisanio?
'T is he and Cloten: malice and lucre in them
Have laid this woe here. O, 't is pregnant, preg-
    nant!
The drug he gave me, which he said was pre-
    cious
And cordial to me, have I not found it
Murderous to the senses? that confirms it home:
This is Pisanio's deed, and Cloten's! O!
Give colour to my pale cheek with thy blood,
That we the horrider may seem to those
Which chance to find us. O, my lord, my lord!

Enter Lucius, *a* Captain, *and other* Officers, *and
a* Soothsayer.

  Cap. To them, the legions garrisoned in Gallia,
After your will, have crossed the sea; attending
You here at Milford-Haven, with your ships:
They are here in readiness.
  Luc.   But what from Rome?
  Cap. The senate hath stirred up the confiners,
And gentlemen of Italy; most willing spirits,
That promise noble service; and they come
Under the conduct of bold Iachimo,
Sienna's brother.
  Luc.   When expect you them?
  Cap. With the next benefit o' the wind.
  Luc.   This forwardness
Makes our hopes fair. Command our present
    numbers
Be mustered; bid the captains look to 't.—Now,
    sir,
What have you dreamed of late, of this war's pur-
    pose?
  Sooth. Last night the very gods shewed me a
    vision
(I fast' and prayed for their intelligence): Thus:
I saw Jove's bird, the Roman eagle, winged
From the spongy south to this part of the west,
There vanished in the sunbeams: which portends
(Unless my sins abuse my divination)
Success to the Roman host.
  Luc.   Dream often so,
And never false.—Soft, ho! what trunk is here,
Without his top? The ruin speaks that sometime
It was a worthy building.—How! a page!
Or dead, or sleeping on him? But dead, rather:
For nature doth abhor to make his bed
With the defunct, or sleep upon the dead.
Let's see the boy's face.

  Cap.   He is alive, my lord.
  Luc. He'll then instruct us of this body.—Young
    one,
Inform us of thy fortunes; for it seems
They crave to be demanded. Who is this
Thou mak'st thy bloody pillow? or who was he
That, otherwise than noble nature did,
Hath altered that good picture? What's thy
    interest
In this sad wreck? how came it? who is it?
What art thou?
  Imo.   I am nothing: or if not,
Nothing to be were better. This was my master,
A very valiant Briton, and a good,
That here by mountaineers lies slain.—Alas!
There are no more such masters: I may wander
From east to occident, cry out for service,
Try many, all good, serve truly, never
Find such another master.
  Luc.   'Lack, good youth,
Thou mov'st no less with thy complaining, than
Thy master in bleeding: say his name, good
    friend.
  Imo. Richard du Champ.—If I do lie, and do
No harm by it, though the gods hear, I hope
They'll pardon it [*aside*]. Say you, sir?
  Luc.   Thy name?
  Imo.   Fidele, sir.
  Luc. Thou dost approve thyself the very same:
Thy name well fits thy faith; thy faith thy
    name.
Wilt take thy chance with me? I will not say
Thou shalt be so well mastered; but be sure,
No less beloved. The Roman emperor's letters,
Sent by a consul to me, should not sooner
Than thine own worth prefer thee: go with me.
  Imo. I'll follow, sir. But first, an 't please the
    gods,
I'll hide my master from the flies, as deep
As these poor pickaxes can dig: and when
With wild wood-leaves and weeds I have strewed
    his grave,
And on it said a century of prayers,
Such as I can, twice o'er, I'll weep and sigh;
And, leaving so his service, follow you,
So please you entertain me.
  Luc.   Ay, good youth;
And rather father thee, than master thee.—
My friends,
The boy hath taught us manly duties: let us
Find out the prettiest daisied plot we can,
And make him with our pikes and partisans
A grave: come, arm him.—Boy, he is preferred
By thee to us; and he shall be interred
As soldiers can. Be cheerful; wipe thine eyes:
Some falls are means the happier to arise.
                        [*Exeunt.*

SCENE III.—*A Room in* CYMBELINE'S *Palace.*

Enter CYMBELINE, Lords, *and* PISANIO.

Cym. Again; and bring me word how 'tis with
    her.
A fever with the absence of her son;
A madness, of which her life's in danger.—
    Heavens,
How deeply you at once do touch me! Imogen,
The great part of my comfort, gone; my queen
Upon a desperate bed; and in a time
When fearful wars point at me, her son gone,
So needful for this present: it strikes me past
The hope of comfort.—But for thee, fellow,
Who needs must know of her departure, and
Dost seem so ignorant, we'll enforce it from thee
By a sharp torture.

Pisa.   Sir, my life is yours,
I humbly set it at your will: but, for my mistress,
I nothing know where she remains, why gone,
Nor when she purposes return. 'Beseech your
    highness,
Hold me your loyal servant.

1st Lord.   Good my liege,
The day that she was missing he was here:
I dare be bound he's true, and shall perform
All parts of his subjection loyally.
For Cloten,
There wants no diligence in seeking him,
And will, no doubt, be found.

Cym.   The time is troublesome:
We'll slip you for a season; but our jealousy
                       [*To* PISANIO.
Does yet depend.

1st Lord.   So please your majesty,
The Roman legions, all from Gallia drawn,
Are landed on your coast; with a supply
Of Roman gentleman, by the senate sent.

Cym. Now for the counsel of my son and
    queen!
I am amazed with matter.

1st Lord.   Good my liege,
Your preparation can affront no less
Than what you hear of: come more, for more
    you're ready.
The want is, but to put those powers in motion
That long to move.

Cym.   I thank you: let's withdraw;
And meet the time, as it seeks us. We fear not
What can from Italy annoy us; but
We grieve at chances here. Away. [*Exeunt.*

Pisa. I heard no letter from my master since
I wrote him Imogen was slain: 'tis strange:
Nor hear I from my mistress, who did promise
To yield me often tidings: neither know I
What is betid to Cloten; but remain
Perplexed in all. The heavens still must work.
Wherein I am false, I am honest; not true, to be
    true.
These present wars shall find I love my country,
Even to the note o' the king, or I'll fall in them.
All other doubts, by time let them be cleared:
Fortune brings in some boats that are not steered.
                         [*Exit.*

SCENE IV.—*Before the Cave.*

Enter BELARIUS, GUIDERIUS, *and* ARVIRAGUS.

Gui. The noise is round about us.

Bel.   Let us from it.

Arv. What pleasures, sir, find we in life, to lock it
From action and adventure?

Gui.   Nay, what hope
Have we in hiding us? this way, the Romans
Must or for Britons slay us, or receive us
For barbarous and unnatural revolts,
During their use, and slay us after.

Bel.   Sons,
We'll higher to the mountains; there secure us.
To the king's party there's no going: newness
Of Cloten's death (we being not known, not mus-
    tered
Among the bands) may drive us to a render
Where we have lived; and so extort from us
That which we've done, whose answer would be
    death
Drawn on with torture.

Gui.   This is, sir, a doubt,
In such a time, nothing becoming you,
Nor satisfying us.

Arv.   It is not likely,
That when they hear the Roman horses neigh,
Behold their quartered fires, have both their eyes
And ears so cloyed importantly as now,
That they will waste their time upon our note,
To know from whence we are.

Bel.   O, I am known
Of many in the army: many years,
Though Cloten then but young, you see not wore
    him
From my remembrance. And besides, the king
Hath not deserved my service, nor your loves;
Who find in my exile the want of breeding,
The certainty of this hard life; aye hopeless
To have the courtesy your cradle promised;
But to be still hot summer's tanlings, and
The shrinking slaves of winter.

Gui.   Than be so,
Better to cease to be. Pray, sir, to the army:
I and my brother are not known; yourself,
So out of thought, and thereto so o'ergrown,
Cannot be questioned.

Arv.   By this sun that shines,
I 'll thither.   What thing is it that I never
Did see man die? scarce ever looked on blood,
But that of coward hares, hot goats, and venison?
Never bestrid a horse, save one, that had
A rider like myself, who ne'er wore rowel
Nor iron on his heel?   I am ashamed
To look upon the holy sun, to have
The benefit of his blessed beams, remaining
So long a poor unknown.
   Gui.   By heavens, I 'll go:
If you will bless me, sir, and give me leave,
I 'll take the better care; but if you will not,

The hazard therefore due fall on me, by
The hands of Romans!
   Arv.   So say I: amen.
   Bel.   No reason I, since on your lives you set
So slight a valuation, should reserve
My cracked one to more care.   Have with you,
   boys:
If in your country wars you chance to die,
That is my bed too, lads, and there I 'll lie:
Lead, lead!—The time seems long; their blood
      thinks scorn,   [*Aside.*
Till it fly out, and shew them princes born.
                      [*Exeunt.*

ACT V.

SCENE I.—*A Field between the British and Roman Camps.*

Enter POSTHUMUS, *with a bloody handkerchief.*

Post. Yea, bloody cloth, I'll keep thee; for I
　　wished
Thou shouldst be coloured thus.　You married
　　ones,
If each of you would take this course, how many
Must murder wives much better than them-
　　selves,
For wrying but a little!—O, Pisanio!
Every good servant does not all commands:
No bond, but to do just ones.—Gods! if you
Should have ta'en vengeance on my faults, I
　　never
Had lived to put on this: so had you saved
The noble Imogen to repent; and struck
Me, wretch, more worth your vengeance.　But
　　alack,
You snatch some hence for little faults; that's
　　love,
To have them fall no more: you some permit
To second ills with ills, each elder worse;
And make them dread it to the doer's thrift.
But Imogen is your own.　Do your best wills,
And make me blessed to obey!—I am brought
　　hither
Among the Italtan gentry, and to fight
Against my lady's kingdom: 'tis enough
That, Britain, I have killed thy mistress: peace!
I'll give no wound to thee.　Therefore, good
　　heavens,
Hear patiently my purpose: I'll disrobe me
Of these Italian weeds, and suit myself
As does a Briton peasant: so I'll fight
Against the part I come with; so I'll die
For thee, O Imogen, even for whom my life
Is, every breath, a death: and thus, unknown,
Pitied nor hated, to the face of peril
Myself I'll dedicate.　Let me make men know
More valour in me than my habits shew.
Gods, put the strength o' the Leonati in me!
To shame the guise o' the world, I will begin
The fashion less without, and more within. [*Exit·*

SCENE II.—*The same.*

Enter, at one side, LUCIUS, IACHIMO, *and the Roman army ; at the other side, the British army ;*
LEONATUS POSTHUMUS *following it, like a poor*

*Soldier. They march over, and go out. Alarums.
Then enter again in skirmish,* IACHIMO *and*
POSTHUMUS; *he vanquisheth and disarmeth*
IACHIMO, *and then leaves him.*

Iach. The heaviness and guilt within my bosom
Takes off my manhood : I have belied a lady,
The princess of this country, and the air on 't
Revengingly enfeebles me ; or could this carl,
A very drudge of nature's, have subdued me
In my profession ? Knighthoods and honours,
    borne
As I wear mine, are titles but of scorn.
If that thy gentry, Britain, go before
This lout, as he exceeds our lords, the odds
Is that we scarce are men, and you are gods.
                         [*Exit.*

The battle continues ; the Britons *fly ;* CYMBELINE
is taken ; then enter, to his rescue, BELARIUS,
GUIDERIUS, *and* ARVIRAGUS.

Bel. Stand, stand ! We have the advantage of
    the ground ;
The lane is guarded : nothing routs us but
The villany of our fears.

Gui.)
Arv.)   Stand, stand, and fight !

Enter POSTHUMUS, *and seconds the* Britons: *they
rescue* CYMBELINE, *and exeunt. Then enter*
LUCIUS, IACHIMO, *and* IMOGEN.

Luc. Away, boy, from the troops, and save
    thyself :
For friends kill friends, and the disorder 's such
As war were hoodwinked.

Iach.   'T is their fresh supplies.

Luc. It is a day turned strangely :—or betimes
Let 's reinforce, or fly.   [*Exeunt.*

SCENE III.—*Another Part of the Field.*

Enter POSTHUMUS *and a British* Lord.

Lord. Cam'st thou from where they made the
    stand ?
Post.   I did :
Though you, it seems, come from the fliers.
Lord.   I did.
Post. No blame be to you, sir ; for all was lost
But that the heavens fought. The king himself
Of his wings destitute, the army broken,
And but the backs of Britons seen, all flying
Through a strait lane ; the enemy full-hearted,
Lolling the tongue with slaughtering, having
    work
More plentiful than tools to do 't, struck down

Some mortally, some slightly touched, some
    falling
Merely through fear ; that the strait pass was
    dammed
With dead men hurt behind, and cowards living
To die with lengthened shame.
Lord.   Where was this lane ?
Post. Close by the battle, ditched, and walled
    with turf ;
Which gave advantage to an ancient soldier,—
An honest one, I warrant ; who deserved
So long a breeding as his white beard came to,
In doing this for his country ;—athwart the
    lane,
He, with two striplings (lads more like to run
The country base than to commit such slaughter ;
With faces fit for masks, or rather fairer
Than those for preservation cased, or shame),
Made good the passage ; cried to those that fled,
" Our Britain's harts die flying, not our men :
To darkness fleet, souls that fly backwards !
    Stand ;
Or we are Romans, and will give you that
Like beasts, which you shun beastly ; and may
    save,
But to look back in frown. Stand, stand !"—These
    three,
Three thousand confident, in act as many
(For three performers are the file when all
The rest do nothing), with this word, "Stand,
    stand !"
Accommodated by the place, more charming
With their own nobleness (which could have
    turned
A distaff to a lance), gilded pale looks,
Part, shame,—part, spirit renewed ; that some,
    turned coward
But by example (O, a sin in war
Damned in the first beginners !), 'gan to look
The way that they did, and to grin like lions
Upon the pikes o' the hunters. Then began
A stop i' the chaser, a retire ; anon,
A rout, confusion thick : forthwith, they fly
Chickens, the way which they stooped eagles ;
    slaves,
The strides they victors made. And now our
    cowards
(Like fragments in hard voyages) became
The life o' the need : having found the back-door
    open
Of the unguarded hearts, Heavens, how they
    wound !
Some, slain before ; some, dying ; some, their
    friends
O'er-borne i' the former wave : ten, chaced by
    one,
Are now each one the slaughter-man of twenty :

Those that would die or ere resist, are grown
The mortal bugs o' the field.

　　Lord.　　　　This was strange chance:
A narrow lane! an old man, and two boys!

　　Post. Nay, do not wonder at it: you are
　　　　made
Rather to wonder at the things you hear,
Than to work any.　Will you rhyme upon 't,
And vent it for a mockery? here is one:
" Two boys, an old man twice a boy, a lane,
Preserved the Britons, was the Romans' bane."

　　Lord. Nay, be not angry, sir.

　　Post.　　　　'Lack, to what end?
Who dares not stand his foe, I 'll be his friend:
For if he 'll do as he is made to do,
I know he 'll quickly fly my friendship too.
You have put me into rhyme.

　　Lord.　　　　Farewell; you are angry. [*Exit.*

　　Post. Still going?—This is a lord! O noble
　　　　misery!
To be i' the field, and ask, what news, of me!—
To-day, how many would have given their ho-
　　　　nours
To have saved their carcasses? took heel to do 't,
And yet died too? I, in mine own woe charmed,
Could not find Death where I did hear him groan,
Nor feel him where he struck: being an ugly
　　　　monster,
'T is strange he hides him in fresh cups, soft
　　　　beds,
Sweet words; or hath more ministers than we
That draw his knives i' the war.—Well, I will find
　　　　him:
For being now a favourer to the Roman,
No more a Briton, I have resumed again
The part I came in: fight I will no more,
But yield me to the veriest hind that shall
Once touch my shoulder.　Great the slaugh-
　　　　ter is
Here made by the Romans; great the answer
　　　　be
Britons must take: for me, my ransom 's death;
On either side I come to spend my breath;
Which neither here I 'll keep, nor bear again,
But end it by some means for Imogen.

Enter two British Captains, *and* Soldiers.

　　1st Cap. Great Jupiter be praised! Lucius is
taken. 'T is thought the old man and his sons
were angels.

　　2nd Cap. There was a fourth man, in a silly
　　　　habit,
That gave the front with them.

　　1st Cap.　　　　So 't is reported:
But none of them can be found.—Stand! who is
　　　　there?

　　Post. A Roman;

Who had not now been drooping here, if seconds
Had answered him.

　　2nd Cap.　　　　Lay hands on him; a dog!
A leg of Rome shall not return to tell
What crows have pecked them here. He brags his
　　　　service
As if he were of note: bring him to the king.

Enter CYMBELINE, *attended;* BELARIUS, GUI-
　　DERIUS, ARVIRAGUS, PISANIO, *and Roman*
　　Captives.　*The* Captains *present* POSTHUMUS
　　to CYMBELINE, *who delivers him over to a*
　　Gaoler; *after which, all go out.*

SCENE IV.—*A Prison.*

Enter POSTHUMUS, *and two* Gaolers.

　　1st Gaol. You shall not now be stolen; you have
　　　　locks upon you;
So graze, as you find pasture.

　　2nd Gaol.　　　　Ay, or a stomach.
　　　　　　　　　　[*Exeunt* Gaolers.

　　Post. Most welcome, bondage! for thou art a
　　　　way,
I think, to liberty: yet am I better
Than one that 's sick o' the gout: since he had
　　　　rather
Groan so in perpetuity, than be cured
By the sure physician, Death, who is the key
To unbar these locks.　My conscience! thou art
　　　　fettered
More than my shanks and wrists: you good gods,
　　　　give me
The penitent instrument, to pick that bolt,
Then, free for ever! Is 't enough I am sorry?
So children temporal fathers do appease;
Gods are more full of mercy.　Must I repent?
I cannot do it better than in gyves,
Desired more than constrained: to satisfy,
If of my freedom 'tis the main part, take
No stricter render of me than my all.
I know you are more clement than vile men,
Who of their broken debtors take a third,
A sixth, a tenth, letting them thrive again
On their abatement; that 's not my desire:
For Imogen's dear life, take mine; and though
'T is not so dear, yet 't is a life; you coined it:
'Tween man and man they weigh not every
　　　　stamp,
Though light, take pieces for the figure's sake:
You rather mine, being yours: and so great
　　　　powers,
If you will take this audit, take this life,
And cancel these cold bonds.　O Imogen!
I 'll speak to thee in silence.　　[*He sleeps.*

Solemn Music. Enter, as an apparition, SICILIUS
LEONATUS, *father to* POSTHUMUS, *an old man,
attired like a warrior; leading in his hand an
ancient Matron, his wife, and mother to* POST-
HUMUS, *with music before them. Then, after
other music, follow the two young* LEONATI,
brothers to POSTHUMUS, *with wounds, as they
died in the wars. They circle* POSTHUMUS
round, as he lies sleeping.

Sici. No more, thou thunder-master, shew
    Thy spite on mortal flies:
  With Mars fall out, with Juno chide,
    That thy adulteries
      Rates and revenges.
  Hath my poor boy done aught but well,
    Whose face I never saw?
  I died whilst in the womb he stayed,
    Attending Nature's law.
  Whose father then (as men report
    Thou orphans' father art)
  Thou shouldst have been, and shielded him
    From this earth-vexing smart.

Moth. Lucina lent not me her aid,
    But took me in my throes;
  That from me was Posthumus ript,
    Came crying 'mongst his foes,
      A thing of pity!

Sici. Great nature, like his ancestry,
    Moulded the stuff so fair,
  That he deserved the praise o' the world,
    As great Sicilius' heir.

1st Bro. When once he was mature for man,
    In Britain where was he
  That could stand up his parallel;
    Or fruitful object be
  In eye of Imogen, that best
    Could deem his dignity?

Moth. With marriage wherefore was he mocked,
    To be exiled, and thrown
  From Leonati' seat, and cast
    From her his dearest one,
      Sweet Imogen?

Sici. Why did you suffer Iachimo,
    Slight thing of Italy,
  To taint his nobler heart and brain
    With needless jealousy;
  And to become the geck and scorn
    O' the other's villany?

2nd Bro. For this, from stiller seats we came,
    Our parents, and us twain,
  That, striking in our country's cause,
    Fell bravely, and were slain;
  Our fealty, and Tenantius' right,
    With honour to maintain.

1st Bro. Like hardiment Posthumus hath
    To Cymbeline performed:

  Then, Jupiter, thou king of gods,
    Why hast thou thus adjourned
  The graces for his merits due;
    Being all to dolours turned?

Sici. Thy crystal window ope; look out;
    No longer exercise,
  Upon a valiant race, thy harsh
    And potent injuries:

Moth. Since, Jupiter, our son is good,
    Take off his miseries.

Sici. Peep through thy marble mansion; help!
    Or we poor ghosts will cry
  To the shining synod of the rest,
    Against thy deity.

2nd Bro. Help, Jupiter; or we appeal,
    And from thy justice fly.

JUPITER *descends in thunder and lightning, sitting
upon an eagle; he throws a thunder-bolt. The
Ghosts fall on their knees.*

Jup. No more, you petty spirits of region low,
  Offend our hearing; hush!—How dare you, ghosts,
Accuse the thunderer, whose bolt you know,
  Sky-planted, batters all rebelling coasts?
Poor shadows of Elysium, hence; and rest
  Upon your never-withering banks of flowers:
Be not with mortal accidents oppressed;
  No care of yours it is; you know t' is ours.
Whom best I love, I cross; to make my gift,
  The more delayed, delighted. Be content;
Your low-laid son our godhead will uplift:
  His comforts thrive, his trials well are spent.
Our Jovial star reigned at his birth, and in
  Our temple was he married.—Rise, and fade!
He shall be lord of lady Imogen,
  And happier much by his affliction made.
This tablet lay upon his breast; wherein
  Our pleasure his full fortune doth confine;
And so, away: no farther with your din
  Express impatience, lest you stir up mine.—
Mount, eagle, to my palace crystalline. [*Ascends.*

Sici. He came in thunder: his celestial breath
Was sulphurous to smell: the holy eagle
Stooped, as to foot us; his ascension is
More sweet than our blessed fields: his royal bird
Prunes the immortal wing, and cloys his beak,
As when his god is pleased.

All.   Thanks, Jupiter!

Sici. The marble pavement closes, he is entered
His radiant roof. Away! and, to be blessed,
Let us with care perform his great behest.
              [*Ghosts vanish.*

Post. [*waking*]. Sleep, thou hast been a grand-
    sire, and begot
A father to me; and thou hast created
A mother and two brothers: but (O scorn!)
Gone! they went hence so soon as they were born.

And so I am awake.—Poor wretches that depend
On greatness' favour, dream as I have done;
Wake, and find nothing.—But, alas, I swerve:
Many dream not to find, neither deserve,
And yet are steeped in favours; so am I,
That have this golden chance, and know not why.
What fairies haunt this ground? A book? O
      rare one!
Be not, as is our fangled world, a garment
Nobler than that it covers: let thy effects
So follow, to be most unlike our courtiers,
As good as promise.

Reads.

"When as a lion's whelp shall, to himself unknown, without seeking, find, and be embraced by
a piece of tender air; and when from a stately cedar
shall be lopped branches, which, being dead many
years, shall after revive, be jointed to the old stock,
and freshly grow; then shall Posthumus end his
miseries, Britain be fortunate, and flourish in peace
and plenty."

'Tis still a dream; or else such stuff as madmen
Tongue, and brain not: either both, or nothing:
Or senseless speaking, or a speaking such
As sense cannot untie. Be what it is,
The action of my life is like it, which
I'll keep, if but for sympathy.

Re-enter Gaolers.

Gaol. Come, sir, are you ready for death?
Post. Over-roasted rather: ready long ago.
Gaol. Hanging is the word, sir; if you be ready
for that, you are well cooked.
Post. So, if I prove a good repast to the spectators, the dish pays the shot.
Gaol. A heavy reckoning for you, sir: but the
comfort is, you shall be called to no more pay-
ments, fear no more tavern bills; which are
often the sadness of parting, as the procuring of
mirth: you come in faint for want of meat, depart reeling with too much drink: sorry that
you have paid too much, and sorry that you are
paid too much; purse and brain both empty:
the brain the heavier for being too light, the
purse too light, being drawn of heaviness: O!

of this contradiction you shall now be quit.—O,
the charity of a penny cord! it sums up thousands in a trice: you have no true debitor and
creditor but it; of what's past, is, and to come,
the discharge:—your neck, sir, is pen, book,
and counters; so the acquittance follows.

Post. I am merrier to die than thou art to live.

Gaol. Indeed, sir, he that sleeps feels not the tooth-ache : but a man that were to sleep your sleep, and a hangman to help him to bed, I think he would change places with his officer ; for, look you, sir, you know not which way you shall go.

Post. Yes, indeed do I, fellow.

Gaol. Your death has eyes in 's head then ; I have not seen him so pictured : you must either be directed by some that take upon them to know ; or take upon yourself that which I am sure you do not know ; or jump the after-inquiry on your own peril : and how you shall speed in your journey's end, I think you 'll never return to tell one.

Post. I tell thee, fellow, there are none want eyes to direct them the way I am going, but such as wink, and will not use them.

Gaol. What an infinite mock is this, that a man should have the best use of eyes, to see the way of blindness ! I am sure hanging 's the way of winking.

Enter a Messenger.

Mess. Knock off his manacles ; bring your prisoner to the king.

Post. Thou bringest good news : I am called to be made free.

Gaol. I 'll be hanged, then.

Post. Thou shalt be then freer than a gaoler ; no bolts for the dead.

[*Exeunt* POSTHUMUS *and* Messenger.

Gaol. Unless a man would marry a gallows, and beget young gibbets, I never saw one so prone. Yet, on my conscience, there are verier knaves desire to live, for all he be a Roman : and there be some of them too that die against their wills ; so should I, if I were one. I would we were all of one mind, and one mind good ; O, there were desolation of gaolers and gallowses ! I speak against my present profit ; but my wish hath a preferment in 't.   [*Exeunt.*

SCENE V.—CYMBELINE'S *Tent.*

Enter CYMBELINE, BELARIUS, GUIDERIUS, ARVIRAGUS, PISANIO, Lords, Officers, *and* Attendants.

Cym. Stand by my side, you whom the gods have made
Preservers of my throne. Woe is my heart
That the poor soldier that so richly fought,
Whose rags shamed gilded arms, whose naked breast
Stepped before targe of proof, cannot be found :

He shall be happy that can find him, if
Our grace can make him so.

Bel.   I never saw
Such noble fury in so poor a thing ;
Such precious deeds in one that promised nought
But beggary and poor looks.

Cym.   No tidings of him ?

Pisa. He hath been searched among the dead
        and living,
But no trace of him.

Cym.   To my grief, I am
The heir of his reward ; which I will add
To you, the liver, heart, and brain of Britain,

[*To* BELARIUS, GUIDERIUS, *and* ARVIRAGUS.
By whom, I grant, she lives. 'Tis now the time
To ask of whence you are : report it.

Bel.   Sir,
In Cambria are we born, and gentlemen :
Further to boast were neither true nor modest,
Unless I add, we are honest.

Cym.   Bow your knees :
Arise, my knights o' the battle ; I create you
Companions to our person, and will fit you
With dignities becoming your estates.

Enter CORNELIUS *and* Ladies.

There 's business in these faces.—Why so sadly
Greet you our victory ? you look like Romans,
And not o' the court of Britain.

Cor.   Hail, great king !
To sour your happiness, I must report
The queen is dead.

Cym.   Whom worse than a physician
Would this report become ? But I consider,
By medicine life may be prolonged, yet death
Will seize the doctor too.—How ended she ?

Cor. With horror, madly dying, like her life ;
Which, being cruel to the world, concluded
Most cruel to herself. What she confessed
I will report, so please you : these her women
Can trip me, if I err ; who, with wet cheeks,
Were present when she finished.

Cym.   Pr'y thee, say.

Cor. First, she confessed she never loved you ;
        only
Affected greatness got by you, not you :
Married your royalty ; was wife to your place ;
Abhorred your person.

Cym.   She alone knew this :
And but she spoke it dying, I would not
Believe her lips in opening it. Proceed.

Cor. Your daughter, whom she bore in hand
        to love
With such integrity, she did confess
Was as a scorpion to her sight ; whose life,
But that her flight prevented it, she had
Ta'en off my poison.

Cym.   O most delicate fiend!
Who is't can read a woman?—Is there more?
    Cor. More, sir, and worse. She did confess
        she had
For you a mortal mineral; which, being took,
Should by the minute feed on life, and lingering,
By inches waste you: in which time she purposed,
By watching, weeping, tendance, kissing, to
O'ercome you with her show: yes, and in time
(When she had fitted you with her craft) to work
Her son into the adoption of the crown.
But failing of her end by his strange absence,
Grew shameless-desperate; opened, in despite
Of heaven and men, her purposes; repented
The evils she hatched were not effected; so,
Despairing, died.
    Cym.   Heard you all this, her women?
    Lady. We did, so please your highness.
    Cym.   Mine eyes
Were not in fault, for she was beautiful;
Mine ears, that heard her flattery; nor my heart,
That thought her like her seeming: it had been
        vicious
To have mistrusted her: yet, O my daughter!
That it was folly in me, thou mayst say,
And prove it in thy feeling. Heaven mend all!

Enter LUCIUS, IACHIMO, *the* Soothsayer, *and other
Roman prisoners, guarded:* POSTHUMUS *behind,
and* IMOGEN.

Thou com'st not, Caius, now for tribute; that
The Britons have razed out, though with the loss
Of many a bold one; whose kinsmen have made suit
That their good souls may be appeased with
        slaughter
Of you their captives, which ourself have granted:
So think of your estate.
    Luc. Consider, sir, the chance of war: the day
Was yours by accident; had it gone with us,
We should not, when the blood was cool, have
        threatened
Our prisoners with the sword. But since the gods
Will have it thus, that nothing but our lives
May be called ransom, let it come: sufficeth,
A Roman with a Roman's heart can suffer:
Augustus lives to think on't: and so much
For my peculiar care. This one thing only
I will entreat: my boy, a Briton born,
Let him be ransomed: never master had
A page so kind, so duteous, diligent,
So tender over his occasions, true,
So feat, so nurse-like: let his virtue join
With my request, which, I'll make bold, your
        highness
Cannot deny: he hath done no Briton harm,
Though he have served a Roman: save him, sir,
And spare no blood beside.

Cym.   I have surely seen him;
His favour is familiar to me.——
Boy, thou hast looked thyself into my grace,
And art mine own. I know not why nor wherefore
To say live, boy: ne'er thank thy master; live:
And ask of Cymbeline what boon thou wilt,
Fitting my bounty and thy state, I'll give it;
Yea, though thou do demand a prisoner,
The noblest ta'en.
    Imo.   I humbly thank your highness.
    Luc. I do not bid thee beg my life, good lad;
And yet I know thou wilt.
    Imo.   No, no: alack,
There's other work in hand; I see a thing
Bitter to me as death: your life, good master,
Must shuffle for itself.
    Luc.   The boy disdains me,—
He leaves me, scorns me: briefly die their joys
That place them on the truth of girls and boys.
Why stands he so perplexed?
    Cym.   What wouldst thou, boy?
I love thee more and more; think more and more
What's best to ask. Know'st him thou look'st
        on? Speak,
Wilt have him live? Is he thy kin? thy friend?
    Imo. He is a Roman; no more kin to me
Than I to your highness; who, being born your
        vassal,
Am something nearer.
    Cym.   Wherefore ey'st him so?
    Imo. I'll tell you, sir, in private, if you please
To give me hearing.
    Cym.   Ay, with all my heart,
And lend my best attention. What's thy name?
    Imo. Fidele, sir.
    Cym.   Thou art, my good youth, my page;
I'll be thy master: walk with me; speak freely.
        [CYMBELINE *and* IMOGEN *converse apart.*
    Bel. Is not this boy revived from death?
    Arv.   One sand another
Not more resembles that sweet rosy lad
Who died, and was Fidele. What think you?
    Gui. The same dead thing alive.
    Bel. Peace, peace! see further; he eyes us not;
        forbear;
Creatures may be alike: were't he, I am sure
He would have spoke to us.
    Gui.   But we saw him dead.
    Bel. Be silent; let's see further.
    Pisa.   It is my mistress: [*Aside.*
Since she is living, let the time run on
To good or bad.
        [CYMBELINE *and* IMOGEN *come forward.*
    Cym.   Come, stand thou by our side;
Make thy demand aloud.—Sir [*to* IACHIMO],
        step you forth;
Give answer to this boy, and do it freely;

Or by our greatness, and the grace of it,
Which is our honour, bitter torture shall
Winnow the truth from falsehood.—On ; speak
    to him.
Imo. My boon is, that this gentleman may render
Of whom he had this ring.
    Post.   What's that to him?   [*Aside.*
    Cym. That diamond upon your finger, say
How came it yours?
    Iach. Thou 'lt torture me to leave unspoken that
Which, to be spoke, would torture thee.
    Cym.   How ! me?
    Iach. I am glad to be constrained to utter that
        which
Torments me to conceal.   By villany
I got this ring : 'twas Leonatus' jewel ;
Whom thou didst banish ; and (which more may
        grieve thee,
As it doth me) a nobler sir ne'er lived
'Twixt sky and ground. Wilt thou hear more,
        my lord?
    Cym. All that belongs to this.
    Iach.   That paragon, thy daughter,
For whom my heart drops blood, and my false spirits
Quail to remember,—Give me leave ; I faint.
    Cym. My daughter ! what of her? Renew thy
        strength :
I had rather thou shouldst live while nature will,
Than die ere I hear more : strive, man, and speak.
    Iach. Upon a time (unhappy was the clock
That struck the hour !)—it was in Rome (accursed
The mansion where !)—'twas at a feast (O 'would
Our viands had been poisoned ! or, at least,
Those which I heaved to head !)—the good Post-
        humus
(What should I say? he was too good to be
Where ill men were ; and was the best of all
Amongst the rar'st of good ones), sitting sadly,
Hearing us praise our loves of Italy
For beauty that made barren the swelled boast
Of him that best could speak : for feature, laming
The shrine of Venus, or straight-pight Minerva,
Postures beyond brief nature ; for condition,
A shop of all the qualities that man
Loves woman for; besides, that hook of wiving,
Fairness, which strikes the eye :—
    Cym.   I stand on fire :
Come to the matter.
    Iach.   All too soon I shall,
Unless thou wouldst grieve quickly.—This Post-
        humus
(Most like a noble lord in love, and one
That had a royal lover) took his hint ;
And, not dispraising whom we praised (therein
He was as calm as virtue), he began
His mistress' picture ; which by his tongue being
        made,

And then a mind put in 't, either our brags
Were cracked of kitchen trulls, or his description
Proved us unspeaking sots.
    Cym.   Nay, nay, to the purpose.
    Iach. Your daughter's chastity—there it begins !
He spake of her as Dian had hot dreams,
And she alone were cold : whereat, I, wretch !
Made scruple of his praise ; and wagered with him
Pieces of gold, 'gainst this, which then he wore
Upon his honoured finger, to attain
In suit the place of his bed, and win this ring
By hers and mine adultery : he, true-knight,
No lesser of her honour confident
Than I did truly find her, stakes this ring ;
And would so had it been a carbuncle
Of Phœbus' wheel ; and might so safely, had it
Been all the worth of his car. Away to Britain
Post I in this design : well may you, sir,
Remember me at court, where I was taught
Of your chaste daughter the wide difference
'Twixt amorous and villanous.   Being thus
        quenched
Of hope, not longing, mine Italian brain
'Gan in your duller Britain operate
Most vilely ! for my vantage, excellent ;
And, to be brief, my practice so prevailed,
That I returned with simular proof enough
To make the noble Leonatus mad,
By wounding his belief in her renown
With tokens, thus and thus ; averring notes
Of chamber-hanging, pictures, this her bracelet
(O, cunning, how I got it !), nay, some marks
Of secret on her person, that he could not
But think her bond of chastity quite cracked,
I having ta'en the forfeit.   Whereupon,—
Methinks I see him now,—
    Post.   Ay, so thou dost,
                        [*Coming forward.*
Italian fiend !—Ah me, most credulous fool,
Egregious murderer, thief, anything
That's due to all the villains past, in being,
To come ! O, give me cord, or knife, or poison,
Some upright justicer !   Thou, king, send out
For torturers ingenious : it is I
That all the abhorréd things o' the earth amend,
By being worse than they. I am Posthumus,
That killed thy daughter :—villain-like, I lie ;
That caused a lesser villain than myself,
A sacrilegious thief, to do 't :—the temple
Of virtue was she ; yea, and she herself.
Spit and throw stones, cast mire upon me, set
The dogs o' the street to bay me : every villain
Be called Posthumus Leonatus ; and
Be villany less than 'twas !—O Imogen !
My queen, my life, my wife ! O Imogen !
Imogen, Imogen !
    Imo.   Peace, my lord ; hear, hear !

Post. Shall's have a play of this? Thou scorn-
     ful page.
There lie thy part.   [*Striking her : she falls.*
  Pisa.   O, gentlemen, help
Mine and your mistress. O, my lord Posthumus!
You ne'er killed Imogen till now.—Help, help!
Mine honoured lady!
  Cym.   Does the world go round?
  Post. How come these staggers on me?
  Pisa.   Wake, my mistress!
  Cym. If this be so, the gods do mean to strike me
To death with mortal joy.
  Pisa.   How fares my mistress?
  Imo. O, get thee from my sight;
Thou gav'st me poison : dangerous fellow, hence!
Breathe not where princes are.
  Cym.   The tune of Imogen!
  Pisa. Lady,
The gods throw stones of sulphur on me, if
That box I gave you was not thought by me
A precious thing. I had it from the queen.
  Cym. New matter still!
  Imo.   It poisoned me.
  Cor.   O gods!—
I left out one thing which the queen confessed,

Which must approve thee honest : " If Pisanio
Have," said she, " given his mistress that confection
Which I gave him for cordial, she is served
As I would serve a rat."
  Cym.   What's this, Cornelius?
  Cor. The queen, sir, very oft importuned me
To temper poisons for her; still pretending
The satisfaction of her knowledge only
In killing creatures vile, as cats and dogs
Of no esteem : I, dreading that her purpose
Was of more danger, did compound for her
A certain stuff, which, being ta'en, would cease
The present power of life; but, in short time,
All offices of nature should again
Do their due functions.—Have you ta'en of it?
  Imo. Most like I did, for I was dead.
  Bel.   My boys,
There was our error.
  Gui.   This is, sure, Fidele.
  Imo. Why did you throw your wedded lady
      from you?
Think that you are upon a rock; and now
Throw me again.   [*Embracing* POSTHUMUS.
  Post. Hang there like fruit, my soul,
Till the tree die!

Cym.   How now, my flesh, my child?
What mak'st thou me a dullard in this act?
Wilt thou not speak to me?
    Imo.   Your blessing, sir.   [*Kneeling.*
    Bel. Though you did love this youth, I blame
         ye not; [*To* Guiderius *and* Arviragus.
You had a motive for it.
    Cym.   My tears that fall
Prove holy water on thee! Imogen,
Thy mother's dead.
    Imo.   I am sorry for 't, my lord.
    Cym. O, she was naught; and 'long of her it was
That we meet here so strangely: but her son
Is gone, we know not how nor where.
    Pisa.   My lord,
Now fear is from me, I 'll speak truth. Lord Cloten,
Upon my lady's missing, came to me
With his sword drawn; foamed at the mouth, and
         swore
If I discovered not which way she was gone,
It was my instant death: by accident
I had a feignéd letter of my master's
Then in my pocket; which directed him
To seek her on the mountains near to Milford;
Where, in a frenzy, in my master's garments,
Which he inforced from me, away he posts
With unchaste purpose, and with oaths to violate
My lady's honour: what became of him,
I further know not.
    Gui.   Let me end the story:
I slew him there.
    Cym.   Marry, the gods forefend!
I would not thy good deeds should from my lips
Pluck a hard sentence: pr'ythee, valiant youth,
Deny 't again.
    Gui.   I have spoke it, and I did it.
    Cym. He was a prince.
    Gui. A most uncivil one. The wrongs he did me
Were nothing prince-like; for he did provoke me
With language that would make me spurn the se.
If it could so roar to me. I cut off 's head;
And am right glad he is not standing here
To tell this tale of mine.
    Cym.   I am sorry for thee:
By thine own tongue thou art condemned, and must
Endure our law: thou art dead.
    Imo.   That headless man
I thought had been my lord.
    Cym.   Bind the offender,
And take him from our presence.
    Bel.   Stay, sir king;
This man is better than the man he slew;
As well descended as thyself; and hath
More of thee merited than a band of Clotens
Had ever scar for.—Let his arms alone;
                  [*To the* Guard.
They were not born for bondage.

    Cym.   Why, old soldier,
Wilt thou undo the worth thou art unpaid for,
By tasting of our wrath?—How of descent
As good as we?
    Arv.   In that he spake too far.
    Cym. And thou shalt die for 't.
    Bel.   We will die all three:
But I will prove that two of us are as good
As I have given out him.—My sons, I must,
For mine own part, unfold a dangerous speech,
Though, haply, well for you.
    Arv.   Your danger's ours.
    Gui. And our good his.
    Bel.   Have at it, then.—
By leave:—thou hadst, great king, a subject who
Was called Belarius.
    Cym.   What of him? he is
A banished traitor.
    Bel.   He it is that hath
Assumed this age: indeed, a banished man;
I know not how a traitor.
    Cym.   Take him hence;
The whole world shall not save him.
    Bel.   Not too hot:
First pay me for the nursing of thy sons;
And let it be confiscate all, so soon
As I have received it.
    Cym.   Nursing of my sons?
    Bel. I am too blunt and saucy: here's my
         knee:
Ere I arise, I will prefer my sons;
Then spare not the old father. Mighty sir,
These two young gentlemen, that call me father,
And think they are my sons, are none of mine;
They are the issue of your loins, my liege,
And blood of your begetting.
    Cym.   How! my issue?
    Bel. So sure as you your father's. I, old Morgan,
Am that Belarius whom you sometime banished:
Your pleasure was my mere offence, my punish-
         ment
Itself, and all my treason; that I suffered,
Was all the harm I did. These gentle princes
(For such and so they are), these twenty years
Have I trained up: those arts they have as I
Could put into them; my breeding was, sir, as
Your highness knows. Their nurse, Euriphile,
Whom for the theft I wedded, stole these children
Upon my banishment: I moved her to 't;
Having received the punishment before
For that which I did then: beaten for loyalty
Excited me to treason: their dear loss,
The more of you 'twas felt, the more it shaped
Unto my end of stealing them. But, gracious sir,
Here are your sons again: and I must lose
Two of the sweet'st companions in the world.
The benediction of these covering heavens

Fall on their heads like dew! for they are worthy
To inlay heaven with stars.

Cym. Thou weep'st and speak'st,
The service that you three have done, is more
Unlike than this thou tellest. I lost my children:
If these be they, I know not how to wish
A pair of worthier sons.

Bel. Be pleased a while.—
This gentleman, whom I call Polydore,
Most worthy prince, as yours, is true Guiderius:
This gentleman, my Cadwal, Arviragus,
Your younger princely son; he, sir, was lapped
In a most curious mantle, wrought by the hand
Of his queen mother, which, for more probation,
I can with ease produce.

Cym. Guiderius had
Upon his neck a mole, a sanguine star;
It was a mark of wonder.

Bel. This is he;
Who hath upon him still that natural stamp;
It was wise nature's end in the donation,
To be his evidence now.

Cym. O, what, am I
A mother to the birth of three? Ne'er mother
Rejoiced deliverance more!—Blessed may you be,
That, after this strange starting from your orbs,
You may reign in them now!—O Imogen,
Thou hast lost by this a kingdom.

Imo. No, my lord;
I have got two worlds by't.—O, my gentle
brothers,
Have we thus met? O, never say hereafter
But I am truest speaker: you called me brother,
When I was but your sister; I you brothers,
When you were so indeed.

Cym. Did you e'er meet?

Arv. Ay, my good lord.

Gui. And at first meeting loved;
Continued so, until we thought he died.

Cor. By the queen's dram she swallowed.

Cym. O rare instinct!
When shall I hear all through? This fierce abridgment
Hath to it circumstantial branches, which
Distinction should be rich in.—Where? how
lived you?
And when came you to serve our Roman captive?
How parted with your brothers? how first met
them?
Why fled you from the court; and whither? These,
And your three motives to the battle, with
I know not how much more, should be demanded;
And all the other by-dependencies,
From chance to chance; but nor the time, nor
place,
Will serve our long inter'gatories. See,
Posthumus anchors upon Imogen;

And she, like harmless lightning, throws her eye
On him, her brothers, me, her master; hitting
Each object with a joy; the counterchange
Is severally in all. Let's quit this ground,
And smoke the temple with our sacrifices.—
Thou art my brother; so we'll hold thee ever.

[*To* BELARIUS.

Imo. You are my father too; and did relieve me,
To see this gracious season.

Cym. All o'erjoyed,
Save these in bonds: let them be joyful too,
For they shall taste our comfort.

Imo. My good master,
I will yet do you service.

Luc. Happy be you!

Cym. The forlorn soldier that so nobly fought,
He would have well becomed this place, and graced
The thankings of a king.

Post. I am, sir,
The soldier that did company these three,
In poor beseeming; 'twas a fitment for
The purpose I then followed.—That I was he,
Speak, Iachimo; I had you down, and might
Have made you finish.

Iach. I am down again; [*Kneeling.*
But now my heavy conscience sinks my knee,
As then your force did. Take that life, 'beseech you,
Which I so often owe: but your ring first;
And here the bracelet of the truest princess
That ever swore her faith.

Post. Kneel not to me:
The power that I have on you, is to spare you;
The malice towards you, to forgive you: live,
And deal with others better.

Cym. Nobly doomed:
We'll learn our freeness of a son-in-law:
Pardon's the word to all.

Arv. You holp us, sir,
As you did mean indeed to be our brother;
Joyed are we that you are.

Post. Your servant, princes.—Good my lord of
Rome,
Call forth your soothsayer. As I slept, methought
Great Jupiter, upon his eagle back,
Appeared to me, with other spritely shows
Of mine own kindred: when I waked, I found
This label on my bosom; whose containing
Is so from sense in hardness, that I can
Make no collection of it: let him shew
His skill in the construction.

Luc. Philarmonus,—

Sooth. Here, my good lord.

Luc. Read, and declare the meaning.

Soothsayer reads.

"When as a lion's whelp shall, to himself unknown, without seeking, find, and be embraced by a

piece of tender air; and when from a stately cedar
shall be lopped branches, which, being dead many
years, shall after revive, be jointed to the old stock,
and freshly grow; then shall Posthumus end his
miseries, Britain be fortunate, and flourish in peace
and plenty."

Thou, Leonatus, art the lion's whelp;
The fit and apt construction of thy name,
Being Leo-natus, doth import so much:
The piece of tender air, thy virtuous daughter,
　　　　　　　　　　　　[*To* Cymbeline.
Which we call *mollis aer;* and *mollis aer*
We term it *mulier:* which *mulier,* I divine,
Is this most constant wife; who, even now,
Answering the letter of the oracle,
Unknown to you, unsought, were clipped about
With this most tender air.

　　Cym.　　　This hath some seeming.
　　Sooth. The lofty cedar, royal Cymbeline,
Personates thee: and thy lopped branches point
Thy two sons forth; who, by Belarius stolen,
For many years thought dead, are now revived,
To the majestic cedar joined; whose issue
Promises Britain peace and plenty.

　　Cym.　　　Well,
My peace we will begin. And, Caius Lucius,
Although the victor, we submit to Cæsar,

And to the Roman empire; promising
To pay our wonted tribute, from the which
We were dissuaded by our wicked queen;
Whom heavens, in justice (both on her and hers),
Have laid most heavy hand.

　　Sooth. The fingers of the powers above do tune
The harmony of this peace. The vision
Which I made known to Lucius ere the stroke
Of this yet scarce-cold battle, at this instant
Is full accomplished: for the Roman eagle,
From south to west on wing soaring aloft,
Lessened herself, and in the beams o' the sun
So vanished: which foreshewed our princely eagle,
The imperial Cæsar, should again unite
His favour with the radiant Cymbeline,
Which shines here in the west.

　　Cym.　　　Laud we the gods;
And let our crooked smokes climb to their nostrils
From our blessed altars! Publish we this peace
To all our subjects. Set we forward: let
A Roman and a British ensign wave
Friendly together: so through Lud's town march:
And in the temple of great Jupiter
Our peace we'll ratify; seal it with feasts.
Set on there.—Never was a war did cease,
Ere bloody hands were washed, with such a peace.

　　　　　　　　　　　　　　　[*Exeunt.*

NOTES.

——" *His father*
Was called Sicilius, who did join his honour
Against the Romans, with Cassibelan;
But had his titles by Tenantius."—Act I., Scene 1.

Tenantius was the father of Cymbeline, and nephew of Cassibelan, being the younger son of Cassibelan's elder brother Lud, on whose death Cassibelan was admitted king. He repulsed the Romans on their first attack; but, being vanquished on Cæsar's second invasion, he agreed to pay an annual tribute to Rome. After his death, Tenantius, Lud's younger son (the elder brother, Androgeus, having fled to Rome), was established on the throne, of which they had been deprived by their uncle. According to some authorities, Tenantius quietly paid the tribute stipulated by Cassibelan: according to others, he refused to pay it, and warred with the Romans. Shakspere supposes the last account to be the true one.

" *Enter the* QUEEN, POSTHUMUS, *and* IMOGEN."
Act I., Scene 2.

Holinshed's "CHRONICLE" probably supplied Shakspere with the beautiful name "Imogen." In the old black letter, it is scarcely distinguishable from "Innogen," the wife of Brute, King of Britain. From the same source, the Poet may have derived the name of Cloten, who, when the line of Brute became extinct, was one of the five kings that governed Britain. Cloten, or Cloton, was King of Cornwall. —Leonatus (the prefix of Posthumus) is a name found in Sydney's "ARCADIA." It is that of the legitimate son of the blind King of Paphlagonia, on whose story is formed the episode of Glo'ster, Edgar, and Edmund, in "KING LEAR."

" *A man worth any woman; overbuys me*
Almost the sum he pays."—Act I., Scene 2.

That is—the most minute portion of his worth would be too high a price for the wife he has acquired.

—— " *If he should write,*
And I not have it, 'twere a paper lost,
As offered mercy is."—Act I., Scene 4.

The meaning probably is, that the loss of that paper would prove as fatal to her (Imogen) as the loss of a pardon to a condemned criminal. A thought resembling this occurs in "ALL'S WELL THAT ENDS WELL:"—

" Like a remorseful pardon slowly carried."

" *Enter* PHILARIO, IACHIMO, *a* Frenchman, *a* Dutchman,
and a Spaniard."—Act I., Scene 5.

The name of Giacomo occurs in the "TWO GENTLEMEN OF VENICE," a novel which immediately follows that of "ROMEO AND JULIETTA," in the second tome of Painter's "PALACE OF PLEASURE."—The behaviour of the Spaniard and the Dutchman, who are stated to be present during this animated scene, is in humorous accordance with the apathy and taciturnity usually attributed to their countrymen. Neither the Don nor Mynheer utters a syllable. "What was Imogen to them, or they to Imogen, that they should speak of her?"

—— " *Your highness*
Shall from this practice but make hard your heart."
Act I., Scene 6.

Johnson's indignant comment on these lines is highly honourable to his feelings. It tends to justify Goldsmith's remark, that he had nothing of the bear but the skin:— "There is in this passage nothing that much requires a note, yet I cannot forbear to push it forward into observation. The thought would probably have been more amplified, had our author lived to be shocked with such experiments as have been published in later times, by a race of men that have practised tortures without pity, and are yet suffered to erect their heads among human beings."

To what particular "experiments" the moralist alluded, we are not at present aware: but the great duty which both he and the Poet seek to inculcate, that of mercy towards the inferior creatures, is of imperishable application.

———

" *Was there ever man had such luck! when I kissed the*
jack upon an up-cast, to be hit away!"—Act II., Scene 1.

Cloten is here describing his fate at bowls. The subject is mentioned in the notes to "TROILUS AND CRESSIDA." It is objected by Steevens to the character of Cloten, that " he is represented at once as brave and dastardly, civil and brutish, sagacious and cruel, without that subtilty of distinction, and those shades of gradation between sense and folly, virtue and vice, which constitute the excellence of such mixed characters as Polonius in 'HAMLET,' and the Nurse in 'ROMEO AND JULIET.'"—Such inconsistency is, however, far more puzzling than unnatural. Miss Seward (as quoted by Mr. Singer) assures us, in one of her letters, that singular as the character of Cloten may appear, it is the exact prototype of a being she once knew:—" The unmeaning frown of the countenance; the shuffling gait; the burst of voice; the bustling insignificance; the fever and ague fits of valour; the froward techiness; the unprincipled malice; and, what is most curious, those occasional gleams of good sense amidst the floating clouds of folly which generally darkened and confused the man's brain, and which, in the character of Cloten, we are apt to impute to a violation of unity of character; but in the sometime Captain C—n I saw the portrait of Cloten was not out of nature."

" *Swift, swift, you dragons of the night!*"—Act II., Scene 2.

The task of drawing the chariot of night was assigned to dragons, on account of their supposed watchfulness. Milton mentions "the dragon yoke of night" in "IL PENSEROSO;" and in his "MASQUE AT LUDLOW CASTLE" we find "the dragon womb of Stygian darkness."

" *Hark! hark! the lark at heaven's gate sings.*"
Act II., Scene 3.

The same highly poetic hyperbole occurs in Milton's "PARADISE LOST," (book v.):—

—— " Ye birds,
That, singing, up to heaven's gate ascend."

Also in Shakspere's 29th Sonnet:—

" Like to the lark, at break of day arising
    From sullen earth, sings hymns at heaven's gate."

And again in "VENUS AND ADONIS:"—

" Lo, here the gentle lark, weary of rest,
    From his moist cabinet mounts up on high,
    And wakes the morning, from whose silver breast
    The sun ariseth in his majesty."

——" Your mother too :
She 's my good lady."—Act II., Scene 3.

This is said ironically. " My good lady " is equivalent to
" my good friend." So in " HENRY IV.," Part 2, Falstaff
says to Prince John:—" And when you come to court, stand
my good lord, pray, in your good report."

—— " The story,
Proud Cleopatra, when she met her Roman,
And Cydnus swelled above the banks, or for
The press of boats, or pride."—Act II., Scene 4.

Johnson observes of this scene, that "Iachimo's language
is such as a skilful villain would naturally use,—a mixture
of airy triumph and serious deposition. His gaiety shews
his seriousness to be without anxiety; and his seriousness
proves his gaiety to be without art."

—— " Her andirons
(I had forgot them) were two winking Cupids
Of silver, each on one foot standing, nicely
Depending on their brands."—Act II., Scene 4.

The andirons of our ancestors were sometimes costly
pieces of furniture; the *standards* were often, as in this
instance, of silver, representing some terminal figure or
device; the transverse or horizontal pieces, upon which the
wood was supported, were what Shakspere here calls the
brands, properly *brandirons.* Upon these the Cupids which
formed the standards "nicely depended," seeming to stand
on one foot.

—— " Her attendants are
All sworn and honourable."—Act II., Scene 4.

It was anciently the custom for attendants on the nobility
(as it is now for the servants of the sovereign) to take an oath
of fidelity, on their entrance into office.

—— " Under her breast
(Worthy the pressing)."—Act II., Scene 4.

The original folio reads, "worthy *her* pressing." Rowe
made the correction. We mention the matter merely as it
affords an opportunity of saying, in justice to Rowe, that in
his edition he made many other verbal emendations of un-
questionable taste and correctness, which are now incorporated with the received text.

" Is there no way for men to be, but women
Must be half-workers."—Act II., Scene 5.

This bitter sarcasm of Posthumus (which, by the way, is
in reality caused by the villany of a man, not by the frailty
of a woman) probably suggested the similar sentiment th •
Milton has put into the mouth of Adam:—

—— " O why did God,
Creator wise, that peopled highest heaven
With spirits masculine, create at last
This novelty on earth, this fair defect
Of nature, and not fill the world at once
With men, as angels, without feminine,
Or find some other way to generate
Mankind?"

" Mulmutius made our laws,
Who was the first of Britain which did put
His brows within a golden crown, and called
Himself a king."—Act III., Scene 1.

The title of the first chapter of Holinshed's third book of
the " HISTORY OF ENGLAND," is :—" Of Mulmutius, the first
King of Britain who was crowned with a golden crown, his
laws, his foundations, &c.

" Mulmutius, the son of Cloten, got the upper hand of
the other dukes or rulers; and, after his father's decease,
began his reign over the whole monarchy of Britain in the
year of the world 3529. He made many good laws, which
were long after used, called Mulmutius' laws, turned out of
the British speech into Latin by Gildas Priscus, and long
time after translated out of Latin into English by Alfred,
King of England, and mingled in his statutes. After he had
established his land, he ordained him, by the advice of his
lords, a crown of gold, and caused himself with great solemnity to be crowned:—and because he was the first that bare
a crown here in Britain, after the opinion of some writers,
he is named the first king of Britain, and all the other
before rehearsed are named rulers, dukes, or governors.
Among other of his ordinances, he appointed weights and
measures, with the which men should buy and sell: and
further, he caused sore and strait orders for the punishment
of theft."

—— " Thou art welcome, Caius.
Thy Cæsar knighted me : my youth I spent
Much under him."—Act III., Scene 1.

Holinshed throws light on this passage also :—" Kymbeline (as some write) was brought up at Rome, and there
was made knight by Augustus Cæsar, under whom he served
in the wars, and was in such favour with him that he was at
liberty to pay his tribute or not.——Yet we find in the
Roman writers, that after Julius Cæsar's death, when Augustus had taken upon him the rule of the empire, the
Britons refused to pay that tribute.——But whether the
controversy which appeared to fall forth between the Britons and Augustus was occasioned by Kymbeline, I have
not a vouch.——Kymbeline reigned thirty-five years, leaving
behind him two sons, Guiderius and Arviragus."

—— " Good wax, thy leave. Blessed be,
You bees, that make these locks of counsel ! Lovers
And men in dangerous bonds pray not alike :
Though forfeiters you cast in prison, yet
You clasp young Cupid's tables."—Act III., Scene 2.

The meaning is, that the bees are not blessed by the man
who is sent to prison for forfeiting a bond, which is sealed
with their product—wax, as they are by lovers, for whom the
same substance performs the more pleasing office of sealing
letters.

—— " What should we speak of,
When we are old as you."—Act III., Scene 3.

This dread of an old age unsupplied with matter for discourse and meditation, is a sentiment natural and noble.
No state can be more destitute than that of him who, when
the delights of sense forsake him, has no pleasures of the
mind.—JOHNSON.

—— " If it be summer news,
Smile to 't before."—Act III., Scene 4.

A similar phrase occurs in the Poet's 98th Sonnet :—

" Yet not the lays of birds, nor the sweet smell
    Of different flowers in odour and in hue,
    Could make me any summer's story tell."

—— " Some jay of Italy,
Whose mother was her painting, hath betrayed him."
Act III., Scene 4.

Meaning, some beauty made by art; the creature, not of
nature, but of painting. " In this sense," says Johnson,
" painting may be not improperly termed her mother."

" *Poor I am stale, a garment out of fashion;*
And, for I am richer than to hang by the walls,
I must be ripped: to pieces with me! "
Act III., Scene 4.

Clothes were not formerly, as at present, made of slight materials; they were not kept in drawers, or given away as soon as lapse of time or change of fashion had impaired their value. On the contrary, they were hung up on wooden pegs, in a room appropriated to the sole purpose of receiving them; and though such cast-off things as were composed of *rich* substances were occasionally *ripped* for domestic uses, articles of inferior quality were suffered to *hang by the wall* till age and moths had destroyed what pride would not permit to be worn by servants or poor relations. When Queen Elizabeth died, she was found to have left above three thousand dresses behind her. Steevens states himself to have seen, at an ancient mansion in Suffolk, one of these dress repositories, which had been preserved with superstitious reverence for almost a century and a half.

" *Come, here's my heart:—*
Something's afore't: soft, soft; we'll no defence."
Act III., Scene 4.

In this passage, we have another of Rowe's happy verbal corrections. The original copy reads, "Something's *afoot*."

" *Hath Britain all the sun that shines? Day, night,*
Are they not but in Britain?"—Act III., Scene 4.

It seems probable that here, as also on a similar occasion in "RICHARD II.," Shakspere had in his thoughts a passage in Lily's "EUPHUES:"—" Nature hath given to no man a country, no more than she hath house, or lands, or living. Plato would never account him banished that had the sun, air, water, and earth, that he had before: where he felt the winter's blast, and the summer's blaze; where the same sun and the same moon shined: whereby he noted that every place was a country to a wise man, and all parts a palace to a quiet mind."

" *True to thee,*
Were to prove false (which I will never be)
To him that is most true."—Act III., Scene 5.

Pisanio, notwithstanding his master's letter commanding the murder of Imogen, considers him true; supposing, as he has already said to her, that Posthumus was abused by some villain, equally an enemy to them both.

" *The bird is dead*
That we have made so much on."
Act IV., Scene 2.

The sweet and wholesome pathos of this scene has been thus noted by Mrs. Radcliffe:—" No master ever knew how to touch the accordant springs of sympathy by small circumstances, like our own Shakspere. In 'CYMBELINE,' for instance, how finely such circumstances are made use of to awaken, at once, solemn expectation and tenderness, and, by recalling the softened remembrance of a sorrow long past, to prepare the mind to melt at one that was approaching; mingling at the same time, by means of a mysterious occurrence, a slight tremor of awe with our pity. Thus, when Belarius and Arviragus return to the cave where they had left the unhappy and worn-out Imogen to repose, while they are yet standing before it, and Arviragus—speaking of her with tenderest pity as 'poor sick Fidele'—goes out to inquire for her, solemn music is heard from the cave, sounded by that harp of which Guiderius says, 'Since the death of my dearest mother, it did not speak before. All solemn things should answer solemn accidents.' Immediately Arviragus enters with Fidele senseless in his arms:—

'*Arv.* The bird is dead that we have made so much on.* * *
Bel. How found you him?
Arv. Stark, as you see: thus smiling.

* * * I thought he slept; and put
My clouted brogues from off my feet, whose rudeness
Answered my steps too loud.
 Gui. Why, he but sleeps. * * *
 Arv. With fairest flowers,
While summer lasts, AND I LIVE HERE, FIDELE,
I'll sweeten thy sad grave.'

Tears alone can speak the touching simplicity of the whole scene."

" *The ruddock would*
With charitable bill."—Act IV., Scene 2.

The ruddock is the redbreast. It is so called by Chaucer and Spenser. The office of covering the dead is likewise ascribed to this bird by Drayton, in his poem called "THE OWL" (1604):—

" Covering with moss the dead's uncloséd eye,
The little redbreast teacheth charity."

" *Reverence*
(That angel of the world)."—Act IV., Scene 2.

Reverence, or due regard to subordination, is the power that keeps peace and order in the world.—JOHNSON.

" *Fear no more the heat o' the sun,*
Nor the furious winter's rages;
Thou thy worldly task hast done,
Home art gone, and ta'en thy wages."
Act IV., Scene 2.

"This," says Warburton, "is the topic of consolation that nature dictates to all men on these occasions. The same farewell we have over the dead body in Lucian."—In the same strain of regret and tender envy, it may be added, Macbeth speaks of his slaughtered victim Duncan: feeling, at the very instant when he should rejoice in the consummation of his wishes, the utter nothingness of perturbed earthly pleasures, when compared with the peaceful slumbers of the innocent dead.

Collins has given an imitation, rather than a version, of this beautiful dirge. It exhibits his usual exquisite taste and felicity of expression, although inferior to the original in condensation and characteristic simplicity:—

" To fair Fidele's grassy tomb
 Soft maids and village hinds shall bring
Each opening sweet of earliest bloom,
 And rifle all the breathing spring.

" No wailing ghost shall dare appear
 To vex with shrieks this quiet grove;
But shepherd lads assemble here,
 And melting virgins own their love.

" No withered witch shall here be seen;
 No goblins lead their nightly crew:
The female fays shall haunt the green,
 And dress thy grave with pearly dew.

" The redbreast oft, at evening hours,
 Shall kindly lend his little aid,
With hoary moss and gathered flowers,
 To deck the ground where thou art laid.

" When howling winds and beating rain
 In tempests shake the sylvan cell;
Or, midst the chase, on every plain,
 The tender thought on thee shall dwell.

" Each lonely scene shall thee restore;
 For thee the tear be truly shed;
Beloved till life can charm no more,
 And mourned till pity's self be dead."

" *Yea, bloody cloth, I'll keep thee; for I wished*
Thou shouldst be coloured thus."—Act V., Scene 1.

The handkerchief spoken of is the token of Imogen's death, which Pisanio, in the foregoing Act, determined to send to Posthumus.—This is a soliloquy of nature, uttered when the effervescence of a mind agitated, and perturbed, spontaneously and inadvertently discharges itself in words. The speech, throughout all its tenour, if the last conceit be excepted, seems to issue warm from the heart. He first condemns his own violence; then tries to disburden himself, by imputing part of the crime to Pisanio; he next soothes his mind to an artificial and momentary tranquillity, by trying to think that he has been only an instrument of the gods for the happiness of Imogen. He is now grown reasonable enough to determine that, having done so much evil, he will do no more; that he will not fight against the country which he has already injured; but, as life is not longer supportable, he will die in a just cause, and die with the obscurity of a man who does not think himself worthy to be remembered.—JOHNSON.

> —— " *Athwart the lane,*
> *He, with two striplings (lads more like to run*
> *The country base than to commit such slaughter).*"
> Act V., Scene 3.

This stoppage of the Roman army by three persons is probably an allusion to the story of the Hays, as related by Holinshed, in his " HISTORY OF SCOTLAND :"—

" There was, near to the place of the battle, a long lane, fenced on the sides with ditches and walls made of turf, through the which the Scots which fled were beaten down by the enemies on heaps. Here Hay, with his sons, supposing they might best stay the flight, placed themselves overthwart the lane, beat them back whom they met fleeing, and spared neither friend nor foe, but down they went all such as came within their reach; wherewith divers hardy personages cried unto their fellows to return back unto the battle."

> " JUPITER *descends in thunder and lightning.*"
> Act V., Scene 4.

It appears from "ACOLASTUS," a comedy by T. Palsgrave, chaplain to King Henry VIII. (bl. l. 1540), that the descent of deities was common to our stage in its earliest state :—" Of which the like thing is used to be shewed now-a-days in stage-plays, when some god or some saint is made to appear forth of a cloud, and succoureth the parties which seemed to be towards some great danger through the Soudan's cruelty."

In reference to this scene of the apparitions, Schlegel ingeniously reasons thus :—" Pope, as is well known, w. strongly disposed to declare whole scenes to be interpolations of the players; but his opinions were not much listened to. However, Steevens still accedes to the opinion of Pope, respecting the apparition of the ghosts and of Jupiter in Cymbeline, while Posthumus is sleeping in the dungeon. But Posthumus finds, on waking, a tablet on his breast, with a prophecy on which the *dénouement* of the piece depends. Is it to be imagined that Shakspere would require of his spectators the belief in a wonder without a visible cause? Is Posthumus to dream this tablet with the prophecy? But these gentlemen do not descend to this objection. The verses which the apparitions deliver do not appear to them good enough to be Shakspere's. I imagine I can discover why the Poet has not given them more of the splendour of diction. They are the aged parents and brothers of Posthumus, who, from concern for his fate, return from the world below: they ought, consequently, to speak the language of more simple olden time, and their voices ought also to appear as a feeble sound of wailing, when contrasted with the thundering oracular language of Jupiter. For this reason, Shakspere chose a syllabic measure, which was very common before his time, but which was then getting out of fashion, though it still continued to be frequently used, especially in translations of classical poets. In some such

manner might the shades express themselves in the then existing translations of Homer and Virgil. The speech of Jupiter is, on the other hand, majestic; and in form and style bears a complete resemblance to the Sonnets of Shakspere."

> " *Why did you throw your wedded lady from you?*
> *Think that you are upon a rock; and now*
> *Throw me again.*"—Act V., Scene 5.

On this little loving incident a pleasant comment has been written by Mr. Pye:—" Imogen comes up to Posthumus, as soon as she knows that the error is cleared up; and, hanging fondly on him, says (not as upbraiding him, but with kindness and good-humour), ' How could you treat your wife thus?'—in that endearing tone which most readers who are fathers and husbands will understand, who will add *poor* to *wife*. She then adds, ' Now you know who I am, suppose we were on the edge of a precipice, and throw me from you:'—meaning, in the same endearing irony, to say, ' I am sure it is as impossible for you to be intentionally unkind to me, as it is for you to kill me.' Perhaps some very wise persons may smile at part of this note: but however much black-letter books may be necessary to elucidate Shakspere, there are others which require some acquaintance with those familiar pages of the book of nature,

> ' Which learning may not understand,
> And wisdom may disdain to hear.' "

———

Something approaching to an adequate eulogy is also given by Schlegel to the general merits of "CYMBELINE." He pronounces it to be "one of Shakspere's most wonderful compositions, in which the Poet has contrived to blend together, into one harmonious whole, the social manners of the latest times with heroic deeds, and even with appearances of the gods. In the character of Imogen not a feature of female excellence is forgotten :—her chaste tenderness, her softness, and her virgin pride; her boundless resignation, and her magnanimity towards her mistaken husband, by whom she is unjustly persecuted; her adventures in disguise, her apparent death, and her recovery,—form altogether a picture equally tender and affecting.

" The two princes, Guiderius and Arviragus, both educated in the wilds, form a noble contrast to Miranda and Perdita. In these two young men, to whom the chase has imparted vigour and hardihood, but who are unacquainted with their high destination, and have always been kept far from human society, we are enchanted by a *naïve* heroism, which leads them to anticipate and to dream of deeds of valour, till an occasion is offered which they are irresistibly impelled to embrace. When Imogen comes in disguise to their cave; when Guiderius and Arviragus form an impassioned friendship, with all the innocence of childhood, for the tender boy (in whom they neither suspect a female nor their own sister); when, on returning from the chase, they find her dead, sing her to the ground, and cover the grave with flowers;—these scenes might give a new life for poetry to the most deadened imagination.

" The wise and virtuous Belarius, who, after living long as a hermit, again becomes a hero, is a venerable figure;—the dexterous dissimulation and quick presence of mind of the Italian, Iachimo, is quite suitable to the bold treachery he plays;—Cymbeline, the father of Imogen (and even her husband, Posthumus), during the first half of the piece, are somewhat sacrificed, but this could not be otherwise;—the false and wicked Queen is merely an instrument of the plot; she and her stupid son Cloten, whose rude arrogance is pourtrayed with much humour, are got rid of, by merited punishment, before the conclusion."

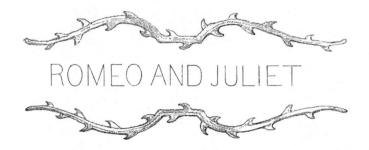

ROMEO AND JULIET

OVE, the universal inspirer of poetry and enthusiasm, has found in the young, impassioned Capulet and Montague, the truest exponents of his divinest and profoundest oracles. Their names are identified with his purest, most fervid worship; and "Juliet and her Romeo" can never die while sympathy controls the youthful heart, or glorious intellect asserts its genial sway o'er all mankind. Victims to the senseless feuds of their families, the lovers perish like twin roses in a tempest; but the memory of their transient passion, their keen delights and keener agonies, embalmed in Shakspere's verse, is destined to flourish, fragrant and immortal.

To relieve the weight of woe that this sad tale of blighted love is calculated to engender, the generous Poet, pursuing his usual plan of shewing human life in all its phases, has conjured up the sprightly antidote, Mercutio: "a fellow" certainly "of infinite jest, of most excellent fancy;" but, unluckily, as ready for a fray as even the fiery and brutal Tybalt. Their encounter is the bitter spring from whence flow Romeo's banishment, and all the suffering of the gentle, hapless pair:—even as the harmless, glittering pinnace, freighted with joy and beauty, perishes by a random shot, from its unsought proximity to two contending burly ships of war.—Peace, however, to the brave Mercutio: he meets his early fate with characteristic gaiety; and, remembering his riotous spirits, and glowing picture of Queen Mab, it is impossible to think of him as "a grave man," despite his own prediction to the contrary.

The Friar, like others of his profession, as delineated by Shakspere, presents a grateful relief to the perturbed and clashing elements at work around him. He looks with compassionate interest on the woes and contentions of active life,—its fierce and feverish alternations,—from which the rules of his order, and his own calm good sense, alike contribute to secure himself. The freshness of innocence and early day seems odorous to the moral sense, in the cell soliloquy, when, in his own sweet phrase,—

> " The grey-eyed morn smiles on the frowning night,
> Checkering the eastern clouds with streaks of light,"—

And the benevolent Friar goes forth to moralise, and to collect his medicinal herbs and precious flowers,—

> " Now ere the sun advance his burning eye,
> The day to cheer, and night's dank dew to dry."

In the Nurse, we have an instance of the falseness of those conventional and stilted notions that would confine the language of tragedy to eminent persons and sounding rhythm. The garrulity and coarseness of this ignorant, half-kind, half-selfish old crone, bring out with double force the grace and purity that wait on Juliet.—The numerous other subordinate characters of the drama, are all essential to the plot, and, whether grave or gay, are invariably supported with unflagging spirit.

There were several separate editions of "ROMEO AND JULIET," previous to its appearance in the original folio. The first was published in 1597, with this title: "An excellent conceited Tragedie of Romeo and Juliet. As it hath been often (with great applause) plaid publiquely by the Right Hon. the L. of Hunsdon his seruants." The second edition appeared in 1599, "Newly corrected, augmented, and amended." There were also three other separate editions, all mainly founded on that of 1599. In addition to these strongest evidences of public liking, a passage in Marston's tenth satire (1599) tends to shew that the play at once acquired that unbounded popularity which has ever since attended it :—

> " Luscus, what's played to-night?—I' faith, now I know :
> I see thy lips abroach, from whence doth flow
> Nought but pure Juliet and Romeo."

Lord Byron states that, " Of the truth of Juliet's story, they," the Veronese, " seem tenacious to a degree ; insisting on the fact, giving a date (1303), and shewing a tomb. It is a plain, open, and partly decayed sarcophagus, with withered leaves in it, in a wild and desolate conventual garden, once a cemetery, now ruined to the very graves."—Some mention will be found in the Notes, of the various sources from which the Poet derived suggestions for the plot of this great effort of dramatic genius.

PERSONS REPRESENTED.

ESCALUS, Prince of VERONA.
PARIS, a young Nobleman, Kinsman to the Prince.
MONTAGUE, } Heads of two Houses, at variance
CAPULET, } with each other.
An Old Man, Uncle to CAPULET.
ROMEO, Son to MONTAGUE.
MERCUTIO, Kinsman to the Prince, and Friend
    to ROMEO.
BENVOLIO, Nephew to MONTAGUE, and Friend
    to ROMEO.
TYBALT, Nephew to LADY CAPULET.
FRIAR LAURENCE, a Franciscan.
FRIAR JOHN, of the same order.
BALTHASAR, Servant to ROMEO.
SAMPSON, }
GREGORY, } Servants to CAPULET.
PETER, }
ABRAM, Servant to MONTAGUE.
An Apothecary.
Three Musicians.
Chorus.
Boy.
Page to PARIS.
An Officer.

LADY MONTAGUE, Wife to MONTAGUE.
LADY CAPULET, Wife to CAPULET.
JULIET, Daughter to CAPULET.
Nurse to JULIET.

Citizens of VERONA: several Men and Women,
    relations to both Houses; Maskers, Guards,
    Watchmen, and Attendants.

———

SCENE. During the greater part of the play, in
    VERONA; once, in the Fifth Act, at MANTUA.

PROLOGUE

Two households, both alike in dignity,
 In fair Verona, where we lay our scene,
From ancient grudge break to new mutiny,
 Where civil blood makes civil hands unclean.
From forth the fatal loins of these two foes
 A pair of star-crossed lovers take their life;
Whose misadventured piteous overthrows
 Do, with their death, bury their parents' strife.—
The fearful passage of their death-marked love,
 And the continuance of their parents' rage,
Which, but their children's end, nought could remove,
 Is now the two hours' traffick of our stage;
The which, if you with patient ears attend,
What here shall miss, our toil shall strive to mend.

ROMEO AND JULIET.

ACT

SCENE I.—*A public Place.*

Enter SAMPSON *and* GREGORY, *armed with swords and bucklers.*

Sam. Gregory, o' my word, we'll not carry coals.

Gre. No, for then we should be colliers.

Sam. I mean, an we be in choler, we'll draw.

Gre. Ay, while you live draw your neck out of the collar.

Sam. I strike quickly, being moved.

Gre. But thou art not quickly moved to strike.

Sam. A dog of the house of Montague moves me.

Gre. To move, is to stir; and to be valiant, is to stand: therefore, if thou art moved, thou runn'st away.

Sam. A dog of that house shall move me to stand: I will take the wall of any man or maid of Montague's.

Gre. That shews thee a weak slave; for the weakest goes to the wall.

Sam. True; and therefore women, being the weaker vessels, are ever thrust to the wall:— therefore I will push Montague's men from the wall, and thrust his maids to the wall.

Gre. The quarrel is between our masters, and us their men.

Sam. 'T is all one; I will shew myself a tyrant:

when I have fought with the men, I will be cruel
with the maids; I will cut off their heads.

Gre. The heads of the maids?

Sam. Ay, the heads of the maids, or their
maidenheads: take it in what sense thou wilt.

Gre. They must take it in sense, that feel it.

Sam. Me they shall feel, while I am able to
stand: and 't is known I am a pretty piece of
flesh.

Gre. 'T is well thou art not fish: if thou hadst,
thou hadst been Poor John. Draw thy tool; here
comes two of the house of the Montagues.

Enter ABRAM *and* BALTHASAR.

Sam. My naked weapon is out: quarrel; I will
back thee.

Gre. How? turn thy back, and run?

Sam. Fear me not.

Gre. No, marry.—I fear thee!

Sam. Let us take the law of our sides; let
them begin.

Gre. I will frown as I pass by; and let them
take it as they list.

Sam. Nay, as they dare. I will bite my
thumb at them; which is a disgrace to them, if
they bear it.

Abr. Do you bite your thumb at us, sir?

Sam. I do bite my thumb, sir.

Abr. Do you bite your thumb at us, sir?

Sam. Is the law on our side, if I say "Ay?"

Gre. No.

Sam. No, sir, I do not bite my thumb at you,
sir; but I bite my thumb, sir.

Gre. Do you quarrel, sir?

Abr. Quarrel, sir? no, sir.

Sam. If you do, sir, I am for you: I serve as
good a man as you.

Abr. No better.

Sam. Well, sir.

Enter BENVOLIO, *at a distance.*

Gre. Say—better: here comes one of my
master's kinsmen.

Sam. Yes, better.

Abr. You lie.

Sam. Draw, if you be men.—Gregory, remember thy swashing blow.   [*They fight.*

Ben. Part, fools; put up your swords; you know not what you do. [*Beats down their swords.*

Enter TYBALT.

Tyb. What, art thou drawn among these heartless hinds?

Turn thee, Benvolio, look upon thy death.

Ben. I do but keep the peace: put up thy sword,

Or manage it to part these men with me.

Tyb. What, draw, and talk of peace? I hate the word,

As I hate hell, all Montagues, and thee:

Have at thee, coward!   [*They fight.*

Enter several Partisans *of both houses, who join the fray: then enter* Citizens, *with clubs.*

1st Cit. Clubs, bills, and partizans! strike! beat them down!

Down with the Capulets!—down with the Montagues!

Enter CAPULET, *in his gown;* and LADY CAPULET.

Cap. What noise is this?—Give me my long-sword, ho!

Lady C. A crutch, a crutch!—Why call you for a sword?

Cap. My sword, I say!—Old Montague is come,

And flourishes his blade in spite of me.

Enter MONTAGUE *and* LADY MONTAGUE.

Mon. Thou villain, Capulet!—Hold me not; let me go.

Lady M. Thou shalt not stir a foot to seek a foe.

Enter PRINCE, *with* Attendants.

Prin. Rebellious subjects, enemies to peace,

Profaners of this neighbour-stainéd steel,—

Will they not hear?—What, ho! you men, you beasts,

That quench the fire of your pernicious rage

With purple fountains issuing from your veins!

On pain of torture, from those bloody hands

Throw your mistempered weapons to the ground,

And hear the sentence of your movéd Prince.—

Three civil brawls, bred of an airy word,

By thee, old Capulet and Montague,

Have thrice disturbed the quiet of our streets;

And made Verona's ancient citizens

Cast by their grave beseeming ornaments,

To wield old partizans, in hands as old,

Cankered with peace, to part your cankered hate:

If ever you disturb our streets again,

Your lives shall pay the forfeit of the peace.

For this time, all the rest depart away:

You, Capulet, shall go along with me;

And, Montague, come you this afternoon,

To know our farther pleasure in this case,

To old Free-town, our common judgment-place.

Once more, on pain of death, all men depart.

[*Exeunt* PRINCE *and* Attendants; CAPULET, LADY CAPULET, TYBALT, Citizens, *and* Servants.

Mon. Who set this ancient quarrel new abroach?—

Speak, nephew, were you by when it began?

Ben. Here were the servants of your adversary,

And yours, close fighting ere I did approach:

I drew to part them: in the instant came

The fiery Tybalt, with his sword prepared;

Which, as he breathed defiance to my ears,

He swung about his head, and cut the winds,

Who, nothing hurt withal, hissed him in scorn:

While we were interchanging thrusts and blows,

Came more and more, and fought on part and part,

Till the Prince came, who parted either part.

Lady M. O, where is Romeo?—saw you him to-day?

Right glad am I he was not at this fray.

Ben. Madam, an hour before the worshipped sun

Peered forth the golden window of the east,

A troubled mind drave me to walk abroad;

Where, underneath the grove of sycamore

That westward rooteth from the city's side,

So early walking did I see your son:

Towards him I made; but he was 'ware of me,

And stole into the covert of the wood:

I, measuring his affections by my own,

That most are busied when they are most alone,

Pursued my humour, not pursuing his,

And gladly shunned who gladly fled from me.

Mon. Many a morning hath he there been seen,

With tears augmenting the fresh morning's dew,

Adding to clouds more clouds with his deep sighs:

But all so soon as the all-cheering sun

Should in the farthest east begin to draw

The shady curtains from Aurora's bed,

Away from light steals home my heavy son,

And private in his chamber pens himself;

Shuts up his windows, locks fair daylight out,

And makes himself an artificial night.

Black and portentous must this humour prove,

Unless good counsel may the cause remove.

Ben. My noble uncle, do you know the cause?

Mon. I neither know it, nor can learn of him.

Ben. Have you impórtuned him by any means?

Mon. Both by myself and many other friends:

But he, his own affections' counsellor,

Is to himself—I will not say, how true—

But to himself so secret and so close,

So far from sounding and discovery,

As is the bud bit with an envious worm,
Ere he can spread his sweet leaves to the air,
Or dedicate his beauty to the sun.
Could we but learn from whence his sorrows grow,
We would as willingly give cure as know.

Enter Romeo, *at a distance.*

Ben. See where he comes: so please you,
    step aside;
I 'll know his grievance, or be much denied.

Mon. I would thou wert so happy by thy stay,
To hear true shrift.—Come, madam, let 's away.
    [*Exeunt* Montague *and* Lady Montague.

Ben. Good morrow, cousin.

Rom.   Is the day so young?

Ben. But new struck nine.

Rom.   Ah me! sad hours seem long.
Was that my father that went hence so fast?

Ben. It was. What sadness lengthens Romeo's
    hours?

Rom. Not having that which, having, makes
    them short.

Ben. In love?

Rom. Out—

Ben. Of love?

Rom. Out of her favour where I am in love.

Ben. Alas, that love, so gentle in his view,
Should be so tyrannous and rough in proof!

Rom. Alas, that love, whose view is muffled still,
Should without eyes see pathways to his will!
Where shall we dine?—O me!—What fray was
    here?
Yet tell me not, for I have heard it all.
Here 's much to do with hate, but more with love:
Why then, O brawling love! O loving hate!
O anything, of nothing first create!
O heavy lightness! serious vanity!
Misshapen chaos of well-seeming forms!
Feather of lead, bright smoke, cold fire, sick health!
Still-waking sleep, that is not what it is!
This love feel I, that feel no love in this.—
Dost thou not laugh?

Ben.   No, coz, I rather weep.

Rom. Good heart, at what?

Ben.   At thy good heart's oppression.

Rom. Why, such is love's trangression.
Griefs of mine own lie heavy in my breast;
Which thou wilt propagate, to have it prest
With more of thine: this love that thou hast
    shewn
Doth add more grief to too much of mine own.
Love is a smoke raised with the fume of sighs;
Being purged, a fire sparkling in lovers' eyes;
Being vexed, a sea nourished with lovers' tears:
What is it else? a madness most discreet,
A choking gall, and a preserving sweet.
Farewell, my coz.   [*Going.*

Ben.   Soft, I will go along:
An if you leave me so, you do me wrong.

Rom. Tut, I have lost myself; I am not here;
This is not Romeo; he 's some other where.

Ben. Tell me in sadness, who she is you love.

Rom. What, shall I groan, and tell thee?

Ben.   Groan? why, no;
But sadly tell me who.

Rom. Bid a sick man in sadness make his will:—
Ah, word ill urged to one that is so ill!
In sadness, cousin, I do love a woman.

Ben. I aimed so near when I supposed you loved.

Rom. A right good marksman!—And she 's
    fair I love.

Ben. A right fair mark, fair coz, is soonest hit.

Rom. Well, in that hit you miss: she 'll not be hit
With Cupid's arrow: she hath Dian's wit;
And, in strong proof of chastity well armed,
From love's weak childish bow she lives un-
    harmed.
She will not stay the siege of loving terms,
Nor bide the encounter of assailing eyes,
Nor ope her lap to saint-seducing gold.
O, she is rich in beauty: only poor,
That, when she dies, with beauty dies her store!

Ben. Then she hath sworn that she will still
    live chaste?

Rom. She hath; and in that sparing makes
    huge waste:
For beauty, starved with her severity,
Cuts beauty off from all posterity.
She is too fair, too wise, wisely too fair,
To merit bliss by making me despair:
She hath forsworn to love; and in that vow
Do I live dead, that live to tell it now.

Ben. Be ruled by me; forget to think of her.

Rom. O, teach me how I should forget to think.

Ben. By giving liberty unto thine eyes:
Examine other beauties.

Rom.   'T is the way
To call her's, exquisite, in question more.
These happy masks that kiss fair ladies' brows,
Being black, put us in mind they hide the fair:
He that is strucken blind, cannot forget
The precious treasure of his eyesight lost:
Shew me a mistress that is passing fair,
What doth her beauty serve, but as a note
Where I may read who passed that passing fair?
Farewell: thou canst not teach me to forget.

Ben. I 'll pay that doctrine, or else die in debt.
    [*Exeunt.*

Scene II.—*A Street.*

Enter Capulet, Paris, *and* Servant.

Cap. And Montague is bound as well as I,

In penalty alike; and 't is not hard, I think,
For men so old as we to keep the peace.

Par. Of honourable reckoning are you both;
And pity 't is you lived at odds so long.
But now, my lord, what say you to my suit?

Cap. But saying o'er what I have said before:
My child is yet a stranger in the world,
She hath not seen the change of fourteen years:
Let two more summers wither in their pride,
Ere we may think her ripe to be a bride.

Par. Younger than she are happy mothers made.

Cap. And too soon marred are those so early
made.
The earth hath swallowed all my hopes but she;
She is the hopeful lady of my earth.
But woo her, gentle Paris, get her heart;
My will to her consent is but a part:
An she agree, within her scope of choice
Lies my consent and fair according voice.
This night I hold an old accustomed feast,
Whereto I have invited many a guest,
Such as I love: and you, among the store,
One more, most welcome, makes my number more.
At my poor house look to behold this night
Earth-treading stars, that make dark heaven light.
Such comfort as do lusty young men feel
When well-apparelled April on the heel
Of limping winter treads, even such delight
Among fresh female buds shall you this night
Inherit at my house: hear all, all see,
And like her most whose merit most shall be:
Such, amongst view of many, mine, being one,
May stand in number, though in reckoning none.
Come, go with me.—Go, sirrah, trudge about
Through fair Verona; find those persons out
Whose names are written there [*gives a paper*],
and to them say,
My house and welcome on their pleasure stay.
[*Exeunt* CAPULET *and* PARIS.

Serv. Find them out whose names are written
here? It is written that the shoemaker should
meddle with his yard, and the tailor with his
last, the fisher with his pencil, and the painter
with his nets; but I am sent to find those persons
whose names are here writ, and can never find
what names the writing person hath here writ.
I must to the learned:—In good time.

Enter BENVOLIO *and* ROMEO.

Ben. Tut, man! one fire burns out another's
burning,
One pain is lessened by another's anguish;
Turn giddy, and be holp by backward turning;
One desperate grief cures with another's lan-
guish:
Take thou some new infection to thy eye,
And the rank poison of the old will die.

Rom. Your plaintain leaf is excellent for that.

Ben. For what, I pray thee?

Rom.   For your broken shin.

Ben. Why, Romeo, art thou mad?

Rom. Not mad, but bound more than a madman is:
Shut up in prison, kept without my food,
Whipped and tormented, and—Good-e'en, good
fellow.

Serv. God gi' good-e'en. I pray, sir, can you
read?

Rom. Ay, mine own fortune in my misery.

Serv. Perhaps you have learned it without book:
But I pray, can you read anything you see?

Rom. Ay, if I know the letters and the language.

Serv. Ye say honestly: rest you merry!

Rom. Stay, fellow: I can read.

Reads.

Signior Martino, and his wife and daughters;
County Anselme and his beauteous sisters; the lady
widow of Vitruvio; Signior Placentio and his lovely
nieces; Mercutio and his brother Valentine; mine
uncle Capulet, his wife and daughters; my fair niece
Rosaline; Livia; Signior Valentio and his cousin
Tybalt: Lucio, and the lively Helena.

A fair assembly [*gives back the note*]. Whither
should they come?

Serv. Up.

Rom. Whither?

Serv. To supper; to our house.

Rom. Whose house?

Serv. My master's.

Rom. Indeed I should have asked you that
before.

Serv. Now I 'll tell you without asking: my
master is the great rich Capulet; and if you be
not of the house of Montagues, I pray come and
crush a cup of wine. Rest you merry. [*Exit.*

Ben. At this same ancient feast of Capulet's
Sups the fair Rosaline, whom thou so lov'st;
With all the admiréd beauties of Verona:
Go thither; and, with unattainted eye,
Compare her face with some that I shall shew,
And I will make thee think thy swan a crow.

Rom. When the devout religion of mine eye
Maintains such falsehood, then turn tears to fires!
And these—who, often drowned, could never die—
Transparent heretics, be burnt for liars!
One fairer than my love!—the all-seeing sun
Ne'er saw her match, since first the world begun.

Ben. Tut! you saw her fair, none else being by;
Herself poised with herself in either eye:
But in those crystal scales, let there be weighed
Your lady-love against some other maid
That I will shew you, shining at this feast,
And she shall scant shew well, that now shews best.

Rom. I 'll go along, no such sight to be shewn,
But to rejoice in splendour of mine own. [*Exeunt.*

SCENE III.—*A Room in* CAPULET's *House.*

Enter LADY CAPULET, *and* Nurse.

Lady C. Nurse, where 's my daughter? call
  her forth to me.
Nurse. Now, by my maidenhead—at twelve
  years old—
I bade her come.—What, lamb! what, lady-
  bird !—
God forbid !—where 's this girl? what, Juliet!

Enter JULIET.

Jul. How now; who calls?
Nurse.   Your mother.
Jul.   Madam, I am here.
What is your will ?
  Lady C. This is the matter :—Nurse, give
    leave awhile;
We must talk in secret.—Nurse, come back
  again ;
I have remembered me, thou shalt hear our
  counsel.
Thou know'st my daughter 's of a pretty age.
  Nurse. 'Faith, I can tell her age unto an hour.
  Lady C. She 's not fourteen.
  Nurse. I 'll lay fourteen of my teeth—
And yet, to my teen be it spoken, I have but
  four—
She is not fourteen.   How long is it now
To Lammas-tide?
  Lady C.   A fortnight and odd days.
  Nurse. Even or odd, of all days in the year,
Come Lammas-eve at night, shall she be four-
  teen.
Susan and she—God rest all Christian souls !—
Were of an age.—Well, Susan is with God ;
She was too good for me :—but, as I said,
On Lammas-eve at night, shall she be fourteen ;
That shall she, marry ; I remember it well.
'T is since the earthquake now eleven years ;
And she was weaned—I never shall forget it—
Of all the days of the year, upon that day :
For I had then laid wormwood to my dug,
Sitting in the sun under the dovehouse wall ;
My lord and you were then at Mantua :—
Nay, I do bear a brain :—but, as I said,
When it did taste the wormwood on the nipple
Of my dug, and felt it bitter, pretty fool !
To see it tetchy, and fall out with the dug.
" Shake," quoth the dovehouse : 't was no need,
  I trow,
To bid me trudge.

And since that time it is eleven years :
For then she could stand alone ; nay, by the rood,
She could have run and waddled all about.
For even the day before, she broke her brow :
And then my husband—God be with his soul !
'A was a merry man—took up the child :
" Yea," quoth he, " dost thou fall upon thy face?
Thou wilt fall backward when thou hast more
  wit;
Wilt thou not, Jule?" and, by my holy-dam,
The pretty wretch left crying, and said "Ay :"
To see now, how a jest shall come about!
I warrant, an I should live a thousand years,
I never should forget it : "Wilt thou not, Jule?"
  quoth he :
And, pretty fool, it stinted, and said "Ay."
  Lady C. Enough of this; I pray thee hold thy
    peace.
  Nurse. Yes, madam ; yet I cannot choose but
    laugh
To think it should leave crying, and say "Ay :"
And yet, I warrant, it had upon its brow
A bump as big as a young cockrel's stone :
A parlous knock ; and it cried bitterly.
" Yea," quoth my husband, " fall'st upon thy
  face?
Thou wilt fall backward when thou com'st to
  age ;
Wilt thou not, Jule?" it stinted, and said "Ay."
  Jul. And stint thou too, I pray thee, nurse,
    say I.
  Nurse. Peace ; I have done. God mark thee
    to His grace !
Thou wast the prettiest babe that e'er I nursed :
An I might live to see thee married once,
I have my wish.
  Lady C. Marry, that marry is the very theme
I came to talk of.—Tell me, daughter Juliet,
How stands your disposition to be married?
  Jul. It is an honour that I dream not of.
  Nurse. An honour! were not I thine only
    nurse,
I 'd say thou hadst sucked wisdom from thy
    teat.
  Lady C. Well, think of marriage now : younger
    than you,
Here in Verona, ladies of esteem,
Are made already mothers : by my count,
I was your mother much upon these years
That you are now a maid.   Thus then, in brief :
The valiant Paris seeks you for his love.
  Nurse. A man, young lady ! lady, such a man,
As all the world—why, he 's a man of wax.
  Lady C. Verona's summer hath not such a
    flower.
  Nurse. Nay, he 's a flower ; in faith, a very
    flower.

And, pretty fool, it stinted, and said " Ay."

Lady C. What say you? can you love the
  gentleman?
This night you shall behold him at our feast;
Read o'er the volume of young Paris' face,
And find delight writ there with beauty's pen;
Examine every married lineament,
And see how one another lends content;
And what obscured in this fair volume lies,
Find written in the margin of his eyes.
This precious book of love, this unbound lover,
To beautify him, only lacks a cover:
The fish lives in the sea; and 't is much pride
For fair without the fair within to hide:
That book in many 's eyes doth share the glory,
That in gold clasps locks in the golden story;
So shall you share all that he doth possess,
By having him, making yourself no less.

Nurse. No less? nay, bigger; women grow by
  men.
Lady C. Speak briefly, can you like of Paris'
  love?
Jul. I 'll look to like, if looking liking move:
But no more deep will I endart mine eye
Than your consent gives strength to make it
  fly.

Enter a Servant.

Serv. Madam, the guests are come, supper
served up, you called, my young lady asked for,
the nurse cursed in the pantry, and everything
in extremity. I must hence to wait: I beseech
you, follow straight.
Lady C. We follow thee.—Juliet, the County
  stays.

Nurse. Go, girl, seek happy nights to happy
   days.   [*Exeunt.*

Scene IV.—*A Street.*

Enter Romeo, Mercutio, Benvolio, *with five
or six* Maskers, Torchbearers, *and others.*

  Rom. What, shall this speech be spoke for our
    excuse?
Or shall we on without apology?
  Ben. The date is out of such prolixity.
We 'll have no Cupid hoodwinked with a scarf,
Bearing a Tartar's painted bow of lath,
Scaring the ladies like a crowkeeper;
Nor no without-book prologue, faintly spoke
After the prompter,—for our entrance:
But, let them measure us by what they will,
We 'll measure them a measure, and be gone.
  Rom. Give me a torch: I am not for this am-
    bling:
Being but heavy, I will bear the light.
  Mer. Nay, gentle Romeo, we must have you
    dance.
  Rom. Not I, believe me: you have dancing-shoes,
With nimble soles: I have a soul of lead,
So stakes me to the ground, I cannot move.
  Mer. You are a lover: borrow Cupid's wings,
And soar with them above a common bound.
  Rom. I am too sore empiercéd with his shaft,
To soar with his light feathers; and so bound,
I cannot bound a pitch above dull woe:
Under love's heavy burden do I sink.
  Mer. And, to sink in it, should you burden love:
Too great oppression for a tender thing.
  Rom. Is love a tender thing? it is too rough,
Too rude, too boisterous; and it pricks like thorn.
  Mer. If love be rough with you, be rough with
    love:
Prick love for pricking, and you beat love down.—
Give me a case to put my visage in.
                 [*Putting on a mask.*
A visor for a visor!—what care I
What curious eye doth quote deformities?
Here are the beetle-brows shall blush for me.
  Ben. Come, knock, and enter; and no sooner in,
But every man betake him to his legs.
  Rom. A torch for me: let wantons, light of
    heart,
Tickle the senseless rushes with their heels;
For I am proverbed with a grandsire phrase,—
I 'll be a candle-holder, and look on;—
The game was ne'er so fair, and I am done.
  Mer. Tut! dun's the mouse, the constable's own
    word:
If thou art dun, we 'll draw thee from the mire

Of this (save reverence) love, wherein thou stick'st
Up to the ears.—Come, we burn daylight, ho.
  Rom. Nay, that 's not so.
  Mer.   I mean, sir, in delay
We waste our lights in vain, like lamps by day.
Take our good meaning; for our judgment sits
Five times in that, ere once in our five wits.
  Rom. And we mean well, in going to this mask;
But 't is no wit to go.
  Mer.   Why, may one ask?
  Rom. I dreamt a dream to-night.
  Mer.   And so did I.
  Rom. Well, what was yours?
  Mer. That dreamers often lie.
  Rom. In bed, asleep, while they do dream things
    true.
  Mer. O, then, I see, Queen Mab hath been with
    you.
She is the fairies' midwife; and she comes
In shape no bigger than an agate-stone
On the forefinger of an alderman,
Drawn with a team of little atomies
Athwart men's noses as they lie asleep:
Her wagon-spokes made of long spinners' legs;
The cover, of the wings of grasshoppers;
The traces, of the smallest spider's web;
The collars, of the moonshine's watery beams:
Her whip of cricket's bone; the lash, of film:
Her wagoner, a small grey-coated gnat,
Not half so big as a round little worm
Pricked from the lazy finger of a maid:
Her chariot is an empty hazel-nut,
Made by the joiner squirrel, or old grub,
Time out of mind the fairies' coach-makers.
And in this state she gallops night by night
Through lovers' brains, and then they dream of
    love:
On courtiers' knees, that dream on court'sies
    straight:
O'er lawyers' fingers, who straight dream on fees:
O'er ladies' lips, who straight on kisses dream;
Which oft the angry Mab with blisters plagues,
Because their breaths with sweetmeats tainted are.
Sometimes she gallops o'er a courtier's nose,
And then dreams he of smelling out a suit:
And sometimes comes she with a tithe-pig's tail,
Tickling a parson's nose as 'a lies asleep,
Then dreams he of another benefice:
Sometimes she driveth o'er a soldier's neck,
And then dreams he of cutting foreign throats,
Of breaches, ambuscadoes, Spanish blades,
Of healths five fathom deep; and then anon
Drums in his ear; at which he starts, and
    wakes;
And, being thus frighted, swears a prayer or two,
And sleeps again. This is that very Mab
That plats the manes of horses in the night;

And bakes the elf-locks in foul sluttish hairs,
Which, once untangled, much misfortune bodes.
This is the hag, when maids lie on their backs,
That presses them, and learns them first to bear,
Making them women of good carriage.
This is she—
 Rom.   Peace, peace, Mercutio, peace;
Thou talk'st of nothing.
 Mer.   True, I talk of dreams,
Which are the children of an idle brain,
Begot of nothing but vain fantasy;
Which is as thin of substance as the air;
And more inconstant than the wind, who wooes
Even now the frozen bosom of the north,
And, being angered, puffs away from thence,
Turning his face to the dew-dropping south.
 Ben. This wind you talk of, blows us from
   ourselves:
Supper is done, and we shall come too late.
 Rom. I fear, too early: for my mind misgives,
Some consequence, yet hanging in the stars,
Shall bitterly begin his fearful date
With this night's revels; and expire the term
Of a despiséd life, closed in my breast,
By some vile forfeit of untimely death:
But He that hath the steerage of my course,
Direct my sail!—On, lusty gentlemen.
 Ben. Strike, drum.   [*Exeunt.*

SCENE V.—*A Hall in* CAPULET's *House.*

Musicians *waiting.* *Enter* Servants.

 1st Serv. Where's Potpan, that he helps not
to take away? He shift a trencher! he scrape a
trencher!
 2nd Serv. When good manners shall lie all in
one or two men's hands, and they unwashed too,
't is a foul thing.
 1st Serv. Away with the joint-stools, remove
the court-cupboard, look to the plate:—good
thou, save me a piece of marchpane; and, as
thou lovest me, let the porter let in Susan Grind-
stone and Nell.—Antony and Potpan!
 2nd Serv. Ay, boy; ready.
 1st Serv. You are looked for and called for,
asked for and sought for, in the great chamber.
 2nd Serv. We cannot be here and there too.
—Cheerly, boys; be brisk a while, and the longer
liver take all.   [*They retire behind.*

Enter CAPULET, *&c., with the* Guests *and the*
Maskers.

 Cap. Welcome, gentlemen! ladies that have
   their toes
Unplagued with corns will have a bout with you:—

Ah ha, my mistresses! which of you all
Will now deny to dance? she that makes dainty, she
I'll swear hath corns:—am I come near you now?
You are welcome, gentlemen! I have seen the
   day
That I have worn a visor, and could tell
A whispering tale in a fair lady's ear,
Such as would please:—'t is gone, 't is gone,
   't is gone.
You are welcome, gentlemen!—Come, musicians,
   play.
A hall! a hall! give room, and foot it, girls.
   [*Music plays, and they dance.*
More light, ye knaves; and turn the tables up,
And quench the fire, the room is grown too hot.—
Ah, sirrah, this unlooked-for sport comes well.
Nay, sit, nay, sit, good cousin Capulet;
For you and I are past our dancing days:
How long is 't now since last yourself and I
Were in a mask?
 2nd Cap.   By 'r lady, thirty years.
 1st Cap. What, man! 't is not so much, 't is
   not so much:
'T is since the nuptial of Lucentio,
Come Pentecost as quickly as it will,
Some five and twenty years; and then we masked.
 2nd Cap. 'T is more, 't is more: his son is
   elder, sir;
His son is thirty.
 1st Cap.   Will you tell me that?
His son was but a ward two years ago.
 Rom. What lady's that, which doth enrich
   the hand
Of yonder knight?
 Serv. I know not, sir.
 Rom. O, she doth teach the torches to burn
   bright!
Her beauty hangs upon the cheek of night
Like a rich jewel in an Ethiop's ear:
Beauty too rich for use, for earth too dear!
So shews a snowy dove trooping with crows,
As yonder lady o'er her fellows shews.
The measure done, I'll watch her place of stand,
And, touching hers, make bless'd my rude hand.
Did my heart love till now? forswear it, sight!
For I ne'er saw true beauty till this night.
 Tyb. This, by his voice, should be a Montague:—
Fetch me my rapier, boy:—What! dares the slave
Come hither, covered with an antick face,
To fleer and scorn at our solemnity?
Now, by the stock and honour of my kin,
To strike him dead I hold it not a sin.
 1st Cap. Why, how now, kinsman; where-
   fore storm you so?
 Tyb. Uncle, this is a Montague, our foe;
A villain, that is hither come in spite,
To scorn at our solemnity this night.

1st Cap. Young Romeo is 't?

Tyb.　　'T is he, that villain Romeo.

1st Cap. Content thee, gentle coz, let him alone;
He bears him like a portly gentleman;
And, to say truth, Verona brags of him,
To be a virtuous and well-governed youth:
I would not, for the wealth of all this town,
Here in my house do him disparagement:
Therefore be patient, take no note of him:
It is my will; the which if thou respect,
Shew a fair presence, and put off these frowns,
An ill-beseeming semblance for a feast.

Tyb. It fits, when such a villain is a guest:
I 'll not endure him.

1st Cap.　　He shall be endured.
What, goodman boy!—I say, he shall; go to:
Am I the master here, or you? go to.
You 'll not endure him!—God shall mend my
　　soul—
You 'll make a mutiny among my guests!
You will set cock-a-hoop! you 'll be the man!

Tyb. Why, uncle, 't is a shame.

1st Cap.　　Go to, go to,
You are a saucy boy:—is 't so, indeed?
This trick may chance to scathe you;—I know
　　what.
You must contráry me! marry, 't is time—
Well said, my hearts!—You are a princox; go:—
Be quiet, or—More light, more light.—For
　　shame!—
I 'll make you quiet:—what!—Cheerly, my
　　hearts.

Tyb. Patience perforce, with wilful choler
　　meeting,
Makes my flesh tremble in their different greeting.
I will withdraw: but this intrusion shall,
Now seeming sweet, convert to bitter gall. [*Exit.*

Rom. If I profane with my unworthy hand
　　　　　　　　　　　　　　[*To* JULIET.
This holy shrine, the gentle fine is this,—
My lips, two blushing pilgrims, ready stand
　To smooth that rough touch with a tender kiss.

Jul. Good pilgrim, you do wrong your hand
　　too much,
Which mannerly devotion shews in this;
For saints have hands that pilgrims' hands do
　　touch,
　And palm to palm is holy palmers' kiss.

Rom. Have not saints lips, and holy palmers too?

Jul. Ay, pilgrim, lips that they must use in
　　prayer.

Rom. O then, dear saint, let lips do what
　　hands do:
　They pray; grant thou, lest faith turn to
　　despair.

Jul. Saints do not move, though grant for
　　prayers' sake.

Rom. Then move not while my prayers' effect
　　I take.
Thus from my lips, by thine, my sin is purged.
　　　　　　　　　　　　[*Kissing her.*

Jul. Then have my lips the sin that they
　　have took.

Rom. Sin from my lips? O trespass sweetly
　　urged!
Give me my sin again.

Jul.　　You kiss by the book.

Nurse. Madam, your mother craves a word
　　with you.

Rom. What is her mother?

Nurse.　　Marry, bachelor,
Her mother is the lady of the house,
And a good lady, and a wise, and virtuous:
I nursed her daughter, that you talked withal:
I tell you—he that can lay hold of her,
Shall have the chinks.

Rom.　　Is she a Capulet?
O dear account! my life is my foe's debt.

Ben. Away, begone; the sport is at the best.

Rom. Ay, so I fear; the more is my unrest.

1st Cap. Nay, gentlemen, prepare not to be
　　gone:
We have a trifling foolish banquet towards.—
Is it e'en so? Why, then I thank you all:
I thank you, honest gentlemen; good night:—
More torches here!—Come on, then let 's to
　　bed.
Ah, sirrah [*to* 2nd CAP.], by my fay, it waxes
　　late;
I 'll to my rest. [*Exeunt all but* JULIET *and* Nurse.

Jul. Come hither, nurse: what is yon gen-
　　tleman?

Nurse. The son and heir of old Tiberio.

Jul. What 's he that now is going out of door?

Nurse. Marry, that I think be young Pe-
　　truchio.

Jul. What 's he that follows there, that would
　　not dance?

Nurse. I know not.

Jul. Go, ask his name:—if he be married,
My grave is like to be my wedding bed.

Nurse. His name is Romeo, and a Montague;
The only son of your great enemy.

Jul. My only love sprung from my only hate!
Too early seen unknown, and known too late!
Prodigious birth of love it is to me,
That I must love a loathéd enemy.

Nurse. What 's this; what 's this?

Jul.　　A rhyme I learned even now
Of one I danced withal.
　　　　　　　[*One calls within,* "Juliet."

Nurse.　　Anon, anon:—
Come, let 's away; the strangers all are gone.
　　　　　　　　　　　　[*Exeunt.*

Enter Chorus.

Now old desire doth in his deathbed lie,
　And young affection gapes to be his heir;
That fair for which love groaned for, and would die,
　With tender Juliet matched, is now not fair.
Now Romeo is beloved, and loves again,
　Alike, bewitchéd by the charm of looks;
But to his foe supposed he must complain,
　And she steal love's sweet bait from fearful hooks.
Being held a foe, he may not have access
　To breathe such vows as lovers use to swear;
And she as much in love, her means much less
　To meet her new-belovéd anywhere:
But passion lends them power, time means, to meet,
Temp'ring extremities with extreme sweet.

　　　　　　　　　　　　　　　　　[*Exit.*

ACT II

SCENE I.—*An open Place, adjoining* CAPULET'S
Garden.

Enter ROMEO.

Rom. Can I go forward, when my heart is here?
Turn back, dull earth, and find thy centre out.
　　[*He climbs the wall, and leaps down within it.*

Enter BENVOLIO *and* MERCUTIO.

Ben. Romeo! my cousin Romeo!
Mer.　　　He is wise;
And, on my life, hath stolen him home to bed.
　　Ben. He ran this way, and leaped this orchard
　　　　wall:
Call, good Mercutio.
　　Mer.　　Nay, I'll conjure too.—
Romeo! humours! madman! passion! lover!
Appear thou in the likeness of a sigh,
Speak but one rhyme, and I am satisfied;
Cry but "Ah me!" couple but—love and dove;
Speak to my gossip Venus one fair word,
One nickname for her purblind son and heir,
Young Adam Cupid, he that shot so trim
When King Cophetua loved the beggar-maid.—

He heareth not, he stirreth not, he moveth not:
The ape is dead, and I must conjure him.—
I conjure thee by Rosaline's bright eyes,
By her high forehead, and her scarlet lip,
By her fine foot, straight leg, and quivering thigh,
And the demesnes that there adjacent lie,
That in thy likeness thou appear to us.
　　Ben. An if he hear thee, thou wilt anger him.
　　Mer. This cannot anger him; 't would anger
　　　　him
To raise a spirit in his mistress' circle
Of some strange nature, letting it there stand
Till she had laid it and conjured it down;
That were some spite: my invocation
Is fair and honest; and, in his mistress' name,
I conjure only but to raise up him.
　　Ben. Come, he hath hid himself among these
　　　　trees,
To be consorted with the humorous night:
Blind is his love, and best befits the dark.
　　Mer. If love be blind, love cannot hit the mark.
Now will he sit under a medlar-tree,
And wish his mistress were that kind of fruit
As maids call medlars, when they laugh alone.—

Romeo, good night :—I 'll to my truckle-bed ;
This field-bed is too cold for me to sleep :
Come, shall we go?
    Ben.   Go, then ; for 't is in vain
To seek him here, that means not to be found.
                       [*Exeunt.*

Scene II.—Capulet's *Garden.*

Enter Romeo.

    Rom. He jests at scars, that never felt a wound.
         [Juliet *appears above, at a window.*
But soft! what light through yonder window
    breaks!
It is the east, and Juliet is the sun!—
Arise, fair sun, and kill the envious moon,
Who is already sick and pale with grief,
That thou her maid art far more fair than she :
Be not her maid, since she is envious ;
Her vestal livery is but sick and green,
And none but fools do wear it ; cast it off.—
It is my lady ; O, it is my love :
O, that she knew she were!—
She speaks, yet she says nothing : what of that?
Her eye discourses ; I will answer it.—
I am too bold ; 't is not to me she speaks :
Two of the fairest stars in all the heaven,
Having some business, do entreat her eyes
To twinkle in their spheres till they return.
What if her eyes were there, they in her head?
The brightness of her cheek would shame those
    stars,
As daylight doth a lamp : her eye in heaven
Would through the airy region stream so bright,
That birds would sing, and think it were not night.
See, how she leans her cheek upon her hand!
O, that I were a glove upon that hand,
That I might touch that cheek!
    Jul.   Ah me!
    Rom.   She speaks :—
O, speak again, bright angel! for thou art
As glorious to this night, being o'er my head,
As is a wingéd messenger of heaven
Unto the white-upturnéd wond'ring eyes
Of mortals, that fall back to gaze on him,
When he bestrides the lazy-pacing clouds,
And sails upon the bosom of the air.
    Jul. O Romeo, Romeo! wherefore art thou
    Romeo?
Deny thy father, and refuse thy name :
Or, if thou wilt not, be but sworn my love,
And I 'll no longer be a Capulet.
    Rom. Shall I hear more, or shall I speak at
    this?   [*Aside.*
    Jul. 'T is but thy name that is my enemy ;—
Thou art thyself though, not a Montague.

What 's Montague? it is nor hand, nor foot,
Nor arm, nor face, nor any other part
Belonging to a man. O, be some other name!
What 's in a name? That which we call a rose,
By any other name would smell as sweet :
So Romeo would, were he not Romeo called,
Retain that dear perfection which he owes,
Without that title.—Romeo, doff thy name ;
And for that name, which is no part of thee,
Take all myself.
    Rom.   I take thee at thy word :
Call me but love, and I 'll be new baptized :
Henceforth I never will be Romeo.
    Jul. What man art thou, that, thus bescreened
    in night,
So stumblest on my counsel?
    Rom.   By a name
I know not how to tell thee who I am :
My name, dear saint, is hateful to myself,
Because it is an enemy to thee :
Had I it written, I would tear the word.
    Jul. My ears have not yet drunk a hundred
    words
Of that tongue's utterance, yet I know the sound :
Art thou not Romeo, and a Montague?
    Rom. Neither, fair maid, if either thee dislike.
    Jul. How cam'st thou hither, tell me? and
    wherefore?
The orchard walls are high, and hard to climb ;
And the place death, considering who thou art,
If any of my kinsmen find thee here.
    Rom. With love's light wings did I o'erperch
    these walls ;
For stony limits cannot hold love out :
And what love can do, that dares love attempt ;
Therefore thy kinsmen are no stop to me.
    Jul. If they do see thee, they will murder thee.
    Rom. Alack! there lies more peril in thine eye,
Than twenty of their swords : look thou but sweet,
And I am proof against their enmity.
    Jul. I would not for the world they saw thee
    here.
    Rom. I have night's cloak to hide me from
    their eyes ;
And, but thou love me, let them find me here :
My life were better ended by their hate,
Than death proroguéd, wanting of thy love.
    Jul. By whose direction found'st thou out this
    place?
    Rom. By love, who first did prompt me to in-
    quire :
He lent me counsel, and I lent him eyes.
I am no pilot ; yet, wert thou as far
As that vast shore washed with the farthest sea,
I would adventure for such merchandise.
    Jul. Thou know'st the mask of night is on my
    face ;

Else would a maiden blush bepaint my cheek,
For that which thou hast heard me speak to-night.
Fain would I dwell on form, fain, fain deny
What I have spoke. But farewell compliment!
Dost thou love me? I know thou wilt say "Ay;"
And I will take thy word: yet, if thou swear'st,
Thou mayst prove false: at lovers' perjuries,
They say, Jove laughs. O, gentle Romeo,
If thou dost love, pronounce it faithfully:
Or, if thou think'st I am too quickly won,
I'll frown and be perverse, and say thee nay,
So thou wilt woo; but else, not for the world.
In truth, fair Montague, I am too fond;
And therefore thou mayst think my haviour light:
But trust me, gentleman, I'll prove more true
Than those that have more cunning to be strange.
I should have been more strange, I must confess,
But that thou overheard'st, ere I was ware,
My true love's passion: therefore pardon me;
And not impute this yielding to light love,
Which the dark night hath so discoveréd.
    Rom. Lady, by yonder blesséd moon I swear.
That tips with silver all these fruit-tree tops,—
    Jul. O, swear not by the moon, the inconstant moon,
That monthly changes in her circled orb,
Lest that thy love prove likewise variable.
    Rom. What shall I swear by?
    Jul.   Do not swear at all:
Or, if thou wilt, swear by thy gracious self,
Which is the god of my idolatry,
And I'll believe thee.
    Rom.   If my heart's dear love—
    Jul. Well, do not swear. Although I joy in thee,
I have no joy of this contráct to-night:
It is too rash, too unadvised, too sudden;
Too like the lightning, which doth cease to be
Ere one can say—"It lightens." Sweet, good night!
This bud of love, by summer's ripening breath,
May prove a beauteous flower when next we meet.
Good night, good night! as sweet repose and rest
Come to thy heart, as that within my breast!
    Rom. O, wilt thou leave me so unsatisfied?
    Jul. What satisfaction canst thou have to-night?
    Rom. The exchange of thy love's faithful vow for mine.
    Jul. I gave thee mine before thou didst request it:
And yet I would it were to give again.
    Rom. Wouldst thou withdraw it? for what purpose, love?
    Jul. But to be frank, and give it thee again.
And yet I wish but for the thing I have:
My bounty is as boundless as the sea,
My love as deep; the more I give to thee,

The more I have, for both are infinite.
                [*Nurse calls within.*
I hear some noise within: dear love, adieu!—
Anon, good nurse!—Sweet Montague, be true.
Stay but a little, I will come again.   [*Exit.*
    Rom. O blesséd, blesséd night! I am afeard,
Being in night, all this is but a dream,
Too flattering-sweet to be substantial.

       Re-enter JULIET, *above.*

    Jul. Three words, dear Romeo, and good night, indeed.
If that thy bent of love be honourable,
Thy purpose marriage, send me word to-morrow,
By one that I'll procure to come to thee,
Where and what time thou wilt perform the rite:
And all my fortunes at thy foot I'll lay,
And follow thee my lord throughout the world.
    Nurse [*within*]. Madam!
    Jul. I come anon.—But if thou mean'st not well,
I do beseech thee—
    Nurse [*within*]. Madam!
    Jul.   By and by I come:—
To cease thy suit, and leave me to my grief.
To-morrow will I send.
    Rom.   So thrive my soul—
    Jul. A thousand times good night!   [*Exit.*
    Rom. A thousand times the worse to want thy light.—
Love goes toward love as schoolboys from their books;
But love from love, toward school with heavy looks.   [*Retiring slowly.*

       Re-enter JULIET, *above.*

    Jul. Hist! Romeo, hist!—O, for a falconer's voice,
To lure this tassel-gentle back again!
Bondage is hoarse, and may not speak aloud;
Else would I tear the cave where echo lies,
And make her airy tongue more hoarse than mine
With repetition of my Romeo's name.
    Rom. It is my soul that calls upon my name:
How silver-sweet sound lovers' tongues by night;
Like softest music to attending ears!
    Jul. Romeo!
    Rom.   My sweet!
    Jul.   At what o'clock to-morrow
Shall I send to thee?
    Rom.   At the hour of nine.
    Jul. I will not fail; 'tis twenty years till then.
I have forgot why I did call thee back.
    Rom. Let me stand here till thou remember it.
    Jul. I shall forget, to have thee still stand there,
Remembering how I love thy company.

SCENE III.—FRIAR LAWRENCE's *Cell*.

Enter FRIAR LAWRENCE, *with a basket*.

Fri. The grey-eyed morn smiles on the frown-
    ing night,
Checkering the eastern clouds with streaks of
    light;
And fleckéd darkness like a drunkard reels
From forth day's path and Titan's fiery wheels:
Now, ere the sun advance his burning eye,
The day to cheer, and night's dank dew to dry,
I must up-fill this osier cage of ours,
With baleful weeds, and precious-juicéd flowers.
The earth, that 's nature's mother, is her tomb;
What is her burying grave, that is her womb:
And from her womb, children of divers kind
We sucking on her natural bosom find;
Many for many virtues excellent,
None but for some, and yet all different.
O, mickle is the powerful grace that lies
In herbs, plants, stones, and their true qualities:
For nought so vile that on the earth doth live,
But to the earth some special good doth give;

Rom. And I 'll still stay, to have thee still
    forget,
Forgetting any other home but this.
    Jul. 'T is almost morning; I would have thee
    gone:
And yet no farther than a wanton's bird;
Who lets it hop a little from her hand,
Like a poor prisoner in his twisted gyves,
And with a silk thread plucks it back again,
So loving-jealous of his liberty.
    Rom. I would I were thy bird.
    Jul.   Sweet, so would I:
Yet I should kill thee with much cherishing.
Good night, good night! parting is such sweet
    sorrow,
That I shall say   " Good night," till it be mor-
    row.   [*Exit.*
    Rom. Sleep dwell upon thine eyes, peace in
    thy breast!—
'Would I were sleep and peace, so sweet to rest!
Hence will I to my ghostly friar's close cell;
His help to crave, and my dear hap to tell. [*Exit.*

Nor aught so good, but, strained from that fair use,
Revolts from true birth, stumbling on abuse:
Virtue itself turns vice, being misapplied;
And vice sometime 's by action dignified.
Within the infant rind of this weak flower
Poison hath residence, and med'cine power:
For this, being smelt, with that part cheers each
    part;
Being tasted, slays all senses with the heart.
Two such opposéd Kings encamp them still
In man as well as herbs,—grace and rude will;
And, where the worser is predominant,
Full soon the canker death eats up that plant.

Enter ROMEO.

Rom. Good morrow, father!
Fri.   *Benedicite!*
What early tongue so sweet saluteth me?—
Young son, it argues a distempered head,
So soon to bid good-morrow to thy bed:
Care keeps his watch in every old man's eye,
And where care lodges, sleep will never lie;
But where unbruiséd youth with unstuffed brain
Doth couch his limbs, there golden sleep doth
    reign:
Therefore thy earliness doth me assure
Thou art up-roused by some distemperature;
Or if not so, then here I hit it right—
Our Romeo hath not been in bed to-night.
    Rom. That last is true; the sweeter rest was
      mine.
    Fri. God pardon sin! wast thou with Rosaline?
    Rom. With Rosaline, my ghostly father? no;
I have forgot that name, and that name 's woe.
    Fri. That 's my good son: but where hast
      thou been, then?
    Rom. I 'll tell thee ere thou ask it me again.
I have been feasting with mine enemy;
Where, on a sudden, one hath wounded me,
That 's by me wounded: both our remedies
Within thy help and holy physic lies.
I bear no hatred, blesséd man; for lo,
My intercession likewise steads my foe.
    Fri. Be plain, good son, and homely in thy
      drift:
Riddling confession finds but riddling shrift.
    Rom. Then plainly know, my heart's dear
      love is set
On the fair daughter of rich Capulet:
As mine on hers, so hers is set on mine;
And all combined, save what thou must combine
By holy marriage. When, and where, and how,
We met, we wooed, and made exchange of vow,
I 'll tell thee as we pass: but this I pray,
That thou consent to marry us this day.
    Fri. Holy Saint Francis! what a change 's
    here!

Is Rosaline, that thou didst love so dear,
So soon forsaken? young men's love, then, lies
Not truly in their hearts, but in their eyes.
Jesu Maria! what a deal of brine
Hath washed thy sallow cheeks for Rosaline!
How much salt water thrown away in waste,
To season love, that of it doth not taste!
The sun not yet thy sighs from heaven clears,
Thy old groans ring yet in my ancient ears;
Lo, here upon thy cheek the stain doth sit
Of an old tear, that is not washed off yet:
If e'er thou wast thyself, and these woes thine,
Thou and these woes were all for Rosaline:
And art thou changed? pronounce this sentence,
    then—
"Women may fall, when there 's no strength in
    men."
    Rom. Thou chid'dst me oft for loving Rosaline.
    Fri. For doting, not for loving, pupil mine.
    Rom. And bad'st me bury love.
    Fri.   Not in a grave
To lay one in, another out to have.
    Rom. I pray thee, chide not: she whom I
      love now,
Doth grace for grace, and love for love allow:
The other did not so.
    Fri.   O, she knew well
Thy love did read by rote, and could not spell.
But come, young waverer, come go with me,
In one respect I 'll thy assistant be:
For this alliance may so happy prove,
To turn your households' rancour to pure love.
    Rom. O, let us hence; I stand on sudden haste.
    Fri. Wisely and slow: they stumble that run
      fast.   [*Exeunt.*

SCENE IV.—*A Street.*

Enter BENVOLIO *and* MERCUTIO.

    Mer. Where the devil should this Romeo be?—
Came he not home to-night?
    Ben. Not to his father's: I spoke with his man.
    Mer. Ah, that same pale hard-hearted wench,
      that Rosaline,
Torments him so, that he will sure run mad.
    Ben. Tybalt, the kinsman of old Capulet,
Hath sent a letter to his father's house.
    Mer. A challenge, on my life.
    Ben. Romeo will answer it.
    Mer. Any man that can write may answer a
letter.
    Ben. Nay, he will answer the letter's master,
how he dares, being dared.
    Mer. Alas, poor Romeo, he is already dead!
stabbed with a white wench's black eye; shot
through the ear with a love-song; the very pin

of his heart cleft with the blind bow-boy's butt-shaft:—and is he a man to encounter Tybalt?

Ben. Why, what is Tybalt?

Mer. More than prince of cats, I can tell you. O, he is the courageous captain of compliments. He fights as you sing prick-song; keeps time, distance, and proportion; rests me his minim rest—one, two, and the third in your bosom: the very butcher of a silk button; a duellist, a duellist: a gentleman of the very first house; of the first and second cause. Ah, the immortal passado! the punto reverso! the hay!

Ben. The what?

Mer. The pox of such antic, lisping, affecting fantasticoes; these new tuners of accents! " By Jesu, a very good blade!"—"A very tall man!" —"A very good whore."—Why, is not this a lamentable thing, grandsire, that we should be thus afflicted with these strange flies, these fashion - mongers, these *pardonnez-mois*, who stand so much on the new form that they cannot sit at ease on the old bench? O, their *bons*, their *bons!*

Enter ROMEO.

Ben. Here comes Romeo, here comes Romeo.

Mer. Without his roe, like a dried herring:— O, flesh, flesh, how art thou fishified!—Now is he for the numbers that Petrarch flowed in: Laura, to his lady, was but a kitchen-wench;— marry, she had a better love to be-rhyme her: Dido, a dowdy; Cleopatra, a gipsy; Helen and Hero, hildings and harlots; Thisbé, a grey eye or so, but not to the purpose.—Signior Romeo, *bon jour!* there's a French salutation to your French slop. You gave us the counterfeit fairly last night.

Rom. Good-morrow to you both. What counterfeit did I give you?

Mer. The slip, sir, the slip: can you not conceive?

Rom. Pardon, good Mercutio, my business was great; and in such a case as mine, a man may strain courtesy.

Mer. That's as much as to say, such a case as yours constrains a man to bow in the hams.

Rom. Meaning, to courtesy.

Mer. Thou hast most kindly hit it.

Rom. A most courteous exposition.

Mer. Nay, I am the very pink of courtesy.

Rom. Pink for flower.

Mer. Right.

Rom. Why, then is my pump well-flowered.

Mer. Well said. Follow me this jest now, till thou hast worn out thy pump; that, when the single sole of it is worn, the jest may remain, after the wearing, solely singular.

Rom. O single-soled jest, solely singular for the singleness!

Mer. Come between us, good Benvolio; my wits fail.

Rom. Switch and spurs, switch and spurs; or I'll cry a match.

Mer. Nay, if thy wits run the wildgoose-chace, I have done; for thou hast more of the wild-goose in one of thy wits than, I am sure, I have in my whole five. Was I with you there for the goose?

Rom. Thou wast never with me for anything, when thou wast not there for the goose.

Mer. I will bite thee by the ear for that jest.

Rom. Nay, good goose, bite not.

Mer. Thy wit is a very bitter sweeting; it is a most sharp sauce.

Rom. And is it not well served in to a sweet goose?

Mer. O, here's a wit of cheveril, that stretches from an inch narrow to an ell broad!

Rom. I stretch it out for that word "broad:" which added to the goose, proves thee far and wide a broad goose.

Mer. Why, is not this better now than groaning for love? Now art thou sociable, now art thou Romeo; now art thou what thou art, by art as well as by nature: for this drivelling love is like a great natural, that runs lolling up and down to hide his bauble in a hole.

Ben. Stop there; stop there.

Mer. Thou desirest me to stop in my tale, against the hair.

Ben. Thou wouldst else have made thy tale large.

Mer. O, thou art deceived; I would have made it short: for I was come to the whole depth of my tale: and meant, indeed, to occupy the argument no longer.

Rom. Here's goodly geer!

Enter Nurse *and* PETER.

Mer. A sail, a sail, a sail!

Ben. Two, two; a shirt and a smock.

Nurse. Peter!

Peter. Anon?

Nurse. My fan, Peter.

Mer. Good Peter, to hide her face; for her fan's the fairer face.

Nurse God ye good morrow, gentlemen.

Mer. God ye good den, fair gentlewoman.

Nurse. Is it good den?

Mer. 'T is no less, I tell you; for the bawdy hand of the dial is now upon the prick of noon.

Nurse. Out upon you, what a man are you!

Rom. One, gentlewoman, that God hath made himself to mar.

Nurse. By my troth it is well said : for himself to mar, quoth'a?—Gentlemen, can any of you tell me where I may find the young Romeo?

Rom. I can tell you; but young Romeo will be older when you have found him, than he was when you sought him : I am the youngest of that name, for 'fault of a worse.

Nurse. You say well.

Mer. Yea, is the worst well? very well took, i' faith; wisely, wisely.

Nurse. If you be he, sir, I desire some confidence with you.

Ben. She will indite him to some supper.

Mer. A bawd, a bawd, a bawd! So ho!

Rom. What hast thou found?

Mer. No hare, sir; unless a hare, sir, in a Lenten pie, that is something stale and hoar ere it be spent.

> An old hare hoar,
> And an old hare hoar,
> Is very good meat in Lent :
> But a hare that is hoar
> Is too much for a score,
> When it hoars ere it be spent.—

Romeo, will you come to your father's? we 'll to dinner thither.

Rom. I will follow you.

Mer. Farewell, ancient lady; farewell, " lady, lady, lady." [*Exeunt* MERCUTIO *and* BENVOLIO.

Nurse. Marry, farewell!—I pray you, sir, what saucy merchant was this, that was so full of his ropery?

Rom. A gentleman, nurse, that loves to hear himself talk; and will speak more in a minute than he will stand to in a month.

Nurse. An 'a speak anything against me, I 'll take him down an 'a were lustier than he is, and twenty such Jacks; and if I cannot, I'll find those that shall. Scurvy knave! I am none of his flirt-gills; I am none of his skains-mates!— And thou must stand by too, and suffer every knave to use me at his pleasure!

Pet. I saw no man use you at his pleasure: if I had, my weapon should quickly have been out, I warrant you. I dare draw, as soon as another man, if I see occasion in a good quarrel, and the law on my side.

Nurse. Now, afore God, I am so vexed that every part about me quivers. Scurvy knave!— Pray you, sir, a word: and as I told you, my young lady bade me inquire you out; what she bade me say, I will keep to myself: but first let me tell ye, if ye should lead her into a fool's paradise, as they say, it were a very gross kind of behaviour, as they say: for the gentlewoman is young; and therefore, if you should deal double with her, truly it were an ill thing to be offered to any gentlewoman, and very weak dealing.

Rom. Nurse, commend me to thy lady and mistress. I protest unto thee,—

Nurse. Good heart! and i' faith I will tell her as much. Lord, lord, she will be a joyful woman!

Rom. What wilt thou tell her, nurse? thou dost not mark me.

Nurse. I will tell her sir, that you do protest; which, as I take it, is a gentlemanlike offer.

Rom. Bid her devise some means to come to shrift
This afternoon;
And there she shall, at Friar Laurence' cell
Be shrived, and married. Here is for thy pains.

Nurse. No, truly, sir, not a penny.

Rom. Go to; I say you shall.

Nurse. This afternoon, sir? well, she shall be there.

Rom. And stay, good nurse, behind the abbey-wall:
Within this hour my man shall be with thee;
And bring thee cords made like a tackled stair:
Which to the high top-gallant of my joy
Must be my convoy in the secret night.
Farewell! be trusty, and I'll quit thy pains.
Farewell! commend me to thy mistress.

Nurse. Now God in heaven bless thee!—Hark you, sir.

Rom. What sayst thou, my dear nurse?

Nurse. Is your man secret? Did you ne'er hear say,
Two may keep counsel, putting one away?

Rom. I warrant thee; my man's as true as steel.

Nurse. Well, sir; my mistress is the sweetest lady—Lord, lord! when 'twas a little prating thing—O, there's a nobleman in town, one Paris, that would fain lay knife aboard; but she, good soul, had as lieve see a toad, a very toad, as see him. I anger her sometimes, and tell her that Paris is the properer man; but I'll warrant you, when I say so, she looks as pale as any clout in the varsal world. Doth not rosemary and Romeo begin both with a letter?

Rom. Ay, nurse: what of that? both with an R.

Nurse. Ah, mocker! that's the dog's name: R is for the dog. No; I know it begins with some other letter: and she hath the prettiest sententious of it, of you and rosemary, that it would do you good to hear it.

Rom. Commend me to thy lady.　　*[Exit.*

Nurse. Ay, a thousand times.—Peter!

Pet. Anon?

Nurse. Before, and apace.　　*[Exeunt.*

Scene V.—Capulet's *Garden.*

Enter Juliet.

Jul. The clock struck nine, when I did send the nurse:
In half an hour she promised to return.
Perchance she cannot meet him:—that's not so.—
O, she is lame! love's heralds should be thoughts,
Which ten times faster glide than the sun's beams,
Driving back shadows over lowering hills:
Therefore do nimble-pinioned doves draw love,
And therefore hath the wind-swift Cupid wings.
Now is the sun upon the highmost hill
Of this day's journey; and from nine till twelve
Is three long hours;—yet she is not come.
Had she affections, and warm youthful blood,
She'd be as swift in motion as a ball;
My words would bandy her to my sweet love,
And his to me:
But old folks, many feign as they were dead;
Unwieldy, slow, heavy and pale as lead.

Enter Nurse *and* Peter.

O God, she comes!—O honey nurse, what news?
Hast thou met with him? Send thy man away.

Nurse. Peter, stay at the gate. *[Exit* Peter.

Jul. Now, good sweet nurse;—O lord! why look'st thou sad?
Though news be sad, yet tell them merrily:
If good, thou sham'st the music of sweet news
By playing it to me with so sour a face.

Nurse. I am aweary; give me leave awhile.—
Fie, how my bones ache! What a jaunt have I had!

Jul. I would thou hadst my bones, and I thy news.

Nay, come, I pray thee, speak;—good, good
　　nurse, speak.
　Nurse. Jesu, what haste? can you not stay
　　awhile?
Do you not see that I am out of breath?
　Jul. How art thou out of breath, when thou
　　hast breath
To say to me that thou art out of breath?
The excuse that thou dost make in this delay
Is longer than the tale thou dost excuse.
Is thy news good or bad? answer to that;
Say either, and I 'll stay the circumstance:
Let me be satisfied, is 't good or bad?
　Nurse. Wéll, you have made a simple choice;
you know not how to choose a man. Romeo!
no, not he: though his face be better than any
man's, yet his leg excels all men's; and for a
hand, and a foot, and a body, though they be not
to be talked on, yet they are past compare. He
is not the flower of courtesy, but, I 'll warrant
him, as gentle as a lamb.—Go thy ways, wench;
serve God.—What, have you dined at home?
　Jul. No, no. But all this did I know before:
What says he of our marriage; what of that?
　Nurse. Lord, how my head aches! what a
　　head have I!
It beats as it would fall in twenty pieces.
My back o' t' other side;—O, my back, my back!
Beshrew your heart for sending me about
To catch my death with jaunting up and down!
　Jul. I' faith I am sorry that thou art not well.
Sweet, sweet, sweet nurse, tell me what says my
　　love?
　Nurse. Your love says, like an honest gentle-
　　man,
And a courteous, and a kind, and a handsome,
And, I warrant, a virtuous,—Where is your mo-
　　ther?
　Jul. Where is my mother!—why, she is within:
Where should she be?—How oddly thou repliest:
"Your love says, like an honest gentleman,—
Where is your mother?"
　Nurse. 　　O, God's lady dear!
Are you so hot? Marry, come up, I trow!
Is this the poultice for my aching bones?
Henceforward do your messages yourself.
　Jul. Here 's such a coil!—Come, what says
　　Romeo?
　Nurse. Have you got leave to go to shrift to-
　　day?
　Jul. I have.
　Nurse. Then hie you hence to Friar Laurence'
　　cell;
There stays a husband to make you a wife.
Now comes the wanton blood up in your cheeks:
They 'll be in scarlet straight at any news.
Hie you to church: I must another way,

To fetch a ladder, by the which your love
Must climb a bird's-nest soon, when it is dark.
I am the drudge, and toil in your delight;
But you shall bear the burden soon at night.
Go; I 'll to dinner; hie you to the cell.
　Jul. Hie to high fortune!—honest nurse, fare-
　　well. 　　　　　　　　　[*Exeunt.*

Scene VI.—Friar Laurence's *Cell.*

Enter Friar Laurence *and* Romeo.

　Fri. So smile the heavens upon this holy act,
That after-hours with sorrow chide us not!
　Rom. Amen, amen! but come what sorrow
　　can,
It cannot countervail the exchange of joy
That one short minute gives me in her sight.
Do thou but close our hands with holy words,
Then love-devouring death do what he dare:
It is enough I may but call her mine.
　Fri. These violent delights have violent ends,
And in their triumph die: like fire and powder,
Which, as they kiss, consume. The sweetest
　　honey
Is loathsome in his own deliciousness,
And in the taste confounds the appetite.
Therefore, love moderately: long love doth so:
Too swift arrives as tardy as too slow.

Enter Juliet.

Here comes the lady:—O, so light a foot
Will ne'er wear out the everlasting flint!
A lover may bestride the gossamers
That idle in the wanton summer air,
And yet not fall: so light is vanity.
　Jul. Good even to my ghostly cónfessor.
　Fri. Romeo shall thank thee, daughter, for us
　　both.
　Jul. As much to him, else are his thanks too
　　much.
　Rom. Ah, Juliet, if the measure of thy joy
Be heaped like mine, and that thy skill be more
To blazon it, then sweeten with thy breath
This neighbour air, and let rich music's tongue
Unfold the imagined happiness that both
Receive in either by this dear encounter.
　Jul. Conceit, more rich in matter than in words,
Brags of his substance, not of ornament.
They are but beggars that can count their worth:
But my true love is grown to such excess,
I cannot sum up half my sum of wealth.
　Fri. Come, come with me, and we will make
　　short work:
For, by your leaves, you shall not stay alone
Till holy church incorporate two in one. [*Exeunt.*

SCENE I.—*A Public Place.*

Enter MERCUTIO, BENVOLIO, Page, *and* Servants.

Ben. I pray thee, good Mercutio, let's retire:
The day is hot, the Capulets abroad;
And, if we meet, we shall not 'scape a brawl:
For now, these hot days, is the mad blood stirring.

Mer. Thou art like one of those fellows that,
when he enters the confines of a tavern, claps me
his sword upon the table, and says, "God send
me no need of thee!" and, by the operation of the
second cup, draws it on the drawer, when indeed
there is no need.

Ben. Am I like such a fellow?

Mer. Come, come, thou art as hot a Jack in
thy mood as any in Italy: and as soon moved to
be moody, and as soon moody to be moved.

Ben. And what to?

Mer. Nay, an there were two such, we should
have none shortly, for one would kill the other.
Thou! why, thou wilt quarrel with a man that
hath a hair more or a hair less in his beard than
thou hast. Thou wilt quarrel with a man for
cracking nuts, having no other reason but because thou hast hazel eyes. What eye, but such
an eye, would spy out such a quarrel? Thy head
is as full of quarrels as an egg is full of meat;
and yet thy head hath been beaten as addle as an
egg for quarrelling. Thou hast quarrelled with
a man for coughing in the street, because he hath
wakened thy dog that hath lain asleep in the sun.
Didst thou not fall out with a tailor for wearing
his new doublet before Easter? with another for
tying his new shoes with old riband? and yet
thou wilt tutor me from quarrelling!

Ben. An I were so apt to quarrel as thou art,
any man should buy the fee-simple of my life for
an hour and a quarter.

Mer. The fee-simple? O simple!

Enter TYBALT *and others.*

Ben. By my head, here come the Capulets.

Mer. By my heel, I care not.

Tyb. Follow me close, for I will speak to them.
Gentlemen, good den: a word with one of you.

Mer. And but one word with one of us? Couple it with something; make it a word and a blow.

Tyb. You will find me apt enough to that, sir,
if you will give me occasion.

Mer. Could you not take some occasion without giving?

Tyb. Mercutio, thou consortest with Romeo,—

Mer. Consort! what, dost thou make us minstrels? an thou make minstrels of us, look to hear
nothing but discords: here's my fiddlestick;
here's that shall make you dance. 'Zounds,
consort!

Ben. We talk here in the public haunt of men:
Either withdraw into some private place,
Or reason coldly of your grievances,
Or else depart: here all eyes gaze on us.

Mer. Men's eyes were made to look, and let
    them gaze:
I will not budge for no man's pleasure, I.

Enter ROMEO.

Tyb. Well, peace be with you, sir; here comes
    my man.

Mer. But I'll be hanged, sir, if he wear your
    livery:
Marry, go before to field, he'll be your follower;
Your worship in that sense may call him "man."

Tyb. Romeo, the love I bear thee can afford
No better term than this—Thou art a villain.

Rom. Tybalt, the reason that I have to love
    thee
Doth much excuse the appertaining rage
To such a greeting.—Villain am I none;
Therefore farewell; I see thou know'st me not.

Tyb. Boy, this shall not excuse the injuries
That thou hast done me; therefore turn and draw.

Rom. I do protest I never injured thee;
But love thee better than thou canst devise,
Till thou shalt know the reason of my love:
And so, good Capulet,—which name I tender
As dearly as mine own,—be satisfied.

Mer. O calm, dishonourable, vile submission!
A la stoccata carries it away.— [*Draws.*
Tybalt, you rat-catcher, will you walk?

Tyb. What wouldst thou have with me?

Mer. Good King of Cats, nothing but one of
your nine lives; that I mean to make bold
withal, and, as you shall use me hereafter, dry-
beat the rest of the eight. Will you pluck your
sword out of his pilcher by the ears? make haste,
lest mine be about your ears ere it be out.

Tyb. I am for you. [*Drawing.*

Rom. Gentle Mercutio, put thy rapier up.

Mer. Come, sir, your passado. [*They fight.*

Rom. Draw, Benvolio; beat down their
weapons:—
Gentlemen, for shame! forbear this outrage:—
Tybalt—Mercutio! the Prince expressly hath
Forbidden bandying in Verona streets.
Hold Tybalt;—good Mercutio!
[*Exeunt* TYBALT *and his* Partisans.

Mer. I am hurt.—
A plague o' both the houses!—I am sped.—
Is he gone, and hath nothing?

Ben. What, art thou hurt?

Mer. Ay, ay, a scratch, a scratch: marry, 'tis
enough.—
Where is my page?—go, villain, fetch a surgeon.
[*Exit* Page.

Rom. Courage, man; the hurt cannot be much.

Mer. No, 'tis not so deep as a well, nor so
wide as a church-door; but 'tis enough, 'twill
serve. Ask for me to-morrow, and you shall
find me a grave man. I am peppered, I warrant, for this world.—A plague o' both your
houses!—What, a dog, a rat, a mouse, a cat, to
scratch a man to death! a braggart, a rogue, a
villain, that fights by the book of arithmetic!—

Why the devil came you between us? I was
hurt under your arm.

 Rom. I thought all for the best.

 Mer. Help me into some house, Benvolio,
Or I shall faint.—A plague o' both your houses!
They have made worms'-meat of me:
I have it, and soundly too.—Your houses!

      [*Exeunt* MERCUTIO *and* BENVOLIO.

 Rom. This gentleman, the Prince's near ally,
My very friend, hath got his mortal hurt
In my behalf: my reputation stained
With Tybalt's slander; Tybalt, that an hour
Hath been my cousin:—O sweet Juliet,
Thy beauty hath made me effeminate,
And in my temper softened valour's steel.

    Re-enter BENVOLIO.

 Ben. O Romeo, Romeo, brave Mercutio's
  dead:
That gallant spirit hath aspired the clouds,
Which too untimely here did scorn the earth!

 Rom. This day's black fate on more days doth
  depend:
This but begins the woe; others must end.

    Re-enter TYBALT.

 Ben. Here comes the furious Tybalt back again.

 Rom. Alive! in triumph! and Mercutio slain!
Away to heaven, respective lenity,
And fire-eyed fury be my conduct now!—
Now, Tybalt, take the "villain" back again,
That late thou gav'st me; for Mercutio's soul
Is but a little way above our heads,
Staying for thine to keep him company:
Either thou or I, or both, must go with him.

 Tyb. Thou, wretched boy, that didst consort
  him here,
Shalt with him hence.

 Rom.   This shall determine that.

    [*They fight:* TYBALT *falls.*

 Ben. Romeo, away, be gone!
The citizens are up, and Tybalt slain.
Stand not amazed: the Prince will doom thee death,
If thou art taken:—hence! be gone! away!

 Rom. O, I am fortune's fool!

 Ben.   Why dost thou stay?

        [*Exit* ROMEO.

    Enter Citizens, *&c.*

 1st Cit. Which way ran he that killed Mercutio?
Tybalt, that murderer, which way ran he?

 Ben. There lies that Tybalt.

 1st Cit.   Up, sir, go with me:
I charge thee in the Prince's name, obey.

 Enter PRINCE, *attended;* MONTAGUE, CAPULET,
  their Ladies, *and others.*

 Prin. Where are the vile beginners of this fray?

 Ben. O noble Prince, I can discover all
The unlucky manage of this fatal brawl:—
There lies the man, slain by young Romeo,
That slew thy kinsman, brave Mercutio.

 Lady C. Tybalt, my cousin!—O my brother's
  child!
O Prince,—O cousin,—husband,—the blood is
  spilled
Of my dear kinsman!—Prince, as thou art true,
For blood of ours, shed blood of Montague.—
O cousin, cousin!

 Prin. Benvolio, who began this bloody fray?

 Ben. Tybalt, here slain, whom Romeo's hand
  did slay;
Romeo that spoke him fair, bade him bethink
How nice the quarrel was, and urged withal
Your high displeasure. All this—utteréd
With gentle breath, calm look, knees humbly
  bowed—
Could not take truce with the unruly spleen
Of Tybalt, deaf to peace, but that he tilts
With piercing steel, at bold Mercutio's breast;
Who, all as hot, turns deadly point to point,
And, with a martial scorn, with one hand beats
Cold death aside, and with the other sends
It back to Tybalt, whose dexterity
Retorts it: Romeo he cries aloud,
"Hold, friends! friends, part!" and, swifter
  than his tongue,
His agile arm beats down their fatal points,
And 'twixt them rushes; underneath whose arm
An envious thrust from Tybalt hit the life
Of stout Mercutio, and then Tybalt fled:
But by and by comes back to Romeo,
Who had but newly entertained revenge,
And to 't they go like lightning; for ere I
Could draw to part them, was stout Tybalt slain;
And, as he fell, did Romeo turn and fly.
This is the truth, or let Benvolio die.

 Lady C. He is a kinsman to the Montague;
Affection makes him false, he speaks not true:
Some twenty of them fought in this black strife,
And all those twenty could but kill one life.
I beg for justice; which thou, Prince, must give:
Romeo slew Tybalt; Romeo must not live.

 Prin. Romeo slew him; he slew Mercutio:
Who now the price of his dear blood doth owe?

 Mon. Not Romeo, Prince, he was Mercutio's
  friend:
His fault concludes but what the law should end,
The life of Tybalt.

 Prin.   And for that offence,
Immediately we do exíle him hence.
I have an interest in your hates' proceeding;
My blood for your rude brawls doth lie a-bleeding:
But I'll amerce you with so strong a fine,
That you shall all repent the loss of mine.

I will be deaf to pleading and excuses ;
Nor tears, nor prayers, shall purchase out abuses;
Therefore use none : let Romeo hence in haste,
Else, when he 's found, that hour is his last.—
Bear hence this body, and attend our will :
Mercy but murders, pardoning those that kill.
                                        [Exeunt.

SCENE II.—*A Room in* CAPULET'S *House.*

Enter JULIET.

Jul. Gallop apace, you fiery-footed steeds,
Towards Phœbus' lodging : such a wagoner
As Phaeton would whip you to the west,
And bring in cloudy night immediately.—
Spread thy close curtain, love-performing night,
That runaway's eyes may wink, and Romeo
Leap to these arms, untalked of and unseen !—
Lovers can see to do their amorous rites
By their own beauties : or, if love be blind,
It best agrees with night.—Come, civil night,
Thou sober-suited matron, all in black,
And learn me how to lose a winning match,
Played for a pair of stainless maidenhoods :
Hood my unmanned blood, bating in my cheeks,
With thy black mantle; till strange love, grown
        bold,
Think true love acted, simple modesty.
Come, night !—Come, Romeo ! come, thou day
        in night !
For thou wilt lie upon the wings of night
Whiter than new snow upon a raven's back.—
Come, gentle night ; come, loving, black-browed
        night !
Give me my Romeo : and, when he shall die,
Take him and cut him out in little stars,
And he will make the face of heaven so fine
That all the world will be in love with night,
And pay no worship to the garish sun.—
O, I have bought the mansion of a love,
But not possessed it ; and, though I am sold,
Not yet enjoyed. So tedious is this day
As is the night before some festival
To an impatient child, that hath new robes
And may not wear them.—O, here comes my nurse,

Enter Nurse, *with cords.*

And she brings news; and every tongue that speaks
But Romeo's name, speaks heavenly eloquence.—
Now, nurse, what news? What hast thou there?
        the cords
That Romeo bade thee fetch?
    Nurse.   Ay, ay, the cords.
                            [*Throws them down.*
    Jul. Ah me, what news? why dost thou wring
        thy hands?

    Nurse. Ah, well-a-day ! he 's dead, he 's dead,
        he 's dead !
We are undone, lady, we are undone !
Alack the day !—he 's gone, he 's killed, he 's
        dead !
    Jul. Can heaven be so envious?
    Nurse.   Romeo can,
Though heaven cannot.—O Romeo, Romeo !
Whoever would have thought it ?—Romeo !
    Jul. What devil art thou, that dost torment me
        thus ?
This torture should be roared in dismal hell.
Hath Romeo slain himself? say thou but "Ay,"
And that bare vowel "I" shall poison more
Than the death-darting eye of cockatrice.
I am not I, if there be such an "Ay;"
Or those eyes shut that make thee answer "Ay."
If he be slain, say "Ay ;" or if not, "No :"
Brief sounds determine of my weal or woe.
    Nurse. I saw the wound, I saw it with mine
        eyes,—
God save the mark !—here on his manly breast.
A piteous corse, a bloody piteous corse ;
Pale, pale as ashes, all bedaubed in blood,
All in gore blood !—I swoonéd at the sight.
    Jul. O break, my heart !—poor bankrout, break
        at once !
To prison, eyes ; ne'er look on liberty !
Vile earth, to earth resign ; end motion here ;
And thou and Romeo press one heavy bier !
    Nurse. O Tybalt, Tybalt, the best friend I
        had !
O courteous Tybalt ! honest gentleman !
That ever I should live to see thee dead !
    Jul. What storm is this, that blows so contrary !
Is Romeo slaughtered, and is Tybalt dead?
My dear-loved cousin, and my dearer lord ?—
Then, dreadful trumpet, sound the general doom !
For who is living, if those two are gone ?
    Nurse. Tybalt is gone, and Romeo banishéd;
Romeo, that killed him, he is banishéd.
    Jul. O God !—did Romeo's hand shed Tybalt's
        blood ?
    Nurse. It did, it did; alas the day ! it did.
    Jul. O serpent heart, hid with a flow'ring face !
Did ever dragon keep so fair a cave ?
Beautiful tyrant, fiend angelical !
Dove-feathered raven ! wolvish-ravening lamb !
Despiséd substance of divinest show !
Just opposite to what thou justly seem'st ;
A damnéd saint, an honourable villain !—
O, nature ! what hadst thou to do in hell,
When thou didst bower the spirit of a fiend
In mortal paradise of such sweet flesh ?
Was ever book containing such vile matter
So fairly bound ? O, that deceit should dwell
In such a gorgeous palace !

Nurse.   There's no trust,
No faith, no honesty in men: all perjured,
All forsworn, all naught, all dissemblers.—
Ah, where's my man? give me some *aqua vitæ:*
These griefs, these woes, these sorrows make me
          old.—
Shame come to Romeo!
     Jul.   Blistered be thy tongue
For such a wish! he was not born to shame:
Upon his brow shame is ashamed to sit;
For 't is a throne where honour may be crowned
Sole monarch of the universal earth.
O, what a beast was I to chide at him!
     Nurse. Will you speak well of him that killed
          your cousin?
     Jul. Shall I speak ill of him that is my hus-
          band?
Ah, poor my lord, what tongue shall smooth thy
          name,
When I, thy three-hours' wife, have mangled it?
But wherefore, villain, didst thou kill my cousin?
That villain cousin would have killed my hus-
          band:—
Back, foolish tears, back to your native spring;
Your tributary drops belong to woe,
Which you, mistaking, offer up to joy.
My husband lives, that Tybalt would have slain;
And Tybalt's dead, that would have slain my
          husband:
All this is comfort: wherefore weep I, then?
Some word there was, worser than Tybalt's death,
That murdered me: I would forget it fain;
But O! it presses to my memory,
Like damnéd guilty deeds to sinners' minds:
"Tybalt is dead, and Romeo—banishéd:"
That "banishéd," that one word "banishéd,"
Hath slain ten thousand Tybalts. Tybalt's death
Was woe enough, if it had ended there:
Or, if sour woe delights in fellowship,
And needly will be ranked with other griefs,
Why followed not, when she said, "Tybalt's dead,"
"Thy father," or "thy mother," nay, or both,
Which modern lamentation might have moved?
But, with a rear-ward following Tybalt's death,
"Romeo is banishéd!"—to speak that word,
Is father, mother, Tybalt, Romeo, Juliet,
All slain, all dead:—"Romeo is banishéd!"
There is no end, no limit, measure, bound,
In that word's death; no words can that woe
          sound.—
Where is my father and my mother, nurse?
     Nurse. Weeping and wailing over Tybalt's
          corse:
Will you go to them? I will bring you thither.
     Jul. Wash they his wounds with tears? mine
          shall be spent,
When theirs are dry, for Romeo's banishment.

Take up those cords:—Poor ropes, you are be-
          guiled,
Both you and I; for Romeo is exíled:
He made you for a highway to my bed;
But I, a maid, die maiden-widowéd.
Come, cords; come, nurse; I'll to my wedding-
          bed;
And death, not Romeo, take my maidenhead!
     Nurse. Hie to your chamber: I'll find Romeo
To comfort you: I wot well where he is.
Hark ye, your Romeo will be here at night:
I'll to him; he is hid at Laurence' cell.
     Jul. O find him! give this ring to my true
          knight,
And bid him come to take his last farewell.
                                        [*Exeunt.*

SCENE III.—FRIAR LAURENCE'S *Cell.*

Enter FRIAR LAURENCE *and* ROMEO.

     Fri. Romeo, come forth; come forth, thou
          fearful man:
Affliction is enamoured of thy parts,
And thou art wedded to calamity.
     Rom. Father, what news? what is the Prince's
          doom?
What sorrow craves acquaintance at my hand,
That I yet know not?
     Fri.   Too familiar
Is my dear son with such sour company.
I bring thee tidings of the Prince's doom.
     Rom. What less than doomsday is the Prince's
          doom?
     Fri. A gentler judgment vanished from his
          lips:
Not body's death, but body's banishment.
     Rom. Ha! banishment? Be merciful, say
          "death:"
For exile hath more terror in his look,
Much more than death: do not say "banish-
          ment."
     Fri. Here from Verona art thou banishéd:
Be patient, for the world is broad and wide.
     Rom. There is no world without Verona walls;
But purgatory, torture, hell itself.
Hence banishéd is banished from the world,
And world's exíle is death. Then banishment
Is death mistermed: calling death banishment,
Thou cutt'st my head off with a golden axe,
And smil'st upon the stroke that murders me.
     Fri. O deadly sin! O rude unthankfulness!
Thy fault our law calls death; but the kind Prince,
Taking thy part, hath rushed aside the law,
And turned that black word "death" to "banish-
          ment:"
This is dear mercy, and thou seest it not.

Rom. 'T is torture, and not mercy. Heaven
    is here,
Where Juliet lives; and every cat, and dog,
And little mouse, every unworthy thing,
Live here in heaven, and may look on her;
But Romeo may not.—More validity,
More honourable state, more courtship, lives
In carrion flies than Romeo: they may seize
On the white wonder of dear Juliet's hand,
And steal immortal blessing from her lips;
Who, even in pure and vestal modesty,
Still blush, as thinking their own kisses sin;
But Romeo may not; he is banishéd:
Flies may do this, when I from this must fly:
They are free men, but I am banishéd.
And sayst thou yet that exile is not death?
Hadst thou no poison mixed, no sharp-ground knife,
No sudden mean of death, though ne'er so mean,
But "banishéd," to kill me? "Banishéd!"
O friar, the damnéd use that word in hell;
Howlings attend it. How hast thou the heart,
Being a divine, a ghostly cónfessor,
A sin-absolver, and a friend professed,
To mangle me with that word "banishéd?"
    Fri. Thou fond mad man, hear me but speak
    a word.
    Rom. O, thou wilt speak again of banishment.
    Fri. I 'll give thee armour to keep off that word:
Adversity's sweet milk, philosophy,
To comfort thee, though thou art banishéd.
    Rom. Yet "banishéd?"—Hang up philosophy!
Unless philosophy can make a Juliet,
Displant a town, reverse a Prince's doom;
It helps not, it prevails not: talk no more.
    Fri. O, then I see that madmen have no ears.
    Rom. How should they, when that wise men
    have no eyes?
    Fri. Let me dispute with thee of thy estate.
    Rom. Thou canst not speak of what thou dost
    not feel:
Wert thou as young as I, Juliet thy love,
An hour but married, Tybalt murderéd,
Doting like me, and like me banishéd,
Then mightst thou speak, then mightst thou tear
    thy hair,
And fall upon the ground, as I do now,
Taking the measure of an unmade grave.
    Fri. Arise; one knocks; good Romeo, hide
    thyself.   [*Knocking within.*
    Rom. Not I; unless the breath of heart-sick
    groans,
Mist-like, infold me from the search of eyes.
                      [*Knocking.*
    Fri. Hark, how they knock!—Who 's there?—
    Romeo, arise;
Thou wilt be taken:—Stay awhile:—stand up;
                      [*Knocking.*

Run to my study:—By and by:—God's will!
What wilfulness is this?—I come, I come.
                      [*Knocking.*
Who knocks so hard? whence come you? what 's
    your will?
    Nurse [*within*]. Let me come in, and you shall
    know my errand:
I come from Lady Juliet.
    Fri.   Welcome, then.

Enter Nurse.

    Nurse. O holy friar, O, tell me, holy friar,
Where 's my lady's lord; where 's Romeo?
    Fri. There on the ground, with his own tears
    made drunk.
    Nurse. O, he is even in my mistress' case;
Just in her case!
    Fri.   O woful sympathy!
Piteous predicament!
    Nurse.   Even so lies she,
Blubbering and weeping, weeping and blub-
    bering.—
Stand up, stand up; stand, an you be a man:
For Juliet's sake, for her sake, rise and stand;
Why should you fall into so deep an O?
    Rom. Nurse!
    Nurse. Ah sir! ah sir!—Well, death 's the
    end of all.
    Rom. Spak'st thou of Juliet? how is it with her?
Doth she not think me an old murderer,
Now I have stained the childhood of our joy
With blood removed but little from her own?
Where is she, and how doth she, and what says
My cóncealed lady to our cancelled love?
    Nurse. O, she says nothing, sir, but weeps
    and weeps;
And now falls on her bed; and then starts up,
And Tybalt calls; and then on Romeo cries,
And then down falls again.
    Rom.   As if that name,
Shot from the deadly level of a gun,
Did murder her; as that name's curséd hand
Murdered her kinsman.—O tell me, friar, tell me,
In what vile part of this anatomy
Doth my name lodge? tell me, that I may sack
The hateful mansion.   [*Drawing his sword.*
    Fri.   Hold thy desperate hand!
Art thou a man? thy form cries out thou art:
Thy tears are womanish; thy wild acts denote
The unreasonable fury of a beast:
Unseemly woman, in a seeming man!
Or ill-beseeming beast, in seeming both!
Thou hast amazed me: by my holy order,
I thought thy disposition better tempered.
Hast thou slain Tybalt? wilt thou slay thyself?
And slay thy lady that in thy life lives,
By doing damnéd hate upon thyself?

Why rail'st thou on thy birth, the heaven, and
    earth?
Since birth, and heaven, and earth, all three do
    meet
In thee at once; which thou at once wouldst lose.
Fie, fie! thou sham'st thy shape, thy love, thy
    wit;
Which, like an usurer, abound'st in all,
And usest none in that true use indeed
Which should bedeck thy shape, thy love, thy wit.
Thy noble shape is but a form of wax,
Digressing from the valour of a man:
Thy dear love, sworn, but hollow perjury,
Killing that love which thou hast vowed to
    cherish:
Thy wit, that ornament to shape and love,
Mis-shapen in the conduct of them both,
Like powder in a skill-less soldier's flask,
Is set on fire by thine own ignorance,
And thou dismembered with thine own defence.—
What, rouse thee, man! thy Juliet is alive,
For whose dear sake thou wast but lately dead;
There art thou happy: Tybalt would kill thee,
But thou slew'st Tybalt; there art thou happy too:
The law, that threatened death, becomes thy
    friend,
And turns it to exíle; there art thou happy:
A pack of blessings lights upon thy back;
Happiness courts thee in her best array;
But, like a misbehaved and sullen wench,
Thou frown'st upon thy fortune and thy love:
Take heed, take heed, for such die miserable.
Go, get thee to thy love, as was decreed;
Ascend her chamber; hence and comfort her:
But look thou stay not till the watch be set,
For then thou canst not pass to Mantua;
Where thou shalt live, till we can find a time
To blaze your marriage, reconcile your friends,
Beg pardon of the Prince, and call thee back
With twenty hundred thousand times more joy
Than thou went'st forth in lamentation.—
Go before, nurse: commend me to thy lady;
And bid her hasten all the house to bed,
Which heavy sorrow makes them apt unto:
Romeo is coming.
    Nurse. O, Lord, I could have stayed here all
    the night,
To hear good counsel. O, what learning is!—
My lord, I'll tell my lady you will come.
    Rom. Do so, and bid my sweet prepare to chide.
    Nurse. Here, sir, a ring she bade me give
    you, sir:
Hie you, make haste, for it grows very late.
                       [Exit Nurse.
    Rom. How well my comfort is revived by this!
    Fri. Go hence: good night; and here stands
    all your state:—

Either begone before the watch be set,
Or by the break of day disguised from hence.
Sojourn in Mantua: I'll find out your man,
And he shall signify from time to time
Every good hap to you that chances here.
Give me thy hand; 't is late: farewell; good night.
    Rom. But that a joy past joy calls out on me,
It were a grief so brief to part with thee.
Farewell.   *[Exeunt.*

SCENE IV.—*A Room in* CAPULET'S *House.*

Enter CAPULET, LADY CAPULET, *and* PARIS.

    Cap. Things have fallen out, sir, so unluckily,
That we have had no time to move our daughter.
Look you, she loved her kinsman Tybalt dearly,
And so did I:—well we were born to die.——
'T is very late; she'll not come down to-night.
I promise you, but for your company,
I would have been a-bed an hour ago.
    Par. These times of woe afford no time to woo.
Madam, good night: commend me to your
    daughter.
    Lady C. I will, and know her mind early
    to-morrow;
To-night she's mewed up to her heaviness.
    Cap. Sir Paris, I will make a desperate tender
Of my child's love: I think she will be ruled
In all respects by me; nay more, I doubt it not.
Wife, go you to her ere you go to bed;
Acquaint her here of my son Paris' love;
And bid her, mark you me, on Wednesday next—
But soft,—what day is this?
    Par.   Monday, my lord.
    Cap. Monday? ha! ha! Well, Wednesday is
    too soon;
O' Thursday let it be:—o' Thursday tell her,
She shall be married to this noble earl.—
Will you be ready? do you like this haste?
We'll keep no great ado: a friend or two:
For hark you, Tybalt being slain so late,
It may be thought we held him carelessly,
Being our kinsman, if we revel much:
Therefore we'll have some half-a-dozen friends,
And there an end. But what say you to Thursday?
    Par. My lord, I would that Thursday were
    to-morrow.
    Cap. Well, get you gone: o' Thursday be it,
    then.—
Go you to Juliet ere you go to bed,
Prepare her, wife, against this wedding-day.—
Farewell, my lord.—Light to my chamber, ho!
Afore me, it is so very late that we
May call it early by and by.—Good night.
                          [Exeunt.

Scene V.—Juliet's *Chamber*.

Enter Romeo *and* Juliet.

Jul. Wilt thou be gone? it is not yet near day:
It was the nightingale, and not the lark,
That pierced the fearful hollow of thine ear:
Nightly she sings on yon pomegranate tree.
Believe me, love, it was the nightingale.

Rom. It was the lark, the herald of the morn;
No nightingale. Look, love, what envious streaks
Do lace the severing clouds in yonder east:
Night's candles are burnt out, and jocund day
Stands tiptoe on the misty mountain tops.
I must be gone and live, or stay and die.

Jul. Yon light is not daylight; I know it, I:
It is some meteor that the sun exhales,

To be to thee this night a torchbearer,
And light thee on thy way to Mantua:
Therefore stay yet; thou need'st not to be gone.

Rom. Let me be ta'en, let me be put to death;
I am content, so thou wilt have it so.
I 'll say, yon grey is not the morning's eye,
'T is but the pale reflex of Cynthia's brow;
Nor that is not the lark whose notes do beat
The vaulty heaven so high above our heads.
I have more care to stay than will to go:

Come, death, and welcome! Juliet wills it so.—
How is 't, my soul? let 's talk; it is not day.

Jul. It is, it is: hie hence, be gone, away:
It is the lark that sings so out of tune,
Straining harsh discords and unpleasing sharps.
Some say, the lark makes sweet division;
This doth not so, for she divideth us:
Some say, the lark and loathéd toad change eyes;
O, now I would they had changed voices too
Since arm from arm that voice doth us affray,

Hunting thee hence with hunts-up to the day.
O, now be gone; more light and light it grows.
   Rom. More light and light?—more dark and
     dark our woes.

Enter Nurse.

Nurse. Madam!
Jul. Nurse?
Nurse. Your lady mother's coming to your
     chamber:
The day is broke; be wary, look about.
                   [*Exit* Nurse.
   Jul. Then, window, let day in, and let life out.
   Rom. Farewell, farewell! one kiss, and I'll
     descend.   [ROMEO *descends.*
   Jul. Art thou gone so? love! lord! ay, hus-
     band, friend!
I must hear from thee every day i' the hour,
For in a minute there are many days:
O! by this count I shall be much in years
Ere I again behold my Romeo.
   Rom. Farewell! I will omit no opportunity
That may convey my greetings, love, to thee.
   Jul. O, think'st thou we shall ever meet again?
   Rom. I doubt it not; and all these woes shall
     serve
For sweet discourses in our time to come.
   Jul. O God, I have an ill-divining soul!
Methinks I see thee, now thou art so low,
As one dead in the bottom of a tomb:
Either my eyesight fails, or thou look'st pale.
   Rom. And trust me, love, in my eye so do you:
Dry sorrow drinks our blood. Adieu, adieu!
                   [*Exit* ROMEO.
   Jul. O fortune, fortune; all men call thee fickle:
If thou art fickle, what dost thou with him
That is renowned for faith? Be fickle, fortune;
For then I hope thou wilt not keep him long,
But send him back.
   Lady C. [*within*]. Ho, daughter! are you up?
   Jul. Who is't that calls? is it my lady mother?
Is she not down so late, or up so early?
What unaccustomed cause procures her hither?

Enter LADY CAPULET.

   Lady C. Why, how now, Juliet?
   Jul.   Madam, I am not well.
   Lady C. Evermore weeping for your cousin's
     death?
What, wilt thou wash him from his grave with
     tears?
An if thou couldst, thou couldst not make him
     live;
Therefore have done: some grief shews much
     of love,
But much of grief shews still some want of wit.
   Jul. Yet let me weep for such a feeling loss.

   Lady C. So shall you feel the loss, but not the
     friend
Which you weep for.
   Jul.   Feeling so the loss,
I cannot choose but ever weep the friend.
   Lady C. Well, girl, thou weep'st not so much
     for his death,
As that the villain lives which slaughtered him.
   Jul. What villain, madam?
   Lady C.   That same villain, Romeo.
   Jul. Villain and he are many miles asunder.
God pardon him! I do with all my heart;
And yet no man like he doth grieve my heart.
   Lady C. That is because the traitor murderer
     lives.
   Jul. Ay, madam, from the reach of these my
     hands.
'Would none but I might venge my cousin's death!
   Lady C. We will have vengeance for it, fear
     thou not:
Then weep no more. I'll send to one in Mantua,
Where that same banished runagate doth live,
Shall give him such an unaccustomed dram,
That he shall soon keep Tybalt company:
And then I hope thou wilt be satisfied.
   Jul. Indeed, I never shall be satisfied
With Romeo, till I behold him—dead—
Is my poor heart, so for a kinsman vexed:—
Madam, if you could but find out a man
To bear a poison, I would temper it,
That Romeo should, upon receipt thereof,
Soon sleep in quiet. O, how my heart abhors
To hear him named,—and cannot come to him,—
To wreak the love I bore my cousin
Upon his body that hath slaughtered him!
   Lady C. Find thou the means, and I'll find
     such a man.
But now I'll tell thee joyful tidings, girl.
   Jul. And joy comes well in such a needful time:
What are they, I beseech your ladyship?
   Lady C. Well, well, thou hast a careful father,
     child;
One who, to put thee from thy heaviness,
Hath sorted out a sudden day of joy,
That thou expect'st not, nor I looked not for.
   Jul. Madam, in happy time, what day is that?
   Lady C. Marry, my child, early next Thurs-
     day morn,
The gallant, young, and noble gentleman,
The County Paris, at St. Peter's church,
Shall happily make thee there a joyful bride.
   Jul. Now by Saint Peter's church, and Peter too,
He shall not make me there a joyful bride.
I wonder at this haste; that I must wed
Ere he that should be husband comes to woo.
I pray you, tell my lord and father, madam,
I will not marry yet; and when I do, I swear

It shall be Romeo, whom you know I hate,
Rather than Paris.—These are news indeed!

   Lady C. Here comes your father : tell him
     so yourself,
And see how he will take it at your hands.

      Enter CAPULET *and* Nurse.

   Cap. When the sun sets, the air doth drizzle dew;
But for the sunset of my brother's son,
It rains downright.—
How now! a conduit, girl? what, still in tears?
Evermore showering? In one little body
Thou counterfeit'st a bark, a sea, a wind :
For still thy eyes, which I may call the sea,
Do ebb and flow with tears : the bark thy body is,
Sailing in this salt flood : the winds, thy sighs;
Who, raging with thy tears, and they with them,
Without a sudden calm will overset
Thy tempest-tosséd body.—How now, wife!
Have you delivered to her our decree?

   Lady C. Ay, sir; but she will none, she gives
     you thanks.
I would the fool were married to her grave!

   Cap. Soft, take me with you; take me with
     you, wife.
How! will she none? doth she not give us thanks?
Is she not proud, doth she not count her blessed,
Unworthy as she is, that we have wrought
So worthy a gentleman to be her bridegroom?

   Jul. Not proud you have; but thankful that
     you have.
Proud can I never be of what I hate :
But thankful even for hate that is meant love.

   Cap. How now, how now; chop-logic! What
     is this?
Proud,—and, I thank you,—and, I thank you not—
Thank me no thankings, nor proud me no prouds,
But settle your fine joints 'gainst Thursday next,
To go with Paris to Saint Peter's church,
Or I will drag thee on a hurdle thither.
Out, you green-sickness carrion! out, you bag-
     gage!
You tallow-face!

   Lady C. Fie, fie! what, are you mad?

   Jul. Good father, I beseech you on my knees,
Hear me with patience but to speak a word.

   Cap. Hang thee, young baggage! disobedient
     wretch!
I tell thee what,—get thee to church o'Thursday,
Or never after look me in the face.
Speak not, reply not, do not answer me :
My fingers ʼitch.—Wife, we scarce thought us
     blessed
That God hath lent us but this only child;
But now I see this one is one too much,
And that we have a curse in having her :
Out on her, hilding!

   Nurse.   God in heaven bless her!
You are to blame, my lord, to rate her so.

   Cap. And why, my lady wisdom? Hold your
     tongue,
Good prudence; smatter with your gossips, go.

   Nurse. I speak no treason.

   Cap.   O, God ye good den!

   Nurse. May not one speak?

   Cap.   Peace, you mumbling fool!
Utter your gravity o'er a gossip's bowl,
For here we need it not.

   Lady C.   You are too hot.

   Cap. God's bread! it makes me mad.
Day, night, hour, tide, time, work, play,
Alone, in company, still my care hath been
To have her matched : and having now provided
A gentleman of princely parentage,
Of fair demesnes, youthful, and nobly trained,
Stuffed (as they say) with honourable parts,
Proportioned as one's heart could wish a man,—
And then to have a wretched puling fool,
A whining mammet, in her fortune's tender,
To answer " I 'll not wed," " I cannot love,"
" I am too young," " I pray you pardon me :"—
But an you will not wed, I 'll pardon you :
Graze where you will, you shall not house with me:
Look to 't, think on 't; I do not use to jest.
Thursday is near; lay hand on heart; advise:
An you be mine, I 'll give you to my friend;
An you be not, hang, beg, starve, die i' the streets;
For, by my soul, I 'll ne'er acknowledge thee,
Nor what is mine shall never do thee good.
Trust to 't; bethink you; I 'll not be forsworn.
                          [Exit.

   Jul. Is there no pity sitting in the clouds,
That sees into the bottom of my grief?
O, sweet my mother, cast me not away!
Delay this marriage for a month, a week;
Or, if you do not, make the bridal bed
In that dim monument where Tybalt lies.

   Lady C. Talk not to me, for I 'll not speak a
     word;
Do as thou wilt, for I have done with thee.
                          [Exit.

   Jul. O God!—O nurse, how shall this be
     prevented?
My husband is on earth, my faith in heaven :
How shall that faith return again to earth,
Unless that husband send it me from heaven
By leaving earth?—Comfort me, counsel me.—
Alack, alack, that heaven should practise strata-
     gems
Upon so soft a subject as myself!—
What sayst thou? hast thou not a word of joy?
Some comfort, nurse.

   Nurse.   'Faith, here 't is :—Romeo
Is banishéd; and all the world to nothing

That he dares ne'er come back to challenge you:
Or, if he do, it needs must be by stealth.
Then, since the case so stands as now it doth,
I think it best you married with the County.
O, he's a lovely gentleman!
Romeo's a dishclout to him. An eagle, madam,
Hath not so green, so quick, so fair an eye,
As Paris hath.   Beshrew my very heart,
I think you are happy in this second match,
For it excels your first: or if it did not,
Your first is dead; or 't were as good he were,
As living here, and you no use of him.

    Jul. Speakest thou from thy heart?

    Nurse.   From my soul too;
Or else beshrew them both.

    Jul.   Amen!

    Nurse.   What?

    Jul. Well, thou hast comforted me marvellous
    much.
Go in; and tell my lady I am gone,
Having displeased my father, to Laurence' cell,
To make confession, and to be absolved.

    Nurse. Marry, I will; and this is wisely done.
                           [Exit.

    Jul. Ancient damnation! O most wicked fiend!
Is it more sin to wish me thus forsworn,
Or to dispraise my lord with that same tongue
Which she hath praised him with above compare
So many thousand times?—Go, counsellor;
Thou and my bosom henceforth shall be twain.
I'll to the Friar, to know his remedy:
If all else fail, myself have power to die. *[Exit.*

IV

SCENE I.—FRIAR LAURENCE'S *Cell.*

Enter FRIAR LAURENCE *and* PARIS.

Fri. On Thursday, sir? the time is very short.
Par. My father Capulet will have it so;
And I am nothing slow, to slack his haste.
Fri. You say you do not know the lady's mind:
Uneven is the course; I like it not.
Par. Immoderately she weeps for Tybalt's
     death,
And therefore have I little talked of love;
For Venus smiles not in a house of tears.
Now, sir, her father counts it dangerous
That she doth give her sorrow so much sway,
And in his wisdom hastes our marriage
To stop the inundation of her tears;
Which, too much minded by herself alone,
May be put from her by society.
Now do you know the reason of this haste.
Fri. I would I knew not why it should be
     slowed.   [*Aside.*
Look, sir, here comes the lady towards my cell.

Enter JULIET.

Par. Happily met, my lady and my wife!
Jul. That may be, sir, when I may be a wife.
Par. That may be, must be, love, on Thursday
     next.
Jul. What must be shall be.
Fri.   That's a certain text.
Par. Come you to make confession to this
     father?
Jul. To answer that, were to confess to you.
Par. Do not deny to him that you love me.
Jul. I will confess to you that I love him.
Par. So will you, I am sure, that you love me.
Jul. If I do so, it will be of more price,
Being spoke behind your back, than to your face.
Par. Poor soul, thy face is much abused with
     tears.
Jul. The tears have got small victory by that;
For it was bad enough before their spite.

Par. Thou wrong'st it, more than tears, with
     that report.
Jul. That is no slander, sir, that is a truth;
And what I spake, I spake it to my face.
Par. Thy face is mine, and thou hast slandered it.
Jul. It may be so, for it is not mine own.—
Are you at leisure, holy father, now;
Or shall I come to you at evening mass?
Fri. My leisure serves me, pensive daughter,
     now.—
My lord, we must entreat the time alone.
Par. God shield I should disturb devotion!—
Juliet, on Thursday early will I rouse you:
Till then, adieu! and keep this holy kiss. [*Exit.*
Jul. O, shut the door! and when thou hast
     done so,
Come weep with me; past hope, past cure, past
     help!
Fri. Ah, Juliet, I already know thy grief;
It strains me past the compass of my wits.
I hear thou must, and nothing may prorogue it,
On Thursday next be married to this County.
Jul. Tell me not, friar, that thou hear'st of this,
Unless thou tell me how I may prevent it:
If in thy wisdom thou canst give no help,
Do thou but call my resolution wise,
And with this knife I'll help it presently.
God joined my heart and Romeo's; thou our hands;
And ere this hand, by thee to Romeo sealed,
Shall be the label to another deed,
Or my true heart with treacherous revolt
Turn to another, this shall slay them both:
Therefore, out of thy long-experienced time,
Give me some present counsel; or, behold,
'Twixt my extremes and me this bloody knife
Shall play the umpire; arbitrating that
Which the commission of thy years and art
Could to no issue of true honour bring.—
Be not so long to speak: I long to die,
If what thou speak'st speak not of remedy.
Fri. Hold, daughter: I do spy a kind of hope,
Which craves as desperate an execution

As that is desperate which we would prevent.
If, rather than to marry County Paris,
Thou hast the strength of will to slay thyself,
Then is it likely thou wilt undertake
A thing like death to chide away this shame,
That cop'st with death himself to 'scape from it :
And if thou dar'st, I 'll give thee remedy.

Jul. O, bid me leap, rather than marry Paris,
From off the battlements of yonder tower ;
Or walk in thievish ways ; or bid me lurk
Where serpents are ; chain me with roaring bears ;
Or shut me nightly in a charnel-house,
O'ercovered quite with dead men's rattling bones,
With reeky shanks, and yellow chapless skulls ;

O, shut the door!

Or bid me go into a new-made grave,
And hide me with a dead man in his shroud ;
(Things that, to hear them told, have made me
    tremble ;)
And I will do it without fear or doubt,
To live an unstained wife to my sweet love.

Fri. Hold, then : go home, be merry, give consent
To marry Paris.   Wednesday is to-morrow :
To-morrow night look that thou lie alone,
Let not thy nurse lie with thee in thy chamber :
Take thou this phial, being then in bed,

And this distilléd liquor drink thou off :
When presently through all thy veins shall run
A cold and drowsy humour, which shall seize
Each vital spirit ; for no pulse shall keep
His natural progress, but surcease to beat :
No warmth, no breath, shall testify thou liv'st :
The roses in thy lips and cheeks shall fade
To paly ashes ; thy eyes' windows fall,
Like death when he shuts up the day of life ;
Each part, deprived of supple government,
Shall, stiff and stark and cold, appear like death :

And in this borrowed likeness of shrunk death
Thou shalt remain full two-and-forty hours,
And then awake as from a pleasant sleep.
Now when the bridegroom in the morning comes
To rouse thee from thy bed, there art thou dead:
Then (as the manner of our country is),
In thy best robes, uncovered on the bier,
Thou shalt be borne to that same ancient vault
Where all the kindred of the Capulets lie.
In the mean time, against thou shalt awake,
Shall Romeo by my letters know our drift;
And hither shall he come; and he and I
Will watch thy waking, and that very night
Shall Romeo bear thee hence to Mantua.
And this shall free thee from this present shame;
If no unconstant toy, nor womanish fear,
Abate thy valour in the acting it.

   Jul. Give me, give me! O tell me not of fear.

   Fri. Hold; get you gone, be strong and pros-
      perous
In this resolve: I 'll send a friar with speed
To Mantua, with my letters to thy lord.

   Jul. Love, give me strength! and strength
      shall help afford.
Farewell, dear father!   *[Exeunt.*

Scene II.—*A Room in* Capulet's *House.*

Enter Capulet, Lady Capulet, Nurse, *and*
      Servants.

   Cap. So many guests invite as here are writ.—
            [Exit 1st Servant.
Sirrah, go hire me twenty cunning cooks.

   2nd Serv. You shall have none ill, sir; for I 'll
try if they can lick their fingers.

   Cap. How canst thou try them so?

   2nd Serv. Marry, sir, 't is an ill cook that cannot lick his own fingers: therefore he that cannot
lick his fingers goes not with me.

   Cap. Go, begone.—   *[Exit 2nd* Servant.
We shall be much unfurnished for this time.—
What, is my daughter gone to Friar Laurence?

   Nurse. Ay, forsooth.

   Cap. Well, he may chance to do some good
      on her:
A peevish self-willed harlotry it is.

Enter Juliet.

   Nurse. See where she comes from shrift with
      merry look.

   Cap. How now, my headstrong, where have
you been gadding?

   Jul. Where I have learned me to repent the sin
Of disobedient opposition
To you and your behests; and am enjoined

By holy Laurence to fall prostrate here,
And beg your pardon:—Pardon, I beseech you!
Henceforward I am ever ruled by you.

   Cap. Send for the County; go tell him of this:
I 'll have this knot knit up to-morrow morning.

   Jul. I met the youthful lord at Laurence' cell;
And gave him what becoméd love I might,
Not stepping o'er the bounds of modesty.

   Cap. Why, I am glad on 't; this is well;—
      stand up:
This is as 't should be.—Let me see the County;
Ay marry, go, I say, and fetch him hither.—
Now, afore God, this reverend holy friar,
All our whole city is much bound to him.

   Jul. Nurse, will you go with me into my closet,
To help me sort such needful ornaments
As you think fit to furnish me to-morrow?

   Lady C. No, not till Thursday: there is time
      enough.

   Cap. Go, nurse, go with her:—we 'll to church
      to-morrow. *[Exeunt* Juliet *and* Nurse.

   Lady C. We shall be short in our provision:
'T is now near night.

   Cap.   Tush! I will stir about,
And all things shall be well, I warrant thee, wife.
Go thou to Juliet, help to deck up her:
I 'll not to bed to-night: let me alone;
I 'll play the housewife for this once.—What, ho!—
They are all forth. Well, I will walk myself
To County Paris, to prepare him up
Against to-morrow: my heart is wondrous light,
Since this same wayward girl is so reclaimed.
                       [Exeunt.

Scene III.—Juliet's *Chamber.*

Enter Juliet *and* Nurse.

   Jul. Ay, those attires are best.—But, gentle nurse,
I pray thee leave me to myself to-night;
For I have need of many orisons
To move the heavens to smile upon my state,
Which well thou know'st is cross and full of sin.

Enter Lady Capulet.

   Lady C. What, are you busy? Need you any
      help?

   Jul. No, madam: we have culled such neces-
      saries
As are behovéd for our state to-morrow.
So please you, let me now be left alone,
And let the nurse this night sit up with you;
For I am sure you have your hands full all,
In this so sudden business.

   Lady C.   Good night:
Get thee to bed, and rest; for thou hast need.
          [Exeunt Lady Capulet *and* Nurse.

Jul. Farewell!—God knows when we shall
    meet again.
I have a faint cold fear thrills through my veins,
That almost freezes up the heat of life:
I 'll call them back again to comfort me :—
Nurse!—What should she do here?
My dismal scene I needs must act alone.—
Come, phial.—
What if this mixture do not work at all?
Must I of force be married to the County?
No, no: this shall forbid it :—lie thou there.
    [*Laying down a dagger.*
What if it be a poison, which the Friar
Subtly hath ministered to have me dead;
Lest in this marriage he should be dishonoured,
Because he married me before to Romeo?
I fear it is : and yet methinks it should not,
For he hath still been tried a holy man.
I will not entertain so bad a thought.—
How if, when I am laid into the tomb,
I wake before the time that Romeo
Come to redeem me? There 's a fearful point!
Shall I not then be stifled in the vault,
To whose foul mouth no healthsome air breathes in,
And there die strangled ere my Romeo comes?
Or if I live, is it not very like
The horrible conceit of death and night,
Together with the terror of the place,—
As in a vault, an ancient receptacle,
Where, for these many hundred years, the bones
Of all my buried ancestors are packed :
Where bloody Tybalt, yet but green in earth,
Lies festering in his shroud : where, as they say,
At some hours in the night, spirits resort :
Alack, alack! is it not like that I,
So early waking,—what with loathsome smells,
And shrieks like mandrakes' torn out of the earth,
That living mortals, hearing them, run mad :—
O! if I wake, shall I not be distraught,
Environéd with all these hideous fears;
And madly play with my forefathers' joints;
And pluck the mangled Tybalt from his shroud;
And in this rage, with some great kinsman's bone,
As with a club, dash out my desperate brains?
O, look! methinks, I see my cousin's ghost
Seeking out Romeo, that did spit his body
Upon a rapier's point!—Stay, Tybalt, stay!—
Romeo, I come! this do I drink to thee.
    [*She throws herself upon the bed.*

Scene IV.—Capulet's *Hall.*

Enter Lady Capulet *and* Nurse.

Lady C. Hold, take these keys, and fetch more
    spices, nurse.

Nurse. They call for dates and quinces in the
    pastry.

Enter Capulet.

Cap. Come, stir, stir, stir ! the second cock
    hath crowed,
The curfew-bell hath rung; 'tis three o'clock.—
Look to the baked meats, good Angelica:
Spare not for cost.
Nurse.   Go, go, you cot-quean, go,
Get you to bed : 'faith, you 'll be sick to-morrow,
For this night's watching.
Cap. No, not a whit. What! I have watched
    ere now
All night for lesser cause, and ne'er been sick.
Lady C. Ay, you have been a mouse-hunt in
    your time;
But I will watch you from such watching now.
    [*Exeunt* Lady Capulet *and* Nurse.
Cap. A jealous-hood, a jealous-hood!—Now,
    fellow,
What 's there ?

Enter Servants, *with spits, logs, and baskets.*

1st Serv. Things for the cook, sir; but I know
    not what.
Cap. Make haste, make haste [*Exit* 1st Servant].
    —Sirrah, fetch drier logs:
Call Peter; he will shew thee where they are.
2nd Serv. I have a head, sir, that will find out
    logs,
And never trouble Peter for the matter.   [*Exit.*
Cap. 'Mass, and well said. A merry whore-
    son! ha,
Thou shalt be loggerhead.—Good faith, 'tis day:
The County will be here with music straight,
                [*Music within.*
For so he said he would.   I hear him near.—
Nurse!—Wife!—what, ho!—what, nurse, I say!

Enter Nurse.

Go, waken Juliet; go, and trim her up :
I 'll go and chat with Paris.—Hie ; make haste,
Make haste ! the bridegroom he is come already.
Make haste, I say !   [*Exeunt.*

Scene V.—Juliet's *Chamber;* Juliet *on the bed.*

Enter Nurse.

Nurse. Mistress! what, mistress! Juliet!—
    fast, I warrant her, she.—
Why, lamb! why, lady! fie, you slug-a-bed!
Why, love, I say! madam! sweetheart! why, bride!
What, not a word!—you take your pennyworths
    now :
Sleep for a week ; for the next night, I warrant,

The County Paris hath set up his rest
That you shall rest but little.—God forgive me,
(Marry, and amen!) how sound is she asleep!
I needs must wake her.—Madam, madam, madam!
Ay, let the County take you in your bed;
He'll fright you up, i' faith.—Will it not be?
What, drest, and in your clothes! and down again!
I must needs wake you:—Lady, lady, lady!
Alas, alas!—Help, help! my lady's dead!
O, well-a-day, that ever I was born!—
Some *aqua-vitæ*, ho!—My lord! my lady!

Enter Lady Capulet.

Lady C. What noise is here?
Nurse.   O lamentable day!
Lady C. What is the matter?
Nurse.   Look, look! O heavy day!
Lady C. O me, O me!—my child, my only life,
Revive, look up, or I will die with thee!—
Help, help!—call help.

Enter Capulet.

Cap. For shame; bring Juliet forth: her lord
     is come.
Nurse. She's dead, deceased, she's dead; alack
     the day!
Lady C. Alack the day! she's dead, she's dead,
     she's dead!
Cap. Ha! let me see her:—Out, alas! she's cold;
Her blood is settled, and her joints are stiff:
Life and these lips have long been separated.
Death lies on her, like an untimely frost
Upon the sweetest flower of all the field.
Accursèd time! unfortunate old man!
Nurse. O lamentable day!
Lady C.   O woful time!
Cap. Death, that hath ta'en her hence to make
     me wail,
Ties up my tongue, and will not let me speak.

Enter Friar Laurence *and* Paris, *with*
Musicians.

Fri. Come, is the bride ready to go to church?
Cap. Ready to go, but never to return.
O son, the night before thy wedding-day
Hath death lain with thy bride:—there she lies,
Flower as she was, deflowerèd by him.
Death is my son-in-law, death is my heir;
My daughter he hath wedded! I will die,
And leave him all: life leaving, all is death's.
Par. Have I thought long to see this morn-
     ing's face,
And doth it give me such a sight as this?
Lady C. Accursed, unhappy, wretched, hate-
     ful day!
Most miserable hour that e'er time saw
In lasting labour of his pilgrimage!—
But one, poor one, one poor and loving child,

But one thing to rejoice and solace in,
And cruel death hath catched it from my sight.
Nurse. O woe! O woful, woful, woful day!
Most lamentable day! most woful day,
That ever, ever I did yet behold!
O day, O day, O day! O hateful day!
Never was seen so black a day as this:
O woful day, O woful day!
Par. Beguiled, divorcèd, wrongèd, spited, slain!
Most detestable death, by thee beguiled,
By cruel, cruel thee quite overthrown!—
O love! O life!—not life, but love in death!
Cap. Despised, distressèd, hated, martyred,
     killed!—
Uncomfortable time! why cam'st thou now
To murder, murder, our solemnity?—
O child, O child!—my soul, and not my child!—
Dead art thou!—alack! my child is dead:
And, with my child, my joys are buried.
Fri. Peace, ho, for shame! confusion's cure
     lives not
In these confusions. Heaven and yourself
Had part in this fair maid; now heaven hath all;
And all the better is it for the maid:
Your part in her you could not keep from death;
But Heaven keeps His part in eternal life.
The most you sought was her promotion;
For 't was your heaven she should be advanced:
And weep ye now, seeing she is advanced,
Above the clouds, as high as heaven itself?
O, in this love you love your child so ill,
That you run mad seeing that she is well:
She's not well married that lives married long;
But she's best married that dies married young.
Dry up your tears, and stick your rosemary
On this fair corse; and, as the custom is,
In all her best array bear her to church:
For though fond nature bids us all lament,
Yet nature's tears are reason's merriment.
Cap. All things, that we ordainèd festival,
Turn from their office to black funeral:
Our instruments to melancholy bells;
Our wedding cheer to a sad burial feast;
Our solemn hymns to sullen dirges change;
Our bridal flowers serve for a buried corse,
And all things change them to the contrary.
Fri. Sir, go you in; and, madam, go with him;
And go, sir Paris: every one prepare
To follow this fair corse unto her grave.
The heavens do low'r upon you, for some ill:
Move them no more, by crossing their high will.
          [*Exeunt* Capulet, Lady Capulet, Paris,
                and Friar.
1st Mus. 'Faith, we may put up our pipes, and
be gone.
Nurse. Honest good fellows, ah, put up, put up;
For well you know this is a pitiful case. [*Exit.*

1st Mus. Ay, by my troth, the case may be amended.

Enter PETER.

Pet. Musicians, O musicians, "Heart's-ease, heart's-ease." O, an you will have me live, play "Heart's-ease."

1st Mus. Why "Heart's-ease?"

Pet. O, musicians, because my heart itself plays "My heart is full of woe." O, play me some merry dump to comfort me.

2nd Mus. Not a dump we: 'tis no time to play now.

Pet. You will not, then?

Mus. No.

Pet. I will, then, give it you soundly.

1st Mus. What will you give us?

Pet. No money, on my faith; but the gleek: I will give you the minstrel.

1st Mus. Then will I give you the serving-creature.

Pet. Then will I lay the serving-creature's dagger on your pate. I will carry no crotchets: I 'll *re* you, I 'll *fa* you: do you note me?

1st Mus. An you *re* us and *fa* us, you note us.

2nd Mus. Pray you, put up your dagger, and put out your wit.

Pet. Then have at you with my wit: I will dry-beat you with an iron wit, and put up my iron dagger. Answer me like men :—

"When griping grief the heart doth wound,
  And doleful dumps the mind oppress,
Then music, with her silver sound,"—

Why "silver sound?" why, "music, with her silver sound?"

What say you, Simon Catling?

1st Mus. Marry, sir, because silver hath a sweet sound.

Pet. Pretty! What say you, Hugh Rebeck?

2nd Mus. I say "silver sound," because musicians sound for silver.

Pet. Pretty too! What say you, James Sound-post?

3rd Mus. 'Faith, I know not what to say.

Pet. O, I cry you mercy! you are the singer: I will say for you. It is "music, with her silver sound," because such fellows as you have seldom gold for sounding :—

"Then music, with her silver sound,
  With speedy help doth lend redress."

[*Exit singing.*

1st Mus. What a pestilent knave is this same!

2nd Mus. Hang him, Jack! Come, we 'll in here: tarry for the mourners, and stay dinner.

[*Exeunt.*

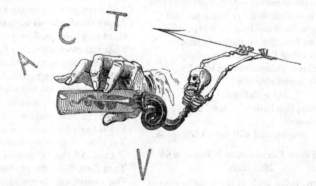

Scene I.—Mantua. *A Street.*

Enter ROMEO.

Rom. If I may trust the flattering truth of sleep,
My dreams presage some joyful news at hand:
My bosom's lord sits lightly in his throne;
And, all this day, an unaccustomed spirit
Lifts me above the ground with cheerful thoughts.
I dreamt my lady came and found me dead
(Strange dream! that gives a dead man leave to
    think),
And breathed such life with kisses in my lips,
That I revived, and was an emperor.
Ah me! how sweet is love itself possessed,
When but love's shadows are so rich in joy!

Enter BALTHASAR.

News from Verona!—How now, Balthasar?
Dost thou not bring me letters from the Friar?
How doth my lady? Is my father well?
How fares my lady Juliet? That I ask again;
For nothing can be ill, if she be well.

Bal. Then she is well, and nothing can be ill:
Her body sleeps in Capels' monument,
And her immortal part with angels lives.
I saw her laid low in her kindred's vault,
And presently took post to tell it you:
O pardon me for bringing these ill news,
Since you did leave it for my office, sir.

Rom. Is it even so? then I defy you, stars!—

Thou know'st my lodging: get me ink and paper,
And hire post-horses: I will hence to-night.

   Bal. Pardon me, sir, I will not leave you thus:
Your looks are pale and wild, and do import
Some misadventure.

   Rom.   Tush, thou art deceived:
Leave me, and do the thing I bid thee do.
Hast thou no letters to me from the friar?

   Bal. No, my good lord.

   Rom.   No matter: get thee gone,
And hire those horses: I 'll be with thee straight.

                               [*Exit* BALTHASAR.

Well, Juliet, I will lie with thee to-night.
Let 's see for means:—O, mischief, thou art
      swift
To enter in the thoughts of desperate men!

I do remember an apothecary,—
And hereabouts he dwells,—whom late I noted
In tattered weeds, with overwhelming brows,
Culling of simples: meagre were his looks;
Sharp misery had worn him to the bones:
And in his needy shop a tortoise hung,
An alligator stuffed, and other skins
Of ill-shaped fishes; and about his shelves
A beggarly account of empty boxes,
Green earthen pots, bladders, and musty seeds,
Remnants of packthread, and old cakes of roses,
Were thinly scattered to make up a show.

Noting this penury, to myself I said,
"An if a man did need a poison now,
Whose sale is present death in Mantua,
Here lives a caitiff wretch would sell it him."
O, this same thought did but forerun my need;
And this same needy man must sell it me.
As I remember, this should be the house:
Being holiday, the beggar's shop is shut.—
What, ho! apothecary!

               Enter Apothecary.

   Apoth.   Who calls so loud?

Rom. Come hither, man.—I see that thou art poor:
Hold, there is forty ducats: let me have
A dram of poison; such soon-speeding geer
As will disperse itself through all the veins,
That the life-weary taker may fall dead,
And that the trunk may be discharged of breath
As violently as hasty powder fired
Doth hurry from the fatal cannon's womb.
   Apoth. Such mortal drugs I have; but Man-
      tua's law
Is death to any he that utters them.
   Rom. Art thou so bare and full of wretchedness,
And fear'st to die? Famine is in thy cheeks,
Need and oppression starveth in thy eyes,
Contempt and beggary hang upon thy back;
The world is not thy friend, nor the world's law:
The world affords no law to make thee rich;
Then be not poor, but break it, and take this.
   Apoth. My poverty, but not my will, consents.
   Rom. I pay thy poverty, and not thy will.
   Apoth. Put this in any liquid thing you will,
And drink it off; and, if you had the strength
Of twenty men, it would despatch you straight.
   Rom. There is thy gold: worse poison to men's
      souls;
Doing more murders in this loathsome world
Than these poor compounds that thou mayst not
      sell:
I sell thee poison; thou hast sold me none.
Farewell; buy food, and get thyself in flesh.—
Come, cordial, and not poison: go with me
To Juliet's grave, for there must I use thee.
        [*Exeunt.*

Scene II.—Friar Laurence's *Cell.*

Enter Friar John.

   John. Holy Franciscan friar! brother, ho!

Enter Friar Laurence.

   Lau. This same should be the voice of Friar
      John.—
Welcome from Mantua. What says Romeo?
Or, if his mind be writ, give me his letter.
   John. Going to find a barefoot brother out,
One of our order, to associate me,
Here in this city visiting the sick,
And finding him,—the searchers of the town,
Suspecting that we both were in a house
Where the infectious pestilence did reign,
Sealed up the doors, and would not let us forth:
So that my speed to Mantua there was stayed.
   Lau. Who bare my letter, then, to Romeo?
   John. I could not send it,—here it is again,—
Nor get a messenger to bring it thee,
So fearful were they of infection.

   Lau. Unhappy fortune! By my brotherhood,
The letter was not nice, but full of charge,
Of dear import; and the neglecting it
May do much danger. Friar John, go hence;
Get me an iron crow, and bring it straight
Unto my cell.
   John. Brother, I'll go and bring it thee.
        [*Exit.*
   Lau. Now must I to the monument alone:
Within this three hours will fair Juliet wake.
She will beshrew me much that Romeo
Hath had no notice of these accidents:
But I will write again to Mantua,
And keep her at my cell till Romeo come:
Poor living corse, closed in a dead man's tomb!
        [*Exit.*

Scene III.—*A Churchyard: in it, a Monument belonging to the* Capulets.

Enter Paris, *and his* Page, *bearing flowers and a torch.*

   Par. Give me thy torch, boy. Hence, and
      stand aloof:—
Yet put it out, for I would not be seen.
Under yon yew-trees lay thee all along,
Holding thine ear close to the hollow ground:
So shall no foot upon the churchyard tread
(Being loose, unfirm, with digging up of graves),
But thou shalt hear it: whistle then to me,
As signal that thou hear'st something approach.
Give me those flowers. Do as I bid thee; go.
   Page. I am almost afraid to stand alone
Here in the churchyard; yet I will adventure.
        [*Retires.*
   Par. Sweet flower, with flowers thy bridal
      bed I strew.
O woe! thy canopy is dust and stones,
Which with sweet water nightly I will dew;
Or, wanting that, with tears distilled by moans:
The obsequies that I for thee will keep,
Nightly shall be, to strew thy grave and weep.
        [*The* Boy *whistles.*
The boy gives warning something doth approach.
What cursèd foot wanders this way to-night,
To cross my obsequies and true love's rites?
What, with a torch!—muffle me, night, a while.
        [*Retires.*

Enter Romeo *and* Balthasar, *with a torch, mattock, &c.*

   Rom. Give me that mattock and the wrench-
      ing-iron.
Hold, take this letter: early in the morning
See thou deliver it to my lord and father.
Give me the light. Upon thy life I charge thee,

Whate'er thou hear'st or seest, stand all aloof,
And do not interrupt me in my course.
Why I descend into this bed of death,
Is partly to behold my lady's face;
But chiefly to take thence from her dead finger
A precious ring; a ring that I must use
In dear employment: therefore hence, begone:
But if thou, jealous, dost return to pry
In what I further shall intend to do,
By heaven, I will tear thee joint by joint,
And strew this hungry churchyard with thy limbs!
The time and my intents are savage-wild;
More fierce, and more inexorable far,
Than empty tigers, or the roaring sea.

  Bal. I will be gone, sir, and not trouble you.

  Rom. So shalt thou shew me friendship.—Take
    thou that:
Live and be prosperous; and farewell, good fellow.

  Bal. For all this same, I 'll hide me hereabout:
His looks I fear, and his intents I doubt. [*Retires.*

  Rom. Thou détestable maw, thou womb of death,
Gorged with the dearest morsel of the earth,
Thus I enforce thy rotten jaws to open :

  [*Breaking open the door of the Monument.*
And, in despite, I 'll cram thee with more food!

  Par. This is that banished haughty Montague,
That murdered my love's cousin ;—with which
    grief
It is supposed the fair creature died ;—
And here is come to do some villanous shame
To the dead bodies.   I will apprehend him.—

    [*Advances.*
Stop thy unhallowed toil, vile Montague:
Can vengeance be pursued farther than death?
Condemnéd villain, I do apprehend thee:
Obey, and go with me; for thou must die.

  Rom. I must indeed, and therefore came I hither.
Good gentle youth, tempt not a desperate man ;
Fly hence and leave me : think upon these gone :
Let them affright thee.   I beseech thee, youth,
Heap not another sin upon my head,
By urging me to fury : O, be gone !
By heaven, I love thee better than myself ;
For I come hither armed against myself.
Stay not, be gone : live, and hereafter say
A madman's mercy bade thee run away.

  Par. I do defy thy conjurations,
And do attach thee as a felon here.

  Rom. Wilt thou provoke me? then have at
    thee, boy.   [*They fight.*

  Page. O lord! they fight: I will go call the
    watch.   [*Exit.*

  Par. O, I am slain! [*Falls.*]—If thou be
    merciful,
Open the tomb, lay me with Juliet.   [*Dies.*

  Rom. In faith, I will. Let me peruse this face:
Mercutio's kinsman, noble County Paris!—

What said my man, when my betosséd soul
Did not attend him, as we rode? I think
He told me Paris should have married Juliet:
Said he not so; or did I dream it so?
Or am I mad, hearing him talk of Juliet,
To think it was so?—O, give me thy hand,
One writ with me in sour misfortune's book!
I 'll bury thee in a triumphant grave :—
A grave? O, no; a lantern, slaughtered youth ;
For here lies Juliet, and her beauty makes
This vault a feasting presence full of light.
Death, lie thou there, by a dead man interred.

  [*Laying* Paris *in the Monument.*
How oft, when men are at the point of death,
Have they been merry! which their keepers call
A lightning before death: O, how may I
Call this a lightning?—O, my love! my wife!
Death, that hath sucked the honey of thy breath,
Hath had no power yet upon thy beauty :
Thou art not conquered: beauty's ensign yet
Is crimson in thy lips and in thy cheeks,
And death's pale flag is not advancéd there.—
Tybalt, liest thou there in thy bloody sheet?
O, what more favour can I do to thee,
Than with that hand that cut thy youth in twain,
To sunder his that was thine enemy?
Forgive me, cousin!—Ah, dear Juliet,
Why art thou yet so fair? Shall I believe
That unsubstantial death is amorous ;
And that the lean abhorréd monster keeps
Thee here in dark to be his paramour?
For fear of that, I will still stay with thee,
And never from this palace of dim night
Depart again: here, here will I remain
With worms that are thy chambermaids.   O, here
Will I set up my everlasting rest,
And shake the yoke of inauspicious stars
From this world-wearied flesh.—Eyes, look your
    last!
Arms, take your last embrace! and lips, O you,
The doors of breath, seal with a righteous kiss
A dateless bargain to engrossing death !—
Come, bitter conduct ; come, unsavoury guide !
Thou desperate pilot, now at once run on
The dashing rocks thy seasick weary bark !
Here 's to my love ! [*Drinks.*]—O, true apothe-
    cary !
Thy drugs are quick.   Thus with a kiss I die.

                    [*Dies.*

Enter, at the other end of the churchyard, Friar
  Laurence, *with a lantern, crow, and spade.*

  Fri. Saint Francis be my speed! how oft to-
    night
Have my old feet stumbled at graves!—Who 's
    there?
Who is it that consorts, so late, the dead?

Bal. Here 's one, a friend, and one that knows
　　you well.

Fri. Bliss be upon you! Tell me, good my
　　friend,
What torch is yond', that vainly lends his light
To grubs and eyeless skulls? As I discern,
It burneth in the Capels' monument.

Bal. It doth so, holy sir; and there 's my master,
One that you love.

Fri.　　　　　Who is it?

Bal.　　　　　Romeo.

Fri. How long hath he been there?

Bal.　　　Full half an hour.

Fri. Go with me to the vault.

Bal.　　　I dare not, sir:
My master knows not but I am gone hence;
And fearfully did menace me with death,
If I did stay to look on his intents.

Fri. Stay, then; I 'll go alone.—Fear comes
　　upon me:
O much I fear some ill unlucky thing.

Bal. As I did sleep under this yew-tree here,
I dreamt my master and another fought,
And that my master slew him.

Fri.　　　Romeo!　　　[*Advances.*
Alack, alack, what blood is this which stains
The stony entrance of this sepulchre?
What mean these masterless and gory swords
To lie discoloured by this place of peace?
　　　　　　[*Enters the Monument.*
Romeo! O, pale!—Who else? what, Paris, too;
And steeped in blood!—Ah, what an unkind hour
Is guilty of this lamentable chance!—
The lady stirs.　　　[JULIET *wakes and stirs.*

Jul. O, comfortable friar, where is my lord?
I do remember well where I should be,
And there I am.—Where is my Romeo?
　　　　　　[*Noise within.*

Fri. I hear some noise.—Lady, come from
　　that nest
Of death, contagion, and unnatural sleep:
A greater Power than we can contradict
Hath thwarted our intents; come, come away:
Thy husband in thy bosom there lies dead;
And Paris too: come, I 'll dispose of thee
Among a sisterhood of holy nuns.
Stay not to question, for the watch is coming:
Come, go, good Juliet. [*Noise again.*]—I dare
　　stay no longer.　　　[*Exit.*

Jul. Go, get thee hence, for I will not away.—
What 's here? a cup, closed in my true love's hand?
Poison, I see, hath been his timeless end.—
O churl! drink all; and leave no friendly drop
To help me after? I will kiss thy lips:
Haply some poison yet doth hang on them,
To make me die with a restorative. [*Kisses him.*
Thy lips are warm!

1st Watch [*within*]. Lead, boy:—which way?

Jul. Yea, noise? then I 'll be brief.—O happy
　　dagger!　　[*Snatching* ROMEO's *dagger.*
This is thy sheath [*Stabs herself*]: there rust,
　　and let me die.
　　　　　　[*Falls on* ROMEO's *body, and dies.*

Enter Watch, *with the* Page *of* PARIS.

Page. This is the place: there, where the torch
　　doth burn.

1st Watch. The ground is bloody: search
　　about the churchyard.
Go, some of you; whoe'er you find, attach.
　　　　　　[*Exeunt some.*
Pitiful sight! here lies the County slain:
And Juliet bleeding, warm, and newly dead,
Who here hath lain these two days buried.
Go, tell the Prince,—run to the Capulets,—
Raise up the Montagues: some others search.
　　　　　　[*Exeunt other* Watchmen.
We see the ground whereon these woes do lie;
But the true ground of all these piteous woes
We cannot without circumstance descry.

Enter some of the Watch, *with* BALTHASAR.

2nd Watch. Here 's Romeo's man; we found
　　him in the churchyard.

1st Watch. Hold him in safety till the Prince
　　come hither.

Enter another Watchman, *with* FRIAR LAURENCE.

3rd Watch. Here is a friar, that trembles,
　　sighs, and weeps:
We took this mattock and this spade from him,
As he was coming from this churchyard side.

1st Watch. A great suspicion: stay the friar too.

Enter the PRINCE *and* Attendants.

Prince. What misadventure is so early up,
That calls our person from our morning's rest?

Enter CAPULET, LADY CAPULET, *and others.*

Cap. What should it be, that they so shriek
　　abroad?

Lady C. The people in the street cry "Romeo;"
Some "Juliet;" and some "Paris:" and all run,
With open outcry, toward our monument.

Prince. What fear is this which startles in our
　　ears?

1st Watch. Sovereign, here lies the County
　　Paris slain;
And Romeo dead; and Juliet, dead before,
Warm and new killed.

Prince. Search, seek, and know how this foul
　　murder comes.

1st Watch. Here is a friar, and slaughtered
　　Romeo's man;

With instruments upon them, fit to open
These dead men's tombs.

    Cap. O, heavens!—O wife! look how our
        daughter bleeds!
This dagger hath mista'en, for lo! his house
Is empty on the back of Montague,
And is mis-sheathéd in my daughter's bosom.

    Lady C. O me! this sight of death is as a
        bell
That warns my old age to a sepulchre.

      Enter MONTAGUE *and others.*

    Prince. Come, Montague; for thou art early
        up,
To see thy son and heir more early down.

    Mon. Alas, my liege, my wife is dead to-night:
Grief of my son's exíle hath stopped her breath:
What further woe conspires against mine age?

    Prince. Look, and thou shalt see.

    Mon. O thou untaught! what manners is in
        this,
To press before thy father to a grave?

    Prince. Seal up the mouth of outrage for a
        while,
Till we can clear these ambiguities,
And know their spring, their head, their true
        descent:
And then will I be general of your woes,
And lead you even to death. Meantime forbear,
And let mischance be slave to patience.—
Bring forth the parties of suspicion.

    Fri. I am the greatest, able to do least,
Yet most suspected, as the time and place
Doth make against me, of this direful murder:
And here I stand, both to impeach and purge
Myself condemnéd and myself excused.

    Prince. Then say at once what thou dost know
        in this.

    Fri. I will be brief; for my short date of breath
Is not so long as is a tedious tale:—
Romeo, there dead, was husband to that Juliet,
And she, there dead, that Romeo's faithful wife:
I married them; and their stolen marriage-day
Was Tybalt's doomsday, whose untimely death
Banished the new-made bridegroom from this city;
For whom, and not for Tybalt, Juliet pined.
You, to remove that siege of grief from her,
Betrothed and would have married her perforce
To County Paris. Then comes she to me;
And with wild looks, bid me devise some means
To rid her from this second marriage,
Or in my cell there would she kill herself.
Then gave I her, so tutored by my art,
A sleeping potion; which so took effect
As I intended, for it wrought on her
The form of death. Meantime I writ to Romeo
That he should hither come as this dire night,

To help to take her from her borrowed grave,
Being the time the potion's force should cease:
But he which bore my letter, Friar John,
Was stayed by accident; and yesternight
Returned my letter back. Then all alone,
At the prefixéd hour of her waking,
Came I to take her from her kindred's vault;
Meaning to keep her closely at my cell
Till I conveniently could send to Romeo:
But when I came (some minute ere the time
Of her awakening), here untimely lay
The noble Paris and true Romeo dead.
She wakes; and I entreated her come forth,
And bear this work of heaven with patience:
But then a noise did scare me from the tomb;
And she, too desperate, would not go with me,
But (as it seems) did violence on herself.
All this I know; and to the marriage
Her nurse is privy. And if aught in this
Miscarried by my fault, let my old life
Be sacrificed some hour before his time,
Unto the rigour of severest law.

    Prince. We still have known thee for a holy
        man.—
Where's Romeo's man? what can he say in this?

    Bal. I brought my master news of Juliet's
        death:
And then in post he came from Mantua
To this same place, to this same monument.
This letter he early bid me give his father;
And threatened me with death, going in the vault,
If I departed not and left him there.

    Prince. Give me the letter; I will look on it.—
Where is the County's page, that raised the
        watch?—
Sirrah, what made your master in this place?

    Page. He came with flowers to strew his lady's
        grave;
And bid me stand aloof, and so I did:
Anon comes one with light, to ope the tomb;
And by and by my master drew on him:
And then I ran away to call the watch.

    Prince. This letter doth make good the friar's
        words;
Their course of love, the tidings of her death:
And here he writes, that he did buy a poison
Of a poor 'pothecary; and therewithal
Came to this vault to die, and lie with Juliet.—
Where be these enemies?—Capulet! Montague!
See what a scourge is laid upon your hate,
That heaven finds means to kill your joys with
        love!
And I, for winking at your discords, too,
Have lost a brace of kinsmen.—All are punished!

    Cap. O, brother Montague, give me thy hand:
This is my daughter's jointure; for no more
Can I demand.

Mon.   But I can give thee more:
For I will raise her statue in pure gold;
That, while Verona by that name is known,
There shall no figure at such rate be set
As that of true and faithful Juliet.
    Cap. As rich shall Romeo by his lady lie:
Poor sacrifices of our enmity!

Prince. A glooming peace this morning with
    it brings:
The sun, for sorrow, will not shew his head.
Go hence, to have more talk of these sad things:
    Some shall be pardoned, and some punishéd:
For never was a story of more woe
Than this of Juliet and her Romeo.   [*Exeunt.*

NOTES.

Gregory, o' my word, we'll not carry coals."—Act I., Scene 1.

This phrase was used proverbially for submitting to insult. Its origin is thus explained by Mr. Gifford:—"In all great houses, but particularly in the royal residences, there were a number of mean and dirty dependents, whose office it was to attend the wood-yard, sculleries, &c. Of these (for in the lowest deep there was a lower still), the most forlorn wretches seem to have been selected to carry coals to the kitchens, halls, &c. To this smutty regiment, who attended the progresses, and rode in the carts with the pots and kettles, which, with every other article of furnitnre, were then moved from palace to palace, the people in derision, gave the name of black-guards; a term since become sufficiently familiar, and never properly explained."

"*Here comes two of the house of the Montagues.*"
Act I., Scene 1.

The partisans of the Montague family wore a token in their hats, in order to distinguish them from their enemies, the Capulets. Hence, throughout the play they are known at a distance. The circumstance is mentioned by Gascoigne, in "A DEVISE OF A MASQUE," written for Lord Mountacute (1575):—

"And for a further proof, he shewed in his hat
This token, which the Mountacutes did bear always, for that
They covet to be known from Capels, where they pass,
For ancient grudge which long ago 'tween these two houses
    was."

"*I will bite my thumb at them; which is a disgrace to them, if they bear it.*"—Act I., Scene 1.

This mode of provoking a quarrel seems to have originated in Italy, but had become common in England at the date of this play. Decker says (speaking of the loungers in St. Paul's Church), "What swearing is there, what shouldering, what justling, what jeering, what biting of thumbs, to beget quarrels!"

Cotgrave thus explains the mode in which this token of contempt was given :—"*Faire la nique.*—To mock by nodding or lifting up of the chin; or, more properly, to threaten or defy by putting the thumb-nail into the mouth, and with a jerk (from the upper teeth) make it to nack."

"*So far from sounding and discovery,
As is the bud bit with an envious worm,
Ere he can spread his sweet leaves to the air,
Or dedicate his beauty to the sun.*"—Act I., Scene 1.

The old copies here, instead of "to the sun," read "to the same." This prosaic termination of so beautiful a passage was altered at the suggestion of Theobald, to whom the received text is, in many instances, indebted, It is highly probable that "same" is a typographical mistake for "sunne," which was often the old orthography of the latter word. Daniel, in one of his sonnets (1594), has a passage somewhat similar :—

"And while thou spread'st unto the rising sun
The fairest flower that ever saw the light,
Now 'joy thy time, before thy sweet be done."

"*For beauty, starved with her severity,
Cuts beauty off from all posterity.*"—Act I., Scene 1.

A similar thought to this is found in Shakspere's third Sonnet :—

"Or who is he so fond will be the tomb
Of his self-love to stop posterity?"

And in his "VENUS AND ADONIS :"—

"What is thy body but a swallowing grave,
Seeming to bury that posterity
Which, by the rights of time, thou needs must have?"

—— "*I remember it well,
'T is since the earthquake now eleven years.*"
Act I., Scene 3.

How comes the Nurse to talk of an earthquake upon this occasion? There is no such circumstance, I believe, mentioned in any of the novels from which Shakspere may be supposed to have drawn his story; and therefore it seems probable that he had in view the earthquake which had really been felt in many parts of England in his own time, viz., on the 6th of April, 1580 (See Stowe's "CHRONICLE," &c.). If so, one may be permitted to conjecture that "ROMEO AND JULIET" was written in 1591.—TYRWHITT.

"*Enter ROMEO, MERCUTIO, &c.*"—Act I., Scene 4.

In Arthur Brooke's heavy rhyming poem of "ROMEUS AND JULIET" (which will be subsequently spoken of), there is the following mention of Mercutio:—

"At th' one side of her chair her lover Romeo,
And on the other side there sat one called Mercutio;—
A courtier that eachwhere was highly had in price,
For he was courteous of his speech and pleasant of device:
Even as a lion would among the lambs be bold,
Such was, among the bashful maids, Mercutio to behold.
With friendly gripe he seized fair Juliet's snowish hand:
A gift he had that nature gave him in his swathing band,—
That frozen mountain ice was never half so cold
As were his hands, though ne'er so near the fire he did them
    hold."

On this slight hint, Shakspere founded the admirable character bearing the same name.

"*Give me a torch : I am not for this ambling.*"—Act I., Scene 4.

A torchbearer seems to have been a constant attendant on every troop of maskers. In "WESTWARD HOE," by Decker and Webster, we find, "He is just like a torchbearer to maskers; he wears good clothes, and is ranked in good company, but he doth nothing."

Henry VIII., when he went masked to visit Wolsey at Whitehall, had sixteen torchbearers. The gentlemen-pensioners of Queen Elizabeth held torches while a play was acted before her, in the chapel of King's College, Cambridge.

"ROM. *The game was ne'er so fair, and I am done.*
MER. *Tut ! 'dun 's the mouse,' the constable's own word.'*
Act I., Scene 4.

"Dun 's the mouse" is a proverbial expression that often occurs in the old comedies; its origin is uncertain: some allusion to the colour of the animal was probably intended, but it was also occasionally used, as in the text, merely to found a quibble on the word "done." Malone observes that the phrase "seems to have meant 'peace, be still:' and hence it is said to be 'the constable's own word;' who may be supposed to be employed in apprehending an offender, and afraid of alarming him by any noise."—The constable may, with at least equal probability, be thought to have appropriated the word or term, from his habit of enjoining silence to others.

"If thou art dun, we'll draw thee from the mire, &c."
Act I., Scene 4.

In this line, the word "dun" is used to signify a dun horse. Mr. Gifford, in a note to Ben Jonson's "MASQUE OF CHRISTMAS," has thus described the rustic sport called "Dun is in the Mire:"—"A log of wood is brought into the room: this is Dun (the cart-horse), and a cry is raised that he is stuck in the mire. Two of the company advance, either with or without ropes, to draw him out. After repeated attempts, they find themselves unable to do it, and call for more assistance. The game continues till all the company take part in it, when "dun" is extricated of course; and the merriment arises from the awkward and affected efforts of the rustics to lift the log, and from sundry arch contrivances to let the ends of it fall on one another's toes."

"Of healths five fathom deep."—Act I., Scene 4.

A passage from "WESTWARD HOE" will best explain the practice here alluded to:—"Troth, sir, my master and Sir Goslin are guzzling: they are dabbling together fathom deep. The knight has drunk so much health to the gentleman, yonder, on his knees, that he hath almost lost the use of his legs."

—— *"This is that very Mab*
That plats the manes of horses in the night."
Act I., Scene 4.

This line alludes to a very singular superstition, not yet forgotten in some parts of the country. It was believed that certain malignant spirits, whose delight was to wander in groves and pleasant places, assumed occasionally the likenesses of women clothed in white; that in this character they sometimes haunted stables in the night-time, carrying in their hands tapers of wax, which they dropped on the horses' manes, thereby platting them in inextricable knots, to the great annoyance of the poor animals and the vexation of their masters. These hags are mentioned in the works of William Auvergne, Bishop of Paris, in the thirteenth century.

There is a very uncommon old print by Hans Burgmair, relating to this subject. A witch enters the stable with a lighted torch; and previously to the operation of entangling the horse's mane, practises her enchantments on the groom, who is lying asleep on his back, and apparently influenced by the nightmare.—DOUCE.

"Nay, sit, nay, sit, good cousin Capulet."—Act I., Scene 5.

The "cousin Capulet" of this scene is doubtless the "uncle Capulet" mentioned in the paper of invitations. Shakspere and his cotemporaries used the word cousin to denote any collateral relation of whatever degree, and sometimes even to denote those of lineal descent. The King calls Hamlet his cousin, although his nephew and step-son; the old Duchess of York, in Richard III., calls her grandson cousin; and in a subsequent scene of this play, Lady Capulet exclaims, "Tybalt, my cousin; O, my brother's child!"

"Her beauty hangs upon the cheek of night
Like a rich jewel in an Ethiop's ear.—Act I., Scene 5.

There is an illustration similar to this in Shakspere's twenty-seventh Sonnet:—

"Which, like a jewel hung in ghastly night,
Makes black night beauteous, and her old face new."

In the passage quoted from the text, all the quartos and the first folio read, "*It seems* she hangs," instead of the more spirited expression, "*Her beauty* hangs." The present phraseology is from the second folio, and is now so consecrated by general use and approval, that it would be both useless and ungracious to attempt to supersede it.

We may here take the opportunity of remarking, that the most rigid sticklers for the authority of the first folio have found it necessary in very many cases (as well in this play as in others) to prefer the readings of the earlier quartos, and in some comparatively few instances, those of the second folio. The reason is this:—we know, unfortunately, as far as the matter is susceptible of proof, that none of Shakspere's plays were published under his own superintendence: we know also, in reference to all the earlier copies, that typographical errors, stage omissions or interpolations, the want of regular editing, and other causes, have contributed to obscure, and, not unfrequently, to destroy the Poet's meaning: it is, therefore, in no irreverent spirit (as is too often inculcated), but rather from a feeling of duty and gratitude, that even the most cautious commentators have felt themselves compelled to depart from the principle of taking any one edition as an invariable guide.

From two or three instances selected in the present play from numerous others, merely as illustrations of the general fact, it will be seen that the reviser who should in every case adopt the readings of the first folio, would bring upon his devoted head the merited anathema of every Shaksperian reader. We have not, however, presumed to vary from its text without anxious consideration, and constant reference to those commentators who have shewn the least disposition to innovate either as to words or versification.

————

"O, mickle is the powerful grace that lies
In herbs, plants, stones, and their true qualities."
Act II., Scene 3.

This eulogium on the hidden powers of nature affords a natural introduction to the Friar's furnishing Juliet with the sleeping potion in Act IV. Here is one of the many instances in which the train of thought was suggested by Brooke's poem:—

"But not in vain, my child, hath all my wandering been:—
What force the stones, the plants, and metals, have to work,
And divers other things that in the bowels of earth do lurk,
With care I have sought out; with pain I did them prove."

"BEN. Why, what is Tybalt?
MER. More than Prince of Cats."—Act II., Scene 4.

This is an allusion to the story-book of "REYNARD THE Fox," in which Tybert is the name given to the Cat. A similar phrase occurs in many old works.

"These fashion-mongers, these pardonnez-mois, who stand
so much on the new form that they cannot sit at ease on the
old bench."—Act II., Scene 4.

It is said that during the ridiculous fashion which prevailed of great "boulstered breeches," it was necessary to cut away hollow places in the benches of the House of Commons, to make room for those monstrous protuberances, without which those "who stood on the new form could not sit at ease on the old bench."—SINGER.

"Thisbé, a grey eye or so."—Act II., Scene 4.

Mercutio means to allow that Thisbé had a very fine eye; for, from various passages, it appears that a grey eye was in our author's time thought eminently beautiful. This may seem strange to those who are not conversant with ancient phraseology; but a grey eye undoubtedly meant what we now denominate a blue eye.—MALONE.

"ROM. *What counterfeit did I give you?*
MER. *The slip, sir, the slip.*"—Act II., Scene 4.

This allusion is to the old counterfeit money called a slip, which is frequently mentioned in writings of the period. Greene, in his "THIEVES FALLING OUT," &c., particularly describes it:—"And therefore he went and got him certain slips, which are counterfeit pieces of money, being brass, and covered over with silver, which the common people call slips."

"*Why, then is my pump well-flowered.*"—Act II., Scene 4.

Here is a vein of wit too thin to be easily found. The fundamental idea is, that Romeo wore pinked pumps; that is, punched with holes in figures."—JOHNSON.

It was the custom to wear ribbands in the shoes, formed into the shape of roses, or of any other flowers. So in the "MASQUE OF GRAY'S INN" (1614):—"Every masker's pump was fastened with a flower suitable to his cap."—STEEVENS.

"*I am none of his skains-mates!*"—Act II., Scene 4.

Skain or skean was the Irish term for a knife or dagger. By "skains-mates," the Nurse probably means swaggering companions. Green, in his "QUIP FOR AN UPSTART COURTIER," describes "an ill-favoured knave, who wore by his side a skein like a brewer's bung-knife."

"*Doth not rosemary and Romeo begin both with a letter?*"
Act II., Scene 4.

By this question, the Nurse means to insinuate that Romeo's image was ever in the mind of Juliet, and that they would be married. Rosemary, being conceived to have the power of strengthening the memory, was an emblem of remembrance and of the affection of lovers; and, for this reason probably, was worn at weddings.

"*Ah, mocker! that's the dog's name: R is for the dog.*"
Act II., Scene 4.

The letter "R" puts the Nurse in mind of that sound which dogs make when they snarl. Ben Jonson, in his "ENGLISH GRAMMAR," says "'R' is the dog's letter, and hirreth in the sound."

"*I pray thee, good Mercutio, let's retire:*
The day is hot, the Capulets abroad."
Act III., Scene 1.

It is observed that, in Italy, almost all assassinations are committed during the heat of summer.—JOHNSON.

"*Alive! in triumph! and Mercutio slain!*"
Act III., Scene 1.

Thus the quarto 1597; for which the quarto 1599 has, "He *gan* in triumph!" This in the subsequent copies wa made, "He *gone*," &c.—MALONE.

"*He is a kinsman to the Montague;*
Affection makes him false, he speaks not true."
Act III., Scene 1.

The charge of falsehood on Benvolio, though produced at hazard, is very just. The author, who seems to intend the character of Benvolio as good, meant perhaps to shew how the best minds, in a state of faction and discord, are detorted to criminal partiality.—JOHNSON.

"*Spread thy close curtain, love-performing night!*
That runaway's eyes may wink, and Romeo
Leap to these arms, untalked of and unseen!"
Act III., Scene 2.

Many attempts have been made to explain the term "runaway," in this passage; but none with success. The most probable solution, it appears to us, is that which sup-

poses the poet to have meant by "runaway," the night; and by its eyes, the stars. It has been proposed to substitute "unawares, eyes may wink," for "runaway's eyes may wink." But this alteration would give a prosaic flatness to the phrase, which—to say nothing of other objections—would alone convince us that it is not the true reading.

"*Give me my Romeo: and, when he shall die,*
Take him and cut him out in little stars."
Act III., Scene 2.

This emendation is drawn from the undated quarto. The quartos of 1599, 1609, and the folio, read, "When *I* shall die."

"*Hath Romeo slain himself? Say thou but 'Ay,'*
And that bare vowel 'I' shall poison more
Than the death-darting eye of cockatrice."
Act III., Scene 2.

In Shakspere's time, the affirmative particle "ay" was usually written "I," and in the above passage the editors have thought it necessary to retain the old spelling. We have, however, ventured to deviate from this unsightly practice, conceiving that there is sufficient similarity between the sounds of "ay" and "I" to point out the intended quibble. This is one of the trivial passages which we easily persuade ourselves have, by some accident or impertinence, been foisted into the genuine text.

"*Wert thou as young as I, Juliet thy love.*"—Act III., Scene 3.

Thus the original copy; for which in the folio we have—

"*Wert thou as young as Juliet my love.*"

I only mention this to shew the very high value of the early quarto editions.—MALONE.

"*Some say the lark and loathèd toad change eyes;*
O, now I would they had changed voices too!
Since arm from arm that voice doth us affray,
Hunting thee hence with hunts-up to the day."
Act III., Scene 5.

The toad having very fine eyes, and the lark very ugly ones, was the occasion of a saying that the lark and toad had changed eyes. This tradition Dr. Johnson states himself to have heard in a rustic rhyme:—

"*To heaven I'd fly,*
But that the toad beguiled me of mine eye."

Juliet means that the croak of the toad would have been no indication of the appearance of day, and consequently no signal for her lover's departure.

The "hunts-up" was the name of the tune anciently played to wake the hunters, and collect them together.

—— "*Ere this hand, by thee to Romeo sealed,*
Shall be the label to another deed."—Act IV., Scene 1.

The seals of deeds were formerly not impressed on the parchment itself, but were appended on distinct slips or labels affixed to it. Hence in "KING RICHARD II.," the Duke of York discovers, by the depending seal, a covenant which his son, the Duke of Aumerle, had entered into:—

"*What seal is that which hangs without thy bosom?*"

"*Then (as the manner of our country is),*
In thy best robes, uncovered on the bier."
Act IV., Scene 1.

The Italian custom here alluded to is still continued. Mr. Rogers, in his poem on Italy, describes a scene of the kind:—

"*But now by fits*
A dull and dismal noise assailed the ear,
A wail, a chant, louder and louder yet:
And now a strange fantastic troop appeared!

Thronging they came, as from the shades below;
All of a ghostly white!—'O say (I cried),
Do not the living here bury the dead?
Do spirits come and fetch them? What are these
That seem not of this world, and mock the day;
Each with a burning taper in his hand?'—
'It is an ancient brotherhood thou seest.
Such their apparel. Through the long, long line,
Look where thou wilt, no likeness of a man:
The living masked, the dead alone uncovered.
But mark!'—And, lying on her funeral couch,
Like one asleep, her eyelids closed, her hands
Folded together on her modest breast,
As 't were her nightly posture, through the crowd
She came at last,—and richly, gaily clad,
As for a birth-day feast!"

" My bosom's lord sits lightly on his throne;
And, all this day, an unaccustomed spirit
Lifts me above the ground with cheerful thoughts."

Act V., Scene 1.

These three lines are very gay and pleasing. But why does Shakspere give Romeo this involuntary cheerfulness just before the extremity of unhappiness? Perhaps to shew the vanity of trusting to those uncertain and casual exaltations or depressions which many consider as certain foretokens of good and evil.—JOHNSON.

" Going to find a barefoot brother out,
One of our order, to associate me."—Act V., Scene 2.

It was customary for friars to travel in pairs, in order that each might be a check upon the behaviour of the other.

The original relater of the story on which this play is formed, was Luigi da Porto, a gentleman of Vicenza, who died in 1529. His novel did not appear till some years after his death; being first printed at Venice, in 1535, under the title of " LA GIULIETTA."

In 1554, Bandello published at Lucca a novel on the same subject (tom. ii., nov. 9); and shortly afterwards Boisteau exhibited one in French, founded on the Italian narratives, but varying from them in many particulars.

From Boisteau's novel the same story was, in 1562, formed into an English poem, with considerable alterations and large additions, by Mr. Arthur Brooke.

Painter, in the second volume of his " PALACE OF PLEASURE" (1567), published a prose translation from the French of Boisteau, which he entitled " RHOMEO AND JULIETTA." Shakspere had probably read Painter's novel, having taken one circumstance from it or from some other prose translation of Boisteau; but his play was undoubtedly formed on the poem of Arthur Brooke.

This is proved decisively by the following circumstances: —1. In the poems, the Prince of Verona is called Escalus: so also in the play. In Painter's translation from Boisteau he is named Signor Escala, and sometimes Lord Bartholomew of Escala.—2. In Painter's novel, the family of Romeo are called the Montesches: in the poem and in the play, the Montagues.—3. The messenger employed by Friar Law-

rence to carry a letter to Romeo, to inform him when Juliet would awake from her trance, is in Painter's translation called Anselme: in the poem and in the play, Friar John is employed in this business.—4. The circumstance of Capulet's writing down the names of the guests whom he invites to supper, is found in the poem and in the play, but is not mentioned by Painter, nor is it found in the original Italian novel.—5. The residence of the Capulets, in the original and in Painter, is called Villa Franca: in the poem and in the play, Freetown.—6. Several passages of Romeo and Juliet appear to have been formed on hints furnished by the poem, of which no traces are found either in Painter's novel, or in Boisteau, or the original.—MALONE.

Romeo and Juliet is a picture of love and its pitiable fate, in a world whose atmosphere is too rough for this tenderest blossom of human life. Two beings, created for each other, feel mutual love at first glance; every consideration disappears before the invisible influence of living in one another: they join themselves secretly, under circumstances in the highest degree hostile to the union, relying merely on the protection of an irresistible power. By unfriendly events following blow upon blow, their heroic constancy is exposed to all manner of trials, till, forcibly separated from each other, they are united in the grave to meet again in another world.

All this is to be found in the beautiful story which Shakspere has not invented; and which, however simply told, will always excite a tender sympathy: but it was reserved for Shakspere to unite purity of heart and the glow of imagination, sweetness and dignity of manners and passionate violence, in one ideal picture. By the manner in which he has handled it, it has become a glorious song of praise on that inexpressible feeling which ennobles the soul, and gives to it its highest sublimity, and which elevates even the senses themselves into soul; and at the same time is a melancholy elegy on its frailty, from its own nature and external circumstances: at once the deification and the burial of love. It appears here like a heavenly spark that, descending to the earth, is converted into a flash of lightning, by which mortal creatures are almost in the same moment set on fire and consumed.

Whatever is most intoxicating in the odour of a southern spring, languishing in the song of the nightingale, or voluptuous in the first opening of the rose, is to be found in this poem. But, even more rapidly than the first blossoms of youth and beauty decay, it hurries on from the first timidly-bold declaration of love and modest return, to the most unlimited passion, to an irrevocable union: then, amidst alternating storms of rapture and despair, to the death of the two lovers, who still appear enviable as their love survives them, and as by their death they have obtained a triumph over every separating power.

The sweetest and the bitterest love and hatred, festivity and dark forebodings, tender embraces and sepulchres, the fulness of life and self-annihilation, are all here brought close to each other: and all these contrasts are so blended, in the harmonious and wonderful work, into a unity of impression, that the echo which the whole leaves behind in the mind resembles a single but endless sigh.—SCHLEGEL.

INTRODUCTORY REMARKS

BUILDING wisely on legendary tale and simple ballad,—those sure foundations for him who seeks to interest the public heart,—the mighty architect has raised, in "LEAR," a structure before whose giant beauties Criticism stands rebuked, in silent and boundless admiration:—as the traveller ascending the Peak of Teneriffe intent to measure its height, suspends his scientific labours in spell-bound contemplation of the magnificent scene that on every side lies spread before him.

The story of the aged monarch, self-willed and impetuous, yet still "more sinned against than sinning," is told, with various modifications, by many ancient writers; but the narrative of Holinshed was probably the immediate source of the poet's inspiration. There is, moreover, an older play than Shakspere's on the subject, called "The true Chronicle History of King Leir and his three Daughters, Gonorill, Ragan, and Cordella." Of this very inferior, although not merit-less effort, he has undoubtedly availed himself, but not to such extent as to impugn the essential originality of his own great work.

It is remarkable that both Holinshed and the older dramatist have given a prosperous termination to the legend, so far at least as Lear himself is implicated. In so doing, they have doubtless fallen in with the general yearning for poetic justice: but whether it were wise to wish that Shakspere had in this respect adhered to his supposed authorities, may well admit of question. The force and splendour of his execution naturally induce the thought that he has chosen for the best in working out his plot: let us, then, be content to inherit the invaluable legacy on such conditions as the donor has imposed, nor seek to tamper with the genuine document. The profane attempts at emendation, by Tate's berouged and smirking muse, are so amusingly vile, that indignation soon relieves itself in laughter. Lear, as a suitable climax to much previous fustian, is made, in the last Act, to call upon the winds to catch certain joyous sounds, "and bear them on their *rosy* wings to heaven." The love passages, too, between the daring laureate's facetiously "wretched Edgar," and no less comical "Cordelia, royal fair," betray a master in the school of unconscious burlesque: they are sacrifices dear to Momus, although Melpomene affects them not.

In Percy's "RELIQUES," there is a reprint of "A lamentable Song of the Death of King Leir and his three Daughters," in which the o'er-afflicted father expires with grief for the loss of Cordelia, who is slain in the battle fought to recover his kingdom. This production was originally published without a date, but is, with great probability, thought to have appeared before the play of Shakspere: and from this popular ballad he may have derived the tragic catastrophe he has deemed it expedient to adopt. The episode of Edmund and Edgar, so skilfully interwoven with the main plot of "LEAR," is founded on the story of the blind King of Paphlagonia, in Sidney's "ARCADIA." The Leonatus of the tale is Edgar in the play.

Shakspere's "LEAR" was first published in 1608, with this "full and particular" title-page:—"Mr. William Shake-speare, his true Chronicle History of the Life and Death of King Lear and his three Daughters. With the unfortunate Life of Edgar, Sonne and Heire to the Earle of Glocester, and his sullen and assumed humour of Tom of Bedlam. As it was plaid before the King's Majesty at White-hall, upon S. Stephens Night, in Christmas Holidaies. By his Majesties Servants playing usually on the Banck-side. Printed for Nathaniel Butter, and are to be sold at his shop in Paul's Churchyard, at the signe of the Pied Bull, neere St. Austin's Gate, 1608." There were two other editions of the play published by the same bookseller, in the same year; but, notwithstanding these indubitable evidences of popularity, "KING LEAR," for some inexplicable reason, was not again reprinted till its appearance in the original folio of 1623.

PERSONS REPRESENTED

LEAR, King of BRITAIN
DUKE OF FRANCE.
DUKE OF BURGUNDY.
DUKE OF CORNWALL.
DUKE OF ALBANY.
EARL OF KENT.
EARL OF GLOSTER.
EDGAR, Son to GLOSTER.
EDMUND, Bastard Son to GLOSTER.
CURAN, a Courtier.
OSWALD, Steward to GONERIL.
Old Man, Tenant to GLOSTER.
Physician.
Fool.
An Officer, employed by EDMUND.
Gentleman, attendant on CORDELIA
A Herald. Servants to CORNWALL.

GONERIL,
REGAN,   } Daughters to LEAR.
CORDELIA.

Knights attending on the KING, Officers, Messengers,
Soldiers, and Attendants

SCENE Britain.

SCENE I.—*A Room of State in* KING LEAR'S *Palace.*

Enter KENT, GLOSTER, *and* EDMUND.

Kent. I thought the King had more affected the Duke of Albany than Cornwall.

Glo. It did always seem so to us: but now, in the division of the kingdom, it appears not which of the dukes he values most; for equalities are so weighed, that curiosity in neither can make choice of either's moiety.

Kent. Is not this your son, my lord?

Glo. His breeding, sir, hath been at my charge: I have so often blushed to acknowledge him, that now I am brazed to it.

Kent. I cannot conceive you.

Glo. Sir, this young fellow's mother could: whereupon she grew round-wombed, and had indeed, sir, a son for her cradle ere she had a husband for her bed. Do you smell a fault?

Kent. I cannot wish the fault undone, the issue of it being so proper.

Glo. But I have, sir, a son by order of law, some year elder than this, who yet is no dearer in my account. Though this knave came somewhat saucily into the world before he was sent for, yet was his mother fair: there was good sport at his making, and the whoreson must be acknowledged. —Do you know this noble gentleman, Edmund?

Edm. No, my lord.

Glo. My lord of Kent: remember him hereafter as my honourable friend.

Edm. My services to your lordship.

Kent. I must love you, and sue to know you better.

Edm. Sir, I shall study deserving.

Glo. He hath been out nine years, and away he shall again.—The King is coming.

[*Trumpets sound within.*

Enter LEAR, CORNWALL, ALBANY, GONERIL, REGAN, CORDELIA, *and* Attendants.

Lear. Attend the lords of France and Burgundy, Gloster.

Glo. I shall, my liege.

[*Exeunt* GLOSTER *and* EDMUND.

Lear. Meantime we shall express our darker purpose.

Give me the map there.—Know that we have divided
In three, our kingdom; and 't is our fast intent
To shake all cares and business from our age;
Conferring them on younger strengths, while we
Unburdened crawl toward death.—Our son of Cornwall,
And you, our no less loving son of Albany,
We have this hour a constant will to publish
Our daughters' several dowers, that future strife
May be prevented now. The princes, France and Burgundy,
Great rivals in our youngest daughter's love,
Long in our court have made their amorous sojourn,
And here are to be answered.—Tell me, my daughters
(Since now we will divest us, both of rule,
Interest of territory, cares of state),
Which of you shall we say doth love us most?
That we our largest bounty may extend
Where merit doth most challenge it.—Goneril,
Our eldest-born, speak first.

Gon. Sir, I
Do love you more than words can wield the matter:
Dearer than eyesight, space, and liberty;
Beyond what can be valued, rich or rare;

No less than life, with grace, health, beauty, honour:
As much as child e'er loved, or father found.
A love that makes breath poor, and speech unable;
Beyond all manner of so much I love you.

Cor. What shall Cordelia do? Love, and be silent. [*Aside.*

Lear. Of all these bounds, even from this line to this,
With shadowy forests and with champains riched,
With plenteous rivers and wide-skirted meads,
We make thee lady. To thine and Albany's issue
Be this perpetual.—What says our second daughter,
Our dearest Regan, wife to Cornwall? Speak.

Reg. I am made of that self metal as my sister,
And prize me at her worth. In my true heart
I find she names my very deed of love:
Only she comes too short,—that I profess
Myself an enemy to all other joys
Which the most precious square of sense possesses,
And find I am alone felicitate
In your dear highness' love.

Cor. Then poor Cordelia! [*Aside.*
And yet not so, since I am sure my love 's
More richer than my tongue.

Lear. To thee and thine, hereditary ever,
Remain this ample third of our fair kingdom;
No less in space, validity, and pleasure,
Than that confirmed on Goneril.—Now, our joy,
Although the last, not least; to whose young love
The vines of France, and milk of Burgundy,
Strive to be interessed; what can you say, to draw
A third more opulent than your sisters? Speak.

Cor. Nothing, my lord.

Lear. Nothing?

Cor. Nothing.

Lear. Nothing can come of nothing: speak again.

Cor. Unhappy that I am, I cannot heave
My heart into my mouth. I love your majesty
According to my bond: nor more, nor less.

Lear. How, how, Cordelia? mend your speech a little,
Lest it may mar your fortunes.

Cor. Good my lord,
You have begot me, bred me, loved me: I
Return those duties back as are right fit;
Obey you, love you, and most honour you.
Why have my sisters husbands, if they say
They love you all? Haply, when I shall wed,
That lord whose hand must take my plight, shall carry
Half my love with him, half my care and duty:
Sure I shall never marry, like my sisters,
To love my father all.

Lear. But goes this with thy heart?

Cor.   Ay, good my lord.

Lear. So young, and so untender?

Cor. So young, my lord, and true.

Lear. Let it be so:—thy truth, then, be thy
          dower:

For, by the sacred radiance of the sun;

The mysteries of Hecate and the night;

By all the operations of the orbs

From whom we do exist, and cease to be,—

Here I disclaim all my paternal care,

Propinquity and property of blood,

And as a stranger to my heart and me

Hold thee, from this, for ever.   The barbarous
          Scythian,

Or he that makes his generation messes

To gorge his appetite, shall to my bosom

Be as well neighboured, pitied, and relieved,

As thou, my sometime daughter.

     Kent.   Good my liege,—

     Lear. Peace, Kent?

Come not between the dragon and his wrath:

I loved her most, and thought to set my rest

On her kind nursery.—Hence, and avoid my sight!

                              [*To* CORDELIA.

So be my grave my peace, as here I give

Her father's heart from her!—Call France:—
          who stirs?

Call Burgundy.—Cornwall and Albany,

With my two daughters' dowers digest this third:

Let pride, which she calls plainness, marry her.

I do invest you jointly with my power,

Pre-eminence, and all the large effects

That troop with majesty.—Ourself, by monthly
          course,

With reservation of an hundred knights,

By you to be sustained, shall our abode

Make with you by due turns.   Only we still retain

The name and all the additions to a king;

The sway,

Revénue, execution of the rest,

Belovéd sons, be yours: which to confirm,

This coronet part between you. [*Giving the crown.*

     Kent.   Royal Lear,

Whom I have ever honoured as my king,

Loved as my father, as my master followed,

As my great patron thought on in my prayers,—

     Lear. The bow is bent and drawn: make from
          the shaft.

Kent. Let it fall rather, though the fork invade
The region of my heart: be Kent unmannerly,
When Lear is mad. What wouldst thou do, old
    man?
Think'st thou that duty shall have dread to speak,
When power to flattery bows? To plainness
    honour 's bound,
When majesty stoops to folly. Reverse thy doom;
And, in thy best consideration, check
This hideous rashness. Answer my life my
    judgment,
Thy youngest daughter does not love thee least;
Nor are those empty-hearted whose low sound
Reverbs no hollowness.

    Lear.   Kent, on thy life, no more.
    Kent. My life I never held but as a pawn
To wage against thine enemies: nor fear to lose it,
Thy safety being the motive.
    Lear.   Out of my sight!
    Kent. See better, Lear; and let me still remain
The true blank of thine eye.
    Lear.   Now, by Apollo,—
    Kent.   Now, by Apollo, King,
Thou swear'st thy gods in vain.
    Lear.   O, vassal! miscreant!
                 [*Laying his hand on his sword.*
Alb.)
      } Dear sir, forbear.
Corn.)
    Kent. Do: kill thy physician, and the fee bestow
Upon the foul disease. Revoke thy gift;
Or, whilst I can vent clamour from my throat,
I 'll tell thee thou dost evil.
    Lear.   Hear me, recreant!
On thine allegiance hear me!—
Since thou hast sought to make us break our vow
(Which we durst never yet) and with strained pride
To come betwixt our sentence and our power
(Which nor our nature nor our place can bear);
Our potency made good, take thy reward.
Five days we do allot thee, for provision
To shield thee from diseases of the world;
And on the sixth to turn thy hated back
Upon our kingdom: if on the tenth day following
Thy banished trunk be found in our dominions,
The moment is thy death. Away! by Jupiter,
This shall not be revoked.
    Kent. Fare thee well, King: since thus thou
          wilt appear,
Freedom lives hence, and banishment is here.—
The gods to their dear shelter take thee, maid,
                 [*To* CORDELIA.
That justly think'st, and hast most rightly said.—
And your large speeches may your deeds approve,
             [*To* REGAN *and* GONERIL.
That good effects may spring from words of love.—
Thus Kent, O princes, bids you all adieu:
He 'll shape his old course in a country new. [*Exit.*

Re-enter GLOSTER; *with* FRANCE, BURGUNDY,
          and Attendants.

    Glo. Here 's France and Burgundy, my noble
          lord.
    Lear. My lord of Burgundy,
We first address towards you, who with this king
Hath rivalled for our daughter:—What, in the
          least,
Will you require in present dower with her,
Or cease your quest of love?
    Bur.   Most royal majesty,
I crave no more than hath your highness offered,
Nor will you tender less.
    Lear.   Right noble Burgundy,
When she was dear to us, we did hold her so;
But now her price is fallen. Sir, there she stands:
If aught within that little, seeming substance,
Or all of it, with our displeasure pieced,
And nothing more, may fitly like your grace,
She 's there, and she is yours.
    Bur.   I know no answer.
    Lear. Sir,
Will you, with those infirmities she owes,
Unfriended, new-adopted to our hate,
Dowered with our curse, and strangered with our
          oath,
Take her, or leave her?
    Bur.   Pardon me, royal sir:
Election makes not up on such conditions.
    Lear. Then leave her, sir: for, by the power
          that made me,
I tell you all her wealth.—For you, great king,
                 [*To* FRANCE.
I would not from your love make such a stray,
To match you where I hate: therefore beseech you
To avert your liking a more worthier way,
Than on a wretch whom nature is ashamed
Almost to acknowledge hers.
    France.   This is most strange!
That she, that even but now was your best object,
The argument of your praise, balm of your age,
Most best, most dearest, should in this trice of time
Commit a thing so monstrous, to dismantle
So many folds of favour! Sure her offence
Must be of such unnatural degree
That monsters it, or your fore-vouched affection
Fall into taint: which to believe of her,
Must be a faith that reason, without miracle,
Could never plant in me.
    Cor.   I yet beseech your majesty
(If for I want that glib and oily art,
To speak and purpose not; since what I well intend,
I 'll do 't before I speak), that you make known
It is no vicious blot, murder, or foulness,
No unchaste action or dishonoured step,
That hath deprived me of your grace and favour:
But even for want of that for which I am richer:

A still-soliciting eye, and such a tongue
That I am glad I have not, though not to have it
Hath lost me in your liking.

Lear.   Better thou
Hadst not been born, than not to have pleased
    me better.

France. Is it but this? a tardiness in nature,
Which often leaves the history unspoke
That it intends to do?—My lord of Burgundy,
What say you to the lady? Love is not love,
When it is mingled with respects that stand
Aloof from the entire point. Will you have her?
She is herself a dowry.

Bur.   Royal Lear,
Give but that portion which yourself proposed,
And here I take Cordelia by the hand,
Duchess of Burgundy.

Lear. Nothing I have sworn : I am firm.

Bur. I am sorry, then, you have so lost a father,
That you must lose a husband. [*To* CORDELIA.

Cor.   Peace be with Burgundy !
Since that respects of fortune are his love.
I shall not be his wife.

France. Fairest Cordelia, that art most rich,
    being poor ;
Most choice, forsaken ; and most loved, despised !
Thee and thy virtues here I seize upon :
Be it lawful, I take up what's cast away.
Gods, gods ! 't is strange, that from their cold'st
    neglect
My love should kindle to inflamed respect.—
Thy dowerless daughter, King, thrown' to my
    chance,
Is queen of us, of ours, and our fair France :
Not all the dukes of waterish Burgundy
Shall buy this unprized precious maid of me.—
Bid them farewell, Cordelia, though unkind :
Thou losest here, a better where to find.

Lear. Thou hast her, France : let her be thine ;
    for we
Have no such daughter, nor shall ever see
That face of hers again :—therefore, be gone,
Without our grace, our love, our benizon.—
Come, noble Burgundy.

    [*Flourish. Exeunt* LEAR, BURGUNDY, CORN-
      WALL, ALBANY, GLOSTER, *and* Attendants.

France. Bid farewell to your sisters.

Cor. The jewels of our father, with washed eyes
Cordelia leaves you : I know you what you are ;
And, like a sister, am most loath to call
Your faults as they are named. Use well our father :
To your professed bosoms I commit him :
But yet, alas ! stood I within his grace,
I would prefer him to a better place.
So farewell to you both.

Gon. Prescribe not us our duties.

Reg.   Let your study

Be to content your lord ; who hath received you
At fortune's alms. You have obedience scanted,
And well are worth the want that you have
    wanted.

Cor. Time shall unfold what plaited cunning
    hides :
Who cover faults, at last shame them derides.
Well may you prosper !

France.   Come, my fair Cordelia.
    [*Exeunt* FRANCE *and* CORDELIA.

Gon. Sister, it is not a little I have to say, of
what most nearly appertains to us both. I think
our father will hence to-night.

Reg. That's most certain, and with you : next
month with us.

Gon. You see how full of changes his age is :
the observation we have made of it hath not
been little. He always loved our sister most :
and with what poor judgment he hath now cast
her off, appears too grossly.

Reg. 'T is the infirmity of his age : yet he
hath ever but slenderly known himself.

Gon. The best and soundest of his time hath
been but rash : then must we look to receive
from his age, not alone the imperfections of
long-engrafted condition, but therewithal the
unruly waywardness that infirm and choleric
years bring with them.

Reg. Such unconstant starts are we like to
have from him, as this of Kent's banishment.

Gon. There is further compliment of leave-
taking between France and him. Pray you, let
us hit together : if our father carry authority
with such dispositions as he bears, this last surrender of his will but offend us.

Reg. We shall further think of it.

Gon. We must do something, and i' the heat.
    [*Exeunt.*

SCENE II.—*A Hall in the* EARL OF GLOSTER'S
Castle.

Enter EDMUND, *with a letter.*

Edm. Thou, nature, art my goddess ; to thy law
My services are bound. Wherefore should I
Stand in the plague of custom ; and permit
The curiosity of nations to deprive me,
For that I am some twelve or fourteen moonshines
Lag of a brother ? Why bastard ; wherefore base ;
When my dimensions are as well compact,
My mind as generous, and my shape as true,
As honest madam's issue ? Why brand they us
With base ; with baseness ; bastardy ; base, base ;
Who, in the lusty stealth of nature, take
More composition and fierce quality
Than doth, within a dull, stale, tired bed,
Go to the creating a whole tribe of fops,

Got 'tween asleep and wake?—Well then,
Legitimate Edgar, I must have your land:
Our father's love is to the bastard Edmund,
As to the legitimate. "Fine word,—legitimate!"
Well, my legitimate, if this letter speed,
And my invention thrive, Edmund the base
Shall top the legitimate. I grow: I prosper.—
Now, gods, stand up for bastards!

Enter GLOSTER.

Glo. Kent banished thus; and France in choler
    parted!
And the king gone to-night: subscribed his power:
Confined to exhibition! All this done
Upon the gad!—Edmund! how now? what news?

Edm. So please your lordship, none.
                [*Putting up the letter.*

Glo. Why so earnestly seek you to put up that
    letter?

Edm. I know no news, my lord.

Glo. What paper were you reading?

Edm. Nothing, my lord.

Glo. No? what needed, then, that terrible
despatch of it into your pocket? the quality of
nothing hath not such need to hide itself. Let's
see: come, if it be nothing, I shall not need
spectacles.

Edm. I beseech you, sir, pardon me. It is a
letter from my brother, that I have not all o'er-
read: for so much as I have perused, I find it
not fit for your over-looking.

Glo. Give me the letter, sir.

Edm. I shall offend either to detain or give
it. The contents, as in part I understand them,
are to blame.

Glo. Let's see, let's see.

Edm. I hope, for my brother's justification,
he wrote this but as an assay or taste of my
virtue.

GLOSTER *reads.*

  "This policy and reverence of age makes the
world bitter in the best of our times; keeps our
fortunes from us till our oldness cannot relish them.
I begin to find an idle and fond bondage in the oppression of aged tyranny; who sways, not as it hath
power, but as it is suffered. Come to me, that of
this I may speak more. If our father would sleep
till I waked him, you should enjoy half his revenue
for ever, and live the beloved of your brother,
                    EDGAR."

Humph!—Conspiracy!—"Sleep till I waked
him—you should enjoy half his revenue!"—My
son Edgar! Had he a hand to write this? a
heart and brain to breed it in?—When came
this to you? who brought it?

Edm. It was not brought me, my lord; there's
the cunning of it: I found it thrown in at the
casement of my closet.

Glo. You know the character to be your
brother's?

Edm. If the matter were good, my lord, I
durst swear it were his; but in respect of that,
I would fain think it were not.

Glo. It is his.

Edm. It is his hand, my lord; but I hope his
heart is not in the contents.

Glo. Hath he never heretofore sounded you
in this business?

Edm. Never, my lord: but I have often heard
him maintain it to be fit, that, sons at perfect
age, and fathers declining, the father should be
as ward to the son, and the son manage his
revenue.

Glo. O villain, villain!—His very opinion in
the letter!—Abhorred villain! Unnatural, detested, brutish villain! worse than brutish!—Go,
sirrah, seek him; I'll apprehend him.—Abominable villain!—Where is he?

Edm. I do not well know, my lord. If it
shall please you to suspend your indignation
against my brother till you can derive from him
better testimony of his intent, you shall run a
certain course: where, if you violently proceed
against him, mistaking his purpose, it would
make a great gap in your own honour, and
shake in pieces the heart of his obedience. I
dare pawn down my life for him that he hath
writ this to feel my affection to your honour,
and to no other pretence of danger.

Glo. Think you so?

Edm. If your honour judge it meet, I will place
you where you shall hear us confer of this, and
by an auricular assurance have your satisfaction;
and that without any further delay than this very
evening.

Glo. He cannot be such a monster.

Edm. Nor is not, sure.

Glo. To his father, that so tenderly and entirely
loves him. Heaven and earth!—Edmund, seek
him out; wind me into him, I pray you: frame
the business after your own wisdom. I would
unstate myself, to be in a due resolution.

Edm. I will seek him, sir, presently; convey
the business as I shall find means, and acquaint
you withal.

Glo. These late eclipses in the sun and moon
portend no good to us. Though the wisdom of
nature can reason it thus and thus, yet nature
finds itself scourged by the sequent affects:—love
cools, friendship falls off, brothers divide: in
cities, mutinies; in countries, discord; in palaces,
treason; and the bond cracked between son
and father. This villain of mine comes under
the prediction; there's son against father: the
king falls from bias of nature; there's father

against child. We have seen the best of our time: machinations, hollowness, treachery, and all ruinous disorders, follow us disquietly to our graves!—Find out this villain, Edmund; it shall lose thee nothing: do it carefully.—And the noble and true-hearted Kent banished! his offence, honesty!—Strange! strange! [*Exit.*

Edm. This is the excellent foppery of the world! that when we are sick in fortune (often the surfeit of our own behaviour), we make guilty of our disasters the sun, the moon, and the stars:—as if we were villains by necessity; fools, by heavenly compulsion; knaves, thieves, and treachers, by spherical predominance; drunkards, liars, and adulterers, by an enforced obedience of planetary influence; and all that we are evil in, by a divine thrusting on. An admirable evasion of whoremaster man, to lay his goatish disposition to the charge of a star! My father compounded with my mother under the dragon's tail, and my nativity was under *ursa major;* so that it follows I am rough and lecherous!—Tut, I should have been that I am, had the maidenliest star in the firmament twinkled on my bastardizing. Edgar—

Enter EDGAR.

And pat he comes, like the catastrophe of the old comedy. My cue is villanous melancholy, with a sigh like Tom o' Bedlam.—O, these eclipses do portend these divisions! fa, sol, la, mi.

Edg. How now, brother Edmund? What serious contemplation are you in?

Edm. I am thinking, brother, of a prediction I read this other day, what should follow these eclipses.

Edg. Do you busy yourself with that?

Edm. I promise you, the effects he writes of succeed unhappily: as of unnaturalness between the child and the parent; death, dearth, dissolutions of ancient amities; divisions in state, menaces and maledictions against king and nobles; needless diffidences, banishment of friends, dissipation of cohorts, nuptial breaches, and I know not what.

Edg. How long have you been a sectary astronomical?

Edm. Come, come; when saw you my father last?

Edg. Why, the night gone by.

Edm. Spake you with him?

Edg. Ay, two hours together.

Edm. Parted you in good terms? found you no displeasure in him, by word or countenance?

Edg. None at all.

Edm. Bethink yourself wherein you may have offended him: and at my entreaty forbear his presence till some little time hath qualified the heat of his displeasure; which at this instant so rageth in him, that with the mischief of your person it would scarcely allay.

Edg. Some villain hath done me wrong.

Edm. That's my fear. I pray you have a continent forbearance till the speed of his rage goes slower; and, as I say, retire with me to my lodging, from whence I will fitly bring you to hear my lord speak. Pray you, go; there's my key.—If you do stir abroad, go armed.

Edg. Armed, brother?

Edm. Brother, I advise you to the best. I am no honest man if there be any good meaning towards you: I have told you what I have seen and heard but faintly: nothing like the image and horror of it. Pray you, away.

Edg. Shall I hear from you anon?

Edm. I do serve you in this business.—

[*Exit* EDGAR.

A credulous father, and a brother noble,
Whose nature is so far from doing harms,
That he suspects none; on whose foolish honesty
My practices ride easy!—I see the business.
Let me, if not by birth, have lands by wit:
All with me's meet, that I can fashion fit. [*Exit.*

SCENE III.—*A Room in the* DUKE OF ALBANY'S *Palace.*

Enter GONERIL *and* Steward.

Gon. Did my father strike my gentleman for chiding of his fool?

Stew. Ay, madam.

Gon. By day and night he wrongs me: every hour
He flashes into one gross crime or other,
That sets us all at odds: I'll not endure it:
His knights grow riotous, and himself upbraids us
On every trifle.—When he returns from hunting
I will not speak with him: say I am sick.
If you come slack of former services,
You shall do well: the fault of it I'll answer.

Stew. He's coming, madam; I hear him.

[*Horns within.*

Gon. Put on what weary negligence you please,
You and your fellows; I'd have it come to question:
If he dislike it, let him to my sister,
Whose mind and mine I know in that are one,
Not to be overruled. Idle old man,
That still would manage those authorities
That he hath given away!—Now, by my life,
Old fools are babes again; and must be used
With checks, as flatteries,—when they are seen abused.
Remember what I have said.

Stew. Very well, madam.

Gon. And let his knights have colder looks
    among you :

What grows of it, no matter : advise your fellows so.
I would breed from hence occasions, and I shall,
That I may speak.—I 'll write straight to my sister,
To hold my very course.—Prepare for dinner.

                        [*Exeunt.*

SCENE IV.—*A Hall in the same.*

Enter KENT, *disguised.*

Kent. If but as well I other accents borrow,
That can my speech diffuse, my good intent
May carry through itself to that full issue
For which I razed my likeness.—Now, banished
    Kent,
If thou canst serve where thou dost stand con-
    demned,
(So may it come !) thy master, whom thou lov'st,
Shall find thee full of labours.

Horns within.   *Enter* LEAR, Knights, *and*
           Attendants.

Lear. Let me not stay a jot for dinner : go,
get it ready. [*Exit an* Attendant.]—How now ;
what art thou ?

Kent. A man, sir.

Lear. What dost thou profess ? what wouldst
thou with us ?

Kent. I do profess to be no less than I seem ;
to serve him truly that will put me in trust ; to
love him that is honest ; to converse with him
that is wise and says little ; to fear judgment ;
to fight when I cannot choose ; and to eat no fish.

Lear. What art thou ?

Kent. A very honest-hearted fellow, and as
poor as the King.

Lear. If thou be as poor for a subject as he is
for a king, thou art poor enough. What wouldst
thou ?

Kent. Service.

Lear. Who wouldst thou serve ?

Kent. You.

Lear. Dost thou know me, fellow ?

Kent. No, sir ; but you have that in your
countenance which I would fain call master.

Lear. What 's that ?

Kent. Authority.

Lear. What services canst thou do ?

Kent. I can keep honest counsel, ride, run,
mar a curious tale in telling it, and deliver a
plain message bluntly : that which ordinary men
are fit for, I am qualified in ; and the best of me
is diligence.

Lear. How old art thou ?

Kent. Not so young, sir, to love a woman for
singing ; nor so old to dote on her for anything.
I have years on my back forty-eight.

Lear. Follow me ; thou shalt serve me : if I
like thee no worse after dinner, I will not part
from thee yet.—Dinner, ho, dinner !—Where 's
my knave ; my fool. Go you, and call my fool
hither.

Enter Steward.

You, you, sirrah, where 's my daughter ?

Stew. So please you,—   [*Exit.*

Lear. What says the fellow there ? Call the
clotpoll back.—Where 's my fool, ho ?—I think
the world 's asleep.—How, now ; where 's that
mongrel ?

Knight. He says, my lord, your daughter is
not well.

Lear. Why came not the slave back to me
when I called him ?

Knight. Sir, he answered me in the roundest
manner, he would not.

Lear. He would not !

Knight. My lord, I know not what the matter
is ; but, to my judgment, your highness is not
entertained with that ceremonious affection as
you were wont : there 's a great abatement of
kindness appears, as well in the general dependants as in the duke himself also, and your
daughter.

Lear. Ha ! sayst thou so ?

Knight. I beseech you pardon me, my lord, if
I be mistaken ; for my duty cannot be silent
when I think your highness is wronged.

Lear. Thou but rememberest me of mine own
conception : I have perceived a most faint neglect of late : which I have rather blamed as
mine own jealous curiosity, than as a very pretence and purpose of unkindness. I will look
further into 't.—But where 's my fool ? I have
not seen him this two days.

Knight. Since my young lady 's going into
France, sir, the fool hath much pined away.

Lear. No more of that ; I have noted it well.
—Go you, and tell my daughter I would speak
with her.—Go you, call hither my fool.

Re-enter Steward.

O, you, sir, you sir, come you hither. Who am
I, sir ?

Stew. My lady 's father.

Lear. My lady 's father ! my lord 's knave :
you whoreson dog ! you slave ! you cur !

Stew. I am none of this, my lord : I beseech
you pardon me.

Lear. Do you bandy looks with me, you
rascal ?   [*Striking him.*

Stew. I 'll not be struck, my lord.

Kent. Nor tripped neither, you base football player.   *[Tripping up his heels.*

Lear. I thank thee, fellow : thou servest me, and I 'll love thee.

Kent. Come, sir, arise, away : I 'll teach you differences : away, away. If you will measure your lubber's length again, tarry ; but away : go to. Have you wisdom ? so.

                    [Pushing the Steward *out.*

Lear. Now, my friendly knave, I thank thee : there 's earnest of thy service.

                  [Giving KENT *money.*

Enter Fool.

Fool. Let me hire him too :—here 's my cox-comb.   *[Giving* KENT *his cap.*

Lear. How now, my pretty knave ; how dost thou ?

Fool. Sirrah, you were best take my coxcomb.

Kent. Why, fool ?

Fool. Why ? for taking one's part that is out of favour. Nay, an thou canst not smile as the wind sits, thou 'lt catch cold shortly : there, take my coxcomb. Why, this fellow has banished two of his daughters, and did the third a bless-ing against his will : if thou follow him, thou must needs wear my coxcomb.—How now, nuncle ? 'Would I had two coxcombs, and two daughters.

Lear. Why, my boy ?

Fool. If I gave them all my living, I 'd keep my coxcombs myself. There 's mine : beg an-other of thy daughters.

Lear. Take heed, sirrah : the whip.

Fool. Truth 's a dog that must to kennel : he must be whipped out, when Lady, the brach, may stand by the fire and stink.

Lear. A pestilent gall to me !

Fool. Sirrah, I 'll teach thee a speech.

Lear. Do.

Fool. Mark it, nuncle :—

Have more than thou shewest,
Speak less than thou knowest,
Lend less than thou owest,
Ride more than thou goest,
Learn more than thou trowest,
Set less than thou throwest ;
Leave thy drink and thy whore,
And keep in-a-door,
And thou shalt have more
Than two tens to a score.

Lear. This is nothing, fool.

Fool. Then 't is like the breath of an unfee'd lawyer : you gave me nothing for 't. Can you make no use of nothing, nuncle ?

Lear. Why, no, boy : nothing can be made out of nothing.

Fool. Pr'y thee, tell him, so much the rent of his land comes to : he will not believe a fool.

Lear. A bitter fool !   *[To* KENT.

Fool. Dost thou know the difference, my boy, between a bitter fool and a sweet fool ?

Lear. No, lad : teach me.

Fool. That lord that counselled thee
    To give away thy land,
Come, place him here by me,—
    Or do thou for him stand :
The sweet and bitter fool
    Will presently appear ;
The one in motley here,
    The other found out there !—

Lear. Dost thou call me fool, boy ?

Fool. All thy other titles thou hast given away : that thou wast born with.

Kent. This is not altogether fool, my lord.

Fool. No, 'faith, lords and great men will not let me ; if I had a monopoly out, they would have part on 't : and ladies, too, they will not let me have all fool to myself ; they 'll be snatching.—Give me an egg, nuncle, and I 'll give thee two crowns.

Lear. What two crowns shall they be ?

Fool. Why, after I have cut the egg i' the middle, and eat up the meat, the two crowns of the egg. When thou clovest thy crown i' the middle, and gavest away both parts, thou borest thine ass on thy back over the dirt : thou hadst little wit in thy bald crown, when thou gavest thy golden one away. If I speak like myself in this, let him be whipped that first finds it so.

Sings.

Fools had ne'er less grace in a year ;
  For wise men are grown foppish ;
And know not how their wits to wear,
  Their manners are so apish.

Lear. When were you wont to be so full of songs, sirrah ?

Fool. I have used it, nuncle, ever since thou madest thy daughters thy mother : for when thou gavest them the rod, and putt'st down thine own breeches,

Sings.

Then they for sudden joy did weep,
  And I for sorrow sung,
That such a king should play bo-peep,
  And go the fools among.

Pr'y thee, nuncle, keep a schoolmaster that can teach thy fool to lie : I would fain learn to lie.

Lear. If you lie, sirrah, we 'll have you whipped.

Fool. I mar'el what kin thou and thy daughters are : they 'll have me whipped for speaking true, thou 'lt have me whipped for lying ; and sometimes I am whipped for holding my peace. I had rather be any kind of thing than a fool : and yet I would not be thee, nuncle ; thou hast pared thy wit o' both sides, and left nothing in the middle. Here comes one o' the parings.

Enter GONERIL.

Lear. How now, daughter, what makes that frontlet on ? Methinks you are too much of late i' the frown.

Fool. Thou wast a pretty fellow when thou hadst no need to care for her frowning : now thou art an O without a figure. I am better than thou art now : I am a fool ; thou art nothing.—Yes, forsooth, I will hold my tongue ; so your face *[To* GONERIL] bids me, though you say nothing. Mum, mum :

He that keeps nor crust nor crum,
  Weary of all, shall want some.—

That 's a shealed peascod.   *[Pointing to* LEAR.

Gon. Not only, sir, this your all-licensed fool,
But other of your insolent retinue
Do hourly carp and quarrel ; breaking forth
In rank and not-to-be-endured riots. Sir,
I had thought, by making this well known unto
    you,
To have found a safe redress ; but now grow
    fearful,
By what yourself too late have spoke and done,
That you protect this course, and put it on
By your allowance : which if you should, the fault
Would not 'scape censure, nor the redresses sleep ;
Which, in the tender of a wholesome weal,
Might in their working do you that offence,
Which else were shame, that then necessity
Will call discreet proceeding.

Fool. For you trow, nuncle,
The hedge-sparrow fed the cuckoo so long,
That it had its head bit off by its young.—
So out went the candle, and we were left darkling.

Lear. Are you our daughter?

Gon. Come, sir, I would you would make use of that good wisdom whereof I know you are fraught; and put away these dispositions, which of late transform you from what you rightly are.

Fool. May not an ass know when the cart draws the horse?—Whoop, Jug! I love thee.

Lear. Does any here know me?—Why this is not Lear: does Lear walk thus? speak thus? Where are his eyes? Either his notion weakens, or his discernings are lethargied.—Sleeping or waking?—Ha! sure 'tis not so.—Who is it that can tell me who I am?—Lear's shadow? I would learn that; for by the marks of sovereignty, knowledge, and reason, I should be false persuaded I had daughters—

Fool. Which they will make an obedient father.

Lear. Your name, fair gentlewoman?

Gon. Come, sir;
This admiration is much o' the favour
Of other your new pranks. I do beseech you
To understand my purposes aright:
As you are old and reverend, you should be wise:
Here do you keep a hundred knights and squires;
Men so disordered, so debauched and bold,
That this our court, infected with their manners,
Shews like a riotous inn: epicurism and lust
Make it more like a tavern or a brothel
Than a graced palace. The shame itself doth speak
For instant remedy: be then desired
By her that else will take the thing she begs,
A little to disquantity your train:
And the remainder that shall still depend,
To be such men as may besort your age,
And know themselves and you.

Lear.   Darkness and devils!—
Saddle my horses; call my train together.—
Degenerate bastard! I'll not trouble thee:
Yet have I left a daughter.

Gon. You strike my people; and your disor-
    dered rabble
Make servants of their betters.

Enter ALBANY.

Lear. Woe, that too late repents!—O, sir, are
    you come?
Is it your will? [*To* ALBANY.] Speak, sir.—Pre-
pare my horses.—
Ingratitude! thou marble-hearted fiend,
More hideous, when thou shew'st thee in a child,
Than the sea-monster!

Alb.   Pray, sir, be patient.

Lear. Detested kite! thou liest: [*To* GONERIL.
My train are men of choice and rarest parts,
That all particulars of duty know,
And in the most exact regard support
The worships of their name.—O most small fault,

How ugly didst thou in Cordelia shew!
Which, like an engine, wrenched my frame of
    nature
From the fixed place; drew from my heart all love,
And added to the gall. O Lear, Lear, Lear!
Beat at this gate, that let thy folly in,
                  [*Striking his head.*
And thy dear judgment out!—Go, go, my people.

Alb. My lord, I am guiltless, as I am ignorant
Of what hath moved you.

Lear.   It may be so, my lord.—
Hear, nature, hear; dear goddess, hear!—
Suspend thy purpose, if thou didst intend
To make this creature fruitful!
Into her womb convey sterility!
Dry up in her the organs of increase;
And from her derogate body never spring
A babe to honour her! If she must teem,
Create her child of spleen; that it may live,
And be a thwart disnatured torment to her!
Let it stamp wrinkles in her brow of youth;
With cadent tears fret channels in her cheeks;
Turn all her mother's pains and benefits
To laughter and contempt: that she may feel
How sharper than a serpent's tooth it is
To have a thankless child!—Away, away! [*Exit.*

Alb. Now, gods that we adore, whereof comes
    this?

Gon. Never afflict yourself to know the cause;
But let his disposition have that scope
That dotage gives it.

Re-enter LEAR.

Lear. What, fifty of my followers at a clap!
Within a fortnight!

Alb. What's the matter, sir?

Lear. I'll tell thee;—Life and death! I am
    ashamed
That thou hast power to shake my manhood thus:
                  [*To* GONERIL.
That these hot tears, which break from me per-
    force,
Should make thee worth them.—Blasts and fogs
    upon thee!
The untented woundings of a father's curse
Pierce every sense about thee!—Old fond eyes,
Beweep this cause again, I'll pluck you out,
And cast you, with the waters that you lose,
To temper clay.—Ha! is it come to this?
Let it be so:—yet have I left a daughter,
Who I am sure is kind and comfortable:
When she shall hear this of thee, with her nails
She'll flay thy wolfish visage. Thou shalt find
That I'll resume the shape which thou dost think
I have cast off for ever; thou shalt, I warrant thee.
       [*Exeunt* LEAR, KENT, *and* Attendants.

Gon. Do you mark that, my lord?

Alb. I cannot be so partial, Goneril,
To the great love I bear you,—

Gon. Pray you, content.—What, Oswald, ho!—
You, sir, more knave than fool, after your master.
                        [*To the* Fool.

Fool. Nuncle Lear, nuncle Lear, tarry; take
the fool with thee.

    A fox, when one has caught her,
    And such a daughter,
    Should sure to the slaughter,
    If my cap would buy a halter:
    So the fool follows after.   [*Exit.*

Gon. This man hath had good counsel!—A
    hundred knights!
'T is politic and safe to let him keep
At point a hundred knights! Yes, that on every
    dream,
Each buz, each fancy, each complaint, dislike,
He may enguard his dotage with their powers,
And hold our lives in mercy.—Oswald, I say!

Alb. Well, you may fear too far.

Gon. Safer than trust too far.
Let me still take away the harms I fear,
Not fear still to be taken. I know his heart:
What he hath uttered I have writ my sister:
If she sustain him and his hundred knights,
When I have shewed the unfitness,—How now,
    Oswald?

Enter Steward.

What, have you writ that letter to my sister?

Stew. Ay, madam.

Gon. Take you some company, and away to
    horse:
Inform her full of my particular fear;
And thereto add such reasons of your own,
As may compact it more. Get you gone;
And hasten your return. [*Exit* Steward.]—No,
    no, my lord,
This milky gentleness and course of yours,
Though I condemn it not, yet, under pardon,
You are much more attasked for want of wisdom
Than praised for harmful mildness.

Alb. How far your eyes may pierce I cannot
    tell:
Striving to better, oft we mar what's well.

Gon. Nay, then,—

Alb. Well, well; the event.   [*Exeunt.*

Scene V.—*Court before the same.*

Enter Lear, Kent, *and* Fool.

Lear. Go you before to Gloster with these
letters: acquaint my daughter no further with
anything you know than comes from her demand out of the letter. If your diligence be not
speedy, I shall be there before you.

Kent. I will not sleep, my lord, till I have
delivered your letter.   [*Exit.*

Fool. If a man's brains were in his heels,
were 't not in danger of kibes?

Lear. Ay, boy.

Fool. Then, I pr'y thee, be merry; thy wit
shall not go slipshod.

Lear. Ha, ha, ha!

Fool. Shalt see thy other daughter will use
thee kindly: for though she's as like this as a
crab is like an apple, yet I can tell what I can tell.

Lear. Why, what canst thou tell, my boy?

Fool. She will taste as like this as a crab
does to a crab.—Thou canst tell why one's nose
stands i' the middle of his face?

Lear. No.

Fool. Why, to keep his eyes on either side his
nose: that what a man cannot smell out, he
may spy into.

Lear. I did her wrong:—

Fool. Canst tell how an oyster makes his shell?

Lear. No.

Fool. Nor I neither: but I can tell why a snail
has a house.

Lear. Why?

Fool. Why, to put his head in: not to give it
away to his daughters, and leave his horns without
a case.

Lear. I will forget my nature.—So kind a father!—Be my horses ready?

Fool. Thy asses are gone about 'em.—The reason why the seven stars are no more than seven,
is a pretty reason.

Lear. Because they are not eight?

Fool. Yes, indeed:—thou wouldst make a good
fool.

Lear. To take it again perforce!—Monster
    ingratitude!

Fool. If thou wert my fool, nuncle, I 'd have
thee beaten for being old before thy time.

Lear. How 's that?

Fool. Thou shouldst not have been old before
thou hadst been wise.

Lear. O let me not be mad, not mad, sweet
    heaven!
Keep me in temper: I would not be mad!

Enter Gentleman.

How now! Are the horses ready?

Gent. Ready, my lord.

Lear. Come, boy.

Fool. She that is maid now, and laughs at my
    departure,
Shall not be a maid long, unless things be cut
    shorter.   [*Exeunt.*

SCENE I.—*A Court within the Castle of the* EARL
OF GLOSTER.

Enter EDMUND *and* CURAN, *meeting.*

Edm. Save thee, Curan.

Cur. And you, sir. I have been with your father; and given him notice that the Duke of
Cornwall, and Regan his duchess, will be here
with him to-night.

Edm. How comes that?

Cur. Nay, I know not.—You have heard of
the news abroad? I mean the whispered ones,
for they are yet but ear-kissing arguments.

Edm. Not I: 'pray you, what are they?

Cur. Have you heard of no likely wars toward,
'twixt the Dukes of Cornwall and Albany?

Edm. Not a word.

Cur. You may then, in time. Fare you well,
sir.   [*Exit.*

Edm. The duke be here to-night! The better;
best:

This weaves itself perforce into my business.
My father hath set guard to take my brother;
And I have one thing, of a queazy question,
Which I must act. Briefness and fortune work!—
Brother, a word: descend.—Brother, I say:

Enter EDGAR.

My father watches.—O sir, fly this place:
Intelligence is given where you are hid;
You have now the good advantage of the night.—
Have you not spoken 'gainst the Duke of Corn-
wall?
He's coming hither; now, i' the night, i' the haste,
And Regan with him. Have you nothing said
Upon his party, 'gainst the Duke of Albany?
Advise yourself.

Edg.   I am sure on 't, not a word,

Edm. I hear my father coming:—Pardon me:
In cunning I must draw my sword upon you:
Draw: seem to defend yourself: now quit you
well.—
Yield; come before my father: light, ho, here!—
Fly, brother.—Torches! torches!—So, farewell.—
                                              [*Exit* EDGAR.
Some blood drawn on me would beget opinion
                                              [*Wounds his arm.*
Of my more fierce endeavour: I have seen
drunkards
Do more than this in sport.—Father! father!
Stop, stop! No help?

Enter GLOSTER *and* Servants, *with torches.*

Glo. Now, Edmund, where's the villain?

Edm. Here stood he in the dark, his sharp
sword out,
Mumbling of wicked charms, conjuring the moon
To stand his auspicious mistress:—

Glo.   But where is he?

Edm. Look, sir, I bleed.

Glo.   Where is the villain, Edmund?

Edm. Fled this way, sir. When by no means
he could,—

Glo. Pursue him, ho! Go after.—[*Exit* Servant.
By no means, what?

Edm. Persuade me to the murder of your
lordship;
But that I told him, the revenging gods
'Gainst parricides did all their thunders bend;
Spoke with how manifold and strong a bond
The child was bound to the father:—Sir, in fine,
Seeing how loathly opposite I stood
To his unnatural purpose, in fell motion,
With his prepared sword, he charges home

My unprovided body, lanced mine arm:
But when he saw my best alarumed spirits,
Bold in the quarrel's right, roused to the encounter,
Or whether ghasted by the noise I made,
Full suddenly he fled.

Glo.   Let him fly far:
Not in this land shall he remain uncaught;
And found, despatch. The noble duke my master,
My worthy arch and patron, comes to-night:
By his authority I will proclaim it
That he which finds him shall deserve our thanks,
Bringing the murderous coward to the stake:
He that conceals him, death.

Edm. When I dissuaded him from his intent,
And found him pight to do it, with curst speech
I threatened to discover him: he replied,
" Thou unpossessing bastard! dost thou think,
If I would stand against thee, would the reposal
Of any trust, virtue, or worth, in thee,
Make thy words faithed? No: what should I deny
(As this I would; ay, though thou didst produce
My very character), I 'd turn it all
To thy suggestion, plot, and damnéd practice:
And thou must make a dullard of the world,
If they not thought the profits of my death
Were very pregnant and potential spurs
To make thee seek it."

Glo.   Strong and fastened villain!
Would he deny his letter?—I never got him.
                         [*Trumpets within.*
Hark, the duke's trumpets! I know not why he
      comes.—
All ports I 'll bar; the villain shall not 'scape:
The duke must grant me that. Besides, his picture
I will send far and near, that all the kingdom
May have due note of him: and of my land,
Loyal and natural boy, I 'll work the means
To make thee capable.

Enter CORNWALL, REGAN, *and* Attendants.

Corn. How now, my noble friend? since I
      came hither
(Which I can call but now), I have heard strange
      news.
Reg. If it be true, all vengeance comes too
      short
Which can pursue the offender. How dost, my
      lord?
Glo. O, madam, my old heart is cracked; it 's
      cracked!
Reg. What, did my father's godson seek your
      life?
He, whom my father named? your Edgar!
Glo. O lady, lady, shame would have it hid!
Reg. Was he not companion with the riotous
      knights
That tend upon my father?

Glo. I know not, madam: 'tis too bad, too bad.
Edm. Yes, madam, he was of that consort.
Reg. No marvel then, though he were ill
      affected:
'T is they have put him on the old man's death,
To have the waste and spoil of his revénues.
I have this present evening from my sister
Been well informed of them; and with such
      cautions,
That, if they come to sojourn at my house,
I 'll not be there.
Corn.   Nor I, assure thee, Regan.—
Edmund, I hear that you have shewn your father
A childlike office.
Edm.   It was my duty, sir.
Glo. He did bewray his practice; and received
This hurt you see, striving to apprehend him.
Corn. Is he pursued?
Glo.   Ay, my good lord.
Corn. If he be taken, he shall never more
Be feared of doing harm: make your own purpose
How in my strength you please.—For you,
      Edmund,
Whose virtue and obedience doth this instant
So much commend itself, you shall be ours:
Natures of such deep trust we shall much need:
You we first seize on.
Edm.   I shall serve you, sir,
Truly, however else.
Glo.   For him I thank your grace.
Corn. You know not why we came to visit you,—
Reg. Thus out of season; threading dark-
      eyed night.
Occasions, noble Gloster, of some poize,
Wherein we must have use of your advice :—
Our father he hath writ, so hath our sister,
Of differences, which I best thought it fit
To answer from our home: the several messengers
From hence attend despatch. Our good old friend,
Lay comforts to your bosom; and bestow
Your needful counsel to our business,
Which craves the instant use.
Glo.   I serve you, madam:
Your graces are right welcome.   [*Exeunt.*

SCENE II.—*Before* GLOSTER'S *Castle.*

Enter KENT *and* Steward, *severally.*

Stew. Good dawning to thee, friend: art of
      the house?
Kent. Ay.
Stew. Where may we set our horses?
Kent. I' the mire.
Stew. Pr'y thee, if thou love me, tell me.
Kent. I love thee not.

Stew. Why, then I care not for thee.

Kent. If I had thee in Lipsbury pinfold, I would make thee care for me.

Stew. Why dost thou use me thus? I know thee not.

Kent. Fellow, I know thee.

Stew. What dost thou know me for?

Kent. A knave; a rascal; an eater of broken meats; a base, proud, shallow, beggarly, three-suited, hundred-pound, filthy worsted-stocking knave; a lily-livered, action-taking knave; a whoreson, glass-gazing, superserviceable, finical rogue; one-trunk-inheriting slave; one that wouldst be a bawd, in way of good service; and art nothing but the composition of a knave, beggar, coward, pander, and the son and heir of a mongrel bitch: one whom I will beat into clamorous whining, if thou deniest the least syllable of thy addition.

Stew. Why, what a monstrous fellow art thou, thus to rail on one that is neither known of thee, nor knows thee!

Kent. What a brazen-faced varlet art thou, to deny thou know'st me! Is it two days ago since I tripped up thy heels and beat thee, before the king? Draw, you rogue; for, though it be night, the moon shines: I 'll make a sop o' the moon-shine of you. Draw, you whoreson cullionly barber-monger; draw.   [*Drawing his sword.*

Stew. Away; I have nothing to do with thee.

Kent. Draw, you rascal: you come with letters against the king, and take vanity the puppet's part against the royalty of her father. Draw, you rogue, or I 'll so carbonado your shanks,—draw, you rascal: come your ways.

Stew. Help, ho! murder! help!

Kent. Strike, you slave: stand, rogue, stand: you neat slave, strike!   [*Beating him.*

Stew. Help, ho! murder; murder!

Enter EDMUND, CORNWALL, REGAN, GLOSTER, *and* Servants.

Edm. How now? What's the matter?—Part!

Kent. With you, goodman boy, if you please: come, I 'll flesh you; come on, young master.

Glo. Weapons! arms! What's the matter here?

Corn. Keep peace, upon your lives:
He dies that strikes again. What is the matter?

Reg. The messengers from our sister and the king.

Corn. What is your difference? speak.

Stew. I am scarce in breath, my lord.

Kent. No marvel, you have so bestirred your valour. You cowardly rascal, nature disclaims in thee: a tailor made thee.

Corn. Thou art a strange fellow: a tailor make a man?

Kent. Ay, a tailor, sir: a stone-cutter or a painter could not have made him so ill, though they had been but two hours at the trade.

Corn. Speak yet, how grew your quarrel?

Stew. This ancient ruffian, sir, whose life I have spared
At suit of his grey beard,—

Kent. Thou whoreson zed! thou unnecessary letter!—My lord, if you will give me leave, I will tread this unbolted villain into mortar, and daub the wall of a jakes with him.—Spare may grey beard, you wagtail!

Corn. Peace, sirrah!
You beastly knave, know you no reverence?

Kent. Yes, sir; but anger has a privilege.

Corn. Why art thou angry?

Kent. That such a slave as this should wear a sword,
Who wears no honesty. Such smiling rogues as these,
Like rats, oft bite the holy cords atwain
Which are too intrinse t' unloose: smooth every passion
That in the natures of their lords rebels;
Bring oil to fire, snow to their colder moods;
Renege, affirm, and turn their halcyon beaks
With every gale and vary of their masters,
As knowing nought, like dogs, but following.—
A plague upon your epileptic visage!
Smile you my speeches, as I were a fool?
Goose, if I had you upon Sarum plain,
I 'd drive ye cackling home to Camelot?

Corn. What, art thou mad, old fellow?

Glo.   How fell you out?
Say that.

Kent. No contraries hold more antipathy
Than I and such a knave.

Corn. Why dost thou call him knave? What 's his offence?

Kent. His countenance likes me not.

Corn. No more, perchance, does mine, or his, or hers.

Kent. Sir, 't is my occupation to be plain:
I have seen better faces in my time
Than stands on any shoulder that I see
Before me at this instant.

Corn.   This is some fellow
Who, having been praised for bluntness, doth affect
A saucy roughness, and constrains the garb
Quite from his nature.—He cannot flatter, he!
An honest mind and plain; he must speak truth:
An they will take it, so; if not, he 's plain.—
These kind of knaves I know, which in this plainness
Harbour more craft and more corrupter ends
That twenty silly ducking observants,
That stretch their duties nicely.

Kent. Sir, in good sooth, in sincere verity,
Under the allowance of your grand aspéct,
Whose influence, like the wreath of radiant fire
On flickering Phœbus' front,—

Corn.   What mean'st by this?

Kent. To go out of my dialect, which you
discommend so much. I know, sir, I am no
flatterer: he that beguiled you in a plain accent,
was a plain knave; which for my part I will
not be, though I should win your displeasure to
entreat me to it.

Corn. What was the offence you gave him?

Stew. I never gave him any.
It pleased the king his master, very late,
To strike at me, upon his misconstruction;
When he, conjunct and flattering his displeasure,
Tripped me behind: being down, insulted, railed,
And put upon him such a deal of man,
That worthy'd him, got praises of the king
For him attempting who was self-subdued:
And, in the fleshment of this dread exploit,
Drew on me here again.

Kent.   None of these rogues and cowards
But Ajax is their fool.

Corn.   Fetch forth the stocks, ho!
You stubborn ancient knave, you reverent
      braggart,
We'll teach you—

Kent.   Sir, I am too old to learn.
Call not your stocks for me: I serve the king;
In whose employment I was sent to you:
You shall do small respect, shew too bold malice
Against the grace and person of my master,
Stocking his messenger.

Corn.   Fetch forth the stocks:
As I have life and honour, there shall he sit till
      noon.

Reg. Till noon! till night, my lord; and all
      night too.

Kent. Why, madam, if I were your father's dog,
You should not use me so.

Reg.   Sir, being his knave, I will.
      [*Stocks brought out.*

Corn. This is a fellow of the self-same colour
Our sister speaks of.—Come, bring away the
      stocks.

Glo. Let me beseech your grace not to do so:
His fault is much, and the good king his master
Will check him for 't:—your purposed low cor-
      rection
Is such as basest and contemned'st wretches,
For pilferings and most common trespasses,
Are punished with. The king must take it ill,
That he, so slightly valued in his messenger,
Should have him thus restrained.

Corn.   I'll answer that.

Reg. My sister may receive it much more worse

To have her gentleman abused, assaulted,
For following her affairs.—Put in his legs.
      [*Kent is put in the stocks.*
Come, my good lord; away.
      [*Exeunt Regan and Cornwall.*

Glo. I am sorry for thee, friend: 'tis the
      duke's pleasure,
Whose disposition, all the world well knows,
Will not be rubbed nor stopped. I'll entreat
      for thee.

Kent. Pray, do not, sir. I have watched and
      travelled hard:
Some time I shall sleep out; the rest I'll whistle.
A good man's fortune may grow out at heels.
Give you good-morrow.

Glo. The duke's to blame in this: 't will be
      ill taken.   [*Exit.*

Kent. Good king, that must approve the com-
      mon saw;
Thou out of heaven's benediction com'st
To the warm sun!—
Approach, thou beacon to this under globe,
That by thy comfortable beams I may
Peruse this letter!—Nothing almost sees miracles,
But misery.—I know 'tis from Cordelia;
Who hath most fortunately been informed
Of my obscuréd course; and shall find time
From this enormous state,—seeking to give
Losses their remedies.—All weary and o'er-
      watched,
Take vantage, heavy eyes, not to behold
This shameful lodging.
Fortune, good night: smile once more; turn
      thy wheel!   [*He sleeps.*

SCENE III.—*A Part of the Heath.*

Enter Edgar.

Edg. I heard myself proclaimed;
And, by the happy hollow of a tree,
Escaped the hunt. No port is free; no place,
That guard and most unusual vigilance
Does not attend my taking. While I may 'scape,
I will preserve myself: and am bethought
To take the basest and most poorest shape
That ever penury, in contempt of man,
Brought near to beast. My face I'll grime with
      filth;
Blanket my loins; elf all my hair in knots;
And with presented nakedness outface
The winds and persecutions of the sky.
The country gives me proof and precedent
Of Bedlam beggars, who, with roaring voices,
Strike in their numbed and mortified bare arms
Pins, wooden pricks, nails, sprigs of rosemary;
And with this horrible object, from low farms,

Poor pelting villages, sheepcotes and mills,
Sometime with lunatic bans, sometime with prayers,
Enforce their charity.—Poor Turlygood! poor
    Tom!
That's something yet:—Edgar I nothing am.
                          [*Exit.*

SCENE IV.—*Before* GLOSTER'S *Castle.*

Enter LEAR, Fool, *and* Gentleman.

Lear. 'T is strange that they should so depart
    from home,
And not send back my messenger.

Gent.   As I learned,

The night before there was no purpose in them
Of this remove.

Kent.   Hail to thee, noble master!

Lear. How!
Mak'st thou this shame thy pastime?

Kent.   No, my lord.

Fool. Ha, ha; look! he wears cruel garters!
Horses are tied by the heads; dogs and bears by
the neck; monkies by the loins, and men by the
legs: when a man is over-lusty at legs, then he
wears wooden nether-stocks.

Lear. What's he that hath so much thy place
    mistook
To set thee here?

Kent.   It is both he and she ;
Your son and daughter.
　Lear. No.
　Kent. Yes.
　Lear. No, I say.
　Kent. I say, yea.
　Lear. No, no ; they would not.
　Kent. Yes, they have.
　Lear. By Jupiter, I swear, no.
　Kent. By Juno, I swear, ay.
　Lear. They durst not do 't ;
They could not, would not do 't : 't is worse than
　　murder,
To do upon respect such violent outrage.
Resolve me, with all modest haste, which way
Thou mightst deserve, or they impose, this usage,
Coming from us.
　Kent.   My lord, when at their home
I did commend your highness' letters to them,
Ere I was risen from the place that shewed
My duty kneeling, came there a reeking post,
Stewed in his haste, half breathless, panting
　　forth,
From Goneril his mistress, salutations :
Delivered letters, spite of intermission,
Which presently they read : on whose contents
They summoned up their meiny, straight took
　　horse ;
Commanded me to follow, and attend
The leisure of their answer ; gave me cold looks :
And meeting here the other messenger,
Whose welcome I perceived had poisoned mine
(Being the very fellow that of late
Displayed so saucily against your highness),
Having more man than wit about me, drew :
He raised the house with loud and coward cries :
Your son and daughter found this trespass worth
The shame which here it suffers.
　Fool. Winter 's not gone yet, if the wild geese
　　fly that way.

　　　Fathers that wear rags
　　　　Do make their children blind ;
　　　But fathers that bear bags
　　　　Shall see their children kind.
　　　Fortune, that arrant whore,
　　　　Ne'er turns the key to the poor.—

But for all this, thou shalt have as many dolours
for thy daughters as thou canst tell in a year.
　Lear. O, how this mother swells up toward
　　my heart !
Hysterica passio !—Down, thou climbing sorrow,
Thy element 's below !—Where is this daughter ?
　Kent. With the earl, sir, here within.
　Lear.   Follow me not :
Stay here.　　　　　　　　　　　　　[*Exit.*
　Gent. Made you no more offence than what
　　you speak of ?

Kent. None.
How chance the king comes with so small a train ?
　Fool. An thou hadst been set i' the stocks for
that question, thou hadst well deserved it.
　Kent. Why, fool ?
　Fool. We 'll set thee to school to an ant, to
teach thee there 's no labouring in the winter.
All that follow their noses are led by their eyes,
but blind men ; and there 's not a nose among
twenty but can smell him that 's stinking.　Let
go thy hold when a great wheel runs down a
hill, lest it break thy neck with following it : but
the great one that goes up the hill, let him draw
thee after.　When a wise man gives thee better
counsel, give me mine again : I would have none
but knaves follow it, since a fool gives it.

　　That sir which serves and seeks for gain,
　　　And follows but for form,
　　Will pack when it begins to rain,
　　　And leave thee in the storm.
　　But I will tarry ; the fool will stay,
　　　And let the wise man fly :
　　The knave turns fool that runs away ;
　　　The fool no knave, perdy.

　Kent. Where learned you this, fool ?
　Fool. Not i' the stocks, fool.

　　　　Re-enter LEAR, *with* GLOSTER.

　Lear. Deny to speak with me ? They are sick ;
　　they are weary ;
They have travelled hard to-night ? Mere fetches ;
The images of revolt and flying off !
Fetch me a better answer.
　Glo.   My dear lord,
You know the fiery quality of the duke ;
How unremovable and fixed he is
In his own course.
　Lear. Vengeance ! plague ! death ! confusion !—
Fiery ! what quality ?—Why, Gloster, Gloster,
I 'd speak with the Duke of Cornwall and his
　　wife.
　Glo. Well, my good lord, I have informed
　　them so.
　Lear. Informed them !　Dost thou understand
　　me, man ?
　Glo. Ay, my good lord.
　Lear. The king would speak with Cornwall :
　　the dear father
Would with his daughter speak ; commands her
　　service :
Are they informed of this ?—My breath and
　　blood !
Fiery ! the fiery duke !—Tell the hot duke, that—
No, but not yet :—may be he is not well :
Infirmity doth still neglect all office
Whereto our health is bound : we are not our-
　　selves,

When nature, being oppressed, commands the
    mind
To suffer with the body. I 'll forbear;
And am fallen out with my more headier will,
To take the indisposed and sickly fit
For the sound man.—Death on my state! where-
    fore   [*Looking on* KENT.
Should he sit here? This act persuades me
That this remotion of the duke and her
Is practice only. Give me my servant forth:
Go, tell the duke and his wife I 'd speak with them,
Now, presently: bid them come forth and hear me,
Or at their chamber door I 'll beat the drum
Till it cry—" Sleep to death."
    Glo. I 'd have all well betwixt you.   [*Exit.*
    Lear. O me, my heart, my rising heart!—but
    down.
    Fool. Cry to it, nuncle, as the cockney did to
the eels when she put them i' the paste alive: she
rapped 'em o' the coxcombs with a stick, and
cried, " Down, wantons, down." 'T was her
brother that, in pure kindness to his horse, but-
tered his hay.

    Enter CORNWALL, REGAN, GLOSTER, *and*
        Servants.

    Lear. Good morrow to you both.
    Corn.   Hail to your grace.
                [KENT *is set at liberty.*
    Reg. I am glad to see your highness.
    Lear. Regan, I think you are: I know what
    reason
I have to think so. If thou shouldst not be glad,
I would divorce me from thy mother's tomb,
Sepúlch'ring an adultress. O, are you free?
                [*To* KENT.
Some other time for that.—Belovéd Regan,
Thy sister's naught. O Regan, she hath tied
Sharp-toothed unkindness, like a vulture, here:—
                [*Points to his heart.*
I can scarce speak to thee: thou 'lt not believe
Of how depraved a quality—O Regan!
    Reg. I pray you, sir, take patience: I have hope
You less know how to value her desert,
Than she to scant her duty.
    Lear.   Say, how is that?
    Reg. I cannot think my sister in the least
Would fail her obligation. If, sir, perchance,
She have restrained the riots of your followers,
'T is on such ground, and to such wholesome end,
As clears her from all blame.
    Lear. My curses on her!
    Reg.   O, sir, you are old:
Nature in you stands on the very verge
Of her confine: you should be ruled and led
By some discretion that discerns your state
Better than you yourself. Therefore I pray you,

That to our sister you do make return:
Say you have wronged her, sir.
    Lear.   Ask her forgiveness!
Do you but mark how this becomes the house:—
" Dear daughter, I confess that I am old:
Age is unnecessary: on my knees I beg
That you 'll vouchsafe me raiment, bed, and food."
    Reg. Good sir, no more: these are unsightly
    tricks.
Return you to my sister.
    Lear.   Never, Regan:
She hath abated me of half my train;
Looked black upon me; struck me with her
    tongue,
Most serpent-like, upon the very heart.—
All the stored vengeances of heaven fall
On her ingrateful top! Strike her young bones,
You taking airs, with lameness!
    Corn.   Fie, sir, fie!
    Lear. You nimble lightnings, dart your blind-
    ing flames
Into her scornful eyes! Infect her beauty,
You fen-sucked fogs, drawn by the powerful sun,
To fall and blast her pride!
    Reg.   O the blest gods!
So will you wish on me, when the rash mood 's on.
    Lear. No, Regan, thou shalt never have my
    curse;
Thy tender-hefted nature shall not give
Thee o'er to harshness: her eyes are fierce, but
    thine
Do comfort, and not burn. 'T is not in thee
To grudge my pleasures, to cut off my train,
To bandy hasty words, to scant my sizes,
And, in conclusion, to oppose the bolt
Against my coming in. Thou better know'st
The offices of nature, bond of childhood,
Effects of courtesy, dues of gratitude:
Thy half o' the kingdom hast thou not forgot,
Wherein I thee endowed.
    Reg.   Good sir, to the purpose.
                [*Trumpets within.*
    Lear. Who put my man i' the stocks?
    Corn.   What trumpet 's that?

    Enter Steward.

    Reg. I know 't; my sister's: this approves
    her letter
That she would soon be here.—Is your lady come?
    Lear. This is a slave whose easy-borrowed pride
Dwells in the fickle grace of her he follows.
Out, varlet, from my sight!
    Corn.   What means your grace?
    Lear. Who stocked my servant? Regan, I
    have good hope
Thou didst not know of 't.—Who comes here?
    O, heavens,

Enter GONERIL.

If you do love old men, if your sweet sway
Allow obedience, if yourselves are old,
Make it your cause; send down, and take my
　　　part!—
Art not ashamed to look upon this beard?—
　　　　　　　　　　　　　　[*To* GONERIL.
O, Regan, wilt thou take her by the hand?
　Gon. Why not by the hand, sir?—How have
　　　I offended?
All 's not offence that indiscretion finds,
And dotage terms so.
　Lear.　　　O, sides, you are too tough!
Will you yet hold?—How came my man i' the
　　　stocks?
　Corn. I set him there, sir : but his own disorders
Deserved much less advancement.
　Lear.　　　You! did you?
　Reg. I pray you, father, being weak, seem so.
If, till the expiration of your month,
You will return and sojourn with my sister,
Dismissing half your train, come then to me :
I am now from home, and out of that provision
Which shall be needful for your entertainment.
　Lear. Return to her, and fifty men dismissed!
No, rather I abjure all roofs, and choose
To wage against the enmity o' the air;
To be a comrade with the wolf and owl :
Necessity's sharp pinch!—Return with her!
Why, the hot-blooded France, that dowerless took
Our youngest born, I could as well be brought
To knee his throne, and, squire-like, pension beg
To keep base life afoot.—Return with her!
Persuade me rather to be slave and sumpter
To this detested groom. [*Looking on the* Steward.
　Gon.　　　At your choice, sir.
　Lear. I pr'y thee, daughter, do not make me
　　　mad :
I will not trouble thee, my child : farewell :
We 'll no more meet; no more see one another.—
But yet thou art my flesh, my blood, my daughter;
Or rather a disease that 's in my flesh,
Which I must needs call mine : thou art a boil,
A plague-sore, an embossèd carbuncle,
In my corrupted blood. But I 'll not chide thee:
Let shame come when it will; I do not call it :
I do not bid the thunder-bearer shoot,
Nor tell tales of thee to high-judging Jove :
Mend when thou canst; be better at thy leisure :
I can be patient; I can stay with Regan,
I and my hundred knights.
　Reg.　　　Not altogether so, sir :
I looked not for you yet, nor am provided
For your fit welcome. Give ear, sir, to my sister:
For those that mingle reason with your passion,
Must be content to think you old, and so—
But she knows what she does.

　Lear.　　　Is this well spoken, now?
　Reg. I dare avouch it, sir. What, fifty fol-
　　　lowers!
Is it not well? What should you need of more?
Yea, or so many; sith that both charge and danger
Speak 'gainst so great a number? How in one
　　　house
Should many people, under two commands,
Hold amity? 't is hard; almost impossible.
　Gon. Why might not you, my lord, receive
　　　attendance
From those that she calls servants, or from mine?
　Reg. Why not, my lord? If then they chanced
　　　to slack you,
We could control them. If you will come to me
(For now I spy a danger), I entreat you
To bring but five-and-twenty : to no more
Will I give place or notice.
　Lear. I gave you all—
　Reg.　　　And in good time you gave it.
　Lear. Made you my guardians, my depositaries;
But kept a reservation to be followed
With such a number. What, must I come to
　　　you
With five-and-twenty, Regan? said you so?
　Reg. And speak it again, my lord: no more
　　　with me.
　Lear. Those wicked creatures yet do look well-
　　　favoured!
When others are more wicked, not being the
　　　worst
Stands in some rank of praise :—I 'll go with thee :
　　　　　　　　　　　　　　[*To* GONERIL.
Thy fifty yet doth double five-and-twenty,
And thou art twice her love.
　Gon.　　　Hear me, my lord :
What need you five-and-twenty, ten, or five,
To follow in a house where twice so many
Have a command to tend you?
　Reg.　　　What need one?
　Lear. O reason not the need : our basest
　　　beggars
Are in the poorest thing superfluous :
Allow not nature more than nature needs,
Man's life is cheap as beast's. Thou art a lady;
If only to go warm were gorgeous,
Why, nature needs not what thou gorgeous wear'st,
Which scarcely keeps thee warm.—But for true
　　　need,—
You heavens, give me that patience, patience
　　　I need!
You see me here, you gods, a poor old man,
As full of grief as age; wretched in both!
If it be you that stir these daughters' hearts
Against their father, fool me not so much
To bear it tamely; touch me with noble anger!
O let not women's weapons, water-drops,

Stain my man's cheeks!—No, you unnatural
   hags,
I will have such revenges on you both
That all the world shall—I will do such things—
What they are yet I know not; but they shall be
The terrors of the earth. You think I 'll weep:
No, I 'll not weep :—
I have full cause of weeping; but this heart
Shall break into a hundred thousand flaws
Or ere I 'll weep.—O, fool, I shall go mad!
    [*Exeunt* LEAR, GLOSTER, KENT, *and* Fool.
  Corn. Let us withdraw : 't will be a storm.
             [*Storm heard at a distance.*
  Reg. This house is little; the old man an
   his people
Cannot be well bestowed.
  Gon. 'T is his own blame : he hath put himself
   from rest,
And must needs taste his folly.
  Reg. For his particular, I 'll receive him
   gladly;
But not one follower.
  Gon.   So am I purposed.
Where is my lord of Gloster?

  Corn. Followed the old man forth.—He is returned.

Re-enter GLOSTER.

  Glo. The King is in high rage.
  Corn.   Whither is he going?
  Glo. He calls to horse ; but will I know not
  whither.
  Corn. 'T is best to give him way; he leads
  himself.
  Gon. My lord, entreat him by no means to stay.
  Glo. Alack, the night comes on, and the bleak
  winds
Do sorely ruffle : for many miles about
There 's scarce a bush.
  Reg.   O, sir, to wilful men,
The injuries that they themselves procure
Must be their schoolmasters. Shut up your doors :
He is attended with a desperate train ;
And what they may incense him to, being apt
To have his ear abused, wisdom bids fear.
  Corn. Shut up your doors, my lord ; 't is a wild
  night :
My Regan counsels well. Come out o' the storm.
                     [*Exeunt.*

SCENE I.—*A Heath.*

A Storm is heard, with thunder and lightning.
Enter KENT *and a* Gentleman, *meeting.*

Kent. Who 's here, beside foul weather?

Gent. One minded like the weather, most un-
    quietly.

Kent. I know you: where 's the King?

Gent. Contending with the fretful element:
Bids the wind blow the earth into the sea,
Or swell the curvéd waters 'bove the main,
That things might change or cease: tears his
    white hair:
Which the impetuous blasts, with eyeless rage,
Catch in their fury, and make nothing of:
Strives in his little world of man to out-scorn
The to-and-fro-conflicting wind and rain.
This night, wherein the cub-drawn bear would
    couch,
The lion and the belly-pinchéd wolf
Keep their fur dry, unbonneted he runs,
And bids what will take all.

Kent.   But who is with him?

Gent. None but the fool; who labours to outjest
His heart-struck injuries.

Kent.   Sir, I do know you;
And dare, upon the warrant of my art,
Commend a dear thing to you. There is division,
Although as yet the face of it be covered
With mutual cunning, 'twixt Albany and Corn-
    wall;
Who have (as who have not, that their great stars
Throned and set high?) servants, who seem no less;
Which are to France the spies and speculations
Intelligent of our state: what hath been seen,

Either in snuffs and packings of the dukes,
Or the hard rein which both of them have borne
Against the old kind king; or something deeper,
Whereof, perchance, these are but furnishings:—
But true it is, from France there comes a power
Into this scattered kingdom; who already,
Wise in our negligence, have secret feet
In some of our best ports, and are at point
To shew their open banner.—Now to you:
If on my credit you dare build so far
To make your speed to Dover, you shall find
Some that will thank you, making just report
Of how unnatural and bemadding sorrow
The King hath cause to plain.
I am a gentleman of blood and breeding;
And, from some knowledge and assurance, offer
This office to you.

    Gent. I will talk further with you.

    Kent.   No, do not.
For confirmation that I am much more
Than my out wall, open this purse, and take
What it contains. If you shall see Cordelia
(As fear not but you shall), shew her this ring;
And she will tell you who your fellow is,
That yet you do not know.—Fie on this storm!
I will go seek the King.

    Gent. Give me your hand: have you no more
         to say?

    Kent. Few words, but to effect more than all
         yet:
That when we have found the King (in which
         your pain
That way; I 'll this), he that first lights on him,
Holla the other.   [*Exeunt severally.*

SCENE II.—*Another part of the Heath. Storm
continues.*

Enter LEAR *and* Fool.

    Lear. Blow, wind, and crack your cheeks
         rage! blow!
You cataracts and hurricanoes, spout
Till you have drenched our steeples, drowned
         the cocks!—
You sulphurous and thought-executing fires,
Vaunt couriers to oak-cleaving thunderbolts,
Singe my white head!—And thou, all-shaking
         thunder,
Strike flat the thick rotundity o' the world!
Crack nature's moulds, all germens spill at once,
That make ingrateful man!

    Fool. O nuncle, court holy-water in a dry
house is better than this rain-water out o' door.
Good nuncle, in, and ask thy daughters' blessing:
here 's a night pities neither wise men nor foo.

    Lear. Rumble thy bellyfull! Spit, fire! spout,
         rain!
Nor rain, wind, thunder, fire, are my daughters:
I tax not you, you elements, with unkindness:
I never gave you kingdom, called you children;
You owe me no subscription: why then let fall
Your horrible pleasure: here I stand your slave,
A poor, infirm, weak, and despised old man:—
But yet I call you servile ministers,
That have with two pernicious daughters joined
Your high-engendered battles 'gainst a head
So old and white as this. O! O! 't is foul!

    Fool. He that has a house to put his head in,
has a good head piece.

         The codpiece that will house
           Before the head has any,
         The head and he shall louse:
           So beggars marry many.

         The man that makes his toe
           What he his heart should make,
         Shall of a corn cry woe,
           And turn his sleep to wake.

—for there was never yet fair woman but she
made mouths in a glass.

    Lear. No, I will be the pattern of all patience;
I will say nothing.

Enter KENT.

    Kent. Who 's there?

    Fool. Marry, here 's grace and a codpiece:
that 's a wise man and a fool.

    Kent. Alas, sir, are you there? Things that
love night,
Love not such nights as these: the wrathful skies
Gallow the very wanderers of the dark,
And make them keep their caves. Since I was man,
Such sheets of fire, such bursts of horrid thunder,
Such groans of roaring wind and rain, I never
Remember to have heard: man's nature cannot
         carry
The affliction nor the fear.

    Lear.   Let the great gods,
That keep this dreadful pudder o'er our heads,
Find out their enemies now. Tremble, thou
         wretch,
That hast within thee undivulgéd crimes,
Unwhipped of justice: hide thee, thou bloody
         hand;
Thou perjured, and thou similar man of virtue
That art incestuous: caitiff, to pieces shake,
That under covert and convenient seeming
Hast practised on man's life!—Close pent-up
         guilts,
Rive your concealing continents, and cry
These dreadful summoners grace!—I am a man
More sinned against than sinning.

    Kent.   Alack, bareheaded!—

Gracious my lord, hard by here is a hovel;
Some friendship will it lend you 'gainst the
tempest:
Repose you there; while I to this hard house
(More hard than is the stone whereof 't is raised;
Which even but now, demanding after you,
Denied me to come in) return and force
Their scanted courtesy.

Lear. My wits begin to turn.—
Come on, my boy. How dost, my boy? art cold?
I am cold myself.—Where is this straw, my fellow?
The art of our necessities is strange,
That can make vile things precious.—Come,
your hovel.
Poor fool and knave, I have one part in my heart
That 's sorry yet for thee.

Fool.

With heigh, ho, the wind and the rain,—
Must make content with his fortunes fit;
For the rain it raineth every day.

Lear. True, my good boy.—Come, bring us
to this hovel. [*Exeunt* LEAR *and* KENT.

Fool. This is a brave night to cool a courtezan.—
I 'll speak a prophecy ere I go:

When priests are more in word than matter;
When brewers mar their malt with water;
When nobles are their tailors' tutors;
No heretics burned but wenches' suitors;
When every case in law is right;
No squire in debt, nor no poor knight;
When slanders do not live in tongues;
Nor cutpurses come not to throngs;
When usurers tell their gold i' the field;
And bawds and whores do churches build;—
Then shall the realm of Albion
Come to great confusion.
Then comes the time, who lives to see 't,
That going shall be used with feet.
This prophecy Merlin shall make; for I live
before his time. [*Exit.*

SCENE III.—*A Room in* GLOSTER'S *Castle.*

Enter GLOSTER *and* EDMUND.

Glo. Alack, alack, Edmund, I like not this
unnatural dealing. When I desired their leave
that I might pity him, they took from me the
use of mine own house; charged me, on pain of
their perpetual displeasure, neither to speak of
him, entreat for him, nor any way sustain him.

Edm. Most savage and unnatural!

Glo. Go to; say you nothing. There is division between the dukes; and a worse matter than
that: I have received a letter this night;—'t is
dangerous to be spoken;—I have locked the
letter in my closet: these injuries the King now
bears will be revenged home; there is part of a
power already footed: we must incline to the
King. I will seek him, and privily relieve him:
go you, and maintain talk with the duke, that
my charity be not of him perceived: if he ask
for me, I am ill, and gone to bed. If I die for
it, as no less is threatened me, the King my old
master must be relieved. There is some strange
thing toward, Edmund; pray you, be careful.
[*Exit.*

Edm. This courtesy, forbid thee, shall the duke
Instantly know; and of that letter too.
This seems a fair deserving, and must draw me
That which my father loses; no less than all:—
The younger rises, when the old doth fall. [*Exit.*

SCENE IV.—*A part of the Heath, with a Hovel.*

Enter LEAR, KENT, *and* Fool.

Kent. Here is the place, my lord; good my
lord, enter:
The tyranny of the open night 's too rough
For nature to endure. [*Storm still.*

Lear. Let me alone.

Kent. Good my lord, enter here.

Lear. Wilt break my heart?

Kent. I 'd rather break mine own. Good my
lord, enter.

Lear. Thou think'st 't is much that this con-
tentious storm
Invades us to the skin: so 't is to thee:
But where the greater malady is fixed,
The lesser is scarce felt. Thou 'dst shun a bear:
But if thy flight lay toward the raging sea,
Thou 'dst meet the bear i' the mouth. When the
mind 's free,
The body 's delicate: the tempest in my mind
Doth from my senses take all feeling else,
Save what beats there.—Filial ingratitude!
Is it not as this mouth should tear this hand
For lifting food to 't?—But I will punish home:—
No, I will weep no more.—In such a night
To shut me out!—Pour on; I will endure:—
In such a night as this! O Regan, Goneril!
Your old kind father, whose frank heart gave all:—
O, that way madness lies; let me shun that;
No more of that!

Kent. Good my lord, enter here.

Lear. Pr'y thee, go in thyself; seek thine own ease:
This tempest will not give me leave to ponder
On things would hurt me more.—But I 'll go in:
In, boy; go first. [*To the* Fool.]—You houseless
poverty,—
Nay, get thee in. I 'll pray, and then I 'll sleep.
[*Fool goes in.*

Poor naked wretches, wheresoe'er you are,
That bide the pelting of this pitiless storm,
How shall your houseless heads and unfed sides,
Your looped and windowed raggedness, defend you
From seasons such as these? O, I have ta'en
Too little care of this! Take physic, pomp:
Expose thyself to feel what wretches feel;
That thou mayst shake the superflux to them,
And shew the heavens more just.
    Edg. [*within*]. Fathom and half, fathom and
      half! Poor Tom!
            [*The* Fool *runs out from the hovel.*

Fool. Come not in here, nuncle; here's a
    spirit:
Help me, help me!
    Kent. Give me thy hand.—Who's there?
    Fool. A spirit, a spirit! he says his name's
    poor Tom.
    Kent. What art thou that dost grumble there
      i' the straw?
Come forth.

    Enter EDGAR, *disguised as a madman.*
    Edg. Away! the foul fiend follows me!—

341

Through the sharp hawthorn blows the cold wind. Humph! go to thy cold bed, and warm thee.

Lear. Hast thou given all to thy two daughters; and art thou come to this?

Edg. Who gives anything to poor Tom? whom the foul fiend hath led through fire and through flame, through ford and whirlpool, over bog and quagmire: that hath laid knives under his pillow, and halters in his pew; set ratsbane by his porridge: made him proud of heart, to ride on a bay trotting-horse over four-inched bridges, to course his own shadow for a traitor.—Bless thy five wits! Tom's a-cold.—O do de, do de, do de.—Bless thee from whirlwinds, star-blasting, and taking! Do poor Tom some charity, whom the foul fiend vexes. There could I have him now,—and there,—and there,—and there again; and there. [*Storm continues.*

Lear. What, have his daughters brought him to this pass?—

Couldst thou save nothing? Didst thou give them all?

Fool. Nay, he reserved a blanket, else we had been all shamed.

Lear. Now, all the plagues that in the pendulous air

Hang fated o'er men's faults, light on thy daughters!

Kent. He hath no daughters, sir.

Lear. Death, traitor! nothing could have subdued nature

To such a lowness but his unkind daughters.—
Is it the fashion that discarded fathers
Should have thus little mercy on their flesh?—
Judicious punishment! 't was this flesh begot
Those pelican daughters.

Edg. Pillicock sat on pillicock's-hill!—
Halloo, halloo, loo, loo!

Fool. This cold night will turn us all to fools and madmen.

Edg. Take heed o' the foul fiend. Obey thy parents; keep thy word justly; swear not; commit not with man's sworn spouse; set not thy sweet heart on proud array.—Tom's a-cold.

Lear. What hast thou been?

Edg. A serving-man, proud in heart and mind; that curled my hair; wore gloves in my cap, served the lust of my mistress's heart, and did the act of darkness with her; swore as many oaths as I spake words, and broke them in the sweet face of heaven: one that slept in the contriving of lust, and waked to do it. Wine loved I deeply; dice dearly; and in woman, out-paramoured the Turk. False of heart, light of ear, bloody of hand: hog in sloth, fox in stealth, wolf in greediness, dog in madness, lion in prey. Let not the creaking of shoes, nor the rustling of silks, betray thy poor heart to women. Keep thy foot out of brothels, thy hand out of plackets, thy pen from lenders' books, and defy the foul fiend.—Still through the hawthorn blows the cold wind: says suum mun, ha no nonny, dolphin my boy, my boy, sessa; let him trot by.

[*Storm still continues.*

Lear. Why, thou wert better in thy grave, than to answer with thy uncovered body this extremity of the skies.—Is man no more than this? Consider him well. Thou owest the worm no silk, the beast no hide, the sheep no wool, the cat no perfume.—Ha! here's three of us are sophisticated! Thou art the thing itself: unaccommodated man is no more but such a poor, bare, forked animal as thou art.—Off, off, you lendings! Come: unbutton here.

[*Tearing off his clothes.*

Fool. Pr'y thee, nuncle, be contented; this is a naughty night to swim in.—Now a little fire in a wild field were like an old lecher's heart; a small spark, all the rest of his body cold.—Look, here comes a walking fire.

Edg. This is the foul fiend Flibbertigibbet: he begins at curfew, and walks till the first cock: he gives the web and the pin, squints the eye, and makes the hare-lip; mildews the white wheat, and hurts the poor creature of earth.

Saint Withold footed thrice the wold;
He met the night-mare and her nine-fold;
 Bid her alight,
 And her troth plight,
And, Aroint thee, witch, aroint thee!

Kent. How fares your grace?

Enter GLOSTER, *with a torch.*

Lear. What's he?

Kent. Who's there? What is 't you seek?

Glo. What are you there? Your names?

Edg. Poor Tom; that eats the swimming frog, the toad, the tadpole, the wall-newt, and the water: that in the fury of his heart, when the foul fiend rages, eats cowdung for sallets; swallows the old rat and the ditch-dog; drinks the green mantle of the standing pool: who is whipped from tything to tything, and stocked, punished, and imprisoned: who hath had three suits to his back, six shirts to his body, horse to ride, and weapon to wear:

But mice, and rats, and such small deer,
Have been Tom's food for seven long year.

Beware my follower.—Peace, Smolkin; peace, thou fiend!

Glo. What, hath your grace no better company?

Edg. The prince of darkness is a gentleman: Modo he's called, and Mahu.

Glo. Our flesh and blood, my lord, is grown
 so vile,
That it doth hate what gets it.

Edg. Poor Tom's a-cold.

Glo. Go in with me: my duty cannot suffer
To obey in all your daughters' hard commands.
Though their injunction be to bar my doors,
And let this tyrannous night take hold upon you,
Yet have I ventured to come seek you out,
And bring you where both fire and food is ready.

Lear. First let me talk with this philosopher.—
What is the cause of thunder?

Kent. Good my lord, take his offer:
Go into the house.

Lear. I'll talk a word with this same learned
 Theban.—
What is your study?

Edg. How to prevent the fiend, and to kill
 vermin.

Lear. Let me ask you one word in private.

Kent. Impórtune him once more to go, my lord;
His wits begin to unsettle.

Glo.   Canst thou blame him?
His daughters seek his death.—Ah, that good
 Kent!
He said it would be thus.—Poor banished man!—
Thou sayst the King grows mad: I'll tell thee,
 friend,
I am almost mad myself. I had a son,
Now outlawed from my blood: he sought my life,
But lately, very late. I loved him, friend;
No father his son dearer: true to tell thee,
      [*Storm continues.*
The grief hath crazed my wits. What a night's
 this!
I do beseech your grace,—

Lear.   O, cry you mercy:—
Noble philosopher, your company.

Edg. Tom's a-cold.

Glo. In, fellow, there, into the hovel: keep
 thee warm.

Lear. Come, let's in all.

Kent.   This way, my lord.

Lear.   With him:
I will keep still with my philosopher.

Kent. Good my lord, soothe him; let him take
 the fellow.

Glo. Take him you on.

Kent. Sirrah, come on; go along with us.

Lear. Come, good Athenian.

Glo.   No words, no words:
Hush.

      Edgar.

Child Rowland to the dark tower came:
 His word was still, Fie, foh, and fum;
 I smell the blood of a British man.
         [*Exeunt.*

Scene V.—*A Room in* Gloster's *Castle.*

Enter Cornwall *and* Edmund.

Corn. I will have my revenge ere I depart
 his house.

Edm. How, my lord, I may be censured that
nature thus gives way to loyalty, something fears
me to think of.

Corn. I now perceive it was not altogether
your brother's evil disposition made him seek
his death; but a provoking merit, set a-work by
a reproveable badness in himself.

Edm. How malicious is my fortune, that I
must repent to be just! This is the letter he
spoke of, which approves him an intelligent
party to the advantages of France. O heavens!
that this treason were not, or not I the detector!

Corn. Go with me to the duchess.

Edm. If the matter of this paper be certain,
you have mighty business in hand.

Corn. True or false, it hath made thee Earl
of Gloster. Seek out where thy father is, that he
may be ready for our apprehension.

Edm. [*aside*]. If I find him comforting the
King, it will stuff his suspicion more fully.—I
will persevere in my course of loyalty, though
the conflict be sore between that and my blood.

Corn. I will lay trust upon thee; and thou
shalt find a dearer father in my love. [*Exeunt.*

Scene VI.—*A Chamber in a Farmhouse, adjoining the Castle.*

Enter Gloster, Lear, Kent, Fool, *and* Edgar.

Glo. Here is better than the open air; take it
thankfully: I will piece out the comfort with what
addition I can. I will not be long from you.

Kent. All the power of his wits has given way
to his impatience.—The gods reward your kindness! [*Exit* Gloster.

Edg. Frateretto calls me; and tells me, Nero
is an angler in the lake of darkness. Pray,
innocent, and beware the foul fiend.

Fool. Pr'y thee, nuncle, tell me whether a
madman be a gentleman or a yeoman?

Lear. A king, a king!

Fool. No; he's a yeoman that has a gentleman to his son: for he's a mad yeoman that sees
his son a gentleman before him.

Lear. To have a thousand with red burning spits
Come hissing in upon them!—

Edg. The foul fiend bites my back.

Fool. He's mad that trusts in the tameness of
a wolf, a horse's health, a boy's love, or a whore's
oath.

Lear. It shall be done; I will arraign them
　　straight :—
Come, sit thou here, most learned justicer ;—
　　　　　　　　　　　　　　　[*To* EDGAR.
Thou, sapient sir, sit here. [*To the* Fool.]—Now,
　　you she-foxes !—
　　Edg. Look, where he stands and glares !—
Wantest thou eyes at trial, madam ?

　　Come o'er the bourn, Bessy, to me :—

　　　　　　　　Fool.

　　　Her boat hath a leak,
　　And she must not speak
Why she dares not come over to thee.

　　Edg. The foul fiend haunts poor Tom in the
voice of a nightingale. Hopdance cries in Tom's
belly for two white herrings. Croak not, black
angel ; I have no food for thee.
　　Kent. How do you, sir ? Stand you not so
amazed :
Will you lie down and rest upon the cushions ?
　　Lear. I 'll see their trial first.—Bring in the
　　evidence.—
Thou robéd man of justice, take thy place ;—
　　　　　　　　　　　　　　[*To* EDGAR.
And thou, his yoke-fellow of equity, [*To the* Fool.
Bench by his side.—You are of the commission ;
Sit you too.　　　　　　　　　　[*To* KENT.
　　Edg. Let us deal justly.

　　Sleepest, or wakest thou, jolly shephérd ?
　　　Thy sheep be in the corn ;
　　And for one blast of thy minikin mouth,
　　　Thy sleep shall take no harm.

Pur ! the cat is grey.
　　Lear. Arraign her first ; 't is Goneril. I here
take my oath before this honourable assembly,
she kicked the poor king her father.
　　Fool. Come hither, mistress. Is your name
Goneril ?
　　Lear. She cannot deny it.
　　Fool. Cry you mercy ; I took you for a joint-
stool.
　　Lear. And here 's another, whose warpéd looks
proclaim
What store her heart is made of.—Stop her there.
Arms, arms, sword, fire !—Corruption in the place !
False justicer, why hast thou let her 'scape ?
　　Edg. Bless thy five wits !
　　Kent. O pity !—Sir, where is the patience now,
That you so oft have boasted to retain ?
　　Edg. My tears begin to take his part so much,
They 'll mar my counterfeiting.　　　[*Aside.*
　　Lear. The little dogs and all,
Tray, Blanch, and Sweetheart, see they bark
　　at me.
　　Edg. Tom will throw his head at them :—
Avaunt, you curs !

Be thy mouth or black or white,
Tooth that poisons, if it bite ;
Mastiff, greyhound, mongrel grim,
Hound or spaniel, brach or lym ;
Or bobtail tike, or trundle-tail ;
Tom will make them weep and wail :
For, with throwing thus my head,
Dogs leap the hatch, and all are fled.
Do de, de de ; sessa. Come, march to wakes
and fairs, and market towns.—Poor Tom, thy
horn is dry.
　　Lear. Then let them anatomise Regan ; see
what breeds about her heart. Is there any cause
in nature that makes these hard hearts ?—You,
sir, I entertain you for one of my hundred ; only
I do not like the fashion of your garments : you
will say they are Persian attire ; but let them be
changed.　　　　　　　　　　[*To* EDGAR.
　　Kent. Now, good my lord, lie here, and rest
awhile.
　　Lear. Make no noise, make no noise ; draw
the curtains : so, so, so. We 'll go to supper
i' the morning : so, so, so.
　　Fool. And I 'll go to bed at noon.

　　　　　Re-enter GLOSTER.

　　Glo. Come hither, friend : where is the King,
　　my master ?
　　Kent. Here, sir : but trouble him not, his wits
　　are gone.
　　Glo. Good friend, I pr'y thee take him in thy
　　arms :
I have o'erheard a plot of death upon him.
There is a litter ready : lay him in 't,
And drive toward Dover, friend, where thou
　　shalt meet
Both welcome and protection. Take up thy master :
If thou shouldst dally half an hour, his life,
With thine, and all that offer to defend him,
Stand in assuréd loss. Take up, take up ;
And follow me, that will to some provision
Give thee quick conduct.
　　Kent.　　　　　　Oppresséd nature sleeps :—
This rest might'yet have balmed thy broken senses,
Which, if convenience will not allow,
Stand in hard cure.—Come, help to bear thy
　　master :
Thou must not stay behind.　　　[*To the* Fool.
　　Glo.　　　Come, come, away.
　　　　[*Exeunt* KENT, GLOSTER, *and the* Fool,
　　　　　　bearing off the KING.
　　Edg. When we our betters see bearing our woes,
We scarcely think our miseries our foes.
Who alone suffers, suffers most i' the mind ;
Leaving free things and happy shows behind :
But then the mind much sufferance doth o'erskip,
When grief hath mates, and bearing fellowship.

How light and portable my pain seems now,
When that which makes me bend makes the
     King bow:
He childed as I fathered!—Tom, away:
Mark the high noises; and thyself bewray,
When false opinion, whose wrong thought defiles
     thee,
In thy just proof repeals and reconciles thee,
What will hap more to-night, safe scape the King!
Lurk, lurk.   [*Exit.*

SCENE VII.—*A Room in* GLOSTER's *Castle.*

Enter CORNWALL, REGAN, GONERIL, EDMUND,
     and Servants.

Corn. Post speedily to my lord your husband;
shew him this letter: the army of France is
landed.—Seek out the villain Gloster.
            [*Exeunt some of the* Servants.
Reg. Hang him instantly.
Gon. Pluck out his eyes.
Corn. Leave him to my displeasure.—Edmund,
keep you our sister company: the revenges we
are bound to take upon your traitorous father
are not fit for your beholding. Advise the duke,
where you are going, to a most festinate preparation: we are bound to the like. Our posts
shall be swift and intelligent betwixt us. Farewell, dear sister: farewell, my lord of Gloster.

Enter Steward.

How now? Where's the King?
     Stew. My lord of Gloster hath conveyed him
         hence:
Some five or six-and-thirty of his knights,
Hot questrists after him, met him at gate;
Who, with some other of the lord's dependants,
Are gone with him towards Dover; where they
     boast
To have well-arméd friends.
     Corn.   Get horses for your mistress.
     Gon. Farewell, sweet lord, and sister.
            [*Exeunt* GONERIL *and* EDMUND.
Corn. Edmund, farewell.—Go, seek the traitor
     Gloster:
Pinion him like a thief; bring him before us.
            [*Exeunt other* Servants.
Though well we may not pass upon his life
Without the form of justice; yet our power
Shall do a courtesy to our wrath, which men
May blame, but not control. Who's there; the
     traitor?

Re-enter Servants, *with* GLOSTER.

Reg. Ingrateful fox! 'tis he.
Corn. Bind fast his corky arms.

Glo. What mean your graces?—Good my
     friends, consider
You are my guests: do me no foul play, friends.
     Corn. Bind him, I say.   [*Servants bind him.*
     Reg.   Hard, hard.—O filthy traitor!
     Glo. Unmerciful lady as you are, I am none.
     Corn. To this chair bind him.—Villain, thou
         shalt find—   [REGAN *plucks his beard.*
     Glo. By the kind gods, 'tis most ignobly done
To pluck me by the beard.
     Reg. So white, and such a traitor!
     Glo.   Naughty lady,
These hairs, which thou dost ravish from my chin,
Will quicken and accuse thee. I am your host:
With robbers' hands, my hospitable favours
You should not ruffle thus. What will you do?
     Corn. Come, sir, what letters had you late
         from France?
     Reg. Be simple-answered, for we know the truth.
     Corn. And what confederacy have you with
         the traitors
Late footed in the kingdom?
     Reg. To whose hands have you sent the lunatic
         king?
Speak.
     Glo. I have a letter guessingly set down,
Which came from one that's of a neutral heart,
And not from one opposed.
     Corn.   Cunning.
     Reg.   And false.
     Corn. Where hast thou sent the King?
     Glo.   To Dover.
     Reg. Wherefore to Dover? Wast thou not
charged at thy peril—
     Corn. Wherefore to Dover? Let him first
answer that.
     Glo. I am tied to the stake, and I must stand
the course.
     Reg. Wherefore to Dover?
     Glo. Because I would not see thy cruel nails
Pluck out his poor old eyes; nor thy fierce sister
In his anointed flesh stick boarish fangs.
The sea, with such a storm as his bare head
In hell-black night endured, would have buoyed
     up,
And quenched the stelléd fires: yet, poor old heart,
He holp the heavens to rain.
If wolves had at thy gate howled that stern time,
Thou shouldst have said "Good porter, turn the
     key:"
All cruels else subscribed.—But I shall see
The wingéd vengeance overtake such children.
     Corn. See it shalt thou never.—Fellows, hold
         the chair.—
Upon these eyes of thine I'll set my foot.
     Glo. He that will think to live till he be old,
Give me some help.—O cruel! O ye gods!

Reg. One side will mock another: the other too.

Corn. If you see vengeance,—

Serv.   Hold your hand, my lord:
I have served you ever since I was a child;
But better service have I never done you
Than now to bid you hold.

Reg.   How now, you dog?

Serv. If you did wear a bear upon your chin,
I 'd shake it on this quarrel.—What do you mean?

Corn. My villain! [*Draws, and runs at him.*

Serv. Nay, then, come on, and take the chance
     of anger.
          [*Draws.* They fight. CORNWALL *is wounded.*

Reg. Give me thy sword.—[*To another* Servant.]
          A peasant stand up thus!
          [*Snatches a sword, comes behind, and stabs
          him.*

Serv. O, I am slain!—My lord, you have one
     eye left
To see some mischief on him.—O!   [*Dies.*

Corn. Lest it see more, prevent it.—Out, vile
     jelly!
Where is thy lustre now?

Glo. All dark and comfortless.—Where 's my
     son Edmund?
Edmund, enkindle all the sparks of nature,
To quit this horrid act.

Reg.   Out, treacherous villain!
Thou call'st on him that hates thee: it was he

That made the overtures of thy treasons to us;
Who is too good to pity thee.

Glo.   O my follies!
Then Edgar was abused.
Kind gods, forgive me that, and prosper him!

Reg. Go, thrust him out at gates, and let him
     smell
His way to Dover.—How is 't, my lord? how
     look you?

Corn. I have received a hurt.—Follow me,
     lady.—
Turn out that eyeless villain;—throw this slave
Upon the dunghill.—Regan, I bleed apace:
Untimely comes this hurt.   Give me your arm.
          [*Exit* CORNWALL, *led by* REGAN. Servants
               unbind GLOSTER, *and lead him out.*

1st Serv. I 'll never care what wickedness I do,
If this man come to good.

2nd Serv.   If she live long,
And in the end meet the old course of death,
Women will all turn monsters.

1st Serv. Let 's follow the old earl, and get the
     Bedlam
To lead him where he would: his roguish madness
Allows itself to anything.

2nd Serv. Go thou: I 'll fetch some flax and
     whites of eggs,
To apply to his bleeding face.   Now, heaven
     help him!   [*Exeunt severally.*

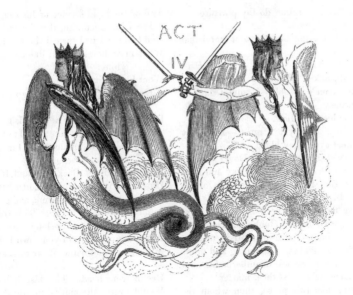

SCENE I.—*The Heath.*

Enter EDGAR.

Edg. Yet better thus, and known to be con-
　　temned,
Than still contemned and flattered. To be worst,
The lowest and most dejected thing of fortune,
Stands still in esperance, lives not in fear:
The lamentable change is from the best;
The worst returns to laughter. Welcome, then,
Thou unsubstantial air that I embrace!
The wretch thou hast blown unto the worst,
Owes nothing to thy blasts.—But who comes
　　here?

Enter GLOSTER, *led by an* Old Man.

My father, poorly led?—World, world, O world!
But that thy strange mutations make us hate thee,
Life would not yield to age.

Old Man. O my good lord, I have been your
tenant, and your father's tenant, these fourscore
years.

Glo. Away, get thee away; good friend, be
　　gone:
Thy comforts can do me no good at all;
Thee they may hurt.

Old Man. Alack, sir, you cannot see your way.

Glo. I have no way, and therefore want no eyes:
I stumbled when I saw. Full oft 't is seen,
Our mean secures us; and our mere defects
Prove our commodities. Ah, dear son Edgar,
The food of thy abused father's wrath!
Might I but live to see thee in my touch,
I 'd say I had eyes again!

Old Man. 　　　How now? Who 's there?

Edg. [*aside*]. O gods! Who is 't can say, "I
　　am at the worst?"
I am worse than e'er I was.

Old Man. 'T is poor mad Tom.

Edg. [*aside*]. And worse I may be yet. The
　　worst is not,
So long as we can say, "This is the worst."

Old Man. Fellow, where goest?

Glo. 　　　Is it a beggar-man?

Old Man. Madman and beggar too.

Glo. He has some reason, else he could not beg.
I' the last night's storm I such a fellow saw;
Which made me think a man a worm. My son
Came then into my mind; and yet my mind
Was then scarce friends with him: I have heard
　　more since.—
As flies to wanton boys, are we to the gods:
They kill us for their sport.

Edg. 　　　How should this be?
Bad is the trade must play the fool to sorrow,
Angering itself and others. [*Aside.*]—Bless thee,
　　master!

Glo. Is that the naked fellow?

Old Man. 　　Ay, my lord.

Glo. Then, pr'y thee, get thee gone. If, for
　　my sake,
Thou wilt o'ertake us, hence a mile or twain,
I' the way to Dover, do it for ancient love;
And bring some covering for this naked soul,
Whom I 'll entreat to lead me.

Old Man. 　　　Alack, sir, he 's mad.

Glo. 'T is the times' plague, when madmen
　　lead the blind.

Do as I bid thee; or rather do thy pleasure:
Above the rest, be gone.

Old Man. I 'll bring him the best 'parel that
    I have,
Come on 't what will.   [*Exit.*

Glo. Sirrah, naked fellow.

Edg. Poor Tom 's a-cold.—I cannot daub it
    further.   [*Aside.*

Glo. Come hither, fellow.

Edg. [*aside*]. And yet I must.—Bless thy
    sweet eyes, they bleed.

Glo. Know'st thou the way to Dover?

Edg. Both stile and gate, horseway and foot-
path. Poor Tom hath been scared out of his
good wits. Bless the good man from the foul
fiend! Five fiends have been in poor Tom at
once: of lust, as Obidicut; Hobbididance, prince
of dumbness; Mahu, of stealing; Modo, of murder; and Flibbertigibbet, of mopping and mowing; who since possesses chambermaids and
waiting women. So, bless thee, master!

Glo. Here, take this purse, thou whom the
        heavens plagues
Have humbled to all strokes: that I am wretched,
Makes thee the happier.—Heavens, deal so still!
Let the superfluous and lust-dieted man,
That slaves your ordinance, that will not see
Because he doth not feel, feel your power quickly:
So distribution should undo excess,
And each man have enough.—Dost thou know
        Dover?

Edg. Ay, master.

Glo. There is a cliff, whose high and bending head
Looks fearfully in the confined deep:
Bring me but to the very brim of it,
And I 'll repair the misery thou dost bear,
With something rich about me. From that place
I shall no leading need.

Edg.   Give me thy arm:
Poor Tom shall lead thee.   [*Exeunt.*

SCENE II.—*Before the* DUKE OF ALBANY's *Palace.*

Enter GONERIL *and* EDMUND; Steward *meeting
        them.*

Gon. Welcome, my lord: I marvel our mild
        husband
Not met us on the way.—Now, where 's your
        master?

Stew. Madam, within; but never man so
        changed.
I told him of the army that was landed:
He smiled at it. I told him you were coming:
His answer was, "The worse." Of Gloster's
        treachery,

And of the loyal service of his son,
When I informed him, then he called me sot,
And told me I had turned the wrong side out.—
What most he should dislike seems pleasant to
        him:
What like, offensive.

Gon.   Then shall you go no further.
                                [*To* EDMUND.
It is the cowish terror of his spirit,
That dares not undertake: he 'll not feel wrongs,
Which tie him to an answer. Our wishes on the
        way
May prove effects. Back, Edmund, to my brother;
Hasten his musters, and conduct his powers:
I must change arms at home, and give the distaff
Into my husband's hands. This trusty servant
Shall pass between us: ere long you are like to hear,
If you dare venture in your own behalf,
A mistress's command. Wear this: spare speech:
                                [*Giving a favour.*
Decline your head. This kiss, if it durst speak,
Would stretch thy spirits up into the air:
Conceive, and fare thee well.

Edm. Yours in the ranks of death.

Gon.   My most dear Gloster!
                                [*Exit* EDMUND.
O, the difference of man and man!
To thee a woman's services are due:
My fool usurps my bed.

Stew.   Madam, here comes my lord. [*Exit.*

Enter ALBANY.

Gon. I have been worth the whistle.

Alb.   O Goneril!
You are not worth the dust which the rude wind
Blows in your face.—I fear your disposition:
That nature which contemns its origin
Cannot be bordered certain in itself:
She that herself will sliver and disbranch
From her material sap, perforce must wither,
And come to deadly use.

Gon. No more: the text is foolish.

Alb. Wisdom and goodness to the vile seem vile:
Filths savour but themselves. What have you
        done?
Tigers, not daughters, what have you performed?
A father, and a gracious agéd man,
Whose reverence the head-lugged bear would lick,
Most barbarous, most degenerate! have you
        madded.
Could my good brother suffer you to do it?
A man, a prince, by him so benefited?
If that the heavens do not their visible spirits
Send quickly down to tame these vile offences,
It will come,
Humanity must perforce prey on itself,
Like monsters of the deep.

Gon.   Milk-livered man!
That bear'st a cheek for blows, a head for wrongs;
Who hast not in thy brows an eye discerning
Thine honour from thy suffering; that not know'st,
Fools do those villains pity who are punished
Ere they have done their mischief! Where's
     thy drum?
France spreads his banners in our noiseless land;
With pluméd helm thy slayer begins threats;
Whilst thou, a moral fool, sitt'st still, and criest,
" Alack! why does he so?"
     Alb.   See thyself, devil!
Proper deformity seems not in the fiend
So horrid as in woman.
     Gon.   O vain fool!
     Alb.   Thou changéd and self-covered thing,
     for shame,
Be-monster not thy feature. Were it my fitness
To let these hands obey my blood,
They are apt enough to dislocate and tear
Thy flesh and bones!—Howe'er thou art a fiend,
A woman's shape doth shield thee.
     Gon. Marry, your manhood now!

     Enter a Messenger.

     Alb. What news?
     Mess. O, my good lord, the Duke of Cornwall's
     dead:
Slain by his servant, going to put out
The other eye of Gloster.
     Alb.   Gloster's eyes!
     Mess. A servant that he bred, thrilled with
     remorse,
Opposed against the act, bending his sword
To his great master; who, thereat enraged,
Flew on him, and amongst them felled him dead:
But not without that harmful stroke, which since
Hath plucked him after.
     Alb.   This shews you are above,
You justicers, that these our nether crimes
So speedily can venge!—But, O poor Gloster!
Lost he his other eye?
     Mess.   Both, both, my lord.—
This letter, madam, craves a speedy answer:
'T is from your sister.
     Gon. [*aside*]. One way I like this well:
But being widow, and my Gloster with her,
May all the building in my fancy pluck
Upon my hateful life. Another way,
The news is not so tart.—I'll read and answer.
         [*Exit.*
     Alb. Where was his son when they did take
     his eyes?
     Mess. Come with my lady hither.
     Alb.   He is not here.
     Mess. No, my good lord: I met him back again.
     Alb. Knows he the wickedness?

     Mess. Ay, my good lord: 't was he informed
     against him;
And quit the house on purpose, that their
     punishment
Might have the freer course.
     Alb.   Gloster, I live
To thank thee for the love thou shew'dst the King,
And to revenge thine eyes.—Come hither, friend:
Tell me what more thou know'st.   [*Exeunt.*

     SCENE III.—*The French Camp, near* Dover.

     Enter KENT *and a* Gentleman.

     Kent. Why the King of France is so suddenly
gone back, know you the reason?
     Gent. Something he left imperfect in the state,
Which since his coming forth is thought of; which
Imports to the kingdom so much fear and danger,
That his personal return was most required
And necessary.
     Kent. Who hath he left behind him general?
     Gent. The Mareschal of France, Monsieur le
     Fer.
     Kent. Did your letters pierce the queen to
any demonstration of grief?
     Gent. Ay, sir: she took them, read them in
     my presence;
And now and then an ample tear trilled down
Her delicate cheek. It seemed she was a queen
Over her passion; who, most rebel-like,
Sought to be king o'er her.
     Kent.   O, then it moved her?
     Gent. Not to a rage: patience and sorrow strove
Who should express her goodliest. You have seen
Sunshine and rain at once: her smiles and tears
Were like a better day. Those happy smilets
That played on her ripe lip, seemed not to know
What guests were in her eyes; which parted
     thence
As pearls from diamonds dropped.—In brief,
     sorrow
Would be a rarity most beloved, if all
Could so become it.
     Kent.   Made she no verbal question?
     Gent. 'Faith, once or twice she heaved the
     name of " father"
Pantingly forth, as if it pressed her heart:
Cried, " Sisters! sisters!—Shame of ladies! sisters!
Kent! father, sisters! What? i' the storm?
     i' the night?
Let pity not be believed!"—There she shook
The holy water from her heavenly eyes,
And clamour moistened: then away she started
To deal with grief alone.
     Kent.   It is the stars,

The stars above us, govern our conditions;
Else one self mate and mate could not beget
Such different issues. You spoke not with her since?
 Gent. No.
 Kent. Was this before the King returned?
 Gent.   No; since.
 Kent. Well, sir; the poor distresséd Lear is
   i' the town:
Who sometime, in his better tune, remembers
What we are come about, and by no means
Will yield to see his daughter.
 Gent.   Why, good sir?
 Kent. A sovereign shame so elbows him. His
   own unkindness,
That stripped her from his benediction, turned her
To foreign casualties, gave her dear rights
To his dog-hearted daughters,—these things sting
His mind so venomously, that burning shame
Detains him from Cordelia.
 Gent.   Alack, poor gentleman!
 Kent. Of Albany's and Cornwall's powers you
   heard not?
 Gent. 'T is so; they are afoot.
 Kent. Well, sir, I 'll bring you to our master
   Lear,
And leave you to attend him. Some dear cause
Will in concealment wrap me up awhile:
When I am known aright, you shall not grieve
Lending me this acquaintance. I pray you, go
Along with me.   *[Exeunt.*

Scene IV.—*The same.* *A Tent.*

Enter Cordelia, Physician, *and* Soldiers.

 Cor. Alack, 'tis he! Why, he was met even now
As mad as the vexéd sea: singing aloud;
Crowned with rank fumiter and furrow weeds,
With harlocks, hemlock, nettles, cuckoo-flowers,
Darnel, and all the idle weeds that grow
In our sustaining corn.—A century send forth:
Search every acre in the high-grown field,
And bring him to our eye. *[Exit an* Officer.
   —What can man's wisdom do,
In the restoring his bereavéd sense?
He that helps him, take all my outward worth.
 Phy. There is means, madam.
Our foster-nurse of nature is repose,
The which he lacks: that to provoke in him,
Are many simples operative, whose power
Will close the eye of anguish.
 Cor.   All blesséd secrets,
All you unpublished virtues of the earth,
Spring with my tears! be aidant and remediate
In the good man's distress!—Seek, seek for him;
Lest his ungoverned rage dissolve the life
That wants the means to lead it.

Enter a Messenger.

 Mess.   News, madam;
The British powers are marching hitherward.
 Cor. 'T is known before: our preparation stands
In expectation of them.—O dear father,
It is thy business that I go about:
Therefore great France
My mourning and important tears hath pitied.
No blown ambition doth our arms incite,
But love, dear love, and our aged father's right:
Soon may I hear and see him! *[Exeunt.*

Scene V.—*A Room in* Gloster's *Castle.*

Enter Regan *and* Steward.

 Reg. But are my brother's powers set forth?
 Stew.   Ay, madam.
 Reg. Himself in person there?
 Stew.   Madam, with much ado:
Your sister is the better soldier.
 Reg. Lord Edmund spake not with your lord
   at home?
 Stew. No, madam.
 Reg. What might import my sister's letter to
   him?
 Stew. I know not, lady.
 Reg. 'Faith, he is posted hence on serious matter.
It was great ignorance, Gloster's eyes being out,
To let him live: where he arrives, he moves
All hearts against us. Edmund I think is gone,
In pity of his misery, to despatch
His nighted life: moreover, to descry
The strength o' the enemy.
 Stew. I must needs after him, madam, with my
   letter.
 Reg. Our troops set forth to-morrow: stay with
   us:
The ways are dangerous.
 Stew.   I may not, madam:
My lady charged my duty in this business.
 Reg. Why should she write to Edmund?—
   Might not you
Transport her purposes by word? Belike,
Something—I know not what:—I 'll love thee
   much,
Let me unseal the letter.
 Stew.   Madam, I had rather—
 Reg. I know your lady does not love her husband;
I am sure of that: and, at her late being here,
She gave strange œiliads and most speaking looks
To noble Edmund. I know you are of her bosom.
 Stew. I, madam!
 Reg. I speak in understanding: you are, I
   know it:
Therefore, I do advise you, take this note:

My lord is dead; Edmund and I have talked;
And more convenient is he for my hand
Than for your lady's:—you may gather more.
If you do find him, pray you, give him this:
And when your mistress hears thus much from
  you,
I pray, desire her call her wisdom to her.
So fare you well.
If you do chance to hear of that blind traitor,
Preferment falls on him that cuts him off.
  Stew. 'Would I could meet him, madam! I
  would shew
What party I do follow.
  Reg.   Fare thee well.   [*Exeunt.*

SCENE VI.—*The Country near* Dover.

Enter GLOSTER, *and* EDGAR *dressed like a peasant.*

  Glo. When shall we come to the top of that same
  hill?
  Edg. You do climb up it now: look how we
  labour.
  Glo. Methinks the ground is even.
  Edg.   Horrible steep:
Hark, do you hear the sea?
  Glo.   No, truly.
  Edg. Why, then your other senses grow im-
  perfect
By your eyes' anguish.
  Glo.   So may it be, indeed:
Methinks thy voice is altered; and thou speak'st
In better phrase and matter than thou didst.
  Edg. You are much deceived: in nothing am
  I changed
But in my garments.
  Glo.   Methinks you are better spoken.
  Edg. Come on, sir; here's the place:—stand
  still.—How fearful
And dizzy 't is to cast one's eyes so low!
The crows and choughs that wing the midway air,
Shew scarce so gross as beetles. Half way down
Hangs one that gathers samphire; dreadful trade!
Methinks he seems no bigger than his head.
The fishermen, that walk upon the beach,
Appear like mice: and yon' tall anchoring bark
Diminished to her cock: her cock, a buoy
Almost too small for sight. The murmuring surge,
That on the unnumbered idle pebbles chafes,
Cannot be heard so high.—I 'll look no more!
Lest my brain turn, and the deficient sight
Topple down headlong.
  Glo.   Set me where you stand.
  Edg. Give me your hand:—You are now
  within a foot
Of the extreme verge: for all beneath the moon
Would I not leap upright.

  Glo.   Let go my hand.
Here, friend, is another purse; in it, a jewel
Well worth a poor man's taking: fairies and gods
Prosper it with thee!—Go thou further off;
Bid me farewell, and let me hear thee going.
  Edg. Now fare you well, good sir. [*Seems to go.*
  Glo.   With all my heart.
  Edg. Why I do trifle thus with his despair,
Is done to cure it.
  Glo.   O you mighty gods!
This world I do renounce; and in your sights
Shake patiently my great affliction off:
If I could bear it longer, and not fall
To quarrel with your great opposeless wills,
My snuff and loathéd part of nature should
Burn itself out. If Edgar live, O bless him!—
Now, fellow, fare thee well.
        [*He leaps and falls along.*
  Edg.   Gone, sir: farewell.—
And yet I know not how conceit may rob
The treasury of life, when life itself
Yields to the theft. Had he been where he thought,
By this had thought been past.—Alive or dead?
Ho, you sir! friend!—Hear you, sir? speak!—
Thus might he pass indeed.—Yet he revives:
What are you, sir?
  Glo.   Away, and let me die.
  Edg. Hadst thou been aught but gossamer,
  feathers, air,
So many fathom down precipitating,
Thou hadst shivered like an egg: but thou dost
  breathe;
Hast heavy substance; bleed'st not; speak'st;
  art sound!
Ten masts at each make not the altitude
Which thou hast perpendicularly fell:
Thy life's a miracle. Speak yet again.
  Glo. But have I fallen, or no?
  Edg. From the dread summit of this chalky bourn.
Look up a-height: the shrill-gorged lark so far
Cannot be seen or heard. Do but look up.
  Glo. Alack, I have no eyes.—
Is wretchedness deprived that benefit
To end itself by death? 'T was yet some comfort
When misery could beguile the tyrant's rage,
And frustrate his proud will.
  Edg.   Give me your arm:
Up:—so.—How is 't? Feel you your legs? You
  stand.
  Glo. Too well, too well.
  Edg. This is above all strangeness!
Upon the crown o' the cliff, what thing was that
Which parted from you?
  Glo.   A poor unfortunate beggar.
  Edg. As I stood here below, methought his eyes
Were two full moons: he had a thousand noses,
Horns whelked, and waved like the enridgéd sea:

It was some fiend. Therefore, thou happy father,
Think that the clearest gods, who make them
    honours
Of men's impossibilities, have preserved thee.

    Glo. I do remember now: henceforth I 'll bear
Affliction, till it do cry out itself,
"Enough, enough," and die. That thing you
    speak of,

I took it for a man: often 't would say,
"The fiend, the fiend!" He led me to that place.
    Edg. Bear free and patient thoughts.—But
    who comes here?

Enter LEAR, *fantastically dressed up with flowers.*

The safer sense will ne'er accommodate
His master thus.
    Lear. No, they cannot touch me for coining:
I am the King himself.

    Edg. O thou side-piercing sight!
    Lear. Nature's above art in that respect.—
There's your press-money.—That fellow handles
his bow like a crowkeeper: draw me a clothier's
yard.—Look, look, a mouse! Peace, peace: this
piece of toasted cheese will do 't.—There's my
gauntlet: I 'll prove it on a giant.—Bring up the
brown bills.—O, well flown, bird! i' the clout,
i' the clout: hewgh!—Give the word.
    Edg. Sweet marjoram.

Lear. Pass.

Glo. I know that voice.

Lear. Ha! Goneril!—with a white beard!—
They flattered me like a dog; and told me I had
white hairs in my beard, ere the black ones were
there. To say, " Ay" and "No" to everything
I said!—"Ay" and "No," too, was no good
divinity. When the rain came to wet me once,
and the wind to make me chatter; when the
thunder would not peace at my bidding; there
I found them, there I smelt them out. Go to,
they are not men o' their words: they told me I
was everything: 't is a lie; I am not ague-proof.

Glo. The trick of that voice I do well remember:
Is 't not the King?

Lear.   Ay, every inch a king:
When I do stare, see how the subject quakes!—
I pardon the man's life.—What was thy cause?—
" Adultery?"—
Thou shalt not die. Die for adultery! No:
The wren goes to 't, and the small gilded fly
Does lecher in my sight.
Let copulation thrive, for Gloster's bastard son
Was kinder to his father than my daughters
Got 'tween the lawful sheets.
To 't, luxury, pell-mell, for I lack soldiers.—
Behold yon' simpering dame,
Whose face between her forks presageth snow;
That minces virtue, and does shake the head
To hear of pleasure's name:
The fitchew, nor the soiléd horse goes to 't
With a more riotous appetite.
Down from the waist they are centaurs,
Though women all above:
But to the girdle do the gods inherit;
Beneath is all the fiends': there 's hell, there 's
darkness, there is the sulphurous pit, burning,
scalding, stench, consumption!—Fie, fie, fie!
pah; pah! Give me an ounce of civet, good
apothecary, to sweeten my imagination: there 's
money for thee.

Glo. O let me kiss that hand!

Lear. Let me wipe it first; it smells of mortality.

Glo. O ruined piece of nature! This great world
Shall so wear out to nought.—Dost thou know me?

Lear. I remember thine eyes well enough.
Dost thou squiny at me? No, do thy worst,
blind Cupid; I 'll not love.—Read thou this
challenge: mark but the penning of it.

Glo. Were all the letters suns, I could not
see one.

Edg. I would not take this from report:—it is,
And my heart breaks at it.

Lear. Read.

Glo. What, with the case of eyes?

Lear. O, ho, are you there with me? No
eyes in your head, nor no money in your purse?
Your eyes are in a heavy case; your purse in a
light: yet you see how this world goes.

Glo. I see it feelingly.

Lear. What, art mad? A man may see how
this world goes, with no eyes. Look with thine
ears: see how yon' justice rails upon yon' simple
thief. Hark, in thine ear:—change places; and,
handy-dandy, which is the justice, which is the
thief?—Thou hast seen a farmer's dog bark at a
beggar?

Glo. Ay, sir.

Lear. And the creature run from the cur?
There thou mightst behold the great image of
authority: a dog 's obeyed in office.—
Thou rascal beadle, hold thy bloody hand:
Why dost thou lash that whore? Strip thine own
          back:
Thou hotly lust'st to use her in that kind
For which thou whipp'st her. The usurer hangs
          the cozener.
Through tattered clothes small vices do appear;
Robes and furred gowns hide all. Plate sin with
          gold,
And the strong lance of justice hurtless breaks:
Arm it in rags, a pigmy's straw doth pierce it.
None does offend; none, I say, none: I 'll able 'em:
Take that of me, my friend, who have the power
To seal the accuser's lips. Get thee glass eyes;
And, like a scurvy politician, seem
To see the things thou dost not.—Now, now,
          now, now:
Pull off my boots:—harder, harder: so.

Edg. O, matter and impertinency mixed!
Reason in madness!

Lear. If thou wilt weep my fortunes, take my
          eyes.
I know thee well enough: thy name is Gloster.
Thou must be patient: we came crying hither.
Thou know'st, the first time that we smell the air,
We wawl and cry.—I will preach to thee: mark
          me.

Glo. Alack, alack the day!

Lear. When we are born, we cry that we are
          come
To this great stage of fools.—This a good block?—
It were a delicate stratagem to shoe
A troop of horse with felt! I 'll put it in proof;
And when I have stolen upon these sons-in-law,
Then kill, kill, kill, kill, kill, kill.

Enter a Gentleman, *with* Attendants.

Gent. O, here he is: lay hand upon him.—Sir,
Your most dear daughter—

Lear. No rescue? What, a prisoner? I am even
The natural fool of fortune.—Use me well:
You shall have ransom. Let me have a surgeon:
I am cut to the brains.

Gent. You shall have anything.

Lear. No seconds? all myself?
Why, this would make a man, a man of salt,
To use his eyes for garden waterpots;
Ay, and for laying autumn's dust.

Gent. Good sir,—

Lear. I will die bravely, like a bridegroom.
What?
I will be jovial.—Come, come: I am a king,
My masters: know you that?

Gent. You are a royal one, and we obey you.

Lear. Then there 's life in it.—Nay, an you get
it, you shall get it by running. Sa, sa, sa, sa!

[*Exit, running; Attendants follow.*

Gent. A sight most pitiful in the meanest wretch;
Past speaking of in a king!—Thou hast one
        daughter,
Who redeems nature from the general curse
Which twain have brought her to.

Edg. Hail, gentle sir.

Gent. Sir, speed you: what 's your will?

Edg. Do you hear aught, sir, of a battle
        toward?

Gent. Most sure and vulgar: every one hears
        that,
Which can distinguish sound.

Edg. But, by your favour,
How near 's the other army?

Gent. Near, and on speedy foot: the main
        descry
Stands on the hourly thought.

Edg. I thank you, sir: that 's all.

Gent. Though that the queen on special cause
        is here,
Her army is moved on.

Edg. I thank you, sir. [*Exit Gentleman.*

Glo. You ever-gentle gods, take my breath
        from me:
Let not my worser spirit tempt me again
To die before you please!

Edg. Well pray you, father.

Glo. Now, good sir, what are you?

Edg. A most poor man, made tame by for-
        tune's blows:
Who, by the art of known and feeling sorrows,
Am pregnant to good pity. Give me your hand,
I 'll lead you to some biding.

Glo. Hearty thanks:
The bounty and the benizon of heaven
To boot, and boot!

Enter Steward.

Stew. A proclaimed prize! Most happy!
That eyeless head of thine was first framed flesh
To raise my fortunes. Thou old unhappy traitor,
Briefly thyself remember. The sword is out
That must destroy thee.

Glo. Now let thy friendly hand
Put strength enough to it. [*Edgar opposes.*

Stew. Wherefore, bold peasant,
Dar'st thou support a published traitor? Hence;
Lest that the infection of his fortune take
Like hold on thee. Let go his arm.

Edg. Ch 'ill not let go, zir, without vurther
        'casion.

Stew. Let go, slave, or thou diest.

Edg. Good gentleman, go your gait, and let
poor volk pass. An ch 'ud ha' been zwaggered
out of my life, 't would not ha' been zo long as
't is by a vortnight. Nay, come not near th' old
man: keep out, che vor' ye, or ise try whether
your costard or my bat be the harder. Ch 'ill
be plain with you.

Stew. Out, dunghill!

Edg. Ch 'ill pick your teeth, zir. Come: no
matter for your foins.

[*They fight; and Edgar knocks him down.*

Stew. Slave, thou hast slain me!—Villain,
        take my purse:
If ever thou wilt thrive, bury my body;
And give the letters which thou find'st about me
To Edmund earl of Gloster: seek him out
Upon the British party.—O untimely death!
[*Dies.*

Edg. I know thee well: a serviceable villain;
As duteous to the vices of thy mistress
As badness would desire.

Glo. What, is he dead?

Edg. Sit you down, father; rest you.—
Let 's see his pockets; these letters that he
        speaks of
May be my friends.—He 's dead: I am only
        sorry
He had no other death's-man.—Let us see:
Leave, gentle wax; and, manners, blame us not:
To know our enemies' minds, we 'd rip their
        hearts;
Their papers, is more lawful.

Reads.

" Let our reciprocal vows be remembered. You
have many opportunities to cut him off: if your
will want not, time and place will be fruitfully
offered. There is nothing done if he return the
conqueror: then am I the prisoner, and his bed my
gaol; from the loathed warmth whereof deliver me,
and supply the place for your labour.

" Your wife (so I would say) and your affectionate
        servant, " GONERIL."

O undistinguished space of woman's will!
A plot upon her virtuous husband's life;
And the exchange, my brother!—Here, in the
        sands,
Thee I 'll rake up, the post unsanctified
Of murderous lechers: and, in the mature time,

With this ungracious paper strike the sight
Of the death-practised duke.   For him 't is well,
That of thy death and business I can tell.

        [Exit EDGAR, *dragging out the body.*

  Glo. The King is mad : how stiff is my vile
      sense,
That I stand up and have ingenious feeling
Of my huge sorrows ! Better I were distract :
So should my thoughts be severed from my
      griefs ;
And woes, by wrong imaginations, lose
The knowledge of themselves.

        Re-enter EDGAR.

  Edg.   Give me your hand :
Far off, methinks, I hear the beaten drum.
Come, father ; I 'll bestow you with a friend.
                       [Exeunt.

SCENE VII.—*A Tent in the French Camp.* LEAR
on a bed, asleep ; Physician, Gentlemen, *and
others, attending.*

      Enter CORDELIA *and* KENT.

  Cor. O thou, good Kent, how shall I live and
      work
To match thy goodness? My life will be too short,
And every measure fail me.
  Kent. To be acknowledged, madam, is o'erpaid.

All my reports go with the modest truth :
Nor more, nor clipped, but so.
  Cor.   Be better suited.
These weeds are memories of those worser hours :
I pr'y thee, put them off.
  Kent.   Pardon me, dear madam :
Yet to be known shortens my made intent.
My boon I make it that you know me not
Till time and I think meet.
  Cor. Then be it so, my good lord.—How does
      the King ?   *[To the* Physician.
  Phys. Madam, sleeps still.
  Cor. O you kind gods,
Cure this great breach in his abusèd nature !
The untuned and jarring senses O wind up
Of this child-changèd father !
  Phys.   So please your majesty
That we may wake the King ? he hath slept long.
  Cor. Be governed by your knowledge, and proceed
I' the sway of your own will.   Is he arrayed ?
  Gent. Ay, madam ; in the heaviness of his sleep
We put fresh garments on him.
  Phys. Be by, good madam, when we do awake
      him :
I doubt not of his temperance.
  Cor.   Very well.
  Phys. Please you, draw near.—Louder the
      music there.
  Cor. O my dear father ! Restoration, hang
Thy medicine on my lips ; and let this kiss

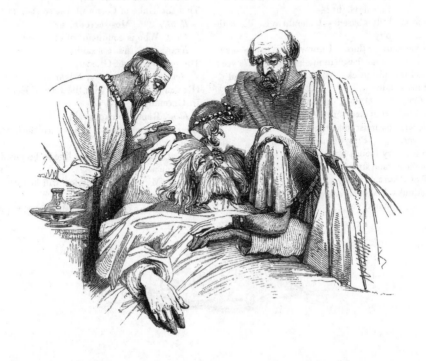

Repair those violent harms that my two sisters
Have in thy reverence made!

Kent. Kind and dear princess!

Cor. Had you not been their father, these
white flakes
Had challenged pity of them. Was this a face
To be exposed against the warring winds?
To stand against the deep dread-bolted thunder?
In the most terrible and nimble stroke
Of quick cross-lightning? to watch (poor perdu!)
With this thin helm?—Mine enemy's dog,
Though he had bit me, should have stood that night
Against my fire: and wast thou fain, poor father,
To hovel thee with swine and rogues forlorn,
In short and musty straw? Alack, alack!
'Tis wonder that thy life and wits at once
Had not concluded all.—He wakes: speak to him.

Phys. Madam, do you; 'tis fittest.

Cor. How does my royal lord? How fares
your majesty?

Lear. You do me wrong to take me out o' the
grave.—
Thou art a soul in bliss; but I am bound
Upon a wheel of fire, that mine own tears
Do scald like molten lead.

Cor. Sir, do you know me?

Lear. You are a spirit, I know. When did
you die?

Cor. Still, still, far wide!

Phys. He's scarce awake: let him alone awhile.

Lear. Where have I been? Where am I?—
Fair daylight?—
I am mightily abused.—I should e'en die with
pity
To see another thus.—I know not what to say:
I will not swear these are my hands. Let's see:
I feel this pin prick. 'Would I were assured
Of my condition.

Cor. O, look upon me, sir,
And hold your hands in benediction o'er me:—
No, sir, you must not kneel.

Lear. Pray do not mock me:
I am a very foolish fond old man,
Fourscore and upward; and, to deal plainly,
I fear I am not in my perfect mind.
Methinks I should know you, and know this
man:

Yet I am doubtful: for I am mainly ignorant
What place this is; and all the skill I have
Remembers not these garments; nor I know not
Where I did lodge last night.—Do not laugh at
me;
For, as I am a man, I think this lady
To be my child Cordelia!

Cor. And so I am; I am.

Lear. Be your tears wet? Yes, 'faith. I pray,
weep not:
If you have poison for me, I will drink it.
I know you do not love me; for your sisters
Have, as I do remember, done me wrong.
You have some cause; they have not.

Cor. No cause, no cause.

Lear. Am I in France?

Kent. In your own kingdom, sir.

Lear. Do not abuse me.

Phys. Be comforted, good madam: the great
rage,
You see, is cured in him; and yet it is danger
To make him even o'er the time he has lost.
Desire him to go in: trouble him no more
Till further settling.

Cor. Will 't please your highness walk?

Lear. You must bear with me:
Pray you now, forget and forgive: I am old and
foolish.

[*Exeunt* LEAR, CORDELIA, Physician, *and*
Attendants.

Gent. Holds it true, sir,
That the Duke of Cornwall was so slain?

Kent. Most certain, sir.

Gent. Who is conductor of his people?

Kent. As 't is said,
The bastard son of Gloster.

Gent. They say, Edgar,
His banished son, is with the Earl of Kent
In Germany.

Kent. Report is changeable.
'Tis time to look about: the powers o' the kingdom
Approach apace.

Gent. The arbitrement is like to be bloody.
Fare you well, sir. [*Exit.*

Kent. My point and period will be throughly
wrought,
Or well, or ill, as this day's battle 's fought? [*Exit.*

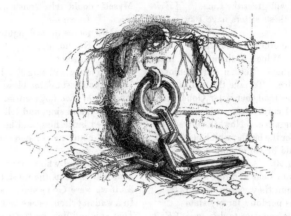

SCENE I.—*The Camp of the British Forces, near Dover.*

Enter, with drum and colours, EDMUND, REGAN, Officers, Soldiers, *and others.*

Edm. Know of the duke if his last purpose hold;
Or whether, since, he is advised by aught
To change the course. He 's full of alteration
And self-reproving : bring his constant pleasure.
                    [*To an* Officer, *who goes out.*
Reg. Our sister's man is certainly miscarried.
Edm. 'T is to be doubted, madam.
Reg.   Now, sweet lord,
You know the goodness I intend upon you :
Tell me,—but truly,—but then speak the truth,
Do you not love my sister?
Edm.   In honoured love.
Reg. But have you never found my brother's
    way
To the forfended place?
Edm.   That thought abuses you.
Reg. I am doubtful that you have been conjunct
And bosomed with her, as far as we call hers.
Edm. No, by mine honour, madam.
Reg. I never shall endure her : dear my lord,
Be not familiar with her.
Edm.   Fear me not :
She and the duke her husband,—

     Enter ALBANY, GONERIL, *and* Soldiers.

Gon. I had rather lose the battle than that sister
Should loosen him and me.   [*Aside.*
Alb. Our very loving sister, well be met.—
Sir, this I hear : the King is come to his daughter,
With others whom the rigour of our state
Forced to cry out. Where I could not be honest,
I never yet was valiant : for this business,
It touches us as France invades our land,
Not bolds the King ; with others, whom, I fear,
Most just and heavy causes make oppose.

Edm. Sir, you speak nobly.
Reg.   Why is this reasoned?
Gon. Combine together 'gainst the enemy :
For these domestic and particular broils
Are not to question here.
Alb.   Let us then determine
With the ancient of war on our proceedings.
Edm. I shall attend you presently at your tent.
Reg. Sister, you 'll go with us?
Gon. No.
Reg. 'T is most convenient : pray you, go with us.
Gon. O, ho, I know the riddle. [*Aside.*]—I
    will go.

 As they are going out, enter EDGAR, *disguised.*

Edg. If e'er your grace had speech with man
      so poor,
Hear me one word.
Alb.   I 'll overtake you.—Speak.
  [*Exeunt* EDMUND, REGAN, GONERIL, Officers,
        Soldiers, *and* Attendants.
Edg. Before you fight the battle, ope this letter.
If you have victory, let the trumpet sound
For him that brought it : wretched though I seem,
I can produce a champion that will prove
What is avouchéd there. If you miscarry,
Your business of the world hath so an end,
And machination ceases. Fortune love you.
Alb. Stay till I have read the letter.
Edg.   I was forbid it.
When time shall serve, let but the herald cry,
And I 'll appear again.   [*Exit.*
Alb. Why, fare thee well : I will o'erlook thy
    paper.

         Re-enter EDMUND.

Edm. The enemy 's in view ; draw up your
    powers.
Here is the guess of their true strength and forces,
By diligent discovery : but your haste
Is now urged on you.

Alb.　　　We will greet the time.　[*Exit.*
Edm. To both these sisters have I sworn my
　　love;
Each jealous of the other, as the stung
Are of the adder.　Which of them shall I take?
Both; one; or neither?　Neither can be enjoyed,
If both remain alive.　To take the widow,
Exasperates, makes mad, her sister Goneril;
And hardly shall I carry out my side,
Her husband being alive.　Now, then, we'll use
His countenance for the battle: which being done,
Let her, who would be rid of him, devise
His speedy taking off.　As for the mercy
Which he intends to Lear and to Cordelia,—
The battle done, and they within our power,
Shall never see his pardon: for my state
Stands on me to defend, not to debate.　[*Exit.*

SCENE II.—*A Field between the two Camps.*

Alarum within.　Enter, with drum and colours,
LEAR, CORDELIA, *and their Forces; and exeunt.*

Enter EDGAR *and* GLOSTER.

Edg. Here, father, take the shadow of this tree
For your good host: pray that the right may thrive.
If ever I return to you again,
I'll bring you comfort.
Glo.　　　Grace go with you, sir.　[*Exit* EDGAR.

Alarums; afterwards a Retreat.　Re-enter EDGAR.

Edg. Away, old man; give me thy hand, away:
King Lear hath lost, he and his daughter ta'en.
Give me thy hand; come on.
Glo. No further, sir: a man may rot even here.
Edg. What, in ill thoughts again?　Men must
　　endure
Their going hence, even as their coming hither:
Ripeness is all.　Come on.
Glo.　　　And that's true too.　[*Exeunt.*

SCENE III.—*The British Camp near* Dover.

Enter, in conquest, with drum and colours, ED-
MUND; LEAR *and* CORDELIA, *as prisoners;*
Officers, Soldiers, &c.

Edm. Some officers take them away: good
　　guard,
Until their greater pleasures first be known
That are to censure them.
Cor.　　　We are not the first
Who, with best meaning, have incurred the worst.
For thee, oppressèd king, am I cast down:

Myself could else out-frown false fortune's
　　frown.—
Shall we not see these daughters and these sisters?
　Lear. No, no, no, no!　Come, let's away to
　　prison:
We two alone will sing like birds i' the cage:
When thou dost ask me blessing, I'll kneel down,
And ask of thee forgiveness.　So we'll live,
And pray, and sing, and tell old tales, and laugh
At gilded butterflies, and hear poor rogues
Talk of court news; and we'll talk with them
　　too,—
Who loses, and who wins; who's in, who's out;
And take upon us the mystery of things,
As if we were God's spies: and we'll wear out,
In a walled prison, packs and sects of great ones,
That ebb and flow by the moon.
　Edm.　　　Take them away.
　Lear. Upon such sacrifices, my Cordelia,
The gods themselves throw incense.　Have I
　　caught thee?
He that parts us shall bring a brand from heaven,
And fire us hence, like foxes.　Wipe thine eyes:
The gougeres shall devour them, flesh and fell,
Ere they shall make us weep: we'll see them
　　starve first.
Come.　[*Exeunt* LEAR *and* CORDELIA, *guarded.*
　Edm. Come hither, captain; hark.
Take thou this note [*giving a paper*]: go, follow
　　them to prison.
One step I have advanced thee: if thou dost
As this instructs thee, thou dost make thy way
To noble fortunes.　Know thou this, that men
Are as the time is: to be tender-minded
Does not become a sword.　Thy great employment
Will not bear question: either say thou'lt do't,
Or thrive by other means.
　Off.　　　I'll do't, my lord.
　Edm. About it; and write happy when thou
　　hast done.
Mark,—I say, instantly: and carry it so
As I have set it down.
　Off. I cannot draw a cart, nor eat dried oats:
If it be man's work, I will do it.　[*Exit* Officer.

Flourish.　Enter ALBANY, GONERIL, REGAN,
Officers, *and* Attendants.

　Alb. Sir, you have shewn to-day your valiant
　　strain,
And fortune led you well.　You have the captives
Who were the opposites of this day's strife:
We do require them of you; so to use them
As we shall find their merits and our safety
May equally determine.
　Edm.　　　Sir, I thought it fit
To send the old and miserable King
To some retention and appointed guard;

Whose age has charms in it, whose title more,
To pluck the common bosom on his side,
And turn our impressed lances in our eyes
Which do command them.   With him I sent the
    queen;
My reason all the same: and they are ready
To-morrow, or at farther space, to appear
Where you shall hold your session.   At this time
We sweat and bleed: the friend hath lost his friend;
And the best quarrels, in the heat, are cursed
By those that feel their sharpness :—
The question of Cordelia and her father
Requires a fitter place.
    Alb.   Sir, by your patience,
I hold you but a subject of this war,
Not as a brother.
    Reg.   That's as we list to grace him.
Methinks our pleasure might have been demanded,
Ere you had spoke so far.   He led our powers;
Bore the commission of my place and person:
The which immediacy may well stand up,
And call itself your brother.
    Gon.   Not so hot:
In his own grace he doth exalt himself,
More than in your advancement.
    Reg.   In my rights,
By me invested, he compeers the best.
    Gon. That were the most, if he should husband
        you.
    Reg. Jesters do oft prove prophets.
    Gon.   Holla, holla!
That eye that told you so looked but a-squint.
    Reg. Lady, I am not well; else I should answer
From a full-flowing stomach.—General,
Take thou my soldiers, prisoners, patrimony:
Dispose of them, of me; the walls are thine.
Witness the world, that I create thee here
My lord and master.
    Gon.   Mean you to enjoy him?
    Alb. The let-alone lies not in your good will.
    Edm. Nor in thine, lord.
    Alb.   Half-blooded fellow, yes.
    Reg. Let the drum strike, and prove my title
        thine.   [*To* EDMUND.
    Alb. Stay yet; hear reason :—Edmund, I ar-
        rest thee
On capital treason; and, in thy arrest,
This gilded serpent. [*Pointing to* GONERIL.—
For your claim, fair sister,
I bar it in the interest of my wife:
'T is she is sub-contracted to this lord,
And I, her husband, contradict your banns.
If you will marry, make your love to me:
My lady is bespoke.
    Gon.   An interlude!
    Alb. Thou art armed, Gloster :—let the trum-
        pet sound:

If none appear to prove upon thy person
Thy heinous, manifest, and many treasons,
There is my pledge : [*Throwing down a glove.*]
        I 'll prove it on thy heart,
Ere I taste bread, thou art in nothing less
Than I have here proclaimed thee.
    Reg.   Sick, O, sick!
    Gon. If not, I 'll ne'er trust poison. [*Aside.*
    Edm. There's my exchange. [*Throwing down
        a glove.*] What in the world he is
That names me traitor, villain-like he lies.
Call by thy trumpet: he, that dares approach,
On him, on you, (who not?) I will maintain
My truth and honour firmly.
    Alb. A herald, ho!
    Edm.   A herald, ho, a herald!
    Alb. Trust to thy single virtue : for thy soldiers,
All levied in my name, have in my name
Took their discharge.
    Reg.   This sickness grows upon me.

Enter a HERALD.

    Alb. She is not well; convey her to my tent.
            [*Exit* REGAN, *led.*
Come hither, herald :—let the trumpet sound,
And read out this.
    Offi. Sound, trumpet.   [*A trumpet sounds.*

HERALD *reads.*

    " If any man of quality, or degree, within the
lists of the army, will maintain upon Edmund, supposed Earl of Gloster, that he is a manifold traitor,
let him appear at the third sound of the trumpet :—
he is bold in his defence."

    Edm. Sound.   [1*st Trumpet.*
    Her. Again.   [2*nd Trumpet.*
    Her. Again.   [3*rd Trumpet.*
            [*Trumpet answers within.*

Enter EDGAR, *armed, preceded by a trumpet.*

    Alb. Ask him his purposes : why he appears
Upon this call o' the trumpet.
    Her.   What are you?
Your name, your quality : and why you answer
This present summons?
    Edg.   Know, my name is lost;
By treason's tooth bare-gnawn, and canker-bit :
Yet am I noble as the adversary
I come to cope withal.
    Alb.   Which is that adversary?
    Edg. What's he that speaks for Edmund
        Earl of Gloster?
    Edm. Himself :—what say'st thou to him?
    Edg.   Draw thy sword ;
That, if my speech offend a noble heart,
Thy arm may do thee justice : here is mine.
Behold, it is the privilege of mine honours,

My oath, and my profession; I protest,
Maugre thy strength, youth, place, and eminence,
Despite thy victor sword and fire-new fortune,
Thy valour, and thy heart,—thou art a traitor:
False to thy gods, thy brother, and thy father;
Conspirant 'gainst this high illustrious prince;
And, from the extremest upward of thy head,
To the descent and dust beneath thy feet.
A most toad-spotted traitor. Say thou, "No,"
This sword, this arm, and my best spirits, are bent
To prove upon thy heart, whereto I speak,
Thou liest.

    Edm.   In wisdom I should ask thy name:
But since thy outside looks so fair and warlike,
And that thy tongue some 'say of breeding
     breathes,
What safe and nicely I might well delay
By rule of knighthood, I disdain and spurn.
Back do I toss these treasons to thy head;
With the hell-hated lie o'erwhelm thy heart;
Which (for they yet glance by, and scarcely bruise)
This sword of mine shall give them instant way,
Where they shall rest for ever.—Trumpets, speak.

    [*Alarums. They fight.* EDMUND *falls.*

    Alb. O save him, save him!

    Gon.   This is mere practice, Gloster:
By the law of arms thou wast not bound to answer
An unknown opposite: thou art not vanquished,
But cozened and beguiled.

    Alb.   Shut your mouth, dame,
Or with this paper shall I stop it.—Hold, sir:—
Thou worse than any name, read thine own evil:—
No tearing, lady; I perceive, you know it.

    [*Gives the letter to* EDMUND.

    Gon. Say if I do: the laws are mine, not thine:
Who shall arraign me for 't?

    Alb.   Most monstrous!
Know'st thou this paper?

    Gon.   Ask me not what I know. [*Exit.*

    Alb. Go after her: she's desperate: govern her.

    [*To an* Officer, *who goes out.*

    Edm. What you have charged me with, that have
     I done;
And more, much more: the time will bring it out:
'T is past, and so am I. But what art thou
That hast this fortune on me? If thou art noble,
I do forgive thee.

    Edg.   Let's exchange charity.
I am no less in blood than thou art, Edmund:
If more, the more thou hast wronged me.
My name is Edgar, and thy father's son.
The gods are just, and of our pleasant vices
Make instruments to scourge us:
The dark and vicious place where thee he got,
Cost him his eyes.

    Edm.   Thou hast spoken right; 't is true:
The wheel is come full circle; I am here.

    Alb. Methought thy very gait did prophecy
A royal nobleness. I must embrace thee:
Let sorrow split my heart, if ever I
Did hate thee, or thy father!

    Edg. Worthy prince, I know it.

    Alb.   Where have you hid yourself?
How have you known the miseries of your father?

    Edg. By nursing them, my lord. List a brief
     tale:
And when 't is told, O that my heart would burst!—
The bloody proclamation t' escape
That followed me so near, (O our lives' sweet-
     ness!
That with the pain of death we 'd hourly die,
Rather than die at once!) taught me to shift
Into a madman's rags; to assume a semblance
That very dogs disdained; and in this habit
Met I my father with his bleeding rings,
Their precious stones new lost; became his guide,
Led him, begged for him, saved him from despair;
Never (O fault!) revealed myself unto him,
Until some half hour past. When I was armed,
Not sure, though hoping, of this good success,
I asked his blessing, and from first to last
Told him my pilgrimage: but his flawed heart,
(Alack, too weak the conflict to support!)
'Twixt two extremes of passion, joy and grief,
Burst smilingly.

    Edm.   This speech of yours hath moved me,
And shall, perchance, do good. But speak you on:
You look as you had something more to say.

    Alb. If there be more, more woful, hold it in;
For I am almost ready to dissolve,
Hearing of this.

    Edg.   This would have seemed a period
To such as love not sorrow: but another
To amplify too much, would make much more,
And top extremity.
Whilst I was big in clamour, came there a man
Who, having seen me in my worst estate,
Shunned my abhorred society; but then, finding
Who 't was that so endured, with his strong arms
He fastened on my neck, and bellowed out
As he 'd burst heaven; threw him on my father;
Told the most piteous tale of Lear and him
That ever ear received: which in recounting
His grief grew puissant, and the strings of life
Began to crack: twice then the trumpet sounded,
And there I left him tranced.

    Alb.   But who was this?

    Edg. Kent, sir, the banished Kent; who in
     disguise
Followed his enemy king, and did him service
Improper for a slave.

Enter a Gentleman *hastily, with a bloody knife.*

    Gent. Help, help! O help!

Edg. What kind of help?

Alb. Speak, man.

Edg. What means that bloody knife?

Gent. 'T is hot, it smokes:

It came even from the heart of—

Alb. Who, man? speak.

Gent. Your lady, sir, your lady:—and her sister
By her is poisoned; she confesses it.

Edm. I was contracted to them both: all three
Now marry in an instant.

Alb. Produce their bodies, be they alive or
dead!—

This judgment of the heavens, that makes us
tremble,

Touches us not with pity. [*Exit* Gentleman.

Enter KENT.

Edg. Here comes, Kent, sir.

Alb. O! 't is he.

The time will not allow the compliment
Which very manners urges.

Kent. I am come
To bid my king and master aye good night:
Is he not here?

Alb. Great thing of us forgot!—
Speak, Edmund, where's the King? and where's
Cordelia?
Seest thou this object, Kent?
[*The bodies of* GONERIL *and* REGAN *are brought in.*

Kent. Alack, why thus?

Edm. Yet Edmund was beloved:
The one the other poisoned for my sake,
And after slew herself.

Alb. Even so.—Cover their faces.

Edm. I pant for life:—some good I mean to do,
Despite of mine own nature. Quickly send,—
Be brief in it,—to the castle; for my writ
Is on the life of Lear and on Cordelia.—
Nay, send in time.

Alb. Run, run; O run!

Edg. To who, my lord? who has the office? send
Thy token of reprieve,

Edm. Well thought on: take my sword;
Give it the captain.

Alb. Haste thee, for thy life. [*Exit* EDGAR.

Edm. He hath commission from thy wife and me
To hang Cordelia in the prison, and
To lay the blame upon her own despair,
That she fordid herself.

Alb. The gods defend her! Bear him hence
awhile. [EDMUND *is borne off.*

Enter LEAR, *with* CORDELIA *dead in his arms:* EDGAR, Officers, *and others.*

Lear. Howl, howl, howl, howl!—O, you are
men of stone!
Had I your tongues and eyes, I'd use them so

That heaven's vault should crack.—O, she is
gone for ever!—
I know when one is dead, and when one lives:
She's dead as earth.—Lend me a looking-glass:
If that her breath will mist or stain the stone,
Why, then she lives.

Kent. Is this the promised end?

Edg. Or image of that horror?

Alb. Fall, and cease!

Lear. This feather stirs: she lives! If it be so,
It is a chance that does redeem all sorrows
That ever I have felt.

Kent. O my good master! [*Kneeling.*

Lear. Pr'y thee, away.

Edg. 'T is noble Kent, your friend.

Lear. A plague upon you, murderous traitors all!
I might have saved her: now she's gone for
ever!—
Cordelia, Cordelia, stay a little. Ha!
What is 't thou say'st?—Her voice was ever soft,
Gentle, and low: an excellent thing in woman:—
I killed the slave that was a hanging thee.

Offi. 'T is true, my lords, he did.

Lear. Did I not, fellow?
I have seen the day, with my good biting faulchion
I would have made them skip: I am old now,
And these same crosses spoil me.—Who are you?
Mine eyes are none o' the best:—I'll tell you
straight.

Kent. If fortune brag of two she loved and
hated,
One of them we behold.

Lear. This is a dull sight: are you not Kent?

Kent. The same:
Your servant Kent. Where is your servant Caius?

Lear. He's a good fellow, I can tell you that;
He'll strike, and quickly too: he's dead and rotten.

Kent. No, my good lord; I am the very man;—

Lear. I'll see that straight.

Kent. That, from your first of difference and
decay,
Have followed your sad steps.

Lear. You are welcome hither.

Kent. Nor no man else: all's cheerless, dark,
and deadly.—
Your eldest daughters have foredoomed themselves,
And desperately are dead.

Lear. Ay, so I think.

Alb. He knows not what he says; and vain it is
That we present us to him.

Edg. Very bootless.

Enter an Officer.

Offi. Edmund is dead, my lord.

Alb. That's but a trifle here.—
You lords and noble friends, know our intent:

What comfort to this great decay may come,
Shall be applied.   For us, we will resign,
During the life of this old majesty,
To him our absolute power:—You, to your rights;
                              [*To* EDGAR *and* KENT.
With boot, and such addition as your honours
Have more then merited.—All friends shall taste
The wages of their virtue, and all foes
The cup of their deservings.—O, see, see!

  Lear. And my poor fool is hanged! No, no, no
    life:
Why should a dog, a horse, a rat, have life,
And thou no breath at all?   O, thou wilt come no
    more:
Never, never, never, never, never!—
Pray you, undo this button.   Thank you, sir.—
Do you see this? Look on her,—look,—her lips,—
Look there, look there!   [*He dies.*

  Edg.   He faints!—My lord, my lord,—
  Kent. Break, heart; I pr'ythee, break!

  Edg.   Look up, my lord.
  Kent. Vex not his ghost: O let him pass! he
    hates him
That would upon the rack of this tough world
Stretch him out longer.

  Edg.   O, he is gone, indeed.
  Kent. The wonder is he hath endured so long:
He but usurped his life.

  Alb. Bear them from hence.—Our present
    business
Is general woe.—Friends of my soul, you twain
                              [*To* KENT *and* EDGAR.
Rule in this realm, and the gored state sustain.

  Kent. I have a journey, sir, shortly to go:
My master calls, and I must not say, no.

  Alb. The weight of this sad time we must obey;
Speak what we feel, not what we ought to say.
The oldest hath borne most: we that are young
Shall never see so much, nor live so long.

                    [*Exeunt, with a dead march.*

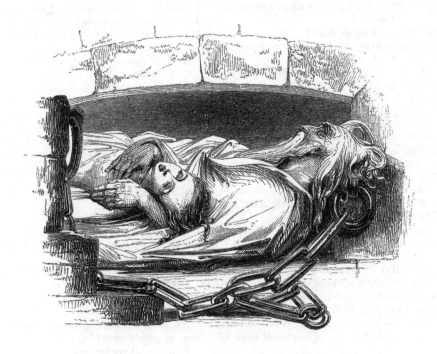

NOTES.

" Meantime we shall express our darker purpose."
Act I., Scene 1.

That is, " We have already made known our desire of parting the kingdom: we will now discover, what has not been told before,—the reasons by which we shall regulate the partition."

" Which of you shall we say doth love us most ?
That we our largest bounty may extend
Where merit doth most challenge it."—Act I., Scene 1.

In Holinshed this incident is thus related :—" He first asked Gonorilla, the eldest, how well she loved him; who, calling her gods to record, protested that she loved him more than her own life, which by right and reason should be most dear unto her. With which answer the father being well pleased, turned to the second, and demanded of her how well she loved him; who answered (confirming her saying with great oaths) that she loved him more than tongue could express, and far above all other creatures of the world.

" Then called he his youngest daughter Cordeilla before him, and asked her what account she made of him: unto whom she made this answer as followeth :—Knowing the great love and fatherly zeal that you have always borne towards me (for the which I may not answer you otherwise than I think and as my conscience leadeth me), I protest unto you that I have loved you ever, and will continually, while I live, love you as my natural father. And if you would more understand of the love I bear you, ascertain yourself that so much as you have so much you are worth; and so much I love you, and no more."

" I am made of that self metal as my sister,
And prize me at her worth."—Act I., Scene 1.

That is, " Estimate me at her value; my love has at least equal claim to your favour: only she comes short of me in this,—that I profess myself an enemy to all other joys which the most precious aggregation of sense can bestow."— The word " square " is here used for the whole complement, as " circle " is now sometimes used.

" O, these eclipses do portend these divisions ! fa, sol, la, mi."
Act I., Scene 2.

Shakspere shews by the context that he was well acquainted with the property of these syllables (fa, sol, la, mi), in solmisation ; which imply a series of sounds so unnatural that ancient musicians prohibited their use. The monkish writers on music say, *mi contra fa, est diabolus :* the interval *fa mi,* including a *tritonus* or sharp fourth, consisting of three tones without the intervention of a semi-tone, expressed in the modern scale by the letters F, G, A, B, would form a musical phrase extremely disagreeable to the ear.—Edmund, speaking of eclipses as portents and prodigies, compares the dislocation of events, the times being out of joint, to the unnatural and offensive sounds, fa, sol, la, mi.—Dr. Burney.

" There, take my coxcomb."—Act I., Scene 4.

By " coxcomb " the fool means his cap; called so, because on the top of it was sewed a piece of red cloth, resembling the comb of a cock. The word has been since used to denote a vain, conceited, meddling fellow.

" That's a shealed peascod."—Act I., Scene 4.

These words, addressed to Lear, signify that he is now a mere husk that contains nothing. The robing of the effigy of Richard II., in Westminster Abbey, is wrought with peascods open and the peas out : perhaps in allusion to his being once in full possession of sovereignty, but reduced to an empty title.

" So out went the candle, and we were left darkling."
Act I., Scene 4.

Shakspere's fools are certainly copied from the life. The originals whom he copied were, no doubt, men of quick parts, lively and sarcastic. Though they were licensed to say anything, it was still necessary, to prevent giving offence, that everything they said should have a playful air. We may suppose, therefore, that they had a custom of taking off the edge of too sharp a speech, by covering it hastily with the end of an old song, or any glib nonsense that came into their mind.—Sir Joshua Reynolds.

In a very old dramatic piece, called " The Longer thou Livest the more Fool thou art," there is this stage direction:—" Entereth Moros, counterfeiting a vain gesture and a foolish countenance, singing the foot of many songs, as fools were wont."

It is but justice to the poet to state that the most offensive passages delivered by the fool in this play occur in the form of *tags* (as they are technically called); that is, phrases or lines spoken in conclusion or on making an exit. Those alluded to were probably interpolations in the first instance and gradually became incorporated with the text of the prompter's book.

" Some blood drawn on me would beget opinion
Of my more fierce endeavour : I have seen drunkards
Do more than this in sport."—Act II., Scene 1.

These drunken feats are mentioned in Marston's " Dutch Courtezan :"—" Have I not been drunk for your health; eat glasses, drunk wine, stabbed arms, and done all offices of protested gallantry for your sake ?"

" If I had thee in Lipsbury pinfold, I would make thee care for me."—Act II., Scene 2.

" Lipsbury pinfold " may, perhaps, like " Lob's pond," be a coined name, but with what allusion does not appear.

" Goose, if I had you upon Sarum plain,
I'd drive ye cackling home to Camelot."—Act II., Scene 2.

In Somersetshire, near Camelot, are many large moors, where are bred great quantities of geese. It was the place where, according to the romances, King Arthur kept his court in the west.

" Good king, that must approve the common saw;
Thou out of heaven's benediction com'st
To the warm sun."—Act II., Scene 2.

That is, from good to worse. Kent is thinking of the King being likely to receive a worse reception from Regan than that which he had already experienced from Goneril. The " common saw " is found in Heywood's " Dialogues on Proverbs :"—

" In your running from him to me, ye run
Out of God's blessing into the warm sun."

" *The country gives me proof and precedent*
Of Bedlam beggars, who, with roaring voices,
Strike in their numbed and mortified bare arms,
Pins, wooden pricks, nails, sprigs of rosemary."
Act II., Scene 3.

In Decker's "BELL-MAN OF LONDON" (1640), there is an
account of a character of this description, under the title
of " Abraham Man :"—

" He swears he hath been in Bedlam, and will talk fran-
ticly of purpose. You see pins stuck in sundry places of his
naked flesh, especially in his arms : which pain he gladly
puts him to, only to make you believe he is out of his wits.
He calls himself by the name of ' Poor Tom ;' and, coming
near anybody, cries out ' Poor Tom is a-cold.' Of these
Abraham-men some be exceeding merry, and do nothing
but sing songs fashioned out of their own brains. Some will
dance, others will do nothing but either laugh or weep :
others are dogged, and so sullen both in look and speech,
that, spying but a small company in a house, they boldly
and bluntly enter, compelling the servants through fear to
give them what they demand."

The cant term, to "sham Abraham," is probably derived
from this source.

" *Poor Turlygood! poor Tom.*"—Act II., Scene 3.

" Turlygood" is supposed to be a corruption of " Tur-
lupin." The Turlupins were a fantastical sect, who appeared on the continent in the thirteenth and fourteenth
centuries, calling themselves Beghards or Beghins. Their
menaces and appearance exhibited the strongest indications
of lunacy and distraction ; and their popular name, Turlupins, was probably derived from the wolfish howlings they
made in their fits of religious raving.

" *Let go thy hold when a great wheel runs down a hill,*" &c.
Act II., Scene 4.

One cannot too much commend the caution which our
moral poet uses on all occasions to prevent his sentime.
from being perversely taken. So here, having given an
ironical commendation of perfidy and base desertion of the
unfortunate,—for fear it should be understood seriously,
though delivered by his buffoon or jester, he has the precau-
tion to add this beautiful corrective, full of fine sense :—" I
would have none but knaves follow it, since a fool gives it."
—WARBURTON.

" *Who gives anything to poor Tom? whom the foul fiend*
hath led through fire and through flame, through ford and
whirlpool, over bog and quagmire: that hath laid knives under
his pillow, and halters in his pew."—Act III., Scene 4.

It is a frequent charge against the fiend that he tempts
to self-destruction. In " DR. FAUSTUS" (1604), we find :—

" Swords, poisons, halters, and envenomed steel,
Are laid before me, to despatch myself."

In Harsenet's " DECLARATION" (a curious work which
is more particularly mentioned in a note on act iv., scene 1),
there is a passage which it is probable the poet had especially in view when writing the quoted passage :—" This
examinant further saith, that one Alexander, an apothecary,
having brought with him from London to Denham, on a
time, a new halter and two blades of knives, did leave the
same upon the gallery floor, in her master's house. A great
search was made in the house to know how the said halter
and knife-blades came thither, till Ma. Mainy, in his next
fit, said, it was reported that the devil laid them in the
gallery, that some of those that were possessed might either
hang themselves with the halter, or kill themselves with the
blades."

" *The foul fiend bites my back.*"—Act III , Scene 6.

All the fine matter commencing with this line, and ending
" False justicer, why hast thou let her 'scape?" appears in
the quartos, but is wanting in the folio editions. This is the
case, also, with the whole of scene 3, act iv. (in which Cordelia's demeanour, on hearing of Lear's sufferings, is so
beautifully painted); it is found only in the quartos. Many
other interesting passages have been restored by the commentators from these editions. In the first folio (which was
published by the players), the tragedy was probably abridged
to some extent, in order to make it more available for stage
purposes; but by whom it is now impossible to ascertain.
The additional matter in this copy is of very small amount.

" *Poor Tom, thy horn is dry.*"—Act III., Scene 6.

The allusion here is to the horn which a " Tom of Bedlam" was in the habit of carrying, to contain such drink as
was given him in charity. See " A PLEASANT DISPUTE
BETWEEN A COACH AND A SEDAN" (1636):—" I have observed when a coach is appendant to but two or three hundred pounds a year, mark it, the dogs are as lean as rakes;
you may tell all their ribs lying by the fire; and Tom of
Bedlam may sooner eat his horn than get it filled with small
drink."

" *See it shalt thou never.—Fellows, hold the chair.—*
Upon these eyes of thine I'll set my foot."
Act III., Scene 7.

In the original copies of " LEAR," there are no indications
as to the manner in which Gloster's eyes are supposed to be
extruded ; and those stage directions which have been
affixed by the commentators give an air of shocking reality
to the deed which was probably avoided in representation :
we have therefore simply adhered to the text, and left the
mode of operation in that obscurity which best befits the
appalling incident.—Tieck, an eminent German critic, thus
comments on the subject, in reference to the construction of
the old theatres :—

" The chair (or seat) in which Gloster is bound is the
same which stood somewhere elevated in the middle of the
scene, and from which Lear delivered his first speech. This
little theatre, in the midst, was, when not in use, concealed
by a curtain, which was again withdrawn when necessary.
Shakspere has, therefore, like all the dramatists of his age,
frequently two scenes at one and the same time. In " HENRY
VIII.," the nobles stand in the ante-chamber; the curtain is
withdrawn, and we are in the chamber of the King. Thus,
also, when Cranmer waits in the ante-chamber, the curtain
then opens to the council-chamber. We have here this
advantage, that, by the pillars which divided this little
central theatre from the proscenium or proper stage, not
only could a double group be presented, but it could be
partially concealed ; and thus two scenes might be played,
which would be wholly comprehended, although not everything in the smaller frame was expressly and evidently seen.
Thus Gloster sat probably concealed, and Cornwall, near
him, is visible. Regan stands below, on the fore-stage, but
close to Cornwall : and on this fore-stage also stand the
servants. Cornwall, horribly enough, tears Gloster's eye out
with his hand; but we do not directly see it, for some of
the servants who hold the chair stand around, and the curtain is only half-withdrawn (for it divided on each side).
The expression which Cornwall uses is only figurative, and
it is certainly not meant that the act of treading on the eye
is actually done.

" During the scornful speeches of Cornwall and Regan,
one of the servants runs up to the upper stage, and wounds
Cornwall. Regan, who is below, seizes a sword from another of the vassals, and stabs him from behind while he is
yet fighting. The groups are all in motion, and become more
concealed; and while the attention is strongly attracted to
the bloody scene, Gloster loses his second eye. We hear
Gloster's complainings, but we see him no more. Thus he
goes off; for this minor stage had also its place of exit.
Cornwall and Regan come again upon the proscenium, and
go off on the side. The servants conclude the scene with
some reflections.

"This I imagine to be the course of the action, and through this the horrors of the scene become somewhat softened. The poet, to be sure, trusted much to the strong minds of his friends, who would be too much affected by the fearfulness of the entire representation of this tragedy to be interrupted by single events, bloody as they were; or, through them, to be frightened back from their conception of the whole."

"Flibbertigibet, of mopping and mowing; who since possesses chambermaids and waiting women."—Act IV., Scene 1.

Shakspere has made Edgar, in his feigned distraction, frequently allude to a vile imposture of some English Jesuits, at that time much the subject of conversation; the history of it having just then been composed with great art and vigour of style and composition by Dr. Harsenet, afterwards Archbishop of York, by order of the Privy Council, in a work entitled "A Declaration of egregious Popish Impostures, to withdraw the Hearts of her Majesty's Subjects from their Allegiance, &c.: practised by Edmunds, alias Weston, a Jesuit, and divers Romish Priests, his wicked Associates:"—printed 1603.

The imposture was in substance this:—While the Spaniards were preparing their Armada against England, the Jesuits here were busy at work to promote it, by making converts: one method they employed was to dispossess pretended demoniacs; by which artifice they made several hundred converts amongst the common people. The principal scene of this farce was laid in the family of Mr. Edward Peckham, a Roman Catholic, where Marwood, a servant of Anthony Babington (who was afterwards executed for treason), Trayford, an attendant upon Mr. Peckham, and Sarah and Friswood Williams, and Anne Smith (three chambermaids in that family), came into the priests' hands for cure. But the discipline of the patients was so long and severe, and the priests so elate and careless with their success, that the plot was discovered on the confession of the parties concerned, and the contrivers of it deservedly punished.

The five devils mentioned in the text are the names of five of those who were made to act in this farce, upon 'he chambermaids and waiting women; and they were genera. so ridiculously nicknamed, that Harsenet has one chapte. "on the strange names of their devils; lest (says he) meeting them otherwise by chance, you mistake them for the names of tapsters or jugglers."—WARBURTON.

"She that herself will sliver and disbranch
From her material sap, perforce must wither,
And come to deadly use."—Act IV., Scene 2.

Alluding to the use that witches and enchanters are said to make of withered branches in their charms. A fine insinuation in Albany that Goneril was ready for the most unnatural mischief; and a preparative of the poet to her plotting with the bastard against her husband's life.—WARBURTON.

So in "MACBETH:"—

"Slips of yew,
Slivered in the moon's eclipse."

"See thyself, devil!
Proper deformity seems not in the fiend
So horrid as in woman."—Act IV., Scene 2.

That is, "Diabolical qualities appear not so horrid in the devil, to whom they belong, as in woman, who unnaturally assumes them."

—— *"This a good block?—*
It were a delicate stratagem to shoe
A troop of horse with felt!"—Act IV., Scene 6.

Upon the King's saying, "I will preach to thee," the poet seems to have meant him to pull off his hat, and keep turning it and feeling it, in the attitude of one of the preachers of those times (whom I have seen represented in ancient prints) till the idea of felt, which the good hat or block was made of, raises the stratagem in his brain of shoeing a troop of horse with the same substance.

Dr. Johnson (with greater probability, as we think) proposes to read "a good flock," instead of "a good block."—"Flocks," he adds, "are wool moulded together. It is very common for madmen to catch an accidental hint, and strain it to the purpose predominant in their minds. Lear picks up a flock, and immediately thinks to surprise his enemies by a troop of horse shod with flocks or felt."

The "delicate stratagem" of so equipping horses, had, it appears from Lord Herbert's "LIFE OF HENRY VIII.," been resorted to, in a tournament held at Lisle in 1513, in order to prevent the animals from slipping on a marble floor.

"Nay, come not near th' old man: keep out, che vor' ye."
Act IV., Scene 6.

"Che vor' ye" means "I warn you." When our ancient writers have occasion to introduce a rustic, they commonly allot him the Somersetshire dialect. Golding, in his translation of the second book of Ovid's "METAMORPHOSES," makes Mercury, assuming the appearance of a clown, speak with the provinciality of Edgar.

"And take upon us the mystery of things,
As if we were God's spies."—Act V., Scene 3.

That is, "as if we were angels, endowed with the power of prying into the original motives of action and the mysteries of conduct."—JOHNSON.

"Trust to thy single virtue."—Act V., Scene 3.

"Virtue" here signifies valour: a Roman sense of the word. Raleigh says, "The conquest of Palestine with singular virtue they achieved."

"Ask him his purposes: why he appears
Upon this call o' the trumpet."—Act V., Scene 3.

This is according to the ceremonials of the trial by combat:—"The appellant and his procurator first come to the gate. The constable and marshal demand, by voice of herald, what he is and why he comes so arrayed."—Selden's "DUELLO."

"KENT. *Is this the promised end?*
EDG. *Or image of that horror?"*—Act V., Scene 3.

Kent, in contemplating the unexampled scene of exquisite affection which was then before him, and the unnatural attempt of Goneril and Regan against their father's life, recollects those passages of St. Mark's Gospel in which Christ foretels to his disciples the end of the world: and hence his question, "Is this the promised end of all things, which has been foretold to us?" to which Edgar adds, "or only a representation or resemblance of that horror?" So Macbeth, when he calls upon Banquo, Malcolm, &c., to view Duncan murdered, says,—

"Up, up, and see
The great doom's image."

There is an allusion to the same passage of Scripture in a speech of Gloster's, in the second scene of the first act.—MASON.

"The weight of this sad time we must obey."
Act V., Scene 3.

This speech, from the authority of the old quarto, is rightly placed to Albany. In the edition by the players it is given to Edgar, by whom, I doubt not, it was of custom spoken; and the case was this: he who played Edgar, being a more favourite actor than he who performed Albany, in spite of decorum it was thought proper he should have the last word.—THEOBALD.

OF this noble tragedy, one of the first productions of the noblest of poets, it is scarcely possible to express our admiration in adequate terms. Whether considered as an effort of art or as a picture of the passions, it is entitled to the highest praise. The two portions of which the fable consists, involving the fate of Lear and his daughters and of Gloster and his sons, influence each other in so many points and are blended with such consummate skill, that whilst the imagination is delighted by diversity of circumstances, the judgment is equally gratified in viewing their mutual cooperation towards the final result; the coalescence being so intimate as not only to preserve the necessary unity of action, but to constitute one of the greatest beauties of the piece.

Such, indeed, is the interest excited by the structure and concatenation of the story, that the attention is not once suffered to flag. By a rapid succession of incidents, by sudden and overwhelming vicissitudes, by the most awful instances of misery and destitution, by the boldest contrariety of characters, are curiosity and anxiety kept progressively increasing, and with an impetus so strong as nearly to absorb every faculty of the mind and every feeling of the heart.

Victims of frailty, of calamity, or of vice, in an age remote and barbarous—the actors in this drama are brought forward with a strength of colouring which, had the scene been placed in a more civilised era, might have been justly deemed too dark and ferocious, but is not discordant with the earliest heathen age of Britain. The effect of this style of characterisation is felt occasionally throughout the entire play, but is particularly visible in the delineation of the vicious personages of the drama; the parts of Goneril, Regan, Edmund, and Cornwall, being loaded not only with ingratitude of the deepest dye, but with cruelty of the most savage and diabolical nature. They are the criminals, in fact, of an age when vice may be supposed to reign with lawless and gigantic power, and in which the extrusion of Gloster's eyes might be such an event as not unfrequently occurred.

Had this mode of casting his characters in the extreme applied to the remainder of the *dramatis personæ*, we should have lost some of the finest lessons of humanity and wisdom that ever issued from the pen of an uninspired writer: but, with the exception of a few coarsenesses, which remind us of the barbarous period to which the story is referred, and of a few instances rather revolting to probability, but which could not be detached from the original narrative, the virtuous agents of the play exhibit the manners and the feelings of civilisation, and are of that mixed fabric which can alone display a just portraiture of the nature and composition of our species.

The characters of Cordelia and Edgar, it is true, approach nearly to perfection; but the filial virtues of the former are combined with such exquisite tenderness of heart, and those of the latter with such bitter humiliation and suffering, that grief, indignation, and pity are instantly excited. Very striking representations are also given of the rough fidelity of Kent and of the hasty credulity of Gloster; but it is in delineating the passions, feelings, and afflictions of Lear that our poet has wrought up a picture of human misery which has never been surpassed and which agitates the soul with the most overpowering emotions of sympathy and compassion.

The conduct of the unhappy monarch having been founded merely on the impulses of sensibility, and not on any fixed principle or rule of action, no sooner has he discovered the baseness of those on whom he had relied, and the fatal mistake into which he had been hurried by the delusions of inordinate fondness and extravagant expectation, than he feels himself bereft of all consolation and resource. Those to whom he had given all, for whom he had stripped himself of dignity and honour, and on whom he had centred every hope of comfort and repose in his old age—his inhuman daughters—having not only treated him with utter coldness and contempt, but sought to deprive him of all the respectability and even of the very means of existence—what, in a mind so constituted as Lear's, the sport of intense and ill-regulated feeling, and tortured by the reflection of having deserted the only child who loved him—what but madness could be expected as the result? It was, in fact, the necessary consequence of the reciprocal action of complicated distress and morbid sensibility: and, in describing the approach of this dreadful infliction, in tracing its progress, its height, and subsidence, our poet has displayed such an intimate knowledge of the workings of the human intellect, under all its aberrations, as would afford an admirable study for the inquirer into mental physiology.

He has also in this play, as in that of "HAMLET," finely discriminated between real and assumed insanity,—Edgar, amidst all the wild imagery which his imagination has accumulated never once touching on the true source of his misery; whilst Lear, on the contrary, finds it associated with every object and every thought, however distant or dissimilar. Not even the Orestes of Euripides, or the Clementina of Richardson, can, as pictures of disordered reason, be placed in competition with this of Lear. It may be pronounced, indeed, from its truth and completeness, beyond the reach of rivalry.—DRAKE'S "SHAKSPEARE AND HIS TIMES."

THE tragedy of "LEAR" is deservedly celebrated among the dramas of Shakspere. There is, perhaps, no play which keeps the attention so strongly fixed; which so much agitates our passions and interests our curiosity. The artful involutions of distinct interests, the striking oppositions of contrary characters, the sudden changes of fortune, and the quick succession of events, fill the mind with a perpetual tumult of indignation, pity, and hope. There is no scene which does not contribute to the aggravation of the distress or conduct of the action, and scarce a line which does not conduce to the progress of the scene. So powerful is the current of the poet's imagination that the mind which once ventures within it is hurried irresistibly along.—JOHNSON.

OTHELLO
THE
MOOR
of
VENICE

INTRODUCTORY

REMARKS

THELLO—noble, generous, and commanding—appeals to the imagination as some grand, elevated tower, overlooking a perturbed and dangerous sea; a fortress indestructible by fair and open arts, but still not proof against the machinations of the subtle, sly, embosomed engineer, who, under pretence of strengthening its defences, labours incessantly to undermine its base. That Iago, the "demi-devil," the "cursed slave," who works the ruin of the high-minded Moor and his gentle, hapless Bride, can be at all endured, in reading or in scenic show, constitutes a higher compliment to intellectual gifts, than even Desdemona's ill-starred passion. Yet, horrible as is the vengeance of the disappointed and malignant Ancient, it is not altogether motiveless: he has the slight excuse of supercession by a junior, and (if his own word is to be taken) less skilful and deserving officer. His denunciation of "the curse of service," where "preferment goes by letter and affection," has been uttered in bitterness by many a better man, and its instructive tendency should never be neglected by superiors, unless with ample cause.

The bland and cordial manners of Iago's successful rival, and intended minor victim, denote the favourite both of intimates and of general society. Nor is Cassio's merit that of mere good-nature simply. His devoted attachment to his General and to Desdemona, seems wholly unpolluted by views of interest on the one hand, or of sensual passion on the other: and his eloquent anathemas against the immediate agent of his disgrace, the "invisible spirit of wine," have anticipated the substance of many a hundred lengthened essays, lectures, and exhortations. The pithy exclamation, "O that men should put an enemy in their mouths, to steal away their brains!" has passed into a proverb.

Desdemona is felt by all to rank among the loveliest of the many lovely female emanations from the Poet's pure and fertile mind. She seems a dew-drop in the traveller's path, glittering and delightful in its little sphere and transient hour, but too ethereal in its texture to endure. Even while he stands to gaze upon its heavenly beauty, the unknowing sun's first fiery glance drinks up its sweet existence!

The first edition of this great drama was published by Thomas Walkley, in 1622, as "The Tragœdy of Othello, the Moore of Venice. As it hath been diverse times acted at the Globe and at the Blackfriars, by his Majesties Servants. Written by William Shakespeare." To this copy is prefixed a brief address from "The Stationer to the Reader," in terms which serve to shew that the Poet was highly appreciated both by the writer and by the public whom he addressed and sought to gratify:—"To set forth a book without an epistle, were like to the old English proverb,—'a blue coat without a badge:' and the author being dead, I thought good to take that piece of work upon me. To commend it, I will not; for that which is good, I hope every man will commend without entreaty: and I am the bolder, because the author's name is sufficient to vent his work. Thus leaving every one to the liberty of judgment, I have ventured to print this play, and leave it to the general censure."—In the following year appeared the first folio collection, of which "THE TRAGEDIE OF OTHELLO, THE MOORE OF VENICE," forms the last part but two in that division of the work. The differences in the copies are for the most part slight.

One of Cinthio's novels, called in the original, "IL MORO DI VENEZIA," furnished a ground-work for the admirable plot of Othello. The incidents of the narrative are generally followed; but its characters are, of course, mere shadows compared with the vital beings of Shakspere's glowing page. Further mention of the original story will be found in the Notes.

The time of the supposed action of the drama is determined with sufficient accuracy. Cyprus was taken from the Venetians by the Turks in 1571. The Republic had then been masters of the island for about a hundred years; and no hostile movement had been made against them previously to that which proved successful. The junction of the Turkish fleets at Rhodes, in order to proceed to the attack, actually occurred in 1570: that year may, therefore, be considered as the era of Othello's fancied government.

In August, 1602, Queen Elizabeth was for three days entertained at Harefield, by Sir Thomas Egerton, afterwards Lord Ellesmere. Among the expenses (accounts of which are preserved at Bridgewater House), mention is made of "£10. to Burbidge's players of Othello." Mr. Collier, who furnishes the fact, reasonably presumes that the play was then both new and popular: no previous allusion to it has been hitherto discovered.—Shakspere was then in his thirty-ninth year: he was born in April, 1564.

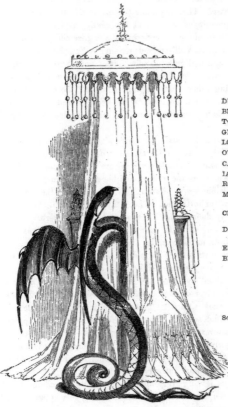

PERSONS REPRESENTED.

DUKE OF VENICE.
BRABANTIO, a Senator.
Two other Senators.
GRATIANO, Brother to BRABANTIO.
LODOVICO, Kinsman to BRABANTIO.
OTHELLO, the Moor.
CASSIO, his Lieutenant.
IAGO, his Ancient.
RODERIGO, a Venetian Gentleman.
MONTANO, OTHELLO's predecessor in the Government
    of Cyprus.
Clown, Servant to OTHELLO Ferald.

DESDEMONA, Daughter to BRABANTIO, and Wife to
    OTHELLO.
EMILIA, Wife to IAGO.
BIANCA, a Courtezan.

Officers, Gentlemen, Messengers, Musicians, Sailors,
Attendants, &c

———————

SCENE. For the First Act, in VENICE; during the rest of
the Play, at a Sea-port in CYPRUS.

SCENE I.—Venice. *A Street.*

Enter Roderigo *and* Iago.

Rod. Tush, never tell me: I take it much un-
kindly,
That thou, Iago, who hast had my purse
As if the strings were thine, shouldst know of this.

Iago. 'Sblood, but you will not hear me.
If ever I did dream of such a matter,
Abhor me.

Rod. Thou told'st me thou didst hold him in
thy hate.

Iago. Despise me if I do not. Three great ones
of the city,

In personal suit to make me his lieutenant,
Oft capped to him: and, by the faith of man,
I know my price; I am worth no worse a place:
But he, as loving his own pride and purposes,
Evades them with a bombast circumstance,
Horribly stuffed with epithets of war;
And, in conclusion, nonsuits my mediators:
"For certes," says he, "I have already
Chosen my officer." And what was he?
Forsooth, a great arithmetician;
One Michael Cassio, a Florentine,
A fellow almost damned in a fair wife:
That never set a squadron in the field,
Nor the division of a battle knows
More than a spinster; unless the bookish theoric,
Wherein the togéd consuls can propose
As masterly as he. Mere prattle, without practice,
Is all his soldiership. But he, sir, had the election:
And I,—of whom his eyes had seen the proof,
At Rhodes, at Cyprus, and on other grounds,
Christian and heathen,—must be be-lee'd and
    calmed
By debitor and creditor; this counter-caster:
He, in good time, must his lieutenant be,
And I (God bless the mark!) his Moorship's
    ancient.
    Rod. By heaven, I rather would have been his
      hangman.
    Iago. But there's no remedy; 't is the curse
      of service:
Preferment goes by letter and affection,
Not by the old gradation, where each second
Stood heir to the first. Now, sir, be judge yourself
Whether I in any just term am affined
To love the Moor.
    Rod.   I would not follow him, then.
    Iago. O, sir, content you;
I follow him to serve my turn upon him:
We cannot all be masters, nor all masters
Cannot be truly followed. You shall mark
Many a duteous and knee-crooking knave,
That, doting on his own obsequious bondage,
Wears out his time, much like his master's ass,
For nought but provender; and when he's old,
    cashiered:
Whip me such honest knaves. Others there are,
Who, trimmed in forms and visages of duty,
Keep yet their hearts attending on themselves;
And, throwing but shows of service on their lords,
Do well thrive by them; and, when they have lined
    their coats,
Do themselves homage: these fellows have some
    soul;
And such a one do I profess myself. For, sir,
It is as sure as you are Roderigo,
Were I the Moor, I would not be Iago.
In following him, I follow but myself:

Heaven is my judge, not I for love and duty,
But seeming so, for my peculiar end:
For when my outward action doth demonstrate
The native act and figure of my heart
In compliment extern, 't is not long after
But I will wear my heart upon my sleeve
For daws to peck at. I am not what I am.
    Rod. What a full fortune does the thick-lips owe,
If he can carry 't thus!
    Iago.   Call up her father;
Rouse him.—Make after him, poison his delight,
Proclaim him in the streets; incense her kinsmen;
And, though he in a fertile climate dwell,
Plague him with flies: though that his joy be joy,
Yet throw such changes of vexation on 't,
As it may lose some colour.
    Rod. Here is her father's house: I'll call
      aloud.
    Iago. Do; with like timorous accent and dire yell
As when (by night and negligence) the fire
Is spied in populous cities.
    Rod. What, ho, Brabantio!—Signior Braban-
      tio, ho!
    Iago. Awake!—what, ho, Brabantio!—thieves,
      thieves, thieves!
Look to your house, your daughter, and your bags!
Thieves, thieves!

BRABANTIO, *above.*

    Bra. What is the reason of this terrible sum-
      mons?
What is the matter there?
    Rod. Signior, is all your family within?
    Iago. Are your doors locked?
    Bra.   Why? wherefore ask you this?
    Iago. 'Zounds, sir, you are robbed:—for shame,
      put on your gown:—
Your heart is burst, you have lost half your soul:
Even now, very now, an old black ram
Is tupping your white ewe. Arise, arise:
Awake the snorting citizens with the bell,
Or else the devil will make a grandsire of you.
Arise, I say.
    Bra.   What, have you lost your wits?
    Rod. Most reverend signior, do you know my
      voice?
    Bra. Not I: what are you?
    Rod. My name is—Roderigo.
    Bra.   The worse welcome:
I have charged thee not to haunt about my doors.
In honest plainness thou hast heard me say,
My daughter is not for thee; and now, in madness,
Being full of supper and distempering draughts,
Upon malicious bravery dost thou come
To start my quiet.
    Rod. Sir, sir, sir, sir,—
    Bra.   But thou must needs be sure

My spirit and my place have in them power
To make this bitter to thee.

Rod.   Patience, good sir.

Bra. What tell'st thou me of robbing? This is Venice:

My house is not a grange.

Rod.   Most grave Brabantio,
In simple and pure soul I come to you.

Iago. 'Zounds, sir, you are one of those that will not serve God, if the devil bid you. Because we come to do you service, you think we are ruffians. You 'll have your daughter covered with a Barbary horse: you 'll have your nephews neigh to you: you 'll have coursers for cousins, and gennets for germans.

Bra. What profane wretch art thou?

Iago. I am one, sir, that comes to tell you your daughter and the Moor are now making the beast with two backs.

Bra. Thou art a villain.

Iago.   You are—a senator.

Bra. This thou shalt answer: I know thee, Roderigo.

Rod. Sir, I will answer anything. But I beseech you,
If 't be your pleasure and most wise consent
(As partly I find it is) that your fair daughter,
At this odd-even and dull watch o' the night,
Transported, with no worse nor better guard
But with a knave of common hire, a gondolier,
To the gross clasps of a lascivious Moor,—
If this be known to you, and your allowance,
We then have done you bold and saucy wrongs:
But if you know not this, my manners tell me
We have your wrong rebuke. Do not believe
That, from the sense of all civility,
I thus would play and trifle with your reverence:
Your daughter,—if you have not given her leave,—
I say again, hath made a gross revolt;
Tying her duty, beauty, wit, and fortunes,
In an extravagant and wheeling stranger,
Of here and everywhere. Straight satisfy yourself:
If she be in her chamber or your house,
Let loose on me the justice of the state
For thus deluding you.

Bra.   Strike on the tinder, ho!
Give me a taper:—call up all my people.—
This accident is not unlike my dream:
Belief of it oppresses me already.—
Light, I say; light!   [*Exit from above.*

Iago.   Farewell; for I must leave you:
It seems not meet, nor wholesome to my place,
To be produced (as if I stay I shall)
Against the Moor. For I do know, the state
(However this may gall him with some check)

Cannot with safety cast him: for he 's embarked
With such loud reason to the Cyprus' wars
(Which even now stand in act), that, for their souls,
Another of his fathom they have not
To lead their business. In which regard,
Though I do hate him as I do hell pains,
Yet, for necessity of present life,
I must shew out a flag and sign of love,
Which is indeed but sign. That you shall surely find him,
Lead to the Sagittary the raiséd search;
And there will I be with him. So farewell. [*Exit.*

Enter, below, BRABANTIO, *and* Servants, *with torches.*

Bra. It is too true an evil: gone she is;
And what 's to come of my despiséd time
Is nought but bitterness.—Now, Roderigo,
Where didst thou see her?—O, unhappy girl!—
With the Moor, say'st thou?—Who would be a father?—
How didst thou know 't was she?—O, thou deceivest me
Past thought!—What said she to you?—Get more tapers;
Raise all my kindred.—Are they married, think you?

Rod. Truly, I think they are.

Bra. O heaven!—How got she out?—O treason of the blood!—
Fathers, from hence trust not your daughters' minds
By what you see them act.—Are there not charms
By which the property of youth and maidhood
May be abused? Have you not read, Roderigo,
Of some such thing?

Rod.   Yes, sir; I have indeed.

Bra. Call up my brother.—O, that you had had her!—
Some one way, some another.—Do you know
Where we may apprehend her and the Moor?

Rod. I think I can discover him; if you please
To get good guard, and go along with me.

Bra. Pray you, lead on. At every house I 'll call;
I may command at most.—Get weapons, ho!
And raise some special officers of night.—
On, good Roderigo: I will deserve your pains.
          [*Exeunt.*

SCENE II.—*The same. Another Street.*

Enter OTHELLO, IAGO, *and* Attendants.

Iago. Though in the trade of war I have slain men,
Yet do I hold it very stuff o' the conscience
To do no contrived murder: I lack iniquity

Sometimes to do me service. Nine or ten times
I had thought to have yerked him here under
    the ribs.
  Oth. 'T is better as it is.
  Iago.   Nay, but he prated,
And spoke such scurvy and provoking terms
Against your honour,
That, with the little godliness I have,
I did full hard forbear him. But I pray, sir,
Are you fast married? for be sure of this,
That the magnifico is much beloved;
And hath in his effect a voice potential,
As double as the Duke's: he will divorce you;
Or put upon you what restraint and grievance
The law (with all his might to enforce it on)
Will give him cable.
  Oth.   Let him do his spite:
My services, which I have done the signiory,
Shall out-tongue his complaints. 'T is yet to know
(Which when I know that boasting is an honour
I shall promulgate) I fetch my life and being
From men of royal siege; and my demerits
May speak unbonneted to as proud a fortune
As this that I have reached. For know, Iago,
But that I love the gentle Desdemona,
I would not my unhoused free condition
Put into circumscription and confine
For the sea's worth.—But, look! what lights come
    yonder?

Enter CASSIO, *at a distance, and certain* Officers
    with torches.

  Iago. These are the raiséd father and his
    friends:
You were best go in.
  Oth.   Not I: I must be found:
My parts, my title, and my perfect soul,
Shall manifest me rightly. Is it they?
  Iago. By Janus, I think no.
  Oth. The servants of the Duke; and my
    lieutenant.—
The goodness of the night upon you, friends:
What is the news?
  Cas.   The Duke does greet you, general;
And he requires your haste post-haste appearance,
Even on the instant.
  Oth.   What is the matter, think you?
  Cas. Something from Cyprus, as I may divine:
It is a business of some heat. The gallies
Have sent a dozen sequent messengers
This very night, at one another's heels:
And many of the consuls, raised and met,
Are at the Duke's already. You have been hotly
    called for;
When, being not at your lodging to be found,
The senate hath sent about three several quests,
To search you out.

  Oth.   'T is well I am found by you.
I will but spend a word here in the house,
And go with you.   [*Exit.*
  Cas.   Ancient, what makes he here?
  Iago. 'Faith, he to-night hath boarded a land
    carack:
If it prove lawful prize, he 's made for ever.
  Cas. I do not understand.
  Iago.   He 's married.
  Cas.   To who?

        Re-enter OTHELLO.

  Iago. Marry, to—Come, captain, will you go?
  Oth.   Have with you.
  Cas. Here comes another troop to seek for you.

Enter BRABANTIO, RODERIGO, *and* Officers *of*
    night, with torches and weapons.

  Iago. It is Brabantio.—General, be advised:
He comes to bad intent.
  Oth.   Holla; stand there!
  Rod. Signior, it is the Moor.
  Bra.   Down with him, thief!
            [*They draw on both sides.*
  Iago. You, Roderigo! Come, sir, I am for you.
  Oth. Keep up your bright swords, for the dew
    will rust them.—
Good signior, you shall more command with years
Than with your weapons.
  Bra. O thou foul thief, where hast thou stowed
    my daughter?
Damned as thou art, thou hast enchanted her:
For I 'll refer me to all things of sense
(If she in chains of magic were not bound),
Whether a maid so tender, fair, and happy,
So opposite to marriage that she shunned
The wealthy curléd darlings of our nation,
Would ever have, to incur a general mock,
Run from her guardage to the sooty bosom
Of such a thing as thou; to fear, not to delight.
Judge me the world, if 't is not gross in sense
That thou hast practised on her with foul charms;
Abused her delicate youth with drugs or minerals
That waken motion. I 'll have it disputed on:
'T is probable, and palpable to thinking.
I therefore apprehend and do attach thee
For an abuser of the world; a practiser
Of arts inhibited and out of warrant.—
Lay hold upon him: if he do resist,
Subdue him at his peril.
  Oth.   Hold your hands,
Both you of my inclining and the rest:
Were it my cue to fight, I should have known it
Without a prompter.—Where will you that I go
To answer this your charge?
  Bra.   To prison: till fit time
Of law, and course of direct session,
Call thee to answer.

Oth. What if I do obey:
How may the Duke be therewith satisfied;
Whose messengers are here about my side,
Upon some present business of the state,
To bring me to him?

Off. 'T is true, most worthy signior:
The Duke 's in council; and your noble self,
I am sure, is sent for.

Bra. How! the Duke in council,
In this time of the night!—Bring him away:
Mine 's not an idle cause. The Duke himself,
Or any of my brothers of the state,
Cannot but feel this wrong as 't were their own:
For if such actions may have passage free,
Bond-slaves and pagans shall our statesmen be.
[*Exeunt.*

SCENE III.—*The same. A Council-Chamber.*

The DUKE *and Senators, sitting;* Officers *attending.*

Duke. There is no composition in these news,
That gives them credit.

1st Sen. Indeed they are disproportioned.
My letters say, a hundred and seven gallies.

Duke. And mine, a hundred and forty.

2nd Sen. And mine, two hundred.
But though they jump not on a just account
(As in these cases where the aim reports,
'T is oft with difference), yet do they all confirm
A Turkish fleet, and bearing up to Cyprus.

Duke. Nay, it is possible enough to judgment.
I do not so secure me in the error,
But the main article I do approve
In fearful sense.

Sailor [*within*]. What ho; what ho; what ho!

Enter an Officer, *with a* Sailor.

Offi. A messenger from the gallies.

Duke. Now: the business?

Sail. The Turkish preparation makes for Rhodes:
So was I bid report here to the state,
By Signior Angelo.

Duke. How say you by this change?

1st Sen. This cannot be,
By no assay of reason: 't is a pageant,
To keep us in false gaze. When we consider
The importancy of Cyprus to the Turk;
And let ourselves again but understand
That, as it more concerns the Turk than Rhodes,
So may he with more facile question bear it,
For that it stands not in such warlike brace,
But altogether lacks th' abilities
That Rhodes is dressed in: if we make thought of this,
We must not think the Turk is so unskilful
To leave that latest which concerns him first:
Neglecting an attempt of ease and gain,
To wake and wage a danger profitless.

Duke. Nay, in all confidence, he 's not for
Rhodes.

Offi. Here is more news.

Enter a Messenger.

Mess. The Ottomites, reverend and gracious,
Steering with due course toward the Isle of Rhodes,
Have there injointed them with an after fleet.

1st Sen. Ay, so I thought:—how many, as you
guess?

Mess. Of thirty sail: and now do they re-stem
Their backward course, bearing with frank ap-
pearance
Their purposes toward Cyprus.—Signior Montano,
Your trusty and most valiant servitor,
With his free duty recommends you thus,
And prays you to believe him.

Duke. 'T is certain, then, for Cyprus.—
Marcus Lucchicos, is not he in town?

1st Sen. He 's now in Florence.

Duke. Write from us: wish him post-post-
haste: despatch.

1st Sen. Here comes Brabantio and the valiant
Moor.

Enter BRABANTIO, OTHELLO, IAGO, RODERIGO,
and Officers.

Duke. Valiant Othello, we must straight em-
ploy you
Against the general enemy Ottoman.—
I did not see you; welcome, gentle signior:
[*To* BRABANTIO.
We lacked your counsel and your help to-night.

Bra. So did I yours. Good your grace, par-
don me:
Neither my place, nor aught I heard of business,
Hath raised me from my bed; nor doth the
general care
Take hold on me; for my particular grief
Is of so flood-gate and o'erbearing nature,
That it engluts and swallows other sorrows,
And it is still itself.

Duke. Why, what 's the matter?

Bra. My daughter! O, my daughter!

Sen. Dead?

Bra. Ay, to me.
She is abused, stolen from me, and corrupted
By spells and medicines bought of mountebanks:
For nature so preposterously to err,
Being not deficient, blind, or lame of sense,
Sans witchcraft, could not.

Duke. Whoe'er he be, that, in this foul pro-
ceeding,
Hath thus beguiled your daughter of herself,
And you of her, the bloody book of law
You shall yourself read in the bitter letter,
After your own sense: yea, though our proper son
Stood in your action.

Bra.   Humbly I thank your grace.
Here is the man, this Moor; whom now, it seems,
Your special mandate, for the state affairs,
Hath hither brought.

Duke. }
Sen.   }   We are very sorry for it.

Duke. What, in your own part, can you say
       to this?   [*To* OTHELLO.

Bra. Nothing, but this is so.

Oth. Most potent, grave, and reverend signiors,
My very noble and approved good masters,—
That I have ta'en away this old man's daughter,
It is most true: true, I have married her:
The very head and front of my offending
Hath this extent,—no more.   Rude am I in my
       speech,
And little blessed with the set phrase of peace;
For since these arms of mine had seven years' pith,
Till now, some nine moons wasted, they have used
Their dearest action in the tented field;
And little of this great world can I speak
More than pertains to feats of broil and battle;
And therefore little shall I grace my cause
In speaking for myself:—yet, by your gracious
       patience,
I will a round unvarnished tale deliver
Of my whole course of love: what drugs, what
       charms,
What conjuration, and what mighty magic
(For such proceeding I am charged withal),
I won his daughter with.

Bra.   A maiden never bold;
Of spirit so still and quiet that her motion
Blushed at herself: and she,—in spite of nature,
Of years, of country, credit, everything,—
To fall in love with what she feared to look on!
It is a judgment maimed and most imperfect
That will confess perfection so could err
Against all rules of nature; and must be driven
To find out practices of cunning hell,
Why this should be.   I therefore vouch again,
That with some mixtures powerful o'er the blood,
Or with some dram conjured to this effect,
He wrought upon her.

Duke.   To vouch this is no proof,
Without more certain and more overt test
Than these thin habits and poor likelihoods
Of modern seeming do prefer against him.

1st Sen. But, Othello, speak:—
Did you, by indirect and forcéd courses
Subdue and poison this young maid's affections;
Or came it by request, and such fair question
As soul to soul affordeth?

Oth.   I do beseech you,
Send for the lady to the Sagittary,

And let her speak of me before her father:
If you do find me foul in her report,
The trust, the office, I do hold of you,
Not only take away, but let your sentence
Even fall upon my life.

Duke. Fetch Desdemona hither.

Oth. Ancient, conduct them: you best know
　　　　the place. [*Exeunt* IAGO *and* Attendants.
And, till she come, as truly as to heaven
I do confess the vices of my blood,
So justly to your grave ears I'll present
How I did thrive in this fair lady's love,
And she in mine.

Duke. Say it, Othello.

Oth. Her father loved me; oft invited me;
Still questioned me the story of my life,
From year to year; the battles, sieges, fortunes,
That I have passed.
I ran it through, even from my boyish days,
To the very moment that he bade me tell it.
Wherein I spoke of most disastrous chances;
Of moving accidents by flood and field;
Of hair-breadth scapes i'the imminent deadly
　　　　breach;
Of being taken by the insolent foe,
And sold to slavery; of my redemption thence,
And with it all my travel's history:
Wherein, of antres vast and deserts idle,
Rough quarries, rocks, and hills whose heads touch
　　　　heaven,
It was my hint to speak; such was the process:
And of the Cannibals that each other eat;
The Anthropophagi, and men whose heads
Do grow beneath their shoulders. These things
　　　　to hear
Would Desdemona seriously incline:
But still the house affairs would draw her thence;
Which ever as she could with haste despatch,
She'd come again, and with a greedy ear
Devour up my discourse. Which I observing,
Took once a pliant hour; and found good means
To draw from her a prayer of earnest heart
That I would all my pilgrimage dilate,
Whereof by parcels she had something heard,
But not intentively. I did consent;
And often did beguile her of her tears,
When I did speak of some distressful stroke
That my youth suffered. My story being done,
She gave me for my pains a world of sighs:
She swore,—In faith, 't was strange, 't was pass-
　　　　ing strange;
'T was pitiful, 't was wondrous pitiful:
She wished she had not heard it; yet she wished
That heaven had made her such a man: she
　　　　thanked me;
And bade me, if I had a friend that loved her,
I should but teach him how to tell my story,

And that would woo her. Upon this hint, I spake:
She loved me for the dangers I had passed;
And I loved her that she did pity them.
This only is the witchcraft I have used.—
Here comes the lady, let her witness it.

Enter DESDEMONA, IAGO, *and* Attendants.

Duke. I think this tale would win my daughter
　　　　too.—
Good Brabantio,
Take up this mangled matter at the best:
Men do their broken weapons rather use,
Than their bare hands.

Bra. I pray you, hear her speak:
If she confess that she was half the wooer,
Destruction on my head if my bad blame
Light on the man!—Come hither, gentle mistress:
Do you perceive, in all this noble company,
Where most you owe obedience?

Des. My noble father,
I do perceive here a divided duty.
To you I am bound for life and education:
My life and education both do learn me
How to respect you: you are the lord of duty;
I am hitherto your daughter. But here's my
　　　　husband:
And so much duty as my mother shewed
To you, preferring you before her father,
So much I challenge that I may profess
Due to the Moor, my lord.

Bra. God be with you! I have done.—
Please it your grace, on to the state affairs:
I had rather to adopt a child than get it.—
Come hither, Moor:
I here do give thee that with all my heart,
Which, but thou hast already, with all my heart
I would keep from thee.—For your sake, jewel,
I am glad at soul I have no other child;
For thy escape would teach me tyranny,
To hang clogs on them.—I have done, my lord.

Duke. Let me speak like yourself, and lay a
　　　　sentence
Which, as a grise or step, may help these lovers
Into your favour.
When remedies are past, the griefs are ended,
By seeing the worst, which late on hopes depended.
To mourn a mischief that is past and gone,
Is the next way to draw new mischief on.
What cannot be preserved when fortune takes,
Patience her injury a mockery makes.
The robbed that smiles steals something from
　　　　the thief:
He robs himself that spends a bootless grief.

Bra. So let the Turk of Cyprus us beguile:
We lose it not so long as we can smile.
He bears the sentence well that nothing bears
But the free comfort which from thence he hears:

But he bears both the sentence and the sorrow,
That, to pay grief, must of poor patience borrow.
These sentences, to sugar or to gall,
Being strong on both sides, are equivocal.
But words are words : I never yet did hear
That the bruised heart was piercéd through the
          ear.——
I humbly beseech you, proceed to the affairs of
     state.
     Duke. The Turk with a most mighty prepara-
tion makes for Cyprus :——Othello, the fortitude
of the place is best known to you : and though
we have there a substitute of most allowed suffi-
ciency, yet opinion, a sovereign mistress of effects,
throws a more safer voice on you :——you must
therefore be content to slubber the gloss of your
new fortunes with this more stubborn and boist-
erous expedition.
     Oth. The tyrant custom, most grave senators,
Hath made the flinty and steel couch of war
My thrice-driven bed of down.   I do agnize
A natural and prompt alacrity
I find in hardness ; and do undertake
These present wars against the Ottomites.
Most humbly therefore bending to your state,
I crave fit disposition for my wife ;
Due reference of place, and exhibition ;
With such accommodation and besort
As levels with her breeding.
     Duke.   If you please,
Be 't at her father's
     Bra.   I will not have it so.
     Oth. Nor I.
     Des.   Nor I.   I would not there reside,
To put my father in impatient thoughts,
By being in his eye.——Most gracious Duke,
To my unfolding lend a gracious ear ;
And let me find a charter in your voice,
To assist my simpleness.
     Duke. What would you, Desdemona ?
     Des. That I did love the Moor to live with
     him,
My downright violence and storm of fortunes
May trumpet to the world. My heart 's subdued
Even to the very quality of my lord :
I saw Othello's visage in his mind ;
And to his honours and his valiant parts
Did I my soul and fortunes consecrate.
So that, dear lords, if I be left behind,
A moth of peace, and he go to the war,
The rights for which I love him are bereft me,
And I a heavy interim shall support
By his dear absence.   Let me go with him.
     Oth. Your voices, lords :——'beseech you, let
     her will
Have a free way.
Vouch with me, heaven, I therefore beg it not

To please the palate of my appetite ;
Nor to comply with heat, the young affects,
In my distinct and proper satisfaction ;
But to be free and bounteous to her mind.
And heaven defend your good souls, that you think
I will your serious and great business scant
For she is with me.   No ; when light-winged toys
Of feathered Cupid seel with wanton dulness
My speculative and active instruments,
That my disports corrupt and taint my business,
Let housewives make a skillet of my helm,
And all indign and base adversities
Make head against my estimation !
     Duke. Be it as you shall privately determine,
Either for her stay or going. The affair cries haste,
And speed must answer it : you must hence to-
          night.
     Des. To-night, my lord ?
     Duke.   This night.
     Oth.   With all my heart.
     Duke. At nine i' the morning here we 'll meet
          again.
Othello, leave some officer behind,
And he shall our commission bring to you ;
With such things else of quality and respect
As doth import you.
     Oth.   Please your grace, my ancient :
A man he is of honesty and trust.
To his conveyance I assign my wife,
With what else needful your good grace shall think
To be sent after me.
     Duke.   Let it be so.
Good night to every one.——And, noble signior,
                    [*To* BRABANTIO.
If virtue no delighted beauty lack,
Your son-in-law is far more fair than black.
     1st Sen. Adieu, brave Moor : use Desdemona
          well.
     Bra. Look to her, Moor ; have a quick eye to see :
She has deceived her father, and may thee.
               [*Exeunt* DUKE, *Senators, Officers, &c.*
     Oth. My life upon her faith.——Honest Iago,
My Desdemona must I leave to thee ;
I pr'y thee let thy wife attend on her ;
And bring them after in the best advantage.——
Come, Desdemona ; I have but an hour
Of love, of worldly matters and direction,
To spend with thee : we must obey the time.
               [*Exeunt* OTHELLO *and* DESDEMONA.
     Rod. Iago.
     Iago. What say'st thou, noble heart ?
     Rod. What will I do, think'st thou ?
     Iago. Why, go to bed and sleep.
     Rod. I will incontinently drown myself.
     Iago. Well, if thou dost, I shall never love
thee after it.   Why, thou silly gentleman !
     Rod. It is silliness to live when to live is a

torment: and then have we a prescription to die, when death is our physician,

Iago. O villanous! I have looked upon the world for four times seven years; and since I could distinguish between a benefit and an injury, I never found a man that knew how to love himself. Ere I would say I would drown myself for the love of a Guinea-hen, I would change my humanity with a baboon.

Rod. What should I do? I confess it is my shame to be so fond; but it is not in virtue to amend it.

Iago. Virtue? a fig!—'t is in ourselves that we are thus or thus. Our bodies are our gardens, to the which our wills are gardeners: so that if we will plant nettles, or sow lettuce; set hyssop, and weed up thyme; supply it with one gender of herbs, or distract it with many; either to have it steril with idleness, or manured with industry,—why, the power and corrigible authority of this lies in our wills. If the balance of our lives had not one scale of reason to poise another of sensuality, the blood and baseness of our natures would conduct us to most preposterous conclusions.—But we have reason to cool our raging motions, our carnal stings, our unbitted lusts; whereof I take this that you call love, to be a sect or scion.

Rod. It cannot be.

Iago. It is merely a lust of the blood and a permission of the will. Come, be a man. Drown thyself! drown cats and blind puppies. I have professed me thy friend, and I confess me knit to thy deserving with cables of perdurable toughness. I could never better stead thee than now. Put money in thy purse: follow these wars; defeat thy favour with an usurped beard: I say, put money in thy purse. It cannot be that Desdemona should long continue her love to the Moor;—put money in thy purse;—nor he his to her: it was a violent commencement, and thou shalt see an answerable sequestration; —put but money in thy purse. These Moors are changeable in their wills;—fill thy purse with money:—the food that to him now is as luscious as locusts, shall be to him shortly as bitter as coloquintida. She must change for youth: when she is sated with his body, she will find the error of her choice. She must have change, she must: therefore put money in thy purse.—If thou wilt needs damn thyself, do it a more delicate way than drowning. Make

all the money thou canst. If sanctimony and a frail vow, betwixt an erring barbarian and a supersubtle Venetian, be not too hard for my wits and all the tribe of hell, thou shalt enjoy her: therefore make money. A pox of drowning thyself! it is clean out of the way: seek thou rather to be hanged in compassing thy joy, than to be drowned and go without her.

Rod. Wilt thou be fast to my hopes, if I depend on the issue?

Iago. Thou art sure of me.—Go, make money. —I have told thee often, and I re-tell thee again and again, I hate the Moor. My cause is hearted; thine hath no less reason. Let us be conjunctive in our revenge against him: if thou canst cuckold him, thou dost thyself a pleasure, and me a sport. There are many events in the womb of time, which will be delivered. Traverse; go; provide thy money. We will have more of this to-morrow. Adieu.

Rod. Where shall we meet i' the morning?

Iago. At my lodging.

Rod. I 'll be with thee betimes.

Iago. Go to; farewell. Do you hear, Roderigo?

Rod. What say you?

Iago. No more of drowning, do you hear.

Rod. I am changed. I 'll sell all my land.

Iago. Go to; farewell: put money enough in your purse. [*Exit* Roderigo.

Thus do I ever make my fool my purse:
For, mine own gainéd knowledge should profane,
If I would time expend with such a snipe,
But for my sport and profit.—I hate the Moor;
And it is thought abroad that 'twixt my sheets
He has done my office: I know not if 't be true;
But I, for mere suspicion in that kind,
Will do as if for surety. He holds me well;
The better shall my purpose work on him.—
Cassio 's a proper man. Let me see now:
To get his place, and to plume up my will:
A double knavery:—how; how? Let me see:—
After some time, to abuse Othello's ear
That he is too familiar with his wife:—
He hath a person and a smooth dispose
To be suspected; framed to make women false.
The Moor is of a free and open nature,
That thinks men honest that but seem to be so;
And will as tenderly be led by th' nose
As asses are.—
I have 't. It is engendered.—Hell and night
Must bring this monstrous birth to the world's
        light. [*Exit.*

ACT II

SCENE I.—*A Sea-port Town in* Cyprus. *A Platform.*

Enter MONTANO *and Two* Gentlemen.

Mon. What from the cape can you discern at sea?

1st Gent. Nothing at all; it is a high-wrought
　　flood:
I cannot 'twixt the heaven and the main
Descry a sail.

Mon. Methinks the wind hath spoke aloud at
　　land;
A fuller blast ne'er shook our battlements:
If it hath ruffianed so upon the sea,
What ribs of oak, when mountains melt on them,
Can hold the mortise? What shall we hear of this?

2nd Gent. A segregation of the Turkish fleet:
For do but stand upon the foaming shore,
The chiding billow seems to pelt the clouds;
The wind-shaked surge, with high and monstro'
　　mane,
Seems to cast water on the burning bear,

And quench the guards of th' ever-fixéd pole:
I never did like molestation view
On the enchaféd flood.

Mon.　　If that the Turkish fleet
Be not ensheltered and embayed, they are
　　drowned:
It is impossible they bear it out.

Enter a Third Gentleman.

3rd Gent. News, lords! our wars are done:
The desperate tempest hath so banged the Turks,
That their designment halts. A noble ship of
　　Venice
Hath seen a grievous wreck and sufferance
On most part of their fleet.

Mon.　　How! is this true?

3rd Gent. The ship is here put in,
A Veronessa.—Michael Cassio,
Lieutenant to the warlike Moor, Othello,
Is come on shore: the Moor himself's at sea,
And is in full commission here for Cyprus.

Mon. I am glad on 't: 't is a worthy governor.

3rd Gent. But this same Cassio, though he
    speak of comfort
Touching the Turkish loss, yet he looks sadly,
And prays the Moor be safe; for they were parted
With foul and violent tempest.

Mon.   'Pray heaven he be;
For I have served him, and the man commands
Like a full soldier. Let's to the sea-side, ho!
As well to see the vessel that's come in,
As throw out our eyes for brave Othello,
Even till we make the main and the aerial blue
An indistinct regard.

3rd Gent.   Come, let's do so:
For every minute is expectancy
Of more arrivance.

Enter CASSIO.

Cas. Thanks to the valiant of this warlike isle,
That so approve the Moor. O, let the heavens
Give him defence against the elements,
For I have lost him on a dangerous sea.

Mon. Is he well shipped?

Cas. His bark is stoutly timbered, and his pilot
Of very expert and approved allowance:
Therefore my hopes, not surfeited to death,
Stand in bold cure.

[*Within.*]   A sail, a sail, a sail!

Enter another Gentleman.

Cas. What noise?

4th Gent. The town is empty; on the brow o'
    the sea
Stand ranks of people, and they cry, " A sail."

Cas. My hopes do shape him for the governor.

2nd Gent. They do discharge their shots of
    courtesy: [*Guns heard.*
Our friends, at least.

Cas.   I pray you, sir, go forth,
And give us truth who 't is that is arrived.

2nd Gent. I shall.   [*Exit.*

Mon. But, good lieutenant, is your general wived?

Cas. Most fortunately: he hath achieved a maid
That paragons description and wild fame:
One that excels the quirks of blazoning pens,
And in the essential vesture of creation
Does bear all excellency.—How now; who has
    put in?

Re-enter Second Gentleman.

2nd Gent. 'T is one Iago, ancient to the general.

Cas. He has had most favourable and happy speed:
Tempests themselves, high seas and howling winds,
The guttered rocks and congregated sands
(Traitors ensteeped to clog the guiltless keel),
As having sense of beauty, do omit
Their mortal natures, letting go safely by
The divine Desdemona.

Mon.   What is she?

Cas. She that I spake of, our great captain's
    captain,
Left in the conduct of the bold Iago;
Whose footing here anticipates our thoughts
A se'nnight's speed.—Great Jove, Othello guard,
And swell his sail with thine own powerful breath;
That he may bless this bay with his tall ship,
Make love's quick pants in Desdemona's arms,
Give renewed fire to our extincted spirits,
And bring all Cyprus comfort!—O, behold,

Enter DESDEMONA, EMILIA, IAGO, RODERIGO,
and Attendants.

The riches of the ship is come on shore!
Ye men of Cyprus, let her have your knees:—
Hail to thee, lady! and the grace of heaven,
Before, behind thee, and on every hand,
Enwheel thee round!

Des.   I thank you, valiant Cassio.
What tidings can you tell me of my lord?

Cas. He is not yet arrived; nor know I aught
But that he 's well, and will be shortly here.

Des. O, but I fear—How lost you company?

Cas. The great contention of the sea and skies
Parted our fellowship. But hark! a sail.

[*Cry within, "A sail, a sail!" Then guns heard.*

2nd Gent. They give their greeting to the citadel:
This likewise is a friend.

Cas.   See for the news. [*Exit* Gentleman.
Good ancient, you are welcome:—Welcome,
    mistress:—   [*To* EMILIA.
Let it not gall your patience, good Iago,
That I extend my manners: 'tis my breeding
That gives me this bold show of courtesy.
    [*Kissing her.*

Iago. Sir, would she give you so much of her lips
As of her tongue she oft bestows on me,
You 'd have enough.

Des.   Alas, she has no speech.

Iago. In faith, too much:
I find it still when I have list to sleep:
Marry, before your ladyship, I grant
She puts her tongue a little in her heart,
And chides with thinking.

Emil.   You have little cause to say so.

Iago. Come on, come on: you are pictures
    out of doors;
Bells in your parlours, wild cats in your kitchens;
Saints in your injuries; devils, being offended;
Players in your housewifery, and housewives in
    your beds.

Des. O, fie upon thee, slanderer!

Iago. Nay it is true, or else I am a Turk:
You rise to play, and go to bed to work.

Emil. You shall not write my praise.

Iago.   No, let me not.

Des. What wouldst thou write of me, if thou
　　shouldst praise me?

Iago. O, gentle lady, do not put me to 't;
For I am nothing if not critical.

Des. Come on, assay.—There 's one gone to
　　the harbour?

Iago. Ay, madam.

Des. I am not merry; but I do beguile

The thing I am by seeming otherwise.—
Come, how wouldst thou praise me?

Iago. I am about it; but indeed my invention
Comes from my pate as birdlime does from frieze,
It plucks out brains and all: but my muse labours,
And thus she is delivered:—
If she be fair and wise,—fairness and wit,
The one 's for use; the other useth it.

Des. Well praised! How if she be black and
witty?

Iago. If she be black, and thereto have a wit,
She 'll find a white that shall her blackness fit.

Des. Worse and worse.

Emil. How if fair and foolish?

Iago. She never yet was foolish that was fair:
For even her folly helped her to an heir.

Des. These are old fond paradoxes, to make
fools laugh i' the alehouse. What miserable
praise hast thou for her that 's foul and foolish?

Iago. There 's none so foul, and foolish thereunto,

But does foul pranks, which fair and wise ones do.

Des. O heavy ignorance!—thou praisest the
worst best. But what praise couldst thou bestow
on a deserving woman indeed? one that, in the
authority of her merit, did justly put on the
vouch of very malice itself?

Iago. She that was ever fair, and never proud;
Had tongue at will, and yet was never loud;
Never lacked gold, and yet went never gay;
Fled from her wish, and yet said,—" Now I
　　may;"
She that, being angered, her revenge being nigh,
Bade her wrong stay, and her displeasure fly;
She that in wisdom never was so frail
To change the cod's head for the salmon's tail;

She that could think, and ne'er disclose her mind;
See suitors following, and not look behind:
She was a wight, if ever such wight were,—

Des. To do what?

Iago. To suckle fools, and chronicle small beer.

Des. O most lame and impotent conclusion!—
Do not learn of him, Emilia, though he be thy
husband.—How say you, Cassio; is he not a most
profane and liberal counsellor?

Cas. He speaks home, madam: you may relish
him more in the soldier than in the scholar.

Iago [*aside*]. He takes her by the palm. Ay,
well said, whisper: with as little a web as this
will I ensnare as great a fly as Cassio. Ay, smile
upon her, do: I will gyve thee in thine own courtship. You say true! 'tis so, indeed. If such
tricks as these strip you out of your lieutenantcy,
it had been better you had not kissed your three
fingers so oft, which now again you are most apt
to play the sir in. Very good: well kissed! an
excellent courtesy! 'tis so, indeed. Yet again
your fingers to your lips? would they were clyster-
pipes for your sake!—[*Trumpet*]. The Moor;
I know his trumpet.

Cas. 'Tis truly so.

Des. Let's meet him, and receive him.

Cas. Lo, where he comes!

Enter OTHELLO, *and* Attendants.

Oth. O my fair warrior!

Des.   My dear Othello!

Oth. It gives me wonder great as my content
To see you here before me. O my soul's joy!
If after every tempest come such calms,
May the winds blow till they have wakened death:
And let the labouring bark climb hills of seas,
Olympus-high; and duck again as low
As hell's from heaven! If it were now to die,
'Twere now to be most happy; for I fear
My soul hath her content so absolute,
That not another comfort like to this
Succeeds in unknown fate.

Des.   The heavens forbid
But that our loves and comforts should increase,
Even as our days do grow!

Oth.   Amen to that, sweet powers!—
I cannot speak enough of this content,
It stops me here; it is too much of joy:
And this, and this, the greatest discords be,
That e'er our hearts shall make! [*Kissing her.*

Iago.   O, you are well tuned now!
But I'll set down the pegs that make this music,
As honest as I am.   [*Aside.*

Oth.   Come, let's to the castle.—
News, friends: our wars are done; the Turks are
        drowned.
How do our old acquaintance of this isle?—

Honey, you shall be well desired in Cyprus;
I have found great love amongst them. O my sweet,
I prattle out of fashion, and I dote
In mine own comforts.—I pr'ythee, good Iago,
Go to the bay, and disembark my coffers:
Bring thou the master to the citadel;
He is a good one, and his worthiness
Does challenge much respect.—Come, Desde-
        mona:
Once more well met at Cyprus.

[*Exeunt* OTHELLO, DESDEMONA, *and* Attendants.

Iago. Do thou meet me presently at the harbour. Come hither:—if thou beest valiant (as
they say, base men, being in love, have then a
nobility in their natures more then is native to
them), list me. The lieutenant to-night watches
on the court of guard:—first, I must tell thee
this—Desdemona is directly in love with him.

Rod. With him! why 'tis not possible.

Iago. Lay thy finger—thus, and let thy soul
be instructed. Mark me with what violence she
first loved the Moor, but for bragging and telling
her fantastical lies: and will she love him still for
prating? let not thy discreet heart think it. Her
eye must be fed; and what delight shall she have
to look on the devil? When the blood is made
dull with the act of sport, there should be, again
to inflame it and to give satiety a fresh appetite,
loveliness in favour; sympathy in years, manners,
and beauties; all which the Moor is defective in.
Now, for want of these required conveniences,
her delicate tenderness will find itself abused,
begin to heave the gorge, disrelish and abhor
the Moor: very nature will instruct her in it,
and compel her to some second choice. Now,
sir, this granted (as it is a most pregnant and
unforced position), who stands so eminently in
the degree of this fortune as Cassio does?—a
knave very voluble; no further conscionable than
in putting on the mere form of civil and humane
seeming, for the better compassing of his salt
and most hidden loose affection—why, none;
why, none. A slippery and subtle knave; a
finder-out of occasions; that has an eye to
stamp and counterfeit advantages, though true
advantage never present itself. A devilish knave!
Besides, the knave is handsome, young, and hath
all those requisites in him that folly and green
minds look after. A pestilent complete knave!
and the woman hath found him already.

Rod. I cannot believe that in her: she is full
of most blessed condition.

Iago. Blessed fig's-end!—the wine she drinks
is made of grapes. If she had been blessed, she
would never have loved the Moor. Blessed
pudding!—Didst thou not see her paddle with
the palm of his hand? didst not mark that?

Rod. Yes, that I did; but that was but courtesy.

Iago. Lechery, by this hand; an index and obscure prologue to the history of lust and foul thoughts. They met so near with their lips that their breaths embraced together. Villanous thoughts, Roderigo! When these mutualities so marshal the way, hard at hand comes the master and main exercise, the incorporate conclusion. Pish!—But, sir, be you ruled by me: I have brought you from Venice. Watch you to-night; for the command, I 'll lay 't upon you. Cassio knows you not:—I 'll not be far from you. Do you find some occasion to anger Cassio; either by speaking too loud, or tainting his discipline, or from what other course you please which the time shall more favourably minister.

Rod. Well.

Iago. Sir, he is rash and very sudden in choler; and haply with his truncheon may strike at you. Provoke him that he may: for even out of that will I cause these of Cyprus to mutiny; whose qualification shall come into no true taste again but by the displanting of Cassio. So shall you have a shorter journey to your desires, by the means I shall then have to prefer them; and the impediment most profitably removed, without the which there were no expectation of our prosperity.

Rod. I will do this, if I can bring it to any opportunity.

Iago. I warrant thee. Meet me by-and-by at the citadel. I must fetch his necessaries ashore. Farewell.

Rod. Adieu.   [*Exit.*

Iago. That Cassio loves her, I do well believe it;
That she loves him, 't is apt and of great credit:
The Moor, howbeit that I endure him not,
Is of a constant, loving, noble nature,
And I dare think he 'll prove to Desdemona
A most dear husband. Now I do love her too;
Not out of absolute lust (though peradventure
I stand accountant for as great a sin),
But partly led to diet my revenge,
For that I do suspect the lusty Moor
Hath leaped into my seat: the thought whereof
Doth, like a poisonous mineral, gnaw my inwards;
And nothing can or shall content my soul
Till I am even with him, wife for wife:
Or, failing so, yet that I put the Moor
At least into a jealousy so strong
That judgment cannot cure. Which thing to do,—
If this poor trash of Venice, whom I trash
For his quick hunting, stand the putting on,
I 'll have our Michael Cassio on the hip;
Abuse him to the Moor in the rank garb,—
For I fear Cassio with my night-cap too:
Make the Moor thank me, love me, and reward me,

For making him egregiously an ass,
And practising upon his peace and quiet
Even to madness.—'T is here, but yet confused:
Knavery's plain face is never seen till used. [*Exit.*

Scene II.—*A Street.*

Enter a Herald, *with a proclamation:* People
following.

Her. It is Othello's pleasure, our noble and valiant general, that, upon certain tidings now arrived, importing the mere perdition of the Turkish fleet, every man put himself into triumph: some to dance, some to make bonfires; each man to what sport and revels his addiction leads him: for, besides these beneficial news, it is the celebration of his nuptials. So much was his pleasure should be proclaimed.—All offices are open, and there is full liberty of feasting from this present hour of five till the bell hath told eleven.—Heaven bless the Isle of Cyprus, and our noble general, Othello!   [*Exeunt.*

Scene III.—*A Hall in the Castle.*

Enter OTHELLO, DESDEMONA, CASSIO, *and*
Attendants.

Oth. Good Michael, look you to the guard tonight:
Let 's teach ourselves that honourable stop,
Not to outsport discretion.

Cas. Iago hath direction what to do:
But, notwithstanding, with my personal eye
Will I look to 't.

Oth. Iago is most honest.
Michael, good night: to-morrow with your earliest,
Let me have speech with you.—Come, my dear love:
The purchase made, the fruits are to ensue;
              [*To* DESDEMONA.
That profit 's yet to come 'twixt me and you.—
Good night.
[*Exeunt* OTHELLO, DESDEMONA, *and* Attendants.

Enter IAGO.

Cas. Welcome, Iago. We must to the watch.

Iago. Not this hour, lieutenant: 't is not yet ten o'clock. Our general cast us thus early, for the love of his Desdemona; whom let us not therefore blame: he hath not yet made wanton the night with her; and she is sport for Jove.

Cas. She 's a most exquisite lady.

Iago. And, I 'll warrant her, full of game.

Cas. Indeed she is a most fresh and delicate creature.

Iago. What an eye she has! methinks it sounds a parley of provocation.

Cas. An inviting eye; and yet methinks right modest.

Iago. And when she speaks, is it not an alarum to love?

Cas. She is indeed perfection.

Iago. Well, happiness to their sheets!—Come, lieutenant, I have a stoop of wine: and here without are a brace of Cyprus gallants, that would fain have a measure to the health of the black Othello.

Cas. Not to-night, good Iago: I have very poor and unhappy brains for drinking. I could well wish courtesy would invent some other custom of entertainment.

Iago. O, they are our friends: but one cup. I 'll drink for you.

Cas. I have drunk but one cup to-night, and that was craftily qualified too; and behold what innovation it makes here! I am unfortunate in the infirmity, and dare not task my weakness with any more.

Iago. What, man! 'tis a night of revels: the gallants desire it.

Cas. Where are they?

Iago. Here at the door: I pray you, call them in.

Cas. I 'll do it; but it dislikes me.   [*Exit.*

Iago. If I can fasten but one cup upon him,
With that which he hath drunk to-night already,
He 'll be as full of quarrel and offence
As my young mistress' dog. Now, my sick fool, Roderigo,
Whom love has turned almost the wrong side outward,
To Desdemona hath to-night caroused
Potations pottle deep: and he 's to watch.
Three lads of Cyprus,—noble swelling spirits,
That holds their honours in a wary distance,
The very elements of this warlike isle,—
Have I to-night flustered with flowing cups:
And they watch too. Now, 'mongst this flock of drunkards,
Am I to put our Cassio in some action
That may offend the isle.—But here they come:
If consequence do but approve my dream,
My boat sails freely, both with wind and stream.

Re-enter CASSIO; *with him* MONTANO *and* Gentlemen.

Cas. 'Fore heaven, they have given me a rouse already.

Mon. Good faith, a little one: not past a pint, as I am a soldier,

Iago. Some wine, ho!

              Sings.

And let me the canakin clink, clink;
   And let me the canakin clink:
     A soldier 's a man;
     A life 's but a span;
   Why then let a soldier drink.

Some wine, boys!   [*Wines brought in.*

Cas. 'Fore heaven, an excellent song.

Iago. I learned it in England, where indeed they are most potent in potting: your Dane, your German, and your swag-bellied Hollander, — Drink, ho!—are nothing to your English.

Cas. Is your Englishman so expert in his drinking?

Iago. Why, he drinks you with facility your Dane dead drunk; he sweats not to overthrow your Almain; he gives your Hollander a vomit ere the next pottle can be filled.

Cas. To the health of our general.

Mon. I am for it, lieutenant; and I 'll do you justice.

Iago. O sweet England!

              Sings.

King Stephen was a worthy peer,
   His breeches cost him but a crown:
He held them sixpence all to dear;
   With that he called the tailor lown.
He was a wight of high renown,
   And thou art but of low degree:
'T is pride that pulls the country down,
   Then take thine auld cloak about thee.

Some wine, ho!

Cas. Why this is a more exquisite song than the other.

Iago. Will you hear it again?

Cas. No; for I hold him to be unworthy of his place, that does those things.—Well, Heaven's above all: and there be souls must be saved, and there be souls must not be saved.

Iago. It 's true, good lieutenant.

Cas. For mine own part,—no offence to the general, nor any man of quality,—I hope to be saved.

Iago. And so do I too, lieutenant.

Cas. Ay, but, by your leave, not before me: the lieutenant is to be saved before the ancient. —Let 's have no more of this: let 's to our affairs. —Forgive us our sins!—Gentlemen, let 's look to our business. Do not think, gentlemen, I am drunk: this is my ancient:—this is my right hand; and this is my left hand.—I am not drunk now: I can stand well enough, and speak well enough.

All. Excellent well.

Cas. Why, very well, then: you must not think, then, that I am drunk.   [*Exit.*

Mon. To the platform, masters: come, let 's set the watch.

Iago. You see this fellow that is gone before:
He is a soldier fit to stand by Cæsar
And give direction: and do but see his vice!
'T is to his virtue a just equinox,
The one as long as th' other: 't is pity of him.
I fear the trust Othello puts him in,
On some odd time of his infirmity,
Will shake this island.

Mon. But is he often thus?

Iago. 'T is evermore the prologue to his sleep.
He 'll watch the horologe a double set,
If drink rock not his cradle.

Mon. It were well
The general were put in mind of it.
Perhaps he sees it not; or his good nature
Prizes the virtue that appears in Cassio,
And looks not on his evils. Is not this true?

Enter RODERIGO.

Iago. How now, Roderigo?   [*Aside.*
I pray you, after the lieutenant : go.
                    [*Exit* RODERIGO.

Mon. And 't is great pity that the noble Moor
Should hazard such a place as his own second,
With one of an ingraft infirmity.
It were an honest action to say
So to the Moor.

Iago. Not I, for this fair island :
I do love Cassio well, and would do much
To cure him of this evil. But hark! what noise?
[*Cry within.*]   Help! help!

Re-enter CASSIO, *driving in* RODERIGO.

Cas. You rogue! you rascal!

Mon. What 's the matter, lieutenant?

Cas. A knave!—teach me my duty!
I 'll beat the knave into a twiggen bottle.

Rod. Beat me?

Cas. Dost thou prate, rogue?
                    [*Striking* RODERIGO.

Mon. Nay, good lieutenant : [*Staying him.*
I pray you, sir, hold your hand.

Cas. Let me go, sir,
Or I 'll knock you o'er the mazzard.

Mon Come, come, you 're drunk.

Cas. Drunk!   [*They fight.*

Iago. Away, I say! go out, and cry, "A mutiny."
                    [*Aside to* RODERIGO, *who goes out.*
Nay, good lieutenant;—alas, gentlemen :—
Help, ho!—Lieutenant;—Sir Montano;—sir :—
Help, masters!—Here 's a goodly watch, indeed!
                    [*Bell rings.*
Who 's that that rings the bell!—Diablo, ho!
The town will rise.—God's will, lieutenant, hold :
You will be shamed for ever.

Enter OTHELLO *and* Attendants.

Oth. What is the matter here?

Mon. I bleed still; I am hurt to the death!—
He dies!

Oth. Hold, for your lives.

Iago. Hold, hold, lieutenant;—Sir Montano;
—gentlemen,—
Have you forgot all sense of place and duty?
Hold, hold; the general speaks to you : hold,
    for shame!

Oth. Why, how now, ho!—from whence ariseth
    this?
Are we turned Turks, and to ourselves do that
Which heaven hath forbid the Ottomites?
For christian shame put by this barbarous brawl :
He that stirs next to carve for his own rage,
Holds his soul light : he dies upon his motion.—
Silence that dreadful bell, it frights the isle
From her propriety.—What is the matter, mas-
    ters?—
Honest Iago, that look'st dead with grieving,
Speak, who began this? on thy love I charge thee.

Iago. I do not know :—friends all but now,
    even now,
In quarter, and in terms like bride and groom
Divesting them for bed : and then, but now
(As if some planet had unwitted men),
Swords out, and tilting one at other's breast,
In opposition bloody. I cannot speak
Any beginning to this peevish odds :
And 'would in action glorious I had lost
These legs that brought me to a part of it!

Oth. How comes it, Michael, you are thus forgot?

Cas. I pray you, pardon me; I cannot speak.

Oth. Worthy Montano, you were wont be civil;
The gravity and stillness of your youth
The world hath noted, and your name is great
In mouths of wisest censure : what 's the matter,
That you unlance your reputation thus,
And spend your rich opinion for the name
Of a night-brawler? Give me answer to it.

Mon. Worthy Othello, I am hurt to danger :
Your officer, Iago, can inform you—
While I spare speech, which something now
    offends me,—
Of all that I do know : nor know I aught
By me that 's said or done amiss this night :
Unless self-charity be sometime a vice;
And to defend ourselves it be a sin,
When violence assails us.

Oth. Now, by heavens,
My blood begins my safer guides to rule;
And passion, having my best judgment collied,
Assays to lead the way. If I once stir,
Or do but lift this arm, the best of you
Shall sink in my rebuke. Give me to know
How this foul rout began, who set it on;
And he that is approved in this offence,
Though he had twinned with me, both at a birth,
Shall lose me.—What! in a town of war,
Yet wild, the people's hearts brimful of fear,
To manage private and domestic quarrel,
In night, and on the court of guard and safety!
'T is monstrous.—Iago, who began it?

Mon. If partially affined, or leagued in office,
Thou dost deliver more or less than truth,
Thou art no soldier.

Iago.　　　Touch me not so near:
I had rather have this tongue cut from my mouth,
Than it should do offence to Michael Cassio;
Yet, I persuade myself to speak the truth
Shall nothing wrong him.—Thus it is, general:
Montano and myself being in speech,

There comes a fellow crying out for help;
And Cassio following him, with determined sword,
To execute upon him.　Sir, this gentleman
Steps in to Cassio, and entreats his pause:
Myself the crying fellow did pursue,
Lest by his clamour (as it so fell out)

The town might fall in fright: he, swift of foot,
Outran my purpose; and I returned the rather
For that I heard the clink and fall of swords,
And Cassio high in oath; which till to-night
I ne'er might say before.　When I came back
(For this was brief), I found them close together,
At blow and thrust; even as again they were
When you yourself did part them.
More of this matter can I not report:—
But men are men; the best sometimes forget.
Though Cassio did some little wrong to him,
As men in rage strike those that wish them best,
Yet surely Cassio, I believe, received
From him that fled some strange indignity,
Which patience could not pass.

Oth.　　　I know, Iago,
Thy honesty and love doth mince this matter,
Making it light to Cassio.—Cassio, I love thee;
But never more be officer of mine.

Enter DESDEMONA, *attended.*

Look if my gentle love be not raised up!—
I 'll make thee an example.
　Des. What is the matter, dear?
　Oth. All 's well now, sweeting:
Come away to bed.—Sir, for your hurts,
Myself will be your surgeon.—Lead him off.
　　　　　[*To* MONTANO, *who is led off.*
Iago, look with care about the town,
And silence those whom this vile brawl distracted.—

Come, Desdemona: 't is the soldiers' life
To have their balmy slumbers waked with strife,
　　　　　　　[*Exeunt all but* IAGO *and* CASSIO.
Iago. What, are you hurt, lieutenant?
Cas. Ay, past all surgery.
Iago. Marry, heaven forbid!
Cas. Reputation, reputation, reputation! O,
I have lost my reputation! I have lost the
immortal part, sir, of myself, and what remains
is bestial.—My reputation, Iago; my reputation!
Iago. As I am an honest man, I thought you
had received some bodily wound: there is
more offence in that than in reputation. Reputation is an idle and most false imposition;
oft got without merit, and lost without deserving.
You have lost no reputation at all, unless you
repute yourself such a loser. What, man! there
are ways to recover the general again. You
are but now cast in his mood; a punishment
more in policy than in malice: even so as one
would beat his offenceless dog, to affright an
imperious lion. Sue to him again, and he 's
your's.
Cas. I will rather sue to be despised, than to
deceive so good a commander with so slight, so
drunken, and so indiscreet an officer. Drunk;
and speak parrot; and squabble; swagger;
swear; and discourse fustian with one's own
shadow!—O thou invisible spirit of wine, if
thou hast no name to be known by, let us
call thee devil!
Iago. What was he that you followed with
your sword? What had he done to you?
Cas. I know not.
Iago. Is it possible?
Cas. I remember a mass of things, but nothing
distinctly: a quarrel, but nothing wherefore.—O
that men should put an enemy in their mouths
to steal away their brains! that we should, with
joy, revel, pleasure, and applause, transform ourselves into beasts!
Iago. Why, but you are now well enough:
how came you thus recovered?
Cas. It hath pleased the devil drunkenness to
give place to the devil wrath: one imperfectness
shews me another, to make me frankly despise
myself.
Iago. Come, you are too severe a moraler.
As the time, the place, and the condition of this
country stands, I could heartily wish this had
not befallen: but since it is as it is, mend it for
your own good.
Cas. I will ask him for my place again: he
shall tell me I am a drunkard! Had I as many
mouths as Hydra, such an answer would stop
them all.—To be now a sensible man, by-and-by
a fool, and presently a beast! O strange!—

Every inordinate cup is unblessed, and the ingredient is a devil.
Iago. Come, come, good wine is a good familiar creature, if it be well used: exclaim no more
against it. And, good lieutenant, I think you
think I love you.
Cas. I have well approved it, sir.—I drunk!
Iago. You or any man living may be drunk
at some time, man. I 'll tell you what you shall
do. Our general's wife is now the general:—I
may say so in this respect, for that he hath
devoted and given up himself to the contemplation, mark, and denotement of her parts and
graces. Confess yourself freely to her; importune her: she 'll help to put you in your place
again. She is of so free, so kind, so apt, so
blessed a disposition, that she holds it a vice in
her goodness not to do more than she is requested. This broken joint between you and
her husband entreat her to splinter; and, my
fortunes against any lay worth naming, this
crack of your love shall grow stronger than it
was before.
Cas. You advise me well.
Iago. I protest, in the sincerity of love and
　　　　　honest kindness.
Cas. I think it freely; and betimes in the morning I will beseech the virtuous Desdemona to undertake for me. I am desperate of my fortunes,
if they check me here.
Iago. You are in the right. Good night, lieute-
nant: I must to the watch.
Cas. Good night, honest Iago.　　　　[*Exit.*
Iago. And what 's he, then, that says I play
　　　　　the villain;
When this advice is free I give, and honest,
Probal to thinking, and, indeed, the course
To win the Moor again? For 't is most easy
The inclining Desdemona to subdue
In any honest suit: she 's framed as fruitful
As the free elements. And then, for her
To win the Moor,—were 't to renounce his baptism,
All seals and symbols of redeeméd sin,—
His soul is so enfettered to her love
That she may make, unmake, do what she list,
Even as her appetite shall play the god
With his weak function. How am I, then, a villain,
To counsel Cassio to this parallel course,
Directly to his good?—Divinity of hell!
When devils will the blackest sins put on,
They do suggest at first with heavenly shows;
As I do now. For while this honest fool
Plies Desdemona to repair his fortunes,
And she for him pleads strongly to the Moor,
I 'll pour this pestilence into his ear,—
That she repeals him for her body's lust:
And by how much she strives to do him good,

She shall undo her credit with the Moor.
So will I turn her virtue into pitch,
And out of her own goodness make the net
That shall enmesh them all.—How now, Roderigo?

Enter RODERIGO.

Rod. I do follow here in the chase, not like a
hound that hunts, but one that fills up the cry.
My money is almost spent; I have been to-night
exceedingly well cudgelled; and I think the issue will be,—I shall have so much experience
for my pains : and so, with no money at all, and
a little more wit, return to Venice.

Iago. How poor are they that have not
    patience !
What wound did ever heal but by degrees?
Thou know'st we work by wit, and not by
    witchcraft ;

And wit depends on dilatory time.
Does 't not go well? Cassio hath beaten thee,
And thou by that small hurt hast cashiered Cassio.
Though other things grow fair against the sun,
Yet fruits that blossom first will first be ripe :
Content thyself awhile.—By the mass, 't is
    morning :
Pleasure and action make the hours seem short.—
Retire thee : go where thou art billetted.
Away, I say ; thou shalt know more hereafter.
Nay, get thee gone. [*Exit* RODERIGO.]—Two
    things are to be done :
My wife must move for Cassio to her mistress ;
I 'll set her on :
Myself, the while, to draw the Moor apart,
And bring him jump when he may Cassio find
Soliciting his wife.—Ay, that 's the way :
Dull not device by coldness and delay.   [*Exit.*

SCENE I.—*Before the Castle.*

Enter CASSIO, *and some* Musicians.

Cas. Masters, play here (I will content your
    pains)
Something that 's brief ; and bid, "Good-morrow,
    general."   [*Music.*

Enter Clown.

Clo. Why, masters, have your instruments been
at Naples, that they speak i' the nose thus?
1st Mus. How, sir, how?
Clo. Are these, I pray you, called wind instruments ?
1st Mus. Ay, marry are they, sir.
Clo. O, thereby hangs a tail.
1st Mus. Whereby hangs a tale, sir?
Clo. Marry, sir, by many a wind instrument
that I know. But, masters, here 's money for
you : and the general so likes your music, that
he desires you, of all loves, to make no more
noise with it.
1st Mus. Well, sir, we will not.

Clo. If you have any music that may not be
heard, to 't again : but, as they say, to hear
music the general does not greatly care.
1st Mus. We have none such, sir.
Clo. Then put up your pipes in your bag, for
I 'll away. Go ; vanish into air ; away.
                  [*Exeunt* Musicians.
Cas. Dost thou hear, my honest friend?
Clo. No, I hear not your honest friend ; I
hear you.
Cas. Pr'y thee, keep up thy quillets. There 's
a poor piece of gold for thee : if the gentlewoman
that attends the general's wife be stirring, tell
her there 's one Cassio entreats her a little favour
of speech. Wilt thou do this?
Clo. She is stirring, sir : if she will stir hither,
I shall seem to notify unto her.   [*Exit.*

Enter IAGO.

Cas. Do, good my friend.—In happy time, Iago.
Iago. You have not been abed, then?
Cas. Why, no : the day had broke
Before we parted.   I have made bold, Iago,

To send in to your wife: my suit to her
Is, that she will to virtuous Desdemona
Procure me some access.

   Iago.   I 'll send her to you, presently;
And I 'll devise a mean to draw the Moor
Out of the way, that your converse and business
May be more free.   [*Exit.*

   Cas. I humbly thank you for 't.—I never knew
A Florentine more kind and honest.

Enter EMILIA.

   Emil. Good-morrow, good lieutenant: I am
      sorry
For your displeasure; but all will soon be well.
The general and his wife are talking of it;
And she speaks for you stoutly. The Moor replies,
That he you hurt is of great fame in Cyprus,
And great affinity; and that, in wholesome
      wisdom,
He might not but refuse you: but he protests
      he loves you,
And needs no other suitor but his likings
To take the saf'st occasion by the front,
To bring you in again.

   Cas.   Yet, I beseech you
(If you think fit, or that it may be done),
Give me advantage of some brief discourse
With Desdemona alone.

   Emil.   Pray you, come in:
I will bestow you where you shall have time
To speak your bosom freely.

   Cas.   I am much bound to you. [*Exeunt.*

SCENE II.—*A Room in the Castle.*

Enter OTHELLO, IAGO, *and* Gentlemen.

   Oth. These letters give, Iago, to the pilot;
And by him do my duties to the state.
That done, I will be walking on the works:
Repair there to me.

   Iago.   Well, my good lord, I 'll do 't.

   Oth. This fortification, gentlemen, shall we see 't?

   Gent. We 'll wait upon your lordship. [*Exeunt.*

SCENE III.—*Before the Castle.*

Enter DESDEMONA, CASSIO, *and* EMILIA.

   Des. Be thou assured, good Cassio, I will do
All my abilities in thy behalf.

   Emil. Good madam, do: I know it grieves
      my husband
As if the case were his.

   Des. O, that 's an honest fellow.—Do not
      doubt, Cassio,
But I will have my lord and you again
As friendly as you were.

   Cas.   Bounteous madam,
Whatever shall become of Michael Cassio,
He 's never anything but your true servant.

   Des. O, sir, I thank you. You do love my lord:
You have known him long: and be you well assured
He shall in strangeness stand no further off
Than in a politic distance.

   Cas.   Ay, but, lady,
That policy may either last so long,
Or feed upon such nice and waterish diet,
Or breed itself so out of circumstance,
That, I being absent, and my place supplied,
My general will forget my love and service.

   Des. Do not doubt that: before Emilia here,
I give thee warrant of thy place: assure thee,
If I do vow a friendship I 'll perform it
To the last article. My lord shall never rest;
I 'll watch him tame, and talk him out of patience:
His bed shall seem a school, his board a shrift:
I 'll intermingle everything he does
With Cassio's suit. Therefore be merry, Cassio;
For thy solicitor shall rather die
Than give thy cause away.

Enter OTHELLO *and* IAGO, *at a distance.*

   Emil.   Madam, here comes
My lord.

   Cas.   Madam, I 'll take my leave.

   Des.   Why, stay,
And hear me speak.

   Cas. Madam, not now: I am very ill at ease;
Unfit for mine own purposes.

   Des. Well, do your discretion. [*Exit* CASSIO.

   Iago.   Ha! I like not that.

   Oth. What dost thou say?

   Iago. Nothing, my lord: or if—I know not what.

   Oth. Was not that Cassio parted from my wife?

   Iago. Cassio, my lord? No, sure, I cannot think it,
That he would steal away so guilty-like,
Seeing you coming.

   Oth.   I do believe 't was he.

   Des. How now, my lord?
I have been talking with a suitor here,
A man that languishes in your displeasure.

   Oth. Who is 't you mean?

   Des. Why, your lieutenant Cassio. Good my
      lord,
If I have any grace or power to move you,
His present reconciliation take:
For if he be not one that truly loves you,
That errs in ignorance and not in cunning,
I have no judgment in an honest face.
I pr'ythee call him back.

   Oth.   Went he hence now?

   Des. Ay, sooth; so humbled,
That he hath left part of his grief with me:
I suffer with him. Good love, call him back.

Oth. Not now, sweet Desdemona: some other
    time.

Des. But shall 't be shortly?

Oth.   The sooner, sweet, for you.

Des. Shall 't be to-night at supper?

Oth.   No, not to-night.

Des. To-morrow dinner, then?

Oth.   I shall not dine at home:
I meet the captains at the citadel.

   Des. Why then, to-morrow night; or Tuesday
    morn;

Or Tuesday noon, or night; or Wednesday
    morn:—

I pray thee, name the time; but let it not
Exceed three days. In faith, he 's penitent:
And yet his trespass, in our common reason
(Save that they say the wars must make examples
Out of their best), is not almost a fault
To incur a private check. When shall he come?
Tell me, Othello. I wonder in my soul
What you could ask me that I should deny,
Or stand so mammering on. What! Michael
    Cassio,

That came a wooing with you; and so many a
    time,

When I have spoke of you dispraisingly,
Hath ta'en your part: to have so much to do
To bring him in! Trust me, I could do much,—

Oth. Pr'y thee, no more: let him come when
    he will:
I will deny thee nothing.

   Des.   Why, this is not a boon:
'T is as I should entreat you wear your gloves,
Or feed on nourishing dishes, or keep you warm;
Or sue to you to do peculiar profit
To your own person. Nay, when I have a suit
Wherein I mean to touch your love indeed,
It shall be full of poize and difficulty,
And fearful to be granted.

   Oth.   I will deny thee nothing:
Whereon, I do beseech thee grant me this,
To leave me but a little to myself.

   Des. Shall I deny you? no. Farewell, my lord.

   Oth. Farewell, my Desdemona: I will come
    to thee straight.

   Des. Emilia, come.—Be it as your fancies
    teach you:
Whate'er you be, I am obedient. [*Exit with* EMILIA.

   Oth. Excellent wretch! Perdition catch my soul
But I do love thee! and, when I love thee not,
Chaos is come again.

   Iago. My noble lord,—

   Oth.   What dost thou say, Iago?

   Iago. Did Michael Cassio, when you wooed
    my lady,
Know of your love?

Oth. He did, from first to last. Why dost thou ask?

Iago. But for a satisfaction of my thought:
No further harm.

Oth.   Why of thy thought, Iago?

Iago. I did not think he had been acquainted
   with her.

Oth. O yes; and went between us very oft.

Iago. Indeed?

Oth. Indeed! ay, indeed.—Discern'st thou
   aught in that?
Is he not honest?

Iago.   Honest, my lord?

Oth.   Honest!—Ay, honest.

Iago. My lord, for aught I know.

Oth. What dost thou think?

Iago.   Think, my lord?

Oth.   Think, my lord!
By heaven, he echoes me,
As if there were some monstér in his thought
Too hideous to be shewn.—Thou dost mean some-
     thing:
I heard thee say but now,—Thou lik'dst not that,
When Cassio left my wife. What didst not like?
And when I told thee he was of my counsel
In my whole course of wooing, thou criedst,
   "Indeed?"
And didst contract and purse thy brow together,
As if thou then hadst shut up in thy brain
Some horrible conceit. If thou dost love me,
Shew me thy thought.

Iago. My lord, you know I love you.

Oth.   I think thou dost:
And, for I know thou art full of love and honesty,
And weigh'st thy words before thou giv'st them
     breath,
Therefore these stops of thine fright me the more:
For such things in a false disloyal knave
Are tricks of custom; but in a man that's just,
They are close denotements working from the heart,
That passion cannot rule.

Iago.   For Michael Cassio,
I dare be sworn I think that he is honest.

Oth. I think so too.

Iago.   Men should be what they seem;
Or, those that be not, 'would they might seem none.

Oth. Certain, men should be what they seem.

Iago. Why then, I think Cassio's an honest man.

Oth. Nay, yet there's more in this:
I pray thee, speak to me as to thy thinkings,
As thou dost ruminate; and give thy worst of
     thoughts
The worst of words.

Iago.   Good my lord, pardon me:
Though I am bound to every act of duty,
I am not bound to all that slaves are free to.
Utter my thoughts! Why, say they are vile and
     false,—

As where's that palace whereinto foul things
Sometimes intrude not?—who has a breast so pure
But some uncleanly apprehensions
Keep leets and law-days, and in session sit
With meditations lawful?

Oth. Thou dost conspire against thy friend, Iago,
If thou but think'st him wronged, and mak'st his
     ear
A stranger to thy thoughts.

Iago.   I do beseech you,
Though I perchance am vicious in my guess
(As I confess it is my nature's plague
To spy into abuses; and oft my jealousy
Shapes faults that are not),—I entreat you then,
From one that so imperfectly conjects,
You'd take no notice; nor build yourself a trouble
Out of his scattering and unsure observance.
It were not for your quiet nor your good,
Nor for my manhood, honesty, or wisdom,
To let you know my thoughts.

Oth.   What dost thou mean?

Iago. Good name, in man and woman, dear
   my lord,
Is the immediate jewel of their souls:
Who steals my purse, steals trash: 'tis some-
     thing, nothing;
'T was mine, 'tis his, and has been slave to thou-
     sands:
But he that filches from me my good name,
Robs me of that which not enriches him,
And makes me poor indeed.

Oth. By heaven, I'll know thy thought.

Iago. You cannot, if my heart were in your hand;
Nor shall not, whilst 'tis in my custody.

Oth. Ha!

Iago.   O beware, my lord, of jealousy:
It is the green-eyed monster which doth make
The meat it feeds on. That cuckold lives in bliss,
Who, certain of his fate, loves not his wronger:
But O, what damnéd minutes tells he o'er,
Who dotes, yet doubts; suspects, yet strongly loves!

Oth. O misery!

Iago. Poor and content is rich, and rich enough:
But riches, fineless, is as poor as winter,
To him that ever fears he shall be poor.
Good heaven, the souls of all my tribe defend
From jealousy!

Oth.   Why! why is this?
Think'st thou I'd make a life of jealousy,
To follow still the changes of the moon
With fresh suspicions? No: to be once in doubt,
Is—once to be resolved. Exchange me for a goat,
When I shall turn the business of my soul
To such exsufflicate and blown surmises,
Matching thy inference. 'T is not to make me
     jealous,
To say my wife is fair, feeds well, loves company;

Is free of speech; sings, plays, and dances well:
Where virtue is, these are more virtuous.
Nor from mine own weak merits will I draw
The smallest fear or doubt of her revolt:
For she had eyes, and chose me. No, Iago:
I 'll see before I doubt; when I doubt, prove:
And, on the proof, there is no more but this,—
Away at once with love or jealousy.

   Iago. I am glad of this; for now I shall have
       reason
To shew the love and duty that I bear you
With franker spirit: therefore, as I am bound,
Receive it from me:—I speak not yet of proof:—
Look to your wife; observe her well with Cassio:
Wear your eye thus,—not jealous, nor secure.
I would not have your free and noble nature,
Out of self-bounty, be abused: look to 't.
I know our country disposition well:
In Venice they do let heaven see the pranks
They dare not shew their husbands: their best
       conscience
Is not to leave undone, but keep unknown.

   Oth. Dost thou say so?

   Iago. She did deceive her father, marrying you;
And when she seemed to shake and fear your looks,
She loved them most.

   Oth.　　　　And so she did.

   Iago.　　　　　　　Why, go to, then:
She that so young could give out such a seeming,
To seel her father's eyes up close as oak,—
He thought 't was witchcraft:—but I am much
       to blame:
I humbly do beseech you of your pardon,
For too much loving you.

   Oth.　　　　I am bound to thee for ever.

   Iago. I see this hath a little dashed your spirits.

   Oth. Not a jot, not a jot.

   Iago.　　　　Trust me, I fear it has.
I hope you will consider what is spoke
Comes from my love.—But I do see you are
      moved:
I am to pray you not to strain my speech
To grosser issues nor to larger reach
Than to suspicion.

   Oth. I will not.

   Iago.　　　　Should you do so, my lord,
My speech should fall into such vile success
As my thoughts aim not at. Cassio 's my worthy
      friend:—
My lord, I see you are moved.

   Oth.　　　　No, not much moved:
I do not think but Desdemona 's honest.

   Iago. Long live she so: and long live you to
      think so.

   Oth. And yet, how nature erring from itself,—

   Iago. Ay, there 's the point:—as (to be bold
      with you)

Not to affect many proposéd matches
Of her own clime, complexion, and degree;
Whereto we see in all things nature tends:
Foh! one may smell in such a will most rank,
Foul disproportion, thoughts unnatural:—
But pardon me: I do not in position
Distinctly speak of her: though I may fear,
Her will, recoiling to her better judgment,
May fall to match you with her country forms,
And, happily, repent.

   Oth.　　　　Farewell, farewell.
If more thou dost perceive, let me know more:
Set on thy wife to observe. Leave me, Iago.

   Iago. My lord, I take my leave. 　[*Going.*

   Oth. Why did I marry?—This honest creature,
      doubtless,
Sees and know more, much more, than he unfolds.

   Iago. My lord, I would I might entreat your
      honour
To scan this thing no further: leave it to time.
And though it be fit that Cassio have his place
(For sure he fills it up with great ability),
Yet if you please to hold him off awhile,
You shall by that perceive him and his means.
Note, if your lady strain his entertainment
With any strong or vehement importunity:
Much will be seen in that. In the meantime,
Let me be thought too busy in my fears
(As worthy cause I have to fear I am),
And hold her free, I do beseech your honour.

   Oth. Fear not my government.

   Iago. I once more take my leave. 　[*Exit.*

   Oth. This fellow 's of exceeding honesty,
And knows all qualities, with a learnéd spirit,
Of human dealings.—If I do prove her haggard,
Though that her jesses were my dear heart-strings,
I 'd whistle her off, and let her down the wind,
To prey at fortune.—Haply for I am black,
And have not those soft parts of conversation
That chamberers have: or, for I am declined
Into the vale of years;—yet that 's not much:—
She 's gone; I am abused; and my relief
Must be to loath her.—O curse of marriage,
That we can call these delicate creatures ours,
And not their appetites! I had rather be a toad,
And live upon the vapour of a dungeon,
Than keep a corner in the thing I love
For others' uses. Yet 't is the plague of great ones;
Prerogatived are they less than the base:
'T is destiny unshunnable, like death:
Even then this forkéd plague is fated to us,
When we do quicken.—Desdemona comes:

     Enter DESDEMONA *and* EMILIA.

If she be false, O then heaven mocks itself!—
I 'll not believe it.

   Des.　　　　How now, my dear Othello?

Your dinner, and the generous islanders
By you invited, do attend your presence.

    Oth. I am to blame.

    Des. Why is your speech so faint? are you not
        well?

    Oth. I have a pain upon my forehead here.

    Des. Faith, that 's with watching; 't will away
        again:
Let me but bind it hard, within this hour
It will be well.

    Oth.   Your napkin is too little:

    [*He puts the handkerchief from him, and
        it drops.*
Let it alone. Come, I 'll go in with you.

    Des. I am very sorry that you are not well.

    [*Exeunt* OTHELLO *and* DESDEMONA.

    Emil. I am glad I have found this napkin:
This was her first remembrance from the Moor.
My wayward husband hath a hundred times
Wooed me to steal it; but she so loves the token
(For he conjúred her she would ever keep it),
That she reserves it evermore about her,
To kiss and talk to. I 'll have the work ta'en out,
And give it Iago:
What he 'll do with it, heaven knows, not I;
I nothing, but to please his fantasy.

Enter IAGO.

    Iago. How now! what do you here alone?

    Emil. Do not you chide: I have a thing for you.

    Iago. A thing for me? It is a common thing,—

    Emil. Ha!

    Iago. To have a foolish wife.

    Emil. O, is that all? What will you give me now
For that same handkerchief?

    Iago.   What handkerchief?

    Emil. What handkerchief?
Why that the Moor first gave to Desdemona;
That which so often you did bid me steal.

    Iago. Hast stolen it from her?

    Emil. No, faith; she let it drop by negligence;
And, to the advantage, I, being here, took it up.
Look, here it is.

    Iago.   A good wench: give it me.

    Emil. What will you do with it, that you have
        been so earnest
To have me filch it?

    Iago.   Why, what 's that to you?

    [*Snatching it.*

    Emil. If it be not for some purpose of import,
Give it me again. Poor lady! she 'll run mad
When she shall lack it.

    Iago. Be not you known of 't: I have use for it.
Go, leave me.   [*Exit* EMILIA.
I will in Cassio's lodging lose this napkin,
And let him find it. Trifles light as air
Are to the jealous confirmations strong

As proofs of holy writ. This may do something.
The Moor already changes with my poison:
Dangerous conceits are in their nature poisons,
Which at the first are scarce found to distaste;
But, with a little act upon the blood,
Burn like the mines of sulphur.—I did say so:
Look where he comes!—Not poppy, nor man-
    dragora,
Nor all the drowsy syrups of the world,
Shall ever medicine thee to that sweet sleep
Which thou ow'dst yesterday.

Enter OTHELLO.

    Oth.   Ha, ha! false to me? to me?

    Iago. Why, how now, general? no more of that.

    Oth. Avaunt; be gone! thou hast set me on
        the rack:
I swear 't is better to be much abused,
Than but to know 't a little.

    Iago.   How now, my lord?

    Oth. What sense had I of her stolen hours of
        lust?
I saw it not, thought it not, it harmed not me:
I slept the next night well, was free and merry:
I found not Cassio's kisses on her lips.
He that is robbed, not wanting what is stolen,
Let him not know it, and he 's not robbed at all,

    Iago. I am sorry to hear this.

    Oth. I had been happy if the general camp,
Pioneers and all, had tasted her sweet body,
So I had nothing known.—O now, for ever,
Farewell the tranquil mind: farewell content!
Farewell the pluméd troop, and the big wars,
That make ambition virtue! O, farewell!
Farewell the neighing steed, and the shrill trump,
The spirit-stirring drum, the ear-piercing fife,
The royal banner; and all quality,
Pride, pomp, and circumstance of glorious war!
And O you mortal engines, whose rude throats
The immortal Jove's dread clamours counterfeit,
Farewell!—Othello's occupation 's gone!

    Iago. Is it possible? My lord,—

    Oth. Villain, be sure thou prove my love a
        whore:
Be sure of it; give me the ocular proof;

    [*Taking him by the throat.*
Or, by the worth of mine eternal soul,
Thou hadst been better have been born a dog,
Than answer my waked wrath.

    Iago.   Is it come to this?

    Oth. Make me to see it: or, at the least, so
        prove it
That the probation bear no hinge nor loop
To hang a doubt on: or woe upon thy life!

    Iago. My noble lord,—

    Oth. If thou dost slander her and torture me,
Never pray more: abandon all remorse:

On horror's head horrors accumulate :
Do deeds to make heaven weep, all earth amazed :
For nothing canst thou to damnation add
Greater than that !
    Iago.   O grace ! O heaven defend me !
Are you a man ? have you a soul or sense ?—
God be with you : take mine office.—O wretched
         fool,
That liv'st to make thine honesty a vice !—
O monstrous world ! Take note, take note, O world,
To be direct and honest is not safe.—
I thank you for this profit ; and from hence
I 'll love no friend, since love breeds such offence.
    Oth. Nay, stay.—Thou shouldst be honest.
    Iago. I should be wise ; for honesty 's a fool,
And loses that it works for.
    Oth.   By the world,
I think my wife be honest, and think she is not ;
I think that thou art just, and think thou art not :
I 'll have some proof. Her name, that was as fresh

As Dian's visage, is now begrimed and black
As mine own face.—If there be cords or knive
Poison or fire, or suffocating streams,
I 'll not endure it.—Would I were satisfied !
    Iago. I see, sir, you are eaten up with passior
I do repent me that I put it to you.
You would be satisfied ?
    Oth.   Would ! nay, I will.
    Iago. And may. But, how ; how satisfied, n
         lord ?
Would you, the supervisor, grossly gape on :
Behold her tupped ?
    Oth. Death and damnation ! O !
    Iago. It were a tedious difficulty, I think,
To bring them to that prospect : damn them the
If ever mortal eyes do see them bolster,
More than their own !—What then ; how then
What shall I say ? Where 's satisfaction ?
It is impossible you should see this,
Were they as prime as goats, as hot as monkey

As salt as wolves in pride, and fools as gross
As ignorance made drunk. But yet I say,
If imputation and strong circumstances,
Which lead directly to the door of truth,
Will give you satisfaction, you may have it.

   Oth. Give me a living reason she 's disloyal.

   Iago. I do not like the office:
But sith I am entered in this cause so far,
Pricked to it by foolish honesty and love,
I will go on. I lay with Cassio lately;
And being troubled with a raging tooth,
I could not sleep.
There are a kind of men so loose of soul
That in their sleeps will mutter their affairs;
One of this kind is Cassio:
In sleep I heard him say,—"Sweet Desdemona,
Let us be wary; let us hide our loves!"
And then, sir, would he gripe and wring my hand,
Cry,—"O, sweet creature!" and then kiss me hard,
As if he plucked up kisses by the roots,
That grew upon my lips: then laid his leg
Over my thigh, and sighed and kissed; and then
Cried,—"Curséd fate, that gave thee to the Moor!"

   Oth. O monstrous! monstrous!

   Iago.   Nay, this was but his dream.

   Oth. But this denoted a foregone conclusion.

   Iago. 'T is a shrewd doubt, though it be but a
      dream:
And this may help to thicken other proofs,
That do demonstrate thinly.

   Oth.   I 'll tear her all to pieces.

   Iago. Nay, but be wise: yet we see nothing done:
She may be honest yet. Tell me but this:
Have you not sometimes seen a handkerchief
Spotted with strawberries, in your wife's hand?

   Oth. I gave her such a one; 't was my first gift.

   Iago. I know not that: but such a handkerchief
(I am sure it was your wife's) did I to-day
See Cassio wipe his beard with.

   Oth.   If it be that,—

   Iago. If it be that, or any that was her's,
It speaks against her with the other proofs.

   Oth. O, that the slave had forty thousand lives:
One is too poor, too weak for my revenge!
Now do I see 't is true.—Look here, Iago;
All my fond love thus I do blow to heaven:
'T is gone.—
Arise, black vengeance, from the hollow hell!
Yield up, O love, thy crown and hearted throne,
To tyrannous hate! Swell, bosom, with thy fraught,
For 't is of aspics' tongues!

   Iago. Pray, be content.

   Oth.   O, blood, Iago, blood!

   Iago. Patience, I say: your mind, perhaps,
      may change.

   Oth. Never, Iago. Like to the Pontic sea,
Whose icy current and compulsive course

Ne'er feels retiring ebb, but keeps due on
To the Propontic and the Hellespont;
Even so my bloody thoughts, with violent pace,
Shall ne'er look back, ne'er ebb to humble love,
Till that a capable and wide revenge
Swallow them up.—Now, by yond' marble heaven,
In the due reverence of a sacred vow   [*Kneels.*
I here engage my words.

   Iago.   Do not rise yet.   [*Kneels.*
Witness, you ever-burning lights above!
You elements that clip us round about!
Witness that here Iago doth give up
The execution of his wit, hands, heart,
To wronged Othello's service! Let him command,
And to obey shall be in me remorse,
What bloody work soever—

   Oth.   I greet thy love,
Not with vain thanks, but with acceptance boun-
      teous,
And will upon the instant put thee to 't:
Within these three days let me hear thee say
That Cassio 's not alive.

   Iago. My friend is dead; 'tis done at thy request:
But let her live.

   Oth.   Damn her, lewd minx! O, damn her!
Come, go with me apart: I will withdraw,
To furnish me with some swift means of death
For the fair devil. Now art thou my lieutenant.

   Iago. I am your own for ever.   [*Exeunt.*

SCENE IV.—*The same.*

Enter DESDEMONA, EMILIA, *and* Clown.

   Des. Do you know, sirrah, where Lieutenant
Cassio lies?

   Clo. I dare not say he lies any where.

   Des. Why, man?

   Clo. He is a soldier; and for me to say a
      soldier lies, is stabbing.

   Des. Go to: where lodges he!

   Clo. To tell you where he lodges, is to tell
      you where I lie.

   Des. Can anything be made of this?

   Clo. I know not where he lodges; and for
me to devise a lodging, and say he lies here, or
he lies there, were to lie in my own throat.

   Des. Can you inquire him out, and be edified
by report?

   Clo. I will catechise the world for him: that
is, make questions, and by them answer.

   Des. Seek him; bid him come hither: tell
him I have moved my lord in his behalf, and
hope all will be well.

   Clo. To do this is within the compass of
man's wit; and therefore I will attempt the
doing it.   [*Exit.*

Des. Where should I lose that handkerchief,
 Emilia?

Emil. I know not, madam.

Des. Believe me, I had rather have lost my purse
Full of crusadoes. And but my noble Moor
Is true of mind, and made of no such baseness
As jealous creatures are, it were enough
To put him to ill thinking.

Emil.   Is he not jealous?

Des. Who, he? I think the sun where he was born
Drew all such humours from him.

Emil.   Look where he comes.

Des. I will not leave him now till Cassio
Be called to him.—How is 't with you, my lord?

   Enter OTHELLO.

Oth. Well, my good lady:—[*Aside*] O, hardness to dissemble!—
How do you, Desdemona?

Des. Well, my good lord.

Oth. Give me your hand.—This hand is
 moist, my lady.

Des. It yet has felt no age, nor known no sorrow.

Oth. This argues fruitfulness and liberal heart:
Hot, hot, and moist. This hand of yours requires
A sequester from liberty, fasting and prayer,
Much castigation, exercise devout:
For here 's a young and sweating devil here,
That commonly rebels. 'T is a good hand;
A frank one.

Des.   You may, indeed, say so;
For 't was that hand, that gave away my heart.

Oth. A liberal hand. The hearts of old gave
 hands;
But our new heraldry is—hands, not hearts.

Des. I cannot speak of this. Come now,
 your promise.

Oth. What promise, chuck?

Des. I have sent to bid Cassio come speak with
 you.

Oth. I have a salt and sullen rheum offends me:
Lend me thy handkerchief.

Des.   Here, my lord.

Oth. That which I gave you.

Des.   I have it not about me.

Oth. Not?

Des.   No, indeed, my lord.

Oth.   That is a fault:
That handkerchief
Did an Egyptian to my mother give:
She was a charmer, and could almost read
The thoughts of people. She told her, while she
 kept it
'T would make her amiable, and subdue my father
Entirely to her love: but if she lost it,
Or made a gift of it, my father's eye
Should hold her loathly, and his spirits should hunt

After new fancies. She, dying, gave it me:
And bid me, when my fate would have me wive,
To give it her. I did so: and take heed of 't,
Make it a darling like your precious eye:
To lose or give 't away, were such perdition
As nothing else could match.

Des.   Is it possible?

Oth. 'T is true. There 's magic in the web of it:
A sibyl, that had numbered in the world
The sun to make two hundred compasses,
In her prophetic fury sewed the work:
The worms were hallowed that did breed the silk:
And it was dyed in mummy which the skilful
Conserved of maidens' hearts.

Des.   Indeed! is 't true?

Oth. Most veritable; therefore look to 't well.

Des. Then 'would to heaven that I had never
 seen it.

Oth. Ha! wherefore?

Des. Why do you speak so startingly and rash?

Oth. Is 't lost? is 't gone? Speak, is 't out of
 the way?

Des. Heaven bless us!

Oth.   Say you?

Des. It is not lost: but, what an if it were?

Oth. Ha!

Des. I say, it is not lost.

Oth.   Fetch it; let me see it.

Des. Why, so I can, sir, but I will not now:
This is a trick to put me from my suit.
I pray, let Cassio be received again.

Oth. Fetch me that handkerchief.—My mind
 misgives.

Des. Come, come:
You 'll never meet a more sufficient man.

Oth. The handkerchief!

Des.   I pray, talk me of Cassio.

Oth. The handkerchief!

Des.   A man that, all his time,
Hath founded his good fortune on your love;
Shared dangers with you;—

Oth.   The handkerchief?

Des. In sooth you are to blame.

Oth. Away!   [*Exit.*

Emil.   Is not this man jealous?

Des. I ne'er saw this before.
Sure there 's some wonder in this handkerchief:
I am most unhappy in the loss of it.

Emil. 'T is not a year or two shews us a man:
They are all but stomachs, and we all but food:
They eat us hungrily, and when they are full,
They belch us.—Look you! Cassio and my
 husband.

   Enter IAGO *and* CASSIO.

Iago. There is no other way; 't is she must do 't:
And lo, the happiness! Go, and importune her.

Des. How now, good Cassio; what 's the news
    with you?

Cas. Madam, my former suit. I do beseech you
That, by your virtuous means, I may again
Exist, and be a member of his love
Whom I, with all the duty of my heart
Entirely honour.   I would not be delayed:
If my offence be of such mortal kind,
That neither service past, nor present sorrows,
Nor purposed merit in futurity,
Can ransom me into his love again,
But to know so must be my benefit:
So shall I clothe me in a forced content,
And shut myself up in some other course,
To fortune's alms.

Des.   Alas! thrice-gentle Cassio,
My advocation is not now in tune:
My lord is not my lord; nor should I know him
Were he in favour as in humour altered.
So help me every spirit sanctified
As I have spoken for you all my best,
And stood within the blank of his displeasure
For my free speech. You must a while be patient:
What I can do, I will; and more I will
Than for myself I dare.   Let that suffice you.

Iago. Is my lord angry?

Emil.   He went hence but now;
And certainly in strange unquietness.

Iago. Can he be angry? I have seen the cannon
When it hath blown his ranks into the air;
And, like the devil, from his very arm
Puffed his own brother:—and can he be angry?
Something of moment, then. I will go meet him:
There 's matter in 't indeed, if he be angry.

Des. I pr'y thee, do so.—Something, sure, of
    state,   [*Exit* IAGO.
Either from Venice, or some unhatched practice
Made démonstrable here in Cyprus to him,
Had puddled his clear spirit: and in such cases
Men's natures wrangle with inferior things,
Though great ones are their object. 'T is even so:
For let our finger ache, and it indues
Our other healthful members ev'n to that sense
Of pain.   Nay, we must think men are not gods;
Nor of them look for such observances
As fit the bridal.—Beshrew me much, Emilia,
I was (unhandsome warrior as I am)
Arraigning his unkindness with my soul:
But now I find I had suborned the witness,
And he 's indicted falsely.

Emil. Pray heaven it be state matters, as you
    think;
And no conception nor no jealous toy
Concerning you.

Des. Alas, the day! I never gave him cause.

Emil. But jealous souls will not be answered so:
They are not ever jealous for the cause;

But jealous for they are jealous.   'T is a monster
Begot upon itself, born on itself.

Des. Heaven keep that monster from Othello's
    mind!

Emil. Lady, amen.

Des. I will go seek him.—Cassio, walk here-
    about:
If I do find him fit, I 'll move your suit,
And seek to effect it to my uttermost.

Cas. I humbly thank your ladyship.
            [*Exeunt* DESDEMONA *and* EMILIA.

Enter BIANCA.

Bian. Save you, friend Cassio!

Cas.   What make you from home?
How is it with you, my most fair Bianca?
I' faith, sweet love, I was coming to your house.

Bian. And I was going to your lodging, Cassio.
What, keep a week away! seven days and nights;
Eight-score eight hours? and lovers' absent hours,
More tedious than the dial eight-score times:
O weary reckoning!

Cas.   Pardon me, Bianca:
I have this while with leaden thoughts been
    pressed;
But I shall, in a more continuate time,
Strike off this score of absence.   Sweet Bianca,
    [*Giving her* DESDEMONA's *handkerchief.*
Take me this work out.

Bian. O, Cassio, whence came this?
This is some token from a newer friend.
To the felt absence now I feel a cause:
Is it come to this?   Well, well.

Cas.   Go to, woman!
Throw your vile guesses in the devil's teeth,
From whence you have them. You are jealous now
That this is from some mistress, some remem-
    brance:
No, in good truth, Bianca.

Bian.   Why, whose is it?

Cas. I know not, sweet: I found it in my cham-
    ber.
I like the work well: ere it be demanded
(As like enough it will), I 'd have it copied.
Take it, and do 't; and leave me for this time.

Bian. Leave you! wherefore?

Cas. I do attend here on the general;
And think it no addition, nor my wish,
To have him see me womaned.

Bian.   Why, I pray you?

Cas. Not that I love you not.

Bian.   But that you do not love me.
I pray you, bring me on the way a little;
And say if I shall see you soon at night.

Cas. 'T is but a little way, that I can bring you,
For I attend here: but I 'll see you soon.

Bian. 'T is very good: I must be circumstanced.
            [*Exeunt.*

ACT

IV

Scene I.—*Before the Castle.*

Enter Othello *and* Iago.

Iago. Will you think so?
Oth.   Think so, Iago?
Iago.   What,
To kiss in private?
Oth.   An unauthorised kiss.
Iago. Or to be naked with her friend abed,
An hour or more, not meaning any harm?
Oth. Naked abed, Iago, and not mean harm!
It is hypocrisy against the devil:
They that mean virtuously, and yet do so,
The devil their virtue tempts, and they tempt
          heaven.
Iago. So they do nothing, 't is a venial slip:
But if I give my wife a handkerchief,—
Oth. What then?
Iago. Why, then, 't is hers, my lord; and
          being hers,
She may, I think, bestow 't on any man.
Oth. She is protectress of her honour too:
May she give that?
Iago. Her honour is an essence that 's not seen;
They have it very oft, that have it not:
But, for the handkerchief,—
Oth. By heaven, I would most gladly have
          forgot it!
Thou saidst—O, it comes o'er my memory
As doth the raven o'er the infected house,
Boding to all—he had my handkerchief.
Iago. Ay, what of that?
Oth.   That 's not so good, now.
Iago. What if I had said I had seen him do
          you wrong?
Or heard him say—(as knaves be such abroad,
Who having, by their own importunate suit,
Or voluntary dotage of some mistress,

Convinced or supplied them, cannot choose
But they must blab),—
Oth.   Hath he said anything?
Iago. He hath, my lord: but, be you well
          assured,
No more than he 'll unswear.
Oth.   What hath he said?
Iago. 'Faith, that he did—I know not what
          he did.
Oth. What; what?
Iago. Lie—
Oth.   With her?
Iago.   With her; on her: what you will.
Oth. Lie with her! lie on her!—We say, lie
on her, when they belie her. Lie with her!
that 's fulsome.—Handkerchief,—confessions,—
handkerchief!—To confess, and be hanged for
his labour.—First, to be hanged, and then to
confess:—I tremble at it. Nature would not
invest herself in such shadowing passion, without
some instruction. It is not words that shake me
thus.—Pish!—Noses, ears, and lips:—Is it possible?—Confess!—Handkerchief!—O devil!
                              [*Falls in a trance.*
Iago. Work on,
My medicine, work! Thus credulous fools are
          caught;
And many worthy and chaste dames, even thus,
All guiltless meet reproach.—What, ho! my lord!

Enter Cassio.

My lord, I say! Othello!—How now, Cassio?
Cas. What is the matter?
Iago. My lord is fallen into an epilepsy:
This is his second fit; he had one yesterday.
Cas. Rub him about the temples.
Iago.   No, forbear:
The lethargy must have his quiet course:

a

If not, he foams at mouth, and by-and-by
Breaks out to savage madness.   Look, he stirs:
Do you withdraw yourself a little while;
He will recover straight: when he is gone,
I would on great occasion speak with you.—
                         [*Exit* CASSIO.
How is it, general? have you not hurt your head?
  Oth. Dost thou mock me?
  Iago.   I mock you! no, by heaven:
'Would you would bear your fortunes like a man.
  Oth. A hornéd man 's a monster and a beast.

Iago. There 's many a beast, then, in a popu-
             lous city;
And many a civil monster.
  Oth. Did he confess it?
  Iago.   Good sir, be a man:
Think every bearded fellow, that 's but yoked,
May draw with you.   There 's millions now alive
That nightly lie in those unproper beds
Which they dare swear peculiar: your case is
             better.
O, 't is the spite of hell, the fiend's arch-mock,

To lip a wanton in a secure couch,
And to suppose her chaste!—No, let me know:
And, knowing what I am, I know what she shall be.
  Oth. O, thou art wise: 't is certain.
  Iago.   Stand you awhile apart;
Confine yourself but in a patient list.
Whilst you were here, ere while mad with your
             grief
(A passion most unsuiting such a man),
Cassio came hither: I shifted him away,
And laid good 'scuse upon your ecstasy:
Bade him anon return, and here speak with me;
The which he promised.   Do but encave yourself,
And mark the fleers, the gibes, and notable scorns,
That dwell in every region of his face;

For I will make him tell the tale anew,
Where, how, how oft, how long ago, and when
He hath, and is again to cope your wife:
I say, but mark his gesture.   Marry, patience;
Or I shall say you are all in all in spleen,
And nothing of a man.
  Oth.   Dost thou hear, Iago?
I will be found most cunning in my patience;
But (dost thou hear) most bloody.
  Iago.   That 's not amiss;
But yet keep time in all.   Will you withdraw?
                         [OTHELLO *withdraws.*
Now will I question Cassio of Bianca,
A housewife that, by selling her desires,
Buys herself bread and clothes: it is a creature

That dotes on Cassio,—as 'tis the strumpet's plague
To beguile many, and be beguiled by one :
He, when he hears of her, cannot refrain
From the excess of laughter.—Here he comes.
As he shall smile, Othello shall go mad ;
And his unbookish jealousy must construe
Poor Cassio's smiles, gestures, and light behaviour,

Re-enter CASSIO.

Quite in the wrong.—How do you now, lieutenant ?
　Cas. The worser that you give me the addition
Whose want even kills me.
　Iago. Ply Desdemona well, and you are sure of 't.
Now, if this suit lay in Bianca's power,
　　　　　　　　　　　　　　[Speaking lower.
How quickly should you speed !
　Cas.　　　　Alas, poor caitiff !
　Oth. Look, how he laughs already !　*[Aside.*
　Iago. I never knew a woman love man so.
　Cas. Alas, poor rogue, I think, i' faith, she
loves me.
　Oth. Now he denies it faintly, and laughs it out.
　　　　　　　　　　　　　　[Aside.
　Iago. Do you hear, Cassio ?
　Oth.　　　　Now he importunes him
To tell it o'er :—go to ; well said, well said. *[Aside.*
　Iago. She gives it out that you shall marry her :
Do you intend it ?
　Cas.　　　　Ha, ha, ha !
　Oth. Do you triumph, Roman ? do you triumph ?
　　　　　　　　　　　　　　[Aside.
　Cas. I marry her !—what ? a customer ! I pr'y-
thee, bear some charity to my wit ; do not think
it so unwholesome. Ha, ha, ha !
　Oth. So, so, so, so : they laugh that win. *[Aside.*
　Iago. 'Faith, the cry goes that you shall marry
　　her.
　Cas. Pr'ythee, say true.
　Iago. I am a very villain else.
　Oth. Have you scored me ? Well.　*[Aside.*
　Cas. This is the monkey's own giving out : she
is persuaded I will marry her, out of her own love
and flattery, not out of my promise.
　Oth. Iago beckons me : now he begins the story.
　　　　　　　　　　　　　　[Aside.
　Cas. She was here even now : she haunts me
in every place. I was, the other day, talking on
the sea-bank with certain Venetians ; and thither
comes this bauble : by this hand, she falls thus
about my neck,—
　Oth. Crying, " O dear Cassio !" as it were : his
gesture imports it.　　　　　　　*[Aside.*
　Cas. So hangs, and lolls, and weeps upon me ;
so hales and pulls me : ha, ha, ha !
　Oth. Now he tells how she plucked him to my
chamber :—O, I see that nose of yours, but not
that dog I shall throw it to.　　　*[Aside.*

　Cas. Well, I must leave her company.
　Iago. Before me ! look where she comes.

Enter BIANCA.

　Cas. 'T is such another fitchew ! marry, a perfumed one.—What do you mean by this haunting
of me ?
　Bian. Let the devil and his dam haunt you !
What did you mean by that same handkerchief
you gave me even now ? I was a fine fool to take
it. I must take out the whole work !—A likely
piece of work that you should find it in your
chamber, and not know who left it there ! This
is some minx's token, and I must take out the
work ! There,—give it your hobby-horse : where-
soever you had it, I 'll take out no work on 't.
　Cas. How now, my sweet Bianca ? how now ;
how now ?
　Oth. By heaven, that should be my handkerchief !　　　　　　　　　　　　*[Aside.*
　Bian. An you 'll come to supper to-night, you
may : an you will not, come when you are next
prepared for.　　　　　　　　　*[Exit.*
　Iago. After her, after her.
　Cas. 'Faith I must, she 'll rail in the street else.
　Iago. Will you sup there ?
　Cas. 'Faith, I intend so.
　Iago. Well, I may chance to see you ; for I
would very fain speak with you.
　Cas. Pr'ythee, come : will you ?
　Iago. Go to ; say no more.　　*[Exit* CASSIO.
　Oth. How shall I murder him, Iago ?
　Iago. Did you perceive how he laughed at his
　　vice ?
　Oth. O, Iago !
　Iago. And did you see the handkerchief ?
　Oth. Was that mine ?
　Iago. Yours, by this hand : and to see how he
prizes the foolish woman your wife ! she gave it
him, and he hath given it his whore.
　Oth. I would have him nine years a killing.—
A fine woman ! a fair woman ! a sweet woman !
　Iago. Nay, you must forget that.
　Oth. Ay, let her rot and perish, and be damned
to-night ; for she shall not live. No, my heart
is turned to stone : I strike it, and it hurts my
hand.—O, the world hath not a sweeter creature :
she might lie by an emperor's side, and command
him tasks.
　Iago. Nay, that 's not your way.
　Oth. Hang her ! I do but say what she is.—
So delicate with her needle ! An admirable musi-
cian : O, she will sing the savageness out of a bear !
Of so high and plenteous wit and invention !
　Iago. She 's the worse for all this.
　Oth. O, a thousand, a thousand times.—And
then, of so gentle a condition !

Iago. Ay, too gentle.

Oth. Nay, that's certain. But yet the pity of it, Iago!—O, Iago, the pity of it, Iago!

Iago. If you are so fond over her iniquity, give her patent to offend: for if it touch not you, it comes near nobody.

Oth. I will chop her into messes.—Cuckold me!

Iago. O, 't is foul in her.

Oth. With mine officer!

Iago. That's fouler.

Oth. Get me some poison, Iago: this night.— I 'll not expostulate with her, lest her body and beauty unprovide my mind again.—This night, Iago.

Iago. Do it not with poison: strangle her in her bed; even the bed she hath contaminated.

Oth. Good, good: the justice of it pleases: very good.

Iago. And for Cassio, let me be his undertaker. You shall hear more by midnight.

[*A trumpet within.*

Oth. Excellent good.—What trumpet is that same?

Iago. Something from Venice, sure. 'T is Lodovico,
Come from the Duke: and see, your wife is with him.

Enter LODOVICO, DESDEMONA, *and* Attendants.

Lod. 'Save you, worthy general!

Oth. With all my heart, sir.

Lod. The Duke and senators of Venice greet you. [*Gives him a packet.*

Oth. I kiss the instrument of their pleasures.
[*Opens the packet, and reads.*

Des. And what's the news, good cousin Lodovico?

Iago. I am very glad to see you, signior:
Welcome to Cyprus.

Lod. I thank you. How does Lieutenant Cassio?

Iago. Lives, sir.

Des. Cousin, there's fallen between him and my lord
An unkind breach: but you shall make all well.

Oth. Are you sure of that?

Des. My lord?

OTHELLO *reads.*
" This fail you not to do, as you will—"

Lod. He did not call: he 's busy in the paper.
Is there division 'twixt thy lord and Cassio?

Des. A most unhappy one: I would do much
To atone them, for the love I bear to Cassio.

Oth. Fire and brimstone!

Des. My lord?

Oth. Are you wise?

Des. What, is he angry?

Lod. 'May be the letter moved him:
For, as I think, they do command him home,
Deputing Cassio in his government.

Des. By my troth, I am glad on 't.

Oth. Indeed?

Des. My lord?

Oth. I am glad to see you mad.

Des. How, sweet Othello?

Oth. Devil! [*Striking her.*

Des. I have not deserved this.

Lod. My lord, this would not be believed in Venice,
Though I should swear I saw it. 'T is very much:
Make her amends: she weeps.

Oth. O devil, devil!
If that the earth could teem with woman's tears,
Each drop she falls would prove a crocodile.—
Out of my sight!

Des. I will not stay to offend you. [*Going.*

Lod. Truly, an obedient lady.
I do beseech your lordship, call her back.

Oth. Mistress—

Des. My lord?

Oth. What would you with her, sir?

Lod. Who, I, my lord?

Oth. Ay; you did wish that I would make her turn:
Sir, she can turn, and turn, and yet go on,
And turn again: and she can weep, sir, weep:
And she 's obedient, as you say; obedient:
Very obedient.—Proceed you in your tears.—
Concerning this, sir,—O well-painted passion!—
I am commanded home.—Get you away:
I 'll send for you anon.—Sir, I obey the mandate,
And will return to Venice.—Hence, avaunt!
[*Exit* DESDEMONA.
Cassio shall have my place.—And, sir, to-night,
I do entreat that we may sup together.
You are welcome, sir, to Cyprus.—Goats and monkeys! [*Exit.*

Lod. Is this the noble Moor, whom our full senate
Call all-in-all sufficient?—This the noble nature
Whom passion could not shake? whose solid virtue
The shot of accident, nor dart of chance,
Could neither graze nor pierce?

Iago. He is much changed.

Lod. Are his wits safe? is he not light of brain?

Iago. He is that he is: I may not breathe my censure.
What he might be (if what he might he is not),
I would to heaven he were.

Lod. What, strike his wife!

Iago. 'Faith, that was not so well: yet 'would I knew
That stroke would prove the worst.

Lod. 　　　　Is it his use?
Or did the letters work upon his blood,
And new-create this fault?
　Iago. 　　　　Alas, alas!
It is not honesty in me to speak
What I have seen and known. You shall observe
　　him;
And his own courses will denote him so
That I may save my speech. Do but go after,
And mark how he continues.
　Lod. I am sorry that I am deceived in him.
　　　　　　　　　　　　　　　[*Exeunt.*

SCENE II.—*A Room in the Castle.*

Enter OTHELLO *and* EMILIA.

Oth. You have seen nothing, then?
Emil. Nor ever heard; nor ever did suspect.
Oth. Yes, you have seen Cassio and she together.
Emil. But then I saw no harm; and then I heard
Each syllable that breath made up between them.
Oth. What, did they never whisper?
Emil. 　　　　Never, my lord.
Oth. Nor send you out o' the way?
Emil. 　　　　Never.
Oth. To fetch her fan, her gloves, her mask, nor
　　nothing?
Emil. Never, my lord.
Oth. 　　　　That's strange.
Emil. I durst, my lord, to wager she is honest,
Lay down my soul at stake: if you think other,
Remove your thought: it doth abuse your bosom.
If any wretch hath put this in your head,
Let heaven requite it with the serpent's curse!
For if she be not honest, chaste, and true,
There's no man happy; the purest of their wives
Is foul as slander.
Oth. 　　　Bid her come hither: go. [*Exit* EMILIA.
She says enough: yet she's a simple bawd
That cannot say as much. This is a subtle whore,
A closet-lock-and-key of villanous secrets:
And yet she'll kneel and pray: I have seen her do't.

Re-enter EMILIA, *with* DESDEMONA.

Des. My lord, what is your will?
Oth. 　　　　Pray, chuck, come hither.
Des. What is your pleasure?
Oth. 　　　　Let me see your eyes:
Look in my face.
Des. 　　　　What horrible fancy's this?
Oth. Some of your function, mistress:
　　　　　　　　　　　　　　　[*To* EMILIA.
Leave procreants alone, and shut the door:
Cough or cry "hem," if anybody come.
Your mystery, your mystery:—nay, despatch.
　　　　　　　　　　　　　　　[*Exit* EMILIA.

Des. Upon my knees, what doth your speech
　　import?
I understand a fury in your words,
But not the words.
Oth. Why, what art thou?
Des. 　　　　Your wife, my lord: your true
And loyal wife.
Oth. 　　　　Come, swear it; damn thyself:
Lest, being like one of heaven, the devils themselves
Should fear to seize thee: therefore be double-
　　damned:
Swear thou art honest.
Des. 　　　　Heaven doth truly know it.
Oth. Heaven truly knows that thou art false as
　　hell.
Des. To whom, my lord? with whom? How
　　am I false?
Oth. O Desdemona!—away; away; away!
Des. Alas, the heavy day!—Why do you weep?
Am I the occasion of these tears, my lord?
If, haply, you my father do suspect
An instrument of this your calling back,
Lay not your blame on me: if you have lost him,
Why, I have lost him too.
Oth. 　　　　Had it pleased Heaven
To try me with affliction; had he rained
All kinds of sores and shames on my bare head;
Steeped me in poverty to the very lips;
Given to captivity me and my utmost hopes;
I should have found in some part of my soul
A drop of patience: but, alas! to make me
A fixéd figure for the time of scorn
To point his slow unmoving finger at,—
O! O!
Yet could I bear that too: well, very well:
But there where I have garnered up my heart;
Where either I must live or bear no life;
The fountain from the which my current runs,
Or else dries up: to be discarded thence!
Or keep it as a cistern, for foul toads
To knot and gender in!—turn thy complexion
　　there,
Patience, thou young and rose-lipped cherubin:
Ay, there, look grim as hell!
Des. I hope my noble lord esteems me honest.
Oth. O, ay, as summer flies are in the shambles,
That quicken even with blowing. O thou weed,
Who art so lovely fair, and smell'st so sweet,
That the sense aches at thee,—'would thou hadst
　　ne'er been born!
Des. Alas, what ignorant sin have I committed?
Oth. Was this fair paper, this most goodly book,
Made to write "whore" upon?—What committed?
Committed!—O thou public commoner,
I should make very forges of my cheeks,
That would to cinders burn up modesty,
Did I but speak thy deeds!—What committed!

Heaven stops the nose at it, and the moon winks:
The bawdy wind, that kisses all it meets,
Is hushed within the hollow mine of earth,
And will not hear it.—What committed !—
Impudent strumpet !

    Des.   By heaven, you do me wrong.
    Oth. Are not you a strumpet ?

    Des.   No, as I am a Christian :
If to preserve this vessel for my lord,
From any other foul unlawful touch,
Be—not to be a strumpet, I am none.

    Oth. What, not a whore ?
    Des.   No, as I shall be saved.
    Oth. Is it possible ?

    Des. O, heaven forgive us !
    Oth.   I cry you mercy, then :
I took you for that cunning whore of Venice
That married with Othello.—You, mistress,

Re-enter EMILIA.

That have the office opposite to St. Peter,
And keep the gate of hell : you, you, ay, you !
We have done our course : there's money for
       your pains :
I pray you turn the key, and keep our counsel.
                      [*Exit.*

    Emil. Alas, what does this gentleman con-
       ceive ?—
How do you, madam ? how do you, my good lady ?
    Des. 'Faith, half asleep.
    Emil. Good madam, what's the matter with
       my lord ?
    Des. With who ?
    Emil.   Why, with my lord, madam.
    Des. Who is thy lord ?
    Emil.   He that is yours, sweet lady.
    Des. I have none. Do not talk to me, Emilia :

I cannot weep; nor answer have I none,
But what should go by water. Pr'y thee, to-night
Lay on my bed my wedding sheets: remember:—
And call thy husband hither.

    Emil.   Here is a change, indeed! [*Exit.*

    Des. 'Tis meet I should be used so, very meet.
How have I been behaved, that he might stick
The small'st opinion on my great'st abuse?

Re-enter EMILIA, *with* IAGO.

    Iago. What is your pleasure, madam? How
      is it with you?

    Des. I cannot tell. Those that do teach young
      babes,
Do it with gentle means and easy tasks:
He might have chid me so; for, in good faith,
I am a child to chiding.

    Iago.   What's the matter, lady?

    Emil. Alas, Iago, my lord hath so bewhored her,
Thrown such despite and heavy terms upon her,
As true hearts cannot bear.

    Des. Am I that name, Iago?

    Iago.   What name, fair lady?

    Des. Such as she says my lord did say I was.

    Emil. He called her whore:—a beggar, in his
      drink
Could not have laid such terms upon his callet.

    Iago. Why did he so?

    Des. I do not know: I am sure I am none such.

    Iago. Do not weep, do not weep. Alas, the day!

    Emil. Has she forsook so many noble matches,
Her father, and her country, and her friends,
To be called whore? Would it not make one weep?

    Des. It is my wretched fortune.

    Iago.   Beshrew him for it!
How comes this trick upon him?

    Des.   Nay, heaven doth know.

    Emil. I will be hanged, if some eternal villain,
Some busy and insinuating rogue,
Some cogging, cozening slave, to get some office,
Have not devised this slander: I'll be hanged else.

    Iago. Fie, there is no such man: it is impossible.

    Des. If any such there be, heaven pardon him!

    Emil. A halter pardon him; and hell gnaw his
      bones!—
Why should he call her whore? who keeps her
      company?
What place; what time; what form; what like-
      lihood?
The Moor's abused by some most villanous knave,
Some base notorious knave, some scurvy fellow:—
O heaven, that such companions thou'dst unfold;
And put in every honest hand a whip,
To lash the rascal naked through the world,
Even from the east to the west!

    Iago.   Speak within door.

    Emil. O, fie upon him! Some such squire he was

That turned your wit the seamy side without,
And made you to suspect me with the Moor.

    Iago. You are a fool: go to.

    Des.   O good Iago,
What shall I do to win my lord again?
Good friend, go to him; for, by this light of
      heaven,
I know not how I lost him. Here I kneel:—
If e'er my will did trespass 'gainst his love,
Either in discourse of thought, or actual deed;
Or that mine eyes, mine ears, or any sense,
Delighted them in any other form;
Or that I do not yet, and ever did,
And ever will,—though he do shake me off
To beggarly divorcement,—love him dearly,
Comfort forswear me! Unkindness may do much;
And his unkindness may defeat my life,
But never taint my love. I cannot say, whore;
It does abhor me, now I speak the word:
To do the act that might the addition earn,
Not the world's mass of vanity could make me.

    Iago. I pray you, be content; 'tis but his humour:
The business of the state does him offence,
And he does chide with you.

    Des.   If 't were no other,—

    Iago. It is but so, I warrant you. [*Trumpets.*
Hark, how these instruments summon to supper!
And the great messengers of Venice stay.
Go in, and weep not: all things shall be well.
           [*Exeunt* DESDEMONA *and* EMILIA.

Enter RODERIGO.

How now, Roderigo?

    Rod. I do not find that thou deal'st justly
      with me.

    Iago. What in the contrary?

    Rod. Every day thou doff'st me with some de-
vice, Iago; and rather (as it seems to me now)
keep'st me from all conveniency, than suppliest
me with the least advantage of hope. I will, indeed, no longer endure it: nor am I yet persuaded
to put up in peace what already I have foolishly
suffered.

    Iago. Will you hear me, Roderigo?

    Rod. 'Faith, I have heard too much; for your
words and performances are in no kin together.

    Iago. You charge me most unjustly.

    Rod. With nought but truth. I have wasted
myself out of my means. The jewels you have
had from me, to deliver to Desdemona, would half
have corrupted a votarist. You have told me she
has received them, and returned me expectations
and comforts of sudden respect and acquittance:
but I find none.

    Iago. Well: go to: very well.

    Rod. Very well! go to! I cannot go to, man;
nor 'tis not very well. By this hand, I say it is

very scurvy; and begin to find myself fobbed in it.

Iago. Very well.

Rod. I tell you 't is not very well. I will make myself known to Desdemona: if she will return me my jewels, I will give over my suit, and repent my unlawful solicitation: if not, assure yourself I will seek satisfaction of you.

Iago. You have said now.

Rod. Ay, and I have said nothing but what I protest intendment of doing.

Iago. Why, now I see there 's mettle in thee; and even from this instant do build on thee a better opinion than ever before. Give me thy hand, Roderigo: thou hast taken against me a most just exception; but yet I protest I have dealt most directly in thy affair.

Rod. It hath not appeared.

Iago. I grant, indeed, it hath not appeared; and your suspicion is not without wit and judgment. But, Roderigo, if thou hast that within thee indeed which I have greater reason to believe now than ever,—I mean purpose, courage, and valour,—this night shew it: if thou the next night following enjoy'st not Desdemona, take me from this world with treachery, and devise engines for my life.

Rod. Well, what is it? is it within reason and compass?

Iago. Sir, there is especial commission come from Venice, to depute Cassio in Othello's place.

Rod. Is that true? Why, then Othello and Desdemona return again to Venice.

Iago. O, no: he goes into Mauritania, and takes away with him the fair Desdemona, unless his abode be lingered here by some accident: wherein none can be so determinate as the removing of Cassio.

Rod. How do you mean removing of him?

Iago. Why, by making him incapable of Othello's place: knocking out his brains.

Rod. And that you would have me do?

Iago. Ay; if you dare do yourself a profit and a right. He sups to-night with a harlot, and thither will I go to him:—he knows not yet of his honourable fortune. If you will watch his going thence (which I shall fashion to fall out between twelve and one), you may take him at your pleasure: I will be near to second your attempt, and he shall fall between us. Come, stand not amazed at it, but go along with me: I will shew you such a necessity in his death, that you shall think yourself bound to put it on him. It is now high supper-time, and the night grows to waste: about it.

Rod. I will hear further reason for this.

Iago. And you shall, be satisfied. [*Exeunt.*

SCENE III.—*Another Room in the Castle.*

Enter OTHELLO, LODOVICO, DESDEMONA, EMILIA, *and* Attendants.

Lod. I do beseech you, sir, trouble yourself no further.

Oth. O pardon me: 't will do me good to walk.

Lod. Madam, good night: I humbly thank your ladyship.

Des. Your honour is most welcome.

Oth.   Will you walk, sir?—
O,—Desdemona,—

Des.   My lord?

Oth. Get you to bed on the instant; I will be returned forthwith: dismiss your attendant there: look it be done.

Des. I will, my lord.

[*Exeunt* OTHELLO, LODOVICO, *and* Attendants.

Emil. How goes it now? he looks gentler than he did.

Des. He says he will return incontinent:
He hath commanded me to go to bed,
And bade me to dismiss you.

Emil.   Dismiss me!

Des. It was his bidding: therefore, good Emilia,
Give me my nightly wearing, and adieu:
We must not now displease him.

Emil. I would you had never seen him!

Des. So would not I: my love doth so approve him,
That even his stubbornness, his cheeks, and frowns,—
Pr'y thee unpin me,—have grace and favour in them.

Emil. I have laid those sheets you bade me on the bed.

Des. All 's one:—good father, how foolish are our minds!—
If I do die before thee, pr'y thee shroud me
In one of these same sheets.

Emil.   Come, come, you talk.

Des. My mother had a maid called Barbara:
She was in love; and he she loved proved mad,
And did forsake her. She had a song of "willow:"
An old thing 't was, but it expressed her fortune,
And she died singing it. That song, to-night,
Will not go from my mind: I have much to do
But to go hang my head all at one side,
And sing it like poor Barbara. Pr'y thee despatch.

Emil. Shall I go fetch your night-gown?

Des.   No, unpin me here.—
This Lodovico is a proper man.

Emil. A very handsome man.

Des.   And he speaks well.

Emil. I know a lady in Venice would have walked barefoot to Palestine for a touch of his nether lip.

DESDEMONA *sings.*

The poor soul sat sighing by a sycamore tree,
    Sing all a green willow;
Her hand on her bosom, her head on her knee,
    Sing willow, willow, willow:
The fresh streams ran by her, and murmured her moans;
    Sing willow, &c.
Her salt tears fell from her, and softened the stones.
Lay by these.—
    Sing willow, willow, willow.
Pr'y thee, hie thee: he'll come anon.—
    Sing all a green willow must be my garlánd.

Let nobody blame him, his scorn I approve,—
Nay, that's not next.—Hark! who is't that knocks?
  Emil. It is the wind.

DESDEMONA *sings.*

I called my love, false love; but what said he then?
    Sing willow, &c.
If I court mo women, you'll couch with mo men.

So get thee gone: good night. Mine eyes do itch:
Doth that bode weeping?
  Emil.   'T is neither here nor there.
  Des. I have heard it said so.—O, these men,
    these men!—
Dost thou in conscience think,—tell me, Emilia,—
That there be women do abuse their husbands
In such gross kind?
  Emil.   There be some such, no question.
  Des. Wouldst thou do such a deed for all the
    world?
  Emil. Why, would not you?
  Des.   No, by this heavenly light!
  Emil. Nor I neither by this heavenly light:
I might do 't as well i' the dark.
  Des. Wouldst thou do such a deed for all the
    world?
  Emil. The world is a huge thing: 't is a great
price for a small vice.
  Des. Good troth, I think thou wouldst not.

  Emil. By my troth, I think I should; and undo 't when I had done. Marry, I would not do
such a thing for a joint-ring; nor for measures
of lawn; nor for gowns, petticoats, nor caps, nor
any petty exhibition: but for the whole world,—
why, who would not make her husband a cuckold
to make him a monarch? I should venture purgatory for 't.
  Des. Beshrew me if I would do such a wrong
for the whole world.
  Emil. Why, the wrong is but a wrong i' the
world: and, having the world for your labour,
't is a wrong in your own world, and you might
quickly make it right.
  Des. I do not think there is any such woman.
  Emil. Yes, a dozen; and as many to the vantage
As would store the world they played for.
But I do think it is their husbands' faults
If wives do fall. Say that they slack their duties,
And pour our treasures into foreign laps;
Or else break out in peevish jealousies,
Throwing restraint upon us; or say they strike us,
Or scant our former having in despite:
Why, we have galls; and though we have some
    grace,
Yet we have some revenge. Let husbands know
Their wives have sense like them: they see and
    smell,
And have their palates both for sweet and sour,
As husbands have. What is it that they do,
When they change us for others? Is it sport?
I think it is: and doth affection breed it?
I think it doth: is 't frailty that thus errs?
It is so too. And have not we affections;
Desires for sport; and frailty, as men have?
Then let them use us well: else, let them know,
The ills we do, their ills instruct us so.
  Des. Good night, good night. Heaven me such
    usage send,
Not to pick bad from bad; but by bad, mend.
                         [*Exeunt.*

ACT V

SCENE I.—*A Street.*

Enter IAGO *and* RODERIGO.

Iago. Here, stand behind this bulk : straight
    will he come :
Wear thy good rapier bare, and put it home.
Quick, quick ; fear nothing : I 'll be at thy elbow.
It makes us, or it mars us : think on that,
And fix most firm thy resolution.
    Rod. Be near at hand : I may miscarry in 't.
    Iago. Here, at thy hand : be bold, and take thy
        sword.   [*Retires to a little distance.*
    Rod. I have no great devotion to the deed ;
And yet he has given me satisfying reasons :—
'T is but a man gone :—forth, my sword : he dies.
              [*Goes to his stand.*
    Iago. I have rubbed this young quat almost to
        the sense,
And he grows angry. Now, whether he kill Cassio,
Or Cassio him, or each do kill the other,
Every way makes my gain :—live Roderigo,
He calls me to a restitution large
Of gold and jewels, that I bobbed from him,
As gifts to Desdemona :
It must not be :—if Cassio do remain,
He hath a daily beauty in his life
That makes me ugly : and besides, the Moor
May unfold me to him : there stand I in much peril :
No, he must die.—But so ; I hear him coming.

Enter CASSIO.

    Rod. I know his gait ; 't is he :—villain, thou
        diest !
[*Rushes from his post, and makes a pass at* CASSIO.
    Cas. That thrust had been mine enemy indeed,
But that my coat is better than thou think'st :—
I will make proof of thine.
           [*Draws, and wounds* RODERIGO.

    Rod.   O, I am slain !
    [IAGO *rushes from his post, cuts* CASSIO
         behind in the leg, and exit.
    Cas. I am maimed for ever !—Help, ho ! mur-
        der ! murder !   [*Falls.*

Enter OTHELLO, *at a distance.*

    Oth. The voice of Cassio :—Iago keeps his word.
    Rod. O, villain that I am !
    Oth.   Hark ! 't is even so.
    Cas. O, help ! ho ! light ! a surgeon !
    Oth. 'T is he :—O brave Iago, honest, and just,
That hast such noble sense of thy friend's wrong !
Thou teachest me.—Minion, your dear lies dead,
And your fate hies apace.   Strumpet, I come :
Forth of my heart those charms, thine eyes, are
    blotted :
Thy bed, lust-stained, shall with lust's blood be
    spotted.   [*Exit* OTHELLO.

Enter LODOVICO *and* GRATIANO, *at a distance.*

    Cas. What, ho ! No watch ? no passage ? Mur-
        der ! murder !
    Gra. 'T is some mischance : the cry is very direful.
    Cas. O help !
    Lod.   Hark !
    Rod.   O wretched villain !
    Lod. Two or three groan :—it is a heavy night.
These may be counterfeits : let 's think 't unsafe
To come in to the cry, without more help.
    Rod. Nobody come ? then shall I bleed to death.

Enter IAGO, *with a light.*

    Lod. Hark !
    Gra. Here 's one comes in his shirt, with light
        and weapons.
    Iago. Who 's there ? whose noise is this that
        cries on murder ?

Lod. We do not know.

Iago.   Did you not hear a cry?

Cas. Here, here :—for heaven's sake, help me!

Iago.   What's the matter?

Gra. This is Othello's ancient, as I take it.

Lod. The same, indeed : a very valiant fellow.

Iago. What are you here that cry so grievously?

Cas. Iago? O, I am spoiled, undone by villains!
Give me some help.

Iago. O me, lieutenant! what villains have done
     this?

Cas. I think that one of them is hereabout,
And cannot make away.

Iago.   O treacherous villains!—
What are you there? come in, and give some help.
                         [*To* LODOVICO *and* GRATIANO.

Rod. O, help me here!

Cas. That 's one of them.

Iago.   O murderous slave! O villain!
                         [IAGO *stabs* RODERIGO.

Rod. O damned Iago! O inhuman dog!—
O! O! O!

Iago. Kill men i' the dark!—Where be these
     bloody thieves?—
How silent is this town!—Ho! murder! murder!
What may you be? are you of good or evil?

Lod. As you shall prove us, praise us.

Iago.   Signior Lodovico?

Lod. He, sir.

Iago.   I cry you mercy. Here 's Cassio hurt
By villains.

Gra.   Cassio?

Iago.   How is it, brother?

Cas. My leg is cut in two.

Iago.   Marry, heaven forbid!—
Light, gentlemen : I 'll bind it with my shirt.

Enter BIANCA.

Bian. What is the matter, ho? who is 't that
     cried?

Iago. Who is 't that cried?

Bian. O my dear Cassio! my sweet Cassio!
O Cassio, Cassio, Cassio!

Iago. O notable strumpet!—Cassio, may you
     suspect
Who they should be that have thus mangled
     you?

Cas. No.

Gra. I am sorry to find you thus : I have been
to seek you.

Iago. Lend me a garter :—so.—O, for a chair,
To bear him easily hence!

Bian. Alas, he faints!—O Cassio, Cassio, Cassio!

Iago. Gentlemen all, I do suspect this trash
To be a party in this injury.—
Patience awhile, good Cassio.—Come, come :
Lend me a light.—Know we this face, or no?

Alas! my friend and my dear countryman,
Roderigo?—no :—yes, sure :—O heaven, Rode-
     rigo!

Gra. What, of Venice?

Iago. Even he, sir : did you know him?

Gra.   Know him? ay.

Iago. Signior Gratiano?—I cry you gentle
     pardon :
These bloody accidents must excuse my manners,
That so neglected you.

Gra.   I am glad to see you.

Iago. How do you, Cassio?—O, a chair, a chair!

Gra. Roderigo!

Iago. He, he; 'tis he.—O, that 's well said :
     the chair.—   [*A chair brought in.*
Some good man bear him carefully from hence :
I 'll fetch the general's surgeon.—For you, mis-
     tress,   [*To* BIANCA.
Save you your labour.—He that lies slain here,
     Cassio,
Was my dear friend : what malice was between
     you?

Cas. None in the world; nor do I know the man.

Iago. What, look you pale?— [*To* BIANCA.
O, bear him out o' the air.—
          [CASSIO *and* RODERIGO *are borne off.*
Stay you, good gentlemen.—Look you pale,
     mistress?—
Do you perceive the ghastness of her eye?—
Nay, if you stare we shall hear more anon.—
Behold her well; I pray you, look upon her :
Do you see, gentlemen? Nay, guiltiness will speak,
Though tongues were out of use.

Enter EMILIA.

Emil. 'Las, what 's the matter? what 's the
     matter, husband?

Iago. Cassio hath here been set on in the dark,
By Roderigo and fellows that are scaped :
He 's almost slain, and Roderigo dead.

Emil. Alas, good gentleman! alas, good Cassio!

Iago. This is the fruit of whoring.—Pr'y thee,
     Emilia,
Go know of Cassio where he supped to-night :—
What, do you shake at that?

Bian. He supped at my house; but I there-
     fore shake not.

Iago. O, did he so? I charge you go with me.

Emil. Fie, fie upon thee, strumpet!

Bian. I am no strumpet; but of life as honest
As you that thus abuse me.

Emil.   As I? foh! fie upon thee!

Iago. Kind gentlemen, let 's go see poor Cassio
     dressed.—
Come, mistress, you must tell us another tale.—
Emilia, run you to the citadel,
And tell my lord and lady what has happed.—

Will you go on, I pray!—[*Aside.*]—This is the
   night
That either makes me or foredoes me quite.
                              [*Exeunt.*

Scene II.—*A Bedchamber.* Desdemona *in bed,
   asleep. A light burning.*

Enter Othello.

   Oth. It is the cause, it is the cause, my soul :—
Let me not name it to you, you chaste stars !—
It is the cause.—Yet I 'll not shed her blood ;
Nor scar that whiter skin of hers than snow,
And smooth as monumental alabaster.
                              [*Takes off his sword.*
Yet she must die, else she 'll betray more men.
Put out the light, and then—Put out the light !—
If I quench thee, thou flaming minister,
I can again thy former light restore,
Should I repent me :—but once put out thy light,
Thou cunning'st pattern of excelling nature,
I know not where is that Promethean heat
That can thy light relume. When I have plucked
   the rose,
I cannot give it vital growth again ;
It needs must wither :—I 'll smell it on the tree.
                              [*Kissing her.*
O balmy breath, that dost almost persuade
Justice to break her sword !—One more, one
   more.—
Be thus when thou art dead, and I will kill thee,
And love thee after.—One more, and this the last :
So sweet was ne'er so fatal. I must weep,
But they are cruel tears. This sorrow 's heavenly ;
It strikes where it doth love.—She wakes.
   Des. Who 's there ? Othello ?
   Oth.   Ay, Desdemona.
   Des. Will you come to bed, my lord ?
   Oth. Have you prayed to-night, Desdemona ?
   Des.   Ay, my lord.
   Oth. If you bethink yourself of any crime
Unreconciled as yet to heaven and grace,
Solicit for it straight.
   Des. Alas, my lord, what may you mean by that ?
   Oth. Well, do it, and be brief : I will walk by.
I would not kill thy unprepared spirit :
No,—Heaven forefend !—I would not kill thy soul.
   Des. Talk you of killing ?
   Oth.   Ay, I do.
   Des.   Then heaven
Have mercy on me !
   Oth.   Amen, with all my heart !
   Des. If you say so, I hope you will not kill me.
   Oth. Humph !
   Des. And yet I fear you ; for you are fatal then

When your eyes roll so. Why I should fear I
   know not,
Since guiltiness I know not : but yet I feel I fear.
   Oth. Think on thy sins.
   Des.   They are loves I bear to you.
   Oth. Ay, and for that thou diest.
   Des. That death 's unnatural, that kills for
   loving.—
Alas, why gnaw you so your nether lip ?
Some bloody passion shakes your very frame.
These are porténts : but yet I hope, I hope,
They do not point on me.
   Oth.   Peace, and be still !
   Des. I will so :—what 's the matter ?
   Oth. That handkerchief which I so loved, and
   gave thee,
Thou gav'st to Cassio.
   Des.   No, by my life and soul :
Send for the man, and ask him.
   Oth.   Sweet soul, take heed,
Take heed of perjury : thou 'rt on thy deathbed.
   Des. Ay, but not yet to die.
   Oth.   Yes, presently :
Therefore confess thee freely of thy sin ;
For to deny each article with oath
Cannot remove nor choke the strong conception
That I do groan withal. Thou art to die.
   Des. O, heaven have mercy on me !
   Oth.   I say, amen.
   Des. And have you mercy too !—I never did
Offend you in my life : never loved Cassio
But with such general warranty of heaven
As I might love. I never gave him token.
   Oth. By heaven, I saw my handkerchief in his
   hand.
O perjured woman ! thou dost stone my heart,
And mak'st me call what I intend to do
A murder, which I thought a sacrifice.
I saw the handkerchief.
   Des.   He found it, then :
I never gave it him. Send for him hither,
Let him confess a truth.
   Oth.   He hath confessed.
   Des. What, my lord ?
   Oth. That he hath used thee.
   Des.   How ; unlawfully ?
   Oth. Ay.
   Des.   He 'll not say so.
   Oth.   No ; his mouth is stopped :
Honest Iago hath ta'en order for 't.
   Des. My fear interprets, then :—what, is he
   dead ?
   Oth. Had all his hairs been lives, my great revenge
Had stomach for them all.
   Des. Alas ! he is betrayed, and I undone.
   Oth. Out, strumpet ! Weep'st thou for him
   to my face ?

Des. O, banish me, my lord, but kill me not.
Oth. Down, strumpet!
Des. Kill me to-morrow; let me live to-night.
Oth. Nay, if you strive,——

Des.   But half an hour.
Oth.   Being done,
There is no pause.
Des.   But while I say one prayer.

Oth. It is too late.   [*He smothers her.*
Emil. [*within*]. My lord, my lord! What ho!
          my lord, my lord!
Oth. What noise is this?—Not dead! not yet
          quite dead!
I that am cruel, am yet merciful:
I would not have thee linger in thy pain.—
So, so.
    Emil. [*within*]. What ho! my lord, my lord!
    Oth.   Who's there?
    Emil. [*within*]. O, good my lord, I would speak
          a word with you.

Oth. Yes:—'t is Emilia:—by-and-by.—She's
          dead.—
'T is like she comes to speak of Cassio's death:
The noise was high.—Ha! no more moving!
Still as the grave.—Shall she come in? were 't
          good?—
I think she stirs again: no.—What's the best?
If she come in, she'll sure speak to my wife.
My wife! my wife! what wife? I have no
          wife!
O, insupportable! O heavy hour!
Methinks it should be now a huge eclipse

Of sun and moon; and that the affrighted globe
Should yawn at alteration.

  Emil. [*within*]. I do beseech you I may speak
    with you,
O, good my lord!

  Oth. I had forgot thee:—O, come in, Emilia.—
Soft; by-and-by.—Let me the curtains draw.—
Where art thou? What's the matter with thee
    now?   [*Unlocks the door.*

Enter EMILIA.

  Emil. O, good my lord, yonder's foul murder
    done.

  Oth. What, now?

  Emil.   But now, my lord.

  Oth. It is the very error of the moon:
She comes more near the earth than she was
    wont,
And makes men mad.

  Emil. Cassio, my lord, has killed a young Vene-
    tian,
Called Roderigo.

  Oth.   Roderigo killed!
And Cassio killed?

  Emil.   No, Cassio is not killed.

  Oth. Not Cassio killed?—Then murder's out
    of tune,
And sweet revenge grows harsh.

  Des. O, falsely, falsely murdered!

  Emil.   Alas! what cry is that?

  Oth. That! what?

  Emil. Out and alas! that was my lady's voice.—
Help, help! ho! help!—O lady, speak again:
Sweet Desdemona! O, sweet mistress, speak.

  Des. A guiltless death I die.

  Emil.   O, who hath done
This deed?

  Des.   Nobody: I myself: farewell.
Commend me to my kind lord. O, farewell.
                     [*Dies.*

  Oth. Why, how should she be murdered?

  Emil.   Alas, who knows?

  Oth. You heard her say herself it was not I.

  Emil. She said so: I must needs report the
    truth.

  Oth. She's, like a liar, gone to burning hell:—
'T was I that killed her.

  Emil.   O, the more angel she,
And you the blacker devil!

  Oth. She turned to folly, and she was a whore.

  Emil. Thou dost belie her, and thou art a devil.

  Oth. She was false as water.

  Emil.   Thou art rash as fire to say
That she was false: O, she was heavenly true!

  Oth. Cassio did tup her: ask thy husband
    else.
O, I were damned beneath all depth in hell,

But that I did proceed upon just grounds
To this extremity! Thy husband knew it all.

  Emil. My husband?

  Oth. Thy husband.

  Emil. That she was false to wedlock?

  Oth.   Ay, with Cassio.
Nay, had she been true,
If heaven would make me such another world
Of one entire and perfect chrysolite,
I'd not have sold her for it.

  Emil. My husband?

  Oth.   Ay; 't was he that told me first:
An honest man he is, and hates the slime
That sticks on filthy deeds.

  Emil.   My husband?

  Oth. What needs this iterance, woman? I say,
    thy husband.

  Emil. O mistress, villany hath made mocks
    with love!—
My husband say that she was false?

  Oth.   He, woman.
I say, thy husband. Dost understand the word?
My friend, thy husband: honest, honest Iago.

  Emil. If he say so, may his pernicious soul
Rot half a grain a day! he lies to the heart:
She was too fond of her most filthy bargain.

  Oth. Ha!

  Emil.   Do thy worst.
This deed of thine is no more worthy heaven,
Than thou wast worthy her.

  Oth.   Peace, you were best.

  Emil. Thou hast not half the power to do me
    harm
As I have to be hurt. O gull! O dolt!
As ignorant as dirt! thou hast done a deed,—
I care not for thy sword: I'll make thee known,
Though I lost twenty lives:—Help! help, ho! help!
The Moor has killed my mistress; murder! mur-
    der!

Enter MONTANO, GRATIANO, *and* IAGO.

  Mon. What is the matter?—How now, general?

  Emil. O, are you come, Iago? you have done
    well,
That men must lay their murders on your neck.

  Gra. What is the matter?

  Emil. Disprove this villain, if thou beest a
    man.
He says thou told'st him that his wife was false.
I know thou didst not, thou 'rt not such a villain:
Speak, for my heart is full.

  Iago. I told him what I thought; and told no
    more
Than what he found himself was apt and true.

  Emil. But did you ever tell him she was false?

  Iago. I did.

  Emil. You told a lie; an odious, damnéd lie;

Upon my soul, a lie ; a wicked lie.—
She false with Cassio :—did you say, with Cassio?

　Iago. With Cassio, mistress. Go to, charm your
　　　tongue.

　Emil. I will not charm my tongue ; I am bound
　　　to speak :

My mistress here lies murdered in her bed.

　All. O heavens forefend !

　Emil. And your reports have set the murder on.

　Oth. Nay, stare not, masters : it is true, indeed.

　Gra. 'T is a strange truth.

　Mon. O monstrous act !

　Emil. Villany, villany, villany !

I think upon 't,—I think,—I smell 't. O villany !
I thought so then.—I 'll kill myself for grief.—
O villany, villany !

　Iago. What, are you mad ? I charge you, get
　　　you home.

　Emil. Good gentlemen, let me have leave to
　　　speak :

'T is proper I obey him, but not now.—
Perchance, Iago, I will ne'er go home.

　Oth. O ! O ! O !

　Emil.　　　Nay, lay thee down, and roar :

For thou hast killed the sweetest innocent
That e'er did lift up eye.

　Oth.　　　O, she was foul !—

I scarce did know you, uncle. There lies your niece,
Whose breath, indeed, these hands have newly
　　　stopped.

I know this act shews horrible and grim.

　Gra. Poor Desdemona ! I am glad thy father 's
　　　dead :

Thy match was mortal to him, and pure grief
Shore his old thread in twain : did he live now,
This sight would make him do a desperate turn
Yea, curse his better angel from his side,
And fall to reprobation.

　Oth. 'T is pitiful : but yet Iago knows
That she with Cassio hath the act of shame
A thousand times committed. Cassio confessed it :
And she did gratify his amorous works
With that recógnizance and pledge of love
Which I first gave her : I saw it in his hand :
It was a handkerchief ; an antique token
My father gave my mother.

　Emil. O heaven ! O heavenly powers !

　Iago.　　　Come, hold your peace.

　Emil. 'T will out, 't will out !—I hold my peace,
　　　sir ? no :

No, I will speak as liberal as the air :
Let heaven, and men, and devils, let them all,
All, all, cry shame against me, yet I 'll speak.

　Iago. Be wise, and get you home.]

　Emil. I will not.

　　　　　[Iago *offers to stab his Wife.*

　Gra. Fie ! your sword upon a woman !

　Emil. O thou dull Moor, that handkerchief thou
　　　speak'st of

I found by fortune, and did give my husband :
For often, with a solemn earnestness
(More than, indeed, belonged to such a trifle),
He begged of me to steal it.

　Iago.　　　Villanous whore !

　Emil. She give it Cassio ! no, alas ; I found it,
And I did give 't my husband.

　Iago.　　　Filth, thou liest.

　Emil. By heaven, I do not ; I do not, gentle-
　　　men.—

O murderous coxcomb ! what should such a fool
Do with so good a wife ?

　　　　　　[Iago *stabs* Emilia, *then runs out.*

　Oth.　　　Are there no stones in heaven
But what serve for the thunder?—Precious villain !

　Gra. The woman falls ! sure he has killed his
　　　wife.

　Emil. Ay, ay.—O, lay me by my mistress' side.

　Gra. He 's gone, but his wife 's killed.

　Mon. 'T is a notorious villain. Take you this
　　　weapon,

Which I have here recovered from the Moor.
Come, guard the door without : let him not pass
But kill him rather. I 'll after that same villain,
For 't is a damnéd slave.

　　　　　[*Exeunt* Montano *and* Gratiano.

　Oth.　　　I am not valiant neither,
But every puny whipster gets my sword :—
But why should honour outlive honesty ?
Let it go all.

　Emil.　　What did thy song bode, lady ?
Hark, canst thou hear me ? I will play the swan,
And die in music :—" Willow, willow, willow."—
Moor, she was chaste : she loved thee, cruel Moor :
So come my soul to bliss as I speak true :
So speaking as I think, I die ;—I die.　　[*Dies.*

　Oth. I have another weapon in this chamber :
It is a sword of Spain ; the ice-brook's temper :—
O, here it is.—Uncle, I must come forth.

　Gra. [*within*]. If thou attempt it, it will cost
　　　thee dear :

Thou hast no weapon, and perforce must suffer.

　Oth. Look in upon me, then, and speak with me ;
Or, naked as I am, I will assault thee.

　　　　　　Re-enter Gratiano.

　Gra. What is the matter ?

　Oth.　　Behold, I have a weapon :
A better never did itself sustain
Upon a soldier's thigh. I have seen the day
That with this little arm, and this good sword,
I have made my way through more impediments
Than twenty times your stop :—but, O vain boast !
Who can control his fate ? 't is not so now.—
Be not afraid, though you do see me weaponed :

Here is my journey's end, here is my butt,
And very seamark of my utmost sail.
Do you go back dismayed? 'tis a lost fear:
Man but a rush against Othello's breast,
And he retires :—where should Othello go?—
Now, how dost thou look now? O ill-starred
    wench,
Pale as thy smock! When we shall meet at compt,
This look of thine will hurl my soul from heaven,
And fiends will snatch at it! Cold, cold, my girl?
Even like thy chastity.—
O curséd, curséd slave!—Whip me, ye devils,
From the possession of this heavenly sight!
Blow me about in winds! roast me in sulphur!
Wash me in steep-down gulfs of liquid fire!—
O Desdemona! Desdemona! dead?
Dead?—O! O! O!

Enter LODOVICO, MONTANO; CASSIO, *carried in a*
    chair; and Officers, *with* IAGO, *prisoner.*

    Lod. Where is this rash and most unfortunate
      man?
    Oth. That's he that was Othello :—here I am.
    Lod. Where is that viper? bring the villain
      forth.
    Oth. I look down towards his feet;—but that's
    a fable :—
If that thou beest a devil I cannot kill thee.
              [OTHELLO *wounds* IAGO.
    Lod. Wrench his sword from him.
    Iago.   I bleed, sir; but not killed.
    Oth. I am not sorry neither: I'd have thee
    live;
For in my sense, 'tis happiness to die.
    Lod. O thou Othello, that was once so good,
Fallen in the practice of a curséd slave,
What shall be said to thee?
    Oth.   Why, anything:
An honourable murderer, if you will;
For nought I did in hate, but all in honour.
    Lod. This wretch hath part confessed his villany:
Did you and he consent in Cassio's death?
    Oth. Ay.
    Cas. Dear general, I never gave you cause.
    Oth. I do believe it, and I ask your pardon.
Will you, I pray you, demand that demi-devil
Why he hath thus ensnared my soul and body?
    Iago. Demand me nothing: what you know,
      you know:
From this time forth I never will speak word.
    Lod. What, not to pray?
    Gra.   Torments will ope your lips.
    Oth. Well, thou dost best.
    Lod. Sir, you shall understand what hath be-
      fallen;
Which, as I think, you know not:—here is a
    letter

Found in the pocket of the slain Roderigo;
And here another: the one of them imports
The death of Cassio to be undertook
By Roderigo.
    Oth. O villain!
    Cas.   Most heathenish and most gross!
    Lod. Now here's another discontented paper,
Found in his pocket too: and this, it seems,
Roderigo meant to have sent this damnéd villain;
But that belike Iago in the interim
Came in and satisfied him.
    Oth.   O the pernicious caitiff!—
How came you, Cassio, by that handkerchief
That was my wife's?
    Cas.   I found it in my chamber:
And he himself confessed, but even now,
That there he dropped it for a special purpose
Which wrought to his desire.
    Oth.   O fool! fool! fool!
    Cas. There is, besides, in Roderigo's letter,
How he upbraids Iago that he made him
Brave me upon the watch; whereon it came
That I was cast: and even but now he spake,
After long seeming dead,—Iago hurt him,
Iago set him on.
    Lod. You must forsake this room, and go with
    us:
Your power and your command is taken off,
And Cassio rules in Cyprus. For this slave,
If there be any cunning cruelty
That can torment him much and hold him long,
It shall be his. You shall close prisoner rest,
Till that the nature of your fault be known
To the Venetian state.—Come, bring him away.
    Oth. Soft you; a word or two before you go.
I have done the state some service, and they
    know it:
No more of that:—I pray you, in your letters,
When you shall these unlucky deeds relate,
Speak of me as I am: nothing extenuate,
Nor set down aught in malice: then must you
    speak
Of one that loved not wisely, but too well;
Of one not easily jealous, but, being wrought,
Perplexed in the extreme; of one whose hand,
Like the base Júdean, threw a pearl away
Richer than all his tribe; of one whose súbdued
    eyes,
Albeit unuséd to the melting mood,
Drop tears as fast as the Arabian trees
Their médicinal gum.—Set you down this:—
And say, besides, that in Aleppo once,
Where a malignant and a turbaned Turk
Beat a Venetian and traduced the state,
I took by the throat the circumciséd dog,
And smote him—thus.   [*Stabs himself.*
    Lod. O bloody period!

Gra. All that is spoke is marred.

Oth. I kissed thee ere I killed thee :—no way
   but this,   [*Falling upon* DESDEMONA.
Killing myself, to die upon a kiss.   [*Dies.*

Cas. This did I fear, but thought he had no
   weapon ;
For he was great of heart.

Lod.   O Spartan dog,
More fell than anguish, hunger, or the sea !

Look on the tragic loading of this bed : [*To* IAGO.
This is thy work.—The object poisons sight :
Let it be hid.—Gratiano, keep the house,
And seize upon the fortunes of the Moor,
For they succeed to you.—To you, lord governor,
Remains the censure of this hellish villain ;
The time, the place, the torture,—O enforce it !
Myself will straight aboard ; and, to the state,
This heavy act with heavy heart relate. [*Exeunt.*

NOTES.

"*One Michael Cassio, a Florentine,*
A fellow almost damned in a fair wife."

Act I., Scene 1.

If the text in the second line is correct, Iago probably means that Cassio is likely to ruin himself by a marriage with Bianca. On a subsequent occasion (act iv., scene 1), he acquaints Cassio himself that such a report is in circulation.

"*What tell'st thou me of robbing? This is Venice:*
My house is not a grange."—Act I., Scene 1.

That is, we are in a populous city, not in a lone house where a robbery might easily be committed. A grange is, strictly, the farm of a monastery; but in some counties every lone house or farm which stands solitary is called a grange.

"*You'll have your nephews neigh to you.*"—Act I., Scene 1.

Nephew, in this instance, has the power of the Latin word *nepos*, and signifies a grandson or any lineal descendant.

"*Tying her duty, beauty, wit, and fortunes,*
In an extravagant and wheeling stranger."

Act I., Scene 1.

The word "in" is here used in the sense of "to." This is one of the many obsolete peculiarities of ancient phraseology. "Extravagant" has its Latin signification of "wandering." As in "HAMLET:"—"The extravagant and erring spirit hies to his confine."

—— *I fetch my life and being*
From men of royal siege; and my demerits
May speak unbonneted to as proud a fortune
As this that I have reached."—Act I., Scene 2.

The term "men of royal siege" signifies men who have sat upon royal seats or thrones. "Siege" is used for "seat" by many other writers. "Demerits" has here the signification of "merits." As in "CORIOLANUS:"—

"Opinion, that so sticks on Martius, may
Of his demerits rob Cominius."

Mereo and *demereo* had the same meaning in the Latin.

Mr. Fuseli has given the best explanation yet offered of the term "unbonneted:"—"I am his equal or superior in rank: and were it not so, such are my *merits*, that unbonneted, without the addition of patrician or senatorial dignity, they may speak to as proud a fortune," &c.

"*Valiant Othello, we must straight employ you*
Against the general enemy Ottoman."—Act I., Scene 3.

It was part of the policy of the Venetian state never to entrust the command of an army to a native. "By land (says Thomas), they are served of strangers, both for generals, for captains, and for all other men of war; because their law permitteth not any Venetian to be captain over an army by land: fearing, I think, Cæsar's example."

"*Send for the lady to the Sagittary.*"—Act I., Scene 3.

"Sagittary" was the name applied to a fictitious being, compounded of man and horse. As used in the text, it has been generally supposed to be the sign of an inn; but it now appears that it was the residence of the commanding officers of the republic. It is said that the figure of an archer, over the gate, still indicates the spot.

"*The Anthropophagi, and men whose heads*
Do grow beneath their shoulders."—Act I., Scene 3.

Legends of this description had long been popular: the allusion in the text is probably directed in a particular manner to a passage in Raleigh's narrative of his voyage to Guiana:—"Next unto the Arvi are two rivers, Atoica and Caova; and on that branch which is called Caova are a nation of people whose heads appear not above their shoulders: which, though it may be thought a mere fable, yet for mine own part I am resolved it is true, because every child in the province of Arromaia and Canuri affirm the same. They are called Ewaipanoma; they are reported to have their eyes in their shoulders and their mouths in the middle of their breasts, and that a long train of hair groweth backward between their shoulders."

"*A Sea-port Town in Cyprus.*"—Act II., Scene 1.

Nicosia (or Leikosia), the capital city of Cyprus, was situated nearly in the centre of the island, and thirty miles distant from the sea. The principal sea-port town was Famagusta, where there was formerly a strong fort and a commodious haven, the only one of any magnitude in the island; and there undoubtedly the scene should be placed.

"*Seems to cast water on the burning bear,*
And quench the guards of th' ever-fixèd poles."

Act II., Scene 1.

The "burning bear" is the constellation near the pole. The next line alludes to the star Arctophylax, which word signifies the guard of the bear.

"*'T is here, but yet confused:*
Knavery's plain face is never seen till used."

Act II., Scene 1.

An honest man acts upon a plan, and forecasts his designs; but a knave depends upon temporary and local opportunities, and never knows his own purpose but at the time of execution.—JOHNSON.

"*King Stephen was a worthy peer.*"—Act II., Scene 3.

The term "peer" is here used in the sense of "fellow." The stanzas sung by Iago are taken from an excellent old ballad, which is printed in Percy's "RELIQUES."

"*He'll watch the horologe a double set,*
If drink rock not his cradle."—Act II., Scene 3.

That is, if he have no drink he'll keep awake while the clock strikes two rounds, or four-and-twenty hours. Chaucer and other old writers use the term horologe familiarly.

—— "*Sir, for your hurts,*
Myself will be your surgeon.—Lead him off."—Act II., Scene 3.

I am persuaded these words ("Lead him off") were originally a marginal direction. In our old plays, all the stage directions were couched in imperative terms:—"Play music;" "Ring the bell;" "Lead him off."

"*When devils will the blackest sins put on,*
They do suggest at first with heavenly shows."

Act II., Scene 3.

The term "put on" is here and in various other places used in the sense of "urge on." The meaning is, when

416

devils mean to instigate men to commit the most atrocious crimes, they prompt or tempt at first with appearances of virtue.

" *I humbly thank you for 't.—I never knew*
A Florentine more kind and honest."

Act III., Scene 1.

Cassio was undoubtedly a Florentine; and, as Iago was a Venetian, what Cassio means to say, in the quoted passage, is, that he never knew one of his own countrymen more kind and honest.

" (*Save that they say the wars must make examples*
Out of their best)."—Act III., Scene 3.

That is, the severity of military discipline must not spare the best men of the army, when their punishment may afford a wholesome example.

" *Excellent wretch! Perdition catch my soul*
But I do love thee!"—Act III., Scene 3.

The meaning of the word wretch is not generally understood. It is now, in some parts of England, a term of the softest and fondest tenderness. It expresses the utmost degree of amiableness, joined with an idea, which perhaps all tenderness includes, of feebleness, softness, and want of protection.—JOHNSON.

—— " *Who has a breast so pure*
But some uncleanly apprehensions
Keep leets and law-days, and in session sit
With meditations lawful."—Act III., Scene 3.

That is, who has so virtuous a breast that some uncharitable surmises will not sometimes enter into it; hold a session there as in a regular court, and " bench by the side" of authorised and lawful thoughts?

" *O beware, my lord, of jealousy:*
It is the green-eyed monster which doth make
The meat it feeds on."—Act III., Scene 3.

The old copies have "mock." The correction was made by Sir T. Hanmer. I have not the smallest doubt that Shakspere wrote "make," and have, therefore, inserted it in the text. The words "make" and "mocke" (for such was the old spelling) are often confounded in these plays.—MALONE.

I have received Hanmer's emendation: because, "to mock" does not signify "to loathe;" and because, when Iago bids Othello "beware of jealousy, the green-eyed monster," it is natural to tell why he should beware; and, for caution, he gives him two reasons:—that jealousy often creates its own cause, and that, when the causes are real, jealousy is misery.—JOHNSON.

Various passages, both from Shakspere and other writers, are quoted in support of this reading. The chief is what Emilia says of jealousy, in the last scene of this Act —" 'T is a monster begot upon itself, born on itself."

" *She did deceive her father, marrying you:*
And when she seemed to shake and fear your looks,
She loved them most."—Act III., Scene 3.

This and the following argument of Othello ought to be deeply impressed on every reader. Deceit and falsehood, whatever conveniences they may for a time promise or produce, are in the sum of life obstacles to happiness. Those who profit by the cheat distrust the deceiver, and the act by which kindness was sought, puts an end to confidence. The same objection may be made, with a lower degree of strength, against the imprudent generosity of disproportionate marriages. When the first heat of passion is over, it is easily succeeded by suspicion that the same violence of inclination which caused one irregularity, may stimulate to another: and those who have shewn that their passions are too violent

for their prudence, will, with very slight appearances against them, be censured as not very likely to restrain them by their virtue.—JOHNSON.

" *To seel her father's eyes up close as oak.*"—Act III., Scene 3.

" To seel" is an expression from falconry. To seel a hawk was to subject it to the barbarous operation of sewing up its eyelids.—" Close as oak" means, as close as the grain of the oak.

" *Though that her jesses were my dear heart-strings,*
I'd whistle her off, and let her down the wind,
To prey at fortune."—Act III., Scene 3.

" Jesses" are short straps of leather tied about the foot of a hawk, by which she is held on the fist.

" The falconers always let fly the hawk against the wind: if she flies with the wind behind her, she seldom returns. If, therefore, a hawk was for any reason to be dismissed, she was 'let down the wind,' and from that time shifted for herself, and ' preyed at fortune.' "—JOHNSON.

—— " *I'll have the work ta'en out,*
And give it Iago."—Act III., Scene 3.

By having the " work ta'en out," Emilia means that she will have it copied. This is her first thought; but the sudden coming in of Iago, in a surly humour, makes her alter her resolution. The same phrase afterwards occurs between Cassio and Bianca, in the last scene of this Act.

It is impossible not to regret the execrable conduct which the poet (most likely from inadvertence) has assigned to Emilia in this matter of the handkerchief.—In Cinthio's novel, while Desdemona is caressing the child of the Iago of the play, the villain steals the handkerchief, which hung at her girdle, without the knowledge of his wife.

" OTH. *But this denoted a foregone conclusion.*
IAGO. *'T is a shrewd doubt, though it be but a dream.*"

Act III., Scene 3.

The last of these lines is usually given to Othello, on the authority of the folio: the quarto ascribes it to Iago; and we coincide with Warburton in thinking the latter arrangement preferable. Othello believes that the dream leaves no ambiguity about the matter: in his judgment, it " denoted a foregone *conclusion.*" Iago, with affected reluctance, merely admits it " a shrewd doubt."

" *She was in love; and he she loved proved mad,*
And did forsake her."—Act IV., Scene 3.

" Mad" must here be understood in the sense of wild, unruly, fickle. As in " LOVE'S LABOUR'S LOST :"—

" Do you hear, my mad wenches ?"

" *She had a song of 'willow.' *"—Act IV., Scene 3.

The original of this ballad (in two parts) is preserved in Percy's collection.

" *Marry, I would not do such a thing for a joint-ring.*"

Act IV., Scene 3.

A joint-ring was anciently a common token between lovers. Their nature will be best understood by a passage from Dryden's " DON SEBASTIAN :"—

" A curious artist wrought them,
With joints so close as not to be perceived:
Yet are they both each other's counterpart.
Her part had 'Juan' inscribed, and his had 'Zayda'
(You know those names are theirs); and, in the midst,
A heart divided in two halves was placed:—
Now if the rivets of those rings enclosed
Fit not each other, I have forged this lie:
But if they join, you must for ever part."

417

—— "*Pr'y thee, Emilia,*
Go know of Cassio where he supped to-night."
Act V., Scene 1.

In the last scene of the preceding Act, Iago informs Roderigo that Cassio was to sup with Bianca; that he would accompany him to her house, and would take care to bring him away from thence between twelve and one. Cassio, too, had informed Iago that he would sup with Bianca, and Iago had indirectly promised to meet him at her house. The villain, however, thought it safest to waylay his victim, and in the passage quoted professes a politic ignorance of Cassio's motions during the evening.

"*Put out the light, and then—Put out the light!*"
Act V., Scene 2.

The old copy gives the line thus:—

"Put out the light, and then put out the light."

The present regulation of the passage, by which so much beauty and spirit are added to it, was proposed by Mr. Upton; but it is to be found in Ayres's "LIFE OF POPE:" it may therefore have originated with Warburton, who thus explains it:—The meaning is, "I will put out the light, and then proceed to the execution of my purpose." But the expression of putting out the light, bringing to mind the effects of the extinction of the light of life, he breaks short, and questions himself about the effects of this metaphorical extinction, introduced by a repetition of his first words; as much as to say,—"But hold, let me first weigh the reflection which this expression naturally excites."—SINGER.

"*O perjured woman! thou dost stone my heart,*
And mak'st me call what I intend to do
A murder, which I thought a sacrifice."
Act V., Scene 2.

That is, "Thou hast hardened my heart, and mak'st me kill thee with the rage of a murderer, when I thought to have sacrificed thee to justice with the calmness of a priest striking a victim."—JOHNSON.

"*O mistress, villany hath made mocks with love!*"
Act V., Scene 2.

That is, villany hath taken advantage to play upon the weakness of love.

"*Go to, charm your tongue.*"—Act V., Scene 2.

To charm is to conjure, to enchant, to lay or still as with an incantation. So in "KING HENRY V.:"—

"Charming the narrow seas
To give you gentle pass."

"*It was a handkerchief; an antique token*
My father gave my mother."—Act V., Scene 2.

In the third Act, Othello states that this fatal handkerchief was given by his mother to his father. The transposition of giver and receiver, in the passage above quoted, was probably a mere inadvertence either of the poet or the transcriber.

"*Of one whose hand,*
Like the base Júdean, threw a pearl away
Richer than all his tribe."—Act V., Scene 2.

It has been a point much disputed whether "Indian" or "Júdean" is the proper reading of the text in this place. The earliest quarto gives "Indian," and two passages are quoted from other writers which strongly support this version. The first is from Habington ("To Castara weeping"):—

"So the unskilful Indian those bright gems
Which might add majesty to diadems,
'Mong the waves scatters."

The second quotation is from Sir R. Howard's "WOMAN'S CONQUEST:"—

"Behold my queen,
Who with no more concern I'll cast away
Than Indians do a pearl—that ne'er did know
Its value."

"Judean" (or rather Iudean) is the reading of the first folio; and, being now generally received, we have not thought it advisable to make a doubtful alteration, the effect of the passage being, in either case, precisely the same. Those who support this last version suppose the allusion in the text is to Herod and his savage sacrifice of Mariamne.

———

["OTHELLO" furnishes one of the very few instances in which Dr. Johnson has spoken of Shakspere's plays in anything like adequate terms of eulogy. In justice to him, therefore, as well as to the poet, we willingly avail ourselves on this occasion of the critic's cogent "summary remarks."]

THE beauties of this play impress themselves so strongly upon the attention of the reader, that they can draw no aid from critical illustration. The fiery openness of Othello, magnanimous, artless, and credulous, boundless in his confidence, ardent in his affection, inflexible in his resolution, and obdurate in his revenge;—the cool malignity of Iago, silent in his resentment, subtle in his designs, and studious at once of his interest and his vengeance;—the soft simplicity of Desdemona, confident of merit and conscious of innocence; her artless perseverance in her suit, and her slowness to suspect that she can be suspected;—are such proofs of Shakspere's skill in human nature as, I suppose, it is in vain to seek in any modern writer. The gradual progress which Iago makes in the Moor's conviction, and the circumstances which he employs to inflame him, are so artfully natural, that though it will not, perhaps, be said of him, as he says of himself, that he is a man "not easily jealous," yet we cannot but pity him when at last we find him "perplexed in the extreme."—There is always danger lest wickedness, conjoined with abilities, should steal upon esteem, though it misses of approbation: but the character of Iago is so conducted that he is, from the first scene to the last, hated and despised.

Even the inferior characters of this play would be very conspicuous in any other piece, not only for their justness but their strength.—Cassio is brave, benevolent, and honest; ruined only by his want of stubbornness to resist an insidious invitation.—Roderigo's suspicious credulity and impatient submission to the cheats which he sees practised upon him (and which by persuasion he suffers to be repeated), exhibit a strong picture of a weak mind betrayed by unlawful desires to a false friend:—and the virtue of Emilia is such as we often find,—worn loosely, but not cast off; easy to commit small crimes, but quickened and alarmed at atrocious villanies.

The scenes, from the beginning to the end, are busy, varied by happy interchanges, and regularly promoting the progress of the story: and the narrative in the end, though it tells but what is known already, yet is necessary to produce the death of Othello. Had the scene opened in Cyprus, and the preceding incidents been occasionally related, there had little wanting to a drama of the most exact and scrupulous regularity.

———

ALL the passions, all the mind of the play, are Shakspere's. He was indebted to Cinthio for the circumstances of his plot, and some individual traits of Othello's and Iago's characters, particularly of that of the latter. Desdemona he chastened into beauty; and the Captain (Cassio), whose character in the novel is scarcely distinguishable, he invested with qualities exactly correspondent to the purpose he was intended to fulfil. The wife of the Lieutenant (Iago) perhaps the poet had better have left as he found her; for in raising Emilia above insignificance, he unfortunately rendered her inexplicable. Roderigo is his own absolute creation.—SKOTTOWE.

CORIOLANUS.

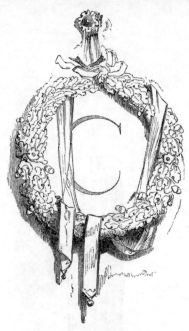

INTRODUCTORY REMARKS

OMING fresh from the perusal of such of Shakspere's plays as exhibit the sparkling treasures of his rare wit, glowing fancy, and surpassing poetry,—the creative power of his far-reaching imagination,—or the convulsive throes, the moral earthquakes and volcanoes, of human passion,—the Drama before us produces an effect almost startling, from the stern, unadorned, and somewhat rugged strength which is its prevailing characteristic. We soon, however, acknowledge the peculiar fitness of the style to the time, the action, and the characters: we recognise in its massive simplicity a grandeur which ornament would injure; in its ruggedness, a power which polish would destroy. In this fitness consists a portion of the value of the Play; a still greater portion in the striking specimen it affords of that "infinite variety" of the writer, which "age cannot wither, nor custom stale;"—and, greatest of all, in its subtle and powerful delineation of human character; that high and extraordinary quality in which all his contemporaries and followers halt so far behind him.

In "CORIOLANUS," as in "MACBETH," the Poet has taken an historical character, belonging to a remote and rude age, the records of whose actions, and of the events that gave birth to them, history borrows from tradition, and perhaps assists by conjecture. From the plain and simple relation of those actions and events, he at once judges of the motives, feelings, and circumstances which actuated and produced them;—and conjures up before the "mind's eye" the very man, a living sentient being, with his moral structure as clearly developed as his outward form would be, were he presented bodily to our senses.

Amongst the many truthful delineations of the human mind which have sprung from Shakspere's teeming brain, none are more exquisitely natural, more nicely discriminated, than the Hero of this stirring Play. Superficially viewed, his character appears repulsive and disagreeable; but study it minutely, and it becomes deeply interesting. Born in a state of society which admitted of no gradual connecting links between the lower and higher classes, no channels to conduct the kindly sympathies of each to the other, Coriolanus naturally inherited the prejudices of his order. But this is not all. He is rendered vain-glorious not alone by the pride of place and ancestry, but likewise by that nobler pride—the consciousness of high desert, of natural nobleness of mind, and of indomitable courage. Viewing all this, and beholding also the selfish, sordid natures, the utter and unredeemed baseness and perfidy of the leaders of that populace with which he is brought into hostile contact;—recollecting, moreover, that he is the spoilt child of success, the boy-warrior, who "at sixteen years"—"fought beyond the mark of others;"—who has thrice won the oaken garland; who has been borne aloft on the shields of a conquering army; greeted by the acclamations of the very populace which afterwards revolts against him;—can we, ought we to feel wonder or disgust at the mingled scorn and rage which, with such heaped measure, he hurls upon the "trades" and "occupations" of Rome? No. His conduct may be somewhat unamiable, but it is perfectly natural. His very faults are but the excesses of his virtues: he sets up a standard of moral perfection derived from the consciousness of his own high qualities, and in his inexperience of the world, its sufferings, mistakes, and accidents, he is indignant that the mass of the community should fall short of that standard.

The character of Volumnia is just what "the honoured mould of Marcius" might be supposed to be: towering grandly above most of the ordinary weaknesses of her sex, but possessing the rest of them in more than ordinary perfection. What an exquisitely natural specimen of the absence of self-knowledge is conveyed in the declaration, "Thy valiantness was mine, thou suck'dst it from me; but owe thy pride thyself!" Now the feeling of pride is to the full as strong in the mother as in her wayward son; but age, experience, and expediency, have modified and checked the free exhibition of it.—Amidst the stir, the turmoil, and the turbulence of this Play, how melodiously the sweet voice of the gentler affections makes itself heard! as though, in the din of arms, the clangour of martial music, and the roar of battle, an occasional pause enabled us to catch the soft breathing of flutes. Around the bold and lofty nature of Marcius, the shoots and tendrils of love are permitted to spring and to twine, shedding a lovely grace, like the clinging leaves of the acanthus round the capital of a Corinthian column; which, while they adorn it with their beauty, rob it not of the least portion of its grandeur or its strength.

"CORIOLANUS" was first published in the original folio. The incidents are derived from Plutarch.

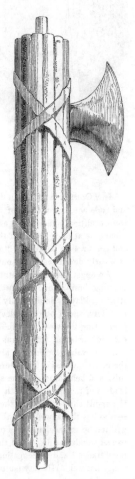

PERSONS REPRESENTED.

CAIUS MARCIUS CORIOLANUS, a noble Roman.
TITUS LARTIUS, } Generals against the Volcians.
COMINIUS, } Generals against the Volcians.
MENENIUS AGRIPPA, Friend to CORIOLANUS.
SICINIUS VELUTUS, } Tribunes of the People.
JUNIUS BRUTUS, } Tribunes of the People.
Young MARCIUS, Son to CORIOLANUS.
A Roman Herald.
TULLUS AUFIDIUS, General of the Volcians.
Lieutenant to AUFIDIUS.
Conspirators with AUFIDIUS.
A Citizen of Antium.
Two Volcian Guards.

VOLUMNIA. Mother to CORIOLANUS.
VIRGILIA, Wife to CORIOLANUS.
VALERIA, Friend to VIRGILIA.
Gentlewoman, attending VIRGILIA.

Roman and Volcian Senators, Patricians, Ædiles,
Lictors, Soldiers, Citizens, Messengers, Servants
to AUFIDIUS, and other Attendants.

———

SCENE. Partly in Rome; and partly in the Territories
of the Volcians and Antiates.

CORIOLI

CORIOLANUS

ACT I

Scene I.—Rome. *A Street.*

Enter a company of mutinous Citizens, *with staves, clubs, and other weapons.*

1st Cit. Before we proceed any farther, hear me speak.

Cit. Speak, speak. [*Several speaking at once.*

1st Cit. You are all resolved rather to die than to famish?

Cit. Resolved, resolved.

1st Cit. First, you know Caius Marcius is chief enemy to the people.

Cit. We know 't; we know 't.

1st Cit. Let us kill him, and we 'll have corn at our own price. Is 't a verdict?

Cit. No more talking on 't: let it be done. Away, away!

2nd Cit. One word, good citizens.

1st Cit. We are accounted poor citizens: the patricians, good. What authority surfeits on, would relieve us: if they would yield us but the superfluity while it were wholesome, we might guess they relieved us humanely: but they think we are too dear. The leanness that afflicts us, the object of our misery, is as an inventory to particularise their abundance: our sufference is a gain to them.—Let us revenge this with our pikes, ere we become rakes: for the gods know I speak this in hunger for bread, not in thirst for revenge.

2nd Cit. Would you proceed especially against Caius Marcius?

Cit. Against him first: he 's a very dog to the commonalty.

2nd Cit. Consider you what services he has done for his country?

1st Cit. Very well: and could be content to give him good report for 't, but that he pays himself with being proud.

2nd Cit. Nay, but speak not maliciously.

1st Cit. I say unto you, what he hath done famously, he did it to that end: though soft-conscienced men can be content to say it was for his country, he did it to please his mother, and to be partly proud: which he is, even to the altitude of his virtue.

2nd Cit. What he cannot help in his nature, you account a vice in him. You must in no way say he is covetous.

1st Cit. If I must not, I need not be barren of accusations: he hath faults, with surplus, to tire in repetition. [*Shouts within.*] What shouts are these? The other side o' the city is risen! Why stay we prating here?—to the Capitol!

Cit. Come, come.

1st Cit. Soft: who comes here?

Enter MENENIUS AGRIPPA.

2nd Cit. Worthy Menenius Agrippa: one that hath always loved the people.

1st Cit. He 's one honest enough. 'Would all the rest were so.

Men. What work 's, my countrymen, in hand? Where go you
With bats and clubs? The matter: speak, I
    pray you.

1st Cit. Our business is not unknown to the senate: they have had inkling this fortnight what we intend to do, which now we 'll shew 'em in deeds. They say, poor suitors have strong breaths: they shall know we have strong arms too.

Men. Why, masters! my good friends, mine
    honest neighbours,
Will you undo yourselves?

1st Cit. We cannot, sir; we are undone already.

Men. I tell you, friends, most charitable care
Have the patricians of you. For your wants,
Your suffering in this dearth, you may as well
Strike at the heaven with your staves, as lift them
Against the Roman state; whose course will on
The way it takes, cracking ten thousand curbs
Of more strong link asunder, than can ever
Appear in your impediment. For the dearth,
The gods, not the patricians, make it; and
Your knees to them, not arms, must help. Alack!
You are transported by calamity
Thither where more attends you; and you slander
The helms o' the state, who care for you like fathers,
When you curse them as enemies.

1st Cit. Care for us!—True, indeed!—They ne'er cared for us yet. Suffer us to famish, and their storehouses crammed with grain; make edicts for usury, to support usurers: repeal daily any wholesome act established against the rich; and provide more piercing statutes daily, to chain up and restrain the poor! If the wars eat us not up, they will: and there 's all the love they bear us.

Men. Either you must
Confess yourselves wondrous malicious,
Or be accused of folly.—I shall tell you
A pretty tale: it may be, you have heard it;
But, since it serves my purpose, I will venture
To scale 't a little more.

1st Cit. Well, I 'll hear it, sir: yet you must not think to fob off our disgrace with a tale: but, an 't please you, deliver.

Men. There was a time when all the body's
    members
Rebelled against the belly; thus accused it:
That only like a gulf it did remain
I' the midst o' the body, idle and inactive,
Still cupboarding the viand, never bearing
Like labour with the rest: where the other in-
    struments
Did see, and hear, devise, instruct, walk, feel,
And, mutually participate, did minister
Unto the appetite and affection common
Of the whole body. The belly answered,—

1st Cit. Well, sir, what answer made the belly?

Men. I shall tell you. With a kind of smile
Which ne'er came from the lungs, but even thus
(For, look you, I may make the belly smile
As well as speak), it tauntingly replied
To the discontented members, the mutinous parts

That envied his receipt: even so most fitly
As you malign our senators, for that
They are not such as you.
    1st Cit.   Your belly's answer.—What!
The kingly-crownéd head, the vigilant eye,
The counsellor heart, the arm our soldier,
Our steed the leg, the tongue our trumpeter,
With other muniments and petty helps
In this our fabric; if that they—
    Men.   What then?—
'Fore me this fellow speaks!—what then; what
    then?
    1st Cit. Should by the cormorant belly be
    restrained,
Who is the sink o' the body,—
    Men.   Well, what then?
    1st Cit. The former agents, if they did complain,
What could the belly answer?
    Men.   I will tell you:
If you 'll bestow a small (of what you have little)
Patience awhile, you 'll hear the belly's answer.
    1st Cit. You are long about it.
    Men.   Note me this, good friend:
Your most grave belly was deliberate,
Not rash like his accusers, and thus answered:—
" True is it, my incorporate friends," quoth he,
" That I receive the general food at first,
Which you do live upon: and fit it is;
Because I am the storehouse and the shop
Of the whole body. But if you do remember,
I send it through the rivers of your blood,
Even to the court, the heart; to the seat o' the brain;
And, through the cranks and offices of man,
The strongest nerves, and small inferior veins,
From me receive that natural competency
Whereby they live. And though that all at once,
You, my good friends," (this says the belly,
    mark me,)—
    1st Cit. Ay, sir: well, well.
    Men.   " Though all at once cannot
See what I do deliver out to each;
Yet I can make my audit up that all
From me do back receive the flour of all,
And leave me but the bran."—What say you to 't?
    1st Cit. It was an answer.—How apply you this?
    Men. The senators of Rome are this good belly,
And you the mutinous members. For, examine
Their counsels and their cares; digest things
    rightly,
Touching the weal o' the common; you shall find,
No public benefit which you receive
But it proceeds or comes from them to you,
And no way from yourselves.—What do you think:
You, the great toe of this assembly?—
    1st Cit. I the great toe!—Why the great toe?
    Men. For that, being one o' the lowest, basest,
    poorest,

Of this most wise rebellion, thou goest foremost:
Thou rascal, that art worst in blood to run,
Lead'st first to win some vantage!
But make you ready your stiff bats and clubs:
Rome and her rats are at the point of battle;
The one side must have bale.—Hail, noble Marcius!

        Enter CAIUS MARCIUS.

    Mar. Thanks.—What 's the matter, you dis-
    sentious rogues,
That rubbing the poor itch of your opinion,
Make yourselves scabs?
    1st Cit.   We have ever your good word.
    Mar. He that will give good words to thee,
    will flatter
Beneath abhorring.—What would you have, you
    curs,
That like nor peace nor war? the one affrights you,
The other makes you proud. He that trusts you,
Where he should find you lions, finds you hares;
Where foxes, geese: you are no surer, no,
Than is the coal of fire upon the ice,
Or hailstone in the sun. Your virtue is
To make him worthy whose offence subdues him,
And curse that justice did it. Who deserves
    greatness,
Deserves your hate: and your affections are
A sick man's appetite, who desires most that
Which would increase his evil. He that depends
Upon your favours, swims with fins of lead,
And hews down oaks with rushes. Hang ye!
    Trust ye?
With every minute you do change a mind;
And call him noble that was now your hate;
Him vile that was your garland. What 's the
    matter,
That in these several places of the city
You cry against the noble senate, who,
Under the gods, keep you in awe, which else
Which feed on one another?—What 's their
    seeking?
    Men. For corn at their own rates: whereof,
    they say,
The city is well stored.
    Mar.   Hang 'em! they say?
They 'll sit by the fire, and presume to know
What 's done i' the Capitol: who 's like to rise,
Who thrives, and who declines: side factions,
    and give out
Conjectural marriages: making parties strong,
And feebling such as stand not in their liking,
Below their cobbled shoes. They say there 's
    grain enough!
Would the nobility lay aside their ruth,
And let me use my sword, I 'd make a quarry
With thousands of these quartered slaves, as high
As I could pick my lance.

Men. Nay, these are almost thoroughly per-
    suaded:
For though abundantly they lack discretion,
Yet are they passing cowardly. But, I beseech you,
What says the other troop?
    Mar.   They are dissolved. Hang 'em!
They said they were an hungry: sighed forth
    proverbs:
That hunger broke stone walls; that dogs must eat;
That meat was made for mouths; that the gods
    sent not
Corn for the rich men only:—with these shreds
They vented their complainings; which being an-
    swered,
And a petition granted them, a strange one
(To break the heart of generosity,
And make bold power look pale), they threw
    their caps
As they would hang them on the horns o' the moon,
Shouting their emulation.
    Men.   What is granted them?
    Mar. Five tribunes, to defend their vulgar wis-
    doms,
Of their own choice. One 's Junius Brutus;
Sicinius Velutus, and I know not—'Sdeath!
The rabble should have first unroofed the city
Ere so prevailed with me: it will in time
Win upon power, and throw forth greater themes
For insurrection's arguing.
    Men.   This is strange.
    Mar. Go, get you home, you fragments!

    Enter a Messenger.

    Mess. Where 's Caius Marcius?
    Mar. Here. What 's the matter?
    Mess. The news is, sir, the Volces are in arms.
    Mar. I am glad on 't: then we shall have means
    to vent
Our musty superfluity.—See, our best elders.

Enter COMINIUS, TITUS LARTIUS, *and other* Senators; JUNIUS BRUTUS *and* SICINIUS VELUTUS.

    1st Sen. Marcius, 't is true that you have lately
    told us:
The Volces are in arms.
    Mar.   They have a leader,
Tullus Aufidius, that will put you to 't.
I sin in envying his nobility:
And were I anything but what I am,
I would wish me only he.
    Com.   You have fought together.
    Mar. Were half to half the world by the ears,
    and he
Upon my party, I 'd revolt, to make
Only my wars with him: he is a lion
That I am proud to hunt.
    1st Sen.   Then, worthy Marcius,
Attend upon Cominius to these wars.

    Com. It is your former promise.
    Mar.   Sir, it is;
And I am constant.—Titus Lartius, thou
Shalt see me once more strike at Tullus' face:
What, art thou stiff? stand'st out!
    Tit. No, Caius Marcius:
I 'll lean upon one crutch, and fight with the othe
Ere stay behind this business.
    Men.   O, true bred!
    1st Sen. Your company to the Capitol: whei
    I know
Our greatest friends attend us.
    Tit.   Lead you on:
Follow, Cominius. We must follow you:
Right worthy you priority.
    Com.   Noble Lartius!
    1st Sen. Hence! To your homes; be gone!
                    [*To the* Citizen
    Mar.   Nay, let them follow.
The Volces have much corn: take these ra
    thither,
To gnaw their garners.—Worshipful mutineers
Your valour puts well forth: pray follow.
    [*Exeunt* Senators, COMINIUS, MARCIUS, LAI
        TIUS, *and* MENENIUS. Citizens *steal awa*
    Sic. Was ever man so proud as is this Marciu:
    Bru. He has no equal.
    Sic. When we were chosen tribunes for tl
    people,—
    Bru. Marked you his lip and eyes?
    Sic.   Nay, but his taunts.
    Bru. Being moved, he will not spare to gii
    the gods.
    Sic. Be-mock the modest moon.
    Bru. The present wars devour him: he is grow
Too proud to be so valiant.
    Sic.   Such a nature,
Tickled with good success, disdains the shadow
Which he treads on at noon. But I do wonde
His insolence can brook to be commanded
Under Cominius.
    Bru.   Fame, at the which he aims,
In whom already he is well graced, cannot
Better be held, nor more attained, than by
A place below the first: for what miscarries
Shall be the general's fault, though he perform
To the utmost of a man; and giddy censure
Will then cry out of Marcius, "O, if he
Had borne the business!"
    Sic.   Besides, if things go well,
Opinion, that so sticks on Marcius, shall
Of his demerits rob Cominius.
    Bru.   Come:
Half all Cominius' honours are to Marcius,
Though Marcius earned them not; and all his faul
To Marcius shall be honours, though indeed
In aught he merit not.

Sic.   Let's hence, and hear
How the despatch is made ; and in what fashion,
More than in singularity, he goes
Upon his present action.

    Bru.   Let's along.   [*Exeunt.*

SCENE II.—Corioli. *The Senate House.*

Enter TULLUS AUFIDIUS *and certain* Senators.

1st Sen. So, your opinion is, Aufidius,
That they of Rome are entered in our counsels,
And know how we proceed.

    Auf.   Is it not yours ?
What ever hath been thought on in this state
That could be brought to bodily act ere Rome
Had circumvention ? 'T is not four days gone
Since I heard thence : these are the words : I think
I have the letter here : yes, here it is :—

          Reads.

" They have pressed a power, but it is not known
Whether for east or west. The dearth is great ;
The people mutinous : and it is rumoured,
Cominius, Marcius your old enemy
(Who is of Rome worse hated than of you),
And Titus Lartius, a most valiant Roman,
These three lead on this preparation
Whither 't is bent. Most likely 't is for you :
Consider of it."

    1st Sen.   Our army 's in the field :
We never yet made doubt but Rome was ready
To answer us.

    Auf.   Nor did you think it folly
To keep your great pretences veiled till when
They needs must shew themselves : which in the
          hatching,
It seemed, appeared to Rome. By the discovery
We shall be shortened in our aim : which was,
To take in many towns ere, almost, Rome
Should know we were afoot.

    2nd Sen.   Noble Aufidius,
Take your commission : hie you to your bands :
Let us alone to guard Corioli.
If they set down before us, for the remove
Bring up your army : but I think you 'll find
They have not prepared for us.

    Auf.   O, doubt not that :
I speak from certainties. Nay, more ;
Some parcels of their powers are forth already,
And only hitherward. I leave your honours.
If we and Caius Marcius chance to meet,
'T is sworn between us we shall ever strike
Till one can do no more.

    All.   The gods assist you.

    Auf. And keep your honours safe.

    1st Sen. Farewell.

    2nd Sen. Farewell.

    All. Farewell.   [*Exeunt.*

SCENE III.—Rome. *An Apartment in* MARCIUS' *House.*

Enter VOLUMNIA *and* VIRGILIA : *they sit down on two low stools, and sew.*

Vol. I pray you, daughter, sing ; or express yourself in a more comfortable sort. If my son were my husband, I should freelier rejoice in that absence wherein he won honour, than in the embracements of his bed, where he would shew most love. When he was but tender-bodied, and the only son of my womb ; when youth with comeliness plucked all gaze his way ; when, for a day of kings' entreaties, a mother should not sell him an hour from her beholding ; I,—considering how honour would become such a person ; that it was no better than picture-like to hang by the wall, if renown made it not stir,—was pleased to let him seek danger where he was like to find fame. To a cruel war I sent him ; from whence he returned, his brows bound with oak. I tell thee, daughter, I sprang not more in joy at first hearing he was a man-child, than now in first seeing he had proved himself a man.

Vir. But had he died in the business, madam ; how then ?

Vol. Then his good report should have been my son : I therein would have found issue. Hear me profess sincerely : had I a dozen sons, each in my love alike, and none less dear than thine and my good Marcius, I had rather had eleven die nobly for their country, than one voluptuously surfeit out of action.

Enter a Gentlewoman.

Gent. Madam, the lady Valeria is come to
      visit you.

Vir. 'Beseech you, give me leave to retire
      myself.

Vol. Indeed you shall not.
Methinks I hear hither your husband's drum ;
See him pluck Aufidius down by the hair ;
As children from a bear, the Volces shunning him :
Methinks I see him stamp thus, and call thus :
" Come on, you cowards, you were got in fear,
Though you were born in Rome." His bloody brow
With his mailed hand then wiping, forth he goes,
Like to a harvest-man that 's tasked to mow
Or all or lose his hire.

Vir. His bloody brow ! O, Jupiter, no blood !

Vol. Away, you fool ! it more becomes a man
Than gilt his trophy. The breasts of Hecuba,
When she did suckle Hector, looked not lovelier
Than Hector's forehead, when it spit forth blood
At Grecian swords contending.—Tell Valeria
We are fit to bid her welcome.

         [*Exit* Gentlewoman.

Vir. Heavens bless my lord from fell Aufidius!

Vol. He 'll beat Aufidius' head below his knee,
And tread upon his neck.

Re-enter Gentlewoman, *with* VALERIA *and her*
Usher.

Val. My ladies both, good day to you.

Vol. Sweet madam,—

Vir. I am glad to see your ladyship.

Val. How do you both? you are manifest housekeepers. What, are you sewing here? A fine spot, in good faith.—How does your little son?

Vir. I thank your ladyship: well, good mada....

Vol. He had rather see the swords and hear a drum, than look upon his schoolmaster.

Val. O' my word, the father's son. I 'll swear 'tis a very pretty boy: o' my troth, I looked upon him o' Wednesday half an hour together. He has such a confirmed countenance! I saw him run after a gilded butterfly; and when he caught it, he let it go again; and after it again; and over and over he comes, and up again; catched it again: or whether his fall enraged him, or

how 'twas, he did so set his teeth and tear it: O, I warrant, how he mammocked it!

Vol. One of his father's moods.

Val. Indeed la, 'tis a noble child.

Vir. A crack, madam.

Val. Come, lay aside your stitchery: I must have you play the idle huswife with me this afternoon.

Vir. No, good madam: I will not out of doors.

Val. Not out of doors!

Vol. She shall, she shall.

Vir. Indeed, no, by your patience. I will not over the threshold till my lord return from the wars.

Val. Fie, you confine yourself most unreasonably. Come, you must go visit the good lady that lies in.

Vir. I will wish her speedy strength, and visit her with my prayers; but I cannot go thither.

Vol. Why, I pray you?

Vir. 'Tis not to save labour, nor that I want love.

Val. You would be another Penelope: yet, they say, all the yarn she spun in Ulysses' absence did but fill Ithaca full of moths. Come: I would your cambric were sensible as your finger, that

you might leave pricking it for pity. Come, you shall go with us.

Vir. No, good madam, pardon me: indeed I will not forth.

Val. In truth, la, go with me; and I 'll tell you excellent news of your husband.

Vir. O, good madam, there can be none yet.

Val. Verily I do not jest with you: there came news from him last night.

Vir. Indeed, madam?

Val. In earnest it 's true: I heard a senator speak it. Thus it is:—The Volces have an army forth; against whom Cominius the general is gone, with one part of our Roman power: your lord and Titus Lartius are set down before their city Corioli: they nothing doubt prevailing, and to make it brief wars. This is true, on mine honour: and so, I pray, go with us.

Vir. Give me excuse, good madam: I will obey you in everything hereafter.

Vol. Let her alone, lady: as she is now, she will but disease our better mirth.

Val. In troth I think she would.—Fare you well, then.—Come, good sweet lady.—Pr'y thee, Virgilia, turn thy solemnness out o' door, and go along with us.

Vir. No: at a word, madam: indeed I must not. I wish you much mirth.

Val. Well then, farewell.   [*Exeunt.*

SCENE IV.—*Before* Corioli.

Enter, with drum and colours, MARCIUS, TITUS LARTIUS, *Officers, and* Soldiers. *To them a* Messenger.

Mar. Yonder comes news.—A wager they have met.

Lart. My horse to yours, no.

Mar.   'T is done.

Lart.   Agreed.

Mar. Say, has our general met the enemy?

Mess. They lie in view; but have not spoke as yet.

Lart. So, the good horse is mine.

Mar.   I 'll buy him of you.

Lart. No, I 'll nor sell nor give him: lend you him I will,

For half a hundred years.—Summon the town.

Mar. How far off lie these armies?

Mess.   Within this mile and half.

Mar. Then shall we hear their 'larum, and they ours.

Now, Mars, I pr'y thee, make us quick in work;
That we with smoking swords may march from hence,

To help our fielded friends!—Come, blow thy
     blast.

They sound a parley. Enter, on the walls, some
Senators, and others.

Tullus Aufidius, is he within your walls?

1st Sen. No, nor a man that fears you less than he;
That 's lesser than a little.—Hark, our drums
               [*Alarums afar off.*
Are bringing forth our youth. We 'll break our
     walls,
Rather than they shall pound us up. Our gates,
Which yet seem shut, we have but pinned with
     rushes:
They 'll open of themselves.—Hark you, far off:
               [*Other alarums.*
There is Aufidius: list what work he makes
Amongst your cloven army.

Mar.   O, they are at it!

Lart. Their noise be our instruction.—Ladders, ho!

The Volces *enter, and pass over the stage.*

Mar. They fear us not, but issue forth their city.
Now put your shields before your hearts, and fight
With hearts more proof than shields.—Advance,
     brave Titus:
They do disdain us much beyond our thoughts;
Which makes me sweat with wrath.—Come on,
     my fellows:
He that retires, I 'll take him for a Volce,
And he shall feel mine edge.

Alarum, and exeunt Romans *and* Volces, *fighting.*
The Romans *are beaten back to their trenches.*
Re-enter MARCIUS.

Mar. All the contagion of the south light on you,
You shames of Rome! you herd of—Boils and
     plagues
Plaster you o'er; that you may be abhorred
Further than seen, and one infect another
Against the wind a mile! You souls of geese
That bear the shapes of men, how have you run
From slaves that apes would beat! Pluto and hell!
All hurt behind: backs red, and faces pale
With flight and agued fear! Mend, and charge
     home,
Or by the fires of heaven I 'll leave the foe,
And make my wars on you: look to 't. Come on:
If you 'll stand fast we 'll beat them to their wives,
As they us to our trenches followed.

Another alarum. The Volces *and* Romans *re-enter,*
and the fight is renewed. The Volces *retire into*
Corioli, *and* MARCIUS *follows them to the gates.*

So, now the gates are ope. Now prove good seconds:

'T is for the followers fortune widens them,
Not for the flyers.   Mark me, and do the like.
        [*He enters the gates, and is shut in.*
1st Sol. Fool-hardiness! not I.
2nd Sol. Nor I.
3rd Sol. See, they have shut him in.
                [*Alarum continues.*
All. To the pot, I warrant him.

      Enter Titus Lartius.

Lart. What is become of Marcius?
All.   Slain, sir, doubtless.
1st Sol. Following the flyers at the very heels,
With them he enters: who, upon the sudden,
Clapped-to their gates.   He is himself alone,
To answer all the city.
Lart.   O noble fellow,
Who, sensible, outdares his senseless sword,
And, when it bows, stands up!—Thou art left,
    Marcius:
A carbuncle entire, as big as thou art,
Were not so rich a jewel.   Thou wast a soldier
Even to Cato's wish: not fierce and terrible
Only in strokes; but with thy grim looks, and
The thunder-like percussion of thy sounds,
Thou mad'st thine enemies shake, as if the world
Were feverous and did tremble.

  Re-enter Marcius, *bleeding, assaulted by the
             enemy.*

1st Sol. Look, sir!
Lart. O, 't is Marcius:
Let 's fetch him off, or make remain alike.
      [*They fight, and all enter the city.*

    Scene V.—*Within the Town.   A Street.*

    Enter certain Romans, *with spoils.*

1st Rom. This will I carry to Rome.
2nd Rom. And I this.
3rd Rom. A murrain on 't!   I took this for
    silver. [*Alarum still continues afar off.*

Enter Marcius *and* Titus Lartius, *with a
            trumpet.*

Mar. See here these movers, that do prize their
    hours
At a cracked drachm!—Cushions, leaden spoons,
Irons of a doit, doublets that hangmen would
Bury with those that wore them, these base slaves,
Ere yet the fight be done, pack up!—Down with
    them.—
And hark, what noise the general makes!—To
    him.—
There is the man of my soul's hate, Aufidius,
Piercing our Romans.   Then, valiant Titus, take

Convenient numbers to make good the city;
Whilst I, with those that have the spirit, will haste
To help Cominius.
Lart.   Worthy sir, thou bleed'st:
Thy exercise hath been too violent for
A second course of fight.
Mar.   Sir, praise me not:
My work hath not yet warmed me.   Fare you well.
The blood I drop is rather physical
Than dangerous to me.   To Aufidius thus
I will appear, and fight.
Lart.   Now the fair goddess Fortune
Fall deep in love with thee; and her great charms
Misguide thy opposers' swords!   Bold gentleman,
Prosperity be thy page!
Mar.   Thy friend no less
Than those she placeth highest!   So, farewell.
Lart. Thou worthiest Marcius!—
                [*Exit* Marcius.
Go, sound thy trumpet in the market-place:
Call thither all the officers of the town,
Where they shall know our mind.   Away.
                   [*Exeunt.*

   Scene VI.—*Near the Camp of* Cominius.

  Enter Cominius *and* Forces, *retreating.*

Com. Breathe you, my friends.   Well fought:
    we are come off
Like Romans, neither foolish in our stands,
Nor cowardly in retire.   Believe me, sirs,
We shall be charged again.   Whiles we have struck,
By interims and conveying gusts we have heard
The charges of our friends:—the Roman gods
Lead their successes as we wish our own;
That both our powers, with smiling fronts en-
    countering,
May give you thankful sacrifice!—Thy news?

      Enter a Messenger.

Mess. The citizens of Corioli have issued,
And given to Lartius and to Marcius battle:
I saw our party to their trenches driven,
And then I came away.
Com.   Though thou speak'st truth,
Methinks thou speak'st not well.   How long is 't
    since?
Mess. Above an hour, my lord.
Com. 'T is not a mile: briefly we heard their
    drums:
How couldst thou in a mile confound an hour,
And bring thy news so late?
Mess.   Spies of the Volces
Held me in chase, that I was forced to wheel
Three or four miles about: else had I, sir,
Half an hour since brought my report.

Enter MARCIUS.

Com.   Who's yonder,
That does appear as he were flayed? O gods!
He has the stamp of Marcius; and I have
Beforetime seen him thus.

Mar.   Come I too late?

Com. The shepherd knows not thunder from a
          tabor,
More than I know the sound of Marcius' tongue
From every meaner man's.

Mar.   Come I too late?

Com. Ay, if you come not in the blood of others,
But mantled in your own.

Mar.   O! let me clip you,
In arms as sound as when I wooed: in heart
As merry as when our nuptial day was done,
And tapers burned to bedward.

Com.   Flower of warriors,
How is 't with Titus Lartius?

Mar. As with a man busied about decrees:
Condemning some to death, and some to exile;
Ransoming him, or pitying; threatening the other:
Holding Corioli in the name of Rome,
Even like a fawning greyhound in the leash,
To let him slip at will.

Com.   Where is that slave
Which told me they had beat you to your trenches?
Where is he? Call him hither.

Mar.   Let him alone;
He did inform the truth. But for our gentlemen,
The common file—(A plague! Tribunes for
          them!)—
The mouse ne'er shunned the cat as they did budge
From rascals worse than they.

Com.   But how prevailed you?

Mar. Will the time serve to tell? I do not think—
Where is the enemy? Are you lords o' the field?
If not, why cease you till you are so?

Com.   Marcius,
We have at disadvantage fought,
And did retire, to win our purpose.

Mar. How lies their battle? Know you on
          which side
They have placed their men of trust?

Com.   As I guess, Marcius,
Their bands in the vaward are the Antiates,
Of their best trust: o'er them Aufidius,
Their very heart of hope.

Mar.   I do beseech you,
By all the battles wherein we have fought,
By the blood we have shed together, by the vows
We have made to endure friends, that you directly
Set me against Aufidius and his Antiates:
And that you not delay the present; but,
Filling the air with swords advanced, and darts,
We prove this very hour.

Com.   Though I could wish

You were conducted to a gentle bath,
And balms applied to you, yet dare I never
Deny your asking: take your choice of those
That best can aid your action.

Mar.   Those are they
That most are willing.—If any such be here
(As it were sin to doubt) that love this painting
Wherein you see me smeared; if any fear
Lesser his person than an ill report;
If any think brave death outweighs bad life,
And that his country's dearer than himself,
Let him, alone, or so many so minded,
Wave thus [*waving his hand*], to express his dis-
          position,
And follow Marcius.

[*They all shout, and wave their swords; take him
          up in their arms, and cast up their caps.*

O me, alone! Make you a sword of me?
If these shows be not outward, which of you
But is four Volces? None of you but is
Able to bear against the great Aufidius
A shield as hard as his. A certain number
(Though thanks to all) must I select from all:
The rest shall bear the business in some other fight,
As cause will be obeyed.—Please you to march;
And four shall quickly draw out my command,
Which men are best inclined.

Com.   March on, my fellows:
Make good this ostentation, and you shall
Divide in all with us.   [*Exeunt.*

SCENE VII.—*The Gates of* Corioli.

TITUS LARTIUS, *having set a guard upon* Corioli,
          going with a drum and trumpet toward COMINIUS
          and CAIUS MARCIUS, *enters with a* Lieutenant,
          a party of Soldiers, *and a* Scout.

Lart. So, let the ports be guarded: keep your
          duties
As I have set them down. If I do send, despatch
Those centuries to our aid: the rest will serve
For a short holding. If we lose the field,
We cannot keep the town.

Lieu.   Fear not our care, sir.

Lart. Hence, and shut your gates upon us.—
Our guider, come; to the Roman camp conduct us.
          [*Exeunt.*

SCENE VIII.—*A Field of Battle between the*
          Roman *and the* Volcian *Camps.*

Alarum.   Enter MARCIUS *and* AUFIDIUS.

Mar. I'll fight with none but thee; for I do
          hate thee
Worse than a promise-breaker.

Auf.   We hate alike :
Not Afric owns a serpent I abhor
More than thy fame and envy.   Fix thy foot.
    Mar. Let the first budger die the other's slave ;
And the gods doom him after !
    Auf.   If I fly, Marcius,
Halloo me like a hare.
    Mar.   Within these three hours, Tullus,
Alone I fought in your Corioli walls,
And made what work I pleased. 'T is not my blood
Wherein thou seest me masked : for thy revenge,
Wrench up thy power to the highest.
    Auf.   Wert thou the Hector
That was the whip of your bragged progeny,
Thou shouldst not 'scape me here.—

        [*They fight, and certain* Volces *come to
            the aid of* AUFIDIUS.

Officious, and not valiant—you have shamed me
In your condemnéd seconds.

        [*Exeunt fighting, driven in by* MARCIUS.

SCENE IX.—*The* Roman *Camp.*

*Alarum. A retreat is sounded. Flourish. Enter
    at one side,* COMINIUS *and* Romans : *at the
    other side,* MARCIUS, *with his arm in a scarf,
    and other* Romans.

    Com. If I should tell thee o'er this thy day's work,
Thou 'lt not believe thy deeds : but I 'll report it
Where senators shall mingle tears with smiles :
Where great patricians shall attend and shrug ;
I' the end, admire : where ladies shall be frighted,
And, gladly quaked, hear more : where the dull
            Tribunes,
That, with the fusty plebeians, hate thine honours,
Shall say, against their hearts,—" We thank the
            gods
Our Rome hath such a soldier ! "—
Yet cam'st thou to a morsel of this feast,
Having fully dined before.

Enter TITUS LARTIUS, *with his power, from the
            pursuit.*

    Lart.   O general,
Here 's the steed ; we the caparison.
Hadst thou beheld—
    Mar.   Pray now, no more : my mother,
Who has a charter to extol her blood,
When she does praise me, grieves me. I have done
As you have done ; that 's what I can : induced
As you have been ; that 's for my country.
He that has but effected his good will,
Hath overta'en mine act.
    Com.   You shall not be
The grave of your deserving : Rome must know

The value of her own : 't were a concealment
Worse than a theft, no less than a traducement,
To hide your doings ; and to silence that
Which, to the spire and top of praises vouched,
Would seem but modest. Therefore, I beseech you
(In sign of what you are, not to reward
What you have done), before our army hear me.
    Mar. I have some wounds upon me, and they
            smart
To hear themselves remembered.
    Com.   Should they not,
Well might they fester 'gainst ingratitude,
And tent themselves with death. Of all the horses
(Whereof we have ta'en good and good store), of all
The treasure in this field achieved, and city,
We render you the tenth ; to be ta'en forth
Before the common distribution,
At your only choice.
    Mar.   I thank you, general ;
But cannot make my heart consent to take
A bribe to pay my sword.   I do refuse it,
And stand upon my common part with those
That have beheld the doing.

        [*A long flourish. They all cry,* " MARCIUS !
            MARCIUS ! " *cast up their caps and lances.*
            COMINIUS *and* LARTIUS *stand bare.*

    Mar. May these same instruments, which you
            profane,
Never sound more !—When drums and trum-
            pets shall
I' the field prove flatterers, let courts and cities be
Made all of false-faced soothing ! When steel grows
Soft as the parasite's silk, let him be made
An overture for the wars !—No more, I say !—
For that I have not washed my nose that bled,
Or foiled some debile wretch (which, without note,
Here's many else have done), you shout me forth
In acclamations hyperbolical :
As if I loved my little should be dieted
In praises sauced with lies.
    Com.   Too modest are you ;
More cruel to your good report than grateful
To us that give you truly.   By your patience,
If 'gainst yourself you be incensed, we 'll put you
(Like one that means his proper harm) in ma-
            nacles ;
Then reason safely with you.—Therefore, be it
            known,
As to us, to all the world, that Caius Marcius
Wears this war's garland : in token of the which,
My noble steed, known to the camp, I give him,
With all his trim belonging : and from this time,
For what he did before Corioli, call him,
With all the applause and clamour of the host,
" Caius Marcius Coriolanus ! "—
Bear the addition nobly ever.

        [*Flourish. Trumpets sound, and drums.*

All. Caius Marcius Coriolanus!

Cor. I will go wash;
And when my face is fair, you shall perceive
Whether I blush or no. Howbeit, I thank you.
I mean to stride your steed; and at all times
To undercrest your good addition,
To the fairness of my power.

Com.   So, to our tent:
Where, ere we do repose us, we will write
To Rome of our success.—You, Titus Lartius,
Must to Corioli back: send us to Rome
The best, with whom we may articulate
For their own good and ours.

Lart.   I shall, my lord.

Cor. The gods begin to mock me. I, that now
Refused most princely gifts, am bound to beg
Of my lord general.

Com.   Take it: 't is yours.—What is 't?

Cor. I sometime lay, here in Corioli,
At a poor man's house; he used me kindly.
He cried to me: I saw him prisoner;
But then Aufidius was within my view,
And wrath o'erwhelmed my pity. I request you
To give my poor host freedom.

Com.   O, well begged!
Were he the butcher of my son, he should
Be free as is the wind. Deliver him, Titus.

Lart. Marcius, his name?

Cor.   By Jupiter, forgot!—
I am weary; yea, my memory is tired.—
Have we no wine here?

Com.   Go we to our tent:
The blood upon your visage dries: 't is time
It should be looked to. Come.   [*Exeunt.*

SCENE X.—*The Camp of the* Volces.

A flourish. Cornets. Enter TULLUS AUFIDIUS,
bloody, with two or three Soldiers.

Auf. The town is ta'en!

1st Sol. 'T will be delivered back on good
condition.

Auf. Condition!
I would, I were a Roman; for I cannot,
Being a Volce, be that I am.—Condition!
What good condition can a treaty find
I' the part that is at mercy? Five times, Marcius,
I have fought with thee: so often hast thou beat
me;
And wouldst do so, I think, should we encounter
As often as we eat.—By the elements,
If e'er again I meet him beard to beard,
He is mine or I am his. Mine emulation
Hath not that honour in 't it had: for where
I thought to crush him in an equal force
(True sword to sword), I 'll potch at him some
way:
Or wrath or craft may get him.

1st Sol.   He 's the devil.

Auf. Bolder, though not so subtle. My valour 's
poisoned
With only suffering stain by him; for him
Shall fly out of itself. Nor sleep, nor sanctuary;
Being naked, sick; nor fane, nor Capitol;
The prayers of priests, nor times of sacrifice
(Embarquements all of fury), shall lift up
Their rotten privilege and custom 'gainst
My hate to Marcius: where I find him, were it
At home, upon my brother's guard, even there,
Against the hospitable canon, would I
Wash my fierce hand in 's heart.—Go you to the
city:
Learn how 't is held; and what they are that must
Be hostages for Rome.

1st Sol.   Will not you go?

Auf. I am attended at the cypress grove:
I pray you
('T is south the city mills), bring me word thither
How the world goes; that to the pace of it
I may spur on my journey.

1st Sol.   I shall, sir.   [*Exeunt.*

SCENE I.—Rome. *A public Place.*

Enter MENENIUS, SICINIUS, *and* BRUTUS.

Men. The augurer tells me we shall have news to-night.

Bru. Good or bad?

Men. Not according to the prayer of the people; for they love not Marcius.

Sic. Nature teaches beasts to know their friends.

Men. Pray you, who does the wolf love?

Sic. The lamb.

Men. Ay, to devour him; as the hungry plebeians would the noble Marcius.

Bru. He's a lamb indeed, that baes like a bear.

Men. He's a bear, indeed, that lives like a lamb. You two are old men: tell me one thing that I shall ask you.

Both Trib. Well, sir.

Men. In what enormity is Marcius poor, that you two have not in abundance?

Bru. He's poor in no one fault, but stored with all.

Sic. Especially in pride.

Bru. And topping all others in boasting.

Men. This is strange now! Do you two know how you are censured here in the city: I mean of us o' the right-hand file? Do you?

Both Trib. Why, how are we censured?

Men. Because you talk of pride now,—will you not be angry?

Both Trib. Well, well, sir, well.

Men. Why, 't is no great matter; for a very little thief of occasion will rob you of a great deal of patience. Give your disposition the reins, and be angry at your pleasures: at the least, if you take it as a pleasure to you in being so. You blame Marcius for being proud?

Bru. We do it not alone, sir.

Men. I know you can do very little alone; for your helps are many, or else your actions would grow wondrous single: your abilities are too infant-like for doing much alone. You talk of pride: O that you could turn your eyes towards the napes of your necks, and make but an interior survey of your good selves: O that you could!

Bru. What then, sir?

Men. Why, then you should discover a brace of unmeriting, proud, violent, testy magistrates (alias fools) as any in Rome.

Sic. Menenius, you are known well enough too.

Men. I am known to be a humorous patrician, and one that loves a cup of hot wine with not a drop of allaying Tyber in 't: said to be something imperfect in favouring the first complaint: hasty and tinder-like upon too trivial motion: one that converses more with the buttock of the night than with the forehead of the morning. What I think I utter; and spend my malice in my breath. Meeting two such weals-men as you are (I cannot call you Lycurguses), if the drink you give me touch my palate adversely, I make a crooked face at it. I cannot say your worships have delivered the matter well, when I find the ass in compound with the major part of your syllables: and though I must be content to bear with those that say you are reverend grave men, yet they lie deadly that tell you have good faces. If you see this in the map of my microcosm, follows it that I am known well enough too? What harm can your bisson conspectuities glean out of this character, if I be known well enough too?

Bru. Come, sir, come, we know you well enough.

Men. You know neither me, yourselves, nor anything. You are ambitious for poor knaves' caps and legs; you wear out a good wholesome forenoon in hearing a cause between an orange-wife and a fosset-seller; and then rejourn the

controversy of threepence to a second day of audience.—When you are hearing a matter between party and party, if you chance to be pinched with the cholic, you make faces like mummers; set up the bloody flag against all patience; and, in roaring for a chamber-pot, dismiss the controversy bleeding, the more entangled by your hearing: all the peace you make in their cause is, calling both the parties knaves. You are a pair of strange ones!

Bru. Come, come, you are well understood to be a perfecter giber for the table than a necessary bencher in the Capitol.

Men. Our very priests must become mockers if they shall encounter such ridiculous subjects as you are. When you speak best unto the purpose, it is not worth the wagging of your beards; and your beards deserve not so honourable a grave as to stuff a botcher's cushion, or to be entombed in an ass's packsaddle. Yet you must be saying, Marcius is proud; who, in a cheap estimation, is worth all your predecessors since Deucalion; though, peradventure, some of the best of them were hereditary hangmen. Good e'en to your worships: more of your conversation would infect my brain, being the herdsmen of the beastly plebeians. I will be bold to take my leave of you.

[BRUTUS *and* SICINIUS *retire up the scene.*

Enter VOLUMNIA, VIRGILIA, VALERIA, &c.

How now, my as fair as noble ladies (and the moon, were she earthly, no nobler), whither do you follow your eyes so fast?

Vol. Honourable Menenius, my boy Marcius approaches: for the love of Juno, let's go.

Men. Ha! Marcius coming home?

Vol. Ay, worthy Menenius; and with most prosperous approbation.

Men. Take my cap, Jupiter, and I thank thee:—Hoo! Marcius coming home!

Two Ladies. Nay, 't is true.

Vol. Look, here 's a letter from him: the state hath another, his wife another; and I think there 's one at home for you.

Men. I will make my very house reel to-night:—A letter for me!

Vir. Yes, certain there 's a letter for you: I saw it.

Men. A letter for me! It gives me an estate of seven years' health; in which time I will make a lip at the physician: the most sovereign prescription in Galen is but empiricutic, and, to this preservative, of no better report than a horse-drench.—Is he not wounded? he was wont to come home wounded.

Vir. O, no, no, no.

Vol. O, he is wounded; I thank the gods for 't.

Men. So do I too, if it be not too much:—Brings 'a victory in his pocket?—The wounds become him.

Vol. On his brows, Menenius: he comes the third time home with the oaken garland.

Men. Has he disciplined Aufidius soundly?

Vol. Titus Lartius writes, they fought together, but Aufidius got off.

Men. And 't was time for him too, I 'll warrant him that: an he had stayed by him, I would not have been so fidiused for all the chests in Corioli, and the gold that 's in them. Is the senate possessed of this?

Vol. Good ladies, let 's go.—Yes, yes, yes: the senate has letters from the general, wherein he gives my son the whole name of the war: he hath in this action outdone his former deeds doubly.

Val. In troth, there 's wondrous things spoke of him.

Men. Wondrous? Ay, I warrant you, and not without his true purchasing.

Vir. The gods grant them true!

Vol. True! pow, wow.

Men. True! I 'll be sworn they are true.—Where is he wounded?—God save your good worships! [*To the* Tribunes, *who come forward.*] Marcius is coming home: he has more cause to be proud.—Where is he wounded?

Vol. I' the shoulder and i' the left arm: there will be large cicatrices to shew the people when he shall stand for his place. He received in the repulse of Tarquin seven hurts i' the body.

Men. One in the neck, and two in the thigh; —there 's nine that I know.

Vol. He had, before this last expedition, twenty-five wounds upon him.

Men. Now it 's twenty-seven: every gash was an enemy's grave. [*A shout and flourish.*] Hark! the trumpets.

Vol. These are the ushers of Marcius: before him He carries noise, and behind him he leaves tears: Death, that dark spirit, in 's nervy arm doth lie; Which being advanced, declines; and then men die.

A Sennet. Trumpets sound. Enter COMINIUS *and* TITUS LARTIUS; *between them,* CORIOLANUS, *crowned with an oaken garland; with* Captains, Soldiers, *and a* Herald.

Her. Know, Rome, that all alone Marcius did fight
Within Corioli' gates; where he hath won,
With fame, a name to Caius Marcius: these
In honour follows,—Coriolanus.
Welcome to Rome, renowned Coriolanus!
                                        [*Flourish.*

All. Welcome to Rome, renowned Coriolanus!

Cor. No more of this; it does offend my heart:
Pray now, no more.

Com.   Look, sir, your mother,—

Cor. O! you have, I know, petitioned all the gods
For my prosperity.   [*Kneels.*

Vol.   Nay, my good soldier, up!
My gentle Marcius, worthy Caius,
And, by deed-achieving honour newly named,—
What is it?—Coriolanus, must I call thee?—
But O, thy wife—

Cor.   My gracious silence, hail!
Wouldst thou have laughed had I come coffined home,
That weep'st to see me triumph?—Ah, my dear,
Such eyes the widows in Corioli wear,
And mothers that lack sons.

Men.   Now the gods crown thee!

Cor. And live you yet?—O my sweet lady, pardon.   [*To* VALERIA.

Vol. I know not where to turn:—O welcome home;
And welcome, general: and you are welcome all.

Men. A hundred thousand welcomes! I could weep,
And I could laugh: I am light and heavy. Welcome!
A curse begin at very root of his heart
That is not glad to see thee!—You are three
That Rome should dote on: yet, by the faith of men,
We have some old crabtrees here at home that will not
Be grafted to your relish. Yet welcome, warriors:
We call a nettle but a nettle, and
The faults of fools but folly.

Com.   Ever right.

Cor. Menenius, ever, ever.

Her. Give way there, and go on.

Cor. Your hand, and yours.

       [*To his wife and mother.*

Ere in our own house I do shade my head,

The good patricians must be visited;

From whom I have received not only greetings,

But with them change of honours.

  Vol. I have lived

To see inherited my very wishes

And the buildings of my fancy:

Only there's one thing wanting, which I doubt not

But our Rome will cast upon thee.

  Cor. Know, good mother,

I had rather be their servant in my way,

Than sway with them in theirs.

  Com. On to the Capitol.

  [*Flourish. Cornets. Exeunt in state, as before.*

   The Tribunes *remain.*

  Bru. All tongues speak of him, and the bleared

   sights

Are spectacled to see him. Your prattling nurse

Into a rapture lets her baby cry,

While she chats him: the kitchen malkin pins

Her richest lockram 'bout her reechy neck,

Clambering the walls to eye him. Stalls, bulks,

   windows,

Are smothered up, leads filled, and ridges horsed

With variable complexions, all agreeing

In earnestness to see him. Seld-shewn flamens

Do press among the popular throngs, and puff

To win a vulgar station: our veiled dames

Commit the war of white and damask in

Their nicely-gawded cheeks, to the wanton spoil

Of Phœbus' burning kisses. Such a pother,

As if that whatsoever god who leads him

Were slily crept into his human powers,

And gave him graceful posture.

  Sic. On the sudden,

I warrant him consul.

  Bru. Then our office may,

During his power, go sleep.

  Sic. He cannot temperately transport his honours

From where he should begin and end; but will

Lose those that he hath won.

  Bru. In that there's comfort.

  Sic. Doubt not, the commoners, for whom we

   stand,

But they, upon their ancient malice, will

Forget, with the least cause, these his new honours:

Which that he'll give them, make I as little ques-

   tion

As he is proud to do 't.

  Bru. I heard him swear,

Were he to stand for consul, never would he

Appear i' the market place, nor on him put

The napless vesture of humility;

Nor, shewing (as the manner is) his wounds

To the people, beg their stinking breaths.

  Sic. 'T is right.

  Bru. It was his word. O, he would miss it rather

Than carry it but by the suit o' the gentry to him,

And the desire of the nobles.

  Sic. I wish no better

Than have him hold that purpose, and to put it

In execution.

  Bru. 'T is most like he will.

  Sic. It shall be to him, then, as our good wills:

A sure destruction.

  Bru. So it must fall out

To him, or our authorities. For an end,

We must suggest the people in what hatred

He still hath held them: that, to his power, he

   would

Have made them mules, silenced their pleaders,

And dispropertied their freedoms: holding them,

In human action and capacity,

Of no more soul nor fitness for the world

Than camels in the war; who have their provand

Only for bearing burdens, and sore blows

For sinking under them.

  Sic. This, as you say,—suggested

At some time when his soaring insolence

Shall teach the people (which time shall not want

If he be put upon 't; and that's as easy

As to set dogs on sheep),—will be his fire

To kindle their dry stubble; and their blaze

Shall darken him for ever.

    Enter a Messenger.

  Bru. What's the matter?

  Mess. You are sent for to the Capitol.

'T is thought that Marcius shall be consul:

I have seen the dumb men throng to see him,

And the blind to hear him speak: matrons flung

   gloves,

Ladies and maids their scarfs and handkerchiefs,

Upon him as he passed: the nobles bended

As to Jove's statue; and the commons made

A shower and thunder, with their caps and shouts!

I never saw the like.

  Bru. Let's to the Capitol,

And carry with us ears and eyes for the time,

But hearts for the event.

  Sic. Have with you. [*Exeunt.*

  SCENE II.—*The same. The Capitol.*

  Enter two Officers, *to lay cushions.*

  1st Off. Come, come, they are almost here.

How many stand for consulships?

  2nd Off. Three, they say: but 't is thought of

every one Coriolanus will carry it.

1st Offi. That's a brave fellow; but he's vengeance proud, and loves not the common people.

2nd Offi. 'Faith, there have been many great
men that have flattered the people, who ne'er
loved them; and there be many that they have
loved they know not wherefore: so that if they
love they know not why, they hate upon no better
ground. Therefore, for Coriolanus neither to
care whether they love or hate him, manifests
the true knowledge he has in their disposition;
and, out of his noble carelessness, lets them
plainly see 't.

1st Offi. If he did not care whether he had
their love or no, he waved indifferently 'twixt
doing them neither good nor harm: but he seeks
their hate with greater devotion than they can
render it him, and leaves nothing undone that
may fully discover him their opposite. Now, to
seem to affect the malice and displeasure of the
people, is as bad as that which he dislikes,—to
flatter them for their love.

2nd Offi. He hath deserved worthily of his
country: and his ascent is not by such easy degrees as those who, having been supple and
courteous to the people, bonneted without any
further deed to have them at all into their estimation and report: but he hath so planted his
honours in their eyes, and his actions in their
hearts, that for their tongues to be silent and
not confess so much were a kind of ingrate. l
injury: to report otherwise were a malice that,
giving itself the lie, would pluck reproof and
rebuke from every ear that heard it.

1st Offi. No more of him: he is a worthy man.
Make way; they are coming.

A Sennet. Enter, with lictors before them, Cominius *the* Consul, Menenius, Coriolanus, *many
other* Senators, Sicinius *and* Brutus. *The Senators take their places; the Tribunes take
theirs also by themselves.*

Men. Having determined of the Volces, and
To send for Titus Lartius, it remains,
As the main point of this our after-meeting,
To gratify his noble service that
Hath thus stood for his country. Therefore, please
    you,
Most reverend and grave elders, to desire
The present consul, and last general
In our well-found successes, to report
A little of that worthy work performed
By Caius Marcius Coriolanus: whom
We meet here both to thank and to remember
With honours like himself.

1st Sen.   Speak, good Cominius:
Leave nothing out for length, and make us think,
Rather our state's defective for requital,

Than we to stretch it out.—Masters o' the people,
We do request your kindest ears: and (after)
Your loving motion toward the common body,
To yield what passes here.

Sic.   We are convented
Upon a pleasing treaty, and have hearts
Inclinable to honour and advance
The theme of our assembly.

Bru.   Which the rather
We shall be blessed to do, if he remember
A kinder value of the people than
He hath hereto prized them at.

Men.   That's off, that's off:
I would you rather had been silent. Please you
To hear Cominius speak?

Bru.   Most willingly:
But yet my caution was more pertinent
Than the rebuke you give it.

Men.   He loves your people;
But tie him not to be their bedfellow.—
Worthy Cominius, speak.—Nay, keep your place.
    [Coriolanus *rises, and offers to go away.*

1st Sen. Sit, Coriolanus: never shame to hear
What you have nobly done.

Cor.   Your honours' pardon:
I had rather have my wounds to heal again
Than hear say how I got them.

Bru.   Sir, I hope
My words disbenched you not.

Cor.   No, sir: yet oft,
When blows have made me stay, I fled from words.
You soothed not, therefore hurt not: but your
    people,
I love them as they weigh.

Men.   Pray now, sit down.

Cor. I had rather have one scratch my head
        i' the sun,
When the alarum was struck, than idly sit
To hear my nothings monstered.   [*Exit.*

Men.   Masters o' the people,
Your multiplying spawn how can he flatter
(That's thousand to one good one), when you
        now see
He had rather venture all his limbs for honour
Than one of his ears to hear it?—Proceed, Co-
        minius.

Com. I shall lack voice: the deeds of Corio-
        lanus
Should not be uttered feebly.—It is held
That valour is the chiefest virtue, and
Most dignifies the haver: if it be,
The man I speak of cannot in the world
Be singly counterpoised. At sixteen years,
When Tarquin made a head for Rome, he fought
Beyond the mark of others: our then dictator,
Whom with all praise I point at, saw him fight,
When with his Amazonian chin he drove

The bristled lips before him : he bestrid
An o'erpressed Roman, and i' the consul's view
Slew three opposers : Tarquin's self he met,
And struck him on his knee. In that day's feats,
When he might act the woman in the scene,
He proved best man i' the field, and for his meed
Was brow-bound with the oak. His pupil age
Man-entered thus, he waxéd like a sea ;
And, in the brunt of seventeen battles since,
He lurched all swords o' the garland.——For this
          last,
Before and in Corioli, let me say,
I cannot speak him home. He stopped the fliers,
And by his rare example made the coward
Turn terror into sport : as weeds before
A vessel under sail, so men obeyed,
And fell below his stem. His sword (death's stamp),
Where it did mark, it took : from face to foot
He was a thing of blood, whose every motion
Was timed with dying cries. Alone he entered
The mortal gate o' the city, which he painted
With shunless destiny : aidless came off,
And with a sudden reinforcement struck
Corioli like a planet :——now all 's his :
When by-and-by the din of war 'gan pierce
His ready sense : then straight his doubled spirit
Requickened what in flesh was fatigate,
And to the battle came he ; where he did
Run reeking o'er the lives of men, as if
'T were a perpetual spoil : and, till we called
Both field and city ours, he never stood
To ease his breast with panting.

Men.   Worthy man !

1st Sen. He cannot but with measure fit the
          honours
Which we devise him.

Com.   Our spoils he kicked at,
And looked upon things precious as they were
The common muck o' the world. He covets less
Than misery itself would give : rewards
His deeds with doing them ; and is content
To spend the time, to end it.

Men.   He 's right noble :
Let him be called for.

1st Sen.   Call for Coriolanus.

Off. He doth appear.

Re-enter CORIOLANUS.

Men. The senate, Coriolanus, are well pleased
To make thee consul.

Cor.   I do owe them still
My life and services.

Men.   It then remains,
That you do speak to the people.

Cor.   I do beseech you,
Let me o'erleap that custom ; for I cannot
Put on the gown, stand naked, and entreat them,

For my wounds' sake, to give their suffrage. Please
          you
That I may pass this doing.

Sic.   Sir, the people
Must have their voices ; neither will they bate
One jot of ceremony.

Men.   Put them not to 't :——
Pray you, go fit you to the custom ;
And take to you, as your predecessors have,
Your honour with your form.

Cor.   It is a part
That I shall blush in acting, and might well
Be taken from the people.

Bru.   Mark you that ?   [*To* SICINIUS.

Cor. To brag unto them,——thus I did, and
          thus ;
Shew them the unaching scars which I should hide,
As if I had received them for the hire
Of their breath only !

Men.   Do not stand upon 't.——
We recommend to you, tribunes of the people,
Our purpose to them :——and to our noble consul
Wish we all joy and honour.

Sen. To Coriolanus come all joy and honour !
          [*Flourish.   Then exeunt* Senators.

Bru. You see how he intends to use the people.

Sic. May they perceive his intent ! He will
          require them
As if he did contemn what he requested
Should be in them to give.

Bru.   Come, we 'll inform them
Of our proceedings here : on the market-place
I know they do attend us.   [*Exeunt.*

SCENE III.——*The same.   The* Forum.

Enter several Citizens.

1st Cit. Once, if he do require our voices, we
ought not to deny him.

2nd Cit. We may, sir, if we will.

3rd Cit. We have power in ourselves to do
it, but it is a power that we have no power to
do : for if he shew us his wounds and tell us his
deeds, we are to put our tongues into those
wounds, and speak for them : so, if he tell us
his noble deeds, we must also tell him our noble
acceptance of them. Ingratitude is monstrous :
and for the multitude to be ingrateful, were to
make a monster of the multitude ; of the which
we being members, should bring ourselves to be
monstrous members.

1st Cit. And to make us no better thought of
a little help will serve : for once, when we stood
up about the corn, he himself stuck not to call
us the many-headed multitude.

3rd Cit. We have been called so of many: not that our heads are some brown, some black, some auburn, some bald, but that our wits are so diversely coloured. And truly I think, if all our wits were to issue out of one skull, they would fly east, west, north, south; and their consent of one direct way should be at once to all the points o' the compass.

2nd Cit. Think you so? Which way do you judge my wit would fly?

3rd Cit. Nay, your wit will not so soon out as another man's will; 'tis strongly wedged up in a block-head: but if it were at liberty, 'twould sure southward.

2nd Cit. Why that way?

3rd Cit. To lose itself in a fog; where being three parts melted away with rotten dews, the fourth would return for conscience' sake, to help to get thee a wife.

2nd Cit. You are never without your tricks:— you may, you may.

3rd Cit. Are you all resolved to give your voices? But that's no matter; the greater part carries it. I say, if he would incline to the people, there was never a worthier man.

Enter Coriolanus *and* Menenius.

Here he comes, and in the gown of humility: mark his behaviour. We are not to stay all together, but to come by him where he stands, by ones, by twos, and by threes. He's to make his requests by particulars: wherein every one of us has a single honour, in giving him our own voices with our own tongues. Therefore follow me, and I'll direct you how you shall go by him.

All. Content, content.　　　[*Exeunt* Citizens.

Men. O sir, you are not right: have you not known

The worthiest men have done't?

Cor.　　　　What must I say?—
" I pray, sir,"—Plague upon't! I cannot bring
My tongue to such a pace:—" Look, sir; my wounds:
I got them in my country's service, when
Some certain of your brethren roared, and ran
From the noise of our own drums."

Men.　　　　O me, the gods!
You must not speak of that: you must desire them
To think upon you.

Cor.　　　　Think upon me? Hang 'em!
I would they would forget me, like the virtues
Which our divines lose by them.

Men.　　　　You'll mar all:
I'll leave you. Pray you, speak to them, I pray you,
In wholesome manner.　　　　　　　[*Exit.*

Enter two Citizens.

Cor.　　　Bid them wash their faces,
And keep their teeth clean.—So, here comes a brace.—
You know the cause, sir, of my standing here.

1st Cit. We do, sir: tell us what hath brought you to 't.

Cor. Mine own desert.

2nd Cit. Your own desert?

Cor. Ay, not mine own desire.

1st Cit. How! not your own desire?

Cor. No, sir: 'twas never my desire yet to trouble the poor with begging.

1st Cit. You must think, if we give you anything, we hope to gain by you.

Cor. Well then, I pray, your price o' the consulship?

1st Cit. The price is, sir, to ask it kindly.

Cor. Kindly, sir? I pray, let me ha't: I have wounds to shew you, which shall be yours in private.—Your good voice, sir: what say you?

2nd Cit. You shall have it, worthy sir.

Cor. A match, sir.—There is in all two worthy voices begged.—I have your alms: adieu.

1st Cit. But this is something odd!

2nd Cit. An 'twere to give again,—but 'tis no matter.　　　　　　[*Exeunt* Citizens.

Enter two other Citizens.

Cor. Pray you now, if it may stand with the tune of your voices that I may be consul, I have here the customary gown.

3rd Cit. You have deserved nobly of your country, and you have not deserved nobly.

Cor. Your enigma?

3rd Cit. You have been a scourge to her enemies; you have been a rod to her friends: you have not, indeed, loved the common people.

Cor. You should account me the more virtuous that I have not been common in my love. I will, sir, flatter my sworn brother the people, to earn a dearer estimation of them: 'tis a condition they account gentle: and since the wisdom of their choice is rather to have my hat than my heart, I will practise the insinuating nod, and be off to them most counterfeitly: that is, sir, I will counterfeit the bewitchment of some popular man, and give it bountifully to the desirers. Therefore, beseech you I may be consul.

4th Cit. We hope to find you our friend; and therefore give you our voices heartily.

3rd Cit. You have received many wounds for your country.

Cor. I will not seal your knowledge with shewing them. I will make much of your voices, and so trouble you no further.

Both Cit. The gods give you joy, sir, heartily!
　　　　　　　　　　　　　[*Exeunt* Citizens.

COR. Your enigma?

Cor. Most sweet voices!—
Better it is to die, better to starve,
Than crave the hire which first we do deserve.
Why in this woolvish toge should I stand here,
To beg of Hob and Dick, that do appear,
Their needless vouches? Custom calls me to 't!
What custom wills, in all things should we do 't,
The dust on antique time would lie unswept,
And mountainous error be too highly heaped
For truth to overpeer.—Rather than fool it so,
Let the high office and the honour go
To one that would do thus.—I am half through:
The one part suffered, the other will I do.

Enter three other Citizens.

Here come more voices.—
Your voices: for your voices I have fought:
Watched for your voices; for your voices bear
Of wounds two dozen odd; battles thrice six
I have seen and heard of; for your voices
  have
Done many things, some less, some more.—Your
  voices:
Indeed I would be consul.

 5th Cit. He has done nobly, and cannot go
without any honest man's voice.

 6th Cit. Therefore let him be consul. The

441

gods give him joy, and make him good friend
to the people!

All. Amen, amen.—God save thee, noble
    consul!   [*Exeunt* Citizens.

Cor. Worthy voices!

Re-enter MENENIUS, *with* BRUTUS *and* SICINIUS.

Men. You have stood your limitation; and
    the tribunes
Endue you with the people's voice.
Remains that, in the official marks invested,
You anon do meet the senate.

Cor.   Is this done?

Sic. The custom of request you have discharged:
The people do admit you; and are summoned
To meet anon, upon your approbation.

Cor. Where? at the senate-house?

Sic.   There, Coriolanus.

Cor. May I change these garments?

Sic.   You may, sir.

Cor. That I'll straight do; and, knowing my-
    self again,
Repair to the senate-house.

Men. I'll keep you company.—Will you along?

Bru. We stay here for the people.

Sic.   Fare you well.
         [*Exeunt* CORIOLANUS *and* MENENIUS.
He has it now; and, by his looks, methinks
'T is warm at his heart.

Bru.   With a proud heart he wore
His humble weeds. Will you dismiss the people?

Re-enter CITIZENS.

Sic. How now, my masters: have you chose
    this man?

1st Cit. He has our voices, sir.

Bru. We pray the gods he may deserve your
    loves.

2nd Cit. Amen, sir. To my poor unworthy
    notice,
He mocked us when he begged our voices.

3rd Cit. Certainly he flouted us downright.

1st Cit. No, 't is his kind of speech: he did
    not mock us.

2nd Cit. Not one amongst us, save yourself,
    but says
He used us scornfully. He should have shewed us
His marks of merit; wounds received for his
    country.

Sic. Why, so he did, I am sure.

Cit. No, no; no man saw 'em. [*Several speak.*

3rd Cit. He said he had wounds, which he
    could shew in private:
And with his hat, thus waving it in scorn,
" I would be consul," says he: " aged custom,
But by your voices, will not so permit me:
Your voices therefore." When we granted that,

Here was,—" I thank you for your voices;—
    thank you;—
Your most sweet voices! Now you have left
    your voices,
I have no further with you."—Was not this
    mockery?

Sic. Why, either were you ignorant to see't,
Or, seeing it, of such childish friendliness
To yield your voices?

Bru.   Could you not have told him,
As you were lessoned,—when he had no power,
But was a petty servant to the state,
He was your enemy; ever spake against
Your liberties, and the charters that you bear
I' the body of the weal: and now, arriving
A place of potency, and sway o' the state,
If he should still malignantly remain
Fast foe to the plebeii, your voices might
Be curses to yourselves?—You should have said,
That as his worthy deeds did claim no less
Than what he stood for, so his gracious nature
Would think upon you for your voices, and
Translate his malice towards you into love,
Standing your friendly lord.

Sic.   Thus to have said,
As you were fore-advised, had touched his spirit
And tried his inclination: from him plucked
Either his gracious promise, which you might,
As cause had called you up, have held him to;
Or else it would have galled his surly nature,
Which easily endures not article
Tying him to aught: so putting him to rage,
You should have ta'en the advantage of his choler,
And passed him unelected.

Bru.   Did you perceive
He did solicit you in free contempt
When he did need your loves; and do you think
That his contempt shall not be bruising to you
When he hath power to crush? Why, had your
    bodies
No heart among you; or had you tongues to cry
Against the rectorship of judgment?

Sic.   Have you,
Ere now, denied the asker; and now again,
On him that did not ask, but mock, bestow
Your sued-for tongues?

3rd Cit. He's not confirmed; we may deny
    him yet.

2nd Cit. And will deny him:
I'll have five hundred voices of that sound.

1st Cit. I twice five hundred, and their friends
    to piece 'em.

Bru. Get you hence instantly; and tell those
    friends
They have chose a consul that will from them
    take
Their liberties; make them of no more voice

Than dogs, that are as often beat for barking
As therefore kept to do so.

Sic. Let them assemble;
And on a safer judgment, all revoke
Your ignorant election. Enforce his pride,
And his old hate unto you: besides, forget not
With what contempt he wore the humble weed;
How in his suit he scorned you: but your loves,
Thinking upon his services, took from you
The apprehension of his present portance,
Which most gibingly, ungravely, he did fashion
After the inveterate hate he bears you.

Bru. Lay a fault on us, your tribunes; that
  we laboured
(No impediment between) but that you must
Cast your election on him.

Sic. Say you chose him
More after our commandment, than as guided
By your own true affections; and that, your minds
Pre-occupied with what you rather must do
Than what you should, made you against the grain
To voice him consul. Lay the fault on us.

Bru. Ay, spare us not. Say we read lectures
  to you
How youngly he began to serve his country,
How long continued: and what stock he springs of,
The noble house o' the Marcians; from whence
  came
That Ancus Marcius (Numa's daughter's son)

Who, after great Hostilius, here was king.
Of the same house Publius and Quintus were,
That our best water brought by conduits hither:
And Censorinus, darling of the people
(And nobly named so, twice being censor),
Was his great ancestor.

Sic. One thus descended,
That hath beside well in his person wrought
To be set high in place, we did commend
To your remembrances: but you have found,
Scaling his present bearing with his past,
That he's your fixéd enemy; and revoke
Your sudden approbation.

Bru. Say you ne'er had done 't
(Harp on that still) but by our putting on:
And presently, when you have drawn your number,
Repair to the Capitol.

Cit. We will so:—almost all [*Several speak*]
repent in their election. [*Exeunt* Citizens.

Bru. Let them go on:
This mutiny were better put in hazard,
Than stay, past doubt, for greater,
If, as his nature is, he fall in rage
With their refusal, both observe and answer
The vantage of his anger.

Sic. To the Capitol; come.
We will be there before the stream o' the people;
And this shall seem, as partly 't is, their own,
Which we have goaded onward. [*Exeunt.*

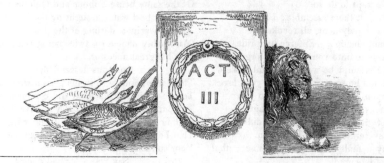

Scene I.—Rome. *A Street.*

Cornets. Enter Coriolanus, Menenius, Cominius, Titus Lartius, Senators, *and* Patricians.

Cor. Tullus Aufidius, then, had made new head?

Lart. He had, my lord : and that it was which
caused
Our swifter composition.

Cor. So, then, the Volces stand but as at first;
Ready, when time shall prompt them, to make road
Upon us again.

Com.   They are worn, lord consul, so
That we shall hardly in our ages see
Their banners wave again.

Cor.   Saw you Aufidus?

Lart. On safeguard he came to me; and did curse
Against the Volces for they had so vilely
Yielded the town.   He is retired to Antium.

Cor. Spoke he of me?

Lart. He did, my lord.

Cor. How? what?

Lart. How often he had met you, sword to sword:
That, of all things upon the earth, he hated
Your person most : that he would pawn his fortunes
To hopeless restitution, so he might
Be called your vanquisher.

Cor.   At Antium lives he?

Lart. At Antium.

Cor. I wish I had a cause to seek him there,
To oppose his hatred full.—Welcome home.
[*To* Lartius.

Enter Sicinius and Brutus.

Behold : these are the tribunes of the people ;
The tongues o' the common mouth !   I do despise them,
For they do prank them in authority
Against all noble sufferance.

Sic.   Pass no further.

Cor. Ha! what is that?

Bru. It will be dangerous to go on : no further.

Cor. What makes this change?

Men. The matter?

Com. Hath he not passed the noble and the
common?

Bru. Cominius, no.

Cor. Have I had children's voices?

1st Sen. Tribunes, give way : he shall to the
market-place.

Bru. The people are incensed against him.

Sic. Stop, or all will fall in broil.

Cor. Are these your herd?—
Must these have voices, that can yield them now,
And straight disclaim their tongues?—What are
your offices?
You being their mouths, why rule you not their
teeth?
Have you not set them on?

Men.   Be calm, be calm.

Cor. It is a purposed thing, and grows by plot,
To curb the will of the nobility.
Suffer it, and live with such as cannot rule,
Nor ever will be ruled.

Bru.   Call 't not a plot.
The people cry, you mocked them; and of late,
When corn was given them gratis, you repined :
Scandalled the suppliants for the people : called
them
Time-pleasers, flatterers, foes to nobleness.

Cor. Why, this was known before.

Bru. Not to them all.

Cor. Have you informed them since?

Bru. How! I inform them?

Cor. You are like to do such business.

Bru. Not unlike, each way, to better yours.

Cor. Why, then, should I be consul?—By yon
clouds,
Let me deserve so ill as you, and make me
Your fellow-tribune.

Sic.   You shew too much of that
For which the people stir.   If you will pass
To where you are bound, you must inquire your way
(Which you are out of) with a gentler spirit ;

Or never be so noble as a consul,
Nor yoke with him for tribune.
   Men.   Let's be calm.
   Com. The people are abused; set on.—This
          paltering
Becomes not Rome; nor has Coriolanus
Deserved this so dishonoured rub, laid falsely
I' the plain way of his merit.
   Cor.   Tell me of corn!
This was my speech, and I will speak 't again :—
   Men. Not now, not now.
   1st Sen.   Not in this heat, sir, now.
   Cor. Now, as I live, I will.—My nobler friends,
I crave their pardons :
For the mutable, rank-scented many,
Let them regard me as I do not flatter,
And therein behold themselves :—I say again,
In soothing them we nourish 'gainst our senate
The cockle of rebellion, insolence, sedition,
Which we ourselves have ploughed for, sowed and
          scattered,
By mingling them with us, the honoured number,
Who lack not virtue, no, nor power, but that
Which they have given to beggars.
   Men.   Well, no more.
   1st Sen. No more words, we beseech you.
   Cor.   How! no more?
As for my country I have shed my blood,
Not fearing outward force, so shall my lungs
Coin words till their decay against those meazels,
Which we disdain should tetter us, yet sought
The very way to catch them.
   Bru.   You speak o' the people
As if you were a god to punish; not
A man of their infirmity.
   Sic. 'Twere well we let the people know 't.
   Men. What, what? his choler?
   Cor. Choler!
Were I as patient as the midnight sleep,
By Jove 't would be my mind.
   Sic.   It is a mind
That shall remain a poison where it is,
Not poison any further.
   Cor.   Shall remain!—
Hear you this Triton of the minnows? mark you
His absolute " shall?"
   Com.   'T was from the canon.
   Cor.   " Shall!"—
O good, but most unwise patricians, why,
You grave but reckless senators, have you thus
Given Hydra here to choose an officer,
That with his peremptory " shall," being but
The horn and noise o' the monsters, wants not spirit
To say he'll turn your current in a ditch,
And make your channel his? If he have power,
Then vail your ignorance : if none, awake
Your dangerous lenity. If you are learnéd,

Be not as common fools : if you are not,
Let them have cushions by you. You are plebeians,
If they be senators : and they are no less,
When, both your voices blended, the greatest taste
Most palates theirs. They choose their magistrate!
And such a one as he who puts his " shall,"
His popular " shall," against a graver bench
Than ever frowned in Greece!—By Jove himself,
It makes the consuls base! and my soul aches
To know, when two authorities are up,
Neither supreme, how soon confusion
May enter 'twixt the gap of both, and take
The one by the other.
   Com.   Well: on to the market-place.
   Cor. Whoever gave that counsel to give forth
The corn o' the storehouse gratis, as 't was used
Sometime in Greece,—
   Men.   Well, well, no more of that.
   Cor. (Though there the people had more
          absolute power),
I say they nourished disobedience, fed
The ruin of the state.
   Bru.   Why shall the people give
One that speaks thus, their voice?
   Cor.   I 'll give my reasons,
More worthier than their voices. They know
          the corn
Was not our recompense; resting well assured
They ne'er did service for 't. Being pressed to
          the war,
Even when the navel of the state was touched,
They would not thread the gates. This kind of
          service
Did not deserve corn gratis. Being i' the war,
Their mutinies and revolts, wherein they shewed
Most valour, spoke not for them. The accusation
Which they have often made against the senate,
All cause unborn, could never be the native
Of our so frank donation.—Well, what then?
How shall this bosom multiplied digest
The senate's courtesy? Let deeds express
What 's like to be their words : " We did request it:
We are the greater poll; and in true fear
They gave us our demands."—Thus we debase
The nature of our seats, and make the rabble
Call our cares, fears : which will in time break ope
The locks o' the senate, and bring in the crows
To peck the eagles.
   Men.   Come, enough.
   Bru. Enough, with over-measure.
   Cor   No; take more :
What may be sworn by, both divine and human,
Seal what I end withal!—This double worship,—
Where one part does disdain with cause, the other
Insult without all reason; where gentry, title,
          wisdom,
Cannot conclude but by the yea and no

Of general ignorance,—it must omit
Real necessities, and give way the while
To unstable slightness. Purpose so barred, it
　　follows
Nothing is done to purpose. Therefore, beseech
　　you,—
You that will be less fearful than discreet;
That love the fundamental part of state
More than you doubt the change of 't; that prefer
A noble life before a long; and wish
To jump a body with a dangerous physic,
That 's sure of death without it,—at once pluck out
The multitudinous tongue; let them not lick
The sweet which is their poison. Your dishonour
Mangles true judgment, and bereaves the state
Of that integrity which should become it:
Not having the power to do the good it would,
For the ill which doth control it.

　　Bru.　　　　　He has said enough.
　　Sic. He has spoken like a traitor, and shall
　　　　answer
As traitors do.

　　Cor. Thou wretch! despite o'erwhelm thee!—
What should the people do with these bald tri-
　　　　bunes?
On whom depending, their obedience fails
To the greater bench. In a rebellion,
When what 's not meet, but what must be, was law,
Then were they chosen: in a better hour,
Let what is meet be said " it must be meet,"
And throw their power i' the dust.

　　Bru. Manifest treason!
　　Sic.　　　　　This a consul? no.
　　Bru. The ædiles, ho!—Let him be appre-
　　　　hended.

　　Sic. Go, call the people: [*Exit* Brutus]—in
　　　　whose name, myself
Attach thee, as a traitorous innovator;
A foe to the public weal. Obey, I charge thee,
And follow to thine answer.

　　Cor.　　　　Hence, old goat!
　　Sen. }
　　Pat. }　We 'll surety him.
　　Com.　　　Agéd sir, hands off.
　　Cor. Hence, rotten thing, or I shall shake thy
　　　　bones
Out of thy garments!
　　Sic.　　　　Help, ye citizens!

Re-enter Brutus, *with the* Ædiles, *and a rabble*
　　　　of Citizens.

　　Men. On both sides more respect.
　　Sic. Here 's he that would take from you all
　　　　your power.
　　Bru. Seize him, ædiles.
　　Cit. Down with him! down with him!
　　　　　　　　　　　　　　　　[*Several speak.*

　　2nd Sen. Weapons, weapons, weapons!
　　　　[*They all bustle about* Coriolanus.
Tribunes,—patricians,—citizens!—what, ho!—
Sicinius,—Brutus,—Coriolanus,—citizens!
　　Cit. Peace, peace, peace! stay, hold, peace!
　　Men. What is about to be?—I am out of breath:
Confusion 's near: I cannot speak.—You, tribunes
To the people,—Coriolanus, patience :—
Speak, good Sicinius.
　　Sic.　　　Hear me, people :—Peace!
　　Cit. Let 's hear our tribune.—Peace! Speak,
　　　　speak, speak!
　　Sic. You are at point to lose your liberties.
Marcius would have all from you: Marcius,
Whom late you have named for consul.
　　Men.　　　　Fie, fie, fie!
This is the way to kindle, not to quench.
　　1st Sen. To unbuild the city, and to lay all flat.
　　Sic. What is the city but the people?
　　Cit. True; the people are the city.
　　Bru. By the consent of all, we were established
The people's magistrates.
　　Cit.　　　You so remain.
　　Men. And so are like to do.
　　Cor. That is the way to lay the city flat;
To bring the roof to the foundation ;
And bury all, which yet distinctly ranges,
In heaps and piles of ruin.
　　Sic.　　　This deserves death.
　　Bru. Or let us stand to our authority,
Or let us lose it.—We do here pronounce,
Upon the part o' the people, in whose power
We were elected theirs, Marcius is worthy
Of present death.
　　Sic.　　　Therefore lay hold of him :
Bear him to the rock Tarpeian, and from thence
Into destruction cast him.
　　Bru.　　　Ædiles, seize him.
　　Cit. Yield, Marcius, yield.
　　Men.　　　Hear me one word :
Beseech you, tribunes, hear me but a word.
　　Æd. Peace, peace!
　　Men. Be that you seem, truly your country's
　　　　friend,
And temperately proceed to what you would
Thus violently redress.
　　Bru.　　　Sir, those cold ways,
That seem like prudent helps, are very poisonous
Where the disease is violent.—Lay hands upon
　　　　him,
And bear him to the rock.
　　Cor. No: I 'll die here. [*Drawing his sword.*
There 's some among you have beheld me fighting :
Come, try upon yourselves what you have seen me.
　　Men. Down with that sword!—Tribunes, with-
　　　　draw awhile.
　　Bru. Lay hands upon him.

Men. Help Marcius : help,
You that be noble : help him, young, and old !
Cit. Down with him, down with him !
    [*In this mutiny, the* Tribunes, *the* Ædiles,
                and the people, are all beat in.
Men. Go, get you to your house : be gone, away !
All will be naught else.
  2nd Sen.   Get you gone.
  Cor.   Stand fast :
We have as many friends as enemies.
  Men. Shall it be put to that ?
  1st Sen.   The gods forbid !
I pr'y thee, noble friend, home to thy house :
Leave us to cure this cause.
  Men.   For 't is a sore upon us
You cannot tent yourself. Begone, 'beseech you.
  Com. Come, sir, along with us.
  Cor. I would they were barbarians (as they are,
Though in Rome littered), not Romans (as they
      are not,
Though calved i' the porch of the Capitol),—
  Men.   Be gone :
Put not your worthy rage into your tongue :
One time will owe another.
  Cor.   On fair ground,
I could beat forty of them.
  Men.   I could myself
Take up a brace of the best of them : yea, the
      two tribunes.
  Com. But now 't is odds beyond arithmetic :
And manhood is called foolery when it stands
Against a falling fabric.—Will you hence
Before the tag return ? whose rage doth rend
Like interrupted waters, and o'erbear
What they are used to bear.
  Men.   Pray you, be gone :
I 'll try whether my old wit be in request
With those that have but little. This must be patched
With cloth of any colour.
  Com.   Nay, come away.
    [*Exeunt* Coriolanus, Cominius, *and others.*
  1st Pat. This man has marred his fortune.
  Men. His nature is too noble for the world :
He would not flatter Neptune for his trident,
Or Jove for his power to thunder. His heart 's
      his mouth :
What his breast forges, that his tongue must vent :
And being angry, does forget that ever
He heard the name of death. [*A noise within.*
Here 's goodly work !
  2nd Pat.   I would they were abed !
  Men. I would they were in Tyber !—What,
      the vengeance,
Could he not speak them fair ?

Re-enter Brutus *and* Sicinius, *with the rabble.*

  Sic.   Where is this viper,

That would depopulate the city, and
Be every man himself ?
  Men.   You worthy tribunes,—
  Sic. He shall be thrown down the Tarpeian rock
With rigorous hands. He hath resisted law ;
And therefore law shall scorn him further trial
Than the severity of the public power,
Which he so sets at nought.
  1st Cit.   He shall well know
The noble tribunes are the people's mouths,
And we their hands.
  Cit. He shall, sure on 't. [*Several speak together.*
  Men. Sir, sir,—
  Sic. Peace !
  Men. Do not cry " havock," where you should
      but hunt
With modest warrant.
  Sic.   Sir, how comes it that you
Have holp to make this rescue ?
  Men.   Hear me speak :—
As I do know the consul's worthiness,
So can I name his faults :—
  Sic.   Consul ! what consul ?
  Men. The consul Coriolanus.
  Bru.   He a consul !
  Cit. No, no, no, no, no !
  Men. If, by the tribunes' leave, and yours, good
      people,
I may be heard, I 'd crave a word or two ;
The which shall turn you to no further harm
Than so much loss of time.
  Sic.   Speak briefly, then ;
For we are peremptory to despatch
This viperous traitor. To eject him hence
Were but one danger ; and to keep him here
Our certain death : therefore it is decreed
He dies to-night.
  Men.   Now the good gods forbid
That our renownéd Rome, whose gratitude
Towards her deservéd children is enrolled
In Jove's own book, like an unnatural dam,
Should now eat up her own !
  Sic. He 's a disease that must be cut away.
  Men. O, he 's a limb that has but a disease :
Mortal to cut it off ; to cure it easy.
What has he done to Rome that 's worthy death ?
Killing our enemies ? The blood he hath lost
(Which I dare vouch is more than that he hath,
By many an ounce) he dropped it for his country :
And what is left, to lose it by his country,
Were to us all that do 't and suffer it
A brand to the end o' the world.
  Sic.   This is clean kam.
  Bru. Merely awry.—When he did love his
      country,
It honoured him.
  Men.   The service of the foot,

Being once gangrened, is not then respected
For what before it was?

Bru.   We 'll hear no more.—
Pursue him to his house, and pluck him thence:
Lest his infection, being of catching nature,
Spread further.

Men.   One word more; one word:
This tiger-footed rage, when it shall find
The harm of unscanned swiftness, will too late
Tie leaden pounds to his heels.   Proceed by
      process:
Lest parties (as he is beloved) break out,
And sack great Rome with Romans.

Bru.   If it were so,—
Sic. What do ye talk?
Have we not had a taste of his obedience?
Our ædiles smote! ourselves resisted!—Come.

Men. Consider this: he has been bred i' the wars
Since he could draw a sword, and is ill schooled
In boulted language; meal and bran together
He throws without distinction.   Give me leave,
I 'll go to him, and undertake to bring him
Where he shall answer, by a lawful form,
(In peace), to his utmost peril.

1st Sen.   Noble tribunes,
It is the humane way: the other course
Will prove too bloody; and the end of it
Unknown to the beginning.

Sic.   Noble Menenius,
Be you, then, as the people's officer.—
Masters, lay down your weapons.

Bru.   Go not home.
Sic. Meet on the market-place.—We 'll attend
      you there:
Where, if you bring not Marcius, we 'll proceed
In our first way.

Men.   I 'll bring him to you.—
Let me desire your company. [*To the* Senators.
       He must come,
Or what is worst will follow.

1st Sen.   Pray you, let 's to him.
                         [*Exeunt.*

SCENE II.—*A Room in* CORIOLANUS'S *House.*

Enter CORIOLANUS *and* Patricians.

Cor. Let them pull all about mine ears;
      present me
Death on the wheel, or at wild horses' heels;
Or pile ten hills on the Tarpeian rock,
That the precipitation might down stretch
Below the beam of sight,—yet will I still
Be thus to them.

1st Pat.   You do the nobler.

Enter VOLUMNIA.

Cor. I muse my mother

Does not approve me further, who was wont
To call them woollen vassals; things created
To buy and sell with groats; to shew bare heads
In congregations, to yawn, be still, and wonder,
When one but of my ordinance stood up
To speak of peace or war.—I talk of you:
                     [*To* VOLUMNIA.
Why did you wish me milder? Would you have me
False to my nature? Rather say, I play
The man I am.

Vol.   O, sir, sir, sir,
I would have had you put your power well on,
Before you had worn it out.

Cor.   Let go.
Vol. You might have been enough the man
       you are,
With striving less to be so.   Lesser had been
The thwartings of your dispositions, if
You had not shewed them how you were disposed
Ere they lacked power to cross you.

Cor.   Let them hang.
Vol. Ay, and burn too.

Enter MENENIUS *and* Senators.

Men. Come, come, you have been too rough;
      something too rough:
You must return, and mend it.

1st Sen.   There 's no remedy:
Unless, by not so doing, our good city
Cleave in the midst, and perish.

Vol.   Pray be counselled.
I have a heart as little apt as yours,
But yet a brain that leads my use of anger
To better vantage.

Men.   Well said, noble woman!
Before he should thus stoop to the herd, but that
The violent fit o' the time craves it as physic
For the whole state, I would put mine armour on,
Which I can scarcely bear.

Cor. What must I do?
Men.   Return to the tribunes.
Cor. Well, what then? what then?
Men.   Repent what you have spoke.
Cor. For them?—I cannot do it to the gods:
Must I, then, do 't to them?

Vol.   You are too absolute:
Though therein you can never be too noble,
But when extremities speak. I have heard you say,
Honour and policy, like unsevered friends,
I' the war do grow together. Grant that, and tell
      me,
In peace what each of them by th' other lose,
That they combine not there.

Cor. Tush, tush!
Men. A good demand.
Vol. If it be honour, in your wars, to seem
The same you are not (which for your best ends

You adopt your policy), how is it less or worse
That it shall hold companionship in peace
With honour, as in war; since that to both
It stands in like request?

    Cor.   Why force you this?

    Vol. Because that now it lies on you to speak
To the people: not by your own instruction,
Nor by the matter which your heart prompts you,
But with such words that are but roted in
Your tongue, though but bastards and syllables
Of no allowance to your bosom's truth.
Now, this no more dishonours you at all
Than to take in a town with gentle words,
Which else would put you to your fortune and
The hazard of much blood.—
I would dissemble with my nature, where
My fortunes and my friends, at stake, required
I should do so in honour. I am in this,
Your wife,—your son, these senators, the nobles:
And you will rather shew our general louts
How you can frown, than spend a fawn upon them
For the inheritance of their loves, and safeguard
Of what that want might ruin!

    Men.   Noble lady!—
Come, go with us: speak fair: you may salve so,
Not what is dangerous present, but the loss
Of what is past.

    Vol.   I pr'y thee now, my son,
Go to them, with this bonnet in thy hand:
And thus far having stretched it (here be with
    them),
Thy knee bussing the stones (for in such business
Action is eloquence, and the eyes of the ignorant,
More learnéd than their ears), waving thy head,
Which often,—thus,—correcting thy stout heart,
Now humble as the ripest mulberry,
That will not hold the handling. Or say to them,
Thou art their soldier, and being bred in broils,
Hast not the soft way which, thou dost confess,
Were fit for thee to use, as they to claim,
In asking their good loves: but thou wilt frame
Thyself, forsooth, hereafter theirs, so far
As thou hast power and person.

    Men.   This but done,
Even as she speaks, why all their hearts were
    yours:

For they have pardons, being asked, as free
As words to little purpose.
    Vol.   Pr'y thee now,
Go, and be ruled: although I know thou hadst
    rather
Follow thy enemy in a fiery gulf,
Than flatter him in a bower.—Here is Cominius.

Enter Cominius.

    Com. I have been i' the market-place: and, sir,
't is fit
You make strong party, or defend yourself
By calmness or by absence: all 's in anger.
    Men. Only fair speech.
    Com.   I think 't will serve, if he
Can thereto frame his spirit.
    Vol.   He must and will.—
Pr'y thee now, say you will; and go about it.
    Cor. Must I go shew them my unbarbed sconce?
    Must I,
With my base tongue, give to my noble heart
A lie that it must bear?—Well, I will do 't:
Yet were there but this single plot to lose,
This mould of Marcius, they to dust should grind it,
And throw it against the wind.—To the market-
    place :—
You have put me now to such a part which never
I shall discharge to the life.
    Com.   Come, come; we 'll prompt you.
    Vol. I pr'y thee now, sweet son, as thou hast said
My praises made thee first a soldier, so,
To have my praise for this, perform a part
Thou hast not done before.
    Cor.   Well, I must do 't.—
Away, my disposition, and possess me
Some harlot's spirit! My throat of war be turned
(Which quiréd with my drum) into a pipe
Small as an eunuch, or the virgin voice
That babies lulls asleep! The smiles of knaves
Tent in my cheeks; and schoolboys' tears take up
The glasses of my sight! A beggar's tongue
Make motion through my lips! and my armed
    knees,
Who bowed but in my stirrup, bend like his
That hath received an alms!—I will not do 't!
Lest I surcease to honour mine own truth,
And by my body's action teach my mind
A most inherent baseness.
    Vol.   At thy choice, then :
To beg of thee it is my more dishonour,
Than thou of them. Come all to ruin: let
Thy mother rather feel thy pride than fear
Thy dangerous stoutness: for I mock at death
With as big heart as thou. Do as thou list.
Thy valiantness was mine, thou suck'dst it from
    me :
But owe thy pride thyself.

    Cor.   Pray be content.
Mother, I am going to the market-place :
Chide me no more. I 'll mountebank their loves,
Cog their hearts from them, and come home
    beloved
Of all the trades in Rome. Look, I am going :
Commend me to my wife. I 'll return consul :
Or never trust to what my tongue can do
I' the way of flattery, further.
    Vol.   Do your will.   [*Exit.*
    Com. Away! the tribunes do attend you. Arm
    yourself
To answer mildly : for they are prepared
With accusations, as I hear, more strong
Than are upon you yet.
    Cor. The word is, mildly.—Pray you, let us go.
Let them accuse me by invention; I
Will answer in mine honour.
    Men.   Ay, but mildly.
    Cor. Well, mildly be it then : mildly! [*Exeunt.*

Scene III.—*The same. The* Forum.

Enter Sicinius *and* Brutus.

    Bru. In this point charge him home, that he
    affects
Tyrannical power. If he evade us there,
Enforce him with his envy to the people;
And that the spoil got on the Antiates
Was ne'er distributed.

Enter an Ædile.

What, will he come?
    Æd. He 's coming.
    Bru. How accompanied?
    Æd. With old Menenius, and those senators
That always favoured him.
    Sic.   Have you a catalogue
Of all the voices that we have procured,
Set down by the poll?
    Æd.   I have; 't is ready here.
    Sic. Have you collected them by tribes?
    Æd.   I have.
    Sic. Assemble presently the people hither :
And when they hear me say, " It shall be so
I' the right and strength o' the commons" (be it
    either
For death, for fine, or banishment), then let them,
If I say "fine," cry "fine;" if " death," cry
    " death :"
Insisting on the old prerogative
And power i' the truth o' the cause.
    Æd.   I shall inform them.
    Bru. And when such time they have begun to
    cry,

Let them not cease, but with a din confused
Enforce the present execution
Of what we chance to sentence.
    Æd.   Very well.
    Sic. Make them be strong and ready for this hint,
When we shall hap to give 't them.
    Bru. Go about it.   [*Exit Ædile.*
Put him to choler straight. He hath been used
Ever to conquer, and to have his worth
Of contradiction:—being once chafed, he cannot
Be reined again to temperance: then he speaks
What's in his heart; and that is there which looks
With us to break his neck.
    Sic. Well, here he comes.

    Enter CORIOLANUS, MENENIUS, COMINIUS,
        Senators, *and* Patricians.

    Men.   Calmly, I do beseech you.
    Cor. Ay, as an ostler, that for the poorest piece
Will bear the knave by the volume.—The ho-
        noured gods
Keep Rome in safety, and the chairs of justice
Supplied with worthy men: plant love among us:
Throng our large temples with the shows of peace,
And not our streets with war!
    1st Sen.   Amen, amen!
    Men. A noble wish.

    Re-enter Ædile, *with* Citizens.

    Sic. Draw near, ye people.
    Æd. List to your tribunes: audience. Peace,
        I say!
    Cor. First hear me speak.
    Both Tri.   Well, say.—Peace, ho!
    Cor. Shall I be charged no further than this
        present?
Must all determine here?
    Sic.   I do demand
If you submit you to the people's voices,
Allow their officers, and are content
To suffer lawful censure for such faults
As shall be proved upon you?
    Cor.   I am content.
    Men. Lo, citizens, he says he is content.
The warlike service he has done consider:
Think on the wounds his body bears, which shew
Like graves i' the holy churchyard.
    Cor.   Scratches with briars;
Scars to move laughter only.
    Men.   Consider further,
That when he speaks not like a citizen,
You find him like a soldier. Do not take
His rougher accents for malicious sounds,
But, as I say, such as become a soldier,
Rather than envy you.
    Com.   Well, well, no more.
    Cor. What is the matter,

That, being passed for consul with full voice,
I am so dishonoured that the very hour
You take it off again?
    Sic.   Answer to us.
    Cor. Say, then: 'tis true I ought so.
    Sic. We charge you, that you have contrived to
        take
From Rome all seasoned office, and to wind
Yourself into a power tyrannical:
For which you are a traitor to the people.
    Cor. How! Traitor?
    Men.   Nay; temperately:—your promise.
    Cor. The fires i' the lowest hell fold in the people!
Call me their traitor!—Thou injurious tribune!
Within thine eyes sat twenty thousand deaths,
In thy hands clutched as many millions, in
Thy lying tongue both numbers, I would say
"Thou liest!" unto thee, with a voice as free
As I do pray the gods.
    Sic.   Mark you this, people?
    Cit. To the rock! to the rock with him!
    Sic. Peace!—
We need not put new matter to his charge:
What you have seen him do, and heard him
        speak,—
Beating your officers, cursing yourselves,
Opposing laws with strokes, and here defying
Those whose great power must try him,—even this,
So criminal, and in such capital kind,
Deserves the extremest death.
    Bru. But since he hath served well for Rome,—
    Cor. What, do you prate of service?
    Bru. I talk of that, that know it.
    Cor. You!
    Men. Is this the promise that you made your
        mother?
    Com.   Know, I pray you,—
    Cor. I'll know no further!
Let them pronounce the steep Tarpeian death,
Vagabond exile, flaying: pent to linger
But with a grain a day, I would not buy
Their mercy at the price of one fair word;
Nor check my courage for what they can give,
To have it with saying, "Good morrow."
    Sic.   For that he has
(As much as in him lies) from time to time
Envied against the people, seeking means
To pluck away their power; as now at last
Given hostile strokes, and that not in the presence
Of dreaded justice, but on the ministers
That do distribute it;—in the name o' the people,
And in the power of us the tribunes, we,
Even from this instant, banish him our city:
In peril of precipitation
From off the rock Tarpeian, never more
To enter our Rome gates.—I' the people's name,
I say it shall be so.

Cit. It shall be so ; it shall be so ! let him away.
He 's banished, and it shall be so !

    Com. Hear me, my masters, and my common
        friends :—

    Sic. He 's sentenced : no more hearing.

    Com.   Let me speak :
I have been consul, and can shew, for Rome,
Her enemies' marks upon me.   I do love
My country's good with a respect more tender,
More holy and profound, than mine own life,
My dear wife's estimate, her womb's increase,
And treasure of my loins.   Then if I would
Speak that—

    Sic.   We know your drift:—speak what ?

    Bru. There 's no more to be said, but he is
      banished,
As enemy to the people and his country.
It shall be so.

    Cit.   It shall be so ; it shall be so !

    Cor. You common cry of curs ! whose breath I
      hate
As reek o' the rotten fens, whose loves I prize
As the dead carcasses of unburied men
That do corrupt my air,—I banish you :—
And here remain with your uncertainty.

Let every feeble rumour shake your hearts !
Your enemies, with nodding of their plumes,
Fan you into despair !   Have the power still
To banish your defenders : till at length
Your ignorance (which finds not till it feels),
Making but reservation of yourselves
(Still your own foes), deliver you,
As most abated captives, to some nation
That won you without blows !—Despising,
For you, the city, thus I turn my back :
There is a world elsewhere.

    [*Exeunt* Coriolanus, Cominius, Menenius,
          Senators, *and* Patricians.

    Æd. The people's enemy is gone, is gone !

    Cit. Our enemy is banished ! he is gone !—Hoo !
      hoo !

    [*The people shout, and throw up their caps.*

    Sic. Go, see him out at gates, and follow him,
As he hath followed you, with all despite :
Give him deserved vexation.—Let a guard
Attend us through the city.

    Cit. Come, come, let 's see him out at gates :
      come.
The gods preserve our noble tribunes !—Come.
                   [*Exeunt.*

ACT IV.

SCENE I.—Rome. *Before the Gate of the City.*

Enter CORIOLANUS, VOLUMNIA, VIRGILIA, MENE-
NIUS, COMINIUS, *and several young* Patricians.

  Cor. Come, leave your tears: a brief farewell.
      The beast
With many heads butts me away.—Nay, mother,
Where is your ancient courage? you were used
To say, extremity was the trier of spirits;
That common chances common men could bear;
That, when the sea was calm, all boats alike
Shewed mastership in floating: fortune's blows
When most struck home, being gentle, wounded,
      craves
A noble cunning: you were used to load me
With precepts that would make invincible
The heart that conned them.
  Vir. O heavens! O heavens!
  Cor.   Nay, I pr'y thee, woman,—
  Vol. Now the red pestilence strike all trades in
      Rome,
And occupations perish!
  Cor.   What, what, what!
I shall be loved when I am lacked. Nay, mo-
      ther,
Resume that spirit when you were wont to say,
If you had been the wife of Hercules,
Six of his labours you'd have done, and saved
Your husband so much sweat.—Cominius,
Droop not: adieu.—Farewell, my wife; my mo-
      ther:
I'll do well yet.—Thou old and true Menenius,
Thy tears are salter than a younger man's,

And venomous to thine eyes.—My sometime ge-
      neral,
I have seen thee stern, and thou hast oft beheld
Heart-hardening spectacles: tell these sad women
'T is fond to wail inevitable strokes,
As 't is to laugh at them.—My mother, you wot
      well
My hazards still have been your solace: and
Believe 't not lightly (though I go alone,
Like to a lonely dragon that his fen
Makes feared and talked of more than seen), your
      son
Will or exceed the common, or be caught
With cautelous baits and practice.
  Vol.   My first son,
Whither wilt thou go? Take good Cominius
With thee awhile: determine on some course,
More than a wild exposure to each chance
That starts in the way before thee.
  Cor.   O the gods!
  Com. I'll follow thee a month, devise with thee
Where thou shalt rest, that thou mayst hear of us,
And we of thee. So, if the time thrust forth
A cause for thy repeal, we shall not send
O'er the vast world to seek a single man;
And lose advantage, which doth ever cool
I' the absence of the needer.
  Cor.   Fare ye well:
Thou hast years upon thee, and thou art too full
Of the wars' surfeits to go rove with one
That's yet unbruised: bring me but out at gate.—
Come, my sweet wife, my dearest mother, and
My friends of noble touch, when I am forth

Bid me farewell, and smile. I pray you, come.
While I remain above the ground, you shall
Hear from me still ; and never of me aught
But what is like me formerly.

Men. That's worthily
As any ear can hear.—Come, let's not weep.—
If I could shake off but one seven years
From these old arms and legs, by the good gods,
I'd with thee every foot.

Cor. Give me thy hand.—Come.
[*Exeunt.*

SCENE II.—*The same. A Street near the Gate.*

Enter SICINIUS, BRUTUS, *and an* Ædile.

Sic. Bid them all home : he's gone, and we'll
no further.
The nobility are vexed, who, we see, have sided
In his behalf.

Bru. Now we have shewn our power,
Let us seem humbler after it is done
Than when it was a doing.

Sic. Bid them home :
Say their great enemy is gone, and they
Stand in their ancient strength.

Bru. Dismiss them home. [*Exit* Ædile.
Here comes his mother.

Enter VOLUMNIA, VIRGILIA, *and* MENENIUS.

Sic. Let's not meet her.

Bru. Why ?

Sic. They say she's mad.

Bru. They have ta'en note of us :
Keep on your way.

Vol. O, you're well met. The hoarded plague
o' the gods
Requite your love !

Men. Peace, peace : be not so loud.

Vol. If that I could for weeping, you should
hear,—
Nay, and shall hear some.—Will you be gone ?
[*To* BRUTUS.

Vir. You shall stay too [*To* SICINIUS]: I
would I had the power
To say so to my husband !

Sic. Are you mankind ?

Vol. Ay, fool : is that a shame ?—Note but
this fool :—
Was not a man my father ? Hadst thou fox-
ship
To banish him that struck more blows for Rome
Than thou hast spoken words ?

Sic. O blesséd heavens !

Vol. More noble blows than ever thou wise
words ;

And for Rome's good.—I'll tell thee what :—
yet go :—
Nay, but thou shalt stay too :—I would my son
Were in Arabia, and thy tribe before him,
His good sword in his hand.

Sic. What then ?

Vir. What then !
He'd make an end of thy posterity.

Vol. Bastards and all.—
Good man, the wounds that he does bear for
Rome !

Men. Come, come, peace.

Sic. I would he had continued to his country
As he began ; and not unknit himself
The noble knot he made.

Bru. I would he had.

Vol. "I would he had !" 'T was you incensed
the rabble :
Cats, that can judge as fitly of his worth
As I can of those mysteries which heaven
Will not have earth to know.

Bru. Pray let us go.

Vol. Now pray, sir, get you gone :
You have done a brave deed ! Ere you go, hear
this :
As far as doth the Capitol exceed
The meanest house in Rome, so far my son
(This lady's husband here, this, do you see),
Whom you have banished, does exceed you
all.

Bru. Well, well, we'll leave you.

Sic. Why stay we to be baited
With one that wants her wits ?

Vol. Take my prayers with you.—
I would the gods had nothing else to do
But to confirm my curses !—[*Exeunt* Tribunes.
Could I meet them
But once a day, it would unclog my heart
Of what lies heavy to 't.

Men. You have told them home ;
And, by my troth, you have cause. You'll sup
with me ?

Vol. Anger's my meat : I sup upon myself,
And so shall starve with feeding.—Come, let's
go :
Leave this faint puling, and lament as I do,
In anger, Juno-like.—Come, come, come.

Men. Fie, fie, fie ! [*Exeunt.*

SCENE III.—*A Highway between* Rome *and*
Antium.

Enter a Roman *and a* Volce, *meeting.*

Rom. I know you well, sir, and you know
me : your name, I think, is Adrian.

Volc. It is so, sir: truly, I have forgot you.

Rom. I am a Roman; and my services are, as you are, against them. Know you me yet?

Volc. Nicanor?—No.

Rom. The same, sir.

Volc. You had more beard when I last saw you; but your favour is well appeared by your tongue. What's the news in Rome? I have a note from the Volcian state to find you out there: you have well saved me a day's journey.

Rom. There hath been in Rome strange insurrection: the people against the senators, patricians, and nobles.

Volc. Hath been! Is it ended, then? Our state thinks not so: they are in a most warlike preparation, and hope to come upon them in the heat of their division.

Rom. The main blaze of it is past, but a small thing would make it flame again. For the nobles receive so to heart the banishment of that worthy Coriolanus, that they are in a ripe aptness to take all power from the people, and to pluck from them their tribunes for ever. This lies glowing, I can tell you, and is almost mature for the violent breaking out.

Volc. Coriolanus banished?

Rom. Banished, sir.

Volc. You will be welcome with this intelligence, Nicanor.

Rom. The day serves well for them now. I have heard it said, the fittest time to corrupt a man's wife is when she's fallen out with her husband. Your noble Tullus Aufidius will appear well in these wars; his great opposer, Coriolanus, being now in no request of his country.

Volc. He cannot choose. I am most fortunate thus accidentally to encounter you: you have ended my business, and I will merrily accompany you home.

Rom. I shall, between this and supper, tell you most strange things from Rome; all tending to the good of their adversaries. Have you an army ready, say you?

Volc. A most royal one: the centurions and their charges, distinctly billeted, already in the entertainment, and to be on foot at an hour's warning.

Rom. I am joyful to hear of their readiness, and am the man, I think, that shall set them in present action. So, sir, heartily well met, and most glad of your company.

Volc. You take my part from me, sir: I have the most cause to be glad of yours.

Rom. Well, let us go together. [*Exeunt.*

SCENE IV.—Antium. *Before* AUFIDIUS's *House.*

Enter CORIOLANUS, *in mean apparel, disguised and muffled.*

Cor. A goodly city is this Antium.—City,
'T is I that made thy widows: many an heir
Of these fair edifices, 'fore my wars,
Have I heard groan and drop: then know me not;
Lest that thy wives with spits, and boys with stones,

Enter a Citizen.

In puny battle slay me.—Save you, sir.

Cit. And you.

Cor.   Direct me, if it be your will,
Where great Aufidius lies. Is he in Antium?

Cit. He is, and feasts the nobles of the state
At his house this night.

Cor.   Which is his house, 'beseech you?

Cit. This, here before you.

Cor. Thank you, sir: farewell. [*Exit* Citizen.
O world, thy slippery turns! Friends now fast sworn,
Whose double bosoms seem to wear one heart,
Whose hours, whose bed, whose meal, and exercise,
Are still together, who twin, as 't were, in love
Unseparable, shall within this hour,
On a dissention of a doit, break out
To bitterest enmity: so fellest foes,
Whose passions and whose plots have broke their sleep
To take the one the other, by some chance,
Some trick not worth an egg, shall grow dear friends,
And interjoin their issues. So with me:
My birth-place hate I, and my love's upon
This enemy town.—I'll enter: if he slay me,
He does fair justice: if he give me way,
I'll do his country service. [*Exit.*

SCENE V.—*The same. A Hall in* AUFIDIUS's *House.*

Music within. Enter a Servant.

1st Serv. Wine, wine, wine! What service is here!
I think our fellows are asleep. [*Exit.*

Enter another Servant.

2nd Serv. Where's Cotus? my master calls for him.—Cotus! [*Exit.*

Enter CORIOLANUS.

Cor. A goodly house. The feast smells well; but I
Appear not like a guest.

Re-enter the first Servant.

1*st Serv.* What would you have, friend? whence are you? Here's no place for you: pray go to the door.

Cor. I have deserved no better entertainment, In being Coriolanus.

Re-enter second Servant.

2*nd Serv.* Whence are you, sir? Has the porter his eyes in his head, that he gives entrance to such companions? pray get you out.

Cor. Away!

2*nd Serv.* "Away!"—Get you away.

Cor. Now thou art troublesome.

2*nd Serv.* Are you so brave? I'll have you talked with anon.

Enter a third Servant. *The first meets him.*

3*rd Serv.* What fellow's this?

1*st Serv.* A strange one as ever I looked on: I cannot get him out o' the house. Pr'y thee call my master to him.

3*rd Serv.* What have you to do here, fellow? Pray you avoid the house,

Cor. Let me but stand: I will not hurt your hearth.

3*rd Serv.* What are you?

Cor. A gentleman.

3*rd Serv.* A marvellous poor one.

Cor. True, so I am.

3*rd Serv.* Pray you, poor gentleman, take up some other station: here's no place for you. Pray you avoid: come.

Cor. Follow your function, go! and batten on cold bits.   [*Pushes him away.*

3*rd Serv.* What, will you not?—Pr'y thee tell my master what a strange guest he has here.

2*nd Serv.* And I shall.   [*Exit.*

3*rd Serv.* Where dwellest thou?

Cor. Under the canopy.

3*rd Serv.* Under the canopy?

Cor. Ay.

3*rd Serv.* Where's that?

Cor. I' the city of kites and crows.

3*rd Serv.* I' the city of kites and crows?— What an ass it is!—Then thou dwellest with daws too?

Cor. No, I serve not thy master.

3*rd Serv.* How, sir! do you meddle with my master?

Cor. Ay, 't is an honester service than to meddle with thy mistress.—Thou prat'st and prat'st: serve with thy trencher: hence!   [*Beats him away.*

Enter AUFIDIUS *and the second* Servant.

Auf. Where is this fellow?

2*nd Serv.* Here, sir. I'd have beaten him like a dog, but for disturbing the lords within.

Auf. Whence com'st thou? what wouldst thou? Thy name?—
Why speak'st not? Speak, man: what's thy name?

Cor.   If, Tullus,   [*Unmuffling.*
Not yet thou know'st me, and seeing me dost not
Think me for the man I am, necessity
Commands me name myself.

Auf. What is thy name?   [*Servants retire.*

Cor. A name unmusical to the Volcians' ears,
And harsh in sound to thine.

Auf.   Say, what's thy name?
Thou hast a grim appearance, and thy face
Bears a command in 't: though thy tackle's torn,
Thou shew'st a noble vessel. What's thy name?

Cor. Prepare thy brow to frown.—Know'st thou
me yet?

Auf. I know thee not: thy name?

Cor. My name is Caius Marcius, who hath done
To thee particularly, and to all the Volces,
Great hurt and mischief: thereto witness may
My surname, Coriolanus. The painful service,
The extreme dangers, and the drops of blood
Shed for my thankless country, are requited
But with that surname: a good memory,
And witness of the malice and displeasure
Which thou shouldst bear me!—Only that name
remains:
The cruelty and envy of the people,
Permitted by our dastard nobles, who
Have all forsook me, hath devoured the rest;
And suffered me, by the voice of slaves, to be
Whooped out of Rome. Now, this extremity
Hath brought me to thy hearth. Not out of hope
(Mistake me not) to save my life; for if
I had feared death, of all the men i' the world
I would have 'voided thee: but in mere spite,
To be full quit of those my banishers,
Stand I before thee here. Then if thou hast
A heart of wreak in thee, that will revenge
Thine own particular wrongs, and stop those
maims
Of shame seen through thy country, speed thee
straight,
And make my misery serve thy turn: so use it
That my revengeful services may prove
As benefits to thee: for I will fight
Against my cankered country with the spleen
Of all the under fiends. But if so be
Thou dar'st not this, and that to prove more
fortunes
Thou art tired, then, in a word, I also am
Longer to live most weary, and present
My throat to thee and to thy ancient malice:
Which not to cut would shew thee but a fool:
Since I have ever followed thee with hate,

Drawn tuns of blood out of thy country's breast,
And cannot live but to thy shame, unless
It be to do thee service.

   Auf.   O Marcius, Marcius!
Each word thou hast spoke hath weeded from my
      heart
A root of ancient envy.   If Jupiter
Should from yon cloud speak divine things, and
      say,
" 'T is true," I 'd not believe them more than
      thee,
All-noble Marcius.—Let me twine
Mine arms about that body, where against
My grainéd ash an hundred times hath broke,
And scared the moon with splinters! Here I clip
The anvil of my sword; and do contest
As hotly and as nobly with thy love
As ever, in ambitious strength, I did

Contend against thy valour.   Know thou first,
I loved the maid I married; never man
Sighed truer breath : but that I see thee here,
Thou noble thing! more dances my rapt heart
Than when I first my wedded mistress saw
Bestride my threshold.   Why, thou Mars! I tell
      thee
We have a power on foot; and I had purpose
Once more to hew thy target from thy brawn,
Or lose mine arm for 't.   Thou hast beat me out
Twelve several times, and I have nightly since
Dreamt of encounters 'twixt thyself and me :
We have been down together in my sleep,
Unbuckling helms, fisting each other's throat,
And waked half dead with nothing.   Worthy
      Marcius,
Had we no quarrel else to Rome but that
Thou art thence banished, we would muster all

From twelve to seventy; and, pouring war
Into the bowels of ungrateful Rome,
Like a bold flood o'erbeat.   O come, go in,
And take our friendly senators by the hands;
Who are now here, taking their leaves of me,
Who am prepared against your territories,
Though not for Rome itself.
    Cor.   You bless me, gods!
    Auf. Therefore, most absolute sir, if thou wilt have
The leading of thine own revenges, take
The one half of my commission; and set down,
As best thou art experienced (since thou know'st
Thy country's strength and weakness), thine own
           ways:
Whether to knock against the gates of Rome,
Or rudely visit them in parts remote,
To fright them ere destroy.   But come in:

Let me commend thee first to those that shall
Say "Yea" to thy desires.   A thousand welcomes!
And more a friend than e'er an enemy:
Yet, Marcius, that was much.   Your hand: most
           welcome!
            [*Exeunt* CORIOLANUS *and* AUFIDIUS.
    1st Serv. [*advancing*]. Here's a strange alteration!
    2nd Serv. By my hand, I had thought to have strucken him with a cudgel; and yet my mind gave me his clothes made a false report of him.
    1st Serv. What an arm he has!   He turned me about with his finger and his thumb as one would set up a top.
    2nd Serv. Nay, I knew by his face that there was something in him: he had, sir, a kind of face, methought,—I cannot tell how to term it.

    1st Serv. He had so: looking, as it were,— 'Would I were hanged but I thought there was more in him than I could think.
    2nd Serv. So did I, I'll be sworn: he is simply the rarest man i' the world.
    1st Serv. I think he is; but a greater soldier than he you wot one.
    2nd Serv. Who; my master?
    1st Serv. Nay, it's no matter for that.
    2nd Serv. Worth six of him.
    1st Serv. Nay, not so neither: but I take him to be the greater soldier.
    2nd Serv. 'Faith, look you, one cannot tell how to say that: for the defence of a town, our general is excellent.
    1st Serv. Ay, and for an assault too.

Re-enter third Servant.

    3rd Serv. O slaves, I can tell you news: new you rascals!
    1st Serv. } What, what, what? let's partak
    2nd Serv. }
    3rd Serv. I would not be a Roman, of ɛ
           nations:
I had as lieve be a condemned man.
    1st Serv. } Wherefore? wherefore?
    2nd Serv. }
    3rd Serv. Why, here's he that was wont thwack our general;—Caius Marcius.
    1st Serv. Why do you say, thwack our genera
    3rd Serv. I do not say, thwack our genera but he was always good enough for him.
    2nd Serv. Come, we are fellows and friends :-

he was ever too hard for him : I have heard him say so himself.

1st Serv. He was too hard for him directly, to say the truth on 't : before Corioli he scotched him and notched him like a carbonado.

2nd Serv. An he had been cannibally given, he might have broiled and eaten him too.

1st Serv. But more of thy news ?

3rd Serv. Why, he is so made on here within as if he were son and heir to Mars : set at upper end o' the table : no question asked him by any of the senators but they stand bald before him. Our general himself makes a mistress of him ; sanctifies himself with 's hand, and turns up the white o' the eye to his discourse. But the bottom of the news is, our general is cut i' the middle, and but one half of what he was yesterday : for the other has half, by the entreaty and grant of the whole table. He 'll go, he says, and sowle the porter of Rome gates by the ears : he will mow down all before him, and leave his passage polle

2nd Serv. And he 's as like to do 't as any man I can imagine.

3rd Serv. Do 't ? he will do 't. For look you, sir, he has as many friends as enemies : which friends, sir (as it were), durst not (look you, sir) shew themselves (as we term it) his friends whilst he 's in directitude.

1st Serv. Directitude ! what 's that ?

3rd Serv. But when they shall see, sir, his crest up again, and the man in blood, they will out of their burrows like conies after rain, and revel all with him.

1st Serv. But when goes this forward ?

3rd Serv. To-morrow : to-day : presently. Yo. shall have the drum struck up this afternoon : 't is, as it were, a parcel of their feast, and to be executed ere they wipe their lips.

2nd Serv. Why, then we shall have a stirring world again. This peace is nothing but to rust iron, increase tailors, and breed ballad-makers.

1st Serv. Let me have war, say I : it exceeds peace as far as day does night : it 's sprightly, waking, audible, and full of vent. Peace is a very apoplexy, lethargy ; mulled, deaf, sleepy, insensible ; a getter of more bastard children than wars a destroyer of men.

2nd Serv. 'T is so : and as wars, in some sort, may be said to be a ravisher, so it cannot be denied but peace is a great maker of cuckolds.

1st Serv. Ay, and it makes men hate one another.

3rd Serv. Reason ; because they then less need one another. The wars for my money : I hope to see Romans as cheap as Volcians.—They are rising, they are rising.

All. In, in, in, in ! [*Exeunt.*

SCENE VI.—Rome. *A public Place.*

Enter SICINIUS *and* BRUTUS.

Sic. We hear not of him, neither need we fear him :
His remedies are tame i' the present peace
And quietness o' the people, which before
Were in wild hurry. Here do we make his friends
Blush that the world goes well : who rather had
(Though they themselves did suffer by 't) behold
Dissentious numbers pestering streets, than see
Our tradesmen singing in their shops, and going
About their functions friendly.

Bru. We stood to 't in good time.—Is this
Menenius ?

Enter MENENIUS.

Sic. 'T is he, 't is he. O he is grown most
kind of late.—Hail, sir !

Men. Hail to you both !

Sic. Your Coriolanus, sir, is not much missed
But with his friends : the commonwealth doth
stand ;
And so would do were he more angry at it.

Men. All 's well ; and might have been much
better
If he could have temporised.

Sic.　　　　Where is he, hear you ?

Men. Nay, I hear nothing : his mother and
his wife
Hear nothing from him.

Enter three or four Citizens.

Cit. The gods preserve you both !

Sic.　　　　Good-e'en, our neighbours.

Bru. Good-e'en to you all : good-e'en to you
all.

1st Cit. Ourselves, our wives, and children, on
our knees
Are bound to pray for you both.

Sic.　　　　Live and thrive !

Bru. Farewell, kind neighbours. We wished
Coriolanus
Had loved you as we did.

Cit.　　　　Now the gods keep you !

Both Tri. Farewell, farewell.

[*Exeunt* Citizens.

Sic. This is a happier and more comely time
Than when these fellows ran about the streets,
Crying "Confusion ! "

Bru.　　　　Caius Marcius was
A worthy officer i' the war : but insolent,
O'ercome with pride, ambitious past all thinking,
Self-loving,—

Sic.　　　　And affecting one sole throne,
Without assistance.

Men.　　　　I think not so.

Sic. We should by this, to all our lamentation,
If he had gone forth consul, found it so.
    Bru. The gods have well prevented it, and
        Rome
Sits safe and still without him.

Enter Ædile.

    Æd.   Worthy tribunes,
There is a slave, whom we have put in prison,
Reports, the Volces with two several powers
Are entered in the Roman territories,
And with the deepest malice of the war
Destroy what lies before them.
    Men.   'T is Aufidius;
Who, hearing of our Marcius' banishment,
Thrusts forth his horns again into the world;
Which were inshelled when Marcius stood for
    Rome,
And durst not once peep out.
    Sic. Come, what talk you of Marcius?
    Bru. Go see this rumourer whipped.—It can-
        not be
The Volces dare break with us.
    Men.   Cannot be!
We have record that very well it can;
And three examples of the like have been
Within my age. But reason with the fellow,
Before you punish him, where he heard this:
Lest you should chance to whip your informa-
    tion,
And beat the messenger who bids beware
Of what is to be dreaded.
    Sic.   Tell not me:
I know this cannot be.
    Bru.   Not possible.

Enter a Messenger.

    Mess. The nobles, in great earnestness, are
        going
All to the senate-house: some news is come in
That turns their countenances.
    Sic.   'T is this slave:—
Go whip him 'fore the people's eyes:—his raising!
Nothing but his report!
    Mess.   Yes, worthy sir,
The slave's report is seconded: and more,
More fearful, is delivered.
    Sic.   What more fearful?
    Mess. It is spoke freely out of many mouths
(How probable I do not know) that Marcius,
Joined with Aufidius, leads a power 'gainst Rome,
And vows revenge as spacious as between
The young'st and oldest thing.
    Sic.   This is most likely!
    Bru. Raised only, that the weaker sort may
        wish
Good Marcius home again.

    Sic.   The very trick on 't.
    Men. This is unlikely:
He and Aufidius can no more atone
Than violentest contrariety.

Enter another Messenger.

    Mess. You are sent for to the senate.
A fearful army, led by Caius Marcius,
Associated with Aufidius, rages
Upon our territories; and have already
O'erborne their way, consumed with fire, and took
What lay before them.

Enter Cominius.

    Com. O, you have made good work!
    Men.   What news? what news?
    Com. You have holp to ravish your own daugh-
        ters, and
To melt the city leads upon your pates:
To see your wives dishonoured to your noses:—
    Men. What's the news? what's the news?
    Com. Your temples burned in their cement; and
Your franchises, whereon you stood, confined
Into an augre's bore.
    Men.   Pray now, your news?—
You have made fair work, I fear me.—Pray,
        your news?
If Marcius should be joined with Volcians,—
    Com.   If!—
He is their god: he leads them like a thing
Made by some other deity than nature,
That shapes man better: and they follow him,
Against us brats, with no less confidence
Than boys pursuing summer butterflies,
Or butchers killing flies.
    Men.   You have made good work,
You and your apron-men: you that stood so much
Upon the voice of occupation, and
The breath of garlick-eaters!
    Com. He'll shake your Rome about your ears.
    Men. As Hercules did shake down mellow fruit.
You have made fair work!
    Bru. But is this true, sir?
    Com.   Ay; and you'll look pale
Before you find it other. All the regions
Do smilingly revolt; and who resist
Are only mocked for valiant ignorance,
And perish constant fools. Who is't can blame him?
Your enemies and his find something in him.
    Men. We are all undone, unless
The noble man have mercy.
    Com.   Who shall ask it?
The tribunes cannot do't for shame: the people
Deserve such pity of him as the wolf
Does of the shepherds:—for his best friends, if they
Should say, "Be good to Rome," they charged
        him even

As those should do that had deserved his hate,
And therein shewed like enemies.

Men.   'T is true:
If he were putting to my house the brand
That should consume it, I have not the face
To say, "Beseech you, cease."—You have made
        fair hands,
You and your crafts: you have crafted fair!

Com.   You have brought
A trembling upon Rome such as was never
So incapable of help.

Tri.   Say not, we brought it.

Men. How! Was it we? We loved him; but,
      like beasts
And cowardly nobles, gave way to your clusters,
Who did hoot him out o 'the city.

Com.   But I fear
They 'll roar him in again. Tullus Aufidius,
The second name of men, obeys his points
As if he were his officer:—desperation
Is all the policy, strength, and defence,
That Rome can make against them.

      Enter a Troop of Citizens.

Men.   Here come the clusters.—
And is Aufidius with him?—You are they
That made the air unwholesome, when you cast
Your stinking, greasy caps, in hooting at
Coriolanus' exile. Now he 's coming;
And not a hair upon a soldier's head
Which will not prove a whip: as many coxcombs
As you threw caps up will he tumble down,
And pay you for your voices. 'T is no matter:
If he could burn us all into one coal,
We have deserved it.

Cit. 'Faith, we hear fearful news.

1st Cit.   For mine own part,
When I said "Banish him," I said 't was pity.

2nd Cit. And so did I.

3rd Cit. And so did I: and, to say the truth,
so did very many of us. That we did, we did
for the best: and though we willingly consented
to his banishment, yet it was against our will.

Com. You are goodly things, you voices!

Men.   You have made
Good work, you and your cry!—Shall us to the
      Capitol?

Com. O, ay: what else?
           [*Exeunt* COMINIUS *and* MENENIUS.

Sic. Go, masters, get you home: be not dis-
      mayed:
These are a side that would be glad to have
This true which they so seem to fear. Go home,
And shew no sign of fear.

1st Cit. The gods be good to us! Come,
masters, let 's home. I ever said we were i' the
wrong when we banished him.

2nd Cit. So did we all. But come, let 's home.
               [*Exeunt* Citizens.

Bru. I do not like this news.

Sic. Nor I.

Bru. Let 's to the Capitol.—'Would half my
      wealth
Would buy this for a lie!

Sic.   Pray let us go.   [*Exeunt.*

SCENE VII.—*A Camp; at a small distance from*
Rome.

Enter AUFIDIUS *and his* Lieutenant.

Auf. Do they still fly to the Roman?

Lieu. I do not know what witchcraft's in him:
      but
Your soldiers use him as the grace 'fore meat,
Their talk at table, and their thanks at end;
And you are darkened in this action, sir,
Even by your own.

Auf.   I cannot help it now;
Unless, by using means, I lame the foot
Of our design. He bears himself more proudlier,
Even to my person, than I thought he would
When first I did embrace him. Yet his nature
In that 's no changeling; and I must excuse
What cannot be amended.

Lieu.   Yet I wish, sir
(I mean for your particular), you had not
Joined in commission with him: but either
Had borne the action of yourself, or else
To him had left it solely.

Auf. I understand thee well: and be thou sure,
When he shall come to his account, he knows not
What I can urge against him. Although it seems,
And so he thinks, and is no less apparent
To the vulgar eye, that he bears all things fairly,
And shews good husbandry for the Volcian state;
Fights dragon-like, and does achieve as soon
As draw his sword: yet he hath left undone
That which shall break his neck, or hazard mine,
When'er we come to our account.

Lieu. Sir, I beseech you, think you he 'll carry
      Rome?

Auf. All places yield to him ere he sits down;
And the nobility of Rome are his:
The senators and patricians love him too:
The tribunes are no soldiers; and their people
Will be as rash in the repeal as hasty
To expel him thence. I think he 'll be to Rome
As is the osprey to the fish, who takes it
By sovereignty of nature.—First he was
A noble servant to them; but he could not
Carry his honours even. Whether 't was pride,
Which out of daily fortune ever taints

The happy man : whether defect of judgment,
To fail in the disposing of those chances
Which he was lord of : or whether nature
Not to be other than one thing,—not moving
From the casque to the cushion, but commanding
　　　peace
Even with the same austerity and garb
As he controlled the war :—but one of these
(As he hath spices of them all, not all,
For I dare so far free him) made him feared ;
So hated, and so banished.　But he has a merit

To choke it in the utterance.　So our virtues
Lie in the interpretation of the time :
And power, unto itself most commendable,
Hath not a tomb so evident as a chair
To extol what it hath done.
One fire drives out one fire ; one nail, one nail :
Rights by rights fouler, strength by strengths,
　　　do fail.
Come, let 's away.—When, Caius, Rome is thine,
Thou art poor'st of all : then shortly art thou
　　　mine.　　　　　　　　　　　　[*Exeunt.*

SCENE I.—Rome. *A public Place.*

Enter MENENIUS, COMINIUS, SICINIUS, BRUTUS,
and others.

Men. No, I 'll not go: you hear what he hath
     said
Which was sometime his general; who loved him
In a most dear particular. He called me father:
But what o' that?—Go, you that banished him,
A mile before his tent fall down, and knee
The way into his mercy. Nay, if he coyed
To hear Cominius speak, I 'll keep at home.

Com. He would not seem to know me.

Men.   Do you hear?

Com. Yet one time he did call me by my name.
I urged our old acquaintance, and the drops
That we have bled together. Coriolanus
He would not answer to: forbad all names:
He was a kind of nothing, titleless,
Till he had forged himself a name i' the fire
Of burning Rome.

Men.   Why, so; you have made good work:
A pair of tribunes that have racked for Rome,
To make coals cheap. A noble memory!

Com. I minded him how royal 't was to pardon
When it was less expected: he replied,
It was a base petition of a state
To one whom they had punished.

Men.   Very well:
Could he say less?

Com. I offered to awaken his regard
For his private friends. His answer to me was,
He could not stay to pick them in a pile
Of noisome, musty chaff: he said 't was folly,
For one poor grain or two, to leave unburnt,
And still to nose the offence.

Men.   For one poor grain or two?
I am one of those: his mother, wife, his child,
And this brave fellow too, we are the grains:
You are the musty chaff; and you are smelt
Above the moon. We must be burnt for you.

Sic. Nay, pray be patient: if you refuse your aid
In this so never-heeded help, yet do not
Upbraid us with our distress. But sure, if you
Would be your country's pleader, your good tongue,
More than the instant army we can make,
Might stop our countryman.

Men.   No; I 'll not meddle.

Sic. I pray you, go to him.

Men.   What should I do?

Bru. Only make trial what your love can do
For Rome, towards Marcius.

Men.   Well, and say that Marcius
Return me, as Cominius is returned,
Unheard: what then?—
But as a discontented friend, grief-shot
With his unkindness: say 't be so?

Sic.   Yet your good will
Must have that thanks from Rome after the mea-
        sure
As you intended well.

Men.   I 'll undertake it:
I think he 'll hear me:—yet to bite his lip
And hum at good Cominius, much unhearts me.—
He was not taken well; he had not dined:
The veins unfilled, our blood is cold, and then
We pout upon the morning; are unapt
To give or to forgive: but when we have stuffed
These pipes and these conveyances of our blood
With wine and feeding, we have suppler souls
Than in our priest-like fasts.   Therefore I 'll
        watch him
Till he be dieted to my request,
And then I 'll set upon him.

Bru. You know the very road into his kindness,
And cannot lose your way.

Men.   Good faith, I 'll prove him,
Speed how it will. I shall ere long have knowledge
Of my success.   *[Exit.*

Com.   He 'll never hear him.

Sic.   Not?

Com. I tell you, he does sit in gold; his eye
Red as 't would burn Rome; and his injury
The gaoler to his pity. I kneeled before him:
'T was very faintly he said, "Rise:" dismissed me
Thus, with his speechless hand. What he would do,
He sent in writing after me: what he would not,
Bound with an oath to yield to his conditions.
So that all hope is vain,
Unless his noble mother and his wife;
Who, as I hear, mean to solicit him
For mercy to his country. Therefore, let 's hence,
And with our fair entreaties haste them on.
                        [Exeunt.

SCENE II.—*An advanced Post of the Volcian Camp
before* Rome.   *The* Guard *at their stations.*

Enter to them MENENIUS.

1st Gua. Stay: whence are you?

2nd Gua.   Stand, and go back.

Men. You guard like men; 't is well: but, by
        your leave,
I am an officer of state, and come

To speak with Coriolanus.

1st Gua.   From whence?

Men.   From Rome.

1st Gua. You may not pass; you must return:
        our general
Will no more hear from thence.

2nd Gua. You 'll see your Rome embraced
        with fire, before
You 'll speak with Coriolanus.

Men.   Good my friends,
If you have heard your general talk of Rome,
And of his friends there, it is lots to blanks
My name hath touched your ears:—it is Mene-
        nius.

1st Gua. Be it so; go back: the virtue of your
        name
Is not here passable.

Men.   I tell thee, fellow,
Thy general is my lover: I have been
The book of his good acts, whence men have read
His fame unparalleled; haply amplified:
For I have ever verified my friends
(Of whom he 's chief) with all the size that verity
Would without lapsing suffer: nay, sometimes,
Like to a bowl upon a subtle ground,
I have tumbled past the throw; and in his praise
Have almost stamped the leasing.   Therefore,
        fellow,
I must have leave to pass.

1st Gua. Faith, sir, if you had told as many
lies in his behalf as you have uttered words in
your own, you should not pass here: no, though
it were as virtuous to lie as to live chastely.
Therefore, go back.

Men. Pr'y thee, fellow, remember my name
is Menenius, always factionary on the party of
your general.

2nd Gua. Howsoever you have been his liar
(as you say you have), I am one that, telling true
under him, must say, you cannot pass. Therefore, go back.

Men. Has he dined, canst thou tell? for I
would not speak with him till after dinner.

1st Gua. You are a Roman, are you?

Men. I am as thy general is.

1st Gua. Then you should hate Rome, as he
does. Can you, when you have pushed out your
gates the very defender of them, and in a violent
popular ignorance given your enemy your shield,
think to front his revenges with the easy groans
of old women, the virginal palms of your daughters, or with the palsied intercession of such a
decayed dotant as you seem to be? Can you
think to blow out the intended fire your city is
ready to flame in, with such weak breath as this?
No, you are deceived: therefore, back to Rome,
and prepare for your execution: you are con-

demned: our general has sworn you out of reprieve and pardon.

Men. Sirrah, if thy captain knew I were here, he would use me with estimation.

2nd Gua. Come, my captain knows you not.

Men. I mean, thy general.

1st Gua. My general cares not for you. Back, I say, go; lest I let forth your half pint of blood. Back:—that's the utmost of your having. Back!

Men. Nay, but fellow, fellow,—

Enter CORIOLANUS *and* AUFIDIUS.

Cor. What's the matter?

Men. Now, you companion, I'll say an errand for you: you shall know now that I am in estimation: you shall perceive that a Jack guardant cannot office me from my son Coriolanus. Guess but by my entertainment with him if thou standst not i'the state of hanging, or of some death more long in spectatorship and crueller in suffering. Behold now presently, and swoon for what's to come upon thee.—The glorious gods sit in hourly synod about thy particular prosperity, and love thee no worse than thy old father Menenius does! O, my son, my son! thou art preparing fire for us: look thee, here's water to quench it. I was hardly moved to come to thee: but being assured none but myself could move thee, I have been blown out of your gates with sighs: and conjure thee to pardon Rome and thy petitionary countrymen. The good gods assuage thy wrath, and turn the dregs of it upon this varlet here:—this, who like a block hath denied my access to thee.

Cor. Away!

Men. How! away?

Cor. Wife, mother, child, I know not. My affairs
Are servanted to others: though I owe
My revenge properly, my remission lies
In Volcian breasts. That we have been familiar,
Ingrate forgetfulness shall poison, rather
Than pity note how much.—Therefore, be gone:
Mine ears against your suits are stronger than
Your gates against my force. Yet, for I loved thee,
Take this along: I writ it for thy sake,
[*Gives a letter.*
And would have sent it. Another word, Menenius,
I will not hear thee speak.—This man, Aufidius,
Was my beloved in Rome: yet thou behold'st—

Auf. You keep a constant temper.

[*Exeunt* CORIOLANUS *and* AUFIDIUS.

1st Gua. Now, sir, is your name Menenius?

2nd Gua. 'Tis a spell, you see, of much power. You know the way home again.

1st Gua. Do you hear how we are shent for keeping your greatness back?

2nd Gua. What cause do you think I have to swoon?

Men. I neither care for the world nor your general: for such things as you, I can scarce think there's any, you are so slight. He that hath a will to die by himself, fears it not from another: let your general do his worst. For you, be that you are long, and your misery increase with your age! I say to you, as I was said to, "Away!" [*Exit.*

1st Gua. A noble fellow, I warrant him.

2nd Gua. The worthy fellow is our general: he is the rock, the oak not to be wind-shaken.
[*Exeunt.*

SCENE III.—*The Tent of* CORIOLANUS.

Enter CORIOLANUS, AUFIDIUS, *and others.*

Cor. We will before the walls of Rome to-morrow
Set down our host.—My partner in this action,
You must report to the Volcian lords how plainly
I have borne this business.

Auf.   Only their ends
You have respected: stopped your ears against
The general suit of Rome: never admitted
A private whisper; no, not with such friends
That thought them sure of you.

Cor.   This last old man,
Whom with a cracked heart I have sent to Rome,
Loved me above the measure of a father:
Nay, godded me, indeed. Their latest refuge
Was to send him: for whose old love I have
(Though I shewed sourly to him) once more offered
The first conditions which they did refuse,
And cannot now accept; to grace him only,
That thought he could do more: a very little
I have yielded, too. Fresh embassies and suits,
Nor from the state nor private friends, hereafter
Will I lend ear to.—Ha! what shout is this?
[*Shout within.*
Shall I be tempted to infringe my vow
In the same time 't is made? I will not.—

Enter, in mourning habits, VIRGILIA; VOLUMNIA,
leading young MARCIUS; VALERIA, *and At-tendants.*

My wife comes foremost: then the honoured mould
Wherein this trunk was framed; and in her hand
The grandchild to her blood. But out, affection!
All bond and privilege of nature, break!
Let it be virtuous to be obstinate.—
What is that curtesy worth; or those dove's eyes,
Which can make gods forsworn?—I melt, and am not

Of stronger earth than others.—My mother bows:
As if Olympus to a molehill should
In supplication nod! and my young boy
Hath an aspéct of intercession, which
Great nature cries, "Deny not."—Let the Volces
Plough Rome and harrow Italy: I 'll never
Be such a gosling to obey instinct; but stand
As if a man were author of himself,
And knew no other kin.

    Vir.　　　　My lord and husband!

    Cor. These eyes are not the same I wore in
    Rome.

    Vir. The sorrow that delivers us thus changed
Makes you think so.

    Cor.　　　　Like a dull actor now,
I have forgot my part, and I am out,
Even to a full disgrace.—Best of my flesh,
Forgive my tyranny; but do not say,
For that, " Forgive our Romans.''—O, a kiss
Long as my exile, sweet as my revenge!
Now, by the jealous queen of heaven, that kiss
I carried from thee, dear, and my true lip
Hath virgined it e'er since.—You gods! I prate,
And the most noble mother of the world
Leave unsaluted! Sink, my knee, i' the earth:
Of thy deep duty more impression shew
Than that of common sons.

    Vol.　　　　O, stand up blessed!
Whilst, with no softer cushion than the flint,
I kneel before thee; and unproperly
Shew duty, as mistaken all the while
Between the child and parent.

    Cor.　　　　What is this?
Your knees to me! to your corrected son!
Then let the pebbles on the hungry beach
Fillip the stars; then let the mutinous winds
Strike the proud cedars 'gainst the fiery sun:
Murdering impossibility, to make
What cannot be, slight work!

    Vol.　　　　Thou art my warrior:
I holp to frame thee. Do you know this lady?

    Cor. The noble sister of Publicola:
The moon of Rome: chaste as the icicle
That 's curded by the frost from purest snow,
And hangs on Dian's temple. Dear Valeria!

    Vol. This is a poor epitome of yours,
Which by the interpretation of full time
May shew like all yourself.

    Cor.　　　　The god of soldiers,
With the consent of supreme Jove, inform
Thy thoughts with nobleness; that thou mayst
    prove
To shame unvulnerable, and stick i' the wars
Like a great sea-mark, standing every flaw,
And saving those that eye thee!

    Vol.　　　　Your knee, sirrah.

    Cor. That 's my brave boy.

    Vol. Even he, your wife, this lady, and myself,
Are suitors to you.

    Cor.　　　　I beseech you, peace:
Or if you 'd ask, remember this before,—
The things I have forsworn to grant, may never
Be held by you denials. Do not bid me
Dismiss my soldiers, or capitulate
Again with Rome's mechanics. Tell me not
Wherein I seem unnatural: desire not
To allay my rages and revenges, with
Your colder reasons.

    Vol.　　　　O, no more, no more!
You have said you will not grant us anything:
For we have nothing else to ask but that
Which you deny already. Yet we will ask;
That, if you fail in our request, the blame
May hang upon your hardness: therefore hear us.

    Cor. Aufidius, and you Volces, mark: for we 'll
Hear nought from Rome in private.—Your re-
    quest?

    Vol. Should we be silent and not speak, our
    raiment
And state of bodies would bewray what life
We have led since thy exile. Think with thyself
How more unfortunate than all living women
Are we come hither: since that thy sight, which
    should
Make our eyes flow with joy, hearts dance with
    comforts,
Constrains them weep, and shake with fear and
    sorrow:
Making the mother, wife, and child, to see
The son, the husband, and the father, tearing
His country's bowels out. And to poor we
Thine enmity 's most capital: thou barr'st us
Our prayers to the gods; which is a comfort
That all but we enjoy. For how can we,
Alas! how can we for our country pray,
Whereto we are bound, together with thy victory,
Whereto we are bound? Alack! or we must lose
The country, our dear nurse; or else thy person,
Our comfort in the country. We must find
An evident calamity, though we had
Our wish which side should win: for either thou
Must, as a foreign recreant, be led
With manacles thorough our streets, or else
Triumphantly tread on thy country's ruin,
And bear the palm for having bravely shed
Thy wife and children's blood. For myself, son,
I purpose not to wait on fortune till
These wars determine: if I cannot persuade thee
Rather to shew a noble grace to both parts
Than seek the end of one, thou shalt no sooner
March to assault thy country than to tread
(Trust to 't, thou shalt not) on thy mother's womb,
That brought thee to this world.

    Vir.　　　　Ay, and on mine,

That brought you forth this boy, to keep your name
Living to time.
    Boy.   He shall not tread on me:
I 'll run away till I am bigger, but then I 'll fight.
    Cor. Not of a woman's tenderness to be,
Requires nor child nor woman's face to see.
I have sat too long.   [*Rising.*
    Vol.   Nay, go not from us thus.
If it were so that our request did tend
To save the Romans, thereby to destroy
The Volces whom you serve, you might condemn
    us,
As poisonous of your honour:—no; our suit
Is that you reconcile them: while the Volces
May say, "This mercy we have shewed;" the
    Romans,
"This we received;" and each in either side
Give the all-hail to thee, and cry, "Be blessed
For making up this peace!"—Thou know'st, great
    son,
The end of war 's uncertain: but this certain,
That if thou conquer Rome, the benefit
Which thou shalt thereby reap is such a name
Whose repetition will be dogged with curses;
Whose chronicle thus writ: "The man was noble,
But with his last attempt he wiped it out;
Destroyed his country; and his name remains
To the ensuing age abhorred."—Speak to me, son:
Thou hast affected the fine strains of honour,
To imitate the graces of the gods;
To tear with thunder the wide cheeks o' the air,
And yet to charge thy sulphur with a bolt
That should but rive an oak. Why dost not speak?
Think'st thou it honourable for a noble man
Still to remember wrongs?—Daughter, speak
    you:
He cares not for your weeping. Speak thou, boy:
Perhaps thy childishness will move him more
Than can our reasons.—There is no man in the
    world
More bound to his mother; yet here he lets me
    prate
Like one i' the stocks! Thou hast never in thy life
Shewed thy dear mother any courtesy;
When she (poor hen!), fond of no second brood,
Has clucked thee to the wars, and safely home,
Loaden with honour. Say my request 's unjust,
And spurn me back: but if it be not so,
Thou art not honest; and the gods will plague thee
That thou restrain'st from me the duty which
To a mother's part belongs.—He turns away:
Down, ladies; let us shame him with our knees.
To his surname Coriolanus 'longs more pride
Than pity to our prayers. Down: an end:
This is the last. So we will home to Rome,
And die among our neighbours.—Nay, behold us:
This boy, that cannot tell what he would have,

But kneels and holds up hands for fellowship,
Does reason our petition with more strength
Than thou hast to deny 't.—Come, let us go:
This fellow had a Volcian to his mother;
His wife is in Corioli, and his child
Like him by chance.—Yet give us our despatch:
I am hushed until our city be afire,
And then I 'll speak a little.
    Cor.   O mother, mother!
          [*Holding* VOLUMNIA *by the hands, silent.*
What have you done? Behold, the heavens do ope,
The gods look down, and this unnatural scene
They laugh at. O my mother, mother! O!
You have won a happy victory to Rome:
But for your son,—believe it, O believe it,
Most dangerously you have with him prevailed,
If not most mortal to him. But let it come.—
Aufidius, though I cannot make true wars,
I 'll frame convenient peace. Now, good Aufidius,
Were you in my stead, would you have heard
A mother less: or granted less, Aufidius?
    Auf. I was moved withal.
    Cor.   I dare be sworn you were:
And, sir, it is no little thing to make
Mine eyes to sweat compassion. But, good sir,
What peace you 'll make advise me. For my part,
I 'll not to Rome; I 'll back with you: and pray you
Stand to me in this cause.—O mother! wife!
    Auf. I am glad thou hast set thy mercy and
         thy honour
At difference in thee: out of that I 'll work
Myself a former fortune.   [*Aside.*
         [*The* Ladies *make signs to* CORIOLANUS.
    Cor. Ay, by-and-by:
           [*To* VOLUMNIA, VIRGILIA, *&c.*
But we will drink together; and you shall bear
A better witness back than words, which we,
On like conditions, will have counter-sealed.
Come, enter with us. Ladies, you deserve
To have a temple built you: all the swords
In Italy, and her confederate arms,
Could not have made this peace.   [*Exeunt.*

SCENE IV.—Rome. *A public Place.*

Enter MENENIUS *and* SICINIUS.

    Men. See you yond' coign o' the Capitol:
yond' corner-stone?
    Sic. Why, what of that?
    Men. If it be possible for you to displace it
with your little finger, there is some hope the
ladies of Rome, especially his mother, may prevail with him. But I say there is no hope
in 't: our throats are sentenced, and stay upon
execution.

Sic. Is't possible that so short a time can alter the condition of a man?

Men. There is differency between a grub and a butterfly; yet your butterfly was a grub. This Marcius is grown from man to dragon: he has wings; he's more than a creeping thing.

Sic. He loved his mother dearly.

Men. So did he me: and he no more remembers his mother now than an eight-year-old horse. The tartness of his face sours ripe grapes: when he walks, he moves like an engine, and the ground shrinks before his treading: he is able to pierce a corslet with his eye; talks like a knell, and his hum is a battery: he sits in his state as a thing made for Alexander: what he bids be done, is finished with his bidding. He wants nothing of a god but eternity, and a heaven to throne in.

Sic. Yes, mercy, if you report him truly.

Men. I paint him in the character. Mark what mercy his mother shall bring from him. There is no more mercy in him than there is milk in a male tiger: that shall our poor city find: and all this is 'long of you.

Sic. The gods be good unto us!

Men. No, in such a case the gods will not be good unto us. When we banished him, we respected not them: and he returning to break our necks, they respect not us.

Enter a Messenger.

Mess. Sir, if you'd save your life, fly to you house:
The plebeians have got your fellow-tribune,
And hale him up and down: all swearing, if
The Roman ladies bring not comfort home,
They'll give him death by inches.

Enter another Messenger.

Sic. What's the news?

Mess. Good news; good news!—The ladies have prevailed;
The Volces are dislodged, and Marcius gone.
A merrier day did never yet greet Rome:
No, not the expulsion of the Tarquins!

Sic. Friend,
Art thou certain this is true? is it most certain?

Mess. As certain as I know the sun is fire:
Where have you lurked, that you make doubt of it?
Ne'er through an arch so hurried the blown tide,
As the recomforted through the gates. Why,
hark you!
[*Trumpets and hautboys sounded, and drums beaten, all together. Shouting also within.*
The trumpets, sackbuts, psalteries, and fifes,
Tabors, and cymbals, and the shouting Romans,
Make the sun dance. Hark you! [*Shouting again.*

Men. This is good news:
I will go meet the ladies. This Volumnia
Is worth, of consuls, senators, patricians,
A city full: of tribunes such as you,
A sea and land full. You have prayed well to-day
This morning for ten thousand of your throats
I'd not have given a doit.—Hark how they joy
[*Shouting and musi*

Sic. First, the gods bless you for your tidings next,
Accept my thankfulness.

Mess. Sir, we have all
Great cause to give great thanks.

Sic. They are near the city?

Mess. Almost at point to enter.

Sic. We will meet them,
And help the joy. [*Going*

Enter the Ladies, *accompanied by* Senators, Patri cians, *and* People. *They pass over the stage.*

1st Sen. Behold our patroness, the life of Rome
Call all your tribes together, praise the gods,
And make triumphant fires: strew flowers befor them:
Unshout the noise that banished Marcius:
Repeal him with the welcome of his mother:
Cry,—Welcome, ladies, welcome!

All. Welcome, ladies! welcome!
[*A flourish with drums and trumpets.—Exeunt*

SCENE V.—Antium. *A public Place.*

Enter Tullus Aufidius, *with* Attendants.

Auf. Go tell the lords of the city I am here:
Deliver them this paper: having read it,
Bid them repair to the market-place; where I,
Even in theirs and in the commons' ears,
Will vouch the truth of it. Him I accuse
The city ports by this hath entered, and
Intends to appear before the people, hoping
To purge himself with words. Despatch.
[*Exeunt Attendants*

Enter three or four Conspirators *of* Aufidius' *faction.*

Most welcome!

1st Con. How is it with our general?

Auf. Even so
As with a man by his own alms empoisoned,
And with his charity slain.

2nd Con. Most noble sir,
If you do hold the same intent wherein
You wished us parties, we'll deliver you
Of your great danger.

Auf. Sir, I cannot tell:
We must proceed as we do find the people.

3rd Con. The people will remain uncertain whilst
'Twixt you there 's difference; but the fall of either
Makes the survivor heir of all.

Auf.　　　I know it:
And my pretext to strike at him admits
A good construction. I raised him, and I pawned
Mine honour for his truth: who being so heightened,
He watered his new plants with dews of flattery,
Seducing so my friends: and to this end
He bowed his nature, never known before
But to be rough, unswayable, and free.

3rd Con. Sir, his stoutness
When he did stand for consul, which he lost
By lack of stooping,—

Auf.　　　That I would have spoken of:—
Being banished for 't, he came unto my hearth;
Presented to my knife his throat. I took him:
Made him joint servant with me: gave him way
In all his own desires; nay, let him choose
Out of my files, his projects to accomplish,
My best and freshest men: served his designments
In mine own person: holp to reap the fame
Which he did end all his; and took some pride
To do myself this wrong: till at the last
I seemed his follower, not partner; and
He waged me with his countenance, as if
I had been mercenary.

1st Con.　　　So he did, my lord:
The army marvelled at it. And in the last,
When he had carried Rome, and that we looked
For no less spoil than glory,—

Auf.　　　There was it:
For which my sinews shall be stretched upon him.
At a few drops of women's rheum, which are
As cheap as lies, he sold the blood and labour
Of our great action. Therefore shall he die,
And I 'll renew me in his fall. But hark!

　　　*[Drums and trumpets sound, with great
　　　　shouts of the people.*

1st Con. Your native town you entered like a
　　　post,
And had no welcomes home: but he returns
Splitting the air with noise.

2nd Con.　　　And patient fools,
Whose children he hath slain, their base throats
　　　tear
With giving him glory.

3rd Con.　　　Therefore, at your vantage,
Ere he express himself, or move the people
With what he would say, let him feel your sword,
Which we will second. When he lies along,
After your way his tale pronounced shall bury
His reasons with his body.

Auf.　　　Say no more:
Here come the lords.

　　　Enter the Lords *of the City.*

Lords. You are most welcome home.

Auf.　　　I have not deserved it:
But, worthy lords, have you with heed perused
What I have written to you?

Lords.　　　We have.

1st Lord.　　　And grieve to hear it.
What faults he made before the last, I think
Might have found easy fines: but there to end
Where he was to begin, and give away
The benefit of our levies, answering us
With our own charge; making a treaty where
There was a yielding: this admits of no excuse.

Auf. He approaches: you shall hear him.

　　　Enter CORIOLANUS, *with drums and colours; a
　　　　crowd of* Citizens *with him.*

Cor. Hail, lords! I am returned your soldier:
No more infected with my country's love
Than when I parted hence, but still subsisting
Under your great command. You are to know
That prosperously I have attempted, and
With bloody passage led your wars even to
The gates of Rome. Our spoils we have brought
　　　home
Do more than counterpoise, a full third part,
The charges of the action. We have made peace,
With no less honour to the Antiates
Than shame to the Romans: and we here deliver,
Subscribéd by the consuls and patricians,
Together with the seal o' the senate, what
We have compounded on.

Auf.　　　Read it not, noble lords;
But tell the traitor, in the highest degree
He hath abused your powers.

Cor. Traitor! How now?

Auf.　　　Ay, traitor, Marcius.

Cor.　　　Marcius!

Auf. Ay, Marcius; Caius Marcius. Dost thou
　　　think
I 'll grace thee with that robbery, thy stolen name
Coriolanus in Corioli?—
You lords and heads of the state, perfidiously
He has betrayed your business, and given up
For certain drops of salt your city Rome
(I say your city) to his wife and mother:
Breaking his oath and resolution like
A twist of rotten silk: never admitting
Counsel o' the war; but at his nurse's tears
He whined and roared away your victory,
That pages blushed at him, and men of heart
Looked wondering each at other.

Cor.　　　Hear'st thou, Mars?

Auf. Name not the god, thou boy of tears!

Cor. Ha!

Auf. No more.

Cor. Measureless liar, thou hast made my heart

Too great for what contains it.—Boy! O slave!—
Pardon me, lords, 't is the first time that ever
I was forced to scold. Your judgments, my grave
  lords,
Must give this cur the lie: and his own notion
(Who wears my stripes impressed on him; that
  must bear
My beating to his grave) shall join to thrust
The lie unto him.

 1st Lord. Peace, both, and hear me speak.
 Cor. Cut me to pieces, Volces; men and
  lads,
Stain all your edges on me.—Boy! False hound!
If you have writ your annals true, 't is there
That, like an eagle in a dovecote, I
Fluttered your Volces in Corioli:
Alone I did it.—Boy!

 Auf. Why, noble lords,
Will you be put in mind of his blind fortune,
Which was your shame, by this unholy braggart,
'Fore your own eyes and ears?

 Con. Let him die for 't. [*Several speak at once.*
 Cit. [*Speaking promiscuously*]. Tear him to
pieces; do it presently. He killed my son:—
my daughter:—he killed my cousin Marcus:
—he killed my father.—

 2nd Lord. Peace, ho!—no outrage:—peace!
The man is noble, and his fame folds in
This orb o' the earth. His last offences to us
Shall have judicious hearing.—Stand, Aufidius,
And trouble not the peace.

 Cor. O that I had him,
With six Aufidiuses, or more, his tribe
To use my lawful sword!

 Auf. Insolent villain!
 Con. Kill, kill, kill, kill, kill him!

 [Aufidius *and the* Conspirators *draw and kill*
  Coriolanus, *who falls, and* Aufidius
  stands on him.
 Lords. Hold, hold, hold, hold!
 Auf. My noble masters, hear me speak.
 1st Lord. O Tullus!—
 2nd Lord. Thou hast done a deed whereat
  valour will weep.
 3rd Lord. Tread not upon him.—Masters all,
  be quiet:
Put up your swords.

 Auf. My lords, when you shall know (as in
  this rage,
Provoked by him, you cannot) the great danger
Which this man's life did owe you, you 'll rejoice
That he is thus cut off. Please it your honours
To call me to your senate, I 'll deliver
Myself your loyal servant, or endure
Your heaviest censure.

 1st Lord. Bear from hence his body,
And mourn you for him: let him be regarded
As the most noble corse that ever herald
Did follow to his urn.

 2nd Lord. His own impatience
Takes from Aufidius a great part of blame.
Let 's make the best of it.

 Auf. My rage is gone,
And I am struck with sorrow.—Take him up:
Help, three o' the chiefest soldiers; I 'll be one.—
Beat thou the drum that it speak mournfully:
Trail your steel pikes.—Though in this city he
Hath widowed and unchilded many a one,
Which to this hour bewail the injury,
Yet he shall have a noble memory.—
Assist. [*Exeunt, bearing the body of* Coriolanus.
  A dead march sounded.

" We are accounted poor citizens : the patricians, good."
Act I., Scene 1.

The word "good" is here used in the sense of rich or prosperous. As in the "MERCHANT OF VENICE :—

" Antonio's a good man."

" To a cruel war I sent him ; from whence he returned, his brows bound with oak."—Act I., Scene 3.

The first time he went to the wars, being but a stripling, was when Tarquin, surnamed the Proud (that had been King of Rome, and was driven out for his pride, after many attempts made by sundry battles to come in again, wherein he was ever overcome), did come to Rome with all the aid of the Latins and many other people of Italy, even, as it were, to set up his whole rest upon a battle by them, who, with a great and mighty army, had undertaken to put him into his kingdom again, not so much to pleasure him as to overthrow the power of the Romans, whose greatness they both feared and envied.

In this battle, wherein were many hot and sharp encounters of either party, Martius valiantly fought in the sight of the Dictator; and a Roman soldier being thrown to the ground even hard by him, Martius straight bestrid him, and slew the enemy with his own hands that had before overthrown the Roman. Hereupon, after the battle was won, the Dictator did not forget so noble an act; and therefore, first of all, he crowned Martius with a garland of oaken boughs : for whosoever saveth the life of a Roman, it is a manner among them to honour him with such a garland.— PLUTARCH's "Life of Coriolanus;" North's Translation.

[Sir Thomas North's translation of PLUTARCH (1579) was, doubtless, the main source whence Shakspere derived the incidents of his Roman plays. The closeness with which he has followed them, and the admirable skill he has shewn in working them into a dramatic shape, will appear from occasional short specimens of the biographer's narrative, as rendered in North's picturesque version.]

" What, are you sewing here ? A fine spot, in good faith."
Act I., Scene 3.

The term "fine spot" relates to the embroidery. "Spotted muslin" is a phrase still in use.

—— " Thou wast a soldier
Even to Cato's wish."—Act I., Scene 4.

In the country of the Volces, against whom the Romans made war at that time, there was a principal city, and of most fame, that was called Corioles; before the which the consul Cominius did lay siege. Whereupon all the other Volces, fearing lest that city should be taken by assault, they came from all parts of the country to save it, intending to give the Romans battle before the city, and to give an onset on them in two several places. The consul Cominius, understanding this, divided his army also into two parts; and, taking the one part with himself, he marched towards them that were drawing to the city out of the country: and the other part of his army he left in the camp with Titus Lartius (one of the valiantest men the Romans had at that time), to resist those that would make any sally out of the city upon them.

So the Coriolans, making small account of them that lay in camp before the city, made a sally out upon them; in the which at the first the Coriolans had the better, and drove the Romans back again into the trenches of their camp. But Martius being there at that time, running out of the camp with a few men with him, he slew the first enemies he met withal, and made the rest of them stay upon the sudden; crying out to the Romans that had turned their backs, and calling them again to fight, with a loud voice. For he was even such another as Cato would have a soldier and a captain to be :—not only terrible and fierce to lay about him, but to make the enemy afeard with the sound of his voice and grimness of his countenance.—PLUTARCH.

It will be seen, that in speaking of Marcius as "a soldier even to Cato's wish," the poet inadvertently attributes to Lartius, what was in fact a remark of the biographer. The old copy has "*Calues* wish ;" but this is, doubtless, a misprint.

—— " Please you to march ;
And four shall quickly draw out my command,
Which men are best inclined."—Act I., Scene 6.

Coriolanus may here mean that he would appoint four persons, to select, for his particular command (or party), those soldiers who were best inclined : and in order to save time, he proposes to have this choice made while the army is marching forward. There is probably some error in the text.

" If I should tell thee o'er this thy day's work,
Thou'lt not believe thy deeds."—Act I., Scene 9.

There the consul Cominius, going up to his chair of state, in the presence of the whole army, gave thanks to the gods for so great, glorious, and prosperous a victory. Then he spoke to Martius, whose valiantness he commended beyond the moon, both for that he himself saw him do with his eyes, as also for that Lartius had reported unto him.

So in the end he willed Martius that he should choose, out of all the horses they had taken of their enemies, and of all the goods they had won (whereof there was great store), ten of every sort which he liked best, before any distribution should be made to others. Besides this great, honourable offer he had made him, he gave him, in testimony that he had won that day the price of prowess above all other, a goodly horse with a caparison, and all furniture to him ; which the whole army beholding, did marvellously praise and commend. But Martius, stepping forth, told the consul he most thankfully accepted the gift of his horse, and was a glad man, besides, that his services had deserved his general's recommendation : and as for his other offer, which was rather a mercenary reward than an honourable recompense, he would have none of it, but was contented to have his equal part with the other soldiers.—PLUTARCH.

" SIC. *Nature teaches beasts to know their friends.*
MEN. *Pray you, who does the wolf love ?"*
Act II., Scene 1.

Menenius probably means to infer that the tribune's rule is not without an exception; and that the people are not, in the particular referred to, more discriminating than the wolf.

" You are ambitious for poor knaves' caps and legs."
Act II., Scene 1.

To "make a leg," was the phrase for bowing. It probably alluded to the practice (still preserved in the representation of rustics) of scraping backward with the left leg, at the time of bending the body.

---- *" It then remains,*
That you do speak to the people."—Act II., Scene 2.

Shortly after this, Martius stood for the consulship; and the common people favoured his suit, thinking it would be a shame to them to deny and refuse the chiefest nobleman of blood and most worthy person of Rome; and especially him that had done so great service and good to the Commonwealth. For the custom of Rome was at that time, that such as did sue for any office should, for certain days before, be in the market-place, only with a poor gown on their backs, and without any coat underneath, to pray the citizens to remember them at the day of election: which was thus devised, either to move the people the more, by requesting them in such mean apparel, or else, because they might shew them their wounds they had gotten in the wars, in the service of the Commonwealth, as manifest marks and testimonies of their valiantness.—PLUTARCH.

" Why in this woolvish toge should I stand here," &c.
Act II., Scene 3.

The first folio has "tongue," instead of "toge." The same error occurs in that version of "OTHELLO," where "tongued consuls" is printed for "toged consuls." The meaning of the term "woolvish" has occasioned much controversy: it appears most probable that the poet supposed, whether erroneously or not, that the candidate had to stand in a garment of woollen material—"the gown of humility."

---- *" What stock he springs of,*
The noble house o' the Marcians; from whence came
That Ancus Marcius (Numa's daughter's son)
Who, after great Hostilius, here was king.
Of the same house Publius and Quintus were,
That our best water brought by conduits hither :
And Censorinus, darling of the people
(And nobly named so, twice being censor),
Was his great ancestor."—Act II., Scene 3.

The house of the Martians at Rome was of the number of the patricians, out of the which have sprung many noble personages; whereof Ancus Martius was one (King Numa's daughter's son), who was King of Rome after Tullus Hostilius. Of the same house was Publius and Quintus, who brought to Rome their best water they had, by conduits. Censorinus also came of that family, that was so surnamed because the people had chosen him censor twice; through whose persuasion they made a law that no man from thenceforth might require or enjoy the censorship twice.—PLUTARCH.

The poet, in the quoted passage, failed to note accurately the expressions of the biographer. Publius and Quintus and Censorinus were not the ancestors of Coriolanus, but his descendants. The line—

" And Censorinus, darling of the people,"

was supplied by Pope; an evident deficiency occurring in the original edition.

" In soothing them we nourish 'gainst our senate
The cockle of rebellion, insolence, sedition."
Act III., Scene 1.

Cockle is a weed which grows up with and chokes the corn. The word is found in "NORTH'S PLUTARCH," as also the general tenour of the speech in which it is used.

---- *" So shall my lungs*
Coin words till their decay, against those menzels."
Act III, Scene 1.

Meazel, or mesell, is the old term for a leper; from the French *meselle.*

---- *" The accusation*
Which they have often made against the senate,
All cause unborn, could never be the native
Of our so frank donation."—Act III., Scene 1.

For "native," in this passage, it has been plausibly proposed to read "motive." If the text is correct, "native" must be understood in the sense of "native cause," or "natural parent."

---- *" In a better hour,*
Let what is meet be said 'it must be meet,'
And throw their power i' the dust."—Act III., Scene 1.

That is, "let it be said by you, that what is *meet* to be done, *must* be done; i. e. *shall* be done."—MALONE.

" Our renownèd Rome, whose gratitude
Towards her deservèd children is enrolled
In Jove's own book."—Act III., Scene 1.

"Deserved" is here used for "deserving." As in "OTHELLO," we have "delighted" for "delighting." These discrepancies of termination were frequent before the language was finally formed.

" This is clean kam."—Act III., Scene 1.

"Kam" is an obsolete word, signifying crooked or awry. In the text, the term is used figuratively, meaning "not to the purpose."

---- *" Waving thy head,*
Which often,—thus,—correcting thy stout heart."
Act III., Scene 2.

"Waving thy head" seems here meant to express the act of bending. As in "HAMLET:"—

" And thrice his head thus waving up and down."

In the second line of the quotation, Volumnia must be supposed to express in action the gesture she recommends to her son.

" Must I go shew them my unbarbed sconce ?"
Act III., Scene 2.

"Unbarbed" signifies unarmed or uncovered. A barbed steed was one covered with trappings.

" First hear me speak."—Act III., Scene 3.

So Martius came and presented himself to answer their accusations against him; and the people held their peace, and gave attentive ear to hear what he would say. But where they thought to have heard very humble and lowly words come from him, he began not only to use his wonted boldness of speaking (which of itself was very rough and unpleasant, and did more aggravate his accusation than purge his innocency), but also gave himself in his words to thunder, and look therewithal so grimly as though he made no reckoning of the matter.

This stirred coals among the people, who were in wonderful fury at it; and their hate and malice grew so toward him, that they could no longer bear nor endure his bravery and careless boldness. Whereupon Sicinius, the cruellest and stoutest of the Tribunes, after he had whispered a little with his companions, did openly pronounce, in the face of all the people, Martius as condemned by the Tribunes to die. Then presently he commanded the ædiles to apprehend him, and carry him straight to the rock Tarpeian, and to cast him headlong down the same. When the ædiles came to lay hands upon Martius to do what they were commanded, divers of the people themselves thought it too cruel and violent a deed.—PLUTARCH.

" *I have been consul, and can shew, for Rome,*
Her enemies' marks upon me."—Act III., Scene 3.

The old copy here reads " from Rome." There can scarcely be a doubt of the propriety of the alteration. In other parts of the play we find:—

" So banish him that struck more blows for Rome."

And again:—

" Good man! the wounds that he does bear for Rome."

" *You common cry of curs!*"—Act III., Scene 3.

" Cry" here signifies a troop or pack. " A cry of hounds" was formerly a common term.

—— " *Have the power still*
To banish your defenders: till at length
Your ignorance (which finds not till it feels),
Making but reservation of yourselves
(Still your own foes), deliver you,
As most abated captives, to some nation
That won you without blows!"—Act III., Scene 3.

That is, " Still retain the power of banishing your defenders, till your undiscerning folly leave none in the city but yourselves; when, for want of skilful leaders, you will become an easy prey to any hostile force."

—— " *Fortune's blows*
When most struck home, being gentle, wounded, craves
A noble cunning."—Act IV., Scene 1.

The sense is, When fortune strikes her hardest blows, to be wounded, and yet continue calm, requires a generous policy. Coriolanus calls calmness cunning, because it is the effect of reflection and philosophy.—JOHNSON.

Cunning is here, as was generally the case in former times, used synonymously with skill or wisdom.

" SIC. *Are you mankind?*
VOL. *Ay, fool: is that a shame?—Note but this fool:—*
Was not a man my father?"—Act IV., Scene 2.

The term " mankind," as applied to women, meant fierce or ferocious. It is so used in the " WINTER'S TALE," where Leontes calls Paulina " a mankind witch."—Volumnia, in her reply, takes the word in its present received sense.

" *A goodly city is this Antium.—City,*
'*T is I that made thy widows.*"—Act IV., Scene 4.

It was even twilight when he entered the city of Antium, and many people met him in the streets, but no man knew him. So he went directly to Tullus Aufidius' house; and when he came thither, he got him up straight to the chimney-hearth, and sat him down, and spake not a word to any man, his face all muffled over. They of the house spying him, wondered what he should be, and yet they durst not bid him rise. For ill-favouredly muffled and disguised as he was, yet there appeared a certain majesty in his countenance and in his silence. Whereupon they went to Tullus, who was at supper, to tell him of the strange disguising of this man. Tullus rose presently from the board, and coming towards him, asked him what he was, and wherefore he came. Then Martius unmuffled himself; and after he had paused awhile (making no answer), he said unto him, " If thou knowest me not yet, Tullus, and, seeing me, dost not perhaps believe me to be the man I am indeed, I must of necessity betray myself to be that I am. I am Caius Marsius, who hath done to thyself particularly, and to all the Volces generally, great hurt and mischief; which I cannot deny, for my surname of Coriolanus that I bear: for I never had other benefit nor recompense of the true and painful service I have done, and the extreme dangers I have been in, but this only surname: a good memory and witness of the malice and displeasure thou shouldst bear me. Indeed, the name only remaineth with me: for the rest the envy and cruelty of the people of Rome have taken from me, by the sufferance of the dastardly nobility and magistrates, who have forsaken me, and let me be banished by the people."—PLUTARCH.

" *O world, thy slippery turns! Friends now fast sworn,*" &c.
Act IV., Scene 4.

This fine picture of common friendship is an artful introduction to the sudden league which the poet makes Coriolanus enter into with Aufidius; and a no less artful apology for his commencing enemy to Rome.—WARBURTON.

—— " *Here I clip*
The anvil of my sword."—Act IV., Scene 5.

To clip is to embrace. Aufidius calls Coriolanus the anvil of his sword, because he had formerly laid as heavy blows on him as a smith strikes on his anvil.

—— " *I think he'll be to Rome*
As is the osprey to the fish, who takes it
By sovereignty of nature."—Act IV., Scene 7.

There was formerly a popular notion that the osprey exercised a fascinating power over his finny prey. Drayton alludes to it:—

" Turning their bellies up, as though their death they saw,
They at his pleasure lie, to stuff his gluttonous maw."

" *First he was*
A noble servant to them; but he could not
Carry his honours even. Whether 't was pride," &c.
Act IV., Scene 7.

Aufidius assigns three probable reasons for the miscarriage of Coriolanus:—pride, which easily follows an uninterrupted train of success: unskilfulness to regulate the consequences of his own victories: a stubborn uniformity of nature, which could not make the proper transition " from the casque to the cushion," or chair of civil authority, but acted with the same despotism in peace as in war.—JOHNSON.

—— " *But he has a merit*
To choke it in the utterance. So our virtues
Lie in the interpretation of the time:
And power, unto itself most commendable,
Hath not a tomb so evident as a chair
To extol what it hath done."—Act IV., Scene 7.

That is, He has a merit for no other purpose than to destroy it by boasting it.—JOHNSON.

Of the latter part of the quotation, Warburton says:—
" The sense is, the virtue which delights to commend itself, will find the surest tomb in that chair wherein it holds forth its own commendations." There is probably some corruption in the original text.

—— " *Go, you that banished him,*
A mile before his tent fall down, and knee
The way into his mercy."—Act V., Scene 1.

In reference to the word " knee" in this passage, it is stated by an intelligent, though sometimes hasty contemporary, that " the second folio, which has been followed *in all other editions*, has the less expressive word *kneel*." The point is of very little importance, but it so happens that we have immediately at hand two copies in which the word *knee* is used, and not *kneel*. These are, a reprint of Malone's edition of 1790 (Dublin, 1794); and Ayscough's (1791). The number might, no doubt, be easily multiplied to any required amount.

Our contemporary is entitled to credit for perfect good faith; but he appears to be inadvertently in the habit of supposing many defects universal, or nearly so, which in fact appertain to those versions only that are too confidently founded on the later editions of Steevens and Reed: the last more especially, which was published in 1803.

> " *He was not taken well ; he had not dined :*
> *The veins unfilled, our blood is cold,*" &c.
> Act V., Scene 1.

This observation is not only from nature, and finely expressed, but admirably befits the mouth of one, who, in the beginning of the play, had told us that he loved convivial doings.—WARBURTON.

> ——" *What he would do,*
> *He sent in writing after me : what he would not,*
> *Bound with an oath to yield to his conditions.*"
> Act V., Scene 1.

No satisfactory solution has been given of the latter part of this passage. Probably "his conditions" may mean the conditions he had before prescribed. Mr. Singer plausibly proposes to read "no conditions." A misprint in the original copy may reasonably be suspected.

> ——" *Nay, sometimes,*
> *Like to a bowl upon a subtle ground,*
> *I have stumbled past the throw ; and in his praise*
> *Have almost stamped the leasing.*"—Act V., Scene 2.

By a subtle ground, is probably meant a deceiving ground. " Stamped the leasing," means, " I have almost given the lie such a sanction as to render it current."

> " *My wife comes foremost : then the honoured mould*
> *Wherein this trunk was framed ; and in her hand*
> *The grandchild to her blood.*"—Act V., Scene 3.

She (Volumnia) took her daughter-in-law, and Martius's children with her ; and, being accompanied with all the other Roman ladies, they went in troop together into the Volces' camp : whom when they saw, they of themselves did both pity and reverence her, and there was not a man amongst them that once durst say a word unto her. Now was Martius set then in his chair of state, with all the honours of a general ; and when he had spied the women coming afar off, he marvelled what the matter meant : but afterwards, knowing his wife, which came foremost, he determined at the first to persist in his obstinate and inflexible rancour. But, overcome in the end with natural affection, and being altogether altered to see them, his heart would not serve him to tarry their coming to his chair, but, coming down in haste, he went to meet them : and first he kissed his mother and embraced her a pretty while ; then his wife and little children ; and nature so wrought with him that the tears fell from his eyes, and he could not keep himself from making much of them, but yielded to the affection of his blood, as if he had been violently carried with the fury of a most swift-running stream.—PLUTARCH.

> " COR. *These eyes are not the same I wore in Rome.*
> VIR. *The sorrow that delivers us thus changed*
> *Makes you think so.*"—Act V., Scene 3.

Virgilia makes a voluntary misinterpretation of her husband's words. He says, " These eyes are not the same ;" meaning that he saw things with other eyes or other dispositions. She lays hold on the word eyes, to turn his attention to their present appearance.—JOHNSON.

> " *Like a great sea-mark, standing every flaw,*
> *And saving those that eye thee !*"—Act V., Scene 3.

A flaw is a violent blast or sudden gust of wind. The word is not obsolete, as stated in Todd's " JOHNSON." It will be found in the interesting " Journal" of Captain Hall (1824, vol. i., p. 4) ; and in Captain Lyon's " Narrative of his attempt to reach Repulse Bay" (1824).—SINGER.

Hamlet, it will be recollected, speaks of "the winter's flaw."

> —— " *Ladies, you deserve*
> *To have a temple built you.*"—Act V., Scene 3.

Plutarch states, that a temple, dedicated to the " Fortune of the Ladies," was built on this occasion by order of the senate.

> " *He waged me with his countenance, as if*
> *I had been mercenary.*"—Act V. Scene 5.

To wage, formerly meant to pay or reward. The meaning is, he prescribed to me with an air of authority, and gave me his countenance for my wages :—thought me sufficiently rewarded with good looks.

> " *Hail, lords ! I am returned your soldier :*
> *No more infected with my country's love*
> *Than when I parted hence.*"—Act V., Scene 5.

Now when Martius was returned again into the city of Antium from his voyage, Tullus, that hated and could no longer abide him, for the fear he had of his authority, sought divers means to make him away ; thinking that, if he let slip that present time, he should never recover the like and fit occasion again. Wherefore Tullus, having procured many other of his confederacy, required Martius might be deposed from his estate, to render up account to the Volces of his charge and government. Martius, fearing to become a private man again, under Tullus, being general (whose authority was greater otherwise than any other among all the Volces), answered he was willing to give up his charge, and would resign it into the hands of the lords of the Volces if they did all command him, as by all their commandment he received it : and moreover, that he would not refuse even at that present to give up an account unto the people, if they would tarry the hearing of it. The people hereupon called a common council, in which assembly there were certain orators appointed that stirred up the common people against him : and when they had told their tales, Martius rode up to make them answer.—Now, notwithstanding the mutinous people made a marvellous great noise, yet when they saw him, for the reverence they bare unto his valiantness, they quieted themselves, and gave him audience to allege with leisure what he could for his purgation. Moreover, the honestest men of the Antiates, and who most rejoiced in peace, shewed by their countenance that they would hear him willingly, and judge also according to their conscience. Whereupon Tullus,—fearing that if he did let him speak, he would prove his innocency to the people, because, amongst other things, he had an eloquent tongue : besides that the first good service he had done to the people of the Volces did win him more favour than these last accusations could purchase him displeasure : and furthermore, the offence they laid to his charge was a testimony of the goodwill they owed him (for they would never have thought he had done them wrong for that he took not the city of Rome, if they had not been very near taking it by means of his approach and conduction) :—for these causes, Tullus thought he might no longer delay his pretence and enterprise, neither to tarry for the mutinying and rising of the common people against him. Wherefore those that were of the conspiracy began to cry out that he was not to be heard, and that they would not suffer a traitor to usurp tyrannical power over the tribe of the Volces ; who would not yield up his state and authority. And in saying these words, they all fell upon him and killed him in the market-place, none of the people once offering to rescue him.—PLUTARCH.

JULIUS
CÆSAR

INTRODUCTORY REMARKS

ULIUS CÆSAR, like Coriolanus, belongs to that class of dramas which represent action and character, and stands conspicuously prominent amongst the many similar productions of Shakspere's wondrous mind. What an elevated tone of thought, feeling, and expression, pervades the whole of this play: how admirably suited to the scene of action, and to the great men who were the actors: how fitly does all seem to belong to the stern, the awful glories of old Rome!—We can almost fancy that we stand upon the Capitoline Hill, and behold the splendours of the eternal city spreading far and wide beneath us: that we see the procession of Cæsar to the Lupercalian games, and the toged senators mounting the steps of the senate-house: that we hear the uproarious shoutings of the mighty mob of Rome:—

> "That Tyber trembles underneath her banks,
> To hear the replication of their sounds
> Made in her concave shores."

But superior even to the reality of the general effect,—to the power of carrying back the imagination to remote ages and events,—is the remarkable individuality of character exhibited in this great tragedy: one of the most distinguished characteristics of the mighty master's mind, but never more powerfully and subtly displayed. Observe all the principal characters: and, without any violent contrasts (the easy and too common trick of dramatic writing), see how completely distinctive in their natures, how delicately and skilfully discriminated, each from the others, they are, in thought, sentiment, and diction! How soon do we perceive the striking difference of nature and disposition between Brutus and Cassius, and the immense superiority of Brutus! Cassius is evidently actuated, in his hostility to Cæsar, quite as much by envy of the man, as by a patriotic dread of the consequences of his overgrown power. The mere existence of that power he evidently thinks less dangerous to the commonweal, than that it should be vested in one man; he appears to have a lurking wish to be a sharer in it. Brutus is the living personification of all that is noble, elevated, kindly, and generous in human nature; never appearing to think of self but in connexion with his kind: but Cassius, with all his high qualities, is well described by Cæsar as one of those who are "never at heart's ease, whiles they behold a greater than themselves." Brutus, perceiving no stains on the bright surface of his own clear mind, suspects them not in that of his fellows: but Cassius, conscious that much of the world's craft enters into his composition, is quick to detect craft in others.

With the same masterly skill are drawn the characters of Julius Cæsar and Marc Antony, as far as the plan of the play allowed: the scene in which Antony delivers his oration over Cæsar's body has ever been regarded as one of the poet's master-pieces in dramatic effect, vigour, and subtlety. The intense reality of this scene is truly marvellous. It is as though the author had been on the actual spot, heard the actual words, and beheld the actual effects he has so vividly recorded. We can *see* the influence of Antony's most artful harangue gradually diffuse itself over the rude multitude. With what consummate tact and address does he at first command their attention, and conciliate their regards, by eulogising "Brutus and the rest"—the very men against whom he wishes to raise that "flood of mutiny" he so artfully affects to deprecate! How admirably, too, he times the reproduction of Cæsar's will, when they, in their excited rage, have forgotten it;—in order that no one motive should be wanting to incite them against the conspirators: so managing, as to make it the uppermost idea in their minds, that they were hastening to avenge the death of their especial benefactor.

Amidst all our admiration of this entire play, Brutus must, however, always rank as its greatest and most interesting character. Farewell to thee, noble, gentle Brutus! deeply, bitterly, must all true lovers of thy humane philosophy regret, that thy great and kindly mind should ever have become engaged in the violent and turbulent scenes of the times in which thou hadst the misfortune to live; scenes so unsuited to thy good and gracious nature: and heartily must all join in the poet's estimate of thy character—

> "This was the noblest Roman of them all!"

Plutarch's Lives of Brutus, Antony, and Cæsar, furnished the incidents of this surpassing drama: the period of time comprised in the action is about two years. "Julius Cæsar" was first published in the original folio, and is obviously a production of the Poet's intellect in its maturer years.

PERSONS REPRESENTED.

JULIUS CÆSAR,
OCTAVIUS CÆSAR,
MARCUS ANTONIUS,
M. ÆMIL. LEPIDUS,
} Triumvirs after the death of
JULIUS CÆSAR.

CICERO, PUBLIUS, POPILIUS LENA, Senators.

MARCUS BRUTUS,
CASSIUS,
CASCA,
TREBONIUS,
LIGARIUS,
DECIUS BRUTUS,
METELLUS CIMBER,
CINNA,
} Conspirators against JULIUS
CÆSAR.

FLAVIUS and MARULLUS, Tribunes.
ARTEMIDORUS, a Sophist of Cnidos
A Soothsayer.
CINNA, a Poet
Another Poet.
LUCILIUS, TITINIUS, MESSSALA, Young CATO, and
VOLUMNIUS, Friends to BRUTUS and Cassius.
VARRO, CLITUS, CLAUDIUS, STRATO, LUCIUS, DAR-
DANIUS, Servants to BRUTUS.
PINDARUS, Servant to CASSIUS.

CALPHURNIA, Wife to CÆSAR.
PORTIA, Wife to BRUTUS.

Senators, Citizens Guards, Attendants, &c.

_____

SCENE. During a great part of the Play, at ROME; afterwards at SARDIS; and near PHILIPPI.

JULIUS CÆSAR

ACT
I

SCENE I.—Rome. *A Street.*

Enter FLAVIUS, MARULLUS, *and a Rabble of*
Citizens.

Flav. Hence: home, you idle creatures; get
    you home.
Is this a holiday? What! know you not,
Being mechanical, you ought not walk
Upon a labouring day without the sign
Of your profession?—Speak, what trade art thou?
  1st Cit. Why, sir, a carpenter.

Mar. Where is thy leather apron and thy rule?
What dost thou with thy best apparel on?—
You, sir; what trade are you?
  2nd Cit. Truly, sir, in respect of a fine work-
    man,
I am but, as you would say, a cobbler.
  Mar. But what trade art thou? Answer me
    directly.
  2nd Cit. A trade, sir, that I hope I may use with
a safe conscience: which is indeed, sir, a mender
of bad soles.

Mar. What trade, thou knave? thou naughty knave, what trade?

2nd Cit. Nay, I beseech you, sir, be not out with me: yet if you be out, sir, I can mend you.

Mar. What meanest thou by that? Mend me, thou saucy fellow?

2nd Cit. Why, sir, cobble you.

Flav. Thou art a cobbler, art thou?

2nd Cit. Truly, sir, all that I live by is with the awl: I meddle with no tradesman's matters, nor women's matters, but with awl. I am indeed, sir, a surgeon to old shoes: when they are in great danger, I re-cover them. As proper men as ever trod upon neats-leather have gone upon my handy-work.

Flav. But wherefore art not in thy shop to-day? Why dost thou lead these men about the streets?

2nd Cit. Truly, sir, to wear out their shoes, to get myself into more work. But indeed, sir, we make holiday to see Cæsar, and to rejoice in his triumph.

Mar. Wherefore rejoice? What conquest brings he home?
What tributaries follow him to Rome,
To grace in captive bonds his chariot-wheels?—
You blocks, you stones, you worse than senseless things!
O you hard hearts, you cruel men of Rome!
Knew you not Pompey?—Many a time and oft
Have you climbed up to walls and battlements,
To towers and windows, yea to chimney-tops,
Your infants in your arms, and there have sat
The live-long day, with patient expectation,
To see great Pompey pass the streets of Rome:
And when you saw his chariot but appear,
Have you not made an universal shout,
That Tiber trembled underneath her banks,
To hear the replication of your sounds
Made in her concave shores?
And do you now put on your best attire;
And do you now cull out a holiday;
And do you now strew flowers in his way
That comes in triumph over Pompey's blood?—
Be gone!
Run to your houses, fall upon your knees;
Pray to the gods to intermit the plague
That needs must light on this ingratitude.

Flav. Go, go, good countrymen; and for this fault
Assemble all the poor men of your sort;
Draw them to Tyber banks, and weep your tears
Into the channel, till the lowest stream
Do kiss the most exalted shores of all.
[*Exeunt* Citizens.
See, whe'r their basest metal be not moved!
They vanish, tongue-tied in their guiltiness.
Go you down that way towards the Capitol;

This way will I: disrobe the images,
If you do find them decked with ceremonies.

Mar. May we do so?
You know it is the feast of Lupercal.

Flav. It is no matter: let no images
Be hung with Cæsar's trophies. I'll about,
And drive away the vulgar from the streets:
So do you too, where you perceive them thick.
These growing feathers plucked from Cæsar's wing
Will make him fly an ordinary pitch;
Who else would soar above the view of men,
And keep us all in servile fearfulness. [*Exeunt.*

SCENE II.—*The same. A public Place.*

Enter, in procession, with music, CÆSAR; ANTONY,
for the course; CALPHURNIA, PORTIA, DECIUS,
CICERO, BRUTUS, CASSIUS, *and* CASCA; *a great
Crowd following; among them a Soothsayer.*

Cæs. Calphurnia,—

Casca. Peace, ho! Cæsar speaks. [*Music ceases.*

Cæs. Calphurnia:—

Cal. Here, my lord.

Cæs. Stand you directly in Antonius' way,
When he doth run his course.—Antonius:—

Ant. Cæsar, my lord.

Cæs. Forget not, in your speed, Antonius,
To touch Calphurnia: for our elders say,
The barren, touchéd in this holy chase,
Shake off their steril curse.

Ant.   I shall remember:
When Cæsar says, "Do this," it is performed.

Cæs. Set on, and leave no ceremony out. [*Music.*

Sooth. Cæsar!

Cæs. Ha! who calls?

Casca. Bid every noise be still:—peace yet again.   [*Music ceases.*

Cæs. Who is it in the press that calls on me?
I hear a tongue, shriller than all the music,
Cry, "Cæsar." Speak: Cæsar is turned to hear.

Sooth. Beware the ides of March!

Cæs.   What man is that?

Bru. A soothsayer bids you beware the ides of March.

Cæs. Set him before me; let me see his face.

Cas. Fellow, come from the throng: look upon Cæsar.

Cæs. What say'st thou to me now? Speak once again.

Sooth. Beware the ides of March.

Cæs. He is a dreamer; let us leave him:—pass.
[*Sennet. Exeunt all but* BRUTUS *and* CASSIUS.

Cas. Will you go see the order of the course?

Bru. Not I.

Cas. I pray you do.

Bru. I am not gamesome : I do lack some part
Of that quick spirit that is in Antony.
Let me not hinder, Cassius, your desires :
I 'll leave you.

Cas. Brutus, I do observe you now of late :
I have not from your eyes that gentleness
And show of love as I was wont to have :
You bear too stubborn and too strange a hand
Over your friend that loves you.

Bru.　　　　Cassius,
Be not deceived : if I have veiled my look,
I turn the trouble of my countenance
Merely upon myself.　Vexed I am
Of late with passions of some difference,
Conceptions only proper to myself,
Which give some soil, perhaps, to my behaviours :
But let not therefore, my good friends be grieved
(Among which number, Cassius, be you one),
Nor construe any further my neglect,
Than that poor Brutus, with himself at war,
Forgets the shows of love to other men.

Cas. Then, Brutus, I have much mistook your
　　　　passion :
By means whereof this breast of mine hath buried
Thoughts of great value, worthy cogitations.
Tell me good Brutus, can you see your face ?

Bru. No, Cassius : for the eye sees not itself,
But by reflection, by some other things.

Cas. 'T is just :
And it is very much lamented, Brutus,
That you have no such mirrors as will turn
Your hidden worthiness into your eye,
That you might see your shadow.　I have heard
Where many of the best respect in Rome
(Except immortal Cæsar), speaking of Brutus,
And groaning underneath this age's yoke,
Have wished that noble Brutus had his eyes.

Bru. Into what dangers would you lead me,
　　　　Cassius,
That you would have me seek into myself
For that which is not in me ?

Cas. Therefore, good Brutus, be prepared to
　　　　hear :
And since you know you cannot see yourself
So well as by reflection, I (your glass)
Will modestly discover to yourself
That of yourself which you yet know not of.
And be not jealous of me, gentle Brutus :
Were I a common laugher, or did use
To stale with ordinary oaths my love
To every new protester ; if you know
That I do fawn on men and hug them hard,
And after scandal them ; or if you know
That I profess myself in banqueting
To all the rout, then hold me dangerous.
　　　　　　　　　　　[*Flourish and shout.*

Bru. What means this shouting ? I do fear the
　　　　people
Choose Cæsar for their king.

Cas.　　　　Ay, do you fear it ?
Then must I think you would not have it so.

Bru. I would not, Cassius : yet I love him
　　　　well,—
But wherefore do you hold me here so long ?
What is it that you would impart to me ?
If it be aught toward the general good,
Set honour in one eye, and death i' the other,
And I will look on both indifferently :
For let the gods so speed me as I love
The name of honour more than I fear death.

Cas. I know that virtue to be in you, Brutus,
As well as I do know your outward favour.
Well, honour is the subject of my story.—
I cannot tell what you and other men
Think of this life : but, for my single self,
I had as lief not be as live to be
In awe of such a thing as I myself.
I was born free as Cæsar ; so were you :
We both have fed as well ; and we can both
Endure the winter's cold as well as he.
For once, upon a raw and gusty day,
The troubled Tyber chafing with her shores,
Cæsar said to me,—" Dar'st thou, Cassius, now
Leap in with me into this angry flood,
And swim to yonder point ?"—Upon the word,
Accoutred as I was, I plungéd in,
And bade him follow : so indeed he did.
The torrent roared, and we did buffet it
With lusty sinews ; throwing it aside
And stemming it with hearts of controversy.
But ere we could arrive the point proposed,
Cæsar cried,—" Help me, Cassius, or I sink."
I, as Æneas, our great ancestor,
Did from the flames of Troy upon his shoulder
The old Anchises bear, so from the waves of
　　　　Tyber
Did I the tired Cæsar.　And this man
Is now become a god ! and Cassius is
A wretched creature, and must bend his body
If Cæsar carelessly but nod on him !
He had a fever when he was in Spain,
And, when the fit was on him, I did mark
How he did shake :—'t is true, this god did shake :
His coward lips did from their colour fly ;
And that same eye whose bend doth awe the world
Did lose his lustre : I did hear him groan :
Ay, and that tongue of his, that bade the Romans
Mark him, and write his speeches in their books,
Alas ! it cried,—" Give me some drink, Titinius :"
As a sick girl !　Ye gods, it doth amaze me
A man of such a feeble temper should
So get the start of the majestic world,
And bear the palm alone.　　[*Shout. Flourish.*

Bru. Another general shout!
I do believe that these applauses are
For some new honours that are heaped on Cæsar.
    Cas. Why, man, he doth bestride the narrow
        world
Like a Colossus; and we petty men
Walk under his huge legs, and peep about
To find ourselves dishonourable graves.
Men at some time are masters of their fates:
The fault, dear Brutus, is not in our stars,
But in ourselves, that we are underlings.
Brutus and Cæsar: what should be in that Cæsar?
Why should that name be sounded more than
        yours?
Write them together, yours is as fair a name;
Sound them, it doth become the mouth as well;
Weigh them, it is as heavy; conjure with them,
Brutus will start a spirit as soon as Cæsar: [*Shout.*

Now in the names of all the gods at once,
Upon what meat doth this our Cæsar feed,
That he is grown so great? Age, thou art shamed:
Rome, thou has lost the breed of noble bloods!
When went there by an age, since the great flood,
But it was famed with more than with one man?
When could they say till now, that talked of Rome,
That her wide walks encompassed but one man?
Now is it Rome indeed, and room enough,
When there is in it but one only man.
O! you and I have heard our fathers say,
There was a Brutus once, that would have brooked
The eternal devil to keep his state in Rome,
As easily as a king.
    Bru. That you do love me, I am nothing jealous;
What you would work me to, I have some aim:
How I have thought of this, and of these times,
I shall recount hereafter: for this present,

I would not, so with love I might entreat you,
Be any further moved. What you have said,
I will consider; what you have to say,
I will with patience hear; and find a time
Both meet to hear and answer such high things.
Till then, my noble friend, chew upon this:
Brutus had rather be a villager,
Than to repute himself a son of Rome
Under these hard conditions as this time
Is like to lay upon us.

   Cas. I am glad that my weak words
Have struck but thus much show of fire from
     Brutus.

Re-enter CÆSAR *and his* Train.

   Bru. The games are done, and Cæsar is returning.

   Cas. As they pass by, pluck Casca by the sleeve;
And he will, after his sour fashion, tell you
What hath proceeded worthy note to day.

   Bru. I will do so.—But look you, Cassius,
The angry spot doth glow on Cæsar's brow,
And all the rest look like a chidden train:
Calphurnia's cheek is pale: and Cicero
Looks with such ferret and such fiery eyes
As we have seen him in the Capitol,
Being crossed in conference by some senators.

   Cas. Casca will tell us what the matter is.

   Cæs. Antonius:

   Ant. Cæsar.

   Cæs. Let me have men about me that are fat;
Sleekheaded men, and such as sleep o'nights:
Yond' Cassius has a lean and hungry look:
He thinks too much: such men are dangerous.

   Ant. Fear him not, Cæsar; he's not dangerous:
He is a noble Roman, and well given.

   Cæs. 'Would he were fatter:—but I fear him not:
Yet if my name were liable to fear,
I do not know the man I should avoid
So soon as that spare Cassius. He reads much;
He is a great observer, and he looks
Quite through the deeds of men: he loves no plays,
As thou dost, Antony; he hears no music:
Seldom he smiles; and smiles in such a sort
As if he mocked himself, and scorned his spirit
That could be moved to smile at anything.
Such men as he be never at heart's ease
Whiles they behold a greater than themselves;
And therefore are they very dangerous.
I rather tell thee what is to be feared,
Than what I fear; for always I am Cæsar.
Come on my right hand (for this ear is deaf),
And tell me truly what thou think'st of him.

   [*Exeunt* CÆSAR *and his* Train. CASCA *stays
     behind.*

   Casca. You pulled me by the cloak: would
you speak with me?

   Bru. Ay, Casca: tell us what hath chanced
     to-day,
That Cæsar looks so sad?

   Casca. Why, you were with him, were you not?

   Bru. I should not then ask Casca what hath
chanced.

   Casca. Why, there was a crown offered him:
and being offered him, he put it by with the
back of his hand,—thus: and then the people
fell a-shouting.

   Bru. What was the second noise for?

   Casca. Why, for that too.

   Cas. They shouted thrice: what was the last
     cry for?

   Casca. Why, for that too.

   Bru. Was the crown offered him thrice?

   Casca. Ay, marry, was't, and he put it by thrice;
every time gentler than other: and at every putting by, mine honest neighbours shouted.

   Cas. Who offered him the crown?

   Casca. Why, Antony.

   Bru. Tell us the manner of it, gentle Casca.

   Casca. I can as well be hanged as tell the
manner of it: it was mere foolery; I did not
mark it. I saw Mark Antony offer him a
crown;—yet 't was not a crown neither, 't was
one of these coronets;—and, as I told you, he
put it by once: but for all that, to my thinking
he would fain have had it. Then he offered it
to him again; then he put it by again: but to
my thinking he was very loath to lay his fingers
off it. And then he offered it the third time;
he put it the third time by: and still, as he refused it, the rabblement hooted, and clapped
their chapped hands, and threw up their sweaty
nightcaps, and uttered such a deal of stinking
breath because Cæsar refused the crown, that it
had almost choked Cæsar; for he swooned and
fell down at it: and for mine own part, I durst
not laugh, for fear of opening my lips and receiving the bad air.

   Cas. But soft, I pray you:—what! did Cæsar
     swoon?

   Casca. He fell down in the market-place,
and foamed at mouth and was speechless.

   Bru. 'T is very like: he hath the falling-
     sickness.

   Cas. No, Cæsar hath it not; but you and I,
And honest Casca, we have the falling-sickness.

   Casca. I know not what you mean by that;
but I am sure Cæsar fell down. If the tag-rag
people did not clap him and hiss him, according
as he pleased and displeased them, as they use
to do the players in the theatre, I am no true
man.

   Bru. What said he when he came unto himself?

   Casca. Marry, before he fell down, when he

perceived the common herd was glad he refused the crown, he plucked me ope his doublet, and offered them his throat to cut:—an I had been a man of any occupation, if I would not have taken him at a word, I would I might go to hell among the rogues:—and so he fell. When he came to himself again, he said, if he had done or said anything amiss, he desired their worships to think it was his infirmity. Three or four wenches, where I stood, cried, "Alas, good soul!" and forgave him with all their hearts. But there's no heed to be taken of them: if Cæsar had stabbed their mothers, they would have done no less.

Bru. And after that, he came thus sad away?

Casca. Ay.

Cas. Did Cicero say anything?

Casca. Ay, he spoke Greek.

Cas. To what effect?

Casca. Nay, an I tell you that, I 'll ne'er look you i' the face again. But those that understood him smiled at one another, and shook their heads: but for mine own part, it was Greek to me. I could tell you more news too: Marullus and Flavius, for pulling scarfs off Cæsar's images, are put to silence. Fare you well. There was more foolery yet, if I could remember it.

Cas. Will you sup with me to-night, Casca?

Casca. No, I am promised forth.

Cas. Will you dine with me to-morrow?

Casca. Ay, if I be alive, and your mind hold, and your dinner worth the eating.

Cas. Good: I will expect you.

Casca. Do so: farewell both. [*Exit.*

Bru. What a blunt fellow is this grown to be! He was quick mettle when he went to school.

Cas. So is he now in execution Of any bold or noble enterprise, However he puts on this tardy form. This rudeness is a sauce to his good wit, Which gives men stomach to digest his words With better appetite.

Bru. And so it is. For this time I will leave you: To-morrow, if you please to speak with me, I will come home to you: or, if you will, Come home to me, and I will wait for you.

Cas. I will do so:—till then, think of the world. [*Exit* BRUTUS.

Well, Brutus, thou art noble: yet I see Thy honourable metal may be wrought From that it is disposed. Therefore 't is meet That noble minds keep ever with their likes: For who so firm that cannot be seduced? Cæsar doth bear me hard; but he loves Brutus: If I were Brutus now, and he were Cassius, He should not humour me.—I will this night,

In several hands, in at his windows throw, As if they came from several citizens, Writings, all tending to the great opinion That Rome holds of his name; wherein obscurely Cæsar's ambition shall be glancéd at: And after this let Cæsar seat him sure; For we shall shake him, or worse days endure. [*Exit.*

SCENE III.—*The same. A Street.*
Thunder and lightning.

Enter, from opposite sides, CASCA, *with his sword drawn, and* CICERO.

Cic. Good even, Casca: brought you Cæsar home? Why are you breathless; and why stare you so?

Casca. Are not you moved, when all the sway of earth Shakes like a thing unfirm? O Cicero, I have seen tempests when the scolding winds Have rived the knotty oaks; and I have seen The ambitious ocean swell and rage and foam, To be exalted with the threatening clouds: But never till to-night, never till now, Did I go through a tempest dropping fire. Either there is a civil strife in heaven; Or else the world, too saucy with the gods, Incenses them to send destruction.

Cic. Why, saw you anything more wonderful?

Casca. A common slave (you know him well by sight) Held up his left hand, which did flame and burn Like twenty torches joined; and yet his hand, Not sensible of fire, remained unscorched. Besides (I have not since put up my sword), Against the Capitol I met a lion, Who glared upon me, and went surly by, Without annoying me. And there were drawn Upon a heap a hundred ghastly women, Transforméd with their fear: who swore they saw Men all in fire walk up and down the streets. And yesterday the bird of night did sit, Even at noon-day, upon the market-place, Hooting and shrieking. When these prodigies Do so conjointly meet, let not men say, "These are their reasons;—they are natural:" For I believe they are portentous things Unto the climate that they point upon.

Cic. Indeed it is a strange-disposéd time: But men may construe things, after their fashion, Clean from the purpose of the things themselves. Comes Cæsar to the Capitol to-morrow?

Casca. He doth; for he did bid Antonius Send word to you he would be there to-morrow.

Cic. Good night, then, Casca; this disturbéd sky
Is not to walk in.

    Casca.   Farewell, Cicero. [*Exit* Cicero.

       Enter Cassius.

  Cas. Who's there?
  Casca.   A Roman.
  Cas.   Casca, by your voice.
  Casca. Your ear is good. Cassius, what night
    is this?
  Cas. A very pleasing night to honest men.
  Casca. Who ever knew the heavens menace so?
  Cas. Those that have known the earth so full
    of faults.
For my part, I have walked about the streets,
Submitting me unto the perilous night;
And thus unbracéd, Casca, as you see,
Have bared my bosom to the thunder-stone:

And when the cross blue lightning seemed to open
The breast of heaven, I did present myself
Even in the aim and very flash of it.
  Casca. But wherefore did you so much tempt
    the heavens?
It is the part of men to fear and tremble,
When the most mighty gods, by tokens, send
Such dreadful heralds to astonish us.
  Cas. You are dull, Casca; and those sparks
    of life
That should be in a Roman you do want,
Or else you use not. You look pale, and gaze,
And put on fear, and cast yourself in wonder,
To see the strange impatience of the heavens:
But if you would consider the true cause
Why all these fires, why all these gliding ghosts,
Why birds and beasts, from quality and kind;
Why old men, fools, and children calculate;

Why all these things change from their ordinance,
Their natures, and pre-formed faculties,
To monstrous quality;—why, you shall find
That heaven hath infused them with these spirits,
To make them instruments of fear and warning
Unto some monstrous state.—Now could I, Casca,
Name to thee a man most like this dreadful night,
That thunders, lightens, opens graves, and roars
As doth the lion in the Capitol:
A man no mightier than thyself or me
In personal action; yet prodigious grown,
And fearful, as these strange eruptions are.

Casca. 'T is Cæsar that you mean: is it not,
Cassius?

Cas. Let it be who it is: for Romans now
Have thews and limbs like to their ancestors;
But, woe the while! our father's minds are dead,
And we are governed with our mothers' spirits:
Our yoke and sufferance shew us womanish.

Casca. Indeed they say the senators to-morrow
Mean to establish Cæsar as a king:
And he shall wear his crown by sea and land,
In every place, save here in Italy.

Cas. I know where I will wear this dagger,
then:
Cassius from bondage will deliver Cassius.
Therein, ye gods, you make the weak most strong;
Therein, ye gods, you tyrants do defeat:
Nor stony tower, nor walls of beaten brass,
Nor airless dungeon, nor strong links of iron,
Can be retentive to the strength of spirit:
But life, being weary of these worldly bars,
Never lacks power to dismiss itself.
If I know this, know all the world besides,
That part of tyranny that I do bear
I can shake off at pleasure.

Casca. So can I:
So every bondman in his own hand bears
The power to cancel his captivity.

Cas. And why should Cæsar be a tyrant, then?
Poor man! I know he would not be a wolf,
But that he sees the Romans are but sheep:
He were no lion were not Romans hinds.
Those that with haste will make a mighty fire,
Begin it with weak straws: what trash is Rome,
What rubbish, and what offal, when it serves
For the base matter to illuminate
So vile a thing as Cæsar!—But, O grief!
Where hast thou led me? I perhaps speak this
Before a willing bondman. Then I know
My answer must be made: but I am armed,
And dangers are to me indifferent.

Casca. You speak to Casca, and to such a man
That is no fleering tell-tale. Hold my hand:
Be factious for redress of all these griefs;
And I will set this foot of mine as far
As who goes farthest.

Cas. There 's a bargain made.
Now know you, Casca, I have moved already
Some certain of the noblest-minded Romans
To undergo with me an enterprise
Of honourable-dangerous consequence;
And I do know, by this they stay for me
In Pompey's porch: for now, this fearful night,
There is no stir or walking in the streets;
And the complexion of the element
Is favoured like the work we have in hand,
Most bloody, fiery, and most terrible.

Enter CINNA.

Casca. Stand close awhile, for here comes one
in haste.

Cas. 'T is Cinna; I do know him by his gait:
He is a friend.—Cinna, where haste you so?

Cin. To find out you. Who 's that? Metellus
Cimber?

Cas. No, it is Casca: one incorporate
To our attempts. Am I not stayed for, Cinna?

Cin. I am glad on 't. What a fearful night is
this!
There 's two or three of us have seen strange
sights.

Cas. Am I not stayed for? Tell me.

Cin. Yes, you are.
O, Cassius, if you could but win the noble Brutus
To our party—

Cas. Be you content. Good Cinna, take this
paper,
And look you lay it in the prætor's chair,
Where Brutus may but find it: and throw this
In at his window: set this up with wax
Upon old Brutus' statue. All this done,
Repair to Pompey's porch, where you shall
find us.
Is Decius Brutus and Trebonius there?

Cin. All but Metellus Cimber; and he 's gone
To seek you at your house. Well, I will hie,
And so bestow these papers as you bade me.

Cas. That done, repair to Pompey's theatre.
[*Exit* CINNA.
Come, Casca, you and I will yet, ere day,
See Brutus at his house: three parts of him
Is ours already; and the man entire,
Upon the next encounter, yields him ours.

Casca. O, he sits high in all the people's hearts:
And that which would appear offence in us,
His countenance, like richest alchymy,
Will change to virtue and to worthiness.

Cas. Him and his worth, and our great need
of him,
You have right well conceited. Let us go,
For it is after midnight: and, ere day,
We will awake him and be sure of him.
[*Exeunt.*

Scene I.—Rome. Brutus's *Orchard.*

Enter Brutus.

Bru. What, Lucius: ho!—
I cannot, by the progress of the stars,
Give guess how near to day.—Lucius, I say!—
I would it were my fault to sleep so soundly.—
When, Lucius, when? awake, I say. What,
　　　Lucius!

Enter Lucius.

Luc. Called you, my lord?
Bru. Get me a taper in my study, Lucius:
When it is lighted, come and call me here.
Luc. I will, my lord.　　　　　　　[*Exit.*
Bru. It must be by his death: and, for my part,
I know no personal cause to spurn at him,
But for the general. He would be crowned:
How that might change his nature, there 's the
　　　question.
It is the bright day that brings forth the adder,
And that craves wary walking. Crown him?—
　　　That—
And then, I grant, we put a sting in him
That at his will he may do danger with.
The abuse of greatness is when it disjoins
Remorse from power. And, to speak truth of
　　　Cæsar,
I have not known when his affections swayed
More than his reason. But 't is a common proof
That lowliness is young ambition's ladder,
Whereto the climber-upward turns his face:
But when he once attains the upmost round,
He then unto the ladder turns his back,
Looks in the clouds, scorning the base degrees
By which he did ascend. So Cæsar may:
Then, lest he may, prevent. And, since the quarrel
Will bear no colour for the thing he is,
Fashion it thus: that what he is, augmented,
Would run to these and these extremities:
And therefore think him as a serpent's egg,
Which hatched, would, as his kind, grow mis-
　　　chievous;
And kill him in the shell.

Re-enter Lucius.

Luc. The taper burneth in your closet, sir.
Searching the window for a flint, I found
This paper, thus sealed up; and I am sure
It did not lie there when I went to bed.
Bru. Get you to bed again; it is not day.
Is not to-morrow, boy, the ides of March?
Luc. I know not, sir.
Bru. Look in the calendar, and bring me
　　　word.
Luc. I will, sir.　　　　　　　　　[*Exit.*
Bru. The exhalations, whizzing in the air,
Give so much light that I may read by them.

Opens the letter, and reads.

" Brutus, thou sleep'st: awake, and see thyself.
　　Shall Rome, &c. Speak, strike, redress!
　　Brutus, thou sleep'st: awake!"—

Such instigations have been often dropped
Where I have took them up.
"Shall Rome, &c." Thus must I piece it out:
Shall Rome stand under one man's awe? What,
        Rome!
My ancestors did from the streets of Rome
The Tarquin drive, when he was called a king.
" Speak, strike, redress!"—Am I entreated
To speak and strike?—O Rome! I make thee
        promise,
If the redress will follow, thou receiv'st
Thy full petition at the hand of Brutus!

Re-enter Lucius.

Luc. Sir, March is wasted fourteen days.
                                [*Knock within.*

Bru. 'T is good.   Go to the gate: somebody
        knocks.   [*Exit* Lucius.
Since Cassius first did whet me against Cæsar,
I have not slept.
Between the acting of a dreadful thing
And the first motion, all the interim is
Like a phantasma, or a hideous dream:
The genius and the mortal instruments
Are then in council; and the state of man,
Like to a little kingdom, suffers then
The nature of an insurrection.

Re-enter Lucius.

Luc. Sir, 't is your brother Cassius at the door,
Who doth desire to see you.
Bru.   Is he alone?

Luc. No, sir, there are more with him.
Bru.   Do you know them?
Luc. No, sir: their hats are plucked about
        their ears,
And half their faces buried in their cloaks,
That by no means I may discover them
By any mark of favour.
Bru.   Let them enter.
                                [*Exit* Lucius.
They are the faction.   O Conspiracy!
Sham'st thou to shew thy dangerous brow by night,
When evils are most free?   O then, by day
Where wilt thou find a cavern dark enough
To mask thy monstrous visage?   Seek none,
        Conspiracy;
Hide it in smiles and affability:

For if thou path thy native semblance on,
Not Erebus itself were dim enough
To hide thee from prevention.

Enter Cassius, Casca, Decius, Cinna, Metel-
        lus Cimber, *and* Trebonius.

Cas. I think we are too bold upon your rest:
Good-morrow, Brutus: do we trouble you?
Bru. I have been up this hour; awake all night.
Know I these men that come along with you?
Cas. Yes, every man of them; and no man here
But honours you: and every one doth wish
You had but that opinion of yourself
Which every noble Roman bears of you.
This is Trebonius.
Bru.   He is welcome hither.

Cas. This Decius Brutus.
Bru   He is welcome too.
Cas. This Casca; this Cinna;
And this Metellus Cimber.
Bru.   They are all welcome.
What watchful cares do interpose themselves
Betwixt your eyes and night?
Cas. Shall I entreat a word? [*They whisper.*
Dec. Here lies the east: doth not the day
    break here?
Casca. No.
Cin. O pardon, sir, it doth: and yon grey lines
That fret the clouds are messengers of day.
Casca. You shall confess that you are both
    deceived.
Here, as I point my sword, the sun arises;
Which is a great way growing on the south,
Weighing the youthful season of the year.
Some two months hence, up higher toward the
    north
He first presents his fire; and the high east
Stands, as the Capitol, directly here.
Bru. Give me your hands all over, one by one.
Cas. And let us swear our resolution.
Bru. No, not an oath. If not the face of men,
The sufferance of our souls, the time's abuse,—
If these be motives weak, break off betimes,
And every man hence to his idle bed:
So let high-sighted tyranny range on
Till each man drop by lottery. But if these
(As I am sure they do) bear fire enough
To kindle cowards, and to steel with valour
The melting spirits of women: then, countrymen,
What need we any spur but our own cause
To prick us to redress: what other bond
Than secret Romans, that have spoke the word,
And will not palter: and what other oath
Than honesty to honesty engaged
That this shall be, or we will fall for it?
Swear priests and cowards, and men cautelous,
Old feeble carrions, and such suffering souls
That welcome wrongs: unto bad causes swear
Such creatures as men doubt: but do not stain
The even virtue of our enterprise,
Nor the insuppressive mettle of our spirits,
To think that or our cause or our performance
Did need an oath, when every drop of blood
That every Roman bears, and nobly bears,
Is guilty of a several bastardy
If he do break the smallest particle
Of any promise that hath passed from him.
Cas. But what of Cicero: shall we sound him?
I think he will stand very strong with us.
Casca. Let us not leave him out.
Cin.   No, by no means.
Met. O let us have him; for his silver hairs
Will purchase us a good opinion,

And buy men's voices to commend our deeds.
It shall be said his judgment ruled our hands;
Our youths and wildness shall no whit appear,
But all be buried in his gravity.
Bru. O, name him not; let us not break with
    him:
For he will never follow anything
That other men begin.
Cas.   Then leave him out.
Casca. Indeed he is not fit.
Dec. Shall no man else be touched but only
    Cæsar?
Cas. Decius, well urged.—I think it is not meet
Marc Antony, so well beloved of Cæsar,
Should outlive Cæsar. We shall find of him
A shrewd contriver: and you know his means,
If he improve them, may well stretch so far
As to annoy us all: which to prevent,
Let Antony and Cæsar fall together.
Bru. Our course will seem too bloody, Caius
    Cassius,
To cut the head off and then hack the limbs;
Like wrath in death, and envy afterwards:
For Antony is but a limb of Cæsar.
Let us be sacrificers, but not butchers, Caius.
We all stand up against the spirit of Cæsar,
And in the spirit of men there is no blood:
O, that we then could come by Cæsar's spirit,
And not dismember Cæsar! But alas,
Cæsar must bleed for it! And, gentle friends,
Let's kill him boldly, but not wrathfully;
Let's carve him as a dish fit for the gods,
Not hew him as a carcase fit for hounds:
And let our hearts, as subtle masters do,
Stir up their servants to an act of rage
And after seem to chide them. This shall make
Our purpose necessary, and not envious:
Which so appearing to the common eyes,
We shall be called purgers, not murderers.
And for Marc Antony, think not of him;
For he can do no more than Cæsar's arm,
When Cæsar's head is off.
Cas.   Yet I fear him:
For in the ingrafted love he bears to Cæsar,—
Bru. Alas, good Cassius, do not think of him:
If he love Cæsar, all that he can do
Is to himself;—take thought, and die for Cæsar:
And that were much he should; for he is given
To sports and wildness, and much company.
Treb. There is no fear in him; let him not die:
For he will live, and laugh at this hereafter.
                      [*Clock strikes.*
Bru. Peace: count the clock.
Cas.   The clock hath stricken three.
Treb. 'T is time to part.
Cas.   But it is doubtful yet
Whe'r Cæsar will come forth to-day or no:

For he is superstitious grown of late;
Quite from the main opinion he held once
Of fantasy, of dreams, and ceremonies.
It may be these apparent prodigies,
The unaccustomed terror of this night,
And the persuasion of his augurers,
May hold him from the Capitol to-day.

   Dec. Never fear that. If he be so resolved,
I can o'ersway him; for he loves to hear
That unicorns may be betrayed with trees,
And bears with glasses, elephants with holes,
Lions with toils, and men with flatterers:
But when I tell him he hates flatterers,
He says he does; being then most flattered.
Let me work:
For I can give his humour the true bent,
And I will bring him to the Capitol.

   Cas. Nay, we will all of us be there to fetch
     him.

   Bru. By the eighth hour: is that the uttermost?

   Cin. Be that the uttermost, and fail not then.

   Met. Caius Ligarius doth bear Cæsar hard,
Who rated him for speaking well of Pompey:
I wonder none of you have thought of him.

   Bru. Now, good Metellus, go along by him.
He loves me well, and I have given him reasons:
Send him but hither, and I'll fashion him.

   Cas. The morning comes upon us. We'll leave
     you, Brutus:—
And, friends, disperse yourselves: but all remem-
     ber
What you have said, and shew yourselves true
     Romans.

   Bru. Good gentlemen, look fresh and merrily:
Let not our looks put on our purposes:
But bear it, as our Roman actors do,
With untired spirits and formal constancy:
And so, good-morrow to you every one.

                 [Exeunt all but BRUTUS.
Boy: Lucius!—Fast asleep! It is no matter:
Enjoy the honey-heavy dew of slumber.
Thou hast no figures nor no fantasies,
Which busy care draws in the brains of men:
Therefore thou sleep'st so sound.

          Enter PORTIA.

   Por.   Brutus, my lord!

   Bru. Portia, what mean you: wherefore rise
     you now?
It is not for your health, thus to commit
Your weak condition to the raw-cold morning.

   Por. Nor for yours neither. You have un-
     gently, Brutus,
Stole from my bed: and yesternight, at supper,
You suddenly arose and walked about,
Musing and sighing, with your arms across:
And when I asked you what the matter was,

You stared upon me with ungentle looks:
I urged you further; then you scratched your
     head,
And too impatiently stamped with your foot:
Yet I insisted, yet you answered not;
But, with an angry wafture of your hand,
Gave sign for me to leave you: so I did;
Fearing to strengthen that impatience
Which seemed too much enkindled; and withal
Hoping it was but an effect of humour,
Which sometime hath his hour with every man.
It will not let you eat, nor talk, nor sleep:
And could it work so much upon your shape
As it hath much prevailed on your condition,
I should not know you, Brutus. Dear, my lord,
Make me acquainted with your cause of grief.

   Bru. I am not well in health, and that is
     all.

   Por. Brutus is wise, and were he not in
     health
He would embrace the means to come by it.

   Bru. Why, so I do.—Good Portia, go to bed.

   Por. Is Brutus sick; and is it physical
To walk unbracéd, and suck up the humours
Of the dank morning? What, is Brutus sick;
And will he steal out of his wholesome bed
To dare the vile contagion of the night,
And tempt the rheumy and unpurgéd air
To add unto his sickness? No, my Brutus;
You have some sick offence within your mind,
Which, by the right and virtue of my place,
I ought to know of: and upon my knees
I charm you, by my once-commended beauty,
By all your vows of love, and that great vow
Which did incorporate and make us one,
That you unfold to me,—yourself, your half,—
Why you are heavy; and what men to-night
Have had resort to you: for here have been
Some six or seven, who did hide their faces
Even from darkness.

   Bru.   Kneel not, gentle Portia.

   Por. I should not need, if you were gentle
     Brutus.
Within the bond of marriage, tell me, Brutus,
Is it excepted I should know no secrets
That appertain to you? Am I yourself
But, as it were, in sort or limitation:
To keep with you at meals, comfort your bed,
And talk to you sometimes? Dwell I but in the
     suburbs
Of your good pleasure? If it be no more,
Portia is Brutus' harlot, not his wife.

   Bru. You are my true and honourable wife:
As dear to me as are the ruddy drops
That visit my sad heart.

   Por. If this were true, then should I know this
     secret.

I grant I am a woman; but withal
A woman that lord Brutus took to wife:
I grant I am a woman; but withal
A woman well-reputed,—Cato's daughter.
Think you I am no stronger than my sex,
Being so fathered and so husbanded?
Tell me your counsels; I will not disclose them:
I have made strong proof of my constancy,
Giving myself a voluntary wound
Here in the thigh. Can I bear that with patience,
And not my husband's secrets?

Bru. O ye gods,
Render me worthy of this noble wife!

        [Knocking within.

Hark, hark! one knocks. Portia, go in awhile;
And by and by thy bosom shall partake
The secrets of my heart.
All my engagements I will construe to thee;
All the charáctery of my sad brows.—
Leave me with haste.   *[Exit* PORTIA.

Enter LUCIUS *and* LIGARIUS.

Lucius, who's that knocks?

Luc. Here is a sick man that would speak
  with you.

Bru. Caius Ligarius, that Metellus spake of.—
Boy, stand aside.—Caius Ligarius! how?

Lig. Vouchsafe good-morrow from a feeble
  tongue.

Bru. O what a time have you chose out, brave
  Caius,
To wear a kerchief! 'Would you were not sick.

Lig. I am not sick, if Brutus have in hand
Any exploit worthy the name of honour.

Bru. Such an exploit have I in hand, Ligarius,
Had you a healthful ear to hear of it.

Lig. By all the gods that Romans bow before,
I here discard my sickness. Soul of Rome!
Brave son, derived from honourable loins!
Thou, like an exorcist, hast conjured up
My mortified spirit. Now bid me run,
And I will strive with things impossible;
Yea, get the better of them. What's to do?

Bru. A piece of work that will make sick men
  whole.

Lig. But are not some whole that we must
  make sick?

Bru. That must we also. What it is, my
  Caius,
I shall unfold to thee as we are going
To whom it must be done.

Lig.   Set on your foot;
And, with a heart new-fired, I follow you,
To do I know not what: but it sufficeth
That Brutus leads me on.

Bru.   Follow me, then. *[Exeunt.*

SCENE II.—*The same. A Room in* CÆSAR'S *Palace.*

Thunder and lightning. Enter CÆSAR, *in his night-gown.*

Cæs. Nor heaven nor earth have been at peace
  to-night:
Thrice hath Calphurnia in her sleep cried out,
"Help, ho! they murder Cæsar!"—Who's within?

Enter a Servant.

Serv. My lord?

Cæs. Go bid the priests do present sacrifice,
And bring me their opinions of success.

Serv. I will, my lord.   *[Exit.*

Enter CALPHURNIA.

Cal. What mean you, Cæsar? Think you to
  walk forth?
You shall not stir out of your house to-day.

Cæs. Cæsar shall forth. The things that
  threatened me
Ne'er looked but on my back: when they shall see
The face of Cæsar, they are vanishéd.

Cal. Cæsar, I never stood on ceremonies;
Yet now they fright me. There is one within
(Besides the things that we have heard and seen)
Recounts most horrid sights seen by the watch.
A lioness hath whelpéd in the streets;
And graves have yawned and yielded up their
  dead:
Fierce fiery warriors fight upon the clouds,
In ranks and squadrons and right form of war,
Which drizzled blood upon the Capitol:
The noise of battle hurtled in the air;
Horses do neigh, and dying men did groan;
And ghosts did shriek and squeal about the streets.
O Cæsar! these things are beyond all use,
And I do fear them.

Cæs.   What can be avoided,
Whose end is purposed by the mighty gods?
Yet Cæsar shall go forth: for these predictions
Are to the world in general as to Cæsar.

Cal. When beggars die there are no comets seen:
The heavens themselves blaze forth the death of
  princes.

Cæs. Cowards die many times before their
  deaths:
The valiant never taste of death but once.
Of all the wonders that I yet have heard,
It seems to me most strange that men should
  fear:
Seeing that death, a necessary end,
Will come when it will come.

Re-enter Servant.

What say the augurers?

Serv. They would not have you to stir forth
     to-day.
Plucking the entrails of an offering forth,
They could not find a heart within the beast.

    Cæs. The gods do this in shame of cowardice:
Cæsar should be a beast without a heart,
If he should stay at home to day for fear.
No, Cæsar shall not. Danger knows full well
That Cæsar is more dangerous than he.
We were two lions littered in one day,
And I the elder and more terrible:
And Cæsar shall go forth.

    Cal.   Alas, my lord,
Your wisdom is consumed in confidence.
Do not go forth to-day: call it my fear
That keeps you in the house, and not your own.
We 'll send Marc Antony to the senate-house,
And he shall say you are not well to-day.
Let me, upon my knee, prevail in this.

    Cæs. Marc Antony shall say I am not well;
And, for thy humour, I will stay at home.

Enter DECIUS.

Here 's Decius Brutus: he shall tell them so.

    Dec. Cæsar, all hail! Good morrow, worthy
     Cæsar:
I come to fetch you to the senate-house.

    Cæs. And you are come in very happy time,
To bear my greeting to the senators,
And tell them that I will not come to-day.
Cannot is false; and that I dare not, falser.
I will not come to-day: tell them so, Decius.

    Cal. Say he is sick.

    Cæs.   Shall Cæsar send a lie?
Have I in conquest stretched mine arm so far,
To be afeard to tell greybeards the truth?
Decius, go tell them Cæsar will not come.

    Dec. Most mighty Cæsar, let me know some
     cause,
Lest I be laughed at when I tell them so.

    Cæs. The cause is in my will; I will not come.
That is enough to satisfy the senate:
But for your private satisfaction,
Because I love you, I will let you know:
Calphurnia here, my wife, stays me at home:
She dreamt to-night she saw my statue,
Which, like a fountain with a hundred spouts,
Did run pure blood; and many lusty Romans
Came smiling, and did bathe their hands in it.
And these does she apply for warnings, portents,
And evils imminent; and on her knee
Hath begged that I will stay at home to-day.

    Dec. This dream is all amiss interpreted:
It was a vision fair and fortunate:
Your statue spouting blood in many pipes,
In which so many smiling Romans bathed,
Signifies that from you great Rome shall suck

Reviving blood; and that great men shall press
For tinctures, stains, relics, and cognizance.
This by Calphurnia's dream is signified.

    Cæs. And this way have you well expounded it.

    Dec. I have, when you have heard what I can
     say:
And know it now:—the senate have concluded
To give this day a crown to mighty Cæsar.
If you shall send them word you will not come,
Their minds may change. Besides, it were a
     mock
Apt to be rendered, for some one to say,
" Break up the senate till another time
WhenCæsar's wife shall meet with better dreams."
If Cæsar hide himself, shall they not whisper,
" Lo, Cæsar is afraid ? "
Pardon me, Cæsar : for my dear, dear love
To your proceeding bids me tell you this;
And reason to my love is liable.

    Cæs. How foolish do your fears seem now,
     Calphurnia ?
I am ashaméd I did yield to them.—
Give me my robe, for I will go :—
And look where Publius is come to fetch me.

Enter PUBLIUS, BRUTUS, LIGARIUS, METELLUS,
     CASCA, TREBONIUS, *and* CINNA.

    Pub. Good-morrow, Cæsar.

    Cæs.   Welcome, Publius.—
What, Brutus, are you stirred so early too ?—
Good-morrow, Casca.—Caius Ligarius,
Cæsar was ne'er so much your enemy
As that same ague which hath made you lean.—
What is 't o'clock ?

    Bru.   Cæsar, 't is strucken eight.

    Cæs. I thank you for your pains and courtesy.

Enter ANTONY.

See ! Antony, that revels long o' nights,
Is notwithstanding up :—good-morrow, Antony.

    Ant. So to most noble Cæsar.

    Cæs. Bid them prepare within :
I am to blame to be thus waited for.—
Now, Cinna: now, Metellus: what, Trebonius !
I have an hour's talk in store for you:
Remember that you call on me to-day:
Be near me, that I may remember you.

    Treb. Cæsar, I will :—and so near will I be,
         [*Aside.*
That your best friends shall wish I had been
     further.

    Cæs. Good friends, go in, and taste some wine
     with me ;
And we, like friends, will straightway go together.

    Bru. That every like is not the same, O Cæsar,
The heart of Brutus yearns to think upon !
         [*Exeunt.*

SCENE III.—*The same.   A Street near the*
Capitol.

Enter ARTEMIDORUS, *reading a paper.*

"Cæsar, beware of Brutus; take heed of Cassius;
come not near Casca; have an eye to Cinna; trust
not Trebonius; mark well Metellus Cimber; Decius
Brutus loves thee not; thou hast wronged Caius
Ligarius. There is but one mind in all these men,
and it is bent against Cæsar.   If thou beest not immortal, look about you: security gives way to conspiracy. The mighty gods defend thee! Thy lover,
                              "ARTEMIDORUS."

Here will I stand till Cæsar pass along,
And as a suitor will I give him this.
My heart laments that virtue cannot live
Out of the teeth of emulation.

If thou read this, O Cæsar, thou mayst live:
If not, the fates with traitors do contrive. [*Exit.*

SCENE IV.—*The same. Another part of the same
Street, before the House of* BRUTUS.

Enter PORTIA *and* LUCIUS.

Por. I pr'y thee, boy, run to the senate-house:
Stay not to answer me, but get thee gone :—
Why dost thou stay?

Luc.   To know my errand, madam.

Por. I would have had thee there and here again,
Ere I can tell thee what thou shouldst do there.—

O constancy, be strong upon my side :
Set a huge mountain 'tween my heart and tongue!
I have a man's mind, but a woman's might.
How hard it is for women to keep counsel!—
Art thou here yet?

Luc.   Madam, what should I do?
Run to the Capitol, and nothing else:
And so return to you, and nothing else?

Por. Yes; bring me word, boy, if thy lord look
well,
For he went sickly forth. And take good note
What Cæsar doth: what suitors press to him.
Hark, boy! what noise is that?

Luc. I hear none, madam.

Por.   Pr'y thee, listen well :
I heard a bustling rumour, like a fray,
And the wind brings it from the Capitol.

Luc. Sooth, madam, I hear nothing.

Enter Soothsayer.

Por. Come hither, fellow :
Which way hast thou been ?

Sooth.   At mine own house, good lady.

Por. What is 't o'clock ?

Sooth.   About the ninth hour, lady.

Por. Is Cæsar yet gone to the Capitol?

Sooth. Madam, not yet : I go to take my stand
To see him pass on to the Capitol

Por. Thou hast some suit to Cæsar, hast thou not?

Sooth. That I have, lady : if it will please Cæsar
To be so good to Cæsar as to hear me,
I shall beseech him to befriend himself.

Por. Why, know'st thou any harm 's intended
     towards him ?

Sooth. None that I know will be ; much that
     I fear may chance.
Good-morrow to you. Here the street is narrow :
The throng that follows Cæsar at the heels,
Of senators, of prætors, common suitors,
Will crowd a feeble man almost to death :
I 'll get me to a place more void, and there
Speak to great Cæsar as he comes along. [*Exit.*

Por. I must go in.—Ah me, how weak a thing
The heart of woman is ! O Brutus,
The heavens speed thee in thine enterprise !
Sure the boy heard me :—Brutus hath a suit
That Cæsar will not grant.—O, I grow faint !—
Run, Lucius, and commend me to my lord :
Say I am merry. Come to me again,
And bring me word what he doth say to thee.

                             [*Exeunt.*

Scene I. — Rome. *The* Capitol; *the* Senate
sitting.

*A crowd of people in the street leading to the
Capitol; among them* Artemidorus *and the*
Soothsayer. *Flourish. Enter* Cæsar, Brutus,
Cassius, Casca, Decius, Metellus, Trebo-
nius, Cinna, Antony, Lepidus, Popilius,
Publius, *and others.*

Cæs. The ides of March are come.

Sooth. Ay, Cæsar; but not gone.

Art. Hail, Cæsar!—Read this schedule.

Dec. Trebonius doth desire you to o'er-read,
At your best leisure, this his humble suit.

Art. O Cæsar, read mine first; for mine 's a
     suit
That touches Cæsar nearer. Read it, great Cæsar.

Cæs. What touches us ourself shall be last
     served.

Art. Delay not, Cæsar : read it instantly.

Cæs. What, is the fellow mad ?

Pub.   Sirrah, give place.

Cas. What, urge you your petitions in the street?
Come to the Capitol.

Cæsar *enters the* Capitol, *the rest following. All the* Senators *rise.*

Pop. I wish your enterprise to-day may thrive.

Cas. What enterprise, Popilius?

Pop. Fare you well. [*Advances to* Cæsar.

Bru. What said Popilius Lena?

Cas. He wished, to-day, our enterprise might thrive.

I fear our purpose is discovered.

Bru. Look how he makes to Cæsar: mark him.

Cas. Casca, be sudden, for we fear prevention.—

Brutus, what shall be done? If this be known,

Cassius or Cæsar never shall turn back,

For I will slay myself.

Bru. Cassius, be constant:

Popilius Lena speaks not of our purposes;

For look, he smiles, and Cæsar doth not change.

Cas. Trebonius knows his time; for look you, Brutus,

He draws Marc Antony out of the way.

[*Exeunt* Antony *and* Trebonius. Cæsar *and the* Senators *take their seats.*

Dec. Where is Metellus Cimber? Let him go,

And presently prefer his suit to Cæsar.

Bru. He is addressed: press near, and second him.

Cin. Casca, you are the first that rears your hand.

Cæs. Are we all ready? what is now amiss,

That Cæsar and his senate must redress?

Met. Most high, most mighty, and most puissant Cæsar.

Metellus Cimber throws before thy seat

An humble heart:— [*Kneeling.*

Cæs. I must prevent thee, Cimber.

These couchings and these lowly courtesies

Might fire the blood of ordinary men,

And turn pre-ordinance and first decree

Into the law of children. Be not fond,

To think that Cæsar bears such rebel blood

That will be thawed from the true quality

With that which melteth fools: I mean, sweet words,

Low-crookéd curt'sies, and base spaniel fawning.

Thy brother by decree is banishéd;

If thou dost bend and pray and fawn for him,

I spurn thee like a cur out of my way.

Know, Cæsar doth not wrong: nor without cause

Will he be satisfied.

Met. Is there no voice more worthy than my own,

To sound more sweetly in great Cæsar's ear,

For the repealing of my banished brother?

Bru. I kiss thy hand, but not in flattery, Cæsar;

Desiring thee that Publius Cimber may

Have an immediate freedom of repeal.

Cæs. What, Brutus!

Cas. Pardon Cæsar; Cæsar, pardon!

As low as to thy foot doth Cassius fall,

To beg enfranchisement for Publius Cimber.

Cæs. I could be well moved if I were as you:

If I could pray to move, prayers would move me:

But I am constant as the northern star,

Of whose true-fixed and resting quality

There is no fellow in the firmament.

The skies are painted with unnumbered sparks;

They are all fire, and every one doth shine:

But there's but one in all doth hold his place.

So in the world: 't is furnished well with men;

And men are flesh and blood, and apprehensive;

Yet, in the number, I do know but one

That unassailable holds on his rank,

Unshaked of motion: and that I am he

Let me a little shew it, even in this:

That I was constant Cimber should be banished,

And constant do remain to keep him so.

Cin. O Cæsar!—

Cæs. Hence! wilt thou lift up Olympus?

Dec. Great Cæsar!—

Cæs. Doth not Brutus bootless kneel?

Casca. Speak, hands, for me.

[Casca *stabs* Cæsar *in the neck.* Cæsar *catches hold of his arm. He is then stabbed by several other* Conspirators, *and at last by* Marcus Brutus.

Cæs. Et tu, Brute?—Then fall, Cæsar! [*Dies.*

[*The* Senators *and* People *retire in confusion.*

Cin. Liberty! Freedom! Tyranny is dead!—

Run hence, proclaim, cry it about the streets.

Cas. Some to the common pulpits, and cry out,

" Liberty, freedom, and enfranchisement! "

Bru. People and senators, be not affrighted;

Fly not; stand still:—ambition's debt is paid.

Casca. Go to the pulpit, Brutus.

Dec. And Cassius too.

Bru. Where's Publius?

Cin. Here, quite confounded with this mutiny.

Met. Stand fast together, lest some friend of Cæsar's

Should chance—

Bru. Talk not of standing:—Publius, good cheer;

There is no harm intended to your person,

Nor to no Roman else: so tell them, Publius.

Cas. And leave us, Publius; lest that the people,

Rushing on us, should do your age some mischief.

Bru. Do so;—and let no man abide this deed

But we the doers.

Et tu, Brute?

Re-enter Trebonius.

 Cas. Where is Antony?

 Tre. Fled to his house amazed:
Men, wives, and children, stare, cry out, and run,
As it were doomsday.

 Bru. Fates! we will know your pleasures.—
That we shall die we know: 'tis but the time,
And drawing days out, that men stand upon.

 Cas. Why he that cuts off twenty years of life,
Cuts off so many years of fearing death.

 Bru. Grant that, and then is death a benefit:
So are we Cæsar's friends, that have abridged
His time of fearing death.—Stoop, Romans, stoop,
And let us bathe our hands in Cæsar's blood
Up to the elbows, and besmear our swords:
Then walk we forth, even to the market-place;

And waving our red weapons o'er our heads,
Let 's all cry, " Peace, freedom, and liberty !"

Cas. Stoop, then, and wash.—How many ages
hence
Shall this our lofty scene be acted over,
In states unborn and accents yet unknown !

Bru. How many times shall Cæsar bleed in
sport,
That now on Pompey's basis lies along,
No worthier than the dust !

Cas. So oft as that shall be,
So often shall the knot of us be called
The men that gave their country liberty.

Dec. What, shall we forth ?

Cas. Ay, every man away :
Brutus shall lead ; and we will grace his heels
With the most boldest and best hearts of Rome.

Enter *a* Servant.

Bru. Soft, who comes here ? A friend of
Antony's.

Serv. Thus, Brutus, did my master bid me kneel;
Thus did Marc Antony bid me fall down ;
And, being prostrate, thus he bade me say :—
Brutus is noble, wise, valiant, and honest ;
Cæsar was mighty, bold, royal, and loving :
Say, I love Brutus, and I honour him ;
Say, I feared Cæsar, honoured him, and loved him.
If Brutus will vouchsafe that Antony
May safely come to him, and be resolved
How Cæsar hath deserved to lie in death,
Marc Antony shall not love Cæsar dead
So well as Brutus living ; but will follow
The fortunes and affairs of noble Brutus,
Thorough the hazards of this untrod state,
With all true faith.—So says my master Antony.

Bru. Thy master is a wise and valiant Roman :
I never thought him worse.
Tell him, so please him come unto this place,
He shall be satisfied ; and, by my honour,
Depart untouched.

Serv. I 'll fetch him presently.

[*Exit* Servant.

Bru. I know that we shall have him well to
friend.

Cas. I wish we may : but yet have I a mind
That fears him much ; and my misgiving still
Falls shrewdly to the purpose.

Bru. But here comes Antony.—Welcome,
Marc Antony.

Re-enter ANTONY.

Ant. O mighty Cæsar ! dost thou lie so low ?
Are all thy conquests, glories, triumphs, spoils,
Shrunk to this little measure ?—Fare thee well.—
I know not, gentlemen, what you intend ;
Who else must be let blood, who else is rank :

If I myself, there is no hour so fit
As Cæsar's death's hour ; nor no instrument
Of half that worth as those your swords, made rich
With the most noble blood of all this world.
I do beseech ye, if ye bear me hard,
Now, whilst your purpled hands do reek and smoke,
Fulfil your pleasure. Live a thousand years,
I shall not find myself so apt to die :
No place will please me so, no mean of death,
As here by Cæsar, and by you cut off,
The choice and master spirits of this age.

Bru. O Antony ! beg not your death of us.
Though now we must appear bloody and cruel,
As, by our hands and this our present act,
You see we do ; yet see you but our hands,
And this the bleeding business they have done :
Our hearts you see not : they are pitiful ;
And pity to the general wrong of Rome
(As fire drives out fire, so pity, pity)
Hath done this deed on Cæsar. For your part,
To you our swords have leaden points, Marc
Antony :
Our arms, in strength of malice, and our hearts,
Of brothers' temper, do receive you in
With all kind love, good thoughts, and reverence.

Cas. Your voice shall be as strong as any man's
In the disposing of new dignities.

Bru. Only be patient till we have appeased
The multitude, beside themselves with fear,
And then we will deliver you the cause
Why I, that did love Cæsar when I struck him,
Have thus proceeded.

Ant. I doubt not of your wisdom.
Let each man render me his bloody hand :—
First, Marcus Brutus, will I shake with you :
Next, Caius Cassius, do I take your hand :
Now, Decius Brutus, yours : now yours, Metellus :
Yours, Cinna : and, my valiant Casca, yours :
Though last, not least in love, yours, good Tre-
bonius.
Gentlemen all,—alas ! what shall I say ?
My credit now stands on such slippery ground,
That one of two bad ways you must conceit me,
Either a coward or a flatterer.—
That I did love thee, Cæsar, O 't is true :
If then thy spirit look upon us now,
Shall it not grieve thee dearer than thy death,
To see thy Antony making his peace,
Shaking the bloody fingers of thy foes,
Most noble ! in the presence of thy corse ?
Had I as many eyes as thou hast wounds,
Weeping as fast as they stream forth thy blood,
It would become me better than to close
In terms of friendship with thine enemies.
Pardon me, Julius !—Here wast thou bayed,
brave hart ;
Here didst thou fall : and here thy hunters stand,

Signed in thy spoil, and crimsoned in thy lethe.
O world! thou wast the forest to this hart:
And this indeed, O world, the heart of thee.—
How like a deer, stricken by many princes,
Dost thou here lie!

    Cas. Marc Antony,—

    Ant.   Pardon me, Caius Cassius:
The enemies of Cæsar shall say this;
Then in a friend it is cold modesty.

    Cas. I blame you not for praising Cæsar so:
But what compact mean you to have with us?
Will you be pricked in number of our friends;
Or shall we on, and not depend on you?

    Ant. Therefore I took your hands; but was,
        indeed,
Swayed from the point by looking down on Cæsar.
Friends am I with you all, and love you all;
Upon this hope, that you shall give me reasons
Why and wherein Cæsar was dangerous.

    Bru. Or else were this a savage spectacle.
Our reasons are so full of good regard,
That were you, Antony, the son of Cæsar,
You should be satisfied.

    Ant.   That's all I seek:
And am moreover suitor that I may
Produce his body to the market-place;
And in the pulpit, as becomes a friend,
Speak in the order of his funeral.

    Bru. You shall, Marc Antony.

    Cas. [*aside*].   Brutus, a word with you.—
You know not what you do: do not consent
That Antony speak in his funeral.
Know you how much the people may be moved
By that which he will utter?

    Bru.   By your pardon:
I will myself into the pulpit first,
And shew the reason of our Cæsar's death.
What Antony shall speak, I will protest
He speaks by leave and by permission:
And that we are contented Cæsar shall
Have all true rites and lawful ceremonies.
It shall advantage more than do us wrong.

    Cas. I know not what may fall: I like it not.

    Bru. Marc Antony, here, take you Cæsar's
        body.
You shall not in your funeral speech blame us,
But speak all good you can devise of Csæar;
And say you do't by our permission:
Else shall you not have any hand at all
About his funeral. And you shall speak
In the same pulpit whereto I am going,
After my speech is ended.

    Ant.   Be it so:
I do desire no more.

    Bru. Prepare the body, then, and follow us.
        [*Exeunt all but* ANTONY.

    Ant. O pardon me, thou bleeding piece of earth,

That I am meek and gentle with these butchers!
Thou art the ruins of the noblest man,
That ever lived in the tide of times.
Woe to the hand that shed this costly blood!
Over thy wounds now do I prophesy
(Which, like dumb mouths, do ope their ruby lips
To beg the voice and utterance of my tongue),
A curse shall light upon the limbs of men:
Domestic fury and fierce civil strife
Shall cumber all the parts of Italy:
Blood and destruction shall be so in use,
And dreadful objects so familiar,
That mothers shall but smile when they behold
Their infants quartered with the hands of war;
All pity choaked with custom of fell deeds:
And Cæsar's spirit, ranging for revenge,
With Até by his side, come hot from hell,
Shall in these confines, with a monarch's voice,
Cry "Havock!" and let slip the dogs of war:
That this foul deed shall smell above the earth
With carrion men, groaning for burial.

           Enter a Servant.

You serve Octavius Cæsar, do you not?

    Serv. I do, Marc Antony.

    Ant. Cæsar did write for him to come to Rome.

    Serv. He did receive his letters, and is coming:
And bid me say to you by word of mouth,—
O Cæsar!—   [*Seeing the body.*

    Ant. Thy heart is big, get thee apart and weep.
Passion, I see is catching; for mine eyes,
Seeing those beads of sorrow stand in thine,
Began to water. Is thy master coming?

    Serv. He lies to-night within seven leagues
        of Rome.

    Ant. Post back with speed, and tell him what
        hath chanced.
Here is a mourning Rome, a dangerous Rome,
No Rome of safety for Octavius yet:
Hie hence, and tell him so. Yet stay awhile:
Thou shalt not back till I have borne this corse
Into the market-place: there shall I try,
In my oration, how the people take
The cruel issue of these bloody men:
According to the which thou shalt discourse
To young Octavius of the state of things.
Lend me your hand.
        [*Exeunt, with* CÆSAR'S *body.*

SCENE II.—*The same. The* Forum.

Enter BRUTUS *and* CASSIUS, *and a throng of*
Citizens.

    Cit. We will be satisfied: let us be satisfied!

    Bru. Then follow me, and give me audience,
        friends.—

Cassius, go you into the other street,
And part the numbers.—
Those that will hear me speak, let them stay here:
Those that will follow Cassius, go with him:
And public reasons shall be renderéd
Of Cæsar's death.

1st Cit.   I will hear Brutus speak.

2nd Cit. I will hear Cassius: and compare their
        reasons,
When severally we hear them renderéd.

        [*Exit* CASSIUS, *with some of the* Citizens.
            BRUTUS *goes into the* Rostrum.

3rd Cit. The noble Brutus is ascended: silence!

Bru. Be patient till the last.

Romans, countrymen, and lovers! hear me for
my cause; and be silent, that you may hear:
believe me for mine honour; and have respect
to mine honour, that you may believe: censure
me in your wisdom; and awake your senses, that
you may the better judge. If there be any in
this assembly, any dear friend of Cæsar's, to him
I say that Brutus' love to Cæsar was not less
than his. If, then, that friend demand why Brutus
rose against Cæsar, this is my answer,—Not that
I loved Cæsar less, but that I loved Rome more.
Had you rather Cæsar were living, and die all
slaves, than that Cæsar were dead, to live all
free men?—As Cæsar loved me, I weep for
him: as he was fortunate, I rejoice at it: as he
was valiant, I honour him: but, as he was ambitious, I slew him. There is tears for his love;
joy for his fortune; honour for his valour; and
death for his ambition.—Who is here so base
that would be a bondman? If any, speak; for
him have I offended. Who is here so rude that
would not be a Roman? If any, speak; for him
have I offended. Who is here so vile that will
not love his country? If any, speak; for him
have I offended.—I pause for a reply.

Cit. None, Brutus, none.

            [*Several speaking at once.*

Bru. Then none have I offended. I have done
no more to Cæsar than you should do to Brutus.
The question of his death is enrolled in the Capitol: his glory not extenuated, wherein he was
worthy; nor his offences enforced, for which he
suffered death.

Enter ANTONY *and others, with* CÆSAR'S *body.*

Here comes his body, mourned by Marc Antony; who, though he had no hand in his death,
shall receive the benefit of his dying,—a place
in the commonwealth: as which of you shall
not?—With this I depart: that, as I slew my best
lover for the good of Rome, I have the same
dagger for myself when it shall please my country
to need my death.

Cit. Live, Brutus, live! live!

1st Cit. Bring him with triumph home unto
        his house.

2nd Cit. Give him a statue with his ancestors.

3rd Cit. Let him be Cæsar.

4th Cit.   Cæsar's better parts
Shall now be crowned in Brutus.

1st Cit. We 'll bring him to his house with
        shouts and clamours.

Bru. My countrymen,—

2nd Cit. Peace; silence! Brutus speaks.

1st Cit. Peace, ho!

Bru. Good countrymen, let me depart alone,
And for my sake stay here with Antony.
Do grace to Cæsar's corpse, and grace his speech
Tending to Cæsar's glories: which Marc Antony,
By our permission, is allowed to make.
I do entreat you not a man depart,
Save I alone, till Antony have spoke.   [*Exit.*

1st Cit Stay, ho! and let us hear Marc Antony.

3rd Cit. Let him go up into the public chair:
We 'll hear him.—Noble Antony, go up.

Ant. For Brutus' sake I am beholden to you.

4th Cit. What does he say of Brutus?

3rd Cit.   He says, for Brutus' sake
He finds himself beholden to us all.

4th Cit. 'T were best to speak no harm of
        Brutus here.

1st Cit. This Cæsar was a tyrant.

3rd Cit.   Nay that 's certain:
We are blessed that Rome is rid of him.

2nd Cit. Peace: let us hear what Antony can
        say.

Ant. You gentle Romans,—

Cit.   Peace, ho! let us hear him.

Ant. Friends, Romans, countrymen, lend me
        your ears.
I come to bury Cæsar, not to praise him:
The evil that men do lives after them;
The good is oft interréd with their bones:
So let it be with Cæsar. The noble Brutus
Hath told you Cæsar was ambitious:
If it were so, it was a grievous fault;
And grievously hath Cæsar answered it.
Here, under leave of Brutus and the rest,
(For Brutus is an honourable man;
So are they all, all honourable men;)
Come I to speak in Cæsar's funeral.
He was my friend, faithful and just to me:
But Brutus says he was ambitious;
And Brutus is an honourable man.
He hath brought many captives home to Rome,
Whose ransoms did the general coffers fill:
Did this in Cæsar seem ambitious?
When that the poor have cried, Cæsar hath wept:
Ambition should be made of sterner stuff:
Yet Brutus says he was ambitious;

And Brutus is an honourable man.
You all did see that, on the Lupercal,
I thrice presented him a kingly crown;
Which he did thrice refuse. Was this ambition?
Yet Brutus says he was ambitious;
And sure he is an honourable man.
I speak not to disprove what Brutus spoke,
But here I am to speak what I do know.
You all did love him once; not without cause:
What cause withholds you, then, to mourn
       for him?
O judgment, thou art fled to brutish beasts,
And men have lost their reason!—Bear with
       me:
My heart is in the coffin there with Cæsar,
And I must pause till it come back to me.

    1st Cit. Methinks there is much reason in
       his sayings.
    2nd Cit. If thou consider rightly of the
       matter,
Cæsar has had great wrong.
    3rd Cit.   Has he, masters?
I fear there will a worse come in his place.
    4th Cit. Marked ye his words? He would
       not take the crown:
Therefore 't is certain he was not ambitious.
    1st Cit. If it be found so, some will dear abide it.
    2nd Cit. Poor soul! his eyes are red as fire with
       weeping.
    3rd Cit. There's not a nobler man in Rome
       than Antony.
    4th Cit. Now mark him; he begins again to
       speak.
    Ant. But yesterday the word of Cæsar might
Have stood against the world: now lies he there,
And none so poor to do him reverence.
O masters! if I were disposed to stir
Your hearts and minds to mutiny and rage,
I should do Brutus wrong, and Cassius wrong,
Who, you all know, are honourable men.
I will not do them wrong: I rather choose
To wrong the dead, to wrong myself, and you,
Than I will wrong such honourable men.

But here's a parchment, with the seal of Cæsar:
I found it in his closet; 't is his will:
Let but the commons hear this testament
(Which, pardon me, I do not mean to read),
And they would go and kiss dead Cæsar's wounds,
And dip their napkins in his sacred blood;
Yea, beg a hair of him for memory,
And, dying, mention it within their wills;
Bequeathing it, as a rich legacy,
Unto their issue.

    4th Cit. We 'll hear the will. Read it, Marc
        Antony.

    Cit. The will; the will! we will hear Cæsar's
        will.

    Ant. Have patience, gentle friends: I must
        not read it:
It is not meet you know how Cæsar loved you.
You are not wood, you are not stones, but men:
And being men, hearing the will of Cæsar,
It will inflame you; it will make you mad.
'T is good you know not that you are his heirs:
For if you should, O what would come of it!

    4th Cit. Read the will: we will hear it, Antony.
You shall read us the will: Cæsar's will!

    Ant. Will you be patient? will you stay awhile?
I have o'ershot myself to tell you of it.
I fear I wrong the honourable men
Whose daggers have stabbed Cæsar: I do fear it.

    4th Cit. They were traitors. Honourable men!

    Cit. The will! the testament!

    2nd Cit. They were villains; murderers. The
        will! read the will!

    Ant. You will compel me, then, to read the will?
Then make a ring about the corpse of Cæsar,
And let me shew you him that made the will.
Shall I descend; and will you give me leave?

    Cit. Come down.

    2nd Cit. Descend. [*He comes from the pulpit.*

    3rd Cit. You shall have leave.

    4th Cit. A ring: stand round!

    1st Cit. Stand from the hearse; stand from
        the body!

    2nd Cit. Room for Antony: most noble Antony!

    Ant. Nay, press not so upon me: stand far off.

    Cit. Stand back! room! bear back!

    Ant. If you have tears, prepare to shed them
        now.
You all do know this mantle: I remember
The first time ever Cæsar put it on;
'T was on a summer's evening, in his tent:
That day he overcame the Nervii:—
Look! in this place ran Cassius' dagger through:
See what a rent the envious Casca made:
Through this the well-belovéd Brutus stabbed;
And, as he plucked his cursèd steel away,
Mark how the blood of Cæsar followed it,
As rushing out of doors, to be resolved

If Brutus so unkindly knocked or no:
For Brutus, as you know, was Cæsar's angel:
Judge, O you gods, how dearly Cæsar loved him!
This was the most unkindest cut of all:
For when the noble Cæsar saw him stab,
Ingratitude, more strong than traitors' arms,
Quite vanquished him. Then burst this mighty
        heart:
And, in his mantle muffling up his face,
Even at the base of Pompey's statue,
Which all the while ran blood, great Cæsar fell.
O what a fall was there, my countrymen!
Then I, and you, and all of us, fell down,
Whilst bloody treason flourished over us!
O now you weep, and I perceive you feel
The dint of pity: these are gracious drops.
Kind souls! what, weep you when you but behold
Our Cæsar's vesture wounded?—Look you here!
Here is himself, marred as you see with traitors.

    1st Cit. O piteous spectacle!

    2nd Cit. O noble Cæsar!

    3rd Cit. O woful day!

    4th Cit. O traitors, villains!

    1st Cit. O most bloody sight!

    2nd Cit. We will be revenged. Revenge!
about,—seek,—burn,—fire,—kill,—slay! Let
not a traitor live!

    Ant. Stay, countrymen.

    1st Cit. Peace there! hear the noble Antony.

    2nd Cit. We 'll hear him; we 'll follow him;
        we 'll die with him!

    Ant. Good friends, sweet friends, let me not
        stir you up
To such a sudden flood of mutiny.
They that have done this deed are honourable:
What private griefs they have, alas, I know not,
That made them do it: they are wise and
        honourable,
And will, no doubt, with reasons answer you.
I come not, friends, to steal away your hearts:
I am no orator, as Brutus is:
But, as you know me all, a plain blunt man,
That love my friend: and that they know full well
That gave me public leave to speak of him:
For I have neither wit, nor words, nor worth,
Action, nor utterance, nor the power of speech,
To stir men's blood. I only speak right on:
I tell you that which you yourselves do know:
Shew you sweet Cæsar's wounds, (poor, poor
        dumb mouths!)
And bid them speak for me. But were I Brutus,
And Brutus Antony, there were an Antony
Would ruffle up your spirits, and put a tongue
In every wound of Cæsar, that should move
The stones of Rome to rise and mutiny.

    Cit. We 'll mutiny!

    1st Cit. We 'll burn the house of Brutus!

3rd Cit. Away, then : come, seek the con-
    spirators !

Ant. Yet hear me, countrymen : yet hear me
    speak.

Cit. Peace, ho ! hear Antony ; most noble
    Antony !

Ant. Why, friends, you go to do you know not
    what ?
Wherein hath Cæsar thus deserved your loves ?
Alas ! you know not :—I must tell you, then :—
You have forgot the will I told you of.

    Cit. Most true :—the will ! let 's stay, and hear
    the will.

Ant. Here is the will, and under Cæsar's seal.
To every Roman citizen he gives,
To every several man, seventy-five drachmas.

    2nd Cit. Most noble Cæsar ! we 'll revenge his
    death.

    3rd Cit. O royal Cæsar !

Ant. Hear me with patience.

Cit. Peace, ho !

Ant. Moreover, he hath left you all his
    walks,
His private arbours and new-planted orchards,
On this side Tyber : he hath left them you,
And to your heirs for ever : common pleasures,
To walk abroad and recreate yourselves.
Here was a Cæsar ! when comes such another ?

    1st Cit. Never, never !—Come, away, away !
We 'll burn his body in the holy place,
And with the brands fire the traitors' houses.
Take up the body.

    2nd Cit. Go, fetch fire !

    3rd Cit. Pluck down benches !

    4th Cit. Pluck down forms, windows, anything !
        [*Exeunt* Citizens *with the body.*

Ant. Now let it work ! Mischief, thou art
    afoot ;
Take thou what course thou wilt.—How now,
    fellow ?

Enter a Servant.

Serv. Sir, Octavius is already come to Rome.

Ant. Where is he ?

Serv. He and Lepidus are at Cæsar's house.

Ant. And thither will I straight to visit him :
He comes upon a wish. Fortune is merry,
And in this mood will give us anything.

Serv. I heard him say, Brutus and Cassius
Are rid like madmen through the gates of Rome.

Ant. Belike they had some notice of the people
How I had moved them. Bring me to Octavius.
        [*Exeunt.*

SCENE III.—*The same. A Street.*

Enter CINNA, *the Poet.*

Cin. I dreamt to-night that I did feast with
    Cæsar,
And things unluckily charge my fantasy.
I have no will to wander forth of doors,
Yet something leads me forth.

Enter Citizens.

1st Cit. What is your name ?

2nd Cit. Whither are you going ?

3rd Cit. Where do you dwell ?

4th Cit. Are you a married man or a bachelor ?

2nd Cit. Answer every man directly ?

1st Cit. Ay, and briefly.

4th Cit. Ay, and wisely.

3rd Cit. Ay, and truly ; you were best.

Cin. What is my name : whither am I going :
where do I dwell : am I a married man or a bachelor ? Then, to answer every man directly
and briefly, wisely and truly :—wisely, I say I am
a bachelor.

2nd Cit. That 's as much as to say they are
fools that marry : you 'll bear me a bang for that,
I fear. Proceed ; directly.

Cin. Directly, I am going to Cæsar's funeral.

1st Cit. As a friend or an enemy ?

Cin. As a friend.

2nd Cit. That matter is answered directly.

4th Cit. For your dwelling ; briefly.

Cin. Briefly, I dwell by the Capitol.

3rd Cit. Your name, sir ; truly.

Cin. Truly, my name is Cinna.

1st Cit. Tear him to pieces ! he 's a conspirator.

Cin. I am Cinna the poet ; I am Cinna the poet.

4th Cit. Tear him for his bad verses ; tear him
for his bad verses !

Cin. I am not Cinna the conspirator.

2nd Cit. It is no matter : his name 's Cinna :
pluck but his name out of his heart, and turn
him going !

3rd Cit. Tear him : tear him !—Come, brands,
ho ! firebrands. To Brutus', to Cassius' : burn
all ! Some to Decius' house, and some to Casca's ;
some to Ligarius'. Away, go !

ACT IV

Scene I.—Rome. *A Room in* Antony's *House.*

Antony, Octavius, *and* Lepidus, *seated at a table.*

Ant. These many, then, shall die: their names are
    pricked.

Oct. Your brother, too, must die: consent you,
    Lepidus?

Lep. I do consent—

Oct.   Prick him down, Antony.

Lep. Upon condition Publius shall not live,
Who is your sister's son, Marc Antony.

Ant. He shall not live: look, with a spot I damn
    him.
But, Lepidus, go you to Cæsar's house:
Fetch the will hither, and we will determine
How to cut off some charge in legacies.

Lep. What, shall I find you here?

Oct. Or here or at the Capitol.

                [Exit Lepidus.

Ant. This is a slight unmeritable man,
Meet to be sent on errands. Is it fit,
The threefold world divided, he should stand
One of the three to share it?

Oct.   So you thought him;
And took his voice who should be pricked to die
In our black sentence and proscription.

Ant. Octavius, I have seen more days than you:
And though we lay these honours on this man
To ease ourselves of divers slanderous loads,
He shall but bear them as the ass bears gold,
To groan and sweat under the business,
Either led or driven as we point the way:

And having brought our treasure where we will,
Then take we down his load, and turn him off,
Like to the empty ass, to shake his ears,
And graze in commons.

Oct.   You may do your will;
But he 's a tried and valiant soldier.

Ant. So is my horse, Octavius; and for that
I do appoint him store of provender.
It is a creature that I teach to fight,
To wind, to stop, to run directly on:
His corporal motion governed by my spirit.
And, in some taste, is Lepidus but so:
He must be taught, and trained, and bid go forth.
A barren-spirited fellow: one that feeds
On objects, arts, and imitations;
Which, out of use, and staled by other men,
Begin his fashion. Do not talk of him
But as a property. And now, Octavius,
Listen great things:—Brutus and Cassius
Are levying powers: we must straight make head:
Therefore, let our alliance be combined,
Our best friends made, and our best means
    stretched out;
And let us presently go sit in council
How covert matters may be best disclosed,
And open perils surest answered.

Oct. Let us do so: for we are at the stake,

And bayed about with many enemies:
And some that smile have in their hearts, I fear,
Millions of mischief.   [*Exeunt.*

SCENE II.—*Before* BRUTUS' *Tent, in the Camp
near* Sardis.

Drum. Enter BRUTUS, LUCILIUS, LUCIUS, *and* Soldiers: TITINIUS *and* PINDARUS *meeting them.*

Bru. Stand, ho!

Luc. Give the word, ho! and stand.

Bru. What now, Lucilius: is Cassius near?

Luc. He is at hand; and Pindarus is come
To do you salutation from his master.
           [PINDARUS *gives a letter to* BRUTUS.

Bru. He greets me well.—Your master, Pin-
darus,
In his own change or by ill officers,
Hath given me some worthy·cause to wish
Things done, undone: but if he be at hand
I shall be satisfied.

Pin.   I do not doubt
But that my noble master will appear
Such as he is, full of regard and honour.

Bru. He is not doubted.—A word, Lucilius:
How he received you let me be resolved.

Luc. With courtesy and with respect enough;
But not with such familiar instances,
Nor with such free and friendly conference,
As he hath used of old.

Bru.   Thou hast described
A hot friend cooling. Ever note, Lucilius,
When love begins to sicken and decay,
It useth an enforcéd ceremony.
There are no tricks in plain and simple faith:
But hollow men, like horses hot at hand,
Make gallant show and promise of their mettle;
But when they should endure the bloody spur
They fall their crests, and like deceitful jades
Sink in the trial. Comes his army on?

Luc. They mean this night in Sardis to be
quartered:
The greater part, the horse in general,
Are come with Cassius.
                    [*March within.*

Bru.   Hark! he is arrived:—
March gently on to meet him.
           Enter CASSIUS *and* Soldiers.

Cas. Stand, ho!

Bru. Stand, ho!—Speak the word along.

Within. Stand.

Within. Stand.

Within. Stand.

Cas. Most noble brother, you have done me
wrong.

Bru. Judge me, you gods! wrong I mine
enemies?
And if not so, how should I wrong a brother?

Cas. Brutus, this sober form of yours hides
wrongs:
And when you do them—

Bru.   Cassius, be content:
Speak your griefs softly:—I do know you well:—
Before the eyes of both our armies here,
Which should perceive nothing but love from us,
Let us not wrangle. Bid them move away:
Then in my tent, Cassius, enlarge your griefs,
And I will give you audience.

Cas.   Pindarus,
Bid our commanders lead their charges off
A little from this ground.

Bru. Lucilius, do you the like; and let no man
Come to our tent till we have done our conference.
Let Lucius and Titinius guard our door.
                    [*Exeunt.*

SCENE III.—*Within the Tent of* BRUTUS.

LUCIUS *and* TITINIUS *at some distance from it.*

Enter BRUTUS *and* CASSIUS.

Cas. That you have wronged me doth appear
in this:
You have condemned and noted Lucius Pella,
For taking bribes here of the Sardians:
Wherein my letters, praying on his side,
Because I knew the man, were slighted off.

Bru. You wronged yourself to write in such
a case.

Cas. In such a time as this it is not meet
That every nice offence should bear his comment.

Bru. Let me tell you, Cassius, you yourself
Are much condemned to have an itching palm:
To sell and mart your offices for gold,
To undeservers.

Cas.   I an itching palm!
You know that you are Brutus that speak this,
Or by the gods this speech were else your last.

Bru. The name of Cassius honours this corruption,
And chastisement doth therefore hide his head.

Cas. Chastisement!

Bru. Remember March, the ides of March
remember!
Did not great Julius bleed for justice' sake?
What villain touched his body, that did stab,
And not for justice? What, shall one of us
That struck the foremost man of all this world,
But for supporting robbers, shall we now
Contaminate our fingers with base bribes,
And sell the mighty space of our large honours
For so much trash as may be graspéd thus?—

I had rather be a dog, and bay the moon,
Than such a Roman.
   Cas.   Brutus, bait not me :
I'll not endure it. You forget yourself,
To hedge me in : I am a soldier, I,
Older in practice, abler than yourself
To make conditions.
   Bru.   Go to : you are not, Cassius.
   Cas. I am.
   Bru. I say you are not.
   Cas. Urge me no more ; I shall forget myself :
Have mind upon your health ; tempt me no further.
   Bru. Away, slight man.
   Cas. Is 't possible !
   Bru.   Hear me, for I will speak.
Must I give way and room to your rash choler ?
Shall I be frighted when a madman stares ?
   Cas. O ye gods, ye gods ! must I endure all this?
   Bru. All this? ay, more.   Fret till your proud
     heart break :
Go shew your slaves how choleric you are,
And make your bondmen tremble. Must I budge ;
Must I observe you ; must I stand and crouch
Under your testy humour ? By the gods,
You shall digest the venom of your spleen,
Though it do split you : for from this day forth
I 'll use you for my mirth, yea for my laughter,
When you are waspish.
   Cas.   Is it come to this ?
   Bru. You say you are a better soldier :
Let it appear so ; make your vaunting true,
And it shall please me well. For mine own part,
I shall be glad to learn of noble men.
   Cas. You wrong me every way ; you wrong me,
     Brutus :
I said, an elder soldier, not a better.—
Did I say, better ?
   Bru.   If you did, I care not.
   Cas. When Cæsar lived, he durst not thus have
moved me.
   Bru. Peace, peace : you durst not so have
     tempted him.
   Cas. I durst not ?
   Bru. No.
   Cas. What ! durst not tempt him ?
   Bru.   For your life you durst not.
   Cas. Do not presume too much upon my love :
I may do that I shall be sorry for.
   Bru. You have done that you should be sorry
     for.
There is no terror, Cassius, in your threats :
For I am armed so strong in honesty,
That they pass by me as the idle wind,
Which I respect not. I did send to you
For certain sums of gold, which you denied me :—
For I can raise no money by vile means :
By heaven, I had rather coin my heart,

And drop my blood for drachmas, than to wring
From the hard hands of peasants their vile trash
By any indirection !—I did send
To you for gold to pay my legions ;
Which you denied me. Was that done like Cas-
     sius?
Should I have answered Caius Cassius so?
When Marcus Brutus grows so covetous
To lock such rascal counters from his friends,
Be ready, gods, with all your thunderbolts,
Dash him to pieces !
   Cas.   I denied you not.
   Bru. You did.
   Cas.   I did not : he was but a fool
That brought my answer back.—Brutus hath
     rived my heart :
A friend should bear his friend's infirmities ;
But Brutus makes mine greater than they are.
   Bru. I do not till you practise them on me.
   Cas. You love me not.
   Bru.   I do not like your faults.
   Cas. A friendly eye could never see such faults.
   Bru. A flatterer's would not, though they do
     appear
As huge as high Olympus.
   Cas. Come, Antony, and young Octavius, come ;
Revenge yourselves alone on Cassius ;
For Cassius is aweary of the world :
Hated by one he loves ; braved by his brother ;
Checked like a bondman ; all his faults observed,
Set in a notebook, learned and conned by rote,
To cast into my teeth ! O, I could weep
My spirit from mine eyes !—There is my dagger,
And here my naked breast : within, a heart
Dearer than Plutus' mine, richer than gold :
If that thou beest a Roman, take it forth :
I, that denied thee gold, will give my heart.
Strike as thou didst at Cæsar : for I know,
When thou didst hate him worst, thou lovedst
     him better
Than ever thou lovedst Cassius.
   Bru.   Sheath your dagger.
Be angry when you will, it shall have scope :
Do what you will, dishonour shall be humour.
O Cassius, you are yokéd with a lamb,
That carries anger as the flint bears fire :
Who, much enforcéd, shews a hasty spark,
And straight is cold again.
   Cas.   Hath Cassius lived
To be but mirth and laughter to his Brutus,
When grief and blood ill-tempered vexeth him ?
   Bru. When I spoke that, I was ill-tempered too.
   Cas. Do you confess so much ? Give me your
     hand.
   Bru. And my heart too.
   Cas.   O Brutus !—
   Bru.   What 's the matter ?

Cas. Have you not love enough to bear with
    me,
When that rash humour which my mother gave
    me
Makes me forgetful?
    Bru. Yes, Cassius; and from henceforth,
When you are over-earnest with your Brutus,
He'll think your mother chides, and leave you so.
                     [*Noise within.*
Poet [*within*]. Let me go in to see the generals.
There is some grudge between them: 'tis not
    meet
They be alone.
Luc. [*within*]. You shall not come to them.
Poet [*within*]. Nothing but death shall stay me.

Enter POET.

    Cas. How now; what's the matter?
    Poet. For shame, you generals! what do you
    mean?
Love and be friends, as two such men should be:
For I have seen more years, I am sure, than ye.
    Cas. Ha, ha! how vilely doth this cynic rhyme!
    Bru. Get you hence, sirrah: saucy fellow, hence!
    Cas. Bear with him, Brutus; 'tis his fashion.
    Bru. I'll know his humour when he knows
    his time.
What should the wars do with these jigging fools?
Companion, hence!
    Cas.   Away, away: be gone.
                     [*Exit* POET.

Enter LUCILIUS *and* TITINIUS.

    Bru. Lucilius and Titinius, bid the commanders
Prepare to lodge their companies to-night.
    Cas. And come yourselves, and bring Messala
    with you,
Immediately to us.
          [*Exeunt* LUCILIUS *and* TITINIUS.
    Bru. Lucius, a bowl of wine.
    Cas. I did not think you could have been so
    angry.
    Bru. O Cassius, I am sick of many griefs.
    Cas. Of your philosophy you make no use,
If you give place to accidental evils.
    Bru. No man bears sorrow better:—Portia is
    dead.
    Cas. Ha! Portia?
    Bru. She is dead.
    Cas. How 'scaped I killing when I crossed
    you so?—
O insupportable and touching loss!—
Upon what sickness?
    Bru.   Impatient of my absence;
And grief that young Octavius with Marc Antony
Have made themselves so strong;—for with her
    death

That tidings came:—with this she fell distract,
And, her attendants absent, swallowed fire.
    Cas. And died so?
    Bru. Even so.
    Cas. O ye immortal gods!

Enter LUCIUS, *with wine and tapers.*

    Bru. Speak no more of her.—Give me a bowl
    of wine:
In this I bury all unkindness, Cassius. [*Drinks.*
    Cas. My heart is thirsty for that noble pledge.—
Fill, Lucius, till the wine o'erswell the cup:
I cannot drink too much of Brutus' love. [*Drinks.*

Re-enter TITINIUS *with* MESSALA.

    Bru. Come in, Titinius:—welcome, good
    Messala.—
Now sit we close about this taper here,
And call in question our necessities.
    Cas. Portia, art thou gone?
    Bru.   No more, I pray you.—
Messala, I have here receivéd letters
That young Octavius and Marc Antony
Come down upon us with a mighty power,
Bending their expedition toward Philippi.
    Mes. Myself have letters of the self-same te-
    nour.
    Bru. With what addition?
    Mes. That, by proscription and bills of out-
    lawry,
Octavius, Antony, and Lepidus,
Have put to death an hundred senators.
    Bru. Therein our letters do not well agree:
Mine speak of seventy senators that died
By their proscriptions; Cicero being one.
    Cas. Cicero one?
    Mes.   Cicero is dead,
And by that order of proscription.—
Had you your letters from your wife, my lord?
    Bru. No, Messala.
    Mes. Nor nothing in your letters writ of her?
    Bru. Nothing, Messala.
    Mes. That methinks is strange.
    Bru. Why ask you: hear you aught of her in
    yours?
    Mes. No, my lord.
    Bru. Now, as you are a Roman, tell me true.
    Mes. Then like a Roman bear the truth I tell:
For certain she is dead, and by strange manner.
    Bru. Why farewell, Portia.—We must die,
    Messala:
With meditating that she must die once,
I have the patience to endure it now.
    Mes. Even so great men great losses should
    endure.
    Cas. I have as much of this in art as you;
But yet my nature could not bear it so.

Bru. Well, to our work alive. What do you
　　　think
Of marching to Philippi presently?
　Cas. I do not think it good.
　Bru.　　　　Your reason?
　Cas.　　　　　　This it is:
'T is better that the enemy seek us:
So shall he waste his means, weary his soldiers,
Doing himself offence; whilst we, lying still,
Are full of rest, defence, and nimbleness.
　Bru. Good reasons must, of force, give place
　　　to better.
The people 'twixt Philippi and this ground
Do stand but in a forced affection;
For they have grudged us contribution:
The enemy, marching along by them,

By them shall make a fuller number up,
Come on refreshed, new-added, and encouraged:
From which advantage shall we cut him off,
If at Philippi we do face him there,
These people at our back.
　Cas.　　　Hear me, good brother.
　Bru. Under your pardon.—You must note
　　　beside,
That we have tried the utmost of our friends;
Our legions are brimful, our cause is ripe.
The enemy increaseth every day:
We, at the height, are ready to decline.
There is a tide in the affairs of men,
Which, taken at the flood, leads on to fortune:
Omitted, all the voyage of their life
Is bound in shallows and in miseries.

On such a full sea are we now afloat;
And we must take the current when it serves,
Or lose our ventures.
    Cas.   Then, with your will, go on:
We'll along ourselves, and meet them at Philippi.
    Bru. The deep of night is crept upon our talk,
And nature must obey necessity;
Which we will niggard with a little rest.
There is no more to say?
    Cas.   No more.   Good night:
Early to-morrow we will rise, and hence.
    Bru. Lucius, my gown.   [*Exit* Lucius.
          Farewell, good Messala:—
Good night, Titinius:—Noble, noble Cassius,
Good night and good repose.
    Cas.   O my dear brother,
This was an ill beginning of the night!
Never come such division 'tween our souls!
Let it not, Brutus.
    Bru. Everything is well.
    Cas. Good night, my lord.
    Bru. Good night, good brother.
    Tit. }
    Mes. } Good night, lord Brutus.
    Bru. Farewell, every one.
       [*Exeunt* Cassius, Titinius, *and* Messala.

    Re-enter Lucius, *with the gown.*

Give me the gown.   Where is thy instrument?
    Luc. Here in the tent.
    Bru.   What, thou speak'st drowsily?
Poor knave, I blame thee not: thou art o'er-
    watched.
Call Claudius, and some other of my men:
I'll have them sleep on cushions in my tent.
    Luc. Varro and Claudius!

    Enter Varro *and* Claudius.

    Var. Calls my lord?
    Bru. I pray you, sirs, lie in my tent and sleep:
It may be I shall raise you by and by
On business to my brother Cassius.
    Var. So please you, we will stand and watch
    your pleasure.
    Bru. I will not have it so: lie down, good
    sirs:
It may be I shall otherwise bethink me.—
Look, Lucius, here's the book I sought for so:
I put it in the pocket of my gown.
       [*Servants lie down.*
    Luc. I was sure your lordship did not give it
    me.
    Bru. Bear with me, good boy; I am much
    forgetful.
Canst thou hold up thy heavy eyes awhile,
And touch thy instrument a strain or two?
    Luc. Ay, my lord, an it please you.

    Bru.   It does, my boy:
I trouble thee too much, but thou art willing.
    Luc. It is my duty, sir.
    Bru. I should not urge thy duty past thy
    might:
I know young bloods look for a time of rest.
    Luc. I have slept, my lord, already.
    Bru. It was well done; and thou shalt sleep
    again:
I will not hold thee long.   If I do live,
I will be good to thee.

    Music, and a Song.

This is a sleepy tune:—O murderous slumber!
Lay'st thou thy leaden mace upon my boy,
That plays thee music?—Gentle knave, good
    night:
I will not do thee so much wrong to wake thee.
If thou dost nod, thou break'st thy instrument:
I'll take it from thee: and, good boy, good night.
Let me see, let me see: is not the leaf turned
    down
Where I left reading?   Here it is, I think.
       [*He sits down.*
How ill this taper burns!—Ha! who comes
    here?

    Enter the Ghost of Cæsar.

I think it is the weakness of mine eyes
That shapes this monstrous apparition.
It comes upon me!—Art thou anything?
Art thou some god, some angel, or some devil,
That mak'st my blood cold, and my hair to stare?
Speak to me what thou art.
    Ghost. Thy evil spirit, Brutus.
    Bru.   Why com'st thou?
    Ghost. To tell thee thou shalt see me at Phi-
    lippi.
    Bru. Well: then I shall thee again?
    Ghost. Ay, at Philippi.   [*Ghost vanishes.*
    Bru. Why, I will see thee at Philippi, then.—
Now I have taken heart, thou vanishest:
Ill spirit, I would hold more talk with thee.—
Boy! Lucius!—Varro! Claudius! Sirs, awake!—
Claudius!
    Luc. The strings, my lord, are false.
    Bru. He thinks he still is at his instrument.—
Lucius, awake!
    Luc. My lord?
    Bru. Didst thou dream, Lucius, that thou so
    criedst out?
    Luc. My lord, I do not know that I did cry.
    Bru. Yes, that thou didst: didst thou see any-
    thing?
    Luc. Nothing, my lord.
    Bru. Sleep again, Lucius.—Sirrah, Claudius!
Fellow thou, awake!

Clau. My lord!
Var. My lord!
Bru. Why did you so cry out, sirs, in your sleep?
Var. } Did we, my lord?
Clau.
Bru. Ay: saw you anything?
Var. No, my lord, I saw nothing.

Clau. Nor I, my lord.
Bru. Go and commend me to my brother
    Cassius:
Bid him set on his powers betimes before,
And we will follow.
Var. } It shall be done, my lord.   [*Exeunt.*
Clau.

GHOST. Ay, at Philippi.

Scene I.—*The Plains of* Philippi.

Enter Octavius, Antony, *and their Army.*

Oct. Now, Antony, our hopes are answeréd:
You said the enemy would not come down,
But keep the hills and upper regions.
It proves not so: their battles are at hand:
They mean to warn us at Philippi here,
Answering before we do demand of them.

Ant. Tut, I am in their bosoms, and I know
Wherefore they do it. They could be content
To visit other places: and come down
With fearful bravery, thinking by this face
To fasten in our thoughts that they have courage:
But 't is not so.

Enter a Messenger.

Mess.   Prepare you, generals:
The enemy comes on in gallant show;
Their bloody sign of battle is hung out,
And something to be done immediately.

Ant. Octavius, lead your battle softly on
Upon the left hand of the even field.

Oct. Upon the right hand I; keep thou the
        left.

Ant. Why do you cross me in this exigent?

Oct. I do not cross you; but I will do so.
                                        [*March.*

Drum. Enter Brutus, Cassius, *and their Army;*
        Lucinius, Titinius, Messala, *and others.*

Bru. They stand, and would have parley.

Cas. Stand fast, Titinius: we must out and talk.

Oct. Marc Antony, shall we give sign of battle?

Ant. No, Cæsar; we will answer on their charge.
Make forth; the generals would have some
        words.

Oct. Stir not until the signal.

Bru. Words before blows: is it so, country-
        men?

Oct. Not that we love words better, as you do.

Bru. Good words are better than bad strokes,
        Octavius.

Ant. In your bad strokes, Brutus, you give
        good words:
Witness the hole you made in Cæsar's heart,
Crying, "Long live! hail, Cæsar!"

Cas.   Antony,
The posture of your blows are yet unknown:
But for your words, they rob the Hybla bees,
And leave them honeyless.

Ant.   Not stingless too.

Bru. O yes, and soundless too:
For you have stolen their buzzing, Antony,
And very wisely threat before you sting.

Ant. Villains, you did not so when your vile
        daggers

Hacked one another in the sides of Cæsar :
You shewed your teeth like apes, and fawned
    like hounds,
And bowed like bondmen, kissing Cæsar's feet ;
Whilst damnéd Casca, like a cur, behind,
Struck Cæsar on the neck.   O you flatterers !
  Cas. Flatterers !—Now, Brutus, thank yourself :
This tongue had not offended so to-day,
If Cassius might have ruled.
  Oct. Come, come, the cause.   If arguing
    make us sweat,
The proof of it will turn to redder drops.
Look ; I draw a sword against conspirators :
When think you that the sword goes up again?—
Never till Cæsar's three-and-twenty wounds
Be well avenged ; or till another Cæsar
Have added slaughter to the sword of traitors.
  Bru. Cæsar, thou canst not die by traitors'
    hands,
Unless thou bring'st them with thee.
  Oct.   So I hope :
I was not born to die on Brutus' sword.
  Bru. O, if thou wert the noblest of thy strain,
Young man, thou couldst not die more honourable.
  Cas. A peevish schoolboy, worthless of such
    honour ;
Joined with a masker and a reveller.
  Ant. Old Cassius still !
  Oct.   Come, Antony ; away.—
Defiance, traitors, hurl we in your teeth.
If you dare fight to-day, come to the field :
If not, when you have stomachs.
      [*Exeunt* Octavius, Antony, *and their Army.*
  Cas. Why now, blow, wind ; swell, billow ;
    and swim, bark !
The storm is up, and all is on the hazard.
  Bru. Ho, Lucilius ; hark, a word with you.
  Luc. My lord.
      [Brutus *and* Lucilius *converse apart.*
  Cas. Messala,—
  Mes.   What says my general ?
  Cas.   Messala,
This is my birth-day : as this very day
Was Cassius born.   Give me thy hand, Messala :
Be thou my witness that, against my will,
As Pompey was, am I compelled to set
Upon one battle all our liberties.
You know that I held Epicurus strong,
And his opinion : now I change my mind,
And partly credit things that do presage.
Coming from Sardis, on our former ensign
Two mighty eagles fell ; and there they perched,
Gorging and feeding from our soldiers' hands ;
Who to Philippi here consorted us :
This morning are they fled away and gone :
And in their steads, do ravens, crows, and kites,
Fly o'er our heads and downward look on us,

As we were sickly prey : their shadows seem
A canopy most fatal, under which
Our army lies, ready to give up the ghost.
  Mes. Believe not so.
  Cas.   I but believe it partly ;
For I am fresh of spirit, and resolved
To meet all perils very constantly.
  Bru. Even so, Lucilius.
  Cas.   Now, most noble Brutus,
The gods to-day stand friendly ; that we may,
Lovers in peace, lead on our days to age !
But, since the affairs of men rest still incertain,
Let's reason with the worst that may befall.
If we do lose this battle, then is this
The very last time we shall speak together :
What are you then determinéd to do ?
  Bru. Even by the rule of that philosophy
By which I did blame Cato for the death
Which he did give himself :—I know not how,
But I do find it cowardly and vile,
For fear of what might fall, so to prevent
The time of life :—arming myself with patience,
To stay the providence of some high powers
That govern us below.
  Cas.   Then, if we lose this battle,
You are contented to be led in triumph
Thorough the streets of Rome ?
  Bru. No, Cassius, no ! think not, thou noble
    Roman,
That ever Brutus will go bound to Rome :
He bears too great a mind.   But this same day
Must end that work the ides of March began ;
And whether we shall meet again I know not.
Therefore our everlasting farewell take :
For ever and for ever, farewell, Cassius !
If we do meet again, why we shall smile :
If not, why then this parting was well made.
  Cas. For ever and for ever, farewell, Brutus !
If we do meet again, we'll smile indeed :
If not, 'tis true this parting was well made.
  Bru. Why then, lead on.—O, that a man might
    know
The end of this day's business, ere it come !
But it sufficeth that the day will end,
And then the end is known.—Come, ho ! away.
      [*Exeunt.*

SCENE II.—*The same.   The Field of Battle.*

  Alarum.   Enter Brutus *and* Messala.

  Bru. Ride, ride, Messala ! ride, and give these
    bills
Unto the legions on the other side :
      [*Loud alarum.*
Let them set on at once ; for I perceive
But cold demeanour in Octavius' wing,

And sudden push gives them the overthrow.
Ride, ride, Messala! let them all come down.
                                        [*Exeunt.*

SCENE III.—*The same. Another part of the Field.*

    Alarum.   Enter CASSIUS *and* TITINIUS.

    Cas. O look, Titinius! look, the villains fly!
Myself have to mine own turned enemy.
This ensign here of mine was turning back:
I slew the coward, and did take it from him.

Tit. O Cassius, Brutus gave the word too earl
Who, having some advantage on Octavius,
Took it too eagerly: his soldiers fell to spoil,
Whilst we by Antony are all enclosed.

        Enter PINDARUS.

    Pin. Fly further off, my lord; fly further o
Marc Antony is in your tents, my lord!
Fly therefore, noble Cassius; fly far off.
    Cas. This hill is far enough.—Look, loo
        Titinius!
Are those my tents where I perceive the fire?

    Tit. They are, my lord.
    Cas.   Titinius, if thou lov'st me,
Mount thou my horse, and hide thy spurs in him
Till he have brought thee up to yonder troops,
And here again: that I may rest assured
Whether yond' troops are friend or enemy.
    Tit. I will be here again even with a thought.
                                        [*Exit.*
    Cas. Go, Pindarus, get higher on that hill:
My sight was ever thick: regard Titinius,
And tell me what thou not'st about the field.—
                                [*Exit* PINDARUS.
This day I breathéd first; time is come round,
And where I did begin, there I shall end:
My life is run his compass,—Sirrah, what news?
    Pin. [*above*]. O my lord!
    Cas. What news?
    Pin. Titinius is encloséd round about

With horsemen that make to him on the spur
Yet he spurs on.—Now they are almost on hin
Now, Titinius!—Now some 'light:—O, he 'ligl
        too:—
He's ta'en:—and hark! they shout for joy.
                                        [*Sho*
    Cas. Come down: behold no more.—
O, coward that I am, to live so long
To see my best friend ta'en before my face!

        Enter PINDARUS.

Come hither, sirrah:
In Parthia did I take thee prisoner:
And then I swore thee, saving of thy life,
That whatsoever I did bid thee do,
Thou shouldst attempt it. Come now, kee
        thine oath:
Now be a freeman; and with this good sword,

That ran through Cæsar's bowels, search this
    bosom.
Stand not to answer. Here, take thou the hilts:
And when my face is covered, as 't is now,
Guide thou the sword.—Cæsar, thou art revenged,
Even with the sword that killed thee!   [*Dies.*
   Pin. So, I am free: yet would not so have
    been,
Durst I have done my will. O Cassius!
Far from this country Pindarus shall run,
Where never Roman shall take note of him.
                          [*Exit.*

      Re-enter TITINIUS, *with* MESSALA.

   Mes. It is but change, Titinius: for Octavius
Is overthrown by noble Brutus' power,
As Cassius' legions are by Antony.
   Tit. These tidings will well comfort Cassius.
   Mes. Where did you leave him?
   Tit.   All disconsolate,
With Pindarus his bondman, on this hill.
   Mes. Is not that he that lies upon the ground?
   Tit. He lies not like the living. O my heart!
   Mes. Is not that he?
   Tit.   No: this was he, Messala;
But Cassius is no more.—O setting sun!
As in thy red rays thou dost sink to-night,
So in his red blood Cassius' day is set:
The sun of Rome is set! Our day is gone;
Clouds, dews, and dangers come: our deeds are
    done!
Mistrust of my success hath done this deed.
   Mes. Mistrust of good success hath done this
    deed.
O hateful error, melancholy's child!
Why dost thou shew to the apt thoughts of
    men
The things that are not? O error, soon conceived,
Thou never com'st unto a happy birth,
But kill'st the mother that engendered thee!
   Tit. What, Pindarus: where art thou, Pin-
    darus?
   Mes. Seek him Titinius; whilst I go to meet
The noble Brutus, thrusting this report
Into his ears. I may say, thrusting it:
For piercing steel and darts envenoméd
Shall be as welcome to the ears of Brutus
As tidings of this sight.
   Tit.   Hie you, Messala,
And I will seek for Pandarus the while.
                  [*Exit* MESSALA.
Why didst thou send me forth, brave Cassius?
Did I not meet thy friends? and did not they
Put on my brows this wreath of victory,
And bid me give 't thee? Didst thou not hear
    their shouts?
Alas, thou hast misconstrued everything!

But hold thee, take this garland on thy brow:
Thy Brutus bid me give it thee, and I
Will do his bidding.—Brutus, come apace,
And see how I regarded Caius Cassius.—
By your leave, gods :—this is a Roman's part:
Come, Cassius' sword, and find Titinius' heart.
                         [*Dies.*

Alarum. Re-enter MESSALA, *with* BRUTUS, *young*
   CATO, STRATO, VOLUMNIUS, *and* LUCILIUS.

   Bru. Where, where, Messala, doth his body
    lie?
   Mes. Lo, yonder; and Titinius mourning it.
   Bru. Titinius' face is upward.
   Cato. He is slain.
   Bru. O Julius Cæsar, thou art mighty yet!
Thy spirit walks abroad, and turns our swords
In our own proper entrails.   [*Low alarums.*
   Cato.   Brave Titinius!
Look whe'r he have not crowned dead Cassius!
   Bru. Are yet two Romans living such as
    these?
The last of all the Romans, fare thee well!
It is impossible that ever Rome
Should breed thy fellow.—Friends, I owe more
    tears
To this dead man than you shall see me pay.—
I shall find time, Cassius; I shall find time.—
Come, therefore, and to Thassos send his body:
His funeral shall not be in our camp,
Lest it discomfort us.—Lucilius, come;
And come, young Cato: let us to the field.—
Labeo and Flavius, set our battles on.—
'T is three o'clock; and, Romans, yet ere night
We shall try fortune in a second fight. [*Exeunt.*

   SCENE IV.—*Another Part of the Field.*

Alarum. Enter fighting, Soldiers *of both Armies;
   then* BRUTUS, CATO, LUCILIUS, *and others.*

   Bru. Yet, countrymen, O yet hold up your
    heads!
   Cato. What bastard doth not? Who will go
    with me?
I will proclaim my name about the field :—
I am the son of Marcus Cato, ho!
A foe to tyrants, and my country's friend:
I am the son of Marcus Cato, ho!
                 [*Charges the enemy.*
   Bru. And I am Brutus; Marcus Brutus, I:
Brutus, my country's friend: know me for
    Brutus.
    [*Exit, charging the enemy.* CATO *is over-
    powered, and falls.*
   Luc. O young and noble Cato, art thou down?

Why, now thou diest as bravely as Titinius;
And mayst be honoured, being Cato's son.

1st Sold. Yield, or thou diest!

Luc. Only I yield to die:
There is so much that thou wilt kill me straight:
[*Offering money.*
Kill Brutus, and be honoured in his death.

1st Sold. We must not.—A noble prisoner!

2nd Sold. Room, ho! Tell Antony, Brutus is
ta'en.

1st Sold. I'll tell the news.—Here comes the
general:—

Enter ANTONY.

Brutus is ta'en; Brutus is ta'en, my lord.

Ant. Where is he?

Luc. Safe, Antony; Brutus is safe enough:
I dare assure thee that no enemy
Shall ever take alive the noble Brutus:
The gods defend him from so great a shame!
When you do find him, or alive or dead,
He will be found like Brutus, like himself.

Ant. This is not Brutus, friend: but, I assure
you,
A prize no less in worth. Keep this man
safe;
Give him all kindness: I had rather have
Such men my friends than enemies. Go on,
And see whe'r Brutus be alive or dead:
And bring us word unto Octavius' tent
How everything is chanced. [*Exeunt.*

SCENE V.—*Another part of the Field.*

Enter BRUTUS, DARDANIUS, CLITUS, STRATO,
and VOLUMNIUS.

Bru. Come, poor remains of friends, rest on
this rock.

Cli. Statilius shewed the torch-light; but, my
lord,
He came not back: he is or ta'en or slain.

Bru. Sit thee down, Clitus. Slaying is the
word:
It is a deed in fashion. Hark thee, Clitus:—
[*Whispering.*

Cli. What, I, my lord! No, not for all the
world.

Bru. Peace, then; no words.

Cli. I'd rather kill myself.

Bru. Hark thee, Dardanius:—[*Whispers him.*

Dar. Shall I do such a deed!

Cli. O, Dardanius!

Dar. O, Clitus!

Cli. What ill request did Brutus make to
thee?

Dar. To kill him, Clitus. Look, he meditates.

Cli. Now is that noble vessel full of grief,
That it runs over even at his eyes.

Bru. Come hither, good Volumnius: list a
word.

Vol. What says my lord?

Bru. Why this, Volumnius:
The ghost of Cæsar hath appeared to me
Two several times by night: at Sardis once;
And this last night, here in Philippi' fields.
I know my hour is come.

Vol. Not so, my lord.

Bru. Nay, I am sure it is, Volumnius.
Thou seest the world, Volumnius, how it goes;
Our enemies have beat us to the pit:
It is more worthy to leap in ourselves,
Than tarry till they push us. Good Volumnius,
Thou know'st that we two went to school together:
Even for that our love of old, I pray thee
Hold thou my sword-hilts, whilst I run on it.

Vol. That's not an office for a friend, my
lord. [*Alarum still.*

Cli. Fly, fly, my lord! there is no tarrying
here.

Bru. Farewell to you;—and you;—and you,
Volumnius.—
Strato, thou hast been all this while asleep:
Farewell to thee too, Strato.—Countrymen,
My heart doth joy that yet, in all my life,
I found no man but he was true to me.
I shall have glory by this losing day,
More than Octavius and Marc Antony
By this vile conquest shall attain unto.
So, fare you well at once; for Brutus' tongue
Hath almost ended his life's history:
Night hangs upon mine eyes; my bones would
rest,
That have but laboured to attain this hour.
[*Alarum. Cry within; "Fly, fly, fly!"*

Cli. Fly, my lord, fly!

Bru. Hence: I will follow.
[*Exeunt* CLITUS, DARDANIUS, *and* VOLUMNIUS.
I pr'y thee, Strato, stay thou by thy lord.
Thou art a fellow of a good respect;
Thy life hath had some smatch of honour in it:
Hold then my sword, and turn away thy face,
While I do run upon it. Wilt thou, Strato?

Stra. Give me your hand first: fare you well,
my lord.

Bru. Farewell, good Strato.—Cæsar, now be
still:
I killed not thee with half so good a will!
[*He runs on his sword, and dies.*

Alarum. Retreat. Enter OCTAVIUS, ANTONY,
MESSALA, LUCILIUS, *and their Army.*

Oct. What man is that?

Mes. My master's man.—Strato, where is thy master?

Stra. Free from the bondage you are in, Messala:
The conquerors can but make a fire of him:
For Brutus only overcame himself,
And no man else hath honour by his death.

Luc. So Brutus should be found.—I thank thee, Brutus,
That thou hast proved Lucilius' saying true.

Oct. All that served Brutus, I will entertain them.—
Fellow, wilt thou bestow thy time with me?

Stra. Ay, if Messala will prefer me to you.

Oct. Do so, good Messala.

Mes. How died my master, Strato?

Stra. I held the sword, and he did run on it.

Mes. Octavius, then, take him to follow thee,
That did the latest service to my master.

Ant. This was the noblest Roman of them all.
All the conspirators, save only he,
Did that they did in envy of great Cæsar:
He, only, in a general honest thought,
And common good to all, made one of them.
His life was gentle; and the elements
So mixed in him, that Nature might stand up
And say to all the world, "This was a man!"

Oct. According to his virtue let us use him;
With all respect and rites of burial.
Within my tent his bones to-night shall lie,
Most like a soldier, ordered honourably.—
So call the field to rest: and let's away,
To part the glories of this happy day. [*Exeunt.*

" *Have you not made an universal shout,*
  That Tiber trembled underneath her banks."
                                    Act I., Scene 1.

Drayton, in his " POLYOLBION," frequently describes the
rivers of England as females, even when he speaks of the
presiding power of the stream. Spenser, more classically,
represents them as males.

Of the address to the plebeians in which the quoted passage occurs, Mr. Campbell eloquently remarks, " It can be
no great exaggeration to say, that these lines in the speech
of Marullus are among the most magnificent in the English
language. They roll over my mind's ear like the lordliest
notes of a cathedral organ."

—— " *Let no images*
  Be hung with Cæsar's trophies."—Act I., Scene 1.

There were set up images of Cæsar in the city, with diadems on their head like kings. Those the two tribunes went
and pulled down.—PLUTARCH (North's Translation).

" *Let me have men about me that are fat;*
  Sleekheaded men, and such as sleep o' nights."
                                    Act I., Scene 2.

Cæsar also had Cassius in great jealousy, and suspected
him much: whereupon he said on a time to his friends,
" What will Cassius do, think ye? I like not his pale looks."
Another time, when Cæsar's friends complained unto him
of Antonius and Dolabella, that they pretended some mischief towards him, he answered them again, " As for those
fat men and smooth-combed heads (quoth he), I never reckon
of them; but these pale-visaged and carrion-lean people, I
fear them most:" meaning Brutus and Cassius.—PLUTARCH.

" *A common slave (you know him well by sight)*
  Held up his left hand, which did flame and burn."
                                    Act I., Scene 3.

Strabo the philosopher writeth that divers men were seen
going up and down in fire: and furthermore, that there was
a slave of the soldiers that did cast a marvellous burning
flame out of his hand, inasmuch as they that saw it thought
he had been burned; but when the fire was out, it was found
he had no hurt.—PLUTARCH.

—— " *Good Cinna, take this paper,*
  And look you lay it in the prætor's chair,
  Where Brutus may but find it."—Act I., Scene 3.

For Brutus, his friends and countrymen, both by divers
procurements and sundry rumours of the city, and by many
bills also, did openly call and procure him to do that he did.
For under the image of his ancestor Junius Brutus (that
drave the kings out of Rome), they wrote, " O that it pleased
the gods thou wert now alive, Brutus!" And again, " That
thou wert here among us now!" His tribunal, or chair,
where he gave audience during the time he was prætor, was
full of such bills:—" Brutus, thou art asleep, and art not
Brutus indeed!"—PLUTARCH.

" *The genius and the mortal instruments*
  Are then in council."—Act II., Scene 1.

Shakspere is describing what passes in a single bosom;
the insurrection which a conspirator feels agitating the little
kingdom of his own mind, when the genius (or power that
watches for his protection), and the mortal instruments (the
passions) which excite him to a deed of honour and danger,
are in council and debate: when the desire of action, and
the care of safety, keep the mind in continual fluctuation
and disturbance.—JOHNSON.

"*Sir, 't is your brother Cassius at the door.*"—Act II., Scene 1.

Junia, the sister of Brutus, was married to Cassius.

" *I can o'ersway him; for he loves to hear*
  That unicorns may be betrayed with trees,
  And bears with glasses, elephants with holes."
                                    Act II., Scene 1.

Unicorns are said to have been taken by one who, running
behind a tree, eluded the violent push the animal was
making at him; so that the unicorn's horn spent its force on
the trunk, and stuck fast, detaining the animal till he was
despatched by the hunter. There is a similar allusion in
Spenser's " FAERY QUEEN," (b. ii., c. 5). Bears are reported
to have been surprised by means of a mirror, which they
would gaze on, affording their pursuers an opportunity of
taking the surer aim. Elephants were seduced into pitfalls,
lightly covered with hurdles and turf, on which a proper bait
to tempt them was exposed.—STEEVENS.

" *I grant I am a woman; but withal*
  A woman that lord Brutus took to wife."
                                    Act II., Scene 1.

I being, O Brutus (said she), the daughter of Cato, was
married unto thee, not to be thy companion in bed and at
board only, like a harlot; but to be partaker also with thee
of thy good and evil fortune. Now for thyself, I can find no
cause of fault in thee touching our match: but for my part,
how may I shew my duty towards thee, and how much I
would do for thy sake, if I cannot constantly bear a secret
mischance or grief with thee which requireth secrecy and
fidelity? I confess that a woman's wit commonly is too weak
to keep a secret safely: but yet, Brutus, good education and
the company of virtuous men have some power to reform the
defect of nature. And for myself, I have this benefit moreover, that I am the daughter of Cato and wife of Brutus.—
PLUTARCH.

" *And graves have yawned and yielded up their dead.*
                                    Act II., Scene 2.

This line recals a passage in " HAMLET :"—

" A little ere the mightiest Julius fell,
  The graves stood tenantless, and the sheeted dead
  Did squeak and gibber in the Roman streets."

" POR. *I pr'y thee, boy, run to the senate-house:*
  Stay not to answer me, but get thee gone.
  Why dost thou stay?
    LUC. *To know my errand, madam.*"—Act II., Scene 3.

Perturbation of mind is admirably expressed in " KING
RICHARD III.," as here by Portia:—

" *Rich. Dull, unmindful villain!*
Why stay'st thou here, and go'st not to the duke?
  Cat. First, mighty liege, tell me your highness' pleasure."

"Et tu, Brute?—Then fall, Cæsar!"—Act III., Scene 1.

Suetonius relates that, according to some authorities, Cæsar exclaimed in Greek, as Brutus approached to stab him, "And thou, my son?" He makes no mention of the Latin phrase attributed to him in the text, neither does Plutarch, who states that the conspirators "compassed him on every side, with their swords drawn in their hands, that Cæsar turned him nowhere but he was stricken by some. Men report also, that Cæsar did still defend himself against the rest, running every way with his body; but when he saw Brutus with his sword drawn in his hand, then he pulled his gown over his head, and made no more resistance."

The often-quoted words probably appeared for the first time in the earlier Latin play on the subject, by Dr. Eedes.

"There is no harm intended to your person,
Nor to no Roman else."—Act III., Scene 1.

The use of two negatives, not to make an affirmative, but to deny more strongly, is common to Chaucer, Spenser, and other of our ancient writers. Hickes observes that, in the Saxon, even four negatives are sometimes conjoined, and still preserve a negative signification.—STEEVENS.

"Cry 'Havock!' and let slip the dogs of war."
Act III., Scene 1.

In military operations of old, the word "havock" signified that no quarter should be given. By the "dogs of war," are probably meant famine, sword, and fire. As in "KING HENRY V. :"—

"Leashed in like hounds, should famine, sword, and fire,
Crouch for employment."

"Those that will hear me speak, let them stay here."
Act III., Scene 2.

A great number of men being assembled together, one after another, Brutus made an oration unto them, to win the favour of the people, and to justify that they had done. All those that were by, said they had done well, and cried unto them that they boldly come down from the Capitol : whereupon Brutus and his companions came boldly down into the market-place. The rest followed in troop, but Brutus went foremost, very honourably compassed in round about with the noblest men of the city.—PLUTARCH.

"Friends, Romans, countrymen, lend me your ears.
I come to bury Cæsar, not to praise him."
Act III., Scene 2.

Then Antonius, thinking good his testament should be read openly, and also that his body should be honourably buried, and not in hugger-mugger, lest the people might thereby take occasion to be worse offended if they did otherwise, Cassius stoutly spake against it, but Brutus went with the motion, and agreed unto it: wherein it seemeth he committed a second fault : for the first fault he did was when he would not consent to his fellow-conspirators that Antonius should be slain ; and therefore he was justly accused that thereby he had saved and strengthened a strong and grievous enemy of their conspiracy. The second fault was when he agreed that Cæsar's funerals should be as Antonius would have them; the which indeed marred all. For, first of all, when Cæsar's testament was openly read amongst them, whereby it appeared that he bequeathed unto every citizen of Rome, seventy-five drachmas a man, and that he left his gardens and arbours unto the people which he had on this side of the river Tiber, in the place where now the temple of Fortune is built, the people then loved him, and were marvellous sorry for him.—PLUTARCH.

"I am not Cinna the conspirator."—Act III., Scene 3.

"Through a most extraordinary licence, or indolence in the collation of copies, this entire line is omitted in all modern editions."—PICTORIAL SHAKSPERE.

The line in question was first, probably, omitted in the last edition of Steevens and Reed (1803); at least we have found it in all those earlier copies that have hitherto fallen in our way. We will, therefore, merely mention four editions of subsequent date, and of no extraordinary pretensions, in which we have observed the line supposed by our contemporary to be "omitted in all modern editions." These are,—Whittingham's (7 vols., Chiswick, 1814); Hurst and Robinson's (2 vols., 1819); Fraser and Crawford's (Edinb., 1 vol., 1838; Orr, London); Sherwood's (London Stage edition, 1 vol., 1825). These copies have all come casually under our notice, and there are doubtless many others that give the line quoted; at the same time, it must be admitted that we have also seen several in which it is wanting. Our contemporary has unwittingly fallen into so many mistakes as to the supposed errors of *all* preceding modern editions, particularly with reference to the three great Roman plays, that it is but fair towards others to enter a general caution on the subject, without impeaching the special merits of the critic alluded to.

———

"Most noble brother, you have done me wrong."
Act IV., Scene 2.

About this time, Brutus sent to pray Cassius to come to the city of Sardis, and so he did. Brutus understanding of his coming, went to meet him with all his friends. There, both armies being armed, they called them both Emperors.

Now, as it commonly happeneth in great affairs between two persons, both of them having many friends, and so many captains under them, there ran tales and complaints betwixt them. Therefore, before they fell in hand with any other matter, they went into a little chamber together, and bade every man avoid, and did shut the doors to them. They then began to pour out their complaints one to the other, and grew hot and loud, earnestly accusing one another, and at length fell both a-weeping.—PLUTARCH.

"By heaven, I had rather coin my heart,
And drop my blood for drachmas, than to wring
From the hard hands of peasants their vile trash
By any indirection!"—Act IV., Scene 3.

This is a noble sentiment, altogether in character, and expressed in a manner inimitably happy. For "to wring" implies both to get unjustly, and to use force in getting : and "hard hands" signify both the peasant's great labour and pains in acquiring, and his great unwillingness to quit his hold.—WARBURTON.

*"*CAS. *A friend should bear his friend's infirmities ;*
But Brutus makes mine greater than they are.
BRU. *I do not till you practise them on me."*
Act IV., Scene 3.

The meaning is this :—" I do not look for your faults : I only see them, and mention them with vehemence, when you force them into my notice by practising them on me."—JOHNSON.

"What should the wars do with these jigging fools?"
Act IV., Scene 3.

By "jigging fools" is meant silly poets. A jig signified (as mentioned in the notes to "HAMLET," Act ii.) a metrical composition, as well as a dance.

——— *"With this she fell distract,*
And her attendants absent, swallowed fire."
Act IV., Scene 3.

And for Portia, Brutus' wife, Nicolaus the philosopher, and Valerius Maximus do write that she, determining to kill herself (her parents and friends carefully looking to her to keep her from it), took hot burning coals and cast them into her mouth, and kept her mouth so close that she choked herself.—PLUTARCH.

" Bru. *Speak to me what thou art.*
  Ghost. *Thy evil spirit, Brutus.*"—Act IV., Scene 3.

As they prepared to pass over again out of Asia into Europe, there went a rumour that there appeared a wonderful sign unto him.

Brutus was a careful man, and slept very little. * * * After he had slumbered a little after supper, he spent all the rest of the night in despatching of his weightiest causes; and after he had taken order for them, if he had any leisure left him he would read some book till the third watch of the night, at what time the captains, petty captains, and colonels, did use to come unto him.

So, being ready to go into Europe, one night (when all the camp took quiet rest), as he was in his tent with a little light, thinking of weighty matters, he thought he heard one come in to him, and, casting his eye towards the door of his tent, that he saw a wonderful, strange, and monstrous shape of a body coming towards him, and said never a word. So Brutus boldly asked what he was, a god or a man, and what cause brought him thither. The spirit answered him, " I am thy evil spirit, Brutus, and thou shalt see me by the city of Philippes." Brutus, being no otherwise afraid, replied again unto it, " Well, then, I shall see thee again."

The spirit presently vanished away; and Brutus called his men unto him, who told him that they heard no noise, nor saw anything at all. Thereupon Brutus returned again to think on his matters as he did before: and when the day broke he went unto Cassius, to tell him what vision had appeared unto him in the night.—Plutarch.

" *They mean to warn us at Philippi here.*"—Act V., Scene 1.

"To warn" meant formerly to summon, as well as to caution. As in " King John:"—

  " Who is it that hath warned us to the walls *?*"

And in " King Richard III.:"—

  " And sent to warn them to his royal presence."

" *Ride, ride, Messala, ride, and give these bills
  Unto the legions on the other side.*"—Act V., Scene 2.

In the meantime, Brutus, that led the right wing, sent little bills to the colonels and captains of private bands, in which he wrote the order of the battle.—Plutarch.

" *Statilius shewed the torchlight; but, my lord,
  He came not back.*"—Act V., Scene 5.

Furthermore, Brutus thought that there was no great number of men slain in battle; and to know the truth of it there was one, called Statilius, that promised to go through his enemies (for otherwise it was impossible to go see their camp), and from thence, if all were well, that he should lift up a torchlight in the air, and then return again with speed to him. The torchlight was lift up as he had promised, for Statilius went thither. Now Brutus, seeing Statilius tarry long after that, and that he came not again, he said, " If Statilius be alive, he will come again:" but his evil fortune was such that, as he came back, he lighted in his enemies' hands, and was slain.—Plutarch.

" *Sit thee down, Clitus: slaying is the word.*"
                          Act V., Scene 5.

Now the night being far spent, Brutus, as he sat, bowed towards Clitus, one of his men, and told him somewhat in his ear: the other answered him not, but fell a-weeping. Thereupon he proved Dardanus, and said somewhat also to him.

At length he came to Volumnius himself, and, speaking to him in Greek, prayed him for the studies' sake which brought them acquainted together, that he would help him to put his hand to his sword, to thrust it in him to kill him. Volumnius denied his request, and so did many others; and amongst the rest, one of them said there was no tarrying for them there, but that they must needs fly.

Then Brutus, rising up, " We must fly, indeed (said he), but it must be with our hands, not with our feet." Then, taking every man by the hand, he said these words unto them with a cheerful countenance : " It rejoiceth my heart that not one of my friends hath failed me at my need ; and I do not complain of my fortune, but only for my country's sake : for, as for me, I think myself happier than they that have overcome, considering that I leave a perpetual fame of our courage and manhood; the which our enemies, the conquerors, shall never attain unto by force or money : neither can let [hinder] their posterity to say that they, being naughty and unjust men, have slain good men, to usurp tyrannical power not pertaining to them."

Having said so, he prayed every man to shift for themselves; and then he went a little aside with two or three only, among the which Strato was one, with whom he came first acquainted by the study of rhetoric. He came as near to him as he could, and taking his sword by the hilts with both his hands, and falling down upon the point of it, ran himself through. Others say that not he, but Strato (at his request), held the sword in his hand, and turned his head aside, and that Brutus fell down upon it, and so ran himself through, and died presently.—Plutarch.

Gildon long ago remarked that Brutus was the true hero of this tragedy, and not Cæsar. Schlegel makes the same observation. The poet has portrayed the character of Brutus with peculiar care, and developed all the amiable traits, the feeling, and patriotic heroism of it with supereminent skill. He has been less happy in personifying Cæsar, to whom he has given several ostentatious speeches, unsuited to his character, if we may judge from the impressions made upon us by his own Commentaries. The character of Cassius is also touched with great nicety and discrimination, and is admirably contrasted to that of Brutus : his superiority " in independent volition, and his discernment in judging of human affairs, are pointed out;" while the purity of mind and conscientious love of justice in Brutus, unfit him to be the head of a party in a state entirely corrupted : these amiable failings gave, in fact, an unfortunate turn to the cause of the conspirators.

The play abounds in well-wrought and affecting scenes. It is scarcely necessary to mention the celebrated dialogue between Brutus and Cassius, in which the design of the conspiracy is opened to Brutus:—the quarrel between them, rendered doubly touching by the close, when Cassius learns the death of Portia; and which one is surprised to think that any critic susceptible of feeling should pronounce " cold and unaffecting;"—the scene between Brutus and Portia, where she endeavours to extort the secret of the conspiracy from him, in which is that heart-thrilling burst of tenderness which Portia's heroic behaviour awakens :—

  " You are my true and honourable wife :
    As dear to me as are the ruddy drops
    That visit my sad heart."

The speeches of Marc Antony over the dead body of Cæsar, and the artful eloquence with which he captivates the multitude, are justly classed among the happiest effusions of poetic declamation.—Singer.

ANTONY

AND

CLEOPATRA

MBITIOUS, brave, able, and enterprising, Marc Antony, takes rank among the foremost men of action of the second order: that is, of those who, possessing ability to achieve greatness, lack fortitude or the higher genius to use it wisely when obtained. The great criterion of excellence in all pursuits is power in repose; spontaneous, comprehensive, easy-working intellect: and in this cardinal quality the revelling Triumvir proves miserably wanting. While "the mighty Julius" lived, Marc Antony felt himself properly placed, as an active instrument in the hands of that great master-spirit; and under him, in Gaul and at Pharsalia, he served with willing vigour and fidelity. To the colder genius of Octavius, his dæmon, though "noble, high, unmatchable," when alone, yields involuntary homage, and " becomes a Fear, as being overpowered." Antony, in short, is one of those who need incessant stimulus to keep their minds in health; and he falls at length, like many other conquerors in war, some better and some worse, a weak and easy victim to himself, in the languid, trying times of peace.

Yet, after all, the victor of Philippi, the deserter of Actium, was no ordinary mortal. His faults and his virtues—his strong points and his weak ones—lie intermixed in glittering profusion; and Shakspere has achieved one of his greatest triumphs in the delineation of this splendid, though inconsistent, victim of ambition, love, and idleness. The pervading folly of the slave of pleasure is interspersed with intervals of self-reproach, of self-respect, and self-assertion.—Among the amiable traits in the character of Antony is his conduct on learning the defection of Enobarbus, his shrewd and long-devoted monitor. "My fortunes have corrupted honest men!" is his mild, pathetic exclamation; and his only rebuke to the repentant deserter, is to send his treasure, with "gentle adieus and greetings," after him, into the enemy's camp. Antony's anxiety, too, for the safety and welfare of his servants, after the ignominious flight from Actium, speaks something for the natural kindliness of his feelings: and altogether it would be difficult not to rejoice that a glimpse of former heroism and success precedes his final fall.

Cleopatra seems the natural counterpart of Antony: they are but sexual variations of the same bright, luxurious, weak, ambitious being. Gorgeous and munificent in prosperity, they retain the love of their attendants to the last: and the fascinating Egyptian, like her ill-starred slave and lover, shows a courage, tenderness, and constancy, in death, that earns some portion of respect as well as sympathy.

The Octavius of this drama (the all-praised, all-powerful Augustus of a later day) does not appear to us so destitute of good feeling and commanding intellect as has been sometimes thought. In the outset, he seems sincerely desirous of continuing friends with his great compeer, on equal terms: he gives to him the hand of a sister, for whom he entertains the most entire affection: and it is not till the natural revulsion of Antony's debauched appetite leads him to indolence and " his Egyptian dish again" (inducing him to banish an affectionate confiding wife on false pretences), that the pride and outraged feeling of the insulted brother awake to vengeance and implacable hostility.—The admirable scene in Pompey's galley strikingly depicts the totally conflicting intellects and dispositions of the two great future contenders for exclusive universal empire. Antony plays upon the tolerated Lepidus with excellent humour, and finally yields himself a willing shouter in the "Egyptian bacchanals." Octavius is polite and affable, but restrained and self-observant: when urged to drink, he answers,—

> " I could well forbear it.
> It's monstrous labour when I wash my brain
> And it grows fouler."

His anxiety, also, to separate before the personal dignity of the guests shall be too far compromised, is highly characteristic. The great "coming event" of future mastery " throws its shadow before," throughout this exquisite scene of rampant revelry.

Lepidus—the younger Pompey—Enobarbus—Ventidius—and the numerous other minor characters, would be minor only in so great a scene: all combine to excite that overpowering wonder which Coleridge speaks of as his predominant feeling in the perusal of this magnificent drama.

No edition of "ANTONY AND CLEOPATRA" is known to exist, prior to that of the first folio. The incidents, as in the two preceding plays, are derived from Plutarch's interesting narrative.

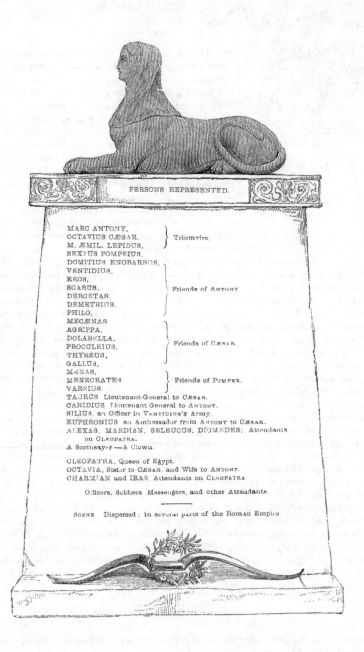

PERSONS REPRESENTED.

MARC ANTONY,
OCTAVIUS CÆSAR, } Triumvirs.
M. ÆMIL. LEPIDUS,
SEXTUS POMPEIUS,
DOMITIUS ENOBARBUS,
VENTIDIUS,
EROS,
SCARUS, } Friends of ANTONY
DERCETAS,
DEMETRIUS,
PHILO,
MECÆNAS,
AGRIPPA,
DOLABELLA,
PROCULEIUS, } Friends of CÆSAR.
THYREUS,
GALLUS,
MENAS,
MENECRATES } Friends of POMPEY.
VARRIUS,
TAURUS, Lieutenant-General to CÆSAR.
CANIDIUS, Lieutenant General to ANTONY.
SILIUS, an Officer in VENTIDIUS's Army.
EUPHRONIUS, an Ambassador from ANTONY to CÆSAR.
ALEXAS, MARDIAN, SELEUCUS, DIOMEDES; Attendants
    on CLEOPATRA.
A Soothsayer — A Clown.

CLEOPATRA, Queen of Egypt.
OCTAVIA, Sister to CÆSAR, and Wife to ANTONY.
CHARMIAN and IRAS, Attendants on CLEOPATRA

    Officers, Soldiers, Messengers, and other Attendants.

    SCENE   Dispersed; in several parts of the Roman Empire

ANTONY

AND

CLEOPATRA.

ACT I.

SCENE I.—Alexandria. *A Room in* CLEOPATRA'S
Palace.

Enter DEMETRIUS *and* PHILO.

Phi. Nay, but this dotage of our general's
O'erflows the measure: those his goodly eyes,
That o'er the files and musters of the war
Have glowed like plated Mars, now bend, now turn,
The office and devotion of their view
Upon a tawny front: his captain's heart,
Which in the scuffles of great fights hath burst
The buckles on his breast, reneges all temper;

And is become the bellows and the fan
To cool a gipsy's lust.—Look, where they come!
Take but good note, and you shall see in him
The triple pillar of the world transformed
Into a strumpet's fool.   Behold and see.

Flourish.   Enter ANTONY *and* CLEOPATRA, *with
their Trains:* Eunuchs *fanning her.*

Cleo. If it be love indeed, tell me how much.
Ant. There 's beggary in the love that can be
reckoned.
Cleo. I 'll set a bourn how far to be beloved.

523

Ant. Then must thou needs find out new heaven, new earth.

Enter an Attendant.

Att. News, my good lord, from Rome :—
Ant.   Grates me :—the sum.
Cleo. Nay, hear them, Antony.
Fulvia perchance is angry : or who knows
If the scarce-bearded Cæsar have not sent
His powerful mandate to you, " Do this, or this :
Take in that kingdom, and enfranchise that :
Perform 't, or else we damn thee."
Ant.   How, my love !
Cleo. Perchance (nay, and most like),
You must not stay here longer : your dismission
Is come from Cæsar : therefore hear it, Antony.—
Where 's Fulvia's process ?—Cæsar's, I would
      say :—both :—
Call in the messengers.—As I am Egypt's queen,
Thou blushest, Antony, and that blood of thine
Is Cæsar's homager : else so thy cheek pays shame
When shrill-tongued Fulvia scolds.—The mes-
      sengers.
Ant. Let Rome in Tyber melt, and the wide arch
Of the ranged empire fall !—Here is my space.
Kingdoms are clay : our dungy earth alike
Feeds beast as man : the nobleness of life
Is to do thus [*Embracing*], when such a mutual
      pair
And such a twain can do 't : in which I bind,
On pain of punishment, the world to weet
We stand up peerless.
Cleo.   Excellent falsehood !
Why did he marry Fulvia, and not love her ?—
I 'll seem the fool I am not : Antony
Will be himself.
Ant.   But stirred by Cleopatra.—
Now, for the love of Love and her soft hours,
Let 's not confound the time with conference harsh :
There 's not a minute of our lives should stretch
Without some pleasure now. What sport to-
      night ?
Cleo. Hear the ambassadors.
Ant.   Fie, wrangling queen,
Whom everything becomes ! to chide, to laugh,
To weep : whose every passion fully strives
To make itself, in thee, fair and admired !
No messenger : but thine, and all alone,
To-night we 'll wander through the streets, and
      note
The qualities of people. Come, my queen :
Last night you did desire it.—Speak not to us.
      [*Exeunt* ANTONY, CLEOPATRA, *and* Train.
Dem. Is Cæsar with Antonius prized so slight ?
Phi. Sir, sometimes, when he is not Antony,
He comes too short of that great property
Which still should go with Antony.

Dem.   I 'm full sorry
That he approves the common liar, who
Thus speaks of him at Rome : but I will hope
Of better deeds to-morrow. Rest you happy !
      [*Exeunt.*

SCENE II.—*The same. Another Room.*

Enter CHARMIAN, IRAS, ALEXAS, *and a* Soothsayer.

Char. Lord Alexas, sweet Alexas, most any-
thing Alexas, almost most absolute Alexas,
where 's the soothsayer that you praised so to
the queen ?—O that I knew this husband which
you say must change his horns with garlands !
Alex. Soothsayer.
Sooth. Your will ?
Char. Is this the man ?—Is 't you, sir, that
know things ?
Sooth. In nature's infinite book of secrecy
A little I can read.
Alex.   Shew him your hand.

Enter ENOBARBUS.

Eno. Bring in the banquet quickly : wine enough,
Cleopatra's health to drink.
Char. Good sir, give me good fortune.
Sooth. I make not, but foresee.
Char. Pray, then, foresee me one.
Sooth. You shall be yet far fairer than you are.
Char. He means, in flesh.
Iras. No ; you shall paint when you are old.
Char. Wrinkles forbid !
Alex. Vex not his prescience : be attentive.
Char. Hush !
Sooth. You shall be more beloving than beloved.
Char. I had rather heat my liver with drinking.
Alex. Nay, hear him.
Char. Good now, some excellent fortune ! Let
me be married to three kings in a forenoon, and
widow them all : let me have a child at fifty, to
whom Herod of Jewry may do homage : find me
to marry me with Octavius Cæsar, and companion
me with my mistress.
Sooth. You shall outlive the lady whom you
serve.
Char. O excellent ! I love long life better than
figs.
Sooth. You have seen and proved a fairer former
fortune than that which is to approach.
Char. Then belike my children shall have no
names. Pr'y thee how many boys and wenches
must I have ?
Sooth. If every of your wishes had a womb,
And fertile every wish, a million.
Char. Out, fool ! I forgive thee for a witch.

Alex. You think none but your sheets are privy to your wishes.

Char. Nay, come, tell Iras hers.

Alex. We 'll know all our fortunes.

Eno. Mine and most of our fortunes, to-night, shall be—drunk to bed.

Iras. There 's a palm presages chastity, if nothing else.

Char. Even as the overflowing Nilus presageth famine.

Iras. Go, you wild bedfellow; you cannot soothsay.

Char. Nay, if an oily palm be not a fruitful prognostication, I cannot scratch mine ear.—Pr'y thee, tell her but a worky-day fortune.

Sooth. Your fortunes are alike.

Iras. But how, but how? give me particulars.

Sooth. I have said.

Iras. Am I not an inch of fortune better than she?

Char. Well, if you were but an inch of fortune better than I, where would you choose it?

Iras. Not in my husband's nose.

Char. Our worser thoughts heavens mend!—Alexas,—come, his fortune, his fortune.—O, let him marry a woman that cannot go, sweet Isis, I beseech thee! And let her die too, and give him a worse: and let worse follow worse, till the worst of all follow him laughing to his grave, fifty-fold a cuckold! Good Isis, hear me this prayer, though thou deny me a matter of more weight: good Isis, I beseech thee!

Iras. Amen. Dear goddess, hear that prayer of the people! for, as it is a heart-breaking to see a handsome man loose-wived, so it is a deadly sorrow to behold a foul-knave uncuckolded.

Therefore, dear Isis, keep decorum, and fortune him accordingly!

Char. Amen.

Alex. Lo now, if it lay in their hands to make me a cuckold, they would make themselves whores but they 'd do 't!

Eno. Hush! here comes Antony.

Char. Not he; the queen.

Enter CLEOPATRA.

Cleo. Saw you my lord?

Eno. No, lady.

Cleo. Was he not here?

Char. No, madam.

Cleo. He was disposed to mirth; but on the sudden
A Roman thought hath struck him.—Enobarbus:

Eno. Madam.

Cleo. Seek him, and bring him hither.— Where's Alexas?

Alex. Here, at your service.—My lord approaches.

Enter ANTONY, *with a* Messenger *and* Attendants.

Cleo. We will not look upon him: go with us.
          [*Exeunt* CLEOPATRA, ENOBARBUS, *&c.*

Mess. Fulvia thy wife first came into the field.

Ant. Against my brother Lucius?

Mess. Ay:
But soon that war had end, and the time's state
Made friends of them, jointing their force 'gainst
          Cæsar:
Whose better issue in the war, from Italy,
Upon the first encounter, drave them.

Ant.   Well, what worst?

Mess. The nature of bad news infects the teller.

Ant. When it concerns the fool or coward.—
          On:
Things that are past are done, with me. 'Tis
          thus:
Who tells me true, though in his tale lie death,
I hear him as he flattered.

Mess.   Labienus
(This is stiff news) hath, with his Parthian force,
Extended Asia from Euphrates;
His conquering banner shook from Syria
To Lydia and to Ionia:
Whilst—

Ant. "Antony," thou wouldst say,—

Mess.   O, my lord!

Ant. Speak to me home, mince not the general
          tongue:
Name Cleopatra as she's called in Rome:
Rail thou in Fulvia's phrase; and taunt my faults
With such full license as both truth and malice
Have power to utter.—O, then we bring forth
          weeds

When our quick winds lie still, and our ills told us
Is as our earing!—Fare thee well awhile.

Mess. At your noble pleasure.   [*Exit.*

Ant. From Sicyon how the news?—Speak there.

1st Att. The man from Sicyon: is there such
          an one?

2nd Att. He stays upon your will.

Ant.   Let him appear.—
These strong Egyptian fetters I must break,

Enter another Messenger.

Or lose myself in dotage.—What are you?

2nd Mess. Fulvia thy wife is dead.

Ant. Where died she?

2nd Mess. In Sicyon:
Her length of sickness, with what else more serious
Importeth thee to know, this bears.
                    [*Gives a letter.*

Ant. Forbear me.   [*Exit* Messenger.
There's a great spirit gone! Thus did I desire it.
What our contempts do often hurl from us,
We wish it ours again: the present pleasure,
By revolution lowering, does become
The opposite of itself. She's good, being gone:
The hand could pluck her back, that shoved her on.
I must from this enchanting queen break off:
Ten thousand harms more than the ills I know,
My idleness doth hatch.—How now; Enobarbus:

Enter ENOBARBUS.

Eno. What's your pleasure, sir?

Ant. I must with haste from hence.

Eno. Why, then, we kill all our women. We see how mortal an unkindness is to them: if they suffer our departure, death's the word.

Ant. I must be gone.

Eno. Under a compelling occasion, let women die: it were pity to cast them away for nothing; though, between them and a great cause, they should be esteemed nothing. Cleopatra, catching but the least noise of this, dies instantly: I have seen her die twenty times upon far poorer moment. I do think there is mettle in death, which commits some loving act upon her; she hath such celerity in dying.

Ant. She is cunning past man's thought.

Eno. Alack, sir, no: her passions are made of nothing but the finest part of pure love. We cannot call her winds and waters, sighs and tears; they are greater storms and tempests than almanacks can report. This cannot be cunning in her: if it be, she makes a shower of rain as well as Jove.

Ant. 'Would I had never seen her!

Eno. O, sir, you had then left unseen a wonderful piece of work; which not to have been blessed withal, would have discredited your travel.

Ant. Fulvia is dead.

Eno. Sir?

Ant. Fulvia is dead.

Eno. Fulvia?

Ant. Dead.

Eno. Why, sir, give the gods a thankful sacrifice. When it pleaseth their deities to take the
wife of a man from him, it shews to man the
tailors of the earth: comforting therein, that
when old robes are worn out, there are members
to make new. If there were no more women
but Fulvia, then had you indeed a cut, and the
case to be lamented: this grief is crowned with
consolation; your old smock brings forth a new
petticoat: and indeed the tears live in an onion
that should water this sorrow.

Ant. The business she hath broachéd in the state
Cannot endure my absence.

Eno. And the business you have broached here
cannot be without you: especially that of Cleopatra's, which wholly depends on your abode.

Ant. No more light answers: let our officers
Have notice what we purpose. I shall break
The cause of our expedience to the queen,
And get her love to part: for not alone
The death of Fulvia, with more urgent touches,
Do strongly speak to us, but the letters too
Of many our contriving friends in Rome
Petition us at home. Sextus Pompeius
Hath given the dare to Cæsar, and commands
The empire of the sea: our slippery people
(Whose love is never linked to the deserver
Till his deserts are past) begin to throw
Pompey the great, and all his dignities,
Upon his son; who, high in name and power,
Higher than both in blood and life, stands up
For the main soldier: whose quality, going on,
The sides o' the world may danger. Much is
      breeding,
Which, like the courser's hair, hath yet but life,
And not a serpent's poison.—Say, our pleasure
(To such whose place is under us) requires
Our quick remove from hence.

Eno. I shall do 't.   *[Exeunt.*

SCENE III.—*Enter* CLEOPATRA, CHARMIAN, IRAS,
and ALEXAS.

Cleo. Where is he?

Char. I did not see him since.

Cleo. See where he is, who's with him, what
      he does:
(I did not send you).—If you find him sad,
Say I am dancing: if in mirth, report
That I am sudden sick. Quick, and return.
          [Exit ALEXAS.

Char. Madam, methinks, if you did love him
      dearly,
You do not hold the method to enforce
The like from him.

Cleo.   What should I do, I do not?

Char. In each thing give him way; cross him
      in nothing.

Cleo. Thou teachest like a fool: the way to
      lose him.

Char. Tempt him not so too far. I wish forbear:
In time we hate that which we often fear.

       Enter ANTONY.

But here comes Antony.

Cleo.   I am sick and sullen.

Ant. I am sorry to give breathing to my pur-
      pose,—

Cleo. Help me away, dear Charmian; I shall fall.
It cannot be thus long; the sides of nature
Will not sustain it.

Ant.   Now, my dearest queen,—

Cleo. Pray you stand further from me.

Ant.   What's the matter?

Cleo. I know by that same eye there's some
      good news.
What says the married woman?—You may go:
'Would she had never given you leave to come!
Let her not say 't is I that keep you here:
I have no power upon you: her's you are.

Ant. The gods best know,—

Cleo.   O, never was there queen
So mightily betrayed! yet at the first
I saw the treasons planted.

Ant.   Cleopatra,—

Cleo. Why should I think you can be mine, and
      true
(Though you in swearing shake the thronéd gods),
Who have been false to Fulvia?—Riotous madness,
To be entangled with those mouth-made vows
Which break themselves in swearing!

Ant.   Most sweet queen,—

Cleo. Nay, pray you seek no colour for your
      going,
But bid farewell and go. When you sued staying,
Then was the time for words! No going then:
Eternity was in our lips and eyes;
Bliss in our brows' bent; none our parts so poor
But was a race of heaven. They are so still,
Or thou, the greatest soldier of the world,
Art turned the greatest liar.

Ant.   How now, lady!

Cleo. I would I had thy inches: thou shouldst
      know
There were a heart in Egypt.

Ant.   Hear me, queen:
The strong necessity of time commands
Our services awhile; but my full heart

Remains in use with you. Our Italy
Shines o'er with civil swords: Sextus Pompeius
Makes his approaches to the port of Rome:
Equality of two domestic powers
Breeds scrupulous faction. The hated, grown
      to strength,
Are newly grown to love: the cóndemned Pompey,
Rich in his father's honour, creeps apace
Into the hearts of such as have not thrived
Upon the present state; whose numbers threaten:
And quietness, grown sick of rest, would purge
By any desperate change. My more particular,
And that which most with you should safe my
      going,
Is Fulvia's death.

    Cleo. Though age from folly could not give
      me freedom,
It does from childishness :—can Fulvia die?

    Ant. She's dead, my queen:
Look here, and at thy sovereign leisure read
The garboils she awaked: at the last, best :—
See when and where she died.

    Cleo.   O most false love!
Where be the secret vials thou shouldst fill
With sorrowful water?—Now I see, I see,
In Fulvia's death, how mine received shall be.

    Ant. Quarrel no more, but be prepared to
      know
The purposes I bear: which are or cease
As you shall give the advice. By the fire
That quickens Nilus' slime, I go from hence
Thy soldier, servant; making peace or war
As thou affect'st.

    Cleo.   Cut my lace, Charmian, come :—
But let it be.—I am quickly ill and well:
So Antony loves!

    Ant.   My precious queen, forbear;
And give true evidence to his love which stands
An honourable trial.

    Cleo.   So Fulvia told me.
I pr'y thee turn aside and weep for her:
Then bid adieu to me, and say the tears
Belong to Egypt. Good now, play one scene
Of excellent dissembling, and let it look
Like perfect honour.

    Ant.   You'll heat my blood: no more.

    Cleo. You can do better yet: but this is meetly.

    Ant. Now, by my sword,—

    Cleo.   And target :—still he mends:
But this is not the best. Look, pr'y thee, Charmian,
How this Herculean Roman does become
The carriage of his chafe.

    Ant.   I'll leave you, lady.

    Cleo. Courteous lord, one word.
Sir, you and I must part;—but that's not it:
Sir, you and I have loved;—but there's not it:
That you know well. Something it is I would :—

O, my oblivion is a very Antony,
And I am all forgotten!

    Ant.   But that your royalty
Holds idleness your subject, I should take you
For idleness itself.

    Cleo.   'T is sweating labour
To bear such idleness so near the heart
As Cleopatra this. But, sir, forgive me;
Since my becomings kill me when they do not
Eye well to you. Your honour calls you hence:
Therefore be deaf to my unpitied folly,
And all the gods go with you: upon your sword
Sit laurelled victory; and smooth success
Be strewed before your feet!

    Ant.   Let us go: come.
Our separation so abides and flies,
That thou, residing here, goest yet with me,
And I, hence fleeting, here remain with thee.
Away !   [*Exeunt.*

SCENE IV.—Rome.   *An Apartment in* CÆSAR'S
                House.

Enter OCTAVIUS, CÆSAR, LEPIDUS, *and* Attendants.

    Cæs. You may see, Lepidus, and henceforth know
It is not Cæsar's natural vice to hate
One great competitor. From Alexandria
This is the news: he fishes, drinks, and wastes
The lamps of night in revel: is not more manlike
Than Cleopatra, nor the Queen of Ptolemy
More womanly than he: hardly gave audience,
Or vouchsafed to think he had partners. You
      shall find there
A man who is the abstract of all faults
That all men follow.

    Lep.   I must not think there are
Evils enough to darken all his goodness:
His faults in him seem as the spots of heaven,
More fiery by night's blackness: hereditary,
Rather than purchased: what he cannot change,
Than what he chooses.

    Cæs. You are too indulgent. Let's grant it
      is not
Amiss to tumble on the bed of Ptolemy;
To give a kingdom for a mirth; to sit
And keep the turn of tippling with a slave;
To reel the streets at noon, and stand the buffet
With knaves that smell of sweat: say this be-
      comes him
(As his composure must be rare indeed
Whom these things cannot blemish), yet must
      Antony
No way excuse his soils, when we do bear
So great weight in his lightness. If he filled
His vacancy with his voluptuousness,

Full surfeits and the dryness of his bones
Call on him for 't: but to confound such time
That drums him from his sport, and speaks as loud
As his own state and ours,—'t is to be chid
As we rate boys, who, being mature in knowledge,
Pawn their experience to their present pleasure,
And so rebel to judgment.

Enter a Messenger.

Lep.   Here 's more news.
Mess. Thy biddings have been done; and
          every hour,
Most noble Cæsar, shalt thou have report
How 't is abroad. Pompey is strong at sea,
And it appears he is beloved of those
That only have feared Cæsar: to the ports
The discontents repair, and men's reports
Give him much wronged.
Cæs.   I should have known no less:
It hath been taught us from the primal state
That he which is was wished, until he were;
And the ebbed man, ne'er loved till ne'er worth
          love,
Comes deared by being lacked. This common body,
Like to a vagabond flag upon the stream,
Goes to and back, lackeying the varying tide,
To rot itself with motion.
Mess.   Cæsar, I bring thee word
Menecrates and Menas, famous pirates,
Make the sea serve them, which they ear and
          wound
With keels of every kind. Many hot inroads
They make in Italy: the borders maritime
Lack blood to think on 't, and flush youth revolt.
No vessel can peep forth but 't is as soon
Taken as seen: for Pompey's name strikes more
Than could his war resisted.
Cæs.   Antony,
Leave thy lascivious wassels. When thou once
Wast beaten from Modena (where thou slew'st
Hirtius and Pansa, consuls), at thy heel
Did famine follow; whom thou fought'st against,
Though daintily brought up, with patience more
Than savages could suffer. Thou didst drink
The stale of horses and the gilded puddle
Which beasts would cough at: thy palate then
          did deign
The roughest berry on the rudest hedge:
Yea, like the stag when snow the pasture sheets,
The barks of trees thou browsed'st: on the Alps,
It is reported, thou didst eat strange flesh
Which some did die to look on. And all this
(It wounds thine honour that I speak it now)
Was borne so like a soldier that thy cheek
So much as lanked not!
Lep.   It is pity of him.
Cæs. Let his shames quickly

Drive him to Rome. 'T is time we twain
Did shew ourselves i' the field; and to that end,
Assemble we immediate council. Pompey
Thrives in our idleness.
Lep.   To-morrow, Cæsar,
I shall be furnished to inform you rightly
Both what by sea and land I can be able,
To front this present time.
Cæs.   Till which encounter
It is my business too. Farewell.
Lep. Farewell, my lord. What you shall
          know meantime
Of stirs abroad, I shall beseech you, sir,
To let me be partaker.
Cæs.   Doubt not, sir:
I knew it for my bond.   [*Exeunt.*

SCENE V.—Alexandria. *A Room in the Palace.*

Enter CLEOPATRA, CHARMIAN, IRAS, *and*
          MARDIAN.

Cleo. Charmian!
Char. Madam.
Cleo. Ha, ha!—
Give me to drink mandragora.
Char. Why, madam?
Cleo. That I might sleep out this great gap of
          time
My Antony is away.
Char.   You think of him too much.
Cleo. O, 't is treason!
Char. Madam, I trust not so.
Cleo. Thou, eunuch: Mardian!
Mar. What 's your highness' pleasure?
Cleo. Not now to hear thee sing: I take no
          pleasure
In aught an eunuch has. 'T is well for thee
That, being unseminared, thy freer thoughts
May not fly forth of Egypt. Hast thou affec-
          tions?
Mar. Yes, gracious madam.
Cleo. Indeed?
Mar. Not in deed, madam; for I can do
          nothing
But what indeed is honest to be done:
Yet have I fierce affections, and think
What Venus did with Mars.
Cleo.   O Charmian,
Where think'st thou he is now? Stands he, or
          sits he;
Or does he walk: or is he on his horse?
O happy horse, to bear the weight of Antony!
Do bravely, horse! for wott'st thou whom thou
          mov'st?
The demi-Atlas of this earth, the arm
And burgonet of men.—He 's speaking now,

Or murmuring, " Where's my serpent of old
    Nile?"
For so he calls me.   Now I feed myself
With most delicious poison !—Think on me,
That am with Phœbus' amorous pinches black,
And wrinkled deep in time ! Broad-fronted Cæsar,
When thou wast here above the ground, I was
A morsel for a monarch : and great Pompey
Would stand and make his eyes grow in my
    brow :
There would he anchor his aspéct, and die
With looking on his life.

Enter ALEXAS.

  Alex. Sovereign of Egypt, hail !
  Cleo. How much unlike art thou Marc Antony !
Yet, coming from him, that great medicine hath
With his tinct gilded thee.—
How goes it with my brave Marc Antony ?
  Alex. Last thing he did, dear queen,
He kissed (the last of many doubled kisses)
This orient pearl :—his speech sticks in my heart.
  Cleo. Mine ear must pluck it thence.
  Alex.   " Good friend (quoth he),
Say, The firm Roman to great Egypt sends
This treasure of an oyster : at whose foot,
To mend the petty present, I will piece
Her opulent throne with kingdoms.   All the
    east
(Say thou) shall call her mistress." So he nodded,
And soberly did mount an arm-gaunt steed,
Who neighed so high that what I would have
    spoke
Was beastly dumbed by him.
  Cleo.   What, was he sad or merry?

  Alex. Like to the time o' the year between the
    extremes
Of hot and cold : he was not sad nor merry.
  Cleo. O well divided disposition !—Note him,
Note him, good Charmian ; 't is the man : but
    note him,
He was not sad ; for he would shine on those
That make their looks by his : he was not merry ;
Which seemed to tell them his remembrance lay
In Egypt with his joy : but between both ;
O heavenly mingle !—Beest thou sad or merry,
The violence of either thee becomes :
So does it no man else.—Mett'st thou my posts ?
  Alex. Ay, madam, twenty several messengers.
Why do you send so thick ?
  Cleo.   Who 's born that day
When I forget to send to Antony,
Shall die a beggar.—Ink and paper, Charmian.—
Welcome, my good Alexas.—Did I, Charmian,
Ever love Cæsar so ?
  Char.   O that brave Cæsar !
  Cleo. Be choked with such another emphasis !
Say, the brave Antony.
  Char.   The valiant Cæsar !
  Cleo. By Isis, I will give thee bloody teeth
If thou with Cæsar paragon again
My man of men.
  Char.   By your most gracious pardon,
I sing but after you.
  Cleo.   My salad days,
When I was green in judgment :—cold in blood,
To say as I said then !—But come, away :
Get me ink and paper : he shall have every day
A several greeting, or I 'll unpeople Egypt.
                           [Exeunt.

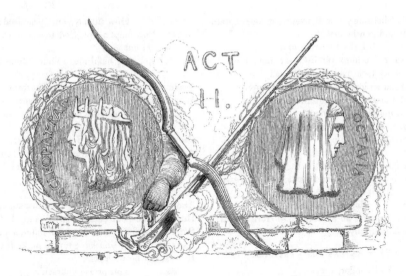

SCENE I.—Messina. *A Room in* POMPEY'S *House.*

Enter POMPEY, MENECRATES, *and* MENAS.

Pom. If the great gods be just, they shall assist
The deeds of justest men.

Mene.   Know, worthy Pompey,
That what they do delay they not deny.

Pom. Whiles we are suitors to their throne,
      decays
The thing we sue for.

Mene.   We, ignorant of ourselves,
Beg often our own harms, which the wise powers
Deny us for our good: so find we profit
By losing of our prayers.

Pom.   I shall do well:
The people love me, and the sea is mine:
My power's a crescent, and my auguring hope
Says it will come to the full.   Marc Antony
In Egypt sits at dinner, and will make
No wars without doors: Cæsar gets money where
He loses hearts: Lepidus flatters both,
Of both is flattered; but he neither loves,
Nor either cares for him.

Men.   Cæsar and Lepidus
Are in the field: a mighty strength they carry.

Pom. Where have you this? 'tis false.

Men.   From Silvius, sir.

Pom. He dreams: I know they are in Rome
      together,
Looking for Antony.   But all charms of love,
Salt Cleopatra, soften thy waned lip!
Let witchcraft join with beauty, lust with both!
Tie up the libertine in a field of feasts;
Keep his brains fuming: Epicurean cooks,
Sharpen with cloyless sauce his appetite,
That sleep and feeding may prorogue his honour
Even till a Lethe'd dulness!—How now, Varrius?

Enter VARRIUS.

Var. This is most certain that I shall deliver:
Marc Antony is every hour in Rome
Expected: since he went from Egypt 'tis
A space for further travel.

Pom.   I could have given less matter
A better ear.—Menas, I did not think
This amorous surfeiter would have donned his helm
For such a petty war: his soldiership
Is twice the other twain: but let us rear
The higher our opinion, that our stirring
Can from the lap of Egypt's widow pluck
The ne'er lust-wearied Antony.

Men.   I cannot hope
Cæsar and Antony shall well greet together:
His wife that's dead did trespasses to Cæsar;
His brother warred upon him: although, I think,
Not moved by Antony.

Pom.   I know not, Menas,
How lesser enmities may give way to greater.
Were't not that we stand up against them all,
'Twere pregnant they should square between
      themselves;
For they have entertainéd cause enough
To draw their swords: but how the fear of us
May cément their divisions, and bind up
The petty difference, we yet not know.
Be it as our gods will have it: it only stands
Our lives upon, to use our strongest hands.
Come, Menas.   [*Exeunt.*

SCENE II.—Rome. *A Room in the House of*
LEPIDUS.

Enter ENOBARBUS *and* LEPIDUS.

Lep. Good Enobarbus, 'tis a worthy deed,

And shall become you well, to entreat your captain
To soft and gentle speech.

Eno.   I shall entreat him
To answer like himself: if Cæsar move him,
Let Antony look over Cæsar's head,
And speak as loud as Mars. By Jupiter,
Were I the wearer of Antonius' beard,
I would not shave 't to-day.

Lep.   'T is not a time
For private stomaching.

Eno.   Every time
Serves for the matter that is then born in it.

Lep. But small to greater matters must give way.

Eno. Not if the small come first.

Lep.   Your speech is passion:
But pray you stir no embers up.—Here comes
The noble Antony.

        Enter ANTONY *and* VENTIDIUS.

Eno. And yonder, Cæsar.

        Enter CÆSAR, MECÆNAS, *and* AGRIPPA.

Ant. If we compose well here, to Parthia:
Hark, Ventidius.

Cæs. I do not know, Mecænas: ask Agrippa.

Lep. Noble friends,
That which combined us was most great, and let not
A leaner action rend us. What's amiss,
May it be gently heard: when we debate
Our trivial difference loud, we do commit
Murder in healing wounds. Then, noble partners
(The rather for I earnestly beseech),
Touch you the sourest points with sweetest terms,
Nor curstness grow to the matter.

Ant.   'T is spoken well:
Were we before our armies, and to fight,
I should do this.

Cæs. Welcome to Rome.

Ant. Thank you.

Cæs. Sit.

Ant. Sit, sir!

Cæs. Nay, then—

Ant. I learn you take things ill which are not so:
Or, being, concern you not.

Cæs.   I must be laughed at
If or for nothing, or a little, I
Should say myself offended: and with you
Chiefly i' the world: more laughed at, that I should
Once name you derogately, when to sound your
          name
It not concerned me.

Ant.   My being in Egypt, Cæsar,
What was 't to you?

Cæs. No more than my residing here at Rome
Might be to you in Egypt: yet if you there
Did practise on my state, your being in Egypt
Might be my question.

Ant.   How intend you "practised?"

Cæs. You may be pleased to catch at mine
          intent
By what did here befal me. Your wife and bro-
          ther
Made wars upon me: and their contestation
Was theme for you; you were the word of war.

Ant. You do mistake your business: my bro-
          ther never
Did urge me in his act: I did inquire it,
And have my learning from some true reports
That drew their swords with you. Did he not
          rather
Discredit my authority with yours,
And make the wars alike against my stomach,
Having alike your cause? Of this my letters
Before did satisfy you. If you 'll patch a quarrel,
As matter whole you have not to make it with,
It must not be with this.

Cæs.   You praise yourself
By laying defects of judgment to me: but
You patched up your excuses.

Ant.   Not so, not so:
I know you could not lack (I am certain on 't)
Very necessity of this thought, that I,
Your partner in the cause 'gainst which he fought,
Could not with graceful eyes attend those wars
Which 'fronted mine own peace. As for my wife,
I would you had her spirit in such another:
The third o' the world is yours; which with a
          snaffle
You may pace easy, but not such a wife.

Eno. ' Would we had all such wives, that the
men might go to wars with the women!

Ant. So much incurbable, her garboils, Cæsar,
Made out of her impatience (which not wanted
Shrewdness of policy too), I grieving grant
Did you too much disquiet: for that, you must
But say I could not help it.

Cæs.   I wrote to you
When rioting in Alexandria: you
Did pocket up my letters, and with taunts,
Did gibe my missive out of audience.

Ant.   Sir,
He fell upon me ere admitted: then
Three kings I had newly feasted, and did want
Of what I was i' the morning: but next day
I told him of myself; which was as much
As to have asked him pardon. Let this fellow
Be nothing of our strife: if we contend,
Out of our question wipe him.

Cæs.   You have broken
The article of your oath; which you shall never
Have tongue to charge me with.

Lep.   Soft, Cæsar.

Ant. No, Lepidus, let him speak:
The honour 's sacred which he talks on now,

Supposing that I lacked it. But on, Cæsar:
The article of my oath,—

Cæs. To lend me arms and aid, when I required them:
The which you both denied.

Ant. Neglected, rather:
And then when poisoned hours had bound me up
From mine own knowledge. As nearly as I may,
I 'll play the penitent to you: but mine honesty
Shall not make poor my greatness, nor my pov
Work without it. Truth is that Fulvia,
To have me out of Egypt, made wars here:
For which myself (the ignorant motive) do
So far ask pardon as befits mine honour
To stoop in such a case.

Lep. 'T is nobly spoken.

Mec. If it might please you to enforce no further
The griefs between ye: to forget them quite,
Were to remember that the present need
Speaks to atone you.

Lep. Worthily spoke, Mecænas.

Eno. Or if you borrow one another's love for
the instant, you may, when you hear no more
words of Pompey, return it again. You shall
have time to wrangle in, when you have nothing
else to do.

Ant. Thou art a soldier only: speak no more.

Eno. That truth should be silent I had almost
forgot.

Ant. You wrong this presence; therefore speak
no more.

Eno. Go to, then: your considerate stone.

Cæs. I do not much dislike the matter, but
The manner of his speech: for it cannot be
We shall remain in friendship, our conditions
So differing in their acts. Yet if I knew
What hoop should hold us staunch, from edge to
edge
O' the world I would pursue it.

Agr. Give me leave, Cæsar,—

Cæs. Speak, Agrippa.

Agr. Thou hast a sister by the mother's side,
Admired Octavia: great Marc Antony
Is now a widower.

Cæs. Say not so, Agrippa:
If Cleopatra heard you, your reproof
Were well deserved of rashness.

Ant. I am not married, Cæsar: let me hear
Agrippa further speak.

Agr. To hold you in perpetual amity,
To make you brothers, and to knit your hearts
With an unslipping knot, take Antony
Octavia to his wife: whose beauty claims
No worse a husband than the best of men;
Whose virtue and whose general graces speak
That which none else can utter. By this marriage,
All little jealousies which now seem great,

And all great fears which now import their dangers,
Would then be nothing: truths would be but tales,
Where now half tales be truths: her love to both
Would each to other, and all loves to both,
Draw after her. Pardon what I have spoke:
For 't is a studied, not a present thought,
By duty ruminated.

Ant. Will Cæsar speak?

Cæs. Not till he hears how Antony is touched
With what is spoke already.

Ant. What power is in Agrippa
If I would say, "Agrippa, be it so,"
To make this good?

Cæs. The power of Cæsar,
And his power unto Octavia.

Ant. May I never
To this good purpose, that so fairly shews,
Dream of impediment!—Let me have thy hand:
Further this act of grace; and from this hour
The heart of brothers govern in our loves,
And sway our great designs!

Cæs. There 's my hand.
A sister I bequeath you whom no brother
Did ever love so dearly: let her live
To join our kingdoms and our hearts; and never
Fly off our loves again!

Lep. Happily, amen!

Ant. I did not think to draw my sword 'gainst
Pompey;
For he hath laid strange courtesies, and great,
Of late upon me. I must thank him only,
Lest my remembrance suffer ill report:
At heel of that, defy him.

Lep. Time calls upon us:
Of us must Pompey presently be sought,
Or else he seeks out us.

Ant. Where lies he?

Cæs. About the Mount Misenum.

Ant. What is his strength by land?

Cæs. Great and increasing:
But by sea he is an absolute master.

Ant. So is the fame.
'Would we had spoke together! Haste we for it:
Yet, ere we put ourselves in arms, despatch we
The business we have talked of.

Cæs. With most gladness;
And do invite you to my sister's view,
Whither straight I will lead you.

Ant. Let us, Lepidus,
Not lack your company.

Lep. Noble Antony,
Not sickness should detain me.

[*Flourish. Exeunt* CÆSAR, ANTONY, *and*
LEPIDUS.

Mec. Welcome from Egypt, sir.

Eno. Half the heart of Cæsar, worthy Mecænas!—my honourable friend Agrippa!

Agr. Good Enobarbus!

Mec. We have cause to be glad that matters are so well digested. You stayed well by it in Egypt.

Eno. Ay, sir; we did sleep day out of countenance, and made the night light with drinking.

Mec. Eight wild boars roasted whole at a breakfast, and but twelve persons there: is this true?

Eno. This was but as a fly by an eagle: we had much more monstrous matter of feasts, which worthily deserved noting.

Mec. She's a most triumphant lady, if report be square to her.

Eno. When she first met Marc Antony, she pursed up his heart, upon the river of Cydnus.

Agr. There she appeared indeed! or my reporter devised well for her.

Eno. I will tell you:—
The barge she sat in, like a burnished throne,
Burned on the water: the poop was beaten gold;
Purple the sails, and so perfumed that
The winds were lovesick with them: the oars
    were silver;
Which to the tune of flutes kept stroke, and made
The water which they beat to follow faster,

As amorous of their strokes. For her own person,
It beggared all description : she did lie
In her pavilion (cloth of gold, of tissue),
O'erpicturing that Venus where we see
The fancy out-work nature : on each side her
Stood pretty dimpled boys, like smiling Cupids,
With divers-coloured fans, whose wind did seem
To glow the delicate cheeks which they did
    cool,
And what they undid did.

   Agr.   O rare for Antony!

   Eno. Her gentlewomen, like the Nereides,
So many mermaids, tended her i' the eyes,
And made their bends adornings : at the helm
A seeming mermaid steers : the silken tackle
Swell with the touches of those flower-soft hands
That yarely frame the office. From the barge
A strange invisible pérfume hits the sense
Of the adjacent wharfs. The city cast
Her people out upon her ; and Antony,
Enthroned in the market-place, did sit alone,
Whistling to the air ; which, but for vacancy,
Had gone to gaze on Cleopatra too,
And made a gap in nature.

   Agr.   Rare Egyptian!

   Eno. Upon her landing, Antony sent tò her ;
Invited her to supper : she replied,
It should be better he became her guest ;
Which she entreated. Our courteous Antony
(Whom ne'er the word of "No" woman heard
    speak),
Being barbered ten times o'er, goes to the feast ;
And for his ordinary pays his heart,
For what his eyes eat only.

   Agr.   Royal wench!
She made great Cæsar lay his sword to bed :
He ploughed her, and she cropped.

   Eno.   I saw her once
Hop forty paces through the public street :
And having lost her breath, she spoke and panted
That she did make defect perfection,
And (breathless) power breathe forth.

   Mec. Now Antony must leave her utterly.

   Eno. Never ; he will not :
Age cannot wither her, nor custom stale
Her infinite variety. Other women
Cloy th' appetites they feed, but she makes hungry
Where most she satisfies : for vilest things
Become themselves in her, that the holy priests
Bless her when she is riggish.

   Mec. If beauty, wisdom, modesty, can settle
The heart of Antony, Octavia is
A blesséd lottery to him.

   Agr.   Let us go.—
Good Enobarbus, make yourself my guest
Whilst you abide here.

   Eno.   Humbly, sir, I thank you. [*Exeunt.*

SCENE III.—*The same. A Room in* Cæsar's *House.*

Enter Cæsar, Antony, Octavia *between them ;*
    Attendants, *and a* Soothsayer.

   Ant. The world and my great office will some-
    times
Divide me from your bosom.

   Octa.   All which time
Before the gods my knee shall bow my prayers
To them for you.

   Ant.   Good night, sir.—My Octavia,
Read not my blemishes in the world's report :
I have not kept my square, but that to come
Shall all be done by the rule. Good night, dear
    lady.—

   Octa. Good night, sir.

   Cæs. Good night.
             [*Exeunt* Cæsar *and* Octavia.

   Ant. Now, sirrah ; you do wish yourself in
    Egypt ?

   Sooth. 'Would I had never come from thence ;
nor you thither!

   Ant. If you can, your reason ?

   Sooth. I see it in my motion ; have it not in
my tongue : but yet hie you to Egypt again.

   Ant.   Say to me,
Whose fortunes shall rise higher, Cæsar's or mine?

   Sooth. Cæsar's.
Therefore, O Antony, stay not by his side :
Thy dæmon (that 's thy spirit which keeps thee) is
Noble, courageous, high, unmatchable,
Where Cæsar's is not ; but near him, thy angel
Becomes a Fear, as being o'erpowered : therefore
Make space enough between you.

   Ant.   Speak this no more.

   Sooth. To none but thee : no more, but when
    to thee.—
If thou dost play with him at any game,
Thou art sure to lose, and of that natural luck
He beats thee 'gainst the odds : thy lustre thickens
When he shines by. I say again, thy spirit
Is all afraid to govern thee near him ;
But he away, 't is noble.

   Ant.   Get thee gone :
Say to Ventidius I would speak with him :—
             [*Exit* Soothsayer.
He shall to Parthia.—Be it art or hap,
He hath spoken true. The very dice obey him,
And in our sports my better cunning faints
Under his chance : if we draw lots, he speeds :
His cocks do win the battle still of mine
When it is all to nought ; and his quails ever
Beat mine, inhooped, at odds. I will to Egypt :
And though I make this marriage for my peace

Enter Ventidius.

I' the east my pleasure lies.—O! come, Ventidius,

You must to Parthia: your commission 's ready:
Follow me and receive it.   [*Exeunt.*

SCENE IV.—*The same. A Street.*

Enter LEPIDUS, MECÆNAS, *and* AGRIPPA.

Lep. Trouble yourselves no further: pray you,
      hasten
Your generals after.
Agr.   Sir, Marc Antony
Will e'en but kiss Octavia, and we 'll follow.
Lep. Till I shall see you in your soldier's dress,
Which will become you both, farewell.
Mec.   We shall,
As I conceive the journey, be at the Mount
Before you, Lepidus.
Lep.   Your way is shorter;
My purposes do draw me much about:
You 'll win two days upon me.
Mec. }
Agr. }   Sir, good success.
Lep. Farewell.   [*Exeunt.*

SCENE V.—Alexandria. *A Room in the Palace.*

Enter CLEOPATRA, CHARMIAN, IRAS, *and* ALEXAS.

Cleo. Give me some music: music, moody food
Of us that trade in love!
Attend. The music, ho!

Enter MARDIAN.

Cleo. Let it alone: let us to billiards. Come,
Charmian.
Char. My arm is sore; best play with Mardian.
Cleo. As well a woman with an eunuch played
As with a woman:—come, you 'll play with me,
      sir?
Mar. As well as I can, madam.
Cleo. And when good will is shewed, though
      it come too short,
The actor may plead pardon.—I 'll none now:
Give me mine angle; we 'll to the river: there,
My music playing far off, I will betray
Tawny-finned fishes: my bended hook shall pierce
Their slimy jaws; and, as I draw them up,
I 'll think them every one an Antony,
And say, "Ah, ah! you 're caught."
Char.   'T was merry when
You wagered on your angling: when your diver
Did hang a salt-fish on his hook, which he
With fervency drew up.
Cleo.   That time!—O times!—
I laughed him out of patience, and that night

I laughed him into patience: and next morn,
Ere the ninth hour, I drunk him to his bed;
Then put my tires and mantles on him, whilst
I wore his sword Philippan.—O! from Italy:—

Enter a Messenger.

Rain thou thy fruitful tidings in mine ears,
That long time have been barren.
Mess.   Madam, madam,—
Cleo. Antony 's dead?—
If thou say so, villain, thou kill'st thy mistress:
But well and free,
If thou so yield him, there is gold, and here
My bluest veins to kiss: a hand that kings
Have lipped, and trembled kissing.
Mess.   First, madam, he 's well.
Cleo. Why, there 's more gold. But, sirrah,
      mark: we use
To say "the dead are well." Bring it to that,
The gold I give thee will I melt, and pour
Down thy ill-uttering throat.
Mess. Good madam, hear me.
Cleo.   Well, go to; I will:
But there 's no goodness in thy face. If Antony
Be free and healthful, why so tart a favour
To trumpet such good tidings? If not well,
Thou shouldst come like a fury crowned with
      snakes;
Not like a formal man.
Mess. Will 't please you hear me?
Cleo. I have a mind to strike thee ere thou
      speak'st:
Yet, if thou say, Antony lives, is well,
Or friends with Cæsar, or not captive to him,
I 'll set thee in a shower of gold, and hail
Rich pearls upon thee.
Mess.   Madam, he 's well.
Cleo.   Well said.
Mess. And friends with Cæsar.
Cleo.   Thou 'rt an honest man.
Mess. Cæsar and he are greater friends than
      ever.
Cleo. Make thee a fortune from me.
Mess.   But yet, madam,—
Cleo. I do not like "but yet;" it does allay
The good precedence: fie upon "but yet:"
"But yet" is as a gaoler to bring forth
Some monstrous malefactor. Pr'y thee, friend,
Pour out the pack of matter to mine ear,
The good and bad together. He 's friends with
      Cæsar,
In state of health, thou sayst; and thou sayst,
      free.
Mess. Free, madam! no; I made no such
      report:
He 's bound unto Octavia.
Cleo.   For what good turn?

Mess. For the best turn i' the bed.
Cleo.   I am pale, Charmian.
Mess. Madam, he 's married to Octavia.
Cleo. The most infectious pestilence upon thee!
                                   [*Strikes him down.*

Mess. Good madam, patience.
Cleo. What say you? [*Strikes him again.*] Hence,
Horrible villain! or I 'll spurn thine eyes
Like balls before me: I 'll unhair thy head:
                                   [*She hales him up and down.*

Thou shalt be whipped with wire, and stewed in
          brine,
Smarting in lingering pickle!
     Mess.   Gracious madam,
I that do bring the news made not the match.
     Cleo. Say 't is not so, a province I will give thee,
And make thy fortunes proud: the blow thou hadst
Shall make thy peace for moving me to rage:
And I will boot thee with what gift beside
Thy modesty can beg.

Mess.   He 's married, madam.
Cleo. Rogue, thou hast lived too long!
                                   [*Draws a dagger.*
Mess. Nay, then I 'll run:—
What mean you, madam? I have made no fault.
                                   [*Exit.*
Char. Good madam, keep yourself within your-
          self:
The man is innocent.
     Cleo. Some innocents 'scape not the thunderbolt.

Melt Egypt into Nile, and kindly creatures
Turn all to serpents!—Call the slave again:˙
Though I am mad, I will not bite him.—Call.

　　Char. He is afeard to come.

　　Cleo.　　　　I will not hurt him:
These hands do lack nobility that they strike
A meaner than myself, since I myself
Have given myself the cause.—Come hither, sir:

Re-enter Messenger.

Though it be honest, it is never good
To bring bad news. Give to a gracious message
An host of tongues: but let ill tidings tell
Themselves when they be felt.

　　Mess.　　　　I have done my duty.

　　Cleo. Is he married?
I cannot hate thee worser than I do,
If thou again say—Yes.

　　Mess.　　　　He is married, madam.

　　Cleo. The gods confound thee! dost thou hold
　　　there still?

　　Mess. Should I lie, madam?

　　Cleo.　　　O, I would thou didst,
So half my Egypt were submerged, and made
A cistern for scaled snakes! Go, get thee hence:
Hadst thou Narcissus in thy face, to me
Thou wouldst appear most ugly. He is married?

　　Mess. I crave your highness' pardon.

　　Cleo.　　　　He is married?

　　Mess. Take no offence that I would not offend you:
To punish me for what you make me do,
Seems much unequal. He is married to Octavia.

　　Cleo. O that his fault should make a knave of
　　　thee,
That art not?—What? thou 'rt sure of 't?—Get
　　thee hence:
The merchandise which thou hast brought from
　　Rome
Are all too dear for me: lie they upon thy hand,
And be undone by 'em!　　*[Exit* Messenger.

　　Char.　　Good your highness, patience.

　　Cleo. In praising Antony, I have dispraised Cæsar.

　　Char. Many times, madam.

　　Cleo.　　　　I am paid for 't now.
Lead me from hence;
I faint: O Iras, Charmian!—'T is no matter.—
Go to the fellow, good Alexas: bid him
Report the feature of Octavia, her years,
Her inclination: let him not leave out
The colour of her hair. Bring me word quickly.—
　　　　　　　　　　　　[Exit ALEXAS.
Let him for ever go!—Let him not—Charmian,
Though he be painted one way like a Gorgon,
T' other way he 's a Mars.—Bid you Alexas
　　　　　　　　　　　　[To MARDIAN.
Bring me word how tall she is.—Pity me, Charmian,
But do not speak to me: lead me to my chamber.
　　　　　　　　　　　　　　　[Exeunt.

SCENE VI.—*Near* Misenum.

Enter POMPEY *and* MENAS, *at one side, with
drum and trumpet: at another,* CÆSAR, LE-
PIDUS, ANTONY, ENOBARBUS, MECÆNAS, *with*
Soldiers *marching.*

　　Pom. Your hostages I have, so have you mine;
And we shall talk before we fight.

　　Cæs.　　　Most meet
That first we come to words; and therefore have we
Our written purposes before us sent:
Which if thou hast considered, let us know
If 't will tie up thy discontented sword,
And carry back to Sicily much tall youth
That else must perish here.

　　Pom.　　　To you all three,
The senators alone of this great world,
Chief factors for the gods,—I do not know
Wherefore my father should revengers want,
Having a son and friends; since Julius Cæsar,
Who at Philippi the good Brutus ghosted,
There saw you labouring for him. What was it
That moved pale Cassius to conspire; and what
Made the all-honoured honest Roman, Brutus,
With the armed rest, courtiers of beauteous free-
　　dom,
To drench the Capitol; but that they would
Have one man but a man? And that is it
Hath made me rig my navy, at whose burden
The angered ocean foams; with which I meant
To scourge the ingratitude that despiteful Rome
Cast on my noble father.

　　Cæs.　　　Take your time.

　　Ant. Thou canst not fear us, Pompey, with
　　　thy sails;
We 'll speak with thee at sea: at land thou know'st
How much we do o'ercount thee.

　　Pom.　　　At land, indeed,
Thou dost o'ercount me of my father's house:
But, since the cuckoo builds not for himself,
Remain in 't as thou mayst.

　　Lep.　　　Be pleased to tell us
(For this is from the present) how you take
The offers we have sent you.

　　Cæs.　　　There 's the point.

　　Ant. Which do not be entreated to, but weigh
What it is worth embraced.

　　Cæs.　　　And what may follow
To try a larger fortune.

　　Pom.　　　You have made me offer
Of Sicily, Sardinia; and I must
Rid all the sea of pirates: then, to send
Measures of wheat to Rome. This 'greed upon,
To part with unhacked edges, and bear back
Our targe undinted.

　　Cæs. ⎫
　　Ant. ⎬　　That 's our offer.
　　Lep. ⎭

Pom.   Know, then,
I came before you here a man prepared
To take this offer: but Marc Antony
Put me to some impatience:—though I lose
The praise of it by telling, you must know,
When Cæsar and your brother were at blows,
Your mother came to Sicily, and did find
Her welcome friendly.

Ant.   I have heard it, Pompey;
And am well studied for a liberal thanks,
Which I do owe you.

Pom.   Let me have your hand:
I did not think, sir, to have met you here.

Ant. The beds i' the east are soft; and thanks
                    to you
That called me, timelier than my purpose, hither:
For I have gained by it.

Cæs.   Since I saw you last
There is a change upon you.

Pom.   Well, I know not
What counts harsh fortune casts upon my face:
But in my bosom shall she never come,
To make my heart her vassal.

Lep.   Well met here.

Pom. I hope so, Lepidus.—Thus we are agreed:
I crave our composition may be written,
And sealed between us.

Cæs.   That's the next to do.

Pom. We'll feast each other ere we part;
                    and let us
Draw lots who shall begin.

Ant.   That will I, Pompey.

Pom. No, Antony, take the lot: but, first
Or last, your fine Egyptian cookery
Shall have the fame. I have heard that Julius Cæsar
Grew fat with feasting there.

Ant.   You have heard much.

Pom. I have fair meanings, sir.

Ant.   And fair words to them.

Pom. Then so much have I heard:
And I have heard Apollodorus carried—

Eno. No more of that: he did so.

Pom.   What, I pray you?

Eno. A certain queen to Cæsar in a mattress.

Pom. I know thee now: how far'st thou, soldier?

Eno.   Well;
And well am like to do; for I perceive
Four feasts are toward.

Pom.   Let me shake thy hand:
I never hated thee. I have seen thee fight
When I have envied thy behaviour.

Eno.   Sir,
I never loved you much; but I have praised you
When you have well deserved ten times as much
As I have said you did.

Pom. Enjoy thy plainness;
It nothing ill becomes thee.—

Aboard my galley I invite you all:
Will you lead, lords?

Cæs.)
Ant. } Shew us the way, sir.
Lep.)

Pom. Come.

[*Exeunt* POMPEY, CÆSAR, ANTONY, LEPIDUS,
                    Soldiers, *and* Attendants.

Men. Thy father, Pompey, would ne'er have
made this treaty [*Aside*].—You and I have
known, sir.

Eno. At sea, I think.

Men. We have, sir.

Eno. You have done well by water.

Men. And you by land.

Eno. I will praise any man that will praise
me: though it cannot be denied what I have
done by land.

Men. Nor what I have done by water.

Eno. Yes, something you can deny for your
own safety: you have been a great thief by sea.

Men. And you by land.

Eno. There I deny my land service. But give
me your hand, Menas: if our eyes had authority,
here they might take two thieves kissing.

Men. All men's faces are true, whatsoe'er
their hands are.

Eno. But there is never a fair woman has a
true face.

Men. No slander: they steal hearts.

Eno. We came hither to fight with you.

Men. For my part, I am sorry it is turned to
a drinking. Pompey doth this day laugh away
his fortune.

Eno. If he do, sure he cannot weep it back again.

Men. You have said, sir. We looked not for
Marc Antony here: pray you is he married to
Cleopatra?

Eno. Cæsar's sister is called Octavia.

Men. True, sir: she was the wife of Caius
Marcellus.

Eno. But she is now the wife of Marcus
Antonius.

Men. Pray you, sir?

Eno. 'Tis true.

Men. Then is Cæsar and he for ever knit
together.

Eno. If I were bound to divine of this unity,
I would not prophesy so.

Men. I think the policy of that purpose made
more in the marriage than the love of the parties.

Eno. I think so too: but you shall find the
band that seems to tie their friendship together,
will be the very strangler of their amity. Octavia
is of a holy, cold, and still conversation.

Men. Who would not have his wife so?

Eno. Not he that himself is not so; which is

Marc Antony. He will to his Egyptian dish again: then shall the sighs of Octavia blow the fire up in Cæsar; and, as I said before, that which is the strength of their amity, shall prove the immediate author of their variance. Antony will use his affection where it is: he married but his occasion here.

Men. And thus it may be. Come, sir, will you aboard? I have a health for you.

Eno. I shall take it, sir: we have used our throats in Egypt.

Men. Come; let 's away.   [*Exeunt.*

SCENE VII.—*On board* POMPEY's *galley, lying near* Misenum.

Music. Enter two or three Servants, *with a banquet.*

1st Serv. Here they 'll be, man. Some o' their plants are ill-rooted already: the least wind i' the world will blow them down.

2nd Serv. Lepidus is high-coloured.

1st Serv. They have made him drink alms-drink.

2nd Serv. As they pinch one another by the disposition, he cries out, "no more:" reconciles them to his entreaty, and himself to the drink.

1st Serv. But it raises the greater war between him and his discretion.

2nd Serv. Why, this it is to have a name in great men's fellowship. I had as lief have a reed that will do me no service, as a partizan I could not heave.

1st Serv. To be called into a huge sphere, and not to be seen to move in 't, are the holes where eyes should be, which pitifully disaster the cheeks.

A Sennet sounded. Enter CÆSAR, ANTONY, POMPEY, LEPIDUS, AGRIPPA, MECÆNAS, ENOBARBUS, MENAS, *with other* Captains.

Ant. Thus do they, sir [*To* CÆSAR]. They take the flow o' the Nile
By certain scales i' the pyramid: they know,
By the height, the lowness, or the mean, if dearth
Or foizon follow: the higher Nilus swells,
The more it promises: as it ebbs, the seedsman
Upon the slime and ooze scatters his grain,
And shortly comes to harvest.

Lep. You have strange serpents there.

Ant. Ay, Lepidus.

Lep. Your serpent of Egypt is bred now of your mud, by the operation of your sun: so is your crocodile.

Ant. They are so.

Pom. Sit; and some wine.—A health to Lepidus.

Lep. I am not so well as I should be, but I 'll ne'er out.

Eno. Not till you have slept: I fear me you 'll be in till then.   [*Aside.*

Lep. Nay, certainly I have heard the Ptolemies' pyramises are very goodly things: without contradiction I have heard that.

Men. Pompey, a word.   [*Aside.*

Pom.   Say in mine ear: what is 't?

Men. Forsake thy seat, I do beseech thee. captain,
And hear me speak a word.

Pom.   Forbear me till anon.—
This wine for Lepidus.

Lep. What manner o' thing is your crocodile?

Ant. It is shaped, sir, like itself, and it is as broad as it hath breadth: it is just so high as it is, and moves with its own organs: it lives by that which nourisheth it; and the elements once out of it, it transmigrates.

Lep. What colour is it of?

Ant. Of its own colour too.

Lep. 'T is a strange serpent!

Ant. 'T is so: and the tears of it are wet.

Cæs. Will this description satisfy him? [*Aside.*

Ant. With the health that Pompey gives him, else he is a very epicure.

Pom. [*To* MENAS *aside*]. Go, hang, sir; hang! Tell me of that? away!
Do as I bid you.—Where 's this cup I called for?

Men. If for the sake of merit thou wilt hear me, Rise from thy stool.   [*Aside.*

Pom.   I think thou 'rt mad. The matter?   [*Walks aside.*

Men. I have ever held my cap off to thy fortunes.

Pom. Thou hast served me with much faith: what 's else to say?—
Be jolly, lords.

Ant.   These quicksands, Lepidus,
Keep off them, or you sink.

Men. Wilt thou be lord of all the world?

Pom.   What sayst thou?

Men. Wilt thou be lord of the whole world? That 's twice.

Pom. How should that be?

Men.   But entertain it,
And, though thou think me poor, I am the man
Will give thee all the world.

Pom.   Hast thou drunk well?

Men. No, Pompey, I have kept me from the cup.
Thou art, if thou dar'st be, the earthly Jove:
Whate'er the ocean pales, or sky inclips,
Is thine, if thou wilt have 't.

Pom.   Shew me which way.

Men. These three world-sharers, these competitors,
Are in thy vessel:—let me cut the cable;
And when we are put off, fall to their throats:
All then is thine.

Pom.   Ah, this thou shouldst have done,
And not have spoke on 't.   In me 'tis villany:
In thee it had been good service.   Thou must know,
'T is not my profit that does lead mine honour:
Mine honour it.   Repent that e'er thy tongue
Hath so betrayed thine act: being done unknown,
I should have found it afterwards well done;
But must condemn it now.   Desist and drink.
    Men. For this,   [*Aside.*
I 'll never follow thy palled fortunes more.
Who seeks, and will not take when once 't is
          offered,
Shall never find it more.
    Pom.   This health to Lepidus.
    Ant. Bear him ashore.—I 'll pledge it for him,
          Pompey.
    Eno. Here 's to thee, Menas.
    Men.   Enobarbus, welcome.
    Pom. Fill till the cup be hid.
    Eno. There 's a strong fellow, Menas.
[*Pointing to the* Attendant *who carries off* LEPIDUS.
    Men. Why?
    Eno. He bears the third part of the world,
man: seest not?
    Men. The third part, then, is drunk: 'would it
were all, that it might go on wheels!
    Eno. Drink thou: increase the reels.
    Men. Come.
    Pom. This is not yet an Alexandrian feast.
    Ant. It ripens towards it.—Strike the ves-
          sels, ho!
Here is to Cæsar.
    Cæs.   I could well forbear it.
It 's monstrous labour when I wash my brain
And it grows fouler.
    Ant.   Be a child o' the time.
    Cæs. Possess it; I 'll make answer:
But I had rather fast from all four days,
Than drink so much in one.
    Eno. Ha, my brave emperor!   [*To* ANTONY.
Shall we dance now the Egyptian Bacchanals,
And celebrate our drink?
    Pom.   Let 's ha 't, good soldier.
    Ant. Come, let us all take hands,

'Till that the conquering wine hath steeped our
          sense
In soft and delicate Lethe.
    Eno.   All take hands.—
Make battery to our ears with the loud music:—
The while I 'll place you.   Then the boy shall sing:
The holding every man shall bear, as loud
As his strong sides can volley.
[*Music plays.*   ENOBARBUS *places them hand in
          hand.*

SONG.

          Come, thou monarch of the vine,
          Plumpy Bacchus, with pink eyne:
          In thy vats our cares be drowned;
          With thy grapes our hairs be crowned.
          Cup us till the world go round:
          Cup us till the world go round!

    Cæs. What would you more?—Pompey, good
          night.—Good brother,
Let me request you off: our graver business
Frowns at this levity.—Gentle lords, let 's part:
You see we have burnt our cheeks: strong Eno-
          barbe
Is weaker than the wine; and mine own tongue
Splits what it speaks: the wild disguise hath almost
Anticked us all.   What needs more words?
          Good night.—
Good Antony, your hand.
    Pom.   I 'll try you o' the shore.
    Ant. And shall, sir: give 's your hand.
    Pom. O Antony, you have my father's house!—
But what? we are friends.   Come down into the
          boat.
    Eno. Take heed you fall not.
[*Exeunt* POMPEY, CÆSAR, ANTONY, & Attendants.
Menas, I 'll not on shore.
    Men. No, to my cabin.—
These drums! these trumpets, flutes! what!—
Let Neptune hear we bid a loud farewell
To these great fellows.   Sound, and be hanged;
          sound out!
          [*A flourish of trumpets, with drums.*
    Eno. Ho, says 'a!—There 's my cap.
    Men. Ho!—noble captain! Come. [*Exeunt.*

SCENE I.—*A Plain in* Syria.

Enter VENTIDIUS, *as after conquest, with* SILIUS,
and other Romans, Officers, *and* Soldiers: *the
dead body of* Pacorus *borne before him.*

Ven. Now, darting Parthia, art thou struck:
                and now
Pleased fortune does of Marcus Crassus' death
Make me revenger.—Bear the king's son's body
Before our army.—Thy Pacorus, Orodes,
Pays this for Marcus Crassus.

Sil.   Noble Ventidius,
Whilst yet with Parthian blood thy sword is
                warm,
The fugitive Parthians follow: spur through
                Media,
Mesopotamia, and the shelters whither
The routed fly: so thy grand captain Antony
Shall set thee on triumphant chariots, and
Put garlands on thy head.

Ven.   O Silius, Silius,
I have done enough. A lower place, note well,
May make too great an act: for learn this,
                Silius:
Better to leave undone, than by our deed
Acquire too high a fame when him we serve 's
                away.
Cæsar and Antony have ever won
More in their officer than person. Sossius,
One of my place in Syria, his lieutenant,
For quick accumulation of renown,
Which he achieved by the minute, lost his fa-
                vour.
Who does i' the wars more than his captain
                can,
Becomes his captain's captain: and ambition,
The soldier's virtue, rather makes choice of loss,
Than gain which darkens him.
I could do more to do Antonius good,
But 't would offend him; and in his offence
Should my performance perish.

Sil.   Thou hast, Ventidius, that
Without the which a soldier and his sword
Grants scarce distinction. Thou wilt write to
                Antony?

Ven. I 'll humbly signify what in his name,
That magical word of war, we have effected:
How with his banners, and his well-paid ranks,
The ne'er-yet beaten horse of Parthia
We have jaded out o' the field.

Sil.   Where is he now?

Ven. He purposeth to Athens: whither, with
                what haste
The weight we must convey with us will permit,
We shall appear before him.—On, there; pass
                along.   [*Exeunt.*

SCENE II.—Rome. *An Antechamber in* CÆSAR'S
                House.

Enter AGRIPPA *and* ENOBARBUS, *meeting.*

Agr. What, are the brothers parted?

Eno. They have despatched with Pompey;
                he is gone:
The other three are sealing. Octavia weeps
To part from Rome: Cæsar is sad: and Lepidus,
Since Pompey's feast, as Menas says, is troubled
With the green sickness.

Agr.   'T is a noble Lepidus.

Eno. A very fine one: O how he loves Cæsar!

Agr. Nay, but how dearly he adores Marc An-
                tony!

Eno. Cæsar? Why, he 's the Jupiter of men.

Agr. What 's Antony? the god of Jupiter.

Eno. Spake you of Cæsar? How! the nonpareil!

Agr. O Antony! O thou Arabian bird!

Eno. Would you praise Cæsar, say "Cæsar!"
go no further.

Agr. Indeed, he plied them both with excel-
                lent praises.

Eno. But he loves Cæsar best:—yet he loves
    Antony :
O ! hearts, tongues, figures, scribes, bards, poets,
    cannot
Think, speak, cast, write, sing, number, ho, his love
To Antony. But as for Cæsar !
Kneel down, kneel down, and wonder.

Agr.   Both he loves.

Eno. They are his shards, and he their beetle.
    So :—   [*Trumpets.*
This is to horse.—Adieu, noble Agrippa.

Agr. Good fortune, worthy soldier ; and fare-
    well.

Enter CÆSAR, ANTONY, LEPIDUS, *and* OCTAVIA.

Ant. No further, sir.

Cæs. You take from me a great part of myself :
Use me well in it.—Sister, prove such a wife
As my thoughts make thee, and as my farthest
    band
Shall pass on thy approof.—Most noble Antony,
Let not the piece of virtue which is set
Betwixt us as the cement of our love,
To keep it builded, be the ram to batter
The fortress of it : for better might we
Have loved without this mean, if on both parts
This be not cherished.

Ant.   Make me not offended
In your distrust.

Cæs.   I have said.

Ant.   You shall not find,
Though you be therein curious, the least cause
For what you seem to fear. So the gods keep you,
And make the hearts of Romans serve your ends !
We will here part.

Cæs. Farewell, my dearest sister ; fare thee well :
The elements be kind to thee, and make
Thy spirits all of comfort ! fare thee well.

Octa. My noble brother !

Ant. The April's in her eyes : it is love's spring,
And these the showers to bring it on.—Be cheerful.

Octa. Sir, look well to my husband's house ; and—

Cæs.   What, Octavia ?

Octa. I 'll tell you in your ear.

Ant. Her tongue will not obey her heart, nor can
Her heart inform her tongue :—the swan's down
    feather,
That stands upon the swell at the full of tide,
And neither way inclines.

Eno. Will Cæsar weep ?   [*Aside to* AGRIPPA.

Agr.   He has a cloud in 's face.

Eno. He were the worse for that were he a horse :
So is he being a man.

Agr.   Why, Enobarbus ?
When Antony found Julius Cæsar dead,
He cried almost to roaring : and he wept
When at Philippi he found Brutus slain.

Eno. That year, indeed, he was troubled with
    a rheum ;
What willingly he did confound, he wailed :
Believe 't till I weep too.

Cæs. No, sweet Octavia.
You shall hear from me still : the time shall not
Outgo my thinking on you.

Ant.   Come, sir, come ;
I 'll wrestle with you in my strength of love :—
Look, here I have you : thus I let you go,
And give you to the gods.

Cæs.   Adieu ; be happy !

Lep. Let all the number of the stars give light
To thy fair way !

Cæs. Farewell, farewell !   [*Kisses* OCTAVIA.

Ant. Farewell !   [*Trumpets sound. Exeunt.*

SCENE III.—Alexandria. *A Room in the Palace.*

Enter CLEOPATRA, CHARMIAN, IRAS, *and* ALEXAS.

Cleo. Where is the fellow ?

Alex.   Half afeard to come.

Cleo. Go to, go to.—Come hither, sir.

Enter a Messenger.

Alex.   Good majesty,
Herod of Jewry dare not look upon you
But when you are well pleased.

Cleo.   That Herod's head
I 'll have : but how ? when Antony is gone,
Through whom I might command it.—Come thou
    near.

Mess. Most gracious majesty,—

Cleo. Didst thou behold Octavia ?

Mess. Ay, dread queen.

Cleo. Where ?

Mess. Madam, in Rome
I looked her in the face, and saw her led
Between her brother and Marc Antony.

Cleo. Is she as tall as me ?

Mess.   She is not, madam.

Cleo. Didst hear her speak ?—is she shrill-
    tongued, or low ?

Mess. Madam, I heard her speak : she is low-
    voiced.

Cleo. That 's not so good : he cannot like her
    long.

Char. Like her ? O Isis ! 't is impossible.

Cleo. I think so, Charmian.—Dull of tongue
    and dwarfish !—
What majesty is in her gait ? Remember,
If e'er thou look'dst on majesty.

Mess.   She creeps :
Her motion and her station are as one :
She shews a body rather than a life ;
A statue than a breather.

Cleo.   Is this certain?

Mess. Or I have no observance.

Char.   Three in Egypt

Cannot make better note.

Cleo.   He 's very knowing;

I do perceive 't.—There 's nothing in her yet:

The fellow has good judgment.

    Char.   Excellent.

Cleo. Guess at her years, I pr'y thee.

Mess. Madam, she was a widow.

Cleo. Widow?—Charmian, hark.

Mess. And I do think she 's thirty.

Cleo. Bear'st thou her face in mind? is it long

      or round?

Mess. Round even to faultiness.

    Cleo.   For the most part, too,

They are foolish that are so.—Her hair, what

      colour?

Mess. Brown, madam: and her forehead is as

      low

As she would wish it.

    Cleo.   There 's gold for thee:

Thou must not take my former sharpness ill.

I will employ thee back again: I find thee

Most fit for business. Go, make thee ready:

Our letters are prepared.   [*Exit* Messenger.

    Char. A proper man.

Cleo. Indeed he is so: I repent me much

That so I harried him. Why, methinks, by him,

This creature 's no such thing.

    Char.   Nothing, madam.

Cleo. The man hath seen some majesty, and

      should know.

Char. Hath he seen majesty? Isis else defend,

And serving you so long!

    Cleo. I have one thing more to ask him yet,

      good Charmian:

But 't is no matter; thou shalt bring him to me

Where I will write. All may be well enough.

    Char. I warrant you, madam.   [*Exeunt.*

SCENE IV.—Athens. *A Room in* ANTONY's *House.*

Enter ANTONY *and* OCTAVIA.

Ant. Nay, nay, Octavia, not only that,—

That were excusable; that, and thousands more

Of semblable import:—but he hath waged

New wars 'gainst Pompey; made his will, and

      read it

To public ear:

Spoke scantly of me: when perforce he could not

But pay me terms of honour, cold and sickly

He vented them: most narrow measure lent me:

When the best hint was given him, he not took 't,

Or did it from his teeth.

Octa.   O my good lord,

Believe not all: or, if you must believe,

Stomach not all. A more unhappy lady,

If this division chance, ne'er stood between,

Praying for both parts:

And the good gods will mock me presently,

When I shall pray, " O, bless my lord and hus-

          band!"

Undo that prayer, by crying out as loud,

" O bless my brother!"—Husband win, win

          brother,

Prays, and destroys the prayer: no midway

'Twixt these extremes at all!

    Ant.   Gentle Octavia,

Let your best love draw to that point which seeks

Best to preserve it. If I lose mine honour,

I lose myself: better I were not yours,

Than yours so branchless. But, as you requested,

Yourself shall go between us: the meantime, lady,

I 'll raise the preparation of a war

Shall stain your brother. Make your soonest haste:

So your desires are yours.

    Octa.   Thanks to my lord.

The Jove of power make me (most weak, most

          weak!)

Your reconciler! Wars 'twixt you twain would be

As if the world should cleave, and that slain men

Should solder up the rift.

    Ant. When it appears to you where this begins,

Turn your displeasure that way: for our faults

Can never be so equal that your love

Can equally move with them. Provide your going;

Choose your own company, and command what

      cost

Your heart has mind to.   [*Exeunt.*

SCENE V.—*The same. Another Room in*

ANTONY's *House.*

Enter ENOBARBUS *and* EROS, *meeting.*

Eno. How now, friend Eros?

Eros. There 's strange news come, sir.

Eno. What, man?

Eros. Cæsar and Lepidus have made wars upon

      Pompey.

Eno. This is old: what is the success?

Eros. Cæsar, having made use of him in the

wars 'gainst Pompey, presently denied him ri-

vality; would not let him partake in the glory

of the action; and not resting here, accuses him

of letters he had formerly wrote to Pompey:

upon his own appeal, seizes him. So the poor

third is up, till death enlarge his confine.

Eno. Then, world, thou hast a pair of chaps;

      no more:

And throw between them all the food thou hast,
They 'll grind the one the other. Where 's Antony?

Eros. He 's walking in the garden—thus; and
spurns
The rush that lies before him: cries, " Fool,
Lepidus!"
And threats the throat of that his officer
That murdered Pompey.

Eno. Our great navy 's rigged.

Eros. For Italy and Cæsar. More, Domitius:
My lord desires you presently. My news
I might have told hereafter.

Eno. 'T will be naught:
But let it be.—Bring me to Antony.

Eros. Come, sir. [*Exeunt.*

SCENE VI.—Rome. *A Room in* CÆSAR's *House.*

Enter CÆSAR, AGRIPPA, *and* MECÆNAS.

Cæs. Contemning Rome, he has done all this.
And more:
In Alexandria,—here 's the manner of it,—
I' the market-place, on a tribunal silvered,
Cleopatra and himself in chairs of gold
Were publicly enthroned: at the feet sat
Cæsarion, whom they call my father's son;
And all the unlawful issue that their lust
Since then hath made between them. Unto her
He gave the 'stablishment of Egypt: made her
Of Lower Syria, Cyprus, Lybia,
Absolute queen.

Mec. This in the public eye?

Cæs. I' the common show-place, where they
exercise.
His sons he there proclaimed "The kings of
kings."
Great Media, Parthia, and Armenia,
He gave to Alexander: to Ptolemy he assigned
Syria, Cilicia, and Phœnicia. She
In the habiliments of the goddess Isis
That day appeared: and oft before gave audience
(As 't is reported) so.

Mec. Let Rome be thus informed.

Agr. Who, queasy with his insolence already,
Will their good thoughts call from him.

Cæs. The people know it; and have now received
His accusations.

Agr. Whom does he accuse?

Cæs. Cæsar: and that, having in Sicily
Sextus Pompeius spoiled, we had not rated him
His part o' the isle: then does he say, he lent me
Some shipping unrestored: lastly, he frets
That Lepidus of the triumvirate
Should be deposed; and, being, that we detain
All his revénue.

Agr. Sir, this should be answered.

Cæs. 'T is done already, and the messenger
gone.
I have told him Lepidus was grown too cruel;
That he his high authority abused,
And did deserve his change: for what I 've con-
quered,
I grant him part: but then, in his Armenia,
And other of his conquered kingdoms,
I demand the like.

Mec. He 'll never yield to that.

Cæs. Nor must not, then, be yielded to in this.

Enter OCTAVIA.

Octa. Hail, Cæsar, and my lord! hail, most
dear Cæsar!

Cæs. That ever I should call thee " cast-away!"

Octa. You have not called me so, nor have you
cause.

Cæs. Why have you stolen upon us thus? You
come not
Like Cæsar's sister. The wife of Antony
Should have an army for an usher, and
The neighs of horse to tell of her approach,
Long ere she did appear: the trees by the way
Should have borne men, and expectation fainted,
Longing for what it had not: nay, the dust
Should have ascended to the roof of heaven,
Raised by your populous troops: but you are come
A market-maid to Rome, and have prevented
The ostent of our love, which left unshewn
Is often left unloved. We should have met you
By sea and land; supplying every stage
With an augmented greeting.

Octa. Good my lord,
To come thus was I not constrained, but did it
On my free will. My lord, Marc Antony,
Hearing that you prepared for war, acquainted
My grieved ear withal: whereon I begged
His pardon for return.

Cæs. Which soon he granted,
Being an obstruct 'tween his lust and him.

Octa. Do not say so, my lord,

Cæs. I have eyes upon him,
And his affairs come to me on the wind.
Where is he now?

Octa. My lord, in Athens.

Cæs. No, my most wronged sister: Cleopatra
Hath nodded him to her. He hath given his
empire
Up to a whore; who now are levying
The kings o' the earth for war. He hath assembled
Bocchus, the King of Lybia; Archelaus,
Of Cappadocia; Philadelphos, King
Of Paphlagonia; the Thracian King, Adallas;
King Malchus of Arabia; King of Pont;
Herod of Jewry; Mithridates, King
Of Comagene; Polemon and Amintas,

The Kings of Mede and Lycaonia; with a
More larger list of sceptres.

Octa.   Ah me, most wretched,
That have my heart parted betwixt two friends
That do afflict each other!

Cæs.   Welcome hither:
Your letters did withhold our breaking forth,
Till we perceived both how you were wrong led,
And we in negligent danger. Cheer your heart:
Be you not troubled with the time, which drives
O'er your content these strong necessities;
But let determined things to destiny
Hold unbewailed their way. Welcome to Rome:
Nothing more dear to me. You are abused
Beyond the mark of thought: and the high gods,
To do you justice, make their ministers
Of us and those that love you. Best of comfort;
And ever welcome to us.

Agr.   Welcome, lady.

Mec. Welcome, dear madam.
Each heart in Rome does love and pity you:
Only the adulterous Antony, most large
In his abominations, turns you off;
And gives his potent regiment to a trull,
That noises it against us.

Octa.   Is it so, sir?

Cæs. Most certain. Sister, welcome: pray you
Be ever known to patience. My dearest sister!
                                  [*Exeunt.*

Scene VII.—Antony's *Camp, near the Promontory of* Actium.

Enter Cleopatra *and* Enobarbus.

Cleo. I will be even with thee, doubt it not.

Eno. But why, why, why?

Cleo. Thou hast forspoke my being in these
      wars;
And sayst it is not fit.

Eno.   Well, is it, is it?

Cleo. Is 't not? Denounce against us, why
      not we
Be there in person?

Eno. [*aside*]. Well, I could reply.
If we should serve with horse and mares together,
The horse were merely lost: the mares would
      bear
A soldier and his horse.

Cleo.   What is 't you say?

Eno. Your presence needs must puzzle Antony;
Take from his heart, take from his brain, from
      his time,
What should not then be spared. He is already
Traduced for levity; and 't is said in Rome
That Photinus an eunuch, and your maids,
Manage this war.

Cleo.   Sink Rome, and their tongues rot
That speak against us! A charge we bear i' the war,
And, as the president of my kingdom, will
Appear there for a man. Speak not against it:
I will not stay behind.

Eno.   Nay, I have done:
Here comes the emperor.

Enter Antony *and* Canidius.

Ant.   Is it not strange, Canidius,
That from Tarentum and Brundusium
He could so quickly cut the Ionian sea,
And take in Toryne!—You have heard on 't,
      sweet?

Cleo. Celerity is never more admired
Than by the negligent.

Ant.   A good rebuke,
Which might have well becomed the best of men,
To taunt at slackness.—Canidius, we
Will fight with him by sea.

Cleo.   By sea! What else?

Can. Why will my lord do so?

Ant.   For he dares us to 't.

Eno. So hath my lord dared him to single fight.

Can. Ay, and to wage this battle at Pharsalia,
Where Cæsar fought with Pompey. But these
      offers,
Which serve not for his vantage, he shakes off:
And so should you.

Eno.   Your ships are not well manned:
Your mariners are muleteers, reapers, people
Ingrossed by swift impress: in Cæsar's fleet
Are those that often have 'gainst Pompey fought.
Their ships are yare: yours heavy. No disgrace
Shall fall you for refusing him at sea,
Being prepared for land.

Ant.   By sea, by sea.

Eno. Most worthy sir, you therein throw away
The absolute soldiership you have by land;
Distract your army, which doth most consist
Of war-marked footmen; leave unexecuted
Your own renownéd knowledge; quite forego
The way which promises assurance; and
Give up yourself merely to chance and hazard,
From firm security.

Ant.   I 'll fight at sea.

Cleo. I have sixty sails, Cæsar none better.

Ant. Our overplus of shipping will we burn;
And with the rest full-manned, from the head
      of Actium
Beat the approaching Cæsar. But if we fail,

Enter a Messenger.

We then can do 't at land.—Thy business?

Mess. The news is true, my lord: he is
      descried:
Cæsar has taken Toryne.

Ant. Can he be there in person? 't is impossible:
Strange that his power should be.—Canidius,
Our nineteen legions thou shalt hold by land,
And our twelve thousand horse.—We 'll to our
　　　ship :

Enter a Soldier.

Away, my Thetis!—How now, worthy soldier?
Sol. O noble emperor, do not fight by sea;
Trust not to rotten planks.　Do you misdoubt
This sword, and these my wounds?　Let the
　　　Egyptians
And the Phœnicians go a ducking : we
Have used to conquer standing on the earth,
And fighting foot to foot.
　　Ant.　　　Well, well, away.
[*Exeunt* ANTONY, CLEOPATRA, *and* ENOBARBUS.
　　Sol. By Hercules, I think I am i' the right.
　　Can. Soldier, thou art; but his whole action
　　　　grows
Not in the power on't : so our leader 's led,
And we are women's men.
　　Sol.　　　You keep by land
The legions and the horse whole, do you not?
　　Can. Marcus Octavius, Marcus Justeius,
Publicola, and Cælius, are for sea :
But we keep whole by land. This speed of Cæsar's
Carries beyond belief.
　　Sol.　　　While he was yet in Rome
His power went out in such distractions
As beguiled all spies.
　　Can.　　　Who 's his lieutenant, hear you?
　　Sol. They say, one Taurus.
　　Can.　　　Well I know the man.

Enter a Messenger.

Mess. The emperor calls Canidius.
Can. With news the time 's with labour, and
　　　throes forth
Each minute some.　　　　　　　　[*Exeunt.*

SCENE VIII.—*A Plain near* Actium.

Enter CÆSAR, TAURUS, Officers, *and others.*

Cæs. Taurus!
Taur.　　My lord.
Cæs.　　　Strike not by land ; keep whole :
Provoke not battle till we have done at sea.
Do not exceed the prescript of this scroll :
Our fortune lies upon this jump.　[*Exeunt.*

Enter ANTONY *and* ENOBARBUS.

Ant. Set we our squadrons on yon side o' the hill,
In eye of Cæsar's battle : from which place
We may the number of the ships behold,
And so proceed accordingly.　　　[*Exeunt.*

Enter CANIDIUS, *marching with his land Army one
way over the stage ; and* TAURUS, *the* Lieutenant
of CÆSAR, *the other way.　After their going in,
is heard the noise of a sea-fight.*

Alarum.　Re-enter ENOBARBUS.

Eno. Naught, naught, all naught ! I can be-
　　　hold no longer :
The Antoniad, the Egyptian admiral,
With all their sixty, fly, and turn the rudder :
To see 't mine eyes are blasted !

Enter SCARUS.

Scar.　　　Gods and goddesses,
All the whole synod of them !
　　Eno.　　　What 's thy passion?
　　Scar. The greater cantle of the world is lost
With very ignorance : we have kissed away
Kingdoms and provinces.
　　Eno.　　　How appears the fight?
　　Scar. On our side like the tokened pestilence,
Where death is sure. Yon' ribald-rid nag of Egypt,
(Whom leprosy o'ertake !) i' the midst o' the fight,
When vantage like a pair of twins appeared,
Both as the same, or rather ours the elder,—
The brize upon her, like a cow in June,
Hoists sails and flies.
　　Eno.　　　That I beheld : mine eyes
Did sicken at the sight, and could not
Endure a further view.
　　Scar.　　　She once being loofed,
The noble ruin of her magic, Antony,
Claps on his sea-wing, and, like a doting mallard,
Leaving the fight in height, flies after her.
I never saw an action of such shame !
Experience, manhood, honour, ne'er before
Did violate so itself.
　　Eno.　　　Alack, alack !

Enter CANIDIUS.

Can. Our fortune on the sea is out of breath,
And sinks most lamentably.　Had our general
Been what he knew himself, it had gone well :
O, he has given example for our flight,
Most grossly, by his own.
　　Eno. Ay, are you thereabouts?　Why then
　　　good night, indeed !　　　　　[*Aside.*
　　Can. Towards Peloponnesus are they fled.
　　Scar. 'T is easy to 't : and there I will attend
What further comes.
　　Can.　　　To Cæsar will I render
My legions and my horse : six kings already
Shew me the way of yielding.
　　Eno.　　　I 'll yet follow
The wounded chance of Antony, though my
　　　reason
Sits in the wind against me.　　　[*Exeunt.*

SCENE IX.—Alexandria. *A Room in the Palace.*

Enter ANTONY *and* Attendants.

Ant. Hark! the land bids me tread no more
    upon 't:
It is ashamed to bear me!—Friends, come hither:
I am so lated in the world that I
Have lost my way for ever. I have a ship

Laden with gold: take that; divide it: fly,
And make your peace with Cæsar.
  Att.   Fly! not we.
  Ant. I have fled myself, and have instructed
    cowards
To run and shew their shoulders.—Friends, be-
    gone:
I have myself resolved upon a course

Which has no need of you: begone.
My treasure's in the harbour; take it.—O,
I followed that I blushed to look upon!
My very hairs do mutiny: for the white
Reprove the brown for rashness, and they them
For fear and doting.—Friends, begone: you shall
Have letters from me to some friends that will
Sweep your way for you. Pray you, look not sad,
Nor make replies of loathness: take the hint
Which my despair proclaims; let that be left
Which leaves itself. To the sea-side straightway:
I will possess you of that ship and treasure.

Leave me, I pray, a little: 'pray you now.—
Nay, do so; for indeed I have lost command;
Therefore I pray you.—I 'll see you by-and-by.
                      [Sits down.

Enter EROS *and* CLEOPATRA, *led by* CHARMIAN
and IRAS.

  Eros. Nay, gentle madam, to him:—comfort him.
  Iras. Do, most dear queen.
  Char. Do! Why, what else?
  Cleo. Let me sit down. O Juno!
  Ant. No, no, no, no, no.

Eros. See you here, sir?

Ant. O fie, fie, fie!

Char. Madam,—

Iras. Madam; O good empress!

Eros. Sir, sir,—

Ant. Yes, my lord, yes:—he at Philippi kept
His sword even like a dancer, while I struck
The lean and wrinkled Cassius; and 't was I
That the mad Brutus ended: he alone
Dealt on lieutenantry, and no practice had
In the brave squares of war: yet now—no matter.

Cleo. Ah, stand by.

Eros. The queen, my lord; the queen.

Iras. Go to him, madam; speak to him:
He is unqualitied with very shame.

Cleo. Well then, sustain me.—O!

Eros. Most noble sir, arise; the queen approaches:
Her head 's declined, and death will seize her; but
Your comfort makes the rescue.

Ant. I have offended reputation:
A most unnoble swerving!

Eros. Sir, the queen.

Ant. O, whither hast thou led me, Egypt? See
How I convey my shame out of thine eyes,
By looking back on what I have left behind
'Stroyed in dishonour.

Cleo. O my lord, my lord,
Forgive my fearful sails! I little thought
You would have followed.

Ant. Egypt, thou knew'st too well
My heart was to thy rudder tied by the strings,
And thou shouldst tow me after. O'er my spirit
Thy full supremacy thou knew'st, and that
Thy beck might from the bidding of the gods
Command me.

Cleo. O, my pardon!

Ant. Now I must
To the young man send humble treaties, dodge
And palter in the shifts of lowness: who
With half the bulk o' the world played as I
pleased,
Making and marring fortunes. You did know
How much you were my conqueror; and that
My sword, made weak by my affection, would
Obey it on all cause.

Cleo. O pardon, pardon!

Ant. Fall not a tear, I say: one of them rates
All that is won and lost! Give me a kiss:
Even this repays me.—We sent our schoolmaster;
Is he come back?—Love, I am full of lead:—
Some wine, within there, and our viands:—fortune knows
We scorn her most, when most she offers blows.

[*Exeunt.*

SCENE X.—Cæsar's *Camp, in* Egypt.

Enter Cæsar, Dolabella, Thyreus, *and others.*

Cæs. Let him appear that 's come from Antony.—
Know you him?

Dol. Cæsar, 't is his schoolmaster:
An argument that he is plucked, when hither
He sends so poor a pinion of his wing,
Which had superfluous kings for messengers,
Not many moons gone by.

Enter Euphronius.

Cæs. Approach, and speak.

Eup. Such as I am, I come from Antony:
I was of late as petty to his ends
As is the morn-dew on the myrtle-leaf
To his grand sea.

Cæs. Be it so: declare thine office.

Eup. Lord of his fortunes he salutes thee, and
Requires to live in Egypt: which not granted,
He lessens his requests, and to thee sues
To let him breathe between the heavens and earth,
A private man, in Athens. This for him.
Next, Cleopatra does confess thy greatness;
Submits her to thy might, and of thee craves
The circle of the Ptolemies for her heirs,
Now hazarded to thy grace.

Cæs. For Antony,
I have no ears to his request. The queen
Of audience nor desire shall fail, so she
From Egypt drive her all disgracéd friend,
Or take his life there: this if she perform,
She shall not sue unheard. So to them both.

Eup. Fortune pursue thee!

Cæs. Bring him through the bands.

[*Exit* Euphronius.
To try thy eloquence now 't is time: [*To* Thyreus.
despatch:
From Antony win Cleopatra: promise,
And in our name, what she requires: add more
(From thine invention) offers. Women are not
In their best fortunes strong; but want will perjure
The ne'er-touched vestal. Try thy cunning, Thyreus:
Make thine own edict for thy pains; which we
Will answer as a law.

Thyr. Cæsar, I go.

Cæs. Observe how Antony becomes his flaw;
And what thou think'st his very action speaks
In every power that moves.

Thyr. Cæsar, I shall. [*Exeunt.*

Scene XI.—Alexandria. *A Room in the Palace.*

Enter Cleopatra, Enobarbus, Charmian, *and*
                        Iras.

Cleo. What shall we do, Enobarbus?
Eno.   Think, and die.
Cleo. Is Antony or we in fault for this?
Eno. Antony only, that would make his will
Lord of his reason. What though you fled
From that great face of war, whose several ranges
Frighted each other, why should he follow?
The itch of his affection should not then
Have nicked his captainship; at such a point,
When half to half the world opposed, he being
The meréd question: 'Twas a shame no less
Than was his loss, to course your flying flags,
And leave his navy gazing.
Cleo.   Pr'y thee, peace.

        Enter Antony, *with* Euphronius.

Ant. Is this his answer?
Eup. Ay, my lord.
Ant. The queen shall, then, have courtesy, so
                        she
Will yield us up.
Eup. He says so.
Ant.   Let her know it.—
To the boy Cæsar send this grizzled head,
And he will fill thy wishes to the brim
With principalities.
Cleo.   That head, my lord?
Ant. To him again. Tell him, he wears the rose
Of youth upon him; from which the world should
                        note
Something particular. His coin, ships, legions,
May be a coward's; whose ministers would prevail
Under the service of a child, as soon
As i' the command of Cæsar. I dare him, therefore,
To lay his gay comparisons apart,
And answer me (declined), sword against sword,
Ourselves alone. I 'll write it: follow me.
            [*Exeunt* Antony *and* Euphronius.
Eno. Yes, like enough high-battled Cæsar will
Unstate his happiness, and be staged to the s.. w
Against a sworder!—I see men's judgments are
A parcel of their fortunes; and things outward
Do draw the inward quality after them,
To suffer all alike. That he should dream,
Knowing all measures, the full Cæsar will
Answer his emptiness!—Cæsar, thou hast subdued
His judgment too.

        Enter an Attendant.

Att.   A messenger from Cæsar.
Cleo. What, no more ceremony?—See, my
                        women!
Against the blown rose may they stop their nose,
That kneeled unto the buds.—Admit him, sir.

Eno. Mine honesty and I begin to square.
                                [*Aside.*
The loyalty well held to fools does make
Our faith mere folly : yet he that can endure
To follow with allegiance a fallen lord,
Does conquer him that did his master conquer,
And earns a place i' the story.

        Enter Thyreus.

Cleo.   Cæsar's will?
Thyr. Hear it apart.
Cleo. None but friends : say boldly.
Thyr. So, haply, are they friends to Antony.
Eno. He needs as many, sir, as Cæsar has;
Or needs not us. If Cæsar please, our master
Will leap to be his friend: for us, you know
Whose he is we are; and that 's Cæsar's.
Thyr.   So.—
Thus then, thou most renowned : Cæsar entreats
Not to consider in what case thou stand'st,
Further than he is Cæsar.
Cleo.   Go on :—right royal.
Thyr. He knows that you embrace not Antony
As you did love, but as you feared him.
Cleo.   O!
Thyr. The scars upon your honour, therefore,
                        he
Does pity as constrainéd blemishes,
Not as deserved.
Cleo.   He is a god, and knows
What is most right : mine honour was not yielded,
But conquered merely.
Eno.   To be sure of that,   [*Aside.*
I will ask Antony.—Sir, sir, thou 'rt so leaky
That we must leave thee to thy sinking; for
Thy dearest quit thee.   [*Exit* Enobarbus.
Thyr.   Shall I say to Cæsar
What you require of him? for he partly begs
To be desired to give. It much would please him
That of his fortunes you should make a staff
To lean upon : but it would warm his spirits
To hear from me you had left Antony,
And put yourself under his shroud,
The universal landlord.
Cleo.   What 's your name?
Thyr. My name is Thyreus.
Cleo.   Most kind messenger,
Say to great Cæsar this :—In deputation
I kiss his conquering hand : tell him I am prompt
To lay my crown at his feet, and there to kneel:
Tell him from his all-obeying breath I hear
The doom of Egypt.
Thyr. 'T is your noblest course.
Wisdom and fortune combating together,
If that the former dare but what it can,
No chance may shake it. Give me grace to lay
My duty on your hand.

Cleo.   Your Cæsar's father
Oft, when he hath mused of taking kingdoms in,
Bestowed his lips on that unworthy place
As it rained kisses.

Re-enter ANTONY *and* ENOBARBUS.

Ant.   Favours, by Jove that thunders!—
What art thou, fellow?
Thyr.   One that but performs
The bidding of the fullest man and worthiest
To have command obeyed.
Eno.   You will be whipped.
Ant. Approach, there:—ay, you kite!—Now
          gods and devils!
Authority melts from me. Of late, when I cried "Ho!"
Like boys unto a muss, kings would start forth,
And cry, "Your will?"—Have you no ears?—I am

Enter Attendants.

Antony yet.—Take hence this Jack, and whip him.
Eno. 'T is better playing with a lion's whelp,
Than with an old one dying.
Ant.   Moon and stars!
Whip him.—Were 't twenty of the greatest tri-
          butaries
That do acknowledge Cæsar, should I find them
So saucy with the hand of she here,—(what's her
          name
Since she was Cleopatra?)—Whip him, fellows,
Till, like a boy you see him cringe his face,
And whine aloud for mercy. Take him hence.
Thyr. Marc Antony,—
Ant.   Tug him away: being whipped,
Bring him again.—This Jack of Cæsar's shall
Bear us an errand to him.—
          [*Exeunt* Attendants *with* THYREUS.
You were half blasted ere I knew you.—Ha!
Have I my pillow left unpressed in Rome,
Forborne the getting of a lawful race,
And by a gem of women, to be abused
By one that looks on feeders?
Cleo.   Good my lord,—
Ant. You have been a boggler ever:—
But when we in our viciousness grow hard,
(O misery on 't!) the wise gods seel our eyes;
In our own filth drop our clear judgments; make us
Adore our errors; laugh at us, while we strut
To our confusion.
Cleo.   O, is it come to this?
Ant. I found you as a morsel cold upon
Dead Cæsar's trencher: nay, you were a fragment
Of Cneius Pompey's: besides what hotter hours,
Unregistered in vulgar fame, you have
Luxuriously picked out: for I am sure,
Though you can guess what temperance should be,
You know not what it is.
Cleo.   Wherefore is this?

Ant. To let a fellow that will take rewards,
And say " God quit you!" be familiar with
My playfellow, your hand; this kingly seal,
And plighter of high hearts!—O, that I were
Upon the hill of Basan, to outroar
The hornéd herd! for I have savage cause;
And to proclaim it civilly were like
A haltered neck which does the hangman thank
For being yare about him.—Is he whipped?

Re-enter Attendants *with* THYREUS.

1st Atten. Soundly, my lord.
Ant.   Cried he, and begged he pardon?
1st Atten. He did ask favour.
Ant. If that thy father live, let him repent
Thou wast not made his daughter; and be thou sorry
To follow Cæsar in his triumph, since
Thou hast been whipped for following him: henceforth
The white hand of a lady fever thee:
Shake thou to look on 't.— Get thee back to Cæsar,
Tell him thy entertainment. Look thou say
He makes me angry with him: for he seems
Proud and disdainful; harping on what I am,
Not what he knew I was. He makes me angry:
And at this time most easy 't is to do it;
When my good stars, that were my former guides,
Have empty left their orbs, and shot their fires
Into the abysm of hell. If he mislike
My speech and what is done, tell him he has
Hipparchus, my enfranchised bondman, whom
He may at pleasure whip, or hang, or torture,
As he shall like, to quit me: urge it thou.
Hence, with thy stripes; begone! [*Exit* THYREUS.
Cleo. Have you done yet?
Ant.   Alack, our terrene moon
Is now eclipsed; and it portends alone
The fall of Antony!
Cleo.   I must stay his time.
Ant. To flatter Cæsar, would you mingle eyes
With one that ties his points?
Cleo.   Not know me yet?
Ant. Coldhearted toward me!
Cleo.   Ah, dear, if I be so,
From my cold heart let heaven engender hail
And poison it in the source, and the first stone
Drop in my neck: as it determines, so
Dissolve my life! The next Cæsarion smite:
Till by degrees the memory of my womb,
Together with my brave Egyptians all,
By the discandering of this pelleted storm,
Lie graveless, till the flies and gnats of Nile
Have buried them for prey!
Ant.   I am satisfied.
Cæsar sits down in Alexandria, where
I will oppose his fate. Our force by land
Hath nobly held; our severed navy too
Have knit again, and fleet, threatening most sealike.

Where hast thou been, my heart?—Dost thou
  hear, lady?
If from the field I shall return once more
To kiss these lips, I will appear in blood;
I and my sword will earn our chronicle:
There 's hope in it yet.

 Cleo. That 's my brave lord!

 Ant. I will be treble-sinewed, hearted, breathed,
And fight maliciously: for when mine hours
Were nice and lucky, men did ransom lives
Of me for jests: but now I 'll set my teeth,
And send to darkness all that stop me.—Come,
Let 's have one other gaudy night: call to me
All my sad captains; fill our bowls; once more
Let 's mock the midnight bell.

 Cleo. It is my birthday:
I had thought to have held it poor: but since
 my lord
Is Antony again, I will be Cleopatra.

 Ant. We 'll yet do well.

 Cleo. Call all his noble captains to my lord.

 Ant. Do so; we 'll speak to them; and to-night
 I 'll force
The wine peep through their scars.—Come on,
 my queen:
There 's sap in 't yet. The next time I do fight,
I 'll make death love me; for I will contend
Even with his pestilent scythe.

 [*Exeunt* ANTONY, CLEOPATRA, *and* Attendants.

 Eno. Now he 'll outstare the lightning. To be
 furious
Is to be frighted out of fear, and in that mood
The dove will peck the estridge: and I see still
A diminution in our captain's brain
Restores his heart. When valour preys on reason,
It eats the sword it fights with. I will seek
Some way to leave him.   [*Exit.*

O my good lord, believe not all.

SCENE I.—Cæsar's *Camp at* Alexandria.

Enter Cæsar, *reading a letter;* Agrippa,
Mecænas, *and others.*

Cæs. He calls me boy, and chides as he had
 power
To beat me out of Egypt : my messenger
He hath whipped with rods ; dares me to personal
 combat,
Cæsar to Antony. Let the old ruffian know
I have many other ways to die ; meantime,
Laugh at his challenge.
 Mec.   Cæsar must think,
When one so great begins to rage, he 's hunted
Even to falling. Give him no breath, but now
Make boot of his distraction. Never anger
Made good guard for itself.
 Cæs. Let our best heads
Know that to-morrow the last of many battles
We mean to fight :—within our files there are
Of those that served Marc Antony but late,
Enough to fetch him in.—See it be done ;
And feast the army : we have store to do 't,
And they have earned the waste.—Poor Antony !
          [*Exeunt.*

SCENE II.—Alexandria. *A Room in the Palace.*

Enter Antony, Cleopatra, Enobarbus, Charmian, Iras, Alexas, *and others.*

Ant. He will not fight with me, Domitius.
Eno. No.
Ant. Why should he not?
Eno. He thinks, being twenty times of better
 fortune,
He is twenty men to one.
 Ant. To-morrow, soldier,
By sea and land I 'll fight : or I will live,
Or bathe my dying honour in the blood
Shall make it live again. Woo't thou fight
 well !
 Eno. I 'll strike, and cry "Take all !"
 Ant. Well said ; come on.—
Call forth my household servants : let 's to night

    Enter Servants.

Be bounteous at our meal.—Give me thy hand ;
Thou hast been rightly honest :—so hast thou ;—

Thou,—and thou,—and thou :—you have served
 me well,
And kings have been your fellows :—
 Cleo. What means this?—
 Eno. 'T is one of those odd tricks which sorrow
  shoots   [*Aside.*
Out of the mind.
 Ant. And thou art honest too.—
I wish I could be made so many men,
And all of you clapped up together in
An Antony ; that I might do you service
So good as you have done.
 Serv. The gods forbid !
 Ant. Well, my good fellows, wait on me to-night ;
Scant not my cups ; and make as much of me
As when mine empire was your fellow too,
And suffered my command.
 Cleo. What does he mean?
 Eno. To make his followers weep.
 Ant. 'Tend me to night :
May be it is the period of your duty :
Haply you shall not see me more ; or if,
A mangled shadow : perchance to-morrow
You 'll serve another master. I look on you
As one that takes his leave. Mine honest friends,
I turn you not away ; but, like a master
Married to your good service, stay till death.
'Tend me to-night two hours ; I ask no more ;
And the gods yield you for 't !

Eno.   What mean you, sir,
To give them this discomfort? Look, they weep;
And I, an ass, am onion-eyed: for shame,
Transform us not to women.
    Ant.   Ho, ho, ho!
Now the witch take me if I meant it thus:
Grace grow where those drops fall!—My hearty
        friends,
You take me in too dolorous a sense:
For I spake to you for your comfort; did desire
        you
To burn this night with torches. Know, my
        hearts,
I hope well of to-morrow, and will lead you
Where rather I'll expect victorious life
Than death and honour. Let's to supper,—come,—
And drown consideration.   [*Exeunt.*

SCENE III.—*The same.   Before the Palace.*

Enter two Soldiers to their guard.

1st Sol. Brother, good night: to-morrow
        the day.
2nd Sol. It will determine one way: fare you
        well.
Heard you of nothing strange about the streets?
1st Sol. Nothing: what news?
2nd Sol. Belike 't is but a rumour: good night
        to you.
1st Sol. Well, sir, good night.

Enter two other Soldiers.

2nd Sol. Soldiers, have careful watch.
3rd Sol. And you.   Good night, good night.
        [*The first two place themselves at their posts.*
4th Sol. Here we: [*they take their posts*]—
        and if to-morrow
Our navy thrive, I have an absolute hope
Our landmen will stand up.
3rd Sol. 'T is a brave army, and full of purpose.
        [*Music of hautboys under the stage.*
4th Sol. Peace: what noise?
1st Sol. List, list!
2nd Sol. Hark!
1st Sol. Music i' the air!
3rd Sol. Under the earth!
4th Sol. It signs well, does it not?
3rd Sol. No.
1st Sol. Peace, I say. What should this mean?
2nd Sol. 'T is the god Hercules, whom Antony
        loved,
Now leaves him.
1st Sol.   Walk: let's see if other watchmen
Do hear what we do.
        [*They advance to another post.*

2nd Sol. How now, masters?
Sol. How now?—How now?—Do you hear this?
        [*Several speaking together.*
1st Sol. Ay: is 't not strange?
3rd Sol. Do you hear, masters; do you hear?
1st Sol. Follow the noise so far as we have
        quarter:
Let's see how 't will give off.
Sol. [*Several speaking*].   Content. 'T is
        strange!   [*Exeunt.*

SCENE IV.—*The same.   A Room in the Palace.*

Enter ANTONY *and* CLEOPATRA; CHARMIAN *and
        others attending.*

Ant. Eros! mine armour, Eros.
Cleo.   Sleep a little.
Ant. No, my chuck.—Eros, come: mine
        armour, Eros.

Enter EROS, *with armour.*

Come, my good fellow, put thine iron on:
If fortune be not ours to-day, it is
Because we brave her.—Come.
Cleo.   Nay, I'll help too.
What's this for?
Ant.   Ah, let be, let be! thou art
The armourer of my heart.—False, false: this,
        this.
Cleo. Sooth, la, I'll help: thus it must be.
Ant.   Well, well:
We shall thrive now.—Seest thou, my good fel-
        low?
Go, put on thy defences.
Eros.   Briefly, sir.
Cleo. Is not this buckled well!
Ant.   Rarely, rarely:
He that unbuckles this till we do please
To doff 't for our repose, shall hear a storm.—
Thou fumblest, Eros, and my queen's a squire
More tight at this than thou: despatch.—O love,
That thou couldst see my wars to-day, and
        knew'st
The royal occupation, thou shouldst see

Enter an Officer, *armed.*

A workman in 't!—Good-morrow to thee: wel-
        come.
Thou look'st like him that knows a warlike charge:
To business that we love we rise betime,
And go to 't with delight.
1st Offi.   A thousand, sir,
Early though it be, have on their rivetted trim,
And at the port expect you.
        [*Shout. Trumpets. Flourish.*

Enter other Officers, *and* Soldiers.

2nd Offi. The morn is fair.—Good-morrow,
     general.
All. Good-morrow, general.
Ant.   'T is well blown, lads.
This morning, like the spirit of a youth
That means to be of note, begins betimes.—
So, so : come, give me that : this way : well said.
Fare thee well, dame : whate'er becomes of
     me :
This is a soldier's kiss [*Kisses her*] : rebukable
And worthy shameful check it were to stand
On more mechanic compliment : I 'll leave
     thee
Now like a man of steel.—You that will fight,
Follow me close : I 'll bring you to 't.—Adieu.
[*Exeunt* ANTONY, EROS, Officers, *and* Soldiers.
Char. Please you, retire to your chamber ?
Cleo.   Lead me.
He goes forth gallantly. That he and Cæsar
     might
Determine this great war in single fight !
Then Antony—but now !—Well, on.   [*Exeunt.*

SCENE V.—ANTONY'S *Camp near* Alexandria.

Trumpets sound.   Enter ANTONY *and* EROS ; *a*
     Soldier *meeting them.*

Sol. The gods make this a happy day to
     Antony !
Ant. 'Would thou and those thy scars had
     once prevailed
To make me fight at land !
Sol.   Hadst thou done so,
The kings that have revolted, and the soldier
That has this morning left thee, would have still
Followed thy heels.
Ant.   Who 's gone this morning ?
Sol.   Who ?
One ever near thee. Call for Enobarbus :
He shall not hear thee ; or from Cæsar's camp
Say, "I am none of thine."
Ant. What sayst thou ?
Sol. Sir, he is with Cæsar.
Eros. Sir, his chests and treasure he has not
     with him.
Ant. Is he gone ?
Sol. Most certain.
Ant. Go, Eros, send his treasure after : do it :
Detain no jot, I charge thee.   Write to him
(I will subscribe) gentle adieus and greetings :
Say that I wish he never find more cause
To change a master.—O, my fortunes have
Corrupted honest men.—Despatch.—Enobarbus !
                              [*Exeunt.*

SCENE VI.—CÆSAR'S *Camp before* Alexandria.

Flourish.   Enter CÆSAR, *with* AGRIPPA,
     ENOBARBUS, *and others.*

Cæs. Go forth, Agrippa, and begin the fight.
Our will is Antony be took alive :
Make it so known.
Agr.   Cæsar, I shall.   [*Exit* AGRIPPA.
Cæs. The time of universal peace is near :
Prove this a prosperous day, the three-nooked
     world
Shall bear the olive freely.

Enter a Messenger.

Mess. Antony is come into the field.
Cæs. Go, charge Agrippa
Plant those that have revolted in the van,
That Antony may seem to spend his fury
Upon himself.   [*Exeunt* CÆSAR *and his Train.*
Eno. Alexas did revolt, and went to Jewry
On affairs of Antony ; there did persuade
Great Herod to incline himself to Cæsar,
And leave his master Antony : for this pains
Cæsar hath hanged him.   Canidius and the
     rest
That fell away have entertainment, but
No honourable trust.   I have done ill :
Of which I do accuse myself so sorely
That I will joy no more.

Enter a Soldier *of* CÆSAR'S.

Sol.   Enobarbus, Antony
Hath after thee sent all thy treasure, with
His bounty overplus.   The messenger
Came on my guard ; and at thy tent is now,
Unloading of his mules.
Eno. I give it you.
Sol.   Mock not, Enobarbus :
I tell you true.   Best that you safed the bringer
Out of the host : I must attend mine office,
Or would have done 't myself.   Your emperor
Continues still a Jove.   [*Exit* Soldier.
Eno. I am alone the villain of the earth,
And feel I am so most.   O Antony,
Thou mine of bounty, how wouldst thou have
     paid
My better service, when my turpitude
Thou dost so crown with gold !   This blows my
     heart :
If swift thought break it not, a swifter mean
Shall outstrike thought : but thought will do 't,
     I feel.
I fight against thee !—No : I will go seek
Some ditch wherein to die : the foul'st best
     fits
My latter part of life.   [*Exit.*

SCENE VII.—*Field of Battle between the Camps.*

Alarum. Drums and Trumpets. Enter AGRIPPA
and others.

Agr. Retire: we have engaged ourselves too far.
Cæsar himself has work, and our oppression
Exceeds what we expected.   [*Exeunt.*

Alarum. Enter ANTONY, *and* SCARUS, *wounded.*

Scar. O my brave emperor, this is fought indeed!
Had we done so at first, we had driven them home
With clouts about their heads.
    Ant.   Thou bleed'st apace.
    Scar. I had a wound here that was like a T;
But now 't is made an H.
    Ant.   They do retire.
    Scar. We 'll beat 'em into bench-holes: I have yet
Room for six scotches more.

            Enter EROS.

    Eros. They are beaten, sir; and our advantage
                serves
For a fair victory.
    Scar.   Let us score their backs,
And snatch 'em up, as we take hares, behind:
'T is sport to maul a runner.
    Ant.   I will reward thee
Once for thy sprightly comfort, and tenfold
For thy good valour. Come thee on.
    Scar.   I 'll halt after.   [*Exeunt.*

SCENE VIII.—*Under the Walls of* Alexandria.

Alarum. Enter ANTONY, *marching;* SCARUS, *and
Forces.*

    Ant. We have beat him to his camp. Run one
                before,
And let the queen know of our guests.—To-
                morrow,
Before the sun shall see us, we 'll spill the blood
That has to-day escaped. I thank you all;
For doughty-handed are you, and have fought
Not as you served the cause, but as 't had been
Each man's like mine: you have shewn all Hectors.
Enter the city, clip your wives, your friends,
Tell them your feats; whilst they with joyful tears
Wash the congealment from your wounds, and
                kiss
The honoured gashes whole.—Give me thy hand:
                            [*To* SCARUS.

        Enter CLEOPATRA, *attended.*
To this great fairy I 'll commend thy acts;
Make her thanks bless thee.—O thou day o' the
                world!
Chain mine armed neck: leap thou, attire and all,

Through proof of harness to my heart, and there
Ride on the pants triumphing.
    Cleo.   Lord of lords!
O infinite virtue! com'st thou smiling from
The world's great snare uncaught?
    Ant.   My nightingale,
We have beat them to their beds. What, girl,
                though grey
Do something mingle with our younger brown;
Yet have we a brain that nourishes our nerves,
And can get goal for goal of youth. Behold this
                man;
Commend unto his lips thy favouring hand:—
Kiss it, my warrior.—He hath fought to-day
As if a god, in hate of mankind, had
Destroyed in such a shape.
    Cleo.   I 'll give thee, friend,
An armour all of gold: it was a king's.
    Ant. He has deserved it, were it carbuncled
Like holy Phœbus' car.—Give me thy hand:
Through Alexandria make a jolly march;
Bear our hacked targets like the men that owe
                them.
Had our great palace the capacity
To camp this host, we all would sup together,
And drink carouses to the next day's fate,
Which promises royal peril.—Trumpeters,
With brazen din blast you the city's ear;
Make mingle with our rattling tabourines;
That heaven and earth may strike their sounds
                together,
Applauding our approach!   [*Exeunt.*

SCENE IX.—CÆSAR'S *Camp.*

Sentinels *on their posts. Enter* ENOBARBUS.

    1st Sol. If we be not relieved within this hour,
We must return to the court of guard. The night
Is shiny, and they say we shall embattle
By the second hour i' the morn.
    2nd Sol. This last day was a shrewd one to us.
    Eno. O, bear me witness, night,—
    3rd Sol. What man is this?
    2nd Sol. Stand close, and list him.
    Eno. Be witness to me, O thou blessèd moon,
When men revolted shall upon record
Bear hateful memory, poor Enobarbus did
Before thy face repent!—
    1st Sol. Enobarbus!
    3rd Sol. Peace: hark further.
    Eno. O sovereign mistress of true melancholy,
The poisonous damp of night disponge upon me,
That life, a very rebel to my will,
May hang no longer on me! throw my heart
Against the flint and hardness of my fault;

Which, being dried with grief, will break to powder,
And finish all foul thoughts.—O Antony!
Nobler than my revolt is infamous,
Forgive me in thine own particular;
But let the world rank me in register
A master-leaver and a fugitive.——
O Antony! O Antony!　　　　　[*Dies.*
　　2nd Sol. Let's speak to him.

　　1st Sol. Let's hear him; for the things he speaks
may concern Cæsar.
　　3rd Sol. Let's do so.　But he sleeps.
　　1st Sol. Swoons rather; for so bad a prayer as
his was never yet for sleep.
　　2nd Sol. Go we to him.
　　3rd Sol. Awake, sir, awake; speak to us.
　　2nd Sol. Hear you, sir!

　　1st Sol. The hand of death hath raught him.—
　　　　Hark! the drums　　[*Drums afar off.*
Demurely wake the sleepers.—Let us bear him
To the court of guard: he is of note.　Our hour
Is fully out.
　　3rd Sol. Come on, then: he may recover yet.
　　　　　　　　　　[*Exeunt with the body.*

SCENE X.—*Between the two Camps.*

Enter ANTONY *and* SCARUS, *with Forces marching.*

　　Ant. Their preparation is to-day by sea:
We please them not by land.
　　Scar.　　For both, my lord.
　　Ant. I would they'd fight i' the fire, or in the air:
We'd fight there too.　But this it is: our foot,
Upon the hills adjoining to the city,
Shall stay with us.　Order for sea is given:
They have put forth the haven.—Further on;

Where their appointment we may best discover,
And look on their endeavour.　　　[*Exeunt.*

Enter CÆSAR *and his Forces, marching.*

　　Cæs. But being charged, we will be still by land;
Which, as I take 't, we shall: for his best force
Is forth to man his gallies.—To the vales,
And hold our best advantage.　　　[*Exeunt.*

Re-enter ANTONY *and* SCARUS.

　　Ant. Yet they're not joined.　Where yond'
　　　　pine does stand
I shall discover all: I'll bring thee word
Straight how 't is like to go.　　　[*Exit.*
　　Scar.　　Swallows have built
In Cleopatra's sails their nests: the augurers
Say they know not,—they cannot tell;—look grimly,
And dare not speak their knowledge.　Antony
Is valiant and dejected; and, by starts,
His fretted fortunes give him hope and fear
Of what he has and has not.

Alarum afar off, as at a sea-fight.

Re-enter ANTONY.

Ant.   All is lost!
This foul Egyptian hath betrayed me:
My fleet hath yielded to the foe; and yonder
They cast their caps up, and carouse together
Like friends long lost.—Triple-turned whore!
          't is thou
Hast sold me to this novice: and my heart
Makes only war on thee.—Bid them all fly:
For when I am revenged upon my charm,
I have done all.—Bid them all fly; be gone!
                              [*Exit* SCARUS.
O sun, thy uprise shall I see no more!
Fortune and Antony part here; even here
Do we shake hands.—All come to this?—The
          hearts
That spanielled me at heels, to whom I gave
Their wishes, do discandy, melt their sweets
On blossoming Cæsar: and this pine is barked,
That overtopped them all. Betrayed I am:
O this false soul of Egypt! this grave charm,—
Whose eye becked forth my wars, and called
          them home;
Whose bosom was my crownet, my chief end,—
Like a right gipsy, hath, at fast and loose,
Beguiled me to the very heart of loss.—
What, Eros, Eros!

Enter CLEOPATRA.

          Ah, thou spell: avaunt!
Cleo. Why is my lord enraged against his
          love?
Ant. Vanish; or I shall give thee thy deserving,
And blemish Cæsar's triumph. Let him take
          thee,
And hoist thee up to the shouting plebeians:
Follow his chariot, like the greatest spot
Of all thy sex: most monster-like, be shewn
For poor'st diminutives, to dolts; and let
Patient Octavia plough thy visage up
With her preparéd nails.   [*Exit* CLEOPATRA.
'T is well thou 'rt gone,
If it be well to live: but better 't were
Thou fell'st into my fury; for one death
Might have prevented many.—Eros, ho!—
The shirt of Nessus is upon me: teach me,
Alcides, thou mine ancestor, thy rage:
Let me lodge Lichas on the horns o' the moon;
And with those hands, that grasped the heaviest
          club,
Subdue my worthiest self. The witch shall die:
To the Roman boy she hath sold me, and I
          fall
Under this plot: she dies for 't.—Eros, ho! [*Exit.*

SCENE XI.—Alexandria. *A Room in the Palace.*

Enter CLEOPATRA, CHARMIAN, IRAS, *and*
          MARDIAN.

Cleo. Help me, my women! O, he is more mad
Than Telamon for his shield: the boar of Thessaly
Was never so embossed.
Char.   To the monument:
There lock yourself, and send him word you are
          dead.
The soul and body rive not more in parting,
Than greatness going off.
Cleo.   To the monument.—
Mardian, go tell him I have slain myself:
Say that the last I spoke was, " Antony:"
And word it, pr'y thee, piteously. Hence,
Mardian; and bring me how he takes my death.—
To the monument.   [*Exeunt.*

SCENE XII.—*The same. Another Room.*

Enter ANTONY *and* EROS.

Ant. Eros, thou yet behold'st me?
Eros.   Ay, noble lord.
Ant. Sometime we see a cloud that 's dragonish;
A vapour sometime like a bear or lion,
A towered citadel, a pendant rock,
A forkéd mountain, or blue promontory
With trees upon 't, that nod unto the world,
And mock our eyes with air:—thou hast seen
          these signs?
They are black vesper's pageants.
Eros.   Ay, my lord.
Ant. That which is now a horse, even with a
          thought
The rack dislimns, and makes it indistinct
As water is in water.
Eros.   It does, my lord.
Ant. My good knave, Eros, now thy captain is
Even such a body: here I am Antony;
Yet cannot hold this visible shape, my knave.
I made these wars for Egypt; and the queen
(Whose heart I thought I had, for she had mine;
Which, whilst it was mine, had annexed unto 't
A million more, now lost)—she, Eros, has
Packed cards with Cæsar, and false played my glory
Unto an enemy's triumph.
Nay, weep not, gentle Eros: there is left us
Ourselves to end ourselves.—O, thy vile lady!

Enter MARDIAN.

She hath robbed me of my sword.
Mar.   No, Antony;
My mistress loved thee, and her fortunes mingled
With thine entirely.

Ant.   Hence, saucy eunuch; peace :
She hath betrayed me, and shall die the death.
     Mar. Death of one person can be paid but once;
And that she has discharged : what thou wouldst do
Is done unto thy hand.   The last she spake
Was, " Antony ! most noble Antony !"
Then in the midst a tearing groan did break
The name of Antony ; it was divided
Between her heart and lips : she rendered life,
Thy name so buried in her.
     Ant.   Dead, then?
     Mar.   Dead.
     Ant. Eros, unarm : the long day's task is done,
And we must sleep.—That thou depart'st hence
                      safe
Does pay thy labour richly : go.—[*Exit* MARDIAN.
          Off, pluck off !—
The sevenfold shield of Ajax cannot keep
The battery from my heart. O cleave, my sides !
Heart, once be stronger than thy continent ;
Crack thy frail case !—Apace, Eros, apace.—
No more a soldier : bruiséd pieces, go ;
You have been nobly borne.—From me awhile.—
                      [*Exit* EROS.
I will o'ertake thee, Cleopatra, and
Weep for my pardon.   So it must be, for now
All length is torture.   Since the torch is out,
Lie down and stray no further : now all labour
Mars what it does ; yea, very force entangles
Itself with strength : seal then, and all is done.—
Eros !—I come, my queen :—Eros !—Stay for me :
Where souls do couch on flowers we'll hand in hand,
And with our sprightly port make the ghosts gaze :
Dido and her Æneas shall want troops,
And all the haunt be ours.—Come, Eros, Eros !

Re-enter EROS.

     Eros. What would my lord ?
     Ant.   Since Cleopatra died,
I have lived in such dishonour that the gods
Detest my baseness.   I, that with my sword
Quartered the world, and o'er green Neptune's
                      back
With ships made cities, condemn myself, to lack
The courage of a woman : less noble mind
Than she, which, by her death, our Cæsar tells,
" I am conqueror of myself." Thou art sworn, Eros,
That, when the exigent should come (which now
Is come indeed), when I should see behind me
The inevitable prosecution of disgrace
And horror, that, on my command, thou then
Wouldst kill me :—do 't ; the time is come :
Thou strik'st not me ; 't is Cæsar thou defeat'st.
Put colour in thy cheek.
     Eros.   The gods withhold me !
Shall I do that which all the Parthian darts,
Though enemy, lost aim, and could not ?

     Ant.   Eros,
Wouldst thou be windowed in great Rome, and see
Thy master thus, with pleached arms, bending
                      down
His corrigible neck, his face subdued
To penetrative shame ; whilst the wheeled seat
Of fortunate Cæsar, drawn before him, branded
His baseness that ensued?
     Eros.   I would not see 't.
     Ant. Come, then; for with a wound I must be
                      cured.
Draw that thy honest sword, which thou hast worn
Most useful for thy country.
     Eros.   O, sir, pardon me.
     Ant. When I did make thee free, swor'st thou
                      not then
To do this when I bade thee?   Do it at once ;
Or thy precedent services are all
But accidents unpurposed.   Draw, and come.
     Eros. Turn from me, then, that noble coun-
                      tenance,
Wherein the worship of the whole world lies.
     Ant. Lo thee.   [*Turning from him.*
     Eros. My sword is drawn.
     Ant.   Then let it do at once
The thing why thou hast drawn it.
     Eros.   My dear master,
My captain, and my emperor, let me say,
Before I strike this bloody stroke, farewell.
     Ant. 'T is said, man ;—and farewell.
     Eros. Farewell, great chief. Shall I strike now?
     Ant.   Now, Eros.
     Eros. Why, there then !— [*Falls on his sword.*
          Thus do I escape the sorrow
Of Antony's death.   [*Dies.*
     Ant.   Thrice nobler than myself !
Thou teachest me, O valiant Eros, what
I should, and thou couldst not.   My queen and Eros
Have, by their brave instruction, got upon me
A nobleness in record : but I will be
A bridegroom in my death, and run into 't
As to a lover's bed.   Come, then ; and, Eros,
Thy master dies thy scholar ; to do thus
I learned of thee [*Falls on his sword.*]—How! not
          yet dead? not dead?—
The guard !—ho !—O, despatch me !

Enter DERCETAS *and* Guard.

     1st Guard. What 's the noise?
     Ant. I have done my work ill, friends : O, make
                      an end
Of what I have begun.
     2nd Guard.   The star is fallen.
     1st Guard. And time is at his period.
     All. Alas, and woe!
     Ant. Let him that loves me strike me dead.
     1st Guard. Not I.

2nd Guard. Nor I,

3rd Guard. Nor any one.   [*Exeunt* Guard.

Der. Thy death and fortunes bid thy followers fly.
This sword but shewn to Cæsar, with this tidings,
Shall enter me with him.

Enter DIOMEDES.

Dio. Where's Antony?

Der.   There, Diomed, there.

Dio. Lives he? wilt thou not answer, man?

[*Exit* DERCETAS.

Ant. Art thou there, Diomed? Draw thy sword,
    and give me
Sufficing strokes for death.

Dio.   Most absolute lord,
My mistress Cleopatra sent me to thee.

Ant. When did she send thee?

Dio. Now, my lord.

Ant. Where is she?

Dio. Locked in her monument. She had a
    prophesying fear
Of what hath come to pass: for when she saw

(Which never shall be found) you did suspect
She had disposed with Cæsar, and that your rage
Would not be purged, she sent you word she was
    dead:
But, fearing since how it might work, hath sent
Me to proclaim the truth; and I am come,
I dread, too late.

Ant. Too late, good Diomed.—Call my guard,
    I pr'y thee.

Dio. What, ho! the emperor's guard! The
    guard! what, ho!
Come: your lord calls.

Enter some of the Guard.

Ant. Bear me good friends, where Cleopatra
    bides:
'T is the last service that I shall command you.

1st Guard. Woe, woe, are we, sir, you may not
    live to wear
All your true followers out.

All.   Most heavy day!

Ant. Nay, good my fellows, do not please
    sharp fate
To grace it with your sorrows: bid that welcome
Which comes to punish us, and we punish it
Seeming to bear it lightly. Take me up:
I have led you oft: carry me now, good friends,
And have my thanks for all.

[*Exeunt, bearing* ANTONY.

SCENE XIII.—*The same.   A Monument.*

Enter above, CLEOPATRA, CHARMIAN, *and* IRAS.

Cleo. O Charmian, I will never go from hence.

Char. Be comforted, dear madam.

Cleo.   No, I will not:
All strange and terrible events are welcome;
But comforts we despise: our size of sorrow,
Proportioned to our cause, must be as great

Enter DIOMEDES.

As that which makes it.—How now; is he dead?

Dio. His death 's upon him, but not dead.
Look out o' the other side your monument;
His guard have brought him hither.

Enter ANTONY, *borne by the* Guard.

Cleo.   O sun,
Burn the great sphere thou mov'st in! darkling
        stand
The varying shore o' the world!—O Antony!
Antony, Antony!—Charmian, help; help, Iras;
Help, friends below: let 's draw him hither.

Ant.   Peace:
Not Cæsar's valour hath o'erthrown Antony;
But Antony's hath triumphed on itself.

Cleo. So it should be, that none but Antony
Should conquer Antony: but woe 't is so!

Ant. I am dying, Egypt, dying: only
I here impórtune death awhile, until
Of many thousand kisses the poor last
I lay upon thy lips.

Cleo.   I dare not, dear
(Dear my lord, pardon); I dare not,
Lest I be taken. Not the imperious show
Of the full-fortuned Cæsar ever shall
Be brooched with me: if knife, drugs, serpents, have
Edge, sting, or operation, I am safe:
Your wife Octavia, with her modest eyes
And still conclusion, shall acquire no honour
Demurring upon me.—But come, come, Antony:—
Help me, my women,—we must draw thee up:—
Assist, good friends.

Ant.   O quick, or I am gone.

Cleo. Here 's sport indeed!—How heavy weighs
        my lord!
Our strength is all gone into heaviness:
That makes the weight!—Had I great Juno's power,
The strong-winged Mercury should fetch thee up,
And set thee by Jove's side. Yet come a little:—
Wishers were ever fools:—O, come, come, come;
                [*They draw* ANTONY *up.*
And welcome, welcome! die where thou hast lived:
Quicken with kissing: had my lips that power,
Thus would I wear them out.

All.   A heavy sight!

Ant. I am dying, Egypt, dying:
Give me some wine, and let me speak a little.

Cleo. No, let me speak; and let me rail so high
That the false housewife Fortune break her wheel,
Provoked by my offence.

Ant.   One word, sweet queen:
Of Cæsar seek your honour with your safety.—O!

Cleo. They do not go together.

Ant.   Gentle, hear me:
None about Cæsar trust but Proculeius.

Cleo. My resolution and my hands I 'll trust:
None about Cæsar.

Ant. The miserable change now at my end
Lament nor sorrow at: but please your thoughts
In feeding them with those my former fortunes,
Wherein I lived the greatest prince o' the world,
The noblest: and do now not basely die,
Nor cowardly; put off my helmet
To my countryman:—a Roman, by a Roman
Valiantly vanquished. Now my spirit is going!
I can no more.   [*Dies.*

Cleo.   Noblest of men, woo't die?
Hast thou no care of me? shall I abide
In this dull world, which in thy absence is
No better than a sty?—O see, my women,
The crown o' the earth doth melt!—My lord!—
O, withered is the garland of the war;
The soldier's pole is fallen: young boys and girls
Are level now with men: the odds is gone,
And there is nothing left remarkable
Beneath the visiting moon!   [*She faints.*

Char. O, quietness, lady!

Iras. She is dead too, our sovereign.

Char. Lady!

Iras. Madam!

Char. O madam, madam, madam!

Iras. Royal Egypt! Empress!

Char. Peace, peace, Iras.

Cleo. No more, but e'en a woman! and com-
        manded
By such poor passion as the maid that milks,
And does the meanest chares.—It were for me
To throw my sceptre at the injurious gods,
To tell them that this world did equal theirs
Till they had stolen our jewel. All 's but naught:
Patience is sottish, and impatience does
Become a dog that 's mad: then is it sin
To rush into the secret house of death,
Ere death dare come to us?—How do you, women?
What, what? good cheer! Why, how now,
        Charmian?
My noble girls!—Ah, women, women! look,
Our lamp is spent; it 's out.—Good sirs, take
        heart.—   [*To the* Guard *below.*
We 'll bury him: and then, what 's brave, what 's
        noble,
Let 's do it after the high Roman fashion,
And make death proud to take us. Come, away:
This case of that huge spirit now is cold.
Ah, women, women! come: we have no friend
But resolution and the briefest end.
[*Exeunt; those above bearing off* ANTONY's *body.*

SCENE I.—CÆSAR's *Camp before* Alexandria.

Enter CÆSAR, AGRIPPA, DOLABELLA, MECÆNAS,
GALLUS, PROCULEIUS, *and others.*

Cæs. Go to him, Dolabella; bid him yield:
Being so frustrate, tell him he mocks us by
The pauses that he makes.
　　Dol.　　　Cæsar, I shall. [*Exit* DOLABELLA.

Enter DERCETAS, *with the sword of* ANTONY.

　　Cæs. Wherefore is that? and what art thou
　　　　that dar'st
Appear thus to us?
　　Der.　　　I am called Dercetas:
Marc Antony I served, who best was worthy
Best to be served: whilst he stood up and spoke
He was my master, and I wore my life
To spend upon his haters.　If thou please
To take me to thee, as I was to him
I 'll be to Cæsar: if thou pleasest not,
I yield thee up my life.
　　Cæs. What is 't thou sayst?
　　Der. I say, O Cæsar, Antony is dead.
　　Cæs. The breaking of so great a thing should
　　　　make
A greater crack: the round world
Should have shook lions into civil streets,
And citizens to their dens.　The death of Antony
Is not a single doom: in the name lay
A moiety of the world.
　　Der. He is dead, Cæsar;
Not by a public minister of justice,
Nor by a hiréd knife: but that self hand
Which writ his honour in the acts it did,
Hath, with the courage which the heart did lend it,
Splitted the heart.—This is his sword;

I robbed his wound of it: behold it stained
With his most noble blood.
　　Cæs.　　　Look you sad, friends?
The gods rebuke me, but it is tidings
To wash the eyes of kings.
　　Agr.　　　And strange it is
That nature must compel us to lament
Our most persisted deeds.
　　Mec.　　　His taints and honours
Waged equal with him
　　Agr.　　　A rarer spirit never
Did steer humanity: but you, gods, will give us
Some faults will make us men.—Cæsar is touched.
　　　　　　　　　　　　　　[*Aside.*
　　Mec. When such a spacious mirror 's set before
　　　　him,
He needs must see himself.
　　Cæs.　　　O Antony,
I have followed thee to this!—But we do lance
Diseases in our bodies: I must perforce
Have shewn to thee such a declining day,
Or look on thine; we could not stall together
In the whole world: but yet let me lament,
With tears as sovereign as the blood of hearts,
That thou, my brother, my competitor
In top of all design, my mate in empire,
Friend and companion in the front of war,
The arm of mine own body, and the heart
Where mine his thoughts did kindle,—that our stars
Unreconcileable, should divide
Our equalness to this.—Hear me, good friends,—
But I will tell you at some meeter season:

Enter a Messenger.

The business of this man looks out of him;
We 'll hear him what he says.—Whence are you?

Mess. A poor Egyptian yet. The queen my
    mistress,
Confined in all she has (her monument),
Of thy intents desires instruction :
That she preparédly may frame herself
To the way she 's forced to.
    Cæs.   Bid her have good heart :
She soon shall know of us, by some of ours,
How honourable and how kindly we
Determine for her : for Cæsar cannot live
To be ungentle.
    Mess.   So the gods preserve thee ! [*Exit.*
    Cæs. Come hither, Proculeius : go, and say
We purpose her no shame : give her what comforts
The quality of her passion shall require ;
Lest, in her greatness, by some mortal stroke
She do defeat us : for her life in Rome
Would be eternal in our triumph. Go ;
And, with your speediest, bring us what she says,
And how you find of her.
    Pro.   Cæsar, I shall. [*Exit* PROCULEIUS.
    Cæs. Gallus, go you along.—Where 's Dolabella,
To second Proculeius ?   [*Exit* GALLUS.
    Agr. }
    Mec. } Dolabella !
    Cæs. Let him alone, for I remember now
How he 's employed : he shall in time be ready.
Go with me to my tent : where you shall see
How hardly I was drawn into this war ;
How calm and gentle I proceeded still
In all my writings. Go with me, and see
What I can shew in this.   [*Exeunt.*

SCENE II.—Alexandria. *A Room in the Monument.*

    Enter CLEOPATRA, CHARMIAN, *and* IRAS.

    Cleo. My desolation does begin to make
A better life. 'T is paltry to be Cæsar :
Not being fortune, he 's but fortune's knave ;
A minister of her will. And it is great
To do that thing that ends all other deeds ;
Which shackles accidents, and bolts up change ;
Which sleeps, and never palates more the dung,
The beggar's nurse and Cæsar's.

    Enter, to the gates of the Monument, PROCULEIUS,
        GALLUS, *and* Soldiers.

    Pro. Cæsar sends greeting to the Queen of
      Egypt ;
And bids thee study on what fair demands
Thou mean'st to have him grant thee.
    Cleo. [*within*].   What 's thy name ?
    Pro. My name is Proculeius.
    Cleo. [*within*].   Antony
Did tell me of you, bade me trust you : but

I do not greatly care to be deceived,
That have no use for trusting. If your master
Would have a queen his beggar, you must tell him
That majesty, to keep decorum, must
No less beg than a kingdom : if he please
To give me conquered Egypt for my son,
He gives me so much of mine own as I
Will kneel to him with thanks.
    Pro.   Be of good cheer ;
You are fallen into a princely hand ; fear nothing :
Make your full reverence freely to my lord,
Who is so full of grace that it flows over
On all that need. Let me report to him
Your sweet dependency : and you shall find
A conqueror that will pray in aid for kindness,
Where he for grace is kneeled to.
    Cleo. [*within*].   Pray you tell him
I am his fortune's vassal, and I send him
The greatness he has got. I hourly learn
A doctrine of obedience, and would gladly
Look him i' the face.
    Pro.   This I 'll report, dear lady.
Have comfort ; for I know your plight is pitied
Of him that caused it.
    Gal. You see how easily she may be surprised.—
[PROCULEIUS *and two of the* Guard *enter the*
    Monument by a ladder placed against a win-
    dow, and come behind CLEOPATRA. *Others*
    unbar and open the gates.
Guard her till Cæsar come.   [*Exit* GALLUS.
    Iras. Royal queen !
    Char. O Cleopatra, thou art taken, queen !
    Cleo. Quick, quick, good hands !
                [*Draws a dagger.*
    Pro. Hold, worthy lady, hold ! [*Disarms her.*
Do not yourself such wrong, who are in this
Relieved, but not betrayed.
    Cleo.   What, of death too,
That rids our dogs of languish ?
    Pro.   Cleopatra,
Do not abuse my master's bounty by
The undoing of yourself : let the world see
His nobleness well acted, which your death
Will never let come forth.
    Cleo.   Where art thou, death ?
Come hither, come ! come, come, and take a queen
Worth many babes and beggars !
    Pro.   O, temperance, lady !
    Cleo. Sir, I will eat no meat ; I 'll not drink, sir :
If idle talk will once be necessary,
I 'll not sleep neither : this mortal house I 'll ruin,
Do Cæsar what he can. Know, sir, that I
Will not wait pinioned at your master's court,
Nor once be chástised with the sober eye
Of dull Octavia. Shall they hoist me up,
And shew me to the shouting varletry
Of censuring Rome ? Rather a ditch in Egypt

Be gentle grave to me: rather on Nilus' mud
Lay me stark naked, and let the water-flies
Blow me into abhorring: rather make
My country's high pyramidés my gibbet,
And hang me up in chains!

Pro. You do extend
These thoughts of horror further than you shall
Find cause in Cæsar.

Enter DOLABELLA.

Dol. Proculeius,
What thou hast done thy master Cæsar knows,
And he hath sent for thee: as for the queen,
I 'll take her to my guard.

Pro. So, Dolabella,
It shall content me best: be gentle to her.—
To Cæsar I will speak what you shall please,
If you 'll employ me to him. [*To* CLEOPATRA.

Cleo. Say, I would die.

[*Exeunt* PROCULEIUS *and* Soldiers.

Dol. Most noble empress, you have heard of
me?

Cleo. I cannot tell.

Dol. Assuredly you know me.

Cleo. No matter, sir, what I have heard or
known.
You laugh when boys or women tell their dreams:
Is 't not your trick?

Dol. I understand not, madam.

Cleo. I dreamed there was an emperor An-
tony:—
O, such another sleep, that I might see
But such another man!

Dol. If it might please you,—

Cleo. His face was as the heavens; and therein
stuck
A sun and moon, which kept their course, and
lighted
The little O, the earth.

Dol. Most sovereign creature,—

Cleo. His legs bestrid the ocean: his reared arm
Crested the world: his voice was propertied
As all the tunéd spheres, and that to friends;
But when he meant to quail and shake the orb,
He was a rattling thunder. For his bounty,
There was no winter in 't; an autumn 't was,
That grew the more by reaping: his delights
Were dolphin-like; they shewed his back above
The element they lived in: in his livery
Walked crowns and crownets; realms and
islands were
As plátes dropped from his pocket.

Dol. Cleopatra,—

Cleo. Think you there was or might be such
a man
As this I dreamed of?

Dol. Gentle madam, no.

Cleo. You lie, up to the hearing of the gods!
But if there be or ever were one such,
It 's past the size of dreaming. Nature wants stuff
To vie strange forms with fancy: yet to imagine
An Antony were nature's piece 'gainst fancy,
Condemning shadows quite.

Dol. Hear me, good madam:
Your loss is as yourself, great; and you bear it
As answering to the weight. 'Would I might
never
O'ertake pursued success but I do feel,
By the rebound of yours, a grief that shoots
My very heart at root.

Cleo. I thank you, sir.
Know you what Cæsar means to do with me?

Dol. I am loth to tell you what I would you
knew.

Cleo. Nay, pray you, sir,—

Dol. Though he be honourable,—

Cleo. He 'll lead me, then, in triumph?

Dol. Madam, he will: I know it.

Within. Make way there:—Cæsar!

Enter CÆSAR, GALLUS, PROCULEIUS, MECÆNAS,
SELEUCUS, *and* Attendants.

Cæs. Which is the Queen of Egypt?

Dol. It is the emperor, madam.

[CLEOPATRA *kneels.*

Cæs. Arise; you shall not kneel.—
I pray you, rise: rise, Egypt.

Cleo. Sir, the gods
Will have it thus: my master and my lord
I must obey.

Cæs. Take to you no hard thoughts:
The record of what injuries you did us,
Though written in our flesh, we shall remember
As things but done by chance.

Cleo. Sole sir o' the world,
I cannot project mine own cause so well
To make it clear: but do confess I have
Been laden with like frailties which before
Have often shamed our sex.

Cæs. Cleopatra, know
We will extenuate rather than enforce.
If you apply yourself to our intents
(Which towards you are most gentle), you shall
find
A benefit in this change: but if you seek
To lay on me a cruelty, by taking
Antony's course, you shall bereave yourself
Of my good purposes, and put your children
To that destruction which I 'll guard them from
If thereon you rely. I 'll take my leave.

Cleo. And may through all the world: 't is
yours; and we,
Your 'scutcheons and your signs of conquest,
shall

Hang in what place you please. Here, my good
    lord :—
  Cæs. You shall advise me in all for Cleopatra.
  Cleo. This is the brief of money, plate, and
    jewels,
I am possessed of : 't is exactly valued ;
Not petty things admitted.—Where 's Seleucus ?
  Sel. Here, madam.
  Cleo. This is my treasurer : let him speak, my
    lord,
Upon his peril, that I have reserved
To myself nothing.—Speak the truth, Seleucus.
  Sel. Madam,
I had rather seel my lips than, to my peril,
Speak that which is not.
  Cleo.   What have I kept back ?
  Sel. Enough to purchase what you have made
    known.
  Cæs. Nay, blush not, Cleopatra : I approve
Your wisdom in the deed.
  Cleo.   See, Cæsar ! O, behold
How pomp is followed !—mine will now be yours :
And, should we shift estates, yours would be
    mine.
The ingratitude of this Seleucus does
Even make me wild :—O slave, of no more trust
Than love that 's hired !—What, go'st thou back ?
    thou shalt
Go back, I warrant thee : but I 'll catch thine eyes,
Though they had wings ! Slave, soulless villain,
    dog !
O rarely base !
  Cæs.   Good queen, let us entreat you.
  Cleo. O Cæsar, what a wounding shame is this,
That thou, vouchsafing here to visit me,
Doing the honour of thy lordliness
To one so meek, that mine own servant should
Parcel the sum of my disgraces by
Addition of his envy ! Say, good Cæsar,
That I some lady trifles have reserved,
Immoment toys, things of such dignity
As we greet modern friends withal ; and say,
Some nobler token I have kept apart
For Livia and Octavia, to induce
Their mediation ; must I be unfolded
With one that I have bred ? The gods ! it smites
    me
Beneath the fall I have.—Pr'y thee, go hence ;
         [*To* Seleucus.
Or I shall shew the cinders of my spirits
Through the ashes of my chance :—wert thou a
    man,
Thou wouldst have mercy on me.
  Cæs. Forbear, Seleucus.   [*Exit* Seleucus.
  Cleo. Be it known that we, the greatest, are
    mis-thought
For things that others do ; and when we fall,

We answer others' merits in our name :
Are therefore to be pitied.
  Cæs.   Cleopatra,
Not what you have reserved, nor what acknow-
    ledged,
Put we i' the roll of conquest : still be it yours,
Bestow it at your pleasure : and believe
Cæsar's no merchant, to make prize with you
Of things that merchants sold. Therefore be
    cheered ;
Make not your thoughts your prisons ; no, dear
    queen ;
For we intend so to dispose you as
Yourself shall give us counsel. Feed and sleep :
Our care and pity is so much upon you,
That we remain your friend : and so adieu.
  Cleo. My master and my lord !
  Cæs. Not so : adieu. [*Exeunt* Cæsar *and* Train.
  Cleo. He words me, girls ; he words me, that
    I should not
Be noble to myself : but hark thee, Charmian.
         [*Whispers* Charmian.
  Iras. Finish, good lady : the bright day is done,
And we are for the dark.
  Cleo.   Hie thee again :
I have spoke already, and it is provided.
Go, put it to the haste.
  Char.   Madam, I will.

        Re-enter Dolabella.

  Dol. Where is the queen ?
  Char. Behold, sir.   [*Exit* Charmian.
  Cleo. Dolabella ?
  Dol. Madam, as thereto sworn by your com-
    mand,
Which my love makes religion to obey,
I tell you this : Cæsar through Syria
Intends his journey, and within three days
You with your children will he send before.
Make your best use of this : I have performed
Your pleasure and my promise.
  Cleo.   Dolabella,
I shall remain your debtor.
  Dol.   I your servant.
Adieu, good queen : I must attend on Cæsar.
  Cleo. Farewell, and thanks. [*Exit* Dolabella.
    Now, Iras, what think'st thou ?
Thou, an Egyptian puppet, shalt be shewn
In Rome, as well as I : mechanic slaves,
With greasy aprons, rules, and hammers, shall
Uplift us to the view : in their thick breaths,
Rank of gross diet, shall we be enclouded,
And forced to drink their vapour.
  Iras.   The gods forbid !
  Cleo. Nay, 'tis most certain, Iras : saucy lictors
Will catch at us like strumpets, and scald rhymers
Ballad us out o' tune : the quick comedians

Extemporally will stage us, and present
Our Alexandrian revels: Antony
Shall be brought drunken forth, and I shall see
Some squeaking Cleopatra boy my greatness
I' the posture of a whore.

Iras. 　　　　O the good gods !

Cleo. Nay, that is certain.

Iras. I 'll never see it; for I am sure my nails
Are stronger than mine eyes.

Cleo. 　　　　Why, that 's the way
To fool their preparation, and to conquer
Their most absurd intents.—Now Charmian?

Enter CHARMIAN.

Shew me, my women, like a queen: go fetch
My best attires: I am again for Cydnus,
To meet Marc Antony.—Sirrah Iras, go.—
Now, noble Charmian, we 'll despatch indeed:
And, when thou hast done this chare, I 'll give
　　　　thee leave
To play till doomsday.—Bring our crown and all.
　　　　　　　　[*Exit* IRAS.—*A noise within.*
Wherefore 's this noise ?

Enter one of the Guard.

Guard. Here is a rural fellow
That will not be denied your highness' presence :
He brings you figs.

Cleo. Let him come in. [*Exit* Guard].—How
　　　　poor an instrument
May do a noble deed! he brings me liberty.
My resolution 's placed, and I have nothing
Of woman in me. Now from head to foot
I am marble-constant: now the fleeting moon
No planet is of mine.

Re-enter Guard, *with a* Clown *bringing a basket.*

Guard. This is the man.

Cleo. Avoid, and leave him.— [*Exit* Guard.
Hast thou the pretty worm of Nilus there,
That kills and pains not ?

Clown. Truly I have him : but I would not be
the party that should desire you to touch him,
for his biting is immortal : those that do die of
it, do seldom or never recover.

Cleo. Remember'st thou any that have died
on 't?

Clown. Very many, men and women too. I
heard of one of them no longer than yesterday :
a very honest woman, but something given to
lie, as a woman should not do but in the way of
honesty : how she died of the biting of it, what
pain she felt ;—truly she makes a very good
report o' the worm : but he that will believe all
that they say, shall never be saved by half that
they do. But this is most fallible,—the worm 's
an odd worm.

Cleo. Get thee hence : farewell.

Clown. I wish you all joy o' the worm.

Cleo. Farewell. 　[Clown *sets down the basket.*

Clown. You must think this, look you, that
the worm will do his kind.

Cleo. Ay, ay : farewell.

Clown. Look you, the worm is not to be trusted
but in the keeping of wise people : for indeed
there is no goodness in the worm.

Cleo. Take thou no care : it shall be heeded.

Clown. Very good : give it nothing, I pray
you ; for it is not worth the feeding.

Cleo. Will it eat me ?

Clown. You must not think I am so simple
but I know the devil himself will not eat a
woman. I know that a woman is a dish for the
gods, if the devil dress her not : but truly these
same whoreson devils do the gods great harm in
their women ; for in every ten that they make,
the devils mar five.

Cleo. Well, get thee gone : farewell.

Clown. Yes, forsooth. I wish you joy of the
worm. 　　　　　　　　　　　　　　[*Exit.*

Re-enter IRAS, *with a robe, crown, &c.*

Cleo. Give me my robe ; put on my crown. I
　　　　have
Immortal longings in me : now no more
The juice of Egypt's grape shall moist this lip.—
Yare, yare, good Iras ; quick.—Methinks I hear
Antony call : I see him rouse himself
To praise my noble act : I hear him mock
The luck of Cæsar, which the gods give men
To excuse their after-wrath.—Husband, I come :
Now to that name my courage prove my title !
I am fire and air ; my other elements
I give to baser life.—So ; have you done ?
Come, then, and take the last warmth of my lips.
Farewell, kind Charmian :—Iras, long farewell.
　　　　　[*Kisses them.* IRAS *falls and dies.*
Have I the aspick in my lips? Dost fall?
If thou and nature can so gently part,
The stroke of death is as a lover's pinch,
Which hurts and is desired. Dost thou lie still?
If thus thou vanishest, thou tell'st the world
It is not worth leave-taking.

Char. Dissolve, thick cloud, and rain : that I
　　　　may say,
The gods themselves do weep !

Cleo. 　　　　This proves me base :
If she first meet the curléd Antony,
He 'll make demand of her ; and spend that kiss
Which is my heaven to have.—Come, thou mortal
　　　　wretch,
　　　[*To the asp, which she applies to her breast.*
With thy sharp teeth this knot intrinsicate
Of life at once untie : poor venomous fool,

Be angry, and despatch. O couldst thou speak!
That I might hear thee call great Cæsar "ass
Unpolicied!"
  Char. O eastern star!

  Cleo. Peace, peace!
Dost thou not see my baby at my breast,
That sucks the nurse asleep?
  Char. O break! O break!

  Cleo. As sweet as balm, as soft as air, as gentle,—
O Antony!—Nay, I will take thee too:—
    [Applying another asp to her arm.
What should I stay— *[Falls on a bed, and dies.*
  Char. In this wild world?—So, fare thee well.—
Now boast thee, death! in thy possession lies
A lass unparalleled.—Downy windows, close;
And golden Phœbus never be beheld
Of eyes again so royal!—Your crown's awry:
I'll mend it, and then play.

    Enter the Guard, *rushing in.*

  1st Guard. Where is the queen?
  Char. Speak softly; wake her not.
  1st Guard. Cæsar hath sent—

  Char. Too slow a messenger. *[Applies the asp.*
O come! apace, despatch! I partly feel thee.
  1st Guard. Approach, ho! all's not well.
  Cæsar's beguiled.
  2nd Guard. There's Dolabella sent from Cæsar:—call him.
  1st Guard. What work is here?—Charmian,
  is this well done?
  Char. It is well done, and fitting for a princess
Descended of so many royal kings.
Ah, soldier!   *[Dies.*

    Enter DOLABELLA.

  Dol. How goes it here?
  2nd Guard. All dead.

Dol.   Cæsar, thy thoughts
Touch their effects in this.   Thyself art coming
To see performed the dreaded act which thou
So sought'st to hinder.

    Within.   A way there; a way for Cæsar!

        Enter Cæsar *and* Attendants.

   Dol. O sir, you are too sure an augurer:
That you did fear is done.

   Cæs.   Bravest at the last!
She levelled at our purposes, and, being royal,
Took her own way.—The manner of their deaths?
I do not see them bleed.

   Dol.   Who was last with them?

   1st Guard. A simple countryman, that brought
       her figs.
This was his basket.

   Cæs.   Poisoned, then.

   1st Guard.   O Cæsar,
This Charmian lived but now; she stood and
       spake.
I found her trimming up the diadem
On her dead mistress: tremblingly she stood,
And on the sudden dropped.

   Cæs.   O noble weakness!

If they had swallowed poison, 't would appear
By external swelling: but she looks like sleep,
As she would catch another Antony
In her strong toil of grace.

   Dol.   Here on her breast
There is a vent of blood, and something blown:
The like is on her arm.

   1st Guard. This is an aspick's trail: and these
       fig-leaves
Have slime upon them, such as the aspick leaves
Upon the caves of Nile.

   Cæs.   Most probable
That so she died; for her physician tells me
She hath pursued conclusions infinite
Of easy ways to die.—Take up her bed,
And bear her women from the monument.
She shall be buried by her Antony:
No grave upon the earth shall clip in it
A pair so famous.—High events as these
Strike those that make them; and their story is
No less in pity than his glory which
Brought them to be lamented.   Our army shall,
In solemn show, attend this funeral;
And then to Rome.—Come, Dolabella, see
High order in this great solemnity.   [*Exeunt.*

NOTES.

" *Take but good note, and you shall see in him*
The triple pillar of the world transformed
Into a strumpet's fool."—Act I., Scene 1.

Triple is here used for third, or one of three; meaning
one of the triumvirs, or masters of the world. The word is
used in the same sense in "ALL 'S WELL THAT ENDS
WELL:"—

" *Which, as the dearest issue of his practice,*
He bade me store up as a triple eye."

" *To-night we'll wander through the streets, and note*
The qualities of people."—Act I., Scene 1.

Sometime also, when he would go up and down the
city disguised like a slave in the night, and would peer into
poor men's windows and their shops, and scold and brawl
with them within the house, Cleopatra would be also in a
chambermaid's array, and amble up and down the streets
with him.—PLUTARCH (North's translation).

" *—— I'm full sorry*
That he approves the common liar, who
Thus speaks of him at Rome."—Act I., Scene 1.

Meaning, that he proves the common liar, Fame, to be a
true reporter in his case.

" *—— Look, pr'y thee, Charmian,*
How this Herculean Roman does become
The carriage of his chafe."—Act I., Scene 3.

Antony professed to trace his descent from Anton, a son
of Hercules.

" *—— When thou once*
Wast beaten from Modena (where thou slew'st
Hirtius and Pansa, consuls), at thy heel
Did famine follow."—Act I., Scene 4.

Cicero, on the other side, being the chiefest man of authority and estimation in the city, he stirred up all men
against Antonius; so that in the end he made the Senate
pronounce him an enemy to his country, and appointed
young Cæsar sergeants to carry axes before him, and such
other signs as were incident to the dignity of a consul or
prætor; and moreover sent Hirtius and Pansa, then consuls, to drive Antonius out of Italy. These two consuls,
together with Cæsar, who also had an army, went against
Antonius, that besieged the city of Modena, and there over-
threw him in battle; but both the consuls were slain there.
Antonius, flying upon this overthrow, fell into great
misery all at once; but the chiefest want of all other, and
that which pinched him most, was famine. Howbeit he was
of such a strong nature, that by patience he would overcome
any adversity; and the heavier fortune lay upon him, the
more constant shewed he himself.

Every man that feeleth want or adversity, knoweth by
virtue and discretion what he should do: but when indeed
they are overlaid with extremity, and be sore oppressed,
few have the hearts to follow that which they praise and
commend, and much less to avoid that they reprove and
mislike; but rather to the contrary, they yield to their accustomed easy life, and through faint heart and lack of

courage do change their first mind and purpose. And
therefore it was a wonderful example to the soldiers to see
Antonius, that was brought up in all fineness and superfluity, so easily to drink puddle-water, and to eat wild fruits
and roots: and moreover it is reported that even, as they
passed the Alps, they did eat the barks of trees, and
such beasts as never man tasted of their flesh before.—
PLUTARCH.

" *—— Let us rear*
The higher our opinion, that our stirring
Can from the lap of Egypt's widow pluck
The ne'er lust-wearied Antony."—Act II., Scene 1.

Cleopatra is styled "Egypt's widow" because Julius
Cæsar had married her to young Ptolemy, who was afterwards drowned.

" *—— Near him, thy angel*
Becomes a Fear, as being o'erpowered."—Act II., Scene 3.

A Fear was a personage in some of the old Moralities.
Fletcher alludes to such an imaginary being in the "MAID's
TRAGEDY," where Aspasia is instructing her servants how,
in needlework, to describe her situation :—

" *—— And then a Fear :*
Do that Fear bravely, wench."

" *His cocks do win the battle still of mine*
When it is all to nought ; and his quails ever
Beat mine, inhooped, at odds."—Act II., Scene 3.

Shakspere derived this from Plutarch. The ancients
used to match quails as we match cocks. Julius Pollux
relates that a circle was made in which the birds were
placed, and he whose quail was first driven out of the circle
lost the stake. We are told by Mr. Marsden that the Su-
matrans practise these quail combats. The Chinese have
always been extremely fond of quail fighting. Mr. Douce
has given a print, from an elegant Chinese miniature painting, which represents some ladies engaged at this amuse-
ment, where the quails are actually inhooped.—SINGER.

Inhooped, means inclosed or confined, that they may be
compelled to fight.

" *They are his shards, and he their beetle.*"—
Act III., Scene 2.

This is spoken of Lepidus. The meaning is that Antony
and Octavius are the wings that raise this heavy lumpish
insect from the ground. In "MACBETH" we find mention
of the "shard-borne beetle."

" ENO. *Will Cæsar weep?*
AGR. *He has a cloud in's face.*
ENO. *He were the worse for that were he a horse.*"—
Act III., Scene 2.

A horse is said to have a cloud in his face when he has
a black or dark-coloured spot in his forehead between his
eyes. This gives him a sour look, and, being supposed to
indicate an ill temper, is of course regarded as a great
blemish.—STEEVENS.

—— " *He at Philippi kept*
His sword even like a dancer."—Act III., Scene 9.

That is, he kept his weapon in the scabbard, like one who dances with a sword, which appears from various passages to have been the custom in Shakspere's time.

—— "'*T was I*
That the mad Brutus ended."—Act III., Scene 9.

Nothing can be more in character, than for an infamous debauched tyrant to call the heroic love of one's country and public liberty, "madness."—WARBURTON.

" *I was of late as petty to his ends*
As is the morn-dew on the myrtle-leaf
To his grand sea."—Act III., Scene 10.

The term " his grand sea" has been supposed by Steevens to be the sea from which the dew-drop was thought to be exhaled.—" The grand sea" and " this grand sea" have both been plausibly proposed as substitutes for the received text, in which there is probably some corruption.

" 1st Sol. *Peace, I say. What should this mean?*
2nd Sol. '*T is the god Hercules, whom Antony loved,*
Now leaves him."—Act IV., Scene 3.

Furthermore, the self-same night, within a little of midnight, when all the city was quiet, full of fear and sorrow, thinking what would be the end and issue of this war, it is said that suddenly they heard a marvellous sweet harmony of sundry sorts of instruments of music, with the cry of a multitude of people, as they had been dancing, and had sung as they had been used in Bacchus' feasts, with movings and turnings, after the manner of the satyrs: and it seemed that this dance went through the city unto the gate that opened to the enemies, and that all the troop that made this noise they heard went out of the city at that gate. Now, such as in reason sought the depth of the interpretation of this wonder, thought that it was the god unto whom Antonius bare singular devotion, to counterfeit and resemble him, that did forsake them.—PLUTARCH.

—— " *How wouldst thou have paid*
My better service, when my turpitude
Thou dost so crown with gold! This blows my heart."—
Act IV., Scene 6.

The word "blows" is here used in the sense of "swells." As in the last scene of this play :—

—— " *On her breast*
There is a vent of blood, and something blown."
And in " KING LEAR :"—

" No blown ambition doth our arms excite."

" *To this great fairy I'll commend thy acts ;*
Make her thanks bless thee."—Act IV., Scene 8.

The term fairy in former times was applied not only to imaginary diminutive beings, but also occasionally to witches and enchanters; in which last sense it is used in the text.

—— " *O, he is more mad*
Than Telamon for his shield."—Act IV., Scene 11.

That is, than Ajax Telamon for the armour of Achilles, the most valuable part of which was the shield.

—— " *Thou hast seen these signs ?*
They are black vesper's pageants."—Act IV., Scene 12.

The beauty both of the expression and the allusion is lost, unless we recollect the frequency and the nature of these shows in Shakspere's age.—WARTON.

This is without doubt one of the finest pieces of poetry in Shakspere. The splendour of the imagery, the semblance of reality, the lofty range of picturesque objects hanging over the world, their evanescent nature, the total uncertainty of what is left behind,—are just like the mouldering schemes of human greatness.—HAZLITT.

" *The miserable change now at my end*
Lament nor sorrow at."—Act IV., Scene 13.

As for himself, she should not lament nor sorrow for the miserable change of his fortune at the end of his days; but rather that she should think him the more fortunate for the former triumphs and honours he had received; considering that while he lived he was the noblest and greatest prince of the world, and that now he was overcome not cowardly, but valiantly; a Roman by another Roman.—PLUTARCH.

" *Wherefore is that ? and what art thou that dar'st*
Appear thus to us ?"—Act V., Scene 1.

After Antonius had thrust his sword into himself, as they carried him into the tombs and monuments of Cleopatra, one of his guard, called Dercetæus, took his sword with which he had stricken himself, and hid it: then he secretly stole away, and brought Octavius Cæsar the first news of his death, and shewed him his sword that was bloodied.

Cæsar, hearing these news, straight withdrew himself into a secret place of his tent, and there burst out with tears, lamenting his hard and miserable fortune that had been his friend and brother-in-law, his equal in the empire, and companion with him in sundry great exploits and battles. Then he called for all his friends, and shewed them the letters Antonius had written to him, and his answers also sent him again, during the quarrel and strife, and how fiercely and proudly the other answered him, to all just and reasonable matters he wrote unto him.

After this, he sent Proculeius, and commanded him to do what he could possible to get Cleopatra alive, fearing lest otherwise all the treasure would be lost: and furthermore, he thought that if he could take Cleopatra, and bring her alive to Rome, she would marvellously beautify and set out his triumph.—PLUTARCH.

" Alexandria. *A Room in the Monument.*"
Act V., Scene 2.

In this scene, as in one of " KING HENRY VIII.," the outside and inside of a building are exhibited at the same time. The old dramatists were enabled to cope with a difficulty of this kind by the aid of the inner or secondary stage, which was also used in " HAMLET," " OTHELLO," &c., and was a constant accompaniment to the principal one.

—— " *Realms and islands were*
As plates dropped from his pocket."—Act V., Scene 2.

The term " plates" was applied to some kind of silver money. As in Marlowe's " JEW OF MALTA :"—

" Ratest thou this Moor but at two hundred plates?"

They are supposed to have been round pieces without stamp or impress, and were probably of fluctuating value.

Of all Shakspere's historical plays, " ANTONY AND CLEOPATRA" is by far the most wonderful.—The highest praise, or rather form of praise, of this play, which I can offer in my own mind, is the doubt which the perusal always occasions in me, whether the " ANTONY AND CLEOPATRA " is not, in all exhibitions of a giant power, in its strength and vigour of maturity, a formidable rival of " MACBETH," " LEAR," " HAMLET," and " OTHELLO."—COLERIDGE.